A COMPARATIVE ATLAS
OF
AMERICA'S GREAT CITIES:
TWENTY
METROPOLITAN REGIONS

ASSOCIATION OF AMERICAN GEOGRAPHERS

# Comparative Metropolitan Analysis Project

Volume 1. *Contemporary Metropolitan America: Twenty Geographical Vignettes.* Cambridge: Ballinger Publishing Company, 1976.

>   Part 1. *Historical Metropolitan Core Cities* (Boston, New York/New Jersey, Philadelphia, Hartford/Central Connecticut)
>
>   Part 2. *19th Century Port Cities* (Baltimore, New Orleans, San Francisco)
>
>   Part 3. *19th Century Inland Cities* (Pittsburgh, St. Louis, Cleveland, Chicago, Detroit, St. Paul/Minneapolis, Seattle)
>
>   Part 4. *20th Century Cities* (Dallas, Miami, Houston, Atlanta, Los Angeles, Washington, D.C.)

Volume 2. *Urban Policymaking and Metropolitan Dynamics: A Comparative Geographical Analysis.* Cambridge: Ballinger Publishing Company, 1976.

Volume 3. *A Comparative Atlas of America's Great Cities: Twenty Metropolitan Regions.* Minneapolis: University of Minnesota Press, 1976.

Ballinger will also publish the following vignettes separately as paperback editions: Boston, New Orleans, St. Paul/Minneapolis, Chicago, New York/New Jersey, Seattle, Los Angeles, Baltimore, Hartford/Central Connecticut, Miami, and Philadelphia.

---

RESEARCH DIRECTOR:

John S. Adams, *University of Minnesota*

ASSOCIATE DIRECTOR AND ATLAS EDITOR:

Ronald Abler, *Pennsylvania State University*

CHIEF CARTOGRAPHER:

Ki-Suk Lee, *University of Minnesota*

STEERING COMMITTEE AND EDITORIAL BOARD:
Brian J. L. Berry, Chairman, *Harvard University*
John R. Borchert, *University of Minnesota*
Frank E. Horton, *Southern Illinois University*
J. Warren Nystrom, Executive Director, *Association of American Geographers*
James E. Vance, Jr., *University of California, Berkeley*
David Ward, *University of Wisconsin*

The Comparative Metropolitan Analysis Project was supported by National Science Foundation Grant No. 3297

# A Comparative Atlas of America's Great Cities

TWENTY METROPOLITAN REGIONS

Published by

THE ASSOCIATION OF AMERICAN GEOGRAPHERS

and

THE UNIVERSITY OF MINNESOTA PRESS

| | |
|---|---|
| ATLAS EDITOR | Ronald Abler |
| ATLAS TEXT | John S. Adams and Ronald Abler |
| CHIEF CARTOGRAPHER | Ki-Suk Lee |
| PRODUCTION DESIGN | Patricia Burwell and Robert Hyde |
| DATA PROCESSING | John Mercer and John Hultquist |
| CARTOGRAPHERS | Sandra J. Haas    Si-Young Park    Cathy L. Smiley |
| | Robert Hyde    Kwai-Shing Poon    Eliahu Stern |
| | Janeen McAllister    Ryan Rudnicki    Su-Chang Wang |
| MAP COMPILATION | Rosella Abler    Audrey J. Jacobson    Paula M. Schmittdiel |
| | Lynne E. Bly    Thomas P. Lutgen    Patricia A. Smith |
| | Monica M. Brinkman    Thomas J. Malterer    Theresa A. Stedman |
| | Katherine Carlson    Margaret C. Peeples    Mary C. Tingerthal |
| | Charlotte W. Cohn    William Porter    Giovanni A. Volpe |
| | Mary M. Dolan |
| PHOTO PROCESSING | Charles F. Gross and John J. Flynn |
| PROJECT SECRETARIES | Patricia A. Kelly and Mary Mace |
| CARTOGRAPHY | Cartographic Laboratory, Department of Geography, University of Minnesota. Sandra J. Haas, Director |

The maps were produced on Keuffel & Esser films using
Keuffel & Esser and Direct Reproduction Company instruments.
The atlas was printed on Northwest Mountie Matte paper by
Harrison Smith-Lund Press and was bound in Columbia Milbank Vellum
by Rand McNally.

Copyright © 1976
by the Association of American Geographers.
All rights reserved.
Printed in the United States of America
at Harrison Smith-Lund Press, Minneapolis, Minnesota
Published in Canada by Burns & MacEachern Limited, Don Mills, Ontario

*Library of Congress Catalog Card Number 76-14268*

*ISBN 0-8166-0753-2*

# Foreword

This *Comparative Atlas of America's Great Cities* is one of three products of the Comparative Metropolitan Analysis Project, an enterprise of the Association of American Geographers funded by the National Science Foundation. It is complemented by two volumes published by the Ballinger Publishing Company, 17 Dunster Street, Cambridge, Massachusetts 02138: *Contemporary Metropolitan America: Twenty Geographical Vignettes* and *Urban Policymaking and Metropolitan Dynamics: A Comparative Geographical Analysis.* In combination, the set represents many things: an attempt to draw together the intellectual resources of a particular field, urban geography, to assess where we stood in 1970 with respect to a range of stated national urban-policy goals; a consistent comparative documentation of a variety of social, economic, political, and physical aspects of the nation's twenty largest urban regions, containing close to half of the total U.S. population; a set of skillfully drawn portraits of each region highlighting both common problems and local individuality; an assessment of the management and performance of these urban regions in twelve major policy areas — in short, a record of what has and has not been accomplished as perceived by a particular research community, a benchmark from which further changes may be documented and evaluated.

The notion of a benchmark at a significant turning point is an important one. Since 1970 the *Current Population Reports* of the Bureau of the Census have documented quite clearly a change in the nature of change, the beginning of a process of counterurbanization. The preceding century had been one of the growth of the industrial metropolis, a product of increasing population concentration, of increasing size and density, of immigrants from many places pouring into the urban melting pot. Yet since 1970 the nation's greatest metropolitan areas have lost population through selective emigration, the populations of their cores have dropped, densities have declined, and the abandonment of old neighborhoods has become contagious. Decreasing size, decreasing density, decreasing heterogeneity, the cooling of the melting pot — all point to a new phase in the nation's settlement history.

What then might be said about the twenty largest urban regions precisely at this significant turning point by representatives of a particular discipline? This atlas documents the geographical outcomes of individual Americans' achievement-orientation and quest for status, their passage through successive stages in the life cycle, their assimilation through the melting pot or their failure to assimilate — outcomes reflected in the internal patterns of each of the twenty great urban regions. Yet it also reveals the major differences that exist between urban regions that grew at different times in the nation's settlement history and the inherent variety resulting from the accidents of site and situation. It suggests where national programs might be fashioned to address common problems and opportunities, yet it also cautions that local initiatives within broad guidelines may be more responsive to individual needs and requirements.

Here one must strike a cautionary note. For if the atlas is a benchmark at a turning point, the geographical patterns it portrays may simply be the symptomatic outcomes of past forces and trends that are no more. To respond to the problems and inequalities portrayed would be, in military idiom, to prepare to fight the last war rather than the next. As a geographical portrait of urban America, the atlas should be a required reference work for concerned citizens, planners, and policymakers at a variety of levels — local, state, and national. As a benchmark, it should be an important point of departure for every student of urban change. As a member of a three-volume set, it represents a serious effort by the research community of urban geographers to contribute to the assessment and improvement of national urban policy. Yet the contribution will be clouded if the response to the maps in the portrait is classical — literal and direct interpretation of deficiencies and inequalities as problems to be cured. To the discerning reader, the message is indirect, a baseline to assess how things are changing and what new opportunities there are that are now developing, to be realized by anticipatory plans and programs, for it is in such anticipatory planning that the hope of further progress in urban (or even counterurban) America resides.

BRIAN J. L. BERRY

Harvard University
July 1976

# Preface

More than two-thirds of the United States' population now resides in Standard Metropolitan Statistical Areas. Consequently, much of the nation's attention to domestic issues during the last 25 years has focused on our large cities. As difficulties emerged, we labeled them *urban* problems, often paying more attention to visible symptoms than to the unseen and poorly understood processes that produced problems among certain people at certain places and times.

Sorting out the causes and effects of urban processes since World War II was particularly difficult because of the rapid pace of postwar city-building and the immediate problems it seemed to create. Our preoccupation with growth and the measures necessary to accommodate it made it easy to neglect the comparative study of our metropolitan regions that might have helped us separate problems *of* cities from those that happen to be located *in* cities because people experiencing certain difficulties are located there.

The early 1970s marked the end of the post-World War II epoch of exuberant metropolitan expansion in the United States. A unique episode in city-building has drawn to a close, its conditions misunderstood and its consequences to be reckoned fully only in the century ahead. It was an era when economic and demographic energies pent up by the depression of the 1930s and World War II exploded in an orgy of city-building that consumed cheap materials, abundant land, and mineral fuels that were virtually free by the standards of the mid-1970s. The epoch is now over. It is unlikely that anything similar will happen again in the United States or elsewhere. Yet we are left with its consequences. In order to respond intelligently to what has happened and to anticipate what will yet occur, we need to know more about what has happened and why.

The national population increased from 140 million in 1945 to 205 million in 1970, while the national territory expanded almost 20 percent as Alaska and Hawaii entered the union. Births per year climbed from a modest 2.6 million in 1940 to over 4.2 million annually in the peak years from 1959 to 1961. Steady economic expansion meant ever-greater consumption of goods and services. Gross national product grew from $210 billion in 1940 to $975 billion in 1970. The nation's real income increased at annual rates averaging 3 percent during the period, resulting in marked increases in family wealth; the median income of white families in constant dollars doubled from 1945 to 1970.

More children and greater prosperity stimulated massive population movements. The children and grandchildren of immigrants, successful in their pursuit of material gains and wanting more space for their growing families, documented their hard-won status and prosperity by relocating to better addresses in more agreeable surroundings. Most of the country participated in the reshuffling. People steadily migrated from old centers in the North and East to new cities in the West and South. Inside metropolitan areas, central-city densities declined as deaths exceeded births near metropolitan cores; the edges flourished and expanded as young households arrived.

As people struggled to achieve, surpass, or keep ahead of ever-rising standards and averages, the young, energetic, resourceful, and ambitious moved to new and more promising parts of the nation and to the peripheries of its metropolitan areas, abandoning places they associated with limited economic opportunities or unpleasant memories. They left behind the elderly, the dependent, the disheartened, the economically impotent, and the socially and politically immobilized components of the metropolitan population. This concentration of needs and human shortcomings created environments of despair in the central cities in the 1960s. Real problems among inner-city residents were compounded by growing expectations, especially among minority groups, that the ever-expanding material bounty of the 1950s and 1960s would increasingly filter down to those in the lower socioeconomic strata.

The poor in the broadest sense are those who lack the resources, health, and skills to cope with metropolitan life in the late 20th century. The poor have always been with us, but the 1960s revealed how much the poor had become geographically isolated in metropolitan cores as better-endowed people moved on to something better someplace else. With the continued departure of the affluent and the concentration of the poor and demoralized, problems of society became identified with the places and regions where the problems were located. Often the impoverished *place or region* was identified as the problem. It is easy to slip from such perceptions to the conclusion that removing the symptoms of poverty from the map will solve the underlying causes. At the regional scale, out-migration of talent, human energy, capital, and leadership focused attention on Appalachia, the upland South, and the cut-over forest and mining areas of the northern Great Lakes states. Inside metropolitan areas, problem places emerged in every core city. Sometimes they were camouflaged, as in rapidly growing centers like Los Angeles, Miami, and Houston, where new housing could not be built fast enough; elsewhere they were starkly displayed, as in St. Louis, Pittsburgh, and Philadelphia.

The perceptions of these problems and the identification of them with certain regions and kinds of places stimulated extended political debate and large-scale programs designed to alleviate or solve them. A long series of housing, urban renewal, antisegregation, and antipoverty legislation culminated in the Great Society programs of the Johnson administration, implicitly promising that human problems concentrated in particular places would be solved quickly. Failure to make good on these promises and to satisfy the expectations they aroused had much to do with the civil disorders that erupted in many metropolitan areas at the end of the 1960s.

After the rhetoric and the riots of the 1960s, it is fair to ask what progress has been made in meeting human needs in the nation's great cities. Promises to solve "the nation's urban problems" have been made. Laws have been passed. Programs have been launched. Billions of dollars have been spent. What are the results? This comparative atlas and its companion volumes examine the nation's 20 most populous metropolitan regions and supply a partial answer.

Part I of the atlas describes how the American metropolitan system emerged, how transportation technology and economic evolution influence the nation's network of cities and their individual internal geographies, and how the cities depend on one another. Part I also contains chapters on sources of information about American cities and the limitations of the census data used in the atlas.

Part II contains 20 chapters, each devoted to the geographical analysis of a single metropolitan region. Maps with identical scales and formats describe each metropolis's setting and physical structure, its housing stock, its people, their socioeconomic characteristics, and topics of special interest within the urban region. The 20 metropolitan regions are centered on Boston, New York and Northern New Jersey, Philadelphia, Hartford and the Connecticut Valley, Baltimore, New Orleans, San Francisco-Oakland, Pittsburgh, St. Louis, Cleveland, Chicago, Detroit, Minneapolis-St. Paul, Seattle, Dallas and Fort Worth, Houston, Los Angeles, Miami, Atlanta, and Washington, D.C.

Part III consists of 23 chapters that compare attributes among the 20 metropolitan regions. In each chapter a series of 20 maps is presented, identical in scale and format. The subjects mapped in Part III are selected aspects of metropolitan physical environments, housing, transportation and communications, population, education, public health, racial and ethnic segregation, employment and poverty, and housing abandonment.

Part IV summarizes the information presented in the atlas in a commentary on past, current, and future policies and policy issues regarding the nation's metropolitan areas.

Our overriding objective has been to provide an accurate comparative assessment of the occurrence and intensity of human problems in the metropolitan regions mapped in the atlas. No city's problems are exactly the same as another city's. Neither are they wholly dissimilar. The same principle applies regarding workable solutions for urban problems. The maps and commentary in Part II emphasize the unique combination of setting, housing, people, and problems in each city. The chapters in Part III illustrate how the same problems appear in different kinds of cities.

The basic processes of urbanization and metropolitan evolution are common to all large cities. Yet regional and temporal variations among American cities have caused urban processes to work themselves out in different ways, producing the metropolitan variety documented in this atlas. Programs and policies that fail to recognize and accommodate the individuality and the underlying similarities among the nation's major metropolitan areas will certainly fail to yield maximum results. Places and people and the differences among them are and will continue to be the critical dimensions of American metropolitan life.

If this atlas and its accompanying volumes provide a better understanding of the interrelationships between places and people in American metropolitan areas, we shall consider the energies invested in this project to be well spent.

Ronald Abler
John S. Adams

# Acknowledgments

Hundreds of people have contributed directly and indirectly to the completion of the atlas and its associated publications. Without their help the work would not have been produced.

Several years of discussion preceded the research proposal that in turn led to the Comparative Metropolitan Analysis Project. Many useful ideas that were later incorporated in the atlas and the project were presented at an A.A.G. (Association of American Geographers) summer institute held in 1970 at which lectures were presented by Robert H. Alexander, Jack Beresford, the Chicago Pollution Control Agency, Kenneth J. Dueker, George Farnsworth, Philip M. Lankford, Philip Rees, Waldo Tobler, William Warntz, and James R. Wray. Attending the institute as participants were Clyde E. Browning, Berenice M. Casper, Robert J. Colenutt, Kenneth E. Corey, Lee Guernsey, John Fraser Hart, Richard D. Hecock, Karel J. Kansky, Michael W. Kuhn, Gopal S. Kulkarni, Harold M. Rose, Lorne H. Russwurm, Carolyn J. Ryan, Paul J. Schwind, and Ranjit A. Tirtha.

In spring 1972, once the project was under way, a letter was sent to all members of the Association of American Geographers interested in urban geography soliciting their advice on atlas design and content. Numerous invaluable suggestions were received from C. Murray Austin, Thomas F. Barton, Emily D. Braneon, Douglas Caruso, Christopher S. Davies, G. E. Alan Dever, David Dnousich, Roland Docter, William E. Dooley, John B. Fieser, Arthur Getis, Norton Ginsburg, Barry Gordon, Keith D. Harries, Richard A. Huck, Frank C. Innes, Harry Kiang, David Lanegran, Walter Lehner, Robert B. McNee, Barry Moriarty, Walt Neliker, John D. Nystuen, Sherry Olson, Risa Palm, Donna J. Pequet, William A. Peterman, Forrest R. Pitts, William Porter, Jr., F. Gerald Rawling, Mark E. Richner, Elizabeth F. Schroeder, H. L. Seyler, Gary W. Shannon, Wendy L. Simpson, David M. Smith, J. A. Soto, Gregory Stein, Russell L. Stubbles, L. A. Swatridge, Mark Wassenich, Thomas R. Weir, and Robert I. Wittick. In addition, Karen Fonstad, Larry Ford, Robert D. Thomson, and Anthony V. Williams volunteered advice on content and design.

In the early stages of atlas design, Canadian participation and the inclusion of Canadian cities were discussed with Harry Swain, Frank C. Innes, and Thomas R. Weir. Unfortunately logistical and financial constraints made Canadian participation impossible. Throughout the last few years, Frederick Broome and Richard H. Schweitzer have been most helpful in keeping us abreast of mapping programs in the U.S. Bureau of the Census.

George F. Jenks, Lawrence Fahey, Joel Morrison, and Arthur Robinson reviewed the plans for cartographic design and production procedures and shared their experience with us. Additional cartographic advice was provided by Borden A. Dent, Mei-Ling Hsu, Judy Olson, Joseph Schwartzberg, and James Wray. David Cuff made several useful suggestions regarding the color scheme. William Beetschen, Michael Czechanski, and Dan G. Snyder gave important tips on production that made our operations more efficient.

Most of the data used in the atlas are derived from the 1970 Censuses of Population and Housing, but transforming the census computer tapes into usable form required the efforts of a number of people. Most of the data extraction was performed at the Institute for Urban and Regional Research at the University of Iowa, which is directed by Kenneth J. Dueker. John Mercer and John Hultquist bore overall responsibility for data processing. Others participating in the work were Robert Aangeenbrug, Bill Clark, Jan Fredricks, Bud Meador, Richard Rhoda, Robert I. Wittick, David Workman, and Michael Wright. Beverly Politzer, of State College, Pennsylvania, also assisted with data processing.

Questions regarding census data and problems in data processing occasioned queries to Marshall L. Turner of the Census Data User Services Staff and to Larry W. Carbaugh and Robert Gignilliat of DUALABS, Inc. We are grateful for the promptness and efficiency with which our queries were answered.

Data on immature births for Chapter 40 were provided by the New York City Department of Health, the Philadelphia Department of Public Health, the Baltimore City Health Department, the Louisiana State Department of Health, the San Francisco County Health Department, the Alameda County Health Department, the Allegheny County Health Department, the Department of Health and Hospitals of the City of St. Louis, the Cleveland City Health Department, the City of Chicago Board of Health, the Minnesota Department of Health, the Seattle-King County Department of Health, the Dallas Department of Public Health, the Houston Department of Public Health, the Georgia Department of Human Resources, and the Department of Human Resources of the District of Columbia.

Land-use maps and data for the generalized land-use maps in the atlas were provided through the courtesy of the Boston Metropolitan Area Planning Council, the Tri-State Regional Planning Commission (New York-Northern New Jersey), the Delaware Valley Regional Planning Commission (Philadelphia), the Capitol City Planning Agency (Hartford), the Regional Planning Council of Baltimore, the New Orleans Regional Planning Commission, the Association of Bay Area Governments (San Francisco), the Southwest Pennsylvania Regional Planning Commission, the East-West Gateway Coordinating Council (St. Louis), the Northeastern Illinois Planning Commission, the Southeastern Michigan Council of Governments, the Twin Cities Metropolitan Council (Minneapolis-St. Paul), the Puget Sound Governmental Conference, the Houston-Galveston Area Council, the Southern California Association of Governments, the Atlanta Regional Planning Commission, and the Metropolitan Washington Council of Governments.

## Acknowledgments

Additional data and literature on a variety of miscellaneous topics were provided by Robert Alexander, Patricia Birdsong, John Blodgett, Jan Breidenbach, Michael R. C. Coulson, Tom Ehlen, Michael O. Filani, Richard Forstall, Edward J. Kaiser, Ephraim Ketchall, James Lewin, the Los Angeles Regional Transportation Study, and the Office of Emergency Preparedness.

Jacqueline A. Gans, the Gulf Oil Company's Tourguide Bureau, Jacob Silver, and Mai Treude were helpful in providing maps used for background information and in the drafting of base maps.

The Comparative Metropolitan Analysis Project produced a series of metropolitan vignettes and urban policy monographs in addition to this atlas. The authors of the monographs and vignettes have provided us with invaluable assistance by reviewing text and maps, suggesting topics for mapping, and providing background information. The respective policy monographs and their authors are:

| | |
|---|---|
| *Land Speculation and Urban Morphology* | Charles S. Sargent, Jr. |
| *Abandoned Housing* | Michael J. Dear |
| *National Progress toward Housing and Urban Renewal Goals* | John Mercer and John Hultquist |
| *Progress toward Environmental Goals for Metropolitan America* | Brian J. L. Berry |
| *Public School Goals and Parochial School Attendance in Twenty American Cities* | John S. Adams and Kathleen Molnar Brown |
| *Geographic Perspectives on Crime and the Impact of Anticrime Legislation* | Gerald F. Pyle |
| *Restructuring the Health Care Delivery System in the United States* | Mary Megee |
| *The Federal Open Space Program: Impacts and Imperatives* | Rutherford H. Platt |
| *Housing and Transportation Problems of the Urban Elderly* | Stephen M. Golant |
| *Metropolitan Governance* | Rex D. Honey |
| *Progress toward Achieving Efficient and Responsive Spatial-Political Systems in Urban America* | David R. Reynolds |
| *Malapportionment and Gerrymandering in the Ghetto* | John O'Loughlin |

The metropolitan vignette titles and authors are:

| | |
|---|---|
| *Boston: A Geographical Portrait* | Michael P. Conzen and George K. Lewis |
| *A Vignette of the New York-New Jersey Metropolitan Region* | George W. Carey |
| *Metropolitan Philadelphia: A Study of Conflicts and Social Cleavages* | Peter O. Muller, Kenneth C. Meyer, and Roman A. Cybriwsky |
| *From Farm to Factory to Urban Pastoralism: Urban Change in Central Connecticut* | David R. Meyer |
| *Baltimore* | Sherry Olson |
| *New Orleans: The Making of an Urban Landscape* | Peirce F. Lewis |
| *The Cities by San Francisco Bay* | Jean Vance |
| *Metropolitan Pittsburgh: Old Trends and New Directions* | Philip H. Vernon and Oswald Schmidt |
| *The St. Louis Daily Urban System* | Dennis K. Ehrhardt |
| *The Northeastern Ohio Urban Complex* | Harold M. Mayer and Thomas Corsi |
| *Chicago: Transformation of an Urban System* | Brian J. L. Berry, Irving Cutler, Edwin H. Draine, Ying-cheng Kiang, Thomas R. Tocalis, and Pierre de Vise |
| *The Regions of Metropolitan Detroit: An Analysis of Spatial Change* | Bryan Thompson and Robert Sinclair |
| *The Twin Cities of St. Paul and Minneapolis* | Ronald Abler, John S. Adams, and John R. Borchert |
| *Seattle* | A. Phillip Andrus, William B. Beyers, Ronald R. Boyce, Jacob J. Eichenbaum, Michael Mandeville, Richard L. Morrill, David Stallings, and David M. Sucher |
| *The Dallas-Fort Worth Region* | Dennis Conway, Kingsley E. Haynes, George Kell, Rodger P. Kester, Ian R. Manners, Dudley L. Poston, and Howard Savage |
| *Houston* | Martha E. Palmer and Marjorie N. Rush |
| *The Los Angeles Metropolitan Experience: Uniqueness, Generality and the Goal of the Good Life* | Howard J. Nelson and W. A. V. Clark |
| *Sunshine and Shadows in Metropolitan Miami* | David B. Longbrake and Woodrow W. Nichols, Jr. |
| *Metropolis in Georgia: Atlanta's Rise as a Major Transaction Center* | Truman A. Hartshorn, Sanford Bederman, Sid Davis, G. E. Alan Dever, and Richard Pillsbury |
| *Washington, D.C.* | Jean-Claude Thomas |

Projects of the magnitude of this atlas and its associated publications require a great deal of administrative flexibility on the part of the professional organizations and educational institutions associated with them, and we are extremely grateful to the Association of American Geographers, the University of Minnesota, and the Pennsylvania State University for smoothing the administrative road to completion of the project. Edward J. Taaffe, Wilbur Zelinsky, and Julian Wolpert were A.A.G. presidents during the project's heydey, and their helpful concern for its ongoing progress is appreciated. Dean John G. Turnbull at the University of Minnesota made it possible for the project to be headquartered there, and Associate Dean John W. Webb assisted with institutional arrangements at Minnesota. Dean Charles Hosler and Geography Department Head Wilbur Zelinsky of The Pennsylvania State University made it possible for the editor to obtain the time needed for the project. Because it was located there, the Geography Department of the University of Minnesota bore the brunt of the project. Ward J. Barrett and Richard H. Skaggs, successive department chairmen, were more than gracious in accommodating numerous inconveniences.

Patricia A. Kelly was project secretary for the bulk of the project's existence. Without her almost incredible efficiency and her unfailing ability to bring order out of several varieties of chaos simultaneously,

## Acknowledgments

the project's directors would no doubt be enjoying an enforced rest cure. When the workload occasionally exceeded her capacity, the department secretaries at Minnesota, Arlette Lindberg, Margaret Rasmussen, Carol Atchley, and Barbara VanDrasek cheerfully pitched in, as did Nina McNeal, Colleen Kristula, and Patty Barnyak at Penn State. We also appreciate the way Elizabeth Beetschen and Pat McKenna kept project paperwork flowing smoothly at the Association of American Geographers' office.

Late in this sequence but first in importance is money. The National Science Foundation support that made the entire project possible and the sympathy and encouragement of Howard Hines are deeply appreciated, as is the courtesy of Harold Rose in making available to us unexpended funds from his National Science Foundation grant.

Throughout the project we received perceptive advice from the steering committee. Its membership is listed opposite the title page.

Above all, it would have been impossible to complete the work without the assistance of the project staff listed on the reverse of the title page. Their dedication to its completion often greatly exceeded the financial compensation we were able to offer.

We are grateful for the patience and understanding of John Ervin, Director of the University of Minnesota Press, in dealing with the many problems the atlas entailed. Because of the complexity and unusual nature of the atlas, the staff of the Press contributed substantially to the final product. We are especially indebted to Beverly Kaemmer, editor, and Robert Taylor, design and production manager.

Given the size and complexity of the atlas and the project, and the number of people who have helped in one way or another, we have doubtless failed to mention people whose names should be listed above, and we apologize for such inadvertent omissions.

# Central Cities, SMSAs, and DUSs Mapped in the Atlas

| Central Cities | SMSAs | DUSs |
|---|---|---|
| Boston | Boston | Boston |
| New York City | New York | New York-Northern New Jersey |
| Philadelphia | Jersey City | Philadelphia |
| Hartford | Newark | Hartford-Connecticut Valley |
| Baltimore | Paterson-Clifton-Passaic | Baltimore |
| New Orleans | Philadelphia | New Orleans |
| San Francisco | Hartford | San Francisco-Oakland |
| Oakland | Baltimore | Pittsburgh |
| Pittsburgh | New Orleans | St. Louis |
| St. Louis | San Francisco-Oakland | Cleveland |
| Cleveland | Pittsburgh | Chicago |
| Chicago | St. Louis | Detroit |
| Detroit | Cleveland | Minneapolis-St. Paul |
| Minneapolis | Chicago | Seattle |
| St. Paul | Detroit | Dallas-Fort Worth |
| Seattle | Minneapolis-St. Paul | Houston |
| Dallas | Seattle | Los Angeles |
| Houston | Dallas | Miami |
| Los Angeles | Fort Worth | Atlanta |
| Long Beach | Houston | Washington, D.C. |
| Miami | Los Angeles | |
| Atlanta | Miami | |
| Washington, D.C. | Atlanta | |
| | Washington, D.C. | |

# Contents

|  | Text | Maps |
|---|---|---|
| Foreword by Brian J. L. Berry, *Chairman of the Steering Committee* | v | |
| Preface | vii | |
| Acknowledgments | ix | |

### Part I: Introduction

| | Text | Maps |
|---|---|---|
| **Chapter 1 How to Use the Atlas** | | |
| The Organization of the Atlas | 1 | |
| Maps and Text | 2 | |
| Reading the Maps and Diagrams | 2 | |
| **Chapter 2 Metropolitan America** | | |
| The Land and the People | 5 | |
| Defining the Metropolis | 5 | |
| The 20 Most Populous Metropolitan Regions | 7 | |
| **Chapter 3 Metropolitan Competition and Interdependence** | | |
| Metropolitan Competition and Growth | 9 | |
| Interdependence among Metropolitan Areas | 9 | |
| Competition, Status, and Urban Problems | 11 | |
| **Chapter 4 Metropolitan Problems: Are There Solutions?** | | |
| The Life Cycle of Urban Neighborhoods | 12 | |
| The Urban League Argument | 12 | |
| The Vacancy Chain Argument | 12 | |
| Population Changes at the Metropolitan and Neighborhood Levels | 13 | |
| Problems of Places; Problems of People | 14 | |
| Metropolitan Problems: Prerequisites for Solutions | 14 | |
| Metropolitan Physical Environments | 14 | |
| Open Space for Metropolitan Amenity and Leisure-Time Use | 14 | |
| Housing | 14 | |
| Transportation and Communication | 14 | |
| Metropolitan Growth | 14 | |
| Education | 14 | |
| Public Health | 15 | |
| Socioeconomic Segregation | 15 | |
| Employment and Poverty | 15 | |
| Urban Renewal and Redevelopment | 15 | |
| Summary and Conclusions | 15 | |

| | Text | Maps |
|---|---|---|
| **Chapter 5 Sources of Information about American Cities** | | |
| What Kinds of Information Do We Need? | 16 | |
| Current Data Sources for the Comparative Geographical Study of American Cities | 16 | |
| Federal Statistics for Local Areas and the 1970 Censuses of Population and Housing | 17 | |
| Sampling People | 17 | |
| Sampling Housing Units | 18 | |
| Collecting the Data | 18 | |
| Processing the Data | 19 | |
| Census Data Products Used in Preparing the Atlas | 19 | |

### Part II: Current Patterns in American Cities

#### A. Cities of the Nation's Historic Metropolitan Core

| | Text | Maps |
|---|---|---|
| **Chapter 6 Boston** | | |
| The Place | | |
| Relief | 21 | 22 |
| Generalized Land Use | 22 | 22 |
| Housing | | |
| Housing Age | 22 | 22 |
| Mobile Homes | 23 | 22 |
| Single-Unit Detached Housing | 23 | 23 |
| Housing Value and Rent | 24 | 23 |
| The People | | |
| Population Density | 25 | 23 |
| Age and the Elderly | 26 | 24 |
| Sex Ratio | 26 | 24 |
| Negroes | 26 | 25 |
| Spanish-Americans | 26 | 25 |
| Chinese-Americans | 26 | 25 |
| Irish-Americans | 26 | 25 |
| Canadian-Americans | 26 | 25 |
| Russian-Americans | 27 | 26 |
| Italian-Americans | 28 | 26 |
| Socioeconomic Characteristics | | |
| Household Size | 29 | 27 |
| Female Headship | 29 | 27 |
| Occupations | 29 | 27 |
| Income | 29 | 27 |

*xiii*

# Contents

|  |  | Text | Maps |
|---|---|---|---|
|  | Topics of Special Interest in the Boston Region |  |  |
|  | Restrictive Zoning | 29 | 28 |
|  | Taxes | 29 | 28 |
|  | Political Fragmentation | 29 | 29 |
| Chapter 7 | New York-Northern New Jersey |  |  |
|  | The Place |  |  |
|  | Relief | 30 | 31 |
|  | Housing |  |  |
|  | Housing Age | 31 | 32-33 |
|  | Mobile Homes | 32 | 33 |
|  | Single-Unit Detached Housing | 32 | 35 |
|  | Housing Value and Rent | 32 | 34 |
|  | The People |  |  |
|  | Population Density | 32 | 35 |
|  | Age and the Elderly | 32 | 36 |
|  | Sex Ratio | 34 | 37 |
|  | Negroes | 36 | 38 |
|  | Spanish-Americans | 36 | 38 |
|  | Chinese-Americans | 37 | 39 |
|  | Japanese-Americans | 37 | 39 |
|  | Irish-Americans | 37 | 40 |
|  | German-Americans | 38 | 40 |
|  | Polish-Americans | 39 | 41 |
|  | Russian-Americans | 39 | 41 |
|  | Italian-Americans | 40 | 42 |
|  | Socioeconomic Characteristics |  |  |
|  | Household Size | 41 | 42 |
|  | Female Headship | 41 | 43 |
|  | Occupations | 41 | 44 |
|  | Income | 42 | 47 |
|  | Topics of Special Interest in the New York Region |  |  |
|  | Young Populations | 43 | 45 |
|  | Population Density | 45 | 46 |
|  | Crowded Housing | 45 | 43 |
| Chapter 8 | Philadelphia |  |  |
|  | The Place |  |  |
|  | Relief | 48 | 49 |
|  | Generalized Land Use | 48 | 49 |
|  | Housing |  |  |
|  | Housing Age | 49 | 50 |
|  | Mobile Homes | 49 | 50 |
|  | Single-Unit Detached Housing | 49 | 51 |
|  | Housing Value and Rent | 49 | 51-52 |
|  | The People |  |  |
|  | Population Density | 51 | 53 |
|  | Age and the Elderly | 52 | 53 |
|  | Sex Ratio | 52 | 54 |
|  | Negroes | 52 | 54 |
|  | Spanish-Americans | 52 | 54 |
|  | Polish-Americans | 52 | 55 |
|  | Russian-Americans | 52 | 55 |
|  | Italian-Americans | 52 | 56 |
|  | Socioeconomic Characteristics |  |  |
|  | Household Size | 55 | 56 |
|  | Female Headship | 55 | 57 |
|  | Occupations | 56 | 58 |
|  | Income | 57 | 59 |

|  |  | Text | Maps |
|---|---|---|---|
|  | Topics of Special Interest in the Philadelphia Region |  |  |
|  | Abandoned Housing | 57 | 59 |
|  | Housing Value | 57 | 59 |
|  | Parochial School Enrollment | 58 | 60 |
|  | Population Change | 58 | 60 |
|  | Negro Neighborhoods | 61 | 61 |
| Chapter 9 | Hartford-Connecticut Valley |  |  |
|  | The Place |  |  |
|  | Relief | 62 | 63 |
|  | Generalized Land Use | 62 | 63 |
|  | Housing |  |  |
|  | Housing Age | 63 | 63 |
|  | Mobile Homes | 63 | 63 |
|  | Single-Unit Detached Housing | 63 | 64 |
|  | Housing Value and Rent | 63 | 64 |
|  | The People |  |  |
|  | Population Density | 64 | 64 |
|  | Age and the Elderly | 65 | 64 |
|  | Sex Ratio | 65 | 64 |
|  | Negroes | 66 | 65 |
|  | Spanish-Americans | 66 | 65 |
|  | Canadian-Americans | 66 | 65 |
|  | Italian-Americans | 66 | 65 |
|  | Polish-Americans | 66 | 65 |
|  | Socioeconomic Characteristics |  |  |
|  | Household Size | 67 | 66 |
|  | Female Headship | 67 | 66 |
|  | Occupations | 67 | 66 |
|  | Income | 67 | 66 |
|  | Topics of Special Interest in the Hartford Region |  |  |
|  | Minority Housing | 68 | 68 |
|  | Housing for the Elderly | 68 | 67 |
|  | Public Transportation | 68 | 67 |

## B. Nineteenth-Century Ports

|  |  | Text | Maps |
|---|---|---|---|
| Chapter 10 | Baltimore |  |  |
|  | The Place |  |  |
|  | Relief | 70 | 71 |
|  | Generalized Land Use | 70 | 71 |
|  | Housing |  |  |
|  | Housing Age | 71 | 71 |
|  | Mobile Homes | 72 | 72 |
|  | Single-Unit Detached Housing | 72 | 72 |
|  | Housing Value and Rent | 72 | 72 |
|  | The People |  |  |
|  | Population Density | 74 | 73 |
|  | Age and the Elderly | 74 | 73 |
|  | Sex Ratio | 74 | 73 |
|  | Negroes | 74 | 74 |
|  | Spanish-Americans | 74 | 74 |
|  | Socioeconomic Characteristics |  |  |
|  | Household Size | 75 | 75 |
|  | Female Headship | 75 | 75 |
|  | Occupations | 75 | 76 |
|  | Income | 76 | 76 |
|  | Topics of Special Interest in the Baltimore Region |  |  |
|  | Population Change and Sewage Disposal | 77 | 77 |
|  | Negroes in New Housing | 78 | 77 |
|  | Automobile Ownership | 78 | 78 |
|  | Rent Stress | 78 | 78 |

xiv

|  | Text | Maps |
|---|---|---|
| **Chapter 11  New Orleans** | | |
| The Place | | |
| Relief | 79 | 80 |
| Generalized Land Use | 83 | 80 |
| Housing | | |
| Housing Age | 83 | 80 |
| Mobile Homes | 83 | 81 |
| Single-Unit Detached Housing | 84 | 81 |
| Housing Value and Rent | 84 | 81 |
| The People | | |
| Population Density | 84 | 82 |
| Age and the Elderly | 84 | 82 |
| Sex Ratio | 85 | 82 |
| Negroes | 85 | 83 |
| Spanish-Americans | 86 | 83 |
| Socioeconomic Characteristics | | |
| Household Size | 86 | 84 |
| Female Headship | 87 | 84 |
| Occupations | 87 | 85 |
| Income | 88 | 85 |
| Topics of Special Interest in the New Orleans Region | | |
| Population Change | 88 | 86 |
| Female Headship and Poverty | 88 | 87 |
| College Enrollments | 88 | 87 |
| Households without Automobiles | 88 | 86 |
| **Chapter 12  San Francisco-Oakland** | | |
| The Place | | |
| Relief | 90 | 90 |
| Generalized Land Use | 90 | 90 |
| Housing | | |
| Housing Age | 90 | 91 |
| Mobile Homes | 95 | 91 |
| Single-Unit Detached Housing | 95 | 92 |
| Housing Value and Rent | 95 | 92 |
| The People | | |
| Population Density | 96 | 93 |
| Age and the Elderly | 96 | 93 |
| Sex Ratio | 97 | 94 |
| Negroes | 97 | 94 |
| Spanish-Americans | 97 | 94 |
| Chinese-Americans | 97 | 95 |
| Japanese-Americans | 98 | 96 |
| Mexican-Americans | 98 | 96 |
| American Indians | 98 | 97 |
| Italian-Americans | 98 | 97 |
| Socioeconomic Characteristics | | |
| Household Size | 99 | 98 |
| Female Headship | 99 | 98 |
| Occupations | 99 | 99 |
| Income | 100 | 100 |
| Topics of Special Interest in the San Francisco-Oakland Region | | |
| Negro Population | 100 | 100 |
| Unemployment | 100 | 101 |
| Negroes in New Housing | 101 | 101 |
| Public Transportation | 101 | 102 |

|  | Text | Maps |
|---|---|---|
| **C. Nineteenth-Century Inland Centers and Ports** | | |
| **Chapter 13  Pittsburgh** | | |
| The Place | | |
| Relief | 105 | 106 |
| Housing | | |
| Housing Age | 106 | 106 |
| Mobile Homes | 107 | 106 |
| Single-Unit Detached Housing | 107 | 108 |
| Housing Value and Rent | 108 | 107 |
| The People | | |
| Population Density | 108 | 109 |
| Age and the Elderly | 108 | 109 |
| Sex Ratio | 108 | 109 |
| Negroes | 110 | 110 |
| Spanish-Americans | 111 | 110 |
| Italian-Americans | 111 | 110 |
| Polish-Americans | 111 | 110 |
| Socioeconomic Characteristics | | |
| Household Size | 113 | 111 |
| Female Headship | 113 | 111 |
| Occupations | 113 | 112 |
| Income | 113 | 112 |
| Topics of Special Interest in the Pittsburgh Region | | |
| Age and the Elderly | 113 | 113 |
| Income and Occupation | 114 | 114 |
| Metropolitan Diversity | 115 | 115 |
| **Chapter 14  St. Louis** | | |
| The Place | | |
| Relief | 116 | 117 |
| Generalized Land Use | 118 | 117 |
| Housing | | |
| Housing Age | 118 | 118 |
| Mobile Homes | 121 | 119 |
| Single-Unit Detached Housing | 121 | 117 |
| Housing Value and Rent | 122 | 119 |
| The People | | |
| Population Density | 123 | 120 |
| Age and the Elderly | 123 | 120-121 |
| Sex Ratio | 123 | 120 |
| Negroes | 123 | 121 |
| Spanish-Americans | 123 | 121 |
| Socioeconomic Characteristics | | |
| Household Size | 124 | 122 |
| Female Headship | 124 | 122 |
| Occupations | 125 | 124 |
| Income | 125 | 123 |
| Topics of Special Interest in the St. Louis Region | | |
| Housing Age | 126 | 125 |
| Quality of Life | 126 | 125-126 |
| **Chapter 15  Cleveland** | | |
| The Place | | |
| Relief | 127 | 128 |
| Housing | | |
| Housing Age | 128 | 128 |
| Mobile Homes | 128 | 128 |
| Single-Unit Detached Housing | 128 | 129 |
| Housing Value and Rent | 129 | 129 |
| The People | | |
| Population Density | 129 | 130 |
| Age and the Elderly | 129 | 130 |

|  | Text | Maps |
|---|---|---|
| Sex Ratio | 130 | 130 |
| Negroes | 131 | 131 |
| Spanish-Americans | 131 | 131 |
| Socioeconomic Characteristics | | |
|     Household Size | 131 | 132 |
|     Female Headship | 131 | 132 |
|     Occupations | 133 | 132 |
|     Income | 133 | 132 |
| Topics of Special Interest in the Cleveland Region | | |
|     Industrial Areas | 133 | 133 |
|     Ethnicity | 133 | 133 |
|     Crime | 133 | 134 |
|     Voting Patterns | 134 | 134 |
|     Crowded Housing | 134 | 134 |
|     Political Fragmentation | 134 | 134 |

## Chapter 16 Chicago

| | Text | Maps |
|---|---|---|
| The Place | | |
|     Relief | 136 | 136 |
| Housing | | |
|     Housing Age | 136 | 137 |
|     Mobile Homes | 136 | 136 |
|     Single-Unit Detached Housing | 136 | 137 |
|     Housing Value and Rent | 136 | 138 |
| The People | | |
|     Population Density | 138 | 139 |
|     Age and the Elderly | 138 | 139 |
|     Sex Ratio | 140 | 140 |
|     Negroes | 141 | 140 |
|     Spanish-Americans | 141 | 141 |
|     American Indians | 141 | 141 |
|     Chinese-Americans | 142 | 142 |
|     Japanese-Americans | 142 | 142 |
|     Irish-Americans | 142 | 142 |
|     German-Americans | 142 | 143 |
|     Polish-Americans | 142 | 143 |
|     Russian-Americans | 144 | 143 |
|     Italian-Americans | 144 | 143 |
| Socioeconomic Characteristics | | |
|     Household Size | 146 | 144 |
|     Female Headship | 146 | 144 |
|     Occupations | 146 | 145 |
|     Income | 146 | 145 |
| Topics of Special Interest in the Chicago Region | | |
|     Residential Change, 1965-1970 | 147 | 146-147 |
|     Labor Force Walking to Work | 147 | 146 |
|     Labor Force Working in the CBD | 147 | 148 |
|     Enrollment in Parochial Elementary Schools | 147 | 147 |
|     Female Headship | 148 | 148 |

## Chapter 17 Detroit

| | Text | Maps |
|---|---|---|
| The Place | | |
|     Relief | 149 | 150 |
|     Generalized Land Use | 149 | 150 |
| Housing | | |
|     Housing Age | 151 | 150 |
|     Mobile Homes | 151 | 150 |
|     Single-Unit Detached Housing | 151 | 151 |
|     Housing Value and Rent | 153 | 151 |
| The People | | |
|     Population Density | 153 | 152 |
|     Age and the Elderly | 153 | 152 |
|     Sex Ratio | 154 | 152 |
|     Negroes | 154 | 153 |
|     Spanish-Americans | 154 | 153 |
|     American Indians | 155 | 154 |
|     Polish-Americans | 155 | 154 |
|     Italian-Americans | 155 | 154 |
| Socioeconomic Characteristics | | |
|     Household Size | 156 | 155 |
|     Female Headship | 157 | 155 |
|     Occupations | 157 | 156 |
|     Income | 157 | 155 |
| Topics of Special Interest in the Detroit Region | | |
|     Unemployment | 158 | 156 |
|     Mean Family Income | 158 | 156 |
|     Negroes | 158 | 157 |
|     Neighborhood Turnover and Population Change | 158 | 157 |
|     Households without Automobiles | 158 | 158 |

## Chapter 18 Minneapolis-St. Paul

| | Text | Maps |
|---|---|---|
| The Place | | |
|     Relief | 159 | 160 |
|     Generalized Land Use | 160 | 160 |
| Housing | | |
|     Housing Age | 160 | 160 |
|     Mobile Homes | 163 | 161 |
|     Single-Unit Detached Housing | 163 | 161 |
|     Housing Value and Rent | 163 | 161 |
| The People | | |
|     Population Density | 163 | 162 |
|     Age and the Elderly | 164 | 162 |
|     Sex Ratio | 164 | 162 |
|     Negroes | 164 | 163 |
|     Spanish-Americans | 164 | 163 |
|     American Indians | 164 | 163 |
| Socioeconomic Characteristics | | |
|     Household Size | 165 | 164 |
|     Female Headship | 165 | 164 |
|     Occupations | 165 | 165 |
|     Income | 166 | 165 |
| Topics of Special Interest in the Twin Cities Region | | |
|     Population Turnover | 166 | 166 |
|     Public Transportation Use | 166 | 166 |
|     Population Density | 166 | 167 |
|     Households without Automobiles | 167 | 167 |
|     Low-Income Home Owners | 167 | 167 |

## Chapter 19 Seattle

| | Text | Maps |
|---|---|---|
| The Place | | |
|     Relief | 169 | 169 |
|     Generalized Land Use | 169 | 169 |
| Housing | | |
|     Housing Age | 169 | 170 |
|     Mobile Homes | 171 | 169 |
|     Single-Unit Detached Housing | 171 | 170 |
|     Housing Value and Rent | 171 | 171 |
| The People | | |
|     Population Density | 171 | 172 |
|     Age and the Elderly | 173 | 172 |
|     Sex Ratio | 174 | 172 |
|     Negroes | 174 | 173 |
|     Spanish-Americans | 174 | 173 |
|     American Indians | 175 | 173 |

|  | Text | Maps |
|---|---|---|
| Chinese-Americans | 176 | 174 |
| Japanese-Americans | 176 | 174 |
| Socioeconomic Characteristics | | |
|   Household Size | 176 | 175 |
|   Female Headship | 176 | 175 |
|   Occupations | 177 | 176 |
|   Income | 178 | 175 |
| Topics of Special Interest in the Seattle Region | | |
|   Poverty | 178 | 177 |
|   Income from Public Sources | 179 | 178 |
|   Population Change | 179 | 178 |
|   Negroes | 179 | 178 |

## D. Twentieth-Century Cities

### Chapter 20 Dallas-Fort Worth

|  | Text | Maps |
|---|---|---|
| The Place | | |
|   Relief | 182 | 182 |
| Housing | | |
|   Housing Age | 182 | 183 |
|   Mobile Homes | 186 | 184 |
|   Single-Unit Detached Housing | 186 | 184 |
|   Housing Value and Rent | 186 | 185 |
| The People | | |
|   Population Density | 186 | 186 |
|   Age and the Elderly | 187 | 188 |
|   Sex Ratio | 187 | 187 |
|   Negroes | 189 | 189 |
|   Spanish-Americans | 189 | 190 |
|   American Indians | 189 | 190 |
| Socioeconomic Characteristics | | |
|   Household Size | 191 | 191 |
|   Female Headship | 191 | 192 |
|   Occupations | 191 | 193 |
|   Income | 192 | 194 |
| Topics of Special Interest in the Dallas-Fort Worth Region | | |
|   Negroes and Negroes in New Housing | 192 | 194-195 |
|   Spanish-Americans | 192 | 195 |
|   Income Deficit | 196 | 196 |

### Chapter 21 Houston

|  | Text | Maps |
|---|---|---|
| The Place | | |
|   Relief | 200 | 198 |
|   Generalized Land Use | 200 | 198 |
| Housing | | |
|   Housing Age | 202 | 199-200 |
|   Mobile Homes | 203 | 201 |
|   Single-Unit Detached Housing | 203 | 201 |
|   Housing Value and Rent | 205 | 202-203 |
| The People | | |
|   Population Density | 206 | 204 |
|   Age and the Elderly | 208 | 205-206 |
|   Sex Ratio | 209 | 204 |
|   Negroes | 209 | 207 |
|   Spanish-Americans | 209 | 207 |
|   Mexican-Americans | 210 | 208 |
| Socioeconomic Characteristics | | |
|   Household Size | 211 | 209 |
|   Female Headship | 211 | 210 |
|   Occupations | 212 | 211-212 |
|   Income | 213 | 213 |
| Topics of Special Interest in the Houston Region | | |
|   Population Change, 1960-1970 | 213 | 214 |
|   Residential Change and New Housing | 214 | 215-216 |
|   Negroes and Spanish-Americans | 214 | 217 |
|   Poverty | 215 | 218 |

### Chapter 22 Los Angeles

|  | Text | Maps |
|---|---|---|
| The Place | | |
|   Relief | 219 | 220 |
|   Generalized Land Use | 222 | 221 |
| Housing | | |
|   Housing Age | 223 | 222 |
|   Mobile Homes | 224 | 221 |
|   Single-Unit Detached Housing | 224 | 221 |
|   Housing Value and Rent | 224 | 223 |
| The People | | |
|   Population Density | 224 | 225 |
|   Age and the Elderly | 224 | 226 |
|   Sex Ratio | 224 | 226 |
|   Negroes | 224 | 228 |
|   Spanish-Americans | 227 | 229 |
|   Mexican-Americans | 227 | 227 |
|   American Indians | 227 | 227 |
|   Chinese-Americans | 227 | 230 |
|   Japanese-Americans | 230 | 230 |
|   Canadian-Americans | 230 | 231 |
|   German-Americans | 230 | 231 |
|   Russian-Americans | 230 | 231 |
|   Italian-Americans | 230 | 232 |
| Socioeconomic Characteristics | | |
|   Household Size | 232 | 233 |
|   Female Headship | 232 | 233 |
|   Occupations | 232 | 234 |
|   Income | 232 | 233 |
| Topics of Special Interest in the Los Angeles-Long Beach Region | | |
|   Residential Turnover | 232 | 235 |
|   Public Transportation Use | 232 | 235 |
|   Households without Automobiles | 232 | 235 |
|   Spanish-Americans | 234 | 236 |
|   The Poverty Population | 234 | 236 |

### Chapter 23 Miami

|  | Text | Maps |
|---|---|---|
| The Place | | |
|   Relief | 237 | 238 |
| Housing | | |
|   Housing Age | 238 | 238 |
|   Mobile Homes | 239 | 238 |
|   Single-Unit Detached Housing | 239 | 239 |
|   Housing Value and Rent | 240 | 239 |
| The People | | |
|   Population Density | 240 | 240 |
|   Age and the Elderly | 241 | 240 |
|   Sex Ratio | 241 | 241 |
|   Negroes | 241 | 242 |
|   Spanish-Americans | 241 | 242 |
|   Cuban-Americans | 242 | 243 |
|   Jews | 242 | 243 |
| Socioeconomic Characteristics | | |
|   Household Size | 242 | 244 |
|   Female Headship | 242 | 244 |
|   Occupations | 243 | 244 |
|   Income | 243 | 244 |

## Contents

|  | Text | Maps |
|---|---|---|
| Topics of Special Interest in the Miami Region | | |
| Negroes | 243 | 245 |
| Spanish-Americans | 243 | 246 |
| Poverty | 245 | 246 |
| Crowded Housing | 245 | 246 |
| **Chapter 24 Atlanta** | | |
| The Place | | |
| Relief | 247 | 248 |
| Generalized Land Use | 249 | 248 |
| Housing | | |
| Housing Age | 249 | 248 |
| Mobile Homes | 249 | 248 |
| Single-Unit Detached Housing | 249 | 249 |
| Housing Value and Rent | 250 | 249 |
| The People | | |
| Population Density | 251 | 250 |
| Age and the Elderly | 251 | 250 |
| Sex Ratio | 251 | 250 |
| Negroes | 251 | 251 |
| Spanish-Americans | 252 | 251 |
| Socioeconomic Characteristics | | |
| Household Size | 252 | 252 |
| Female Headship | 252 | 252 |
| Occupations | 252 | 253 |
| Income | 253 | 253 |
| Topics of Special Interest in the Atlanta Region | | |
| Income from Public Sources | 253 | 254 |
| 20- and 21-Year Olds in School | 254 | 254 |
| Residential Change | 254 | 254 |
| Crowded Housing | 254 | 255 |
| Single-Unit Detached Housing | 254 | 255 |
| Households without Automobiles | 255 | 255 |
| **Chapter 25 Washington, D.C.** | | |
| The Place | | |
| Relief | 256 | 257 |
| Generalized Land Use | 257 | 257 |
| Housing | | |
| Housing Age | 259 | 258 |
| Mobile Homes | 260 | 257 |
| Single-Unit Detached Housing | 260 | 257 |
| Housing Value and Rent | 261 | 258 |
| The People | | |
| Population Density | 261 | 259 |
| Age and the Elderly | 262 | 259 |
| Sex Ratio | 262 | 260 |
| Negroes | 263 | 260 |
| Spanish-Americans | 263 | 260 |
| Chinese-Americans | 263 | 260 |
| Socioeconomic Characteristics | | |
| Household Size | 264 | 261 |
| Female Headship | 264 | 261 |
| Occupations | 265 | 262 |
| Income | 265 | 262 |
| Topics of Special Interest in the Washington Region | | |
| Negroes | 265 | 263 |
| Crowded Housing | 265 | 263 |
| Income Deficit | 265 | 264 |
| Commuting to the Central-City Area | 265 | 264 |

|  | Text | Maps |
|---|---|---|
| **Part III: Metropolitan Problems: Similarities and Differences among Metropolitan Regions** | | |
| **A. Metropolitan Physical Environments** | | |
| **Chapter 26 Private Water Supplies** | | |
| Boston | 267 | 268 |
| New York-Northern New Jersey | 267 | 268 |
| Philadelphia | 267 | 268 |
| Hartford-Connecticut Valley | 268 | 268 |
| Baltimore | 268 | 269 |
| New Orleans | 268 | 269 |
| San Francisco-Oakland | 268 | 269 |
| Pittsburgh | 268 | 270 |
| St. Louis | 268 | 270 |
| Cleveland | 269 | 270 |
| Chicago | 269 | 270 |
| Detroit | 269 | 270 |
| Minneapolis-St. Paul | 269 | 271 |
| Seattle | 269 | 271 |
| Dallas-Fort Worth | 269 | 271 |
| Houston | 270 | 271 |
| Los Angeles | 270 | 272 |
| Miami | 270 | 272 |
| Atlanta | 271 | 272 |
| Washington, D.C. | 272 | 272 |
| **Chapter 27 Private Sewage Disposal** | | |
| Boston | 273 | 274 |
| New York-Northern New Jersey | 273 | 274 |
| Philadelphia | 273 | 274 |
| Hartford-Connecticut Valley | 273 | 274 |
| Baltimore | 274 | 275 |
| New Orleans | 274 | 275 |
| San Francisco-Oakland | 274 | 275 |
| Pittsburgh | 274 | 276 |
| St. Louis | 274 | 276 |
| Cleveland | 275 | 276 |
| Chicago | 275 | 276 |
| Detroit | 275 | 276 |
| Minneapolis-St. Paul | 275 | 277 |
| Seattle | 275 | 277 |
| Dallas-Fort Worth | 275 | 277 |
| Houston | 275 | 277 |
| Los Angeles | 276 | 278 |
| Miami | 276 | 278 |
| Atlanta | 277 | 278 |
| Washington, D.C. | 278 | 278 |
| **B. Open Space for Metropolitan Leisure-Time Use** | | |
| **Chapter 28 Seasonal Housing Units** | | |
| Boston | 279 | 280 |
| New York-Northern New Jersey | 279 | 280 |
| Philadelphia | 280 | 280 |
| Hartford-Connecticut Valley | 280 | 280 |
| Baltimore | 280 | 281 |
| New Orleans | 280 | 281 |
| San Francisco-Oakland | 280 | 281 |
| Pittsburgh | 281 | 282 |
| St. Louis | 281 | 282 |
| Cleveland | 281 | 282 |
| Chicago | 281 | 282 |
| Detroit | 281 | 282 |

|  | Text | Maps |
|---|---|---|
| Minneapolis-St. Paul | 281 | 283 |
| Seattle | 282 | 283 |
| Dallas-Fort Worth | 282 | 283 |
| Houston | 282 | 283 |
| Los Angeles | 283 | 284 |
| Miami | 284 | 284 |
| Atlanta | 284 | 284 |
| Washington, D.C. | 284 | 284 |

### C. Housing in Metropolitan Areas

**Chapter 29 Crowded Housing**

|  | Text | Maps |
|---|---|---|
| Boston | 285 | 286 |
| New York-Northern New Jersey | 285 | 286 |
| Philadelphia | 285 | 286 |
| Hartford | 285 | 286 |
| Baltimore | 287 | 287 |
| New Orleans | 287 | 287 |
| San Francisco-Oakland | 288 | 287 |
| Pittsburgh | 288 | 288 |
| St. Louis | 288 | 288 |
| Cleveland | 288 | 289 |
| Chicago | 288 | 289 |
| Detroit | 289 | 289 |
| Minneapolis-St. Paul | 289 | 290 |
| Seattle | 289 | 290 |
| Dallas-Fort Worth | 289 | 290 |
| Houston | 291 | 291 |
| Los Angeles | 291 | 292 |
| Miami | 291 | 292 |
| Atlanta | 291 | 292 |
| Washington, D.C. | 291 | 292 |

**Chapter 30 Rent in Relation to Income**

|  | Text | Maps |
|---|---|---|
| Boston | 293 | 294 |
| New York-Northern New Jersey | 293 | 294 |
| Philadelphia | 293 | 294 |
| Hartford | 295 | 294 |
| Baltimore | 295 | 295 |
| New Orleans | 296 | 295 |
| San Francisco-Oakland | 296 | 295 |
| Pittsburgh | 296 | 296 |
| St. Louis | 296 | 296 |
| Cleveland | 296 | 297 |
| Chicago | 297 | 297 |
| Detroit | 297 | 297 |
| Minneapolis-St. Paul | 297 | 298 |
| Seattle | 297 | 298 |
| Dallas-Fort Worth | 299 | 298 |
| Houston | 299 | 299 |
| Los Angeles | 299 | 300 |
| Miami | 299 | 300 |
| Atlanta | 299 | 300 |
| Washington, D.C. | 299 | 300 |

**Chapter 31 Housing Value and Income**

|  | Text | Maps |
|---|---|---|
| Boston | 301 | 302 |
| New York-Northern New Jersey | 301 | 302 |
| Philadelphia | 301 | 302 |
| Hartford | 304 | 302 |
| Baltimore | 304 | 303 |
| New Orleans | 304 | 303 |
| San Francisco-Oakland | 304 | 303 |
| Pittsburgh | 304 | 304 |
| St. Louis | 305 | 304 |
| Cleveland | 305 | 305 |
| Chicago | 305 | 305 |
| Detroit | 305 | 305 |
| Minneapolis-St. Paul | 305 | 305 |
| Seattle | 305 | 306 |
| Dallas-Fort Worth | 307 | 306 |
| Houston | 307 | 307 |
| Los Angeles | 307 | 308 |
| Miami | 307 | 308 |
| Atlanta | 307 | 308 |
| Washington, D.C. | 307 | 308 |

### D. Transportation and Communication

**Chapter 32 Population Density**

|  | Text | Maps |
|---|---|---|
| Boston | 309 | 310 |
| New York-Northern New Jersey | 309 | 310 |
| Philadelphia | 309 | 310 |
| Hartford | 309 | 310 |
| Baltimore | 312 | 311 |
| New Orleans | 312 | 311 |
| San Francisco-Oakland | 312 | 311 |
| Pittsburgh | 312 | 312 |
| St. Louis | 312 | 312 |
| Cleveland | 313 | 313 |
| Chicago | 313 | 313 |
| Detroit | 313 | 313 |
| Minneapolis-St. Paul | 313 | 314 |
| Seattle | 313 | 314 |
| Dallas-Fort Worth | 313 | 314 |
| Houston | 313 | 315 |
| Los Angeles | 315 | 316 |
| Miami | 315 | 316 |
| Atlanta | 315 | 316 |
| Washington, D.C. | 315 | 316 |

**Chapter 33 Working in the Central Business District**

|  | Text | Maps |
|---|---|---|
| Boston | 317 | 318 |
| New York-Northern New Jersey | 317 | 318 |
| Philadelphia | 317 | 318 |
| Hartford | 317 | 318 |
| Baltimore | 317 | 319 |
| New Orleans | 320 | 319 |
| San Francisco-Oakland | 320 | 319 |
| Pittsburgh | 320 | 320 |
| St. Louis | 320 | 320 |
| Cleveland | 320 | 321 |
| Chicago | 321 | 321 |
| Detroit | 321 | 321 |
| Minneapolis-St. Paul | 321 | 322 |
| Seattle | 321 | 322 |
| Dallas-Fort Worth | 321 | 322 |
| Houston | 323 | 323 |
| Los Angeles | 323 | 324 |
| Miami | 323 | 324 |
| Atlanta | 323 | 324 |
| Washington, D.C. | 323 | 324 |

**Chapter 34 Public Transportation to Work**

|  | Text | Maps |
|---|---|---|
| Boston | 325 | 326 |
| New York-Northern New Jersey | 325 | 326 |
| Philadelphia | 325 | 326 |
| Hartford | 328 | 326 |
| Baltimore | 328 | 327 |
| New Orleans | 328 | 327 |

Contents

|  | Text | Maps |
|---|---|---|
| San Francisco-Oakland | 328 | 327 |
| Pittsburgh | 328 | 328 |
| St. Louis | 328 | 328 |
| Cleveland | 328 | 329 |
| Chicago | 329 | 329 |
| Detroit | 329 | 329 |
| Minneapolis-St. Paul | 329 | 330 |
| Seattle | 329 | 330 |
| Dallas-Fort Worth | 331 | 330 |
| Houston | 331 | 331 |
| Los Angeles | 331 | 332 |
| Miami | 331 | 332 |
| Atlanta | 331 | 332 |
| Washington, D.C. | 331 | 332 |

Chapter 35 Households without Automobiles
| | | |
|---|---|---|
| Boston | 333 | 334 |
| New York-Northern New Jersey | 333 | 334 |
| Philadelphia | 333 | 334 |
| Hartford | 335 | 334 |
| Baltimore | 336 | 335 |
| New Orleans | 336 | 335 |
| San Francisco-Oakland | 336 | 335 |
| Pittsburgh | 336 | 336 |
| St. Louis | 336 | 336 |
| Cleveland | 336 | 337 |
| Chicago | 337 | 337 |
| Detroit | 337 | 337 |
| Minneapolis-St. Paul | 337 | 338 |
| Seattle | 337 | 338 |
| Dallas-Fort Worth | 339 | 338 |
| Houston | 339 | 339 |
| Los Angeles | 339 | 340 |
| Miami | 339 | 340 |
| Atlanta | 339 | 340 |
| Washington, D.C. | 339 | 340 |

Chapter 36 Households without Telephones
| | | |
|---|---|---|
| Boston | 341 | 342 |
| New York-Northern New Jersey | 341 | 342 |
| Philadelphia | 341 | 342 |
| Hartford | 341 | 342 |
| Baltimore | 341 | 343 |
| New Orleans | 344 | 343 |
| San Francisco-Oakland | 344 | 343 |
| Pittsburgh | 344 | 344 |
| St. Louis | 344 | 344 |
| Cleveland | 344 | 345 |
| Chicago | 344 | 345 |
| Detroit | 345 | 345 |
| Minneapolis-St. Paul | 345 | 346 |
| Seattle | 345 | 346 |
| Dallas-Fort Worth | 345 | 346 |
| Houston | 347 | 347 |
| Los Angeles | 347 | 348 |
| Miami | 347 | 348 |
| Atlanta | 347 | 348 |
| Washington, D.C. | 347 | 348 |

**E. Metropolitan Growth**

Chapter 37 Population Change, 1960-1970
| | | |
|---|---|---|
| Boston | 349 | 350 |
| New York-Northern New Jersey | 349 | 350 |
| Philadelphia | 349 | 350 |

|  | Text | Maps |
|---|---|---|
| Hartford | 349 | 350 |
| Baltimore | 352 | 351 |
| New Orleans | 352 | 351 |
| San Francisco-Oakland | 352 | 351 |
| Pittsburgh | 352 | 352 |
| St. Louis | 352 | 352 |
| Cleveland | 352 | 353 |
| Chicago | 353 | 353 |
| Detroit | 353 | 353 |
| Minneapolis-St. Paul | 353 | 354 |
| Seattle | 353 | 354 |
| Dallas-Fort Worth | 355 | 354 |
| Houston | 355 | 355 |
| Los Angeles | 355 | 356 |
| Miami | 355 | 356 |
| Atlanta | 355 | 356 |
| Washington, D.C. | 355 | 356 |

**F. Education**

Chapter 38 Parochial School Enrollment
| | | |
|---|---|---|
| Boston | 357 | 358 |
| New York City | 357 | 358 |
| Philadelphia | 357 | 358 |
| Hartford | 357 | 358 |
| Baltimore | 359 | 359 |
| New Orleans | 359 | 359 |
| San Francisco-Oakland | 359 | 359 |
| Pittsburgh | 359 | 360 |
| St. Louis | 359 | 360 |
| Cleveland | 359 | 360 |
| Chicago | 361 | 360 |
| Detroit | 361 | 361 |
| Minneapolis-St. Paul | 361 | 361 |
| Seattle | 361 | 361 |
| Dallas | 361 | 362 |
| Houston | 361 | 362 |
| Los Angeles | 361 | 363 |
| Miami | 364 | 364 |
| Atlanta | 364 | 364 |
| Washington, D.C. | 364 | 364 |

Chapter 39 20- and 21-Year-Olds in School
| | | |
|---|---|---|
| Boston | 365 | 366 |
| New York-Northern New Jersey | 365 | 366 |
| Philadelphia | 365 | 366 |
| Hartford | 365 | 366 |
| Baltimore | 365 | 367 |
| New Orleans | 368 | 367 |
| San Francisco-Oakland | 368 | 367 |
| Pittsburgh | 368 | 368 |
| St. Louis | 368 | 368 |
| Cleveland | 368 | 369 |
| Chicago | 368 | 369 |
| Detroit | 369 | 369 |
| Minneapolis-St. Paul | 369 | 370 |
| Seattle | 369 | 370 |
| Dallas-Fort Worth | 371 | 370 |
| Houston | 371 | 371 |
| Los Angeles | 371 | 372 |
| Miami | 371 | 372 |
| Atlanta | 371 | 372 |
| Washington, D.C. | 371 | 372 |

xx

|  | Text | Maps |
|---|---|---|
| **G. Public Health** | | |
| Chapter 40  Immature Births | | |
| Boston | 373 | 374 |
| New York City | 373 | 374 |
| Philadelphia | 373 | 374 |
| Hartford | 373 | 374 |
| Baltimore | 375 | 375 |
| New Orleans | 375 | 375 |
| San Francisco-Oakland | 375 | 375 |
| Pittsburgh | 375 | 376 |
| St. Louis | 375 | 376 |
| Cleveland | 375 | 376 |
| Chicago | 377 | 376 |
| Detroit | 377 | 377 |
| Minneapolis-St. Paul | 377 | 377 |
| Seattle | 377 | 377 |
| Dallas | 377 | 378 |
| Houston | 377 | 378 |
| Los Angeles | 377 | 379 |
| Miami | 377 | 380 |
| Atlanta | 377 | 380 |
| Washington, D.C. | 380 | 380 |
| **H. Socioeconomic Segregation** | | |
| Chapter 41  Negroes and New Single-Family Housing | | |
| Boston | 381 | 382 |
| New York-Northern New Jersey | 381 | 382 |
| Philadelphia | 383 | 382 |
| Hartford | 383 | 382 |
| Baltimore | 383 | 383 |
| New Orleans | 384 | 383 |
| San Francisco-Oakland | 384 | 383 |
| Pittsburgh | 384 | 384 |
| St. Louis | 384 | 384 |
| Cleveland | 384 | 385 |
| Chicago | 385 | 385 |
| Detroit | 385 | 385 |
| Minneapolis-St. Paul | 385 | 386 |
| Seattle | 387 | 386 |
| Dallas-Fort Worth | 387 | 386 |
| Houston | 387 | 387 |
| Los Angeles | 387 | 388 |
| Miami | 387 | 388 |
| Atlanta | 387 | 388 |
| Washington, D.C. | 387 | 388 |
| Chapter 42  Spanish-Americans | | |
| Boston | 389 | 390 |
| New York-Northern New Jersey | 389 | 390 |
| Philadelphia | 389 | 390 |
| Hartford | 389 | 390 |
| Baltimore | 389 | 391 |
| New Orleans | 389 | 391 |
| San Francisco-Oakland | 391 | 391 |
| Pittsburgh | 391 | 392 |
| St. Louis | 391 | 392 |
| Cleveland | 392 | 393 |
| Chicago | 392 | 393 |
| Detroit | 392 | 393 |
| Minneapolis-St. Paul | 392 | 394 |
| Seattle | 392 | 394 |
| Dallas-Fort Worth | 393 | 394 |
| Houston | 393 | 395 |

|  | Text | Maps |
|---|---|---|
| Los Angeles | 393 | 396 |
| Miami | 395 | 396 |
| Atlanta | 395 | 396 |
| Washington, D.C. | 395 | 396 |
| **I. Employment and Poverty** | | |
| Chapter 43  Females in the Labor Force | | |
| Boston | 397 | 398 |
| New York-Northern New Jersey | 397 | 398 |
| Philadelphia | 397 | 398 |
| Hartford | 397 | 398 |
| Baltimore | 397 | 399 |
| New Orleans | 399 | 399 |
| San Francisco-Oakland | 399 | 399 |
| Pittsburgh | 400 | 400 |
| St. Louis | 400 | 400 |
| Cleveland | 400 | 401 |
| Chicago | 400 | 401 |
| Detroit | 400 | 401 |
| Minneapolis-St. Paul | 400 | 402 |
| Seattle | 403 | 402 |
| Dallas-Fort Worth | 403 | 402 |
| Houston | 403 | 403 |
| Los Angeles | 403 | 404 |
| Miami | 403 | 404 |
| Atlanta | 403 | 404 |
| Washington, D.C. | 403 | 404 |
| Chapter 44  Unemployed Males | | |
| Boston | 405 | 406 |
| New York-Northern New Jersey | 405 | 406 |
| Philadelphia | 405 | 406 |
| Hartford | 405 | 406 |
| Baltimore | 407 | 407 |
| New Orleans | 408 | 407 |
| San Francisco-Oakland | 408 | 407 |
| Pittsburgh | 408 | 408 |
| St. Louis | 408 | 408 |
| Cleveland | 408 | 409 |
| Chicago | 408 | 409 |
| Detroit | 409 | 409 |
| Minneapolis-St. Paul | 409 | 410 |
| Seattle | 409 | 410 |
| Dallas-Fort Worth | 409 | 410 |
| Houston | 411 | 411 |
| Los Angeles | 411 | 412 |
| Miami | 411 | 412 |
| Atlanta | 411 | 412 |
| Washington, D.C. | 411 | 412 |
| Chapter 45  The Poverty Population | | |
| Boston | 413 | 414 |
| New York-Northern New Jersey | 413 | 414 |
| Philadelphia | 413 | 414 |
| Hartford | 413 | 414 |
| Baltimore | 415 | 415 |
| New Orleans | 415 | 415 |
| San Francisco-Oakland | 416 | 415 |
| Pittsburgh | 416 | 416 |
| St. Louis | 416 | 416 |
| Cleveland | 416 | 417 |
| Chicago | 416 | 417 |
| Detroit | 416 | 417 |
| Minneapolis-St. Paul | 417 | 418 |

# Contents

|  | Text | Maps |
|---|---|---|
| Seattle | 417 | 418 |
| Dallas-Fort Worth | 417 | 418 |
| Houston | 417 | 419 |
| Los Angeles | 419 | 420 |
| Miami | 419 | 420 |
| Atlanta | 419 | 420 |
| Washington, D.C. | 419 | 420 |

**Chapter 46 Income from Public Payments**

|  | Text | Maps |
|---|---|---|
| Boston | 421 | 422 |
| New York-Northern New Jersey | 421 | 422 |
| Philadelphia | 421 | 422 |
| Hartford | 421 | 422 |
| Baltimore | 421 | 423 |
| New Orleans | 421 | 423 |
| San Francisco-Oakland | 423 | 423 |
| Pittsburgh | 424 | 424 |
| St. Louis | 424 | 424 |
| Cleveland | 424 | 425 |
| Chicago | 424 | 425 |
| Detroit | 424 | 425 |
| Minneapolis-St. Paul | 424 | 426 |
| Seattle | 425 | 426 |
| Dallas-Fort Worth | 425 | 426 |
| Houston | 425 | 427 |
| Los Angeles | 427 | 428 |
| Miami | 427 | 428 |
| Atlanta | 427 | 428 |
| Washington, D.C. | 427 | 428 |

**Chapter 47 Income Deficits**

|  | Text | Maps |
|---|---|---|
| Boston | 429 | 430 |
| New York-Northern New Jersey | 429 | 430 |
| Philadelphia | 429 | 430 |
| Hartford | 429 | 430 |
| Baltimore | 431 | 431 |
| New Orleans | 432 | 431 |
| San Francisco-Oakland | 432 | 431 |
| Pittsburgh | 432 | 432 |
| St. Louis | 432 | 432 |
| Cleveland | 433 | 433 |
| Chicago | 433 | 433 |
| Detroit | 433 | 433 |
| Minneapolis-St. Paul | 433 | 434 |
| Seattle | 433 | 434 |
| Dallas-Fort Worth | 433 | 434 |
| Houston | 435 | 435 |
| Los Angeles | 435 | 436 |
| Miami | 435 | 436 |
| Atlanta | 435 | 436 |
| Washington, D.C. | 435 | 436 |

## J. Urban Renewal and Redevelopment

**Chapter 48 Long-Term Housing Vacancies**

|  | Text | Maps |
|---|---|---|
| Boston | 439 | 438 |
| New York City | 439 | 438 |
| Philadelphia | 439 | 438 |
| Hartford | 439 | 438 |
| Baltimore | 439 | 439 |
| New Orleans | 439 | 439 |
| San Francisco-Oakland | 440 | 439 |
| Pittsburgh | 441 | 440 |
| St. Louis | 441 | 440 |
| Cleveland | 441 | 440 |
| Chicago | 441 | 440 |
| Detroit | 441 | 441 |
| Minneapolis-St. Paul | 441 | 441 |
| Seattle | 441 | 441 |
| Dallas | 441 | 442 |
| Houston | 441 | 442 |
| Los Angeles | 444 | 443 |
| Miami | 444 | 444 |
| Atlanta | 444 | 444 |
| Washington, D.C. | 444 | 444 |

## Part IV: Policy Requisites for American Metropolitan Regions

**Chapter 49 National, State, and Local Policy Considerations**

|  | Text |
|---|---|
| The End and the Beginning | 447 |
| The Post-World War II Era Has Ended | 447 |
| . . . But Troublesome Facts Remain | 448 |
| Problems of People vs. Problems of Places | 448 |
| Obstacles to Effective Government Response to Urban Problems | 449 |
| Policy Considerations | 450 |
| Appendixes: A. Location Maps | 456 |
| B. Data Tables for Part II | 471 |
| C. Technical Notes for Cartographers | 477 |
| Glossary | 485 |
| Index/Gazetteer | 493 |

# PART I

# INTRODUCTION

If we could first know where
we are, and whither we are tending,
we could then better judge what to
do and how to do it.

Abraham Lincoln

# CHAPTER 1

# How to Use the Atlas

This atlas has three purposes. First, it is intended to teach Americans the human geography of the 20 urban areas in which a large fraction of them live (Figure 1.1). Second, the atlas makes it possible for people to make comparisons among the 20 places. Third, and most important of all, the atlas attempts to measure where the nation stood in 1970 with respect to meeting basic human needs in the 20 metropolitan regions.

Cities are like the weather—everybody talks about them, but little is done about them or about the specific issues that provoke discussion. The few attempts to do something substantial have usually backfired because we know little about our cities, great or small. Sam Bass Warner, Jr. puts the matter nicely: "For generations we have dwelt in a self-created urban wilderness of time and space, confounding ourselves with its lusty growth and rising to periodic alarms in the night."[*] We hope our maps provide at least an indication of the way out of the wilderness; they make it possible to study metropolitan areas in a way that has heretofore been impossible. The 45 or more maps assembled here for each of the 20 places are a foundation upon which better urban theory might be built.

Building such knowledge will require that we stop pretending that a city is a city is a city. Few people would confuse Baltimore with Houston. Yet we persist in perpetuating standard mythologies about urban problems and their causes. We also continue—particularly at the federal level—to formulate policies and legislation that apply to Baltimore in the same way they apply to Houston and every other metropolis. Accurate assessments of which places are afflicted by a problem, of variations among the places in the seriousness of the problem, and, most important, of differences in the extent to which a given program might alleviate the problem are prerequisite to intelligent policy making. We have mapped the same phenomena for all 20 places in a way that should help politicians, public officials, businessmen, and scholars design programs and policies that accommodate the individuality as well as the similarities among the nation's metropolitan regions.

People everywhere must have food, water, clothing, shelter, and companionship. They all seek security, good health, knowledge, and recreation. Debates rage over which of these are needs and which are wants, over how much of each is necessary and how much is luxury, and whether some, such as health care, are rights or privileges. Measurements of how well needs and wants are fulfilled vary in availability and quality; there are abundant data on housing characteristics, for example, but no data on crime worth mapping. Within the constraints of available data and the philosophical, conceptual, and practical thickets that surround the definition of, say, an *adequate* income, we have tried to assess the nation's progress toward providing for peoples' needs and wants in metropolitan regions by mapping numerous commonly accepted socioeconomic indicators.

Places and people are the fundamental dimensions of American metropolitan life. The only kind of analysis that will enable policy makers to progress toward the solution of the nation's metropolitan problems is one that is simultaneously sensitive to people, places, and their problems. This atlas tries to describe where we are and whither we are tending, so that those responsible for designing policy can better judge what to do and how to do it.

## THE ORGANIZATION OF THE ATLAS

The atlas is divided into four parts, I through IV. Part I consists of this chapter and four others. They are designed to introduce you first to the atlas and then to some background material about American cities. Designing this atlas raised a host of thorny questions concerning which cities should be included, what topics should be mapped, and how the maps should be made. Part I addresses these questions. In Chapter 2 we provide the rationale for choosing 20 places out of the many we could have selected. How the American metropolitan network developed and how the 20 areas we have included interact with other places in the nation are described in Chapter 3. Comments on the myth and reality of the nation's urban problems, with specific reference to different definitions of what constitutes a problem, are made in Chapter 4. In Chapter 5 we survey sources of information on American cities and describe the data sources used to produce the atlas maps.

A great deal of careful thought has gone into the general design of the atlas, the ways in which the maps and text have been put together, and the mapping techniques described below. Chapter 1 is especially important because it contains a description of the cartographic conventions used in the atlas proper.

Readers who have a good grasp of the nation's settlement history and metropolitan evolution may not find it necessary to read Chapters 2 and 3, although a glance at the illustrations should be worthwhile. Likewise, Chapters 4 and 5 will be review material for those who are up-to-date on urban issues and on the limitations of U.S. Census data. These chapters will help the reader avoid reading too much into the maps.

Part II of the atlas contains 20 chapters, one for each of the 20 areas. Information is provided about problems people have *at places* by bringing together 27 or more maps for each area. Each chapter is divided into four sections. The first includes maps of terrain, land use, and housing characteristics. In the second section the people are described in terms of population density, age-sex structure, and racial and ethnic composition. The third section focuses on household size, family structure, occupation, and income. The final section consists of individually selected maps that highlight topics of special interest in the particular metropolis. The chapters in Part II are arranged so

---

[*]Sam Bass Warner, Jr. *The Urban Wilderness: A History of the American City.* New York: Harper and Row, 1972, p. 267.

*1*

*How to Use the Atlas*

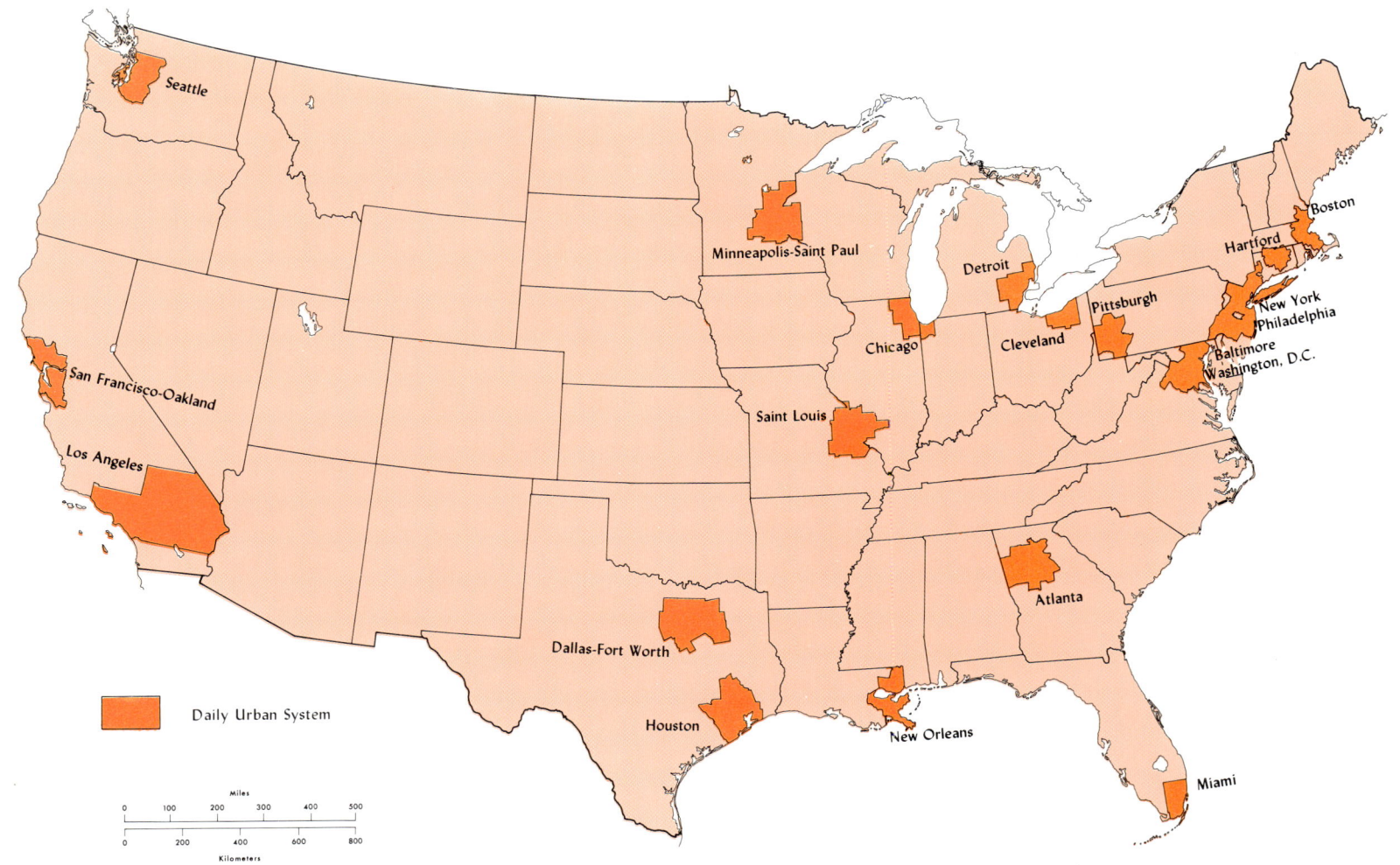

*Figure 1.1. The 20 Largest Daily Urban Systems, 1970.* Each Daily Urban System consists of a central metropolis and the surrounding counties that have at least 5 percent of their labor forces working in the central county or counties. See the glossary for details of the Daily Urban System definition.

that chapters for areas with similar histories (such as Baltimore, New Orleans, and San Francisco) are together. Places with similar histories generally have similar problems, and grouping them in this fashion makes comparisons among similar places easier.

Part III is the truly comparative section. Maps are grouped primarily by topic and only secondarily by area. Part III contains 23 individual map series; each series consists of 20 maps of the same topic, one for each of the 20 metropolitan regions. General topics covered are: metropolitan physical environments, open space, housing, transportation and communication, population change, education, public health, minority-group segregation, employment and poverty, and urban renewal. Part III will be most useful to those concerned with comparing the occurrence and intensity of these problems among the places mapped.

Part IV presents our conclusions. It summarizes what we have learned from the atlas, and how we think our findings bear on public policy making.

## MAPS AND TEXT

The maps and graphs are more than half the atlas, but they are not the whole story. The maps are freestanding. If the reader understands the cartographic conventions, he or she should be able to turn to any map in the atlas and derive a great deal of information directly from the map and its associated histogram. The added time needed to read the commentary is well worth investing, however. The maps and histograms state precisely what is being mapped, but they contain little information about what the variables mean, what inferences can validly be drawn from the maps, and how the information presented on the maps should be qualified.

The commentary in the chapters in Part II forms a running narrative in which each variable mapped and its relation to other variables are discussed. A map of housing age, for example, shows where old housing is located but does not indicate what percentage of the housing stock in the metropolitan area was built before 1940; the fact is given in the text and is important to remember when looking at the pattern of older housing in the city. Also, textual comments on how housing age relates to housing value, another variable that is mapped, may be helpful. The commentary in Part III focuses on the topic as well as on variations among the 20 places. Throughout the commentary there are frequent cross-references to other maps and map series that should be consulted in conjunction with the series being examined. For example, there are several maps of basic housing characteristics in the first section of each chapter in Part II that provide useful background information for the chapters on housing problems in the comparative Part III of the atlas.

The skilled professional who works with maps and census data day in and day out in a planning agency or similar enterprise may find little that is novel in the commentary. Other readers should probably use map and commentary together to obtain optimal yields from the time spent consulting the atlas.

## READING THE MAPS AND DIAGRAMS

Reading maps and graphs productively is not difficult, but it requires some instruction. We have eased the task here by using only a few kinds of maps and common map symbols throughout. More important than learning what the maps say, however, is being aware of what they do not say.

Almost all the maps in the atlas are much like Figure 1.2, the map and histogram of older housing in Boston (they also appear on p. 23). Note, first of all, that the left side of the histogram indicates that census tracts are the basis of the map and histogram. The title below the histogram identifies the specific variable being mapped, for example, the percentage of each tract's total housing stock that was built before 1940. The shape of the histogram is important. In this instance, tracts are spread relatively evenly across the entire range from a single tract in which only 1 percent of the housing was built before 1940 to a cluster of over 100 tracts in which 90 to 100 percent of the housing stock was built before 1940.

The histogram distribution has been divided at 10, 30, 70, and 90 percent, and the areas between these values appear in different shades of orange. In this instance, as in almost all instances, the values of greatest interest are those at the extremes of the range. Tracts containing mostly old housing are more likely to be places where housing is deteriorating than are tracts in which virtually none of the housing is old. In the latter, of course, there may be other problems, such as the payment of high taxes to support schools for the large numbers of school-age children who typically occupy such tracts. In either instance, it is the high or low values that often excite interest and reveal potential problems, although tracts in which 30 to 70 percent of the housing was built before 1940 are also of interest in some places.

The 10-30-70-90 division is used throughout the atlas. The same color scheme is also used throughout. Thus wherever dark orange appears, values are high, and wherever the shading is light, values are low. Some maps, such as those of income, rent, and housing value, are not presented in percentages, but the same scheme applies. High rents are dark orange and lower rents are light orange.

Now the map itself. The map shows the geographical pattern, by tract, of the percentage of housing built before 1940 in the Boston metropolitan area. Isopleths—lines of equal value—connect interpolated points on the map that have the same percentage of housing built before 1940, thereby separating the metropolis into areas above and below those values (10, 30, 70, or 90). There are two critical things to keep in mind concerning this and the other maps in the atlas. First, the

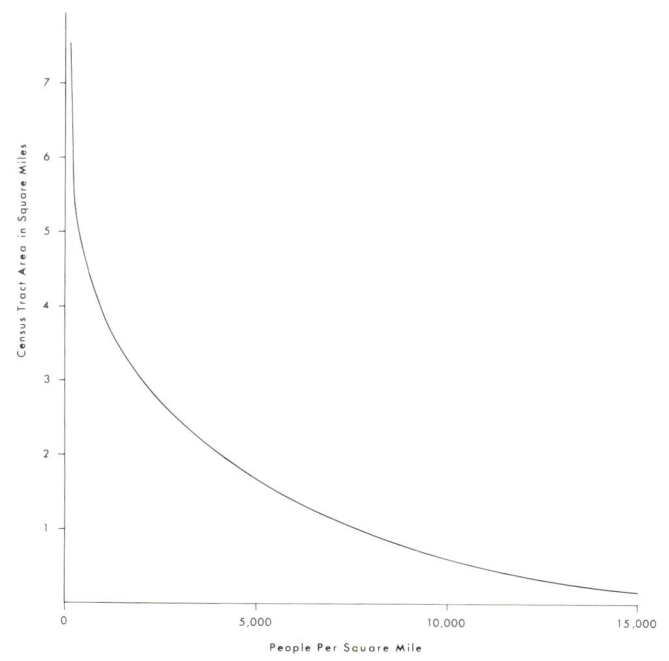

*Figure 1.3. Generalized Relationship between Population Density and Census Tract Area.* Because the Census Bureau tries to keep the populations of census tracts constant (about 4,000 people), census tract areas vary greatly with population density. They are large where population densities are low and small where population densities are high.

maps are highly *generalized*. Within the area shown as having more than 70 percent of its housing built before 1940, for example, there are actually a few tracts in which less than 70 percent of the housing is of that age. Such scattered low values have usually been eliminated when they interrupt generally higher values in areas surrounding them. Because of the small scale of the maps and because we want to simplify comparisons, we have emphasized general patterns rather than fine details throughout the atlas. We believe we have rendered accurate general descriptions of the patterns mapped, but one limitation introduced by generalizing is that no place on any map can be interpreted literally; you cannot put your finger down and say that at that point, over 70 percent or more of the housing was built before 1940. Your finger may have lighted on one of the divergent tracts that was eliminated in the generalization process, or it may be on a cluster of newer housing within a tract in which most of the housing was indeed built before 1940. Either way, the only valid inference that can be made from this and the other maps in the atlas is that the *general* areas, identified by the various shadings, have the values the shadings represent.

The second critical consideration is that tract areas and tract populations vary considerably. In Figure 1.2 areas below 30 percent occupy a large proportion of the map area, whereas the histogram indicates that the number of tracts in that category is small. The disparity occurs because tracts on the outskirts of metropolitan areas are, on the average, much larger than tracts near the centers. Five large tracts at the edge of a city may occupy 20 times the area taken up by 50 tracts at the metropolitan center. Because tract populations also vary (although usually not as widely as tract areas), the 50 central tracts may contain 100 times the population of the 5 peripheral tracts—in fact, tract area is very much a function of population density because the Bureau of the Census attempts to keep populations of tracts relatively constant, allowing area to vary instead (Figure 1.3).

To obtain the correct impression of problems, people, and places, the map and the histogram must be used in close conjunction. Tracts have an average population of 4,000 people, and histograms give a more accurate picture of how many people, households, or housing units have a given characteristic. The map, of course, more effectively shows the locations of characteristics, but the picture it

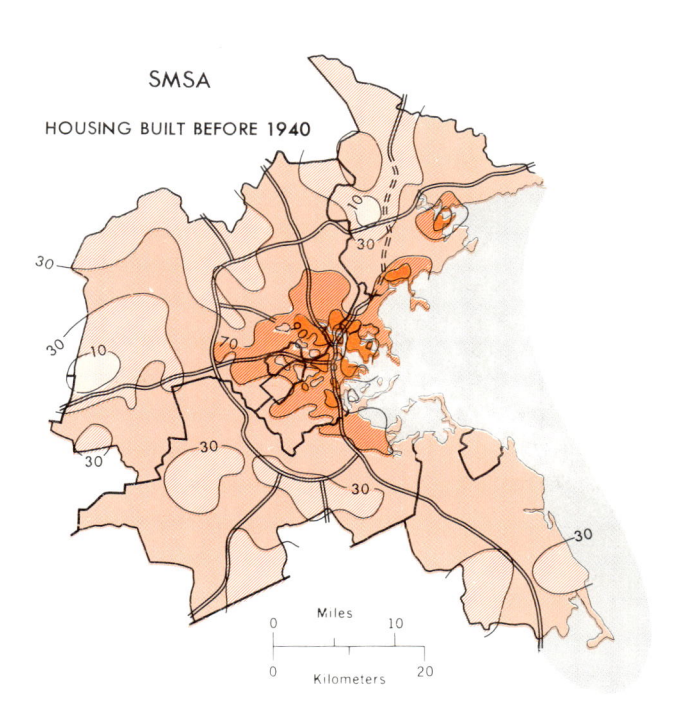

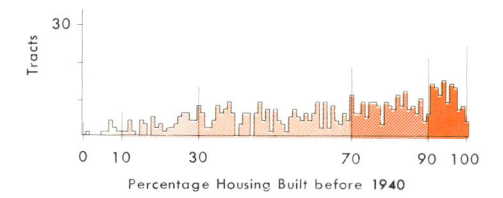

*Figure 1.2. Housing Built before 1940 in the Boston SMSA.* See the accompanying text for an explanation of the cartographic conventions used throughout the atlas.

portrays has to be interpreted in light of what the histogram says about the relative number of people, households, or housing units in each category. A completely false impression of the map may be obtained if map area in each category is equated with the number of people or houses in each category.

Some additional notes on the histograms. The maps of mobile homes in each chapter in Part II and the maps in Chapters 26 to 28 in the comparative section are based on minor civil divisions (cities, villages, townships) rather than census tracts. The units are identified on the vertical scale of the histograms. Histograms are broken when values pile up to the point at which a complete histogram would occupy too much space. The New York histogram on p. 286, for example, would exceed the height of the page if it were not broken. When histograms are broken, additional values are added on the vertical scale to enable readers to estimate the number of tracts omitted.

Finally, information for tracts is sometimes suppressed by the Census Bureau to avoid disclosure of information that might violate the confidentiality of the Census. Suppressions are not usually a problem, but they do affect some variables. The histogram for the map of Spanish-Americans in Philadelphia on p. 54, for example, notes that values for 275 tracts have been suppressed. There are a few Spanish-Americans in each of these 275 tracts, but the number in each is below the suppression threshold (fewer than 6 in this instance) so data are not reported for those tracts. Thus a large number of suppressions indicates there are a few people with the characteristic in each of the suppressed tracts; were there none, the values would be reported as zeros. As a general rule we have not noted suppressions when fewer than 6 tracts are affected. When 6 or more tracts have been suppressed, the number is printed on the histogram. If the number exceeds 20 or 30, the reader should be alert for the effects that the absence of so many tracts may have on his interpretation of the histogram. Generally, suppressions will be mentioned in the commentary when they are important.

Some of the qualifications appropriate to isopleth maps apply also to the dot distribution maps used to show the locations of ethnic groups, income deficits, and housing characteristics. Because the dots represent people, dollars, or houses, some of the possible confusion arising from highly variable population densities among tracts is obviated. But the same caveats about generalization apply. Since one dot may represent 50 Italian-born Americans, 4 or 5 tracts may have to be put together to obtain the 50 people needed to justify putting a dot on the map in areas where there are few Italian-born. When that happens, the dot is placed in the centroid of the aggregated tracts. Thus where dots are sparse, they must be understood to be "spread" over a large area.

Aside from the danger of reading isopleth and dot maps too literally, the atlas presents few conceptual pitfalls. Each chapter in Part II has relief map and a land-use map; both are straightforward. A location map at the beginning of each chapter provides county and city names and highway numbers. In many atlases such information would be repeated on every map. We decided to retain the highway network and political boundaries on all maps but to omit the names. Some maps are quite complicated even though they are generalized; by adding to the general clutter, county names and highway numbers would have further obscured data patterns. Additional locational information will be found in the maps in Appendix A, where the locations of important towns and places within metropolitan regions are mapped.

There are three different kinds of maps for each of the 20 areas. In some instances we have mapped only the central municipality. In others we have mapped the Standard Metropolitan Statistical Area (see Chapter 2 for definition). County names and highway numbers for central-city and SMSA maps are given on the map at the beginning of each chapter. A third metropolitan region, the Daily Urban System (also defined in Chapter 2), is used for the maps of mobile homes in the chapters in Part II and in Chapters 26 to 28 in Part III. Names for counties outside the SMSA but inside the Daily Urban System will be found on the map of mobile homes in the first part of each chapter in Part II. Municipal, county, and state boundaries are shown on atlas maps by lines of differing widths. Boundaries of central cities are shown only on Standard Metropolitan Statistical Area maps where they can be distinguished from county boundaries by the greater thickness of the latter. State boundaries are shown by a heavy broken line on all maps. Only county and state boundaries appear on Daily Urban System maps. Shorelines—indicated by the finest black lines—take precedence where a municipal, county, or state boundary, or some combination thereof, is coincident with the water boundary the shoreline demarcates and where the water body is large enough to be shown in the light gray screen used to identify water. A darker gray screen (see p. 23) is used to show nonresidential areas on the central-city maps of population density in each chapter in Part II.

We shall conclude these prefatory remarks with an important note about scale. Atlas makers frequently fool themselves as much as their readers by using different map scales for maps of different places. To portray correctly the fundamentals of the intersection of people, places, and problems in American metropolitan areas, it must be stressed that some cities have large areas whereas others are small. For that reason, we have maintained a single scale for all central-city maps (1:250,000), another for all SMSA maps (1:1,000,000), and a third for all DUS maps (1:2,000,000). The size differences between Houston and Boston as they are presented in the atlas are enormous but they are accurate.

# CHAPTER 2

# Metropolitan America

Why focus an atlas on 20 places that together comprise less than 5 percent of the nation's territory? America is a metropolitan nation. Two of every three Americans now live in metropolitan areas that occupy only a tenth of the nation's land area. People are concentrated even more in the continuous stretches of built-up areas within metropolitan regions. These areas make up only 1 percent of the nation's territory, but they are home for almost 60 percent of our people.

Population concentrations of this kind are unprecendented in human history, but they are common today in all parts of the world. America is a metropolitan nation in an increasingly metropolitan world. Some problems, such as poverty, would exist whether people congregated in metropolitan areas or not. Other problems, such as those connected with housing, are intensified by the agglomeration of people into large cities and their consequent competition for limited housing. The sheer fact of geographical concentration is threatening and intriguing. No American, regardless of where he or she lives, can afford to be indifferent to the problems and the fortunes of the nation's metropolitan areas.

## THE LAND AND THE PEOPLE

It was not always so. The United States began as a rural nation whose fortunes were far less dependent on the welfare of cities. In 1790, only 5 percent of the nation's people lived in urban places. America's two largest cities, Philadelphia and New York, had only 29,000 and 33,000 people, respectively. Boston took third place with 18,000 inhabitants. By today's standards, such cities are minuscule.

But small cities sufficed for a population huddled along the eastern seaboard. The infant nation made its collective living by farming, so a rural society was inevitable. The proportion of the population in urban places remained below 10 percent until 1840 (Figure 2.1). After 1840 Americans began to urbanize at a steady rate. Interior settlement promoted long-distance trade and related urban services such as warehousing, banking, and shipping. Newly discovered resources and newly developed technologies made manufacturing an important element of many cities' economies. As manufacturing and trade grew and reinforced one another, they produced a general economic expansion that attracted immigrants and fueled continued growth. People follow jobs, and as agricultural productivity increased and fewer people were needed on farms, they sought opportunities in the cities. When new work opportunities diminished in the cities, as they did in the 1870s and 1930s, people stopped coming or returned to the farm temporarily.

Since 1920 white-collar office jobs have expanded more rapidly than the commercial and manufacturing jobs that were mainstays of earlier urban growth. The larger cities that had emerged before 1920 were good locations for conducting the new business of the post-World War II era, and the migration of many young people to urban places during the war ensured that the postwar population boom would increase even more the percentage of the nation's people who lived in large cities. By 1970, three of every four Americans lived in an urban area.

The pattern of urban places resulting from two centuries of growth is uneven (Figure 2.2). The early start and continued advantage of the cities clustered along the Atlantic coast between Boston and Washington are evident in the almost continuous urbanized area between them. Jean Gottmann, suggesting that "metropolis" (mother city) fails to do justice to such an aggregation, called it "Megalopolis" — the great city.* A similar urban belt is emerging between Pittsburgh and Cleveland and extending on to Detroit, Chicago, and Milwaukee. The quadrant of the nation east of the Mississippi and north of the Ohio River and the Pennsylvania-Maryland boundary contains 44 percent of the nation's people.

Elsewhere urbanized areas, cities, and towns are scattered irregularly. Settlement is denser in the Midwest, the South, and along the west coast than it is in the Plains and Mountain states. West of the Mississippi, towns are often strung out along the railroads that originally spawned them. Similar beaded strings connect major midwestern and southern cities. The Pacific Coast states have 13 percent of the nation's population, leaving the remaining 43 percent not living in the Northeast or the Pacific Coast region in the interior West, the west-central area, and the South.

## DEFINING THE METROPOLIS

Clusters of urban places such as Megalopolis present conceptual and practical difficulties to those who monitor problems and change. Cities do not cease growing when they reach municipal boundaries. To cope with early suburbanization, the Census Bureau defined Metropolitan Districts in 1910, each of which consisted of a large city and its environs. Since 1910 Census officials have refined their definitions to make it possible to identify and obtain data for regions that are socially and economically tied to large centers of population. Standard Metropolitan Statistical Areas (SMSAs) were used in the 1960 and 1970 Censuses. As now defined, SMSAs consist of a central population cluster and a surrounding area that is closely linked to that cluster, with a combined population of at least 50,000 people. New SMSAs are established as needed. Given the proportion of the nation's population that is urbanized, SMSAs are distributed much as the population is (Figure 2.3).

SMSAs are useful units for which a good many data are available, but there are drawbacks. For one thing, the SMSAs are greatly disparate in size. In 1970, SMSA populations varied from 11,576,000 in the New York SMSA to 56,000 in the Meriden, Connecticut

*Jean Gottmann, *Megalopolis: The Urbanized Northeastern Seaboard of the United States.* Cambridge: M.I.T. Press, 1964.

*Metropolitan America*

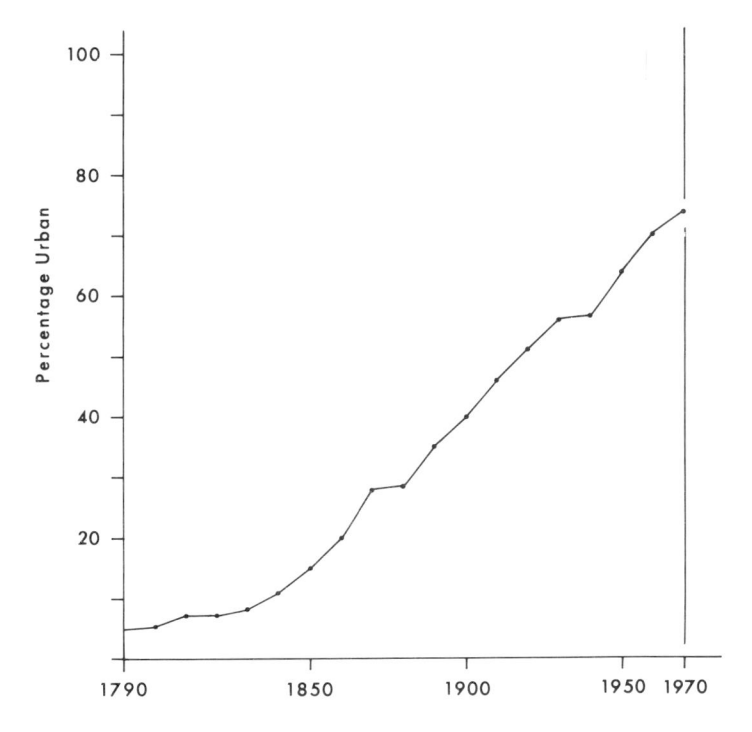

*Figure 2.1. Urbanization in the United States, 1790-1970.* The curve shows the percentage of total population living in towns larger than 2,500 people at each decennial census.

SMSA. Second, SMSAs often contain considerable nonurban territory because their boundaries follow county boundaries. The Duluth-Superior SMSA, for example, extends north to the Canadian border despite the official designation of the northern reaches of St. Louis County, Minnesota as a wilderness area. Finally, and admittedly in sharp contrast to the last point, SMSAs sometimes underbound the true metropolitan community. Outlying counties must be primarily nonagricultural and there must be a large exchange of workers between central counties and outlying counties if the outlying counties are to be included in the SMSA; indeed, a county must send at least 15 percent of its resident workers to a central city to be included in that city's SMSA. Current SMSA definitions understate metropolitan limits most seriously in the eastern states, where SMSAs often abut one another. A single county may be closely tied to more than one SMSA, but it can be included in only one.

Our comments on the defects of SMSA definitions are not meant to be critical of the Census Bureau and the local committees that create SMSAs. The inconsistencies we mention are inescapable consequences of applying a standard definition across a nation as diverse as ours. At the same time, we cannot ignore the conceptual and practical thickets one wanders into when setting out to define cities, gather data about them, and assess their importance in the nation. Quite apart from urban and metropolitan problems themselves, it is hard to formulate appropriate terms and concepts to use when talking about cities and their problems.

Maps often confuse us even more than our terminology does

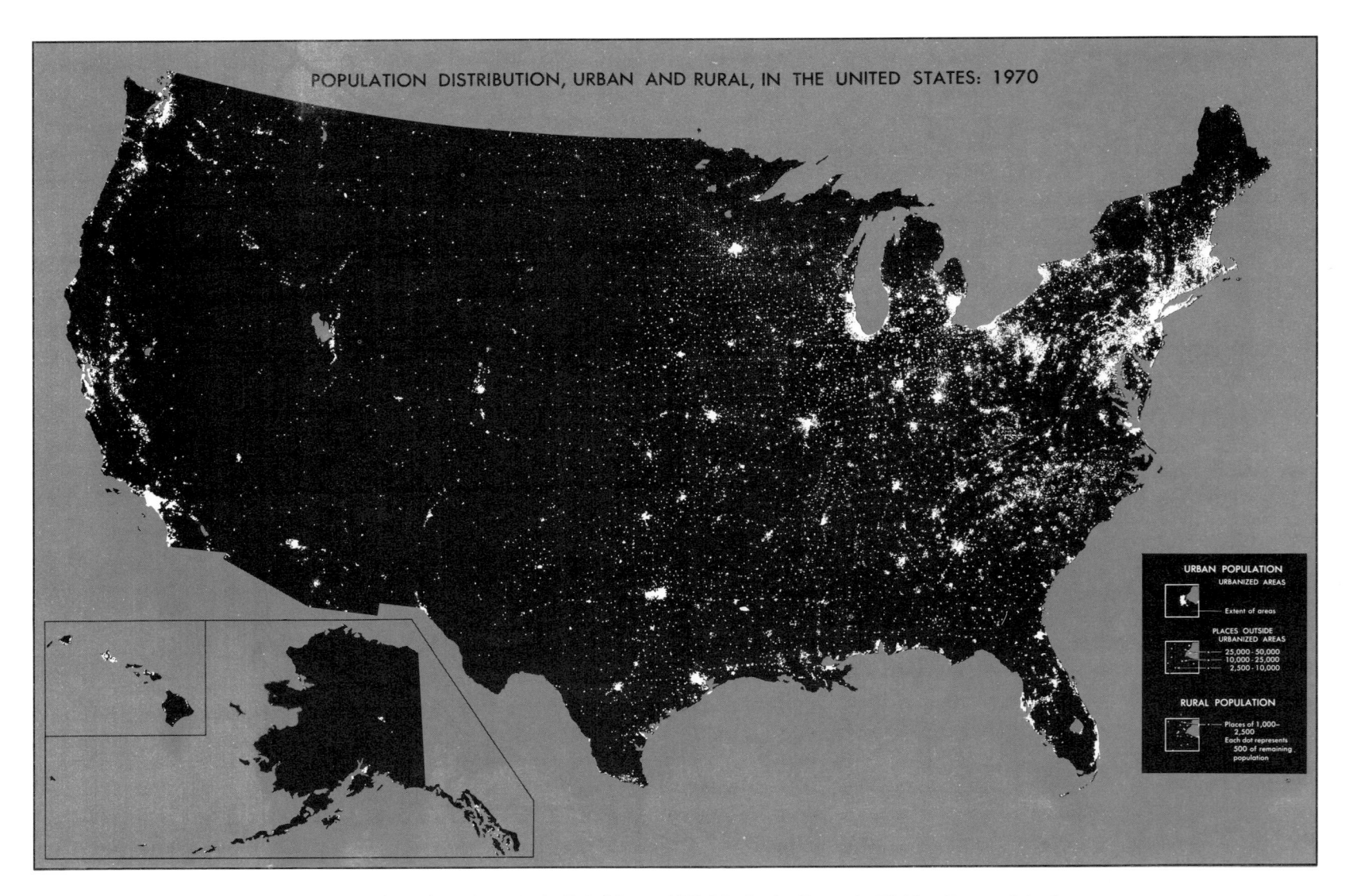

*Figure 2.2. Urban and Rural Population in the United States, 1970.* Map by the Geography Division, Bureau of the Census.

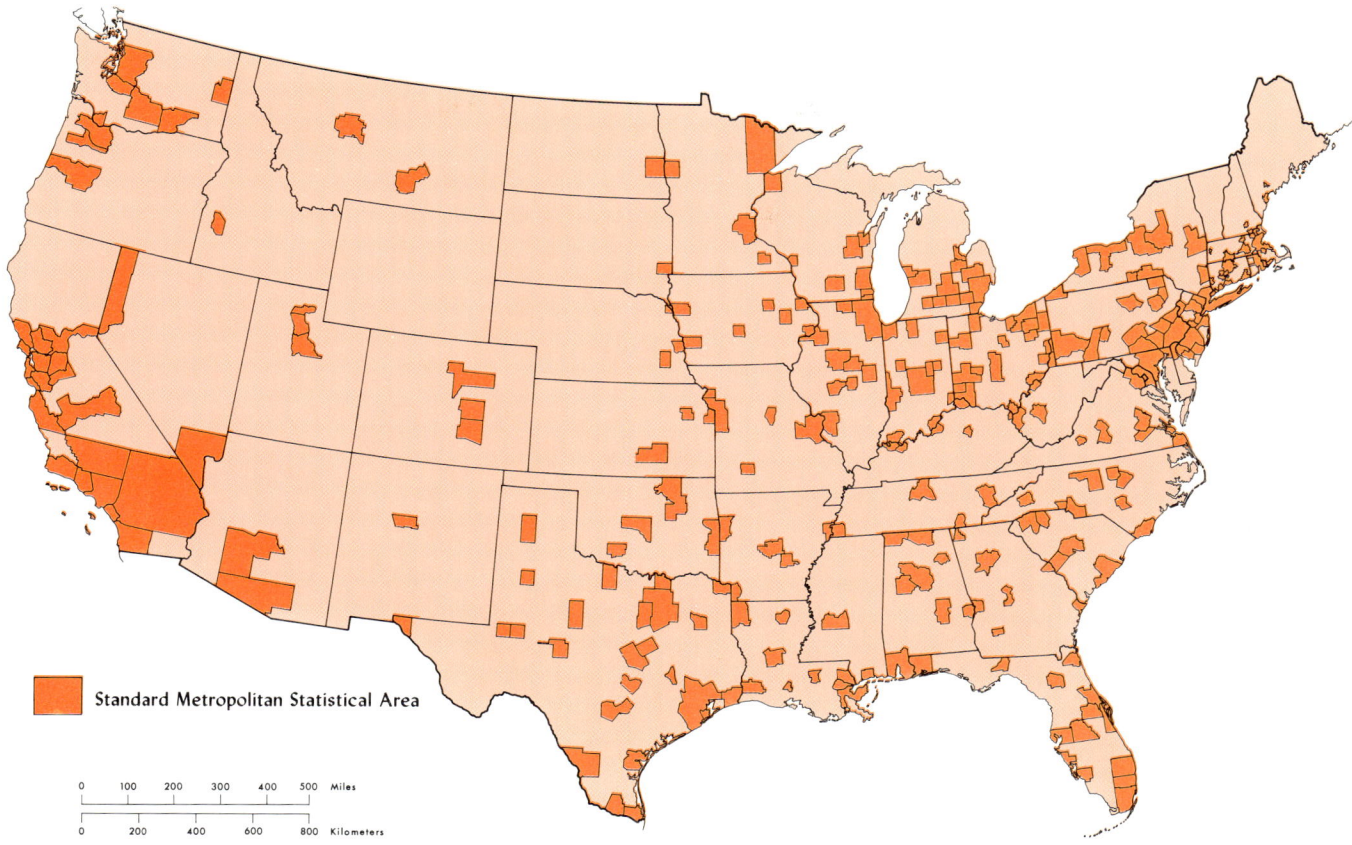

*Figure 2.3. Standard Metropolitan Statistical Areas, 1970.*

because the emphasis is on land instead of people. A good cartographer takes pains to ensure that land areas are given their correct proportion, as the states are presented in Figure 2.3. But when 60 percent of a nation's people live on 1 percent of its land, such maps may mislead more than they enlighten. One alternative is to make areas proportional to their populations instead of to their geographical areas (Figure 2.4). Although most people would describe this map as "distorted," it does highlight differences in population density in a way typical maps cannot. The northeast quadrant occupies 44 percent of the map area, matching the 44 percent of the nation's population that lives there. Similarly, California, Oregon, and Washington constitute 13 percent of the area within the boundaries of the United States. Most striking is the shrinking of the large but relatively empty states of the plains and mountain regions. Nevada and Wyoming almost disappear. Alaska and Hawaii have in fact disappeared, not because they have even smaller populations, but because of problems in programming noncontiguous regions in the computer routine that generated this cartogram. Hawaii would be the same size as New Hampshire, and Alaska would be half the size of North Dakota.

## THE 20 MOST POPULOUS METROPOLITAN REGIONS

In Figure 2.4 we have stressed the size and consequent importance of the 20 metropolitan regions mapped in this atlas by shading areas proportional to the populations of the 20 regions. The nation's 20 most populous metropolitan regions, which include 24 SMSAs, account for a major fraction of the nation's population. Because of widespread suburbanization over the last three decades, the 30 central cities recognized by the Census Bureau within the 24 SMSAs contain only 14 percent of the population in the United States. Adding those persons living in SMSA territories surrounding these 30 cities (only the larger ones are mapped separately) more than doubles the figure: 33 percent of America's people live in the 24 SMSAs. Finally, if we consider the even larger metropolitan zone of the Daily Urban System (DUS), we find that 40 percent of Americans live in the 20 systems.

Each DUS consists of one or more cities, the surrounding SMSA or SMSAs, and any contiguous counties that have more than 5 percent of their labor forces working in the central county or counties of the SMSA. The 20 systems are small in area, but they loom large in the social, economic, and political life of the nation, for they are home to two of every five Americans.

Population distribution is easy to measure and good data are available. Concentrations of people such as those in the 20 Daily Urban Systems are important in and of themselves. Beyond population size, however, there are other features that make the 20 metropolitan regions vital elements in national and international affairs. Many critical activities are even more highly concentrated in metropolitan regions than is population. In 1967, for example, 57 percent of the nation's wholesale trade was conducted within the 20 regions mapped in Figure 1.1.

Each year *Fortune* magazine lists the 500 largest industrial corporations in the nation. In 1970, 370 (75 percent) of the 500 largest corporations and 81 of the 100 largest had their corporate headquarters in the 20 most populous metropolitan regions. Similarly, 42 of the 50 largest commercial banks and 40 of the 50 largest transportation companies had headquarters within these regions. A large percentage of the nation's productive capacity is controlled from the 20 metropolitan regions. Finance and transportation are likewise concentrated. Were the commercial, industrial, and transportation management capacity of these critical nodes crippled or destroyed, the national economy would collapse.

Almost every American's continued prosperity is linked to the fortunes of the nation's great cities. Metropolitanism is the most productive land use man has invented; it permits more people to live at higher income levels than does any alternative. The size of the nation's population is a direct consequence of the prosperity the American metropolis has been instrumental in creating. Americans are now as dependent on sophisticated metropolitan technology as

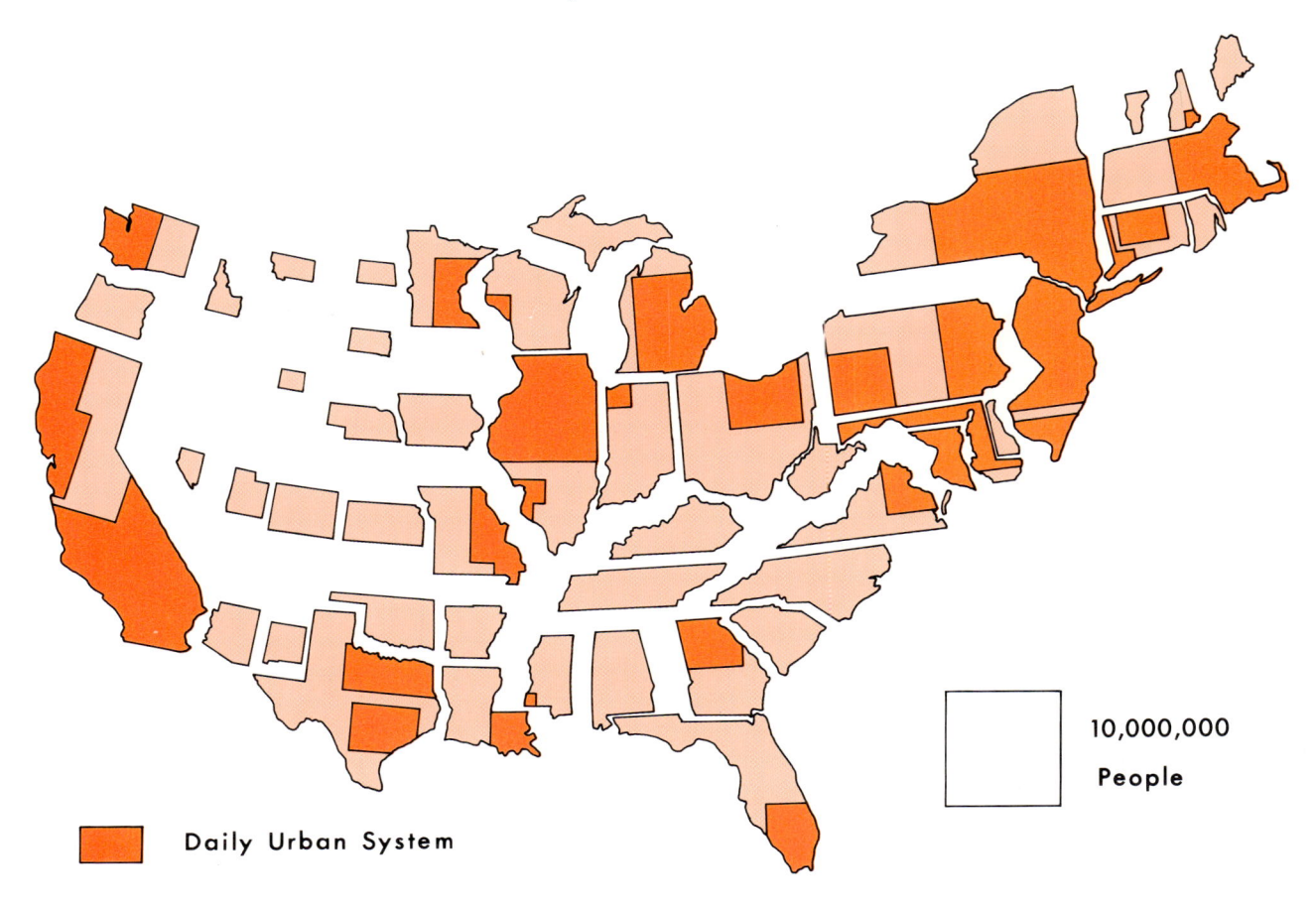

*Figure 2.4. Population Cartogram of the United States, 1970.* The size of each state is proportional to its population. Computer program and plot courtesy of John Longfellow.

they are on intricate agricultural, manufacturing, and transportation technologies. The notion that our metropolitan millions can go back to the land if our great cities sicken and die is romantic nonsense. The clear consequence of the demise of our great cities is political, social, and economic trauma for the entire nation.

Beyond considerations of prosperity and poverty lie the images and the ethos of every great society, which have always been intimately associated with its great cities. Most of us identify France with Paris more than vice versa. Similarly every empire evokes a city that almost overshadows its imperial matrix. The glories of the Muslim empire are inseparable from exotic Baghdad. There may indeed always be an England, but an England without London is unthinkable.

So is an America without New York, Chicago, and Los Angeles. We edify ourselves with images of amber waves of grain and purple mountain majesties above the fruited plain. But our alabaster cities—even considerably dimmed by human tears and smog—are equally important parts of our image of ourselves and of America's image abroad. There is nothing inspiring in the bleak reality of elderly people rummaging garbage cans in south Miami Beach because they are starving on their scandalously inadequate retirement incomes. Such poverty is all the more shameful because of the bejeweled and befurred wealth that thrives only blocks away. A glance northward takes in the fantasy castles of wealthy vacationers; the view across Biscayne Bay to the west reveals Miami's lush opulence. Yet even the most compassionate or outraged observer must marvel at the juxtaposition of such extremes. Thousands of disparities, contradictions, and conflicts permeate our great cities. That any metropolis works at all in the face of them is remarkable.

The variety that exists among metropolitan areas is equally remarkable. Baltimore and Cleveland are the same size, but nobody would ever mistake one for the other. Nor would anyone confuse either with Dallas. The fundamental processes that govern city origins and development may be universal, but they work themselves out in different ways in different places and at different times. In the United States the variety of physical environments in which cities began have given us an especially rich variety of metropolitan regions. The differences among our cities are as intriguing as the range of human experience that exists within any one of them. More than in other nations, America's cultural identities are an amalgam from diverse cities.

By focusing our attention on 20 regions we concentrate on only 10 percent of the nation's metropolitan regions. But we make no serious mistake in doing so. The most populous 20 are diverse enough—internally and among themselves—to incorporate the entire panoply of American metropolitan life. Politically, economically, socially, and culturally, enough of America is inextricably bound up in these 20 places to make it essential that we understand as much about them as we can.

# CHAPTER 3

# Metropolitan Competition and Interdependence

Cities compete with one another at the same time that they depend on each other. To advance beyond a local trade center, a town must offer some product or service that it can produce better than other places. To attain the status of a great metropolis, it must build a considerable array of such comparative advantages. But to realize comparative advantages, a great city must rely on other cities for raw materials, financing, goods, services, and markets. Specialization is the way a city distinguishes itself. The larger and more successful a city becomes, the more it depends on other places to consume its specialized offerings. As a network of great metropolitan regions grows and expands, the entire system becomes more interdependent.

## METROPOLITAN COMPETITION AND GROWTH

In every era some industries expand and others stagnate. Accordingly, places that can attract or promote jobs in expanding industries thrive, while those that cannot, stabilize or decline. Pittsburgh prospered, for example, as long as it was a lynchpin between the East and the interior, and as long thereafter as it manufactured heavy industrial products. When services and consumer goods became the economy's growth industries after World War II, Pittsburgh stagnated. America's urban history consists of thousands of sagas of success and failure. Every city in the United States started from zero population sometime during the last 500 years. Although metropolitan competition is more genteel today than it was during the settlement expansion of the 19th century, it is no less real.

Historically, the dominant economic activity in conjunction with the dominant transportation and communication technologies determined which places were chosen to become large cities or which existing places were favored for new increments of rapid growth. The agrarian economic era in the United States lasted until the 1850s. The chief transportation media were foot and horse overland, boats on streams and canals, and sailing ships on the seas. Population was dispersed to tap the land resource, and among the small cities that existed, the most populous places were ports (Figure 3.1). Cities that had water access to the interior as well as to Europe, such as New York, Philadelphia, Baltimore, Boston, and New Orleans, grew quickly after 1800. Pittsburgh, the major gateway to the interior before 1825, also prospered early.

After 1850, the economy shifted to manufacturing, rail transportation spread rapidly, and new places prospered. Pittsburgh, Cleveland, St. Louis, Detroit, and Chicago all started as interior ports, but they made a successful transition to manufacturing as rail transportation supplanted river and lake routes. They were able to manipulate rail routes to favor their interests at the expense of other places, a game at which Chicago boosters were particularly adept.

Like their older rivals on the seaboard, interior cities depended heavily on their locations between specialized production and consumption regions. The agricultural produce of the Midwest had to be moved to the East and overseas, and return flows of goods and services had to be shipped in the opposite direction. The middlemen in interior metropolises made good profits on both flows and plowed the profits back into local commercial and industrial enterprise. As the settlement frontier progressed farther westward, newer rail and manufacturing centers such as Minneapolis-St. Paul and Dallas-Fort Worth carved out tributary territories and began their rise to metropolitan status. Toward the end of the 19th century, West Coast and Gulf ports such as Seattle and Houston-Galveston began to perform the same role in the West as their earlier counterparts had on the eastern seaboard. San Francisco, of course, got an even earlier start because of its access to the California gold fields.

Since 1920 services—trade, finance, real estate, business, personal and government—have been the economy's growth industries, and automobile and air transportation have replaced railroads. Most established metropolises have continued to grow, but some places have progressed especially rapidly. Detroit's rapid growth has been sustained by the automobile industry. Formerly inaccessible places with climatic amenities such as Miami and Los Angeles advanced rapidly as transportation improved. Los Angeles was the nation's 10th city in 1920; by 1970 it ranked 2nd. After 1940, growth was especially rapid in government centers such as Washington, D.C. Atlanta, Dallas, and Houston all capitalized to some degree on the rapid postwar urban growth in the South, which had previously lagged behind the rest of the nation in urbanization.

Two hundred years of metropolitan growth have produced a mixed bag. None of the 4 most populous places in 1790 have disappeared from today's 20 most populous, but many of the remaining 16 did not exist in 1790. New York has maintained supremacy throughout the nation's history, but the nation's 2nd metropolis, Los Angeles, had but 100,000 people as recently as 1900, when New York had 3,500,000 and Chicago had 1,700,000. Philadelphia and Detroit are the nation's 4th and 5th metropolises. Philadelphia, like New York, has always been one of the nation's largest cities, but Detroit, like Los Angeles, is a comparative newcomer; its 1900 population was 285,000 compared with Philadelphia's 1,300,000. Once established, a great city's political and economic influence usually prevent it from disappearing, but competition can bring about absolute and relative decline.

## INTERDEPENDENCE AMONG METROPOLITAN AREAS

Specialization is, paradoxically, the keystone of both competition and interdependence. An enterpreneur who seeks to advance Chicago's interests by building a $500 million industrial facility, for example, may have to journey to New York City to arrange financing. Similarly, an Atlanta merchant wanting to import inexpensive clothing from Taiwan or Hong Kong will probably have to call upon wholesalers and custom brokers in New York or Los Angeles or both.

A city usually sends it largest outflow of travelers and information to the city upon which it relies most heavily for specialized services that are not locally available. Thus mapping largest outflows from a matrix of interchanges reveals the ways American metropolitan areas depend on one another (Figure 3.2). New York's premier position is especially evident in information flows among the 20 study regions. Fourteen of the 20 places sent more interstate telephone calls to New York City than to any other place in the late 1960s. Only Detroit, St. Louis, Minneapolis-St. Paul, and Seattle are more closely linked to one of the other 20 places. Chicago is clearly the nation's 2nd most dominant metropolis, given the dependence of Minneapolis-St. Paul, St. Louis, and Detroit on it. Los Angeles, the nation's 2nd most populous metropolis, had captured only Seattle's primary attentions in the late 1960s.

Past, present, and future roles of the 20 places on the nation's metropolitan stage are also evident in their connections to surrounding SMSAs that have over 250,000 population. New York, Los Angeles, and Chicago have numerous subordinates, and Atlanta is rapidly becoming the metropolis of the Southeast. Dallas is also profiting from the South's more rapid urban growth via its links with Oklahoma

METROPOLITAN POPULATION, 1790–1970

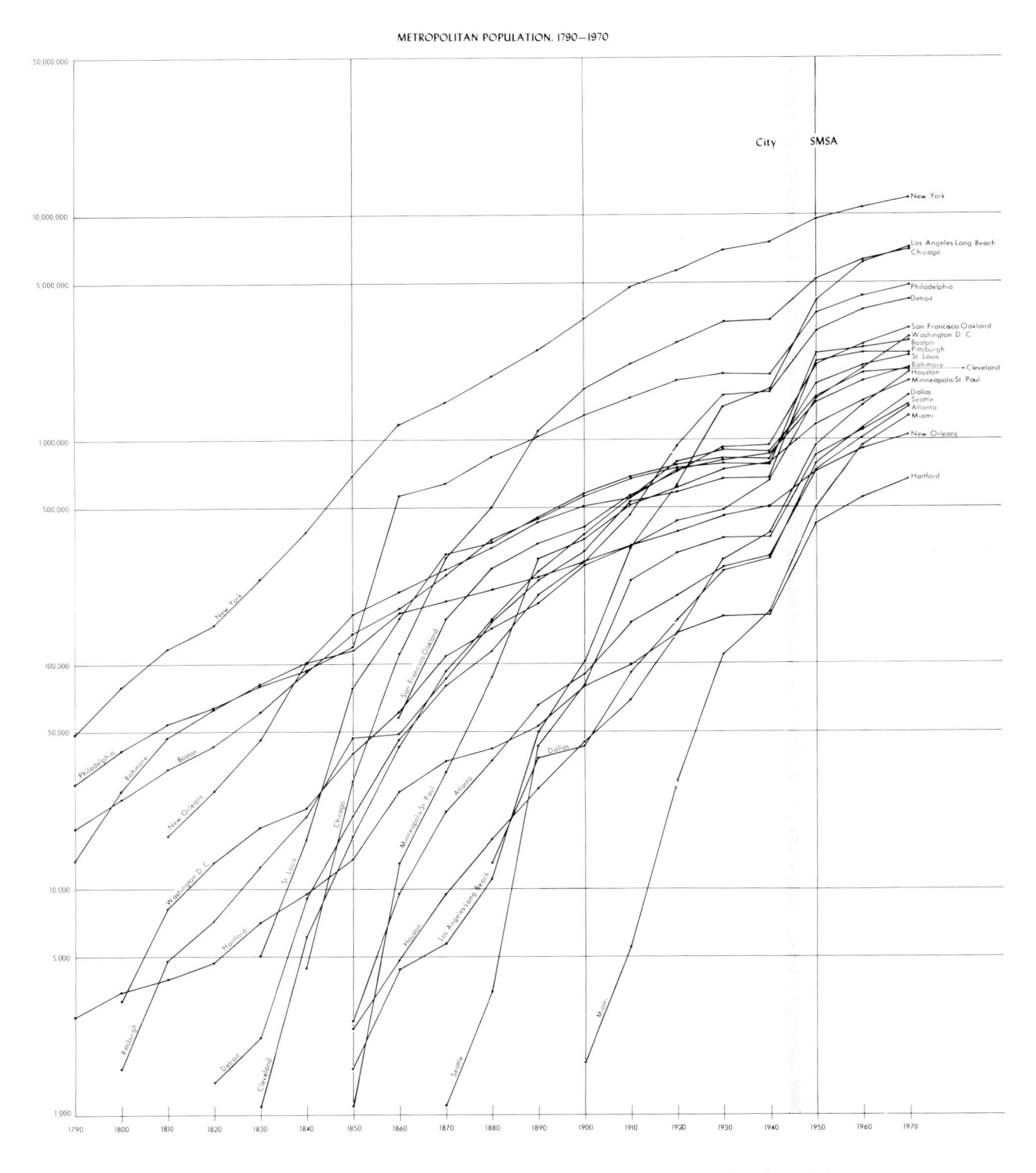

*Figure 3.1. Metropolitan Population, 1790-1970.* Central-city populations are charted from 1790 to 1940. SMSA populations are plotted for 1950, 1960, and 1970. Source: U.S. Bureau of the Census.

*10*

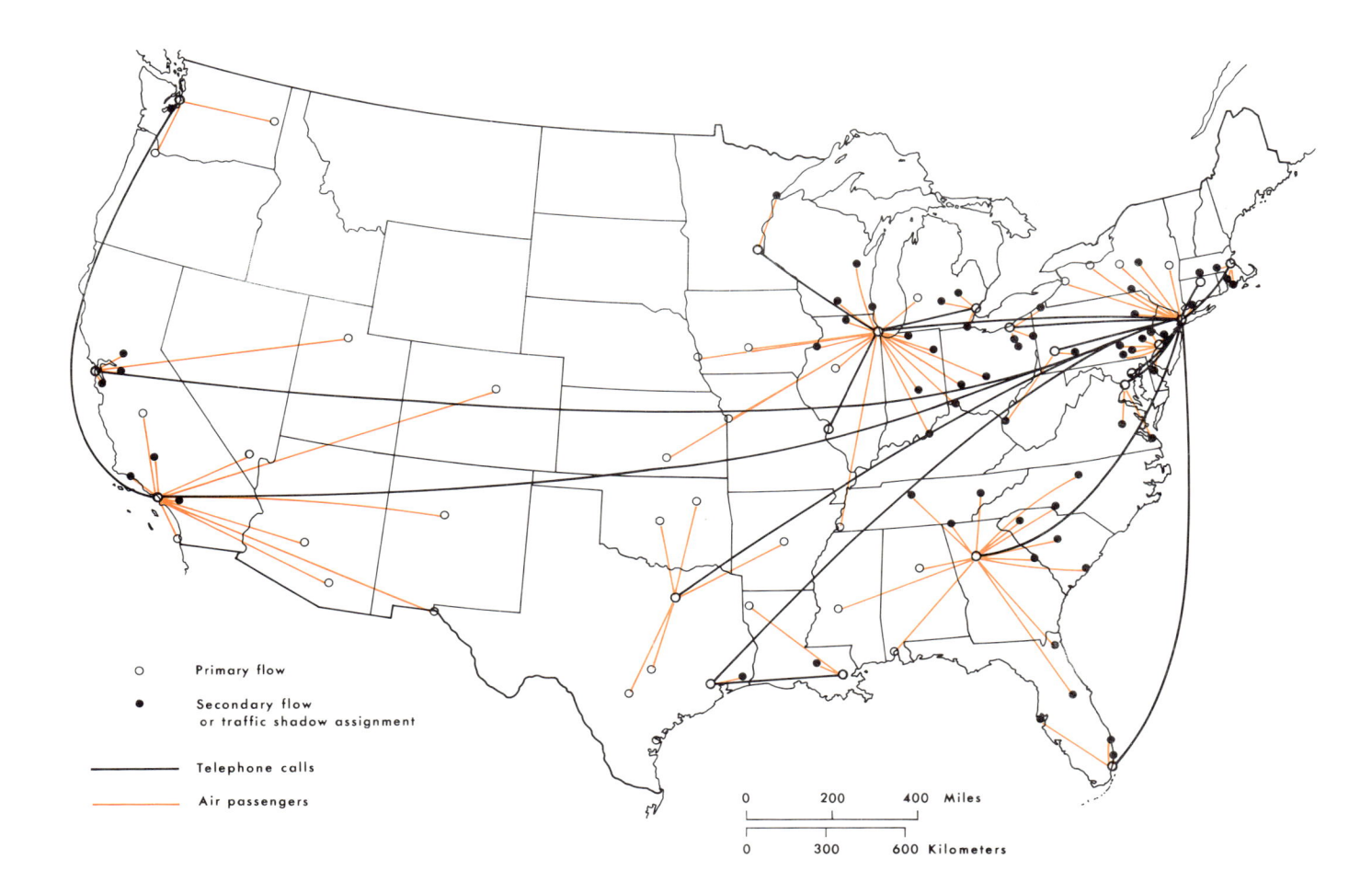

*Figure 3.2 Relationships among America's Most Populous Metropolitan Areas.* Black lines indicate the largest outflows of interstate telephone calls for a sample period in 1968. Orange lines indicate largest or second largest outflows of air passengers from SMSAs over 250,000. SMSAs close to one of the 20 regions have been arbitrarily assigned to the major metropolis if they lie within the air passenger "shadow" (ca. 100 miles) of the larger place or omitted if they are immediately adjacent. The flows mapped from open city symbols are primary flows; flows mapped from solid city symbols are second largest outflows or traffic shadow assignments if they are within about 100 miles of their superordinate. With the exception of places very close to one of the 20 study regions, almost all the places east of the Mississippi for which secondary flows are indicated sent their primary outflow to New York City. Sources: Telephone call data, American Telephone and Telegraph Company, Air Passenger Data, courtesy of Professor Michael O. Filani, University of Ibadan.

and Texas. On the other hand, places like Hartford, Philadelphia, Baltimore, Pittsburgh, Cleveland, and St. Louis have had access to potential client cities cut off by stronger or later rivals. For them, the future promises slow growth or stagnation; their opportunities for expanding the specialized employment that would enable them to attract more people are limited because they have few client cities and lack distinctive environmental amenities. Boston, New Orleans, Seattle, and Detroit face a similar future because their peripheral locations reduce the number of subordinates they might attract. San Francisco's former dominance of West Coast affairs is increasingly eroding in favor of Los Angeles. Minneapolis-St. Paul has only one metropolitan subordinate, but it serves a large and prosperous agrarian hinterland.

Miami, Houston, and Washington, D.C. are unusual cases. Miami is peripheral and has few subordinates, but it has valuable climatic amenities. Washington, almost wholly a creature of the federal government, seems to be insulated from typical metropolitan competition and capable of self-sustaining growth in a way no other city could be. Houston's prosperity and rapid growth are based on a complex of petrochemical and aerospace industries that should provide sustained growth in the decades ahead.

## COMPETITION, STATUS, AND URBAN PROBLEMS

A city's prospects depend on its past and current status in the shifting hierarchy of metropolitan places. A city's age and the time during which it experienced its most rapid growth are the major determinants of how many problems it has and how serious they are. Similarly, its growth prospects are good predictors of how well it can cope with its problems, for human and environmental problems are likely to be more intractable in stagnating places than in places where opportunities are expanding. Agencies that rate municipal bonds determine how much interest a city will pay for the funds it needs to solve or head off problems, for example, and they attach considerable importance to growth.

More important than such external evaluations, however, are the ways in which growth and status are translated into a city's collective feelings about itself, the confidence that the average resident has that problems are soluble, and that staying, rather than moving elsewhere, is the sensible thing to do. For in the final analysis, it is the collective opinions and decisions of average residents—especially regarding moving or staying—that determine whether most metropolitan problems develop and how well they are handled when they do.

# CHAPTER 4

# Metropolitan Problems: Are There Solutions?

## THE LIFE CYCLE OF URBAN NEIGHBORHOODS

Some problems may be experienced collectively by many average citizens, but many more are restricted to particular kinds of neighborhoods. This occurs because urban neighborhoods usually pass through well-defined stages during their life cycle. The cycle starts when formerly rural land is subdivided. Houses are erected and occupied, but as they age and become obsolete they may be neglected, allowed to fall into disrepair, and eventually abandoned and demolished. After World War II vigorous suburban development engulfed the American countryside. Each new subdivision spawned another example of the youthful stage in the neighborhood life cycle.

During a neighborhood's middle years the homes lose their sparkle, some developing a mellow patina while the rest acquire only the cracks and wrinkles of age. A certain number of the first residents stay to grow old with their houses. Others move outward to the suburban frontier, to be replaced by families younger and less affluent than they.

In one critical respect new urban neighborhoods have a common goal with youth: to grow up and mature without getting old. Nevertheless, we cannot tell whether housing abandonment in a 100-year-old neighborhood means the end of the road or merely a rough transition to middle age. Rejuvenation of old inner-city neighborhoods, under way with increasing vigor in many central cities, may mean a burst of genuine vitality or just a final flicker before the flame goes out for good.

The fact of housing and neighborhood abandonment in the nation's major central cities is indisputable. The causes of abandonment are much less certain. One estimate places the gross loss of housing units in the 25 most populous cities during the 1960s at 5 to 10 percent of the 1960 housing stock. In Chicago, to take one important example, residential and commercial structures containing 14,000 housing units, 1.25 percent of the 1970 housing stock, were officially abandoned through demolition court during 1970. Court-processed abandonments in 1971 in areas of minority population exceeded 4 percent of the 1970 housing stock. Two major arguments have been advanced to explain the abandonment process, one by civil-rights activists, the other by housing economists.

### The Urban League Argument

Researchers in civil rights organizations assert that abandonment comes about through a process combining racially inspired social change and conspiratorial behavior by urban institutions.* According to the National Urban League, the abandonment process starts with neighborhood transition. Real estate entrepreneurs subdivide housing units or crowd large families into existing units formerly used by smaller households. The increased rental income is not reinvested to maintain building quality. Instead, the higher rents temporarily inflate property values, thereby encouraging refinancing or quick resale to capture short-term capital gains.

The neighborhood that results from these manipulations is a social disaster. Residents lack the skills and the resources to improve or even maintain their habitats. Public services become scarce. The area becomes an enclave of the aged, the poor, and the young. Those who can flee do so.

The final step before abandonment is disinvestment. Landlords see no future for their properties. Taxes and maintenance costs may exceed rental collections owing to vandalism, nonpayment of rents, or housing-code enforcement. In response, the landlords may end maintenance, cease paying taxes, and default on mortgages.

Abandonment is the last stage in the process outlined by the Urban League. Rent goes unpaid, the damage of unchecked vandalism is not repaired, and most residents leave. The property may be placed in a tax lien, then resold or demolished. Sometimes derelict buildings burn down.

### The Vacancy Chain Argument

There is an alternative to the Urban League's grim view of the neighborhood life cycle.† Vacancies are created when a new housing unit is built, when an old unit is subdivided, when a family dies, or when a household leaves the local market. When a vacancy at address A is filled by a family moving in from B, the vacancy is transmitted from A to the family's previous address at B. The two addresses, A and B, form the first link in a vacancy chain. Address B is vacant until someone moves in from address C. Addresses B and C form the second link in the chain, and so on. The vacancy chain grows outward from the original vacancy, link by link, until the chain ends. A vacancy chain ends when a housing unit is demolished, is consolidated into another unit, or stands permanently vacant. The length of a vacancy chain, measured by the number of links, determines the local impact of a newly created vacancy. If a chain has seven links, seven households were able to acquire housing that was in some way preferable to the housing they occupied previously.

Local markets are connected to national markets; thus new

---

*Center for Community Change and National Urban League. *The National Survey of Housing Abandonment*, 3rd edition, March 1972.

†B.J.L. Berry. "What Really Happens When Tenants Leave." *AIA Journal*, December 1973, pp.36-38.

construction anywhere is linked at least indirectly to vacancy changes and ultimately to housing abandonment. Consider the components of change in the United States housing inventory between 1960 and 1970:

|  | Units |
|---|---|
| U.S. housing inventory in 1960 | 58.3 million |
| Units added from new construction, 1960-1970 | 15.5 million |
| Units added from subdivision and other sources | 1.6 million |
| Units lost from inventory through demolition, consolidation of units, or permanent vacancy | −6.8 million |
| Net increase in the inventory, 1960-1970 | 10.4 million |

The net increase of 10.4 million housing units was absorbed in three ways:

| Net new household formations | 10.4 million |
|---|---|
| Units newly vacant for sale or rent | 0.2 million |
| Formerly vacant units, no longer available | −0.2 million |

Thus as housing demand grew by the addition of over 10 million new households, 6.8 million housing units were withdrawn from the housing inventory. Meanwhile, the number of housing units dilapidated or lacking plumbing facilities dropped 50 percent, from 8.4 to 4.2 million. Most of the decrease was in units withdrawn from the housing stock, many of which were abandoned. Indeed, between 1950 and 1970, over 30 million new units were built while net household growth was slightly over 20 million. During that time the number of substandard units dropped from 17 million to less than 4 million. These facts illustrate that households are moving into better quarters as a steadily improving housing stock filters down to lower-income groups. For each 100 new housing units constructed, between 240 and 350 families move into more satisfactory housing, 100 move into the new units, and the rest move into older units vacated by successive turnover.

Housing vacancy chains set in motion by new construction account for perhaps half of the yearly residential relocations in the United States. The other half are responses to family life-cycle changes (birth, death, marriage, divorce) and job shifts (promotions, relocations, retirements). Imagine the geography involved and compare it with the National Urban League's view of abandonment. Through the 1920s urban housing was always in short supply. After World War II rapid expansion of the housing supply of all metropolitan areas occurred at the suburban fringe. The oldest housing stocks were concentrated around downtown near the core of the central city and were occupied by the poor, especially minority poor. Each additional link in a housing vacancy chain begun by new suburban construction extended deeper into the core of the city. As chains grew from the suburbs inward, they extended from expanding to stable to declining neighborhoods, from white to minority occupancy, and within each ethnic or racial group from child-rearing middle-class families at the outer edge toward the older and poorer households in the inner neighborhoods. Minority groups were major beneficiaries. Their housing improved even though they retained their relative positions behind the white upper classes.

The housing vacancy-chain argument asserts that filtering processes are working. Seen in this light, abandonment becomes the mechanism for removing the worst housing from the market. Housing abandonment is thus not a problem; it is a positive sign that the housing market is working. But problems do result. An ideal filtering process yields its results without adverse effects on neighboring low-income households left behind or on the attractiveness of neighboring housing units. Today, however, housing abandonment is accompanied by abandonment of disadvantaged groups in discarded neighborhoods, which is the human side of the life cycle of urban neighborhoods.

## POPULATION CHANGES AT THE METROPOLITAN AND NEIGHBORHOOD LEVELS

Just as the city's housing stock is steadily transformed by new construction, demolition, and varying rates of deterioration among the components of the stock, each metropolitan area and each neighborhood within it has a distinctive blend of population fluctuations based on migration, birth, and death.

Early in this century, urban populations grew mainly from rural-to-urban migration and from foreign immigration. These migrations combined with natural increase to help all urban centers grow. After World War I net growth from international migration dropped sharply, reaching a rate of 0.4 per 1,000 population in the 1930s. It rose steadily during the 1940s and 1950s and averaged 1.7 per 1,000 in the 1960s. After passage of the more liberal immigration law in 1965, nearly 4 million immigrants arrived in the next decade, pushing the average annual rate close to 2 per 1,000. In contrast, the birthrate rose to over 25 per 1,000 population in the late 1940s, but by the mid-1970s it had dropped to 15 and was moving even lower. The average woman in 1960 would bear 3.7 children during her lifetime, but in 1973 it would be only 2 children. Thus foreign immigration is increasingly important, especially in several large cities of the East Coast (from Europe and elsewhere), in Florida (from Cuba, the rest of the Caribbean, and Latin America), in the Southwest (Mexico), and on the West Coast (Asia).

While immigration and natural increase augment the national population, migration flows among metropolitan areas transform local population structures, with some areas growing at the expense of others. Peter A. Morrison describes this redistribution by comparing the extreme cases of San Jose and St. Louis.* During the 1960s the expanding aerospace and service industries of San Jose attracted new residents at a rate sufficient to enlarge the metropolitan population 66 percent. Two-thirds of the growth was net in-migration and one-third was natural change. The selective in-migration brought young people who were of childbearing age. Thus in-migration augmented natural increase.

The St. Louis metropolitan area has had just the opposite experience, steady out-migration of the young who carry their demographic potential away with them. Between 1960 and 1970 the metropolitan population grew 12 percent, which is substantially lower then the national metropolitan rise of 17 percent. After 1970, the population in metropolitan St. Louis—and in 21 other formerly growing metropolitan areas—began to drop.

The city of St. Louis reached its peak population of 880,000 in the early 1950s, but by 1972 it had shrunk to less than 590,000. During the 1960s when the city population dropped 17 percent, the metropolitan total rose 29 percent. The white population declined because of deaths among the elderly and steady out-migration of the young to the suburbs. During the decade 34 percent of the city's whites moved away. The movers included a large portion of young households in the family-forming years, who, when they left, took their reproductive potential with them.

The picture was quite different for St. Louis blacks during the decade. Migration gains equaled losses, but the black population rose 19.5 percent through natural increase, close to its national rate of 21.6 percent. Annual figures show that the city's nonwhite population peaked in 1968, then started dropping as young black families migrated to the suburbs in increasing numbers.

The persistent migration of whites and then blacks away from St. Louis has drastically altered the structure of the city's population (p. 121). Heavy and prolonged out-migration of young whites drew away potential parents and left behind an older population that could not

*Peter A. Morrison, "Urban Growth and Decline: San Jose and St. Louis in the 1960's." *Science*, vol. 185, 30 August 1974, pp. 757-762.

replace itself. Recently the same process has begun for the black population.

As migration overhauls the distribution of the metropolitan population, the city of St. Louis is fast becoming a repository of the disadvantaged and persons with special needs. In 1959 only 16 percent of the city's families had incomes falling below half the city median; by 1965 the proportion had reached 21 percent. Through selective out-migration, Morrison concludes, problems of dependency and poverty, not exclusively problems *of* St. Louis, have increasingly become located *in* St. Louis.

## PROBLEMS OF PLACES; PROBLEMS OF PEOPLE

San Jose and St. Louis are not unique. They are representative of the wide range of population compositions and change patterns in metropolitan America. The rate of decline in St. Louis may be unusual, but the phenomenon of local population decline is increasingly common. In coping with the local consequences of such decline, the policy dilemma is this: St. Louis officials and their counterparts in other cities are understandably alarmed at the loss of young and prosperous families and the accumulation of the poor and the troubled inside their jurisdictions. Such trends portend a bleak future for the city, its remaining population, and the businesses that depend on local buying power.

Yet from the viewpoint of individual welfare, the people who moved out usually went on to something better. They now enjoy conditions they prefer. Moreover, if there are disadvantages to crowding, the persons left behind benefit from the thinning out of formerly crowded areas. The city may be worse off, but the people may be better off. Statistics can mislead us if they confine our attention to the plight of *places,* when our central concern should be with the well-being of people. It is hard to avoid this difficulty because social and economic statistics are compiled and published mainly by *areas* rather than by groups of people. Thus we can monitor the experiences of places over time, but not of the individuals and groups who live there. The places remain far longer than any resident, beguiling us into defining problems of people as problems of places.

## METROPOLITAN PROBLEMS: PREREQUISITES FOR SOLUTIONS

It is on this moving metropolitan stage of housing stocks in flux and populations migrating that we have tried to conduct a broadly based geographical analysis of the nation's urban structure and its pressing problems. The strategy has been to expand and organize a body of comparative evidence on the structure and the changing geographical organization of the nation's 20 leading metropolitan regions.

Part II of the atlas facilitates that goal. For each place a linked series of socioeconomic variables is presented in the geographical context in which problems of people and place must be considered. Although these chapters often illustrate problems and although the city chapters can be used comparatively by paging from chapter to chapter, the primary purpose of Part II is to provide background knowledge about the 20 places so that the maps in Part III, which are focused on specific topics and problems, can be used to maximum advantage.

In the comparative analysis section (Part III) of this atlas, 10 topics are examined: for each of the identified subjects of interest or concern, one or more indicators—statistical measures of important aspects of the topic—have been identified and mapped.* The map series that follow permit vivid comparisons among places, helping us decide which problems are common enough to justify national-level attention and which are features confined to a small number of comparable urban regions.

*Executive Office of the President, Office of Management and the Budget. *Social Indicators, 1973.* Washington, D.C.: U.S. Government Printing Office, 1973.

### Metropolitan Physical Environments

The physical environment of each urban area is the basic stage on which the metropolitan drama unfolds. Today, in the interests of efficient resource use and protection of fragile environments, urban development is increasingly limited to areas served by public water and sewer systems. The limits of these systems are described in Chapters 26 and 27.

### Open Space for Metropolitan Amenity and Leisure-Time Use

Leisure-time activities can be grouped by location: activities carried on at or near home (television, radio, reading, visiting with family and friends, hobbies), and those away from home (outdoor recreation, commercial entertainment, cultural activities, travel). In an effort to assess one facet of weekend leisure-time use, the geographical distribution of seasonal homes around each major metropolitan region is presented in Chapter 28.

### Housing

The Housing and Urban Development Act of 1968 stated a basic housing goal: that every American family have a decent home and a suitable living environment. One indicator of comfort and living space is the percentage of households living in crowded conditions, usually measured by the proportion of households in units with more than 1.01 persons per room. This variable is mapped and discussed in Chapter 29.

Since many measures of housing and neighborhood quality vary with income levels, we present variations in these housing and neighborhood characteristics in Part II, and we focus in the comparative section on the squeeze experienced by many households as they attempt to rent or maintain standard housing. Chapter 30 presents a map series describing the percentage of tenant households that allocate more than one-fourth of their incomes to rent. Chapter 31 is a cartographic description of the proportion of low-income homeowners (mainly elderly) who attempt to maintain standard housing on their limited resources.

### Transportation and Communication

Every metropolitan resident needs a minimum level of accessibility to the places, people, goods, services, and information that the urban realm provides. Because there are vast differences in physical structure among cities, problems of accessibility vary as well. The subjects of the map series in Chapters 32-36 are population density, the journey to work, the use of public transportation, the availability of cars, and access to the telephone.

### Metropolitan Growth

Housing conditions and mobility determine the long-term as well as the daily movements and contacts of people in metropolitan regions. Chapter 37 describes population changes and redistribution during the 1960s by sketching areas of population increase and decrease. Such redistributions are consequences as well as causes of commercial, office, and professional employment growth in some parts of cities and of commercial contraction near city centers.

### Education

Providing basic education universally and the opportunity for higher education are two central concerns of contemporary Americans. Within metropolitan areas there are important variations in how such educational opportunities are provided; Chapter 38 maps the proportion of elementary school enrollees attending parochial schools in the larger central cities of the 24 SMSAs included in the atlas. Chapter 39 consists of SMSA maps of 20 and 21 year olds attending school.

## Public Health

Although there are many others, four major social concerns are widely acknowledged in health planning: adequate prenatal care and healthy birth, long life, freedom from disability, and access to medical care when it is needed. Good health before and after birth means maximum advantage for healthy growth and maturation. In Chapter 40 public health levels are assessed in the nation's major cities by mapping rates of immature births at the tract and neighborhood level.

## Socioeconomic Segregation

If housing markets in American metropolitan areas were color-blind, minority families could distribute themselves among housing opportunities according to tastes, needs, and ability to pay. During the 1960s, some progress was made in opening metropolitan housing submarkets to racial and ethnic minorities. The map series in Chapter 41 describes the segregation of black Americans and shows the number of housing units built from 1960 to March 1970 that are owned and occupied by blacks. Chapter 42 shows the residential patterns of Spanish-Americans. More than describing progress during the last decade, the two chapters dramatize how far the nation must yet go to achieve unbiased housing markets.

## Employment and Poverty

A topic of increasing concern in the nation is equality of opportunity and financial rewards for women. Some indications of the degree to which women are participating in the nation's economic life are presented in Chapter 43, which maps the proportion of females in the SMSA labor forces. Another important facet of economic opportunity and welfare is simply whether able, willing persons seeking work can find a job. The major indicator of this concern is the unemployment rate, which is mapped in Chapter 44 for males in SMSAs.

Employment does not automatically assure adequate incomes, especially among groups with limited skills and education. Although there are no widely accepted standards for equitable income distribution, a set of minimum standards has been set. Persons whose incomes (personal or family) are below the federally established poverty level are mapped in Chapter 45.

Components of income, regardless of its adequacy, are also important social phenomena. In Chapter 46 the percentage of all income in census tracts received from Social Security (and railroad retirement) and public assistance and welfare payments is mapped for SMSAs. The section on employment and poverty concludes with a discussion showing the locations of income deficits (Chapter 47).

## Urban Renewal and Redevelopment

The comparative map series conclude with a description in Chapter 48 of vacant year-round housing in each of our major cities. We finish where we started, wondering if housing abandonment near the core signals the beginning of the end for large expanses of urban real estate, or whether we are merely watching old, needlessly high-density areas steadily settling to the lower-density uses characteristic of metropolitan areas targeted to remain essentially the same size for the next century or two.

The view in each chapter is retrospective—who would make forecasts for an affluent society that is now on a productivity plateau at the same time that it is trying to live on credit and an ever-expanding money supply? The nation subjects itself to wrenching inflation, while it is pinched between higher energy prices on one side and materials shortages on the other. These new forces suggest that the next few decades will build less, conserve more, and waste less. Increasingly, it will be relatively cheaper to refurbish old buildings than to discard them and build anew. It seems likely that the physical structures of cities will be much more stable in the next quarter-century than they were in the years since 1950.

## SUMMARY AND CONCLUSIONS

Urban residential neighborhoods pass through life cycles that may last much longer than we previously thought. People live from day to day—or paycheck to paycheck—but cities last for centuries, and most American cities are young by world standards. Cities and individuals depend on one another for their vitality, but the life cycle of cities differs significantly from the cycle of individuals. The city is built and transformed by countless decisions of individuals. As the city is remodeled it opens new options for people and eliminates others. New perspectives are needed to help judge whether certain urban problems are part of larger, inexorable adjustments in metropolitan structure and thus not susceptible to short-term, local control. From the standpoint of people rather than places, rapid neighborhood change means progress for those who arrive or who leave. It is those left behind who suffer. The short-term policy might well be to alleviate the suffering rather than to pretend to arrest its causes.

In each topic of public concern, such as housing, employment, and education, every American has some basic level of need that society must guarantee to fill. The comparative maps in this atlas attempt to describe the location and severity of various problems in each major aspect of public concern in our major metropolitan regions.

One issue that cannot be handled is the widespread feeling of relative deprivation, the gap between what people feel they justifiably deserve and what they actually get. Television, movies, advertising, and a pervasive obsession with material consumption can easily push wants beyond incomes. According to Richard Easterlin the pursuit of happiness and the pursuit of money come to much the same thing for most Americans.* But are people who get more money typically happier? It depends. In all societies more money for the individual usually means more happiness or satisfaction. However, raising the incomes of all need not increase the happiness of all, because the general level of needs and wants relative to which material well-being is measured rises along with and as a result of general income growth. If one individual gets more money and others do not, his happiness increases because he advances his rank or position with respect to his peers. But when all incomes gradually increase, no one on the average feels better off.

To the outside observer, Easterlin concludes, economic growth seems to produce an ever more affluent society, but to those inside the process, affluence remains a remote, urgently sought, but never attained goal. The maps in the atlas show the distribution of prosperity and poverty for almost half the population of the richest country in the world. But maps only report the facts; our values determine their meaning.

*Richard A. Easterlin. "Does Money Buy Happiness?" *The Public Interest*, No. 30, Winter 1973, pp. 3-10.

# CHAPTER 5

# Sources of Information about American Cities

## WHAT KINDS OF INFORMATION DO WE NEED?

During the 1960s the nation gradually became aware that it lacked comprehensive statistics reflecting social progress or retrogression. In 1966 President Johnson directed Secretary of Health, Education, and Welfare Wilbur J. Cohen to search for ways to improve the nation's ability to chart its social progress. In particular he asked HEW "to develop the necessary social statistics and indicators to supplement those prepared by the Bureau of Labor Statistics and the Council of Economic Advisers. With these yardsticks, we can better measure the distance we have come and plan for the way ahead."

Cohen's report to the president noted the long-standing availability of a comprehensive set of sensitive, reliable economic indicators.* Annual, quarterly, monthly, and sometimes even weekly reports present statistics on national income and its components: employment and unemployment, retail and wholesale prices, and the balance of payments. These national economic indicators are watched by government officials and private citizens alike as closely as a doctor watches a fever chart for signs of change in a patient's condition. Indeed, the Cohen report noted, economic indicators are now so much a part of our thinking that we tend to equate a rising national income with improved well-being. Yet by the end of the 1960s many were surprised to find unrest and discontent growing in many quarters while the national income was rising rapidly.

Why did income and disaffection increase at the same time? One reason was that general improvements in levels of living, along with new and highly publicized social legislation, generated new expectations, expectations that rose faster than they could be fulfilled. A second reason was that general advances in prosperity were not shared by everyone. The averages rose rapidly, but persons at the lower end of the economic ladder continued to suffer. The third reason for protest by disappointed and disaffected groups was that many serious troubles of a noneconomic nature went unreported. The economic indicators told only part of what was happening across the land.

The principal economic indicators have two important shortcomings: they tend to be national in scope and ignore differences from city to city and from neighborhood to neighborhood where people actually live; second, they fasten our attention to the health of our economy, neglecting to address social, environmental, and other crucial facets of national and local life. Curiosity about these noneconomic conditions would itself justify attempts to assess the social state of the nation. People want to know: Are we getting healthier? Is pollution increasing? Are children doing better in school than they used to? Is crime increasing? Do people feel alienated from society? Just as we need to measure our incomes, so, the Cohen report argues, we need "social indicators" that report on other facets of our lives, to give us a better idea how well off we really are.

In the comparative map series in this atlas, social and environmental indicators are presented side-by-side with economic measures, and the geographical variations in these measures are described at the level at which individual lives are lived—the Daily Urban System, the metropolitan area, the city, and the local neighborhood. Our map sets are not comprehensive, but they do dramatize a method of analysis. They also reveal the important similarities and differences among our 20 most populous metropolitan regions.

Geographical analysis of social and environmental indicators satisfies our curiosity about how well we are doing in our nation's cities. Such analysis improves policy making in at least two ways. It gives problems greater visibility, thereby making informed judgments about the local impact of national policies possible. Moreover, by showing how different measures of national well-being vary from place to place at the local level, comparative geographical analysis helps us evaluate the location and the degree of local change produced by national programs.

## CURRENT DATA SOURCES FOR THE COMPARATIVE GEOGRAPHICAL STUDY OF AMERICAN CITIES

Every measurement and classification system represents a hidden theory. Each data series has a significance based on some issue, argument, or goal. We watch average prices in the stock market because for over 100 years their movements have proved to be reliable forecasts of subsequent movements in the national economy. Manufacturers of toys and superintendents of schools watch the birthrate to anticipate their markets. Careful attention is paid to differential pay and promotion rates between blacks and whites, men and women.

The development of truly useful data series is expensive in time, money, and intellectual energy. For one thing, we may sense the existence of a problem, perhaps something we call "neighborhood deterioration" or "unsatisfactory schools," but we may not know exactly what we mean. Consequently we do not know exactly what to measure. We are reluctant to make hasty choices because in measuring the symptoms of a problem we may beguile ourselves into defining the problem only in terms of its symptoms. Certain diseases may produce a rash, but clearing or covering up the rash is no guarantee of a cure. Similarly, abandoned houses may need paint, repair, and yardwork, but providing these gives little assurance that people will want to live in the houses. The indicators used today gained acceptance in the past but only in response to their proven usefulness with respect to even earlier data needs. In the same sequence, today's needs lead to tomorrow's indicators.

---

*U.S. Department of Health, Education, and Welfare. *Toward a Social Report.* Washington, D.C.: U.S. Government Printing Office, 1969.

In contrast to national data series, local series are useful and reliable, but their formats are unique and thus prohibit comparative analysis. The *Statistical Abstract of the United States: 1974\** contains a guide (pp. 979-981) to state statistical abstracts that lists the most recent state statistical abstracts (including one for Puerto Rico) published since 1965. When no statistical abstract exists for a particular state, near equivalents are given. These sources contain tables on many subjects for the state, its component parts, or both, but no attempt is made to ensure comparability of data among states.

In 1970 the U.S. Bureau of the Census issued a *Directory of Non-Federal Statistics for States and Local Areas: a Guide to Sources, 1969.*[†] It was the first guide to nonfederal sources of current statistics for the 50 states, the District of Columbia, Guam, Puerto Rico, the Virgin Islands, and for some of their component local areas. It is a companion document to the Census's *Directory of Federal Statistics for Local Areas, 1966* and the *Directory of Federal Statistics for States, 1967.*[‡] It describes published sources of nonfederal statistics on social, political, and economic subjects. The 13 major subjects are: population estimates; vital statistics and health; education; housing; public welfare; labor and unemployment; banking; finance and insurance; commerce; transportation and utilities; agriculture and conservation; government and elections; and law enforcement.

The 1966 and 1967 reports describe data collected and published by state agencies, colleges and universities, and private organizations. They may cover an entire state, a significant area within the state, or the subareas of the state. The 1970 report excludes material described in the *Directory of Federal Statistics for Local Areas* and the *Directory of Federal Statistics for States*. An appendix to the 1970 report contains a state-by-state bibliography of supplementary sources even more complete than the one provided annually in the *Statistical Abstract of the United States*.

## FEDERAL STATISTICS FOR LOCAL AREAS AND THE 1970 CENSUSES OF POPULATION AND HOUSING

Most of the maps in this atlas are based on data from the 1970 Censuses of Population and Housing. Much of the background information, such as national and regional averages, is from the *County and City Data Book, 1972* or the earlier edition published in 1967.[§]

Census questions are selected only after a lengthy process.[‖] Each question must conform to guidelines established by Congress. Each potential census question must be submitted to the Office of Management and Budget by the Census Bureau for approval and review to ensure that the data obtained are "valid and appropriate to the purpose intended." Final authority for determining which approved questions will be included is lodged with the Secretary of Commerce.

The Census Bureau decides which questions are most important by consulting people who need the statistics. The needs of government agencies receive top priority, but those of businessmen, labor groups, research workers, and others are also considered—often through the use of advisory committees. In 1966 the Bureau also obtained suggestions and comments through intensive discussion with many individuals, organizations, and federal agency representatives in a series of locally sponsored public meetings in 23 cities across the country. The questions proposed for 1970 are too numerous to present here. Many were dismissed as falling outside the broad public interest, which is the first criterion for possible inclusion. Others were vetoed as too complex or too personal, as more appropriate for a national sample survey than for the Census, or for other reasons.

Among the proposals rejected for one or more of the above-mentioned reasons were questions on exterior building materials of houses, amount of taxes paid, automobile accidents, religion, union membership, ownership of musical instruments, smoking, multiple job holding, distance to shopping areas, stock ownership, and expected family size. The final format of the 1970 census questionnaire represented a balance between meeting the needs of those who use data to carry out program and research responsibilities and avoiding exorbitant costs to citizens and the government.

### Sampling People

Only five questions are asked of all individuals. These "complete count" or "100 percent" items on relationship to household head, sex, race, age, and marital status permit an accurate count of persons in each area as required by the Constitution to determine representation in Congress. All other information concerning individuals is obtained from questions asked of only a sample of the population. There were 15 percent and 5 percent samples in the 1970 Census, and certain questions common to both samples yielded a 20 percent sample:

*100 percent items*
   Relationship to head of household
   Color or race
   Age (month and year of birth)
   Sex
   Marital status

*20 percent items*
   State or country of birth
   Years of school completed
   Number of children ever born
   Activity 5 years ago (working, in Armed forces, attending college)
   Employment status
   Hours worked last week
   Weeks worked last year
   Last year in which worked
   Occupation, industry, and class of worker
   Income last year
      Wage and salary income
      Self-employment income
      Other income

*15 percent items*
   Country of birth of parents
   Mother tongue
   Year moved into this house
   Place of residence 5 years ago
   School or college enrollment (public or private)
   Veteran status
   Place of work
   Means of transportation to work

*5 percent items*
   Mexican or Spanish origin or descent
   Citizenship
   Year of immigration
   Marital history
   Vocational training completed
   Presence and duration of disability
   Occupation-industry 5 years ago

---

*U.S. Bureau of the Census. *Statistical Abstract of the United States: 1974*, 95th edition. Washington, D.C.: U.S. Government Printing Office, 1974.

†The directory was published by the U.S. Government Printing Office in 1970.

‡Both directories were published by the U.S. Government Printing Office, the directory for local areas in 1967 and the directory for states in 1968.

§U.S. Bureau of the Census. *County and City Data Book, 1972*. (A Statistical Abstract Supplement.) Washington, D.C.: U.S. Government Printing Office, 1973.

‖U.S. Bureau of the Census. *1970 Census User's Guide*, Parts 1 and 2. Washington, D.C.: U.S. Government Printing Office, 1970.

The size of the area for which statistics were to be tabulated and published determined in part whether a question was asked of everyone or of a sample of people. Information required for apportionment purposes and data to be tabulated for city blocks were collected on a 100 percent basis; information to be tabulated for larger areas, the smallest being a census tract, was collected on a 15 or 20 percent sample basis. The 5 percent sample provides reliable data for large counties and all states.

Although the average census tract has a population of about 4,000 persons, tracts with as few as 1,000 persons are not unusual. A tract with just 1,000 inhabitants would be expected to have perhaps 300 households (and household heads). For a 5 percent sample this would mean 15 households, of which 10 might be owner-occupied and 5 renter-occupied. When combined for larger areas, such as an entire SMSA, 5 percent data could be expected to be fairly reliable. However, 5 percent sample data for census tracts, available on census summary tapes and used to construct many maps in this atlas, can be used for statistical analysis only with great caution

*Sampling Housing Units*

The basic unit in census sampling is the housing unit. Therefore, the sampling percentages (20, 15, and 5) are the same for housing units as for people. For example, in a household where each person answers 15 percent sample population questions, 15 percent sample housing data are also obtained. There are more complete-count housing questions (15) than population questions because of the need for housing data on a city-block basis where a sample would not be reliable because of the small number of cases. These block data are essential to public and private housing programs, renewal, city planning, and other work related to the physical characteristics of our environment.

*100 percent items*
    Number of units at this address
    Telephone available
    Direct or indirect access to unit
    Kitchen or cooking facilities
    Complete kitchen facilities
    Condition of housing unit
    Rooms
    Water supply
    Flush toilet
    Bathtub or shower
    Basement
    Tenure
    Commercial establishment on property
    Value
    Contract rent
    Vacancy status
    Months vacant

*20 percent items*
    Heating equipment
    Components of gross rent
    Year structure built
    Number of units in structure and whether a trailer
    Farm resident (acreage and sales of farm products)

*15 percent items*
    Source of water
    Sewage disposal
    Bathrooms
    Air conditioning
    Automobiles
    Stories, elevator in structure
    Fuel—heating, cooking, water heating
    Bedrooms

*5 percent items*
    Clothes washing machine
    Clothes dryer
    Dishwasher
    Home food freezer
    Television
    Radio
    Second home

*Collecting the Data*

In 145 of the more populous SMSAs and some rural test counties, householders were asked to fill in questionnaires and return them by mail to the local census field office. Enumerators obtained the necessary information from households that either did not respond or returned incomplete questionnaires. For the balance of the country, the traditional house-to-house canvass was used, supplemented (as in 1960) by the distribution to all households shortly before Census Day of a questionnaire containing the 100 percent population and housing questions.

The major steps in the mail-out/mail-back system were as follows: Over a span of approximately six months in 1969, about 40 million individual address labels were printed out from a computer tape Address Register containing city residential addresses. These addresses were derived from a commercial mailing list. The labels contained apartment designation (in multiunit structures), house number, street name, city, and postal ZIP code; however, they did not contain the name of the householder. Each label was affixed to a card, and the cards were turned over to the Post Office Department for transmittal to their respective letter carriers. Each carrier checked his cards for completeness and accuracy. Nonexistent addresses were marked for deletion, incorrect addresses were corrected, and addresses for which the carrier had not been given a card were listed for addition to the Address Register cards. Lists were then returned to the Census Bureau and the necessary revisions were made on the computer tape.

The corrected tape was then processed through an Address Coding Guide so that each address could be assigned its appropriate geographic identification codes describing its tract, block, ward, city, county, and so forth. Finally, the addresses were identified with the census field control codes for district office, enumeration district (ED), and serial number within the ED. Each address was designated through a random-start serialization technique to receive one of the three types of questionnaires. The three types were the "short form" which contained the 100 percent items and went to 80 of every 100 housing units; the "15 percent long form" which contained the 100, 20, and 15 percent items and went to 15 of every 100 housing units; and the "5 percent long form" which contained the 100, 20, and 5 percent items and went to 5 of every 100 housing units.

The mail-out/mail-back process did not cover entire SMSAs but only the portions receiving city delivery service from the Post Office Department. For the balance of the SMSAs, temporary Census Bureau employees developed Address Registers which were then used to prepare hand-addressed mailing pieces. About 15 March 1970 all mailing pieces—containing questionnaires, instruction booklets, and return envelopes—were transmitted to local post offices. The carriers sorted the mailing pieces to recheck whether any residential addresses had been omitted. The missing addresses were sent to the appropriate local Census Bureau office where they were added to the Address Registers and mailing pieces were prepared. About four days before Census Day—Wednesday, 1 April 1970—all the mailing pieces were delivered. During the delivery process, the carriers made a final check for missing addresses and informed the Census office accordingly.

Householders were requested to fill out and mail back their questionnaires on Census Day. This request was reinforced by a widespread publicity campaign. Within a few days after Census Day, checking and review of the mail returns began. Incomplete questionnaires and nonresponses were followed up. The goal of the operation was to have a completed questionnaire for each address on the Register or an explanation on the Register of why a listed address was not included in the Census (perhaps it was really part of another housing unit or it was not a residential address even though the letter carrier had checked it).

Mail enumeration gave all respondents a chance to answer questions for themselves at their own speed and to check their records if necessary, thus assuring privacy and increasing the likelihood of accuracy. The mail system also permitted the Census Bureau to concentrate its effort on hard-to-enumerate areas by reducing demands on employees' time in areas where respondents were very cooperative about mailing back questionnaires. Nevertheless, certain problems developed during the processing of census questionnaires.

*Processing the Data*

Census Bureau workers had to assign acceptable entries in place of unacceptable or missing entries on a census questionnaire. Such assignments are made when an entry on a given item is missing (e.g., no age is given for a named individual) or when the information reported for a person on an item is inconsistent with other information about the person (e.g., 10 years of schooling for a 6-year-old child). The process begins with a set of items stored in the computer from the most recently processed questionnaire containing the item. Substitutions are then made for missing items using the stored information. For inconsistent schooling, the number of years of schooling reported for the previous 6-year-old child would be substituted for the erroneous 10.

## CENSUS DATA PRODUCTS USED IN PREPARING THE ATLAS

The 1970 Censuses of Population and Housing are sources of a flexible data base from which a variety of data products and services may be obtained. Most maps in the atlas were constructed from this base.

Second Count Summary Tapes were used for basic racial data. These tapes have two file subdivisions. The Second Count file A contains about 3,500 cells of complete-count (i.e., 100 percent count) population and housing data summarized and cross-tabulated for each census tract; file B contains the same number of items of complete-count population and housing data, but they are summarized for states, counties, minor civil divisions (or census county divisions) places (cities, towns, and villages), and SMSAs.

Fourth Count Summary Tapes supplied most of the remaining atlas data. These tapes contain 20, 15, and 5 percent sample population and housing characteristics such as education, occupation, income, citizenship, vocational training, and household equipment and facilities. This count is organized into three file subdivisions. Fourth Count file A contains sample data for census tracts (sample data summaries are not available for areas smaller than census tracts); file B contains minor civil division or census county division sample summaries; and file C includes summaries for states, counties, SMSAs, and places. Files A and B and places in file C have 13,000 data cells summarized for each statistical unit. File C, excluding places, contains 30,000 data cells for each area.

Our use of census data raises two central questions: Does the Census yield data that are appropriate for a geographical analysis of national progress toward urban goals? Are the data accurate and meaningful? The answer to both questions is a qualified yes. Census data are imperfect, but no better alternative is available. Limitations of local and regional data series for comparative analysis are more serious than census data short-comings.

Census data are imperfect tools for measuring national well-being because they do not measure nutrition, health, crime, and perceptions of public safety. Some housing characteristics are measured well, but the ways different people use and react to different kinds of housing are measured only indirectly, which causes difficulty in making the kinds of connections among people, places, and problems we should be making. Whether we could use such data effectively, even if we had them, is another question; considerable theoretical work is prerequisite to acceptable definitions and measures of common concepts such as "neighborhood stability," "environmental quality," and "adequate housing."

As for reliability, data are most dependable for stable neighborhoods in which people are highly literate and prosperous. Neighborhoods in which social disorganization and population turnover are high often return the most unreliable census questionnaires, which is especially unfortunate since they are the places from which we need accurate information most badly. Persistent attempts to remedy undercounting and incomplete returns in inner-city neighborhoods have not been especially successful.

Having said all this, we are still convinced the game has been worth the candle or, perhaps more appropriately, the atlas is worth the price. So long as the qualifications described in Chapter 1 are kept in mind, misinterpretation should be minimal. Some *valid* information, even if it bears on problems of interest only indirectly, is always preferable to none, and we are confident that the generalized pictures we have painted of the socioeconomic geography of the 20 metropolitan regions are both useful and reasonably accurate.

# PART II

# CURRENT PATTERNS

# IN

# AMERICAN CITIES

## A. Cities of the Nation's Historic Metropolitan Core

Boston
New York-Northern New Jersey
Philadelphia
Hartford-Connecticut Valley

# CHAPTER 6

# Boston

*Boston is a state of mind surrounded by water.*

LOCAL PROVERB

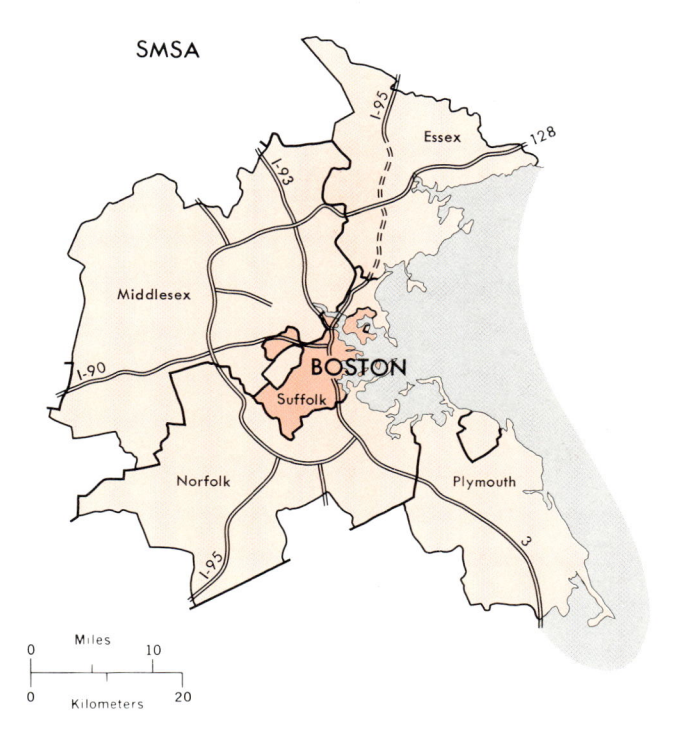

The 2,750,000 people in the Boston Standard Metropolitan Statistical Area (SMSA) form the nation's 8th most populous metropolitan area. The Daily Urban System (DUS) for which Boston serves as center embraces each New England town that daily sends at least 5 percent of its resident labor force to Boston and contiguous municipalities. The DUS has 3,850,000 inhabitants and is the 7th most populous DUS in the nation. Boston is small, with a population of only 640,000, but it is seriously underbounded. Adding the populations of independent cities such as Cambridge and Somerville to Boston's population would provide a more reasonable estimate of the size of the true "central city."

Boston is one of the oldest settlements in Anglo-America. Its proximity to Europe (it is closer to London than it is to Los Angeles) was an early advantage, but nearness to Europe became less important as settlement advanced into the continent. Even before the Revolution, Boston had begun to lose ground in favor of New York and Philadelphia. Boston was still the nation's 3rd city in 1850, but by 1900 it had dropped to 5th behind Chicago and St. Louis as well as New York and Philadelphia. A half century later it was 6th; Detroit and Los Angeles had surpassed it, but Boston had regained its lead over St. Louis (p. 10).

*Note:* All data are from the 1970 Censuses of Population and Housing unless otherwise indicated. Therefore the present tense refers to 1970 data except for income data which are from 1969. Cartographic conventions are explained in Chapter 1.

Boston is now growing slowly. The metropolitan area grew only 6.1 percent during the 1960s compared with the 16.6 percent increase for all SMSAs. The central-city population is falling fast. It has declined by 160,000 from an all-time high of 800,000 in 1950. Net out-migration, the loss of many housing units to urban renewal, demolition of substandard units, and freeway construction are contributing causes.

The SMSA embraces most of eastern Massachusetts. It includes all of Norfolk and Suffolk counties and parts of Essex, Middlesex, and Plymouth counties. In New England, SMSA boundaries often follow town rather than county boundaries. The DUS (p. 22) extends south into Plymouth County to the Rhode Island boundary, west into Worcester County, and north into New Hampshire.

The region is hilly as a result of recent glaciation. Rough, often wooded areas alternate with lakes and marshes. Extensive flat areas are rare except in river valleys or at river mouths. Like most early American settlements, Boston owes its origin to the junction of a river and salt water. The structural basin in which Boston is located and the mouths of the rivers and streams in the basin have been partially drowned by postglacial rises in sea level. In no other large city, except in New York and San Francisco, does the ocean penetrate so deeply into the urban core. Deep tidal estuaries hamper easy movement into and out of Boston in almost every direction.

Boston's older areas are flatter now than they have ever been. Early

*21*

## The Nation's Metropolitan Core: Boston

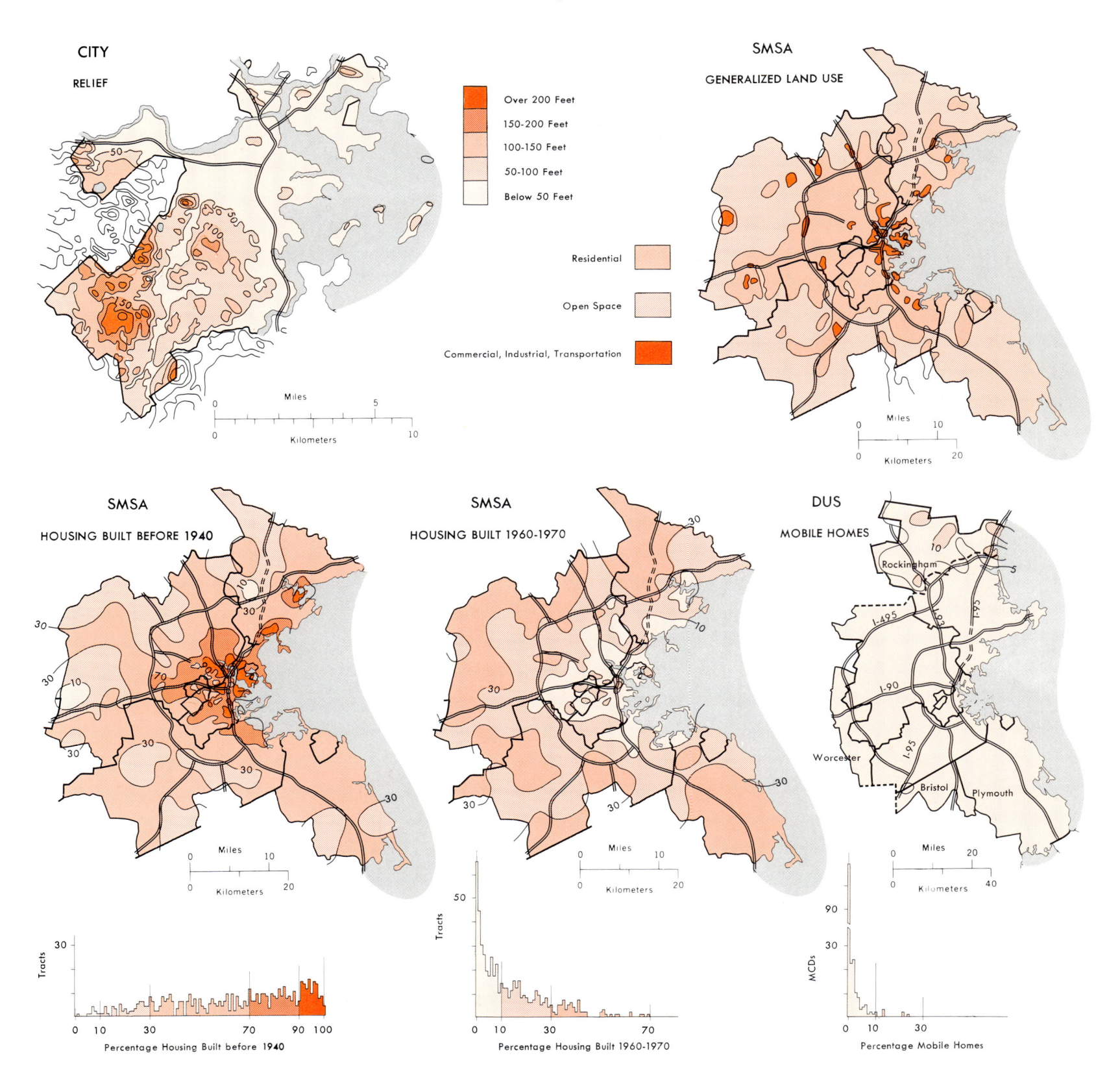

settlers began leveling the land by shoving the tops of hills into the bay, and the practice continued into the 20th century. The northern third of the city is low, with only a few small hills rising more than 50 feet (15 meters) above sea level. Elevations rise southwest and west from the Central Business District (CBD) but not sharply. Only a small area of the city rises above 250 feet (75 meters) at a point four miles (2.5 kilometers) inland. Terrain becomes a barrier to movement and construction outside the immediate confines of the basin, but within the city of Boston it presents few problems.

Land use in the Boston SMSA is governed by the city's historic port function and by transportation routes. Most of the land fronting the bay or the estuaries is given over to docks, warehouses, naval facilities, and the metropolitan airport. Extensive tracts of industrial or commercial land away from the metropolitan core are rare. The typical pattern for Boston is mixed land use; small light-manufacturing firms intermingle with residential and commercial functions. The continuously built-up residential area lies roughly within Boston's circumferential highway (128) with salients extending along Interstate 90 to the west and U.S. 1 to the southwest.

### HOUSING

**Housing Age.** Boston's housing stock is exceptionally old. Of the housing in the SMSA, 64 percent was built before 1940; in the central city the percentage rises to 77. Only 14 percent of the SMSA's housing was built from 1960 to March 1970. Older housing is not inherently bad; soundly built housing will last indefinitely if it is well

22

maintained. But if it is not maintained, an aged housing stock can quickly become a serious urban liability. Patterns of old and new housing in the Boston region are closely tied to transportation routes. There is some clustering of older housing in established outlying towns within the SMSA. The area in which more than 70 percent of the housing dates from before 1940 forms an irregular semicircle around the central core. The 30 percent isopleth is even more irregular, extending farther toward the periphery along some of the major highways and leaving interstices below 30 percent. The map of new housing reverses this pattern, as one would expect in a region in which only 22 percent of the housing dates from the 1940s and 1950s. New housing is now filling in the open areas that were unsettled during the era when people went to work by commuter train or by automobile on pre–World War II highways.

**Mobile Homes.** Mobile homes are of minor importance in the Boston DUS. There are only 1,800 in the entire DUS. In New Hampshire, mobile homes are a larger component of the local housing stock, especially in southern Rockingham County where they exceed 10 percent of all dwelling units in some minor civil divisions.

**Single-Unit Detached Housing.** This is a limited option in most of Boston. Only 12 percent of the city's housing stock consists of such units. Row houses, duplexes, triple-deckers, and apartments are the

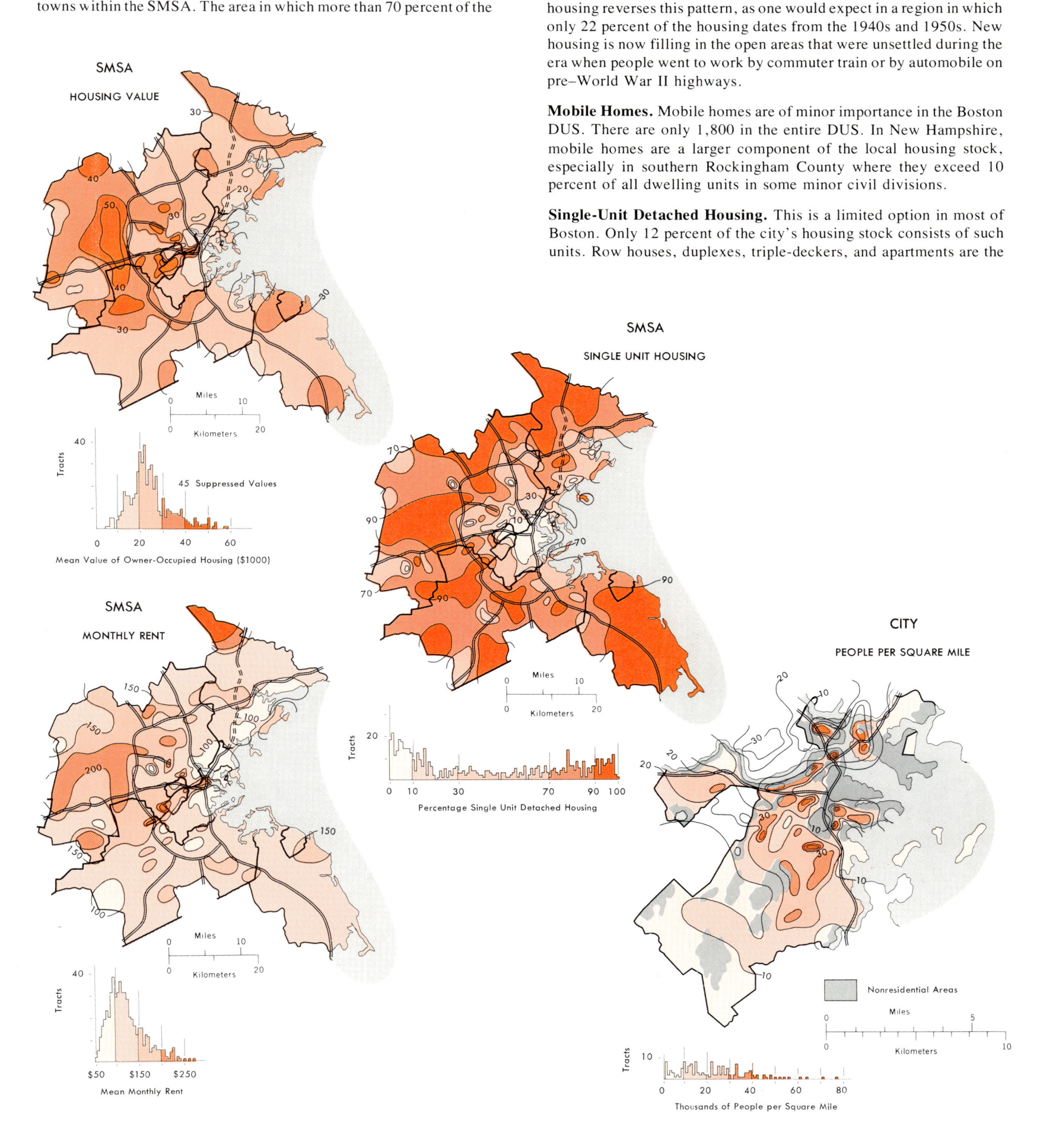

*The Nation's Metropolitan Core Boston*

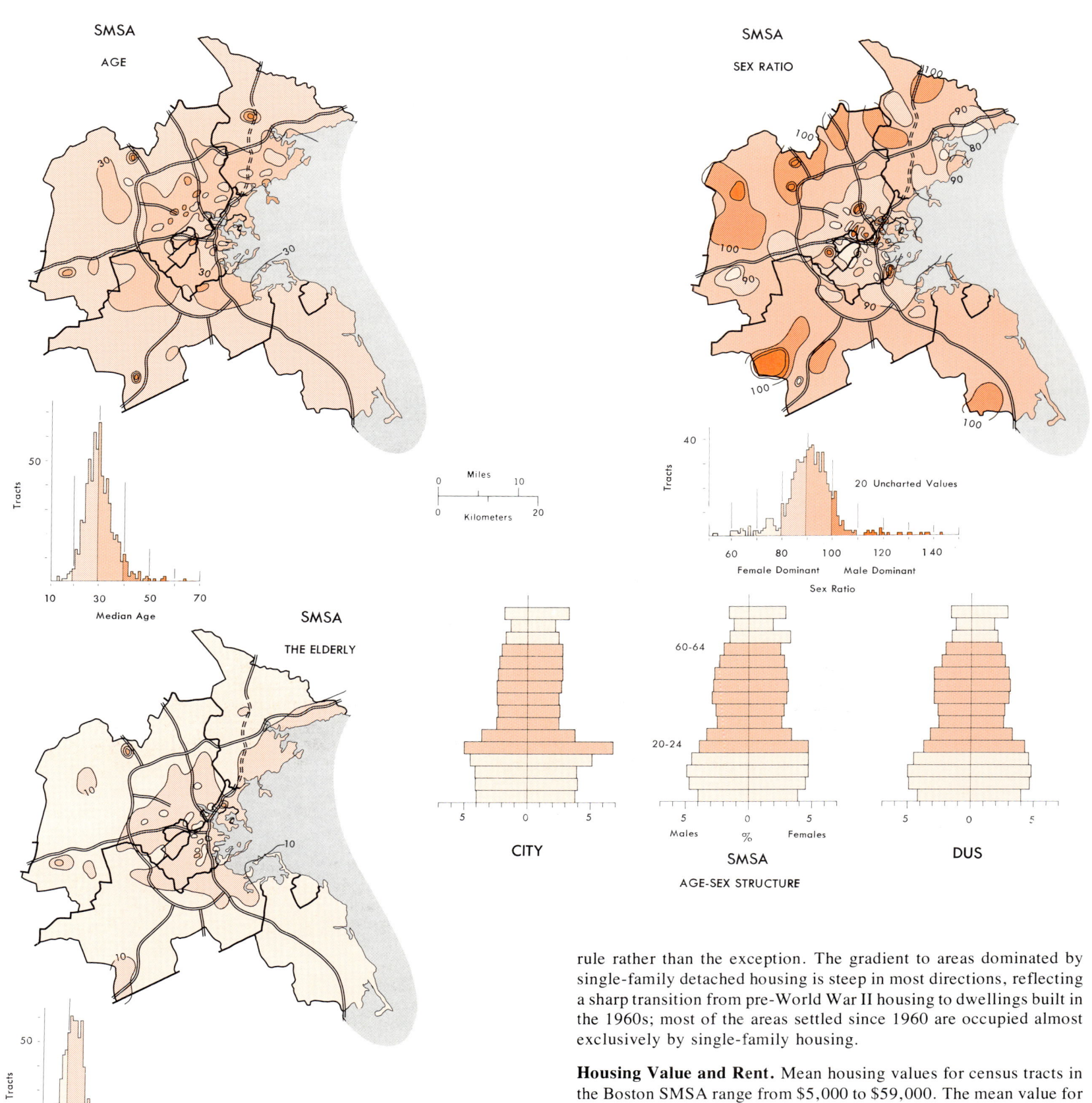

rule rather than the exception. The gradient to areas dominated by single-family detached housing is steep in most directions, reflecting a sharp transition from pre-World War II housing to dwellings built in the 1960s; most of the areas settled since 1960 are occupied almost exclusively by single-family housing.

**Housing Value and Rent.** Mean housing values for census tracts in the Boston SMSA range from $5,000 to $59,000. The mean value for the entire SMSA is $27,000 and for the central city, $21,000. Tracts with high values cluster directly west of the city with a secondary concentration west of the CBD. The historic axis of upper-class residential expansion in Boston has been westward. Mean monthly rents show the same directional bias except for the higher prices commanded by units close to the ocean. The mean rent for all SMSA tracts is $117, with a central-city mean of $111. There is little variation in mean rents among large metropolitan areas, but there is considerable variation at the upper end of the scale. The most expensive tract in Boston has a mean of $290, whereas maximum mean rents in excess of $400 occur in some western cities.

Metropolitan Boston possesses a varied housing stock which our highly generalized maps can depict only in the broadest outlines.

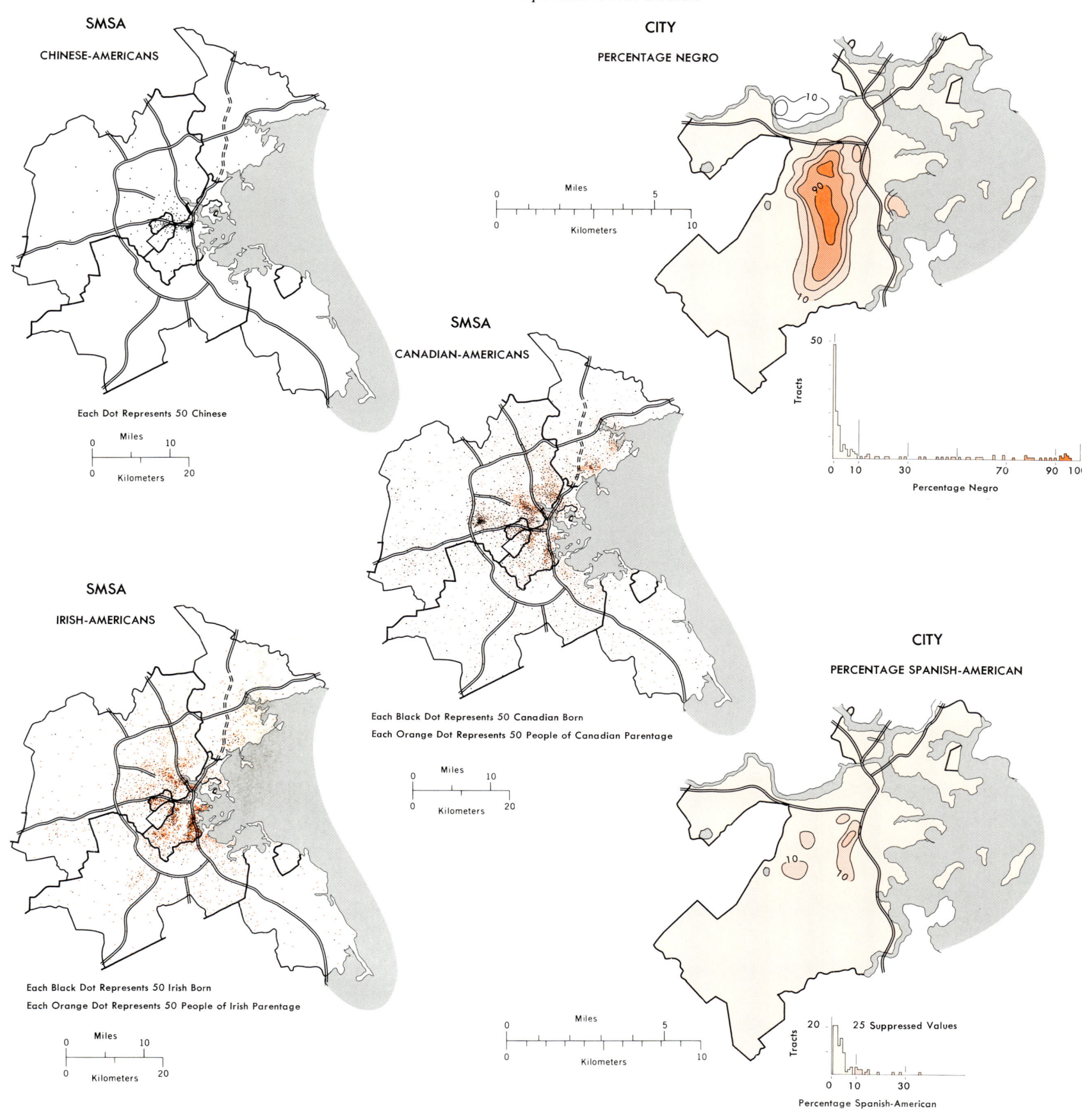

*The Nation's Metropolitan Core: Boston*

## THE PEOPLE

**Population Density.** Boston's overall population density of 14,000 per square mile (5,400 per square kilometer) is high for an American city. Tract population densities range from below 10,000 per square mile (3,900 per square kilometer) in the south of the city to 60,000 and 70,000 per square mile (23,200 to 27,000 per square kilometer) in a few of the tracts adjacent to the CBD. Densities over 50,000 per square mile (19,300 per square kilometer) are consolidated on the map. The southern part of the city is an area of newer, lower-density housing. The northern part of the city around the Boston inner harbor

There is some old housing in almost every portion of the city, but this is not true of new housing. The long-term future of Boston's aged housing stock is unclear. Three-fourths of Boston City housing is rented property, and renters are under increasing financial pressure. Rents throughout the metropolitan area rose 65 percent during the 1960s whereas median income rose only 45 percent (see p. 294 for a map of rent pressure in Boston). High rentals and higher returns to landlords could provide incentives to maintain and preserve the older housing stock, but to the extent that rentals absorb increasingly larger shares of renters' incomes, other problems may develop.

## The Nation's Metropolitan Core: Boston

**SMSA RUSSIAN-AMERICANS**

Each Black Dot Represents 50 Russian Born
Each Orange Dot Represents 50 People of Russian Parentage

**SMSA ITALIAN-AMERICANS**

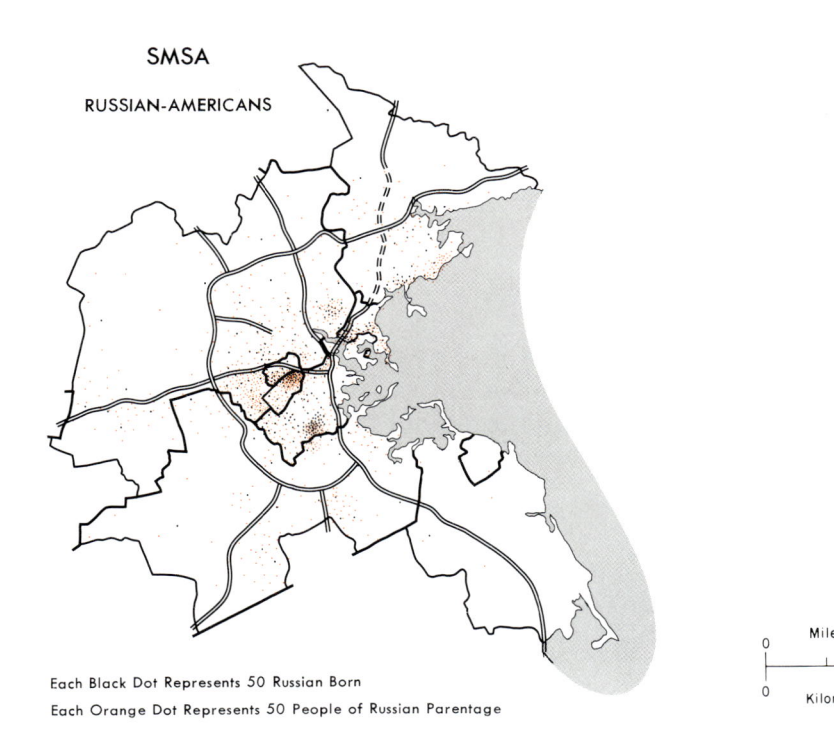

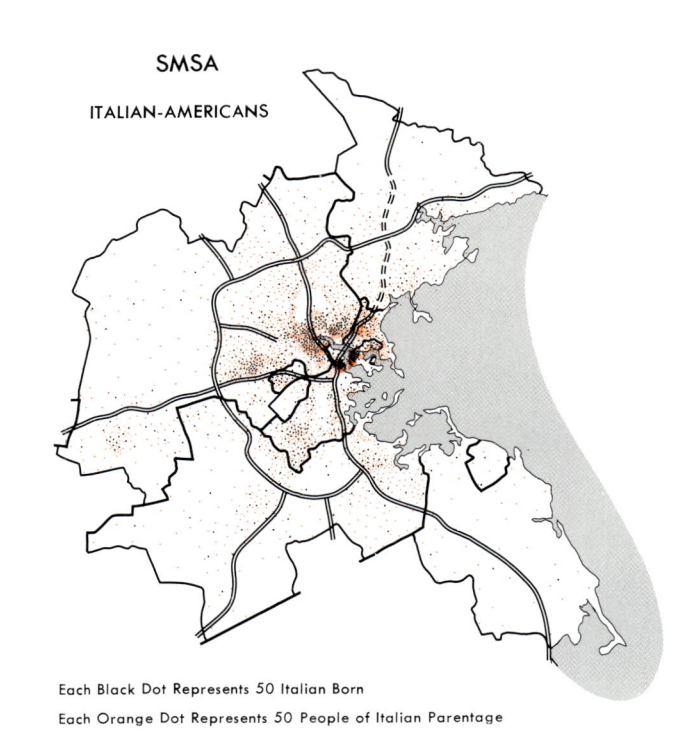

Each Black Dot Represents 50 Italian Born
Each Orange Dot Represents 50 People of Italian Parentage

has densities well over 20,000 per square mile (7,700 per square kilometer). In contrast to many American cities, the predominantly black areas are not the most densely occupied portions of the city (p. 25); rather, densities peak in white ethnic neighborhoods and especially in the South Boston area immediately east of U.S. 1.

**Age and the Elderly.** The median age of the metropolitan population is 29 years, and the central-city median is 28 years. The typical American pattern of an older city population, a younger suburban population, and a higher median age on the metropolitan periphery breaks down in Boston. A large college-student population and stable ethnic neighborhoods with high rates of natural increase produce a central-city population that is younger than usual. The inner ring of suburbs has median ages exceeding 30 years, although there are numerous communities to the north of Boston City where medians fall below 30 years. The small, high median-age tract values on the metropolitan periphery are caused by institutionalized populations.

The elderly constitute 11 percent of the metropolitan population and 13 percent of the city's people. For the most part they are slightly concentrated in the central portion of the metropolitan region and in the coastal areas northeast of Boston City. In few tracts other than those containing institutions is more than 30 percent of the population in the over-64 category.

**Sex Ratio.** There are 1.1 females for every male in the metropolitan region and almost 1.2 females for each male in the city of Boston. There is a surplus of city females in each five-year age cohort over 15 years, but they are especially concentrated in the 15 to 24-year-old group and in the older population. The pyramid suggests that more young women than young men migrate to Boston in search of employment. The surplus of older women is caused largely by the greater longevity of women at all ages past adolescence, although there is also most likely some carryover of the younger female surplus into older age cohorts. The surplus of females is less evident at the metropolitan level, especially in the 15 to 24-year-old group. Only scattered areas in the metropolis are male-dominant. Isolated areas in the central core, usually composed of predominantly male college populations or derelict groups, occasionally have sex ratios (males divided by females times 100) over 100. The male-dominant area on the western edge of the metropolitan region surrounds the U.S. Army installation at Natick. Tracts with values over 110 on the periphery are correctional institutions and a veterans' hospital.

**Negroes.** The 105,000 blacks who live in the city of Boston comprise 16 percent of the city's people and 82 percent of the SMSA's black population. As is true in most metropolitan areas, few blacks live outside the central city (see p. 28). Within Boston, blacks occupy the South Bay and Roxbury areas south of the city center and a public housing project on Columbia Point. Railyards and a freeway separate blacks from white ethnics on the northeast quadrant of the ghetto; elsewhere demarcation is determined less by physical features than by hostility. An SMSA map is on p. 382.

**Spanish-Americans.** There are 36,000 Spanish-speaking people living in Boston. Some are located on the fringes of the black ghetto, although the 25 suppressed tracts and the absence of zero values in the histogram suggest that a few Spanish-Americans live in every tract in the city. Outside the central city, Hispanics are scattered throughout the metropolitan area (see p. 390). About half of the city's Spanish-Americans are Puerto Rican immigrants, most of whom arrived during the 1960s. The remainder are mostly from Central and South America and Cuba.

**Chinese-Americans.** The Census requires nonwhites to identify themselves as members of 1 of 8 "racial" categories: Negro, Indian, Japanese, Chinese, Filipino, Korean, Hawaiian, or Other. Some 12,000 people in the Boston SMSA identified themselves as Chinese. The Chinese are the most rapidly growing ethnic group in Boston. They numbered 2,000 in 1950, and there are now 7,000 in the city and 5,000 elsewhere in the metropolitan area. The city's Chinatown is located just south of the CBD at the junction of the Massachusetts Turnpike and the Fitzgerald Expressway.

**Irish-Americans.** The Boston SMSA has 26,000 Irish-born and 121,000 who have at least one Irish-born parent. The total of the two — Boston's Irish foreign stock — is 5 percent of the metropolitan population. Within the city, Irish foreign stock constitutes 8 percent of the population. There are three major clusters of Irish-Americans: one stretches along the east side of the city; the second is located along the city's western boundary and in Boston's western "appendix"; and the third is across the Charles River in Somerville. Irish-Americans are sparse in the heavily black area of central Boston and in upper-class Brookline.

**Canadian-Americans.** Boston's Canadian foreign stock is scattered throughout the region with some clustering on the north, especially in

## The Nation's Metropolitan Core: Boston

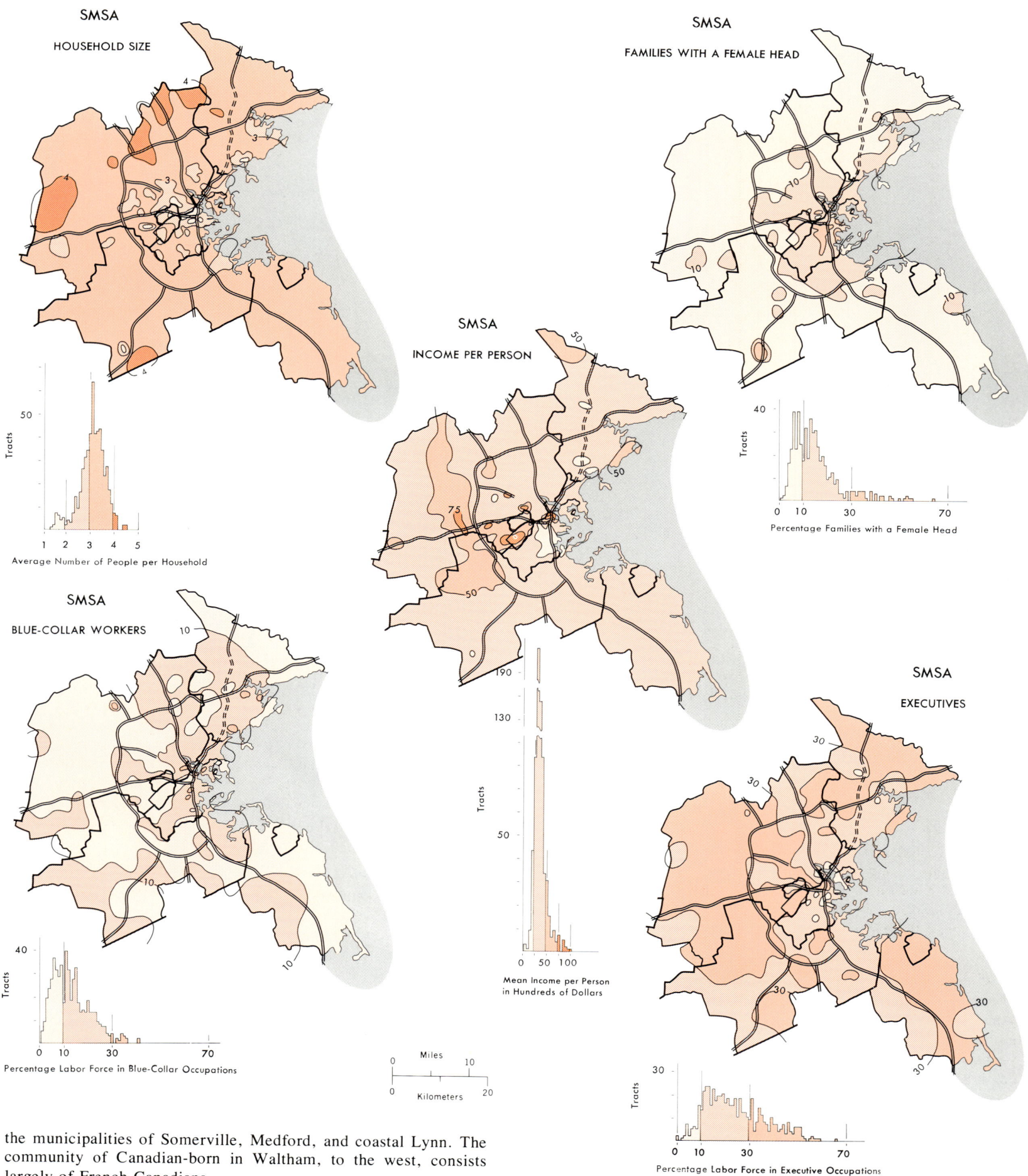

the municipalities of Somerville, Medford, and coastal Lynn. The community of Canadian-born in Waltham, to the west, consists largely of French-Canadians.

**Russian-Americans.** Russians (mostly Jews) began to arrive in large numbers late in the 19th century. By 1910, Russian foreign stock aggregated 9 percent of the city's people. Russian Jews first settled south of the CBD in what is now Chinatown. From there settlement expanded southward along an elevated railway line. As Jews

*The Nation's Metropolitan Core: Boston*

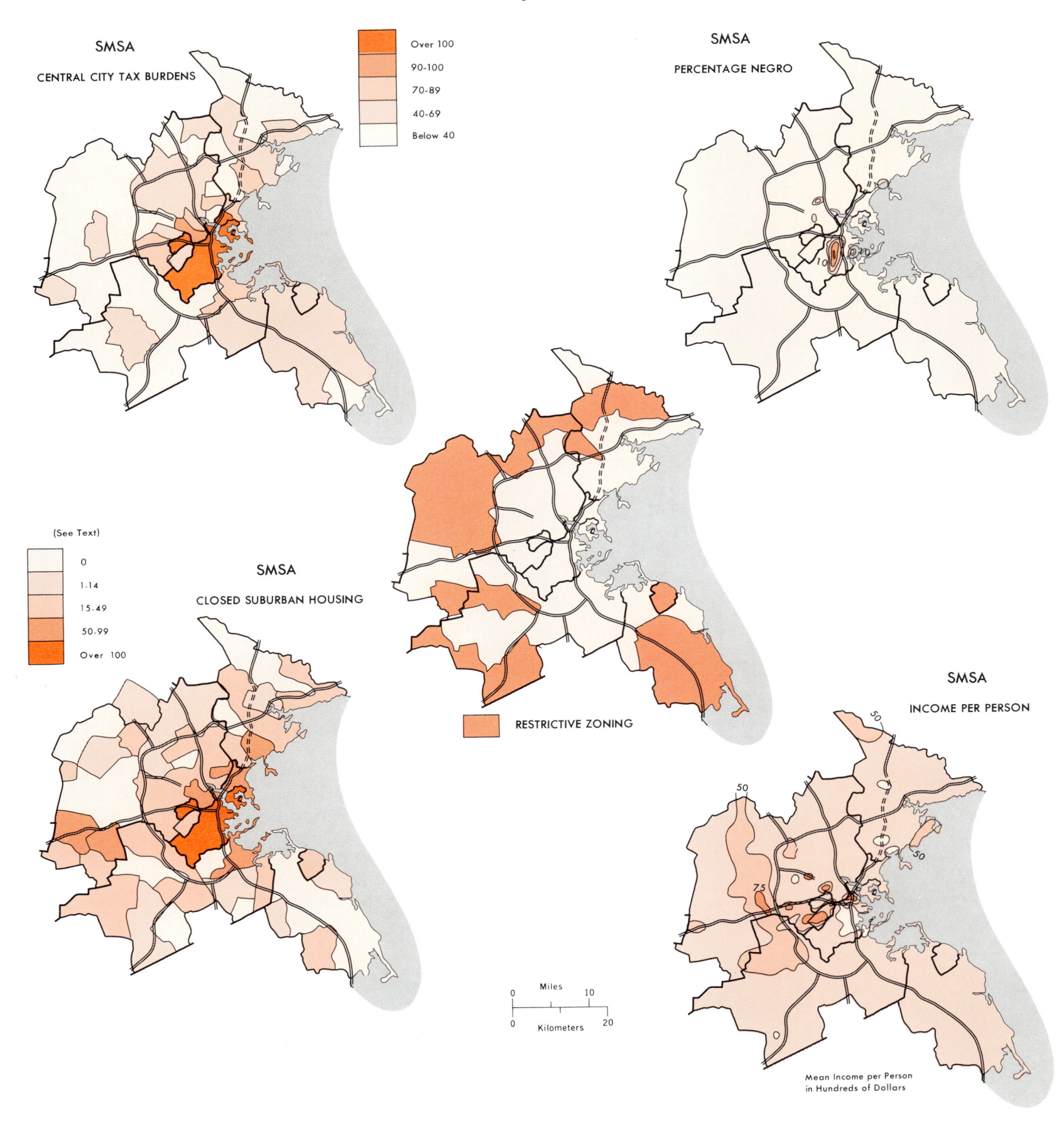

prospered after 1920, they began to leave the area. Some moved farther south and others went west into Brookline and adjacent Newton. A third cluster developed in Chelsea, to the north. The southern extension in the Roxbury neighborhood has now been taken over almost completely by blacks.

**Italian-Americans.** Italian foreign stock numbers 192,000, three-fourths of whom live in Boston City. Concentrations of Italians are still common in the central city — sometimes, as in the North End and East Boston (across the harbor), almost to the exclusion of non-Italians.

Boston's ethnic composition has been a persistent source of conflict. Competition for jobs and housing among Irish, Chinese, Jews, Italians, and blacks has produced a constant shifting of occupations and residences so that some areas of the city have played host to four distinct minority groups during the last century. The North End, for example, was as Irish in the 1800s as it is Italian today.

## SMSA
### POLITICAL FRAGMENTATION

- No Metropolitan Services
- At Least One Metropolitan Service
- All Three Metropolitan Services
- City of BOSTON

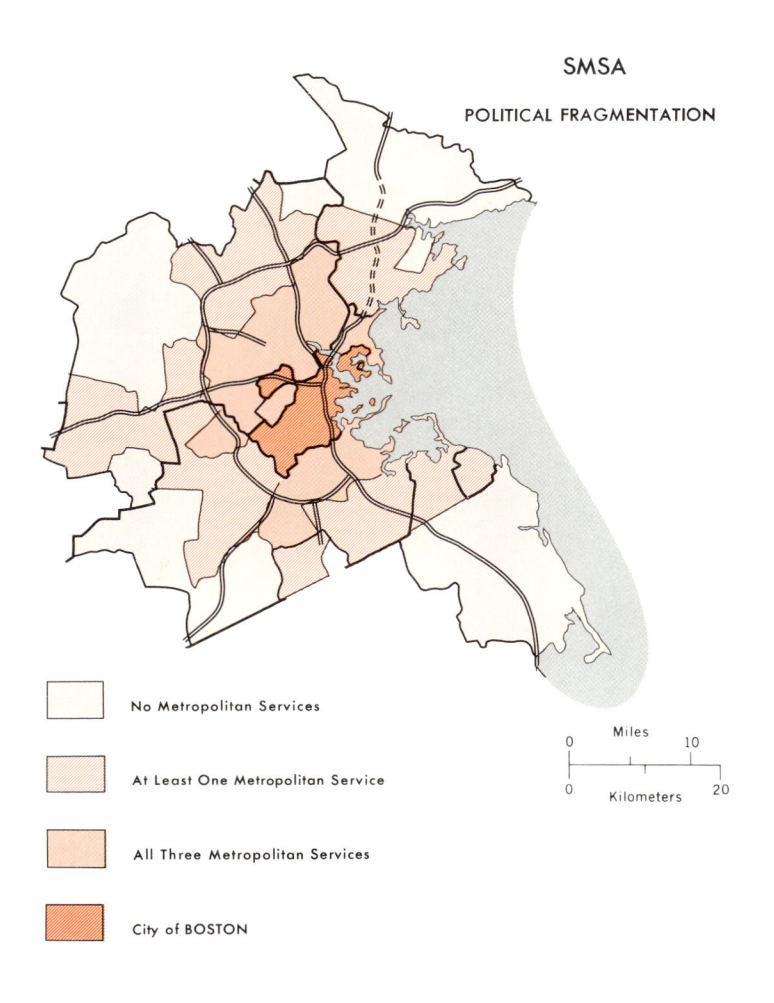

Neighborhoods are taken seriously in Boston. One expert on Boston's fluid settlement geography calls Boston's ethnic neighborhoods "tribal domains."

## SOCIOECONOMIC CHARACTERISTICS

**Household Size.** There are 3.1 persons in the average SMSA household. Boston is typical in having smaller households in the central city and larger households in newer housing on the metropolitan periphery. Tracts in which the average household has fewer than 2 people are in downtown Boston and the adjacent Back Bay area, and around Harvard University across the Charles River. Outlying towns, like Salem and Lynn on the north shore and Quincy on the south, have mean tract values below 3 persons. Elsewhere in the region values fall between 3 and 4 except for the scattered larger households on the SMSA margins.

**Female Headship.** Over 10 percent of all households are headed by females in a broad zone extending from Quincy on the south around to Waltham on the west and then northeast to include Lynn and Salem. Percentages rise well above 30 in central Boston, especially in the black neighborhoods, and there are also values over 30 percent in Irish neighborhoods east of the black ghetto. The high value in the southwest quadrant of the SMSA is a state correctional institution.

**Occupations.** A low proportion (12 percent) of Boston's labor force is in blue-collar (laborers and operatives) occupations. Tracts in which as much as a third of the total labor force is engaged in blue-collar jobs are rare throughout the region.

Executives (engineers, teachers, professionals, managers, proprietors, and administrators) are important components of tract labor-force structures on the northeastern, western, and southeastern sides of the SMSA. One-fourth of the SMSA labor force and a fifth of the central city's labor force work in executive occupations. On Boston's western boundary, the 30 percent isopleth almost follows the municipal boundary that separates higher-status Brookline from Boston. After swinging west, the 30 percent isopleth turns east again to include Cambridge, the Boston Back Bay area, and the CBD in the over-30-percent category.

**Income.** Mean income per person for the entire SMSA is $3,700 per year. The highest tract value of $10,000 occurs in a single tract in the prosperous Back Bay neighborhood immediately southwest of Boston Common (it is too small to map). The prosperity of the Brookline area and the region to the west and northwest of Boston generally is apparent. The high-income area in the northern CBD and the Beacon Hill section in Boston is more difficult to see because it is small, but it and Back Bay are notable as Boston's confirmation of the general rule that some well-to-do households usually live downtown. Tracts with mean per capita incomes below $2,500 are concentrated in eastern Boston. Some of the low-income tracts are located in predominantly black areas, but an almost equal number are in adjacent, heavily Irish neighborhoods.

## TOPICS OF SPECIAL INTEREST IN THE BOSTON REGION

**Restrictive Zoning.** Suburban zoning regulations have helped to exclude low-income housing by requiring large lots and other expensive features. The center map on page 28 shows areas that have one or more of the following regulations: prohibition of multifamily housing; prohibition of two-family housing; 70 percent or more of the local residential land zoned for minimum lots of one acre. A 1969 "antisnob" law requires every Massachusetts civil division to designate a modest percentage of its area for low- and moderate-income housing. It is unclear how effective the legislation will be in the long run for opening the suburbs to low-income groups. As of June 1972, very few places had progressed toward meeting the mandated goal of one-tenth of all housing units for low- and moderate-income families. As indicated on the map of closed suburban housing on page 28, only the city of Boston had achieved the goal and only the older outlying cities were more than halfway there. About half of the suburban areas in the SMSA had made no progress at all.

**Taxes.** Some secondary problems that can emerge when primary problems are seriously malapportioned in a metropolitan region are evident in the map of central-city tax burdens (p. 28). Tax rates equalized for variations in assessment practices are as much as four times higher in Boston than they are in suburban communities. In general, towns with high per capita incomes (p. 27) have low tax rates; the reverse is not necessarily true, for some towns with low tax rates are middle-income rather than high-income areas. As long as blacks (p. 28) and other low-income groups are confined to central cities that are already taxing their citizens at rates far higher than suburban communities, devising strictly local solutions to human problems will be difficult.

**Political Fragmentation.** The Boston area pioneered some kinds of metropolitan government. Metropolitan cooperation started with a Sewerage Board in 1889 and soon spread to park planning and public water networks. Despite such early and continuing efforts, the metropolis of the 1970s is a crazy quilt of metropolitan and nonmetropolitan services. Some places have one or more of the three metropolitan services, whereas others have none.

---

Boston's age is at once the source of some of its problems and a valuable asset. Age bequeaths the city an antiquated housing stock and narrow streets — often arranged almost randomly — that bedevil newcomers and visitors accustomed to more open, orderly vistas. But these same features produce a sense of closeness and neighborhood identity that is often absent in younger cities.

# CHAPTER 7

# New York – Northern New Jersey

*New York lays hands upon a man's bowels; he grows drunk with ecstasy;
he grows young and full of glory; he feels that he can never die.*

THOMAS WOLFE, *The Web and the Rock*, 1937

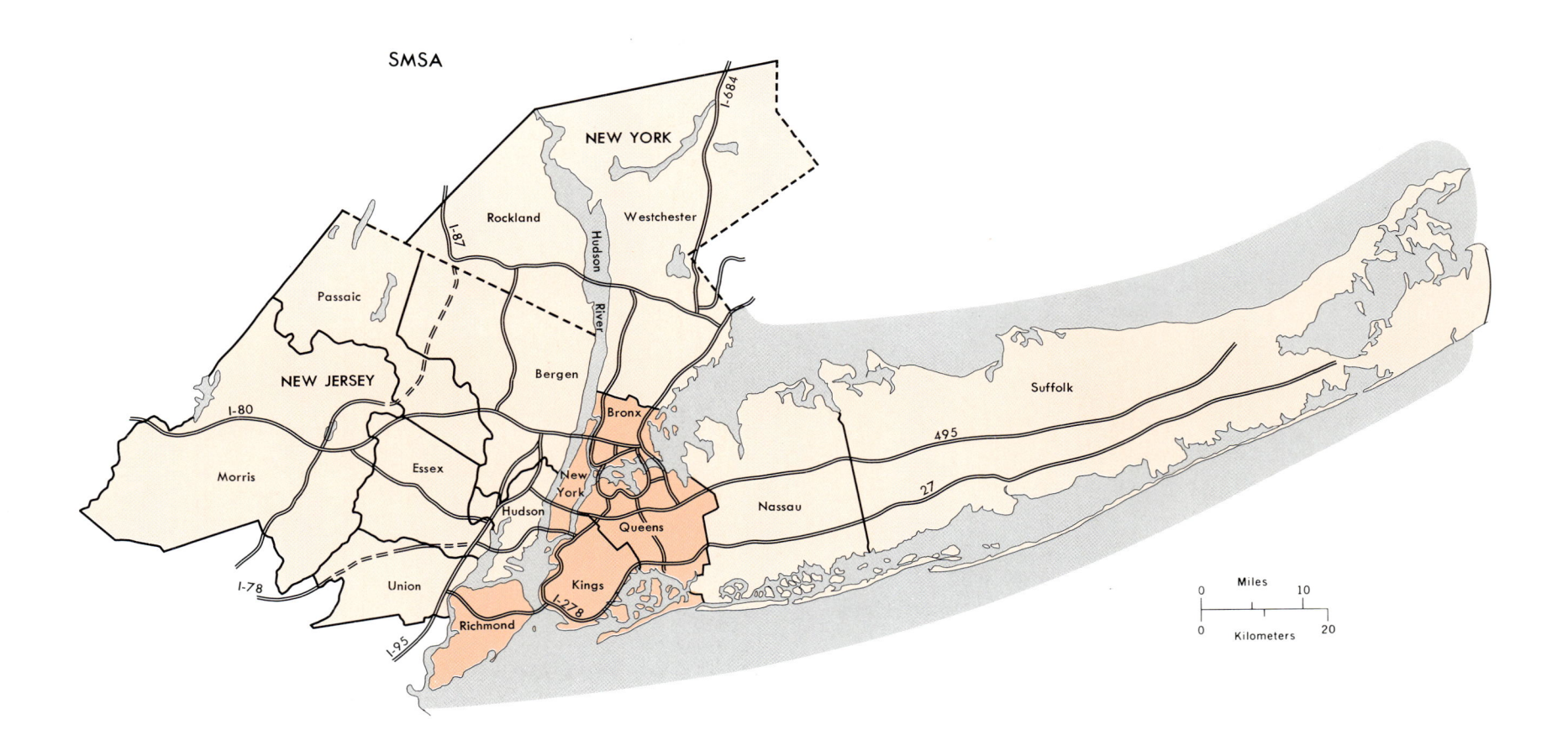

Americans refer to New York City as the Big Apple. The origins of the sobriquet are obscure, but the name is appropriate. New York City has a population of 8,000,000 people. There are four Standard Metropolitan Statistical Areas (SMSAs) in the region (New York City, Jersey City, Paterson-Clifton-Passaic, and Newark), which have a combined population of 15,400,000. The New York City SMSA is the nation's most populous metropolitan area. The commuting region or Daily Urban System (DUS) — consisting of New Jersey and New York counties and Connecticut towns that send at least 5 percent of their labor forces to the metropolitan employment core each day — contains 17,450,000 people (p. 33). It is the most populous DUS in the United States. No other place in the nation begins to compare with the New York metropolitan region in size and economic power. As early as 1800, the New York settlement was the nation's largest city (p. 10). The New York metropolitan complex has always served as the hinge between the United States and the rest of the world. It is America's "world city," equivalent to London, New Delhi, Tokyo, Moscow, and Peking. New York's international position in finance and trade arises naturally out of the city's location and its historic role as the nation's entrepôt.

The metropolitan community spreads over three states and a variety of landscapes. The core area of New York City, Newark, and Jersey City is almost an archipelago. Four of New York City's five boroughs (each of which is a separate county) are located on islands; only Bronx County is part of the mainland. Such penetration is excellent for waterborne commerce, but it hampered landward connections as railroads overtook river and canal transport after 1850. The New Jersey cities, which had grown slowly until then, grew rapidly during the second half of the 19th century on the economic base of landward connections with the rest of the nation.

The city's five boroughs spread across a coastal plain interspersed with low moraines. New York (Manhattan Island) and Bronx counties rise above 200 feet (61 meters) in scattered spots in the northern part of

*Note:* All data are from the 1970 Censuses of Population and Housing unless otherwise indicated. Therefore the present tense refers to 1970 data except for income data which are from 1969. Cartographic conventions are explained in Chapter 1.

*The Nation's Metropolitan Core: New York-Northern New Jersey*

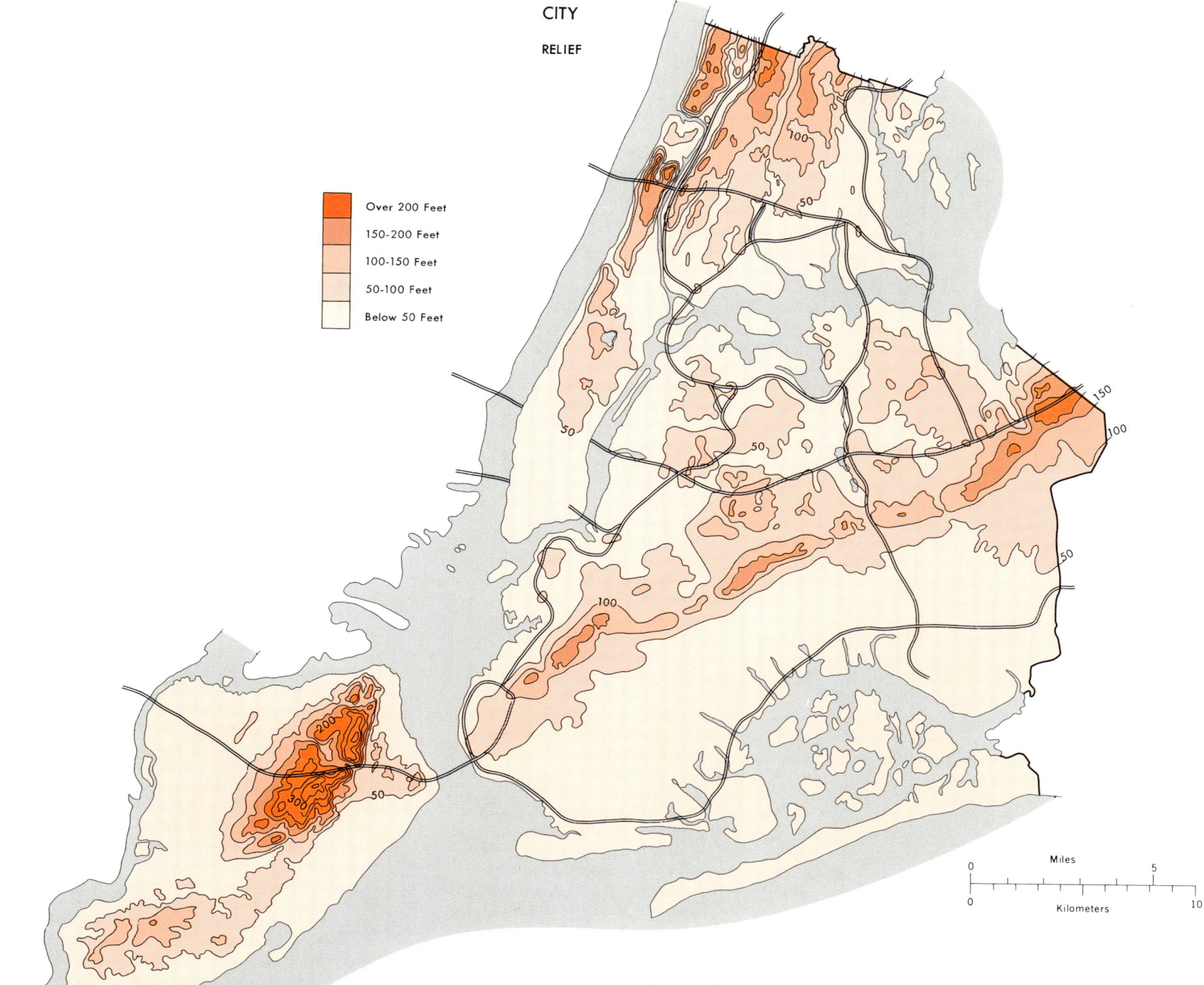

CITY

RELIEF

Over 200 Feet
150-200 Feet
100-150 Feet
50-100 Feet
Below 50 Feet

the city. Elsewhere there is little local relief except in northern Richmond County (Staten Island) where morainic deposits rise to 400 feet (122 meters). The slightly elevated areas along the axis of Long Island are remnants of glacial moraines. Most American cities are built on level, low-lying land, and New York is no exception. Land is at a premium, and some has been manufactured by filling in the harbors, especially on Manhattan, one-fifth of which is made land. Outside the city the terrain is level eastward into Long Island and rolling to rough northward into New York State. To the west, the low Watchung Mountains lie 20 to 25 miles (32 to 40 kilometers) inland. They retarded suburban settlement for some time, but since they were breached by interstate highways in the 1950s and 1960s, settlement has proceeded apace.

HOUSING

**Housing Age.** The region's housing stock is old compared with housing in other American cities. Of the entire region's housing, 53 percent was built before 1940, 17 percent was built from 1960 to March 1970, and the remaining 30 percent dates from 1940 through 1959. Sixty-two percent of New York City's housing dates from before 1940, compared with 77 percent in Boston and 67 percent in Chicago. Public housing projects and private developments of recent vintage, coupled with steady demolition of old units, give New York City a lower percentage of older housing than might otherwise be expected. But 70 percent or more of the housing is pre-1940 in a core area that stretches west into New Jersey from northern Staten Island to include Elizabeth, Newark, Patterson, and Passaic. On the New York side, this core of older housing includes large parts of Bronx, Kings, and Queens counties. Within this zone, pre-1940 housing exceeds 90 percent in many tracts. Within New York City old housing falls below 70 percent in northeastern Bronx County and on the east side of Manhattan. In Manhattan post-World War II apartment construction has produced a newer housing stock. Newer single- and multiple-unit dwellings create lower percentages in the Bronx. Older houses comprise less than 10 percent of the total housing units in some tracts in southeastern Kings County, where space for new development was still available after World War II. Outside the core cities, values over 30 percent occur only in small, older settlement centers and in areas not yet affected by large-scale suburban development.

Compared with other SMSAs, the region's 17 percent housing units built since 1960 is low. In New York City itself, 14 percent of all housing is less than a decade old, which is a high percentage for an eastern central city; some of the new units are in large developments in Richmond, Bronx, and southeastern Brooklyn, but a large number (102,000) are new housing units in Manhattan. Popular accounts of

31

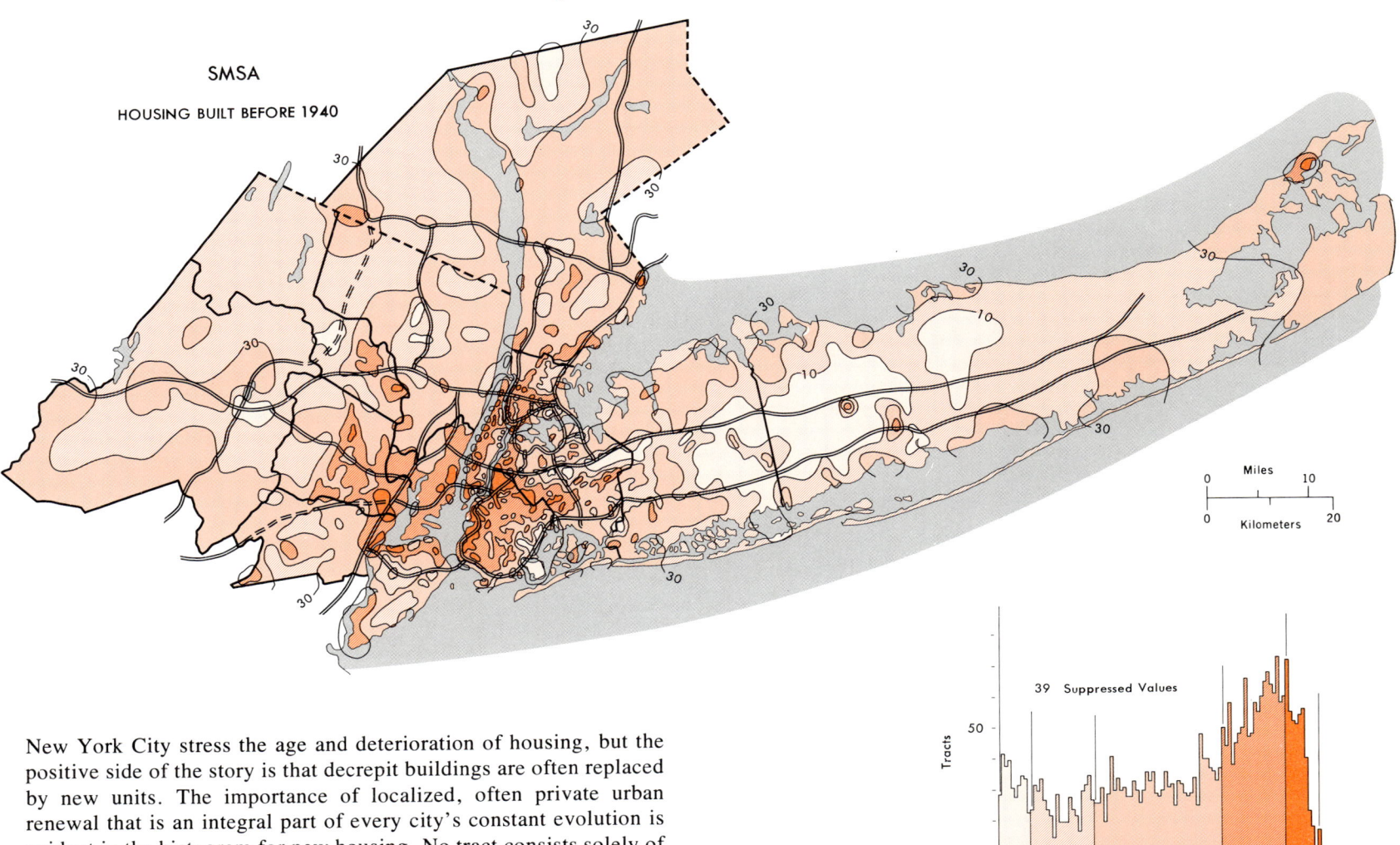

*The Nation's Metropolitan Core: New York–Northern New Jersey*

New York City stress the age and deterioration of housing, but the positive side of the story is that decrepit buildings are often replaced by new units. The importance of localized, often private urban renewal that is an integral part of every city's constant evolution is evident in the histogram for new housing. No tract consists solely of housing built in the last decade, although some come close. More often, tracts have 1 to 50 percent new units sited among older housing. It is true that over 400 of the region's tracts have no housing dating from the 1960s, but there are 3,900 tracts in the SMSAs.

**Mobile Homes.** Most places in the New York–Northern New Jersey commuting region have no mobile homes; some have a few, but mobile homes rarely make up more than 10 percent of the housing stock except in far eastern Long Island and in a few New Jersey towns. Values exceed 30 percent in two mobile-home parks in Middlesex and Monmouth counties in New Jersey. The large area over 5 percent in Ocean County is a portion of New Jersey's Pine Barrens, where low incomes make mobile homes an attractive option.

**Single-Unit Detached Housing.** This type of housing comprises 31 percent of the region's dwellings, the lowest percentage among the 20 areas in the atlas. Because of New York's high population density, in many parts of the region only multiple-unit dwellings can repay high land costs. Only 8 percent of New York City's housing is single-unit detached, and in Manhattan single units are almost nonexistent. The distribution is bimodal; although single- and multiple-unit dwellings are indeed mixed in many tracts, there are large clusters at each end of the histogram. The map mirrors the histogram. The core region with values below 10 percent corresponds to the left side of the histogram, the transition zone from single to multiple units consists of tracts in the center of the histogram, and the suburban-ring tracts cluster on the right side of the histogram.

**Housing Value and Rent.** The mean value of owner-occupied housing in the region is $32,000 — the highest among the 20 regions in the atlas. Mean monthly contract rent is $118, which is not especially high. Intense competition for space and the greater return accruing from rental units cause the high housing values in relation to normal rentals. The area below $20,000 at the center of the housing-value map is questionable; many tracts are suppressed because there are few owner-occupied units at the metropolitan cores, especially east of the Hudson. Outside the low-value core there are sharp transitions to more expensive housing except on the southern part of Long Island, where values below $30,000 predominate. Rentals below $100 per month in the core area give way to higher-cost housing to the east. The contrast between high rents in northern Long Island and lower rents in the southern half is evident, but it is not as marked as the north-south difference on the housing-value map. Rents exceed $300 in two areas on Long Island, on the New York State mainland, and in Midtown Manhattan. Rentals are low in eastern Passaic County, New Jersey, with higher values in areas where the Watchung Mountains provide amenity home and apartment sites.

THE PEOPLE

**Population Density.** New York City's overall population density of 26,350 people per square mile (10,175 per square kilometer) is the highest in the nation. In no other American city do values consistently rise above 60,000 people per square mile (23,200 per square kilometer) nor do they reach the densities over 100,000 (38,600 per square kilometer) found in Manhattan and the Bronx. New York City's extreme densities are functions of the employment opportunities concentrated at the core during the 19th and early 20th centuries and of the inability to spread out because of water barriers. Even today there are 1,600,000 jobs in Manhattan. Fierce competition for space means that only the highest density residential land uses can outbid economic activities. Outside New York City and Newark, New Jersey, population densities decline sharply (p. 46).

**Age and the Elderly.** New York has an older population than most large cities; the median age for the region and the central city is 32

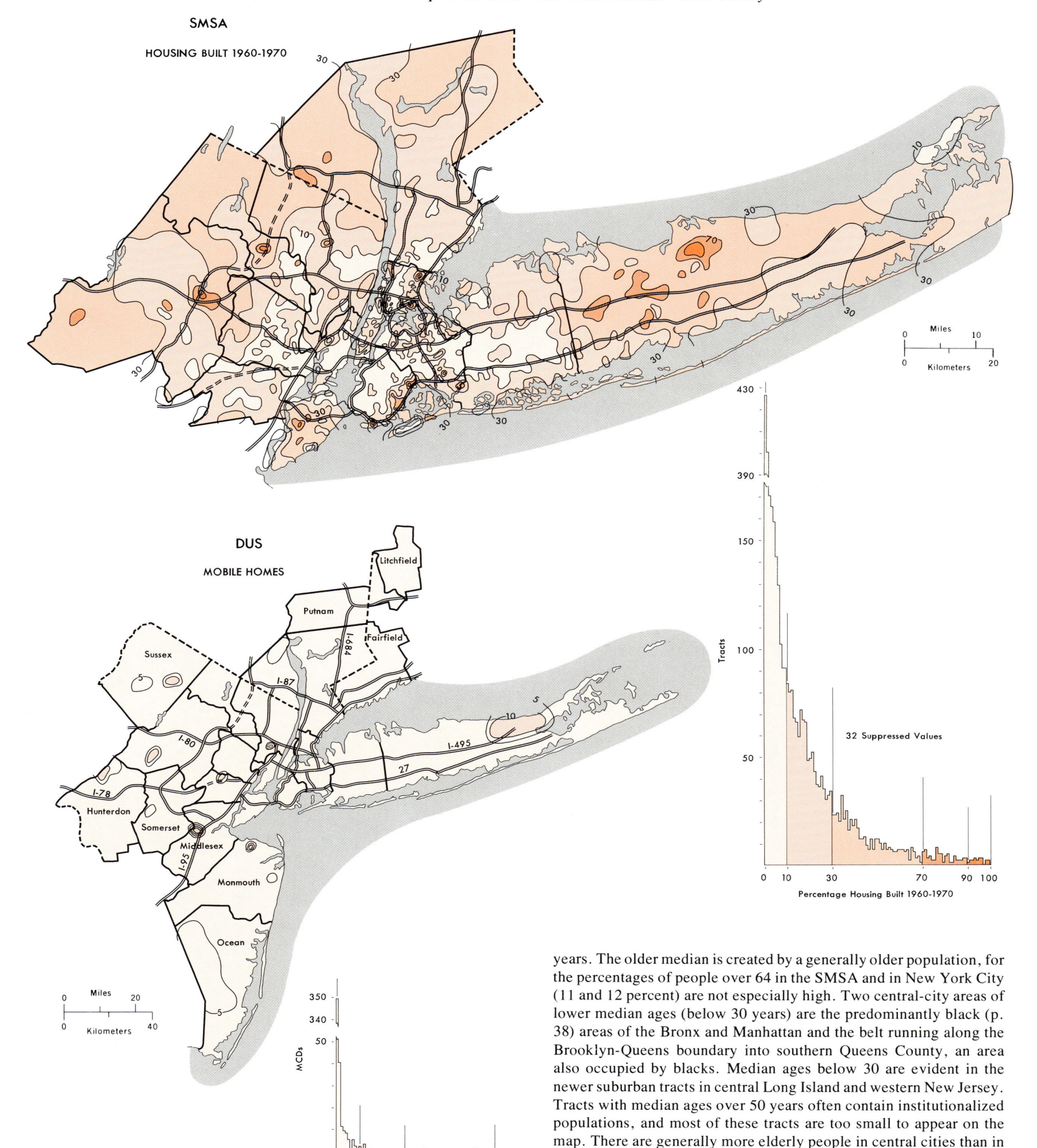

*The Nation's Metropolitan Core: New York-Northern New Jersey*

years. The older median is created by a generally older population, for the percentages of people over 64 in the SMSA and in New York City (11 and 12 percent) are not especially high. Two central-city areas of lower median ages (below 30 years) are the predominantly black (p. 38) areas of the Bronx and Manhattan and the belt running along the Brooklyn-Queens boundary into southern Queens County, an area also occupied by blacks. Median ages below 30 are evident in the newer suburban tracts in central Long Island and western New Jersey. Tracts with median ages over 50 years often contain institutionalized populations, and most of these tracts are too small to appear on the map. There are generally more elderly people in central cities than in suburban areas. People often age with their houses or they move to apartments closer to the metropolitan center when their suburban, child-rearing days are over. People over 64 constitute more than 10 percent of the core area's population except in heavily black or Spanish-American areas, or where inexpensive housing has attracted

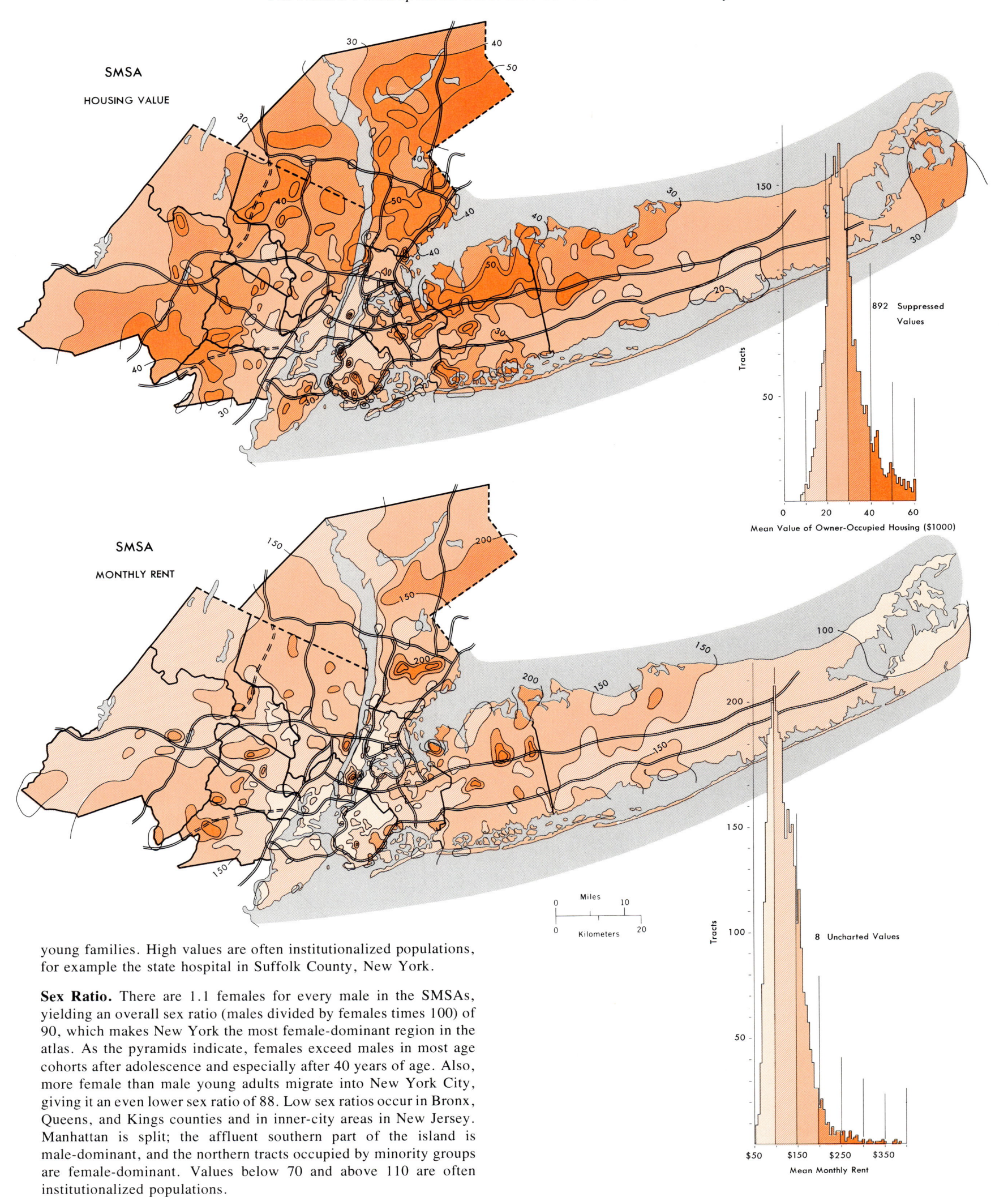

The Nation's Metropolitan Core: New York-Northern New Jersey

SMSA
HOUSING VALUE

SMSA
MONTHLY RENT

young families. High values are often institutionalized populations, for example the state hospital in Suffolk County, New York.

**Sex Ratio.** There are 1.1 females for every male in the SMSAs, yielding an overall sex ratio (males divided by females times 100) of 90, which makes New York the most female-dominant region in the atlas. As the pyramids indicate, females exceed males in most age cohorts after adolescence and especially after 40 years of age. Also, more female than male young adults migrate into New York City, giving it an even lower sex ratio of 88. Low sex ratios occur in Bronx, Queens, and Kings counties and in inner-city areas in New Jersey. Manhattan is split; the affluent southern part of the island is male-dominant, and the northern tracts occupied by minority groups are female-dominant. Values below 70 and above 110 are often institutionalized populations.

34

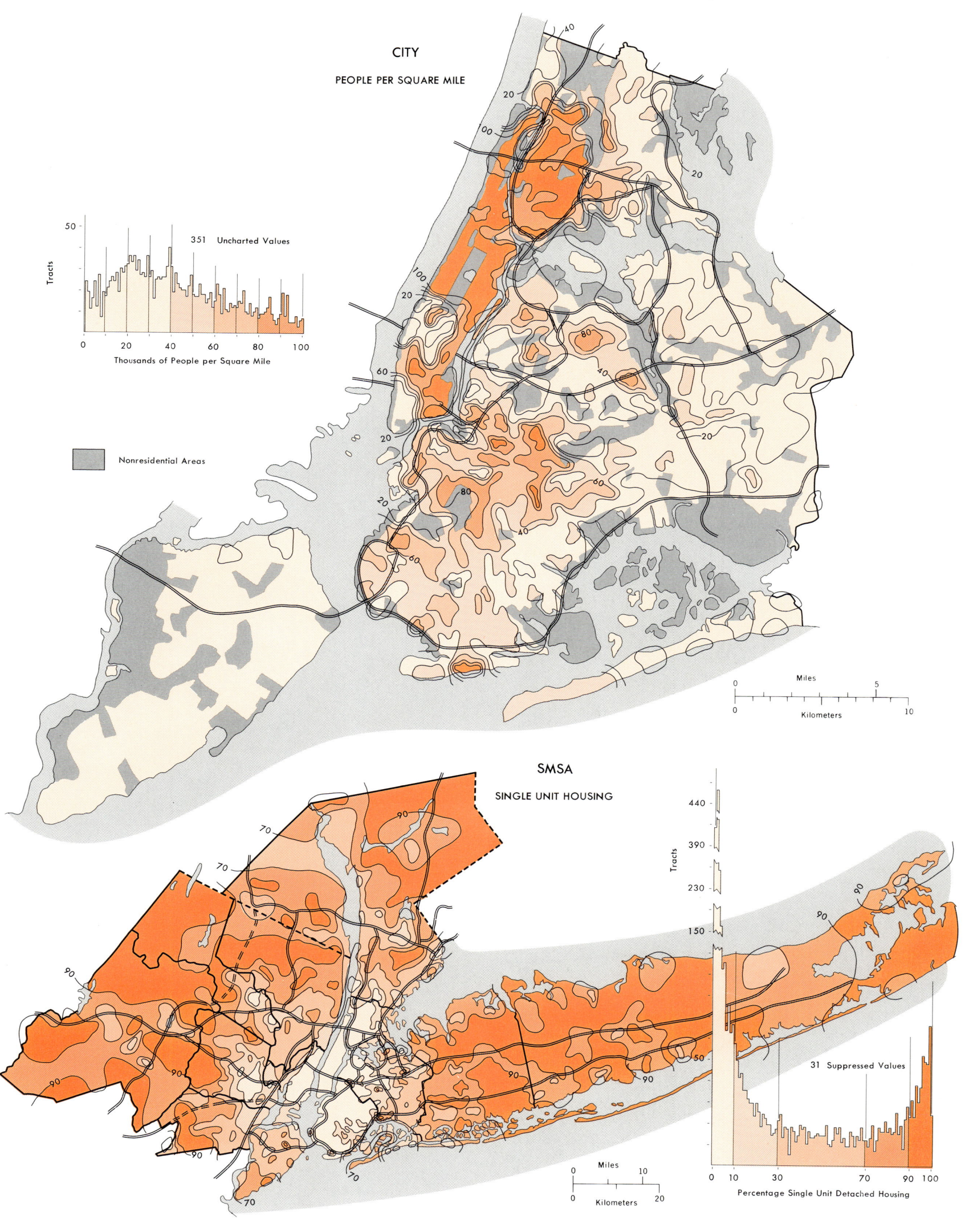

*The Nation's Metropolitan Core: New York-Northern New Jersey*

## CITY
PEOPLE PER SQUARE MILE

351 Uncharted Values

Thousands of People per Square Mile

Nonresidential Areas

## SMSA
SINGLE UNIT HOUSING

31 Suppressed Values

Percentage Single Unit Detached Housing

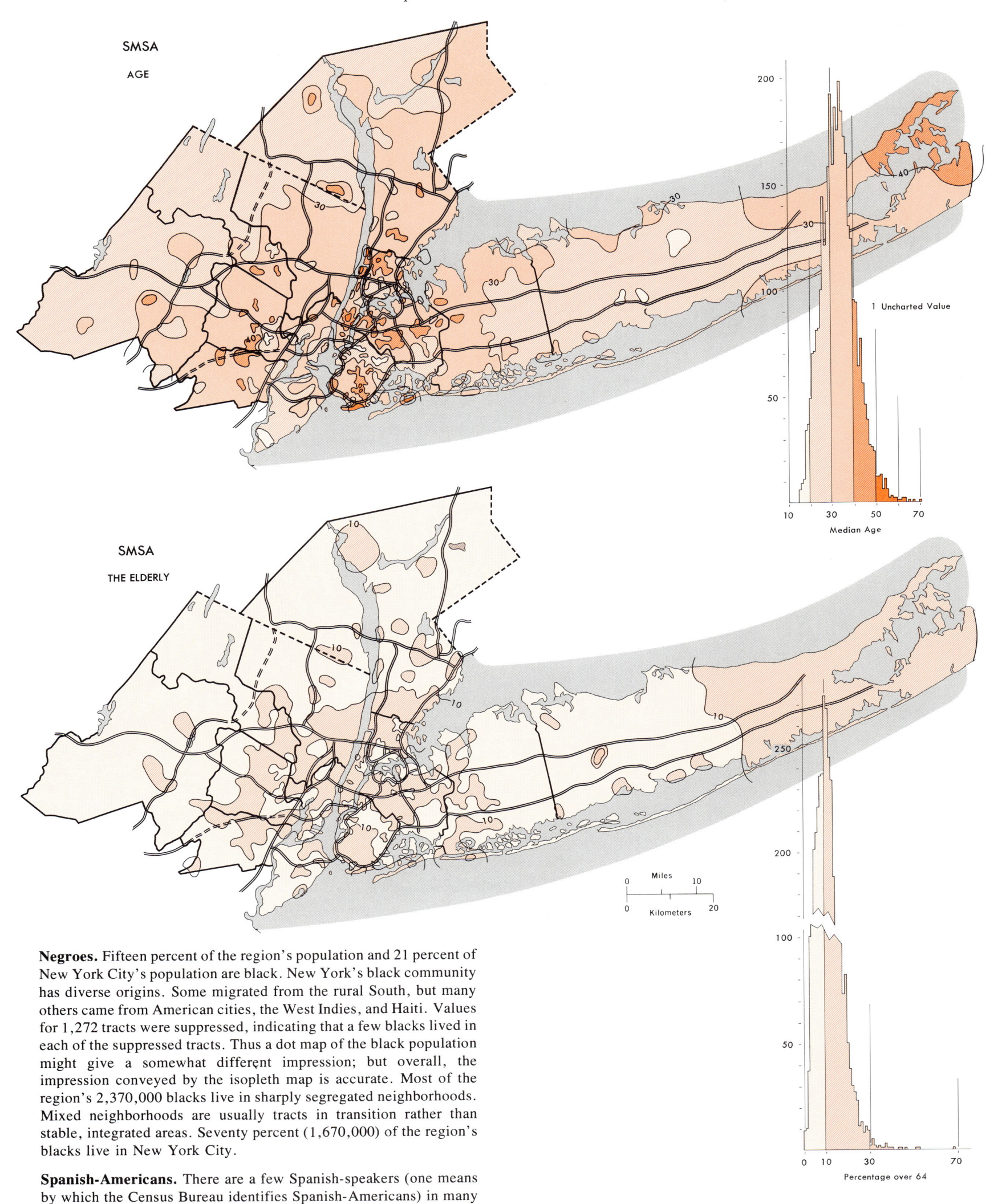

*The Nation's Metropolitan Core: New York-Northern New Jersey*

SMSA

AGE

SMSA

THE ELDERLY

**Negroes.** Fifteen percent of the region's population and 21 percent of New York City's population are black. New York's black community has diverse origins. Some migrated from the rural South, but many others came from American cities, the West Indies, and Haiti. Values for 1,272 tracts were suppressed, indicating that a few blacks lived in each of the suppressed tracts. Thus a dot map of the black population might give a somewhat different impression; but overall, the impression conveyed by the isopleth map is accurate. Most of the region's 2,370,000 blacks live in sharply segregated neighborhoods. Mixed neighborhoods are usually tracts in transition rather than stable, integrated areas. Seventy percent (1,670,000) of the region's blacks live in New York City.

**Spanish-Americans.** There are a few Spanish-speakers (one means by which the Census Bureau identifies Spanish-Americans) in many

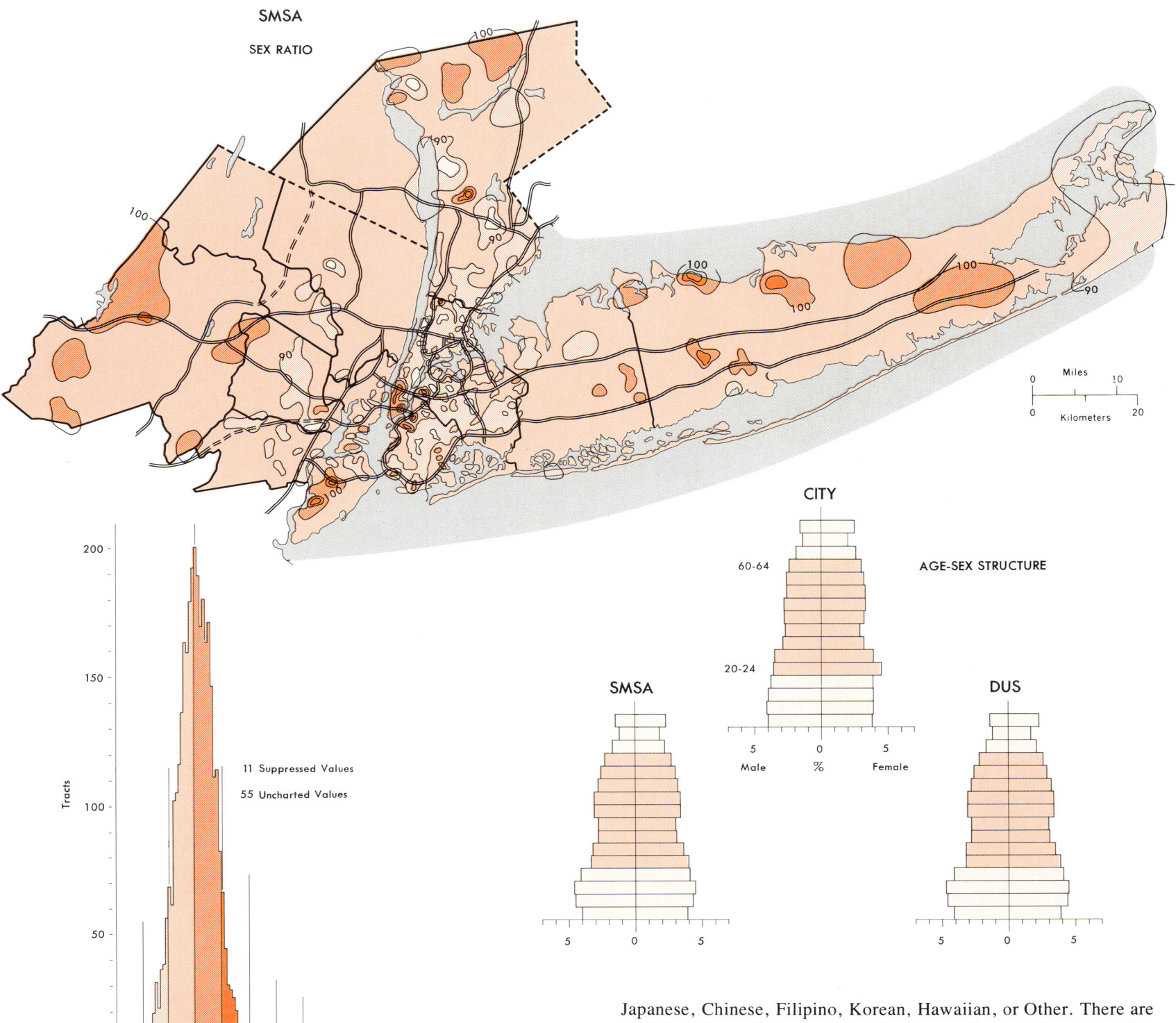

*The Nation's Metropolitan Core: New York-Northern New Jersey*

tracts, but most of New York's Hispanics live in clearly defined areas where they are a significant minority or a majority. Spanish-American neighborhoods are often situated on one side of a black ghetto. Whereas New Jersey contains large numbers of blacks, most Spanish-Americans live in New York. Seventy-nine percent of the region's 1,620,000 Hispanics live in New York City. New York's Spanish-American population is heterogeneous. Puerto Ricans form the largest group, but refugees from the Spanish Civil War, former residents of the Dominican Republic, Cubans, and the children of all three groups have also settled in the city.

**Chinese-Americans.** New York City, in fact, has more Chinese than San Francisco. The Census requires all nonwhites to identify themselves as members of 1 of 8 "racial" categories: Negro, Indian, Japanese, Chinese, Filipino, Korean, Hawaiian, or Other. There are 83,250 Chinese in the region, 83 percent of whom live in the five boroughs. Within the city, Manhattan's Chinatown on the lower east side and the city's west side along and north of Central Park contain by far the largest numbers. There are minor clusters in Kings and northern Queens counties and a few Chinese in the suburbs, but intensely Chinese neighborhoods continue to attract the region's Chinese inhabitants. New York's Chinatown is second in culinary and visual delights only to San Francisco's.

**Japanese-Americans.** The region's 20,259 Japanese are much less clustered than the Chinese. There is some agglomeration on Manhattan's west side, extending north into the Bronx along the Hudson, but other than that and the small community in the Flushing neighborhood of Queens County, Japanese are spread thinly through the region.

**Irish-Americans.** The Irish were one of the first non-English immigrant groups to arrive in New York in large numbers. They have given the city a strong Irish tradition that persists today. There are almost 400,000 Irish stock (Irish-born plus those with at least one Irish-born parent) in the metropolitan region. Most Irish (80 percent)

37

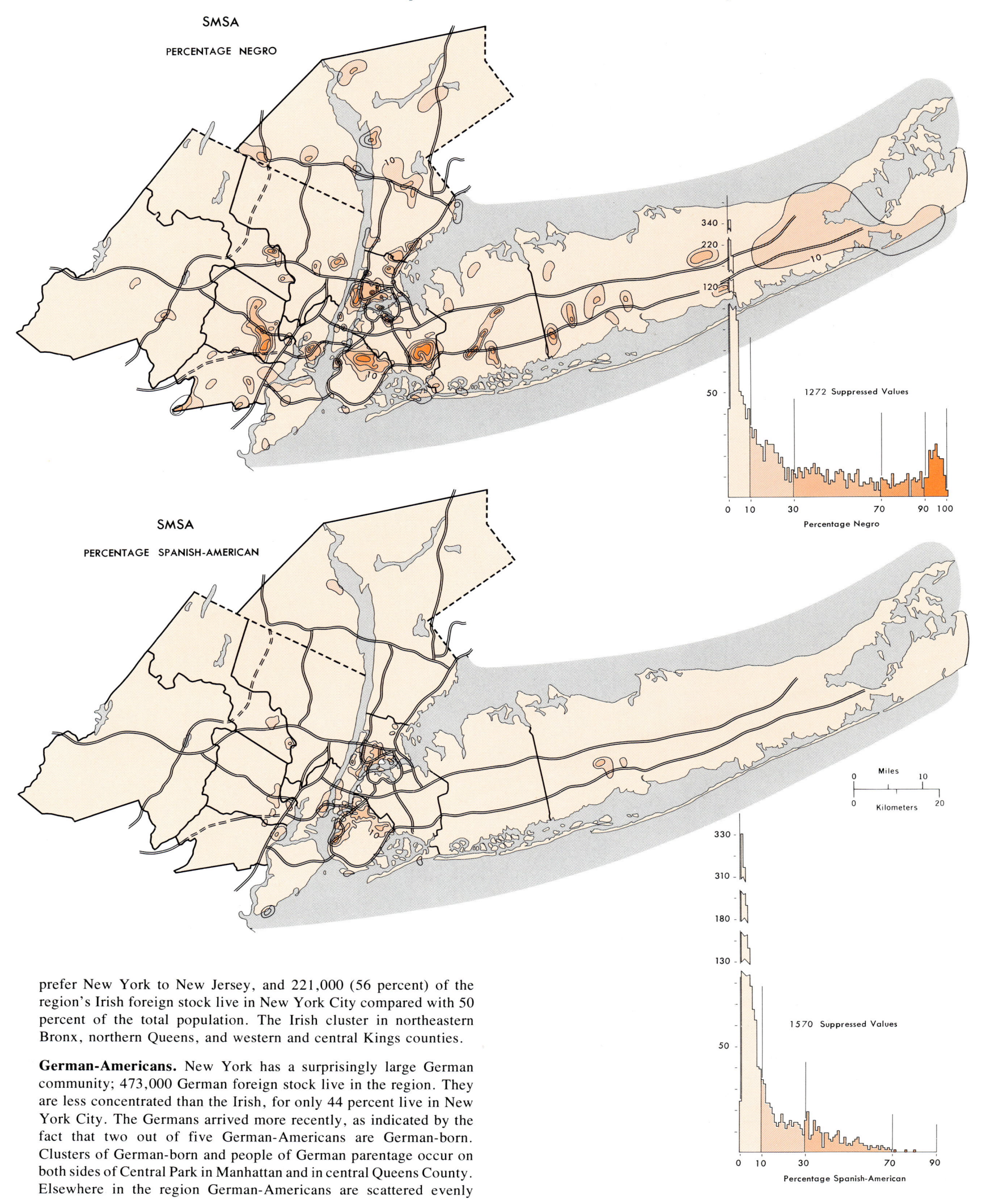

*The Nation's Metropolitan Core: New York-Northern New Jersey*

SMSA

PERCENTAGE NEGRO

SMSA

PERCENTAGE SPANISH-AMERICAN

prefer New York to New Jersey, and 221,000 (56 percent) of the region's Irish foreign stock live in New York City compared with 50 percent of the total population. The Irish cluster in northeastern Bronx, northern Queens, and western and central Kings counties.

**German-Americans.** New York has a surprisingly large German community; 473,000 German foreign stock live in the region. They are less concentrated than the Irish, for only 44 percent live in New York City. The Germans arrived more recently, as indicated by the fact that two out of five German-Americans are German-born. Clusters of German-born and people of German parentage occur on both sides of Central Park in Manhattan and in central Queens County. Elsewhere in the region German-Americans are scattered evenly

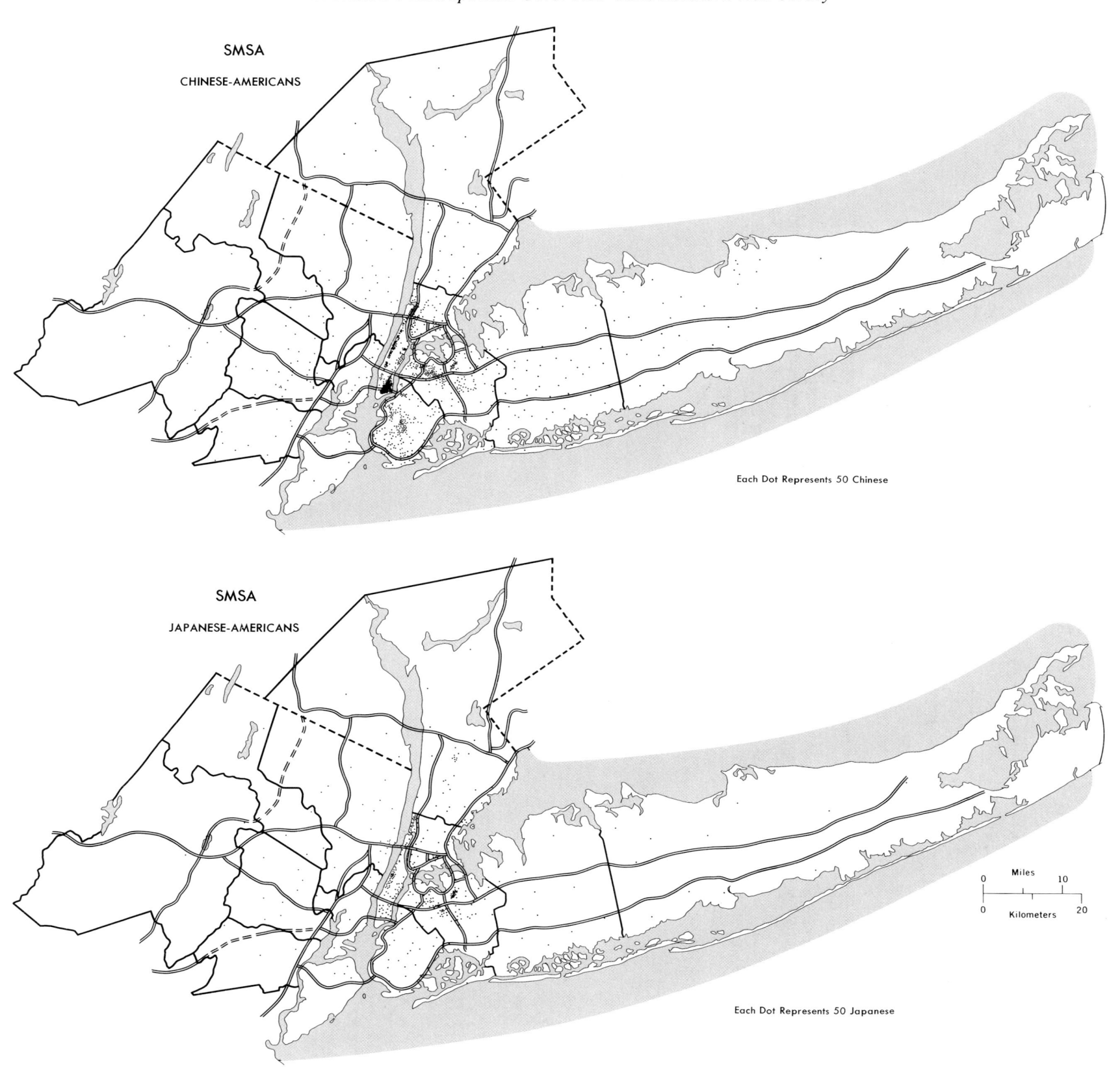

*The Nation's Metropolitan Core: New York-Northern New Jersey*

**SMSA CHINESE-AMERICANS**

Each Dot Represents 50 Chinese

**SMSA JAPANESE-AMERICANS**

Each Dot Represents 50 Japanese

through the population, varying in numbers with population density. The arrival of many German Jews in the 1920s and 1930s is a partial explanation for the high proportion of foreign-born among the German-Americans. It also means the map must be interpreted cautiously. Most of the German-Americans on the west side of Central Park are ethnic Germans, for example, whereas most of those on the east side consider themselves Jewish, not German.

**Polish-Americans.** Poles started arriving in large numbers in the 1880s and 1890s. They now live in New York and New Jersey in proportion to the breakdown of the total population between the two states. The group is differentially concentrated in New York City, however, for the city has 56 percent of the Polish foreign stock but only half the region's population. About a third of the stock is Polish-born. How many of the people the Census lists as Polish-Americans are Polish Jews rather than ethnic Poles is hard to say. It is highly probable that many, if not most, are Jewish rather than Polish, especially considering the overlap between the areas occupied by Polish and Russian foreign stock. In any event, there is little overlap between Polish-Americans and blacks and Spanish-Americans. Ethnic Poles show little inclination to abandon their neighborhoods to blacks and Spanish-Americans, but Jews often have the means and the inclination to move, thereby laying the groundwork for neighborhood succession.

**Russian-Americans.** Most people designated as U.S.S.R. foreign

## SMSA IRISH-AMERICANS

Each Black Dot Represents 50 Irish Born
Each Orange Dot Represents 50 People of Irish Parentage

## SMSA GERMAN-AMERICANS

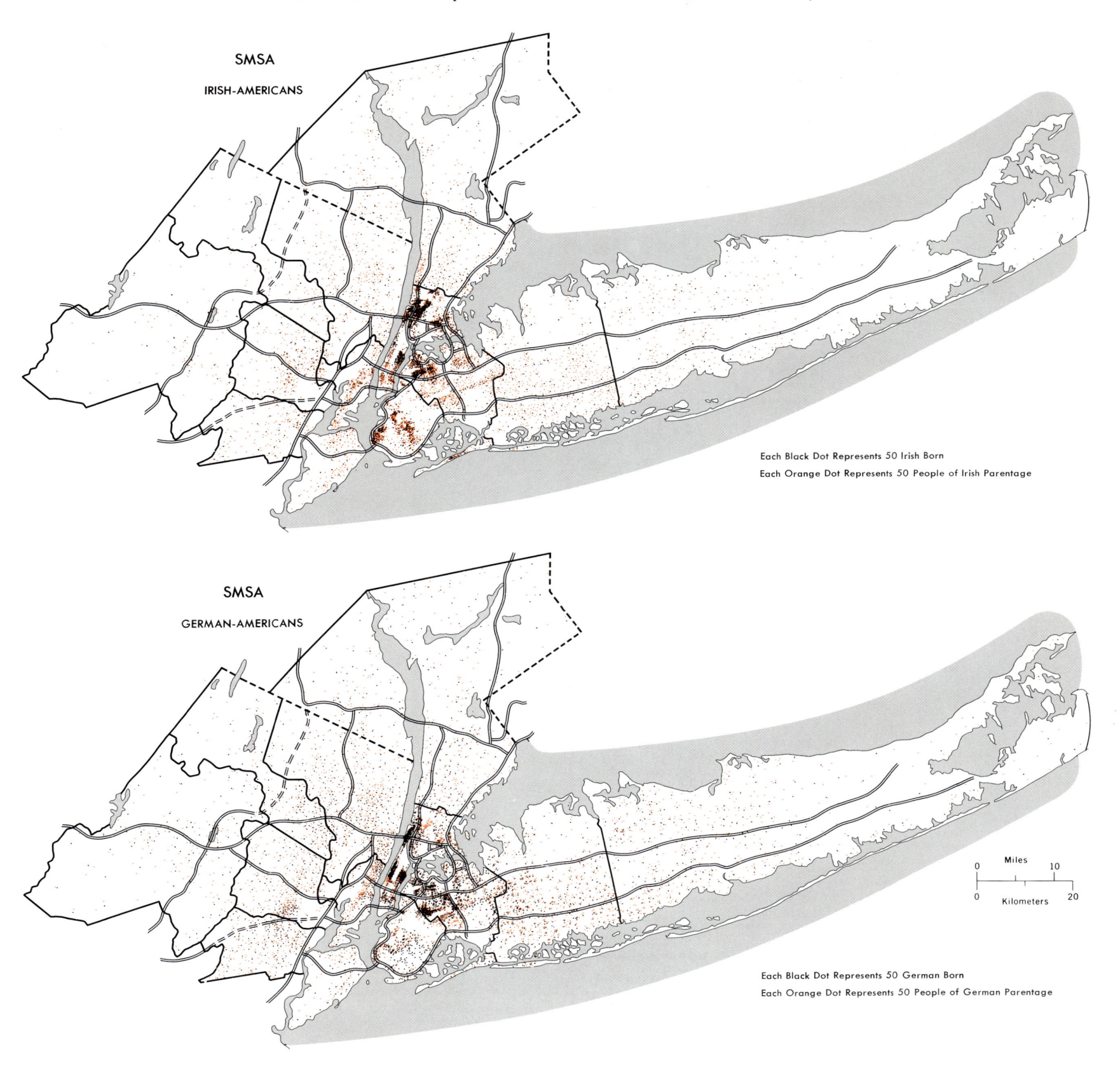

Each Black Dot Represents 50 German Born
Each Orange Dot Represents 50 People of German Parentage

stock by the Census are in fact Russian Jews. They started arriving in large numbers around the turn of this century, and perhaps more than any other ethnic group they have left their distinctive imprint on the city and the metropolitan area. There are more Jews in New York City than in Tel Aviv. Five-sixths of the New York-Northern New Jersey region's 600,000 Russian-Americans live in New York State in contrast to the state's three-fourths share of the region's total population. New York City has 66 percent of the region's Russian foreign stock but only half the total population, indicating selective residence in the central city. The geographical distribution of Russian-Americans is similar to that of Polish-Americans.

**Italian-Americans.** People of Italian origin and descent are the largest single ethnic group in the region, numbering some 1,350,000. Their distribution between New York and New Jersey is identical to that of the total population. In both states they show no particular preference for central-city locations, their numbers in suburban areas being what would be expected on the basis of total population. Though they came about the same time or somewhat after Poles and Russians, they have moved out of the central city in greater numbers than Polish- and Russian-Americans. Like other European ethnic groups, they mingle little with blacks and Spanish-Americans.

Acting as the nation's gateway for several centuries has enabled New York to collect a much richer ethnic composition than is suggested by mapping only the largest groups. The area is home for

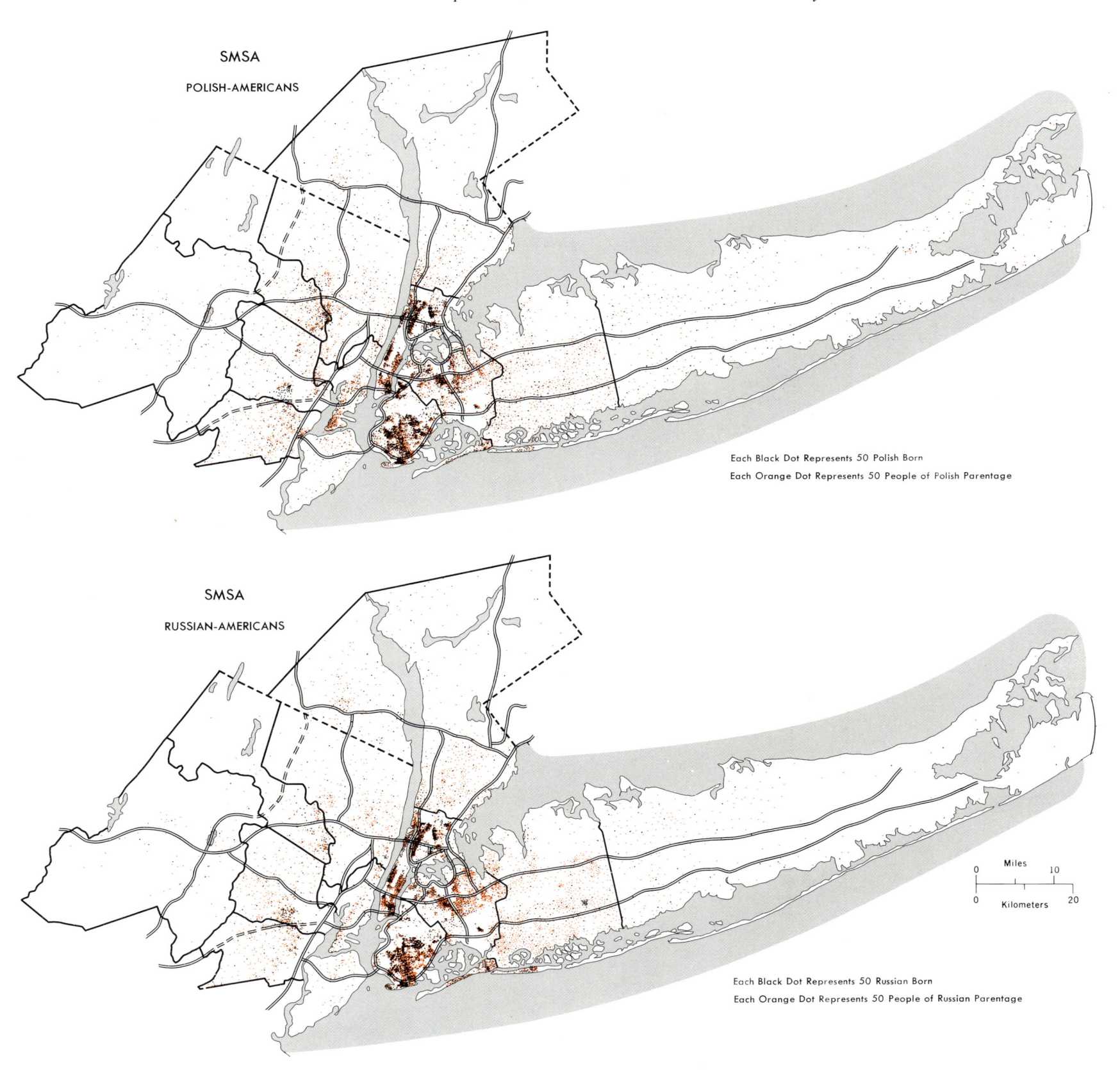

*The Nation's Metropolitan Core: New York-Northern New Jersey*

SMSA
POLISH-AMERICANS

Each Black Dot Represents 50 Polish Born
Each Orange Dot Represents 50 People of Polish Parentage

SMSA
RUSSIAN-AMERICANS

Each Black Dot Represents 50 Russian Born
Each Orange Dot Represents 50 People of Russian Parentage

almost 45,000 people of Romanian stock and 12,500 Portuguese foreign stock, for example, not to mention almost 80,000 Greeks. The city's numerous ethnic enclaves and rich mixture of peoples lend it a cosmopolitan air unmatched elsewhere in the nation.

## SOCIOECONOMIC CHARACTERISTICS

**Household Size.** There are 2.9 persons per household in both the region and New York City. That is low for a metropolitan region, but the city's household size is average. The usual pattern is smaller households in the central city that are more than offset by larger suburban households. Such a pattern does exist in the New York region, but the large number of smaller households at the region's high-density core just balance the large households on Long Island, in Rockland and Westchester counties, and in western New Jersey.

**Female Headship.** Females head 15 percent of the region's families and 17 percent of New York City's families. Compared with other large places, New York City has a low proportion of families headed by females even though tracts with more than 10 percent of such families do dominate the region's core. The highest values occur in predominantly black and Spanish-American areas (p. 38).

**Occupations.** Blue-collar jobs (laborers and operatives) are held by 12 percent of the New York region's labor force and executive occupations (engineers, teachers, professionals, managers, pro-

*41*

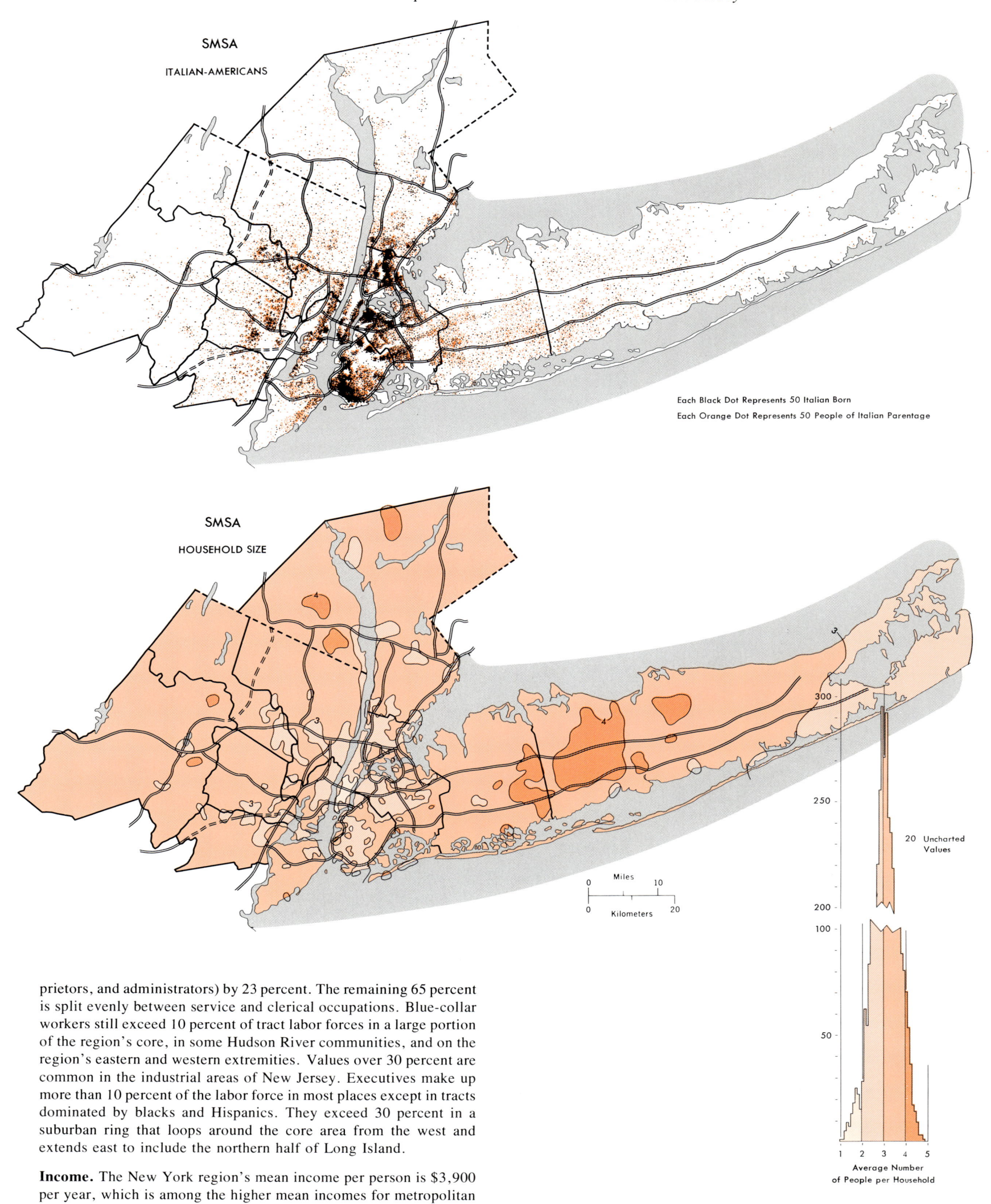

*The Nation's Metropolitan Core: New York-Northern New Jersey*

SMSA
ITALIAN-AMERICANS

Each Black Dot Represents 50 Italian Born
Each Orange Dot Represents 50 People of Italian Parentage

SMSA
HOUSEHOLD SIZE

Average Number of People per Household

prietors, and administrators) by 23 percent. The remaining 65 percent is split evenly between service and clerical occupations. Blue-collar workers still exceed 10 percent of tract labor forces in a large portion of the region's core, in some Hudson River communities, and on the region's eastern and western extremities. Values over 30 percent are common in the industrial areas of New Jersey. Executives make up more than 10 percent of the labor force in most places except in tracts dominated by blacks and Hispanics. They exceed 30 percent in a suburban ring that loops around the core area from the west and extends east to include the northern half of Long Island.

**Income.** The New York region's mean income per person is $3,900 per year, which is among the higher mean incomes for metropolitan

42

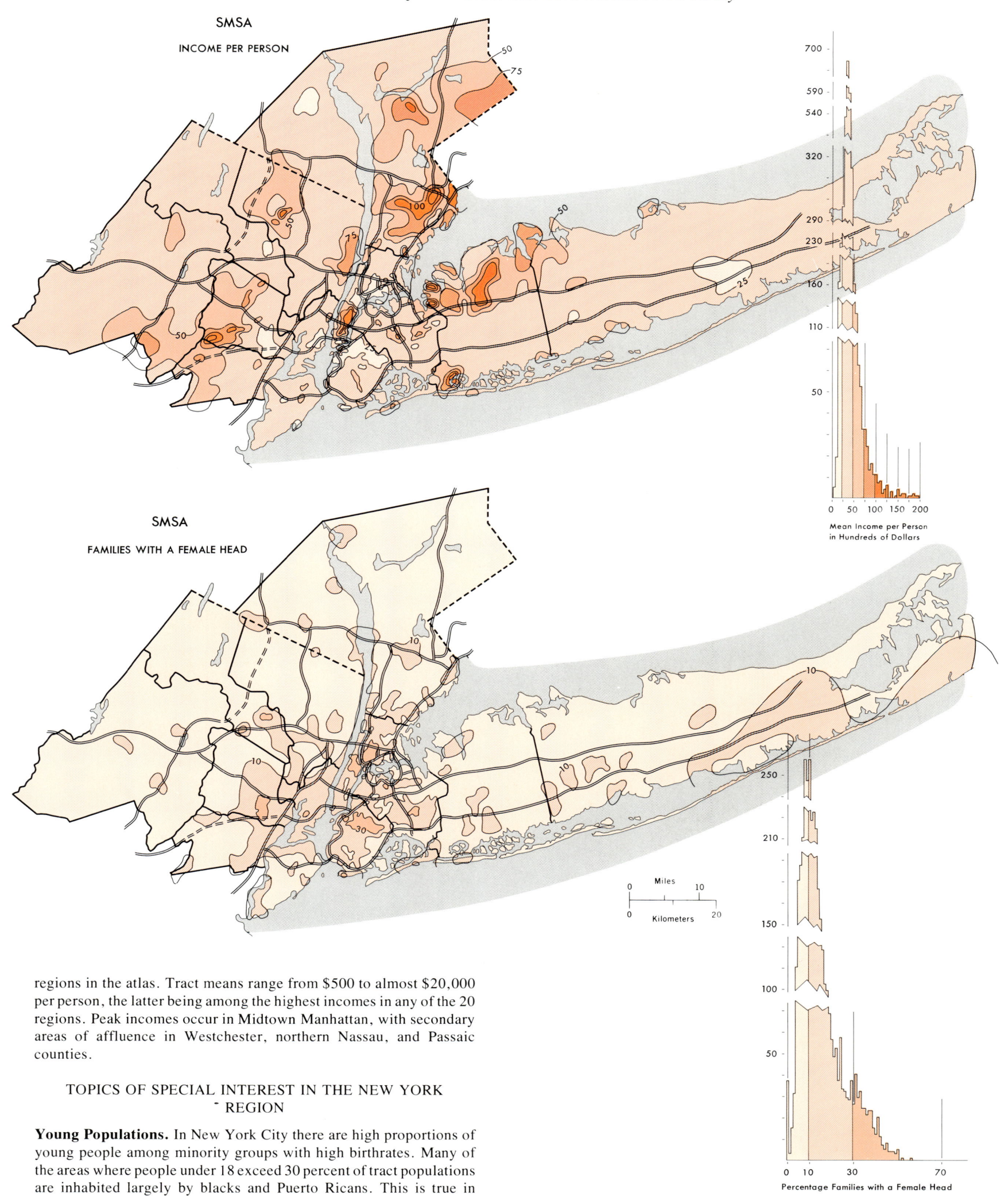

*The Nation's Metropolitan Core: New York-Northern New Jersey*

**SMSA**
INCOME PER PERSON

Mean Income per Person
in Hundreds of Dollars

**SMSA**
FAMILIES WITH A FEMALE HEAD

Percentage Families with a Female Head

regions in the atlas. Tract means range from $500 to almost $20,000 per person, the latter being among the highest incomes in any of the 20 regions. Peak incomes occur in Midtown Manhattan, with secondary areas of affluence in Westchester, northern Nassau, and Passaic counties.

TOPICS OF SPECIAL INTEREST IN THE NEW YORK REGION

**Young Populations.** In New York City there are high proportions of young people among minority groups with high birthrates. Many of the areas where people under 18 exceed 30 percent of tract populations are inhabited largely by blacks and Puerto Ricans. This is true in eastern Manhattan and south-central Bronx County, where the high

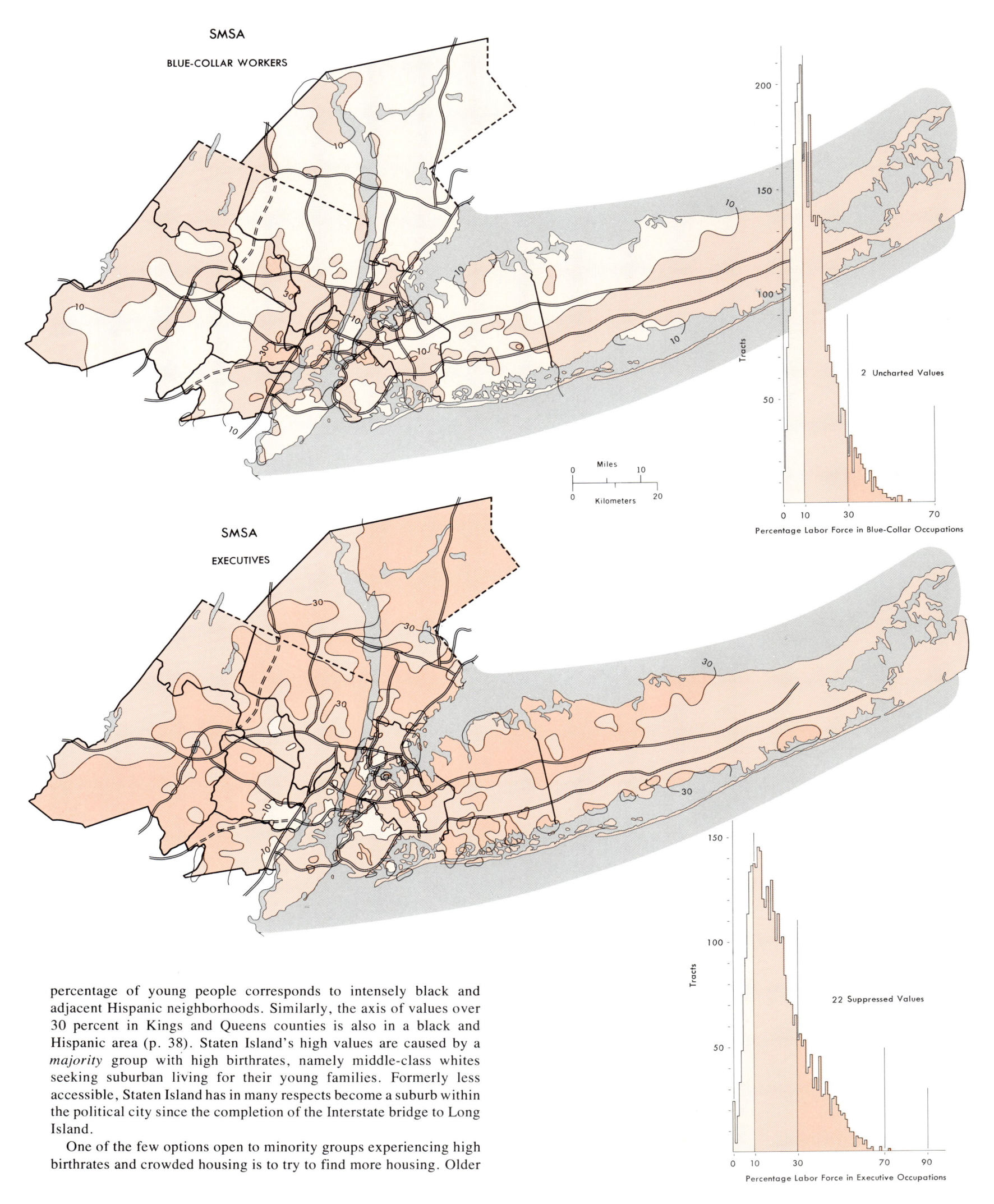

*The Nation's Metropolitan Core: New York-Northern New Jersey*

percentage of young people corresponds to intensely black and adjacent Hispanic neighborhoods. Similarly, the axis of values over 30 percent in Kings and Queens counties is also in a black and Hispanic area (p. 38). Staten Island's high values are caused by a *majority* group with high birthrates, namely middle-class whites seeking suburban living for their young families. Formerly less accessible, Staten Island has in many respects become a suburb within the political city since the completion of the Interstate bridge to Long Island.

One of the few options open to minority groups experiencing high birthrates and crowded housing is to try to find more housing. Older

44

*The Nation's Metropolitan Core: New York-Northern New Jersey*

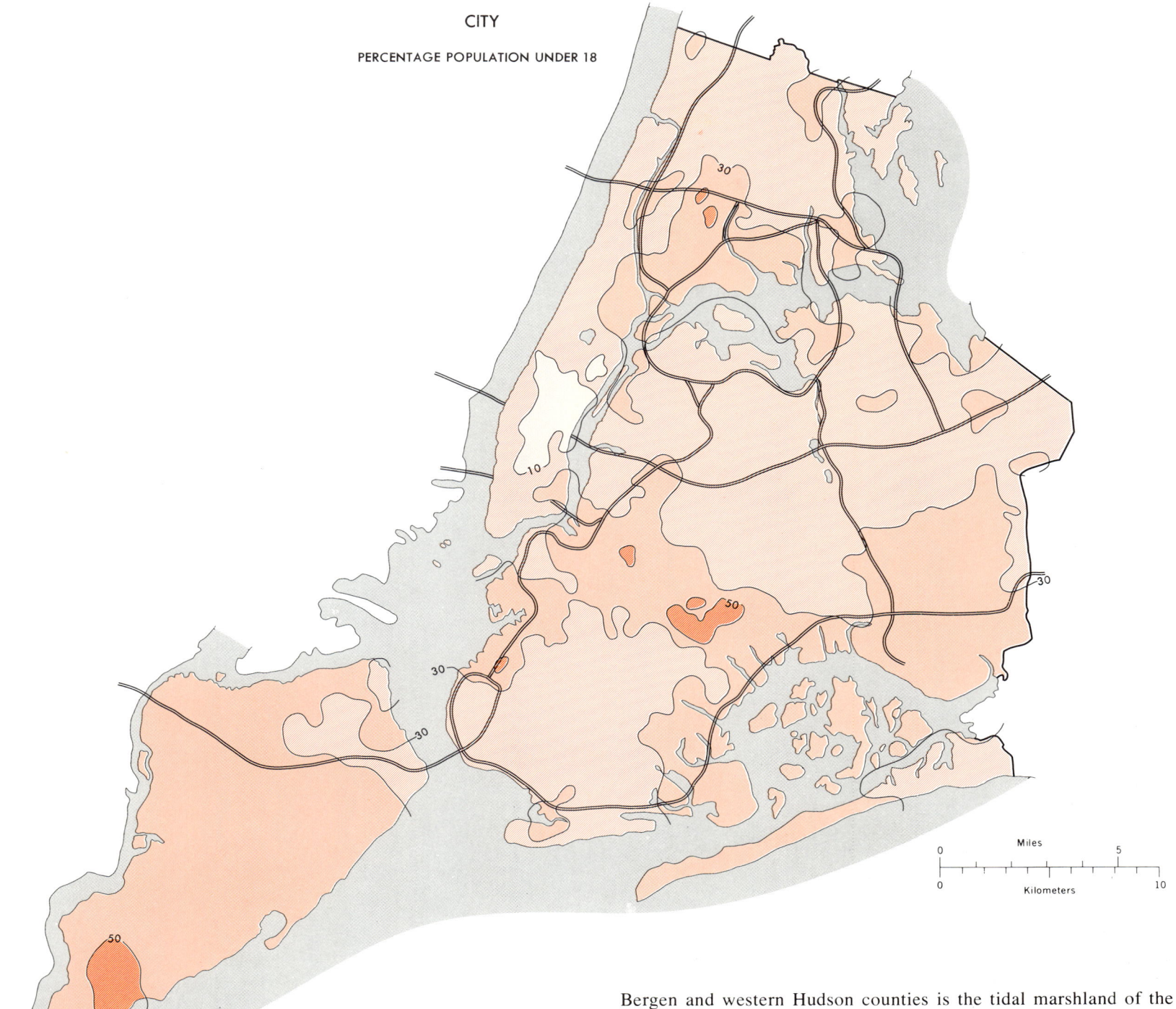

CITY

PERCENTAGE POPULATION UNDER 18

residents may resist such expansion either because they need or want local housing vacancies for themselves or because they fear their prospective neighbors. When minority groups do expand into new areas, older people are often prevented from moving elsewhere because of low income. The aged thus become unwilling residents of much younger neighborhoods they would prefer to abandon.

**Population Density.** (Isopleth interval, 10,000 people per square mile or 3,860 per square kilometer.) New York's population densities are the highest in the nation. Very high densities, in excess of 50,000 people per square mile (19,300 per square kilometer), are confined to New York City and Newark. Densities in Manhattan and the Bronx exceed 100,000 people per square mile (38,600 per square kilometer) over extensive areas (p. 35), whereas densities over 50,000 per square mile (19,300 per square kilometer) are rare in New Jersey. Outside the core counties, density declines sharply; areas settled since World War II are occupied at densities well below 10,000 people per square mile (3,860 per square kilometer). The large low-density area in southern Bergen and western Hudson counties is the tidal marshland of the Jersey Meadows. It remains largely uninhabited despite its proximity to the highest population densities in the nation.

New York's intensive land use is a product of competing demands for commercial and residential space close to the nation's economic heart. Millions of workers are needed to run Manhattan's intricate economic hothouse, and the limited capacity of the region to cope with private automobile transportation means that many workers must live within short distances of their jobs. Because space is at such a premium, commercial and residential land must be developed at high densities to be profitable. Continued high-density development escalates land values even more, forcing yet higher density development. The process is circularly causal.

High densities are not inherently evil. Attempts to indict population density as a cause of social pathologies have failed to withstand rigorous test. High densities do ensure that a local disruption affects many more people than it would at lower densities, but density itself seems to be neutral in relation to human behavior.

**Crowded Housing.** The same cannot be said of crowding, which sometimes accompanies high densities but need not. A commonly accepted measure of overcrowded housing is the percentage of all housing units that have more than one person per room. A comparison of the population density, crowded housing, and income per person

45

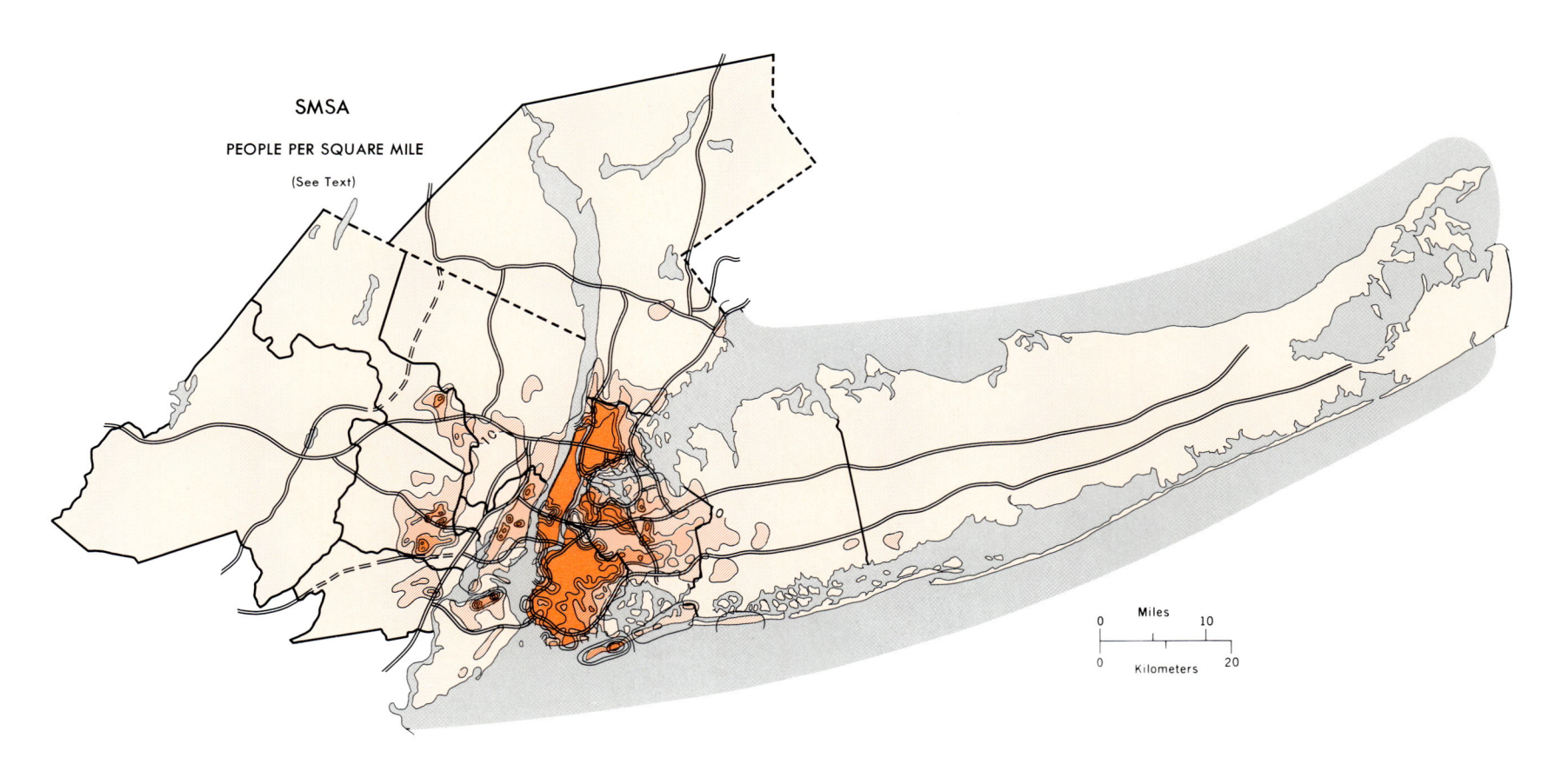

## The Nation's Metropolitan Core: New York-Northern New Jersey

**SMSA**
PEOPLE PER SQUARE MILE
(See Text)

(in hundreds of dollars) maps illustrates the ways prosperity can modify the effect of density and poverty can reinforce them. There are few overcrowded units in wealthy Midtown Manhattan despite densities well in excess of 100,000 people per square mile (38,600 per square kilometer) on the most expensive real estate on earth. But low-income areas of Manhattan, the Bronx, Kings and Queens counties often have crowded units in excess of 10 to 30 percent of the housing stock. Jersey City, Elizabeth, and Newark — all central cities with low incomes — also appear as areas in which crowded housing is far from negligible. The income gradient between the east side of Central Park in Manhattan, where annual per *person* incomes approach $20,000, and Harlem two miles to the north, where incomes drop to less than a tenth of that amount, is probably the sharpest transition in the nation. The map of crowded housing suggests that the two places are poles apart along other dimensions of urban life related to prosperity despite their proximity and similar population densities.

The news from New York is almost always bad, not necessarily because New York is any worse a place to live than most other metropolitan areas in the final analysis but because when anything goes wrong in New York it does so on a colossal scale. Events that would affect thousands or tens of thousands elsewhere inconvenience or threaten hundreds of thousands or millions in New York. The city's numerous problems appear to have become increasingly serious since World War II, but the city has been pronounced dead more than once only to revive just as everyone was consigning it to the morgue. Whether New York City will survive the afflictions of the 1970s and 1980s is debatable. It is doubtful whether the rest of the nation could survive without the invaluable specialized services only a vital, healthy New York City can provide. This is the best insurance that it will.

## The Nation's Metropolitan Core: New York–Northern New Jersey

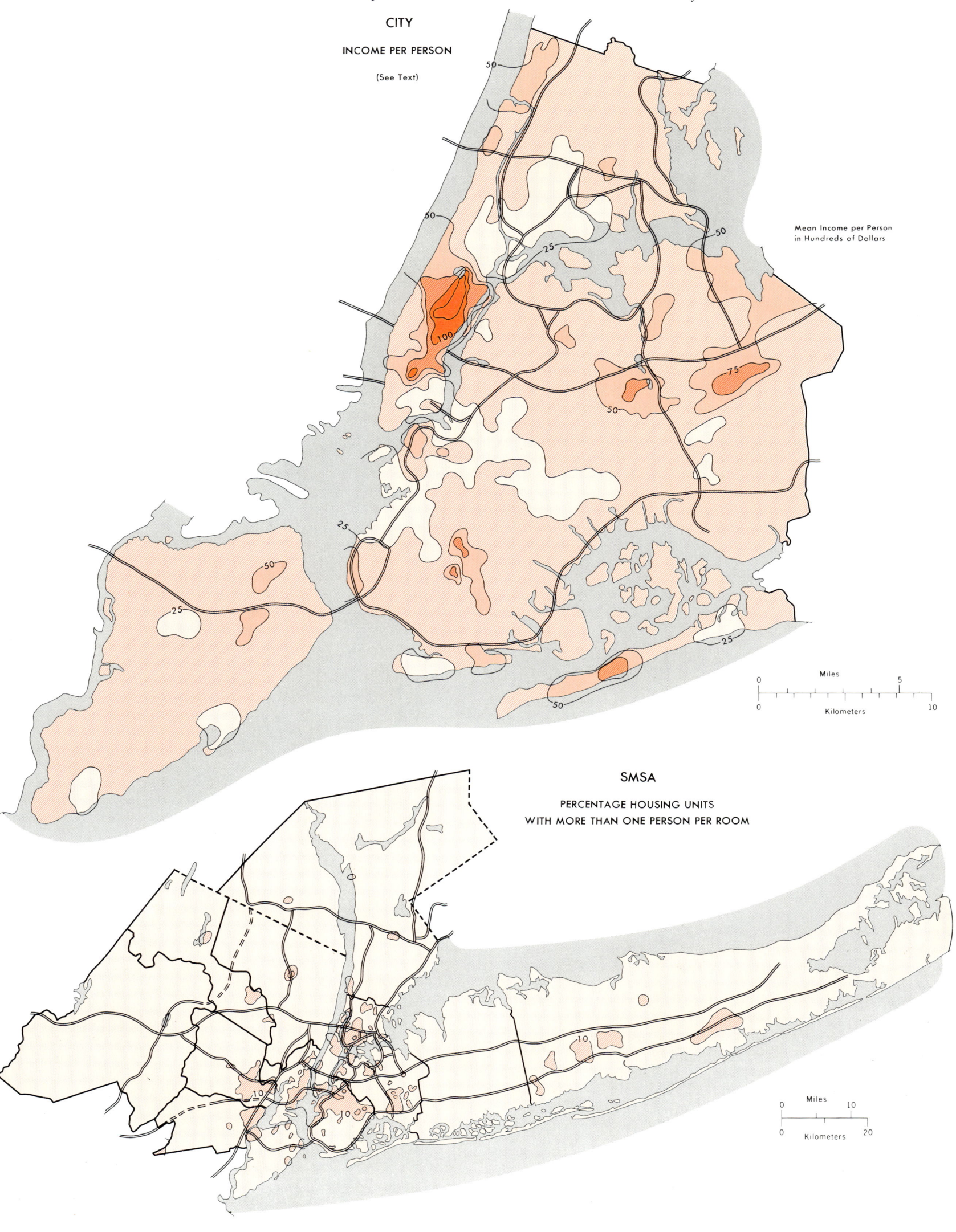

### CITY
#### INCOME PER PERSON
(See Text)

Mean Income per Person in Hundreds of Dollars

### SMSA
#### PERCENTAGE HOUSING UNITS WITH MORE THAN ONE PERSON PER ROOM

47

# CHAPTER 8

# Philadelphia

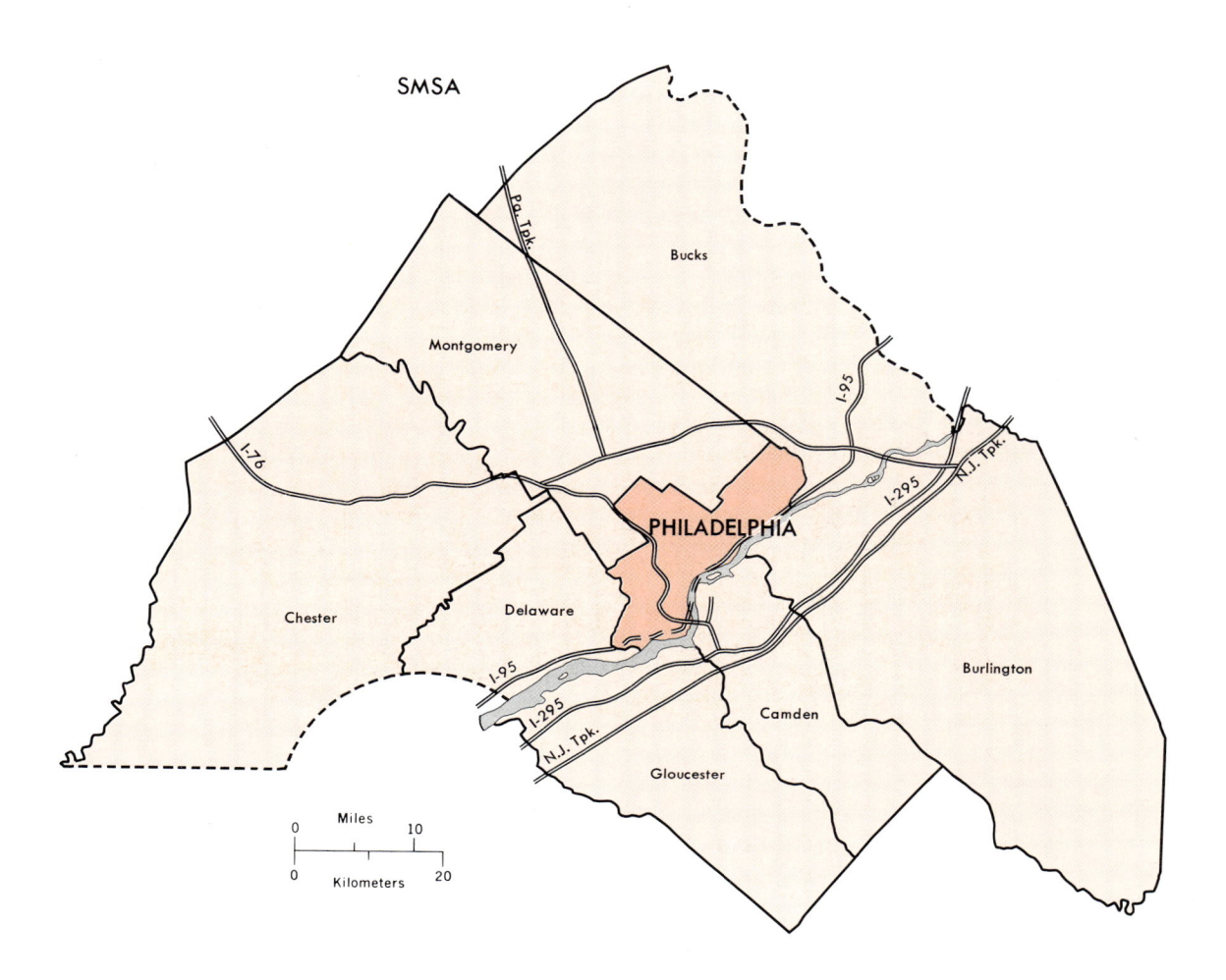

Philadelphia is the nation's 4th most populous metropolis, with a total population of 4,800,000 people in the Standard Metropolitan Statistical Area (SMSA). The commuting region defined by counties that have at least 5 percent of their labor forces working in Philadelphia is coincident with the SMSA. This Daily Urban System (DUS) is the 4th most populous DUS in the nation. Philadelphia has always been one of America's most important cities. It was 2nd only to New York throughout most of the 19th century, slipping behind Chicago after 1880 (p. 10). The city reached its peak population in 1950 when it had 2,100,000 people. Between 1950 and 1970 the city lost 200,000 people. By 1970 only 40 percent of the metropolitan area's population lived in Philadelphia City.

*Note:* All data are from the 1970 Censuses of Population and Housing unless otherwise indicated. Therefore the present tense refers to 1970 data except for income data which are from 1969. Cartographic conventions are explained in Chapter 1.

Philadelphia owes its original settlement to the confluence of the Schuylkill and Delaware rivers. The two rivers provided access to the interior for traders and Indians. River access to the fertile agricultural regions north and west was the basis of Philadelphia's fortunes during the 18th and 19th centuries. The Schuylkill provided water-power sites, and railroads later used both river valleys as routes into and out of the city.

Philadelphia is flat to rolling. The land rises gently away from the Delaware, reaching maximum elevations of over 400 feet (120 meters) in the northwest corner of the city. The land to the west continues to rise and becomes gently rolling, providing sites for expensive suburban housing. New Jersey is flatter than Philadelphia; the nearly level coastal plain extends from Philadelphia to the ocean.

Floodplain areas along the lower Schuylkill and the Delaware have been given over to industrial and shipping activities within

*The Nation's Metropolitan Core: Philadelphia*

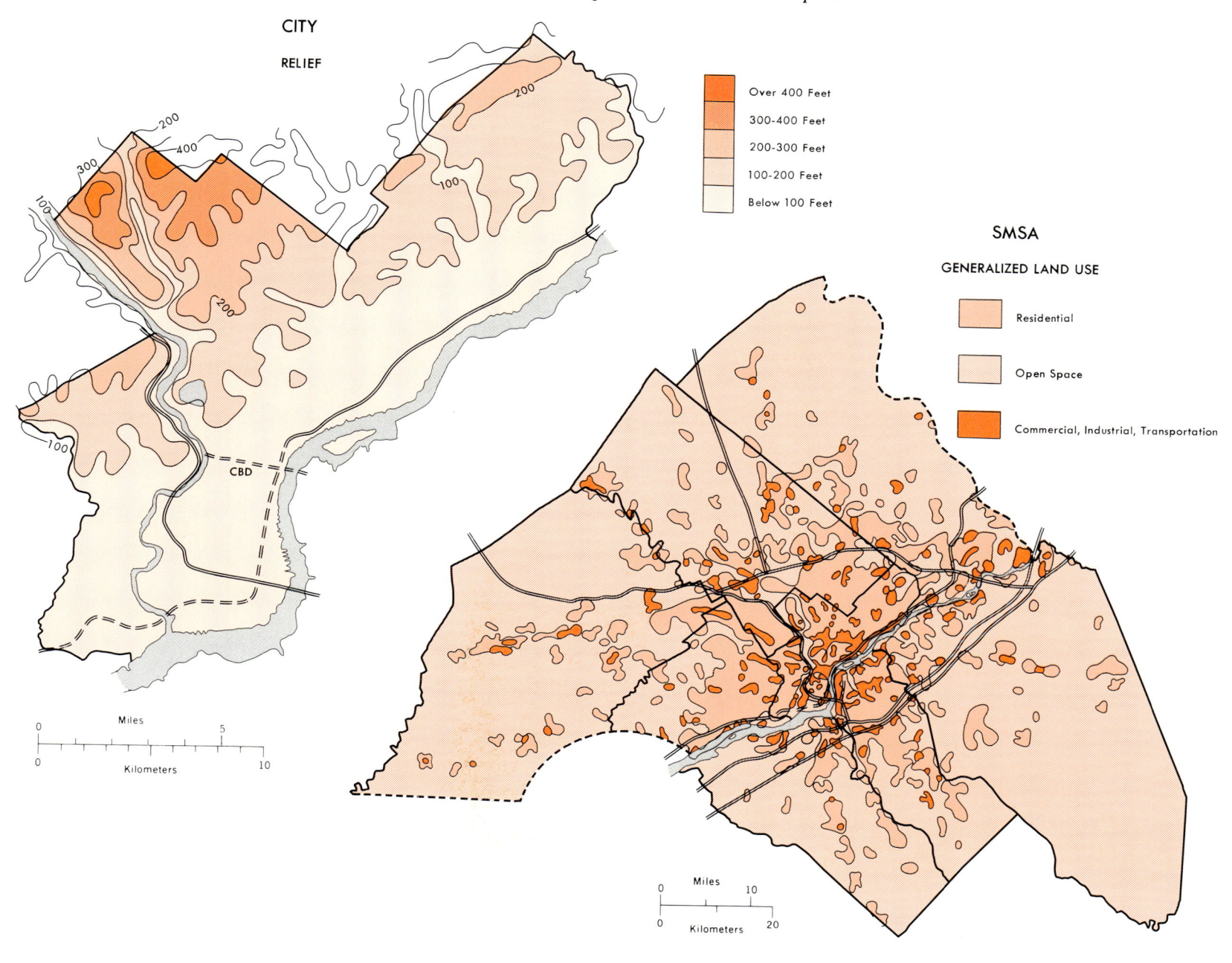

Philadelphia and Camden as well as farther south along the Delaware. The continuously built-up settlement area extends to the north and northwest with a cluster of outliers along the main line of the old Pennsylvania Railroad in Montgomery, Delaware, and Chester counties. Suburbanization is less extensive in New Jersey, but it is increasing more rapidly there than in Pennsylvania; whereas Pennsylvania suburbanization began before 1900, most suburban development in New Jersey has occurred in the last 15 years.

## HOUSING

**Housing Age.** Half the region's housing was built before 1940 and a fifth was built between 1960 and March, 1970. The remaining 30 percent thus dates from 1940 through 1959. Philadelphia contains 460,000 dwellings built before 1940, which constitute 70 percent of the city's units. Older units predominate except in the northwestern and northeastern parts of the city. Northeast Philadelphia is a suburb within the city. A housing project in south Philadelphia and the Central Business District (CBD) renewal area push local percentages of housing built after 1960 over 30 percent.

The concentration of new housing along the Burlington-Camden county line centers on Cherry Hill. As is often true in the region's suburbs, this new housing is clustered around commercial shopping malls and office parks. The Echelon Mall area, near Lindenwold, was linked to downtown Philadelphia by a new high-speed transit line in 1969. Now the region's highest paying jobs can be reached in less than 20 minutes from the Ashland Station of the Lindenwold Speedline.

**Mobile Homes.** These are of minor importance in the central portion of the region, comprising less than 10 percent of all housing units in the immediate vicinity of Philadelphia, except in one small New Jersey municipality. Mobile homes constitute 1 percent (11,000) of the housing units in the Philadelphia SMSA.

**Single-Unit Detached Housing.** Individual dwellings dominate the suburbs but the percentage of such units is unusually low in the central city. In most cities, multiple units are apartments, but in Philadelphia row houses are more common. The core area in which less than 10 percent of all dwellings are single detached units is filled with individual houses built wall to wall. They are usually narrow and deep; lots 20 feet wide are common, and old houses that are 12 and 14 wide are still standing in the city's oldest neighborhoods. Thirty-seven percent of the SMSA's housing is single-unit detached, but only 7 percent of Philadelphia's housing is in that category.

**Housing Value and Rent.** The axis of high-value housing is clearly west of Philadelphia. The Main Line, a series of early commuter suburbs along the main line of the Pennsylvania Railroad, is a high-prestige corridor. The best addresses are Bryn Mawr, Villanova, and Rosemont. Within Philadelphia, Chestnut Hill in the city's

*The Nation's Metropolitan Core: Philadelphia*

SMSA

HOUSING BUILT BEFORE 1940

DUS

MOBILE HOMES

SMSA

HOUSING BUILT 1960-1970

50

The Nation's Metropolitan Core: Philadelphia

northwest corner is an area where mean housing values exceed $40,000. The gradient to less valuable housing immediately to the southeast is sharp. Elsewhere in the region, mean housing values rarely exceed $40,000 except near Cherry Hill and Lindenwold, New Jersey. Lower value housing is concentrated in the central city, where tracts with mean values below $10,000 are numerous.

Rental units are expensive along the Main Line axis, but they are also costly north of the city. Mean monthly rentals exceed $250 in several luxury apartment complexes. In Philadelphia, units generally rent for less than $100 except near the city's center, where they are more expensive.

THE PEOPLE

**Population Density.** The city's overall density of 15,200 people per square mile (5,900 per square kilometer) is high for an American central city. Densities within Philadelphia vary from zero in some industrial areas to 60,000 per square mile (23,200 per square kilometer) in one tract north of the CBD. Outside the industrial areas, densities are low in the northeast and northwest, and high in South Philadelphia, West Philadelphia, and the area north of the CBD, where densities reach peaks of over 50,000 (19,300 per square kilometer). There are sharp differences among the high-density areas. The northern and western areas are predominantly black and beginning to experience rapid deterioration and abandonment (see pp.

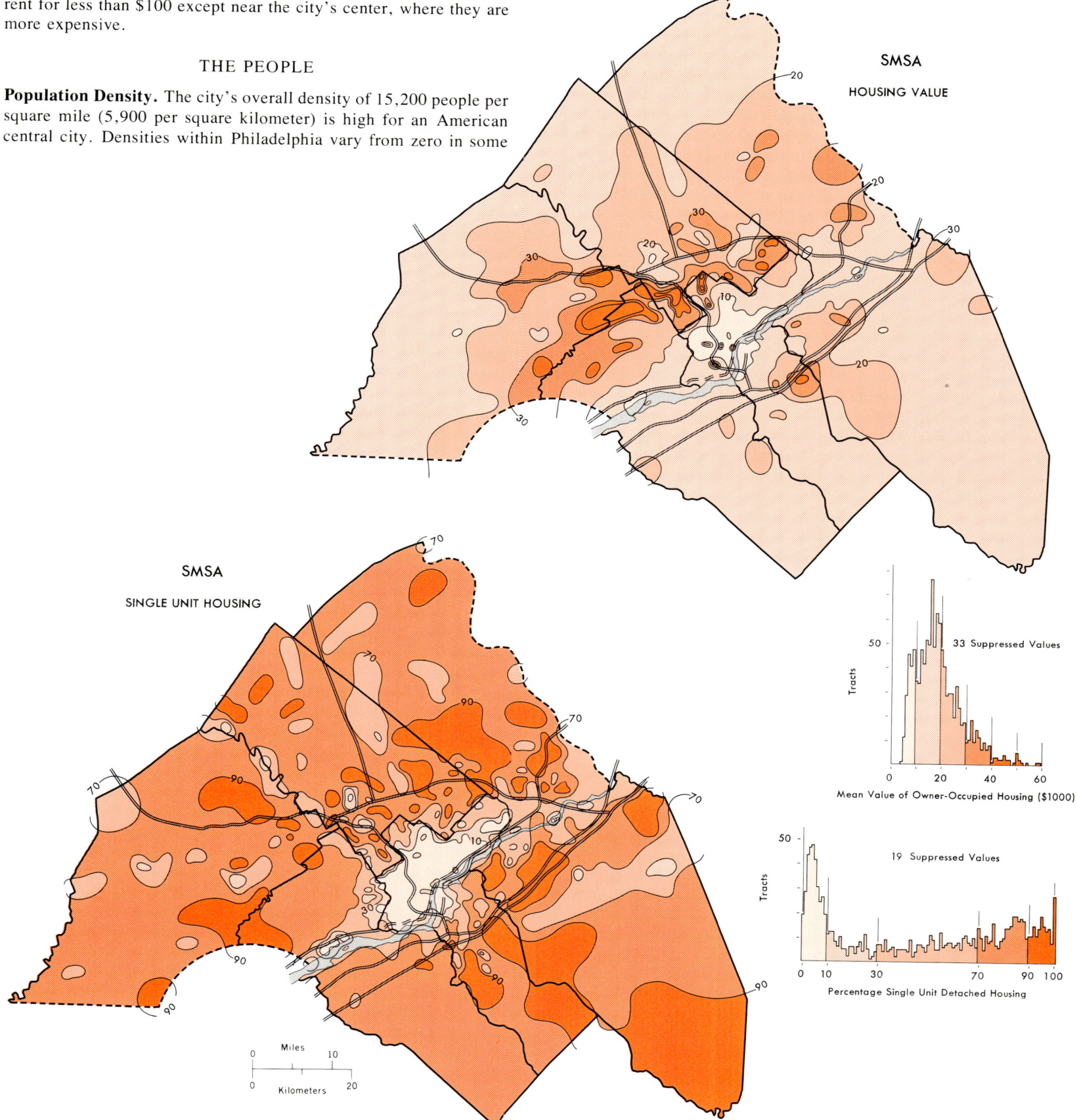

51

## The Nation's Metropolitan Core: Philadelphia

54 and 59). The southern area is largely white, and although some abandonment is occurring, it is not serious. The isopleth that delimits areas above 10,000 (3,900 per square kilometer) in northeast Philadelphia marks the transition from housing built in the 1950s to dwellings erected after 1960 at significantly lower densities (see p. 50). The SMSA map of population density is on p. 310.

**Age and the Elderly.** Median ages in Philadelphia exceed 30 years except for an area in southeast, west, and near-north Philadelphia. Areas inside the city where median ages exceed 40 are ripe for transition as the older families occupying them vacate for apartments or die. Outside Philadelphia, there are clusters of older populations around the industrial towns on the Schuylkill River (the boundary between Montgomery and Chester counties above Valley Forge).

Areas where people over 64 exceed 10 percent of the population are usually caused by out-migration of young people rather than in-migration of old people. Most clusters of the elderly are located in the region's older settlements.

**Sex Ratio.** There are 1.1 females for every male in the SMSA, yielding an overall sex ratio (males divided by females times 100) of 93. The population pyramids for Philadelphia and the SMSA (coincident with the DUS) both show more females than males after age 30. On the map, the prominent male-dominant (over 100) area on the east side of the SMSA is Fort Dix, New Jersey.

**Negroes.** There are 654,000 blacks living in Philadelphia; they constitute 34 percent of the city's people. The absence of suppressed values on the histogram and the 107 zero values indicate that gradients between black and white neighborhoods are sharp; either tracts have no blacks or they are present in reasonably large numbers. Mixed neighborhoods are in transition from white to black rather than stable areas. The income differential between the two groups (black 1969 median family income in Philadelphia was $7,522 whereas the median for whites was $10,783) means whites can more often afford to leave deteriorating neighborhoods. Blacks have more difficulty doing so and a great deal of difficulty leaving the central city, as the SMSA map of black population on p. 61 clearly shows.

**Spanish-Americans.** There are 46,000 Spanish-speaking people living in Philadelphia. The fact that information on their numbers is suppressed for 275 tracts suggests that a very few are scattered in small numbers throughout most of the city. Concentrations occur in north-central Philadelphia where Spanish-Americans (mostly Puerto Rican stock) are intermingled with blacks on the edge of the ghetto. The concentration of Spanish-Americans is not intense; in only two tracts does the percentage rise above 30 percent of the total population. (See the SMSA map of Spanish-Americans on p. 390.)

**Polish-Americans.** In the SMSA there are 17,300 Polish-born and 70,500 people with at least one Polish-born parent. Of the Polish-born, 11,100 (64 percent) live in Philadelphia, where they are most evident in the city's northeastern side. Half of the people of Polish parentage (35,400) live inside the city. They are concentrated in the Kensington and Fishtown neighborhoods northeast of the CBD.

**Russian-Americans.** How many of the people listed as Russian-Americans are Jews is unclear, although most undoubtedly are. In the SMSA there are 29,900 Russian-born and 90,600 people with at least one Russian-born parent. Russian Jews, who have prospered and had smaller than average families, have moved outward from their original immigrant neighborhoods to communities near and over the municipal boundaries. Whereas 78 percent of the Russian-born still live in Philadelphia, only 61 percent of the people of Russian parentage reside there.

**Italian-Americans.** Italian-Americans are dispersed among the general population and concentrated in central-city neighborhoods as well. In the SMSA there are 47,300 Italian-born and 182,000 people with at least one Italian-born parent; together they comprise 11 percent of the SMSA population. Half the Italian-born and 43 percent of the people of Italian parentage reside in Philadelphia, where much of the Italian-American community is concentrated in South Philadelphia. This ethnic community is one of the largest and most vivacious in the nation.

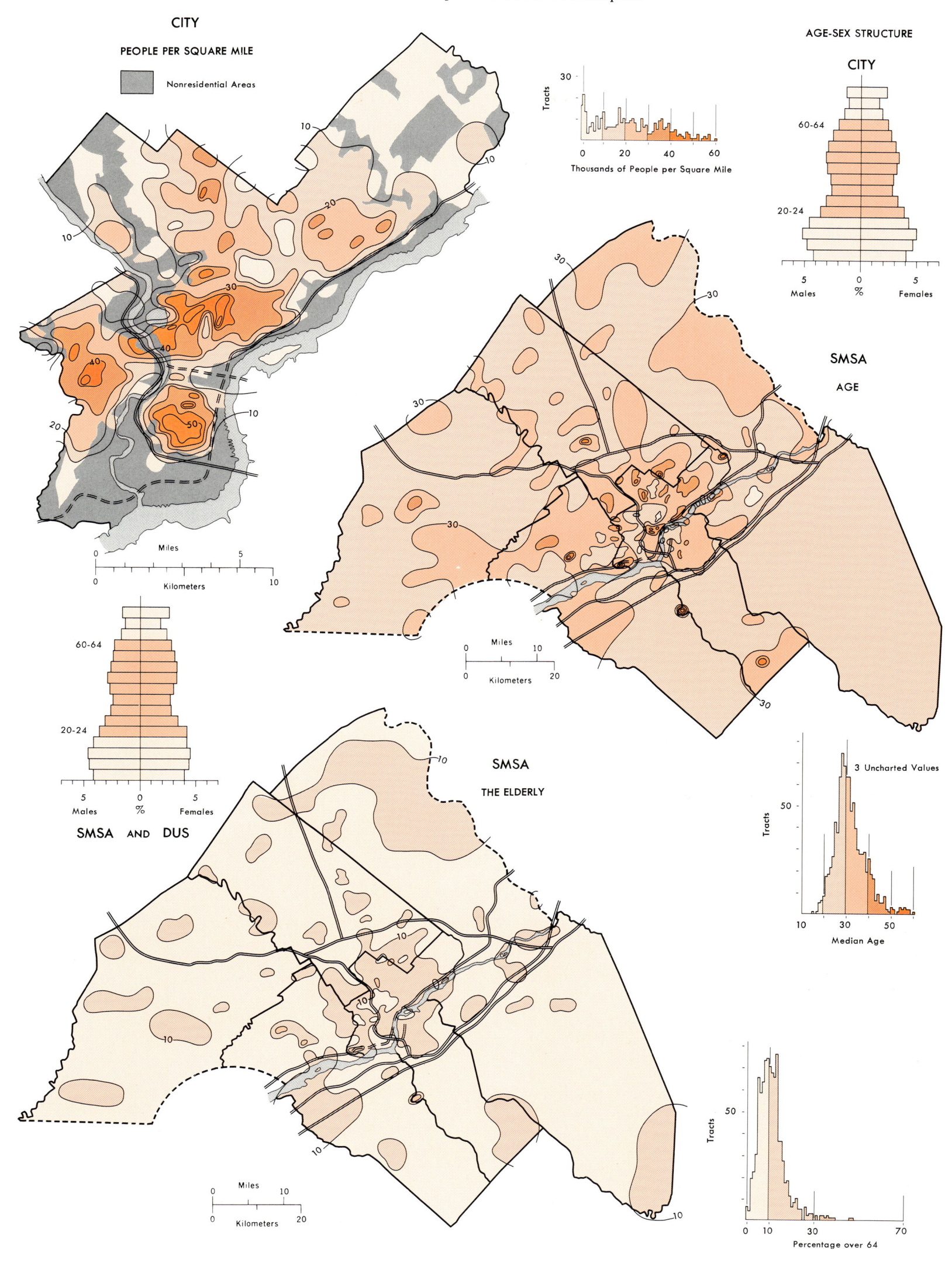

## The Nation's Metropolitan Core: Philadelphia

### CITY
PEOPLE PER SQUARE MILE

Nonresidential Areas

### AGE-SEX STRUCTURE
**CITY**

60-64

20-24

Males / % / Females

### SMSA
AGE

### SMSA
THE ELDERLY

### SMSA AND DUS

60-64

20-24

Males / % / Females

Thousands of People per Square Mile

3 Uncharted Values

Median Age

Percentage over 64

53

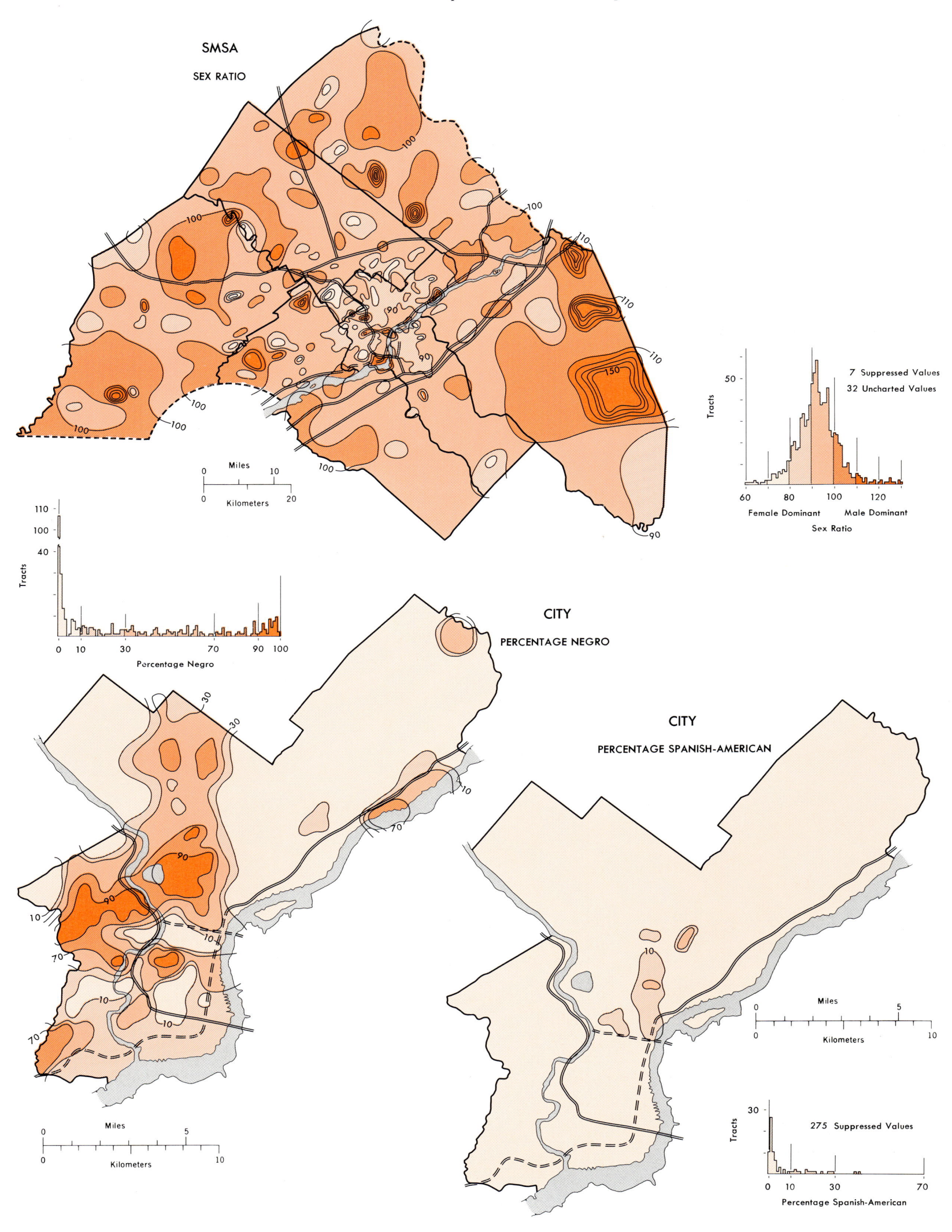

The Nation's Metropolitan Core: Philadelphia

SMSA

SEX RATIO

7 Suppressed Values
32 Uncharted Values

Female Dominant    Male Dominant
Sex Ratio

Percentage Negro

CITY

PERCENTAGE NEGRO

CITY

PERCENTAGE SPANISH-AMERICAN

275 Suppressed Values

Percentage Spanish-American

54

## The Nation's Metropolitan Core: Philadelphia

### SOCIOECONOMIC CHARACTERISTICS

**Household Size.** The average household size in the Philadelphia region is a typical 3.2; the average of 3 in the central city is larger than the norm for a large central city. As the histogram indicates, tracts with average household sizes over 4 or under 2 are rare. Most values lie between 2.5 and 4. Sizes of less than 2 are confined to the CBD area of Philadelphia. Some parts of the city have values below 3, but large areas have more than 3 persons in the average household, especially in South Philadelphia and in the southerly portions of the northeastern sector, where Italians and Poles are numerous. Outside the central city two general patterns should be noted. In some older population centers and inner suburbs on the west, values often fall below 3. To the north and in New Jersey, however, there are several areas where average household size exceeds 4. Housing is less expensive in these areas (p. 51), and the inexpensive single-family housing draws disproportionate numbers of young families with several children. The value over 5 located along the Chester-Montgomery County line is the Pennhurst State School in which the entire population lives in group quarters.

**Female Headship.** These families, like smaller households, are more numerous in central cities than in suburbs or exurbs. Values over 30 percent and as high as 50 or 60 percent occur in the black ghetto in

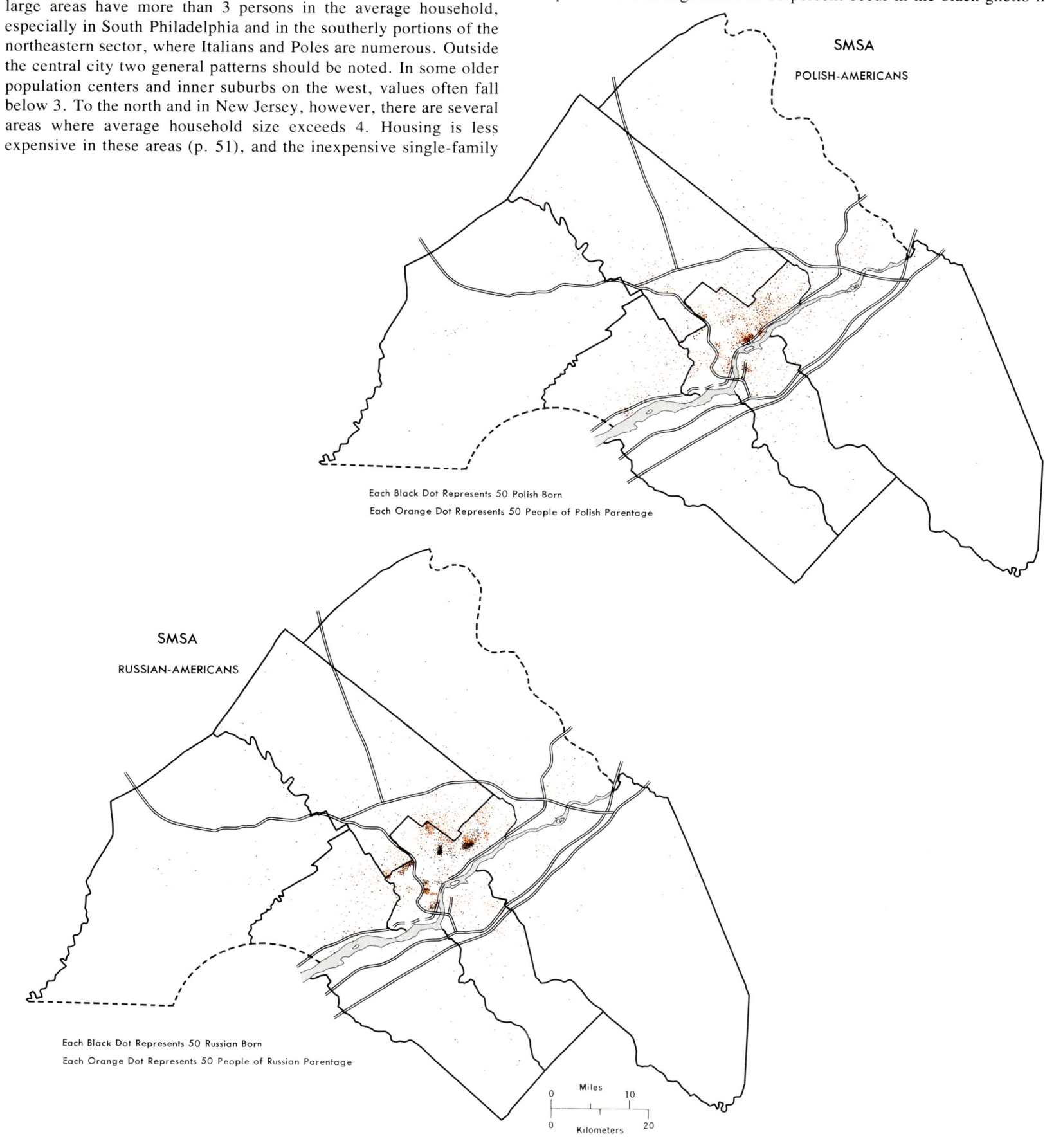

SMSA
POLISH-AMERICANS

Each Black Dot Represents 50 Polish Born
Each Orange Dot Represents 50 People of Polish Parentage

SMSA
RUSSIAN-AMERICANS

Each Black Dot Represents 50 Russian Born
Each Orange Dot Represents 50 People of Russian Parentage

55

north-central Philadelphia and West Philadelphia. For some tracts in the predominantly black areas of Camden (p. 61) a third or more of the families are headed by females. Outside the central city and the immediately adjacent areas, few families are headed by females. In the older towns, values often rise above 10 percent, but outside these older settlement cores values are low. The large area with values over 10 percent in Burlington County, New Jersey, is deceptive; tracts in the region are large and population density is low (p. 310).

**Occupations.** Blue-collar workers are laborers and operatives. The executive category consists of engineers, teachers, professionals, managers, proprietors, and administrators. Tracts with large numbers of blue-collar workers appear intermittently in the central city. Values are low in the CBD and across the Schuylkill around the University of Pennsylvania. The north-central ghetto area has values over 30 percent, as do the working-class neighborhoods along the Delaware on both sides of the river. Inner western and northern suburbs are notable for the low proportions of blue-collar workers living there, as are the newer suburbs of New Jersey, where values are also below 10 percent.

The number of executives is usually larger where the number of blue-collar workers is smaller, but interpretation of the maps is complicated by service and clerical occupations that we have not mapped. The percentage of executives is above 30 in the CBD tracts, but values are below 30 percent throughout most of the city and below

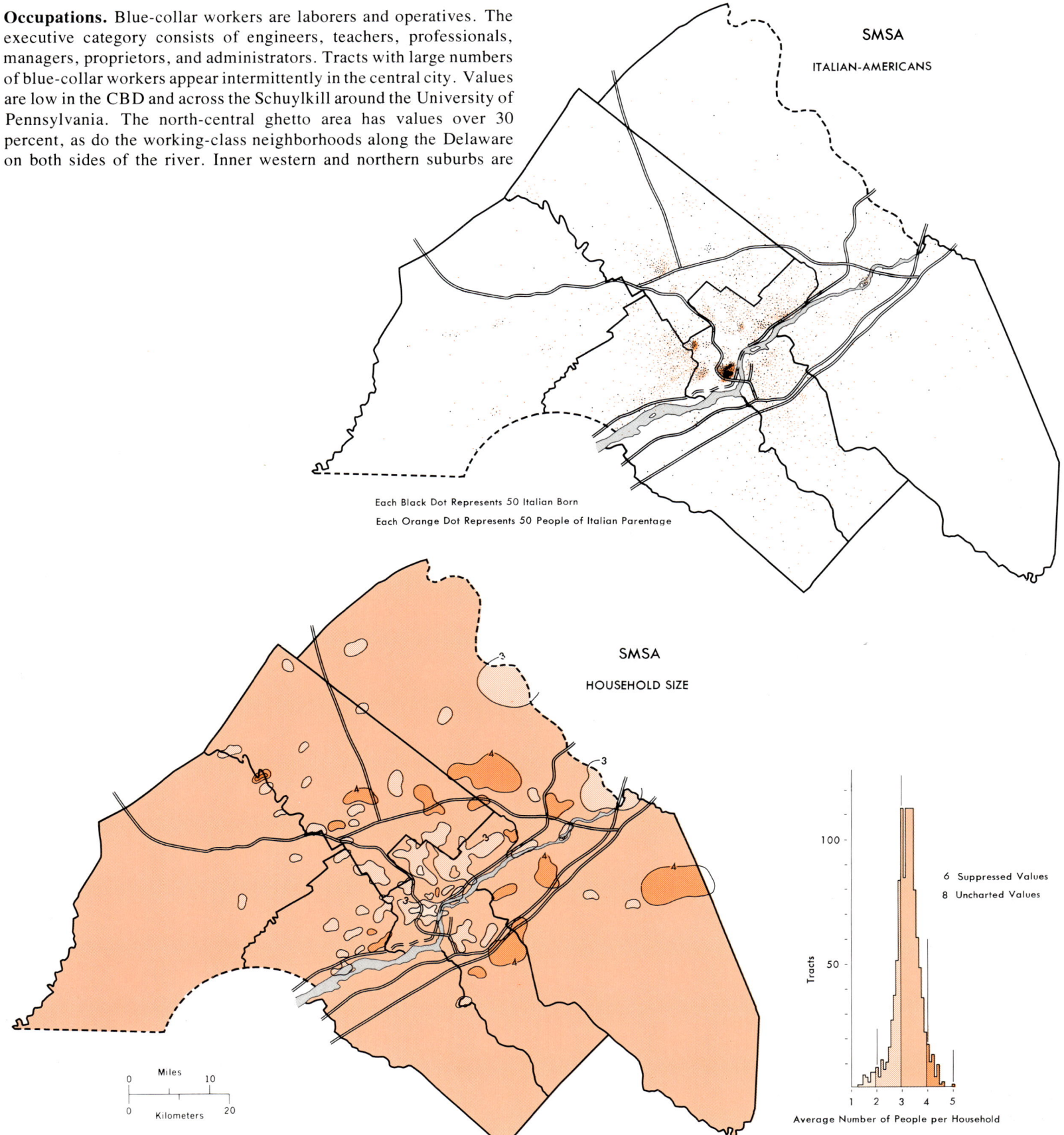

SMSA
ITALIAN-AMERICANS

Each Black Dot Represents 50 Italian Born
Each Orange Dot Represents 50 People of Italian Parentage

SMSA
HOUSEHOLD SIZE

6 Suppressed Values
8 Uncharted Values

Average Number of People per Household

## The Nation's Metropolitan Core: Philadelphia

**SMSA**

**FAMILIES WITH A FEMALE HEAD**

10 Suppressed Values

Percentage Families with a Female Head

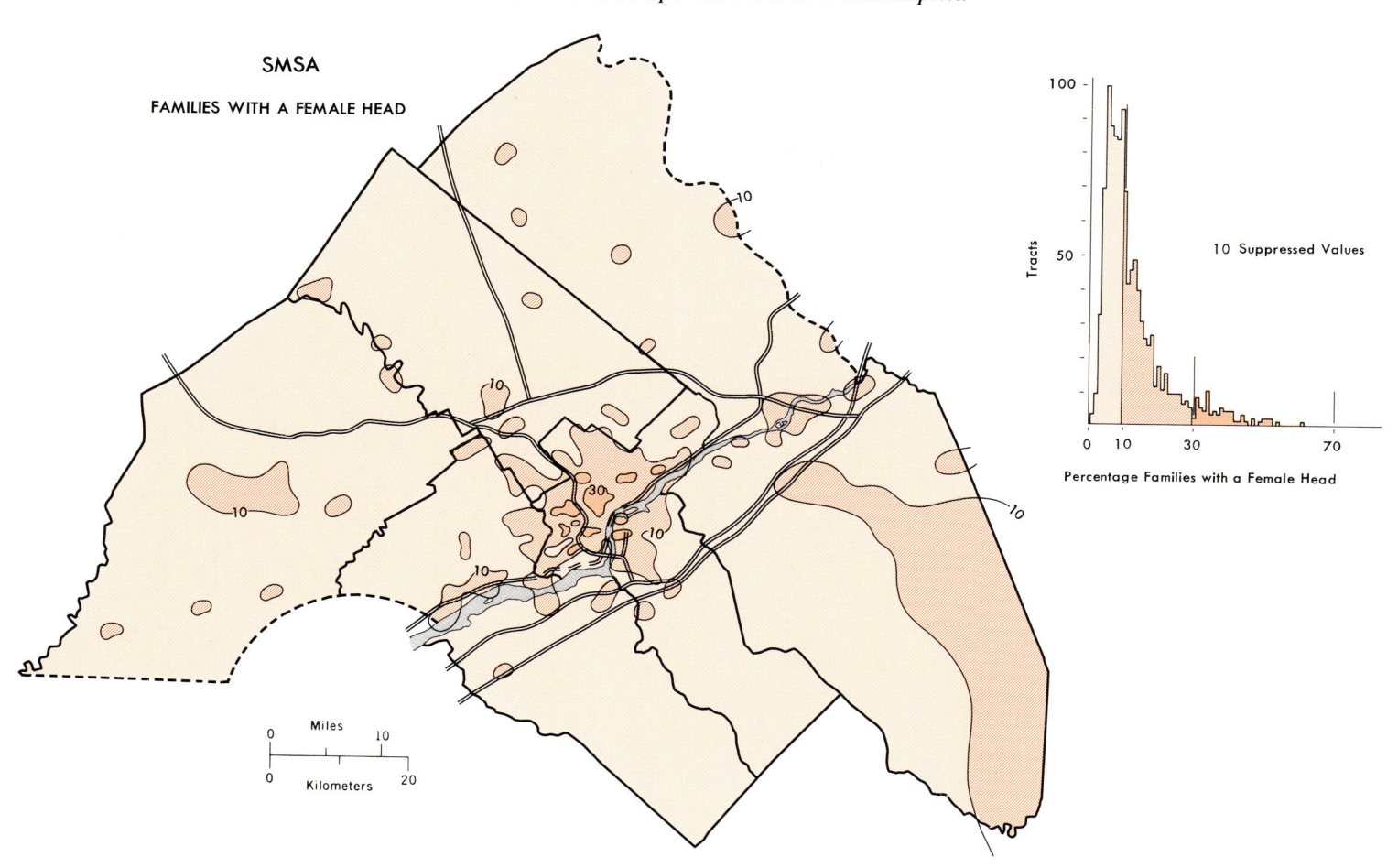

10 percent in the inner city. Values over 30 percent occur in a broad swath of suburban communities that parallels the Delaware River west of Philadelphia. The 100 percent value in Chester County is the Valley Forge Army Hospital, with its large number of resident professionals. In New Jersey, values exceed 30 percent in the newer suburbs and in eastern Burlington County, also the site of a public institution.

**Income.** Tract values for mean income per person per year in Philadelphia range from less than $500 (plotted on the histogram as zero) to more than $17,500 (not plotted). High incomes are concentrated in the wealthy suburbs immediately west of Philadelphia. Main Line communities such as Merion, Bala Cynwyd, Bryn Mawr, Rosemont, and Villanova have incomes over $7,500 per person, with one tract east of Villanova exceeding $10,000. Chestnut Hill in northwestern Philadelphia is even more well-to-do; the tracts with the highest mean per person incomes in the metropolitan area ($13,000, $17,000, and $17,500) are located there. Downtown residents are also well-off, with incomes averaging over $7,500 in some places.

The mean income per person for the Philadelphia region as a whole is $3,450 ($3,050 for the city of Philadelphia) which means that affluent areas are offset by areas with very low incomes. Poorer areas are found in the central city and in a few exurban locations, most notably the eastern portion of Burlington County, New Jersey, part of a region known as the Pine Barrens, a desolate low-lying area of scrub pine forest that offers little economic opportunity for its few inhabitants. Low-income areas within Philadelphia and Camden coincide generally with portions of both cities that are predominantly black.

### TOPICS OF SPECIAL INTEREST IN THE PHILADELPHIA REGION

**Abandoned Housing.** This is becoming an increasingly serious issue in some eastern cities (see pp. 437-444). The map of vacant housing shows the distribution of dwellings that have been vacant for one year or more. Vacancy of that duration is not always indicative of abandonment, but in a thriving housing market such as central-city Philadelphia's, it is diagnostic. Vacant housing is most frequent in the dominantly black areas, with a sparser scattering in the northwestern area that has been the scene of the most recent expansion of the black ghetto (p. 54). This suggests that at least some housing abandonment is in response to anticipated or actual black succession and the consequent pessimism about the neighborhood's long-run prospects.

Philadelphia has an urban homestead program. The city can sell abandoned, structurally sound houses for one dollar to low-income families who are willing to refurbish and occupy them for at least five years. But the number of sound houses acquired is small compared with the quickening pace of abandonment, and the limitation of the program to low-income families causes problems, since the families typically lack the cash and credit necessary to remodel a house if they do acquire one. It is debatable whether eliminating the low-income restriction would help, for the sufficient condition for investment in housing by any family is confidence that the neighborhood will be a viable residential area over the long run. It almost seems that the initial abandonment is a silent but powerful judgment that a neighborhood is doomed.

**Housing Value.** The detailed map of housing value for the city (the SMSA map is on p. 51) shows high housing values in the CBD area and across the Schuylkill around the University of Pennsylvania campus. The western CBD peak is produced by expensive high-rise condominiums, but the even higher eastern peak, where values exceed $40,000, consists largely of completely remodeled single-family row houses in Society Hill, southeast of the CBD, and the Independence Hall area. Many of these row houses date from colonial times; despite their age, and despite the fact that renovation costs often exceeded $50,000 in the mid-1970s, competition for salvageable shells (at prices up to $75,000) remains keen.

In other parts of the inner city the picture is bleak. The high-value area in South Philadelphia consists of housing from the 1940s and 1950s. The high values of Chestnut Hill and the northwest stand out,

## The Nation's Metropolitan Core: Philadelphia

but elsewhere in the city values above $20,000 are rare and values below $10,000 are common. Low housing values are not a problem if the housing in question provides sound, adequate shelter. Too often, however, low-value housing does not, especially in the areas within the $10,000 isopleth.

**Parochial School Enrollment.** The map of percentage elementary enrollment in parochial schools is best considered in conjunction with the city map of percentage Negro (p. 54) and the maps of Polish- and Italian-Americans (pp. 55-56). High enrollments in parochial schools (largely Roman Catholic) are directly correlated with the Catholic minorities and inversely correlated with black populations. Parochial school enrollments rise to more than 70 percent in strongly Polish Kensington in the near northeast and in the minor Italian cluster along the southern boundary of northwest Philadelphia. Parochial schools provide an alternative to the integrated, troubled public schools and keep white ethnics in central-city neighborhoods from which they might otherwise flee. But the schools do so at the cost of perpetuating racial segregation. (See pp. 357-364 for maps of parochial school enrollment in other cities.)

**Population Change.** Constant ebb and flow and the pressure of

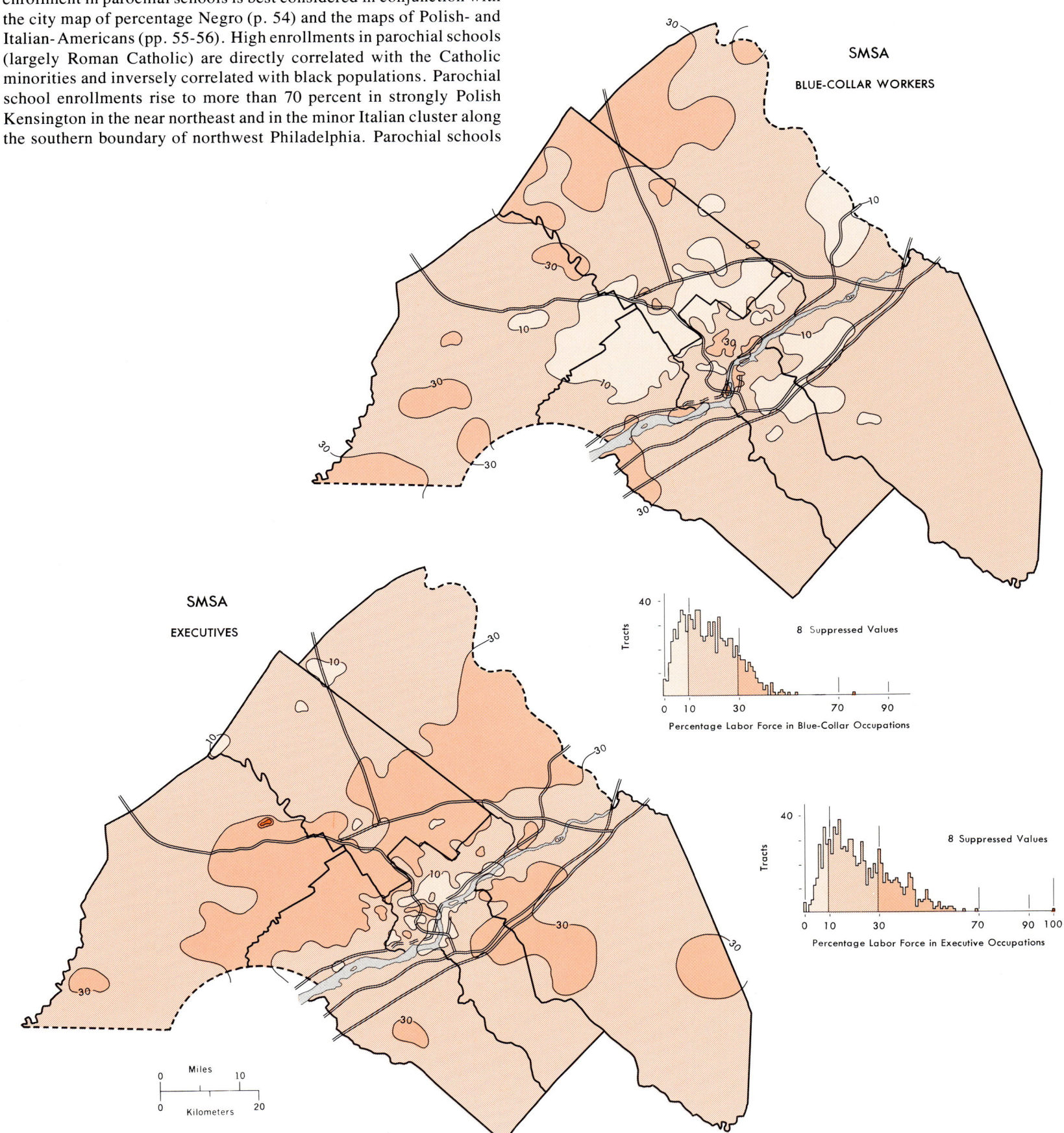

*The Nation's Metropolitan Core: Philadelphia*

SMSA
INCOME PER PERSON

2 Uncharted Values

Mean Income per Person in Hundreds of Dollars

CITY
VACANT HOUSING

Each Dot Represents 10 Vacant Units

CITY
HOUSING VALUE

Mean Value of Owner-Occupied Housing ($1000)

*The Nation's Metropolitan Core: Philadelphia*

**CITY**

PERCENTAGE ELEMENTARY ENROLLMENT IN PAROCHIAL SCHOOLS

**SMSA**

POPULATION CHANGE, 1960-1970

(See Text)

**SMSA**

INCOME PER PERSON

Mean Income per Person in Hundreds of Dollars

*The Nation's Metropolitan Core: Philadelphia*

**SMSA**

**PERCENTAGE NEGRO**

tensions, conflicts, needs, desires, hopes, and fears create the gross patterns of population change mapped on p. 60. The map is produced by dividing each census tract's 1970 population by its 1960 population. If the 1970 population is larger than the 1960 population, a number greater than 1.00 will result. If the tract lost population in the decade, the result will be less than 1.00. The population loss in the central city and the population increases of suburban tracts during the decade are immediately apparent. The city had 2,002,000 people in 1960, but only 1,949,000 in 1970, or a value of 0.93 from the calculation described above. Decline in the central portions of the city was offset by population gains in the northeast, the northwest, and in scattered tracts in South Philadelphia; but the gains were insufficient to wholly offset losses. Outside the central city, the inner ring of suburbs exhibited modest growth. The most rapid suburban growth is occurring in the outer suburbs in Pennsylvania and New Jersey. Although population change results from a complicated mixture of births, deaths, and migrations, it is clear that some suburban growth is occurring at the expense of central-city Philadelphia. (Maps of population change in other metropolitan areas are on pp. 349-56.)

**Negro Neighborhoods.** The economic and social progress blacks made during the 1960s has not enabled them to breach city boundaries; aside from a few scattered clusters in older towns and rural areas, blacks in the Philadelphia area—as in most metropolitan regions (pp. 381-388)—are still confined to the central cities. In 1970, only 18 percent of the metropolitan region's blacks lived outside Philadelphia and Camden.

---

The maps present an almost classic American scenario of a deteriorating central city that is the geographical repository of increasing numbers of disadvantaged people. Yet for all the negative values that seem to stand in sharp contrast to the higher and more positive values of the suburbs, central-city Philadelphia should not be written off, even if that were possible. Visitors are surprised and impressed by the amount of new skyscraper construction downtown, and correctly so, for the continued renewal of Philadelphia's center is a visible sign that many of the region's important powers consider the central city indispensable despite its current difficulties.

CHAPTER 9

# Hartford – Connecticut Valley

*The New Hartford requires a new image to symbolize and to deliver the amenities and promise of a good city.*

THE GREATER HARTFORD PROCESS

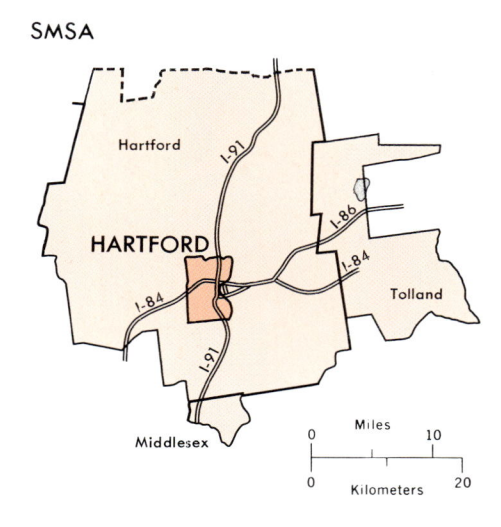

The Hartford Standard Metropolitan Statistical Area (SMSA) is home to 664,000 people, which makes it the 49th most populous SMSA in the nation. SMSAs in New England are underbounded, and therefore the SMSA population understates the size of the social and economic community that focuses on Hartford. When Hartford's commuter region is delimited by including all towns (New England minor civil divisions) that send 5 percent or more of their labor forces into the Hartford core area every day (p. 63), the resulting Daily Urban System (DUS) has an aggregate population of 1,190,000, which is the nation's 19th most populous DUS. Hartford lies in the midst of a cluster of large cities and metropolitan areas such as Springfield, Massachusetts, and Manchester, Meriden, Middletown, New Haven, New London, and Waterbury in Connecticut.

Hartford has historically been the geographical and economic hub of the region. In 1800 Hartford was small compared with Boston, Baltimore, Philadelphia, and New York; but its population of 3,500 made it the nation's 5th largest city, and it was well ahead of its neighbors (p. 10). The site of modern Hartford was the head of navigation on the Connecticut River for ocean vessels; it has been permanently occupied by Caucasoids since 1635. Fertile lowlands along the river were the foundation for the early agrarian economy. Around 1800 manufacturing accelerated in the region, and throughout the 19th century manufacturing sustained rapid population growth and urbanization. Textile, firearms, timepiece, brass, and hardware manufacturing—all leavened well with the region's legendary Yankee ingenuity—provided a secure base for economic expansion and population growth. An unusual combination of manufacturing and office employment—especially office jobs in the insurance industry and state government—provides most of the jobs in the region today.

The city of Hartford occupies low-lying land adjacent to the Connecticut River. Much of the area below the 50-foot (15-meter) contour is floodplain, which has historically been vacant or occupied by industry. The land rises very gently to the west and the south, reaching a maximum elevation over 250 feet (75 meters) in the southwest portion of the city. Thus topography offers neither guidelines nor barriers to growth or movement within the city. Most of the land immediately outside the city is also relatively smooth, for the entire river valley lies in a structural depression. Thus aside from problems encountered in bridging the Connecticut River, rail and highway movement in almost any direction has been relatively easy throughout the central part of the SMSA.

As might be expected in a multinodal region, land-use patterns in the Hartford vicinity are irregular. Numerous settlement cores give rise to clusters of residential land use throughout the region. Solid belts of residential land surround Hartford itself, but elsewhere they occur almost randomly. Away from the river's floodplain, extensive tracts of industrial/commercial/transportation land use are rare. In Hartford, as in most New England cities, manufacturing and commercial enterprises are closely intermingled with residential land use. Such mixed land use is a consequence of the age of New England cities. When people had to walk to work, they necessarily lived close to their jobs.

*Note:* All data are from the 1970 Censuses of Population and Housing unless otherwise indicated. Therefore the present tense refers to 1970 data except for income data which are from 1969. Cartographic conventions are explained in Chapter 1.

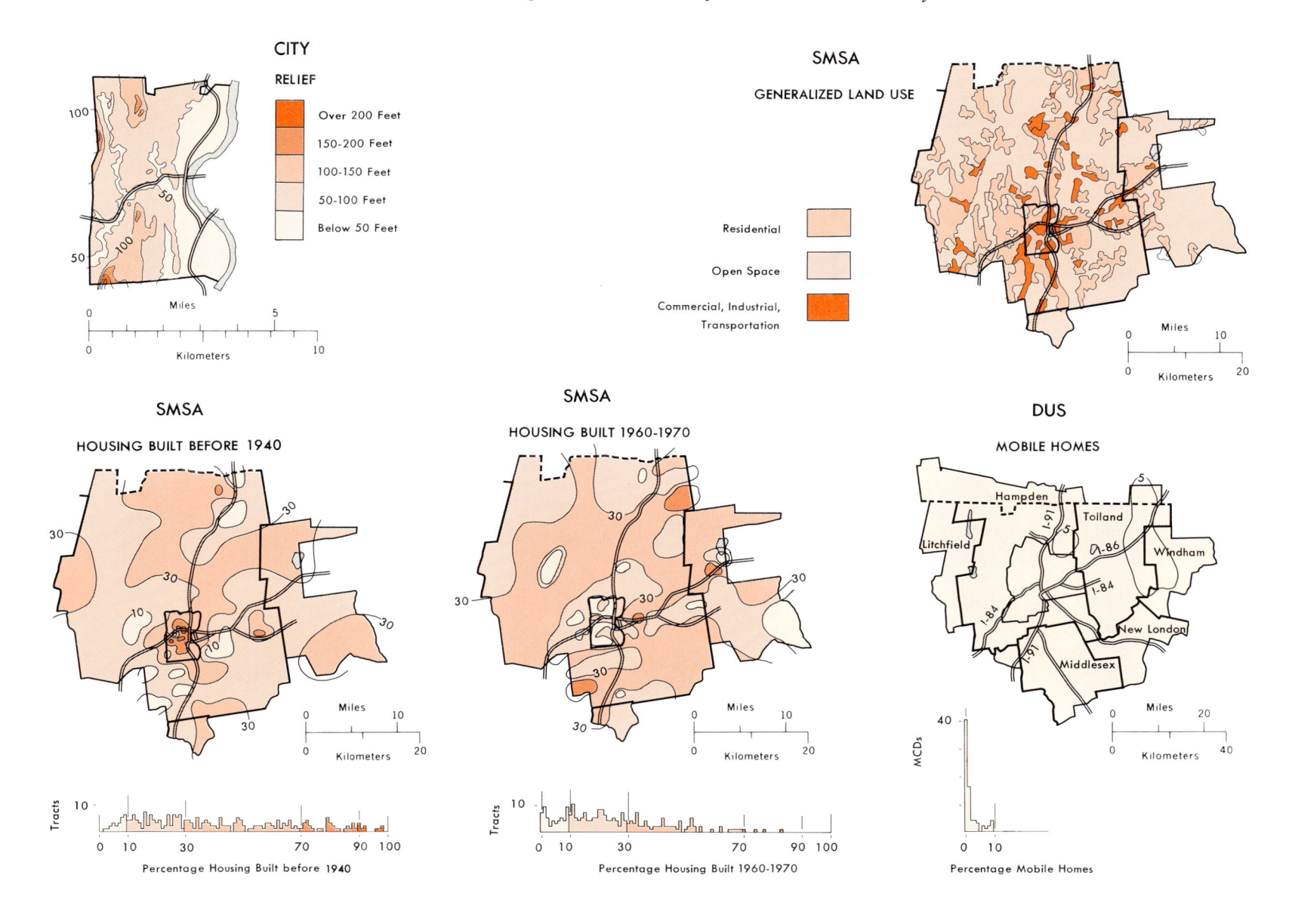

*The Nation's Metropolitan Core: Hartford-Connecticut Valley*

## HOUSING

**Housing Age.** Like its land-use patterns, the housing stock in the SMSA is mixed. Forty percent of the housing was built before 1940, and 25 percent was built from 1960 to March 1970, giving Hartford a young housing-age structure for an eastern city. But local variations within the SMSA complicate the picture in the 67 percent of Hartford City's housing stock that dates from before 1940. High percentages of older housing are at the cores of most settled areas in the region. The areas in which older housing predominates extend in a rough Y pattern from central Hartford to the northeast and northwest. Tracts in which older housing is less than 10 percent lie to the west, the southwest, and the southeast of the city. Tracts in which over 30 percent of the housing units were built between 1960 and 1970 extend southeast and southwest from the city, with two additional extensions to the north and northeast. There are few tracts in which more than 70 percent of the housing was built during the 1960s and no tracts where new housing exceeds 90 percent of the total stock. Older, multifamily housing on narrow lots with little or no yard space is the dominant housing type in central cities like Hartford. Two- and three-family houses are especially common. Remnants of middle- and upper-middle-class residential districts composed of large, well-built houses on tree-lined streets also persist. For the most part, however, middle- and upper-middle-income groups have moved to outlying housing.

**Mobile Homes.** These are unimportant throughout the Hartford DUS. Most towns have no mobile homes or very few. Mobile homes account for as much as 9 percent of the total housing stock in only a few towns in eastern Tolland and western Windham counties that have not adopted the restrictive zoning prohibiting mobile homes.

**Single-Unit Detached Housing.** In Hartford, as in Boston, duplexes and tri-deckers are common forms of multiunit dwellings; a few older row houses also remain. Row houses were built for factory workers in the 19th century, and as other groups have prospered and moved on, the houses have frequently been occupied by blacks and Puerto Ricans. Within the SMSA, 72 percent of the housing stock consists of single-family detached dwellings. In Hartford City, however, only 12 percent of the housing falls into this category. There are sharp contrasts between the older central city and the outlying areas of the SMSA. New housing is being built in the semirural portions of the region at very low densities. Lot sizes averaging one acre per dwelling are common.

**Housing Value and Rent.** There are few extremes on the map of housing value except for the low values in the central city and the high-value belt west of the city. The mean value of owner-occupied housing for the SMSA is $28,000, with individual tract values ranging from a low of $17,000 within Hartford to $57,000 in the prosperous area west of the city. One tract within Hartford exceeds $50,000; the Asylum Avenue neighborhood, west-northwest of the downtown along the city's western boundary, is a high-income, high-prestige area.

The pattern of monthly rents is roughly similar to the pattern of housing value. The average for the SMSA is $119 and for Hartford City it is $109, with total SMSA values ranging from $70 to $350.

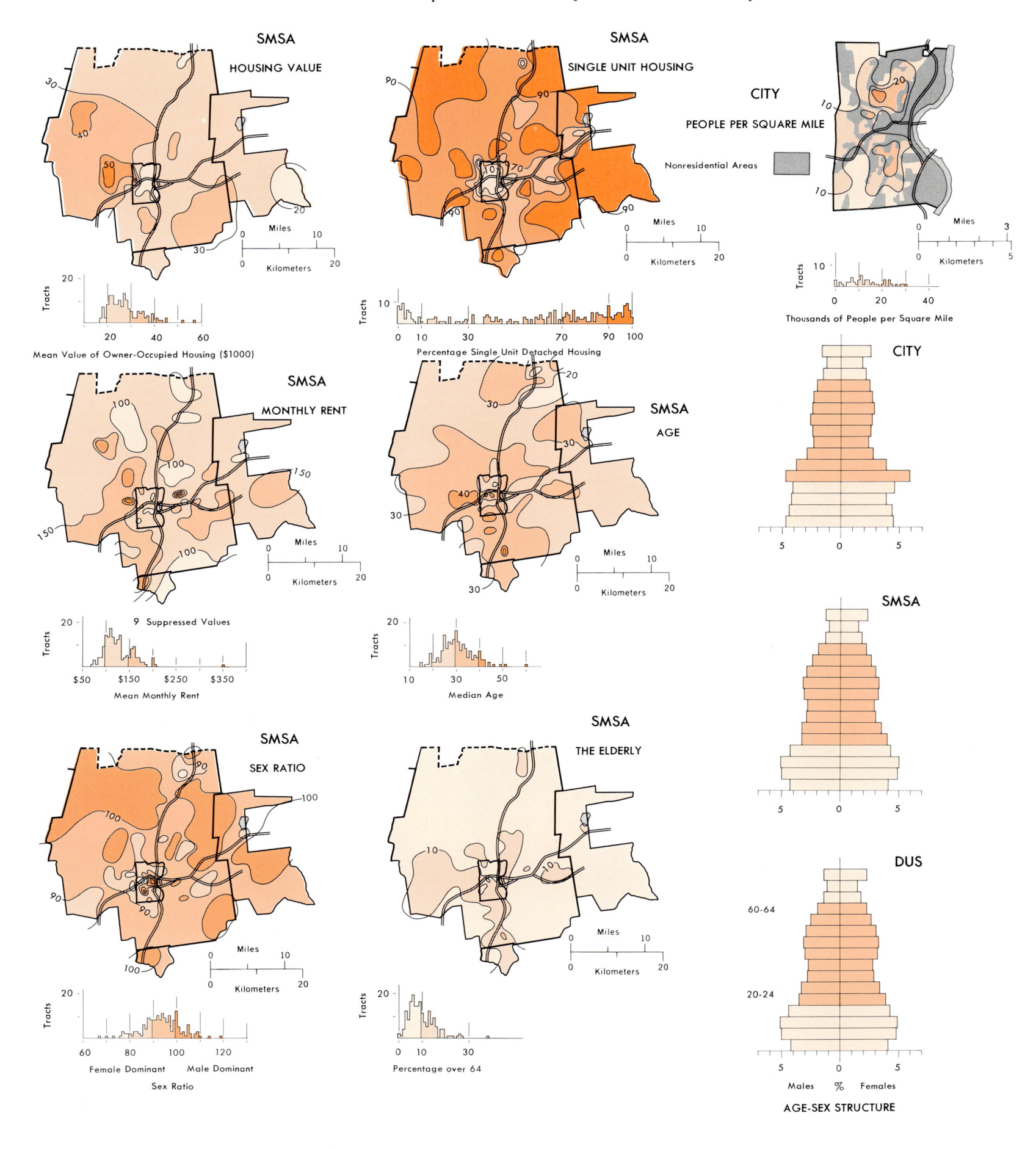

*The Nation's Metropolitan Core: Hartford-Connecticut Valley*

## THE PEOPLE

**Population Density.** Hartford City's people are concentrated in the north-central and south-central portions of the city. Tracts next to the river and broad swaths of land elsewhere contain very few people, being given over to industrial, commercial, or transportation functions. Thus the overall city population density of 9,100 people per square mile (3,500 per square kilometer) is deceptively low. Although

Hartford's western suburbs command higher rents than the rest of the region. The peak value occurs in West Hartford just across the Hartford City line from the Asylum Avenue area. Other tracts with high mean rentals are located northwest of the city and in the northeastern corner of East Hartford Township, across the Connecticut River.

64

*The Nation's Metropolitan Core: Hartford-Connecticut Valley*

**CITY** PERCENTAGE NEGRO

**CITY** PERCENTAGE SPANISH-AMERICAN

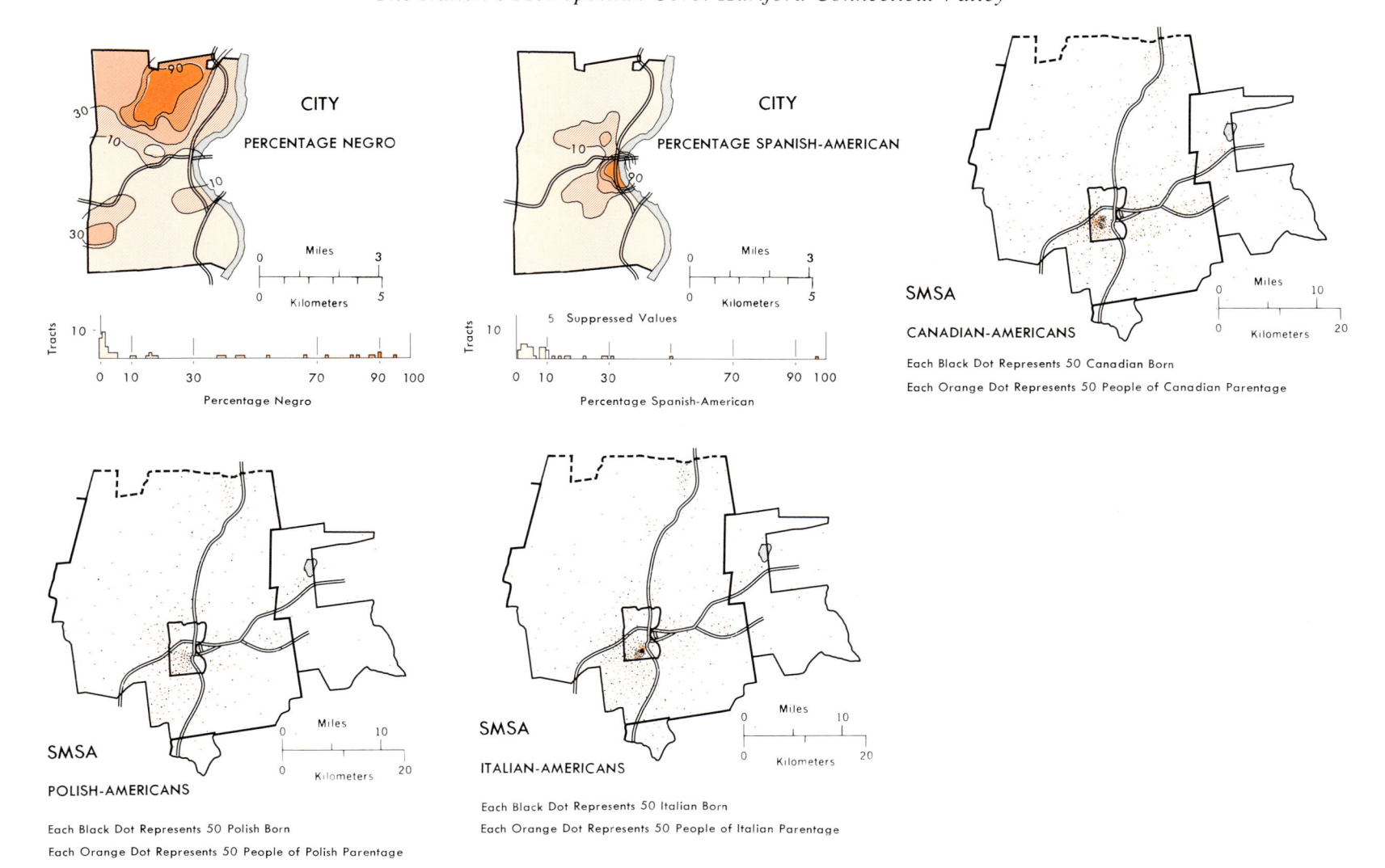

**SMSA** CANADIAN-AMERICANS
Each Black Dot Represents 50 Canadian Born
Each Orange Dot Represents 50 People of Canadian Parentage

**SMSA** POLISH-AMERICANS
Each Black Dot Represents 50 Polish Born
Each Orange Dot Represents 50 People of Polish Parentage

**SMSA** ITALIAN-AMERICANS
Each Black Dot Represents 50 Italian Born
Each Orange Dot Represents 50 People of Italian Parentage

some areas have tract densities below 10,000 (3,900 per square kilometer), population densities in excess of that figure are more common, and the peak value reaches 30,000 per square mile (11,600 per square kilometer) in north-central Hartford. Even so, Hartford's densities are low for a major eastern city. Once again, the polynucleated nature of the central Connecticut urban region is the explanation. Competition for land (and the consequent high densities) is less keen in the region's several urban centers than it would be if the separate populations were aggregated into a single metropolitan region. (A map of SMSA population density appears on p. 310.)

**Age and the Elderly.** The population pyramid of Hartford City is somewhat at odds with the SMSA and DUS pyramids, and the differences reflect the specialized role the city plays in the region. The city has an unusual number of young adults and especially of young females as a result of the migration to Hartford of people in the 20- to 24-year cohort in search of employment. There are 1.2 females for every male in that age cohort because of the many clerical and secretarial jobs in Hartford's insurance industry and state government agencies.

An unusually high proportion of the city's population is in the zero to five-year cohort. Although there are proportionately fewer children in Hartford than in the SMSA or DUS, there are relatively more younger children. SMSA and DUS pyramids narrow at the bases, whereas the city pyramid widens, reflecting the continued high birthrates of Hartford's black and Puerto Rican minorities.

The median age of the SMSA population is 29 years; the median for the city is just a year younger at 28. The northern half of Hartford City is young; the median age in one tract is below 20 years. The area is occupied by blacks and Puerto Ricans who have larger families and higher birthrates than the rest of the region's population. Most of the remainder of the SMSA's southwest quadrant has an older population;

it is occupied by established, more prosperous families who probably had fewer children, many of whom have now established independent households. The higher median ages in the prosperous high-prestige area west of the city are especially apparent, but the highest median ages, over 50 years, occur in two tracts in downtown Hartford. (They could not be shown on the map because the tracts are so small.) As noted earlier, an elderly population—often poor and sometimes derelict—is a standard feature of tracts adjacent to the CBD in most cities. In the northeast portion of the SMSA, median ages below 20 interpenetrate areas with median ages over 30. The areas with older populations are rural tracts or older towns along the Connecticut River. The younger areas are suburban developments midway between Hartford and Springfield, Massachusetts, to the north. An irregular zone of tracts with median ages below 30 runs southeast to northwest across the SMSA in areas where housing values are often below $30,000 and more than a third of the housing was built after 1960. This zone is a preferred location for families of modest means with young children.

Nine percent of the SMSA population is over 64 years old, but the elderly constitute 11 percent of the people in Hartford City. There are few elderly in the northern half of Hartford. Thus, Hartford's racial and ethnic segregation is to some extent age segregation. The southwest quadrant of the SMSA generally has tract values over 10 percent except for the tracts on the southwestern periphery. Manchester to the east and Thompsonville and Enfield to the north, older industrial towns, also have concentrations of the elderly.

**Sex Ratio.** The SMSA sex ratio (males divided by females times 100) is 93 and the city ratio is 89. The SMSA ratio reflects the greater survival rate of females at all ages after the first few years of life. The lower city ratio is a function of female survival in part, but more specifically it reflects selective migration of females to the city. There are few male-dominant tracts in the Hartford SMSA; usually they are either sparsely populated rural areas or older populations near the Hartford CBD.

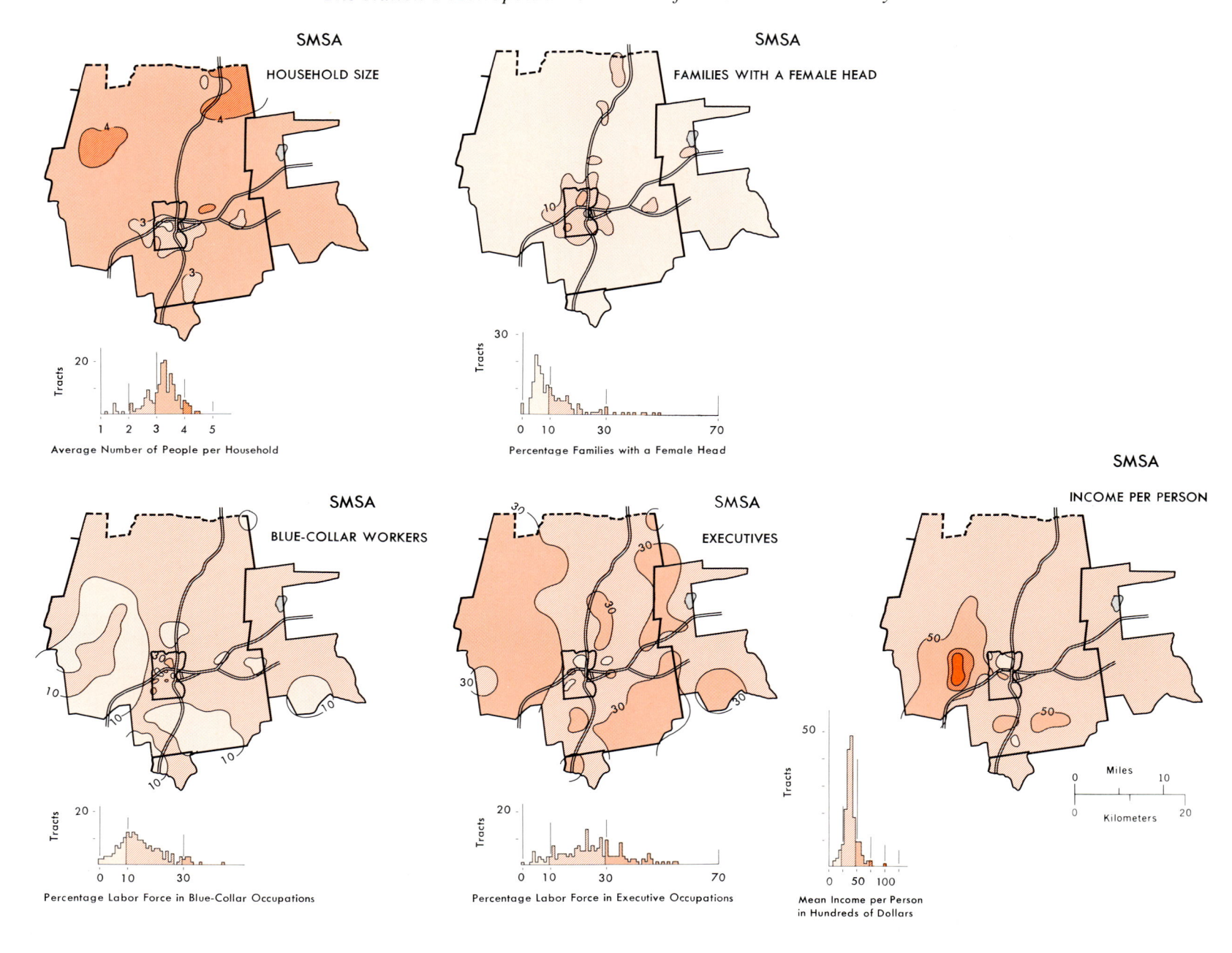

**Negroes.** Blacks constitute 28 percent of Hartford's population but only 8 percent of the SMSA (p. 392) total. Of the SMSA's 50,500 blacks, 44,100 (87 percent) live in Hartford where they cluster in the north-central portion, with one outlier south of the CBD and another in a housing project near the western boundary of the city.

**Spanish-Americans.** There is little overlap between black and Hispanic areas. Spanish-Americans dominate a few tracts in the CBD area; lower-intensity extensions are to the northwest and southwest. Some of the region's Hispanics are migrant laborers who settled in the region instead of making the long return journey to the American Southwest. During the 1960s they were joined by Puerto Ricans. There are 15,000 Spanish-Americans in the SMSA, 11,900 of whom live in Hartford City. Persons of Puerto Rican birth or parentage account for 9,200 of the SMSA (p. 400) total.

**Canadian-Americans.** Like other large New England cities, Hartford has long attracted immigrants from Canada. There are 36,400 Canadian-Americans (9,000 Canadian-born, 26,500 of Canadian parentage) in the SMSA. In many instances they have fewer problems than other immigrant groups. Few linguistic or educational barriers prevent them—French-Canadians excepted—from moving into the mainstream of American life. Hartford's Canadian-Americans are concentrated along the city's western boundary. Outside the city they are distributed relatively evenly among the population; in the SMSA, 40 percent of the Canadian-born and 22 percent of those with at least one Canadian-born parent live in Hartford. There are larger numbers along the axes of high population density to the north, east, and the southwest, as would be expected in a group that melds easily with the general population.

**Italian-Americans.** In the Hartford SMSA, there are 11,300 Italian-born and 27,400 people with at least one Italian-born parent. The total foreign stock is 6 percent of the SMSA population. The concentration of Italian stock is slightly higher in Hartford City (7 percent) than it is in the SMSA. Italian-Americans are heavily clustered in south-central Hartford, but many have settled outside the city. They have moved outward in a highly sectoral manner, shifting southeast from the heavily Italian tracts of the city. Elsewhere clusters of Italian-Americans are located around Manchester on the east and in the Connecticut River Valley towns north of Hartford, roughly in proportion to population density.

**Polish-Americans.** In the Hartford SMSA, there are 6,000 Polish-born and 18,000 people who have at least one Polish-born parent; the Polish foreign stock is 4 percent of the SMSA population. Polish-Americans are spread more evenly through south Hartford City than are the Italian-Americans, but otherwise they occupy the

HOUSING PROJECTS FOR THE NONELDERLY

- Privately Sponsored
- Publicly Sponsored Low Income
- Publicly Sponsored Moderate Income

HOUSING PROJECTS FOR THE ELDERLY

CITY

- Privately Sponsored
- Publicly Sponsored (Hartford Housing Authority)

LOCAL BUS TRANSIT SERVICE AREAS, 1972

SMSA

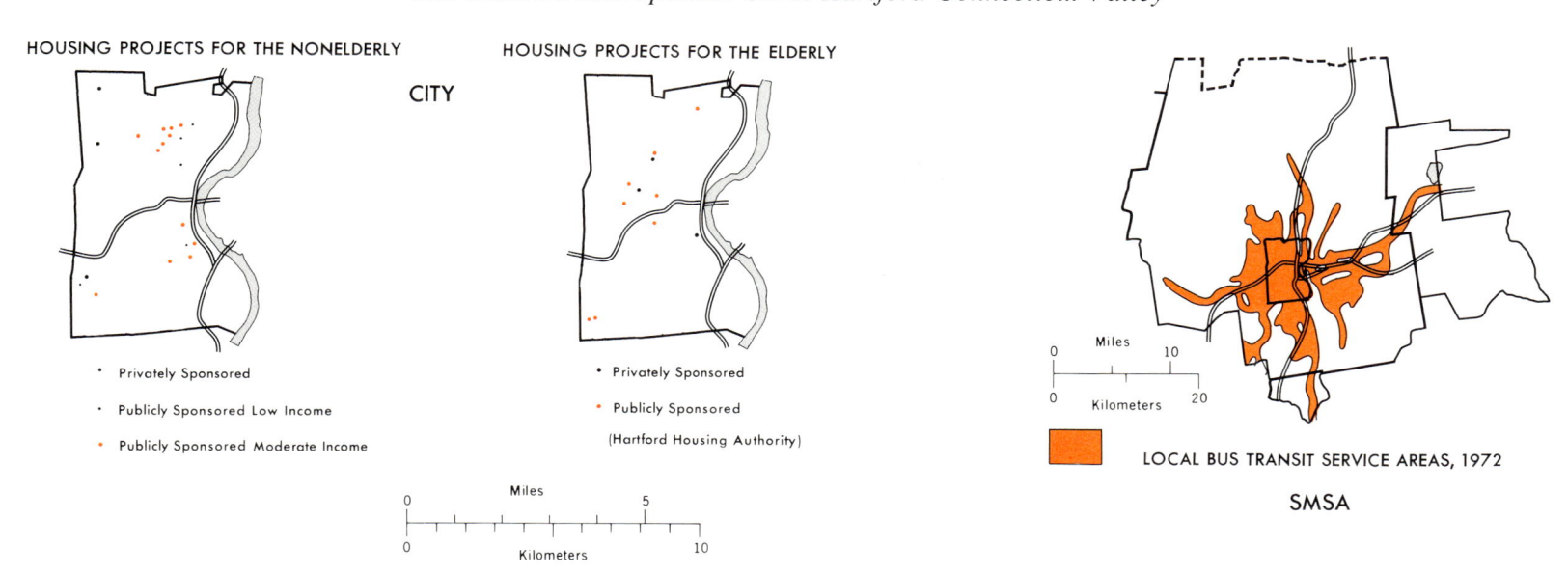

same general parts of the city and the same regions outside Hartford. Both Polish- and Italian-Americans resist penetration of their central-city neighborhoods by blacks and Spanish-Americans. They are conspicuously absent where blacks and Hispanics are present, and vice versa. Unlike some other ethnic groups, Poles and Italians have not done especially well financially, for many continue to specialize in blue-collar occupations. Until recently they also have had larger than average families (p. 66). Thus Polish- and Italian-Americans have fewer opportunities and less inclination to leave central cities for suburban locations than do other ethnic groups. Housing vacancies are scarce in their neighborhoods.

## SOCIOECONOMIC CHARACTERISTICS

**Household Size.** The average household in the Hartford SMSA contains 3.1 persons, a typical metropolitan-area figure. Also typically, the average households are smaller in the central city than in outlying areas; the average for Hartford City is 2.7 persons. The lowest average household sizes are in tracts to the west of the CBD in an area with high proportions of elderly males (p. 64). South Hartford and part of the area to the west that is occupied by a somewhat older population also have smaller than average households. Average households with more than 4 people occur in suburban areas of Springfield, Massachusetts, located in the northwestern corner of Hartford County, and in the western part of the SMSA. Outlying areas where household sizes fall below 3 persons are older settlement centers.

**Female Headship.** There are more families headed by females in population centers than in suburban or exurban areas. Females head 22 percent of Hartford City's households, whereas the proportion is 11 percent for the entire SMSA. The central-city value is somewhat high in comparison with other cities. This is partially a function of the large proportion of blacks in Hartford, for all the tracts in which more than 30 percent of the households are headed by females lie in predominantly black areas of the city. With the exception of one small area near the CBD, females head 10 percent or more of the households throughout the city. There is nothing inherently problematical about families headed by females except that this often means the absence of a well-paid breadwinner, resulting in low income and public assistance. In 1969, for example, 4,600 families had incomes below the poverty level in Hartford City, and 2,800 of them were headed by females.

**Occupations.** Blue-collar workers (laborers and operatives) comprise 14 percent of the SMSA labor force, and executives (engineers, teachers, professionals, managers, proprietors, and administrators) account for 25 percent. The remaining 61 percent is evenly split between service and clerical occupations. Within Hartford City, 21 percent of the labor force works at blue-collar jobs, and only 14 percent is executive. The percentage of blue-collar jobs exceeds 30 in some central-city tracts. Outside the city, values range from 10 to 29 percent in most of the SMSA. One notable exception is the large area to the west where values fall below 10 percent and then rise above that figure again even farther west. Agricultural workers may contribute to the high values, and long-distance commuters with higher than average incomes may occupy low-value areas. In both instances, the tracts are large and the actual numbers of people are small.

The same comment applies to the map of executive workers, although it is easier to relate where executives live to some of the other maps in the chapter. The generally higher percentages of executives in the west and in the Asylum Avenue area within Hartford are expected, given income and housing patterns in the metropolis. Low central-city values make it clear that few blacks have moved into executive and professional ranks. Hartford is not alone in having a population with few executive occupations in close proximity to the cluster of white-collar jobs in its CBD; virtually every city in the atlas shows such an anomaly.

**Income.** Jobs, earning power, and family size eventually translate into income—the most important index of a population's ability to cope with urban life. Incomes in Connecticut and the Hartford region are high. The SMSA's average of $3,950 per person is exceeded only by San Francisco's $4,100 and Washington, D.C.'s $4,250 among the SMSAs in the atlas. It compares well with Baltimore's $3,350 and Pittsburgh's $3,200. But living costs are high in central Connecticut, and incomes are not distributed equally. Hartford City's average is $3,100, $850 lower than the SMSA average income per person. Incomes below $2,500 per person are largely confined to Hartford's black ghetto, emphasizing once again the limited skills and resources of this minority. Much of the rest of the region has tract-level values from $2,500 to $5,000 per person except for the prosperous areas west and southeast of the city. One tract in Farmington Town with an income per capita of $10,000 anchors the larger area of incomes over $5,000 in West Hartford and Avon Towns. The small low-income tract next to the two areas is a veterans' hospital. Exurban areas of newer, low-density housing south of the city have attracted high-income families also.

The contrasts between the central city and the outlying areas evident in these five socioeconomic variables are sharper in Hartford than in other metropolitan areas, but there are similar situations in many American cities. People with means who have no special commitment to a central city have used their resources to leave it. In doing so, they have created vacancies for more recent arrivals, but at the price of increased concentrations in the central city of low-income people with limited skills.

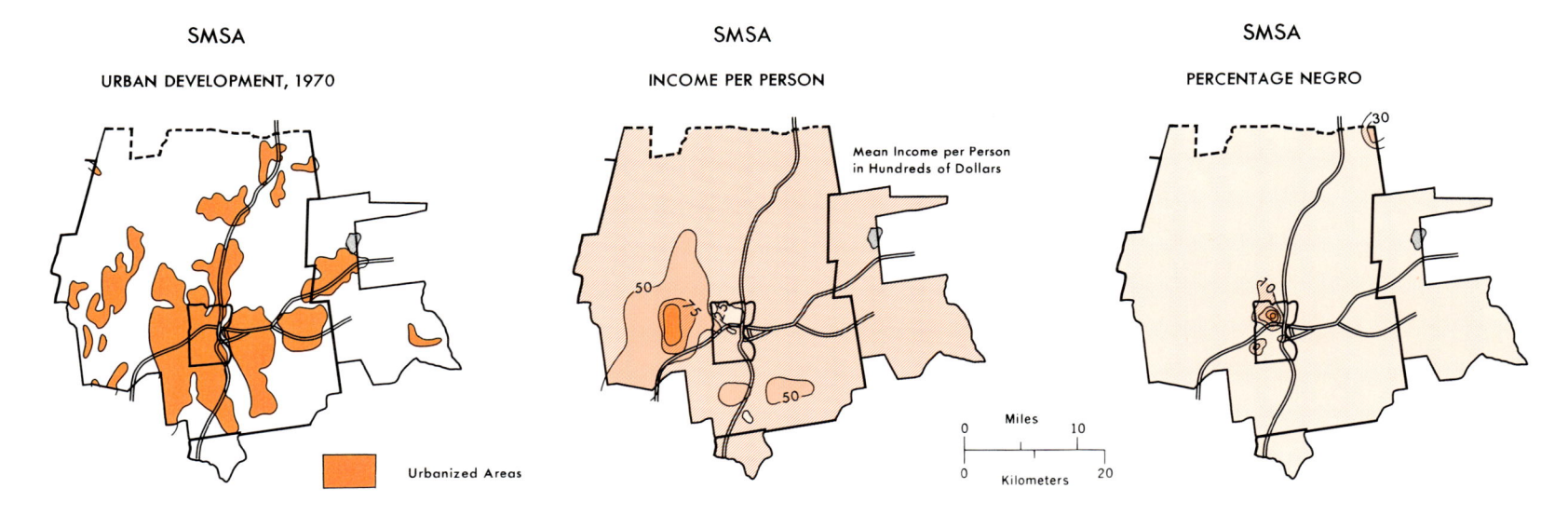

## TOPICS OF SPECIAL INTEREST IN THE HARTFORD REGION

Preserving a quality environment in the Hartford area will require that hard choices be made concerning the nature and location of residential development. The land-use map on page 63 emphasizes how much of the SMSA is affected by low-density urban development. The map of higher-intensity urban development on page 67 is less alarming, but it is far from comforting. The persistent demand for large building lots and the intensity of existing development surrounding Hartford imply continued outward expansion. This in turn implies less open space, less concern for those left behind in the older industrial centers, and greater transportation demand.

**Minority Housing.** Blacks are effectively barred from outward migration by their low incomes and by racial prejudice. Of the SMSA's 50,500 blacks, 44,100 reside in the city of Hartford, and most of the 6,400 blacks living outside the city reside in extensions of black ghettos across the municipal boundary. (The high percentage tract in the SMSA's northeast corner is a correctional institution with a total population of 300 people.) But minority groups are not the only people trapped in central cities. Other poor people and the elderly are often just as immobile.

Attempts to alleviate the housing problems of central-city minority groups have centered on public facilities rather than on income supplements that might permit outward movement. As of 1973, 5,700 units—about 10 percent of the city's housing stock—had been built by the Hartford Housing Authority and private sponsors. Housing for the nonelderly is located in three areas. Facilities for low- and moderate-income families have been built along the city's east side, in the black ghetto, and on the city's western boundary. Projects have not been built in middle- and upper-middle-income areas, so income segregation persists.

**Housing for the Elderly.** The elderly are trapped in the central city by low incomes and limited mobility. Local responses to their housing needs have also centered on public facilities rather than on rent or income supplements. Many housing projects for the elderly are located west of the CBD. Most residents in housing for the elderly are neither black nor Puerto Rican, but those two minorities dominate housing for the nonelderly because facilities for the nonelderly were built in their neighborhoods. Whether the poor are elderly or nonelderly, minority or majority, they will remain trapped in central cities until assistance programs centering on facilities are revised in favor of rent and construction grants that provide low-income people with some of the residential options only money can buy.

**Public Transportation.** Whether in the final analysis the Hartford region can afford much more dispersion of both the poor and the affluent remains to be seen. Providing transit in a dispersed, low-density, multicentered region is a difficult and expensive undertaking. Scattered centers and low densities almost preclude any technology but bus transportation; however, buses serve only a small portion of the SMSA and patronage is dwindling. Proposed improvements stress express buses and some rail service; both would benefit the affluent white-collar worker more than the middle- or lower-income blue-collar worker whose jobs are often more dispersed than white-collar occupations. Such conditions, coupled with the lack of coordination among the 30 bus companies that serve central Connecticut, suggest that many suburbanites and exurbanites—regardless of income—are as irrevocably wed to their increasingly expensive automobiles as Hartford's poor are to their central-city locations.

---

The region's major employers apparently have no intention of writing off the central city as thousands of individuals have done by exercising their suburban and exurban housing options. The region's 30 largest corporations formed the Greater Hartford Process, Incorporated in 1969 to guide change and development in Hartford and the region. "The Process," as it is locally known, is trying to create a "New Hartford" at the same time that it promotes a new community at Coventry, 20 minutes east of the city. The Process has proposed what is probably the largest redevelopment ever planned in an American city. It embraces half the city's area, 40 percent of its population, and 75 percent of its office space. The overall Process goal is to retain Hartford's traditional position as the political, cultural, and economic hub of the central-Connecticut region. Time will tell whether the Process can make good its ambitious plans, but the proposal itself, considering the power of the people and the firms behind it, is an important vote of confidence in the central city's future.

## B. Nineteenth-Century Ports

Baltimore
New Orleans
San Francisco-Oakland

# CHAPTER 10

# Baltimore

*A Baltimorean is not merely John Doe, an isolated individual of* Homo sapiens, *exactly like every other John Doe. He is John Doe of a certain place – of Baltimore.*

H. L. MENCKEN, "On Living in Baltimore," *Prejudices*, 1926

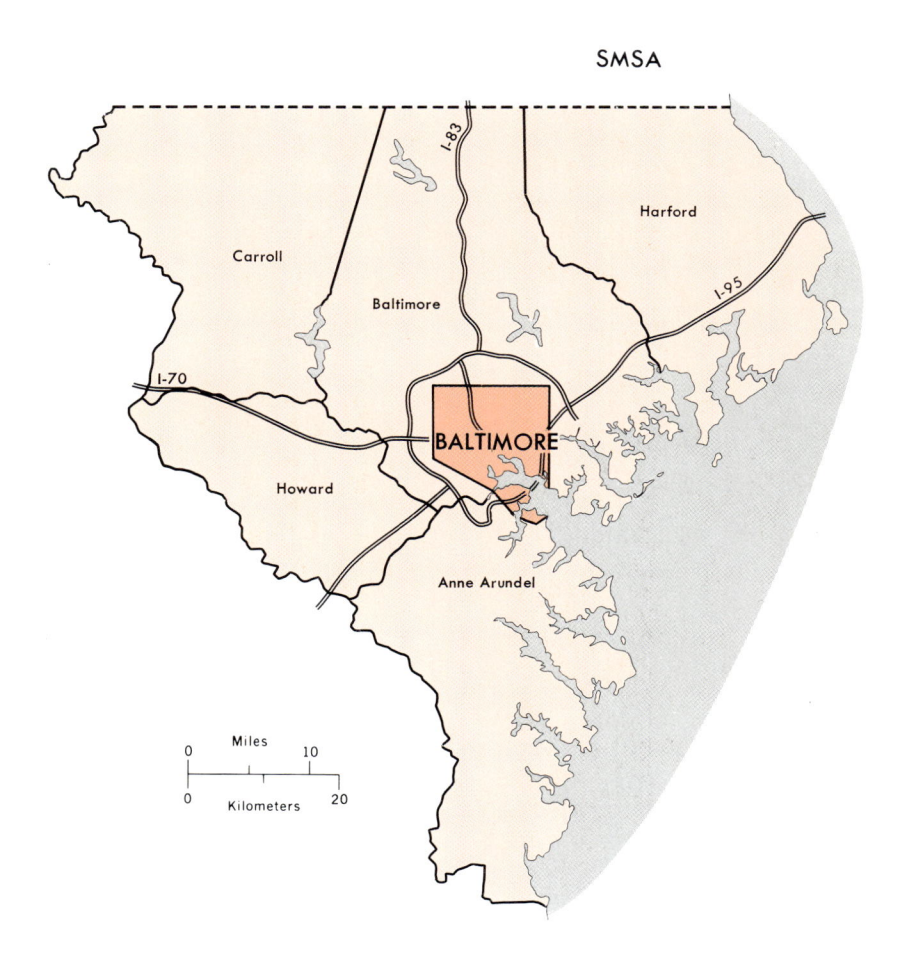

The Baltimore Standard Metropolitan Statistical Area (SMSA) is a community of 2,070,000 people. It is the 11th most populous SMSA in the nation. No county outside the SMSA sends 5 percent of its labor force into the central employment core daily and thus the SMSA and the Daily Urban System (DUS) are coincident. The DUS is the 15th most populous in the nation. Baltimore, which is politically distinct from Baltimore County, has 906,000 residents, or 44 percent of the metropolitan total. Baltimore (620,000), Anne Arundel (298,000), and Harford (115,000) are the most populous counties. Carroll and Howard have 69,000 and 62,000, respectively. Part of Anne Arundel County is more closely linked to Washington, D.C. than it is to Baltimore. Downtown Washington lies about 40 miles southeast of Baltimore's Central Business District (CBD)

*Note:* All data are from the 1970 Censuses of Population and Housing unless otherwise indicated. Therefore the present tense refers to 1970 data except for income data which are from 1969. Cartographic conventions are explained in Chapter 1.

Despite its situation near the head of Chesapeake Bay and its access to a fertile hinterland, Baltimore was never much of a colonial town. It began to prosper during the Revolution and the Napoleonic wars. In 1790 it was the nation's 4th largest city, with 14,000 people (p. 10). In 1828 the city leaders built the nation's first railroad—the Baltimore and Ohio—to compete with the canals that gave its seacoast rivals access to the nation's interior. The city loomed large in national affairs in the mid-years of the 19th century; but growth began to slow during the Civil War.

Baltimore is located on the estuary of the Patapsco River, where numerous stream and creek mouths provide many miles of shoreline for docks, shipyards, steel mills, and grain elevators. The land rises steadily away from the harbor, reaching elevations over 400 feet (120 meters) within 5 miles (8 kilometers) of tidewater. The valleys of Gwynns Falls (northwest) and Jones Falls (north-northwest) become gorges as the land rises. Gwynns Falls valley is largely parkland.

## Nineteenth-Century Ports: Baltimore

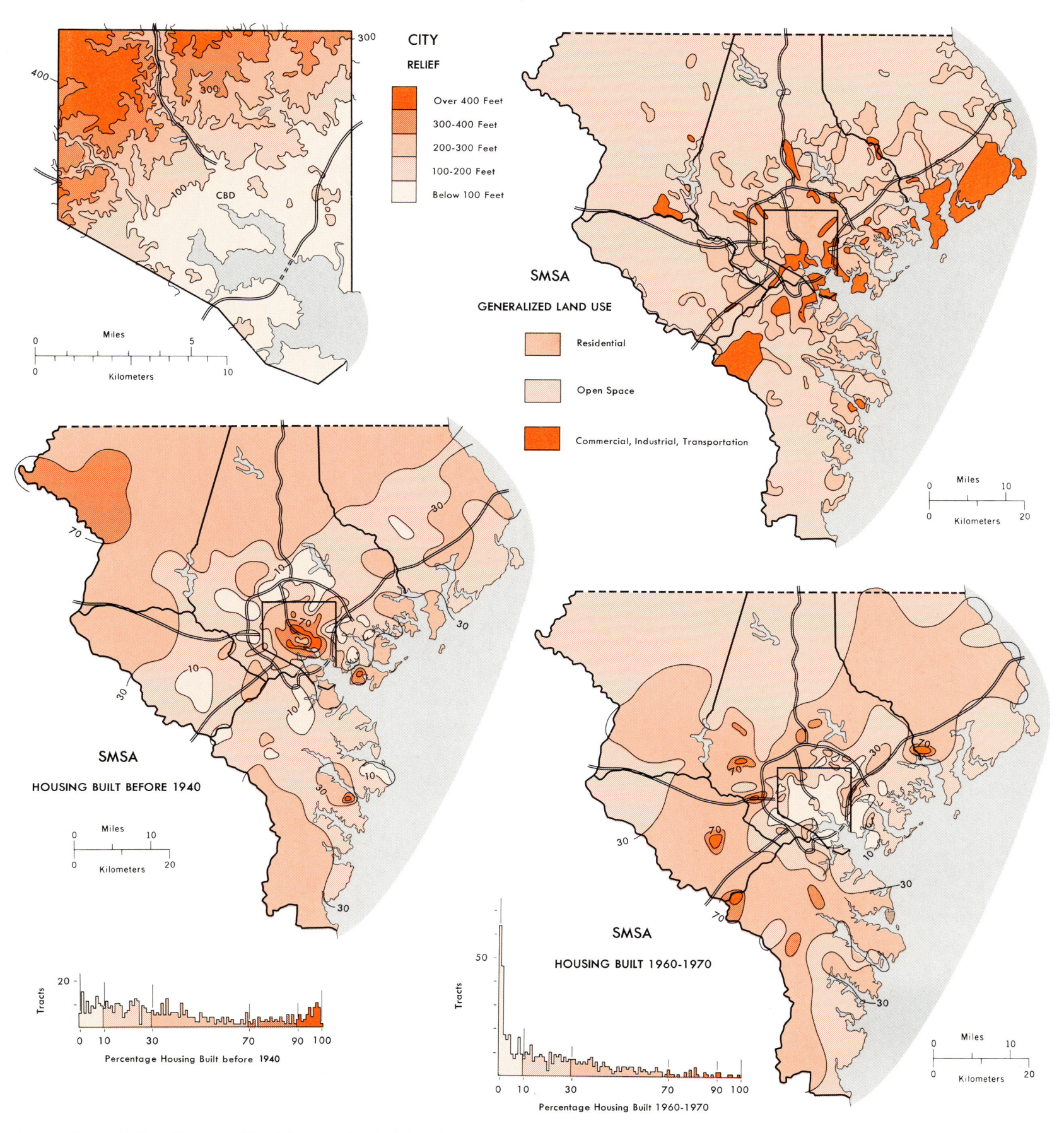

Some of Jones Falls valley is parkland, but small industrial plants and Interstate 83 are also located in the gorge. Most land adjacent to tidewater is given over to shipping and industrial activities. Suburban expansion has traditionally been to the north and northwest, with the most recent push to the northeast and southeast into the Baltimore-Washington corridor.

### HOUSING

**Housing Age.** The SMSA has a young housing stock for an old, eastern city; 40 percent of its units were built before 1940, 37 percent from 1940 to 1959, and 23 percent since 1960. Old housing predominates in central Baltimore where many structures predate 1900. The area below 70 percent at the city's center is a large urban-renewal project. The cluster of older housing in Anne Arundel County centers on Annapolis, the state capitol. New housing exceeds 30 percent of all units in much of the SMSA. The high proportion in Howard County is the planned community of Columbia. The areas over 90 percent in Anne Arundel and Harford counties are new housing adjacent to military installations.

Nineteenth-Century Ports: Baltimore

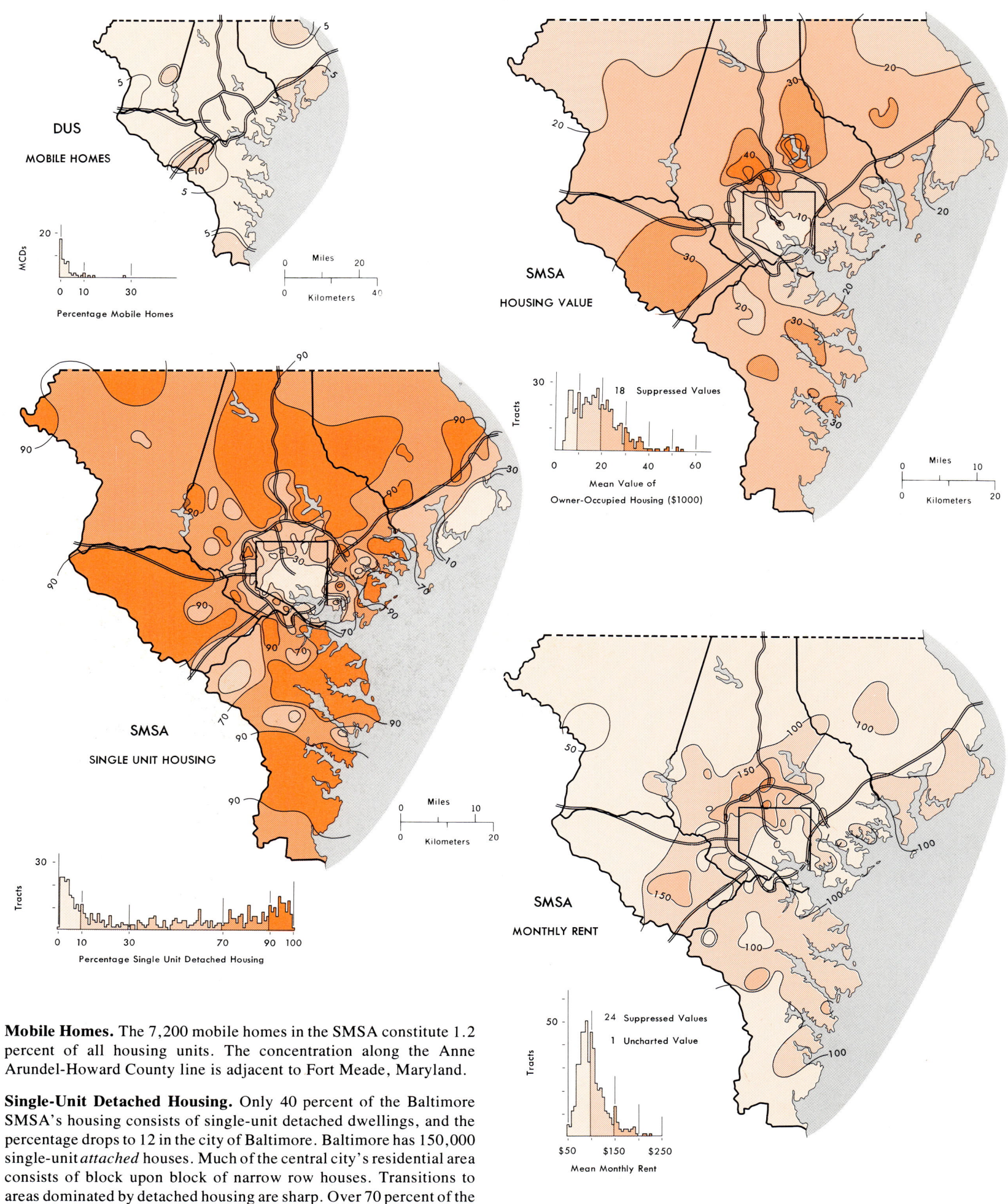

DUS
MOBILE HOMES

SMSA
HOUSING VALUE

SMSA
SINGLE UNIT HOUSING

SMSA
MONTHLY RENT

**Mobile Homes.** The 7,200 mobile homes in the SMSA constitute 1.2 percent of all housing units. The concentration along the Anne Arundel-Howard County line is adjacent to Fort Meade, Maryland.

**Single-Unit Detached Housing.** Only 40 percent of the Baltimore SMSA's housing consists of single-unit detached dwellings, and the percentage drops to 12 in the city of Baltimore. Baltimore has 150,000 single-unit *attached* houses. Much of the central city's residential area consists of block upon block of narrow row houses. Transitions to areas dominated by detached housing are sharp. Over 70 percent of the units are detached single-family residences throughout most of the rest of the region.

**Housing Value and Rent.** The mean value for owner-occupied housing in the SMSA is $18,000, and the mean monthly cost of rental

# Nineteenth-Century Ports: Baltimore

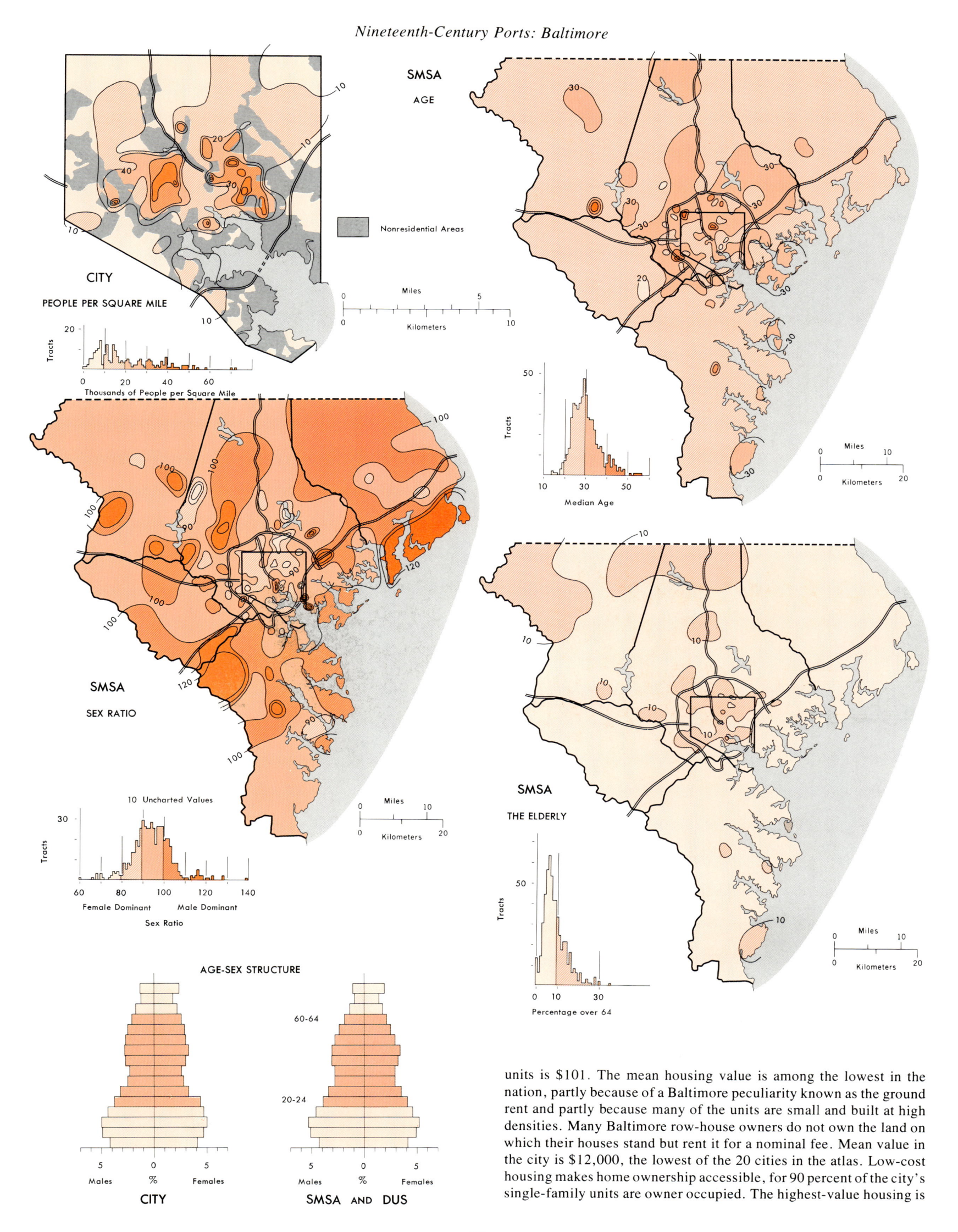

## CITY
### PEOPLE PER SQUARE MILE

## SMSA
### AGE

## SMSA
### SEX RATIO

## SMSA
### THE ELDERLY

### AGE-SEX STRUCTURE
CITY    SMSA AND DUS

units is $101. The mean housing value is among the lowest in the nation, partly because of a Baltimore peculiarity known as the ground rent and partly because many of the units are small and built at high densities. Many Baltimore row-house owners do not own the land on which their houses stand but rent it for a nominal fee. Mean value in the city is $12,000, the lowest of the 20 cities in the atlas. Low-cost housing makes home ownership accessible, for 90 percent of the city's single-family units are owner occupied. The highest-value housing is located north of the city, and some luxury housing is located in the city east of Jones Falls. Monthly rentals are below $100 in much of the city and in outlying areas, except north of the city where some tracts have mean rentals exceeding $200. Rentals drop to $50 at Fort Meade and below $50 in a single low-income tract in Carroll County. (See pp. 78, 295, and 303 for maps relating value and rent to income.)

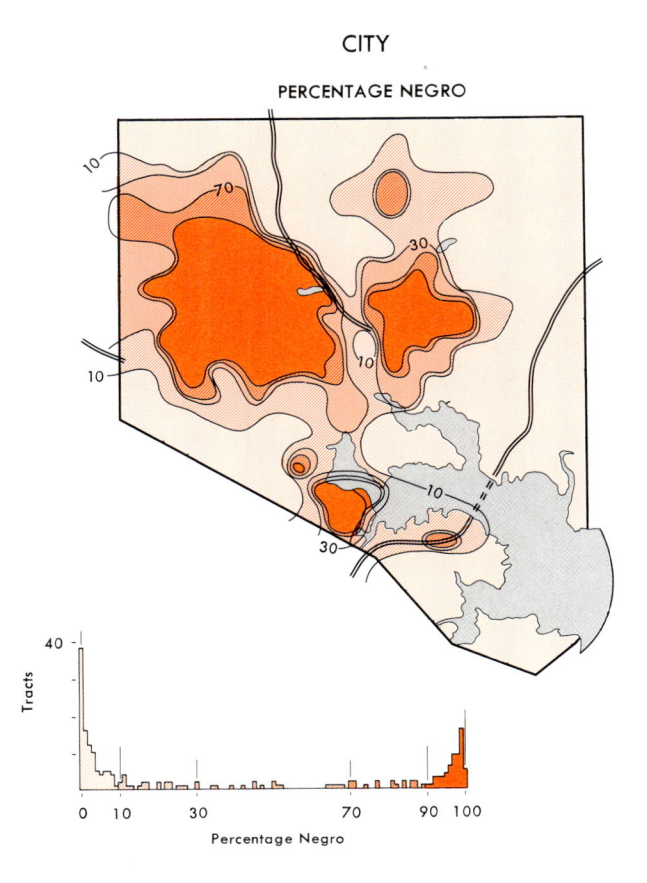

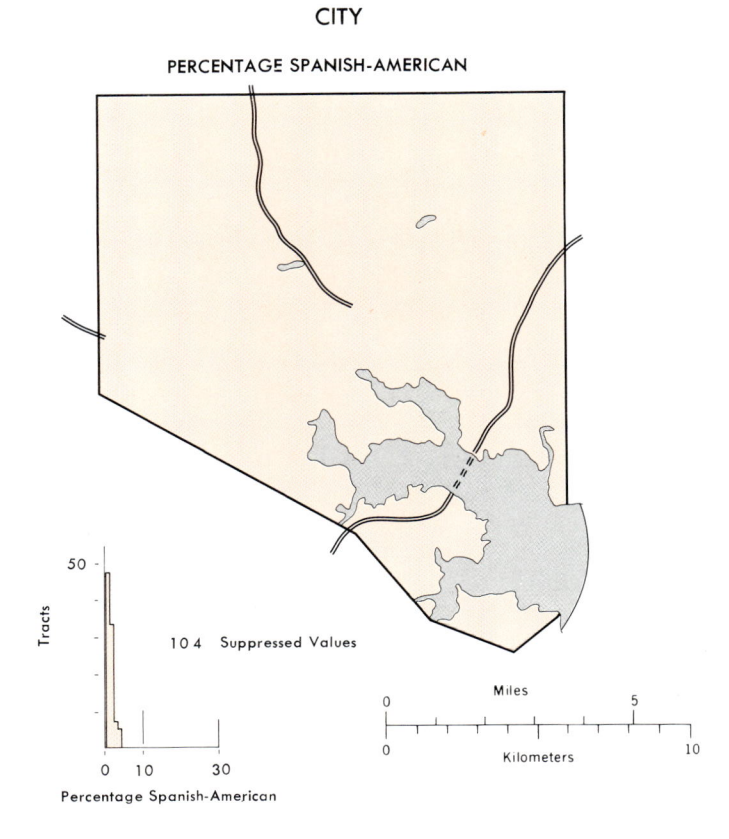

## THE PEOPLE

**Population Density.** Baltimore City has an overall population density of 11,600 people per square mile (4,500 per square kilometer). Neighborhood densities are higher than the city's overall mean suggests because so much of the city's land area is devoted to industrial, educational, and open space. Densities over 40,000 (15,500 people per square kilometer) are common, and two tracts have densities over 70,000 (27,000 per square kilometer). The transitions between neighborhoods built before World War II and the lower-density housing constructed after the war are sharp, and they are often accompanied by racial, income, and occupational transitions. (See p. 311 for an SMSA map of population density.)

**Age and the Elderly.** The SMSA's median age of 28 years and its proportion of people over 64 (8 percent) are typical values for a metropolitan area. Similarly, the respective central-city values of 29 years and 11 percent over 64 are congruent with the usual concentration of old people in central cities.

Median ages for census tracts range from 14 years in some central-city tracts to over 50 in tracts dominated by institutionalized populations. Median ages below 20 occur in the eastern black ghetto within Baltimore and near Fort Meade. Tract medians above 30 years are prevalent in northern Baltimore City and in the suburbs to the west, north, and northeast, except where clusters of new housing attractive to young families have been built. The numerous spots of median ages below 30 years along the circumferential highway are examples.

Tract percentages of people over 64 range from zero to over 30. Some of the rural tracts on the SMSA's periphery exceed 10 percent, but the majority of the region's elderly live in and near the central city; Baltimore has 44 percent of the total population over 64. The area where the elderly exceed 10 percent forms a distorted I that excludes heavily black areas of the central city. The tract near the end of the expressway where the elderly exceed 30 percent contains a home for the aged, and the tract next to the harbor is a skid row area.

**Sex Ratio.** There are 1.05 females for each male in the SMSA, resulting in a sex ratio (males divided by females times 100) of 95. Central cities are usually more female-dominant than are entire metropolitan regions, and this is true in Baltimore; the city sex ratio is 90. Females outnumber males in every age cohort older than 15 years, an imbalance which increases with age because of greater female longevity. Much of northern Baltimore is female-dominant, with sex ratios below 90 extending into some of the near northern suburbs. Scattered tracts within the area have ratios below 80, or 5 females for every 4 males. Sex ratios below 70, like those above 120, usually occur only in institutionalized populations. The more rural areas of the SMSA are male-dominant, but the map is misleading because such areas are disproportionately large on the map compared with the number of tracts and people represented. Comparison with the histogram is essential. Sex ratios exceed 150 near Fort Meade and the Aberdeen Proving Ground.

**Negroes.** Most census tracts are either nearly all black or nearly all white. In the 18th century Baltimore was segregated at the household scale, with servants' quarters over the backyard kitchens. By the 19th century it was streets and alleys of the city block. Starting from three small neighborhoods in the periphery of the CBD, the black ghetto had coalesced into a ring around the downtown by World War II. The south Baltimore ghetto has now been partially demolished by urban renewal, but three distinct nodes remain. Mixed tracts are few and are areas shifting rapidly from white to black rather than stable integrated neighborhoods. There are 490,000 blacks in the SMSA. As the SMSA map indicates (p. 383), most live in Baltimore. The city has 44 percent of the total population but 86 percent (420,000) of the SMSA's black population; it is 46 percent black.

**Spanish-Americans.** Spanish-speaking people are scattered throughout the city. No tract has none, although 104 tracts are suppressed indicating that only a few Spanish-Americans reside within them. Baltimore's remaining tracts have 1 to 4 percent

Spanish-speakers. There are 8,400 Spanish-speaking people in the city. Most central-city Hispanics either are from Latin America or are Mexican-Americans, for only 10 percent are Puerto Rican and only 5 percent are Cuban. (See p. 39 for the SMSA map.)

## SOCIOECONOMIC CHARACTERISTICS

**Household Size.** There are 3.2 people in the average SMSA household and 3.1 in the average central-city household. Tract values range from just over 1 at the city's center to 4.2 in suburban areas. The extreme values are usually caused by populations living in group quarters. The 4.7 value is the tract in Baltimore containing the city jail and a state prison; one of the other high values is the Naval Academy at Annapolis. Smaller households correlate closely with older populations that tend to be composed of smaller families, the children having married and established their own households. The tracts with small households along the city's eastern boundary are old suburban areas. The five small areas within Baltimore where average household sizes exceed 4 people are in predominantly black areas. Blacks have higher birthrates and larger households than whites. The mean household size for blacks in Baltimore is 3.6 as opposed to 3.2 for the total population. Outside the central city, large households are characteristic of new housing developments that attract young families.

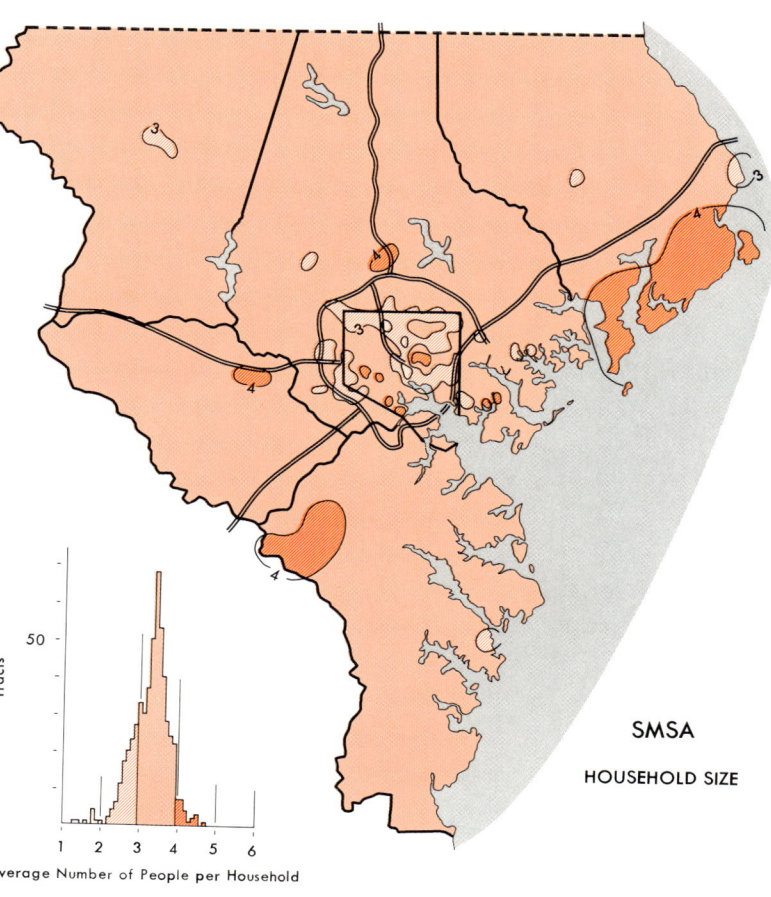

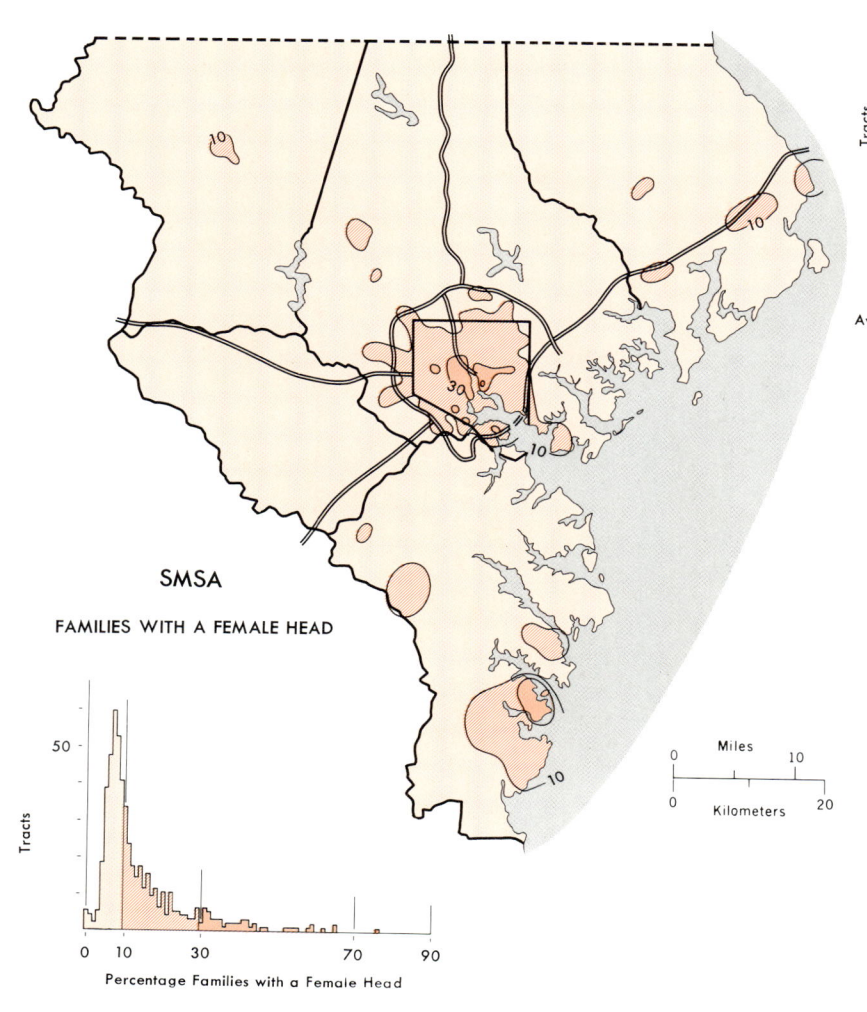

**Female Headship.** The Census Bureau does not define heads of families in terms of the breadwinner's sex; a family headed by a female is one in which no male spouse is present. In the SMSA, 14 percent of all families are headed by females. The proportion rises from 22 percent in Baltimore. Tract values range from zero to 76 percent, with most tracts in the 5 to 35 percent category. The extreme value occurs in a tract that is 99 percent black, where a housing project has an unusual number of families headed by females. Of the tract's 1,100 families, 863 are headed by females, and 567 of that 863 (66 percent) have incomes below the poverty level (see pp. 425, 433, and 441). Dominantly black areas tend to have values well over 10 percent. Families headed by females exceed 10 percent of all families throughout the central city and along the early axes of suburban expansion.

**Occupations.** Of the SMSA labor force, 15 percent works in blue-collar jobs (laborers and operatives) and 21 percent in executive occupations (teachers, engineers, professionals, managers, proprietors, and administrators). The remaining 64 percent is divided between service workers (36 percent) and clerical employees (28 percent). The city has more blue-collar (18 percent) and service (40 percent) workers and comparatively fewer executives (16 percent).

A few tracts have blue-collar percentages over 30; they are either central-city working-class areas or the largely agrarian region in northwestern Carroll County. Some of the inner-city blue-collar areas are black neighborhoods, but the easternmost is a Polish-East European area. Many of its residents work at blue-collar jobs in nearby industrial and shipping facilities. Proportions drop below 10 percent in the area of recent suburban expansion west and north of the city (p. 71) and in the corridor through Anne Arundel County that fans out eastward from Washington.

Executives are rare in inner-city locations and more prevalent in outer suburban areas. Individual tract values range between zero and 70 percent. The highest proportion (not mapped) occurs in a small (266 workers) tract in north-central Baltimore populated by a well-educated labor force. Workers in executive occupations exceed 30 percent of the labor force in central Baltimore and east-central Hartford counties. Executives and other workers there focus on the

## Nineteenth-Century Ports: Baltimore

Baltimore employment market. Values exceed 30 percent in much of Howard and parts of Anne Arundel counties, but some of the executives in these areas are oriented to Washington, D.C. jobs. A third of the labor force in the high-proportion area in northwestern Anne Arundel County, for example, works in the Washington area. Anne Arundel's eastern high-value areas clearly focus on Baltimore, but the two westernmost areas are partially tied to Washington. In Howard County, 6,800 people work in Baltimore City and County, and 5,100 work outside the SMSA. The split is indicative of the progressing coalescence of the two metropolitan areas.

**Income.** The Baltimore SMSA has a mean income per person of $3,350 per year. The city mean income is considerably lower at $2,900. Both are low relative to northern cities. Incomes per person range from $500 in some central-city tracts to a peak of $12,500 per person in a sparsely populated but wealthy tract in north-central Baltimore County. The high value results from a skewed income distribution. Median family income in the tract is $15,500 but the mean family income is $45,000. A sixth of the tract's 300 families have incomes exceeding $50,000 per year. The tract is unusual, but is located in a region of generally higher incomes that extends outward from the northern part of the city.

Most per person incomes in the SMSA range from $2,500 to $5,000; a few tract averages exceed $5,000 in Anne Arundel, Carroll, and Harford counties, but the number of people is small. Incomes are low near Fort Meade in Anne Arundel County, but the largest cluster of low-income people is in Baltimore City, where 50,000 (23 percent) of the 216,000 households have incomes below the poverty level. Most are concentrated in the area within the $2,500 isopleth (see p. 415).

## TOPICS OF SPECIAL INTEREST IN THE BALTIMORE REGION

**Population Change and Sewage Disposal.** The map of population change is produced by dividing the 1970 population figures by 1960 population figures for each census tract. The quotient is less than unity if the tract has lost population during the decade and greater than unity if it has increased. The city lost population (0.96), but the SMSA gained (1.15). Baltimore and Howard counties experienced the most growth, with the population more than tripling in the part of Howard County that is tied to the Washington metropolitan region. The population also tripled north and northwest of Baltimore, and it more than doubled in parts of Anne Arundel County. Areas with increases are usually places where new housing was built during the 1960s (p. 71). Population losses did not occur throughout the city, for the northern and western parts continued to grow. But this growth was more than offset by population losses at the city's center. A few close-in tracts lost as much as half their populations. Population increased in some core-area tracts where replacements were provided for housing units demolished by urban renewal but not enough to counterbalance losses.

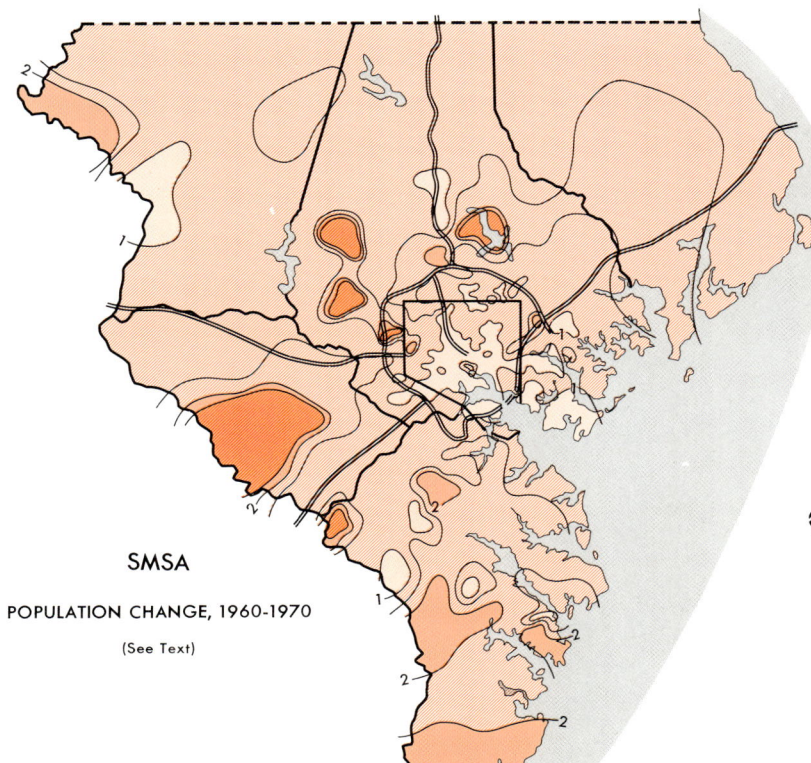

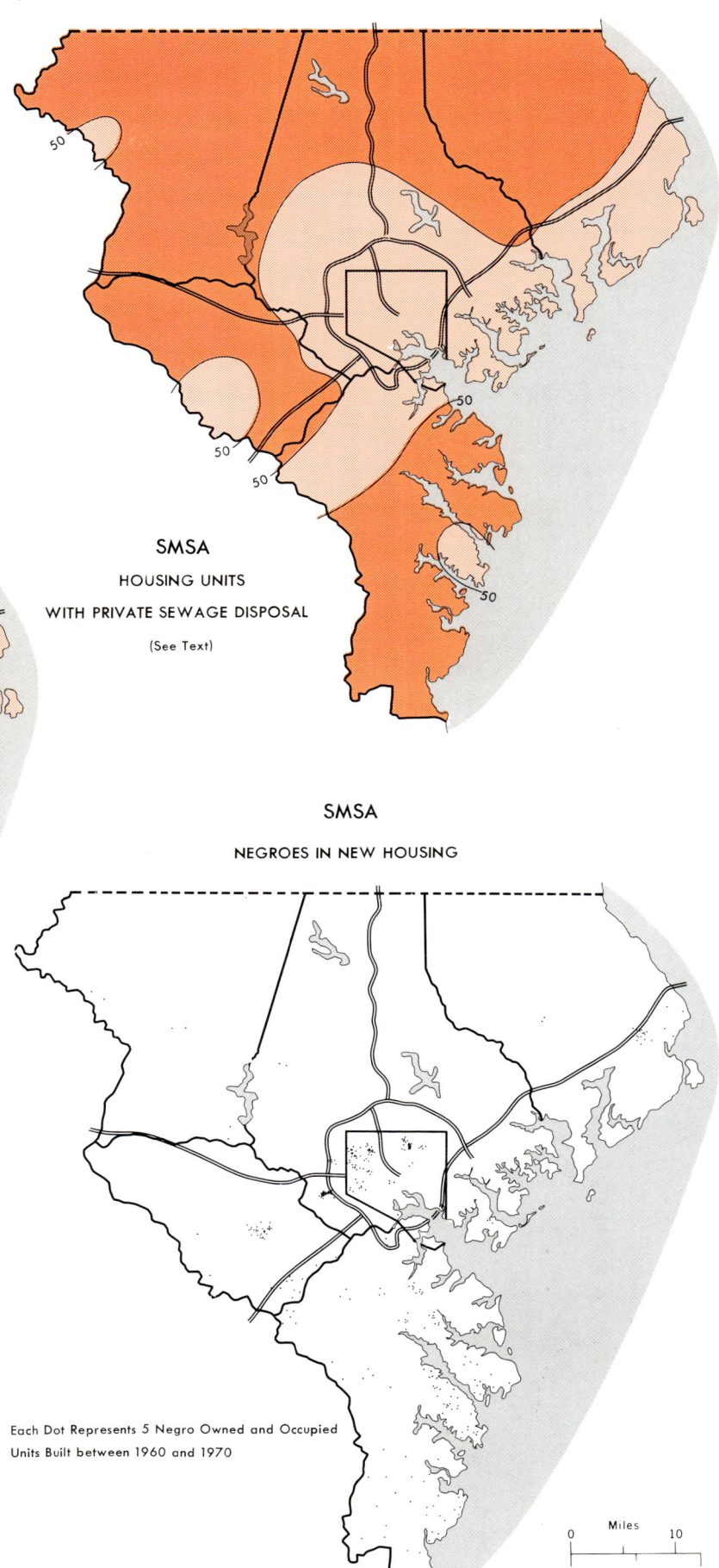

Servicing new developments with sewer and water is desirable but not always possible. When large-scale development occurs in an area without public-sewage collection and treatment facilities, groundwater pollution problems are likely to result, which are especially serious because areas without sewers are often areas without public water (p. 269). New housing often needs the water it is gradually polluting. Sharp population increases in areas where more than half the housing units rely on private sewage disposal are cause for concern.

**Negroes in New Housing.** Baltimore's blacks shared meagerly in suburban and exurban growth. During the 1960s, 150,000 new housing units were built in the SMSA. Blacks own and occupy only 2,900 of them, of which 500 are located within Baltimore. The remaining 2,350 are near military facilities at Fort Meade and Aberdeen, clustered in the new town of Columbia in Howard County and in the Liberty Road corridor west of Baltimore near the Social Security employment center. Only Anne Arundel County has a scattering of blacks in new houses that suggests participation in the general housing market. Elsewhere in the suburbs, as in Baltimore, blacks obtained new housing only on the leading edge of ghetto expansion or under unusual circumstances such as a public housing project.

**Automobile Ownership.** As public transportation deteriorates, people without automobiles become progressively more isolated from housing, recreational, and social opportunities. Households without automobiles exceed 10 percent of all units in a few outlying areas, but the most immobile populations are those living in central-city, predominantly black areas. Such households exceed 70 percent in central Baltimore and 30 percent throughout most of the city. High densities of business establishments, helping facilities, and social contacts in central-city areas moderate but do not eliminate the problem. As jobs and good housing become more scarce in the central city, people lacking the automobile mobility prerequisite to following them to the suburbs will be increasingly disadvantaged.

**Rent Stress.** (Histogram on p. 295.) Households that spend more than 25 percent of their monthly incomes for rent often have problems meeting other expenses. Within the SMSA, 37 percent of the renting households fall into this category. Large areas in the suburbs have values over 30 percent, but the smaller tracts and higher population densities of the central city where similar values prevail mean that the problem is more concentrated in the central city than the map suggests. In fact, 72 percent of the SMSA's households that allocate more than a fourth of their income for rent live in Baltimore. Aside from one low-rental housing project and the prosperous area along the northern city line, most areas of the city have proportions over 30 percent.

---

Baltimore's problems are standard for an eastern city; new jobs, new growth, and general prosperity are favoring the suburbs, leaving the central city as the local repository of the old, the poor, and the black. Baltimore's city fathers are much concerned about the situation, and public and private leaders are working to improve the city's image at the same time they shore up its financial foundations. However, these plans and objectives are often perceived to be inimical to neighborhood needs and desires. An anonymous resident speaking out at an expressway hearing summarized the conflict nicely:

> I say first the city is a place to live in. They
> say first the city is a place to make money in.
> Whether I am right or they are right makes the
> big difference.

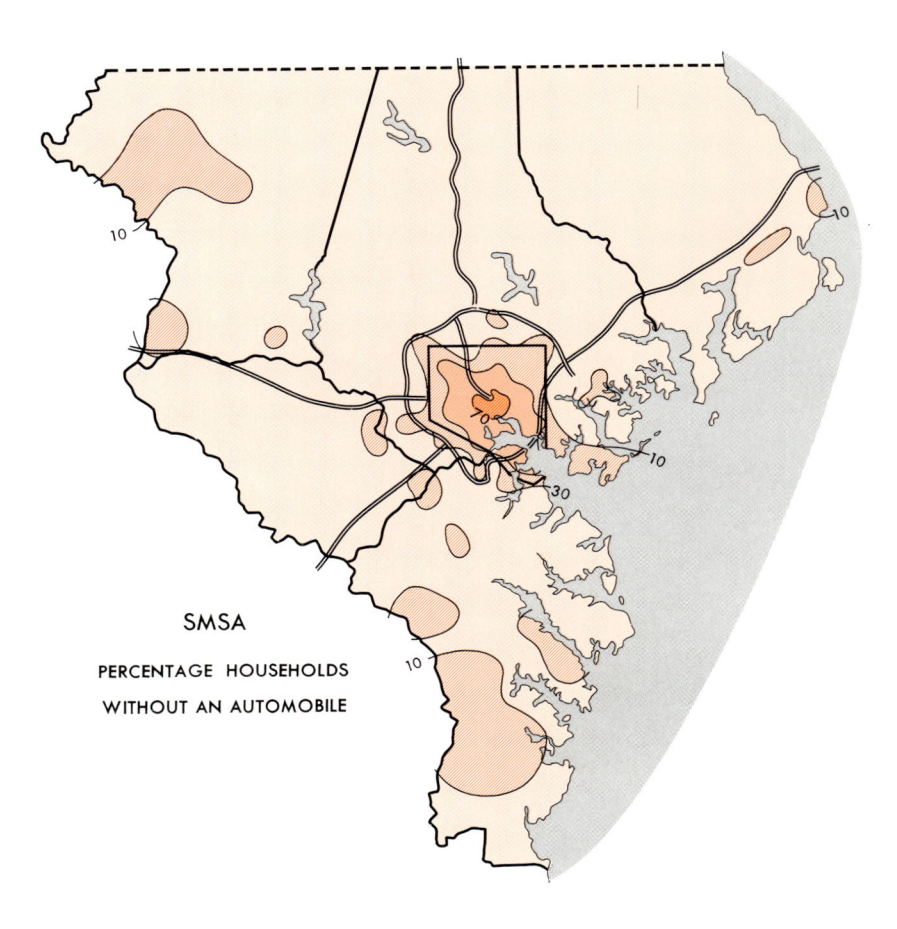

SMSA

PERCENTAGE HOUSEHOLDS WITHOUT AN AUTOMOBILE

SMSA

PERCENTAGE HOUSING UNITS FOR WHICH RENT EXCEEDS ONE-FOURTH INCOME

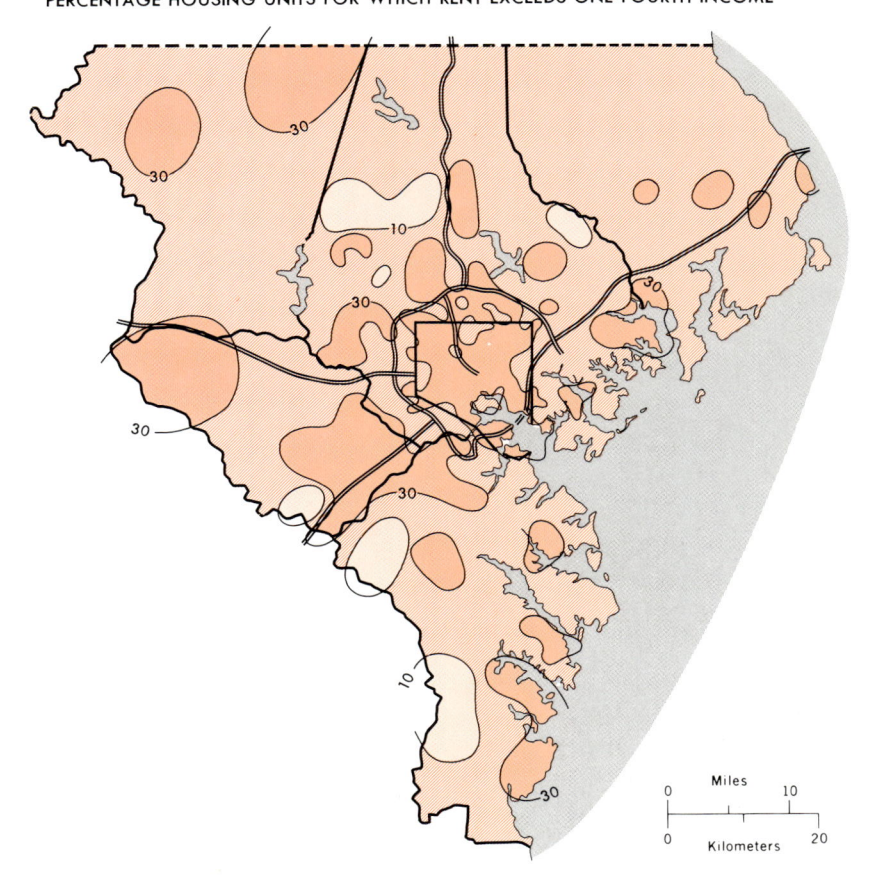

# CHAPTER 11

# New Orleans

*I'm a politician, but I'm also a New Orleanian, and that means I'm different.*

MOON LANDRIEU, Mayor of New Orleans, 1972

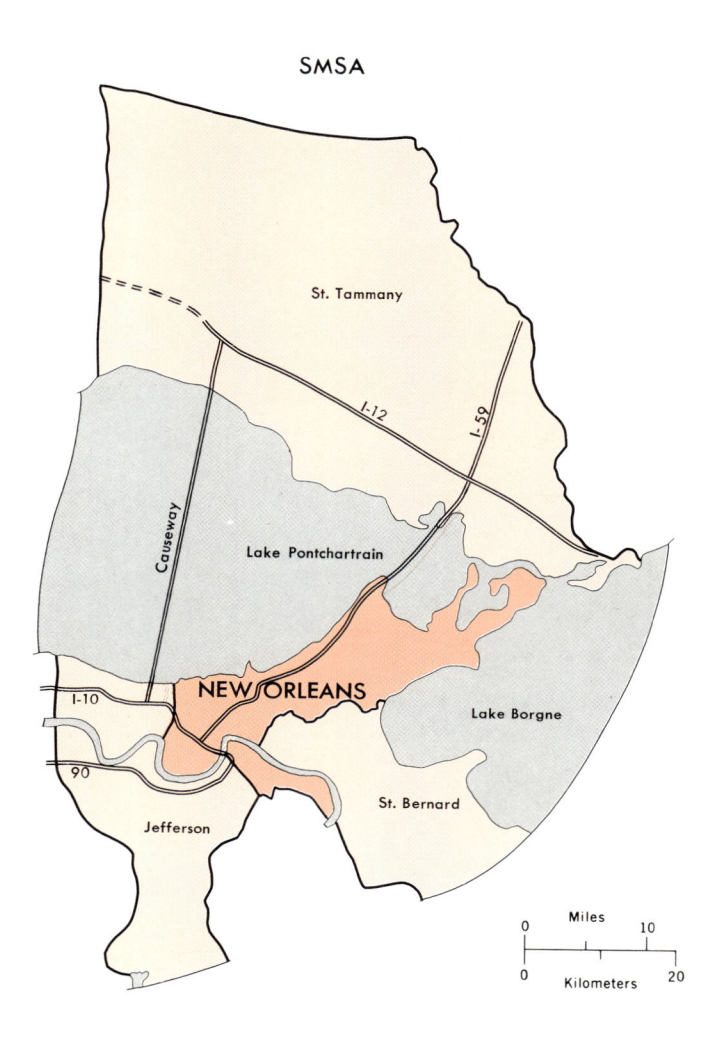

New Orleans is the nation's 31st most populous Standard Metropolitan Statistical Area (SMSA), with a population of 1,046,000 people. Orleans Parish (County), which is coterminous with New Orleans City, is home to 593,000 people (57 percent of the SMSA total). Jefferson Parish is next most populous with 338,000 people (32 percent), and St. Bernard and St. Tammany have 51,000 (5 percent) and 64,000 (6 percent) respectively. The commuting region defined by counties with at least 5 percent of their labor forces working in Orleans County extends to the northeast, west, and south (p. 81). This Daily Urban System (DUS) contains 1,170,000 people, which makes it the 20th most populous DUS in the nation.

New Orleans commands the mouth of the Mississippi-Ohio-Missouri River network. It was already a large city at the time it first appeared in American Census statistics; in 1810 it had 17,000 inhabitants and was the nation's 5th largest city (p. 10). Its dominion over the nation's interior river commerce enabled it to remain 5th until late in the 19th century, when rail transportation rendered riverboats obsolete and relegated towns that depended on them to stagnation. Since 1880 New Orleans has steadily dropped behind more recent, rail-oriented urban centers.

The city is located on a neck of land between the Mississippi and Lake Pontchartrain, where it was easy to portage between the two bodies of water. The only parts of New Orleans that are more than 15 feet (5 meters) above sea level are the levees. Areas of the city are below sea level, and coping with floods and drainage is a way of life. Orleans Parish extends well to the east of the region included on our maps. The omitted areas, like the portions of Jefferson and St.

*Note:* All data are from the 1970 Censuses of Population and Housing unless otherwise indicated. Therefore the present tense refers to 1970 data except for income data which are from 1969. Cartographic conventions are explained in Chapter 1.

Nineteenth-Century Ports: New Orleans

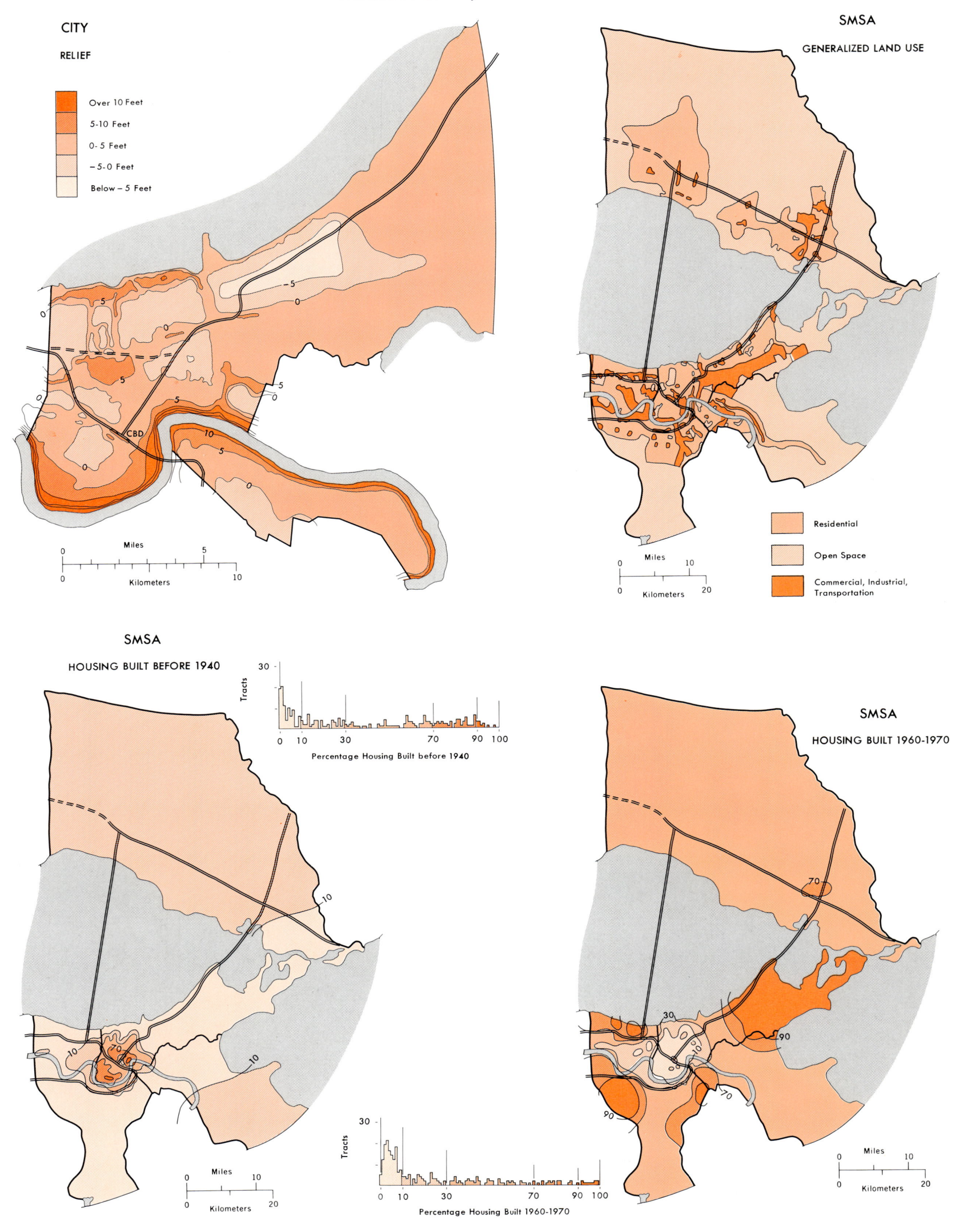

*Nineteenth-Century Ports: New Orleans*

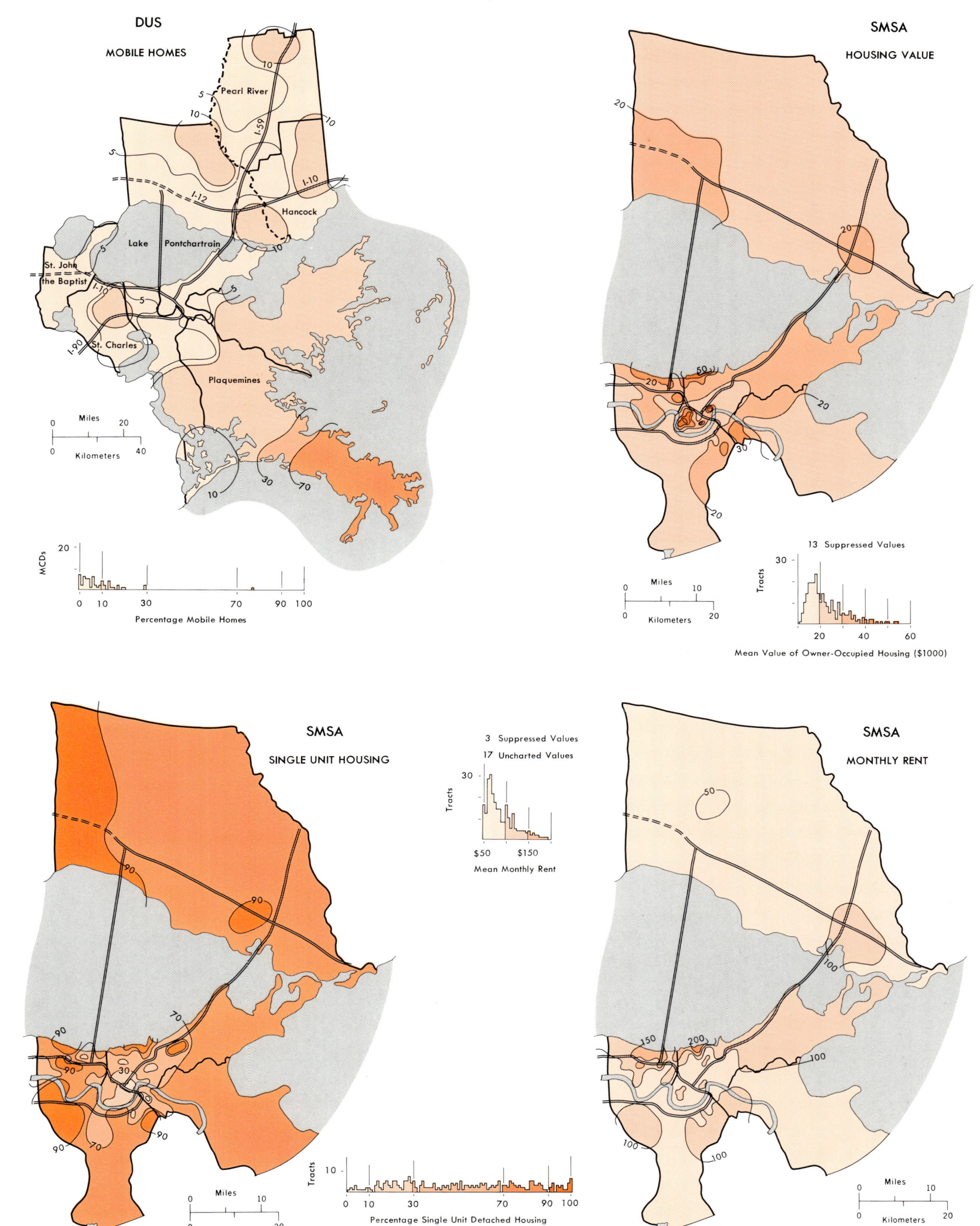

DUS
MOBILE HOMES

SMSA
HOUSING VALUE

Percentage Mobile Homes

Mean Value of Owner-Occupied Housing ($1000)

13 Suppressed Values

SMSA
SINGLE UNIT HOUSING

3 Suppressed Values
17 Uncharted Values

Mean Monthly Rent

SMSA
MONTHLY RENT

Percentage Single Unit Detached Housing

81

## Nineteenth-Century Ports: New Orleans

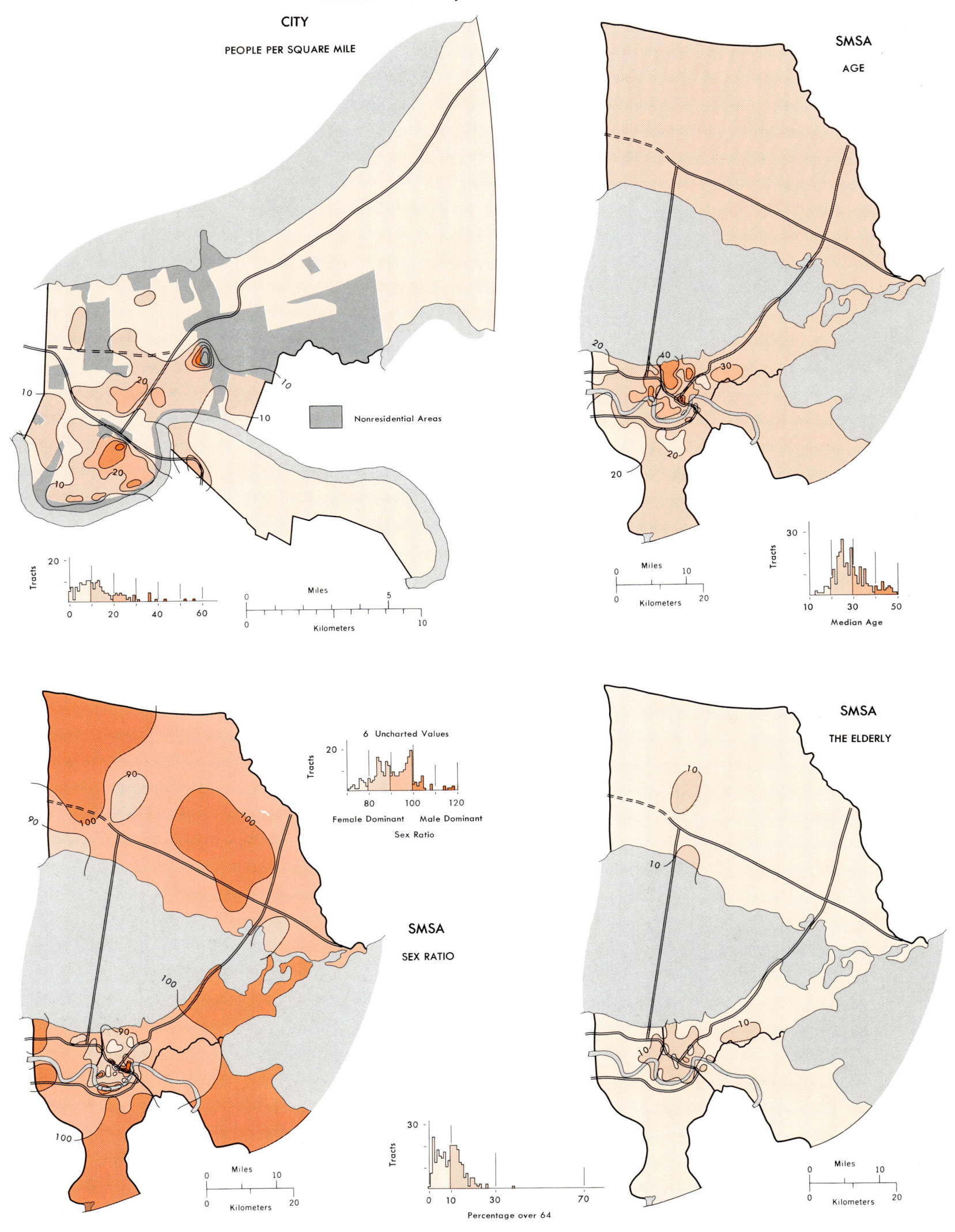

### CITY
PEOPLE PER SQUARE MILE

### SMSA
AGE

### SMSA
SEX RATIO

### SMSA
THE ELDERLY

## Nineteenth-Century Ports: New Orleans

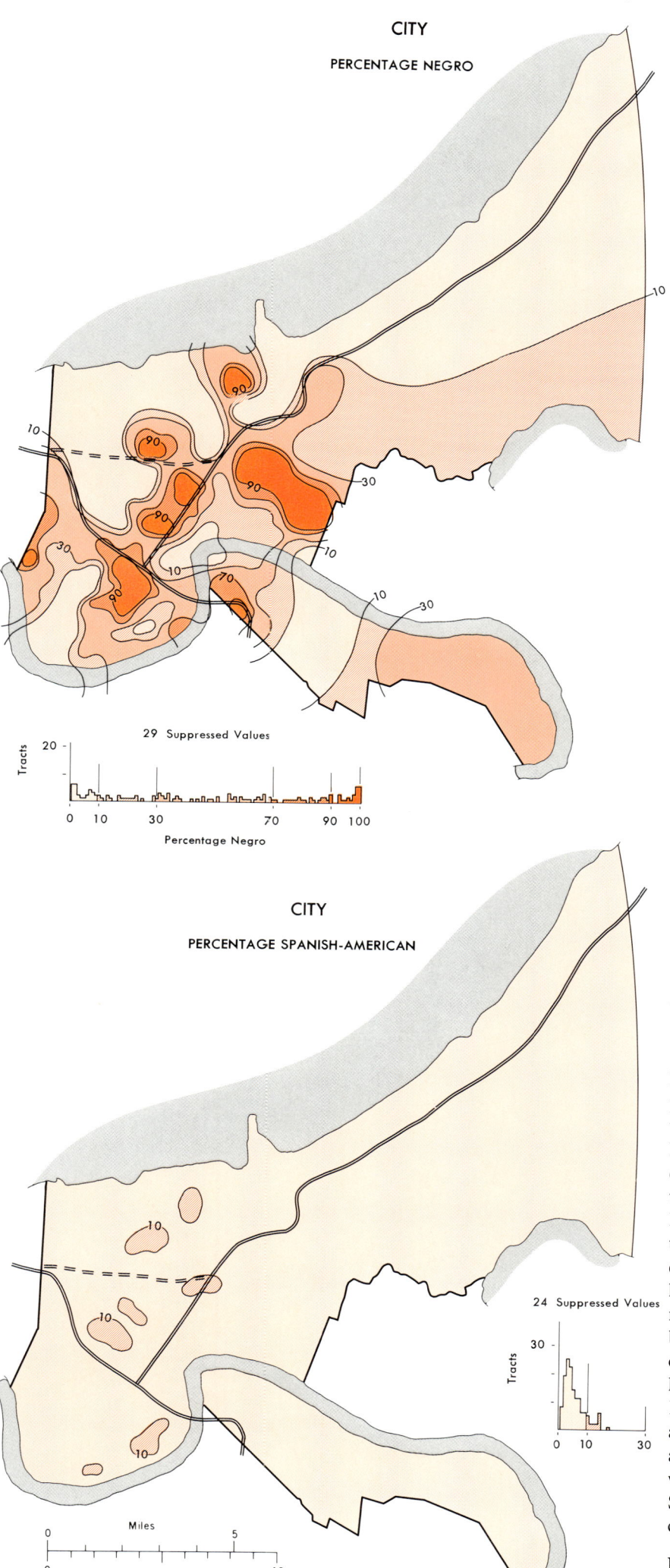

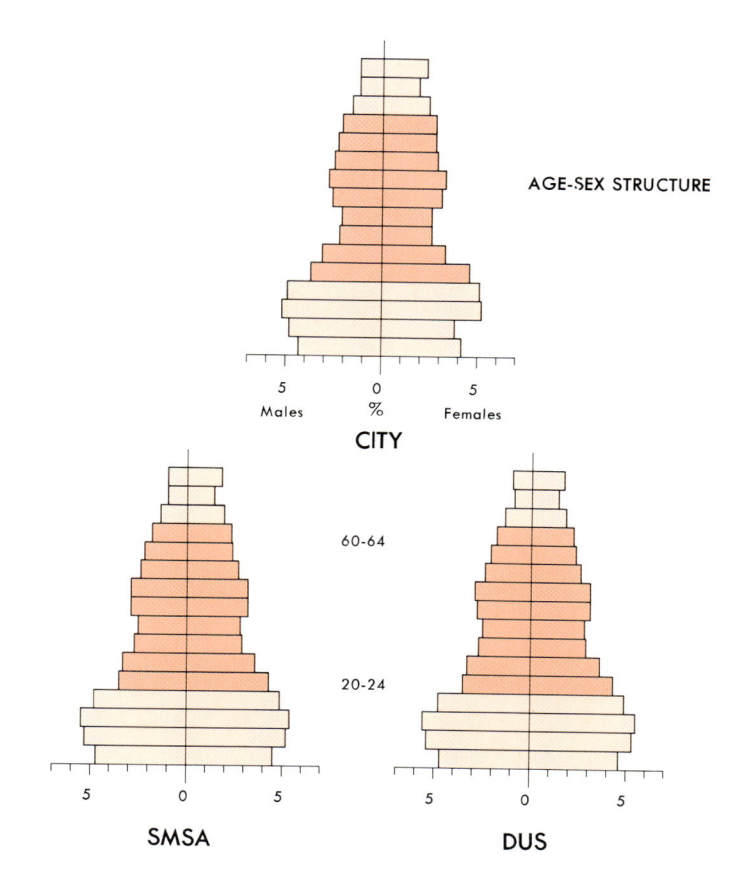

**CITY** — PERCENTAGE NEGRO

**CITY** — PERCENTAGE SPANISH-AMERICAN

AGE-SEX STRUCTURE — CITY, SMSA, DUS

Bernard parishes not included on the SMSA maps, are largely uninhabited swamplands at or slightly under sea level.

Such unusual physical conditions and the city's historic function as entrepôt for America's midwestern interior are the major determinants of land use. Land near the Mississippi and along shipping canals is devoted to shipping facilities. Commercial activities are concentrated in the Central Business District (CBD) and along an old commercial strip that parallels Interstate 10. The rest of the SMSA core consists of medium- and low-density residential areas interspersed with an occasional park. Low-density suburban settlement is now spreading rapidly into St. Tammany Parish from the end of the Interstate causeway. Before completion of highways to St. Tammany Parish, the major axis of residential growth had been westward into Jefferson Parish.

### HOUSING

**Housing Age.** The SMSA has an almost bimodal housing stock; 34 percent of all units were built before 1940, and the remaining two-thirds were built since 1940. Much of the post-World War II housing (27 percent) was constructed in the 1960s. The city's compact core is evident on the map of housing built before 1940; 47 percent of the city's housing is pre-World War II. Gradients between high and low percentages of older housing are steep in every direction except the older axis west into Jefferson County. Away from the core, values exceed 10 percent only where wholesale construction of new housing has not yet overwhelmed prewar units. New housing shows almost a reverse pattern because relatively little of the region's housing was built from 1940 through 1959. New construction has proceeded outward from the older core in a wavelike fashion except for the leapfrogging to the area at the intersection of Interstates 10 and 12. New Orleans City still contains undeveloped land, and some of the areas near Lake Pontchartrain are postwar suburbs even though they are in the central city. Fourteen percent of the city's housing units were built from 1960 to March 1970. Just before the recent opening of St. Tammany and eastern Orleans parishes, the major focus of new construction was northern Jefferson Parish.

**Mobile Homes.** There are 9,500 mobile homes in the DUS; they constitute 2.5 percent of the DUS housing stock. Mobile-home

*Nineteenth-Century Ports: New Orleans*

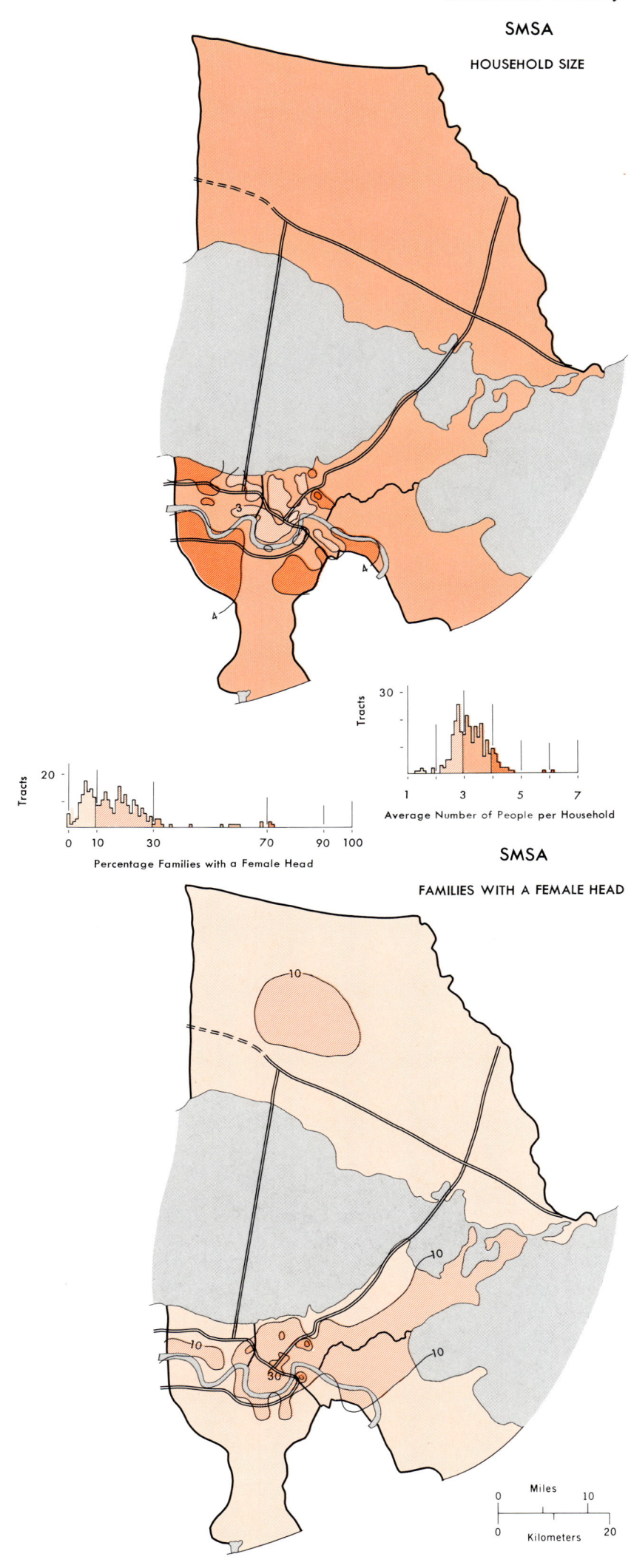

SMSA
HOUSEHOLD SIZE

SMSA
FAMILIES WITH A FEMALE HEAD

proportions over 5 percent penetrate the metropolitan core only in Jefferson Parish.

**Single-Unit Detached Housing.** Single-family houses make up 52 percent of all SMSA housing and 37 percent of the city's housing stock. The city's multiples are mainly duplexes and 3- or 4-unit apartments. Only 17 percent of the city's housing units are in structures containing 5 or more units, for New Orleanians shun apartments. Single-unit detached housing dominates new construction even in the northern part of the city, although some suburban apartment complexes are being built, especially along Interstate 10 in eastern Orleans Parish.

**Housing Value and Rent.** The mean value for owner-occupied housing in the New Orleans SMSA is $23,000. The corresponding figure for the city is $25,000. It is unusual for a central city to have a higher mean housing value than the SMSA. The anomaly is a result of two factors: much of the new construction within Orleans Parish is expensive housing, and housing values outside the Jefferson-Orleans core are low. Neighborhoods of fine older homes in southwestern Orleans Parish still command good prices; one tract has a mean over $50,000. Small pockets of high-value housing east of the CBD and in the historic French Quarter to the CBD's northeast complement the newer high-value housing along the lakefront.

The monthly cost of rental units in New Orleans is low. The SMSA mean is $81 and the city's is $75. The SMSA mean rental is the lowest of the 24 SMSAs included in the atlas. The map of rentals is much the same as the housing-value map. The semiluxury apartment construction in northern Jefferson Parish is more noticeable than the relatively less expensive single-family development in the same tracts. (See pp. 295 and 303 for maps that relate value and rent to income.)

## THE PEOPLE

**Population Density.** The overall population density of New Orleans City is 3,010 people per square mile (1,200 per square kilometer), but because the city contains extensive areas of undeveloped and industrial land, the aggregate statistic seriously understates actual neighborhood densities. Residential areas near the CBD exceed 20,000 people per square mile (7,700 per square kilometer). The highest densities occur in the Desire Housing Project, which occupies two small census tracts at densities over 50,000 people per square mile (19,300 per square kilometer). The suburban character of housing in the city's northern third is evident on the density map; most of the area has densities of fewer than 10,000 per square mile (3,900 per square kilometer). The low-density wedge running from the northwest through the CBD results from railyards and industrial plants near the CBD, and includes the CBD itself. (See the SMSA population-density map on p. 311.)

**Age and the Elderly.** The median age for the SMSA is 26 years. Within New Orleans City, the median is 28 years. Individual tract medians range from 13 to 49 years, with younger tract populations in suburban areas and in heavily black areas, whereas older populations appear in more prosperous northern New Orleans, which is predominantly white. The lowest ages occur in the Desire Housing Project, where 56 percent of the population is less than 15 years of age.

The elderly make up 8 percent of the SMSA population and 11 percent of the city population. In most tracts the proportion of people over 64 is well below 30 percent. The single over-30 tract occurs in a rundown area next to the French Quarter. Tract values in most of the city exceed 10 percent. In many cities, percentages over 64 years fall below 10 in heavily black areas, but this is not true in New Orleans, where blacks are long-time residents rather than migrants to the city. The city contains 74 percent of the SMSA's elderly and only 57 percent of the total population.

## Nineteenth-Century Ports: New Orleans

**Sex Ratio.** There are 1.1 females for each male in the SMSA, which results in a female-dominant sex ratio (males divided by females times 100) of 91. New Orleans has a sex ratio of 87. Female survival rates exceed those for males after adolescence resulting in progressively lower sex ratios in older age cohorts. Thus the central city's higher median age contributes to female dominance. Ratios over 100 are few, although they take up considerable space on the map, for they occur in large, sparsely populated, rural tracts. Older outlying settlements have ratios below 90. Suburban areas have ratios between 90 and 100, whereas most of the city tracts have sex ratios well below 90.

**Negroes.** New Orleans is a racially segregated city, although like other southern cities, the segregation is often at the block rather than the neighborhood scale. Blacks and whites were historically not geographically segregated. First slaves and then servants lived in the household or a separate building behind it. The progressive elimination of master-slave and employer-servant relationships has been accompanied by progressive segregation into dominantly black and dominantly white neighborhoods from what had formerly been a more intermingled pattern. Thus the tract map presented here indicates highly segregated racial areas; but in sharp contrast to most other cities in the nation, the mixed tracts spread across the middle of the histogram represent stable neighborhoods rather than those in racial transition. Yet they are not integrated, for they consist of separate black and white areas that census tracts are too coarse to delimit.

As befits the way segregation developed in southern cities, New Orleans has several ghettos rather than a single predominantly black area. One of special interest is the northernmost area extending to the shores of Lake Pontchartrain. New Orleans had a considerable number of prosperous blacks who were as anxious as anyone else to buy new housing after World War II. Two tracts in the undeveloped part of the city were reserved for black occupancy. Blacks have thus

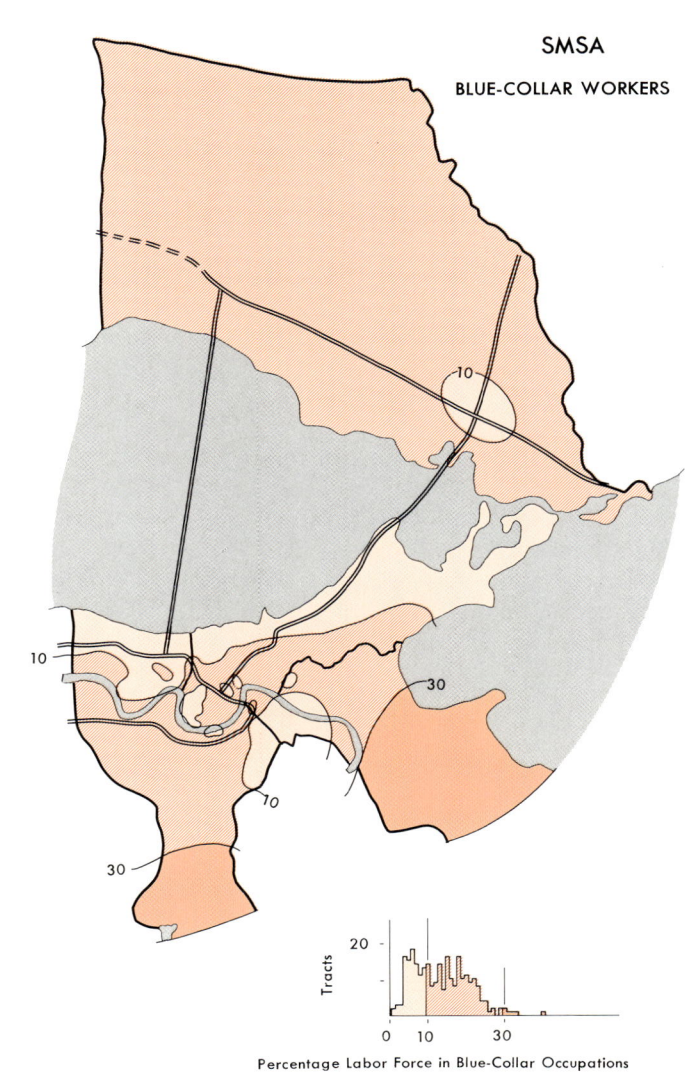

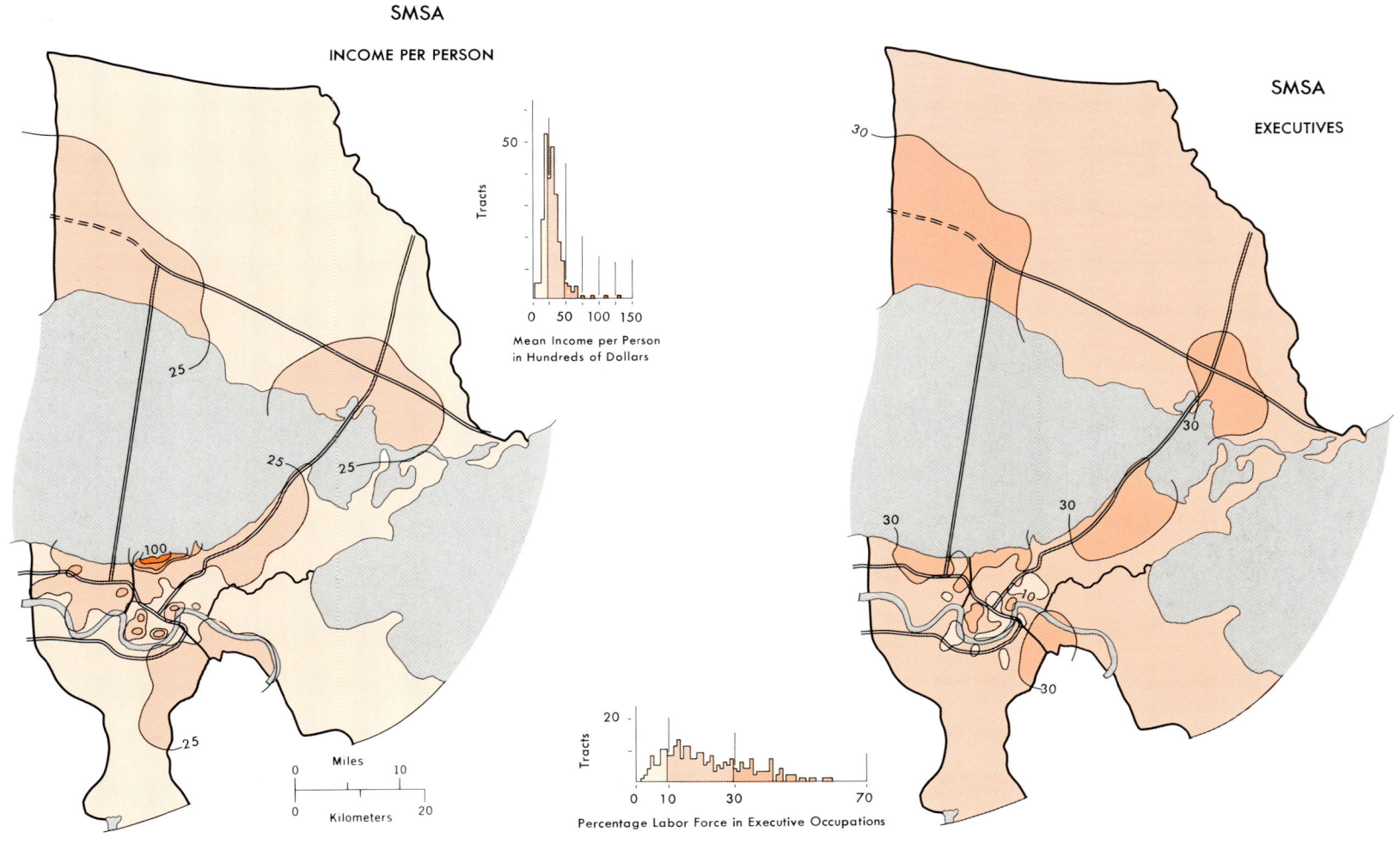

85

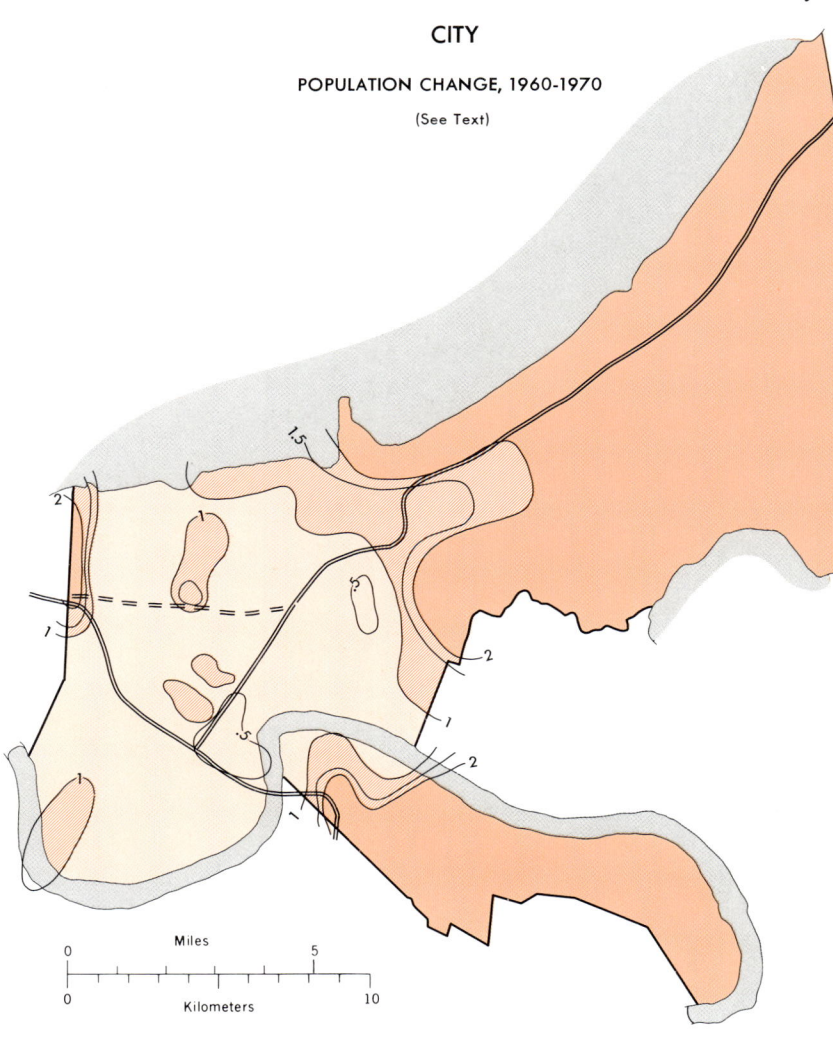

## CITY
### POPULATION CHANGE, 1960-1970
(See Text)

moved into the suburbs within the city, although they have been less successful in breaching the outer suburban walls; 83 percent of the SMSA's blacks live in Orleans Parish. Blacks constitute 31 percent of the SMSA population and 45 percent of New Orleans's people.

**Spanish-Americans.** There are 44,400 Spanish-speaking people in the SMSA, 4.2 percent of the total population. New Orleans contains 26,400, which is 60 percent of the Spanish-speaking population and 4.4 percent of the total city population. Most of the SMSA's Hispanics are of indigenous U.S., Central American, and Latin American origin, although there are 5,200 Cubans and 1,300 Puerto Ricans. Spanish-Americans are scattered in small numbers throughout the city, for there are no zero values and the 24 tracts that are suppressed each have a few.

Italian-Americans are the largest European ethnic group in the SMSA, but the 17,800 Italian foreign stock are but 1.7 percent of the population. No other foreign-stock group accounts for as much as 1 percent of the population, and time and prosperity have diluted even the Italian presence. Distinct ethnic neighborhoods aside from those occupied by blacks are almost nonexistent.

### SOCIOECONOMIC CHARACTERISTICS

**Household Size.** There are 3.2 people in the average SMSA household, and 3 in the average New Orleans City household. Tract means range from just over 1 in New Orleans to 4 or more in some central-city and suburban tracts. The highest values, 5.8 and 6.1, occur in the Desire Housing Project. Household size is closely related to family life cycle. Small households correlate with older populations

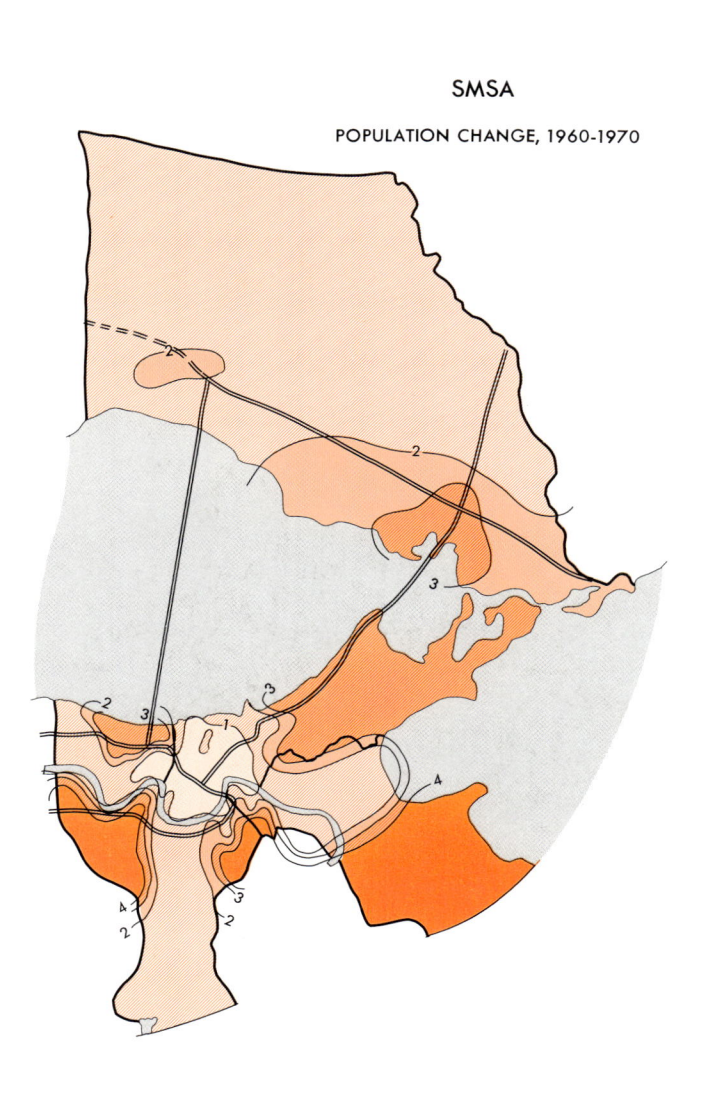

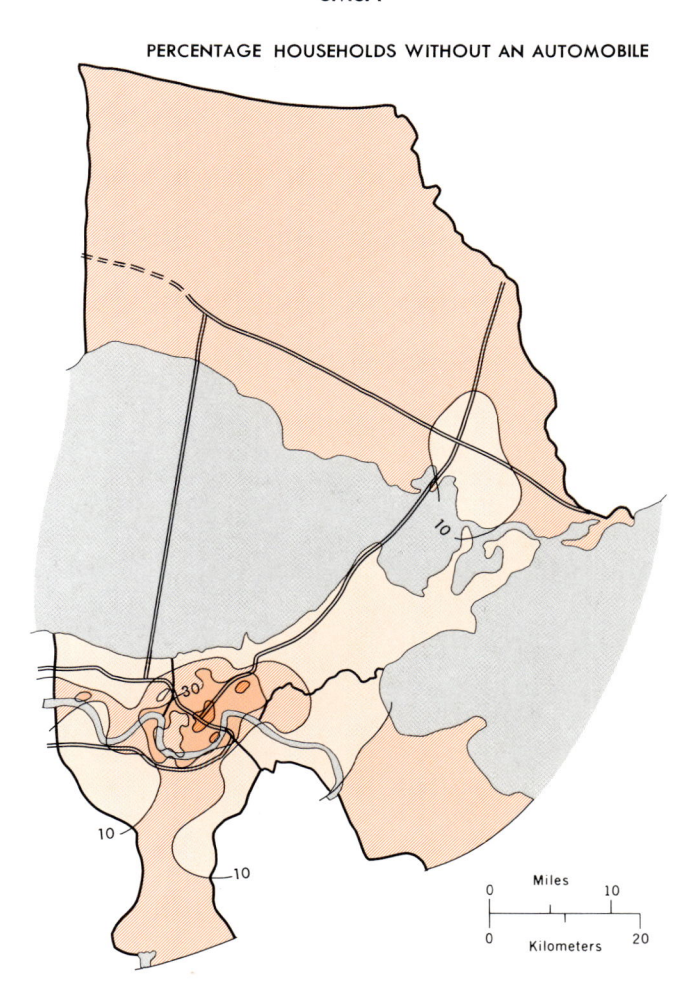

## SMSA
### POPULATION CHANGE, 1960-1970

## SMSA
### PERCENTAGE HOUSEHOLDS WITHOUT AN AUTOMOBILE

## Nineteenth-Century Ports: New Orleans

**CITY**
PERCENTAGE FAMILIES WITH A FEMALE HEAD

**CITY**
PERCENTAGE POPULATION BELOW POVERTY LEVEL

**SMSA**
PERCENTAGE 20-21 YEAR OLDS IN SCHOOL

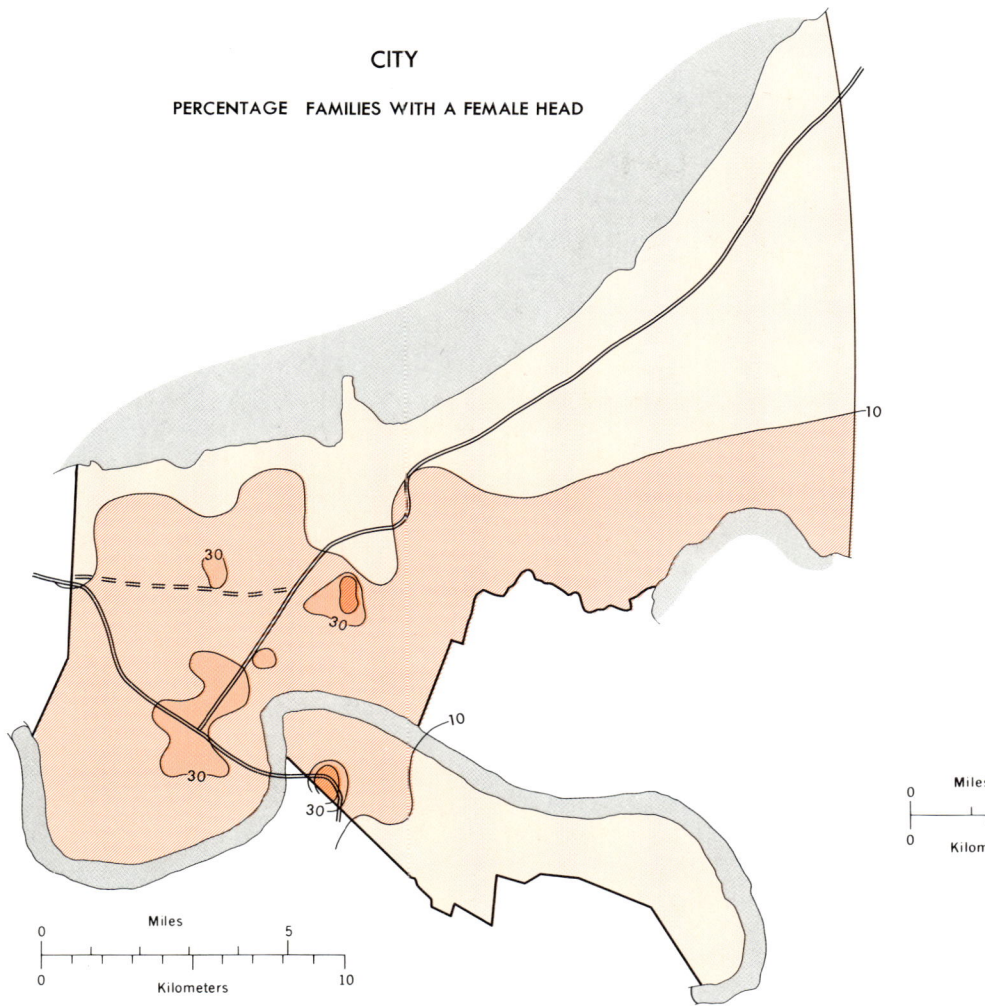

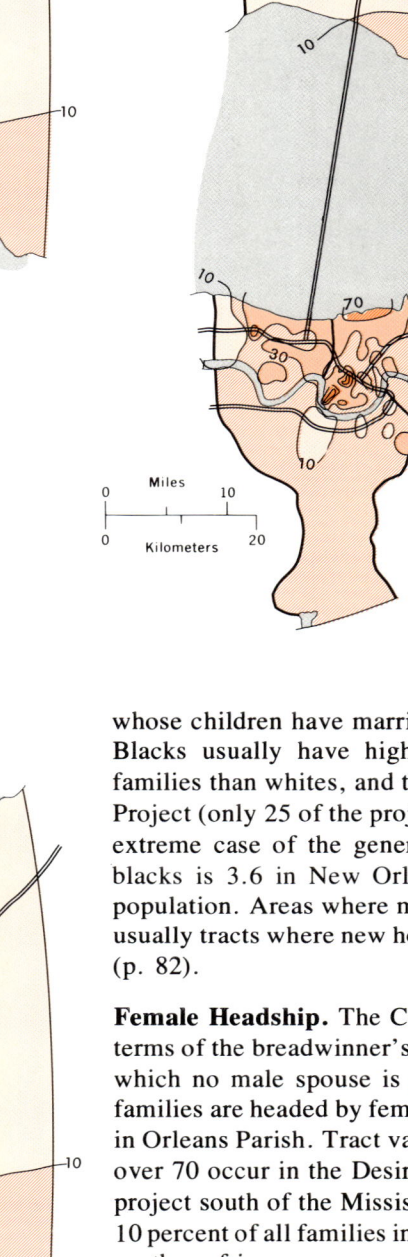

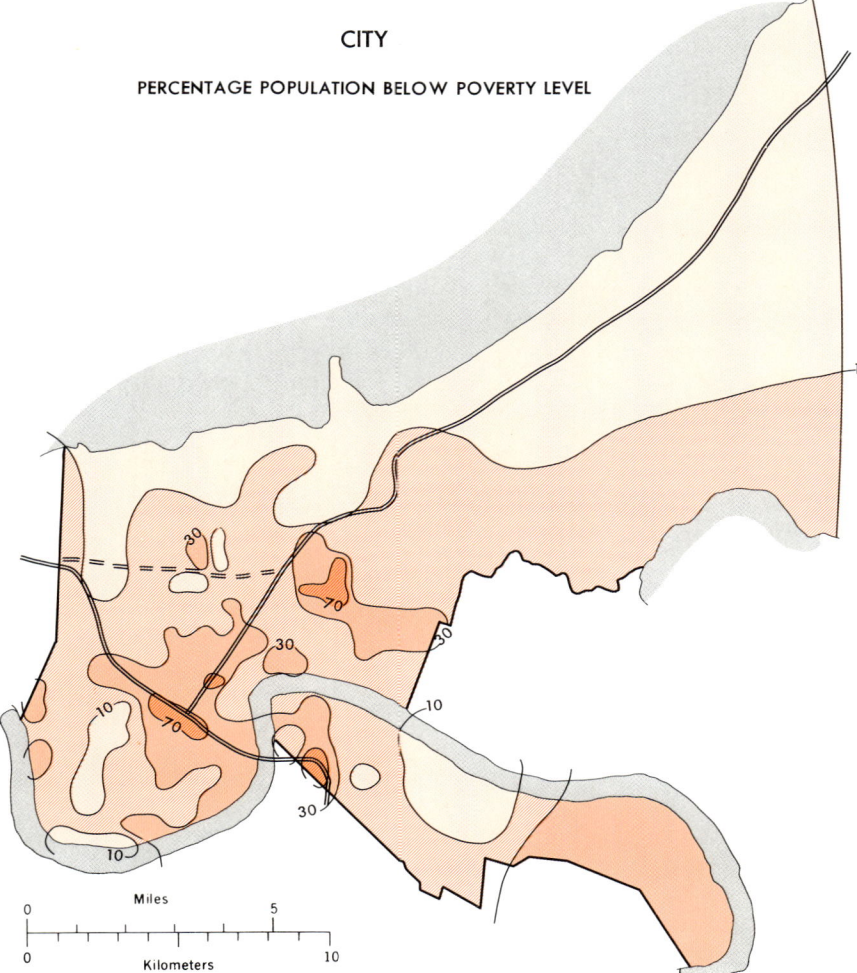

whose children have married and established their own households. Blacks usually have higher birthrates and thus somewhat larger families than whites, and the very high values in the Desire Housing Project (only 25 of the project's 10,755 residents are white) is but an extreme case of the general association. Mean household size for blacks is 3.6 in New Orleans City, as opposed to 3 for the total population. Areas where mean household sizes exceed 4 persons are usually tracts where new housing (p. 80) has attracted young families (p. 82).

**Female Headship.** The Census Bureau does not define headship in terms of the breadwinner's sex; a family headed by a female is one in which no male spouse is present. In the SMSA, 16 percent of all families are headed by females, and the proportion rises to 22 percent in Orleans Parish. Tract values range from zero to 72 percent; values over 70 occur in the Desire Housing Project and in another housing project south of the Mississippi. Families headed by females exceed 10 percent of all families in most of the central-city area except for the northern fringe.

**Occupations.** The SMSA's civilian labor force consists of 368,000 workers; 12 percent engage in blue-collar (laborers and operatives) occupations, and 22 percent are executives (engineers, teachers, professionals, managers, proprietors, and administrators). The remaining 66 percent are service workers (37 percent) and clerical workers (29 percent). The city has the same proportions of blue-collar and executive workers as the SMSA, which is unusual. Most central cities have relatively more blue-collar workers and fewer executives than their SMSAs. The city proportions in service and clerical occupations are also the same as the SMSA breakdown. Tract percentages for blue-collar occupations range from 1 to over 30; high values are in rural areas and in one predominantly black tract across the Mississippi from the CBD. The recently occupied areas of Jefferson and northern Orleans parishes have few blue-collar workers, as do higher-prestige areas near the CBD and in southwestern Orleans Parish.

Executives are evident in large proportions throughout the region. They have established beachheads north of Lake Pontchartrain, but most are located closer to the city. The tracts with values in the 50 percent range are located along Lake Pontchartrain and in southwestern Orleans Parish. Proportions fall well below 10 percent in the heavily black areas of the city. The availability of new housing and the maintenance of fine older homes in southwestern New Orleans has enabled the city to keep its highly paid decision makers, which is a rarity in large American cities. Another factor that keeps executives closer to the city is the concentration of jobs in the CBD; employment suburbanization has not progressed as far in New Orleans as it has in many cities (see p. 319).

**Income.** The SMSA has a mean income per person of $2,800 per year, which is the lowest of the 24 SMSAs included in the atlas. Mean income per capita in the city is $2,700. Tract means range from $500 to $13,000. The highest incomes accrue to those living along Lake Pontchartrain in northern Orleans Parish, and the lowest occur in predominantly black areas. Incomes are below $2,500 per person in much of the older area of New Orleans City except in the traditional prestige residential area in the southwest. The SMSA's low incomes are a function of generally lower wages and salaries, for there is little variation from parish to parish in summary statistics. Thus poor rural areas are not pulling down the metropolitan average. The reason for low incomes is a large poverty population. One-fifth of all people in the SMSA and 27 percent of the city's population have incomes that place them below the poverty level (p. 415). Almost 10 percent of the SMSA's families receive some public assistance (p. 423).

## TOPICS OF SPECIAL INTEREST IN THE NEW ORLEANS REGION

**Population Change.** The population-change maps are produced by dividing the 1970 population by the 1960 population. The quotient is less than unity if an area lost population during the decade and greater than unity if population increased. The New Orleans SMSA increased from 907,000 to 1,460,000 (1.15). The city had 628,000 people in 1960, but only 593,000 in 1970 for an index value of 0.95. The largest absolute increase occurred in Jefferson Parish which grew from 209,000 to 338,000 (1.62). St. Bernard (1.59) and St. Tammany (1.66) grew by similar proportions, but from smaller 1960 bases. Within the city, population losses were widespread in the older areas. Renewal areas in and adjacent to the CBD and the Desire Housing Project (northeast of the CBD) lost over half their populations. A few close-in areas gained population, but most of the places that increased are located to the northwest, northeast, and southeast, where new housing was still being built in the 1960s (p. 80). (A histogram for the SMSA map appears on p. 351.)

**Female Headship and Poverty.** The people who are being left behind as suburban areas grow are largely those who cannot share in metropolitan expansion because of racial barriers, poverty, or both. The nodes of predominantly black population (p. 83) appear on the map of families headed by females as areas of high values. There is one exception: the northernmost node of black population is an affluent, black suburb within the city called Pontchartrain Park. For the city as a whole, 18,500 (60 percent) of the 30,950 families headed by females are black. Female headship is also correlated with poverty, especially among black families. There are 31,000 families with incomes below the poverty level; 15,100 of them are families headed by females and 14,000 (93 percent) of the 15,100 are headed by black females.

**College Enrollments.** Twenty-nine percent of all 20 and 21 year olds in the SMSA are students, a percentage that increases to 34 in the city because of the universities and colleges located there. Away from Tulane and Loyola in southwestern Orleans Parish and from the University of New Orleans on the lakefront, enrollments are highest in affluent areas and low in rural and predominantly black areas. (See p. 367 for the histogram for this variable.)

**Households without Automobiles.** Households without automobile transportation are at a serious disadvantage. Since housing, jobs, commercial establishments, recreational facilities, and even health-care centers are often located with only minimal consideration of how people without cars can reach them, many people are increasingly cut off from such opportunities and services. In New Orleans, 26 percent of the SMSA households and 37 percent of the city households are without automobiles. Such households exceed 30 percent in tracts in the older part of the city except for the affluent southwest. Values decline to less than 10 percent quickly as one moves out in most directions from these older areas. (See p. 335 for the histogram for this variable.)

---

Compared with most American cities, New Orleans is in good shape despite population losses and the increasing concentration of disadvantaged people. The CBD still has a fourth of the metropolitan area's jobs. The French Quarter—a major national, regional, and local tourist attraction—has been rescued from an Interstate highway. Most important, the downtown has the allegiance of a large number of influential citizens who love it and are determined to see it preserved as a civilized, humane place. Whether their affection for the downtown area will be adequate to keep the entire city healthy is uncertain, but their commitment to the older city is a considerable advantage.

# CHAPTER 12

# San Francisco– Oakland

The San Francisco Standard Metropolitan Statistical Area (SMSA), with a population of 3,110,000, is the nation's 6th most populous SMSA. San Francisco (the city and county are coterminous) has 23 percent (716,000) of the region's people. Alameda County is the largest of the counties with 1,073,000 people (35 percent). Oakland, which is located within Alameda County, has a population of 362,000 (12 percent of the SMSA total). Contra Costa and San Mateo counties are almost equal in size with 558,000 and 556,000 (18 percent each), and Marin County is smallest in population with 206,000 people (7 percent). The commuting region defined by counties with at least 5 percent of their labor forces working in San Francisco and Alameda counties brings in 4 more counties (p. 81). This Daily Urban System (DUS) has a population of 4,631,000, which makes it the nation's 6th most populous DUS.

San Francisco's sheltered Bay and access to the interior made it an early point for penetration of northern California and the central valley. By 1852, the California Gold Rush had attracted enough people to make San Francisco almost as large as Chicago, and a decade later it was the 9th city in the nation. It was 7th in 1900, and after the churning of the interwar and postwar years it emerged as 6th in 1960 (p. 10). San Francisco was a major port during the 19th century. As long as connections with the eastern United States were by water, San Francisco was unchallenged. When rail connections to the East were established, its peninsular location made access into San Francisco difficult, whereas the eastern side of the Bay had large expanses of flat land and much easier rail connections to the East. The arrival of railroads stimulated the growth of Oakland and other East Bay towns, and over the years most of the region's port functions have shifted to the East Bay.

*Note:* All data are from the 1970 Censuses of Population and Housing unless otherwise indicated. Therefore the present tense refers to 1970 data except for income data which are from 1969. Cartographic conventions are explained in Chapter 1.

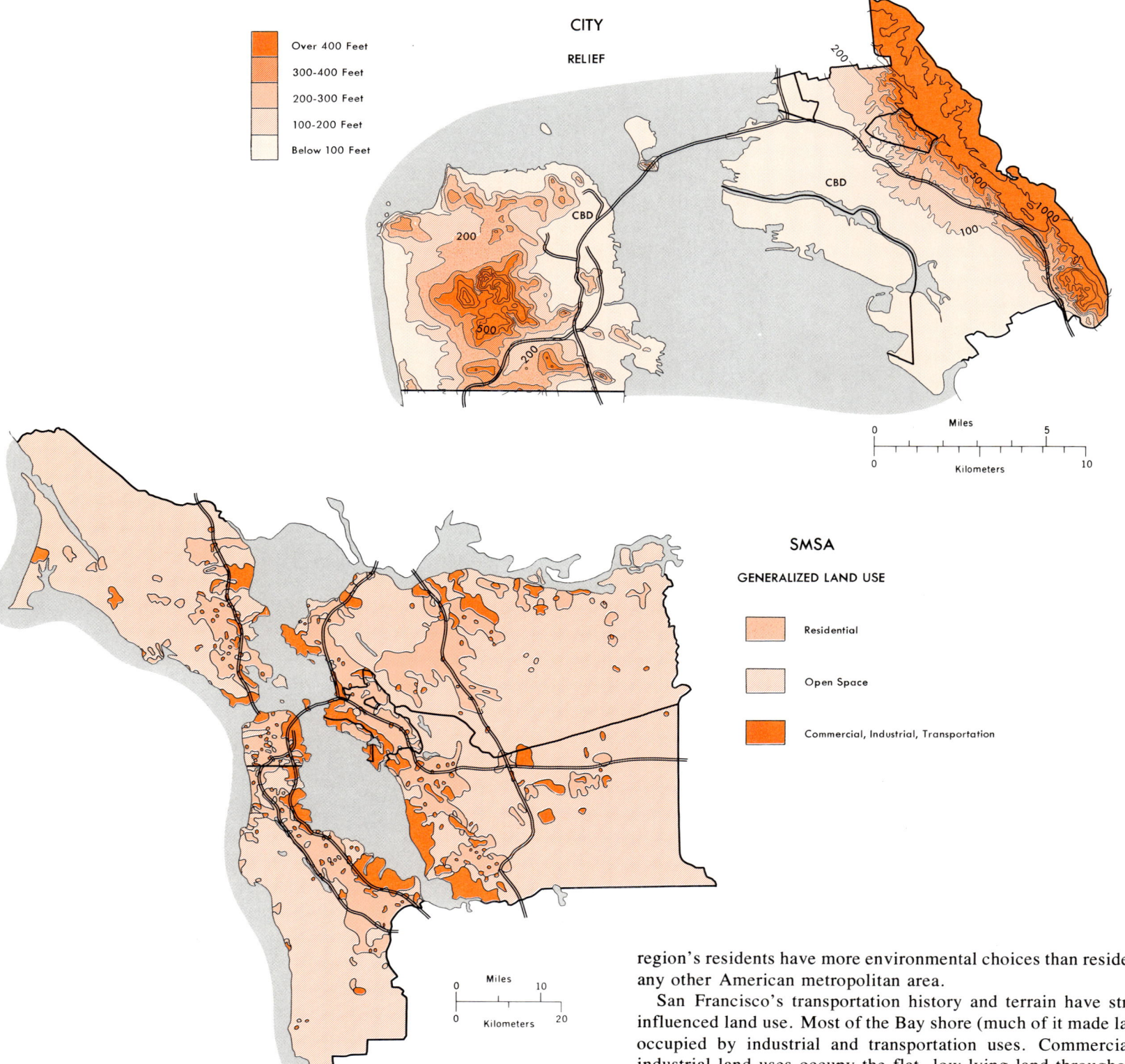

# Nineteenth-Century Ports: San Francisco-Oakland

San Francisco Bay lies in a structural depression in the coast ranges that separate the central valley from the Pacific. Mountains and foothills penetrate San Francisco and Oakland. Elevations over 800 feet (250 meters) above sea level occur within three miles (5 kilometers) of the ocean in San Francisco, producing some of the steep hills for which the city is famous. Much of Oakland is flat and low, but the Berkeley Hills to the east rise to peak elevations of 1,500 feet (450 meters). The rugged terrain and interpenetration of land and sea combine to produce a diversity of physical environments in the SMSA, ranging from the cool, moist climate of San Francisco to the semiarid conditions that prevail east of the Berkeley Hills. The region's residents have more environmental choices than residents in any other American metropolitan area.

San Francisco's transportation history and terrain have strongly influenced land use. Most of the Bay shore (much of it made land) is occupied by industrial and transportation uses. Commercial and industrial land uses occupy the flat, low-lying land throughout the region, and residential uses occupy the slopes, which has the virtue of giving many ordinary homes fine views across the metropolitan region. Residential expansion outside the immediate vicinity of San Francisco and Oakland is highly dependent on highway access to the central employment cores.

## HOUSING

**Housing Age.** The region's housing stock is relatively new. Of the SMSA total, 37 percent was built before 1940, 38 percent was constructed from 1940 through 1959, and 25 percent dates from the 1960s. Much of the older housing is located in San Francisco, with a smaller amount in Oakland; San Francisco has half the SMSA's pre-1940 units and Oakland has 19 percent. Sixty-seven percent of San Francisco's housing stock was built before 1940, as was 53 percent of Oakland's. Peripheral tracts beyond the range of recent suburban growth have 30 percent or more older housing, and the sites of older, separate communities around the Bay and along Carquinez

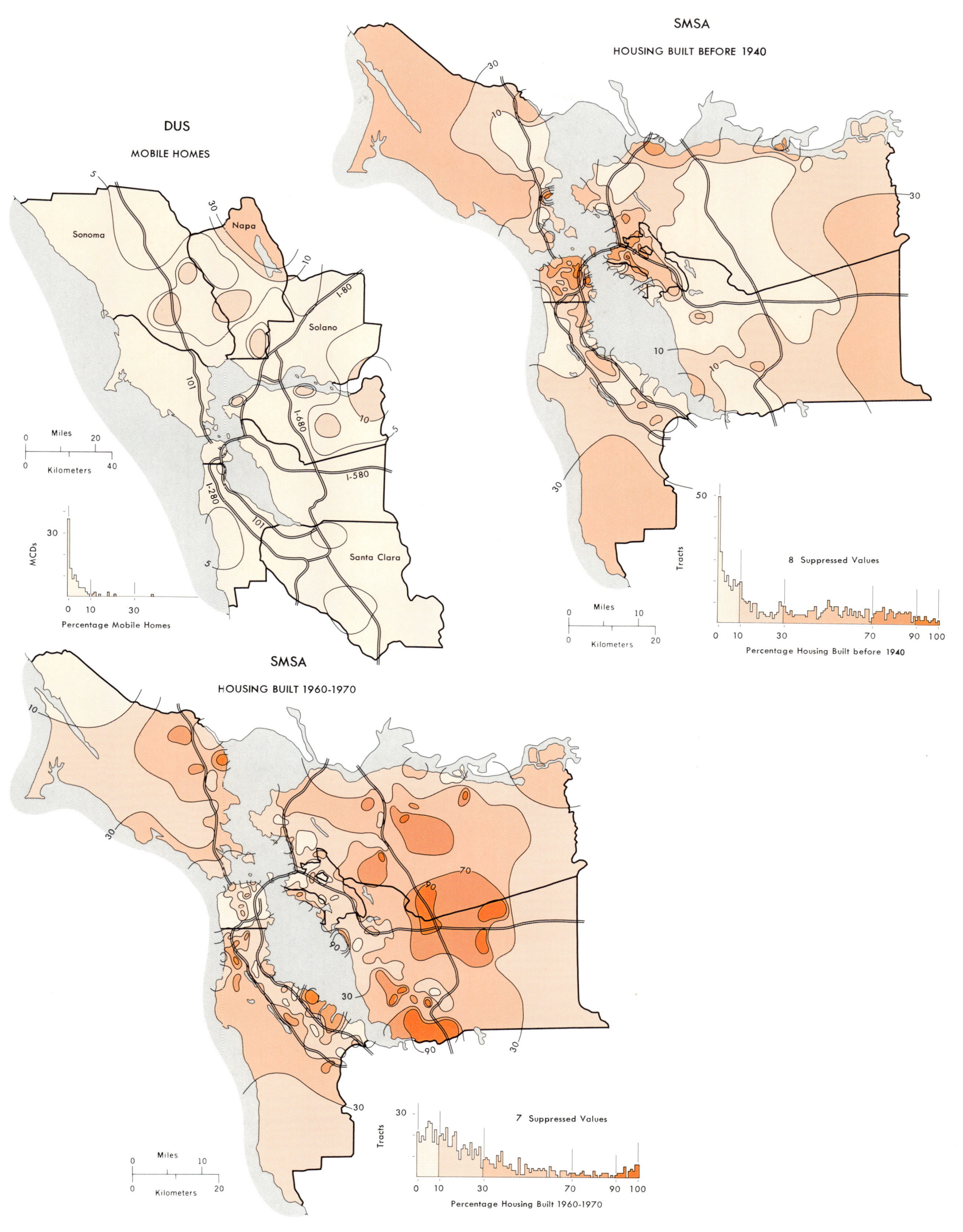

## Nineteenth-Century Ports: San Francisco-Oakland

**DUS** — MOBILE HOMES

**SMSA** — HOUSING BUILT BEFORE 1940

**SMSA** — HOUSING BUILT 1960-1970

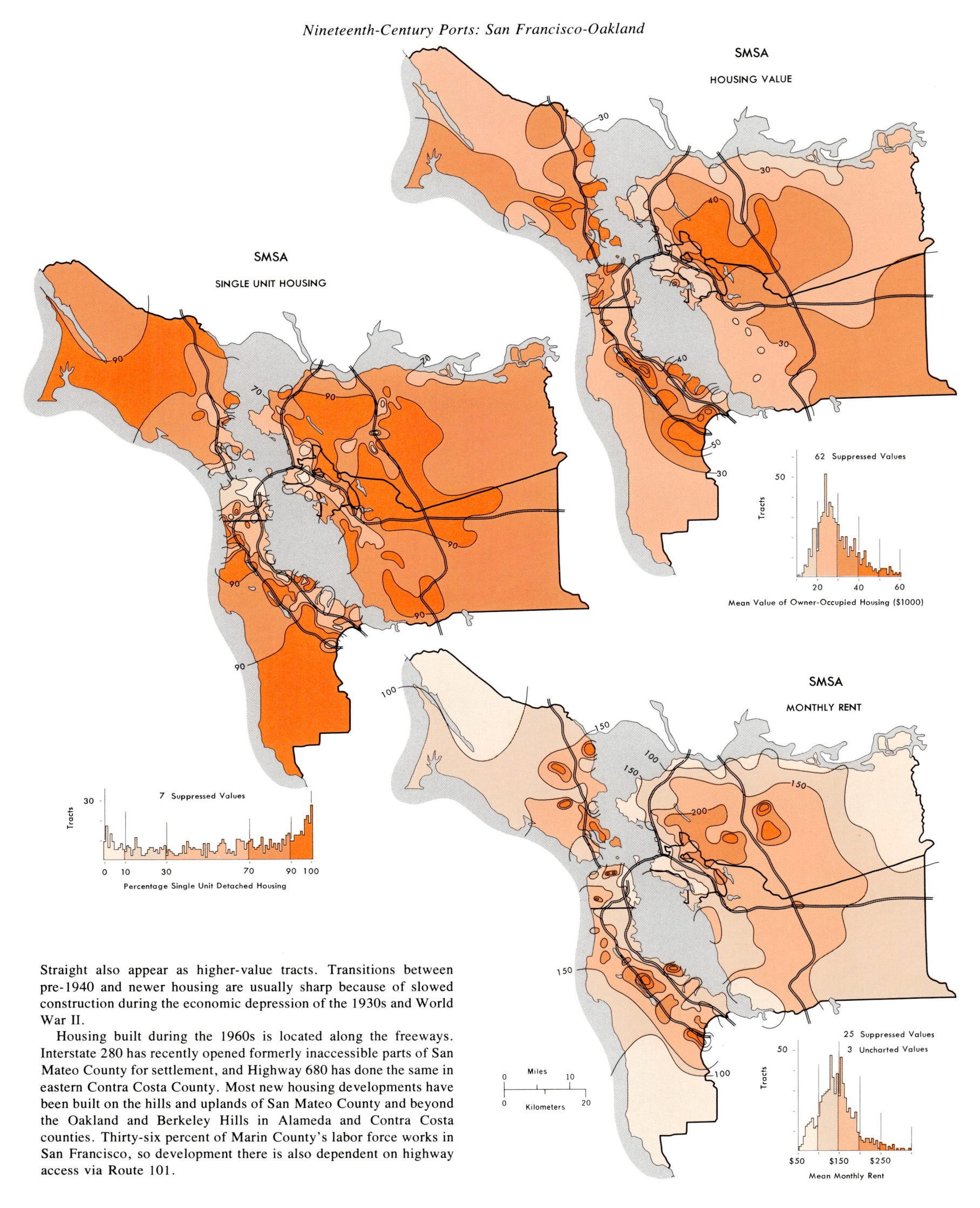

## Nineteenth-Century Ports: San Francisco-Oakland

Straight also appear as higher-value tracts. Transitions between pre-1940 and newer housing are usually sharp because of slowed construction during the economic depression of the 1930s and World War II.

Housing built during the 1960s is located along the freeways. Interstate 280 has recently opened formerly inaccessible parts of San Mateo County for settlement, and Highway 680 has done the same in eastern Contra Costa County. Most new housing developments have been built on the hills and uplands of San Mateo County and beyond the Oakland and Berkeley Hills in Alameda and Contra Costa counties. Thirty-six percent of Marin County's labor force works in San Francisco, so development there is also dependent on highway access via Route 101.

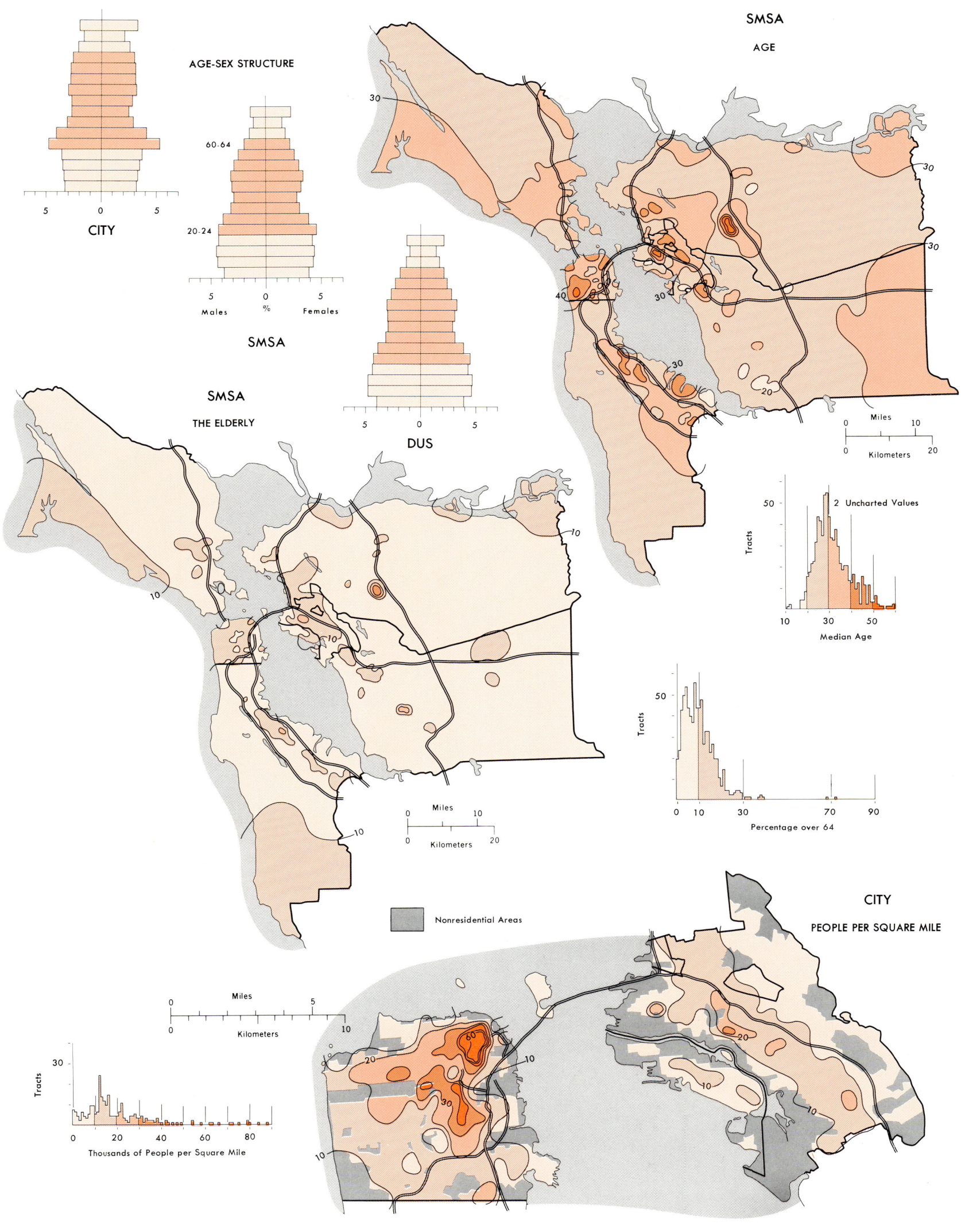

## Nineteenth-Century Ports: San Francisco-Oakland

### AGE-SEX STRUCTURE
CITY
SMSA
DUS

### SMSA AGE

### SMSA THE ELDERLY

### CITY PEOPLE PER SQUARE MILE

93

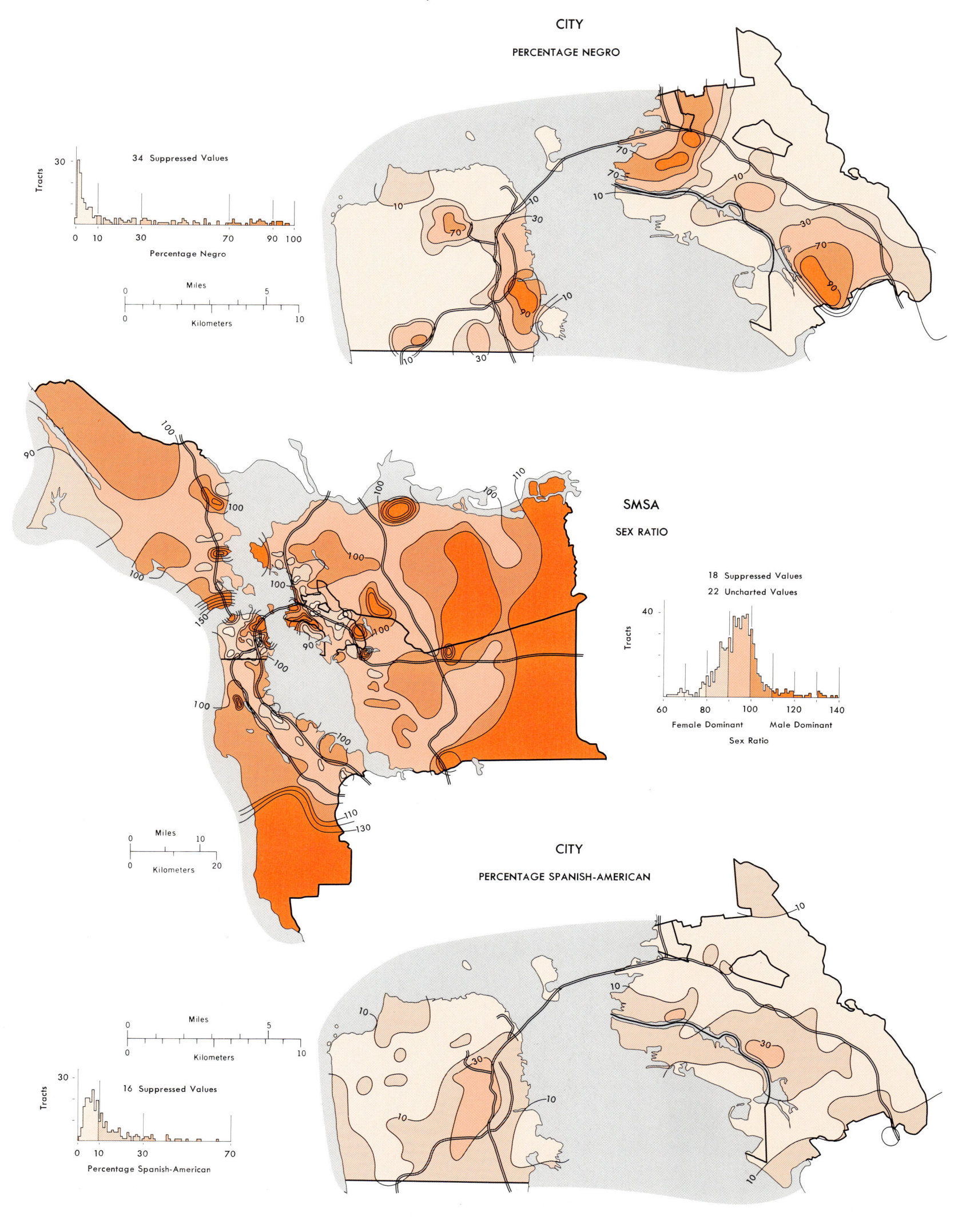

## Nineteenth-Century Ports: San Francisco-Oakland

### CITY
#### PERCENTAGE NEGRO

34 Suppressed Values

### SMSA
#### SEX RATIO

18 Suppressed Values
22 Uncharted Values

Female Dominant — Male Dominant
Sex Ratio

### CITY
#### PERCENTAGE SPANISH-AMERICAN

16 Suppressed Values

*Nineteenth-Century Ports: San Francisco-Oakland*

CITY

CHINESE-AMERICANS

Each Dot Represents 50 Chinese

SMSA

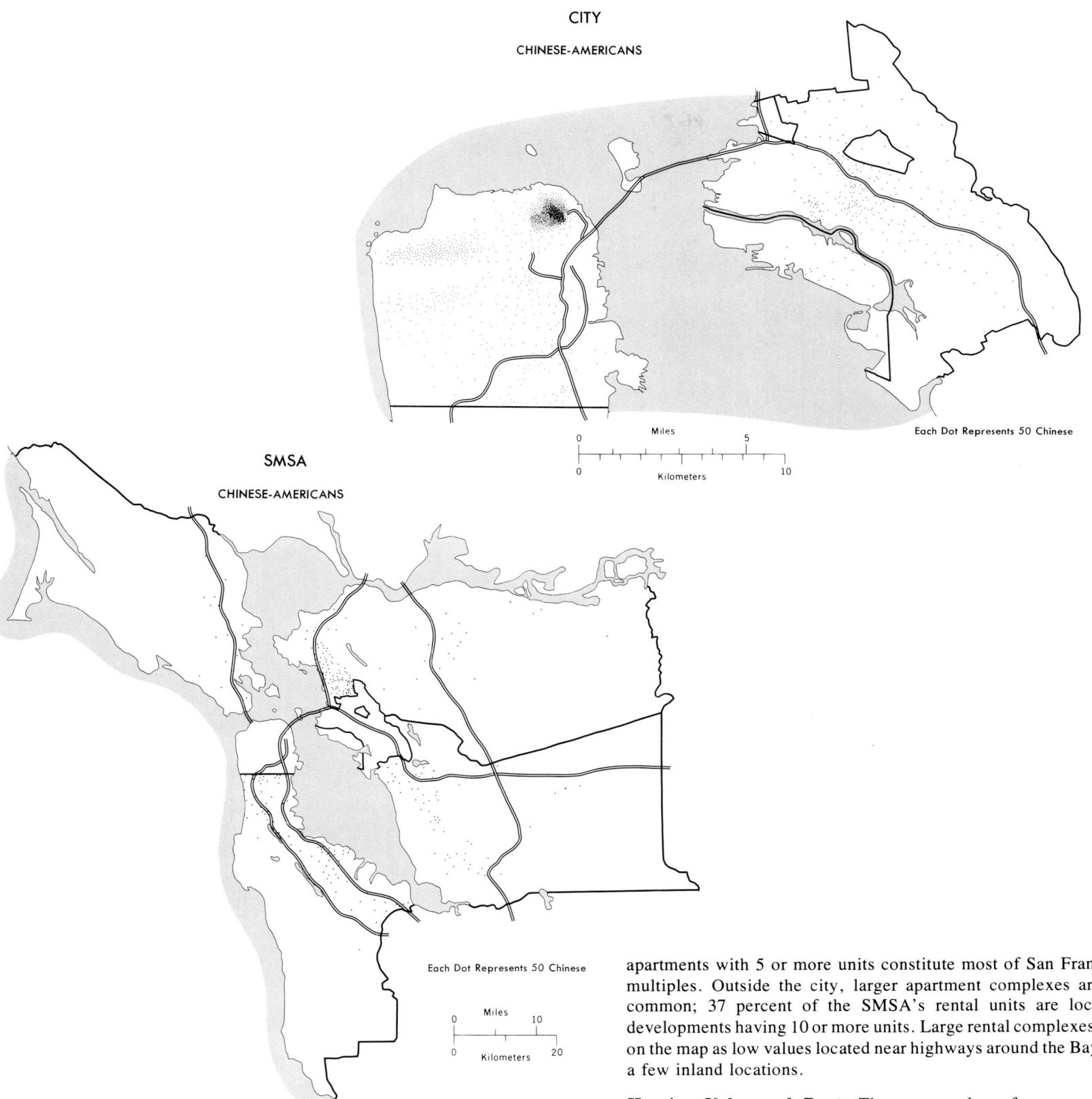

CHINESE-AMERICANS

Each Dot Represents 50 Chinese

**Mobile Homes.** There are 17,800 mobile homes in the DUS; they constitute 1.1 percent of the region's housing stock. Zoning restrictions usually confine mobile homes to the metropolitan periphery. A single sparsely populated area of Napa County has more than 30 percent mobile homes. Values above 10 percent are confined to Napa and Sonoma counties and to small communities with less restrictive zoning in Contra Costa County.

**Single-Unit Detached Housing.** Single-unit detached houses make up 52 percent of the SMSA's housing stock. In San Francisco only 17 percent of the units are single-family detached, whereas in newer and more sparsely populated Oakland, 47 percent are. Row houses and apartments with 5 or more units constitute most of San Francisco's multiples. Outside the city, larger apartment complexes are more common; 37 percent of the SMSA's rental units are located in developments having 10 or more units. Large rental complexes appear on the map as low values located near highways around the Bay and in a few inland locations.

**Housing Value and Rent.** The mean value of owner-occupied housing in the SMSA is $30,000. San Francisco's housing is slightly more expensive at $31,000, whereas Oakland's is cheaper on the average at $25,000. It is unusual for a central city's housing to be more expensive than the regional average. High housing values are concentrated in Marin and San Mateo counties. The East Bay shore has been an area of less expensive housing since cheap ferry service was established in 1878, allowing San Francisco's less affluent workers to avoid expensive housing within San Francisco by commuting across the Bay. Some of Marin County's luxury housing is located close to the Bay, whereas many of San Mateo's high-priced units are well inland. In Alameda and Contra Costa counties, low-value housing is on the level land next to the Bay, and expensive housing is built on the slopes of the hills or inland.

The mean cost of rental units in the SMSA is $133; San Francisco's mean is identical, and Oakland's is $110. Individual tract values range

SMSA
MEXICAN-AMERICANS

SMSA
JAPANESE-AMERICANS

Each Black Dot Represents 50 Mexican Born
Each Orange Dot Represents 50 People of Mexican Parentage

Each Dot Represents 50 Japanese

0   Miles   10
0   Kilometers   20

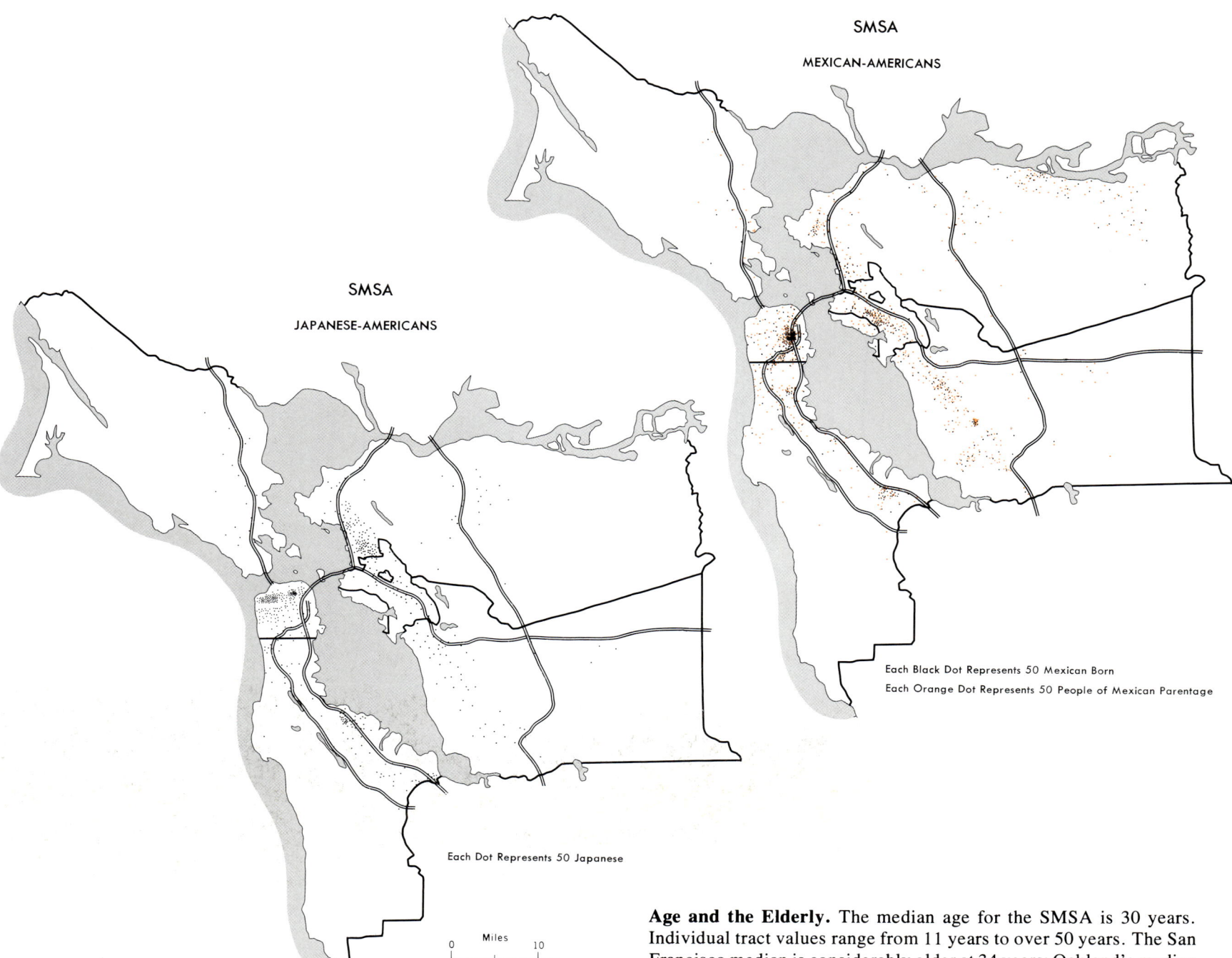

from $55 to over $300. The map of rentals is similar to the housing-value map. Low-cost rental housing is most abundant in Alameda and Contra Costa counties, whereas Marin and San Mateo counties have clusters of expensive rental units. There is a considerable range in San Francisco, where expensive units north and west of the CBD are counterbalanced by the often deteriorating units of the Mission District and Hunter's Point along the city's eastern shore.

## THE PEOPLE

**Population Density.** San Francisco's overall density is 15,800 people per square mile and Oakland's is 6,800 (6,100 versus 2,600 people per square kilometer). Densities exceed 20,000 per square mile (7,700 per square kilometer) and reach intensities of over 80,000 per square mile (30,900 per square kilometer) in San Francisco, whereas Oakland's highest density is a single tract of 36,000 (13,900 per square kilometer). Peak densities are located adjacent to the San Francisco CBD. Part of the area is occupied by San Francisco's Chinatown. An SMSA map of population density appears on p. 311.

**Age and the Elderly.** The median age for the SMSA is 30 years. Individual tract values range from 11 years to over 50 years. The San Francisco median is considerably older at 34 years; Oakland's median is 32. It is usual for a city to have an older median than its SMSA, but the 4-year difference for San Francisco is unusually large. The city population pyramid (based on the combined populations of both cities) indicates that the older median is produced by the presence of relatively few people under 19 years of age and large numbers in the 20- to 35-year age cohorts. Young people evidently find San Francisco and Oakland attractive places to seek employment and mates, but when couples have children they seek housing outside the cities. SMSA and DUS pyramids contain typical proportions of people in the under-19 cohorts.

Median ages over 30 years extend through much of San Francisco and Oakland. Median ages are relatively high in the affluent parts of San Mateo County, but low in comparable areas of Marin County, suggesting that prosperous young families prefer Marin. Young families of limited means live in northern San Mateo County and Alameda County. Most median ages over 50 years are produced by institutionalized populations that are not mapped because they are very small. Two exceptions are the large retirement villages near Walnut Creek in south-central Contra Costa County and the cluster of tracts containing large numbers of old people near the Oakland CBD.

Ten percent of the SMSA's population is over 64 years of age. The elderly make up 14 percent of San Francisco's people and 13 percent of Oakland's population. People often age with their housing, staying in the neighborhood in which they raised their children after the

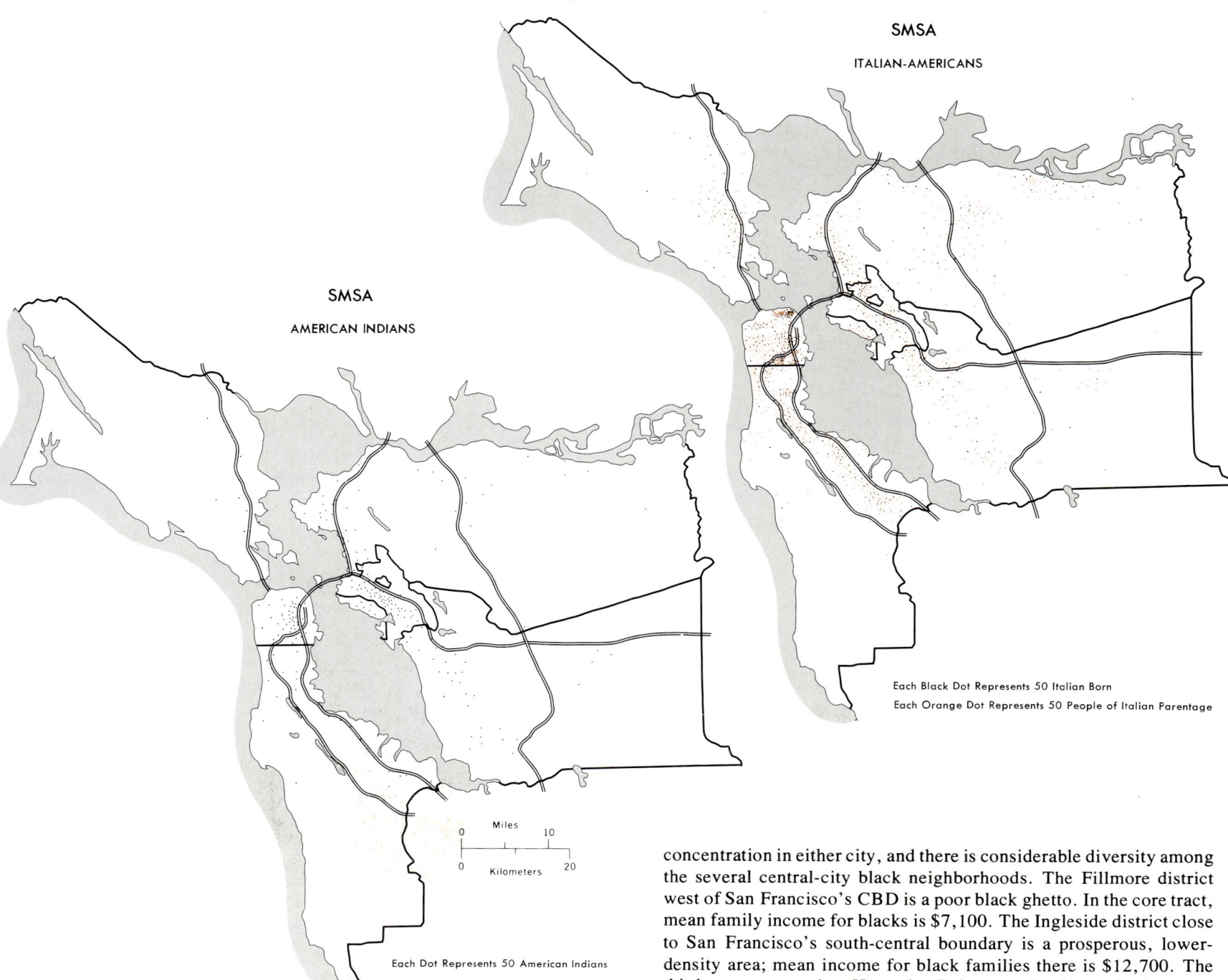

*Nineteenth-Century Ports: San Francisco-Oakland*

SMSA
ITALIAN-AMERICANS

SMSA
AMERICAN INDIANS

Each Black Dot Represents 50 Italian Born
Each Orange Dot Represents 50 People of Italian Parentage

Each Dot Represents 50 American Indians

children leave. Thus the elderly come to be concentrated in central cities. San Francisco and Oakland have half the SMSA's elderly in contrast to 35 percent of the total population. Many older Bay Area communities are identifiable by the clusters of tracts where the elderly exceed 10 percent of the population

**Sex Ratio.** There are 1.05 females for each male in the SMSA, resulting in a sex ratio (males divided by females times 100) of 96. Central cities are usually more female-dominant than metropolitan regions. This is true in San Francisco and Oakland which have sex ratios of 93 and 92. Female survival rates exceed male survival rates after adolescence, resulting in increasingly lower sex ratios in older age cohorts. Thus higher central-city median ages contribute to lower sex ratios. Sex ratios below 70 and above 120 are often caused by sex-segregated institutions. Military facilities produce the high male-dominant sex ratios in northern Contra Costa and San Francisco counties, and in southern Marin County.

**Negroes.** Thirteen percent of San Francisco's population is black, as is 35 percent of Oakland's population. There is no single black concentration in either city, and there is considerable diversity among the several central-city black neighborhoods. The Fillmore district west of San Francisco's CBD is a poor black ghetto. In the core tract, mean family income for blacks is $7,100. The Ingleside district close to San Francisco's south-central boundary is a prosperous, lower-density area; mean income for black families there is $12,700. The third area near the Hunter's Point naval shipyards has two components: Bay View, occupied by middle-income blacks, and Hunter's Point, occupied by low-income blacks. Oakland's black community has been a blue-collar working-class group since its origins. Whereas many blacks were employed as sleeping-car porters and dining-car cooks in the early days, local industry and the Port of Oakland now provide most of their jobs. See p.100 or 383 for the SMSA map.

**Spanish-Americans.** The Census Bureau identifies Spanish-Americans in California and other southwestern states by adding people with Spanish surnames to Spanish-speaking people. By such criteria 35,400 (9.8 percent) of Oakland's people are Spanish-American, as are 101,900 (14.2 percent) of San Francisco's. Spanish-Americans are dispersed in small numbers throughout the cities. Most tracts have values ranging from 4 to 15 percent, and no tracts are without Spanish-American residents. The Mission District, which houses many Spanish-Americans, lies between the Fillmore and Hunter's Point black concentrations in San Francisco. San Francisco and Oakland have 35 percent of the SMSA's total population and 38 percent of its Spanish-American population. See p. 391 for the SMSA map and p. 96 for a map of Mexican foreign stock.

**Chinese-Americans.** The Census requires all nonwhite individuals to

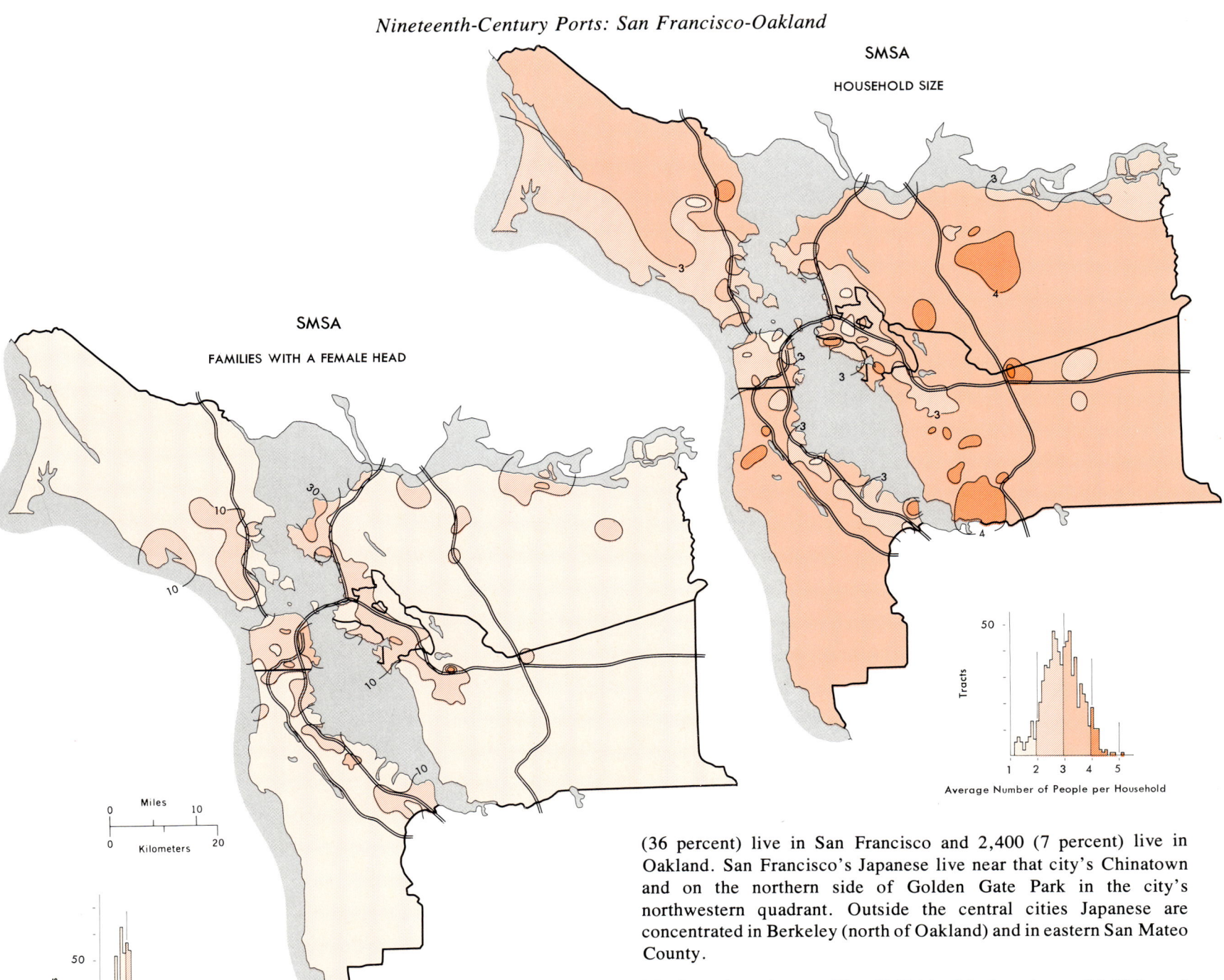

*Nineteenth-Century Ports: San Francisco-Oakland*

identify themselves as members of 1 of 8 "racial" groups: Negro, Indian, Chinese, Japanese, Filipino, Korean, Hawaiian, or Other. There are 88,100 people who identify themselves as Chinese in the SMSA. Sixty-seven percent (58,700) live in San Francisco, and 13 percent (11,300) reside in Oakland. San Francisco's Chinese community is still focused on the original Chinatown along Grant Avenue next to the CBD. Since 1960 Chinatown has spread rapidly toward the northwest. Young professionals and well-educated Chinese are establishing a new community north of Golden Gate Park, several miles west of Chinatown. Oakland's Chinese community is smaller and less concentrated than San Francisco's, but it is also becoming more diffuse as young families leave the traditional core near the CBD. The 20 percent of the SMSA's Chinese that live outside the two central cities are distributed roughly in accordance with population density.

**Japanese-Americans.** The SMSA contains 32,500 Japanese; 11,700 (36 percent) live in San Francisco and 2,400 (7 percent) live in Oakland. San Francisco's Japanese live near that city's Chinatown and on the northern side of Golden Gate Park in the city's northwestern quadrant. Outside the central cities Japanese are concentrated in Berkeley (north of Oakland) and in eastern San Mateo County.

**Mexican-Americans.** The SMSA's Mexican-born (25,800) and people of Mexican parentage (44,400) constitute 2.3 percent of the total SMSA population and 19 percent of the SMSA's Spanish-Americans. Since there are few (10,100) people of Puerto Rican stock and even fewer Cubans (3,600), the majority of the SMSA's Spanish-Americans are Americans of Mexican extraction. Of the SMSA's 364,000 Spanish-Americans, 235,000 (66 percent) are indigenous Americans who neither were born in Mexico nor have one or both Mexican parents. As for the Mexican foreign stock, the major concentration occurs in San Francisco's Mission District. The cluster in southern Alameda County is a Mexican enclave in Union City.

**American Indians.** San Francisco has a sizable Indian minority numbering 12,000 in the SMSA with 2,900 (24 percent) located in San Francisco and an almost identical number in Oakland. Indians are spread generally throughout the central areas of both cities and in proportion to general population densities in the rest of the SMSA.

**Italian-Americans.** There are 23,100 Italian-born and 65,600 people of Italian parentage in the San Francisco SMSA; in aggregate they are 2.9 percent of the SMSA's people. San Francisco contains 29,000 (33 percent) and Oakland contains 7,500 (8.4 percent). Whereas Italian-Americans are dispersed throughout the total population in Oakland and the SMSA, the waning North Beach community is still evident in San Francisco, with a secondary cluster along the city's southern boundary.

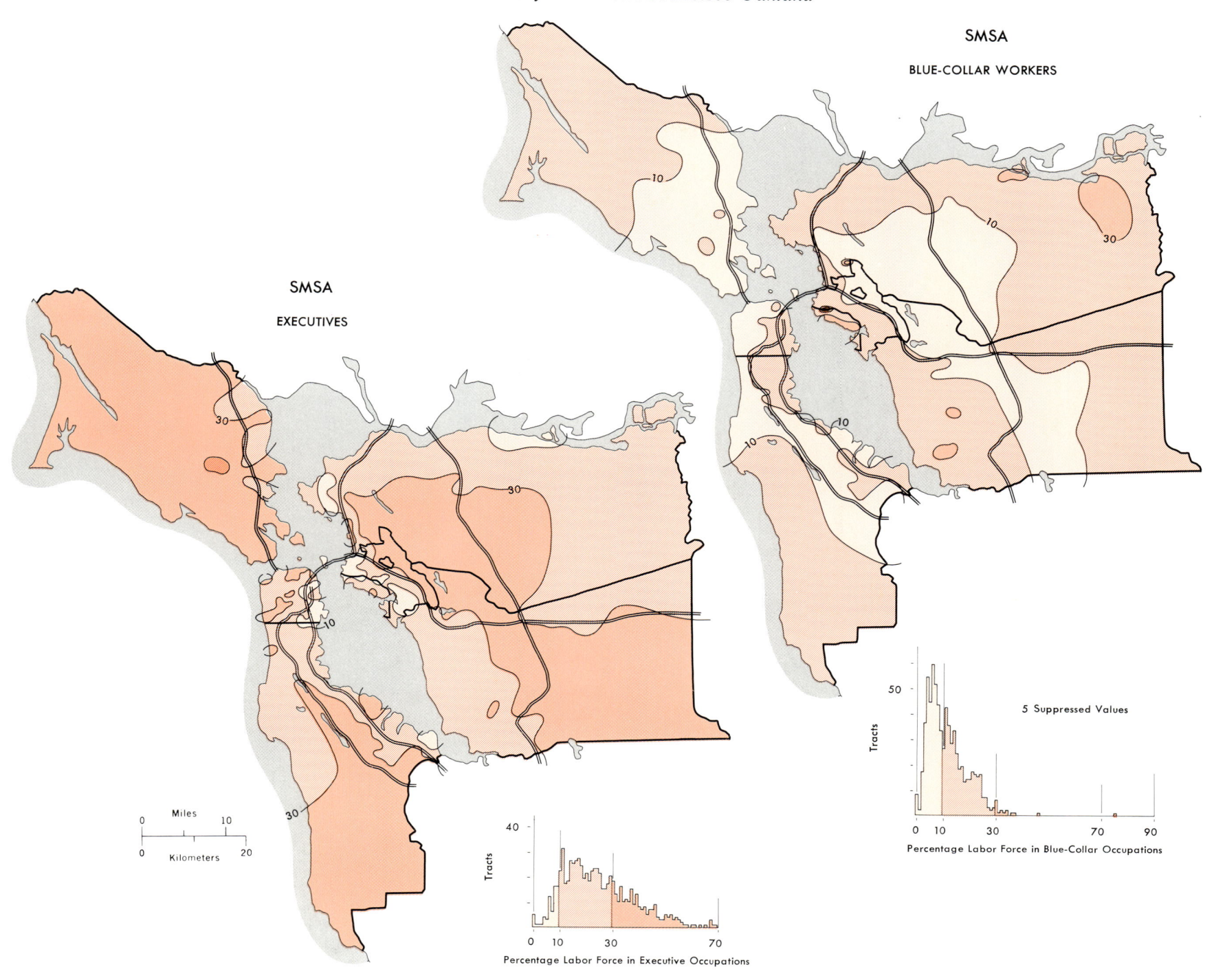

## SOCIOECONOMIC CHARACTERISTICS

**Household Size.** There are 2.8 people in the average SMSA household, 2.3 in the average San Francisco household, and 2.5 in the average Oakland household. West Coast metropolitan areas and central cities have small household sizes. San Francisco's SMSA mean of 2.8 is the same as the average for the Los Angeles SMSA, and the two are the lowest values among the 20 regions mapped in the atlas. The 2.3 mean for San Francisco is the smallest household size among central cities. Individual tracts have mean household sizes from just over one person to 5.1 persons. The high value is a tract consisting almost entirely of large young families in north-central Alameda County. Households are large in areas where there is new housing which attracts young families. The central cities have disproportionate numbers of small households because suburban areas attract families in their child-raising years.

**Female Headship.** The Census Bureau defines a family headed by a female as one in which no male spouse is present, regardless of the sex of the household's breadwinner. Twelve percent of the SMSA's households are headed by females, a percentage that increases to 17 in both San Francisco and Oakland. The two cities have 46 percent of the SMSA's families headed by females. The tendency for female headship to be concentrated in black areas is evident, but less strongly than is true in eastern cities.

**Occupations.** Eleven percent of the SMSA's labor force work at blue-collar occupations (laborers and operatives) and 25 percent are executives (engineers, teachers, professionals, managers, proprietors, and administrators). The remaining 64 percent are service (33 percent) and clerical (31 percent) workers. San Francisco has fewer blue-collar workers (9 percent), reflecting its traditional role as the West Coast's business and financial center; 13 percent of Oakland's labor force work at blue-collar occupations. Executives are more common outside the central cities than within them; whereas 25 percent of the total SMSA labor force are executives, the percentage falls to 22 percent in San Francisco and 21 percent in Oakland. Individual tract values for blue-collar workers range from zero to 75 percent; the latter is a small tract (20 workers) in Oakland's dock area. Executives constitute from zero to 69 percent of tract labor forces, with the highest percentages located near the University of California at Berkeley, (north of Oakland), and in central San Mateo County.

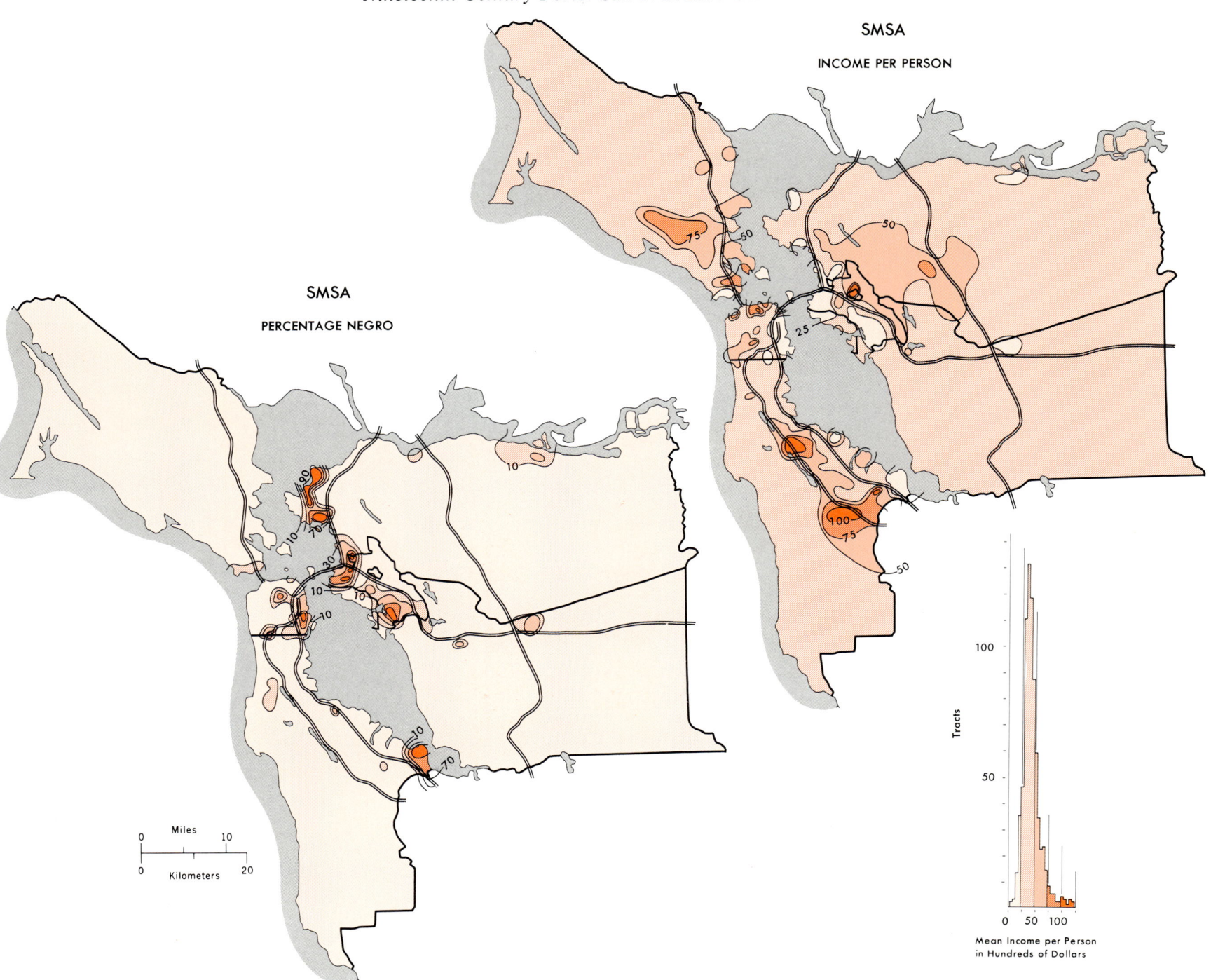

**Income.** The mean SMSA income per person of $4,100 per year is second only to Washington, D.C.'s mean of $4,275 among the 24 SMSAs in the atlas. San Francisco's per person income of $4,300 is higher than any other city's and Oakland's $3,650 ranks among the 5 most affluent. On the whole, the region's residents are well off, but there are large departures from the mean in both directions; individual tract means range from $500 to $12,000. There is considerable diversity within the two cities; both have tracts with incomes under $2,000 and over $10,000. Black areas are often low-income areas, except for the Ingleside community along San Francisco's southern boundary. Affluent residents occupy San Francisco's Pacific Heights and Oakland's enclave of Piedmont. Outside the two cities notable clusters of affluence occur in Marin and central San Mateo counties. See related maps on pp. 415, 423, and 431.

## TOPICS OF SPECIAL INTEREST IN THE SAN FRANCISCO-OAKLAND REGION

**Negro Population.** (The histogram for this map is on p. 383.) Eleven percent of the SMSA population is black, and 67 percent of the SMSA's 330,000 blacks live in San Francisco (29 percent) and Oakland (38 percent). The region's blacks are well off in comparison with the national average: their median family income is $7,970 and the median for all blacks in metropolitan areas is $6,830. Locally blacks are considerably less prosperous than whites, whose median family income is $11,800, or Spanish-Americans, whose median family income is $10,460. For a variety of reasons, blacks remain poor; 20 percent of all black families and 23 percent of all blacks have incomes below the poverty level.

As long as blacks continue to lack the means needed for equitable participation in daily urban life, and, more important, the health, skills, and education prerequisite to earning the means, concentrations of blacks will typically be human problem areas within metropolitan regions. The severity of these problems for Bay Area governments is somewhat reduced by the existence of several distinct clusters of black population. For the most part, black residential neighborhoods are located near blue-collar employment opportunities that occupy the Bay shores. Jobs in the region's shipyards were important in attracting blacks to the Bay Area during World War II.

**Unemployment.** (An SMSA map of this variable is on p. 409.) Forty-six percent of the SMSA's unemployed males live in San

## Nineteenth-Century Ports: San Francisco-Oakland

**CITY**
PERCENTAGE UNEMPLOYED MALES

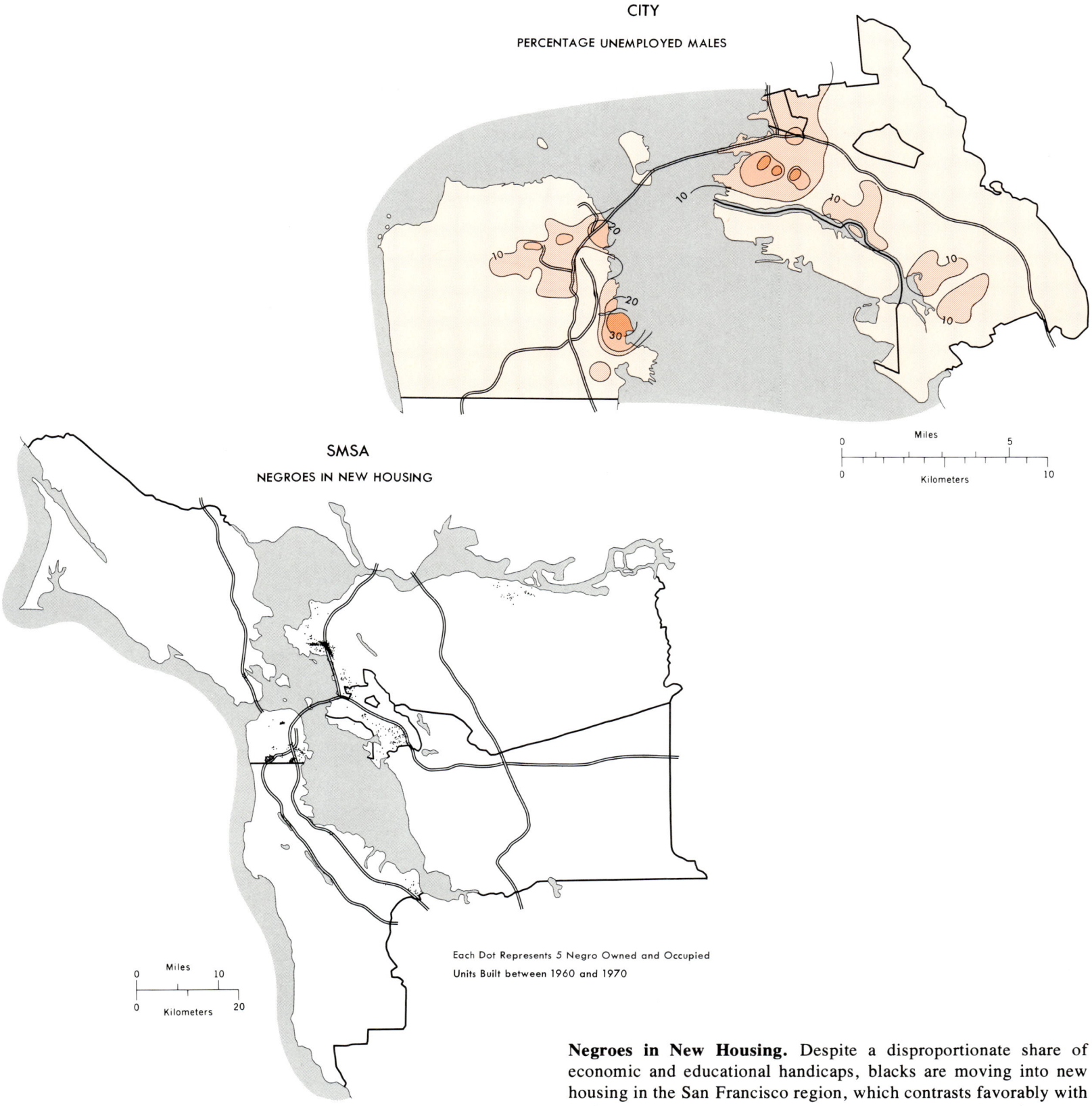

**SMSA**
NEGROES IN NEW HOUSING

Each Dot Represents 5 Negro Owned and Occupied Units Built between 1960 and 1970

Francisco and Oakland. Currently 5,500 (27 percent) of San Francisco-Oakland's 20,700 unemployed are black, whereas blacks are but 20 percent of the two cities' combined populations. The problems faced by the poorly educated (47 percent of blacks 25 years old or over are high-school graduates versus 66 percent of whites in that age group) are emphasized by the incidence of high unemployment rates in black areas. Virtually all tracts where unemployment rates exceed 10 percent are tracts where blacks predominate or are significant minorities. As the SMSA employment base continues to shift toward white-collar work requiring high degrees of literacy and numerical skill, many of those currently unemployed will be increasingly unqualified for jobs in the region's growth industries.

**Negroes in New Housing.** Despite a disproportionate share of economic and educational handicaps, blacks are moving into new housing in the San Francisco region, which contrasts favorably with their absence from such housing in some metropolitan regions (pp. 381-388). Blacks occupy 6 percent of the 280,000 housing units in the SMSA built from 1960 to March 1970, and they *own* and occupy 1.5 percent of them. Most units are in black neighborhoods, but a few are located in suburban tracts away from predominantly black areas. Within central cities and the older black community of Richmond (north of Oakland), many units are replacements for dilapidated housing that has been demolished. Blacks are participating in the general housing market in the Ingleside area along San Francisco's southern boundary and in northern Richmond.

**Public Transportation.** (The histogram for this variable is on p. 319.) The Bay Area has completed a 75-mile (120-kilometer) fixed-rail transportation system whose success is subject to debate. In contrast to other metropolitan areas (pp. 317-324) a large number

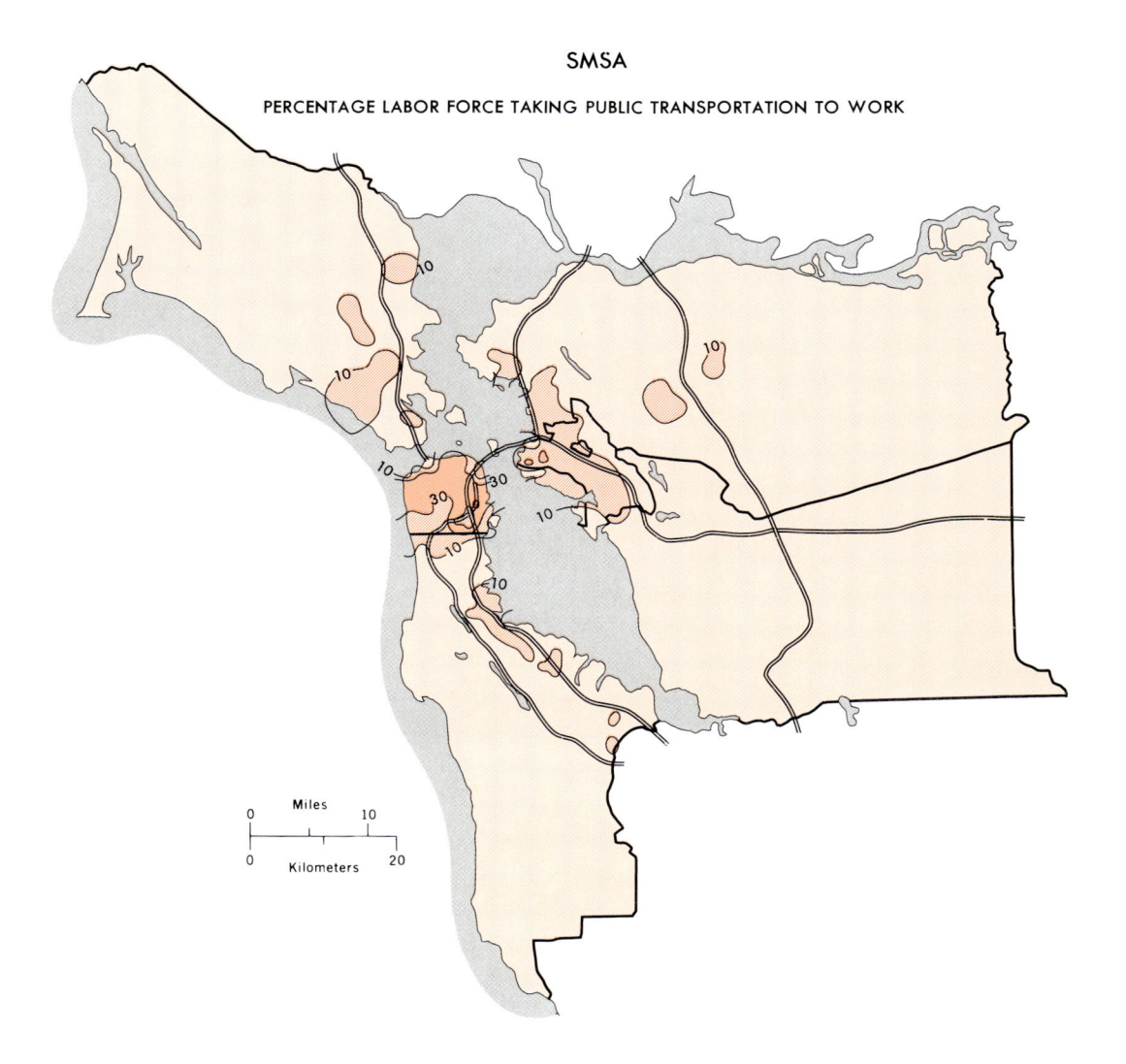

## SMSA
### PERCENTAGE LABOR FORCE TAKING PUBLIC TRANSPORTATION TO WORK

(192,000) of the region's workers currently use public transportation to get to their jobs. Yet that number is only 15 percent of all workers, and it is unclear whether the Bay Area Rapid Transit (BART) trains can lure enough of the region's 929,000 automobile commuters to keep the system from sustaining massive losses. Hopes that the network will succeed are based on the concentration of jobs in San Francisco and the congestion that ensues for people commuting from San Mateo or via the San Francisco-Oakland Bay Bridge from the East Bay Area. San Francisco is the place of work for 36 percent of the SMSA's employees (the CBD contains 12 percent of the metropolitan total). Eight percent (34,500) of Alameda's workers and 10 percent (20,300) of Contra Costa's employees work in San Francisco. On the other hand, 7,000 San Francisco residents work in Alameda County, and 1,050 work in Contra Costa County. The motor vehicle trips and bridge crossings such commuting generated were among the incentives for building BART.

The low percentages of people now using public transportation outside the immediate San Francisco, Oakland, and Berkeley areas suggest that BART's services must be attractive to wean commuters from their cars. The fundamental geographical difficulty is that BART, like all fixed-rail systems, necessarily focuses primarily on serving downtown centers and only San Francisco shows increasing office employment. San Francisco has 36 percent of the region's jobs, but other places, most of which will be poorly served by BART, have the remaining 64 percent. Thus BART may change current commuting habits in areas well served by its trains, but overall patterns may remain much like the current map. For the most part, people who are now using public transportation either have no alternative (see the map of automobile ownership on p. 335), or receive good central-city bus service that BART will have great difficulty matching.

---

As noted at the beginning of the chapter, the San Francisco metropolitan area embraces a wider variety of physical conditions than any other American metropolitan area. Its human geography is a good match for its physical environments. The city of San Francisco is a 19th-century port—like New Orleans and Baltimore—but one that arose amidst a Spanish-speaking population. Railroads stimulated the growth of East Bay communities. Asians, blacks, and large doses of youthful in-migration have produced a heady cultural vintage. It is no accident that much of the social innovation and protest that simultaneously amused, bemused, and perplexed the nation for the last quarter century originated in the Bay Area.

## C. Nineteenth-Century Inland Centers and Ports

Pittsburgh
St. Louis
Cleveland
Chicago
Detroit
Minneapolis-St. Paul
Seattle

# CHAPTER 13

# Pittsburgh

*Pittsburgh is undoubtedly the cockeyedest city in the United States. Physically, it is absolutely irrational.*

ERNIE PYLE, "Home Country," 1947

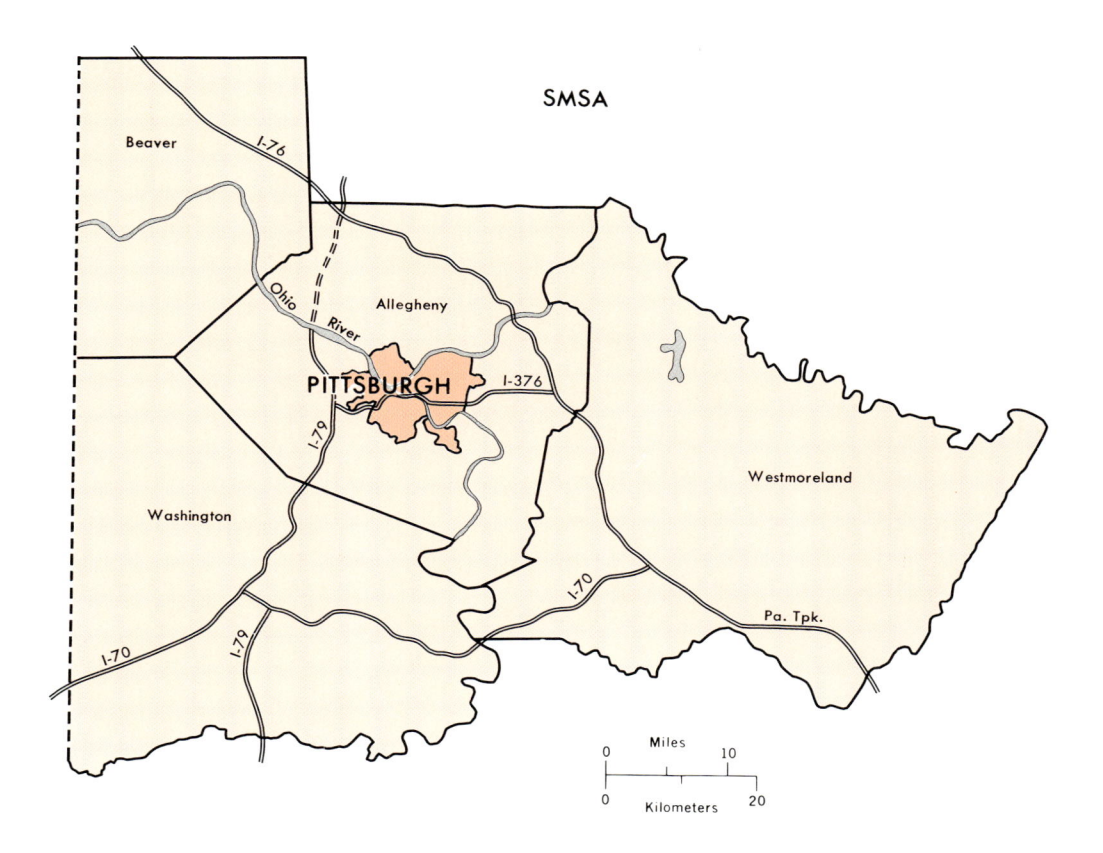

The Pittsburgh Standard Metropolitan Statistical Area (SMSA) is the 9th most populous SMSA in the nation with a population of 2,401,000. Allegheny County (1,605,000 or 67 percent) contains the bulk of the SMSA population with Westmoreland (377,000 or 16 percent), Washington (211,000 or 9 percent), and Beaver (208,000 or 9 percent) counties following in order. The Pittsburgh Daily Urban System (DUS) defined by counties that have at least 5 percent of their labor forces working in Allegheny County includes the four SMSA counties plus Butler, Armstrong, and Fayette counties (p. 106) for a total DUS population of 2,760,000. The Pittsburgh DUS is the 10th largest in the nation.

Pittsburgh is located where the Allegheny and Monongahela rivers meet to form the Ohio. The city's early fortunes were based on its role as the gateway to the Ohio Valley interior. As canal and rail transportation cut into river traffic, Pittsburgh elaborated its traditional manufacturing industries. Some of the richest coal deposits

*Note:* All data are from the 1970 Censuses of Population and Housing unless otherwise indicated. Therefore the present tense refers to 1970 data except for income data which are from 1969. Cartographic conventions are explained in Chapter 1.

in the world are in the area, and Pittsburgh used them—in conjunction first with local iron ores and later with ores imported from the Great Lakes region—to build a heavy industrial economy. In so doing it was able to retain its position near the top of the nation's metropolitan hierarchy throughout the 19th and early 20th centuries (p. 10). The region's specialization in iron and steel, metal fabrication, and machine manufacture was a major asset up to and through World War II, but the national economy has since become more service oriented at the same time that the focus of iron and steel production has shifted toward new markets in the West and South. Pittsburgh was the first large U.S. metropolitan area to decline. The SMSA lost 4,100 people between 1960 and 1970. It dropped from 6th in the nation to its current 9th between 1950 and 1970. Losses in Pittsburgh City have been more serious; Pittsburgh lost 24 percent of its population during the last two decades, the decrease during the 1960s alone being from 604,000 to 520,000. The city now has 22 percent of the SMSA population.

The urban region is located in a deeply dissected area that has hilly terrain with steep gradients between stream bottoms and adjacent uplands. The Laurel Hill uplands on the eastern margin of the SMSA

## Nineteenth-Century Inland Centers and Ports: Pittsburgh

reach elevations of 3,000 feet (900 meters). Elevations within the city range from 700 to 1,300 feet (200 to 400 meters). Large areas of flat land are in limited supply, generally being confined to narrow terraces along the rivers. River lowlands are subject to flooding, but their suitability for large-scale manufacturing operations and the unsuitability of rougher terrain for such activities have produced a "two-story" land-use pattern in which the rivers are lined with heavy industrial facilities and houses cling precariously to the adjacent steep hills. The river valleys act as traps for pollutants generated by the low-lying industries and thus create one of the SMSA's traditional environmental problems.

### HOUSING

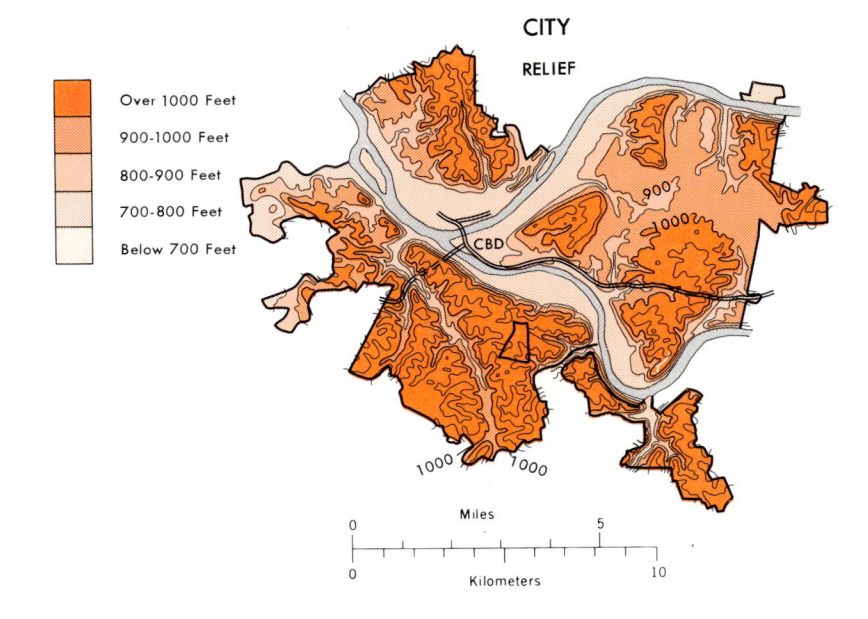

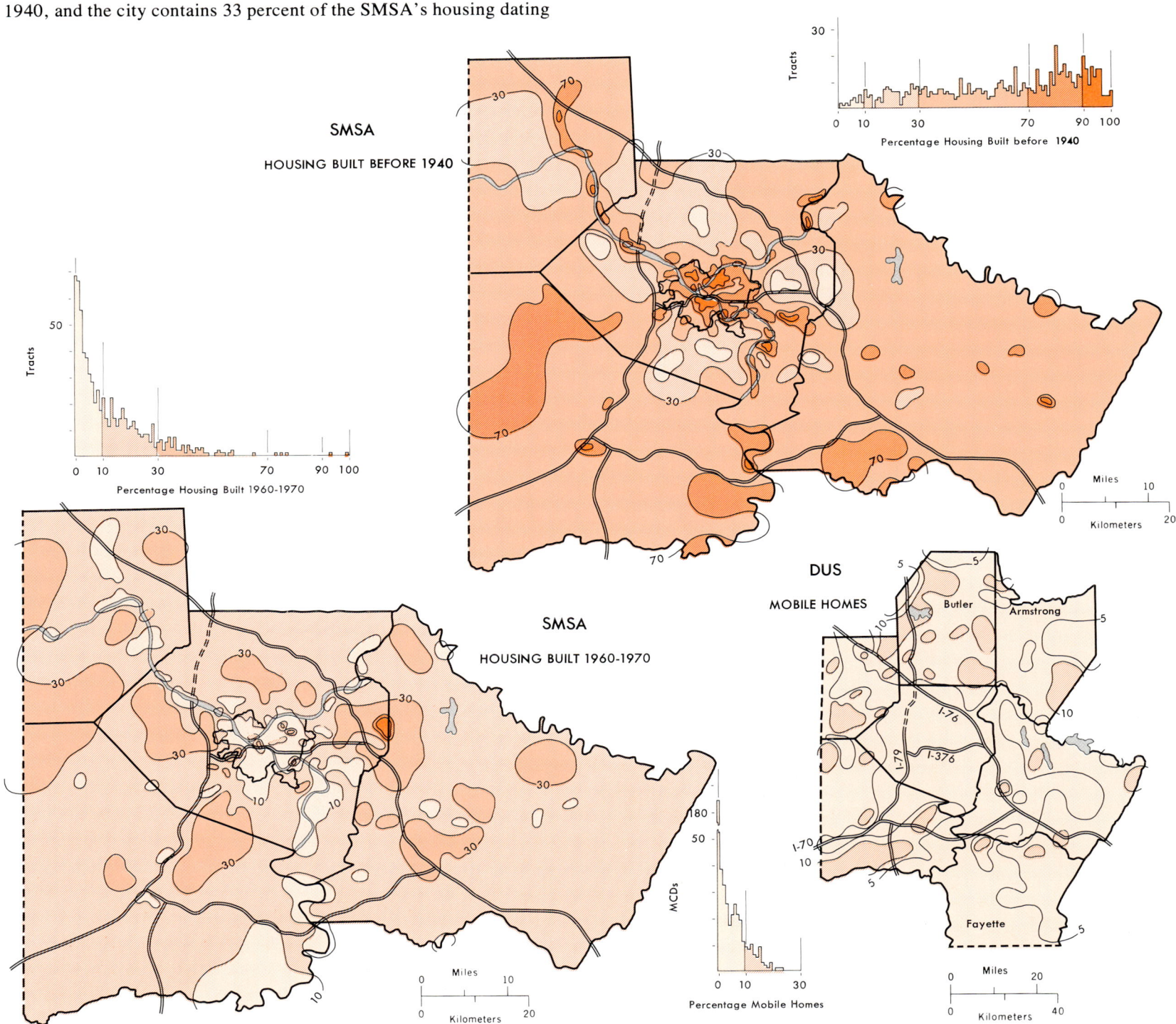

**Housing Age.** Over half (54 percent) of the SMSA's units predate 1940, and only 15 percent were built in the 1960s; the residual 31 percent were constructed from 1940 through 1959. Old housing is concentrated in Pittsburgh and the older industrial towns along the rivers. Three-fourths of Pittsburgh's housing units were built before 1940, and the city contains 33 percent of the SMSA's housing dating from that era. Proportions rise over 70 percent in isolated rural areas of Washington County that have not yet experienced rapid suburban growth. Within Pittsburgh and other industrial towns, row houses built for millworkers in the early 20th century are still in use in some places. Hillside houses, built in high-density patches and connected by publicly maintained stairways, are distinctive of Pittsburgh.

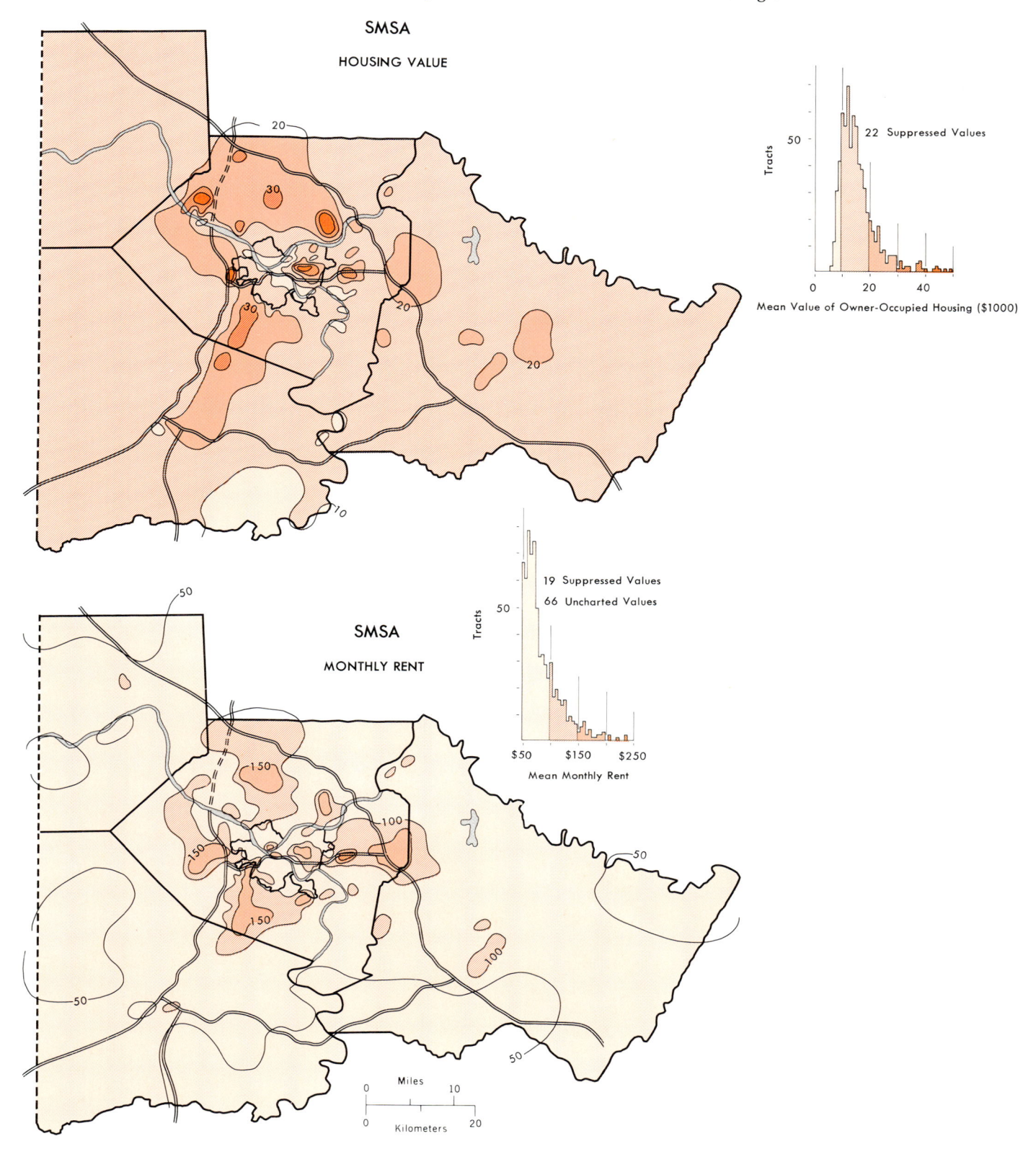

The sixth of the region's housing that was built in the 1960s is almost wholly suburban. Eighty-eight percent of the new housing units were built outside the city. Many of the 13,700 units built in the city in the 1960s are publicly subsidized, and they did not replace the larger number of units that were demolished. The terrain, much of which is unusable because of slope, makes large housing developments impractical; tracts in which more than 30 percent of the housing units were built during the 1960s are rare, and only 5 exceed 70 percent. Patterns of housing age, and patterns of income and life-style that are related to them, occur in fragments rather than in continuous belts.

**Mobile Homes.** There are 15,800 mobile homes in the DUS, comprising 1.7 percent of the region's housing stock. Mobile homes are unimportant in most of the SMSA counties but are a feasible alternative in the next tier of counties outward from the metropolitan core. Mobile homes are 6.1 percent of Armstrong County's housing units, 4.6 of Butler's, and 3.3 percent of Fayette's units.

**Single-Unit Detached Housing.** Single-family houses make up 66 percent of the SMSA's housing stock but only 39 percent of the housing units in Pittsburgh. Row houses (13 percent), duplexes (15 percent), and small apartment buildings (11 percent) provide another

## SMSA
### SINGLE UNIT HOUSING

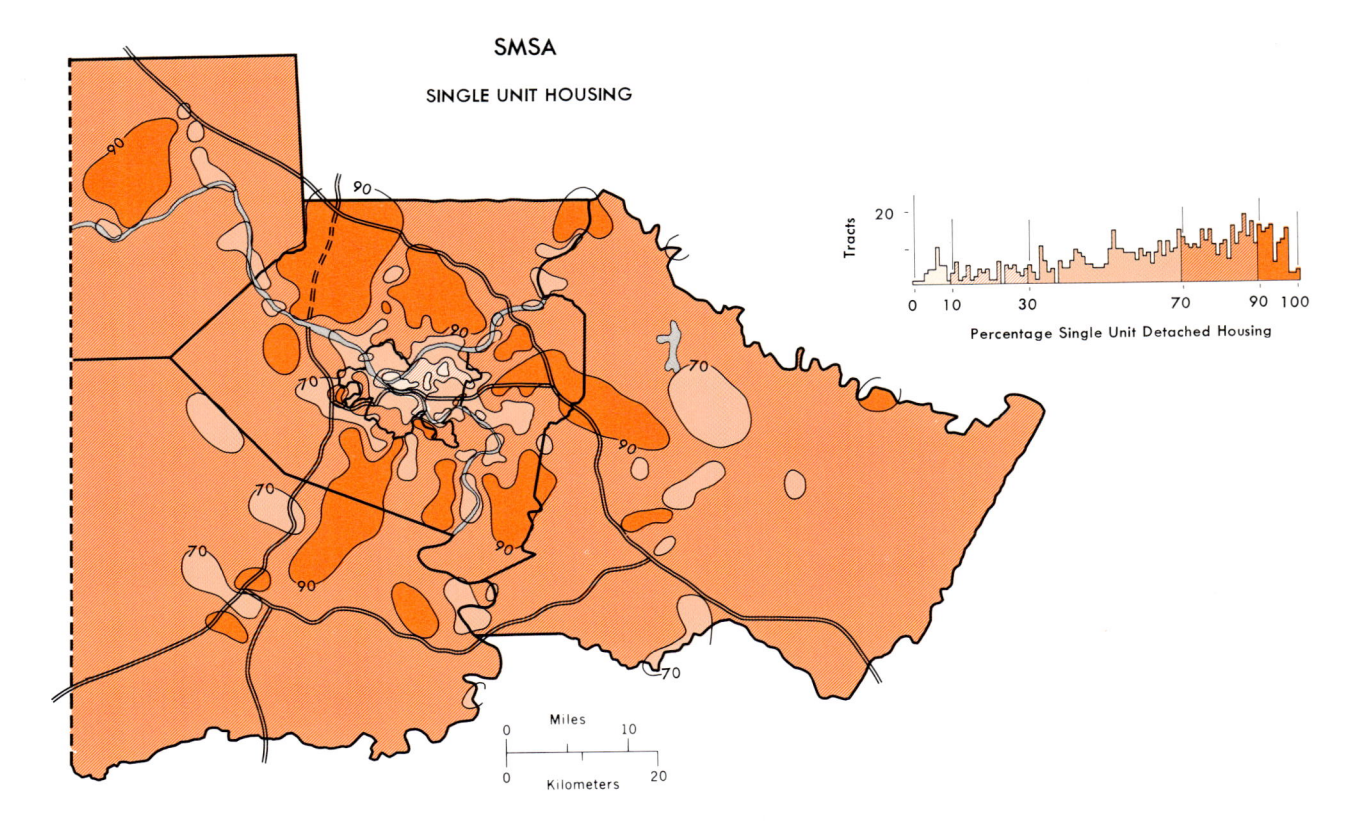

39 percent of the city's units. The remaining 22 percent are in structures with 5 or more units. Outside the central-city area where single-unit dwellings are usually less than 10 percent of all units, high and low values occur in patches. Major clusters of dominantly single-unit tracts are interspersed with smaller areas where values drop below 70 percent. Topography and the peculiarities of the Pittsburgh region's participation in housing cycles have produced irregular pockets of different kinds of housing in contrast to the broad swaths characteristic of other metropolitan areas.

**Housing Value and Rent.** The mean value for owner-occupied housing in the Pittsburgh SMSA is $17,000. The corresponding figure for the city is $15,000. Tract means range from $6,000 to $49,000, with most of the tracts below $10,000 concentrated in Pittsburgh or one of the older industrial river towns. Within Pittsburgh there are sharp value differences between housing along the rivers and the more expensive housing in the eastern part of the city around Squirrel Hill, where some tract means exceed $50,000. Outside the city the axes of high-value housing are clearly to the north, west, and southwest, with very little high-value housing in Westmoreland County to the east. The sectors to the southwest and northwest began in the city, where hilltop sites were often relatively free of pollution because of the prevailing west-to-east winds.

Mean monthly contract rentals average $89 for the SMSA; in Pittsburgh City the average is $95. SMSA rentals are usually higher than central-city rentals. The reverse is true in Pittsburgh because of the large number of tracts with rentals below $50 (the 66 ungraphed tracts) on the SMSA's periphery. The prestige rental areas to the north, northwest, and southwest are evident on the rental map, as is the Squirrel Hill area within the city. But a belt of relatively high-cost housing extending east of the city appears more clearly on the rental map than on the housing-value map. The SMSA's highest rentals are charged in the Churchill area east of the Pittsburgh municipal boundary. (See pp. 296 and 304 for maps that relate value and rent to income.) However, the number of rental units there is small.

## THE PEOPLE

**Population Density.** The overall population density of Pittsburgh City is 9,400 people per square mile (3,600 per square kilometer). Individual tract densities range from less than 1,000 to 34,000 per square mile (386 to 13,100 per square kilometer). The inclusion of nonresidential areas in the density calculations means that actual residential densities in some parts of the city are considerably higher than gross densities. The highest densities occur in the residential areas adjacent to the Central Business District (CBD), across the Allegheny in the North Side and Spring Hill neighborhoods, and in the Point Breeze area on the city's east side. Upland areas away from the rivers are usually settled at lower densities (p. 106), although in some places high-density settlement continues up and down sharp gradients producing vistas of houses clinging to steep slopes. Population densities are highest in the city and fall away rapidly outward from the city boundaries. (The SMSA map is on p. 312.)

**Age and the Elderly.** The Pittsburgh SMSA has a high median age, 32 years. The city's median age of 34 years is second to Miami City's 37. Significant population losses throughout the region since 1950 have left a relatively old population produced by the migration of many young adults out of the region. The city's population pyramid shows large portions of the population in the over-40 and under-20 cohorts. This highly unusual pyramid is partially a function of racial differences in settlement and migration. The elderly population is mostly white and composed of people who prefer to stay or cannot leave the city. The younger population is more likely to be black. Without blacks, the city's median age would be higher than it is. Indeed, most of the tracts with median ages below 20 years are located in areas where blacks form a majority or large minority (p. 110). Median ages for individual tracts range from less than 20 to over 50 years. Tracts with median ages over 50 are usually institutionalized populations.

People 64 years of age and older are 11 percent of the SMSA population and 13 percent of Pittsburgh's people. In old industrial river towns, the elderly are often present in sufficient numbers to raise local median ages over 40 years. Some of the elderly are almost completely dependent on public assistance, and local concentrations can become serious social problems, for a fourth of the SMSA's people over 64 have incomes below the poverty level. (See related maps on pp. 416, 424, and 432.)

**Sex Ratio.** There are 1.1 females for each male in the SMSA, which yields a female-dominant sex ratio (males divided by females times

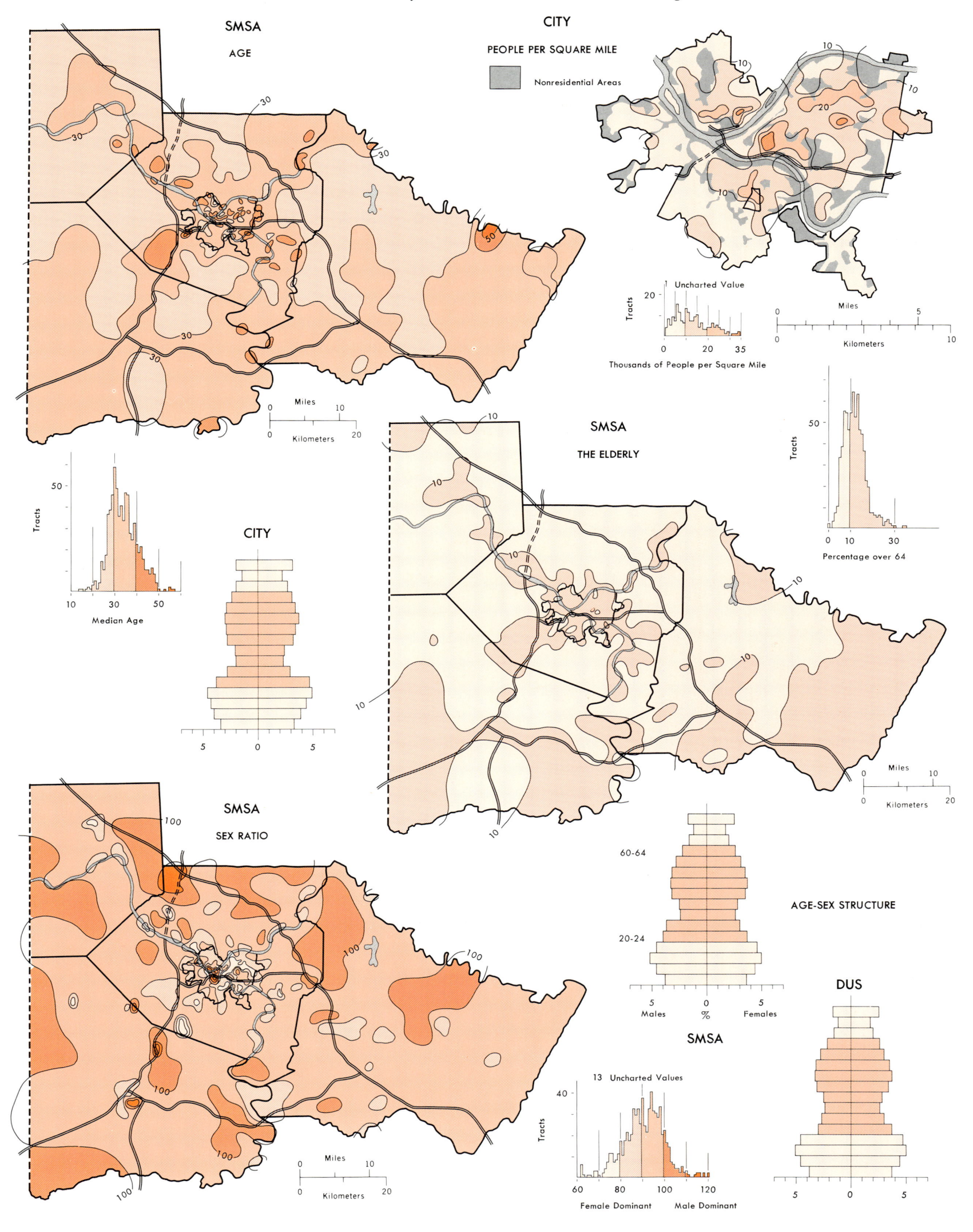

# Nineteenth-Century Inland Centers and Ports: Pittsburgh

## SMSA
### AGE

## CITY
### PEOPLE PER SQUARE MILE
Nonresidential Areas

Thousands of People per Square Mile

Median Age

## CITY

## SMSA
### THE ELDERLY

Percentage over 64

## SMSA
### SEX RATIO

### AGE-SEX STRUCTURE

### DUS

### SMSA
Female Dominant — Male Dominant

109

## Nineteenth-Century Inland Centers and Ports: Pittsburgh

### SMSA
POLISH-AMERICANS

Each Black Dot Represents 50 Polish Born
Each Orange Dot Represents 50 People of Polish Parentage

### CITY
PERCENTAGE NEGRO

63 Suppressed Values

### SMSA
ITALIAN-AMERICANS

Each Black Dot Represents 50 Italian Born
Each Orange Dot Represents 50 People of Italian Parentage

### CITY
PERCENTAGE SPANISH-AMERICAN

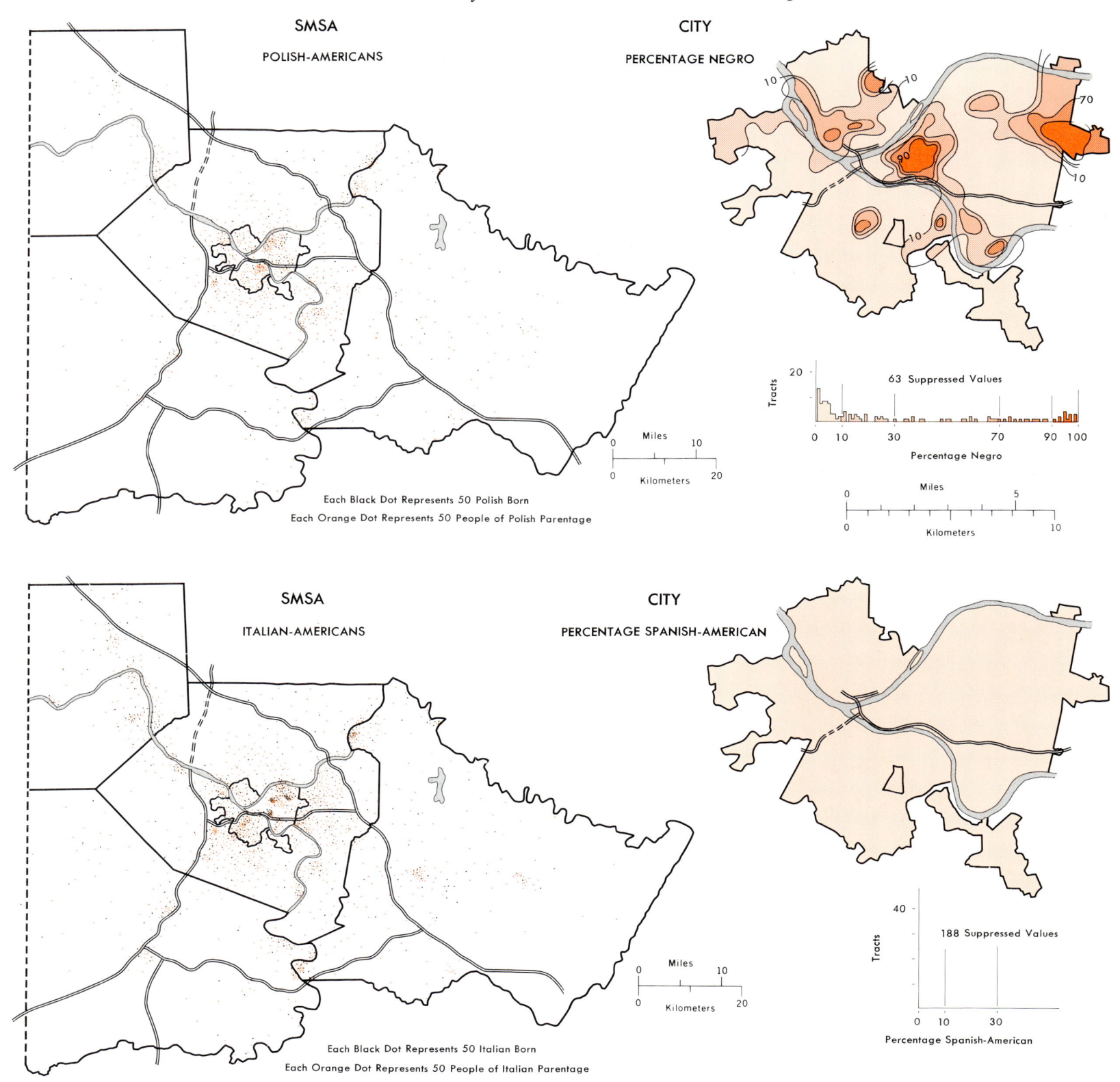

188 Suppressed Values

100) of 91. Pittsburgh's sex ratio is 87. Tract sex ratios range from 62 to well over 120, but ratios less than 70 or over 120 are usually the result of sex-segregated public institutions or military facilities. Outside the central-city area that is below 90, sex ratios are patchy reflections of local housing conditions and settlement history; areas with new housing are less female-dominant than areas with older housing stocks, especially tracts in the industrial towns along the rivers.

**Negroes.** The 105,000 blacks in Pittsburgh make up 20 percent of the city's people. Blacks are highly concentrated in the city, for 62 percent of the SMSA's black population lives in Pittsburgh, which has only 22 percent of the total SMSA population. Blacks make up one to 99 percent of individual tract populations. The 63 suppressed tracts would be rounded zero values if percentages were calculated, but they are suppressed because there are few blacks within them. That blacks and whites are segregated in Pittsburgh is evident in the bimodal nature of the histogram. The few tracts in the middle of the histogram are shifting from white to black and are not stable residential neighborhoods.

Blacks were recruited from the South during the World War I industrial boom. Most blacks took up low-cost central-city housing that was being discarded by European immigrants (especially Jews). The Hill District, east of the CBD, is the largest black neighborhood. It was formerly occupied by Russian Jews who began to leave the area after 1920. The East Liberty-Homewood-Brushton area on the city's east side is the second largest concentration, and the Manchester area north of the Allegheny-Ohio is the third major concentration. The cluster of blacks in the Beltzhoover neighborhood west of the enclave of Mt. Oliver is more affluent than is usually true of black

*110*

## SMSA
### FAMILIES WITH A FEMALE HEAD

Percentage Families with a Female Head

## SMSA
### HOUSEHOLD SIZE

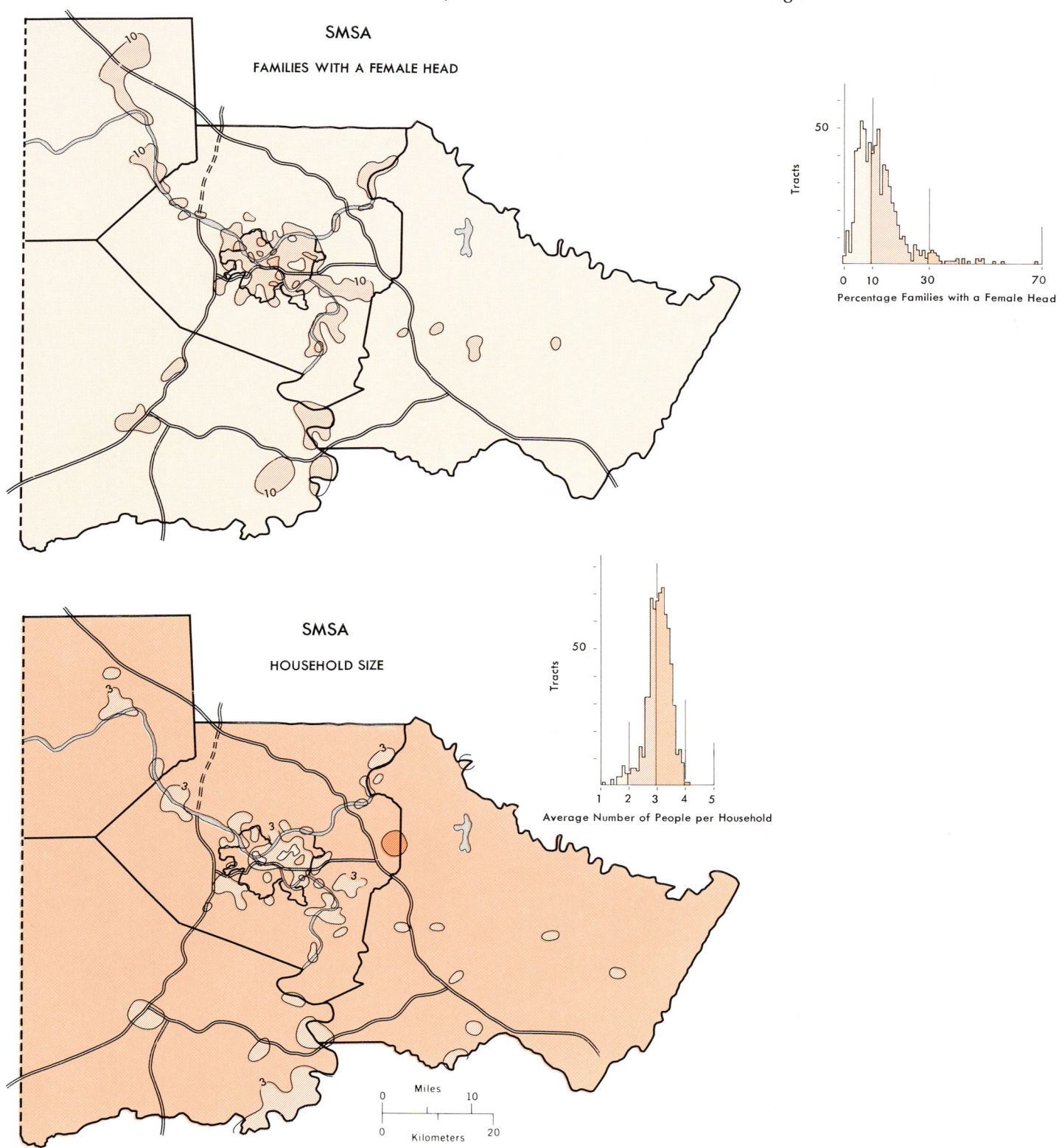

Average Number of People per Household

neighborhoods in Pittsburgh. The two tracts have median family incomes for blacks of $7,500 and $8,800 in contrast to the $6,100 median for all Pittsburgh's black families. Only 16 percent of the two tracts' people have incomes below the poverty level, as opposed to 31 percent of the city's total black population. (The SMSA map of black population is on p. 394.)

**Spanish-Americans.** There are few Spanish-Americans in Pittsburgh; 2,800 live in the city, of whom 120 are of Puerto Rican birth or parentage and 120 are of Cuban stock originally. About 1,500 are Mexican and Latin-American foreign stock, which means that the remaining 1,060 are indigenous Mexican-Americans. No tract contains more than 150 Spanish-Americans, and they never constitute as much as 3 percent of a tract population.

**Italian-Americans.** Italian-born (26,600) and people with at least one Italian-born parent (93,600) are the largest foreign-stock group, comprising 5 percent of the SMSA population. The SMSA's Italian-American community is distributed much the same as is the total population. Pittsburgh contains 21 percent of the SMSA's Italian-Americans and 20 percent of the total population. Within the city, the absence of Italians in predominantly black areas and the dense cluster in the Bloomfield neighborhood are notable.

**Polish-Americans.** There are 9,700 Polish-born and 54,600 people of Polish parentage in the SMSA. Together they constitute 2.7 percent of the SMSA population. There is always some question whether Polish foreign stock are ethnic Poles or Polish Jews. Much more than is true in East Coast cities, Polish foreign stock can safely be designated Polish ethnics in Pittsburgh and Detroit, where employment opportunities in heavy industry attracted the Polish rather than the Jewish component of immigration from central

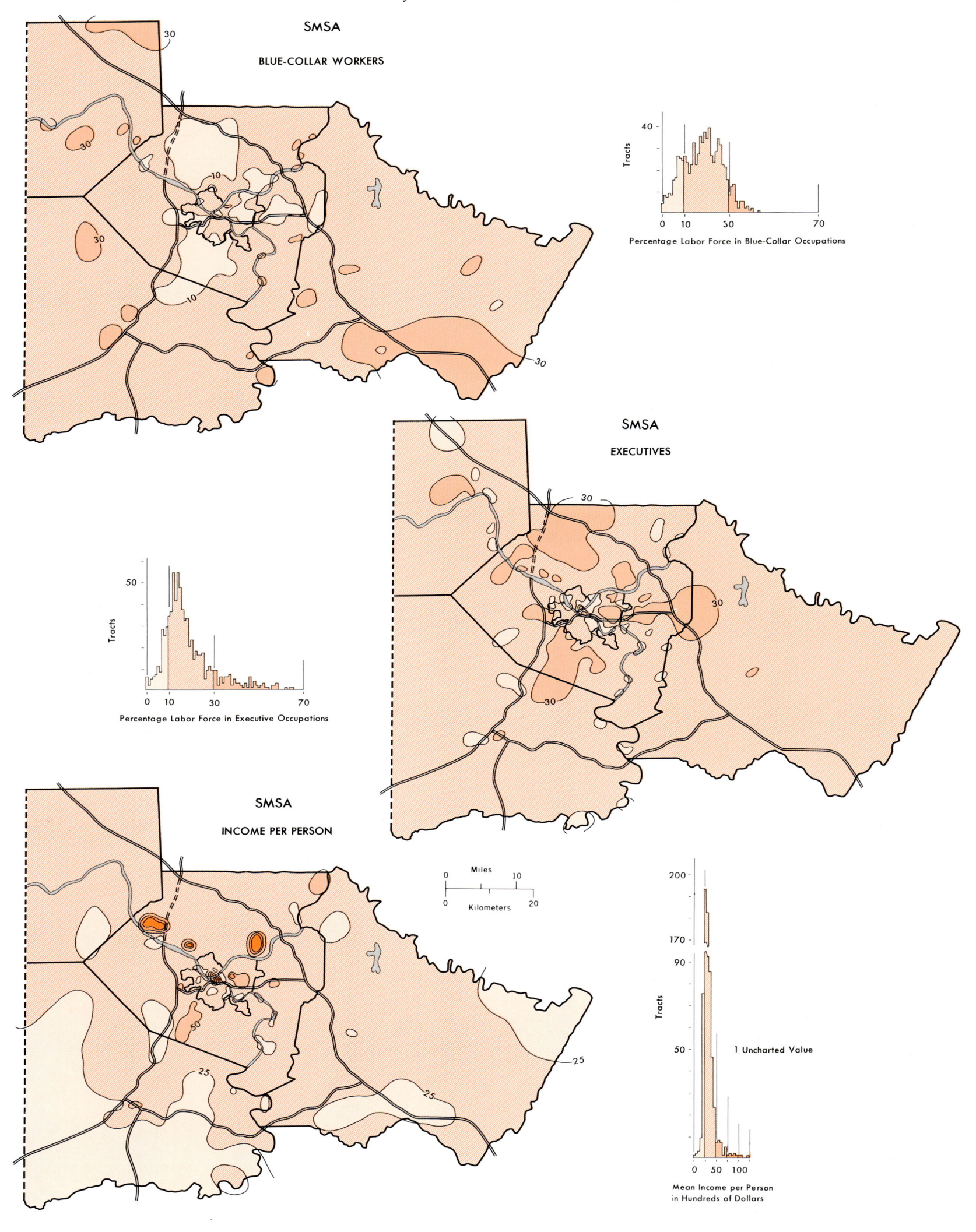

*Nineteenth-Century Inland Centers and Ports: Pittsburgh*

SMSA
BLUE-COLLAR WORKERS

Percentage Labor Force in Blue-Collar Occupations

SMSA
EXECUTIVES

Percentage Labor Force in Executive Occupations

SMSA
INCOME PER PERSON

1 Uncharted Value

Mean Income per Person in Hundreds of Dollars

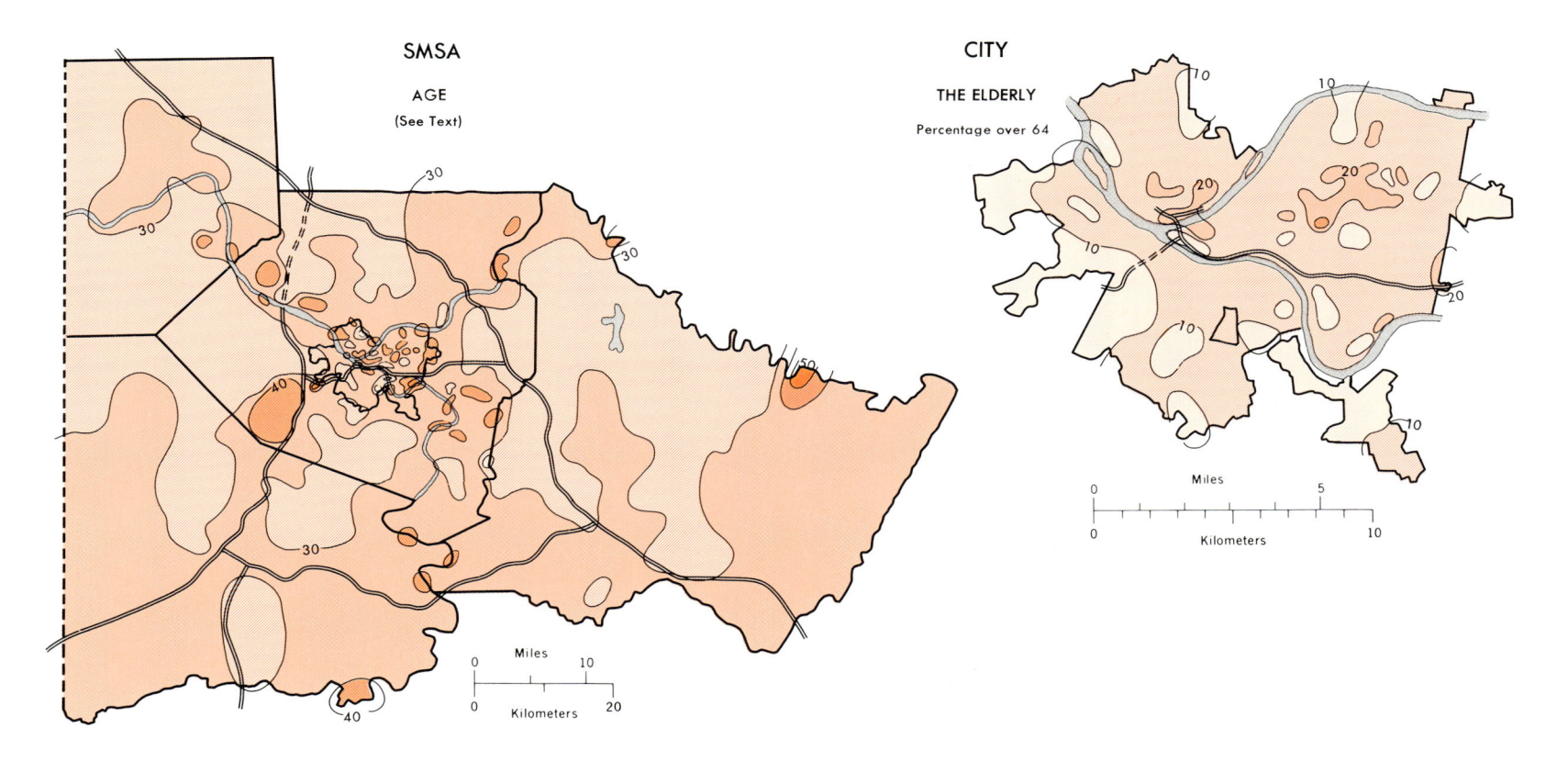

Europe. Poles are slightly concentrated in the city, which has 27 percent of the SMSA Polish foreign stock and 22 percent of the total SMSA population. Like Italians they are sparse in heavily black areas. Outside the city, Polish-Americans are distributed in accordance with total population density.

## SOCIOECONOMIC CHARACTERISTICS

**Household Size.** There are 3.1 people in the average SMSA household and 2.8 in the average Pittsburgh City household. Tract values range from just over 1 near the city's CBD to 4.1 in a heavily black tract (not mapped) on Pittsburgh's north side. Small households are more frequent among young families who have not yet had children and among older populations whose children have married and established their own households. Blacks usually have larger families than whites. At the SMSA level, black households average 3.2 people. In Pittsburgh the black average household of 3.1 people contrasts with the 2.8 average for the total city population. The migration of young people out of the Pittsburgh area is reflected in the narrow range of household sizes in comparison with western cities that are growing rapidly, where values above 4 people are common in tracts of new suburban housing.

**Female Headship.** The Census Bureau defines female headship in terms of the absence of a male spouse rather than by the sex of the household's breadwinner. A family headed by a female is one in which no male is present. In the SMSA, 11 percent of all families are headed by females; the proportion rises to 18 percent in Pittsburgh. Individual tract proportions range from zero to almost 70 percent. Female headship is high in black areas, and the highest value is for the Arlington Heights Housing Project in south-central Pittsburgh, where 302 of the tract's 442 families are headed by females. Of the 442, 225 have incomes below the poverty level. Thirty-four percent of the SMSA's families headed by females live in Pittsburgh, and 72 percent live in Allegheny County.

**Occupations.** The SMSA's civilian labor force totals 910,000 workers; 16 percent work at blue-collar (laborers and operatives) jobs, and 21 percent are executives (engineers, teachers, professionals, managers, proprietors, and administrators). The remaining 63 percent are service (37 percent) and clerical (26 percent) workers. The city has a lower proportion of blue-collar workers (13 percent) than the SMSA, which is unusual. Executives are also less important in the city (18 percent), and the difference appears in the city's larger service (40 percent) and clerical (29 percent) components.

Tract proportions of blue-collar workers range from zero to 43 percent, but percentages less than 5 and over 30 are rare. Most tracts over 30 percent occur in the industrial settlements strung along the river valleys or in rural tracts. Blue-collar workers are less than 10 percent of the labor force in the region's prestigious suburban residential districts (p. 107).

Executives make up between zero and 65 percent of individual tract labor forces. Low values appear in the black areas of Pittsburgh and in the region's industrial river towns. High values occur in and north of the CBD, in the Squirrel Hill area within Pittsburgh, and in the suburbs to the east, north, west, and southwest. Over half the workers in the heart of Squirrel Hill fall into the executive category. The low percentages of executives in Pittsburgh's black neighborhoods, despite their proximity to the many executive jobs in the CBD, are the local instance of a common feature of American cities.

**Income.** The mean income per person in the Pittsburgh SMSA is $3,200 per year, which is a low value for the SMSAs in the atlas; only the New Orleans SMSA ($2,800) is lower. However, the city's mean personal income of $3,150 is similar to means for other central cities in the atlas. Individual tract means range from values that round to zero to $12,000 per person annually. Incomes over $5,000 and approaching $10,000 per person occur in new housing facilities in the CBD renewal area, in the Allegheny Center complex across the river to the north, and in Squirrel Hill. The highest incomes accrue to residents of Fox Chapel, Sewickley Heights, and Edgeworth in Allegheny County. Incomes are less than $2,500 in scattered city tracts and in large parts of the SMSA's periphery.

## TOPICS OF SPECIAL INTEREST IN THE PITTSBURGH REGION

**Age and the Elderly.** (The histogram for the median-age map is on p. 109.) The all-too-frequent implications of being elderly are poverty and dependency. As noted earlier, Pittsburgh's median age is high (SMSA 32; city 34) as a result of selective out-migration and limited

**SMSA**

**MEAN FAMILY INCOME**

Thousands of Dollars

**SMSA**

**PERCENTAGE BLUE-COLLAR WORKERS**

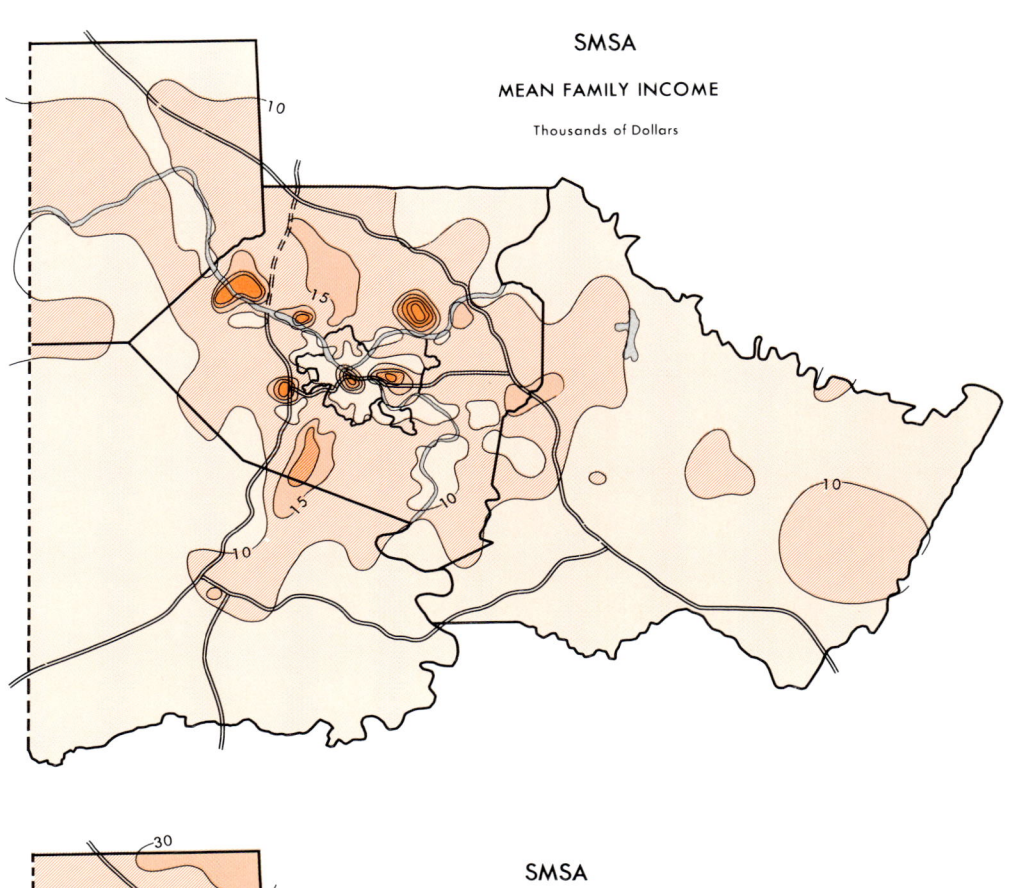

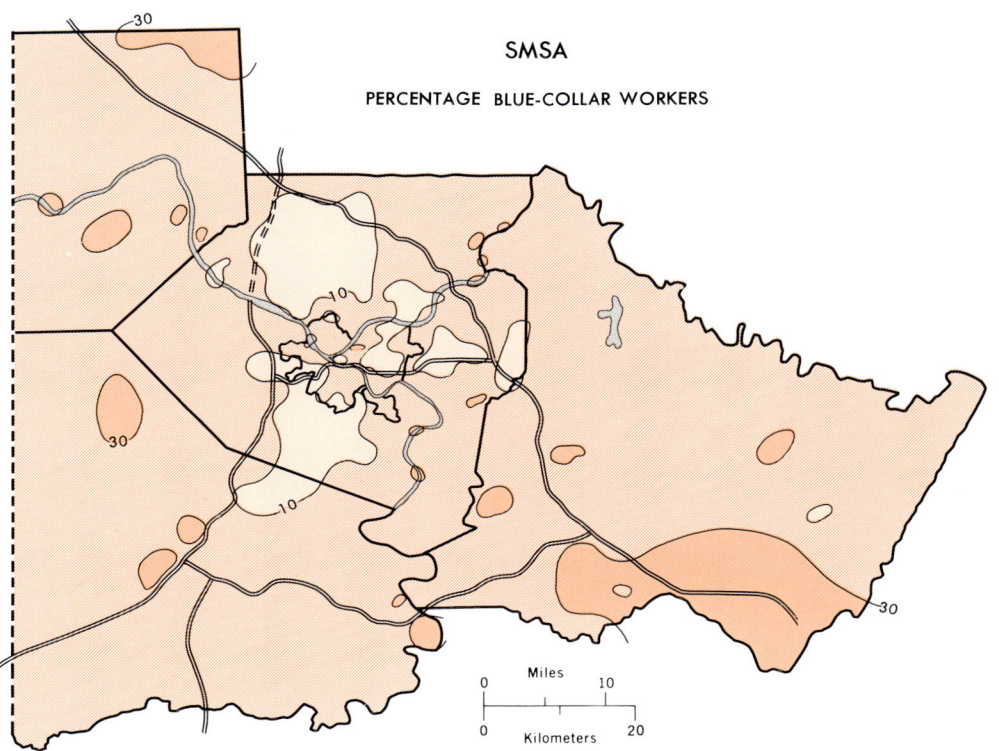

in-migration associated with the economic stagnation since 1950. Migration of young white families out of Pittsburgh City has left behind a population of older whites and young blacks. Median ages are even higher in some of the industrial towns along the river valleys where there are fewer blacks; medians over 40 years are more common in the Pittsburgh SMSA than in any of the other 23 SMSAs mapped in the atlas, with the possible exception of Miami. Older populations are often dependent. When they become concentrated by out-migration of the young they can create problems for the communities in which they live. They are often poor and depend on small fixed incomes, if not public assistance.

Such problems are especially acute among Pittsburgh's elderly. Thirteen percent of the city's population, some 70,000 people, are over 64. Of that number, 17,350 (25 percent) have incomes below the poverty level, and of that 17,350, almost 12,000 are single individuals who are usually most seriously affected by the poverty and immobility age often brings. The elderly are concentrated near the CBD in the older sections of the north side and in several tracts in east-central Pittsburgh. Sheltering, clothing, and often feeding the elderly will be a continuing problem, especially if Pittsburgh and other older population centers continue to lose the younger populations that could shoulder some of the costs of caring for the elderly.

**Income and Occupation.** Income per person (p. 112) takes into account variations in household size. Mean family income does not, but it does recognize that households are the primary consumptive

## Nineteenth-Century Inland Centers and Ports: Pittsburgh

SMSA
PERCENTAGE HOUSING BUILT BEFORE 1940

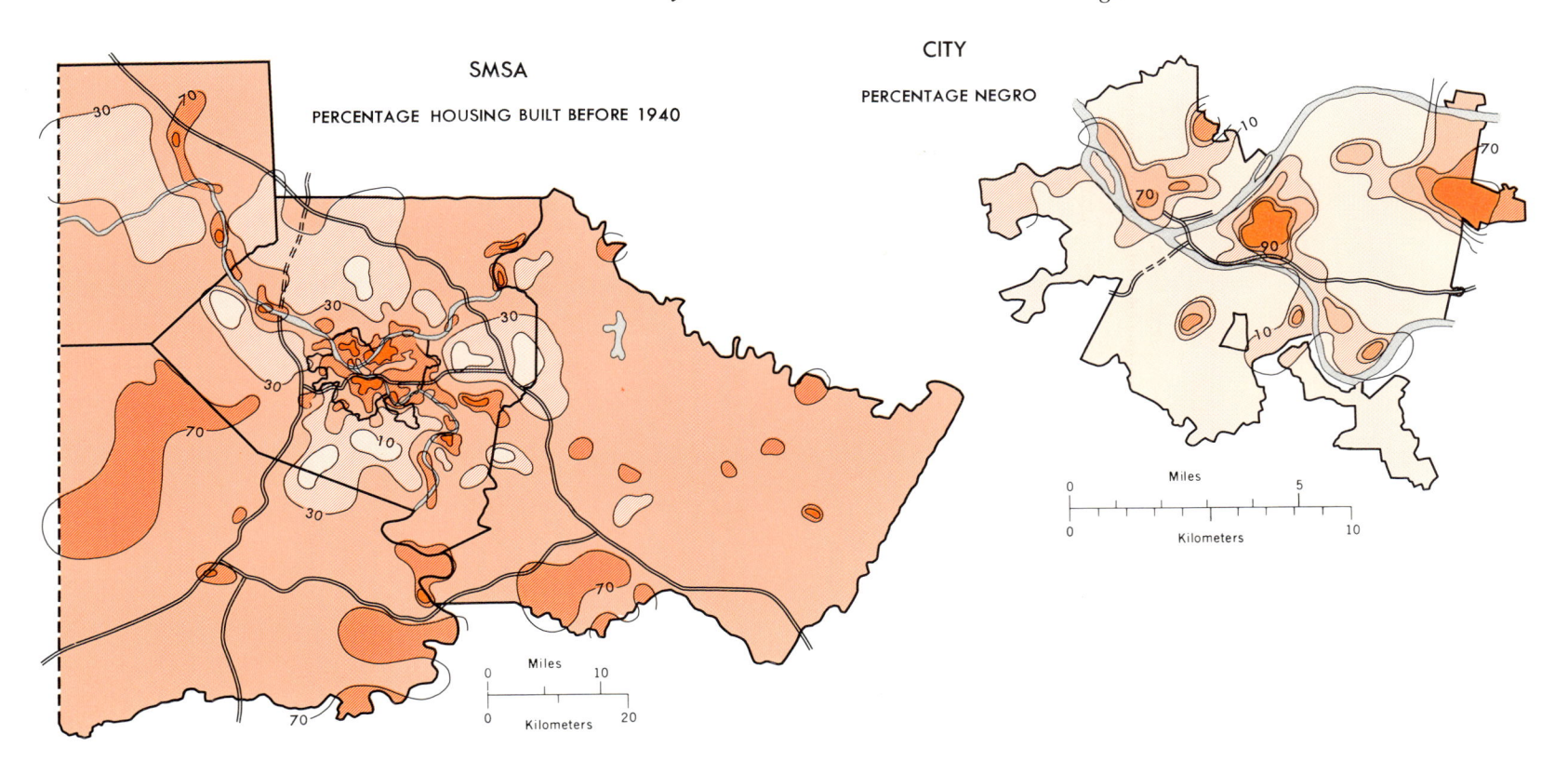

CITY
PERCENTAGE NEGRO

unit. Whichever measure is used, income is usually highly correlated with occupation. The maps of mean family income and percentage in blue-collar occupations (histogram on p. 112) show rather clearly the inverse relationship between the two variables; incomes are high where percentages of the labor force in blue-collar occupations are low. Both maps emphasize once again the fractionalized nature of the Pittsburgh region's socioeconomic geography. There are few continuous zones of either prosperity or poverty; rather, islands of both are interspersed, often in close proximity.

**Metropolitan Diversity.** The ways in which Pittsburgh's older housing stock evolved were mentioned earlier in this chapter. The map of housing built before 1940 (54 percent of the SMSA total and 74 percent of Pittsburgh City's units) repeated here emphasizes one of the SMSA's unique qualities—the many separated settlement centers scattered throughout the region. Each of the small islands of older housing represents an industrial city with its own economic and immigration history. Pittsburgh was one of the first American cities west of the Appalachians, but its human and social geography is as dissimilar from that of East Coast cities as it is from that of cities in the Midwest, where open flat land and different economic bases have produced more regular land-use patterns. The fractionalization evident at the regional scale extends into the inner city as well, for in

contrast to most places, Pittsburgh does not have a single black ghetto. Instead, blacks are scattered in three major and several minor communities that are separated by rivers and topography. The black enclaves often differ among themselves in socioeconomic status. The texture of the city and the Pittsburgh region is fine-grained, partially in response to a physical geography that is unique among large metropolitan areas.

---

How well Pittsburgh and the region will fare in the decades ahead depends on how well the area can shift economic gears. A new and shiny downtown Pittsburgh arose during the 1950s and 1960s when the region's powerful private concerns decided to clean up and rebuild the city center. The thriving Golden Triangle at the river junction and the preservation of the downtown as the business, cultural, and sports (Three Rivers Stadium) center of the metropolitan area bodes well for the city. But Pittsburgh's impressive face-lift and downtown revitalization have not overcome the city's human problems and the metropolitan area's basic dilemma of being out of step with the nation's economic evolution. Unless the region's economic foundations are shored up and population decreases are stemmed, the Golden Triangle will rest on an increasingly insecure base.

# CHAPTER 14

# St. Louis

*St. Louis is a great and prosperous and advancing city, but the river-edge of it seems dead past resurrection.*

MARK TWAIN, *Life on the Mississippi*, 1883

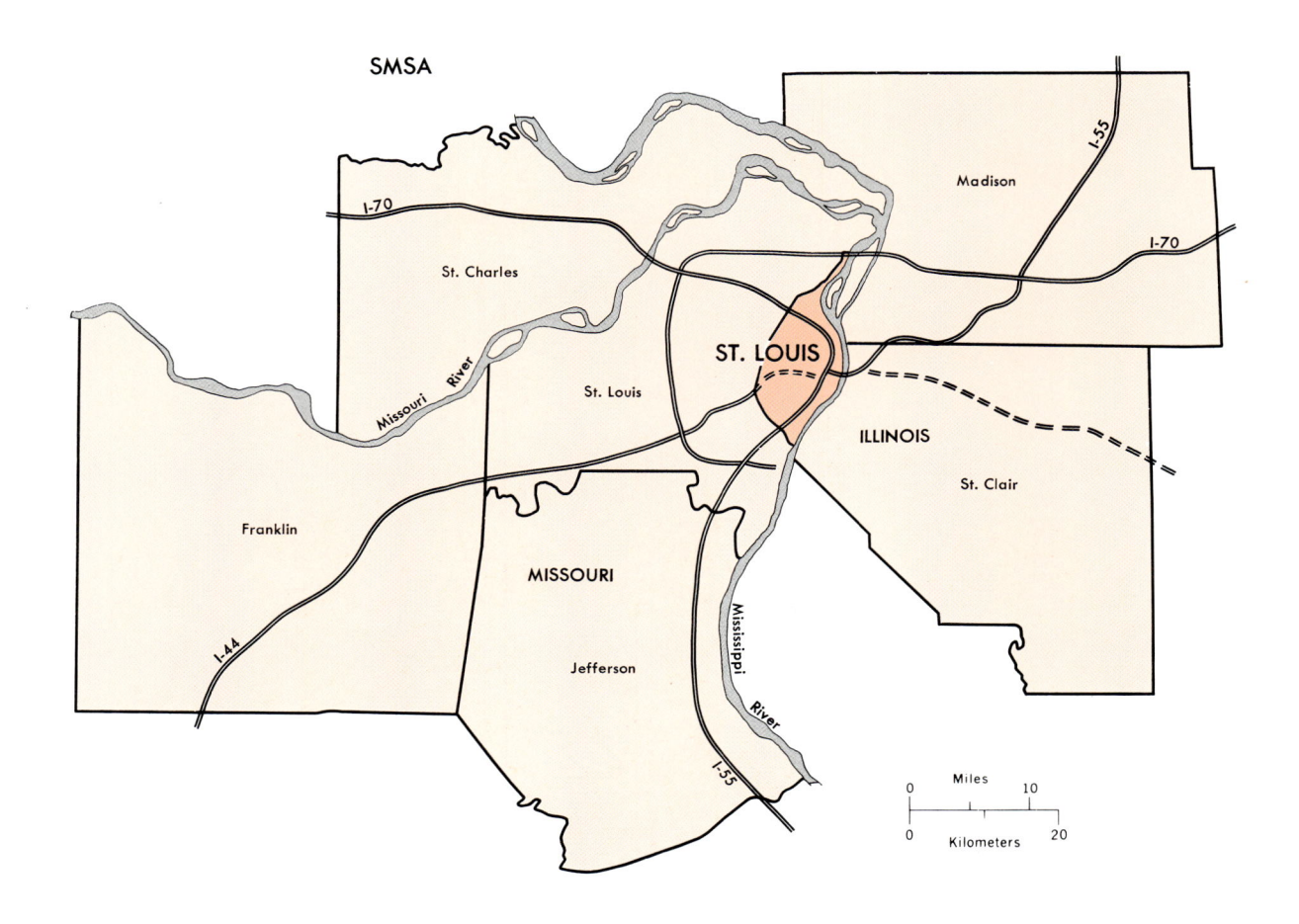

The St. Louis Standard Metropolitan Statistical Area (SMSA) has a population of 2,363,000. It is thus the 10th most populous American SMSA. Twenty-six percent (622,000) of the SMSA's people live in St. Louis City, which is politically and geographically distinct from St. Louis County. The remainder of the SMSA population is divided among the four Missouri counties, which have 1,205,000 (51 percent), and the two Illinois counties where 536,000 (23 percent) live. St. Louis County is the most populous (951,000 or 40 percent of the SMSA total) of the suburban counties. The commuting region defined by counties that have at least 5 percent of their labor forces working in St. Louis City and County extends the boundaries of the functioning economic metropolis outward to include 9 more counties and 180,000 more people (p. 119). This Daily Urban System (DUS) has a population of 2,542,000. It is the nation's 11th most populous DUS.

*Note:* All data are from the 1970 Censuses of Population and Housing unless otherwise indicated. Therefore the present tense refers to 1970 data except for income data which are from 1969. Cartographic conventions are explained in Chapter 1.

St. Louis began as a frontier trading post in 1768. The Louisiana purchase brought the city into the United States in 1804, and St. Louis quickly established itself as a point of embarkation for the continent's interior. In the 1830s the population rose from 5,000 to 17,000 as steamboat traffic began on interior rivers. St. Louis became the break-in-bulk port for large steamers that plied the lower Mississippi and smaller boats that navigated the Missouri, Upper Mississippi, and Ohio rivers. Population boomed (p. 10). From 1850 to 1870 St. Louis and Chicago battled for economic supremacy in the Midwest. St. Louis bet on steamboats and Chicago bet on railroads. The two cities had nearly equal populations in 1870. Thirty years later Chicago had three times the population of St. Louis, which has continued to fall behind later and more perceptive competitors. The SMSA continued to grow during the 1960s, although at a rate substantially lower than the national metropolitan average and to some degree at the expense of the central city. St. Louis reached its peak population of 857,000 in 1950. Since then it has declined 27 percent to its current 622,000.

The city began on a limestone ledge close to the confluence of the

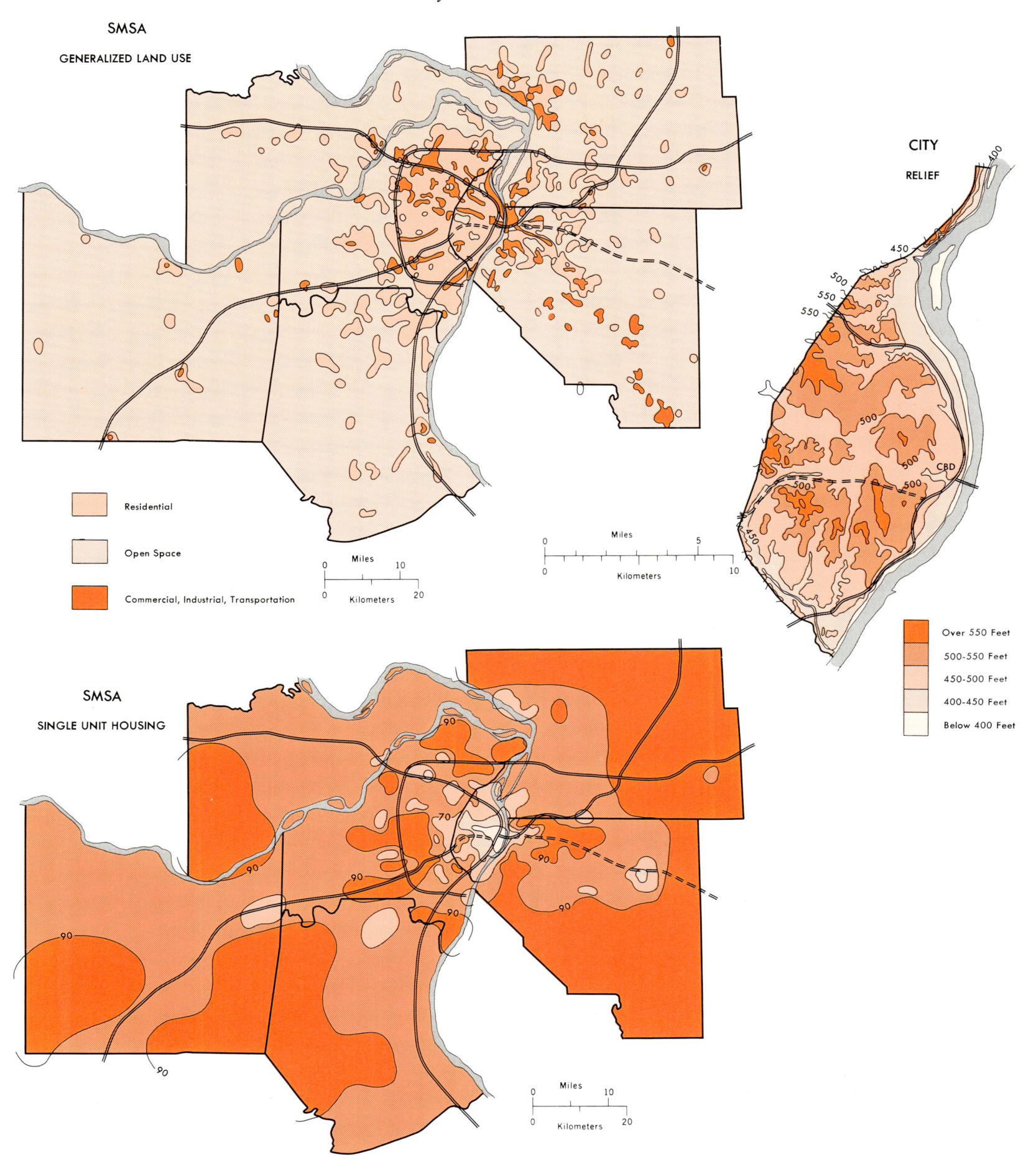

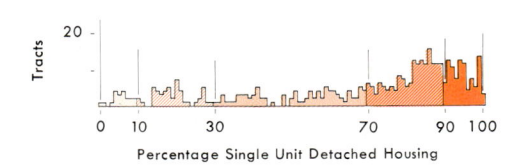

## Nineteenth-Century Inland Centers and Ports: St. Louis

SMSA
GENERALIZED LAND USE

- Residential
- Open Space
- Commercial, Industrial, Transportation

CITY
RELIEF

- Over 550 Feet
- 500-550 Feet
- 450-500 Feet
- 400-450 Feet
- Below 400 Feet

SMSA
SINGLE UNIT HOUSING

Percentage Single Unit Detached Housing

Missouri and Mississippi rivers. The land in Illinois is flat or very gently rolling. In Missouri, terrain becomes increasingly rough away from the Mississippi, especially in the western and southwestern reaches of the SMSA, which extend into the Ozark uplands. Relief within the city is minimal; few places in St. Louis are more than 150 feet (50 meters) above river level. The relatively flat terrain extends into much of St. Louis County, and it has permitted the city to expand

**SMSA HOUSING BUILT BEFORE 1940**

**SMSA HOUSING BUILT 1960-1970**

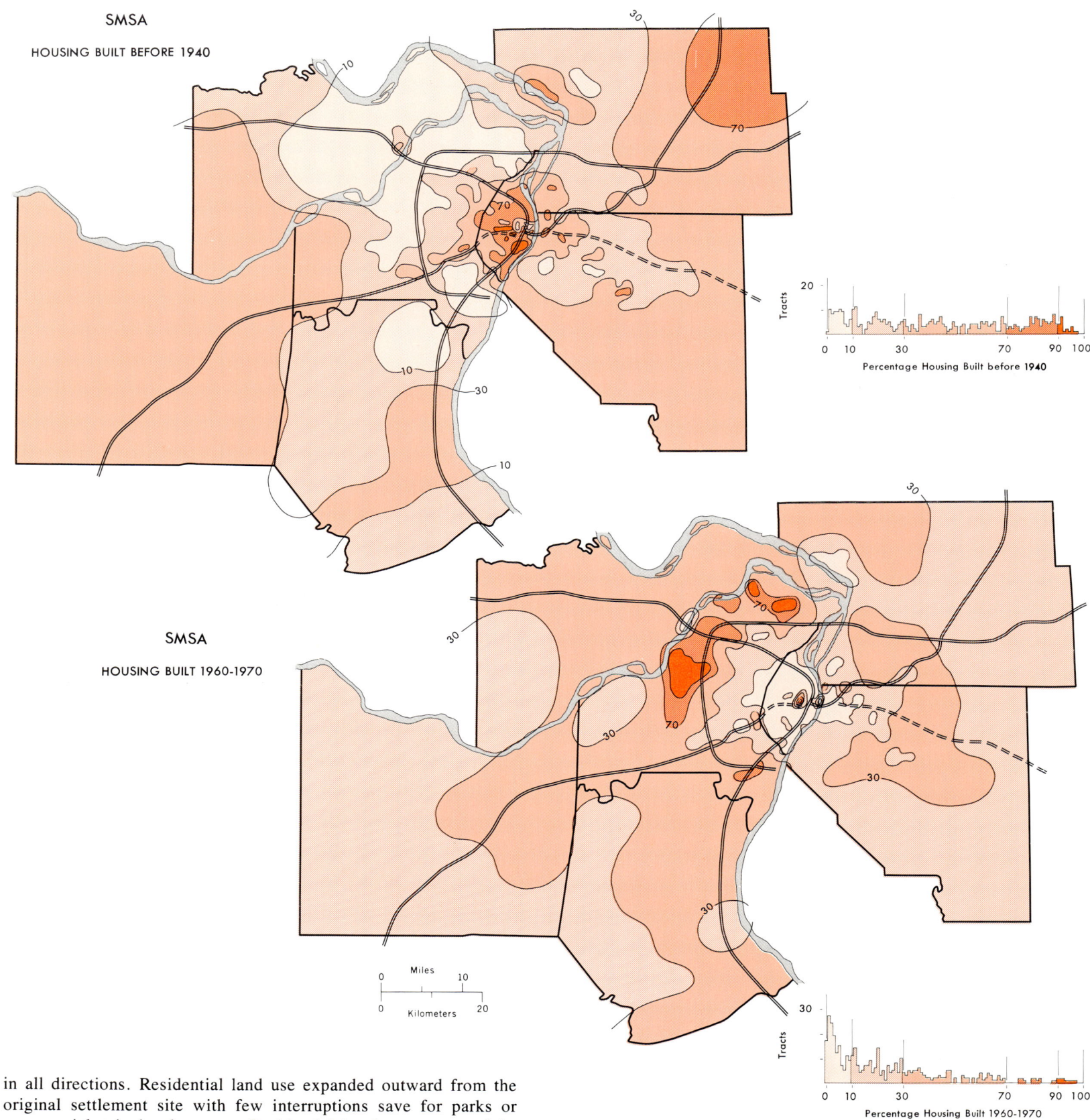

in all directions. Residential land use expanded outward from the original settlement site with few interruptions save for parks or commercial strip developments. Residential development east of the Mississippi is more spotty, reflecting the area's later growth and its dependence on highway access to the East St. Louis employment core. Important outlying settlements are located along Interstate 70 near the old town of St. Charles, at Alton, in Madison County, and at Belleville, in central St. Clair County.

The contrasts in land use and socioeconomic patterns in St. Louis and Pittsburgh could not be more striking. The two cities began about the same time, had similar economic bases — first in trade and then in manufacturing — and thus have similar growth histories. Yet land-use patterns, housing distributions, and maps of social characteristics for St. Louis are regular, whereas maps of the same variables for Pittsburgh are complex and irregular. The fact that urban expansion and economic activities were highly constrained by rough terrain in Pittsburgh and virtually unrestrained in St. Louis explains the differences between two places that should be similar if topography were not a factor.

## HOUSING

**Housing Age.** There are sharp differences in the age of the SMSA housing stock and the age of central-city housing. Forty-two percent of the SMSA's total stock was built before 1940, whereas 74 percent of the city's units are of pre-World War II vintage. Since 25 percent of the SMSA's housing and 6 percent of the city's dwellings were built from 1960 to March 1970, the residuals—33 percent in the SMSA and

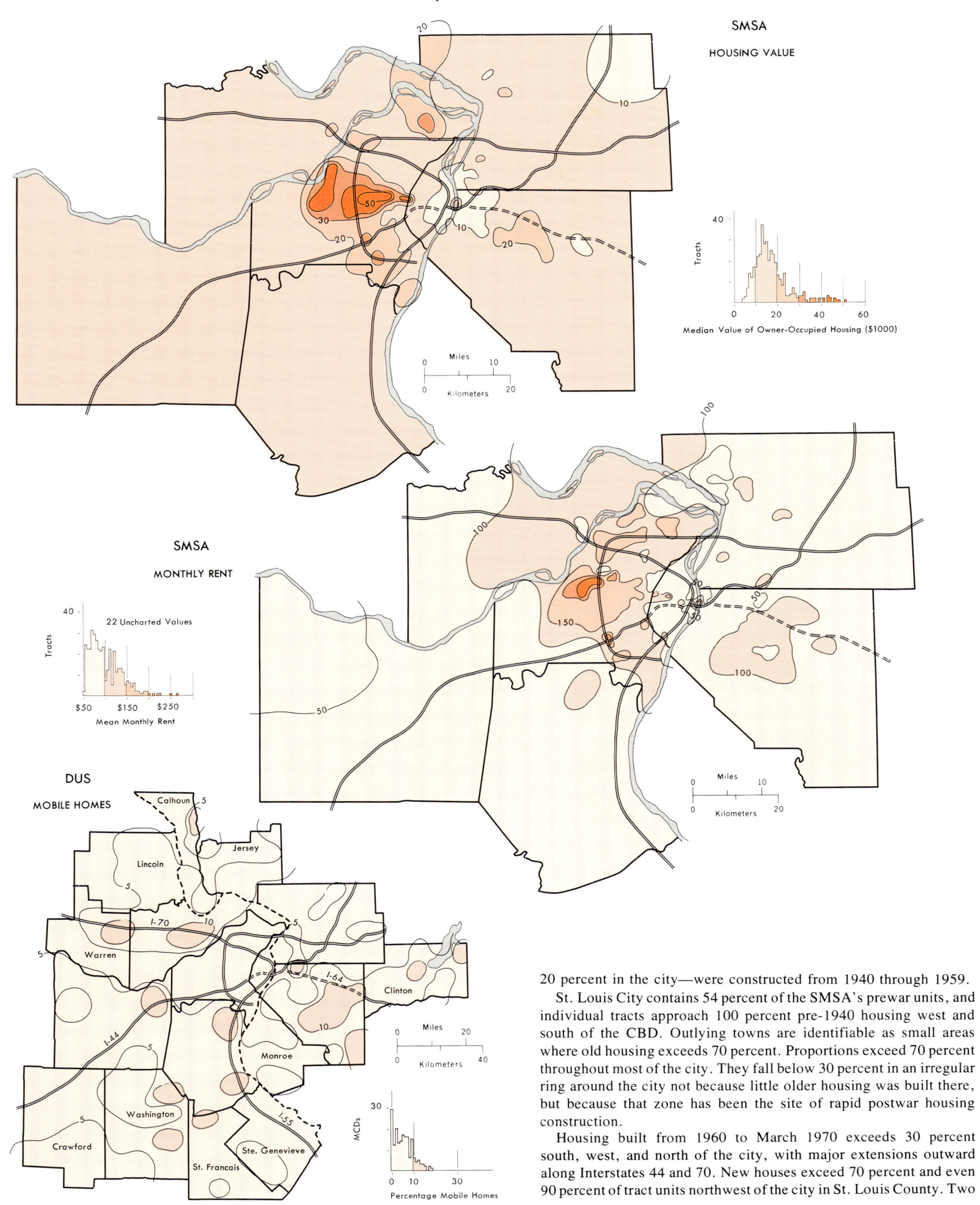

## Nineteenth-Century Inland Centers and Ports: St. Louis

**SMSA HOUSING VALUE**

**SMSA MONTHLY RENT**

**DUS MOBILE HOMES**

20 percent in the city—were constructed from 1940 through 1959.

St. Louis City contains 54 percent of the SMSA's prewar units, and individual tracts approach 100 percent pre-1940 housing west and south of the CBD. Outlying towns are identifiable as small areas where old housing exceeds 70 percent. Proportions exceed 70 percent throughout most of the city. They fall below 30 percent in an irregular ring around the city not because little older housing was built there, but because that zone has been the site of rapid postwar housing construction.

Housing built from 1960 to March 1970 exceeds 30 percent south, west, and north of the city, with major extensions outward along Interstates 44 and 70. New houses exceed 70 percent and even 90 percent of tract units northwest of the city in St. Louis County. Two

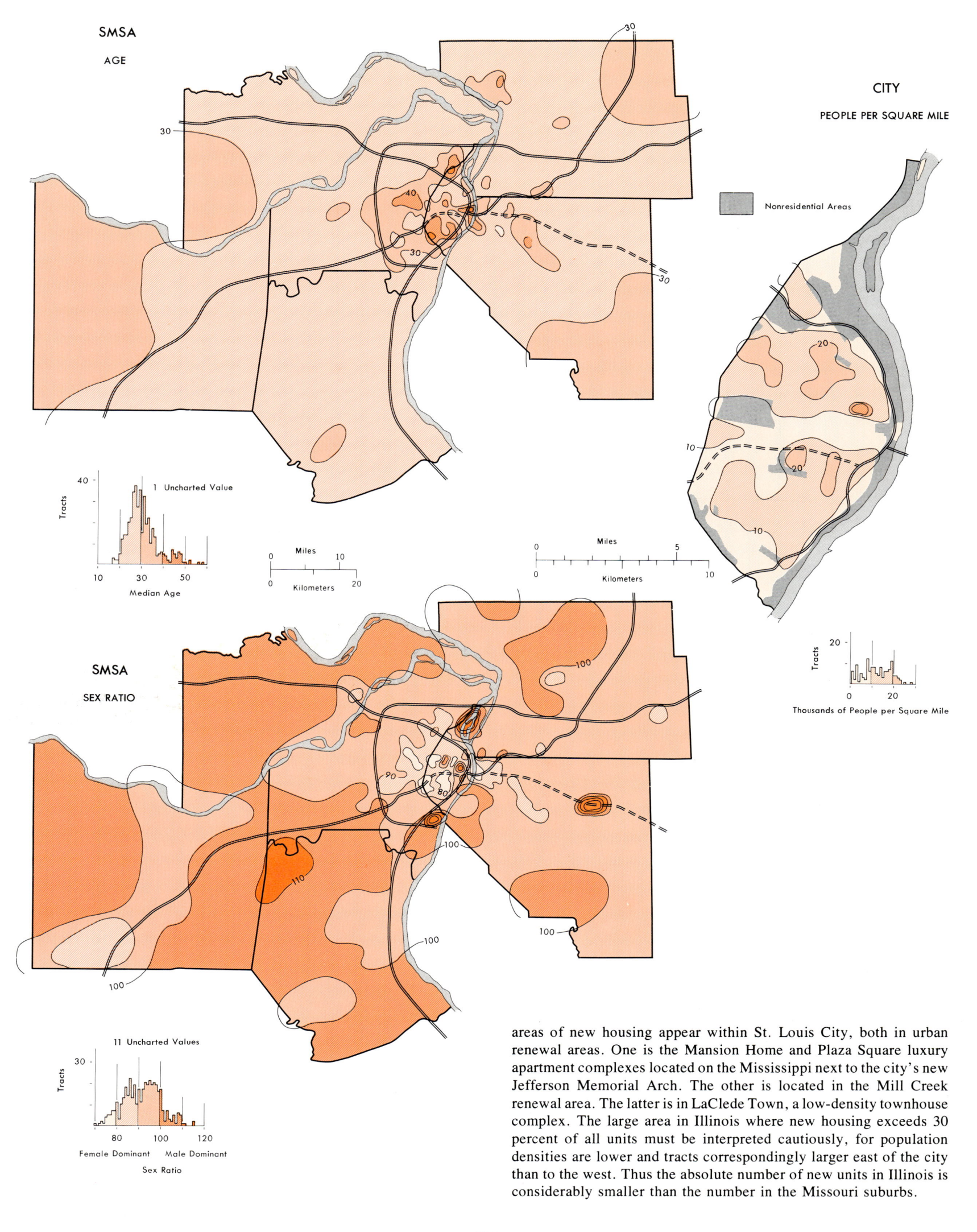

## Nineteenth-Century Inland Centers and Ports: St. Louis

areas of new housing appear within St. Louis City, both in urban renewal areas. One is the Mansion Home and Plaza Square luxury apartment complexes located on the Mississippi next to the city's new Jefferson Memorial Arch. The other is located in the Mill Creek renewal area. The latter is in LaClede Town, a low-density townhouse complex. The large area in Illinois where new housing exceeds 30 percent of all units must be interpreted cautiously, for population densities are lower and tracts correspondingly larger east of the city than to the west. Thus the absolute number of new units in Illinois is considerably smaller than the number in the Missouri suburbs.

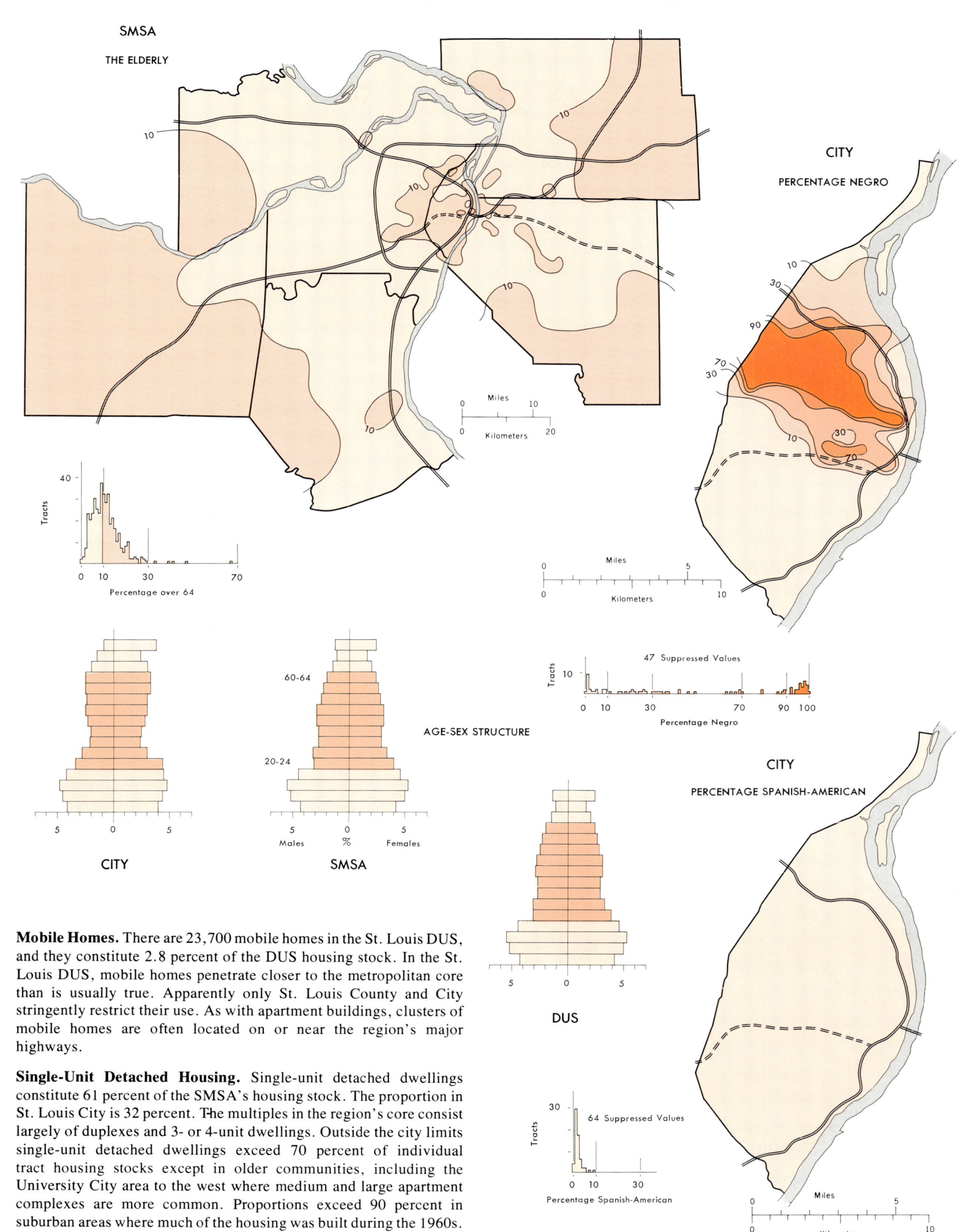

## Nineteenth-Century Inland Centers and Ports: St. Louis

**Mobile Homes.** There are 23,700 mobile homes in the St. Louis DUS, and they constitute 2.8 percent of the DUS housing stock. In the St. Louis DUS, mobile homes penetrate closer to the metropolitan core than is usually true. Apparently only St. Louis County and City stringently restrict their use. As with apartment buildings, clusters of mobile homes are often located on or near the region's major highways.

**Single-Unit Detached Housing.** Single-unit detached dwellings constitute 61 percent of the SMSA's housing stock. The proportion in St. Louis City is 32 percent. The multiples in the region's core consist largely of duplexes and 3- or 4-unit dwellings. Outside the city limits single-unit detached dwellings exceed 70 percent of individual tract housing stocks except in older communities, including the University City area to the west where medium and large apartment complexes are more common. Proportions exceed 90 percent in suburban areas where much of the housing was built during the 1960s.

## SMSA
### HOUSEHOLD SIZE

*Average Number of People per Household*

## SMSA
### FAMILIES WITH A FEMALE HEAD

*Percentage Families with a Female Head*

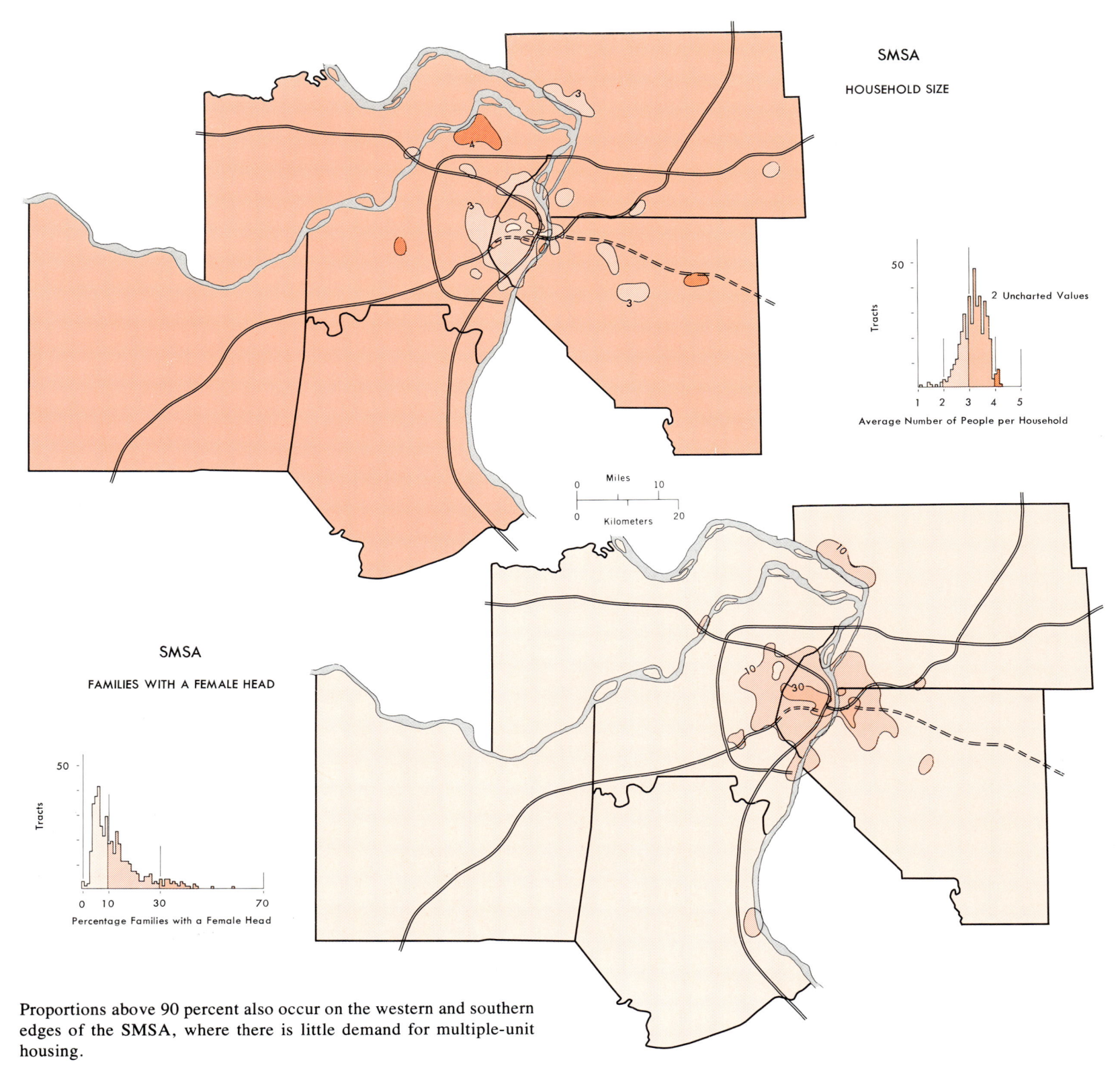

Proportions above 90 percent also occur on the western and southern edges of the SMSA, where there is little demand for multiple-unit housing.

**Housing Value and Rent.** The median value of owner-occupied housing in the SMSA is $16,300; in the city it is $13,200. Tract medians range from $4,000 to $51,000. Most tracts with medians below $10,000 are located in inner St. Louis City and in old, equally dilapidated areas in East St. Louis. The prestige residential area is clearly to the west. Tract medians over $50,000 are located in Ladue, Creve Coeur, and Frontenac. The high-prestige, high-value sector repeats another pattern common to American metropolitan areas: it originates in the fine old mansions located north of Forest Park on the city's western boundary.

Mean monthly contract rentals average $92 in the SMSA and $74 in St. Louis. Both means are low for a large metropolitan area; the city mean is the lowest (under New Orleans by one dollar) of the 20 areas mapped in the atlas. Aside from the area where mean rents exceed $100 in St. Clair County, high rentals are confined to the area west of the Mississippi. Rentals below $100 and below $50 predominate throughout St. Louis City except near Forest Park and in the CBD renewal area.

St. Louis City has had more than its share of housing problems. The city cleared the squalid 475-acre Mill Creek area and built the highly touted Pruitt-Igoe apartments to house low-income families displaced from Mill Creek. Both projects came to grief. Some portions of Mill Creek remained vacant in the early 1970s, 20 years after they had been cleared. Despite the architectural awards garnered by the designers of the Pruitt-Igoe complex, some of the deserted buildings were dynamited in the early 1970s, their inhabitants having fled concentrated misery, inadequate or nonexistent maintenance, and high crime rates in the project. Part of the disaster is attributable to design deficiencies in the project and part to populating the project with a poverty group with little experience in urban, high-density

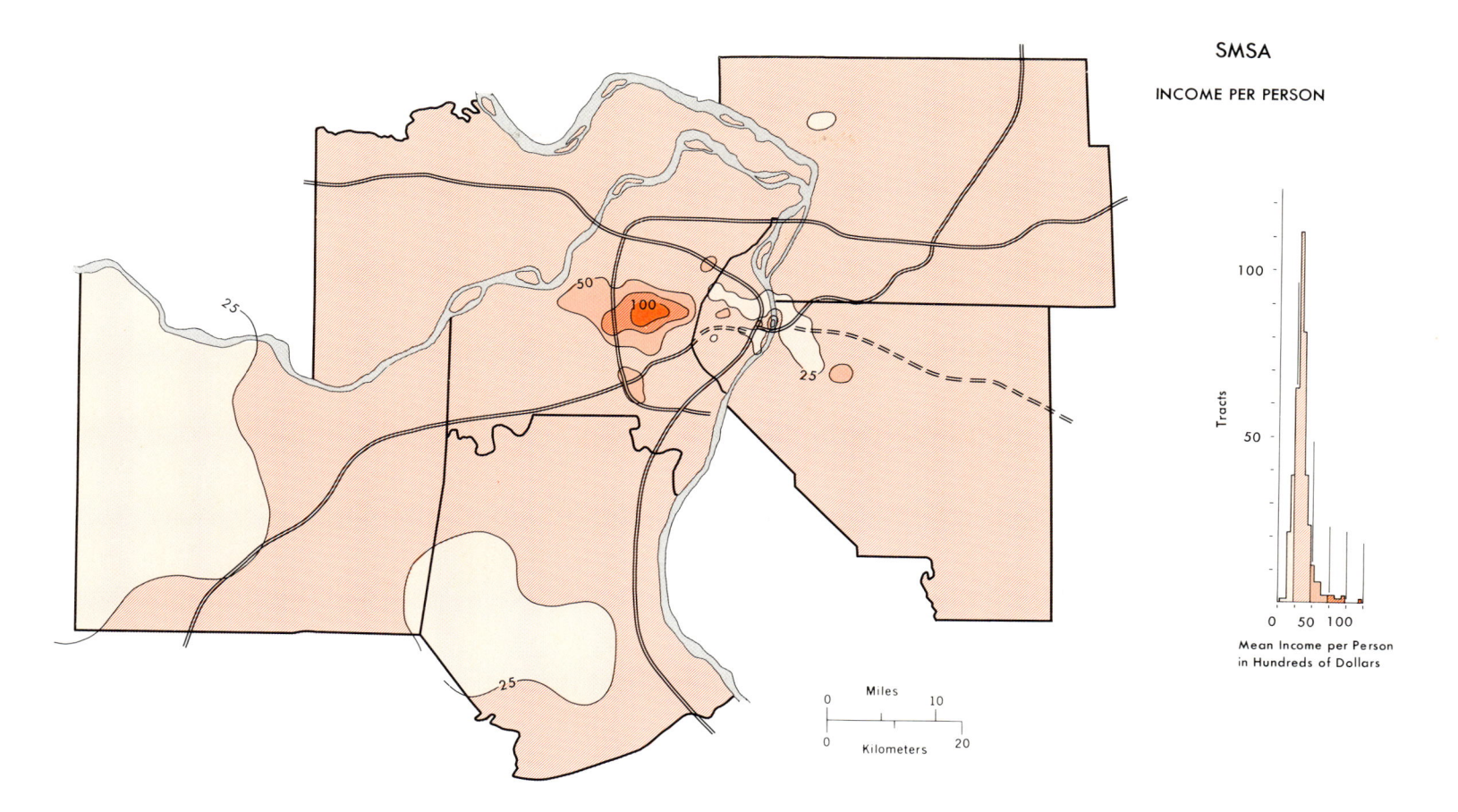

*Nineteenth-Century Inland Centers and Ports: St. Louis*

living. Wherever the responsibility lies, St. Louis is left with its effects, namely, a large net reduction of housing units within the city.

THE PEOPLE

**Population Density.** The overall population density of St. Louis City is 10,200 people per square mile (3,940 per square kilometer). Individual tract densities range from less than 1,000 to 38,000 people per square mile (385 to 14,700 per square kilometer). The inclusion of nonresidential areas in density calculations means that actual densities in some parts of the city are higher than the gross densities mapped here. The highest density occurs in an inner-city tract that is the site of a large public-housing project. It is completely out of character with densities in the rest of the city. Similar or higher densities were at least a contributing factor in the Pruitt-Igoe problems noted above. Densities rarely exceed 10,000 per square mile (3,900 per square kilometer) outside St. Louis City (map on p. 312). City population density has been dropping because of population decreases; in 1950 the city's density was 14,050 people per square mile (5,425 per square kilometer).

**Age and the Elderly.** The median age for the SMSA is 28 years. The city's population is considerably older, with a median age of 32 years. During the 1960s, 34 percent of the city's whites moved away; most of these were young families who took their reproductive potential with them. The white death rate in the city now exceeds the white birthrate, and in the absence of net in-migration of whites, the city can only become more black. The black population grew by almost 20 percent through natural increase. The net effect is a city of young blacks and old whites. Tract medians range from less than 20 years to over 50 years, although values over 50 are usually institutionalized, elderly populations. Median ages exceed 30 years in most of the city and in the northern and western suburbs. The areas with median ages below 30 years within the city are located in the predominantly black neighborhoods. Tracts with median ages below 20 years are scattered areas in the East St. Louis area and in St. Louis City; the latter are usually too small to map.

People 64 years of age and older make up 9 percent of the SMSA population and 15 percent of the city's people. The elderly exceed 10 percent of local populations in the older metropolitan cores and in some of the outlying settlement centers. A few tracts in St. Louis exceed 30 percent. The 67 percent tract is the easternmost of the over-30-percent areas; it contains a home for the elderly.

**Sex Ratio.** There are 1.1 females for each male in the SMSA, which yields a female-dominant sex ratio (males divided by females times 100) of 91. The city's sex ratio is 84, which is the lowest among the central cities in the atlas. Female survival rates exceed those of males after adolescence and especially after middle age, and the large proportion of old people concentrated in St. Louis contributes to the low sex ratio. Tract ratios below 70 (none mapped) and above 120 are usually caused by sex-segregated institutionalized populations. Aside from such extremes, the city and inner suburbs have ratios below 90. Areas where the population is increasing because of the influx of young families into new housing are near equality, and areas that are slightly male-dominant are usually rural areas that have not experienced much suburban growth.

**Negroes.** Selective out-migration of whites and high rates of natural increase among blacks have increased the city's black population from 29 percent in 1960 to 41 percent in 1970. Blacks are highly segregated in the metropolitan area (map on p. 384). Sixty-seven percent of the SMSA's blacks live in the city, whereas it has only 26 percent of the total population. Segregation is the rule within the city also. The few tracts with mixed populations are tracts caught by the Census in transition from white to black. One exception is the LaClede Town Project for lower-middle-income families, which appears on the map as the small area west of the CBD that is less than 30 percent black.

**Spanish-Americans.** The Census identifies Spanish-Americans in St. Louis by counting Spanish-speaking people. The 5,950 so identified constitute less than 1 percent of the city's population. There are few people of Cuban or Puerto Rican birth or parentage in the city; most Spanish speakers are of Mexican (1,130), other Latin-American (760), or indigenous Mexican-American origin. The region's few

123

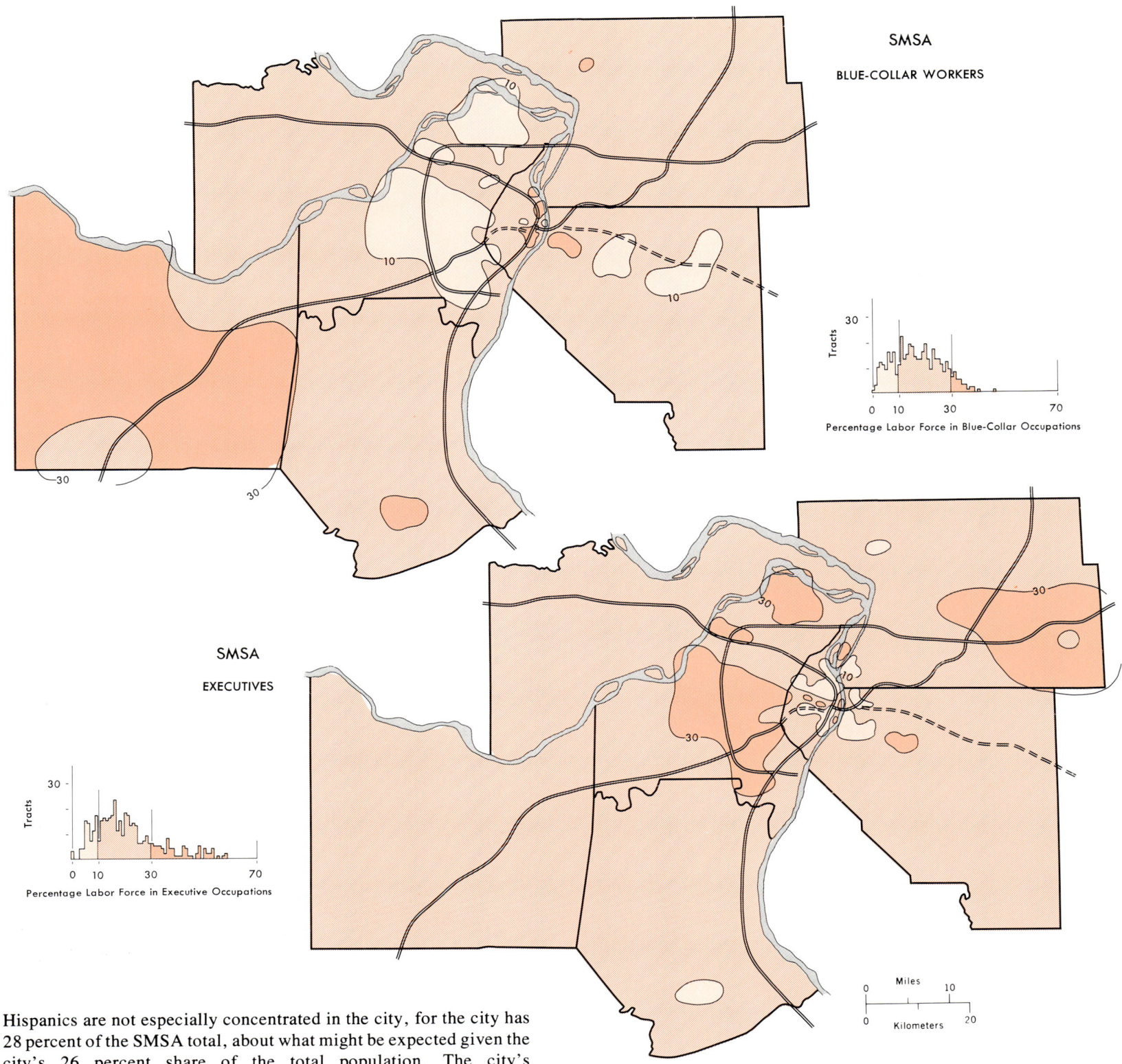

Hispanics are not especially concentrated in the city, for the city has 28 percent of the SMSA total, about what might be expected given the city's 26 percent share of the total population. The city's Spanish-Americans are diffused throughout the city in small numbers; the largest numbers (tract values of 7 and 9 percent) occur in the southern tip of the city.

## SOCIOECONOMIC CHARACTERISTICS

**Household Size.** There are 3.2 people in the average SMSA household and 2.8 in the average St. Louis City household. Tract values range from just over 1 near the city's CBD to 4.2 in a sparsely populated (50 people) tract on the St. Louis waterfront. Household sizes larger than 4 do occur in tracts north and west of the city where much of the housing was constructed recently (p. 118). Large numbers of young couples who have not yet had children and older populations whose children have established their own households explain the smaller household sizes in the city. Blacks have higher birthrates and larger families than whites. The mean number of persons per household for blacks is 3.5 in the SMSA and 3.4 in the city. The slightly smaller city mean suggests that young black families are beginning to emulate the earlier trek of white families to suburbia. The black city average of 3.4 persons contrasts sharply with the white mean of 2.8, and the predominantly black area of St. Louis is accordingly outlined neatly by the 3-person isopleth.

**Female Headship.** The Census Bureau defines female headship in terms of the absence of a male spouse rather than by the sex of the household's breadwinner. In the SMSA, 12 percent of all families are headed by females. The proportion rises to 21 percent in St. Louis City, where 46 percent of the SMSA's families headed by females live. Tract values vary from zero to 58 percent. Female headship is highest in black neighborhoods; the highest value occurs in the housing project that is the location of the city's highest population density (p. 120).

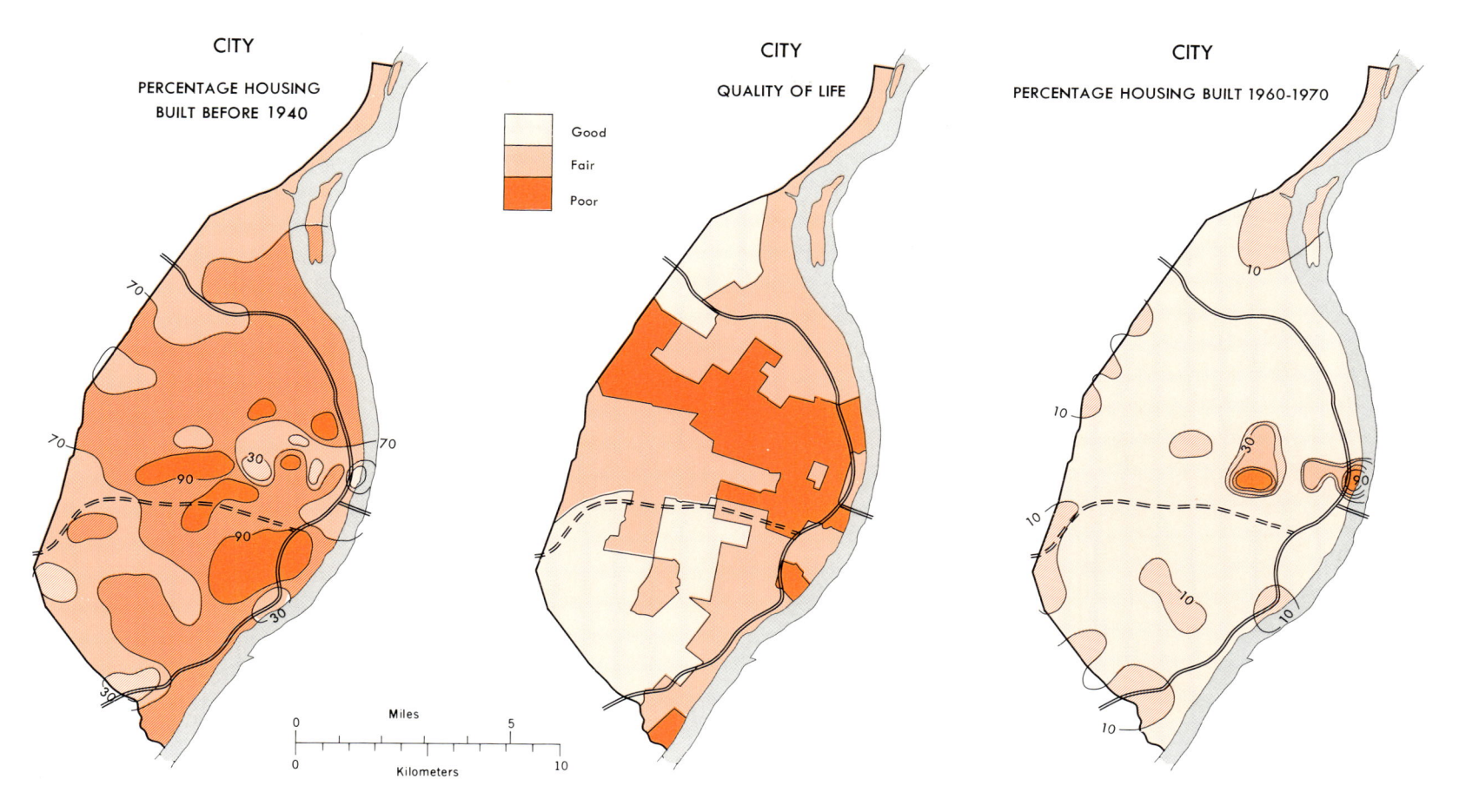

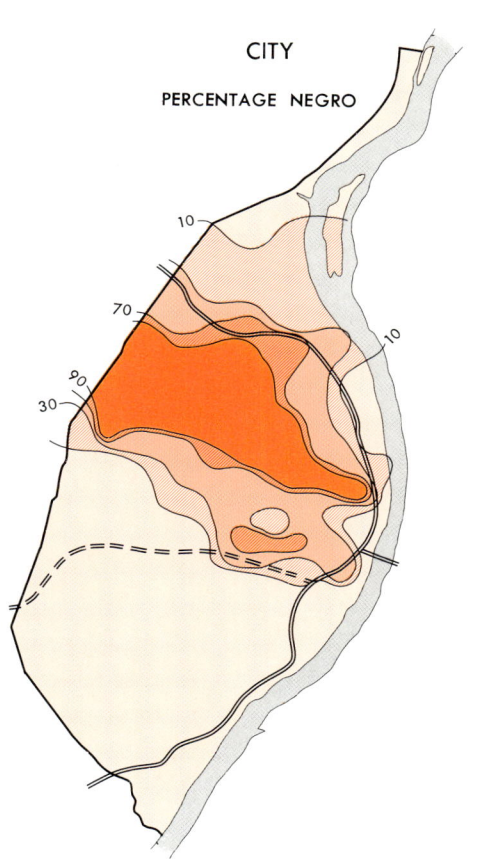

## Nineteenth-Century Inland Centers and Ports: St. Louis

**Occupations.** The SMSA's employed labor force totals 898,000 workers; 16 percent work at blue-collar (laborers and operatives) jobs, and 21 percent are executives (engineers, teachers, professionals, managers, proprietors, and administrators). The remaining 63 percent are service (35 percent) and clerical (28 percent) workers. The city has a higher proportion of blue-collar (20 percent), service (40 percent), and clerical (27 percent) workers, and a correspondingly lower percentage (13) of executives. Proportions of the labor force in blue-collar occupations range from zero to 46 percent; most tracts have percentages ranging from 10 to 30. Proportions fall below 10 in suburban areas, especially to the west and north of the city. Blue-collar workers make up more than 30 percent of local labor forces in a few areas within the city and in industrial East St. Louis. Much of Franklin County lies beyond easy commuting distance to St. Louis employment, and as a result local blue-collar jobs provide many of the county's jobs. Tract proportions of executive occupations range from zero to 58 percent. Tract percentages over 30 ring the city in large and small clusters, and percentages below 10 occupy much of the central portion of St. Louis. Some tracts with values over 30 appear in the downtown renewal areas and near St. Louis University, to the west of the CBD. Large parts of the city of East St. Louis also have few executive residents. The low percentages of executives in the black neighborhoods of St. Louis are the local instance of a common feature of American cities.

**Income.** The mean income per person in the St. Louis SMSA is $3,450 per year. The city's mean is $2,750, which is the second lowest central-city income among the cities in the atlas (New Orleans is lowest at $2,700). The $700 difference between SMSA mean income and city mean income is unusually large and is exceeded only in Cleveland and Hartford. Mean income per person in individual tracts varies from less than $1,000 to $12,000. Low incomes occur in the black ghetto core and across the Mississippi in East St. Louis. Isolated rural areas on the metropolitan periphery also have per person incomes below $2,500; they lie outside the belt of recent metropolitan growth (p. 118). The high-income sector that extends west of the city embraces the prestige suburbs of Clayton, Ladue, Creve Couer, and Westwood, among others. Incomes over $5,000 per person in St. Louis City are confined to small pockets in new housing near the CBD and in the older prestige neighborhood adjacent to Forest Park, west of downtown.

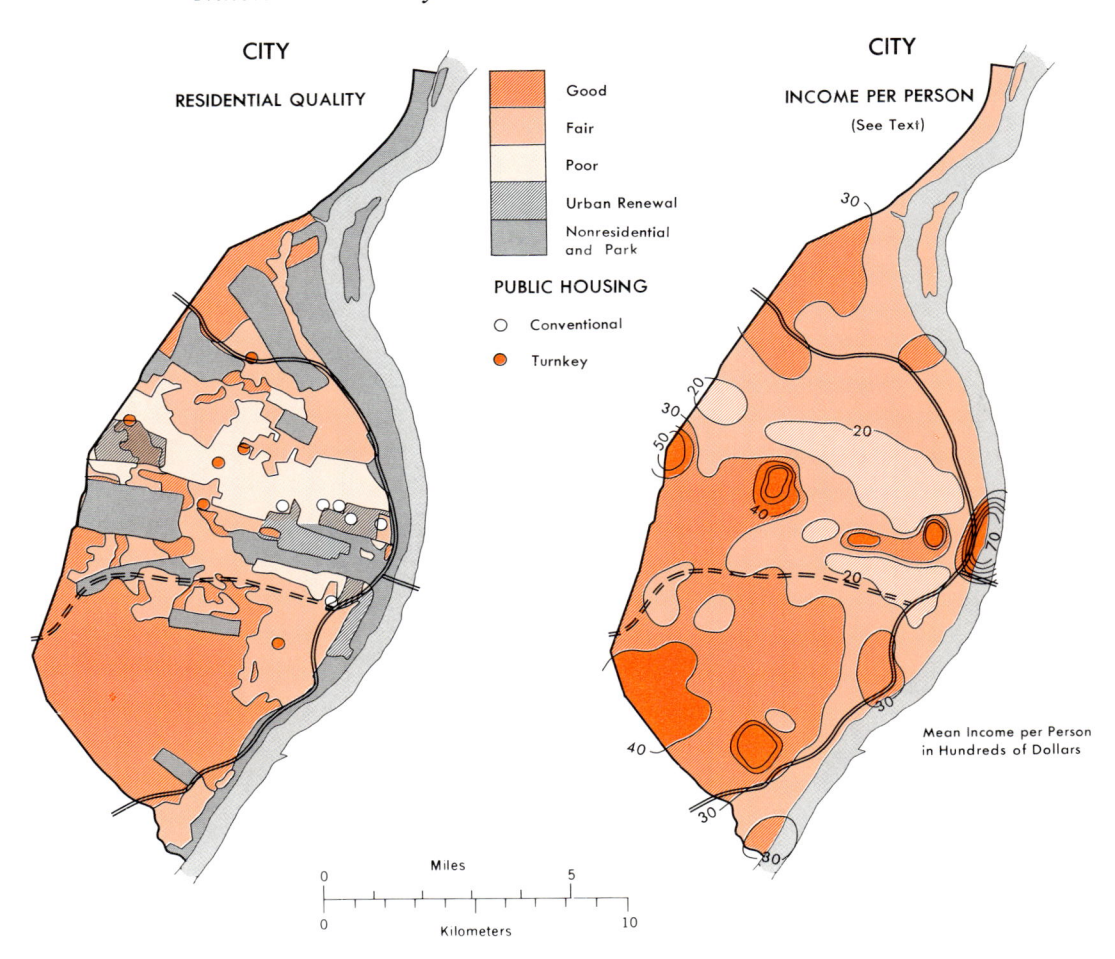

## TOPICS OF SPECIAL INTEREST IN THE ST. LOUIS REGION

**Housing Age.** The city's aged housing stock is intimately associated with several of its most pressing human problems, but the exact role older housing plays in such problems is unclear. Seventy-four percent of the city's housing was built before 1940, 20 percent was built from 1940 through 1959, and the remaining 6 percent dates from 1960 to March 1970. Only the northern and southwestern parts of the city have large areas where less than 70 percent of the housing is of pre-war vintage, and outside the waterfront and Mill Creek redevelopment areas, there are few tracts in which new housing is as much as 10 percent of a neighborhood's units.

**Quality of Life.** Old housing is often related to social problems, although the relationship is one of association rather than causation. High percentages of old housing attract low-income (mapped here in hundreds of dollars per person per year) populations because they offer cheap shelter. But old housing is inexpensive because it is often inadequate, as indicated on the map of residential quality prepared by the St. Louis City Plan Commission. This dilapidated housing is usually attractive to people such as blacks (p. 125) who have few real alternatives. The net effect is concentration in old housing of people with mutually reinforcing problems of minority status, poverty, unemployment, and dependency. Variations in the quality of life (measured on p. 125 by general health reflected in morbidity and mortality rates) correspond closely to geographical patterns of residential quality, income, housing age, and percentage black, taken severally or in varying combinations. The fact that any one of the six maps in this section is similar and related to the other five illustrates the complexity of urban problems in a stagnating city.

The ways in which the characteristics mapped in this series interrelate also bode ill for quick solutions to the human problems documented. The hypothesis that better housing can produce better people was put to the test earlier and on a more massive scale in St. Louis than in other American cities, and it failed. Policy makers still lack the insights necessary to intervene successfully in ongoing metropolitan problems without running a serious risk of doing more harm than good. It is possible to map patterns of residential quality, health, and income, to describe how current patterns came to be, and to speculate about how they interrelate. But programs that will change the behavior that creates them remain elusive.

---

St. Louis has acquired the reputation and has much of the substance of an urban disaster area. Whether the city's grave problems foretell the long-run fate of the metropolitan area is difficult to say, but the SMSA economy relies heavily on defense contracts and automobile assembly, both of which seem increasingly unstable. The SMSA began to lose population after 1970, a trend which is certainly related to the decrease of 61,000 in the total number of jobs in the St. Louis SMSA that occurred between 1970 and 1973. Had the SMSA gained jobs at the national rate during these three years, employment would have risen by 110,000 jobs instead of declining by 61,000. The loss suggests that the city's decline since 1950 may indeed be a harbinger of regional fortunes.

# CHAPTER 15

# Cleveland

*While I was in New Connecticut I laid out a town on the banks of Lake Erie that was called by my name.*

MOSES CLEAVELAND in his report to the Connecticut Land Company, 1796

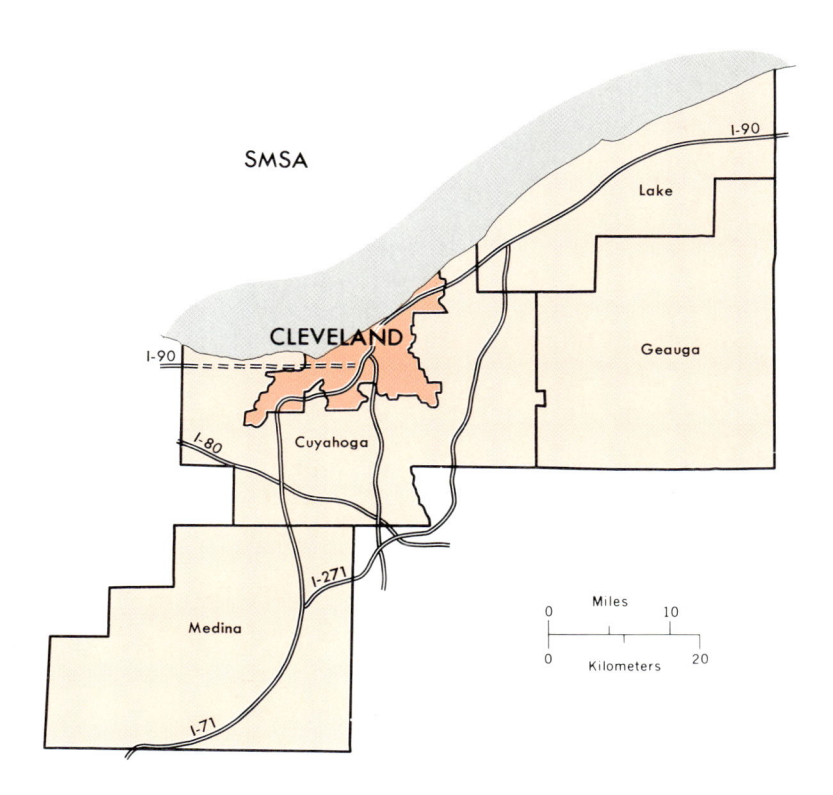

The Cleveland Standard Metropolitan Statistical Area (SMSA) has a population of 2,064,000 people; it is the 12th most populous among the American metropolitan regions. Cleveland contains 36 percent of the SMSA population and another 47 percent live in the remainder of Cuyahoga County. The balance of the SMSA total is divided among Lake (10 percent), Medina (4 percent), and Geauga (3 percent) counties. The Daily Urban System defined by counties that have at least 5 percent of their labor forces working in Cuyahoga County includes the four SMSA counties plus Lorain, Portage, and Summit counties (p. 128). The population of the DUS is 3,000,000, which makes it the 9th most populous DUS in the nation. It is unusual for the DUS population to be almost half again as large as the SMSA, but Cleveland is surrounded by separate SMSAs such as Lorain and Akron which are linked in a complex, multicentered urban region.

Cleveland began as a lake port in Connecticut's Western Reserve. With the opening of the Erie Canal in 1825 Ohio interests built canals to link Lake Erie to the Ohio River. The Ohio and Erie Canal began at Cleveland, went up the Cuyahoga to Akron, and then south via the Muskingum to the Ohio River. The city grew rapidly after 1830 and continued to grow when railroads supplanted canals (p. 10). East-west rail routes skirting the south shore of Lake Erie perforce came through Cleveland. By 1920 Cleveland was the 5th largest city in the nation, based on its location astride north-south and east-west routes, its proximity to the energy resources of Ohio and Pennsylvania, and its access to raw materials via the Great Lakes. Since 1920 economic and population growth in the region have slowed. Cleveland continues to specialize in manufacturing and heavy industry at a time when the economy's growth sectors are service and information-processing industries. The SMSA's population increased by 8.1 percent between 1960 and 1970 compared with a national metropolitan increase of 16.6 percent.

The principal features of the region's terrain are the uplands of the Appalachian Plateau, the Lake Erie shoreline and the valley of the Cuyahoga River, which bisects the city. The plateau is gently to moderately rolling. Its northern edge forms a steep bluff that stands as much as 250 feet (75 meters) above the lake shore. The Cuyahoga and its tributaries have cut back into the bluff in the Cleveland vicinity, thereby widening the coastal plain and building flat land in the Cuyahoga Valley. The Cuyahoga and other incised streams are barriers to movement. Sharp transitions from lowland to upland are often accompanied by equally sharp socioeconomic transitions.

*Note:* All data are from the 1970 Censuses of Population and Housing unless otherwise indicated. Therefore the present tense refers to 1970 data except for income data which are from 1969. Cartographic conventions are explained in Chapter 1.

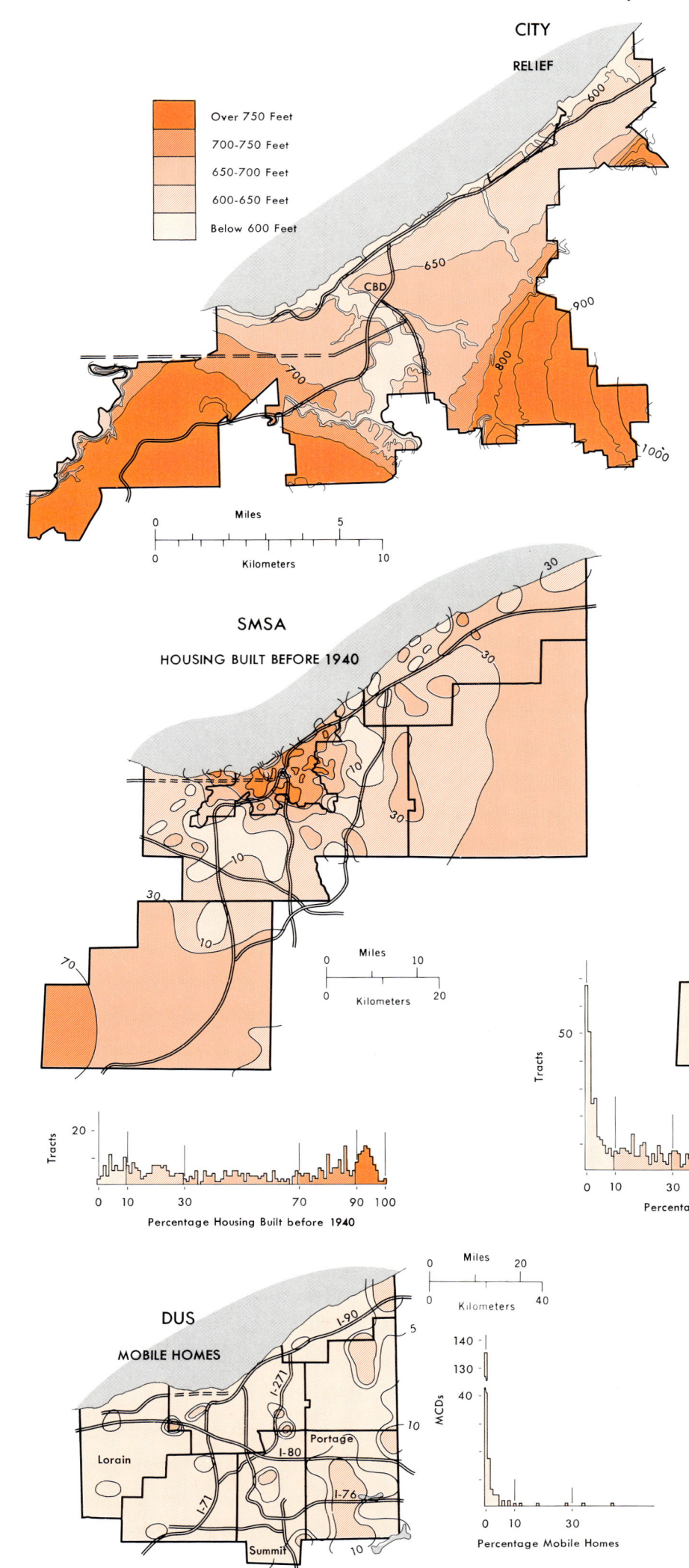

## Nineteenth-Century Inland Centers and Ports: Cleveland

### HOUSING

**Housing Age.** Forty-six percent of the Cleveland SMSA's housing units were built before 1940; 34 percent were built from 1940 through 1959, and the remaining 20 percent were built from 1960 to March 1970. The city has a considerably older housing stock; 73 percent of Cleveland's units were built before 1940 and only 6 percent date from 1960 to March 1970. Individual tract proportions vary from zero to 100 percent housing built before 1940. Most of the city lies within the over-70-percent isopleth; the exception is the southwest corner, which developed after World War II. The inner suburbs that were settled after World War II have less than 10 percent prewar housing. From these low values the percentage of old housing rises beyond the outer limits of easy commuting in southern Medina and eastern Lake and Geauga counties.

The small number of tracts with more than 70 percent new housing is partially attributable to slowed metropolitan growth in the 1960s and partially a function of the absence of large tracts of flat land suitable for the massive developments. Some new housing has been built within the city close to the Central Business District (CBD) and along Lake Erie.

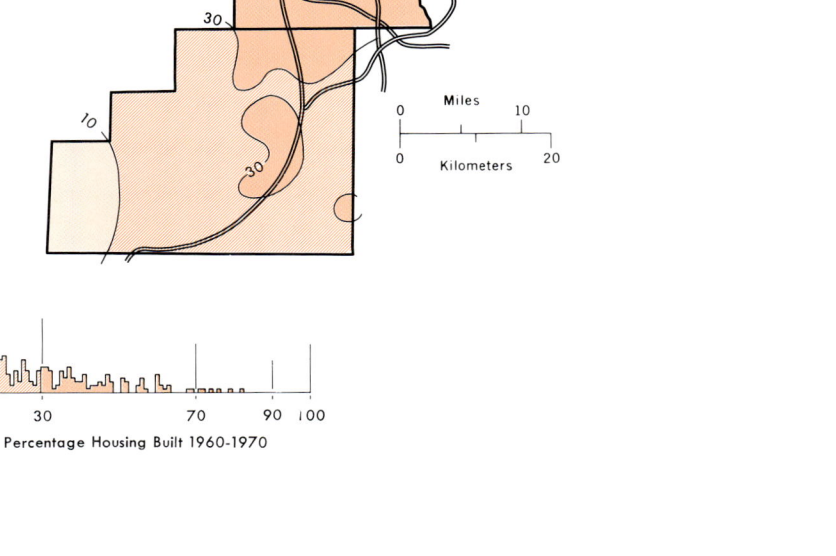

**Mobile Homes.** There are 11,700 mobile homes in the Cleveland DUS; they constitute 1.2 percent of the DUS housing stock. Mobile homes are largely confined to tracts containing mobile-home parks except in Portage, eastern Geauga, and eastern Lake counties.

**Single-Unit Detached Housing.** Single detached houses constitute 57 percent of the SMSA's housing units but only 37 percent of the dwellings in Cleveland City. Tract percentages of single-unit detached housing range from zero to 100 percent, with tracts spread relatively evenly across the entire range. Individual units predominate east and west of Cleveland and throughout Medina County except in old towns. Single-family units are less than 10 percent of local housing stock in the downtown area and in two city tracts that are sites of large housing projects.

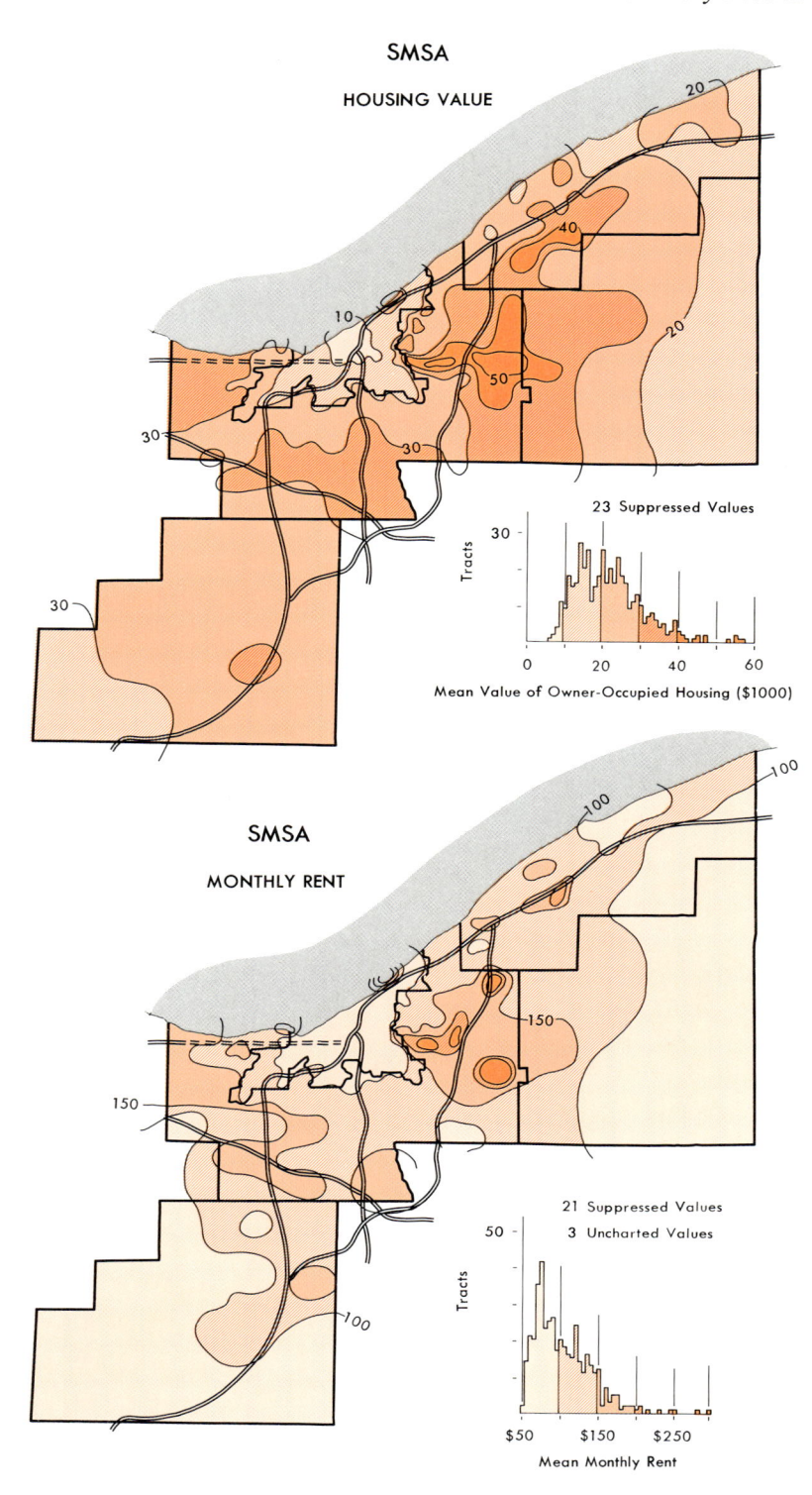

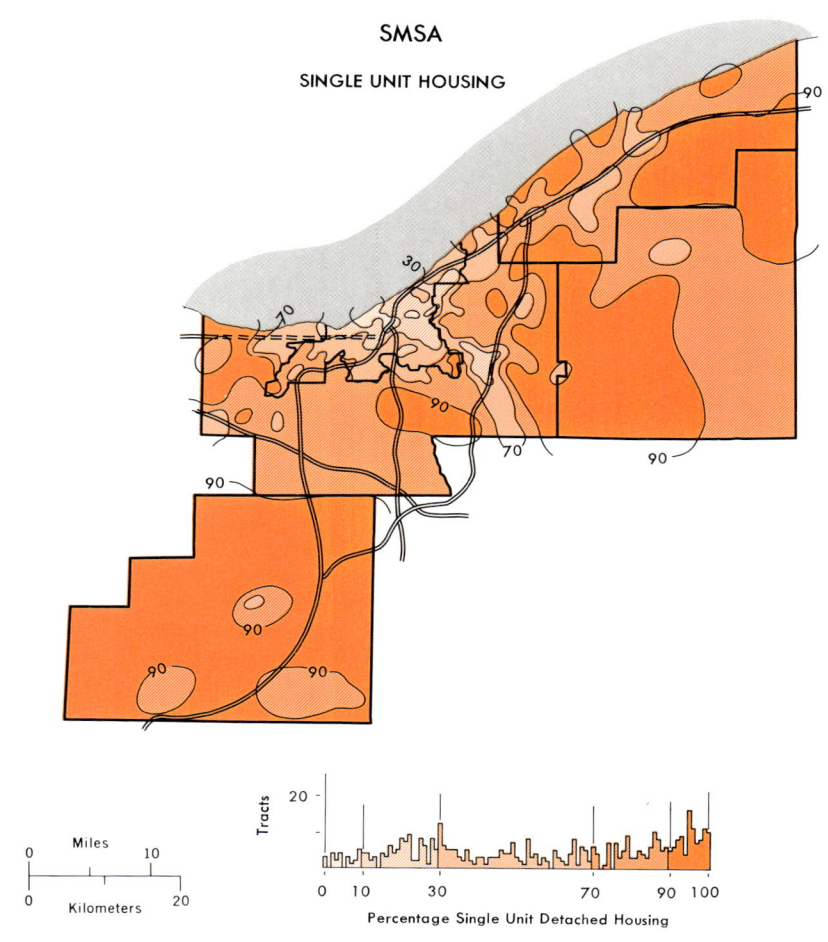

**Housing Value and Rent.** The mean value of owner-occupied housing in the SMSA is $26,000, and the corresponding value for the city is $17,000. The $9,000 gap in Cleveland is extreme; it is the largest central-city/SMSA difference in the atlas. Individual tract means vary from $6,000 to $57,000. Tracts with means below $10,000 are concentrated in Cleveland's core area, and most of the city falls below the $20,000 isopleth. The high-value housing sector is clearly east of the downtown area in Shaker Heights and adjacent communities. The bluffs east and southeast of the city provided amenity housing sites that were attractive to upper-income groups.

Mean monthly contract rentals average $105 in the SMSA and $81 in the city. As is true for housing values, the difference between SMSA and city rentals is unusually large. Mean rents for individual tracts range from less than $50 to $300. Rentals inside the city are less than $100 except in the far west, the southwest, and in the municipal enclave of Bratenahl on the lakeshore.

## THE PEOPLE

**Population Density.** Cleveland City's overall population density is 9,900 people per square mile (3,800 per square kilometer). Individual tract densities vary from less than 1,000 to 47,000 people per square mile (385 to 18,150 per square kilometer). The inclusion of nonresidential areas in density calculations means that actual neighborhood densities in some parts of the city are higher than gross densities. Densities are low in the southwestern part of the city, where housing was built at lower post-World War II densities than is true in the rest of the city. Densities in the old eastern part of the city are higher than they are in the more recently settled area west of the Cuyahoga, but peak densities over 40,000 people per square mile (15,500 per square kilometer) occur in old neighborhoods on both sides of the river. Outside the city (p. 313) population densities rarely exceed 10,000 people per square mile (3,900 per square kilometer).

**Age and the Elderly.** The median age in the Cleveland SMSA is 29 years, and the city's median is identical. A central city's median age is usually older than the SMSA median; this is not true in Cleveland because there are an unusual number of large, young families, many of which are black. The city's population pyramid has a virtually solid base below the 25-29 age cohort. The city pyramid is racially divided to some extent. The 60-64 age cohort, for example, is 26 percent black whereas the 10-14 cohort is 49 percent black. The city lost 14 percent of its population between 1960 and 1970, and much of the loss was caused by out-migration.

Median ages for individual tracts range from 16 to 59 years. Tracts with medians below 20 years are located in the heavily black areas on Cleveland's east side; in most instances they are too small to map. Medians are below 30 throughout eastern Cleveland, and the contrast with the medians over 40 in adjacent prestige suburbs is as striking as the income gradient (p. 132) between the two areas.

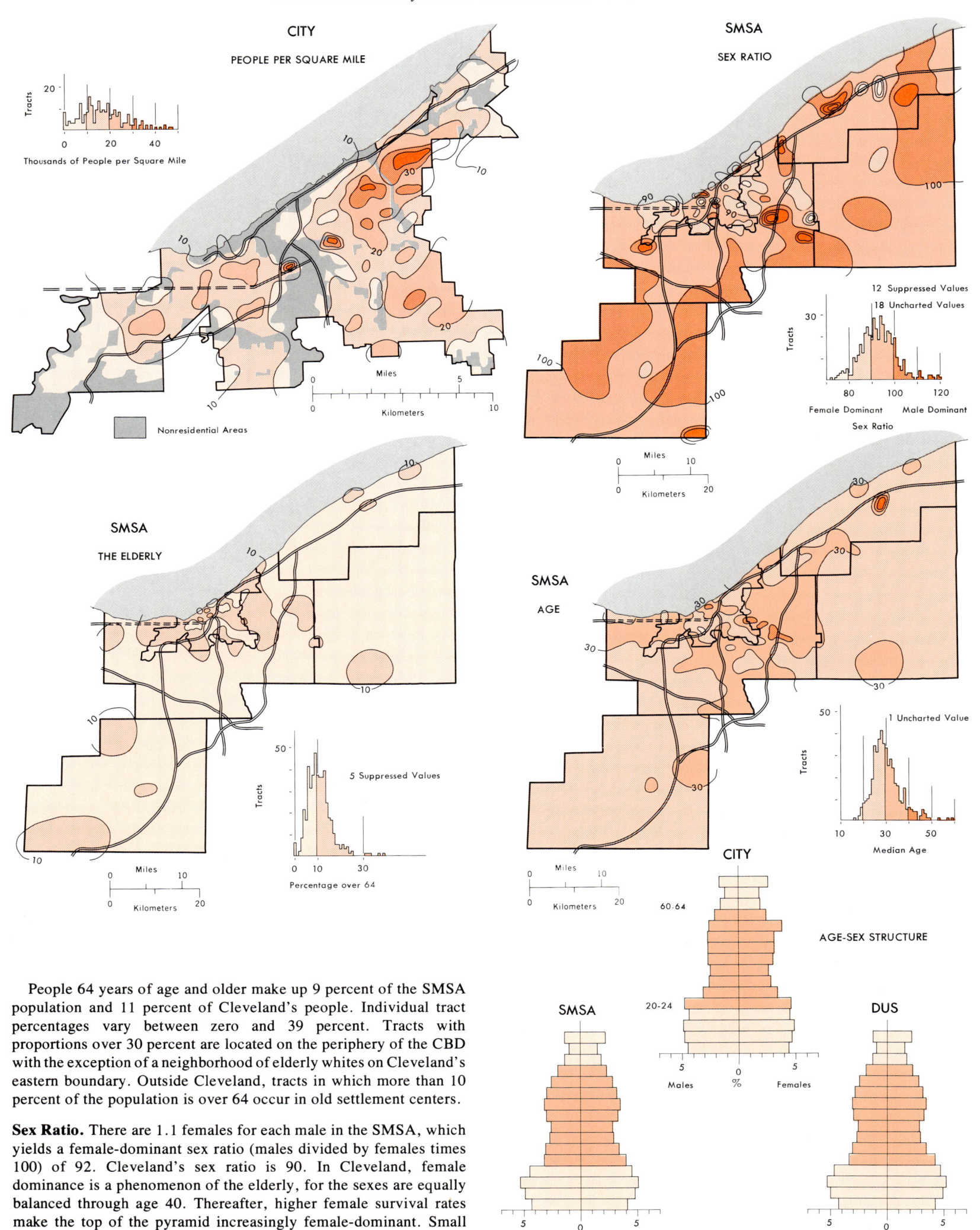

## Nineteenth-Century Inland Centers and Ports: Cleveland

People 64 years of age and older make up 9 percent of the SMSA population and 11 percent of Cleveland's people. Individual tract percentages vary between zero and 39 percent. Tracts with proportions over 30 percent are located on the periphery of the CBD with the exception of a neighborhood of elderly whites on Cleveland's eastern boundary. Outside Cleveland, tracts in which more than 10 percent of the population is over 64 occur in old settlement centers.

**Sex Ratio.** There are 1.1 females for each male in the SMSA, which yields a female-dominant sex ratio (males divided by females times 100) of 92. Cleveland's sex ratio is 90. In Cleveland, female dominance is a phenomenon of the elderly, for the sexes are equally balanced through age 40. Thereafter, higher female survival rates make the top of the pyramid increasingly female-dominant. Small tract populations or sexually segregated institutions produce extreme

130

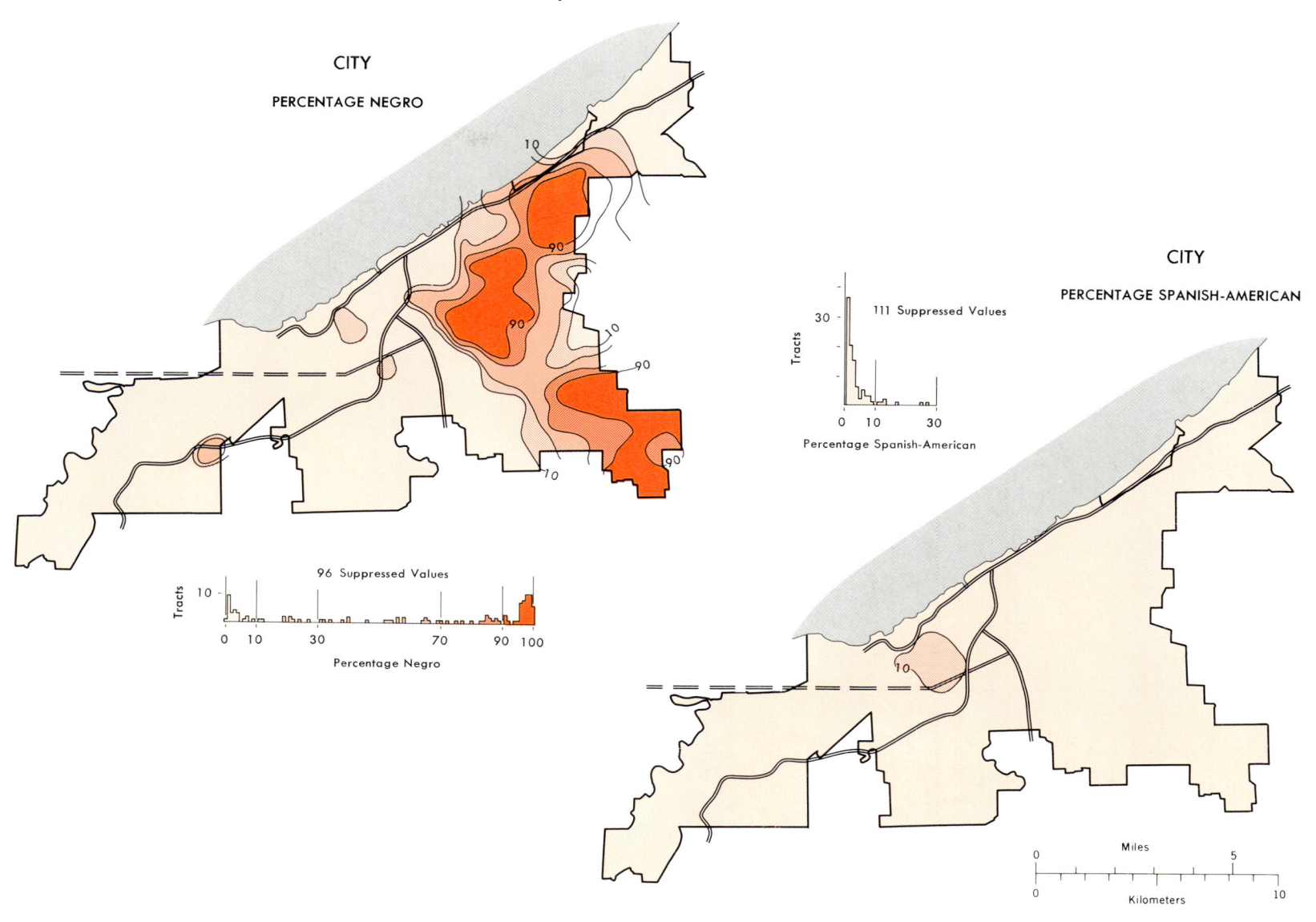

sex ratios. Generally, ratios are low in Cleveland and high on the periphery, but patterns are complicated by an old population in the CBD area and by the institutions that produce unusually high and low values at numerous places on the map.

**Negroes.** Blacks started arriving in large numbers during the 1940s. By 1970, Cleveland's 333,000 blacks were 38 percent of the city population. The SMSA's blacks are highly concentrated in the city (p. 385); Cleveland contains 87 percent of the SMSA total. Almost all blacks in Cleveland live east of the Cuyahoga Valley, where they have expanded eastward from the central area in the wake of residents leaving for housing in the eastern suburbs. Racial gradients are sharp within the city; there are few tracts in the middle of the histogram.

**Spanish-Americans.** There are almost 14,000 Spanish-speaking people in Cleveland, who constitute 1.9 percent of the city population. The large number of suppressions and the absence of zero values suggest that Spanish-Americans are scattered in small numbers throughout the city, with some clustering along Lorain Avenue across the Cuyahoga from downtown Cleveland. Almost 60 percent of the city's Spanish speakers are of Puerto Rican birth or parentage. The remainder are largely Hispanics from the American southwest who were originally attracted to northern Ohio by jobs for migrant laborers in the region's vegetable fields. (An SMSA map is on p. 393.)

Rapid expansion of heavy industry in the late 19th century attracted many immigrants to the Cleveland area. In 1900 three-fourths of the city's population was either foreign-born or of foreign parentage. Cleveland's immigrant stock came mainly from areas now included in Poland, Hungary, Germany, Czechoslovakia, and Italy. Immigration restrictions and aging of the original immigrant stock are diluting Cleveland's ethnicity. Foreign stock now amounts to only 22 percent of the city population, and no single ethnic group makes up more than 3 percent of the city's people.

## SOCIOECONOMIC CHARACTERISTICS

**Household Size.** There are 3.1 people in the average SMSA household and 3 in the average Cleveland household. Individual tract averages vary from 1.2 near the CBD to 4.3 in suburban Medina County. Small households are common in areas populated by families that have not yet had children and by old populations whose children have established their own households. Blacks usually have higher birthrates and larger families than whites. There are 3.3 people in the average SMSA black household. Within the city, black household size is also 3.3, which contrasts with an average of 3 for all city residents. Average household sizes are below 3 throughout much of the city except for the black ghetto.

**Female Headship.** The Census Bureau defines female headship in terms of the absence of male spouse. Twelve percent of all SMSA families are headed by females as are 25 percent of all city families. Cleveland's proportion of female headship is unusually high. It exceeds 10 percent through most of the city, with tract values rising to well over 30 percent in the black ghetto. Outside the city and its immediate suburbs, female headship in excess of 10 percent is rare. Cleveland has 36 percent of the SMSA's total population, but it contains 58 percent of the SMSA's families headed by females.

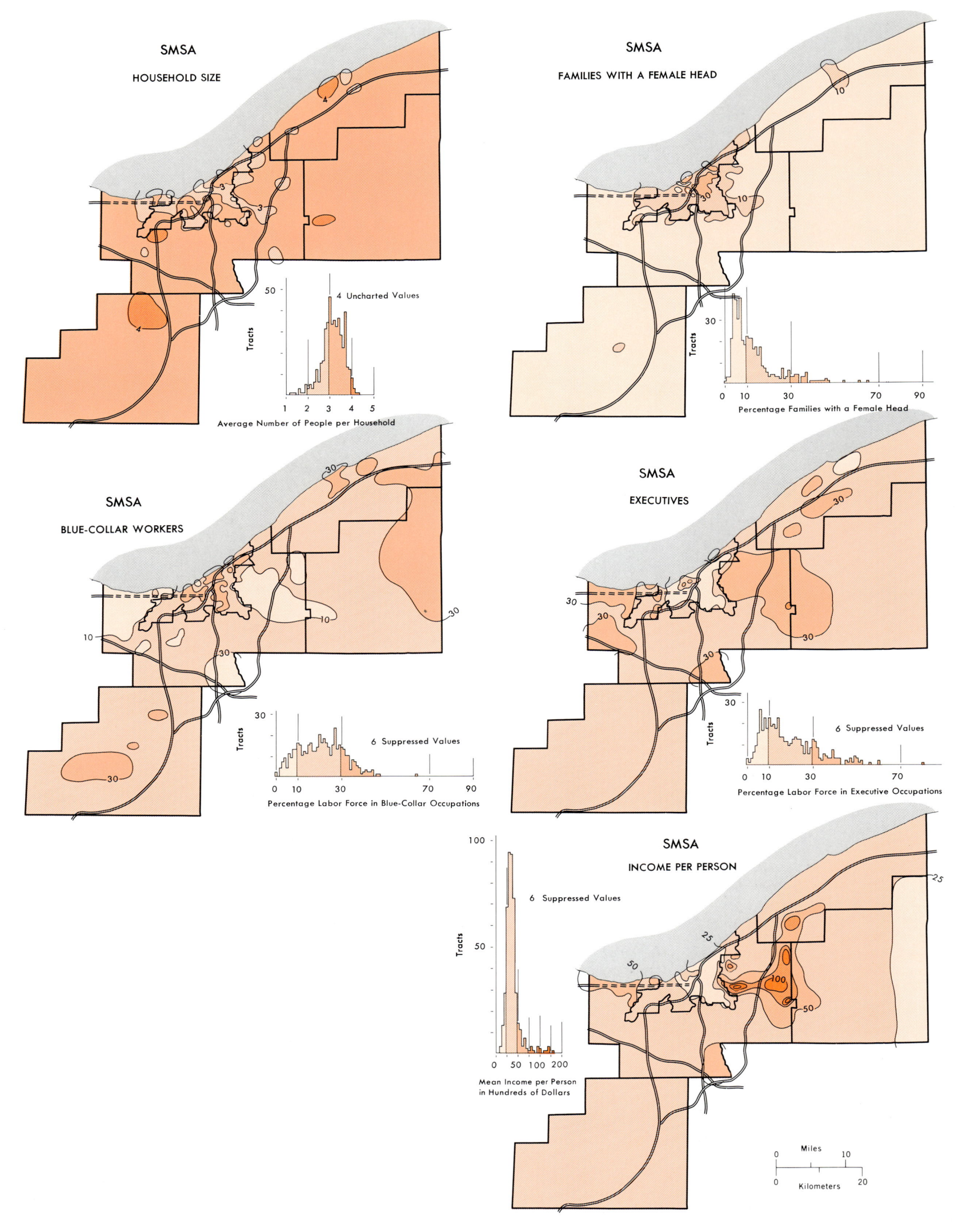

## Nineteenth-Century Inland Centers and Ports: Cleveland

### SMSA
#### HOUSEHOLD SIZE
Average Number of People per Household
4 Uncharted Values

### SMSA
#### FAMILIES WITH A FEMALE HEAD
Percentage Families with a Female Head

### SMSA
#### BLUE-COLLAR WORKERS
Percentage Labor Force in Blue-Collar Occupations
6 Suppressed Values

### SMSA
#### EXECUTIVES
Percentage Labor Force in Executive Occupations
6 Suppressed Values

### SMSA
#### INCOME PER PERSON
Mean Income per Person in Hundreds of Dollars
6 Suppressed Values

## CITY
ITALIAN-AMERICANS

Each Black Dot Represents 50 Italian Born

## CITY

INDUSTRIAL AREAS

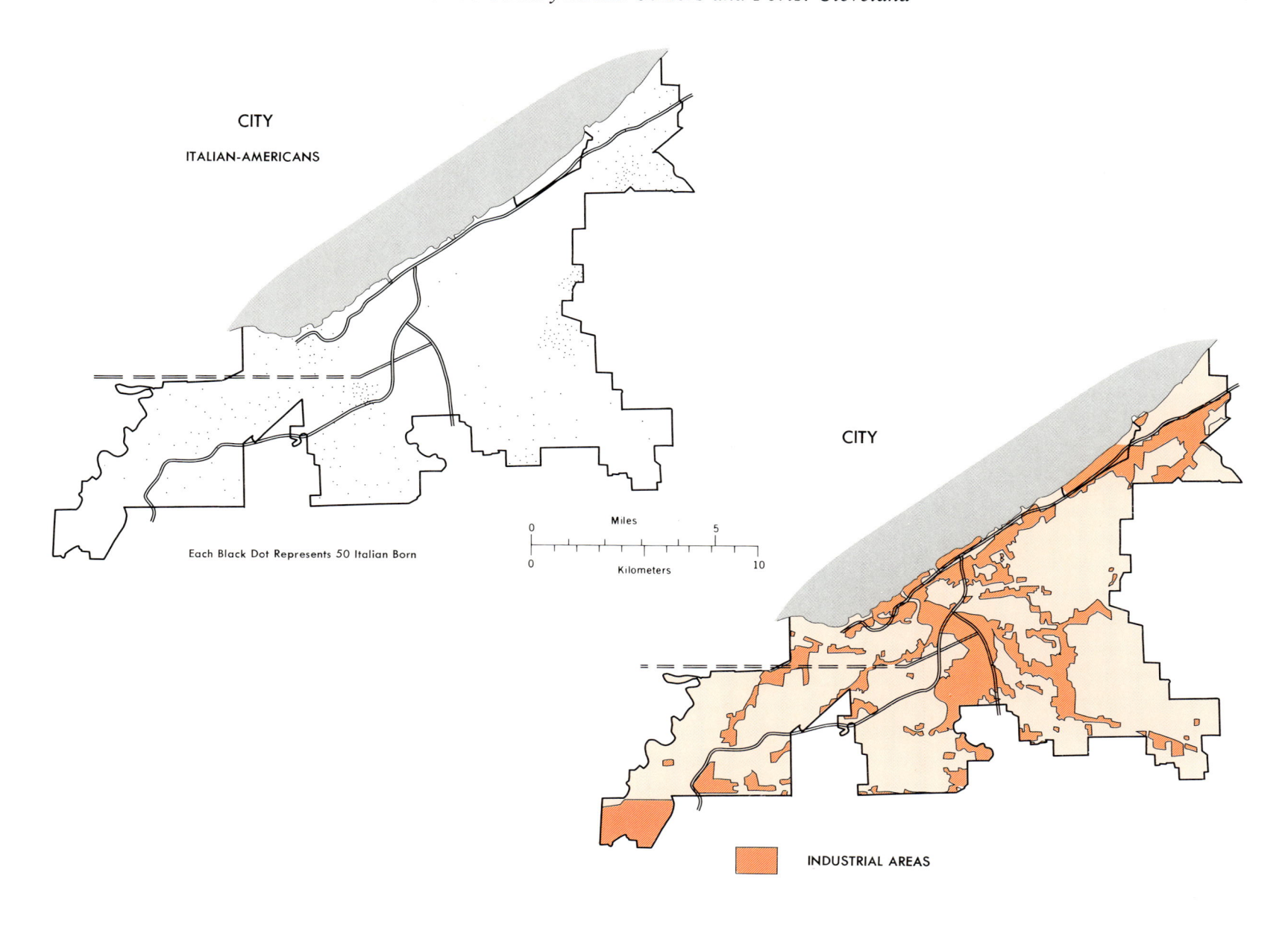

**Occupations.** Eighteen percent of the SMSA labor force work at blue-collar (laborers and operatives) jobs, and 21 percent are executives (engineers, teachers, professionals, managers, proprietors, and administrators). The remaining 61 percent are service (34 percent) and clerical (27 percent) workers. The comparable figures for Cleveland City are: blue-collar, 26 percent; services, 39 percent; clerical, 24 percent; and executive, 11 percent. The proportion of Cleveland's labor force in blue-collar occupations is the highest for the central cities in the atlas, reflecting its heavy industrial economy.

Tract percentages of blue-collar workers range from zero to 64 percent. Percentages exceed 30 in several sections of Cleveland and in rural areas on the metropolitan periphery. Tract percentages fall below 10 in the eastern suburbs and along the lakeshore to the west.

The proportion of tract labor forces in executive occupations varies from zero to 80 percent. Much of Cleveland has percentages below 10 except for an executive population near the CBD that exceeds 30 percent in two tracts. Clusters of values over 30 percent ring the city, with the largest area located in the prestige suburbs to the east and southeast. The peak value of 80 percent is a small (84 workers), wealthy tract along the eastern boundary of Cuyahoga County.

**Income.** The mean income per person in the Cleveland SMSA is $3,700 per year. The city's mean is $2,850. The $850 difference is the largest central-city/SMSA difference among the metropolitan areas in the atlas. Income differentials in the SMSA are sharp. Individual tract means range from less than $1,000 to $13,000. Per person incomes are well below $2,500 in Cleveland's eastern half and in exurban Geauga County. High incomes are concentrated in the prestige suburbs east of the city. The highest per person income area is the small tract mentioned above.

## TOPICS OF SPECIAL INTEREST IN THE CLEVELAND REGION

**Industrial Areas.** Cleveland's industrial areas divide the city into sectors and fragments. Such divisions are not necessarily harmful, for the distinct boundaries they create define neighborhoods and help maintain their identities. But Cleveland's industrial zones—especially because they are so often located along railways or in the Cuyahoga River Valley—also constitute serious obstacles to easy movement in the city.

**Ethnicity.** The map of the 6,060 Italian-born in Cleveland exemplifies the preference of some ethnic groups for neighborhood homogeneity. Italian-American and eastern European resistance to penetration by blacks arises out of local housing shortages and lack of financial means to move to the suburbs. The net effect is to bar blacks (p. 131) from some housing that might be available to them if they were not black.

**Crime.** Urban whites commonly believe that most crimes are committed by blacks against whites. Mapping the total number of major crimes (murder, rape, robbery, assault, and various categories of theft) by census tracts for 1970 makes it clear that crimes are more frequent in black neighborhoods than in predominantly white areas of the city. Nonetheless, the experience of crime in black areas and the

*Nineteenth-Century Inland Centers and Ports: Cleveland*

CITY

CRIME
(See Text)

SMSA

POLITICAL FRAGMENTATION
(See Text)

Central City

Urbanized Areas

VOTING PATTERNS  CITY

STOKES (Black, Democrat)

TAFT (White, Republican)

CITY

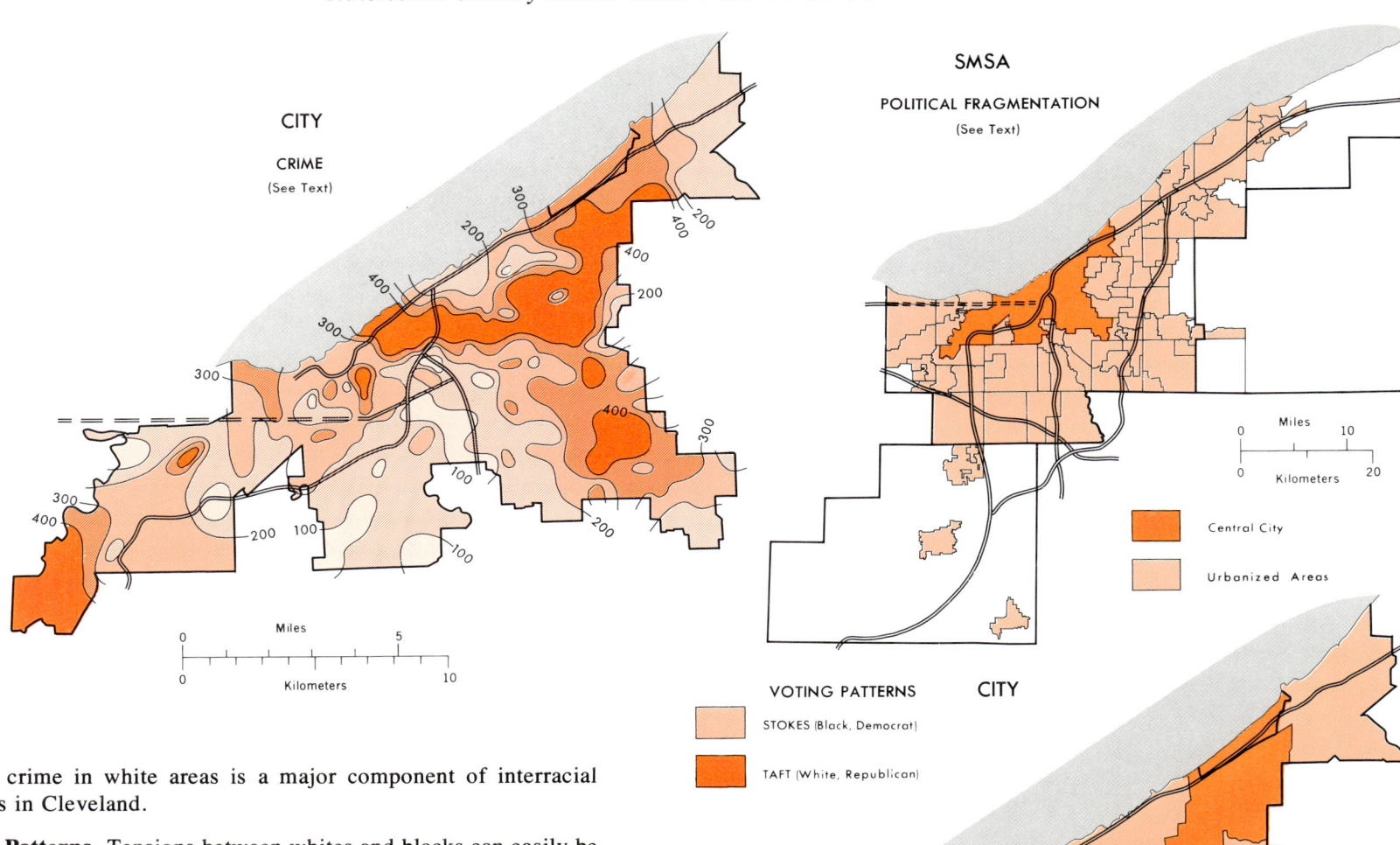

PERCENTAGE HOUSING UNITS
WITH MORE THAN ONE PERSON PER ROOM

fear of crime in white areas is a major component of interracial tensions in Cleveland.

**Voting Patterns.** Tensions between whites and blacks can easily be translated into clearly defined political antagonisms. The map of voting patterns shows the way the city split in a recent mayoral election between a black Democratic candidate (Stokes) and a white Republican candidate. The correspondence of precincts voting for Stokes with black neighborhoods (p. 131) is striking.

**Crowded Housing.** Overcrowded housing and the competition for better housing it stimulates are closely related to ethnic and political patterns. Areas where more than 10 percent of all housing units have more than 1.01 people per room are concentrated in black and Spanish-American (p. 131) neighborhoods. Cleveland's racial riots of the late 1960s broke out in areas where overcrowded housing seemed to be a distinguishing variable among more general conditions such as family disorganization and poverty.

**Political Fragmentation.** The view of Cleveland that emerges from the maps in this chapter is of a metropolis in which the quality of life in the central city stands in especially sharp contrast to life in the suburbs. Cleveland is not alone among American cities in being ringed by many small, antagonistic municipalities, but the fact that Cleveland City differs more sharply from the SMSA as a whole than do any of the other SMSAs mapped in the atlas suggests that suburban opposition to area-wide programs that might alleviate some of Cleveland's problems will be intense.

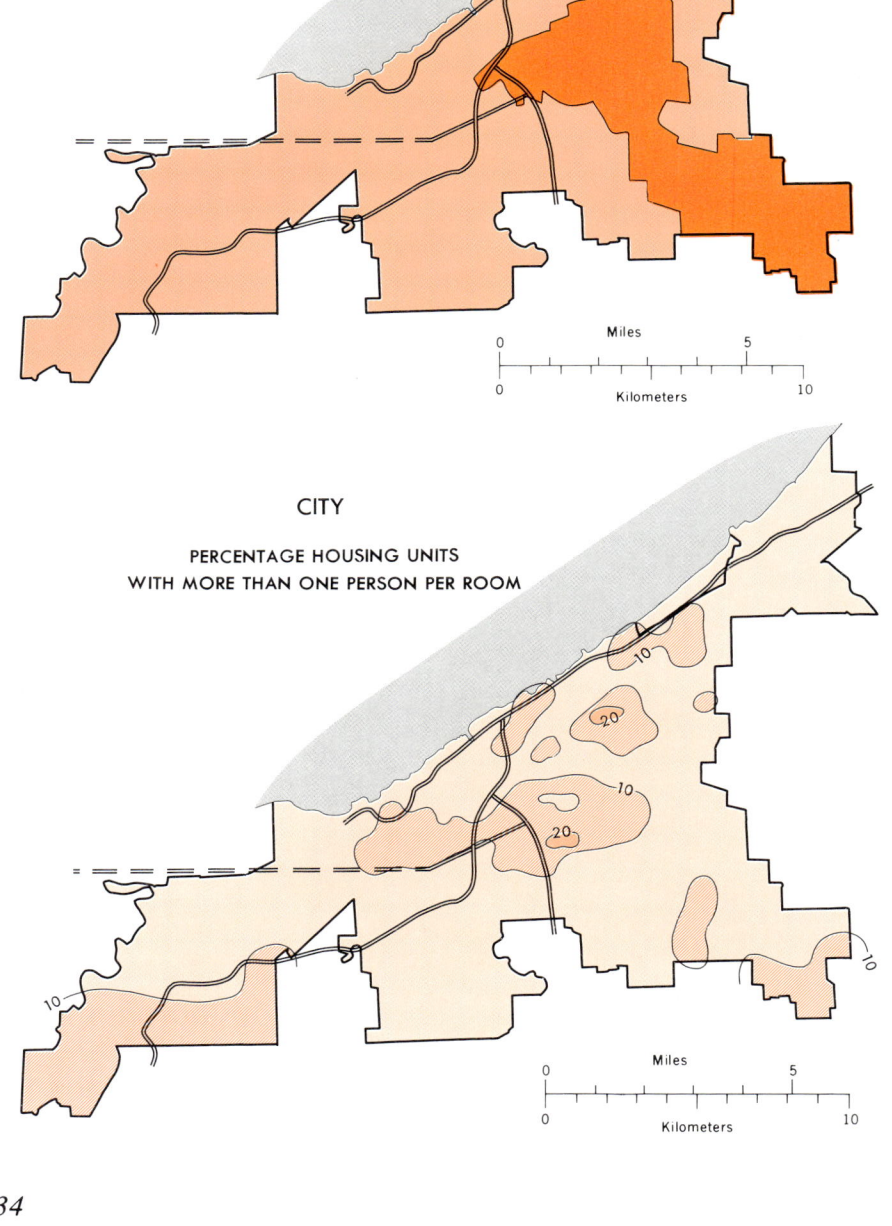

# CHAPTER 16

# Chicago

*. . . a tall bold slugger set vivid against the little soft cities.*

CARL SANDBURG, "Chicago," 1916

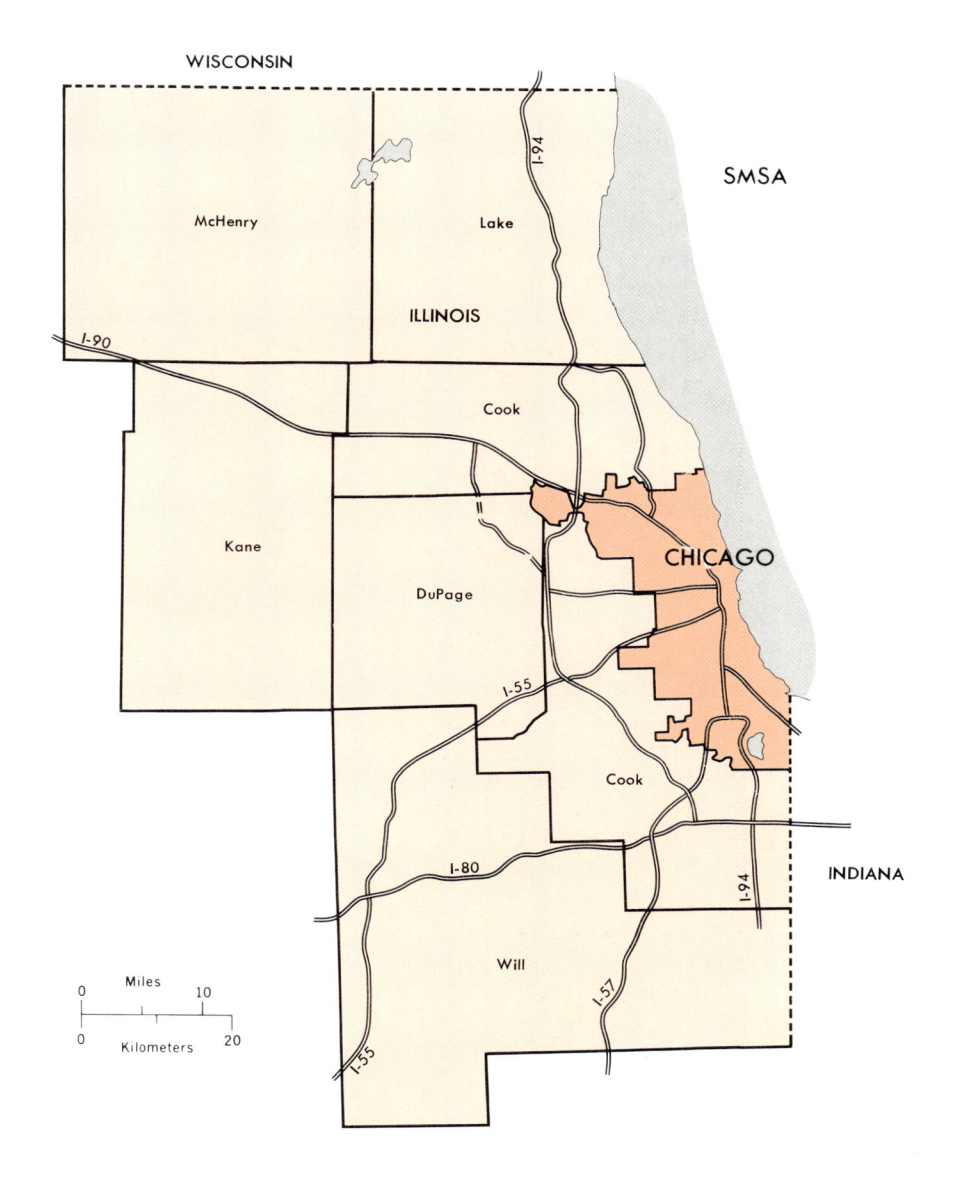

The Chicago Standard Metropolitan Statistical Area (SMSA) is the 3rd most populous in the nation. It has a population of 6,978,000. Chicago has a population of 3,363,000, or 48 percent of the SMSA total. Another 30 percent of the SMSA population lives in the parts of Cook County that are outside Chicago. The remaining 22 percent is divided among DuPage (7 percent), Kane (4 percent), Lake (5 percent), McHenry (2 percent), and Will (4 percent) counties. The

*Note:* All data are from the 1970 Censuses of Population and Housing unless otherwise indicated. Therefore the present tense refers to 1970 data except for income data which are from 1969. Cartographic conventions are explained in Chapter 1.

Daily Urban System (DUS) defined by counties that have at least 5 percent of their labor forces working in Cook County includes the Chicago SMSA and Lake and Porter counties in Indiana (p. 136). The DUS population is 7,611,000, which makes it the nation's 3rd most populous DUS.

Chicago began as a fur trading post at the mouth of the Chicago River in the 1770s. Fort Dearborn was established on the site in 1803. By 1850 Chicago had become the focus of transportation linkages between the East and the West, and by 1860 it had begun to consolidate its position of dominance in the Midwest by sending out

## Nineteenth-Century Inland Centers and Ports: Chicago

10 trunk rail lines in all directions. By the turn of the century it was the nation's 2nd city with 1,700,000 people, a position it has retained since, even though the SMSA slipped behind the Los Angeles SMSA in the 1970 Census (p. 10).

The Chicago region is flat, with low morainic hills inland from the shore of Lake Michigan. The city is built on an almost completely flat lake plain. The low, smooth surface produced serious drainage problems for the city's early residents which were gradually solved by the simple expedient of raising both the land surface and buildings. Once drainage problems were overcome, the smooth surface allowed railroads to proceed in almost any direction, and industrial and urban expansion proceeded radially from the city center. Much of the city burned down in 1871, leaving a third of the population homeless, but the destroyed area was rebuilt quickly. The original grid system was retained except for several radial routes inherited from Indian trails.

### HOUSING

**Housing Age.** Forty-eight percent of the SMSA's housing was built before 1940, 31 percent was built from 1940 through 1959, and 21 percent dates from 1960 to March 1970. Sixty-seven percent of the city's housing was built before 1940, 22 percent was erected from 1940 through 1959, and 11 percent was built from 1960 to March 1970. Chicago has 73 percent of the pre-1940 units in the SMSA in contrast to its 53 percent share of all SMSA housing units. Throughout a large area of central Chicago, pre-1940 housing is more than 70 percent of the housing stock. Old housing is less dominant in the northwest and southern parts of the city, where settlement came late, in some cases after World War II. The low percentages of old housing along the lakeshore north of the Central Business District (CBD) are produced by new high-rise apartment construction in the prestige residential sector. Percentages of old housing are low throughout suburban Cook County. Farther out, proportions of old housing rise above 30 percent in Kane, McHenry, and southern Will counties, where farmland and country towns coexist with suburban growth.

Although 128,000 units (11 percent of the city's total) were built from 1960 to March 1970, they usually exceed 10 percent of tract totals only where public renewal programs or housing projects have fostered new dwellings. An exception occurs along the lakeshore, where lake views provide an incentive for continued private renewal. Over 30 percent of tract units were built during the 1960s in a broad ring that covers northern Will County, outer Cook County, most of DuPage County, and central Lake County.

**Mobile Homes.** There are few mobile homes in the Chicago DUS. The 19,800 units in the region are only 0.8 percent of all DUS dwelling units. The few tracts in which mobile homes exceed 10 percent of all housing units are located in sparsely populated areas.

**Single-Unit Detached Housing.** Individual dwelling units make up 45 percent of the SMSA's housing stock and 24 percent of the city's units. Single-unit detached housing exceeds 70 percent of the units in almost all suburban tracts. Proportions of single units are below 70 percent in most of Chicago and below 10 percent in the old core area. Chicago's multiple-unit housing consists largely of duplexes (19 percent of the total housing stock), 3- and 4-unit buildings (16 percent) and small to medium-size (5 to 49 units) apartment buildings (28 percent). The residual 13 percent is in apartments of 50 or more units. Outside the city percentages of single-unit housing are high except where suburban apartment complexes occur, as is true at the intersection of Interstates 90 and 94 near O'Hare airport.

**Housing Value and Rent.** The mean value of owner-occupied housing in the SMSA is $28,000, and the corresponding figure for Chicago is $23,000. Individual tract means range from $9,000 to

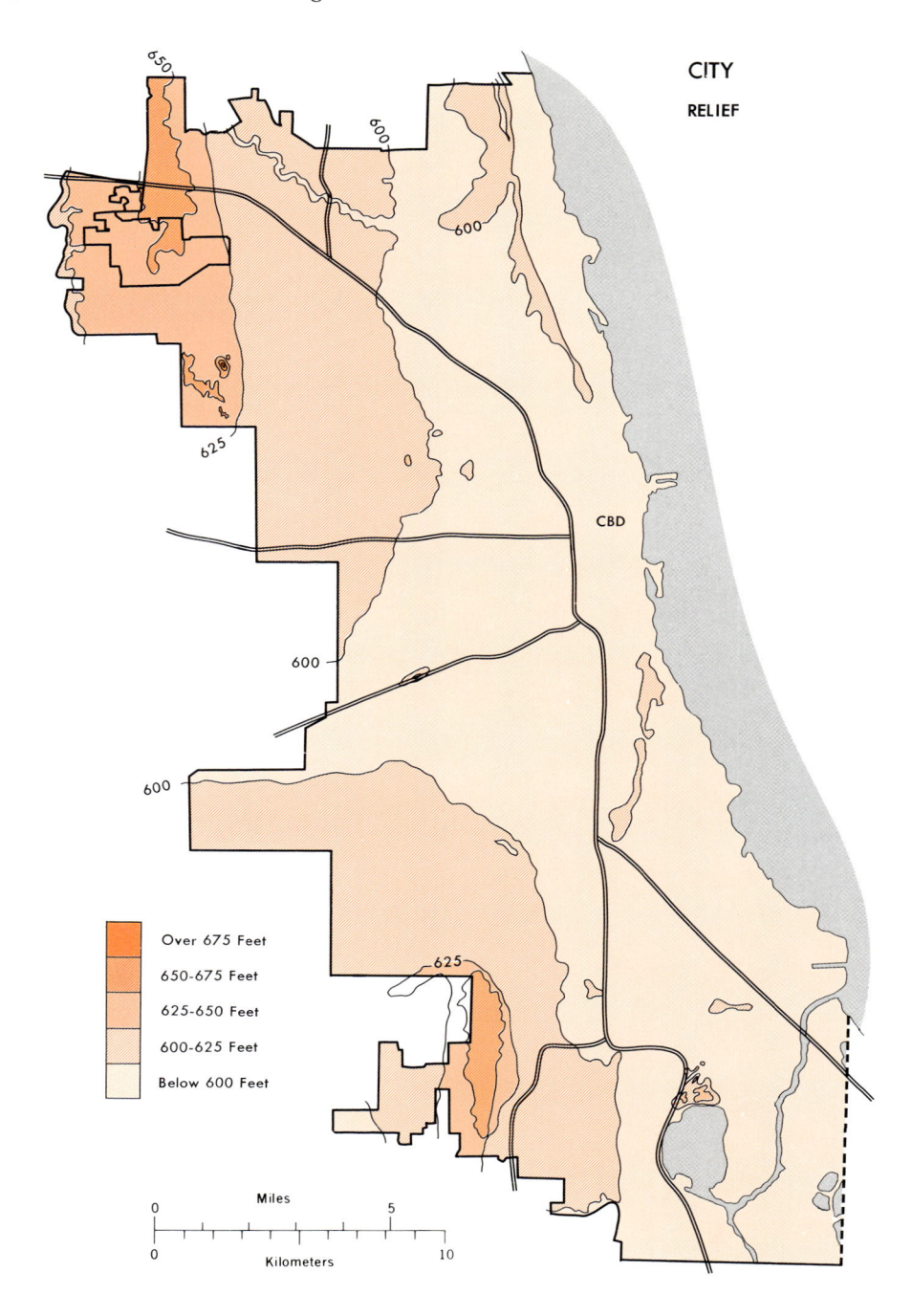

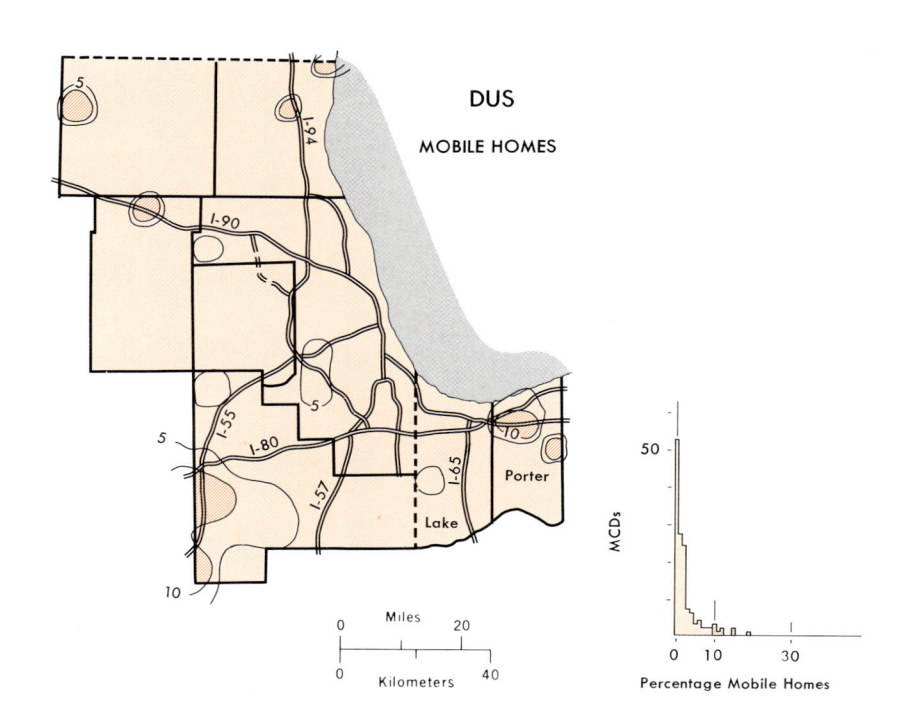

136

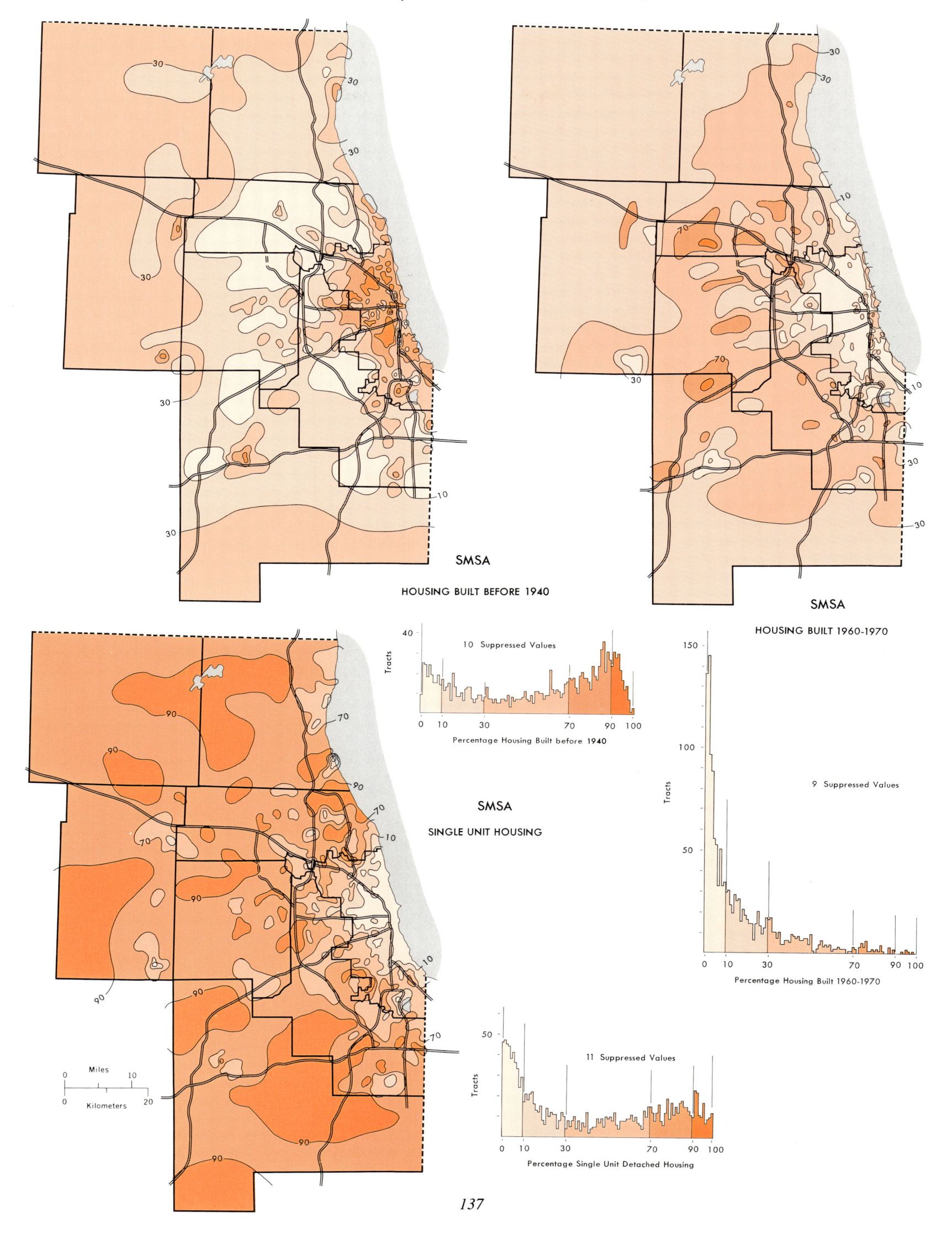

## Nineteenth-Century Inland Centers and Ports: Chicago

SMSA
HOUSING BUILT BEFORE 1940

SMSA
HOUSING BUILT 1960-1970

SMSA
SINGLE UNIT HOUSING

*137*

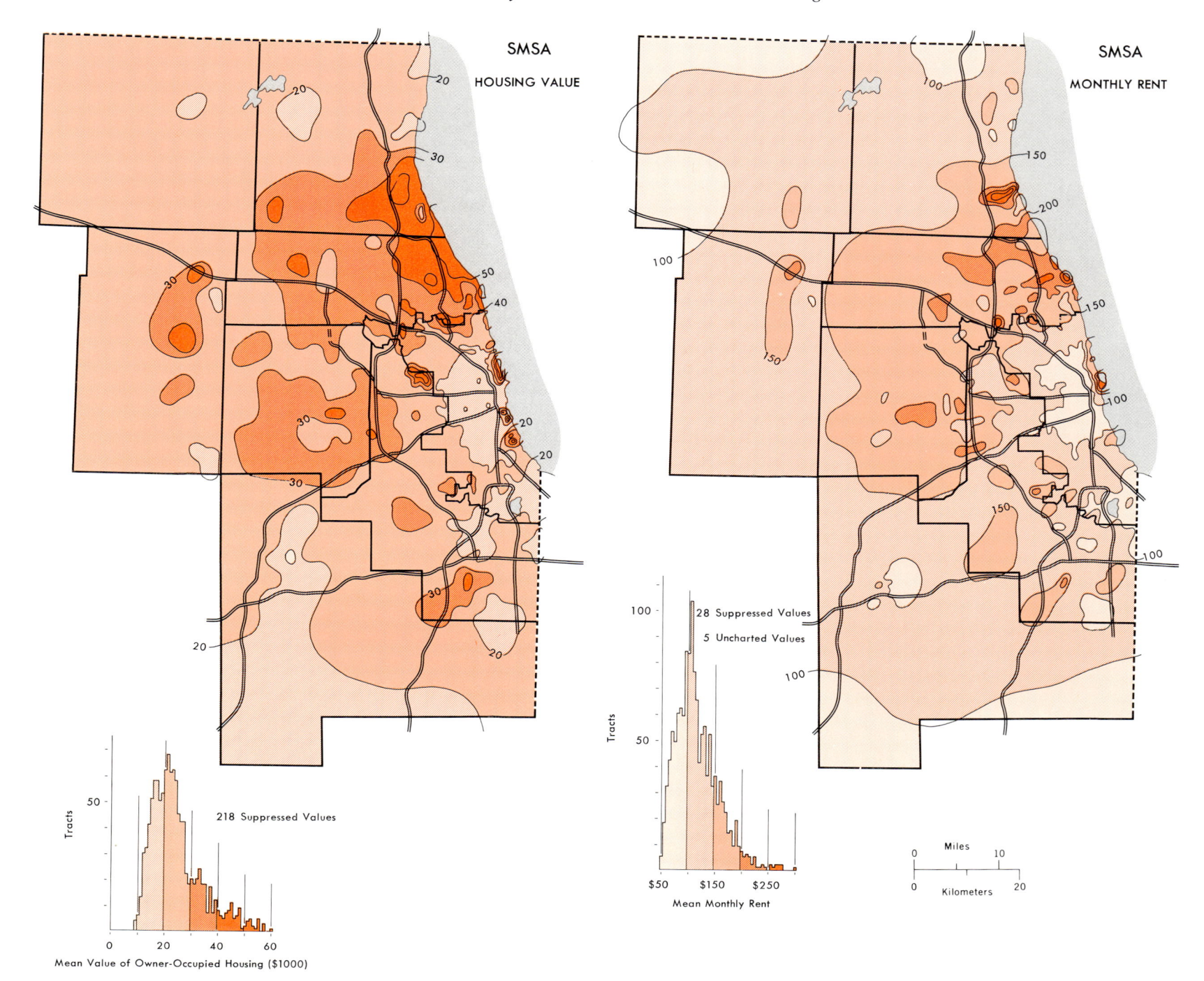

$60,000. The very low-value tracts are scattered in a large area of central Chicago. Mean values over $50,000 occur in Oak Park west of Chicago, along the lakeshore north of the city, and along the Gold Coast north of the CBD. Suburban housing values exceed $40,000 in scattered areas but are usually in the $20,000 to $39,000 range except in southwestern Will County, where values are less than $20,000.

Mean monthly contract rents average $121 for the SMSA and $113 in Chicago. Individual tract means range from less than $50 (not plotted or mapped) to $300. The region's highest rents are paid in Lake Forest, a suburban community along the north shore. Rents on the Gold Coast exceed $250. Similar prices are paid for apartments adjacent to the intersection of Interstates 90 and 94. Housing in the northwestern suburbs is generally more expensive, whether purchased or rented, than it is south and southwest of Chicago.

## THE PEOPLE

**Population Density.** Chicago's overall population density is 15,150 people per square mile (5,800 per square kilometer). Densities are low in the CBD area and in the industrial area that extends northwest from the CBD along Interstate 90. All densities over 40,000 per square mile (15,600 per square kilometer) are consolidated into a single category on the map, but the highest densities occur in predominantly black neighborhoods (p. 140). Densities in the high-rise housing projects built along Interstate 90 south of the CBD are especially high, reaching peaks of 120,000 per square mile (46,000 per square kilometer). Population density is low on the southwest and northwest sides, which were settled later and at lower densities than the core areas. Population densities are low outside Chicago, where they rarely exceed 10,000 people per square mile (3,900 per square kilometer) except in outlying towns (SMSA map on p. 313).

**Age and the Elderly.** The median age of the Chicago SMSA population is 28 years. The city population (median age of 30 years) is older than the SMSA population. Medians in individual tracts range from 11 to 50 years. Along the lakefront and near the CBD, older medians are produced by affluent couples living in apartments and condominiums. Median ages are above 30 years in the southeastern, western, and northern parts of the city and into the inner suburbs. Medians below 30 years are widespread in the outer suburbs and in the densely populated parts of the central city. Central-city medians below 20 years occur in areas where the population is over 90 percent

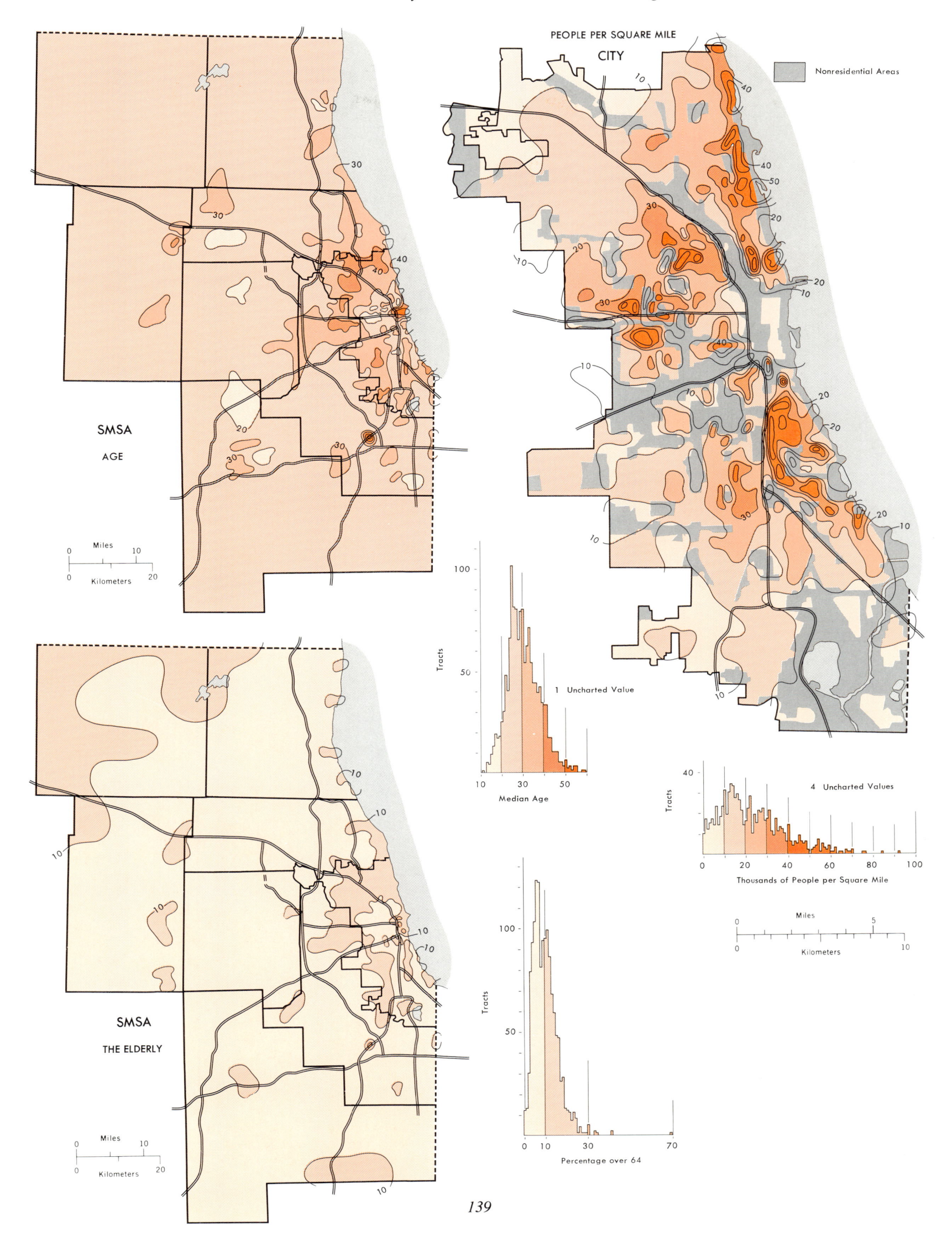

## Nineteenth-Century Inland Centers and Ports: Chicago

PEOPLE PER SQUARE MILE
CITY

Nonresidential Areas

SMSA
AGE

SMSA
THE ELDERLY

1 Uncharted Value
Median Age

4 Uncharted Values
Thousands of People per Square Mile

Percentage over 64

139

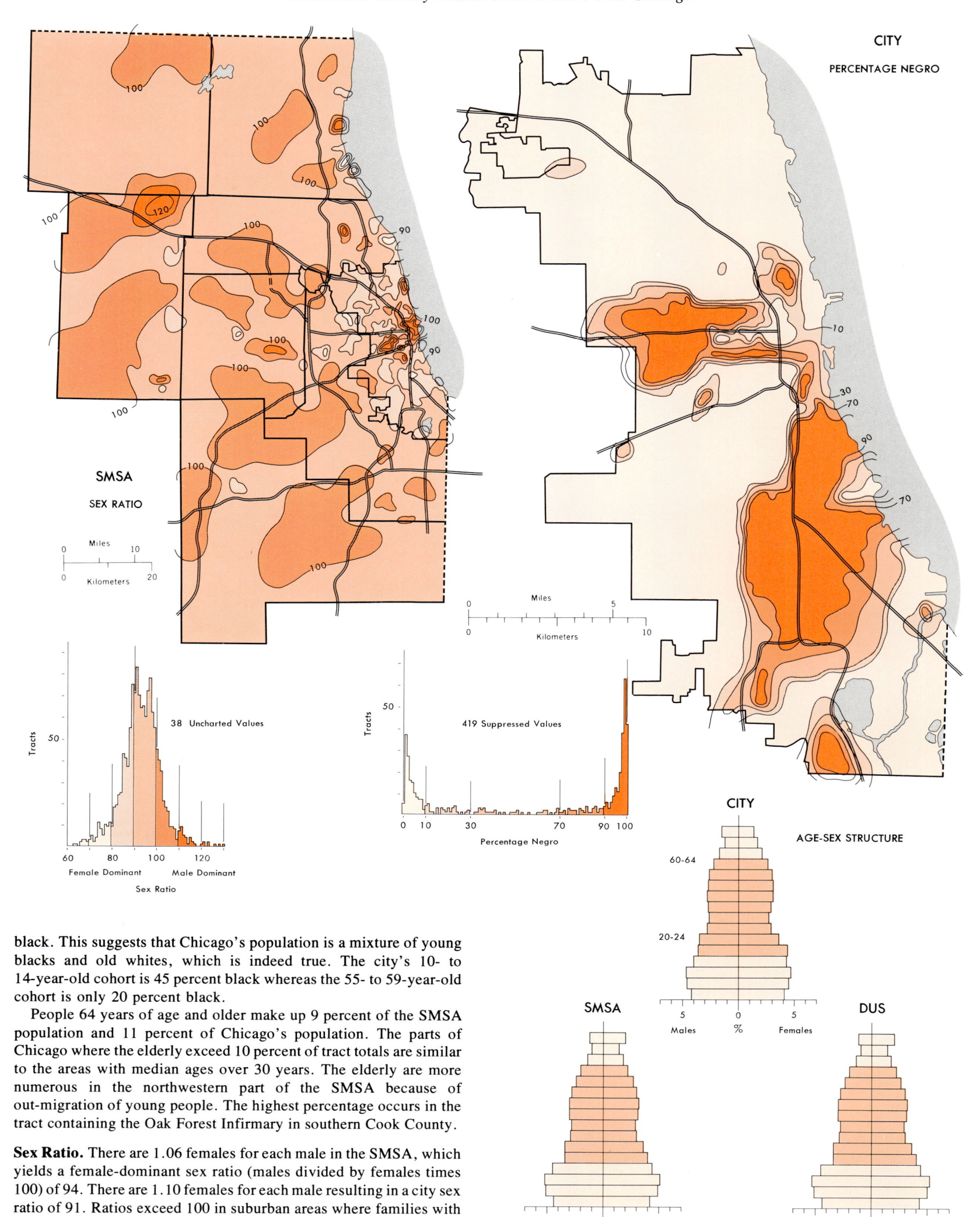

black. This suggests that Chicago's population is a mixture of young blacks and old whites, which is indeed true. The city's 10- to 14-year-old cohort is 45 percent black whereas the 55- to 59-year-old cohort is only 20 percent black.

People 64 years of age and older make up 9 percent of the SMSA population and 11 percent of Chicago's population. The parts of Chicago where the elderly exceed 10 percent of tract totals are similar to the areas with median ages over 30 years. The elderly are more numerous in the northwestern part of the SMSA because of out-migration of young people. The highest percentage occurs in the tract containing the Oak Forest Infirmary in southern Cook County.

**Sex Ratio.** There are 1.06 females for each male in the SMSA, which yields a female-dominant sex ratio (males divided by females times 100) of 94. There are 1.10 females for each male resulting in a city sex ratio of 91. Ratios exceed 100 in suburban areas where families with young children are numerous. Thus young populations in new suburban housing are often male-dominant whereas the older central-city population is female-dominant.

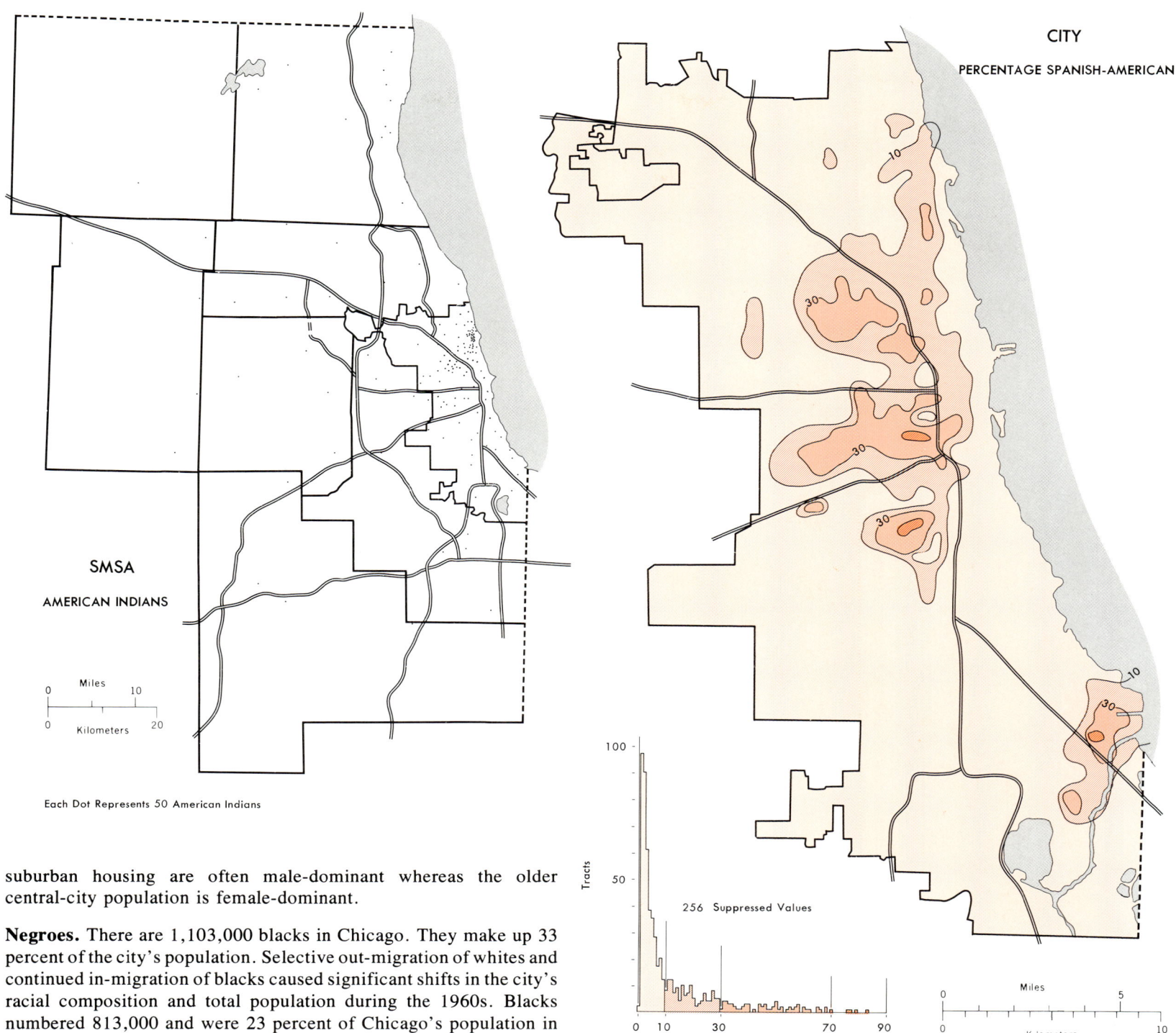

**Negroes.** There are 1,103,000 blacks in Chicago. They make up 33 percent of the city's population. Selective out-migration of whites and continued in-migration of blacks caused significant shifts in the city's racial composition and total population during the 1960s. Blacks numbered 813,000 and were 23 percent of Chicago's population in 1960. Chicago was on the receiving end of a massive migration of blacks from the rural South during the 1950s and early 1960s. The new arrivals sought cheap housing within areas where they were not excluded by restrictive covenants. Blacks now occupy two ghettos, one south and the other west of the CBD. The island of nonblacks along Lake Michigan is the Hyde Park-University of Chicago area. Gradients between heavily black and almost completely white neighborhoods are steep. The 419 suppressed tracts have so few blacks that they fall below the Census suppression threshold. They would swell the cluster of tracts at the left edge of the histogram were percentages calculated for them. There are few blacks outside Chicago (p. 385); the city contains 90 percent of the SMSA's blacks.

**Spanish-Americans.** The Census Bureau estimates the number of Hispanics in Chicago by counting people who speak Spanish. By this reckoning there are 247,000 Spanish-Americans in the city. Tract values range from zero to 85 percent, but the few zero values and the 256 suppressed tracts suggest that some Hispanics live in almost all tracts. The majority, however, are concentrated north and west of the CBD. The two heaviest concentrations of Hispanics are to the north (Puerto Rican) and south (Mexican-American) of the west-side black ghetto, and a third concentration (Mexican-American) is west of the south-side ghetto. The pattern is repeated in the southeast, where both Hispanics and blacks occupy somewhat distinct neighborhoods adjacent to U.S. Steel's South Works.

Puerto Ricans and Mexican-Americans each constitute about a third of Chicago's Hispanic community. The remainder are most likely Cuban (6 percent), foreign stock from South and Central America (8 percent), or indigenous Mexican-Americans. Mexican-Americans came to Chicago in large numbers during the World War I industrial boom. Puerto Ricans began to arrive after World War II, usually via one of the East Coast cities.

**American Indians.** Chicago has one of the nation's large urban Indian populations. The Census Bureau enumerated 9,000 in 1970, which is probably a serious undercount. A few are scattered in suburban areas, but 73 percent of the SMSA's enumerated Indians live in Chicago, where many concentrate near the American Indian Center in the city's north-side Uptown Area.

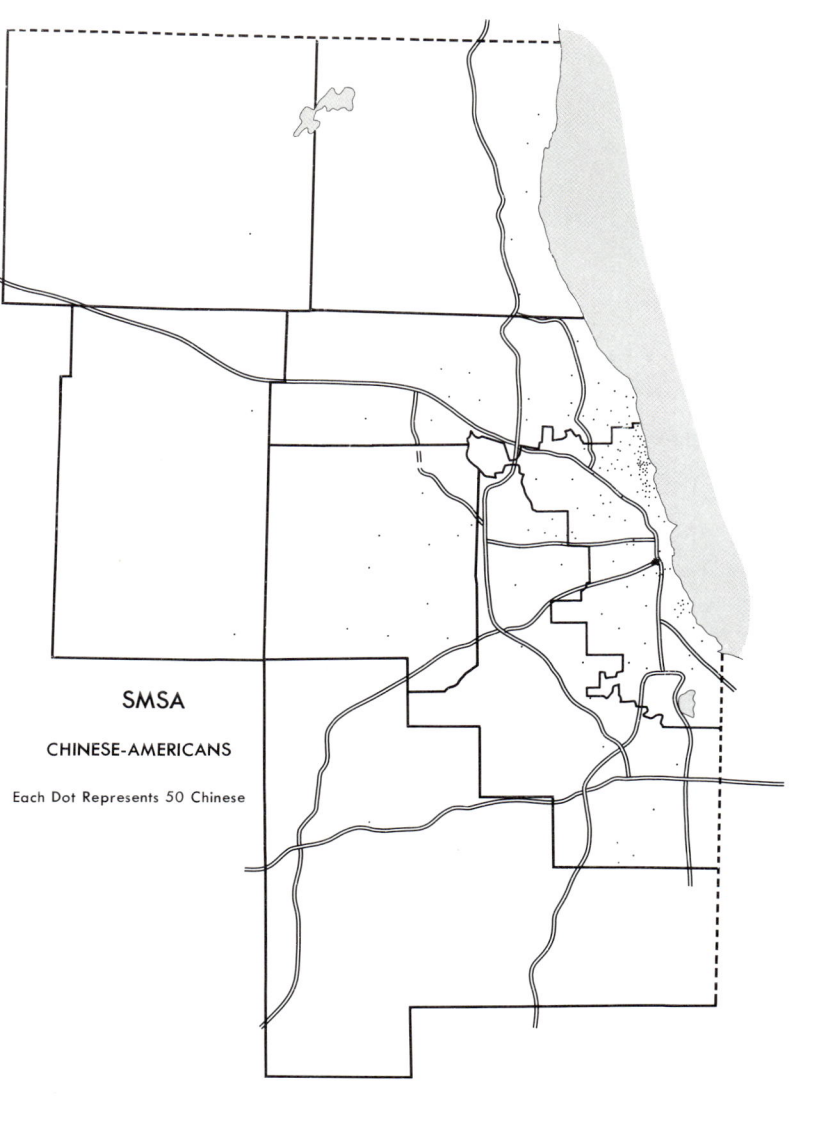

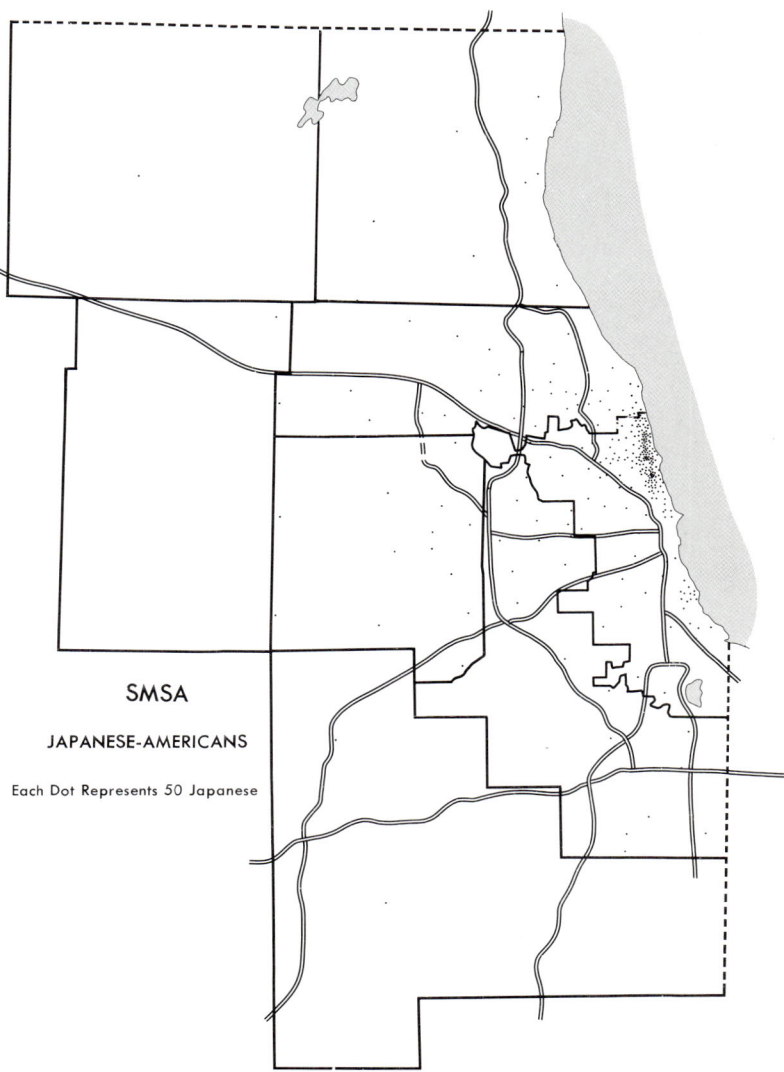

*Nineteenth-Century Inland Centers and Ports: Chicago*

**Chinese-Americans.** The census questionnaire requires nonwhite persons to identify themselves as members of 1 of 8 "racial" categories: Negro, Indian, Japanese, Chinese, Filipino, Korean, Hawaiian, or Other. The SMSA's 12,650 Chinese are concentrated in Chicago, where 74 percent of them live. Many of the city's Chinese-Americans live in the city's south-side Chinatown located at the intersection of Interstates 55 and 94.

**Japanese-Americans.** In the Chicago SMSA, 15,300 said they were Japanese. Seventy-one percent of the SMSA's Japanese live in Chicago, where they cluster on the city's north side.

**Irish-Americans.** There are 18,800 Irish-born and 72,700 people of Irish parentage in the Chicago SMSA. Seventy-three percent of the Irish-born and 59 percent of the people with at least one Irish-born parent live in Chicago. Irish-Americans have migrated outward along well-defined corridors from the central-city neighborhoods they formerly occupied. They are especially concentrated in northern and west-south-central Chicago and the adjacent inner suburbs.

**German-Americans.** The Chicago SMSA has a large Germanic community consisting of 58,100 German-born and 166,500 first-generation German-Americans. German-Americans are more dispersed throughout the SMSA than the other ethnic groups mapped here. Only 54 percent of the German-born and 41 percent of those with at least one German-born parent live in Chicago. German-Americans are spread throughout the SMSA in a way that suggests they have moved into the mainstream of Chicago's economic and social life more successfully than the other ethnic groups mapped here.

**Polish-Americans.** There are 69,400 Polish-born and 214,900 people

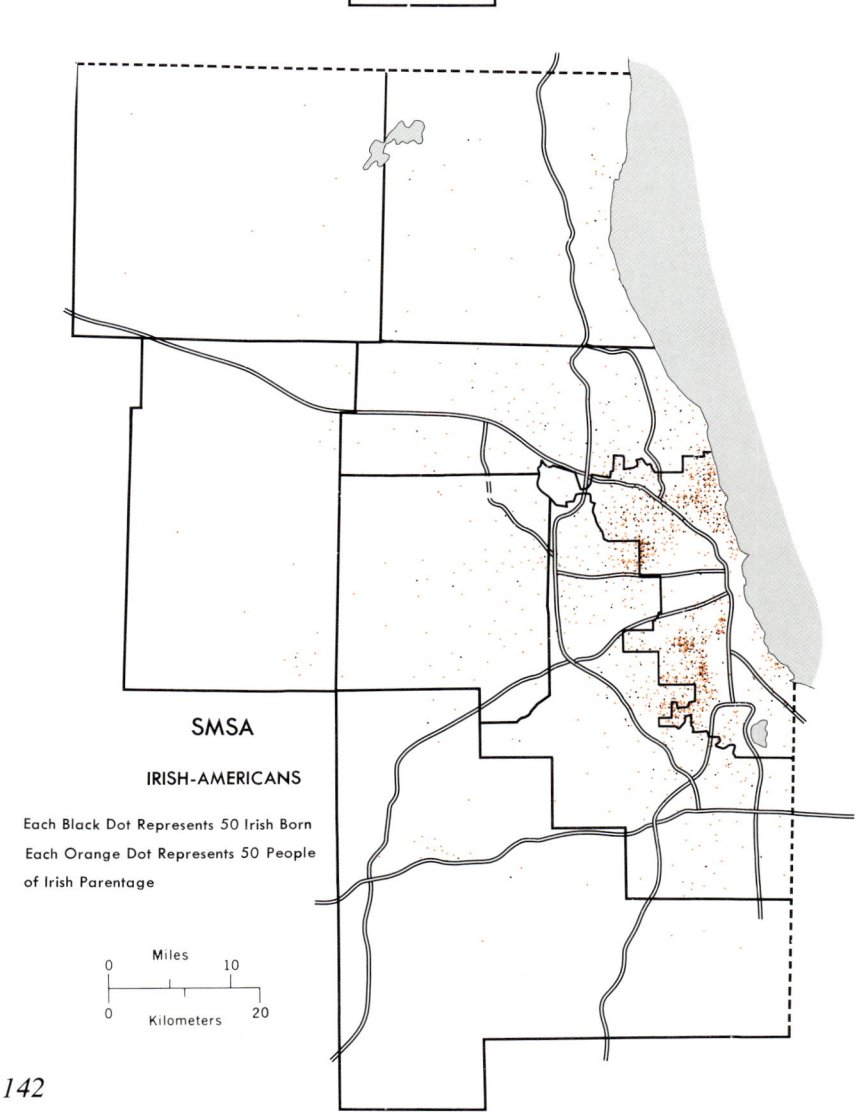

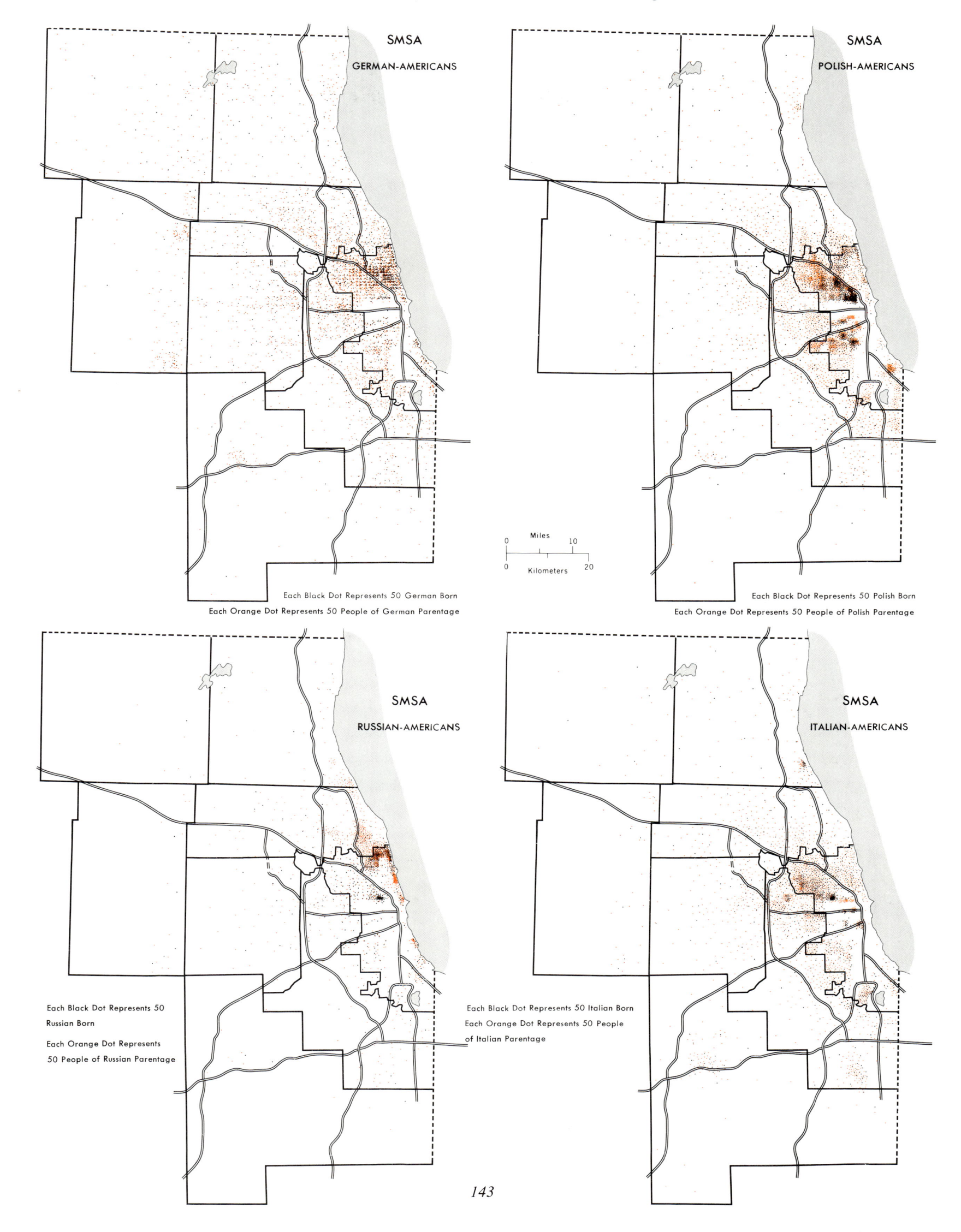

## Nineteenth-Century Inland Centers and Ports: Chicago

SMSA
GERMAN-AMERICANS

Each Black Dot Represents 50 German Born
Each Orange Dot Represents 50 People of German Parentage

SMSA
POLISH-AMERICANS

Each Black Dot Represents 50 Polish Born
Each Orange Dot Represents 50 People of Polish Parentage

SMSA
RUSSIAN-AMERICANS

Each Black Dot Represents 50 Russian Born
Each Orange Dot Represents 50 People of Russian Parentage

SMSA
ITALIAN-AMERICANS

Each Black Dot Represents 50 Italian Born
Each Orange Dot Represents 50 People of Italian Parentage

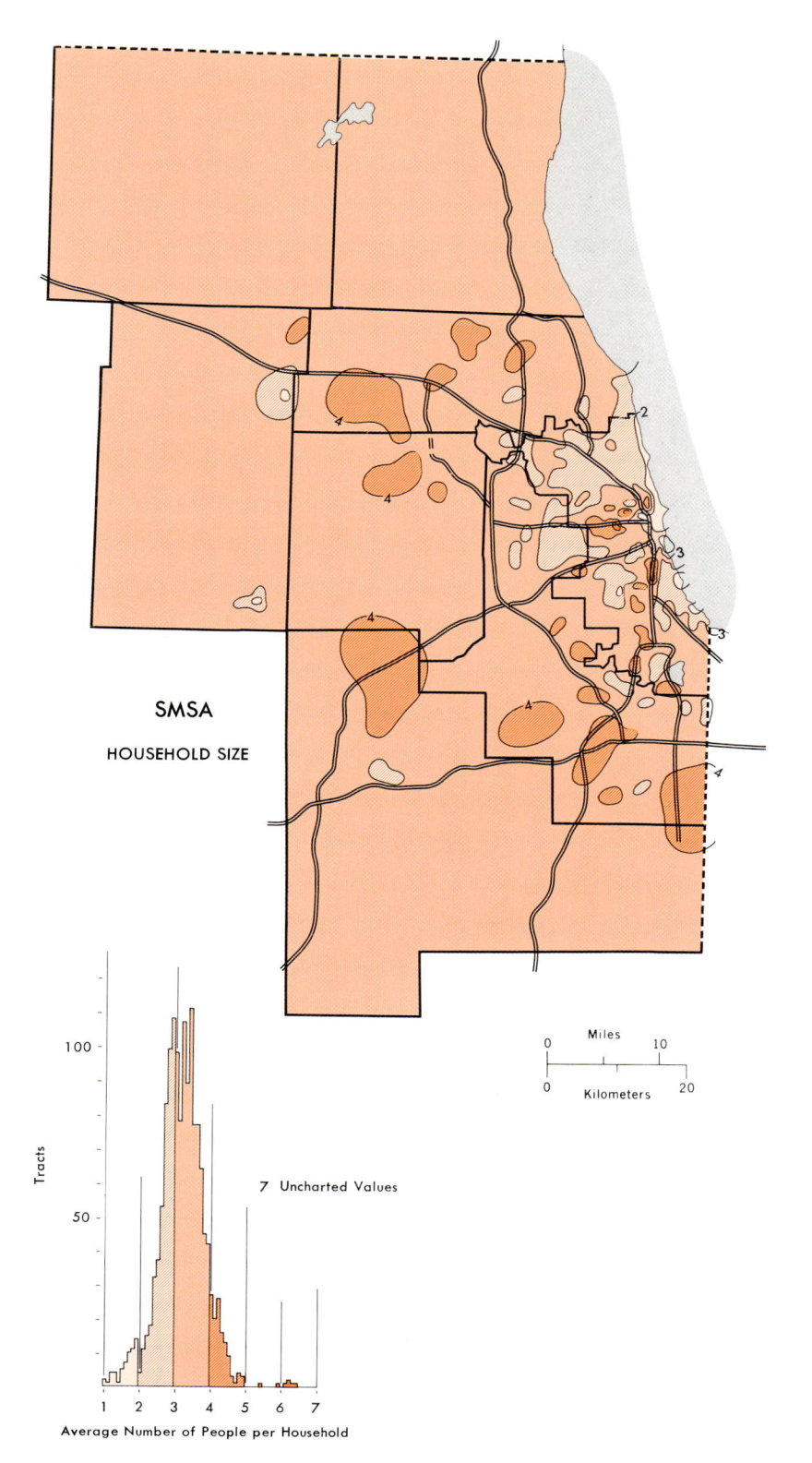

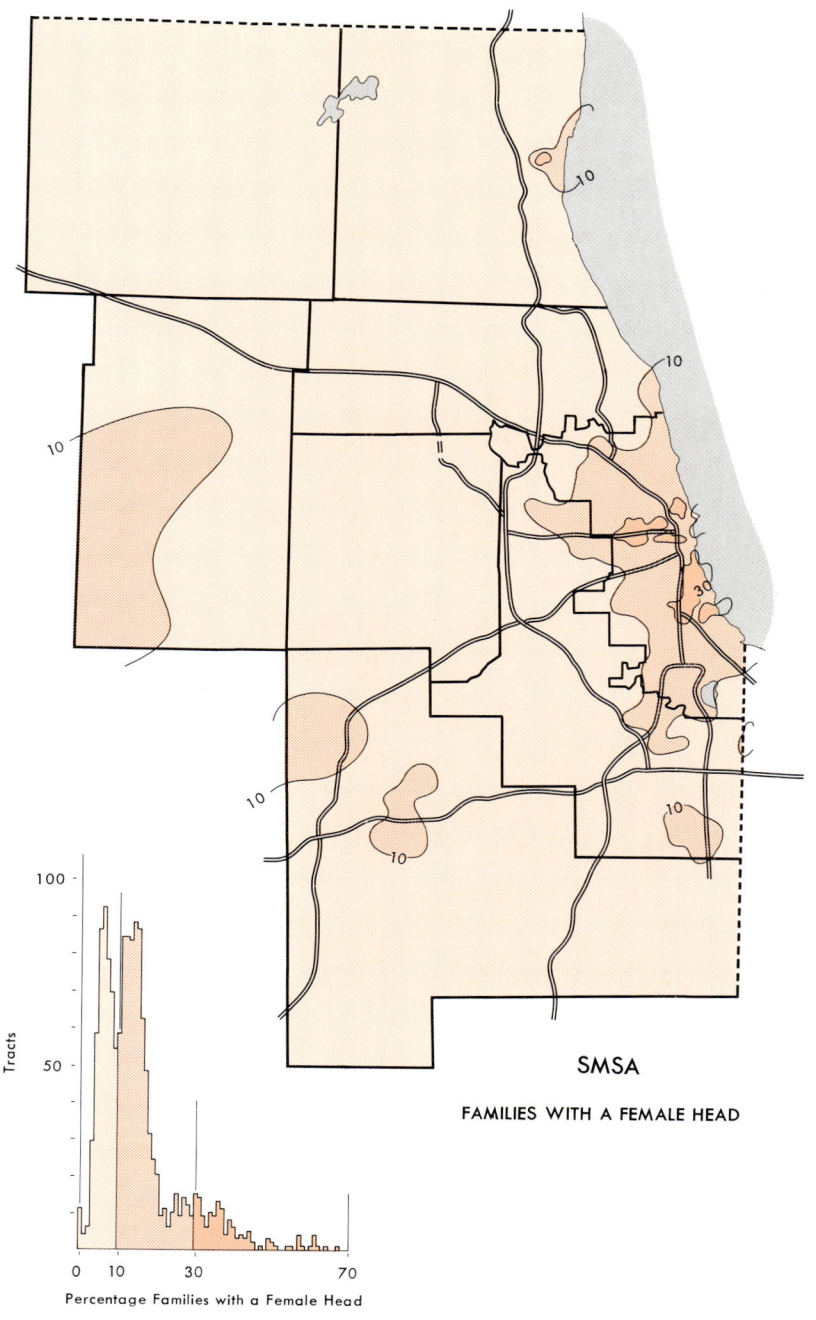

with at least one Polish-born parent in the Chicago SMSA. Eighty percent of the SMSA's Polish-born and 63 percent of its population of Polish parentage reside within the city. Polish-Americans live in three parts of the city: one runs northwest from the CBD just south of Interstate 90-94; the second extends west and southwest from the CBD on both sides of Interstate 55; the third—which has no counterpart among the other ethnic groups mapped here—is one of Chicago's earliest Polish neighborhoods in southeastern Chicago near the steel mills and foundries around Calumet Harbor.

**Russian-Americans.** The SMSA contains 28,700 Russian-born and 76,100 people with at least one Russian-born parent. Seventy-nine percent of the Russian-born live in Chicago in contrast to 55 percent of those of Russian parentage. The majority of Russian foreign stock are Jews rather than ethnic Russians. Many Russian-born occupy one neighborhood on the fringe of the expanding ghetto. People of Russian parentage have taken part in the general shift to northern Chicago and adjacent Skokie, but they have also clustered in several lakeshore communities. Many of the areas now occupied by blacks were formerly Jewish neighborhoods. This succession, common in American cities, is a function of the relatively small family sizes and greater prosperity of Jews, who were starting to leave their original urban housing for better quarters at the same time blacks started arriving in northern cities in large numbers.

**Italian-Americans.** The 53,500 Italian-born and the 143,600 people with at least one Italian-born parent together comprise 2.8 percent of the SMSA population. Sixty-one percent of the SMSA's Italian-born and 45 percent of its people of Italian parentage live inside the city. Italian-Americans are most concentrated on Chicago's northwest and west sides, sharply segregated from blacks.

Chicago was an important destination for immigrants throughout the late 19th and early 20th centuries. In addition to the groups mapped here, Austrians, Czechs, Swedes, and numerous other groups came to Chicago and created ethnic enclaves. The city's grid-street system and the numerous railroads traversing Chicago created clearly defined areas that ethnic groups could identify and occupy. The

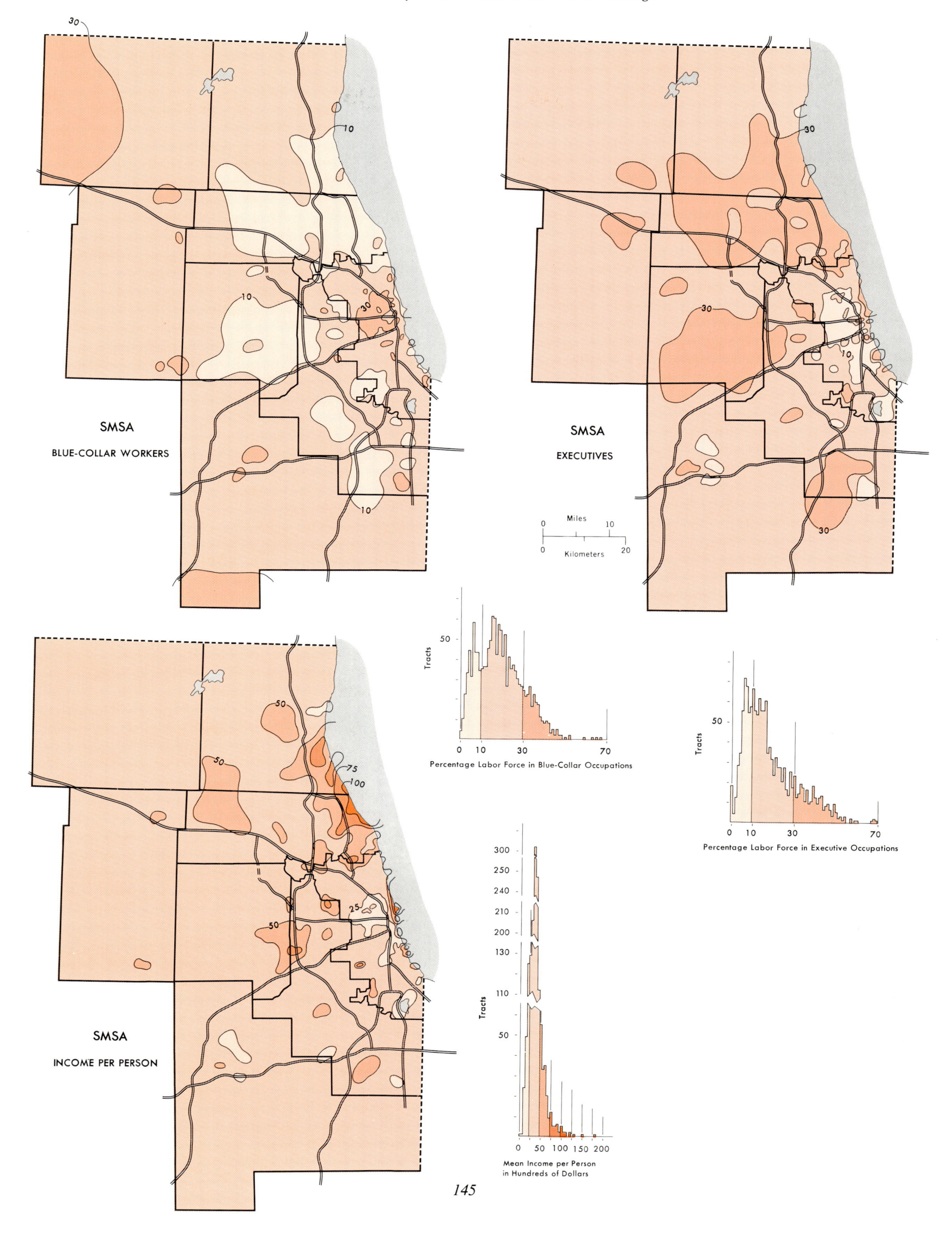

Nineteenth-Century Inland Centers and Ports: Chicago

SMSA
BLUE-COLLAR WORKERS

SMSA
EXECUTIVES

SMSA
INCOME PER PERSON

Percentage Labor Force in Blue-Collar Occupations

Percentage Labor Force in Executive Occupations

Mean Income per Person
in Hundreds of Dollars

**RESIDENTIAL CHANGE, 1965-1970**
(See Text)

SMSA

CITY

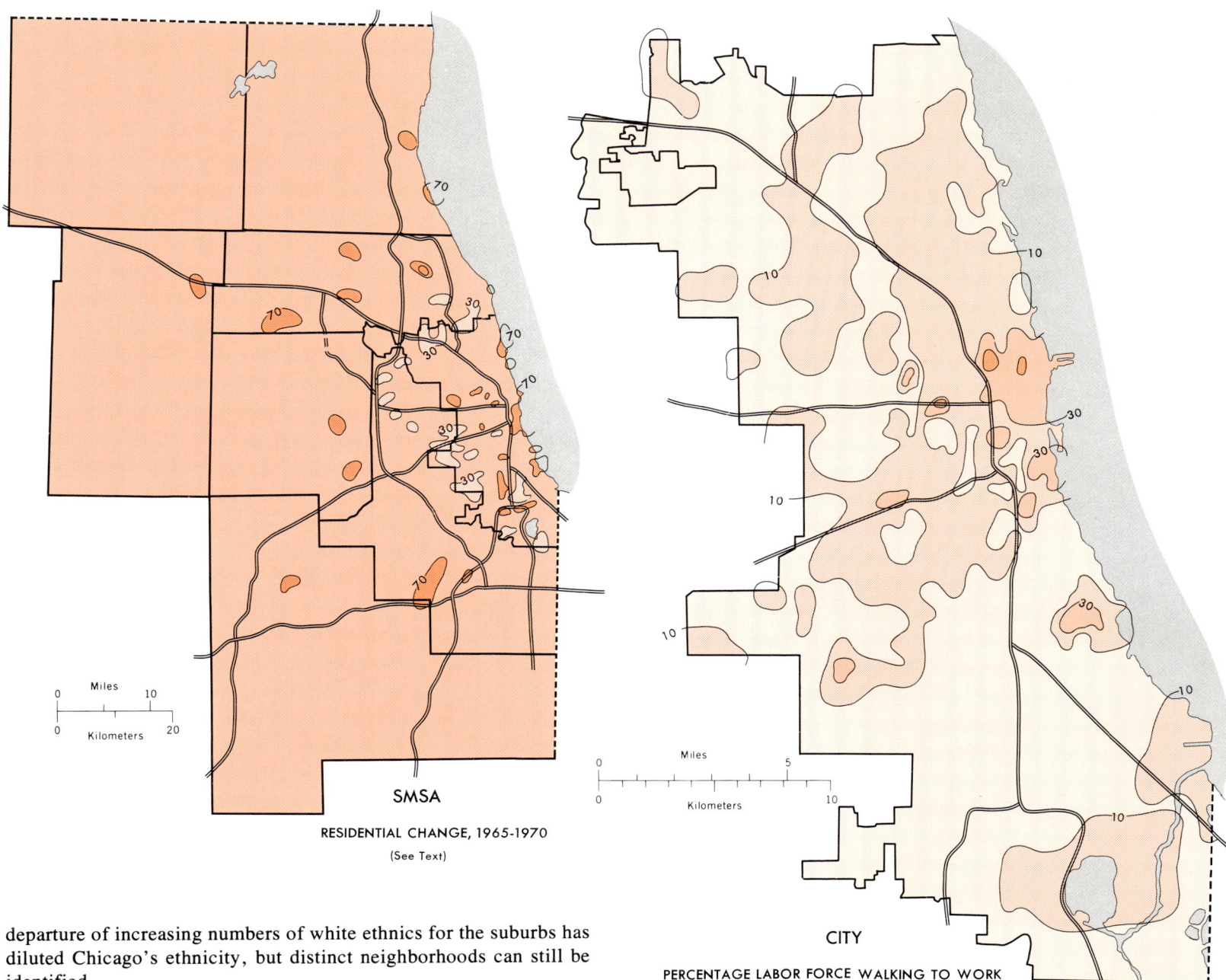

PERCENTAGE LABOR FORCE WALKING TO WORK

departure of increasing numbers of white ethnics for the suburbs has diluted Chicago's ethnicity, but distinct neighborhoods can still be identified.

## SOCIOECONOMIC CHARACTERISTICS

**Household Size.** There are 3.1 people in the average SMSA household and 2.7 in the average Chicago household. Blacks typically have larger families than whites. The average black SMSA household has 3.5 people and the average black household in Chicago consists of 3.4 persons. Individual tract values range from 1 person to over 7 persons per household. Small households are common along the lakeshore, especially north of the CBD. Suburban tracts occupied by young families have larger households, but the largest households, excluding people living in group quarters, occur in the centers of Chicago's black neighborhoods.

**Female Headship.** The Census Bureau defines female headship by the absence of a male spouse regardless of the sex of the family's principal breadwinner. Twelve percent of the SMSA's families and 18 percent of Chicago's families are headed by females. Seventy percent of the SMSA's families headed by females live in Chicago, compared with 48 percent of the total population. Most of the city falls in the over-10-percent category, and values rise well above 30 percent in black neighborhoods. Twenty-two percent of the SMSA's black households and 23 percent of the city's black households are headed by females. Tracts with the highest proportions of female headship are those containing public housing projects inhabited primarily by blacks.

**Occupations.** Sixteen percent of the SMSA's civilian labor force work at blue-collar (laborers and operatives) jobs and 21 percent classify themselves as executives (engineers, teachers, professionals, managers, proprietors, and administrators). The remaining 63 percent are service (33 percent) and clerical (30 percent) workers. The breakdown for the city is: blue-collar, 19 percent; services, 35 percent; clerical, 30 percent; and executive, 16 percent.

Blue-collar workers are less than 10 percent of labor forces in large areas of the inner suburbs. Percentages exceed 30 in rural McHenry and Will counties and in central Chicago, especially in the black and ethnic neighborhoods on the city's near north side. There are few blue-collar workers along the Gold Coast.

The map of executive occupations almost reverses the map of blue-collar workers. Executives are less than 10 percent of tract labor forces throughout large areas of central Chicago with the notable exception of wealthy lakeshore enclaves.

**Income.** Mean income per person in the Chicago SMSA is $3,800 per year, and in Chicago it is $3,400 per year. Individual tract means vary from values that round to zero to $18,000 per person per year. Northern lakeshore communities such as Glencoe, Winnetka, Wilmette, and Evanston generally enjoy high incomes, but the highest accrue to people living along Lake Michigan north of the CBD. The region's lowest incomes are located in black neighborhoods hard by the Gold Coast.

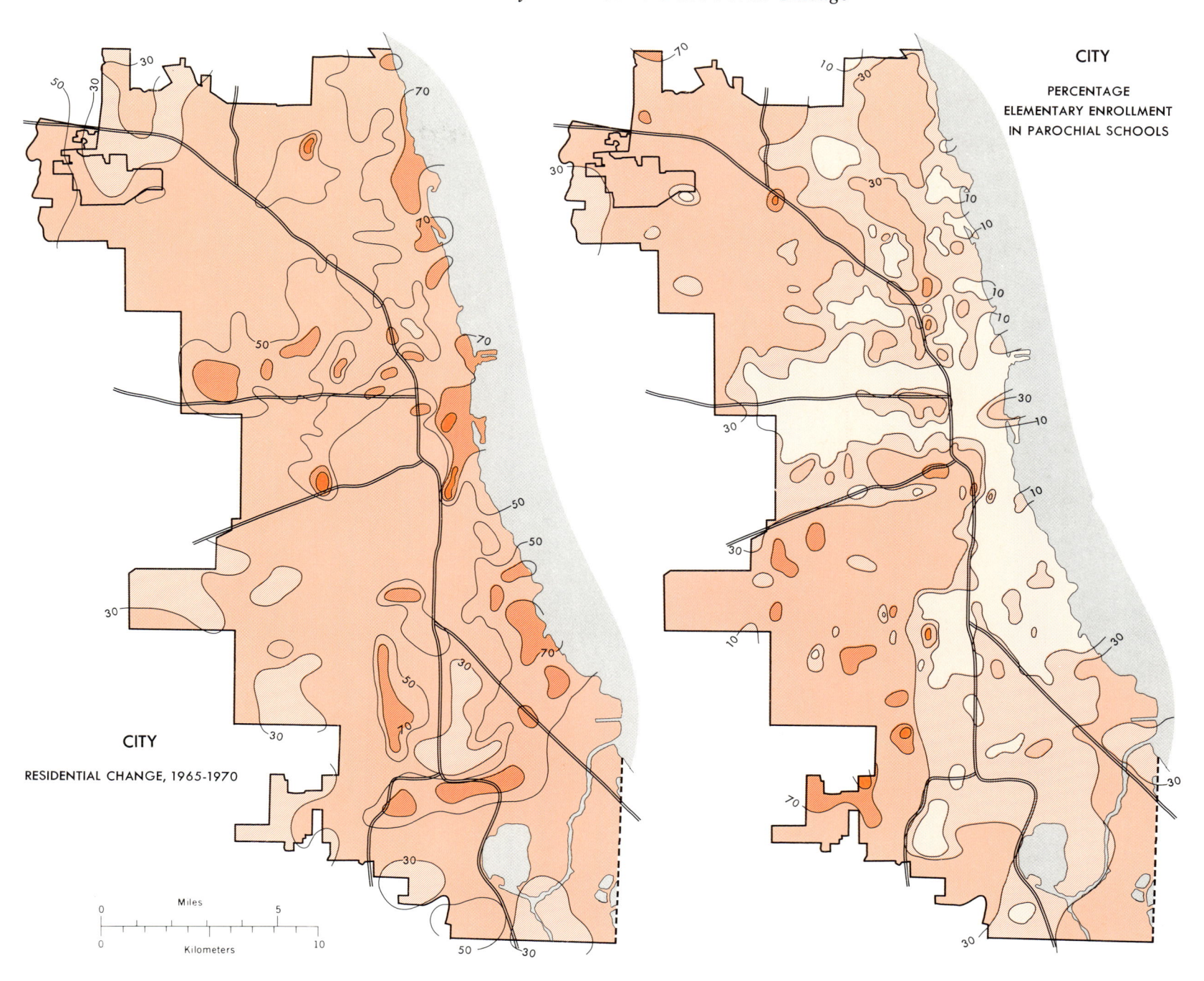

TOPICS OF SPECIAL INTEREST IN THE CHICAGO REGION

**Residential Change, 1965 to 1970.** In 1970, 47 percent of the SMSA's people over 5 years of age were living in different houses from the ones they occupied in 1965. In Chicago, 48 percent lived in different houses. Suburban areas where turnover is high are often new suburbs where much of the population moved into recently constructed housing. Central-city areas with high turnover are sometimes places that have recently changed hands, as in the area now occupied by Chicago's west-side ghetto. High values along the lake and near the CBD reflect healthy competition and turnover among desirable residential properties.

**Labor Force Walking to Work.** Ten percent of Chicago's labor force get to work by walking, taking a taxi, or riding a bicycle. Walking to work requires that people choose a job and residence that are close enough to make walking feasible. Jobs and adequate residence are suitably close to make walking, taking taxis, or riding bicycles feasible for at least 10 percent of tract labor forces in large areas of central and northern Chicago. Proportions exceed 30 percent in a number of areas, among which are the CBD area and the University of Chicago area south of the CBD.

**Labor Force Working in the CBD.** (Histogram on p. 321.) Eight percent of the SMSA's labor force work in Chicago's CBD. The 5 percent isopleth encloses a considerable area. Areas where more than 10 percent of all workers are employed in the CBD are considerably more rare. The two major areas of commuting to the CBD are southwestern Chicago and the north shore, extending as far as southern Lake County. Commuter railroads are important means of access to the CBD from the north shore and many of the western suburbs.

**Enrollment in Parochial Elementary Schools.** (The histogram for this map is on p. 360.) Parochial elementary schools offer a refuge from the often troubled public school system as well as providing religious education. Parochial enrollments exceed 30 percent of the eligible population in the southwest and northwest quadrants of the city, where white ethnics are still numerous. Percentages are low in predominantly black areas (p. 140) of the city because few blacks are Catholic, the denomination that runs most parochial schools. Thus parochial schools usually close as blacks move into the territories they serve, and neighborhood succession is often accompanied by sharply

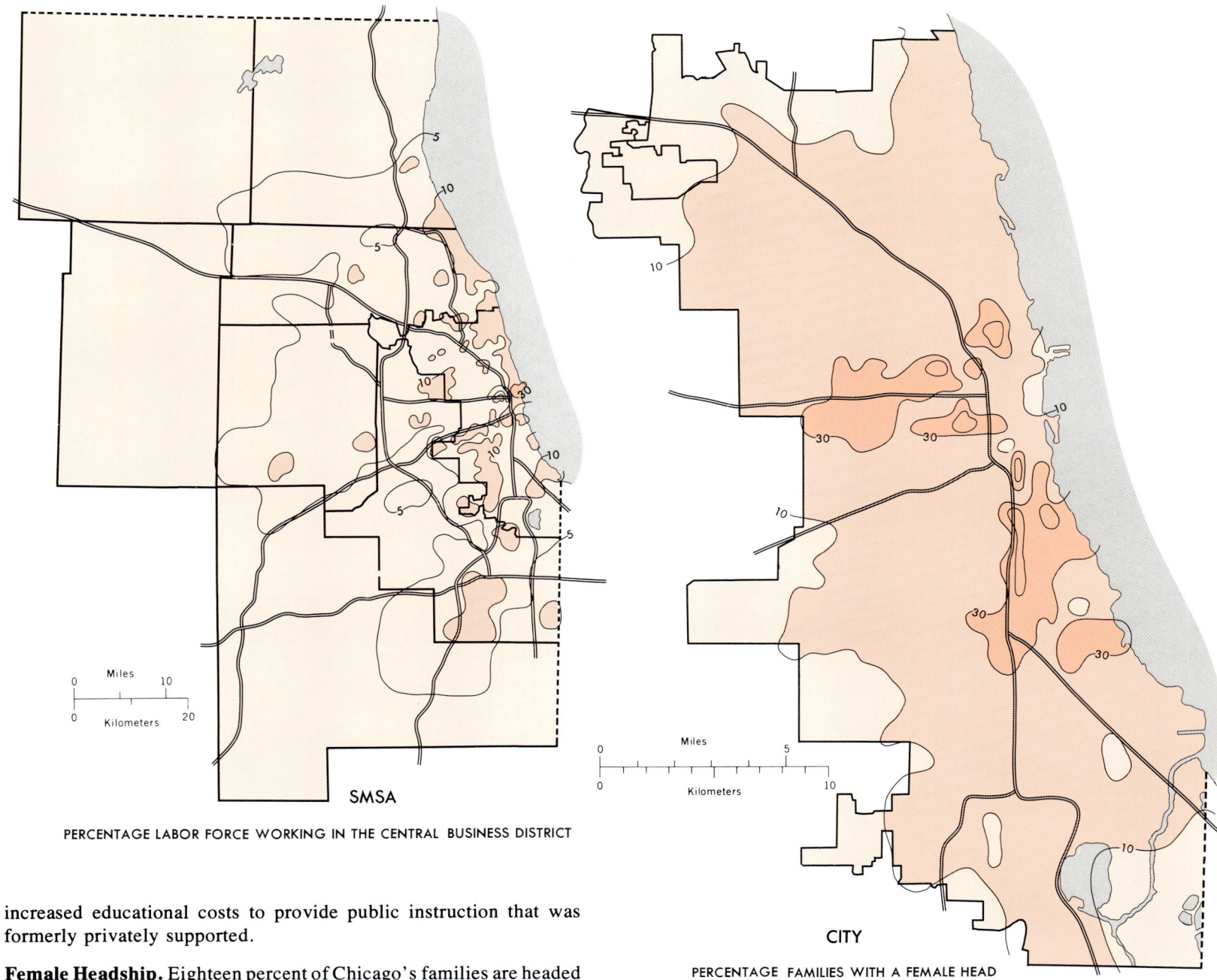

PERCENTAGE LABOR FORCE WORKING IN THE CENTRAL BUSINESS DISTRICT

PERCENTAGE FAMILIES WITH A FEMALE HEAD
(See Text)

increased educational costs to provide public instruction that was formerly privately supported.

**Female Headship.** Eighteen percent of Chicago's families are headed by females, and female headship is especially prevalent in black areas. Each major concentration of blacks (p. 140) has its counterpart on the female-headship map in the form of an area where female headship exceeds 30 percent (supplemental 50 percent isopleths are interpolated inside the 30 percent isopleth). Of the city's 317,000 black families, 71,650 (23 percent) are headed by females. Black female headship often means poverty, for 46 percent of all families headed by female blacks have incomes below the poverty level. Proportions of female headship peak in tracts containing public housing projects.

Despite the concentration of disadvantaged populations in Chicago, and despite the population losses the city has experienced since 1950, Chicago retains the confidence of the SMSA's leading citizens. Population and employment have suburbanized rapidly since World War II, but the downtown area continues to thrive and to attract private renewal and construction projects such as the John Hancock and Standard Oil buildings and the Sears Tower. The decision to push the Sears Tower to a height greater than New York City's World Trade Center is evidence of the persistence in the city of the earthy self-confidence Sandburg captured so well.

# CHAPTER 17

# Detroit

*This fluidity of life, this refusal to "jell" or ever to grow old,
helps to explain why everything that is right or wrong which happens
to our nation seems to break here first.*

MALCOLM W. BINGAY, *Detroit Is My Home Town*, 1946

The Detroit Standard Metropolitan Statistical Area (SMSA) is the 5th most populous in the nation with 4,200,000 people. The city of Detroit, with the municipal enclaves of Hamtramck and Highland Park, has 1,574,000 people (37 percent of the SMSA total). The remainder of Wayne County has 26 percent of the SMSA's people, and Oakland and Macomb counties have 22 and 15 percent respectively. The Daily Urban System (DUS) defined by counties that have at least 5 percent of their labor forces working in Wayne County includes the SMSA and Monroe, Washtenaw, Livingston, and St. Clair counties (p. 150). The DUS population is 4,736,000, which makes it the nation's 5th most populous DUS.

Detroit began as Fort Pontchartrain, a French military post. With the settling of Michigan in the 1820s it became a commercial center and debarkation point for settlers moving west into the territory. The city grew rapidly throughout the 19th century. After 1900, Detroit continued to boom on the economic base of its automobile industry (p. 10). The region was the 5th most populous metropolitan area when the nation emerged from World War II, a position it still retains. Detroit lost population during the 1960s, decreasing 9.5 percent from 1,670,000 to its current size. At the same time, the SMSA increased 11.6 percent, compared with a national metropolitan growth rate of 16.6 percent.

Detroit lies on a lake plain. Relief within the city (p. 150) is less than 100 feet (30 meters), and drainage has been a persistent problem in some areas. Flat terrain has made it possible for transportation routes and residential expansion to proceed in all directions. The land remains flat outside the city as far as the northeast-southwest-trending moraines in Oakland County. There the lake plain gives way to rolling, often swampy terrain interspersed with lakes and ponds. Land uses in the SMSA occur in large, regular zones that are consequences of topographical regularity. Residential expansion has proceeded outward in all directions but particularly into central Oakland County. Industrial and commercial tracts are located along transportation routes and watercourses. The contrast between Detroit's regular land-use patterns and the patchy, irregular distributions in cities with rougher terrain, such as Pittsburgh, is striking.

*Note:* All data are from the 1970 Censuses of Population and Housing unless otherwise indicated. Therefore the present tense refers to 1970 data except for income data which are from 1969. Cartographic conventions are explained in Chapter 1.

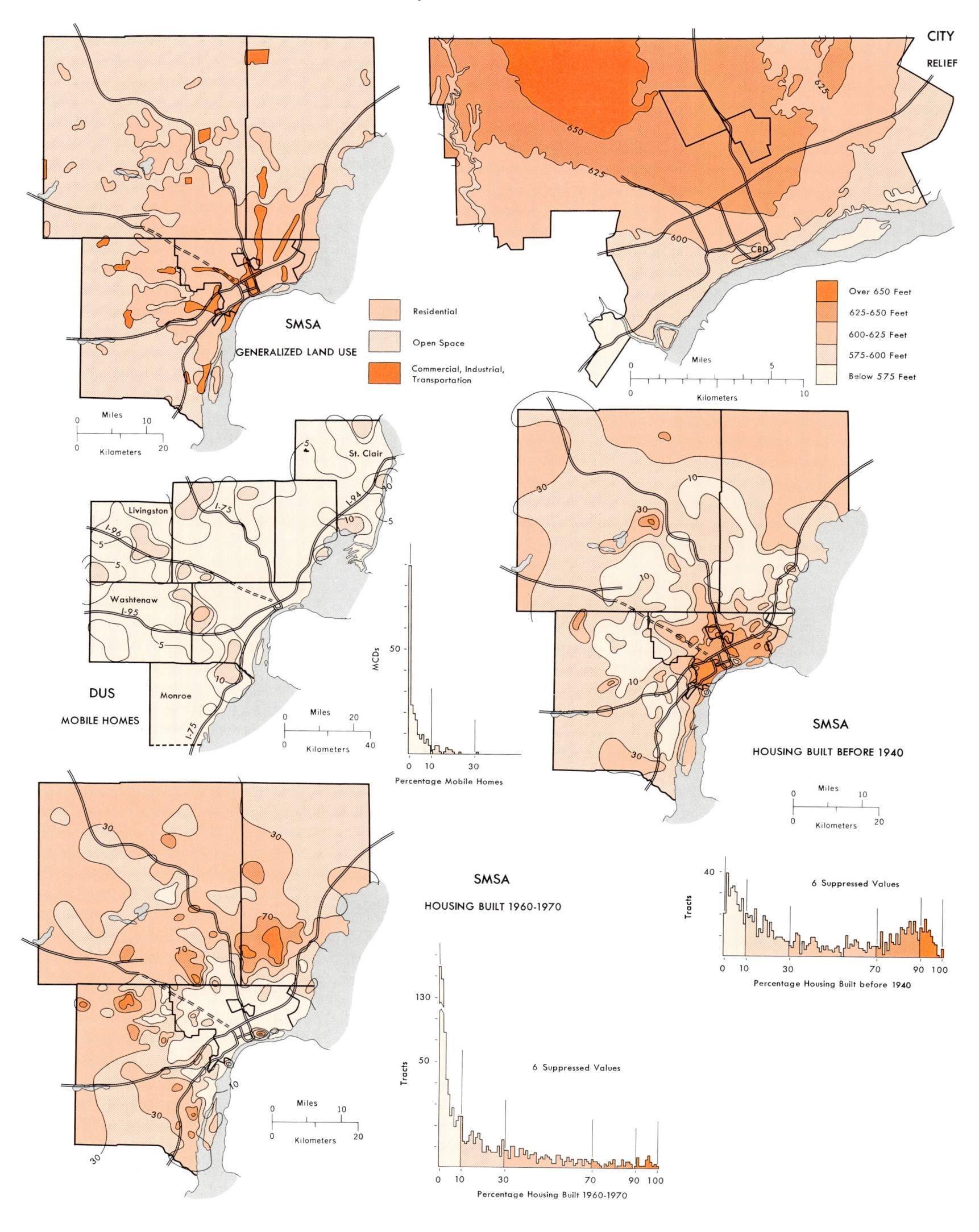

*Nineteenth-Century Inland Centers and Ports: Detroit*

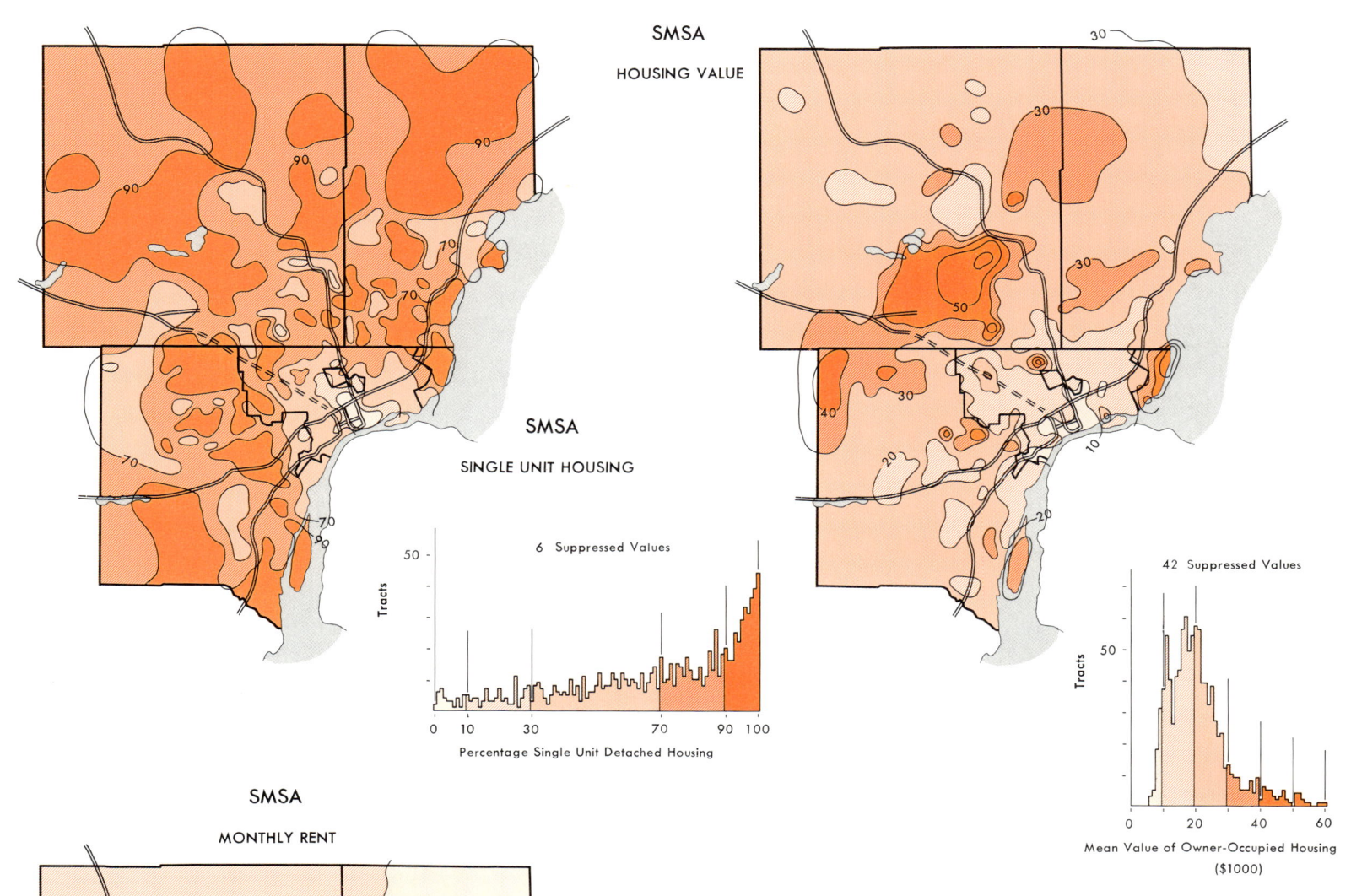

## Nineteenth-Century Inland Centers and Ports: Detroit

### HOUSING

**Housing Age.** Thirty-seven percent of the SMSA's housing was built before 1940, 44 percent was built from 1940 through 1959, and 19 percent dates from 1960 to March 1970. For a midwestern SMSA, a relatively large proportion of the housing stock dates from 1940 through 1959. Detroit's housing stock is older than the SMSA's: 62 percent was built before 1940, 34 percent from 1940 through 1959, and only 4 percent since 1960. Detroit, Hamtramck, and Highland Park have 71 percent of all housing units built before 1940 compared with their 42 percent share of the total housing stock.

Proportions of old housing are high in the city's older core and decrease with distance outward. Values are low in the wedges between major radial arteries where recent settlement has taken place. Old housing becomes more dominant again on the metropolitan periphery beyond the zones of recent housing construction.

Proportions of new housing are below 10 percent in most of Detroit. Only 21,700 housing units were built in the city between 1960 and 1970, many the results of publicly supported urban-renewal programs. New housing is most dominant in southern Macomb and southeastern Oakland counties where the interstices between major arterials were filled in during the 1960s. The Macomb County wedge is middle-income housing whereas housing in the Oakland County sector is more expensive.

**Mobile Homes.** There are 20,350 mobile homes in the Detroit DUS, which make up 1.4 percent of the DUS housing stock. The proportion of mobile homes exceeds 10 percent in a number of minor civil divisions within the SMSA and in the first tier of counties outside the SMSA limits. Mobile homes are most important in Livingston County, where they constitute 8.5 percent of all housing units.

**Single-Unit Detached Housing.** Individual dwelling units make up 69 percent of the SMSA's housing stock and 54 percent of the city's

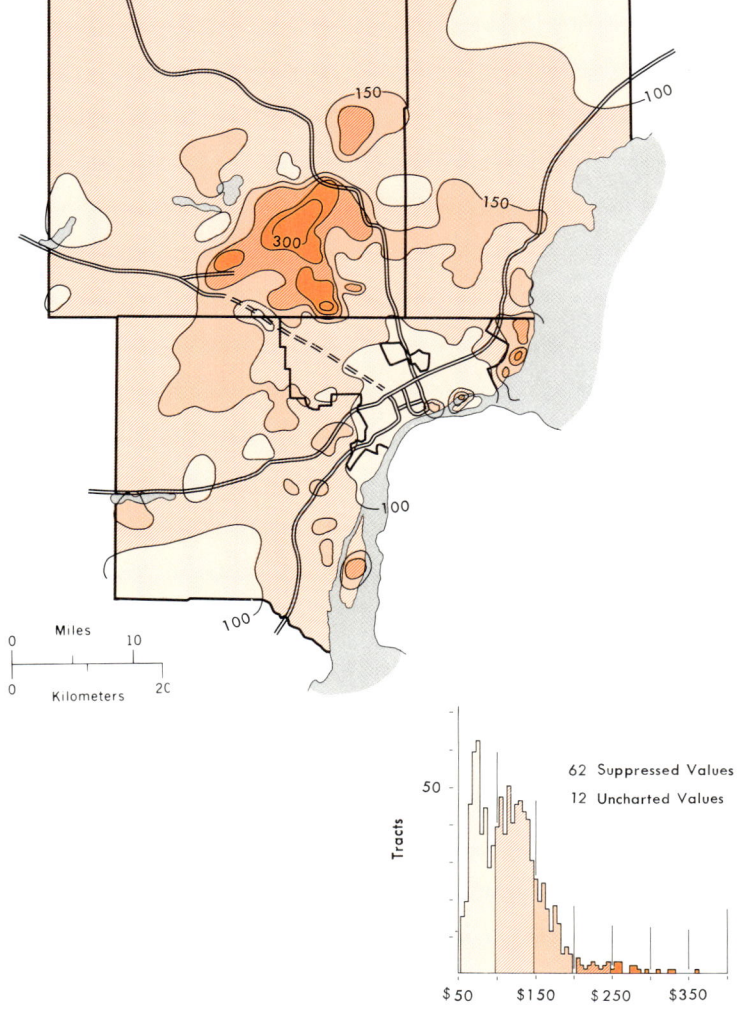

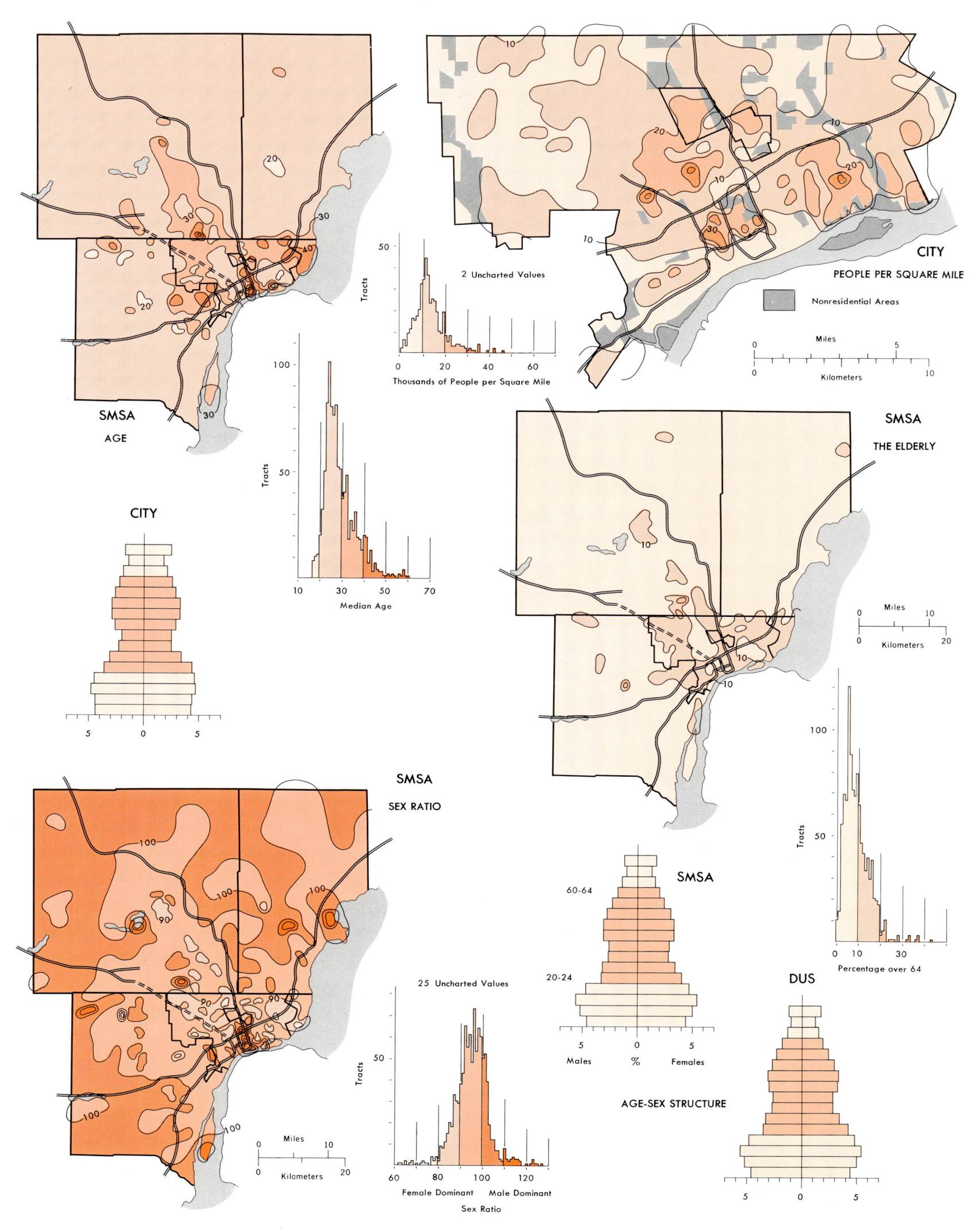

## Nineteenth-Century Inland Centers and Ports: Detroit

SMSA AGE

CITY PEOPLE PER SQUARE MILE

Nonresidential Areas

CITY

SMSA THE ELDERLY

SMSA SEX RATIO

SMSA AGE-SEX STRUCTURE

DUS

152

CITY
PERCENTAGE NEGRO

CITY
PERCENTAGE SPANISH-AMERICAN

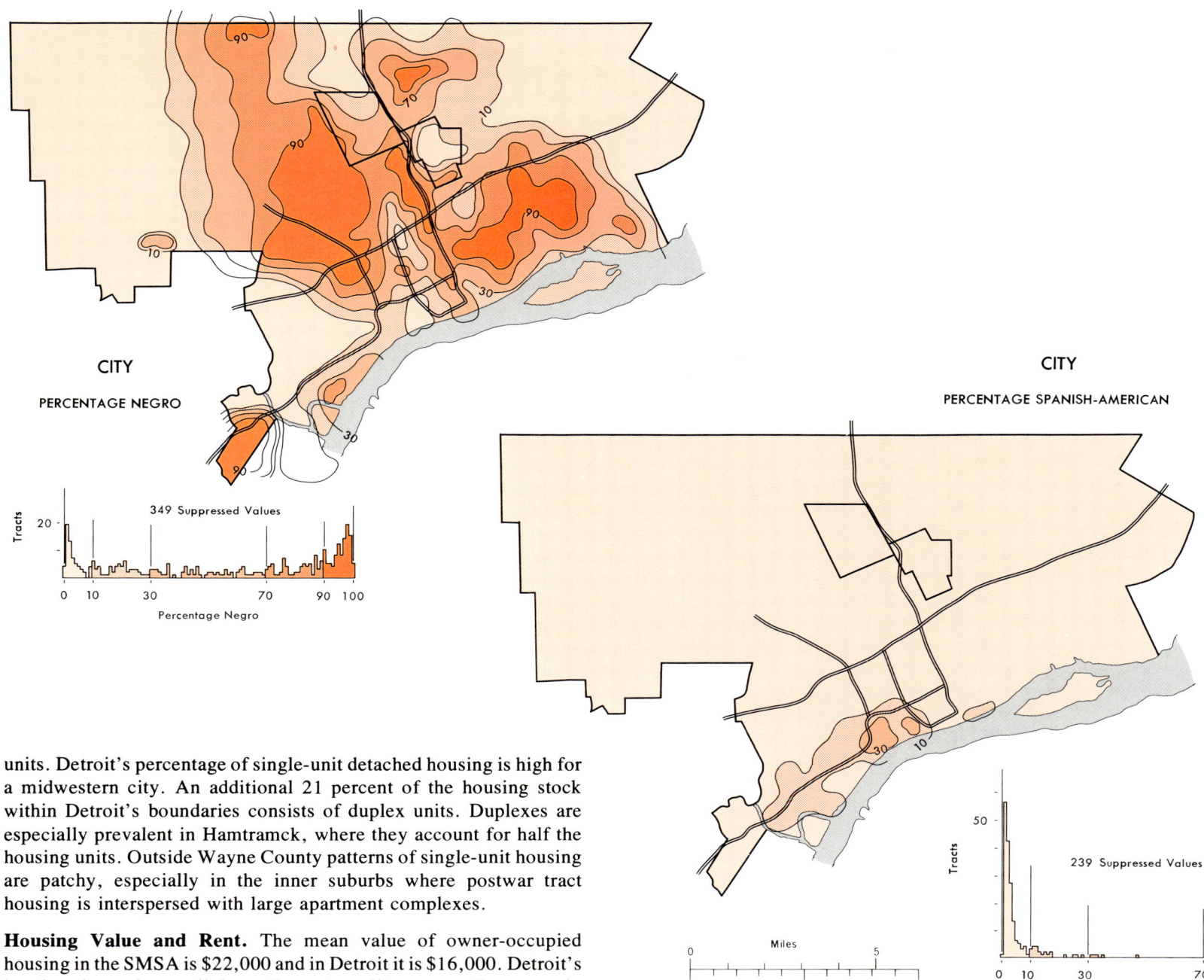

units. Detroit's percentage of single-unit detached housing is high for a midwestern city. An additional 21 percent of the housing stock within Detroit's boundaries consists of duplex units. Duplexes are especially prevalent in Hamtramck, where they account for half the housing units. Outside Wayne County patterns of single-unit housing are patchy, especially in the inner suburbs where postwar tract housing is interspersed with large apartment complexes.

**Housing Value and Rent.** The mean value of owner-occupied housing in the SMSA is $22,000 and in Detroit it is $16,000. Detroit's low housing values pull down the metropolitan mean; the means in Macomb and Oakland counties are considerably higher than the Wayne County average. Individual tract means vary from $5,000 to $60,000. Housing values are lowest in inner-city Detroit and highest in the suburbs of southeastern Oakland County, such as Bloomfield Hills and Birmingham, and in the Grosse Pointe communities in northeastern Wayne County.

Mean monthly contract rents are $107 in the SMSA and $86 in Detroit. Individual tract means range from less than $50 (not plotted or mapped) to $360. Rents are below $100 in central Detroit. An irregular ring of rents over $150 almost surrounds Detroit. The high-rental ring is widest in Oakland County where the SMSA's highest rents occur in the same tracts where housing values peak.

## THE PEOPLE

**Population Density.** Detroit's overall population density is 10,970 people per square mile (4,200 per square kilometer). Individual tract densities range from 1,000 to 39,000 people per square mile (386 to 15,000 per square kilometer). Densities throughout Detroit are low compared with those in the cities already described in the atlas. The low overall densities are a reflection of the proportion of the city's expansion that has taken place since 1900 and the amount of the city's housing that was built at low densities from 1940 through 1959. Densities are less than 10,000 per square mile (3,900 per square kilometer) in the Central Business District (CBD), along the river to the east, and in western Detroit. The few areas where population densities exceed 30,000 (11,600 per square kilometer) are the locations of multiple-unit housing facilities. Population densities are low outside Detroit (p. 314), where they rarely exceed 10,000 people per square mile (3,900 per square kilometer).

**Age and the Elderly.** The median age of the SMSA population is 27 years and of the city is 29 years. Individual tracts have medians varying from 17 to 60 years. Medians exceed 30 years in the outer areas of Detroit, the inner suburbs, and the affluent sector extending into Oakland County. Middle-income suburbs have medians below 20 years. The lowest medians occur in predominantly black areas of Detroit; areas within the city where median ages are below 30 years correspond roughly to the black neighborhoods. Detroit's median age is an average of the age of generally younger blacks and generally older whites. Black families with young children swell the bottom of the city pyramid, which is notably broader than the bottoms of the SMSA and DUS pyramids. In a city in which the total population is 44 percent black, the 10- to 14-year cohort is 54 percent black whereas the 55- to 59-year cohort is 32 percent black.

People 64 years old and older make up 8 percent of the SMSA population and 12 percent of Detroit's people. Detroit has 51 percent

## Nineteenth-Century Inland Centers and Ports: Detroit

SMSA
AMERICAN INDIANS

Each Dot Represents 50 American Indians

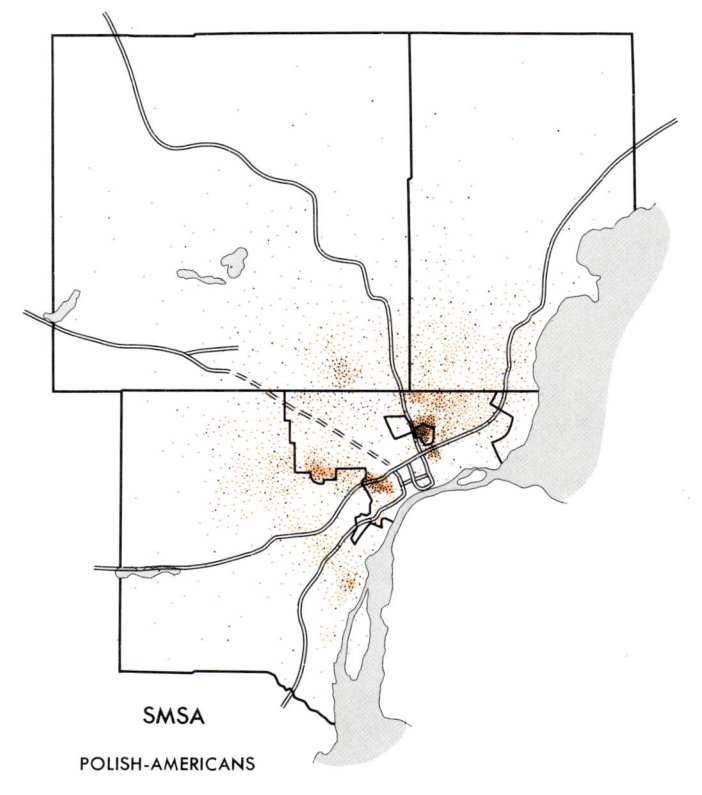

SMSA
POLISH-AMERICANS

Each Black Dot Represents 50 Polish Born
Each Orange Dot Represents 50 People of Polish Parentage

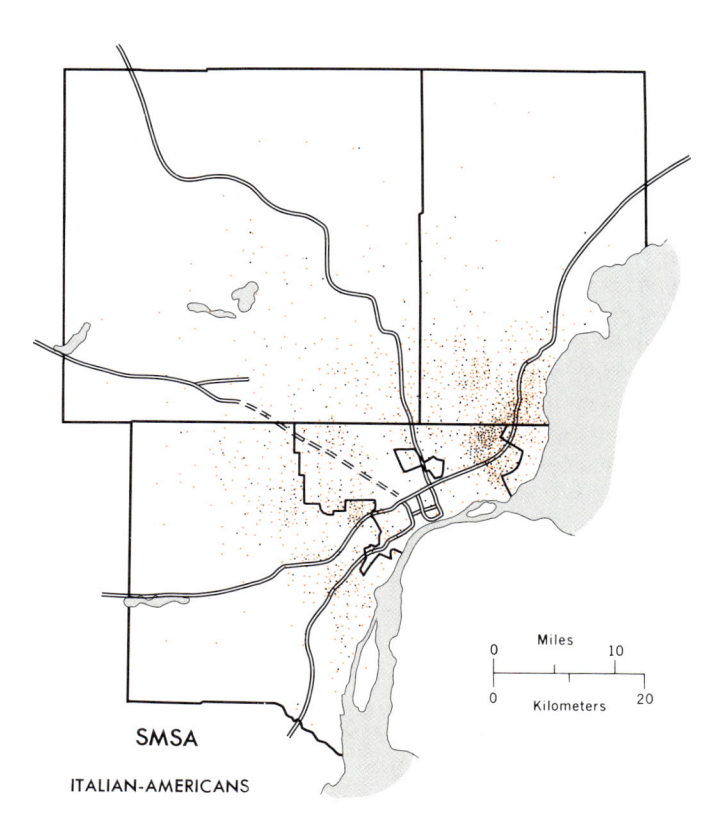

SMSA
ITALIAN-AMERICANS

Each Black Dot Represents 50 Italian Born
Each Orange Dot Represents 50 People of Italian Parentage

of the SMSA's elderly compared with 36 percent of the total population. People over 64 are more than 10 percent of local populations throughout Detroit except in heavily black areas. Most of the remainder of the SMSA has proportions below 10 percent. The tract with more than 30 percent over 64 in west-central Wayne County contains the Eloise State Hospital. The two over-30-percent tracts in southeastern Oakland County are located in apartment complexes near the Northland Shopping Center that have attracted exceptional numbers of the elderly.

**Sex Ratio.** There are 1.06 females for each male in the SMSA which yields a female-dominant sex ratio (males divided by females times 100) of 95. There are 1.09 females for each male in Detroit, resulting in a sex ratio of 92. A typical population is female-dominant. Male-dominant populations occur in largely rural areas, as well as in the CBD area where many elderly males live. Other male-dominant areas are usually special cases such as the Detroit House of Corrections in northwestern Wayne County, the Clinton Valley State Hospital in central Oakland County, and Selfridge Air Force Base in east-central Macomb County.

**Negroes.** There are 660,400 blacks in Detroit. They constitute 44 percent of the city's population. Blacks numbered 483,000 and were 29 percent of Detroit's people in 1960. Out-migration of whites and natural increase among blacks have caused significant changes in the city's racial composition since 1960. Detroit's blacks now occupy a broad swath through the center of the city that leaves the CBD, the area northwest of it, and heavily Polish Hamtramck islands of whites in a ghetto where many tracts are predominantly black. Gradients between completely black and completely white neighborhoods are not as sharp as they are in many cities. Only 10 percent of the SMSA's blacks live outside Detroit, Hamtramck, and Highland Park (map on p. 385).

**Spanish-Americans.** The Census estimates the number of Hispanics in Detroit by counting people who speak Spanish. Using that reckoning there are 27,000 Spanish-Americans in the city; they are 1.8 percent of the population. A few Hispanics are scattered

*154*

## Nineteenth-Century Inland Centers and Ports: Detroit

**SMSA HOUSEHOLD SIZE**

*Average Number of People per Household*

**SMSA INCOME PER PERSON**

*Mean Income per Person in Hundreds of Dollars*

**SMSA FAMILIES WITH A FEMALE HEAD**

*Percentage Families with a Female Head*

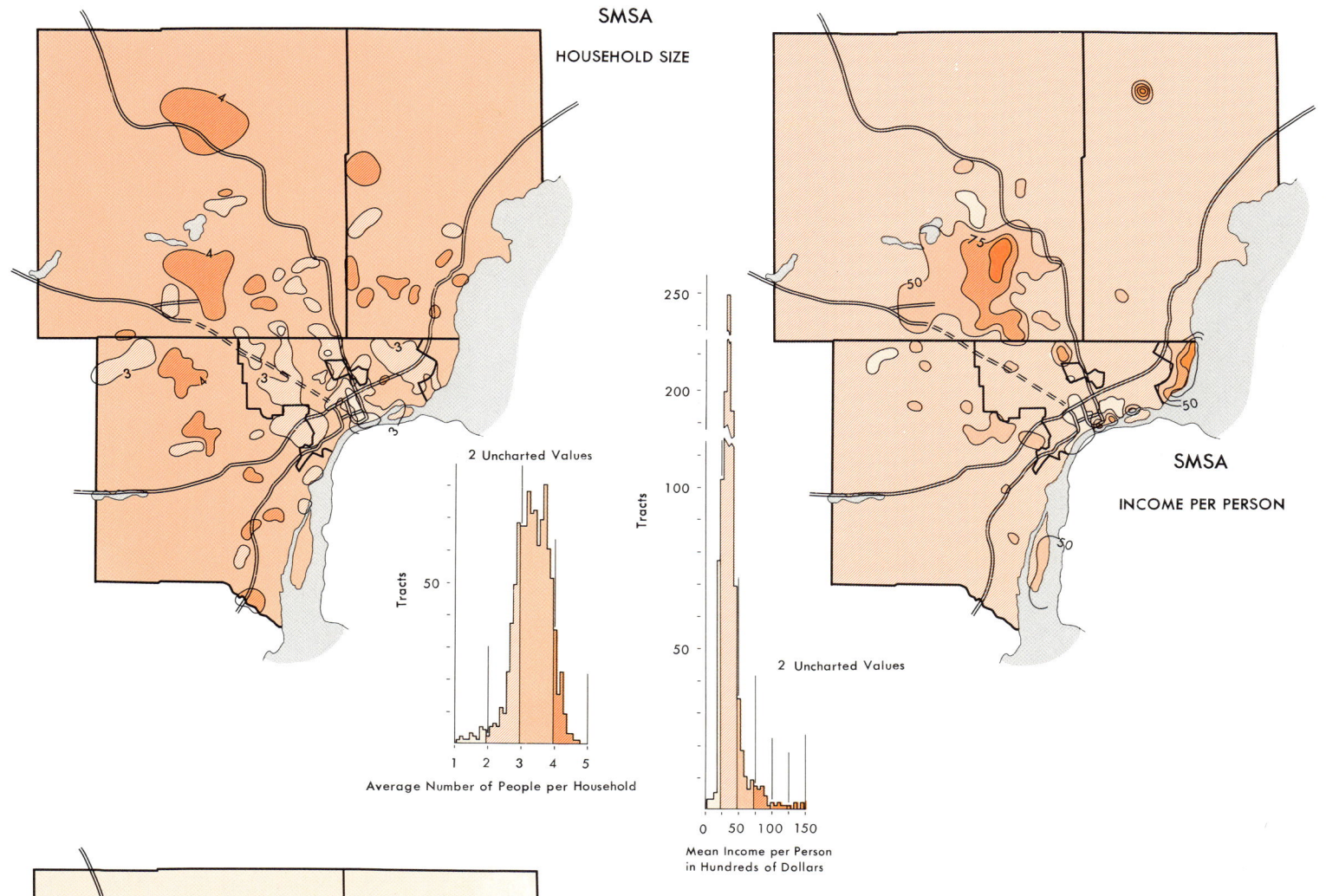

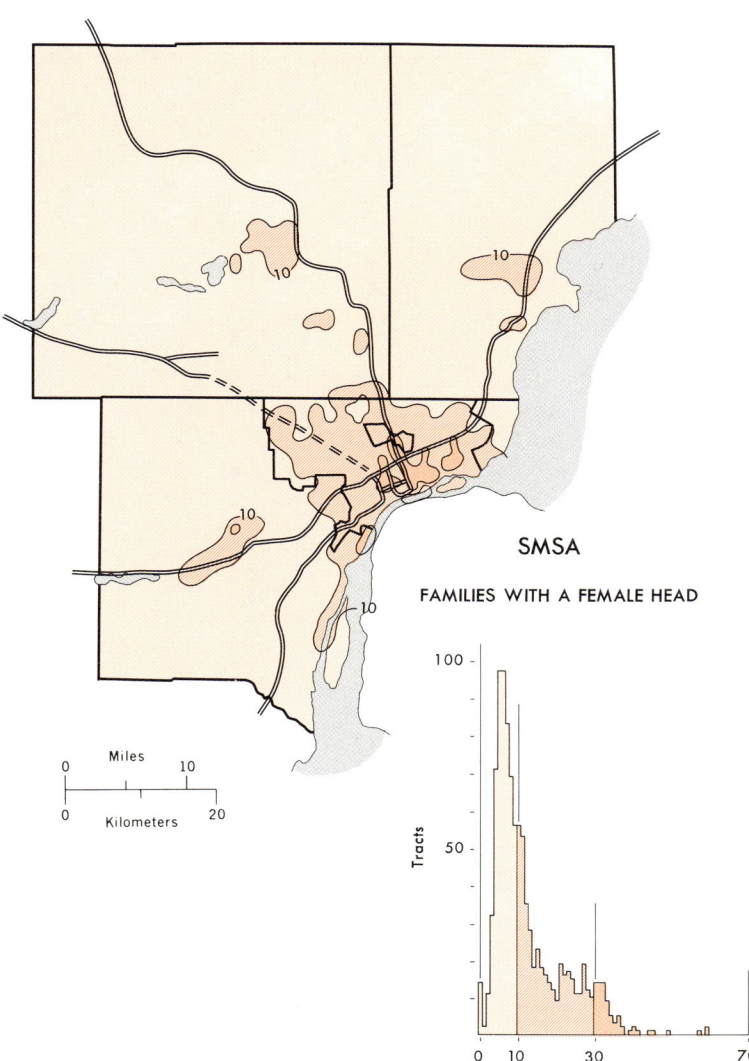

throughout the city; there is but one zero-percentage tract, and each of the 239 suppressed tracts contains a few. But most Spanish-Americans cluster in southwest Detroit. The Hispanic community is of mixed origin. About 8 percent are Puerto Rican, about 3 percent are Cuban, and the remainder are Central and South American foreign stock (16 percent), Mexican foreign stock (31 percent), and indigenous Mexican-Americans (42 percent).

**American Indians.** There are 5,700 American Indians in the Detroit SMSA. Detroit's Indians are scattered throughout the SMSA roughly in accordance with population density, with only slight clustering in the deteriorating neighborhoods near the CBD. Fifty-one percent of the SMSA's Indians live in Detroit, which is more, but not much more, than the 36 percent there would be if Indians were evenly distributed among the total population.

**Polish-Americans.** In the Detroit SMSA, there are 33,700 Polish-born and 126,000 people who have at least one Polish-born parent. They constitute 3.8 percent of the SMSA population. Fifty-one percent of the Polish-born and 40 percent of the people of Polish parentage live in Detroit. Hamtramck and the west Detroit area have traditionally been centers of the Polish community.

**Italian-Americans.** The SMSA's Italian foreign stock consists of 27,000 Italian-born and 66,000 people with at least one Italian-born parent. Together they make up 2.2 percent of the SMSA population. The primary focus of the original Italian community was along Gratiot Street on Detroit's northeast side. With the expansion of the black area, Italian-Americans have moved outward to the northeast. Currently 42 percent of the Italian-born and 29 percent of the first-generation Italian-Americans live in Detroit.

Detroit attracted large numbers of immigrants over the years. Irish, English, Scots, Jews, and Germans have left their mark on the city and

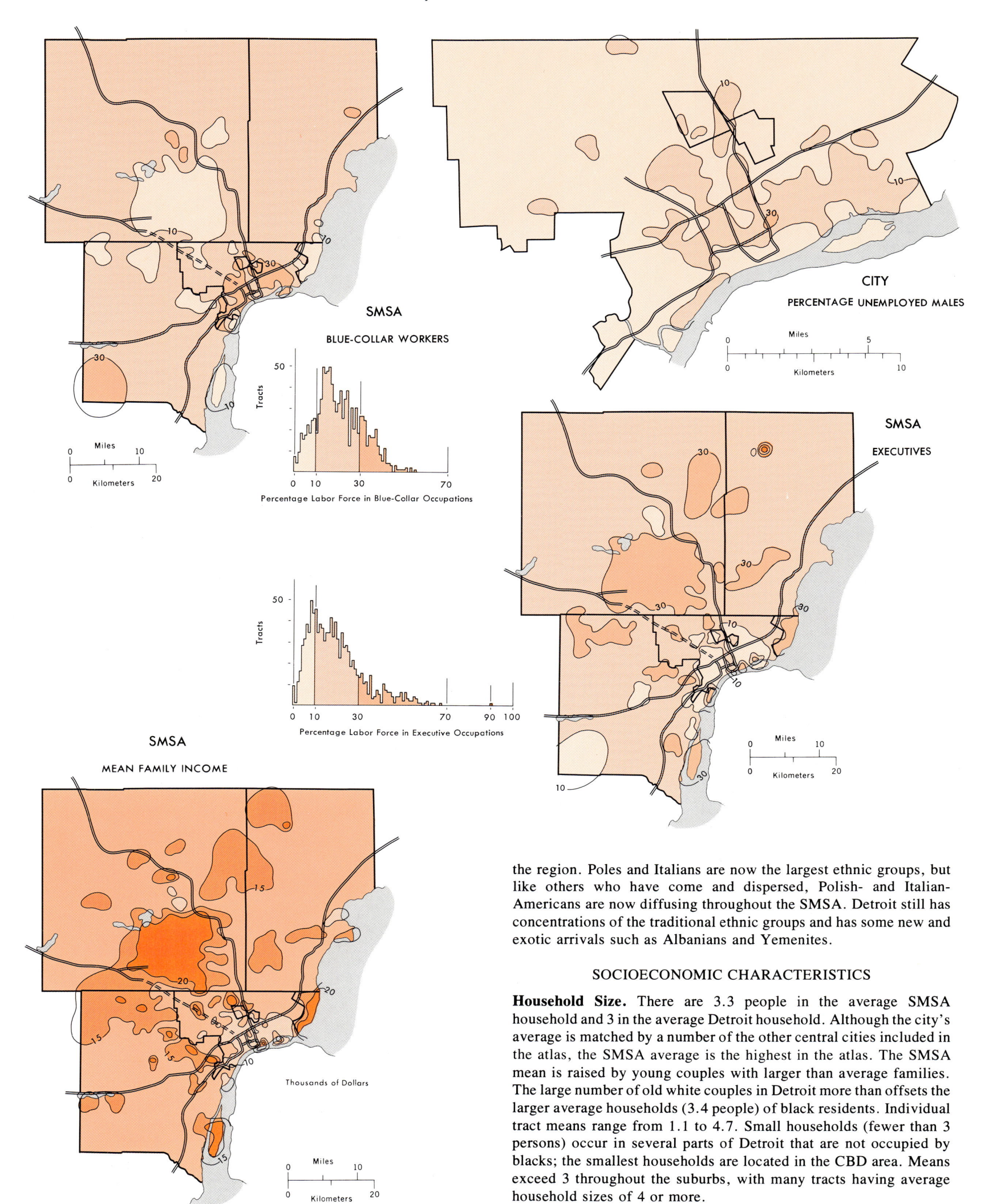

## Nineteenth-Century Inland Centers and Ports: Detroit

**SMSA** — BLUE-COLLAR WORKERS
Percentage Labor Force in Blue-Collar Occupations

**CITY** — PERCENTAGE UNEMPLOYED MALES

**SMSA** — EXECUTIVES
Percentage Labor Force in Executive Occupations

**SMSA** — MEAN FAMILY INCOME
Thousands of Dollars

the region. Poles and Italians are now the largest ethnic groups, but like others who have come and dispersed, Polish- and Italian-Americans are now diffusing throughout the SMSA. Detroit still has concentrations of the traditional ethnic groups and has some new and exotic arrivals such as Albanians and Yemenites.

### SOCIOECONOMIC CHARACTERISTICS

**Household Size.** There are 3.3 people in the average SMSA household and 3 in the average Detroit household. Although the city's average is matched by a number of the other central cities included in the atlas, the SMSA average is the highest in the atlas. The SMSA mean is raised by young couples with larger than average families. The large number of old white couples in Detroit more than offsets the larger average households (3.4 people) of black residents. Individual tract means range from 1.1 to 4.7. Small households (fewer than 3 persons) occur in several parts of Detroit that are not occupied by blacks; the smallest households are located in the CBD area. Means exceed 3 throughout the suburbs, with many tracts having average household sizes of 4 or more.

## Nineteenth-Century Inland Centers and Ports: Detroit

SMSA
RESIDENTIAL CHANGE, 1965-1970
(See Text)

SMSA
POPULATION CHANGE, 1960-1970
(See Text)

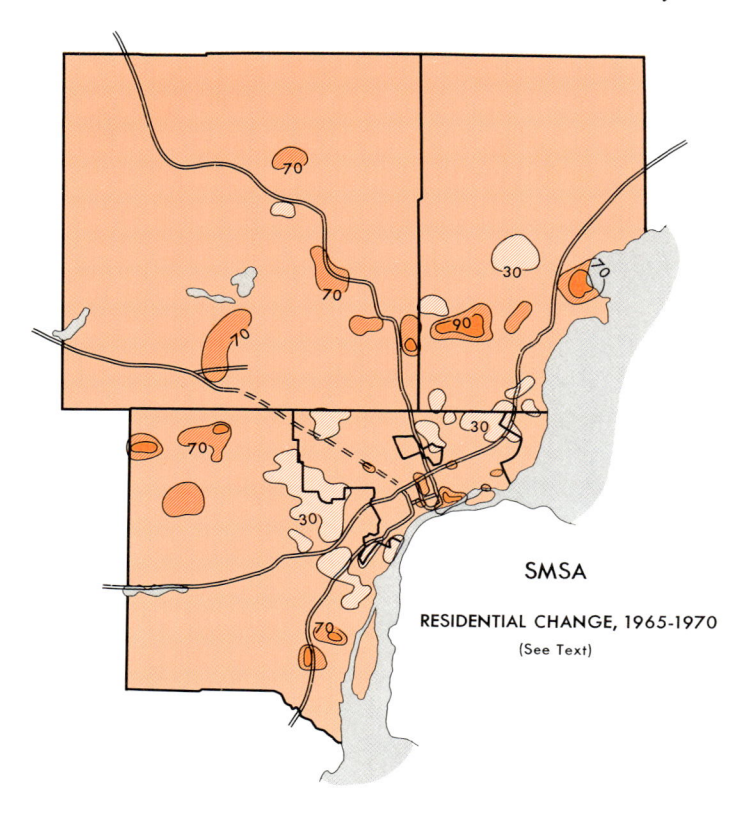

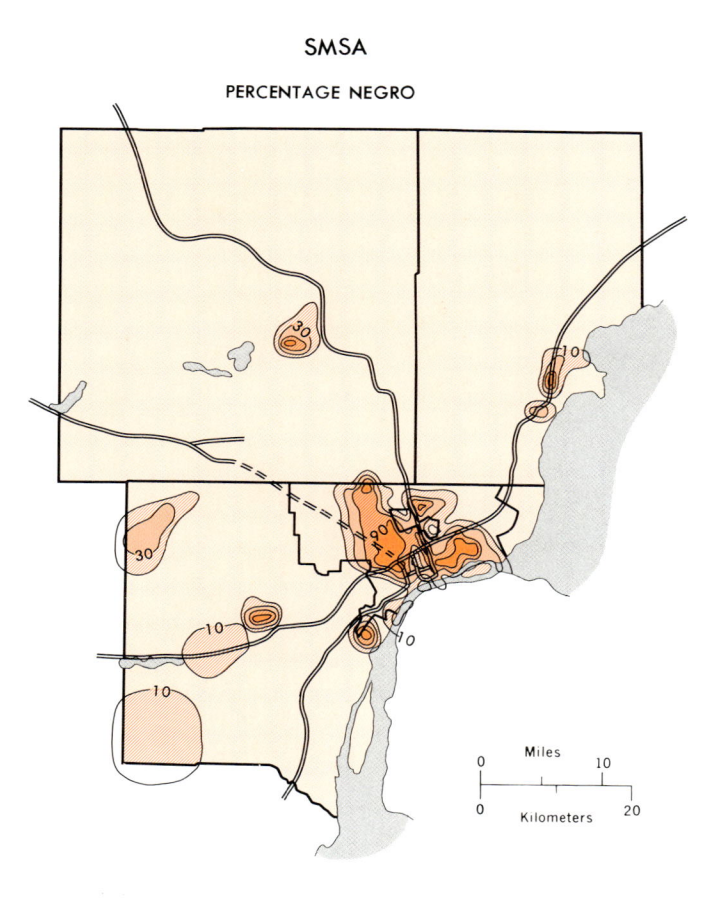

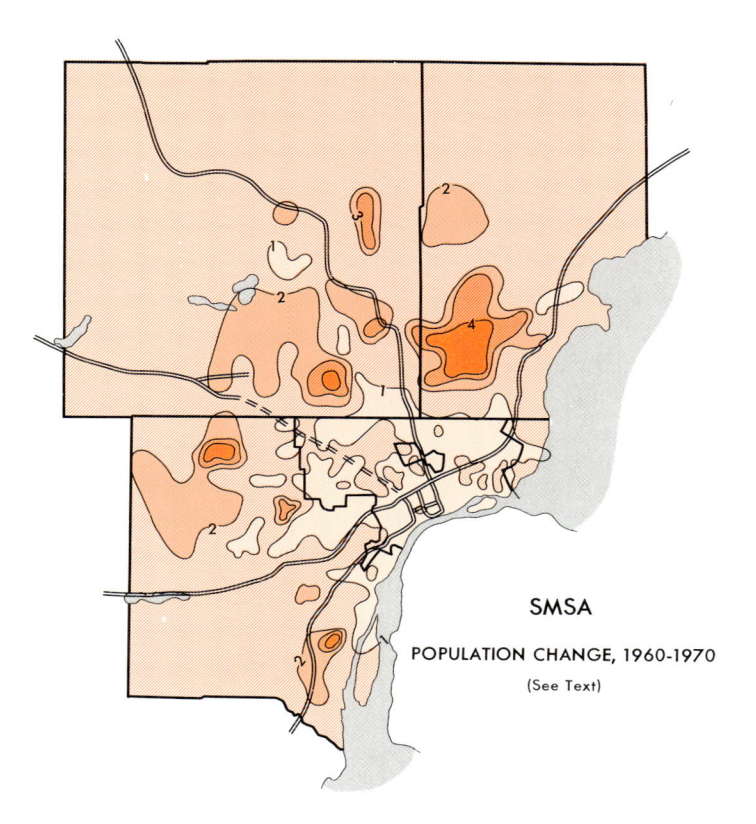

SMSA
PERCENTAGE NEGRO

**Female Headship.** The Census Bureau defines female headship by the absence of a male spouse regardless of the sex of the family's principal breadwinner. Eleven percent of the SMSA's families and 18 percent of Detroit's families are headed by females. Fifty-seven percent of the SMSA's families headed by females reside in the city of Detroit. Individual tract proportions vary from zero to 59 percent. Female headship exceeds 10 percent throughout the city, rising above 30 percent to the highest proportions in dominantly black areas near the city's center. Of the city's 195,000 black families, 39,000 (20 percent) are headed by females, and 17,700 of the black families headed by females have incomes below the poverty level.

**Occupations.** Nineteen percent of the SMSA's civilian labor force work in blue-collar (laborers and operatives) jobs, and 20 percent classify themselves as executives (engineers, teachers, professionals, managers, proprietors, and administrators). The remaining 61 percent are service (35 percent) and clerical (26 percent) workers. The breakdown for Detroit is: blue-collar, 24 percent; service, 37 percent; clerical, 25 percent; and executive, 14 percent.

The Detroit SMSA has the highest proportion of blue-collar workers among the 20 regions in the atlas, which is doubtless a reflection of the importance of the automobile industry in the local economy. Cleveland exceeds Detroit City's 24 percent blue-collar workers by a single percentage, but both are unusually high. Tract proportions vary from zero to 55 percent. Many tracts where proportions exceed 30 percent are located in the city's black areas. Values are low throughout the suburbs and especially in southeastern Oakland County.

Individual tracts have between zero and 90 percent of their labor forces working in executive occupations, and in many areas this map reverses the map of blue-collar workers. Proportions are low in the inner zone of the central city and well over 30 percent in the SMSA's affluent areas. The 90 percent value is a statistical anomaly. The tract is an exclave of Romeo which has only 54 individuals in the labor force, almost all of whom are teachers and professionals.

**Income.** Mean income per person in the Detroit SMSA is $3,750 per year. The comparable figure for Detroit is $3,250. Individual tract means vary from $1,000 to $14,500 per person per year. Incomes in most of the region vary between $2,500 and $5,000. They fall below $2,500 in Detroit's inner-city areas and rise well above $5,000 in the Grosse Pointe communities and in southeastern Oakland County.

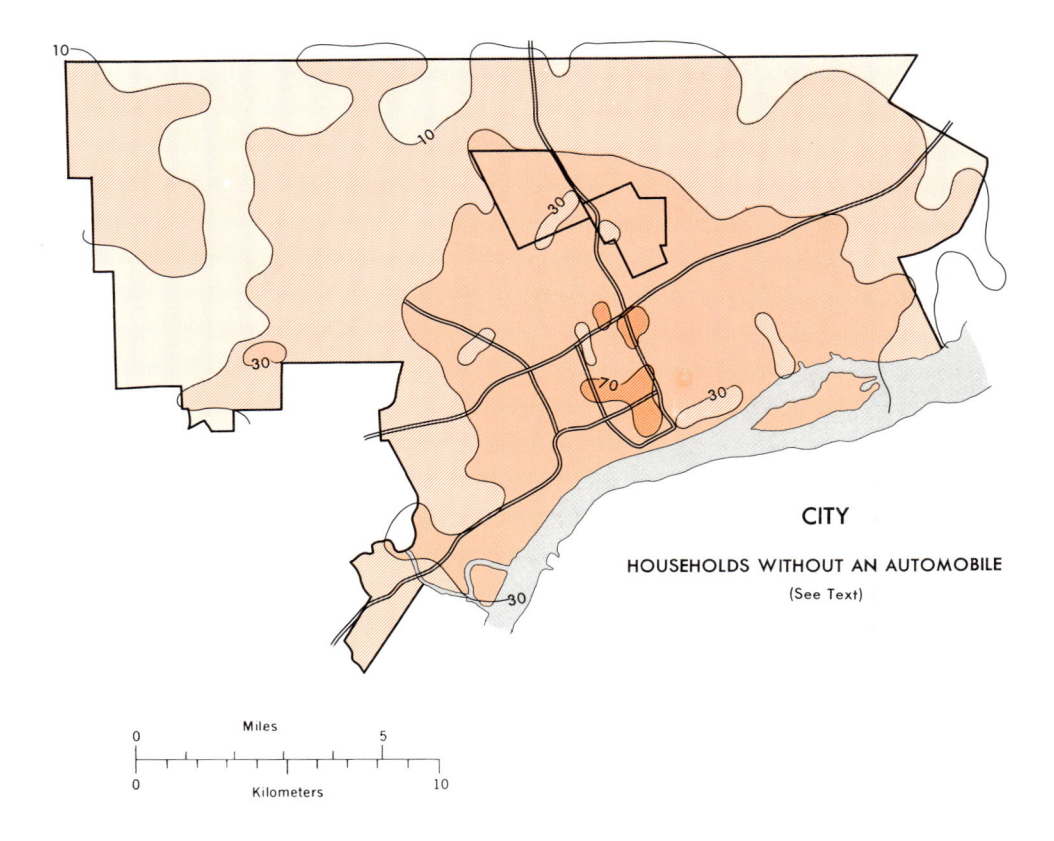

CITY
HOUSEHOLDS WITHOUT AN AUTOMOBILE
(See Text)

## TOPICS OF SPECIAL INTEREST IN THE DETROIT REGION

**Unemployment.** (Histogram on p. 409.) When the 1970 Census was taken in April of that year, 6.9 percent of the city's male labor force was unemployed but seeking work, compared with 4 percent in the nation. The areas where unemployed males exceeded 10 percent of the labor force were disproportionately concentrated in the inner city and in black neighborhoods. Indeed, 14,350 (57 percent) of the unemployed were blacks, which meant that the unemployment rate among black males stood at 9.8 percent while the nonblack rate was 5 percent. Regional and national unemployment rates have changed markedly since 1970, but it is reasonable to expect that Detroit's inner-city areas will continue to be hard hit by unemployment.

**Mean Family Income.** When per person income is measured, family size is taken into account; but when mean family income is measured, the family is considered the primary income-earning and income-consumption unit. The mean family income for the entire SMSA is $13,500; for Detroit it is $11,000. Mean incomes for black families are lower: $9,375 in the city and SMSA. Although this gap between total income and black incomes is far from small, it is smaller than it usually is in American SMSAs, reflecting the accessibility to blacks of the region's high-paying blue-collar jobs. The correspondence of the SMSA map of mean family income with the SMSA map of percentage Negro is not as close as it is in other metropolitan areas.

**Negroes.** (Histogram on p. 385.) Although some blacks do reside in areas outside Detroit, most do not; 90 percent of the SMSA's blacks live in Detroit, Hamtramck, and Highland Park. The black population in central Oakland County lives in central Pontiac. Almost all the blacks in northwestern Wayne County are residents of the Detroit House of Corrections or the Northville State Hospital, and those in west-central Wayne County are sharply segregated in the town of Inkster. Blacks in Detroit are moving into new housing (p. 385), but many suburban areas remain closed to blacks eventhough they have incomes that approach regional averages.

**Neighborhood Turnover and Population Change.** Between 1965 and 1970, 38 percent of the SMSA's population 5 years old and older moved to different houses. Tract proportions exceed 30 percent throughout most of the SMSA, and proportions above 70 and 90 percent occur in the ring of new suburbs occupied during the 1960s. The high values there reflect the movement of population into a previously unsettled area. As the map of population change from 1960 to 1970 (produced by dividing 1970 population by 1960 population for each tract) indicates, population increase has been rapid in such areas; in some, population quadrupled during the decade. Turnover rates below 30 percent occur in an inner ring surrounding Detroit. Comparison with the population-change map indicates that the low-turnover areas lost population or grew slowly during the 1960s. (The histogram for the population-change map is on p. 353.)

**Households without Automobiles.** (Histogram and SMSA map on p. 337.) The irony of the proverb that the cobbler's children are often barefoot is evident in the high proportion (28 percent) of Detroit's households that do not have an automobile. Over 10 percent of all households throughout most of the city lack automobiles, and the proportion exceeds 30 percent in a large part of the old core. Detroit's public transportation is increasingly ineffective in providing efficient access to jobs, shopping, and services, and thus populations without automobile transportation are becoming increasingly isolated.

---

The Detroit area is a culturally diverse region where neighborhood and social differentiation has long been a way of life. Contrasts among ethnic neighborhoods have been augmented by socioeconomic and racial contrasts between central city and suburbs, and among different suburbs. Such diversity has a dual potential: it can enrich or it can generate destructive conflict. Detroit experienced both during the 1960s. Much of the nation's popular music emerged from Detroit's racial and cultural diversity, but so did some of the nation's worst civil disorders and highest crime rates. Detroit's future depends to a large degree on how well all the area's residents can move from socioeconomic separation to mutually enriching interaction.

CHAPTER 18

# Minneapolis—St. Paul

*St. Paul, from lofty bluffs, looks down upon the valley in content.*
*Minneapolis, from its level of a prairie, peers*
*aloft at its twelve-story cornices and ever strives to climb.*

CHARLES KING, "The Twin Cities of the Northwest,"
*The Cosmopolitan Magazine*, vol. ix, October 1890

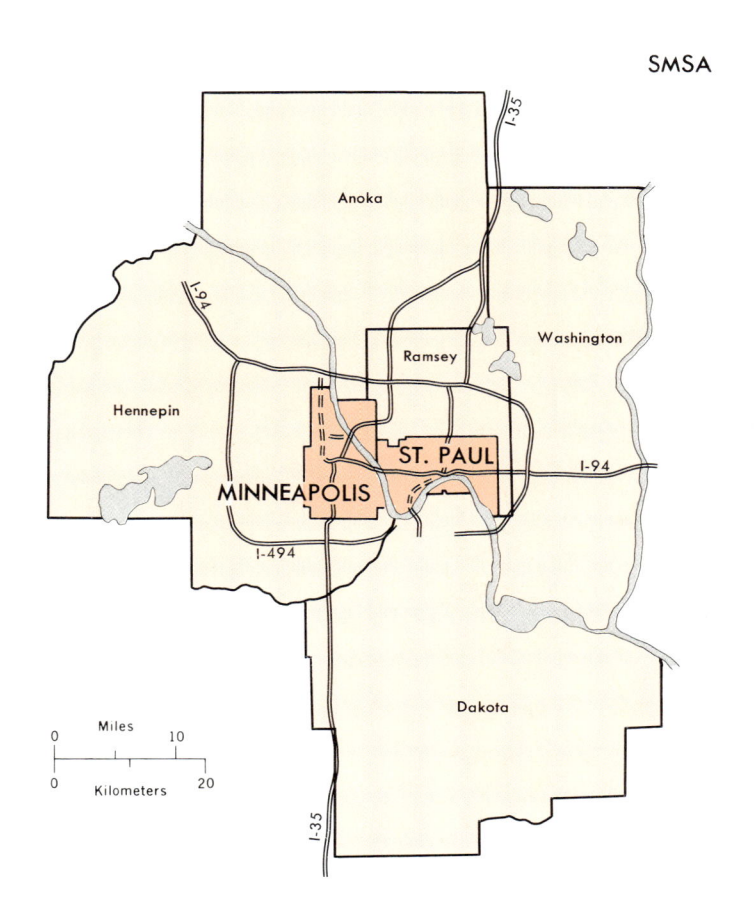

The Minneapolis-St. Paul Standard Metropolitan Statistical Area (SMSA) is the 15th most populous in the nation. It has a population of 1,814,000. Minneapolis and St. Paul are distinct municipalities; their respective populations are 434,000 and 310,000, and their combined population is 41 percent of the metropolitan total. Another 38 percent of the SMSA's people live in suburban Hennepin (29 percent) and suburban Ramsey (9 percent) counties. The remaining 21 percent of the population is divided among Anoka (9 percent), Dakota (8 percent), and Washington (4 percent) counties. The Daily Urban System (DUS) defined by counties that have at least 5 percent of their labor forces working in Hennepin and Ramsey counties includes the 5 SMSA counties and 13 additional counties in Minnesota and Wisconsin (p. 161). The population of the DUS is 2,123,000, which makes it the nation's 14th most populous DUS. The Twin Cities DUS is one of the largest (areally) in the nation.

*Note:* All data are from the 1970 Censuses of Population and Housing unless otherwise indicated. Therefore the present tense refers to 1970 data except for income data which are from 1969. Cartographic conventions are explained in Chapter 1.

Civilian settlement in the Twin Cities began in the 1840s. St. Paul was the head of effective steam navigation on the Mississippi, and Minneapolis possessed a good site for bridging the Mississippi and a superb waterpower site at the Falls of St. Anthony. As the Minnesota territory opened to settlement, St. Paul prospered on trade and Minneapolis boomed in its role as the processor of the region's forest and farm products. Starting from fewer than 1,500 people in 1850, the Twin Cities became the nation's 8th largest settlement in 1900 (p. 10). Rivalry between the two cities was always keen, frequently bitter, and occasionally farcical. As long as trade and river transportation were dominant, St. Paul retained its premier position. By 1880 Minneapolis had surpassed St. Paul by 5,500 residents, for rail transportation and agrarian settlement to the west made Minneapolis a better location for new enterprise.

The region's terrain was sculptured by glaciers that left numerous lakes and hills. Minneapolis and St. Paul lie on relatively flat areas of sand and gravel washed out from the edges of the ice sheets. The two cities are surrounded by rougher areas left behind when glaciers were

159

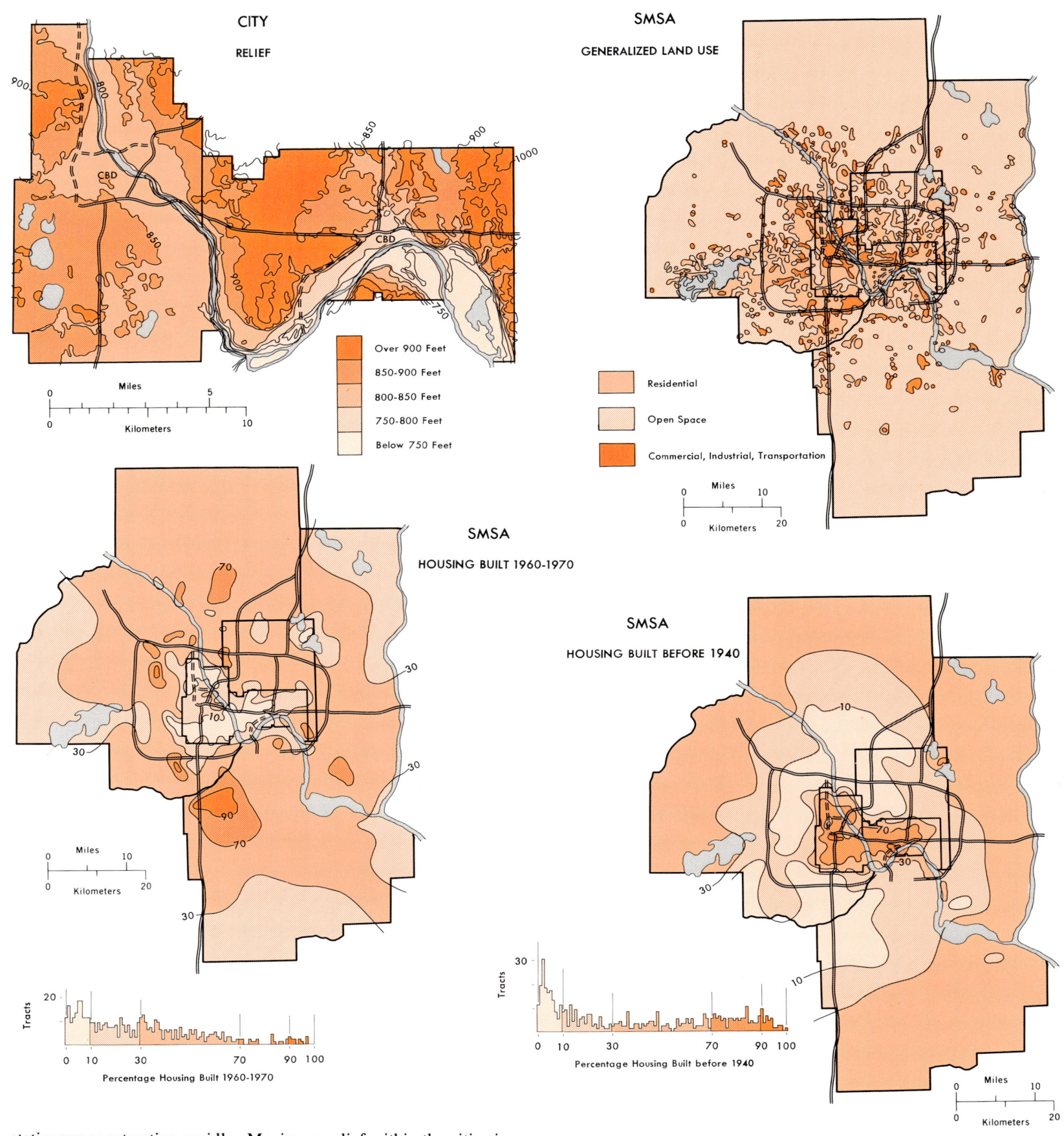

# Nineteenth-Century Inland Centers and Ports: Minneapolis-St. Paul

stationary or retreating rapidly. Maximum relief within the cities is about 200 feet (60 meters). The eastern part of St. Paul and the northern part of Minneapolis are hilly. The most extensive area of flat land runs through south and central Minneapolis into western St. Paul.

The necessity of building railroad tracks and marshaling yards, warehouses, and car shops in both cities has had a strong influence on land use. Industrial areas are fragmented and scattered throughout the cities. The cities' Central Business Districts (CBDs) are separated by almost 10 miles. Residential expansion has proceeded more rapidly south, west, and north of Minneapolis than north, east, or south of St. Paul. Terrain and local tastes combine to produce fragmented residential development in which tracts of suburban housing and areas of open space are interspersed. Patches of open country approach central-city boundaries in many places.

## HOUSING

**Housing Age.** The Twin Cities have relatively young housing stocks for midwestern cities, but there are large variations within the SMSA.

160

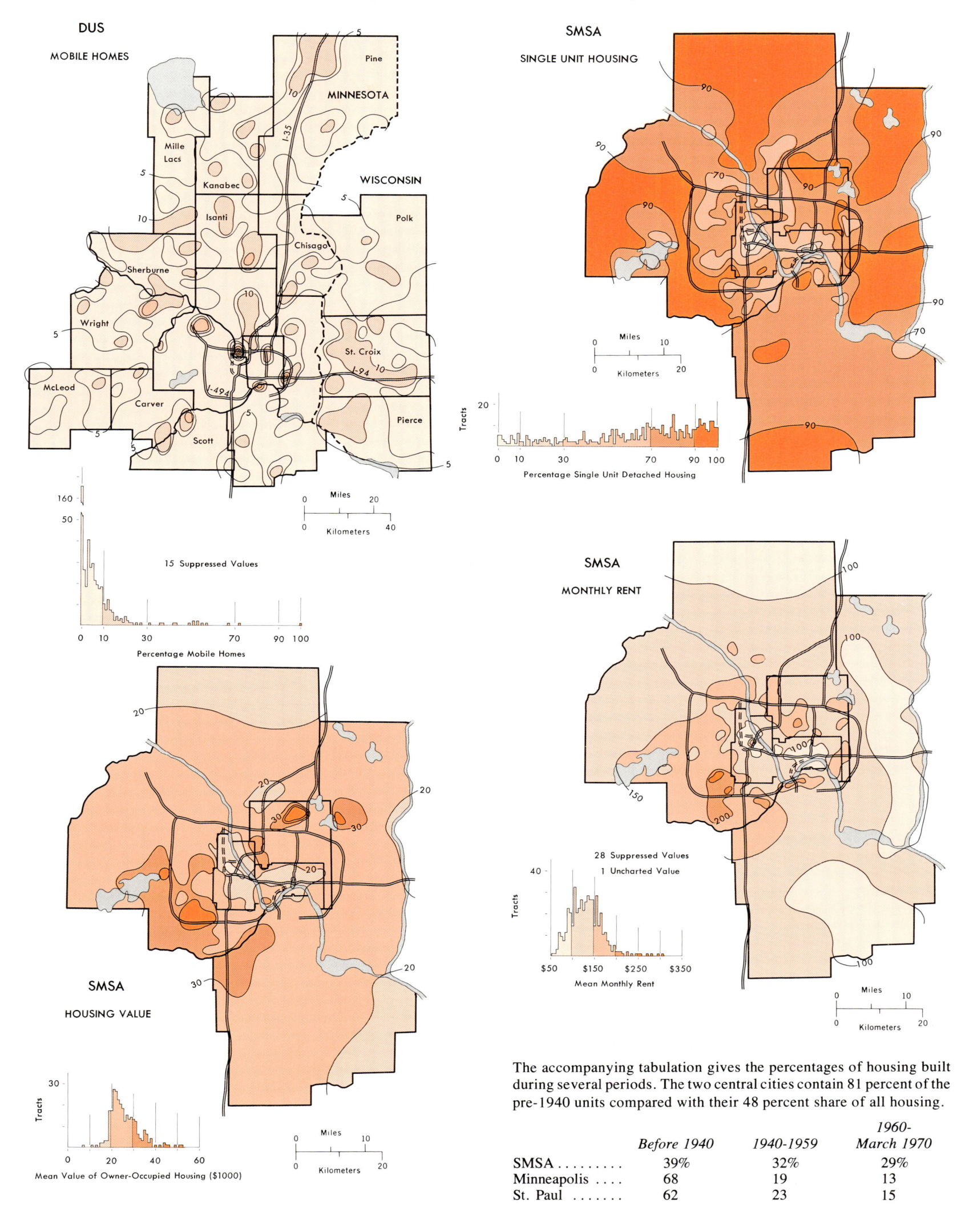

## Nineteenth-Century Inland Centers and Ports: Minneapolis-St. Paul

### DUS
**MOBILE HOMES**

Percentage Mobile Homes
15 Suppressed Values

### SMSA
**SINGLE UNIT HOUSING**

Percentage Single Unit Detached Housing

### SMSA
**HOUSING VALUE**

Mean Value of Owner-Occupied Housing ($1000)

### SMSA
**MONTHLY RENT**

Mean Monthly Rent
28 Suppressed Values
1 Uncharted Value

The accompanying tabulation gives the percentages of housing built during several periods. The two central cities contain 81 percent of the pre-1940 units compared with their 48 percent share of all housing.

|  | Before 1940 | 1940-1959 | 1960-March 1970 |
|---|---|---|---|
| SMSA | 39% | 32% | 29% |
| Minneapolis | 68 | 19 | 13 |
| St. Paul | 62 | 23 | 15 |

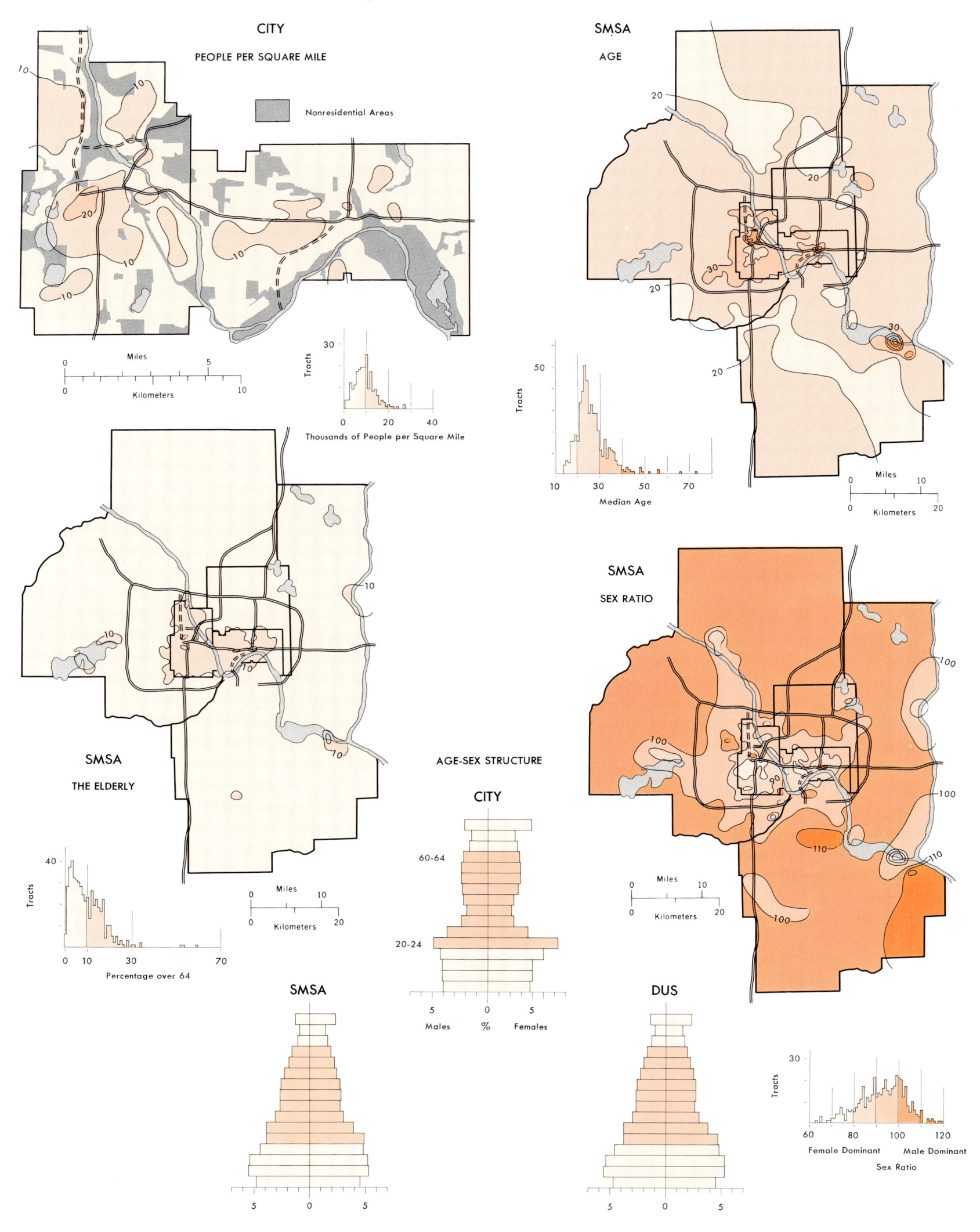

## Nineteenth-Century Inland Centers and Ports: Minneapolis-St. Paul

### CITY
**PEOPLE PER SQUARE MILE**

### SMSA
**AGE**

### SMSA
**THE ELDERLY**

### AGE-SEX STRUCTURE
**CITY**

**SMSA**

**DUS**

### SMSA
**SEX RATIO**

162

# Nineteenth-Century Inland Centers and Ports: Minneapolis-St. Paul

**CITY** — PERCENTAGE NEGRO

**SMSA** — AMERICAN INDIANS

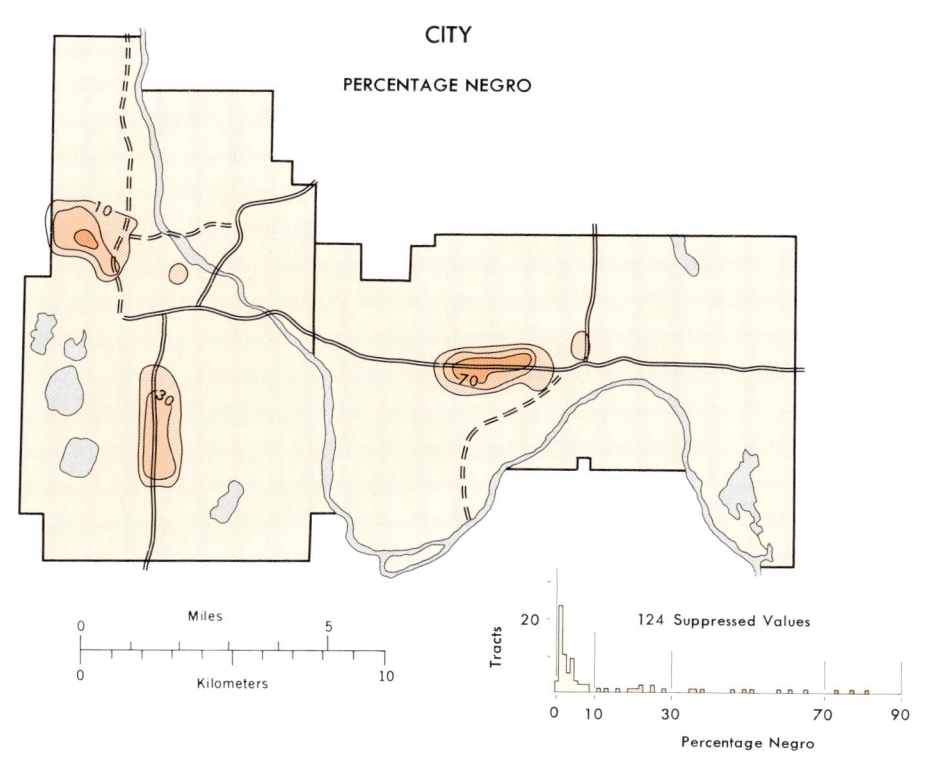

Each Dot Represents 50 American Indians

The decline in proportions of old housing with distance away from the central cities' area is extremely regular. Proportions below 10 percent are concentrated in the northern and southern suburbs where most post-World War II growth occurred. Percentages rise again near the metropolitan periphery, beyond the zone of recent rapid growth.

Proportions of new housing are low in the central cities, except in the downtown Minneapolis renewal area. The highest percentages in suburban areas occur on the frontiers of suburban settlement in central Anoka, northern Dakota, and central Hennepin counties. The presence of only a few high percentages east and north of St. Paul emphasizes by contrast the degree to which growth has occurred around Minneapolis.

**Mobile Homes.** The 12,400 mobile homes in the DUS constitute 1.9 percent of the DUS housing stock. In some areas, such as Wright County, mobile homes are as much as 6.5 percent of all housing units. Zoning restrictions confine mobile homes to trailer parks in the immediate vicinity of the central cities, but they are widespread in the rest of the DUS.

**Single-Unit Detached Housing.** Individual dwellings make up 63 percent of the SMSA's housing stock. The percentages in Minneapolis and St. Paul are 45 and 52, respectively. Proportions rise outward from low percentages in and near each of the downtown areas. More than 70 percent of the housing units in suburban areas are single-family units except along some freeways and arterials, which are preferred locations for large suburban apartment complexes.

**Housing Value and Rent.** The mean value of owner-occupied housing in the SMSA is $24,000 and in both Minneapolis and St. Paul is $20,000. Individual tract means vary from $7,000 to $52,000. The lowest values are located near the two CBDs, and mean housing values below $20,000 are characteristic of large parts of both central cities. Higher housing values are located in amenity residential areas near Lake Minnetonka on the west and in the morainic area north of St. Paul. The highest mean occurs in the exclusive residential community of North Oaks in north-central Ramsey County.

Mean monthly contract rents average $121 in the entire SMSA, $108 in Minneapolis, and $101 in St. Paul. Tract means vary from $55 to $305, although tract means over $200 are rare. The highest mean rent occurs in a tract with a few luxury apartment units in northern Dakota County. Larger numbers of high-cost rental units are available southwest of Minneapolis, but they are not quite as costly as the Dakota County units.

## THE PEOPLE

**Population Density.** The overall population density of Minneapolis and St. Paul is 6,900 people per square mile (2,700 per square kilometer). The cities are almost equal in area, but since Minneapolis has a larger population than St. Paul, its density is correspondingly higher—7,900 versus St. Paul's 5,900 (3,100 versus 2,300 per square kilometer). The two tracts where densities reach 27,000 per square mile (10,500 per square kilometer) are located southwest of the Minneapolis CBD. The Twin Cities' density of 6,900 (2,700) is

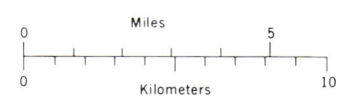

**CITY** — PERCENTAGE SPANISH-AMERICAN

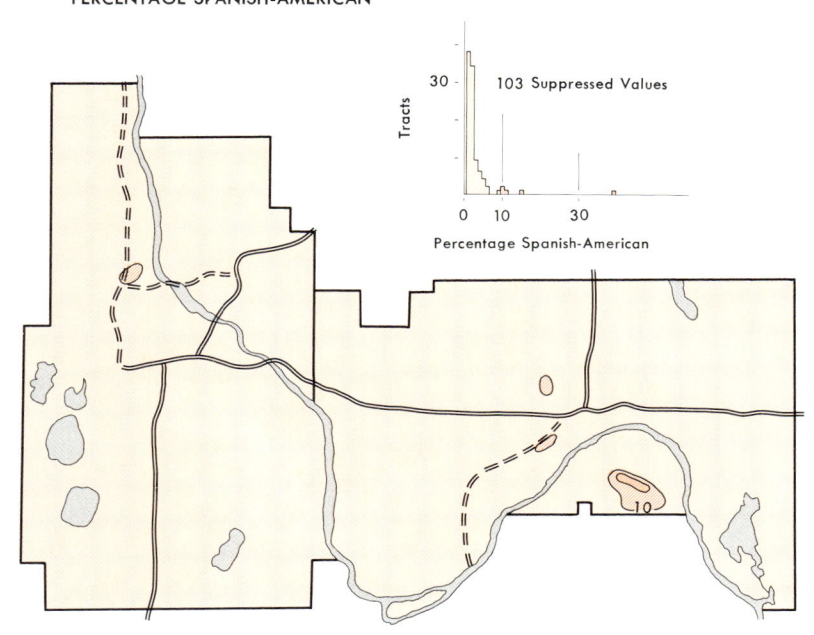

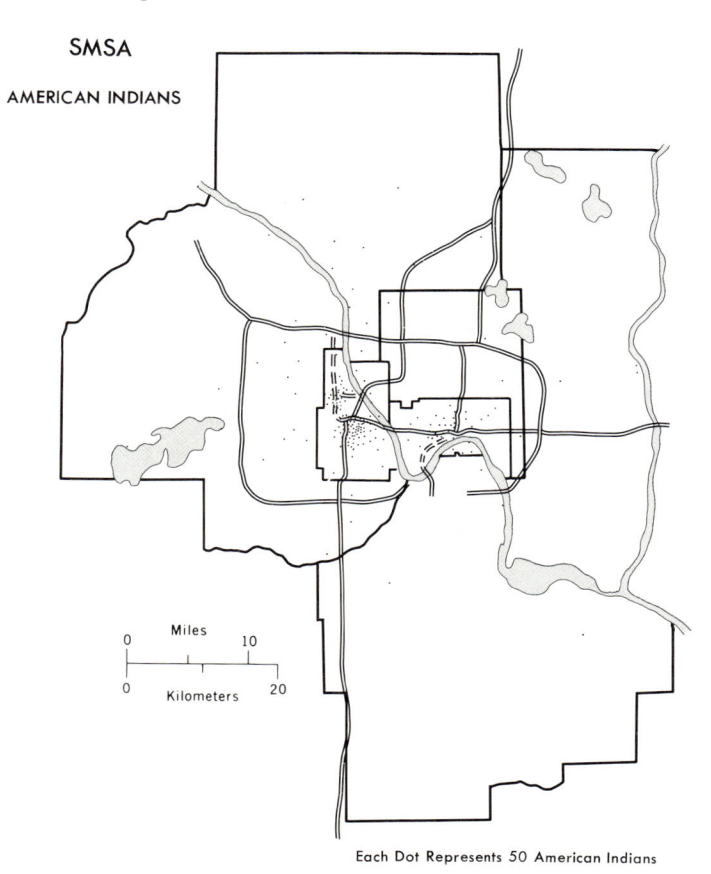

## Nineteenth-Century Inland Centers and Ports: Minneapolis-St. Paul

**SMSA HOUSEHOLD SIZE**

3 Uncharted Values

Average Number of People per Household

**SMSA FAMILIES WITH A FEMALE HEAD**

Percentage Families with a Female Head

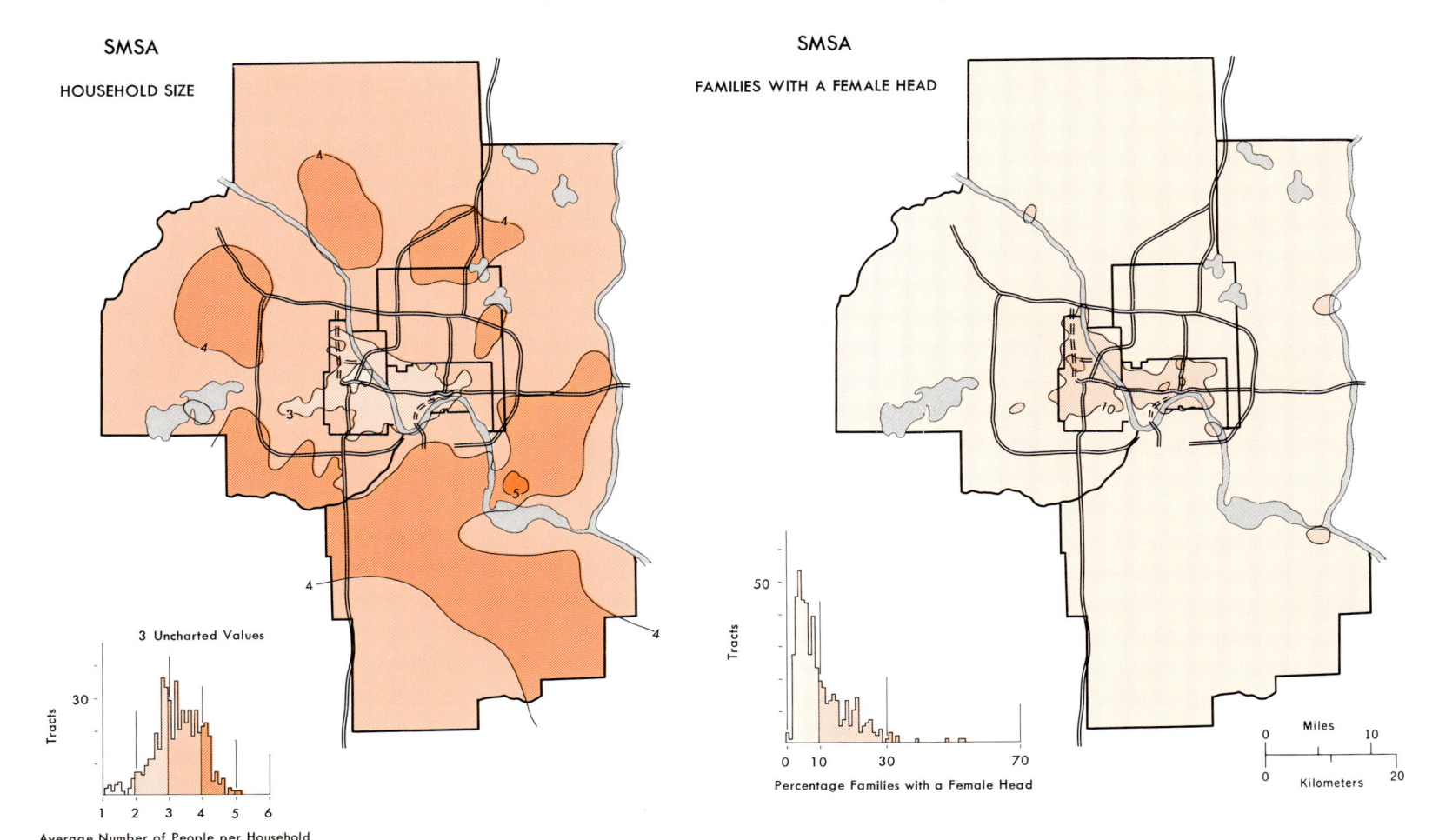

similar to Los Angeles's 6,100 per square mile or 2,400 per square kilometer rather than to Chicago's 15,100 people per square mile or 5,800 per square kilometer. (An SMSA map is on p. 314.)

**Age and the Elderly.** The median age of the Twin Cities SMSA is 26 years. The median ages of the Minneapolis and St. Paul populations are 29 and 28, respectively. Individual tract medians range from 14 to 73 years. Median ages are lowest in the northern and southern suburbs where young families are rearing children. The tract with an over-50 median near the St. Paul CBD has a derelict population.

People 64 years of age and older make up 9 percent of the SMSA population, 15 percent of all Minneapolis residents, and 13 percent of St. Paul's people. There are few places where the proportion of a tract population exceeds 30 percent. The elderly constitute more than 10 percent of tract populations in most of Minneapolis and St. Paul except for a sparsely settled area of northeastern Minneapolis and tracts in eastern and southeastern St. Paul. The highest percentages are derelict populations near the CBDs and institutionalized groups.

**Sex Ratio.** There are 1.07 females for each male in the SMSA resulting in a female-dominant sex ratio (males divided by females times 100) of 93. The sex ratio in Minneapolis is 84, and in St. Paul it is 88. Ratios exceed 100 in rural and suburban areas where young children are numerous, for young populations are often male-dominant. Usual female dominance is reinforced by significant in-migration of young females to Minneapolis and St. Paul in search of employment and education. The imbalance in the 15- to 29-year-old group is clearly evident on the combined population pyramid for Minneapolis and St. Paul.

**Negroes.** There are 30,000 blacks in Minneapolis and St. Paul. They make up 4 percent of the combined population of the cities. Twin Cities' blacks occupy three distinct neighborhoods in Minneapolis and St. Paul. The Twin Cities' early black community was small (4,500 in 1940) and primarily an offshoot of the railroad industry. It is still small; the Twin Cities SMSA has the lowest proportion (1.8 percent) of blacks of any of the 24 SMSAs in the atlas. The impact of blacks in the Twin Cities is further diluted by their separation into three neighborhoods. Few blacks now work for the railroads, but they have not yet moved into well-paying jobs in large numbers. The median family income for blacks in Minneapolis and St. Paul is over $4,000 below that of whites. There are few blacks outside the two central cities (map on p. 386); 93 percent of the SMSA's blacks reside in Minneapolis and St. Paul.

**Spanish-Americans.** The Census Bureau estimates the number of Hispanics in the Twin Cities by counting people who speak Spanish. By that reckoning, there are 10,500 Spanish-Americans in the two cities, 6,500 of whom live in St. Paul. Most are Mexican foreign stock or indigenous Mexican-Americans who originally began to come to Minnesota when sugar beets became an important crop in the Red River Valley. In St. Paul, Hispanics have moved southeast from the neighborhood they formerly occupied on the Mississippi floodplain across from the CBD. The St. Paul cluster is the only notable concentration in the Twin Cities. The remaining population is scattered throughout the cities in small numbers. (An SMSA map is on p. 394.)

**American Indians.** There are 9,850 Indians in the Twin Cities SMSA, which is one of the larger urban Indian concentrations in the nation. The Indian population is clustered in the two central cities. Of the SMSA total, 18 percent live in St. Paul and 56 percent live in Minneapolis. The densest cluster of Indians occurs in south-central Minneapolis in a deteriorating neighborhood. Many of the area's Indians move rather freely back and forth between the Indian reservations in north-central Minnesota and the Twin Cities. Thus the census count of Indians in the Twin Cities is probably low.

The Twin Cities area and Minnesota have a reputation of being strongly Scandinavian, and indeed they once were. But the immigrant groups are disappearing rapidly. Today Swedish foreign stock is the largest ethnic group in the SMSA, but it barely exceeds 3 percent of the total population. Only remnants of what were strong Swedish, German, Irish, Italian, and eastern European neighborhoods remain.

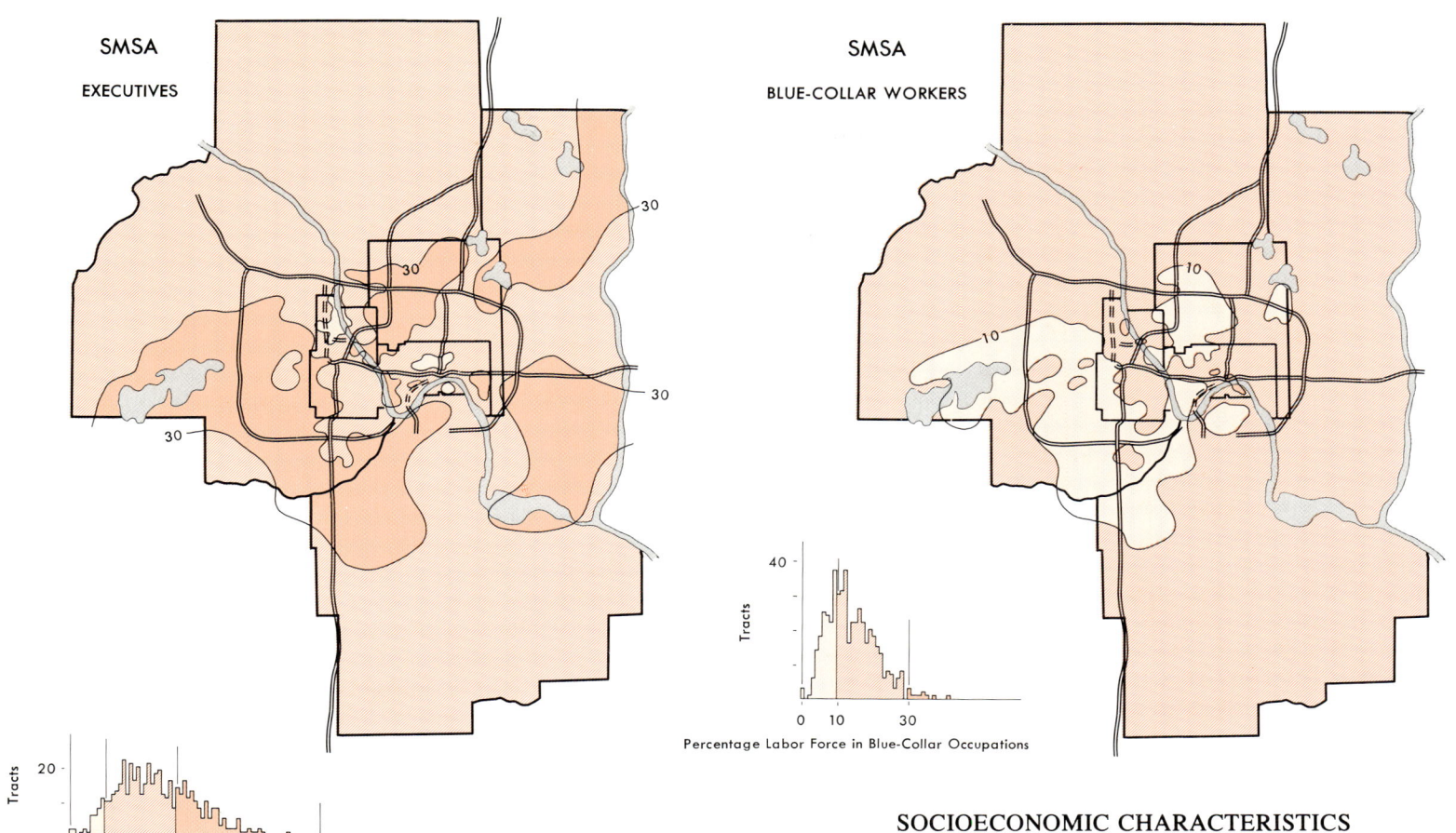

## SOCIOECONOMIC CHARACTERISTICS

**Household Size.** There are 3.2 people in the average SMSA household, 2.6 in the average Minneapolis household, and 2.9 in the average St. Paul household. Individual tract averages vary from 1.1 to 5.1. The largest households are located in new suburbs, and the smallest occur in the CBDs of St. Paul and Minneapolis. Blacks typically have larger households than the total population. The SMSA average for black households is 3.1; it is also 3.1 in Minneapolis, and in St. Paul it is 3.2.

**Female Headship.** The Census Bureau defines female headship by the absence of a male spouse regardless of the sex of the family's principal breadwinner. Nine percent of the SMSA's families, 16 percent of Minneapolis's families, and 14 percent of St. Paul's families are headed by females. Sixty-four percent of the SMSA's families headed by females live in Minneapolis and St. Paul, compared with the 41 percent of the SMSA's total population that live there. Individual tract proportions of female headship range from zero to 53 percent. The highest percentages are located in predominantly black areas and in the Mount Airy housing project north of the St. Paul CBD.

**Occupations.** Thirteen percent of the SMSA's civilian labor force work at blue-collar (laborers and operatives) jobs, and 25 percent classify themselves as executives (engineers, teachers, professionals, managers, proprietors, and administrators). The remaining 62 percent are service (33 percent) and clerical (29 percent) workers. The breakdown for the combined cities is: blue-collar, 14 percent; services, 35 percent; clerical, 31 percent; and executive, 20 percent. The percentages for each city are identical to the combined figures.

The few tracts where proportions of blue-collar workers exceed 30 percent are located in the central cities. Tracts with proportions of less than 10 percent are in suburban areas, with important extensions into the central cities in the Highland Park area of southwestern St. Paul and the area near the lakes in southwestern Minneapolis. The largest low-percentage area extends south and southwest from Minneapolis.

To some extent the map of executives is a reverse of the map of blue-collar workers. The old prestige axis reaching westward toward Lake Minnetonka from Minneapolis is evident, and proportions also

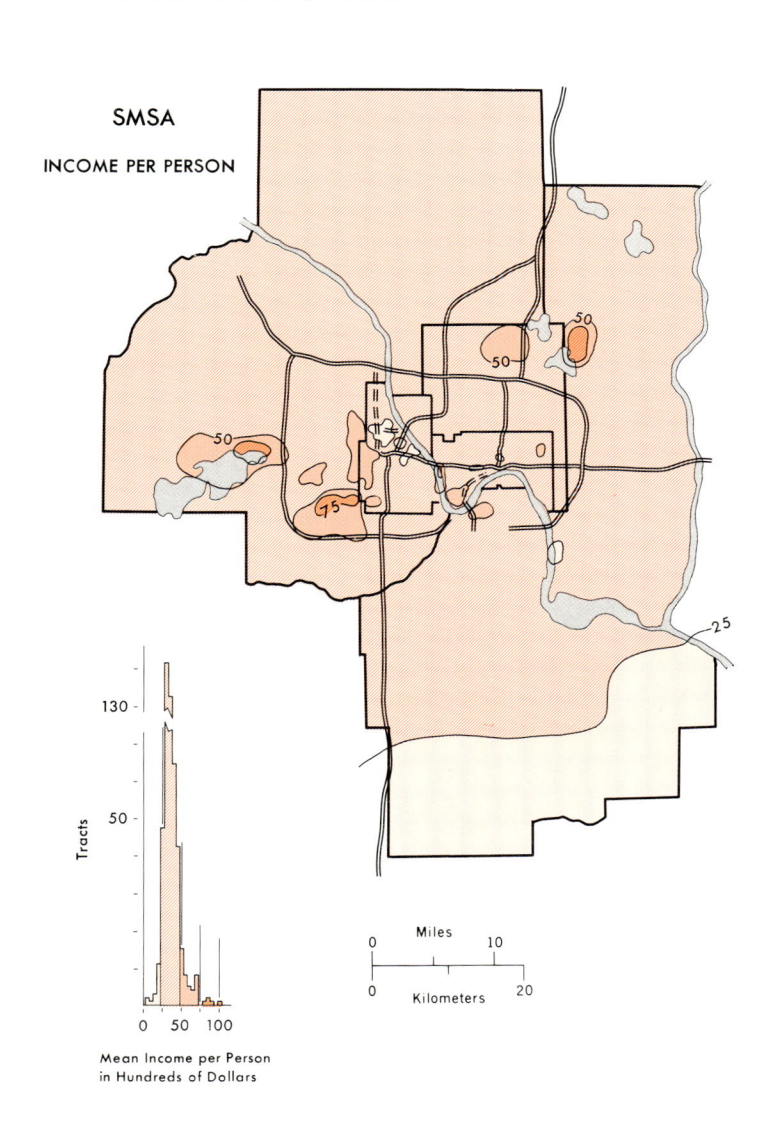

SMSA

LABOR FORCE TAKING PUBLIC TRANSPORTATION TO WORK

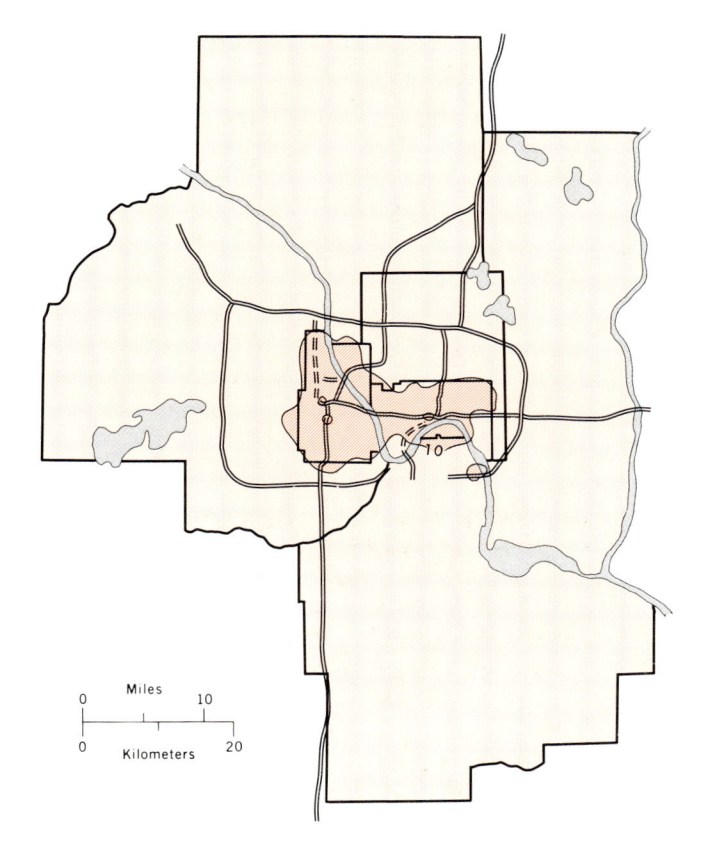

SMSA

RESIDENTIAL CHANGE, 1965-1970
(See Text)

exceed 30 percent in the recently settled areas of northern Dakota County. Other areas favored by people in executive occupations are St. Paul's sparsely settled northern suburbs, especially the sector extending to the northeast that is anchored by White Bear Lake and rural southern Washington County, where working farms are gradually being bought by prosperous people seeking housing in a rural setting.

**Income.** Mean income per person in the Twin Cities SMSA is $3,650 per person per year. Mean incomes per person in Minneapolis and St. Paul are $3,500. This small difference between SMSA and central-city incomes is unusual. Individual tract means vary from $1,000 to $9,800. Means below $2,500 are rare and are concentrated in black areas or where dependent populations cluster adjacent to the two CBDs. Mean per person incomes over $7,500 are even more rare. They occur in the prestige suburb of Edina—west of south Minneapolis—on the edge of Lake Minnetonka, in North Oaks in north-central Ramsey County, and in Dellwood, north of White Bear Lake.

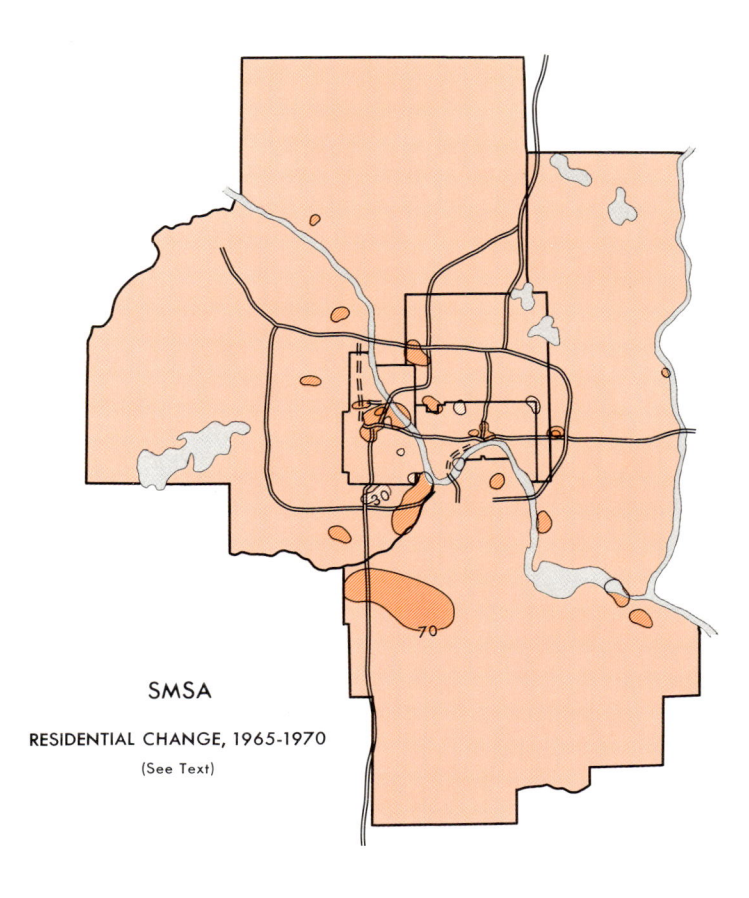

## TOPICS OF SPECIAL INTEREST IN THE TWIN CITIES REGION

**Population Turnover.** Forty-one percent of the population 5 years old and older were living in different houses in 1970 from the ones they occupied in 1965. In Minneapolis 43 percent were in different houses, and in St. Paul, 36 percent. This turnover is average for a large metropolitan area but somewhat unusual because the SMSA summary statistic is more a product of widespread moderate turnover than of high turnover in some tracts offset by low turnover in others. Turnover exceeds 90 percent only in the Landfall Trailer Park on Ramsey County's eastern boundary and in a single tract in downtown Minneapolis.

**Public Transportation Use.** (Histogram on p. 330.) Nine percent of the SMSA's labor force take public transportation to work, but the people who do so are heavily concentrated in Minneapolis (54 percent) and St. Paul (26 percent). There have been recurrent discussions of high-capacity public-transportation facilities in the Twin Cities region, but the dispersion of jobs in two CBDs and two sets of suburbs and the inability of existing bus services to attract ridership greater than 10 percent of local labor forces outside the city's boundaries might make such investment risky.

**Population Density.** (Histogram on p. 314.) Viable public transportation throughout the Twin Cities region would be particularly difficult to effect given the extremely low population densities. The SMSA's overall population density is 860 people per square mile (335 per square kilometer), which is half the density of the Los Angeles SMSA. More important, even in the two central cities, densities over 10,000 people per square mile (3,900 per square kilometer) are rare. Thus the population concentrations that would make conventional forms of transit other than buses feasible do not exist.

# Nineteenth-Century Inland Centers and Ports: Minneapolis-St. Paul

SMSA

PEOPLE PER SQUARE MILE

Thousands of People per Square Mile

SMSA

PERCENTAGE HOUSEHOLDS WITHOUT AN AUTOMOBILE

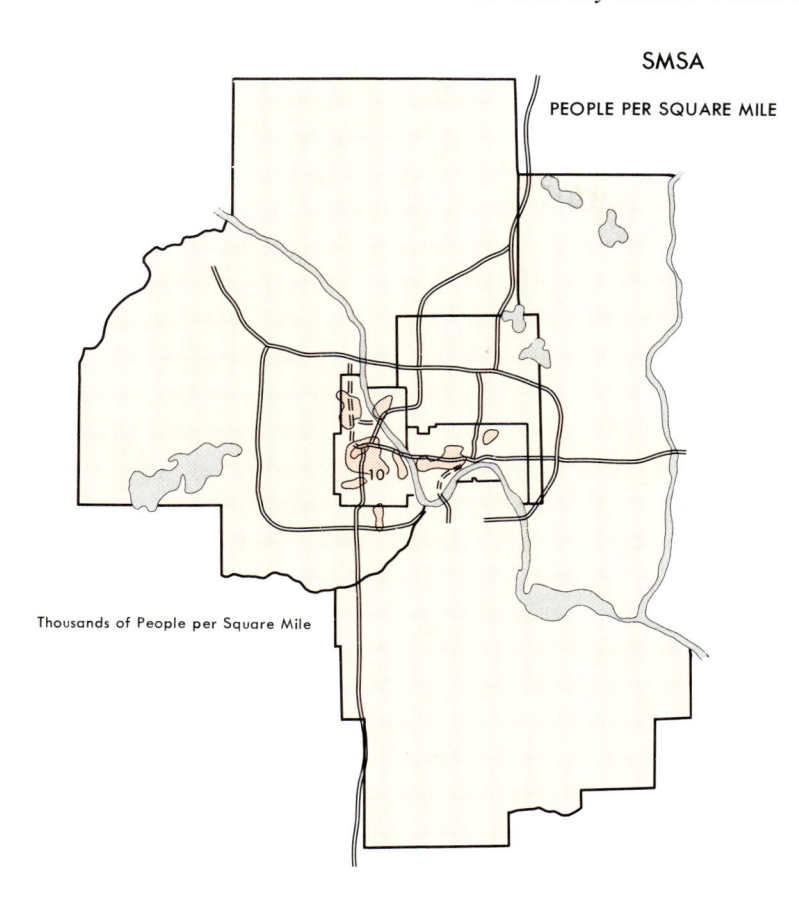

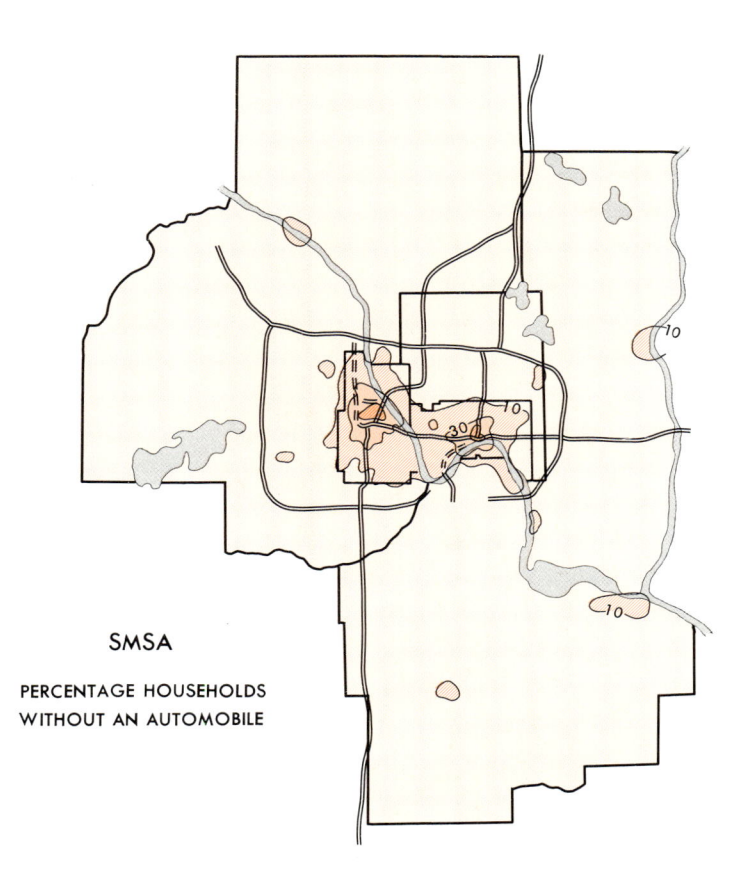

SMSA

PERCENTAGE HOUSING UNITS WORTH MORE THAN $15,000 OCCUPIED BY HOUSEHOLDS WITH INCOMES LESS THAN $5,000

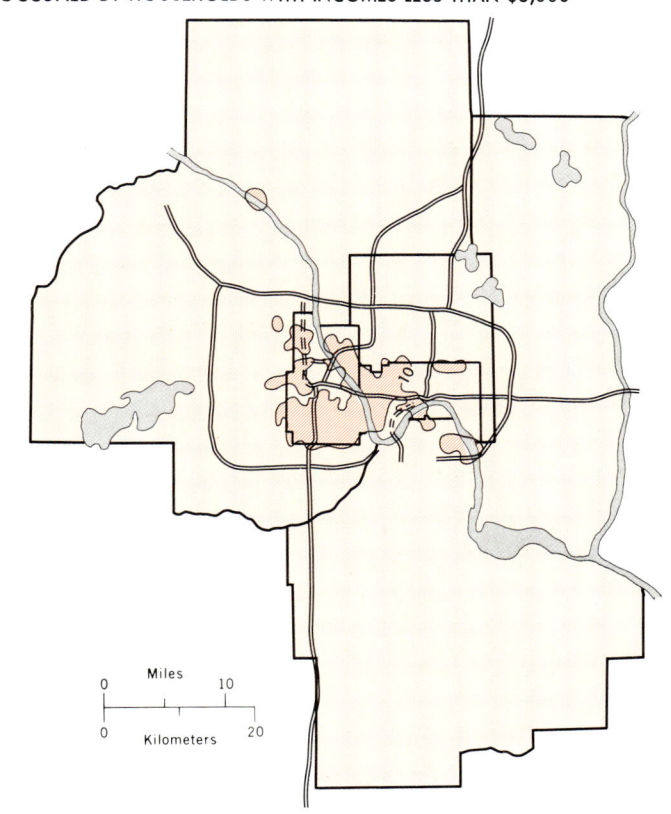

**Households without Automobiles.** (Histogram on p. 338.) In a metropolitan area as dependent on automobile transportation as the Twin Cities region, not having a car can be a serious impediment to obtaining daily needs. Fourteen percent of the SMSA's households do not have an automobile available. In Minneapolis, 27 percent of all households are without automobiles, as are 22 percent of St. Paul's households. Eighty-five percent of the SMSA's households without automobiles are located in Minneapolis and St. Paul. Cause and effect are difficult to separate; households without cars necessarily locate where they have access to public transportation if they have a choice. The most immobile people in the SMSA are probably the small percentage without an automobile in every suburban tract.

**Low-Income Home Owners.** (Histogram on p. 306.) A current difficulty in the Twin Cities SMSA is posed by low-income (but nonpoor) elderly householders who own their homes. Seven percent of the SMSA's owner-occupied houses worth more than $15,000 are occupied by households whose annual income is less than $5,000. With such a small income, the owner either allocates too much of it to taxes and maintenance, and thus has inadequate resources to meet other expenses, or skimps on maintenance. Indeed, both may result. Households in such a predicament are heavily concentrated in the two central cities, and they are potential problem areas from the standpoint of the owners' human needs and of housing deterioration.

The Twin Cities SMSA has remarkably few problems compared with most metropolitan regions of its size. This happy situation is largely a function of the social and economic homogeneity of the metropolitan area's population. Most Twin Cities residents are well educated and well off financially. The sharp social and economic gradients common in many metropolitan areas are absent in the Twin Cities. The Twin Cities have been national pioneers in the realm of metropolitan government, which suggests that any problems that do arise in the future will be dealt with forthrightly and effectively.

# CHAPTER 19

# Seattle

*Railroads and steamers have brought the [Puget Sound] country out of the wilderness and abolished old distances. It is now near to all the world.*

JOHN MUIR, *Steep Trails*, 1918

The Seattle-Everett Standard Metropolitan Statistical Area (SMSA) is the 17th most populous in the nation. It has a population of 1,425,000, of whom 531,000 (37 percent) live in Seattle. The remaining 63 percent is divided between suburban King County (44 percent) and Snohomish County (19 percent). Only the western sides of King and Snohomish counties are densely settled; the central and eastern portions of the SMSA are sparsely populated forested lowlands and the Cascade Mountains. The Daily Urban System (DUS) defined by counties that have at least 5 percent of their labor forces working in King County adds only Kitsap and Pierce

*Note:* All data are from the 1970 Censuses of Population and Housing unless otherwise indicated. Therefore the present tense refers to 1970 data except for income data which are from 1969. Cartographic conventions are explained in Chapter 1.

counties to the DUS (p. 169), because King and Snohomish counties are so large. The DUS population is 1,937,000, and the increase over the SMSA population is largely accounted for by the 411,000 people in the Tacoma SMSA (Pierce County). The DUS is the 16th most populous in the nation.

Seattle had but 3,500 residents in 1880, most of whom made their living by small-scale exportation of lumber to San Francisco. Connection to the East by transcontinental railroads in 1883, 1893, and 1906 opened new markets for the region's forest products and brought immigrants from the Midwest and Europe. Seattle prospered anew with the Alaskan gold rush of the late 1890s. As the Alaskan boom faded, World War I shipbuilding picked up the slack. The city's population was 81,000 in 1900 and 315,000 in 1920 (p. 10). Seattle

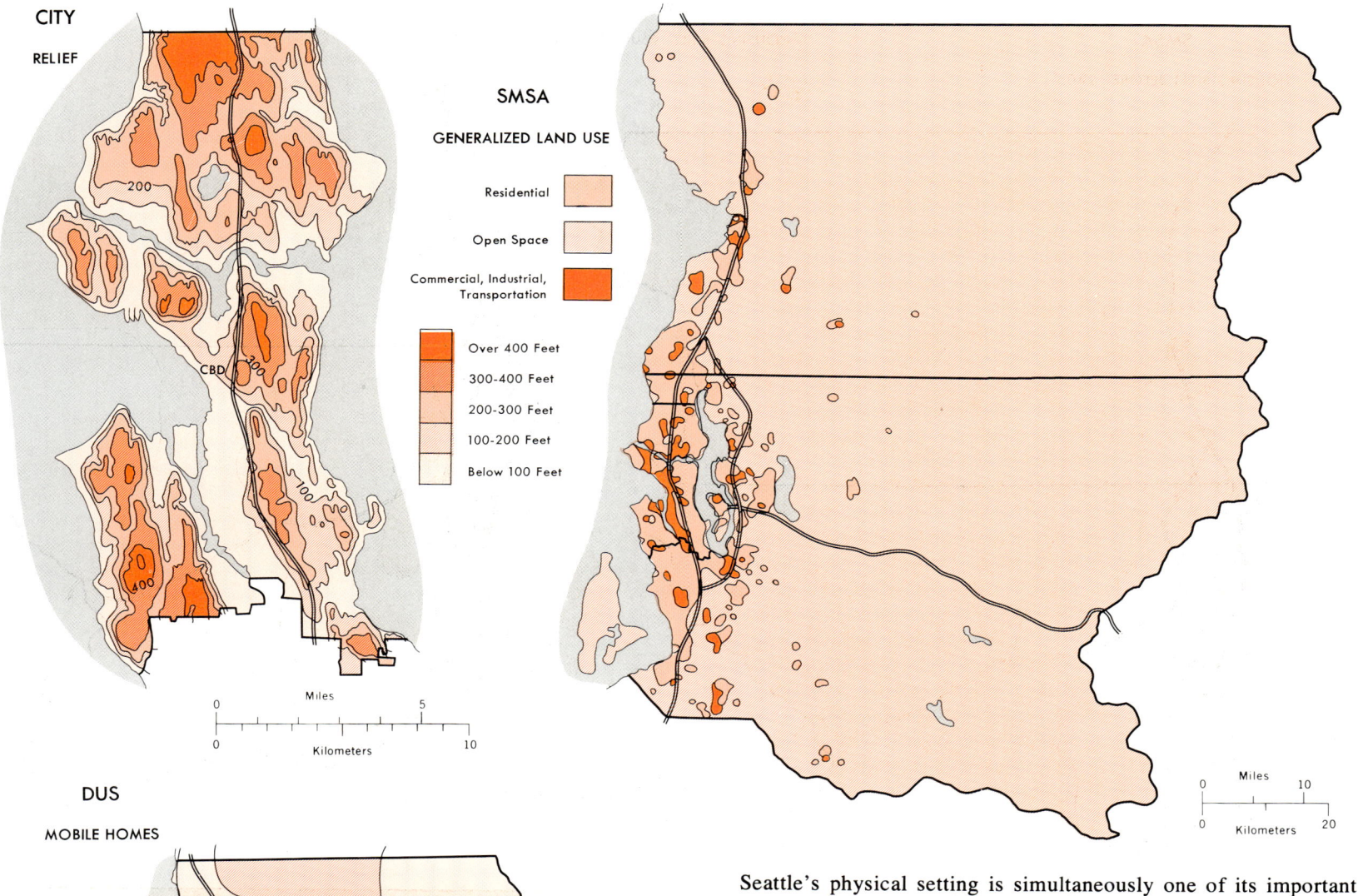

## Nineteenth-Century Inland Centers and Ports: Seattle

Seattle's physical setting is simultaneously one of its important amenities and the cause of early isolation. The Cascades begin to rise 25 miles (40 kilometers) inland from Puget Sound, forming a barrier to land transportation. The Puget Sound shore is rugged, for the region was glaciated during the Pleistocene epoch and the morainic deposits left behind have had little time to erode. Elevations exceed 400 feet (120 meters) within two miles (3 kilometers) of Puget Sound in Seattle. The only flat area of any consequence is the floodplain at the Duwamish River mouth. Seattle is now less rugged than it was originally, since many hilltops were sluiced into the bay to make land and even out the terrain. Although the hills and Lake Washington make movement around the Seattle area difficult, the combination provides many homesites with fine views of the lake or the Sound. Even the steepest slopes are often occupied.

The Duwamish lowlands are given over to commercial and industrial land uses associated with the Seattle Central Business District (CBD) and the city's important shipping business. The area of urban residential land use extends over 50 miles from southern King County north to Everett in Snohomish County. The narrow settled strip gives way quickly to the private and National Forests of the Cascade Range on the east.

boomed again during World War II as shipbuilding and aircraft manufacturing flourished. The city had 368,000 people in 1950 and 557,000 in 1960. Since 1950 the city population has declined 24 percent to its current size. The SMSA population increased 28.7 percent during the 1960s, compared with a national metropolitan growth rate of 16.6 percent. Population growth slowed in the late 1960s and early 1970s owing to cutbacks at the Boeing aircraft company, the region's major employer.

### HOUSING

**Housing Age.** Thirty percent of the SMSA's housing was built before 1940, 36 percent from 1940 through 1959, and 34 percent from 1960 to March 1970. In Seattle, 48 percent dates from before 1940, 36 percent was erected from 1940 through 1959, and the remaining 16 percent was built during the 1960s. Although Seattle is not usually viewed as one of the recent cities of the West and South, the age structure of its housing stock suggests it is. The identical proportions of city and SMSA housing built from 1940 through 1959 and the relatively large percentage of the SMSA's housing erected since 1960

169

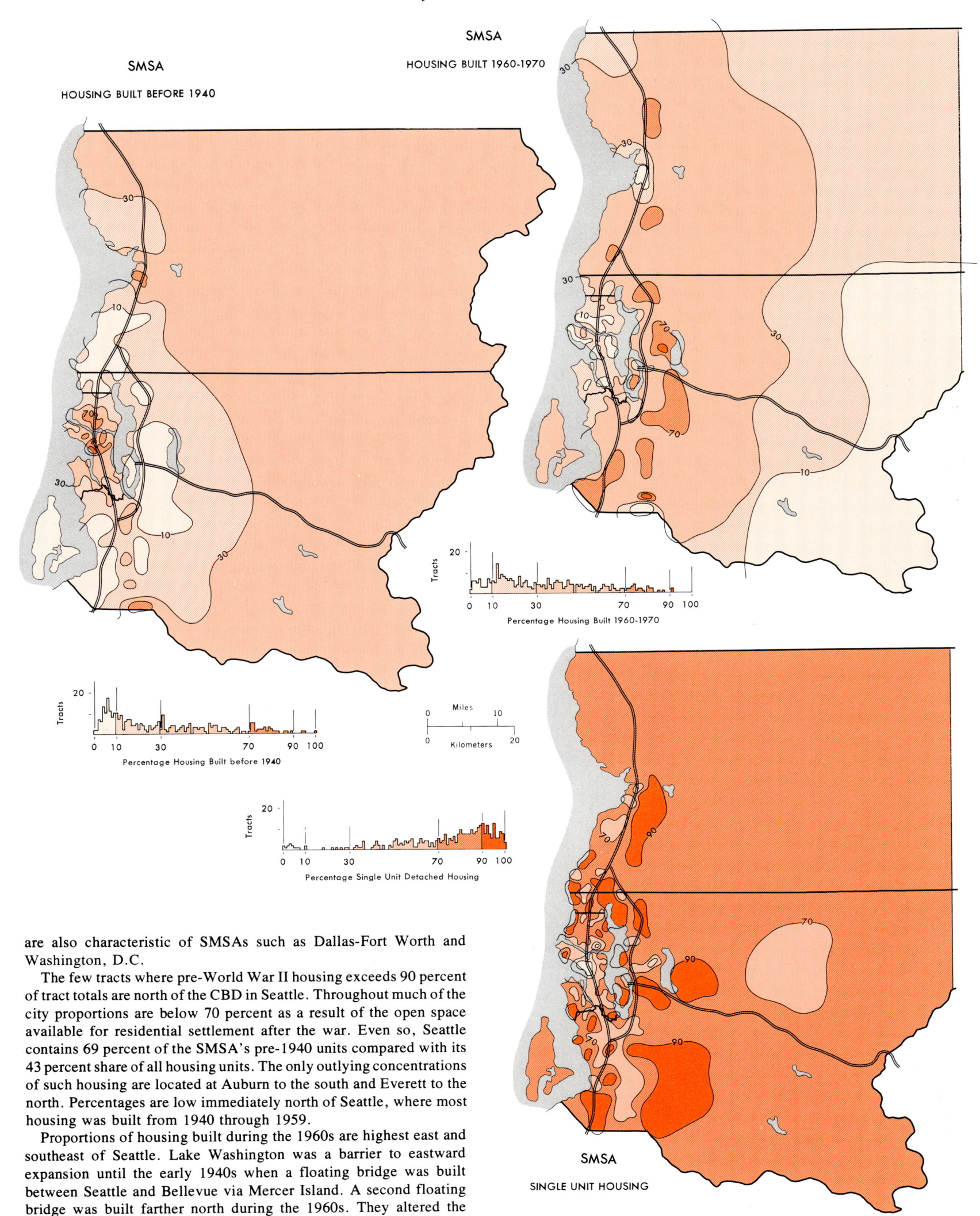

## Nineteenth-Century Inland Centers and Ports: Seattle

**SMSA**
HOUSING BUILT BEFORE 1940

**SMSA**
HOUSING BUILT 1960-1970

**SMSA**
SINGLE UNIT HOUSING

are also characteristic of SMSAs such as Dallas-Fort Worth and Washington, D.C.

The few tracts where pre-World War II housing exceeds 90 percent of tract totals are north of the CBD in Seattle. Throughout much of the city proportions are below 70 percent as a result of the open space available for residential settlement after the war. Even so, Seattle contains 69 percent of the SMSA's pre-1940 units compared with its 43 percent share of all housing units. The only outlying concentrations of such housing are located at Auburn to the south and Everett to the north. Percentages are low immediately north of Seattle, where most housing was built from 1940 through 1959.

Proportions of housing built during the 1960s are highest east and southeast of Seattle. Lake Washington was a barrier to eastward expansion until the early 1940s when a floating bridge was built between Seattle and Bellevue via Mercer Island. A second floating bridge was built farther north during the 1960s. They altered the

170

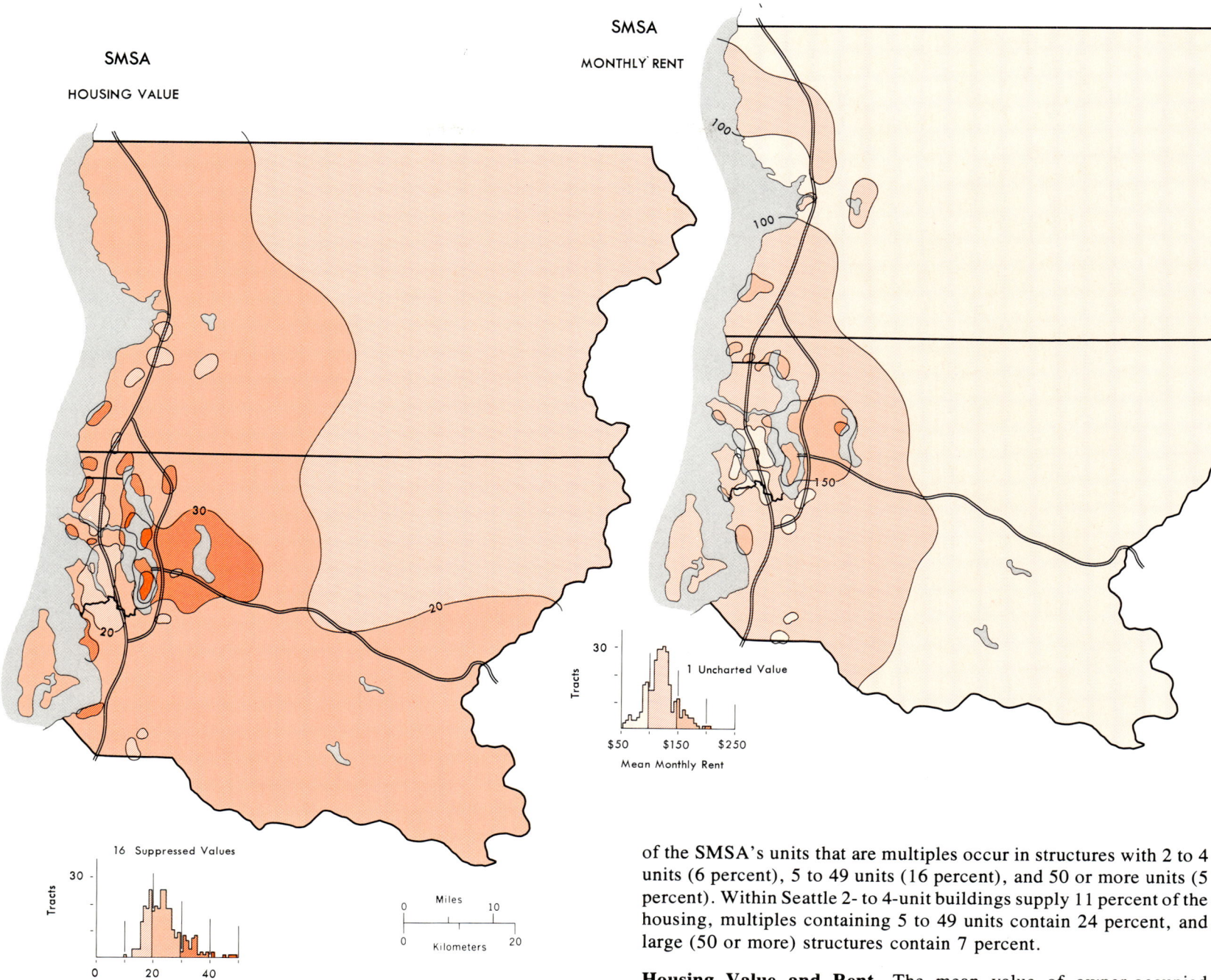

## Nineteenth-Century Inland Centers and Ports: Seattle

**SMSA HOUSING VALUE**

**SMSA MONTHLY RENT**

16 Suppressed Values
Mean Value of Owner-Occupied Housing ($1000)

1 Uncharted Value
Mean Monthly Rent

traditional north-south axis of residential expansion, producing explosive growth east of Lake Washington. Bellevue is now Washington's 4th largest city with a population of 62,000. (See the map of population change, p. 178.) The area in southwestern King County in which more than 70 percent of the housing was built during the 1960s is more closely tied to Tacoma than to Seattle.

**Mobile Homes.** There are 19,900 mobile homes in the Seattle DUS; they constitute 2.9 percent of the DUS's housing units. Mobile homes are more than 5 percent of local housing stocks throughout most of the DUS except in Seattle, Everett, Tacoma, and a narrow zone along the Sound. Proportions exceed 10 percent inland in sparsely settled areas.

**Single-Unit Detached Housing.** Individual dwelling units make up 73 percent of the SMSA's housing stock and 59 percent of Seattle's housing units. Both percentages are high compared with other places included in the atlas. Tracts that have less than 30 percent single-unit detached housing are located near downtown Seattle and near the University of Washington. Percentages exceed 70 throughout the region except for a strip running south from central Seattle. Outside the strip, the pattern is spotty reflecting a mix between single-family and multiple-unit dwellings in postwar construction. The 27 percent of the SMSA's units that are multiples occur in structures with 2 to 4 units (6 percent), 5 to 49 units (16 percent), and 50 or more units (5 percent). Within Seattle 2- to 4-unit buildings supply 11 percent of the housing, multiples containing 5 to 49 units contain 24 percent, and large (50 or more) structures contain 7 percent.

**Housing Value and Rent.** The mean value of owner-occupied housing in the SMSA is $24,000 and the corresponding figure for Seattle is $23,000. Individual tract means range from $10,000 to $49,000. Tracts with mean housing values below $20,000 are located in central and southern Seattle, in the suburbs immediately south of the city, in and near Everett in Snohomish County, and in the sparsely populated eastern part of the SMSA. Housing near Lakes Washington and Sammamish commands higher prices, with peak values located on southern Mercer Island.

Mean monthly contract rents average $115 for the SMSA and $109 for Seattle. Individual tract means vary from $55 to $205; the region's highest mean rents are in Bellevue on the shores of Lake Sammamish. The pattern of rents is roughly similar to that of mean values of owner-occupied housing; both are more expensive north and east of Seattle, and lower in Seattle and its southern suburbs. Much of the housing immediately south of Seattle was built during and immediately after World War II, and it is now less desirable than the newer, more spacious dwellings built during the 1950s and 1960s.

### THE PEOPLE

**Population Density.** Seattle's overall population density is 6,350 people per square mile (2,500 per square kilometer). Seattle is settled at about the same density as Los Angeles and at half the density of Washington, D.C. Individual tract densities vary from 1,000 to 36,000 people per square mile (385 to 13,900 per square kilometer).

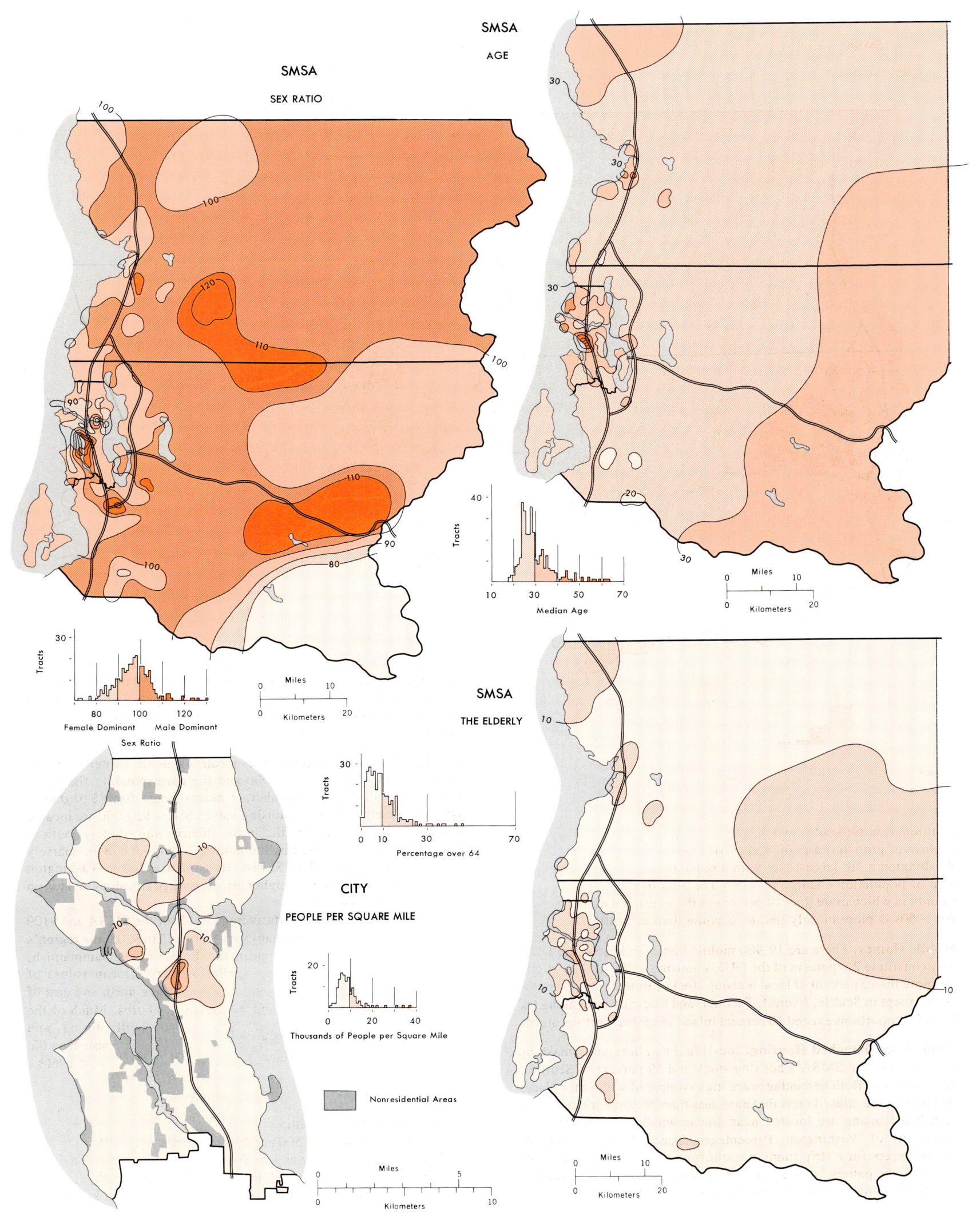

## Nineteenth-Century Inland Centers and Ports: Seattle

SMSA
SEX RATIO

SMSA
AGE

SMSA
THE ELDERLY

CITY
PEOPLE PER SQUARE MILE

The highest densities are located just east of the CBD, but the three tracts over 30,000 per square mile (11,600 per square kilometer) are small in area. Gross densities in excess of 10,000 people per square mile (3,900 per square kilometer) are infrequent within Seattle and almost nonexistent in the rest of the SMSA (p. 314).

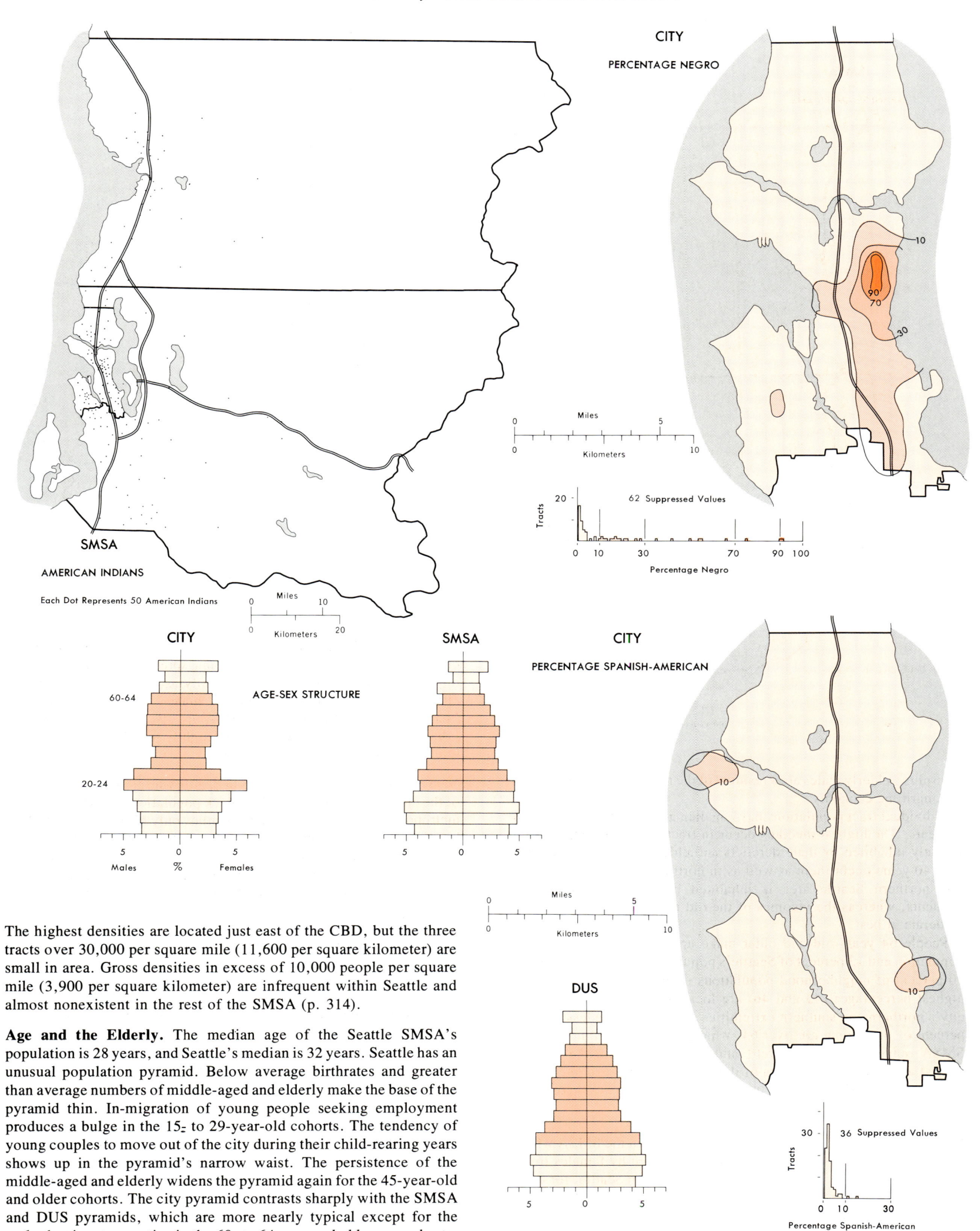

**Age and the Elderly.** The median age of the Seattle SMSA's population is 28 years, and Seattle's median is 32 years. Seattle has an unusual population pyramid. Below average birthrates and greater than average numbers of middle-aged and elderly make the base of the pyramid thin. In-migration of young people seeking employment produces a bulge in the 15- to 29-year-old cohorts. The tendency of young couples to move out of the city during their child-rearing years shows up in the pyramid's narrow waist. The persistence of the middle-aged and elderly widens the pyramid again for the 45-year-old and older cohorts. The city pyramid contrasts sharply with the SMSA and DUS pyramids, which are more nearly typical except for the male-dominant sex ratios in the 60- to 64-year and older age cohorts.

## Nineteenth-Century Inland Centers and Ports: Seattle

**SMSA JAPANESE-AMERICANS**

Each Dot Represents 50 Japanese

**SMSA CHINESE-AMERICANS**

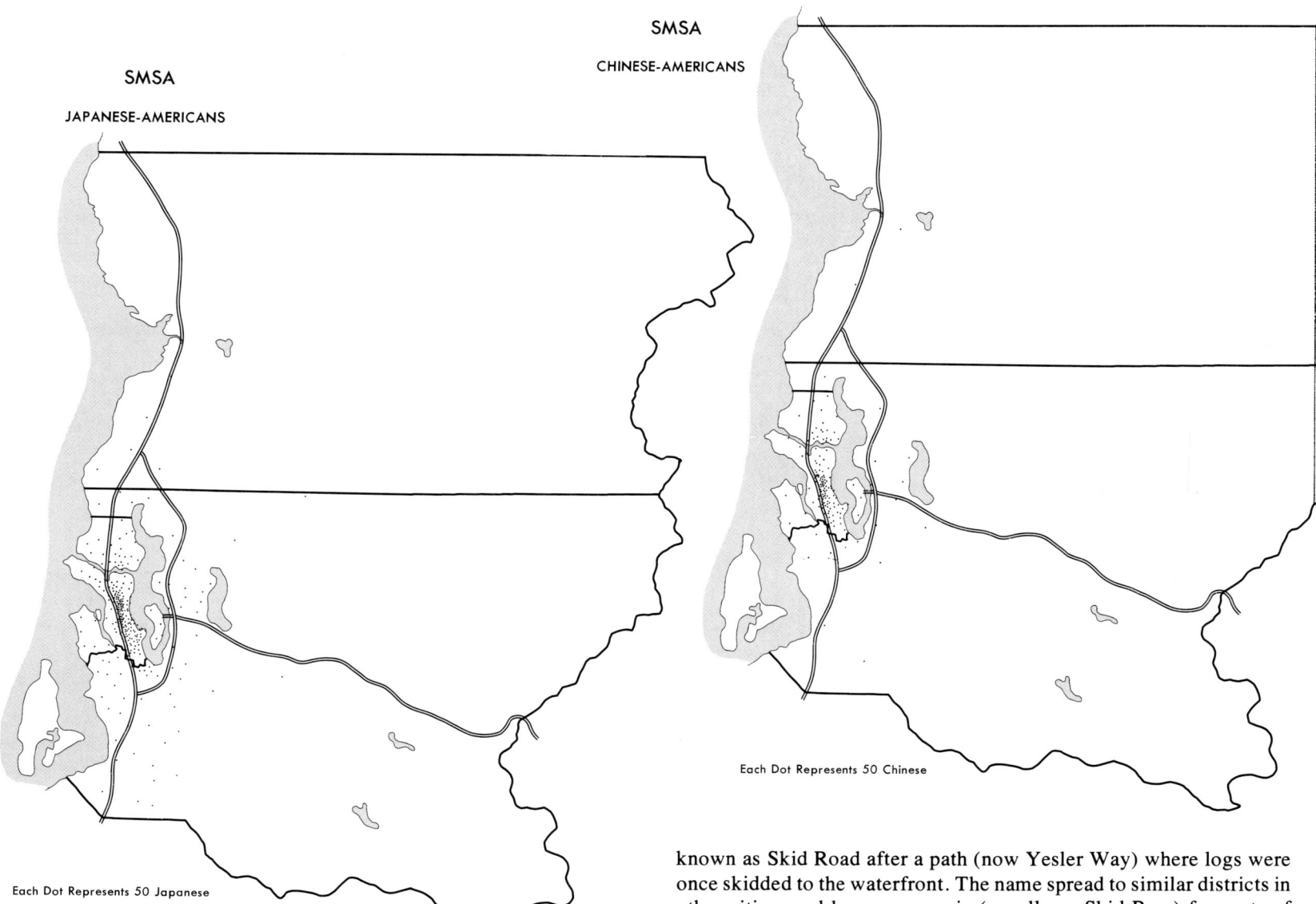

Each Dot Represents 50 Chinese

"Surplus" elderly males are a residual of the region's early lumbering and maritime economy.

Individual tract populations have median ages that vary from 18 to 63 years. The highest medians occur in tracts adjacent to the CBD, sparsely inhabited by male derelicts and elderly poor. Median ages over 40 years occur there as well as in northern Seattle and Everett. The northern Seattle area is inhabited by upper-middle-income residents, whereas the incomes of the old population in Everett are moderate at best.

People 64 years old and older make up 9 percent of the SMSA population and 13 percent of Seattle's population. The elderly exceed 10 percent of neighborhood populations in most of Seattle, and the highest percentages (43 and 46) are located in the CBD area. The city's northern and southern extremities are areas where less than 10 percent of the people are over 64, which is also true in most of the SMSA outside Seattle, Everett, and the sparsely populated east-central and northwestern parts of the region. Seattle is home for 57 percent of the SMSA's elderly in contrast to its 37 percent share of the total population.

**Sex Ratio.** There are 1.04 females for each male in the SMSA which yields a female-dominant sex ratio (males divided by females times 100) of 96. There are 1.09 females for each male in Seattle, for a sex ratio of 92. The dominantly male population of Seattle's CBD area raises the area's sex ratio to 130. The commercial establishments in the vicinity also serve transients from the rest of the region. The area is known as Skid Road after a path (now Yesler Way) where logs were once skidded to the waterfront. The name spread to similar districts in other cities, and became generic (usually as Skid Row) for parts of cities occupied by derelicts, elderly males, and camp followers. Sparsely populated parts of the SMSA are also male-dominant. The urbanized strip along Puget Sound is slightly female-dominant; most tracts have sex ratios in the high 90s.

**Negroes.** There are 37,900 blacks in Seattle who comprise 7.1 percent of the city's population. Seattle's black population is small for a large metropolitan area; of the cities in the atlas, only Minneapolis-St. Paul has a smaller proportion of blacks (4 percent) than Seattle. During the 1890s a black businessman received a parcel of land northeast of the CBD in payment of a debt. He settled there and attracted other black residents. The city's black population was swelled by new arrivals during World Wars I and II, and it gradually filled in an area east of the CBD, taking up housing that was being vacated by Jews and Asians moving to the suburbs. The region's black population is heavily concentrated (91 percent of the SMSA total) in Seattle. (An SMSA map is on p. 178.)

**Spanish-Americans.** The Census Bureau estimates the number of Hispanics in Seattle by counting people who speak Spanish. By this reckoning, there are 10,800 Spanish-Americans in Seattle. Spanish-Americans exceed 10 percent in only two tracts. One was the Fort Lawton army base when the 1970 Census was taken (it is now Discovery Park); the other is the tract on Lake Washington that is 15 percent Spanish-American. The absence of zero values and the 36 suppressed tracts suggest that Hispanics are spread in small numbers throughout the city. Almost 70 percent of the city's Spanish-Americans are indigenous citizens of Mexican descent. Only 15 percent are from Central and South America, no more than 11 percent are Mexican foreign stock (Mexican-born or with at least one Mexican-born parent) and the remaining 4 percent are Cubans and

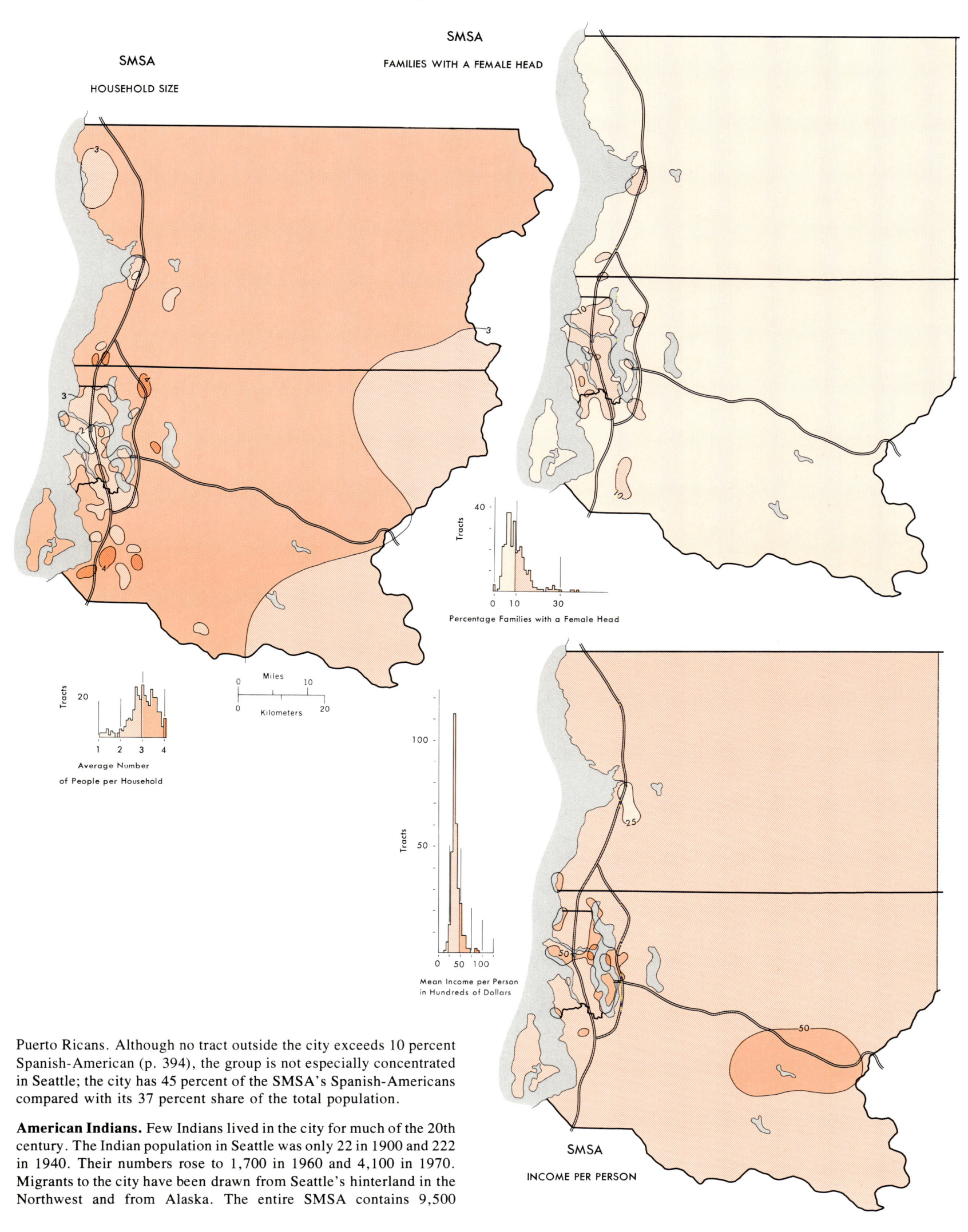

## Nineteenth-Century Inland Centers and Ports: Seattle

**SMSA**
HOUSEHOLD SIZE

**SMSA**
FAMILIES WITH A FEMALE HEAD

**SMSA**
INCOME PER PERSON

Puerto Ricans. Although no tract outside the city exceeds 10 percent Spanish-American (p. 394), the group is not especially concentrated in Seattle; the city has 45 percent of the SMSA's Spanish-Americans compared with its 37 percent share of the total population.

**American Indians.** Few Indians lived in the city for much of the 20th century. The Indian population in Seattle was only 22 in 1900 and 222 in 1940. Their numbers rose to 1,700 in 1960 and 4,100 in 1970. Migrants to the city have been drawn from Seattle's hinterland in the Northwest and from Alaska. The entire SMSA contains 9,500

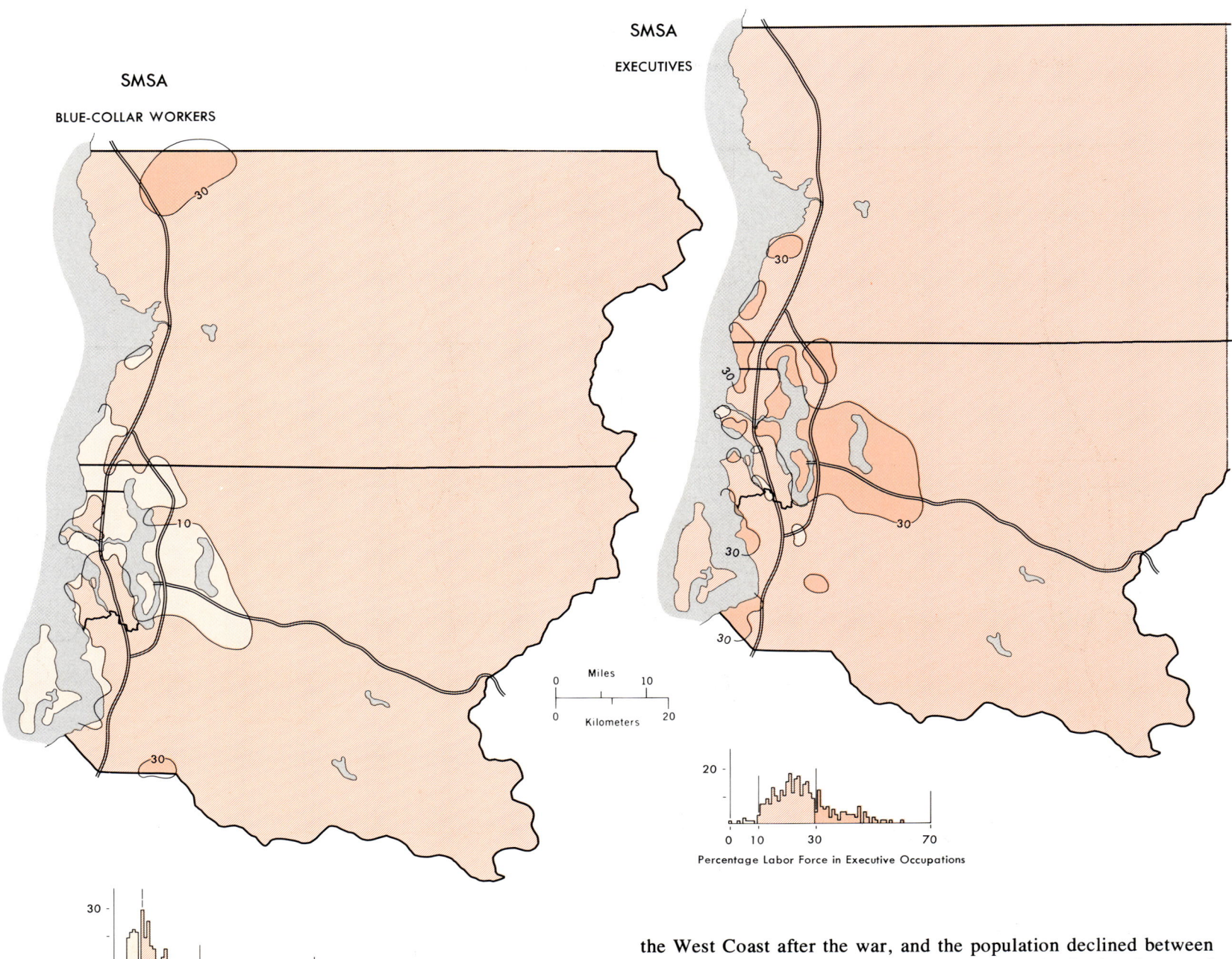

## Nineteenth-Century Inland Centers and Ports: Seattle

**SMSA BLUE-COLLAR WORKERS**

*Percentage Labor Force in Blue-Collar Occupations*

**SMSA EXECUTIVES**

*Percentage Labor Force in Executive Occupations*

Indians. In Seattle and the rest of the SMSA, Indians are distributed roughly in accordance with total population density.

**Chinese-Americans.** The Census questionnaire requires that every nonwhite person identify himself as a member of 1 of 8 "racial" categories: Negro, Indian, Japanese, Chinese, Filipino, Korean, Hawaiian, or Other. In the Seattle SMSA, 7,400 people identified themselves as Chinese. Chinese began to arrive in Seattle in the 1870s. Their numbers increased with the completion of the transcontinental railroads and the release of the Chinese laborers they employed. An area southeast of the CBD remains the cultural and commercial center of the Chinese community, but few of the city's Chinese now live there; most have dispersed east and south. Eighty-four percent of the SMSA's Chinese reside within Seattle.

**Japanese-Americans.** Japanese arrived in Seattle in sizable numbers only after 1890, and most were small businessmen rather than laborers. The community increased in size through World War I until postwar legislation practically halted immigration. During World War II all Japanese living west of the Cascades and the Sierras were forcibly evacuated to the nation's interior. Many chose not to return to the West Coast after the war, and the population declined between 1940 and 1950. Since 1950 the Japanese community has increased steadily; it now numbers 13,900. Like the Chinese, the Japanese have dispersed, but 72 percent of the SMSA's Japanese live in Seattle.

Seattle has a Filipino community as large as its Chinese minority, and when Seattle's unusually heavy concentrations of Indians, Japanese, Chinese, Filipinos, and the remnants of its once strong Scandinavian and German areas are added to the city's complement of blacks and Spanish-Americans, the whole is more diverse than someone unfamiliar with local history might expect.

### SOCIOECONOMIC CHARACTERISTICS

**Household Size.** There are 2.9 people in the average SMSA household and 2.5 in the average Seattle household. Birthrates have long been below the national average in the region, resulting in small households despite the attractions of the area for young families. Most of Seattle and the southern suburbs have mean household sizes of fewer than 3 persons. The smallest households are located in and near the Seattle CBD, and the largest occur in suburban tracts with many young families. Seattle's average household size is 2nd smallest of the central cities included in the atlas; only San Francisco's 2.3 average is smaller.

**Female Headship.** The Census Bureau defines female headship by the absence of a male spouse regardless of the sex of the family's principal breadwinner. Nine percent of the SMSA's families and 13

*176*

## SMSA
### THE ELDERLY

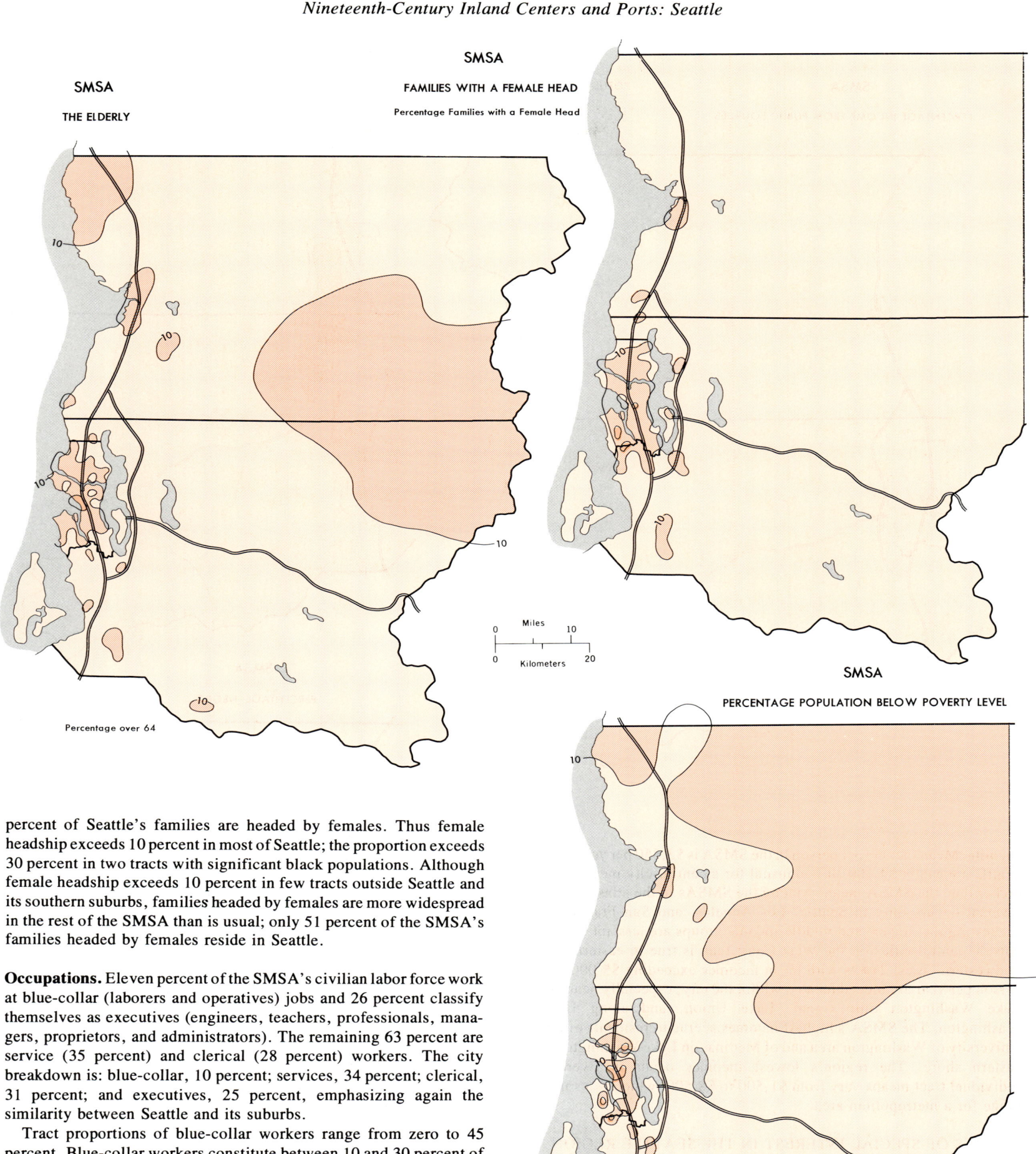

Percentage over 64

## SMSA
### FAMILIES WITH A FEMALE HEAD
Percentage Families with a Female Head

## SMSA
### PERCENTAGE POPULATION BELOW POVERTY LEVEL

percent of Seattle's families are headed by females. Thus female headship exceeds 10 percent in most of Seattle; the proportion exceeds 30 percent in two tracts with significant black populations. Although female headship exceeds 10 percent in few tracts outside Seattle and its southern suburbs, families headed by females are more widespread in the rest of the SMSA than is usual; only 51 percent of the SMSA's families headed by females reside in Seattle.

**Occupations.** Eleven percent of the SMSA's civilian labor force work at blue-collar (laborers and operatives) jobs and 26 percent classify themselves as executives (engineers, teachers, professionals, managers, proprietors, and administrators). The remaining 63 percent are service (35 percent) and clerical (28 percent) workers. The city breakdown is: blue-collar, 10 percent; services, 34 percent; clerical, 31 percent; and executives, 25 percent, emphasizing again the similarity between Seattle and its suburbs.

Tract proportions of blue-collar workers range from zero to 45 percent. Blue-collar workers constitute between 10 and 30 percent of tract labor forces in most parts of the SMSA except in northern Seattle and the northern and eastern suburbs, where values below 10 percent are common.

Between zero and 60 percent of individual tract labor forces work at executive occupations. Most tracts where more than 30 percent of the labor force are executives are located along Puget Sound or in the Lake Washington-Lake Sammamish area to the east. Only a few tracts in and south of the city have less than 10 percent of their labor forces in executive occupations.

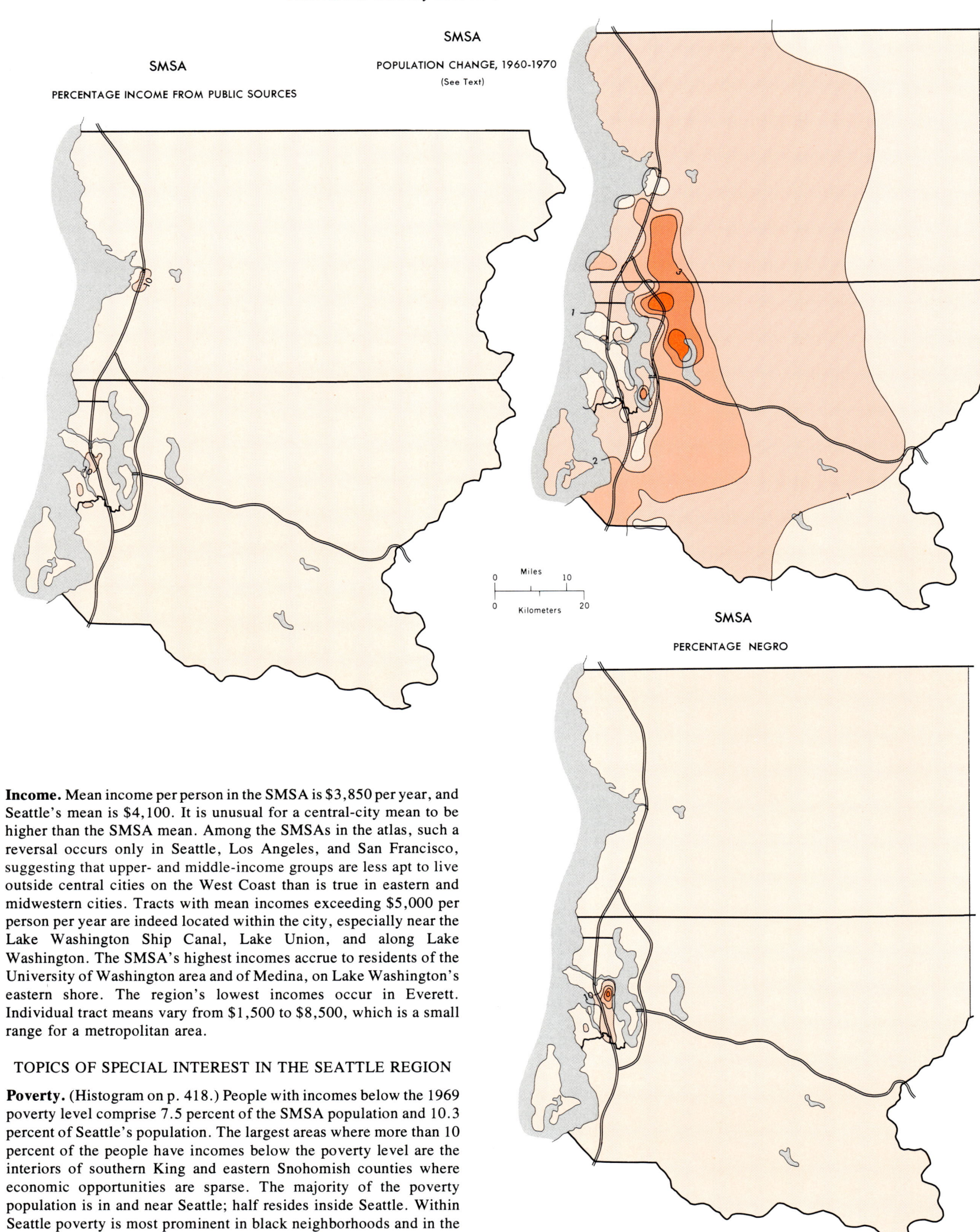

## Nineteenth-Century Inland Centers and Ports: Seattle

SMSA
PERCENTAGE INCOME FROM PUBLIC SOURCES

SMSA
POPULATION CHANGE, 1960-1970
(See Text)

SMSA
PERCENTAGE NEGRO

**Income.** Mean income per person in the SMSA is $3,850 per year, and Seattle's mean is $4,100. It is unusual for a central-city mean to be higher than the SMSA mean. Among the SMSAs in the atlas, such a reversal occurs only in Seattle, Los Angeles, and San Francisco, suggesting that upper- and middle-income groups are less apt to live outside central cities on the West Coast than is true in eastern and midwestern cities. Tracts with mean incomes exceeding $5,000 per person per year are indeed located within the city, especially near the Lake Washington Ship Canal, Lake Union, and along Lake Washington. The SMSA's highest incomes accrue to residents of the University of Washington area and of Medina, on Lake Washington's eastern shore. The region's lowest incomes occur in Everett. Individual tract means vary from $1,500 to $8,500, which is a small range for a metropolitan area.

### TOPICS OF SPECIAL INTEREST IN THE SEATTLE REGION

**Poverty.** (Histogram on p. 418.) People with incomes below the 1969 poverty level comprise 7.5 percent of the SMSA population and 10.3 percent of Seattle's population. The largest areas where more than 10 percent of the people have incomes below the poverty level are the interiors of southern King and eastern Snohomish counties where economic opportunities are sparse. The majority of the poverty population is in and near Seattle; half resides inside Seattle. Within Seattle poverty is most prominent in black neighborhoods and in the small population of elderly males living near the CBD.

**Income from Public Sources.** (Histogram on p. 426.) In 1969 3.3 percent of the SMSA's total income came from public sources, 2.7 percent was Social Security and railroad retirement benefits, and .6 percent came from public assistance and welfare payments. Comparable figures for Seattle are 3.8 percent and .8 percent. Areas where such public payments exceed 10 percent of tract incomes are confined to central-city tracts in Seattle and Everett populated by small groups of elderly males. Dependence on such income, especially public assistance, is low in Seattle and the SMSA compared with other metropolitan regions.

**Population Change.** (Histogram on p. 354.) The map of population change is produced by dividing each tract's 1970 population by its 1960 population. The quotient is greater than 1 if the population grew and less than 1 if it declined. Population declined throughout Seattle during the decade except in its northern and southern extremities. East of Lake Washington population doubled and in some areas tripled and quadrupled. Before the second bridging of Lake Washington in the 1960s, development east of the lake was restricted and suburban growth was forced into the strip along Puget Sound.

**Negroes.** (Histogram on p. 386.) The SMSA's 41,600 blacks make up only 2.9 percent of the total population. The SMSA's blacks are highly concentrated in Seattle, where 91 percent now reside. Median family income for blacks in the SMSA is $8,700 versus $11,700 for the total population. Comparable figures for Seattle are $8,500 and $11,000. Seattle's black family incomes are among the highest in the nation, and the difference between black incomes and those of the total population is one of the smallest in the country.

---

The general picture of the Seattle SMSA that emerges from the maps in this chapter is one of a stable metropolitan area in which sharp socioeconomic gradients are rare despite a diverse ethnic and racial mix, especially in Seattle. Differences between Seattle and the rest of the SMSA are small, especially on the critical dimensions of housing, income, and occupations. Compared with other places Seattle seems to have few serious problems, and those it has are less easily identifiable as central-city problems or suburban problems than is often true elsewhere.

## D. Twentieth-Century Cities

Dallas-Fort Worth
Houston
Los Angeles
Miami
Atlanta
Washington, D.C.

# CHAPTER 20

# Dallas – Fort Worth

*The most striking symbol of these new national [rail] connections upon the geography of Texas was the rise of Dallas.*

DONALD MEINIG, *Imperial Texas*, 1969

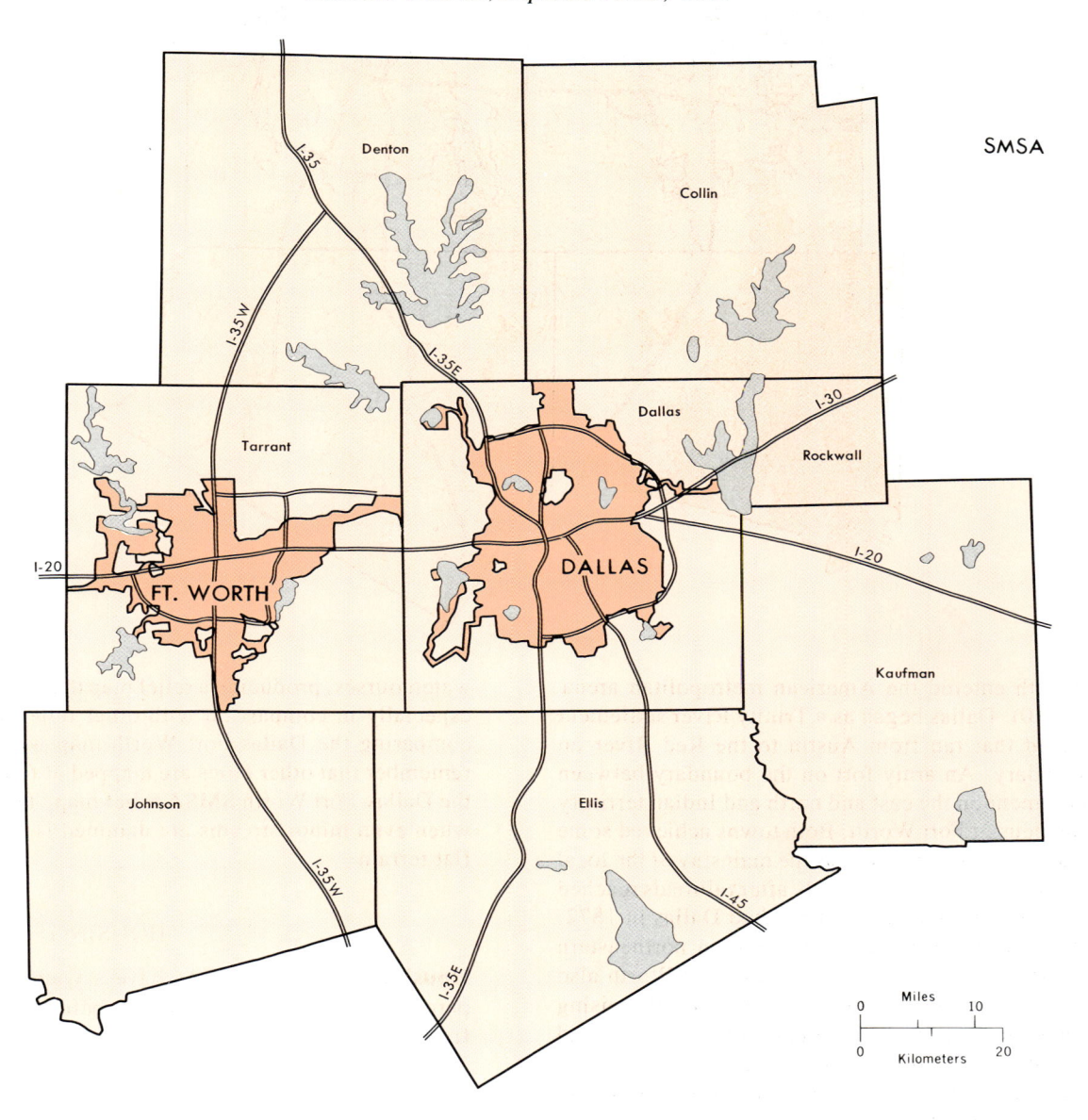

Dallas and Fort Worth were separate Standard Metropolitan Statistical Areas (SMSAs) in the 1970 Census. They have since been combined into a single SMSA. Had they been combined in 1970, their total population of 2,318,000 (Dallas, 1,556,000; Fort Worth, 762,000) would have made the region 11th in population size among American SMSAs. Separately, Dallas was the 16th most populous, and Fort Worth ranked 43rd. The combined SMSAs mapped here consist of 8 counties; all are sparsely populated except for Dallas and Tarrant counties, which together contain 88 percent of the region's total population. Dallas City has a population of 844,000 (35 percent of the regional total), and Fort Worth's population is 393,000 (17 percent). The Fort Worth SMSA consists of Johnson and Tarrant counties; the remaining 6 form the Dallas SMSA. The two SMSAs are mapped together throughout this chapter.

The Daily Urban System (DUS) defined by counties that have at least 5 percent of their labor forces working in Dallas and Tarrant counties (p. 184) adds 9 more counties to the combined SMSAs but only 186,000 people; the DUS total is 2,504,000. The Dallas-Fort Worth DUS is the nation's 12th most populous DUS.

*Note:* All data are from the 1970 Censuses of Population and Housing unless otherwise indicated. Therefore the present tense refers to 1970 data except for income data which are from 1969. Cartographic conventions are explained in Chapter 1.

*Twentieth-Century Cities: Dallas-Fort Worth*

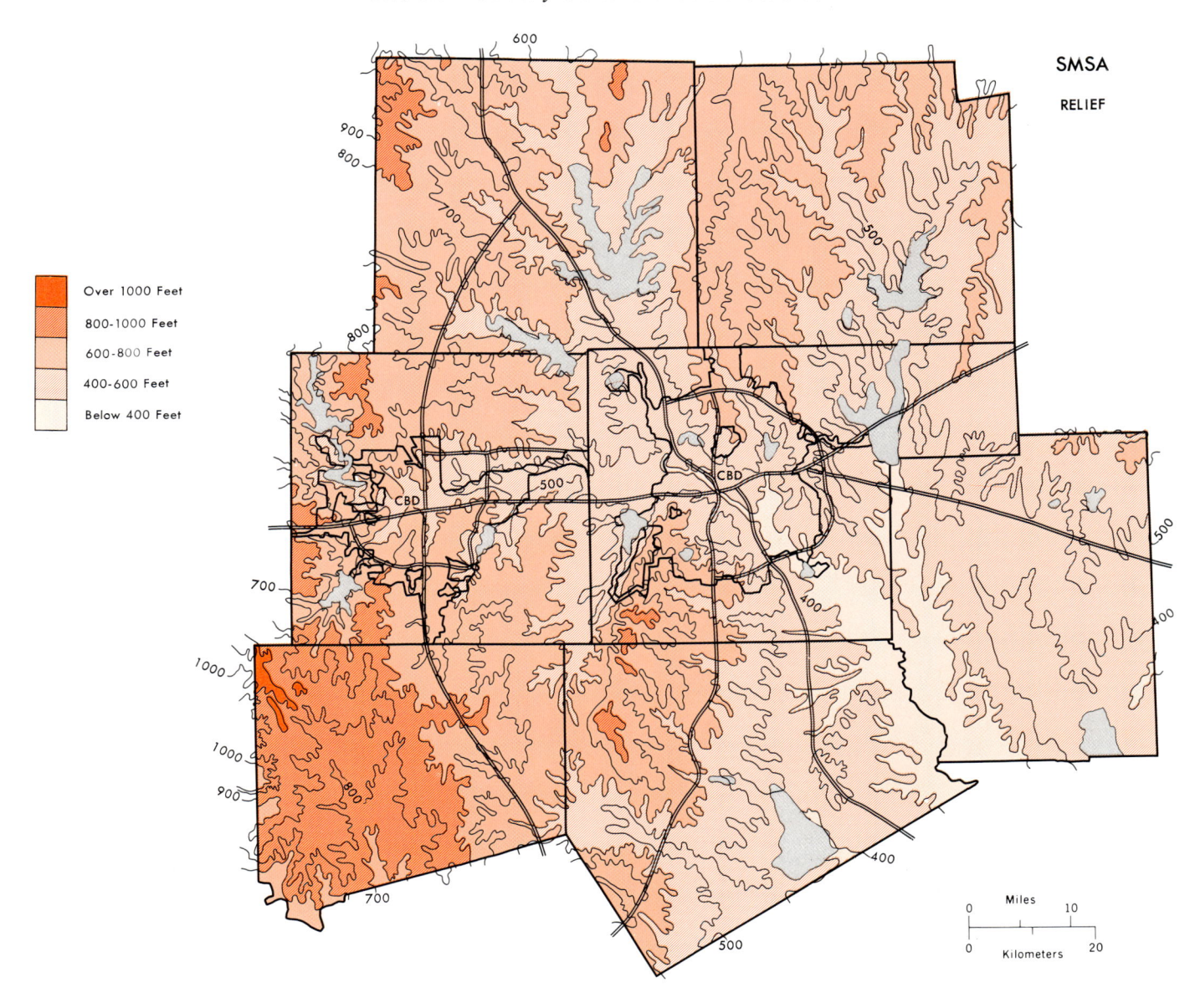

Dallas and Fort Worth entered the American metropolitan arena relatively recently (p. 10). Dallas began as a Trinity River settlement along the Preston Road that ran from Austin to the Red River on Texas's northern boundary. An army fort on the boundary between Anglo-American settlement on the east and north and Indian territory to the west was the nucleus of Fort Worth. Both towns achieved some growth during the era when cattle export was the mainstay of the local economy, but large-scale growth occurred only after railroads reached the region. The Houston and Texas Central reached Dallas in 1872, and the city soon became the dominant rail center in northeastern Texas. As railroads extended their lines westward, Fort Worth also obtained service and connections to national markets. Cattle raising and agriculture became the basis of the regional economy. Swift and Armour built packing plants in Fort Worth in 1903, and they were the city's major employers until oil was discovered west of Fort Worth in 1917. Refining and the construction associated with the oil boom of the 1920s created greater economic diversification. The discovery of the East Texas oil field in 1930 brought oil money and related activities to Dallas. Dallas spurted ahead of Fort Worth after 1920. Competition between the two places was keen, but Dallas had better rail connections than Fort Worth. As services and information-processing activities became growth sectors of the national economy after World War II, Dallas, with better political and commercial connections with the rest of the nation, expanded its competitive edge.

Dallas and Fort Worth are situated where the prairies of the Texas coastal plain give way to the higher plains of north-central Texas. Topography in the SMSA is flat to gently rolling, with the land rising in elevation from east to west. Local relief is rarely more than 200 feet (60 meters), but streams have dissected the region along even minor watercourses, producing a relief map that looks more rugged than it is, especially in comparison with other relief maps in the atlas. When comparing the Dallas-Fort Worth map with other city relief maps, remember that other cities are mapped at five times the scale used for the Dallas-Fort Worth SMSA relief map. The size of the lakes created when even minor streams are dammed is indicative of the generally flat terrain.

### HOUSING

**Housing Age.** The SMSAs have a young housing stock. Eighteen percent of their housing was built before 1940, 44 percent was built from 1940 through 1959, and 38 percent dates from 1960 to March 1970. There is little difference between the housing-age structures of the two SMSAs except that slightly more of the Fort Worth SMSA's housing was built from 1940 through 1959 and slightly less was erected from 1960 to March 1970 than in Dallas, reflecting the rapid growth of the Dallas SMSA in the 1960s.

Individual tract proportions of housing built before 1940 vary from zero to 88 percent, with a cluster of tracts at the lower end of the range. Proportions exceed 70 percent in scattered tracts in Dallas and Fort Worth and are below 30 percent in large parts of both cities. Most tracts on the periphery have less than 30 percent pre-1940 housing except for a few outlying towns. Thirty-eight percent of the pre-1940 housing in the SMSA is located in Dallas, and 25 percent is located in Fort Worth, compared with their respective shares of 38 and 18 percent of all housing units. Old and new housing are more evenly distributed throughout the region than is usual, for old housing is often disproportionately concentrated in central cities. One reason this is

*Twentieth-Century Cities: Dallas-Fort Worth*

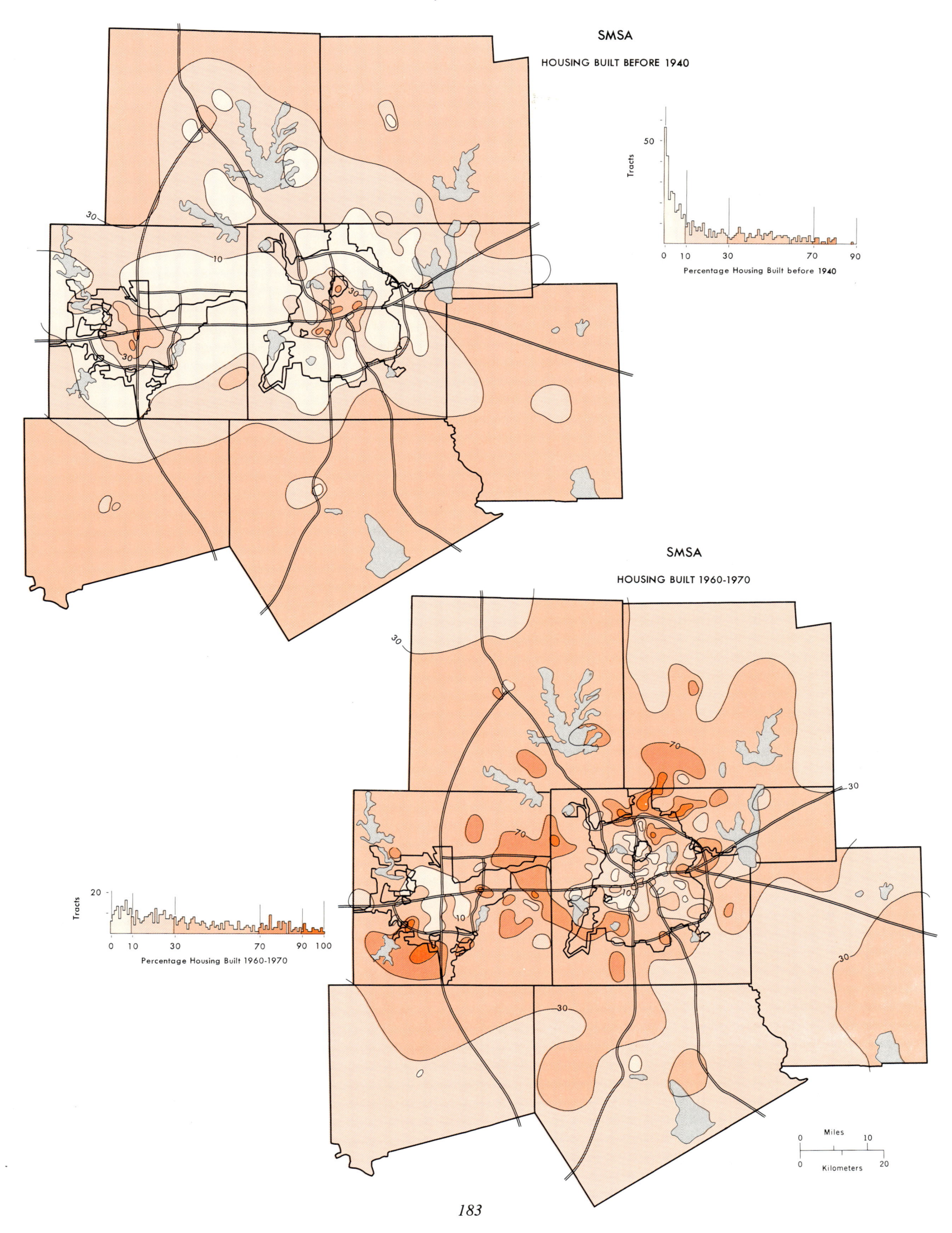

SMSA

HOUSING BUILT BEFORE 1940

Percentage Housing Built before 1940

SMSA

HOUSING BUILT 1960-1970

Percentage Housing Built 1960-1970

183

*Twentieth-Century Cities: Dallas-Fort Worth*

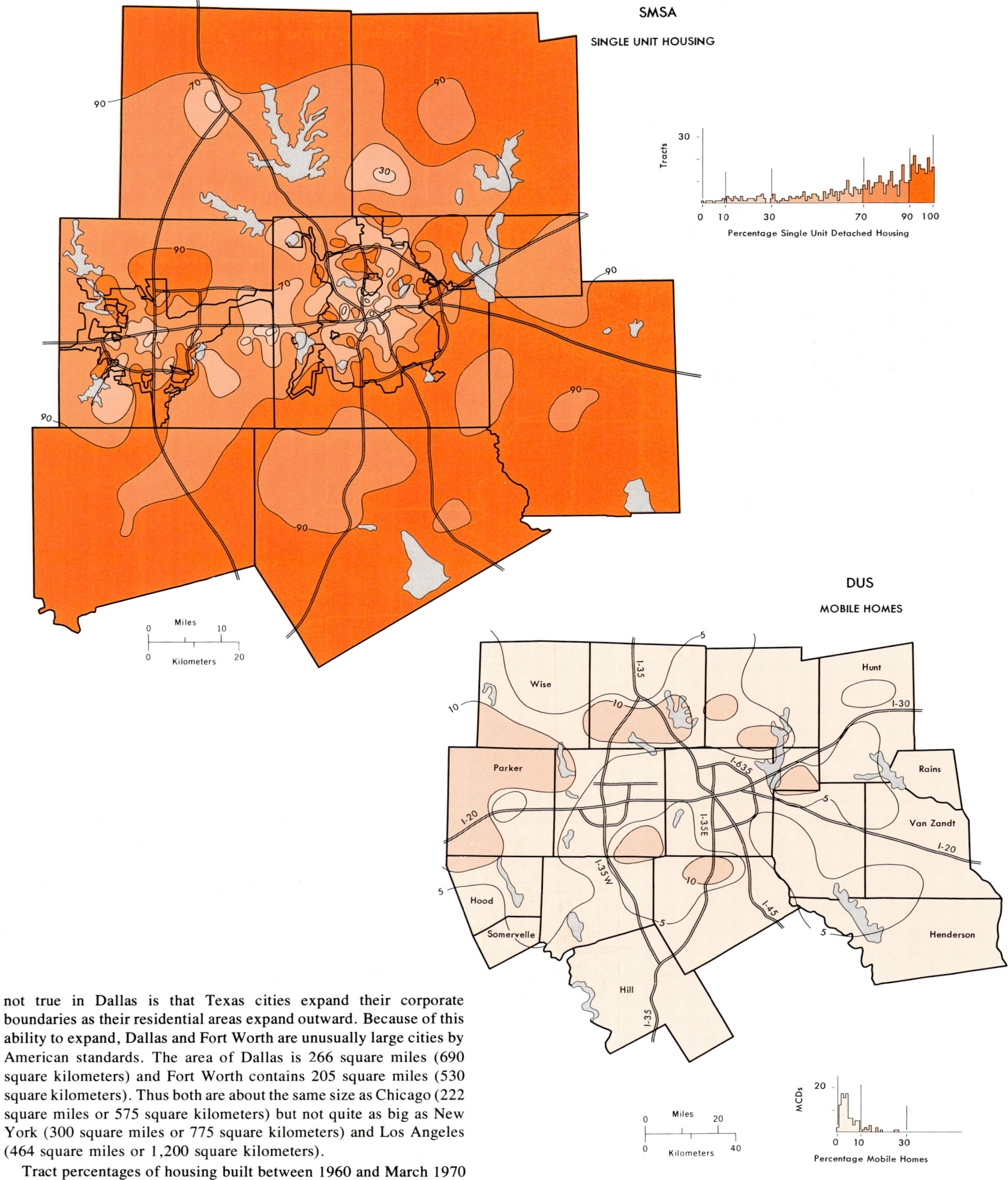

SMSA

SINGLE UNIT HOUSING

DUS

MOBILE HOMES

not true in Dallas is that Texas cities expand their corporate boundaries as their residential areas expand outward. Because of this ability to expand, Dallas and Fort Worth are unusually large cities by American standards. The area of Dallas is 266 square miles (690 square kilometers) and Fort Worth contains 205 square miles (530 square kilometers). Thus both are about the same size as Chicago (222 square miles or 575 square kilometers) but not quite as big as New York (300 square miles or 775 square kilometers) and Los Angeles (464 square miles or 1,200 square kilometers).

Tract percentages of housing built between 1960 and March 1970 range from zero to 100. The highest percentages are located north of Dallas, between Dallas and Fort Worth, and south of Fort Worth. There has been little recent residential expansion south or east of

184

*Twentieth-Century Cities: Dallas-Fort Worth*

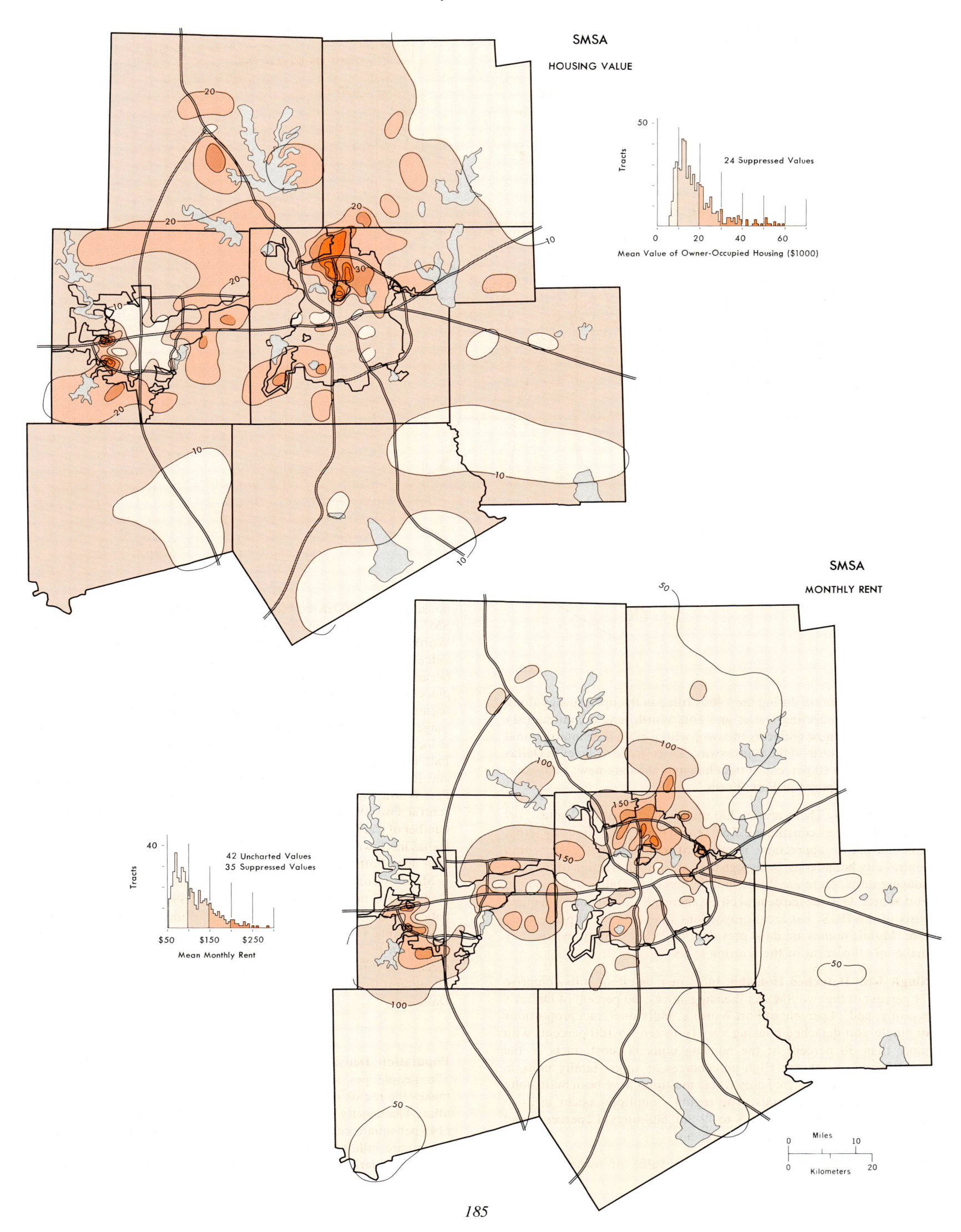

SMSA
HOUSING VALUE

SMSA
MONTHLY RENT

## Twentieth-Century Cities: Dallas-Fort Worth

### SMSA
PEOPLE PER SQUARE MILE

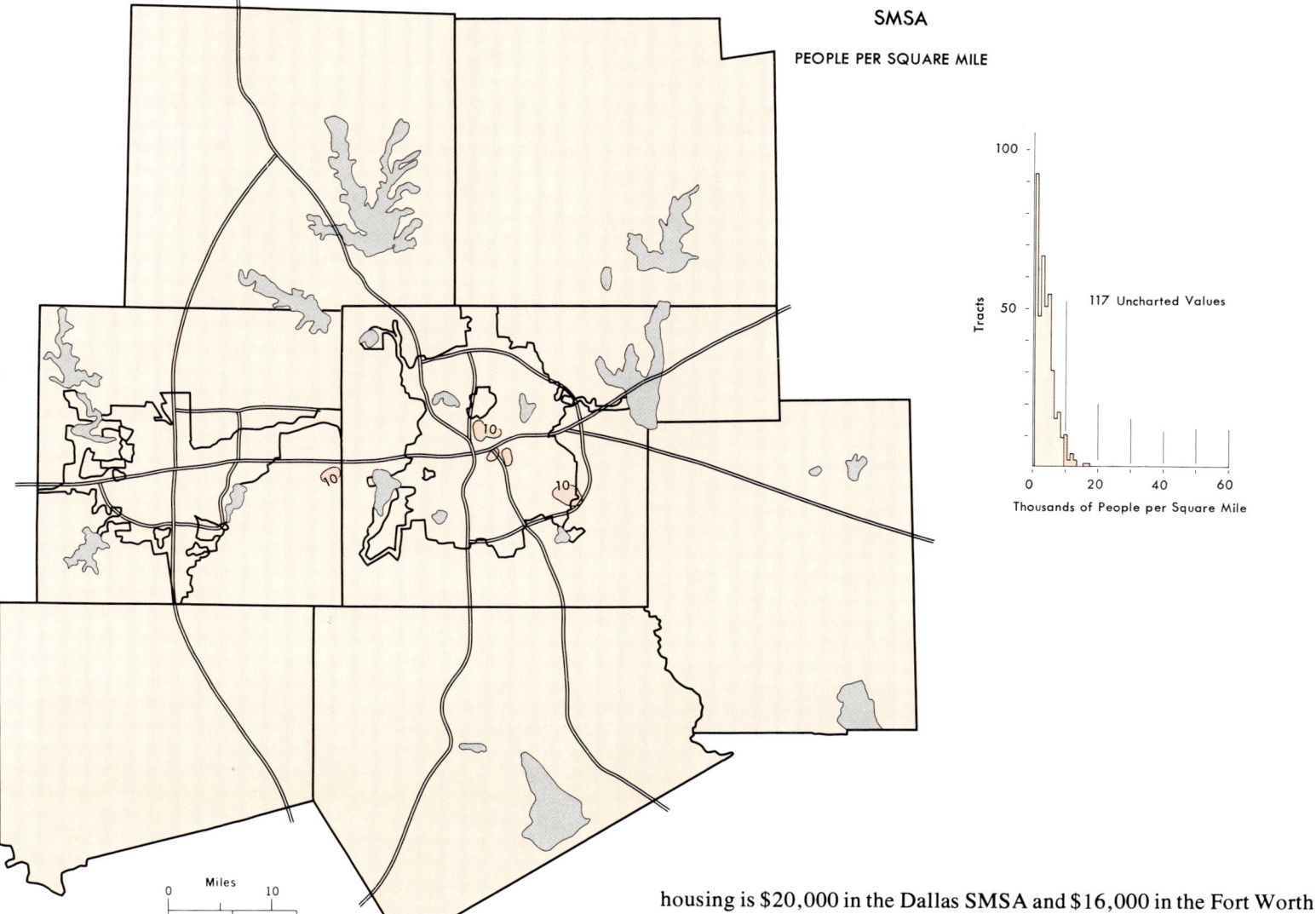

Dallas. Construction during the 1960s filled in the open spaces along the turnpike connecting Dallas and Fort Worth, and a continuously urbanized strip now connects the two, with a giant new international airport located north of the expressway. There are few places in Dallas where less than 10 percent of tract housing units are new; such areas are more widespread in Fort Worth.

**Mobile Homes.** There are 19,300 mobile homes in the Dallas-Fort Worth DUS. They constitute 2.2 percent of the region's housing units. It is unusual for appreciable numbers of mobile homes to be within central-city boundaries. Although they are a small fraction of the total housing units, there are 2,000 mobile homes in Dallas and 1,400 in Fort Worth. Outside the central cities, there are mobile homes in many parts of the DUS, but local proportions in excess of 10 percent are rare. Mobile homes are most prevalent in Parker County, where they make up 10 percent of the housing stock.

**Single-Unit Detached Housing.** Individual dwelling units comprise 71 percent of the two SMSAs' housing stocks, 60 percent of Dallas's housing, and 74 percent of Fort Worth's. Individual tract proportions of single-unit detached housing vary from zero to 100 percent, with more than 30 percent of the housing units in most tracts in the single-family category. High percentages of single-family units in outlying areas are lowered only where multiples have been built along freeways or major arterials. The region's multiples occur in 2- to 4-unit buildings (13 percent), 5- to 49-unit buildings (12 percent), and large (50 or more) structures (5 percent).

**Housing Value and Rent.** The mean value of owner-occupied housing is $20,000 in the Dallas SMSA and $16,000 in the Fort Worth SMSA. The corresponding figures for the cities of Dallas and Fort Worth are $21,000 and $14,000 respectively. Central-city mean values are typically lower as in Fort Worth. This is not true in Dallas, because it is so large; new housing that would be suburban in other places has been built in Dallas. Also the most expensive housing in the region is located in Dallas. Mean housing values for individual tracts range from $6,000 to $59,000. The region's most expensive housing is located in and adjacent to Dallas's Highland Park and University Park municipal enclaves and in Fort Worth's Westover Hills enclave and Ridglea neighborhood. Housing values are generally high on Fort Worth's west side and on the north side of Dallas. A large area of central Fort Worth has tract mean values below $10,000, as do a number of tracts on the metropolitan periphery. Despite its larger size, Dallas has fewer (25,500 versus 32,900) units worth less than $10,000 than does Fort Worth.

Monthly contract rents average $116 in the Dallas SMSA, $119 in Dallas, $103 in the Fort Worth SMSA, and $96 in the Fort Worth. The patterns of high and low rents are roughly similar to those of high and low housing values except for the somewhat more complicated rent pattern in the area between the two central cities. Individual tract means vary from less than $50 (mapped but not plotted on the histogram) to $285. The highest rents are paid for units in northern Dallas.

### THE PEOPLE

**Population Density.** Overall density of the combined SMSAs is 376 people per square mile (145 per square kilometer), which makes the region one of the lowest-density metropolitan areas in the atlas. The density of the Dallas SMSA is 340 people per square mile (145 per square kilometer) and of the Fort Worth SMSA is 474 people per square mile (185 per square kilometer); the difference depends more on the larger number of counties and the consequent greater land area of the Dallas SMSA than on major differences in the way land is occupied in the two parts of the region. The population density of Dallas City is 3,200 people per square mile compared with Fort Worth's 1,900 (1,200 versus 730 per square kilometer). Although the difference is not inconsequential, both densities are extremely low compared with central-city densities in other parts of the nation. Even Los Angeles, for example, has a central-city density of 6,100 people per square mile (2,400 per square kilometer), almost twice that of Dallas. Low densities are important dimensions of the cost of providing municipal services and public transportation. When an entire city is settled at densities that usually characterize suburbia, the cost of providing services can increase sharply.

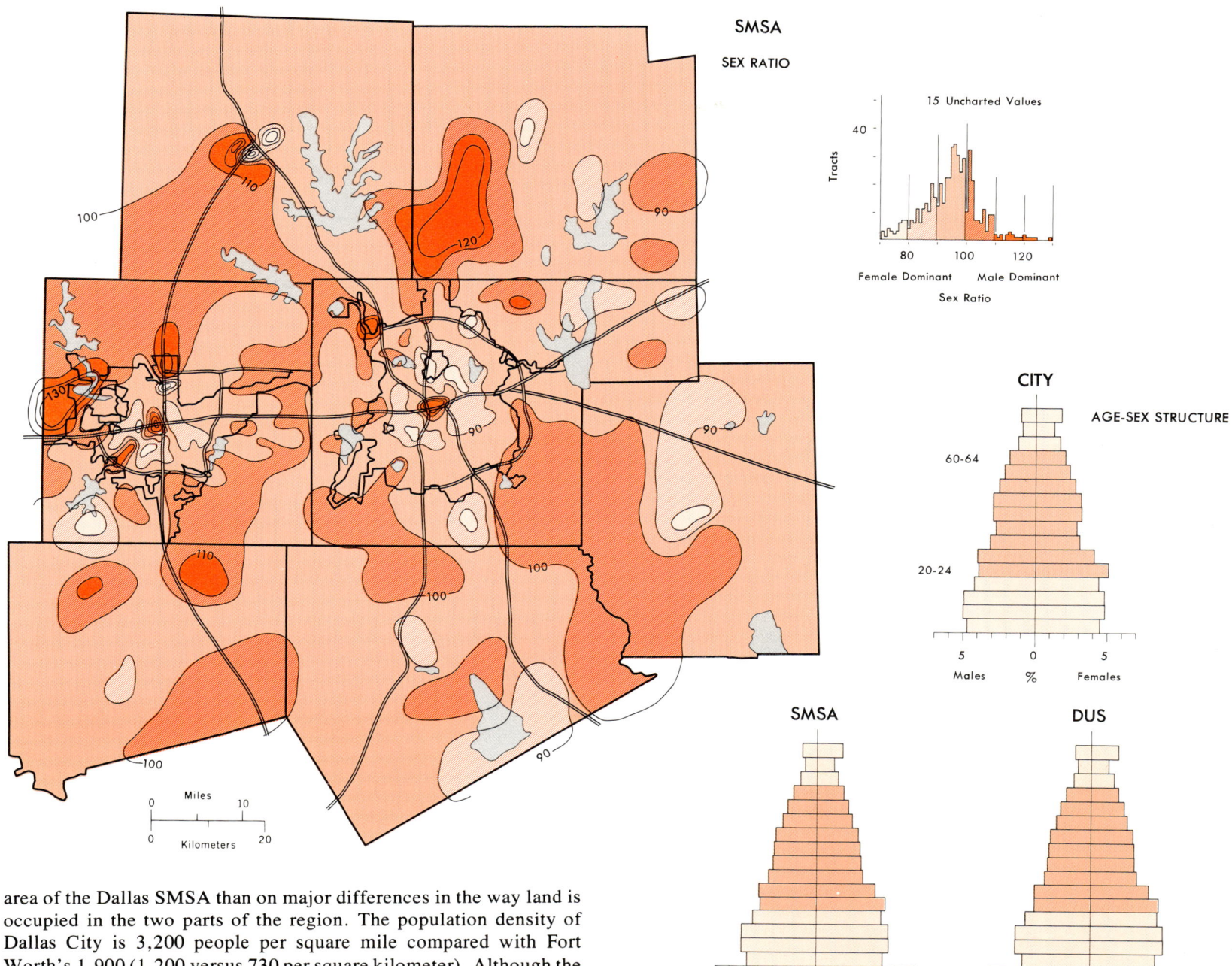

**Age and the Elderly.** The median age of the combined SMSA populations is 27 years, and the individual medians for the Dallas and Fort Worth SMSAs are identical, as are the medians for the two central cities. Median ages for tract populations vary from 13 to 66 years. Median ages are high in the central cities, low in outlying areas of the cities and inner suburban areas, and high again on the metropolitan periphery. Tracts where median ages exceed 50 years occur in both CBDs. The largest areas within the cities where median ages exceed 30 years are a low- to middle-income area in Fort Worth and the well-to-do area in northern Dallas.

The identical median age throughout the region suggests that central-city and suburban populations are similar, and the city (combined Dallas and Fort Worth), SMSA, and DUS population pyramids confirm this. In contrast to the sharply different age-sex structures in many metropolitan areas where city, SMSA, and DUS pyramids are different, the shapes of the three pyramids in the Dallas-Fort Worth region are nearly identical.

People over 64 years of age make up 7 percent of the combined and individual SMSA populations, 8 percent of the Dallas population, and 10 percent of the Fort Worth population. The elderly are only slightly concentrated in the central cities. Thirty-nine percent of the combined SMSAs' total population over 64 live in Dallas and 21 percent reside in Fort Worth, compared with the cities' 35 and 17 percent shares of the total population. In the two cities, the elderly are concentrated near the cores, where percentages exceed 10; in a few tracts more than 30 percent of the people are over 64 years of age. Outside the core areas, percentages are below 10 in the cities and the inner suburbs. Proportions exceed 10 percent on the metropolitan periphery beyond the areas where the influx of young families with links to Dallas and Fort Worth have reduced the elderly to small proportions of tract populations. An unusual concentration of 400 elderly people in a tract with but 950 people produces the high value southwest of Fort Worth.

**Sex Ratio.** There are 1.06 females for each male in the combined SMSAs, yielding a female-dominant regional sex ratio of 94. The Dallas SMSA is slightly more female-dominant than the Fort Worth SMSA. The central cities are more female-dominant than the SMSAs. The sex ratio in Dallas is 91, and Fort Worth's is 93. Sex ratios range from 60 to 120 in the absence of unusual circumstances. Most of the

*Twentieth-Century Cities: Dallas-Fort Worth*

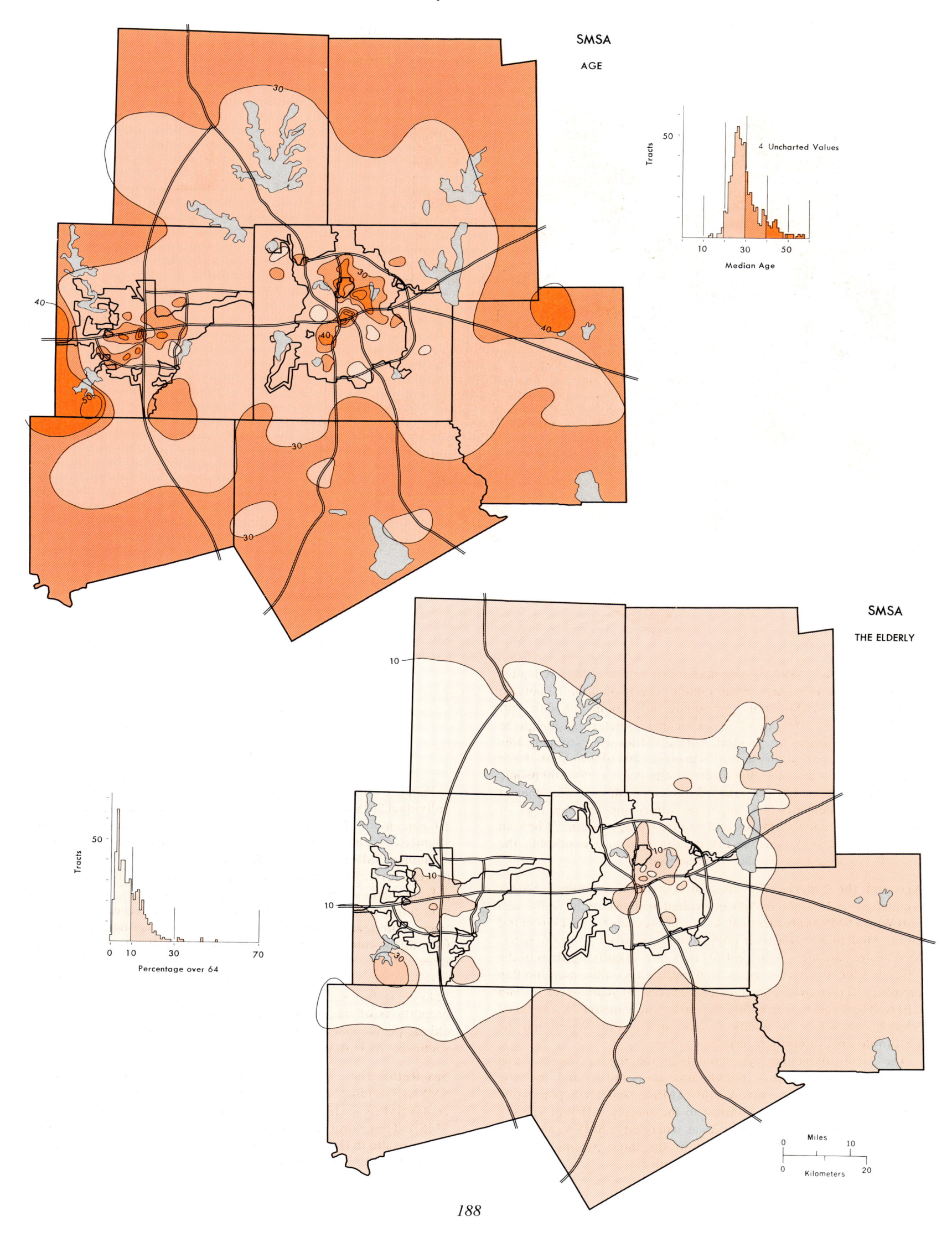

SMSA

AGE

SMSA

THE ELDERLY

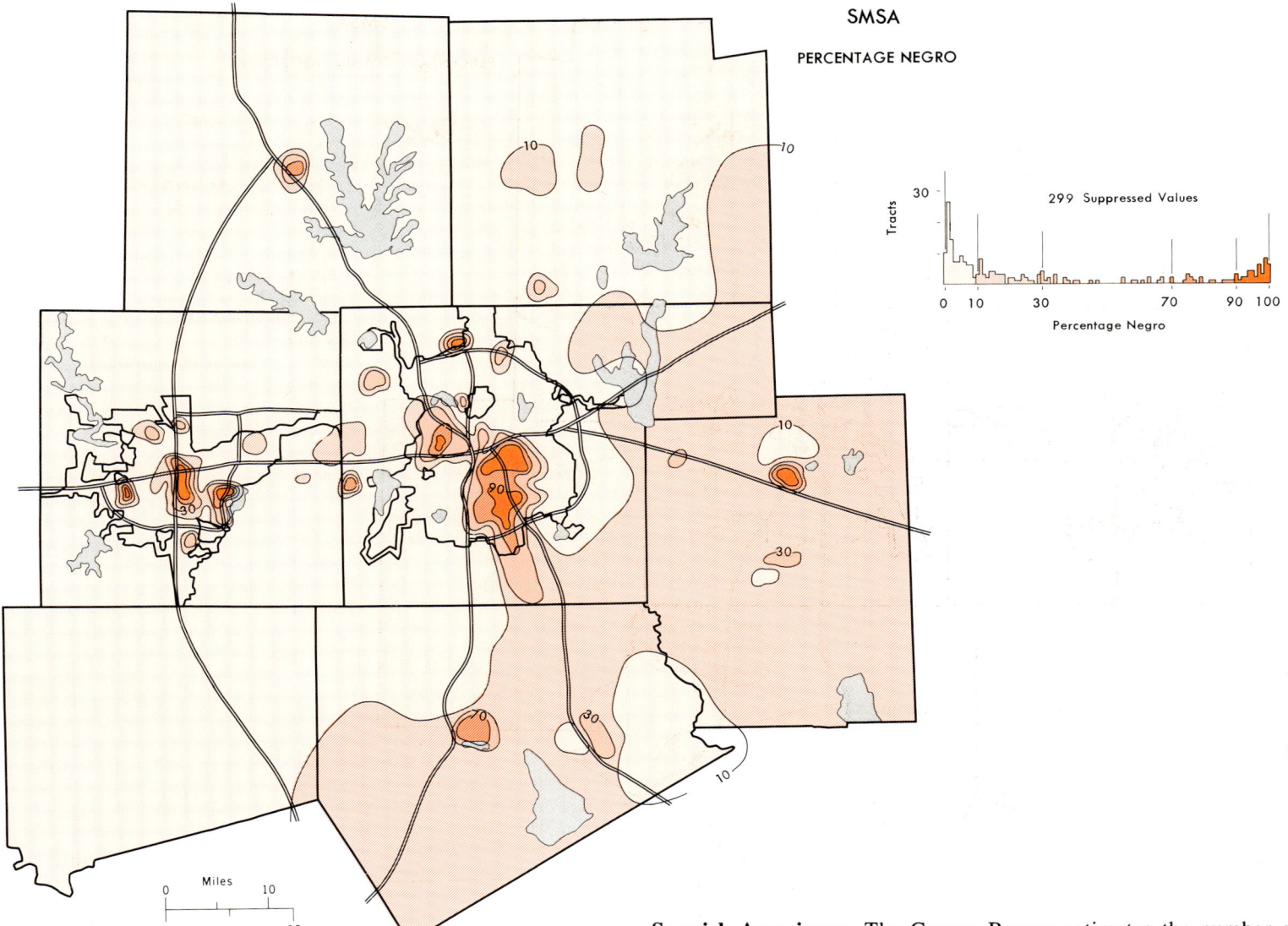

SMSA is female-dominant, but there are a number of areas where males exceed females. Elderly male populations produce high sex ratios in both CBDs. In Denton County, where Interstate 35 divides, sexually segregated institutions produce extreme sex ratios on both ends of the scale. Military bases in Fort Worth cause high sex ratios. Slightly male-dominant populations in suburban areas are usually attributable to the presence of families with young children, since they are often male-dominant. The male-dominant area north of Dallas in Collin County looms large on the map, but the area is sparsely populated. The imbalance is a result of a small group of men in group quarters in a large tract with a small population.

**Negroes.** There are 330,000 blacks in the combined SMSAs, who make up 14 percent of the total population. The percentage of blacks in the Fort Worth SMSA is 15 and in the Dallas SMSA is 11. Blacks are disproportionately concentrated in the central cities. The 210,000 blacks in Dallas are 64 percent of the combined SMSA total, and Fort Worth's 82,500 blacks are 25 percent of that total. These proportions are considerably higher than the two cities' percentages (35 and 17) of the total population. The bimodal histogram and the steep gradients between heavily black and predominantly white areas suggest sharp segregation within the cities. However, the small number of zero-percentage tracts and the 299 tracts with so few blacks that they fall below the suppression threshold suggest that a few blacks live everywhere in the metropolitan area. Blacks are intermingled with the total population only in the southeastern quadrant of the metropolitan area. Elsewhere, concentrations of blacks usually appear as small islands in predominantly white areas. Johnson and Denton counties have few (6 and 3 percent) blacks. Proportions are higher in other outlying counties.

**Spanish-Americans.** The Census Bureau estimates the number of Hispanics in the five southwestern states by counting the people who speak Spanish and adding to them people who have certain Spanish surnames but who have not identified themselves as Spanish speakers. By this reckoning, there are 146,500 Spanish-Americans in the combined SMSAs, of whom 133,600 speak Spanish and 12,900 have Spanish surnames. The Spanish-Americans thus identified make up 6.2 percent of the population in the combined SMSAs. Proportions in the individual SMSAs are about the same. Only 30 percent of the region's Hispanics live outside the cities of Dallas and Fort Worth, which have 47 and 23 percent of the combined SMSA totals. Proportions exceed 10 percent in much of Ellis County; elsewhere in the region concentrations of Spanish-Americans are rare outside Dallas and Fort Worth.

Most of the region's Spanish-Americans are indigenous Americans of Mexican descent or of Mexican foreign stock (Mexican-born or with at least one Mexican-born parent). There are only 2,500 Cubans, 3,750 Central and South Americans, and 1,250 Puerto Ricans in the combined SMSAs.

**American Indians.** There are 6,600 American Indians in the combined SMSAs; 1,600 reside in the Fort Worth SMSA and 5,000 live in the Dallas SMSA. The region's Indians are concentrated in Dallas, which has 52 percent of the Indian population of the combined SMSAs. Fort Worth has fewer than would be expected given its 17 percent share of the total population, for it has only 13 percent of the region's Indian population. Less than 8 percent of the region's Indians live outside Dallas and Tarrant counties.

Southern cities attracted few European immigrants. In Dallas and Fort Worth, German-Americans are the largest foreign-stock group after Mexican-Americans, but they comprise less than 1 percent of the region's total population.

*Twentieth-Century Cities: Dallas-Fort Worth*

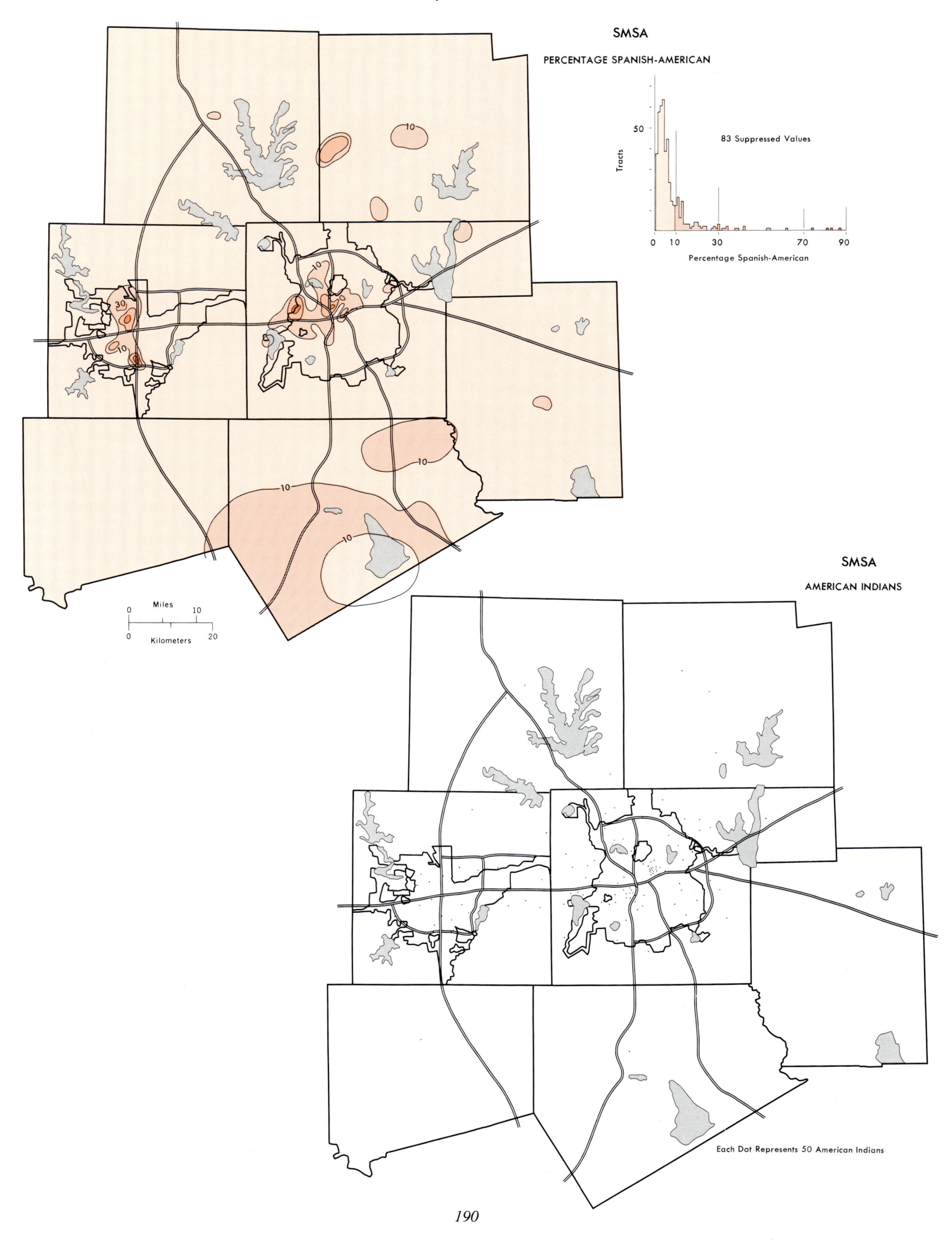

SMSA

PERCENTAGE SPANISH-AMERICAN

83 Suppressed Values

SMSA

AMERICAN INDIANS

Each Dot Represents 50 American Indians

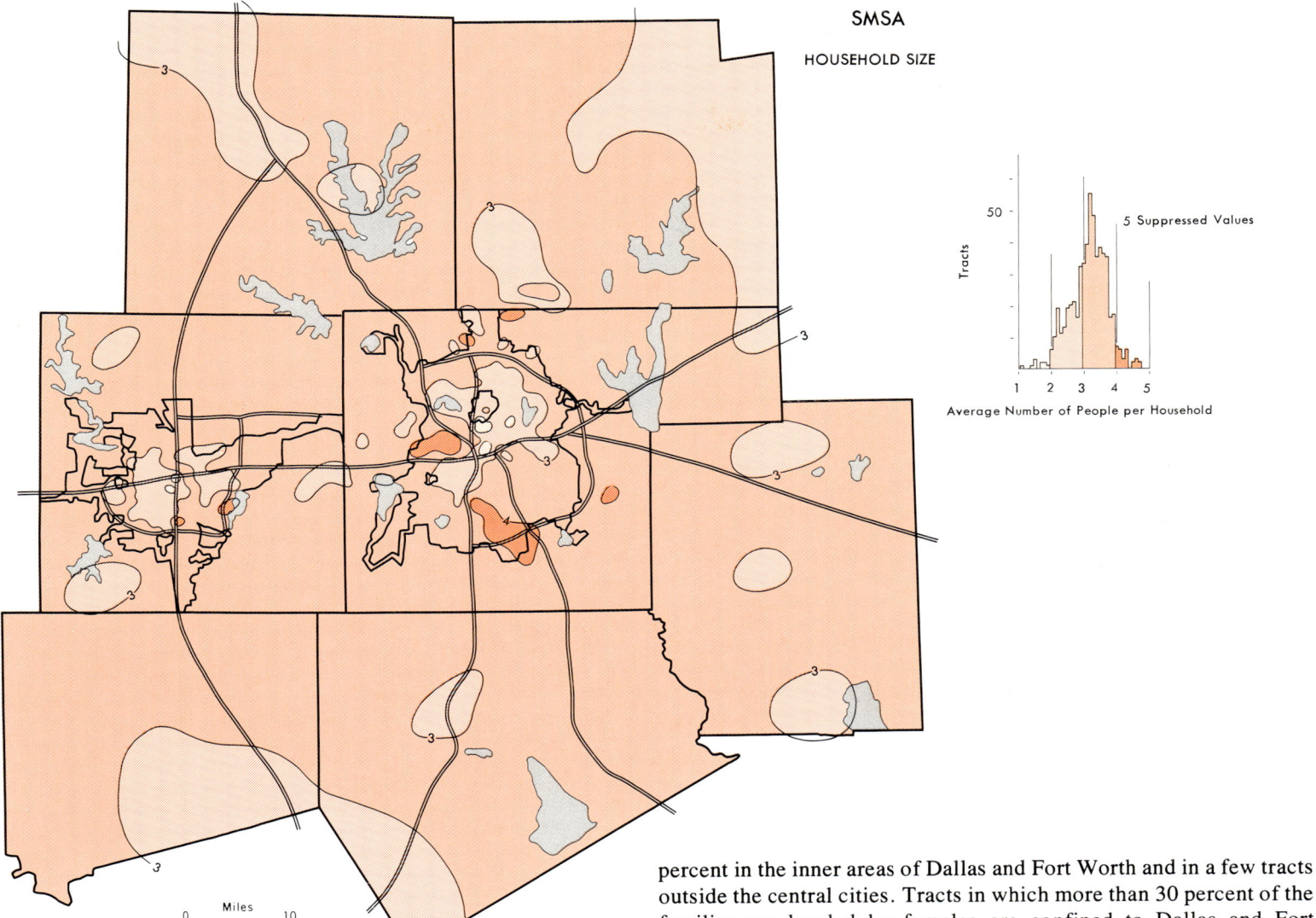

## SOCIOECONOMIC CHARACTERISTICS

**Household Size.** There are 3.1 people in the average SMSA household and 3 in the average Dallas and Fort Worth households. Individual tract averages vary from just over 1 person per household to 4.7. Small households are most frequent among young families that have not yet had children and among older populations whose children have established their own households. The differences between the central-city averages and the SMSA mean are unusually small. They reflect the similarity of central cities and suburban areas that results from recent urban growth. The smallest households are located in and near the CBDs, where elderly people often live alone. Some tracts with more than 4 persons per household are scattered on the periphery of Dallas and Fort Worth; they are usually tracts in which families with young children predominate. Other tracts with high averages are located in predominantly black and Spanish-American areas, especially in western Dallas. The average size of black households in Dallas is 3.6 people, and the average Spanish-American household has 4.1 people. SMSA averages for blacks and Spanish-Americans are similar. Most tracts have averages of 3 to 4 persons per household outside the central areas of Dallas and Fort Worth, but household sizes are below 3 persons on the metropolitan margins.

**Female Headship.** The Census Bureau defines female headship by the absence of a male spouse regardless of the sex of the family's principal breadwinner. Ten percent of the combined SMSAs' families, 14 percent of the families in Dallas, and 12 percent of those in Fort Worth are headed by females. Female headship exceeds 10 percent in the inner areas of Dallas and Fort Worth and in a few tracts outside the central cities. Tracts in which more than 30 percent of the families are headed by females are confined to Dallas and Fort Worth, and they are usually located in the predominantly black areas of the cities. Twenty percent of the black households in the combined SMSAs are headed by females, which is also true in the central cities. Female headship is less prevalent among Spanish-Americans than it is among the total population. In Dallas, 9.6 percent of all Spanish-American households are headed by females, and in Fort Worth the proportion is 8.1 percent. Because of the concentration of blacks in the central cities and the high rates of female headship in black households, 49 percent of the region's families headed by females reside in Dallas and 20 percent live in Fort Worth.

**Occupations.** The occupational breakdown in percentages for the combined SMSAs and the two central cities is given in the accompanying tabulation. The entire region is homogeneous in terms of occupation, except for the somewhat higher percentage of blue-collar (laborers and operatives) workers in Fort Worth and the correspondingly lower proportions of clerical workers and executives (engineers, teachers, professionals, managers, proprietors, and administrators).

|  | *SMSAs* | *Dallas* | *Fort Worth* |
|---|---|---|---|
| Blue-Collar | 14 | 13 | 17 |
| Service | 34 | 33 | 35 |
| Clerical | 29 | 32 | 27 |
| Executive | 23 | 22 | 21 |

Tract proportions of blue-collar workers range from zero to 49 percent. In Fort Worth and surrounding areas, generally more than 10 percent of the local labor forces are in blue-collar occupations; some tracts exceed 30 percent and tracts with less than 10 percent are exceptions. In Dallas the situation is reversed; blue-collar percentages in the Dallas area are generally under 10, and higher proportions

## SMSA
### FAMILIES WITH A FEMALE HEAD

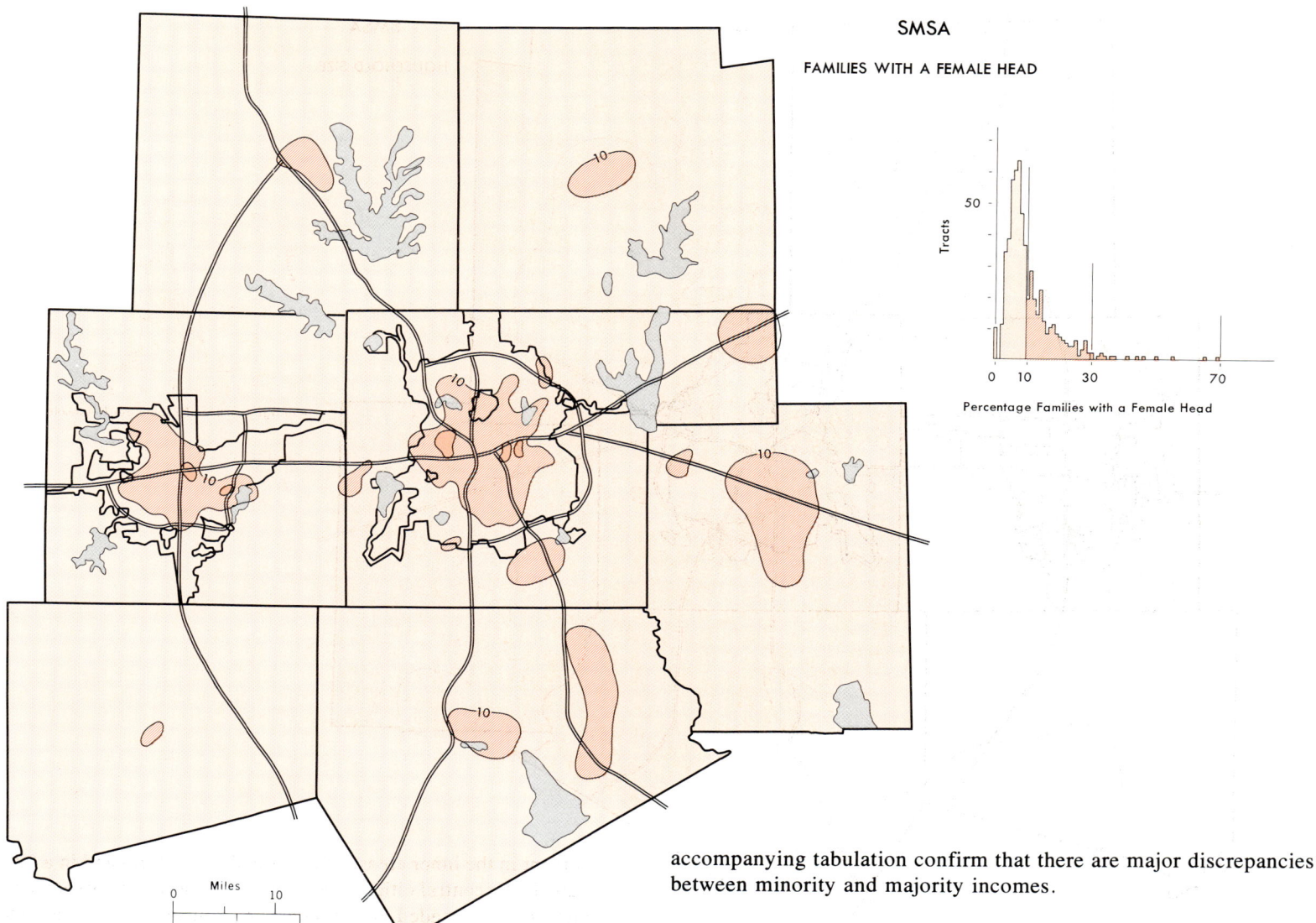

appear as islands. The area within Dallas where blue-collar workers are more than 10 percent (and occasionally 30 percent) of the labor force corresponds roughly with the black and Spanish-American parts of the city.

Individual tracts have between zero and 82 percent of their labor forces working in executive occupations, although proportions over 50 percent are rare. The preferred locations for executive workers are clearly northern Dallas and the northern suburbs, and southwest Fort Worth and its adjacent areas. A third area where executives make up more than 30 percent of tract labor forces is the zone between Dallas and Fort Worth, where such values occur in scattered patches rather than in the larger zones characteristic of the other two areas. Executives are less than 30 percent of local labor forces in much of Dallas and Fort Worth, and less than 10 percent in black and Spanish-American areas.

**Income.** Mean incomes per person per year in the region vary from less than $1,000 to $19,600 (not graphed or mapped). Summary statistics are: Dallas SMSA, $3,550; Dallas, $3,750; Fort Worth SMSA, $3,300; and Fort Worth, $3,250. It is unusual for a central-city mean to be higher than the SMSA mean, which is true in Dallas; the anomaly results because the region's highest incomes are in the northern part of the city, where several tracts exceed $12,500 per person annually. Incomes are nearly as high in Fort Worth's municipal enclave of Westworth.

It is clear from the map of income per person that the lowest incomes are in areas occupied by blacks and Spanish-Americans, and summary statistics for 1969 mean family income given in the accompanying tabulation confirm that there are major discrepancies between minority and majority incomes.

|  | Dallas | | Fort Worth | |
| --- | --- | --- | --- | --- |
|  | SMSA | City | SMSA | City |
| White | $13,100 | $14,000 | $11,800 | $11,800 |
| Spanish-American | 9,400 | 9,200 | 9,200 | 8,700 |
| Black | 6,900 | 7,100 | 7,100 | 7,100 |

### TOPICS OF SPECIAL INTEREST IN THE DALLAS-FORT WORTH REGION

**Negroes and Negroes in New Housing.** The region's 330,000 blacks are disproportionately concentrated in Dallas (210,000 or 64 percent) and Fort Worth (82,500 or 25 percent); only 11 percent live outside the two cities. Open space for new residential construction within Dallas and Fort Worth and the existence of significant income differences within the generally poor black community results in opportunities for blacks to purchase new housing. Blacks own and occupy 4,300 housing units built between 1960 and March 1970 in Dallas, and 2,000 in Fort Worth. These new units comprise 4.1 percent of the total 1960-1970 construction in Dallas and 6.8 percent in Fort Worth. An additional 1,450 new units owned and occupied by blacks are located outside Dallas and Fort Worth. In the combined SMSAs, blacks own and occupy 2.6 percent of the units erected between 1960 and March 1970. Thus blacks are participating in the general market for new housing in Dallas and Fort Worth to a greater degree than they are in some other cities.

**Spanish-Americans.** Although Spanish-Americans (people who speak Spanish plus those with Spanish surnames who do not speak Spanish) outnumber blacks in Texas, there are usually more blacks than Spanish-Americans in Texas metropolitan areas. In Texas as a whole, almost 20 percent of the population are Spanish-Americans and 13 percent are blacks. As noted earlier, in the Dallas-Fort Worth area there are 145,500 Spanish-Americans who comprise 6.2 percent

*Twentieth-Century Cities: Dallas-Fort Worth*

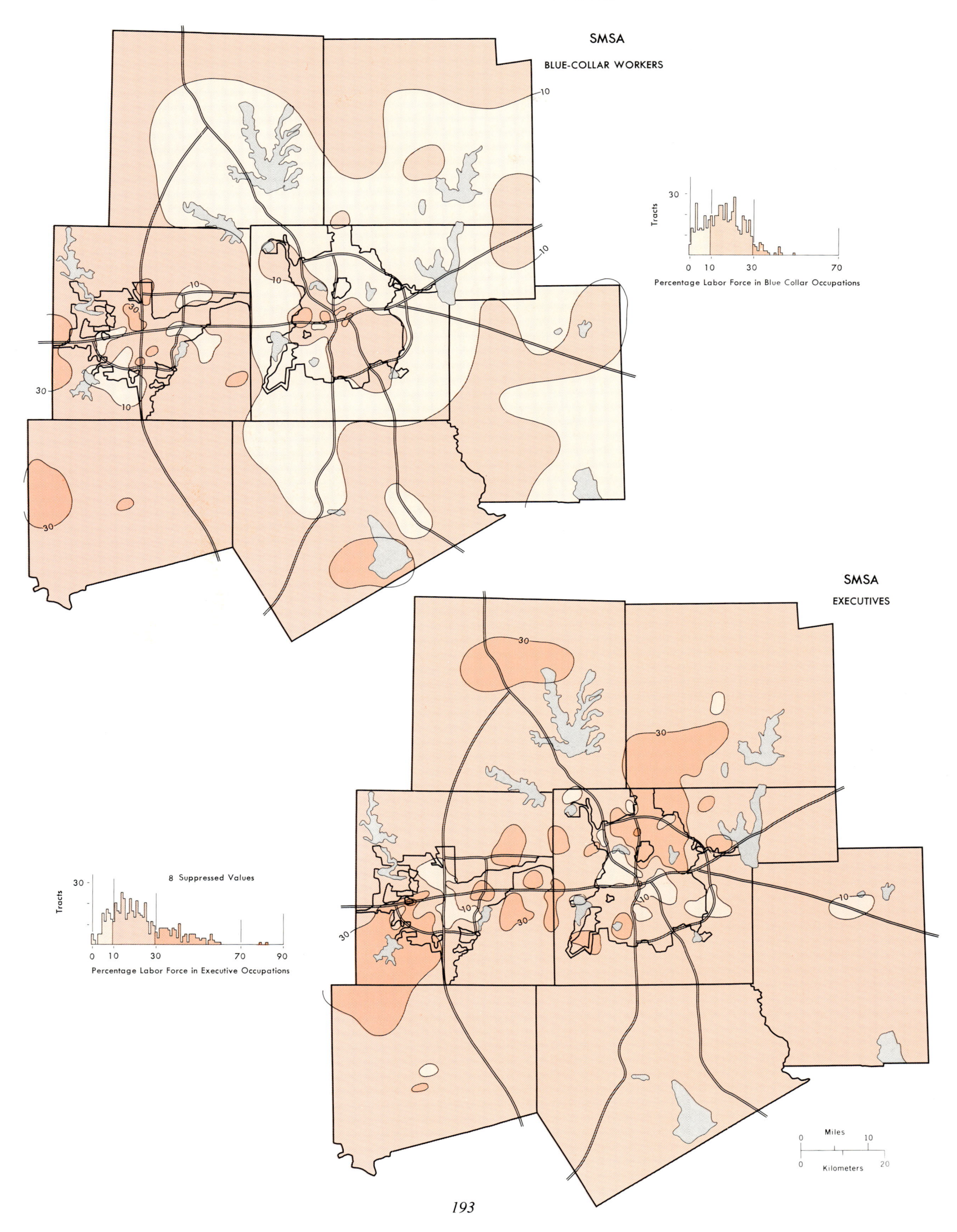

SMSA
BLUE-COLLAR WORKERS

Percentage Labor Force in Blue Collar Occupations

SMSA
EXECUTIVES

8 Suppressed Values

Percentage Labor Force in Executive Occupations

*Twentieth-Century Cities: Dallas-Fort Worth*

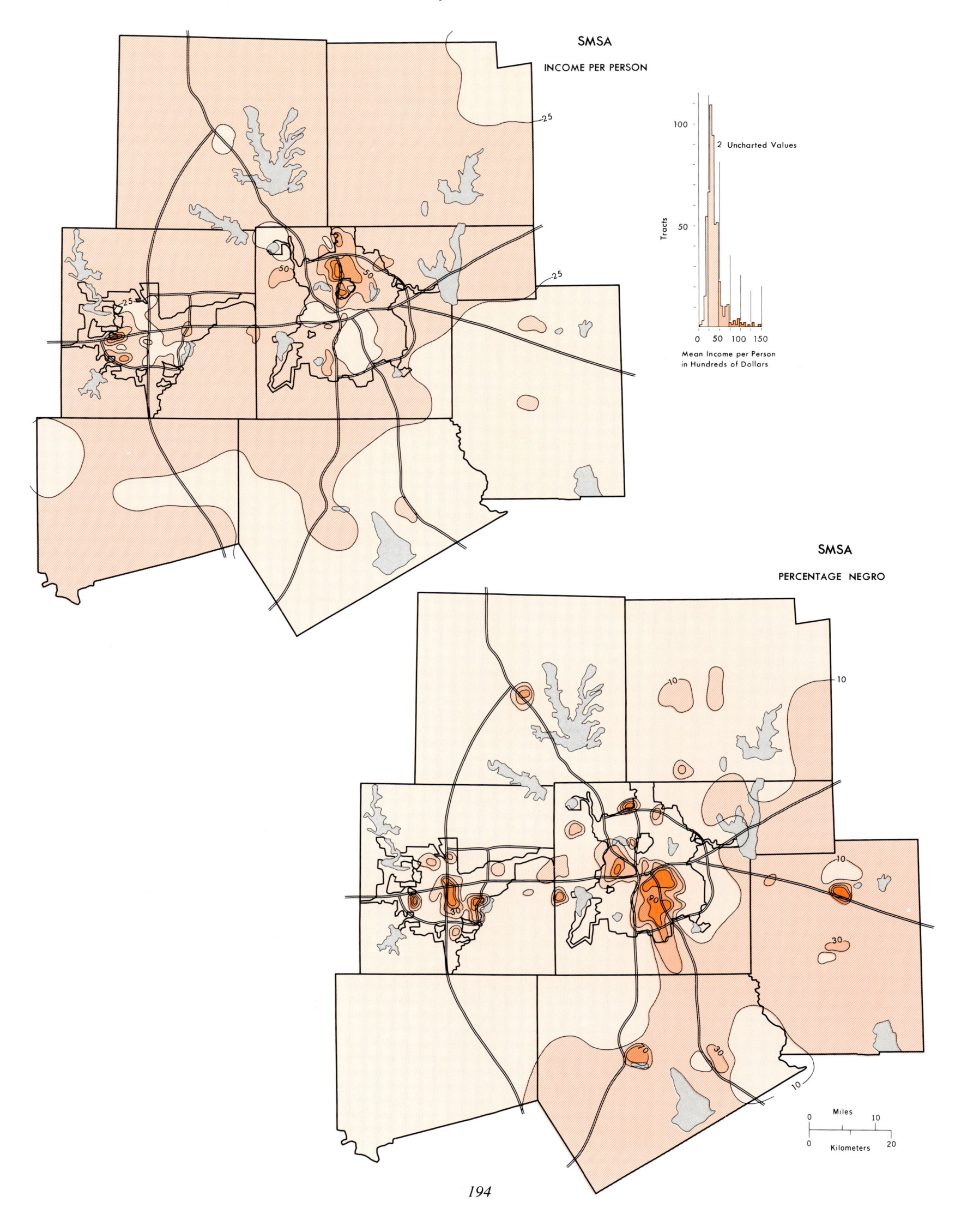

SMSA

INCOME PER PERSON

Mean Income per Person in Hundreds of Dollars

SMSA

PERCENTAGE NEGRO

194

*Twentieth-Century Cities: Dallas-Fort Worth*

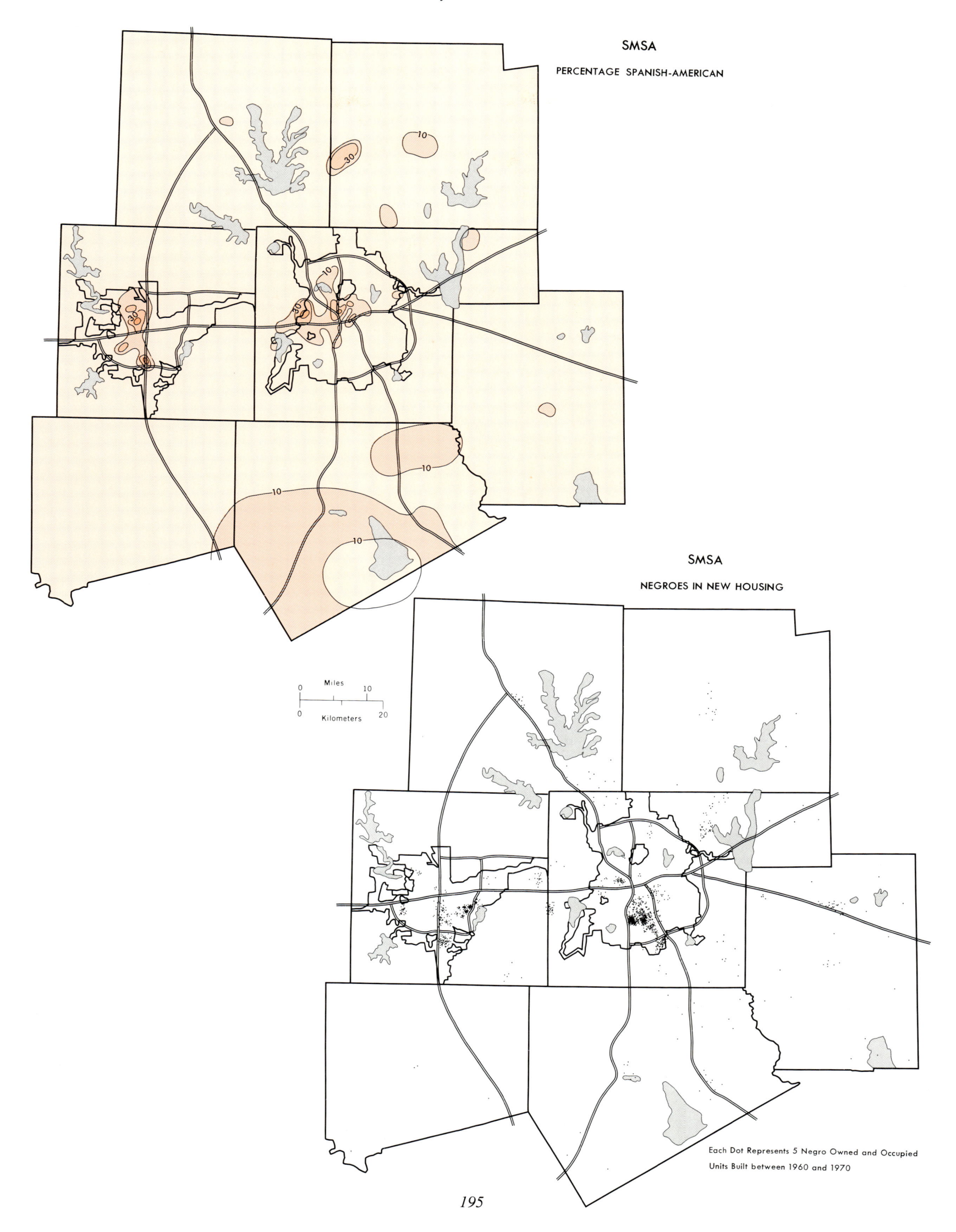

SMSA

PERCENTAGE SPANISH-AMERICAN

SMSA

NEGROES IN NEW HOUSING

Each Dot Represents 5 Negro Owned and Occupied Units Built between 1960 and 1970

195

## SMSA

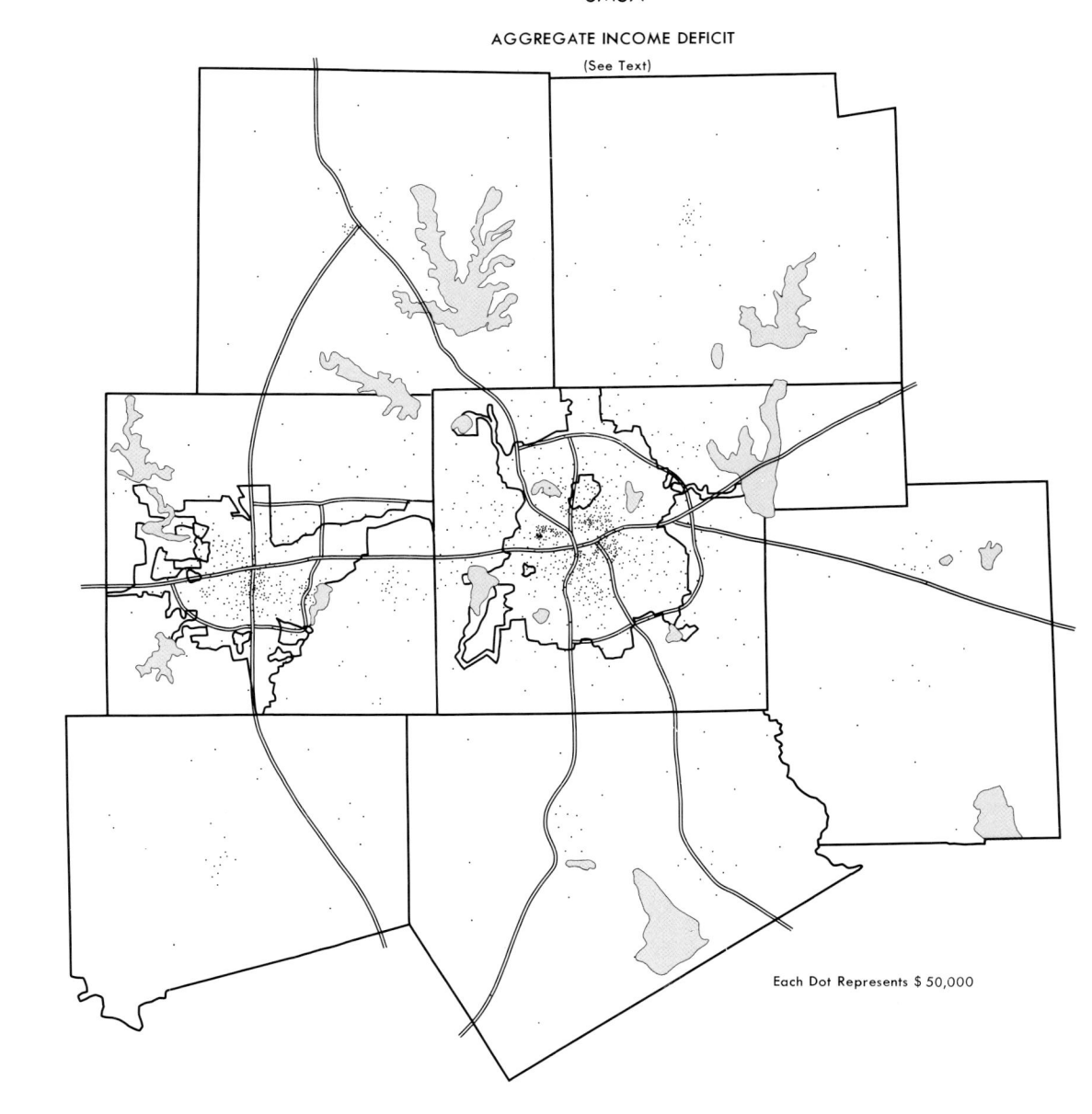

### AGGREGATE INCOME DEFICIT
(See Text)

Each Dot Represents $50,000

of the population of the combined SMSAs. The Hispanic community is not as highly concentrated in the central cities as the black population, but the distribution is disproportionate; 47 percent of the region's Hispanics live in Dallas and 23 percent live in Fort Worth compared with their 35 and 17 percent shares of the total population. An additional 20 percent live in suburban Dallas and Tarrant counties. Most of the remaining 10 percent live in Collin (2.9 percent), Denton (2.0 percent), and Ellis (2.8 percent) counties.

**Income Deficit.** The amount by which 1969 incomes fall below the poverty level in the combined SMSAs totaled $128,735,000, a per capita deficit (total population) of $55.50. This deficit is somewhat higher in the Dallas SMSA ($57.00) than in the Fort Worth SMSA ($52.60). The income deficits are somewhat concentrated in the central cities. The deficit in Dallas is 44 percent of the regional total and the Fort Worth deficit is 21 percent. As might be expected, the deficit is concentrated in the black and Spanish-American areas, but it is important to note that deficits are not confined to these neighborhoods. There are some dots (each dot represents $50,000 of the deficit) in almost every area where people live in appreciable numbers. Elderly people on limited, fixed incomes often account for much of the deficit in prosperous areas not usually associated with poverty.

---

Many of the city-suburb differences usually evident in American SMSAs are absent in Dallas. This results not so much from the area's recent growth as from the ability of Texas cities to annex unincorporated territory and to control independent incorporation outside their boundaries. Such control and annexation power allow cities like Dallas and Fort Worth to keep the boundaries of the functioning economic city congruent with those of the political city. Expansion is not totally unconstrained; expanding municipalities must provide public utilities in the areas they annex. But expansion can proceed to a degree that is largely impossible elsewhere. In most states, central-city annexation is virtually, if not totally, impossible. The annexation powers held by Dallas and Fort Worth should help them avoid some of the problems that develop when it is possible for affluent individuals and economic activities to abandon central cities and their problems by moving to independent municipalities.

# CHAPTER 21

# Houston

*The town of Houston is located at a point on the river which must ever command the trade of the largest and richest portion of Texas.*

Telegraph and Texas Register, 1836

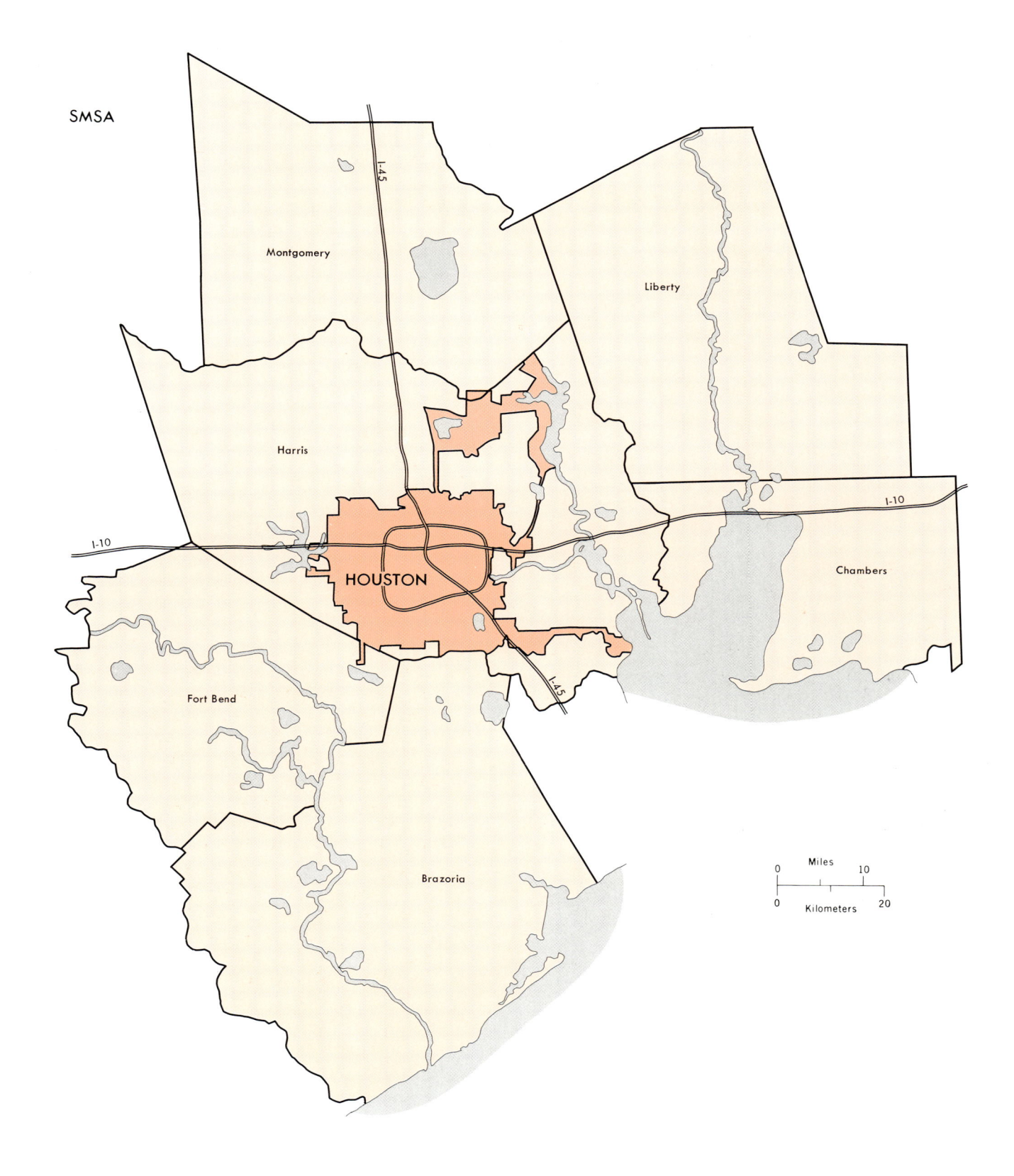

*Twentieth-Century Cities: Houston*

SMSA
GENERALIZED LAND USE

- Residential
- Open Space
- Commercial, Industrial, Transportation

CITY
RELIEF

- Over 75 Feet
- 50-75 Feet
- 25-50 Feet
- Below 25 Feet

*Twentieth-Century Cities: Houston*

SMSA

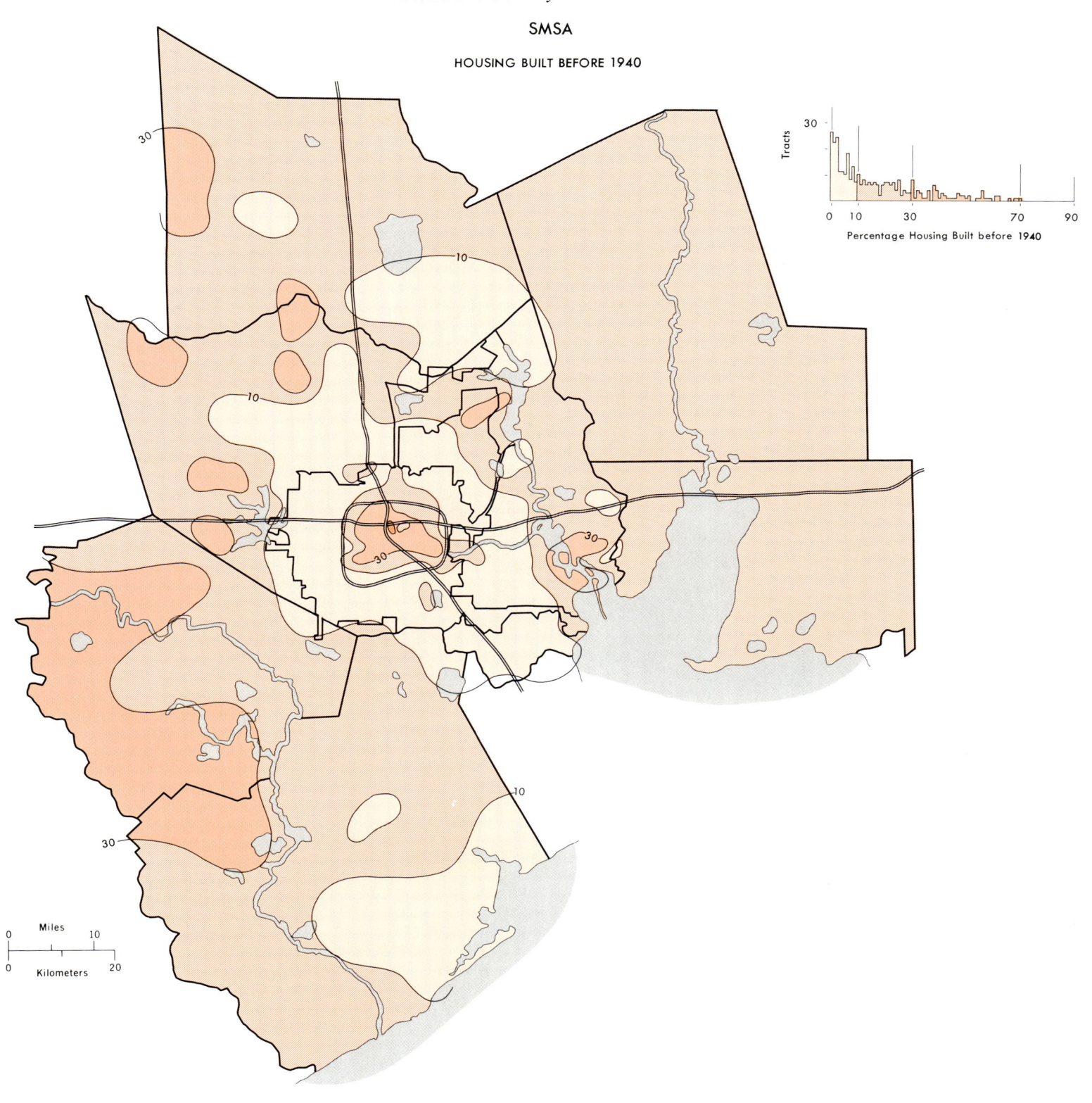

HOUSING BUILT BEFORE 1940

The Houston Standard Metropolitan Statistical Area (SMSA), with a population of 1,985,000, is the 13th most populous metropolitan area in the United States. It is an extremely large SMSA, extending over 6,300 square miles (10,150 square kilometers) in 6 large counties. The city of Houston is the largest incorporated place in the nation. Its 434 square miles (700 square kilometers) contain 1,233,000 people or 62 percent of the metropolitan total. Another 509,000 people (26 percent of the SMSA total) live in Harris County outside Houston. The remaining 12 percent of the SMSA population is divided among Brazoria (5 percent), Fort Bend (3 percent), Liberty (2 percent), and Montgomery (2 percent) counties. The Daily Urban System (DUS) defined by counties that have at least 5 percent of their labor forces working in Harris County consists of the SMSA counties plus Austin, Galveston, San Jacinto, Walker, and Waller counties (p. 201). The DUS population is 2,230,000 people. Most of the 245,000 increase over the SMSA population results from the inclusion of Galveston County's 170,000 people. It is the 13th most populous DUS in the nation.

Houston was established to link interior settlements with the Gulf Coast. Interior cities were separated from the coast by a vast, poorly drained plain which was hard to cross in wet periods. Numerous settlements tried to interconnect the interior with tidewater. Before railroads were built, most achieved limited success. Houston, established at the confluence of the Buffalo and White Oaks bayous, had a larger and better connection to tidewater shipping and was therefore able to take the lead. After the 1850s, railroads spreading out from Houston to the rest of the region put the city in a strong

*Note:* All data are from the 1970 Censuses of Population and Housing unless otherwise indicated. Therefore the present tense refers to 1970 data except for income data which are from 1969. Cartographic conventions are explained in Chapter 1.

## Twentieth-Century Cities: Houston

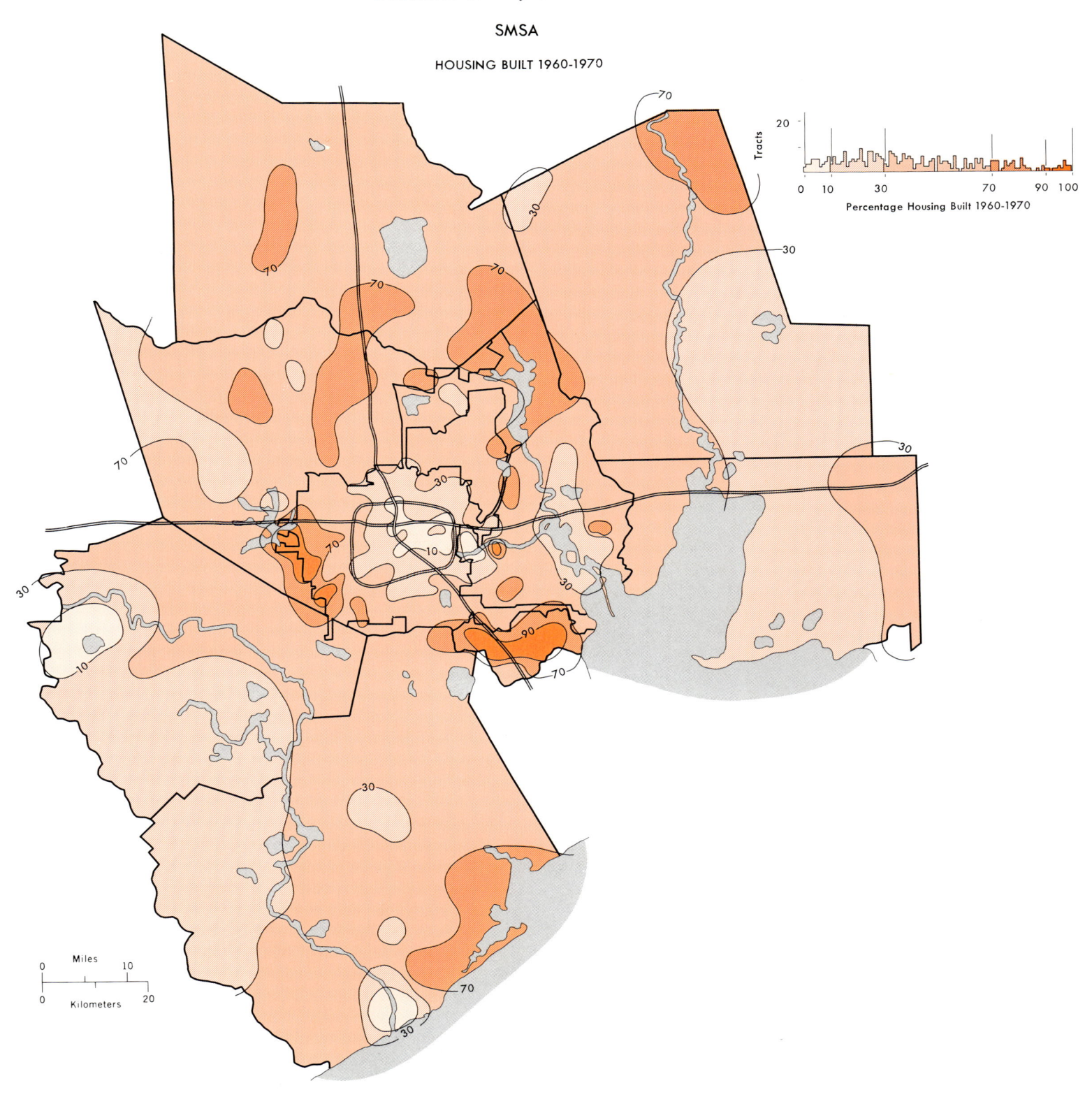

### SMSA
#### HOUSING BUILT 1960-1970

competitive position and enabled it to capture much of the trade and shipping that had formerly moved through Galveston. The hurricane that destroyed much of Galveston in 1900 accelerated the rise of Houston and the relative decline of Galveston. Buffalo Bayou was deepened and transformed into the Houston Ship Channel, complete with a turning basin. The discovery of oil north of Houston stimulated refinery construction along the bayou and elsewhere in the region, since it was convenient to convert petroleum into higher-value refined products before loading them onto tankers.

Houston was an important port by 1920, and the combination of shipping, petroleum refining, and petrochemicals manufacture, and more recently commerce and federal space agency employment, underlies the continuous and rapid growth of the region since 1850 (p. 10). After 1960, spectacular growth became a way of life in Houston.

Between 1960 and 1970 the Houston SMSA increased its population 40 percent, compared with the national metropolitan growth rate of 16.6 percent.

Houston is situated on a flat plain that presents few physical restrictions or natural barriers to movement and urban expansion. Local relief throughout the area is well under 100 feet (30 meters), the only minor topographic features being the courses of the bayous. The level topography and persistent land subsidence make water slow to run off, and downpours are inevitably followed by flooding along the bayous. Because most growth occurred recently when automobile transportation was available and single-family housing on large lots was preferred, the city has spread at low densities. It is served by an extensive freeway system that makes most parts of the city easily accessible by car.

## Twentieth-Century Cities: Houston

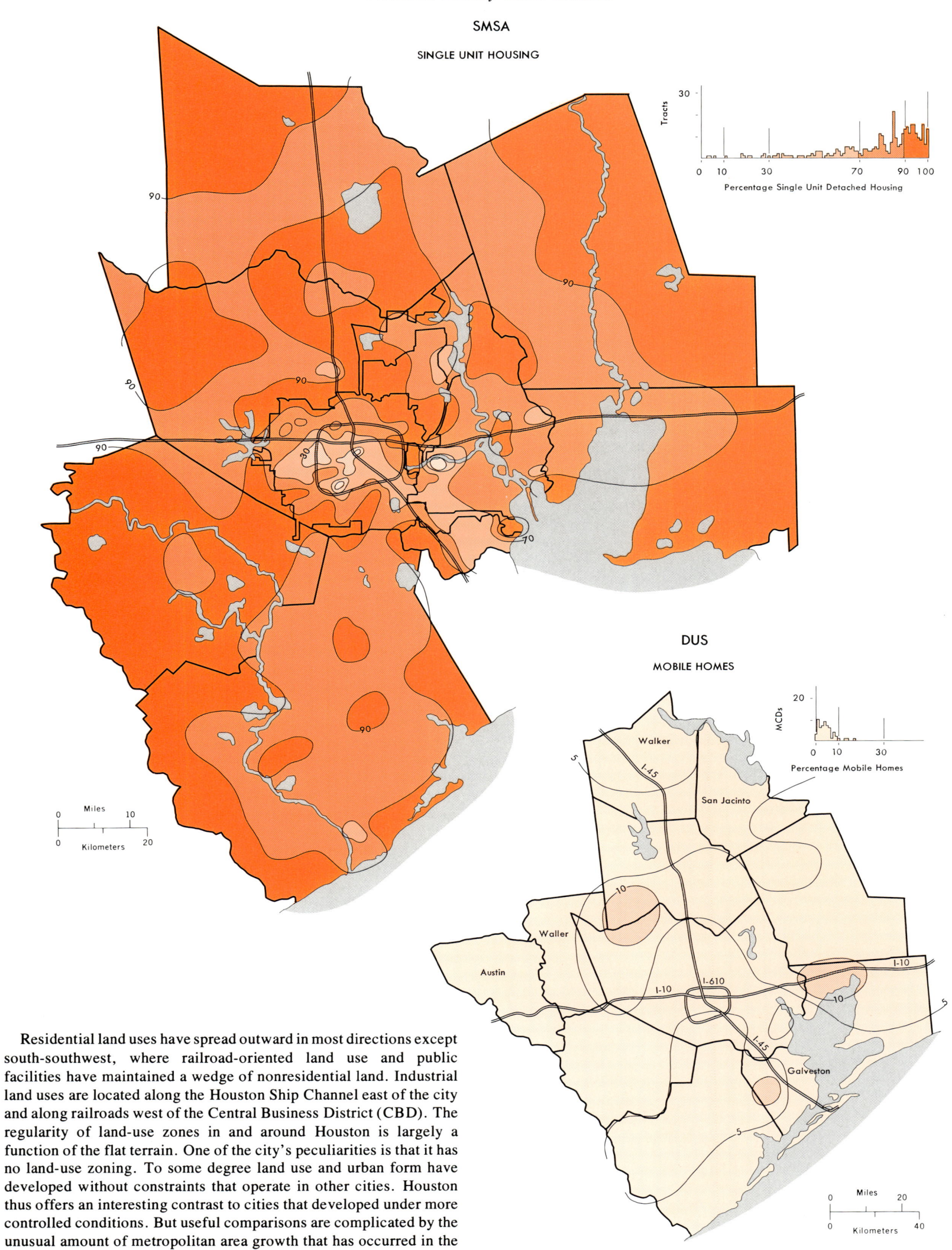

### SMSA
#### SINGLE UNIT HOUSING

### DUS
#### MOBILE HOMES

Residential land uses have spread outward in most directions except south-southwest, where railroad-oriented land use and public facilities have maintained a wedge of nonresidential land. Industrial land uses are located along the Houston Ship Channel east of the city and along railroads west of the Central Business District (CBD). The regularity of land-use zones in and around Houston is largely a function of the flat terrain. One of the city's peculiarities is that it has no land-use zoning. To some degree land use and urban form have developed without constraints that operate in other cities. Houston thus offers an interesting contrast to cities that developed under more controlled conditions. But useful comparisons are complicated by the unusual amount of metropolitan area growth that has occurred in the

*Twentieth-Century Cities: Houston*

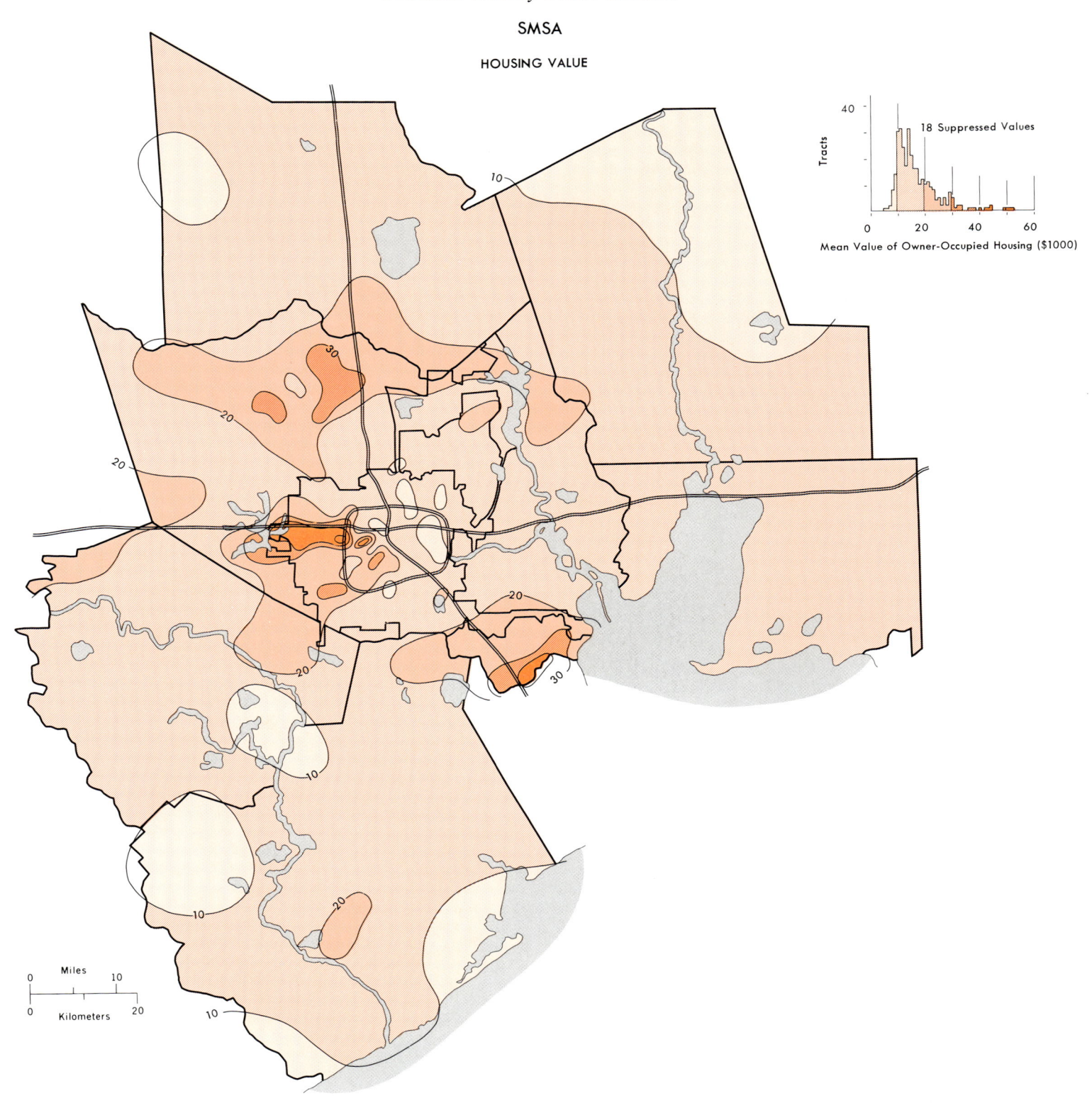

## SMSA
### HOUSING VALUE

last decade, for which there are few counterparts. Also, land use in Houston is partially controlled by restrictive deed covenants, which can be more effective in forestalling land-use changes than are zoning laws.

Another Houston peculiarity is evident in the city's form. Texas law gives Houston the power to place all land within 5 miles of its city limits under extraterritorial jurisdiction. Only Houston may annex in the extraterritorial area, and no settlement may incorporate there without Houston's permission. The city may annex annually up to 10 percent of its total area as of the previous January 1. Houston has used the law to maximize its control over the surrounding areas by incorporating 10-foot-wide strips along highways, which extend control farther than if annexation proceeded by tiers. These strips have been omitted from base maps in the atlas, except for those connecting the city to its northern "exclave" that contains the Houston Intercontinental Airport.

## HOUSING

**Housing Age.** Only 15 percent of the SMSA's housing was built before 1940, 47 percent was built from 1940 through 1959, and 38 percent dates from 1960 to March 1970. The Houston SMSA has more new housing and less old housing than any of the other SMSAs in the atlas. The city's housing stock has a similar age structure: 17 percent was built before 1940, 49 percent was built from 1940 through 1959, and 34 percent was erected during the 1960s. Of the pre-1940 units, 73 percent are located in the city of Houston.

The proportion of old housing decreases steadily away from downtown Houston in all directions until it begins to rise again on the metropolitan periphery and in other areas where new housing construction has been minimal. The area at the confluence of the San Jacinto River and Galveston Bay where pre-1940 housing exceeds 30 percent consists of the old, separate settlements of Baytown and Morgans Point. Individual tract proportions of old housing vary from

*Twentieth-Century Cities: Houston*

SMSA

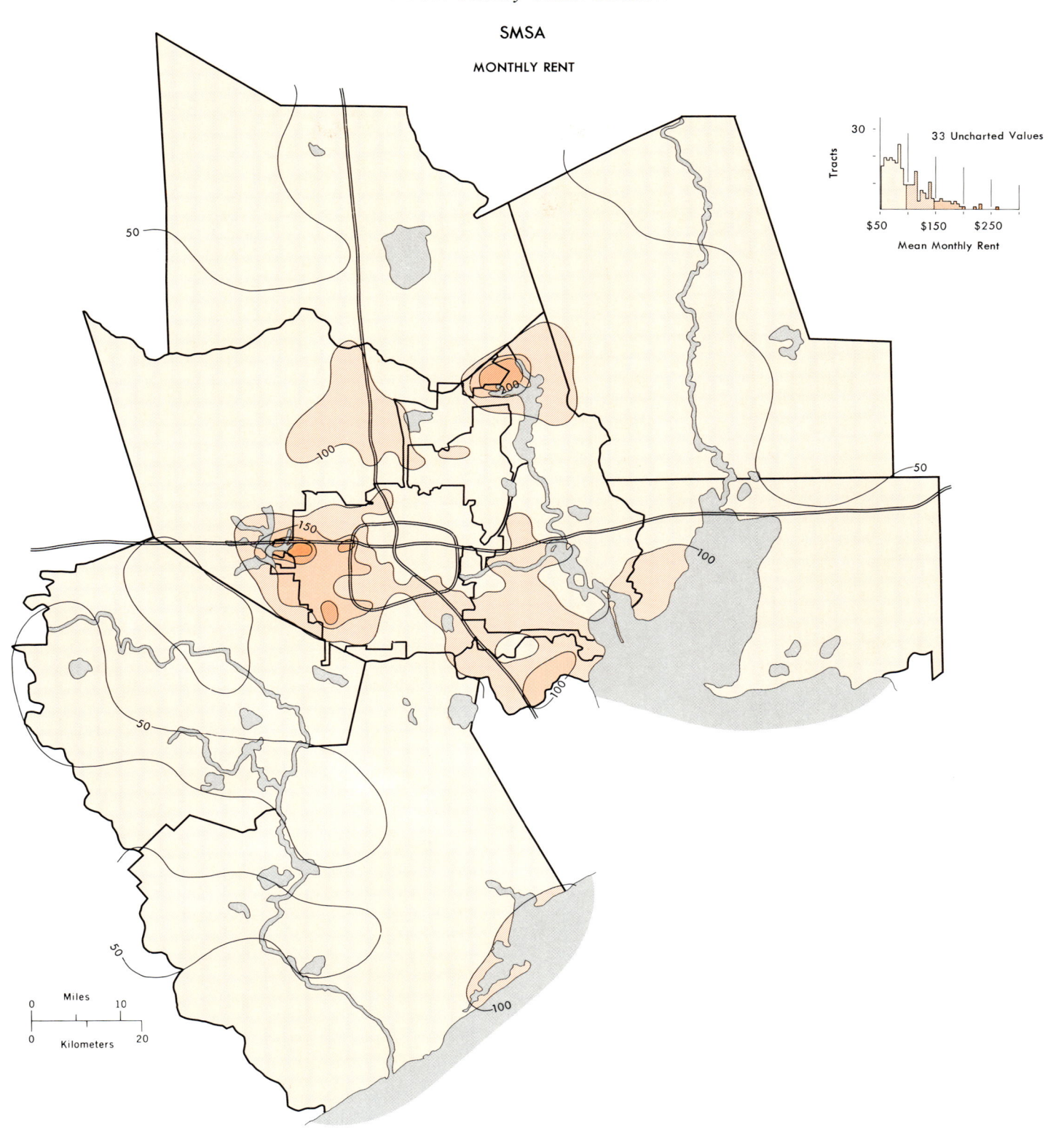

MONTHLY RENT

zero to 70 percent with many more low than high percentages. The highest percentages are located in the downtown core of the city.

Tract percentages of housing built from 1960 to March 1970 vary from zero to 99, with an even distribution of tracts across the range. New housing is being built all around Houston except for narrow corridors on the south and east. The refineries and petrochemical plants clustered along the Houston Ship Channel (Buffalo Bayou) discourage residential expansion eastward, and the dominantly black area in south-central Houston makes the suburban sector due south of the CBD unattractive to white suburbanites. The most rapid expansion during the 1960s occurred to the southeast near Ellington Air Force Base and the National Aeronautics and Space Administration's Manned Spacecraft Center, and to the west, which is Houston's traditional high-prestige residential axis. New dwellings also dominate local housing inventories along the Gulf Coast in southern Brazoria County.

**Mobile Homes.** The 17,750 mobile homes in the Houston DUS comprise 2.4 percent of the DUS housing stock. Mobile homes make up more than 10 percent of local housing inventories in only a few places at some distance from Houston. In contrast to most eastern cities, there are many (5,050) mobile homes within the central city. They constitute 1.2 percent of Houston's housing stock. Mobile homes are most in use in Brazoria and Montgomery counties, where they are 6 percent of county housing inventories.

**Single-Unit Detached Housing.** Individual dwellings constitute 72 percent of the SMSA's housing stock and 69 percent of Houston's housing. Both percentages are the highest proportions of single-unit detached housing among the 24 regions mapped in the atlas. The predominance of single-unit housing in the Houston region is largely due to the recent growth of the area. Single-unit detached housing has been the preferred form of housing since World War II when the bulk

## Twentieth-Century Cities: Houston

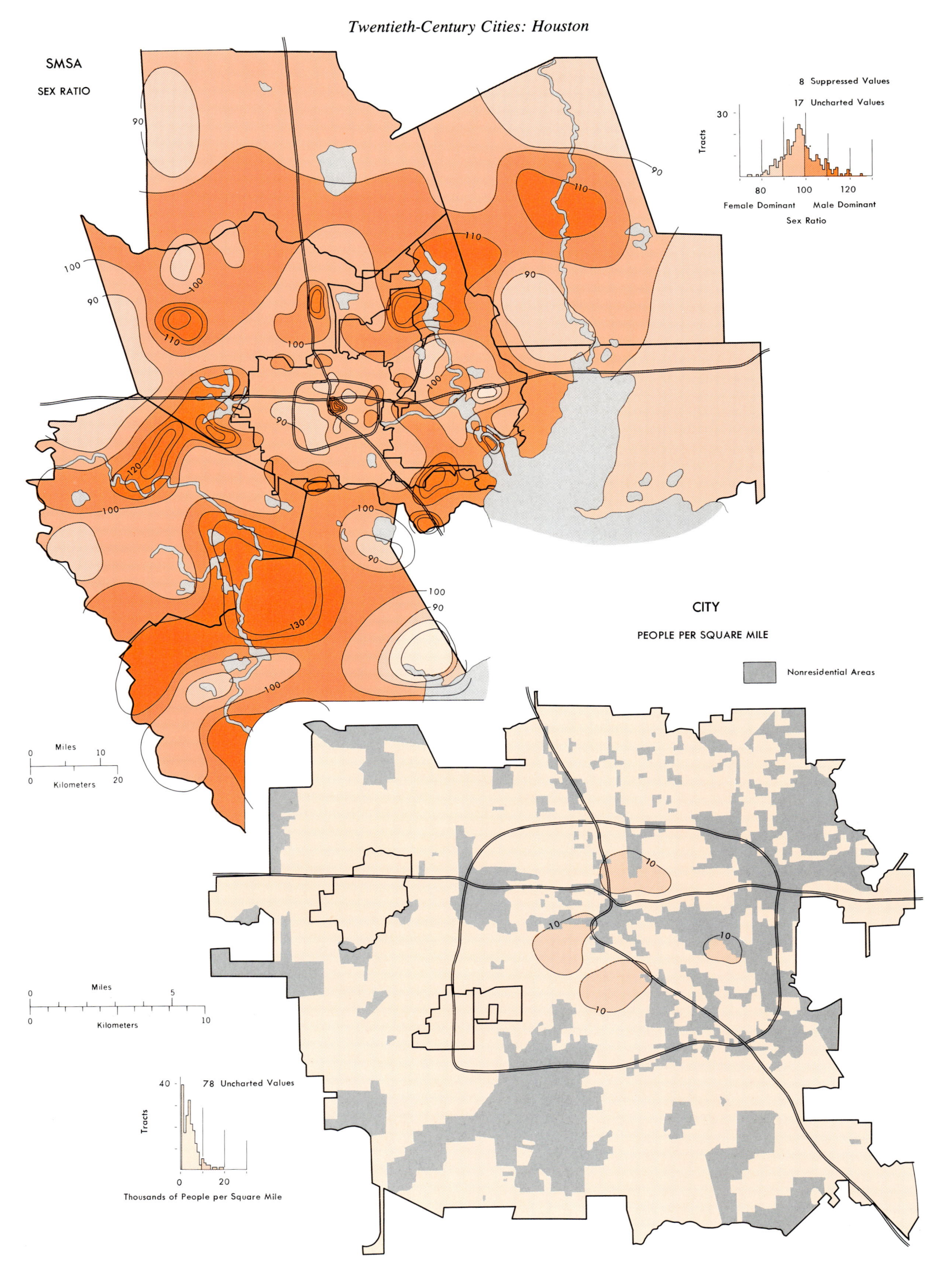

**SMSA**
SEX RATIO

**CITY**
PEOPLE PER SQUARE MILE

## Twentieth-Century Cities: Houston

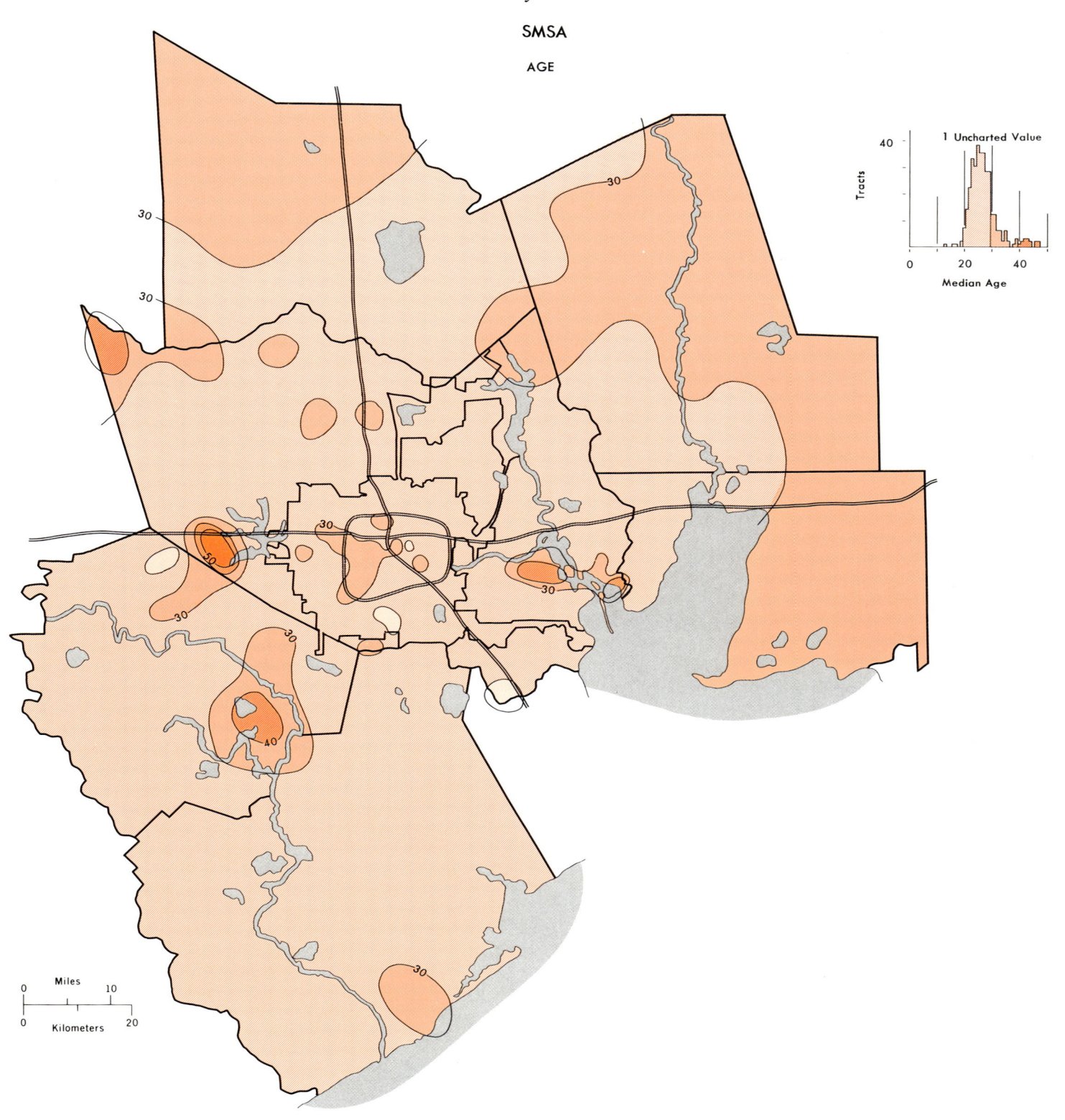

### SMSA
### AGE

of the region's housing was built, and, by and large, people have been able to afford their preferences. Tract percentages of single-unit housing range from 3 to 100, but tracts in which less than half the housing is single-unit detached dwellings are now rare, for most of the SMSA's tracts are clustered at the higher end of the range. Multiple-unit structures are common in center-city tracts, in a tract in Pasadena (south of the Houston Ship Channel), where almost all the housing units are recently built apartments, and in a tract in south-central Houston adjacent to the Astrodome Stadium, which is also the site of new apartment construction. Outside central Houston, proportions of single-unit detached housing exceed 70 percent with few exceptions. Multiples constitute 31 percent of Houston's housing stock: duplexes (4 percent); 3- and 4-unit structures (5 percent); 5- to 49-unit buildings (12 percent); and structures containing 50 or more dwellings (10 percent).

**Housing Value and Rent.** The mean value of owner-occupied housing in the SMSA and in Houston is $18,000. Individual tract means range from $5,000 to $52,000. Mean values below $10,000 occur on the metropolitan periphery and in several neighborhoods in eastern Houston. The SMSA's prestige residential area is clearly directly west of downtown Houston where mean tract values over $40,000 are common and where the peaks over $50,000 occur. A secondary cluster of expensive housing is located in southeastern Harris County, near the Manned Space Center. Although its highest housing values equal those of most SMSAs, the Houston mean values are low by metropolitan standards. Low summary statistics are not necessarily an indication of lower-quality housing than obtains elsewhere, for good housing is less expensive to build in Houston than it is in other parts of the nation. Few houses have basements, and there is no need for insulation and central heating, which raise the prices of

*Twentieth-Century Cities: Houston*

SMSA

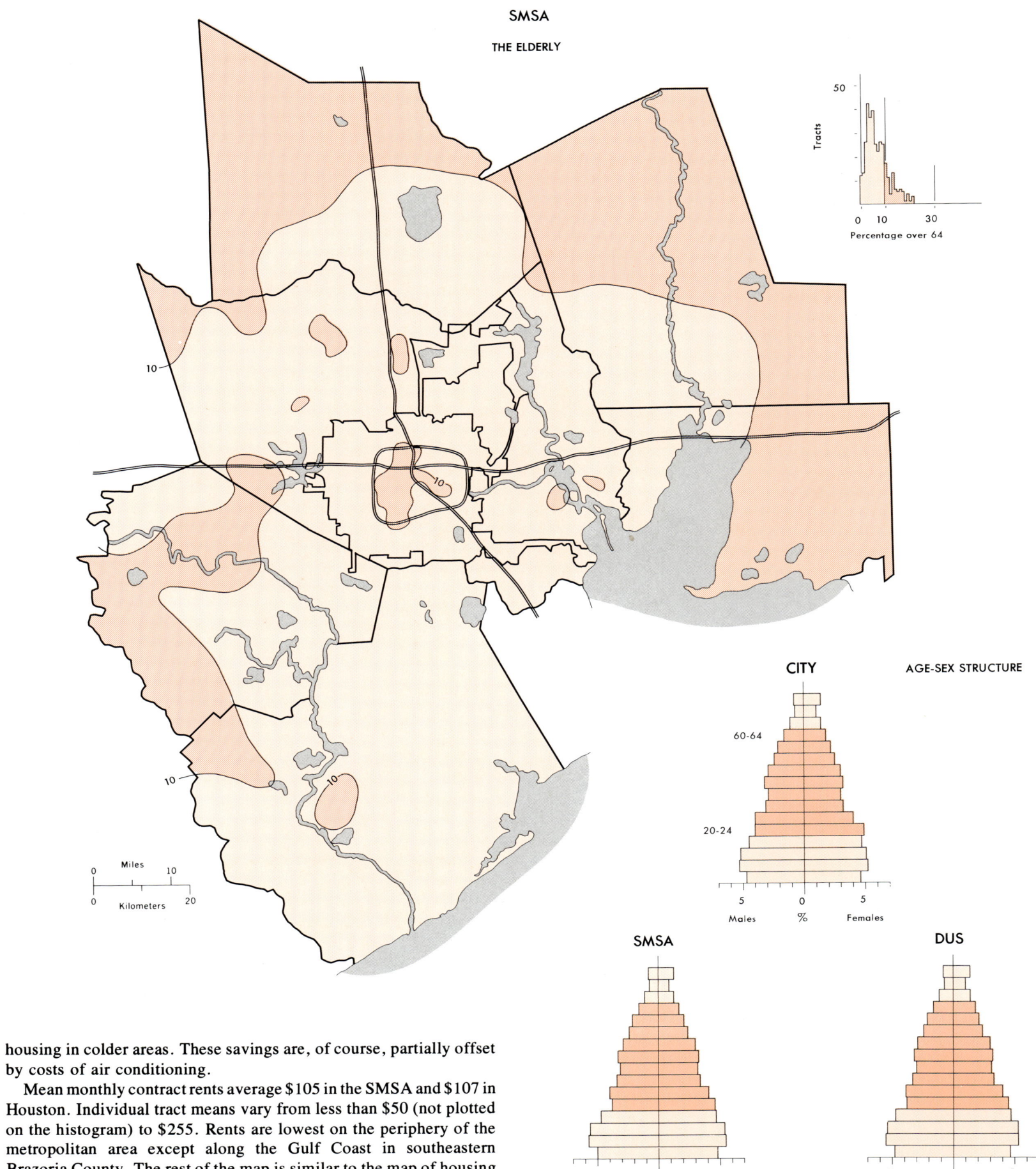

THE ELDERLY

AGE-SEX STRUCTURE

housing in colder areas. These savings are, of course, partially offset by costs of air conditioning.

Mean monthly contract rents average $105 in the SMSA and $107 in Houston. Individual tract means vary from less than $50 (not plotted on the histogram) to $255. Rents are lowest on the periphery of the metropolitan area except along the Gulf Coast in southeastern Brazoria County. The rest of the map is similar to the map of housing values; both western Houston and the area near the Manned Space Center have high rentals. One high-rental area that has no counterpart on the housing-value map is the area north of the Houston Intercontinental Airport where 70 units rent for a mean cost over $200.

## THE PEOPLE

**Population Density.** Houston's overall population density is 2,850

*Twentieth-Century Cities: Houston*

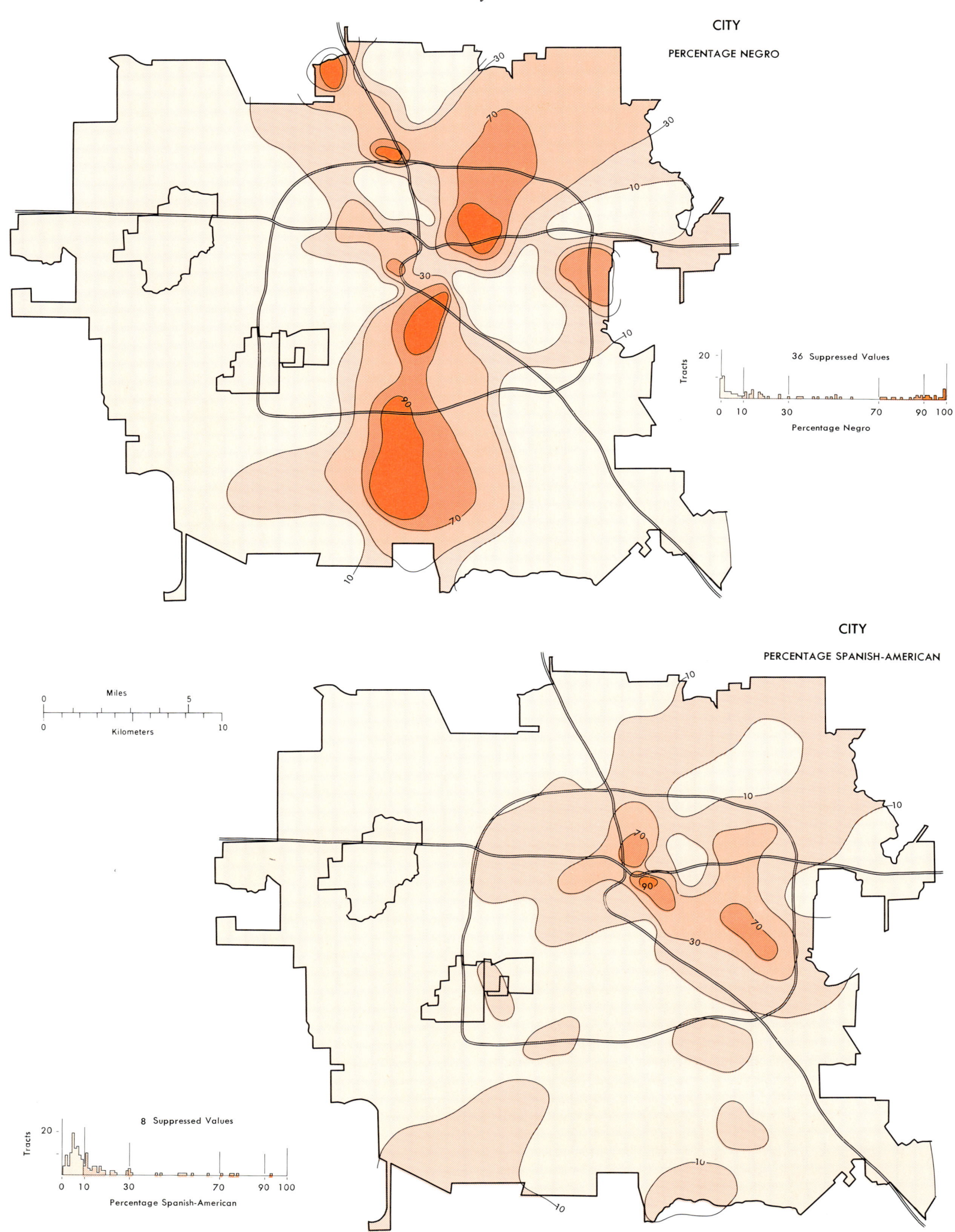

CITY

PERCENTAGE NEGRO

CITY

PERCENTAGE SPANISH-AMERICAN

207

*Twentieth-Century Cities: Houston*

SMSA

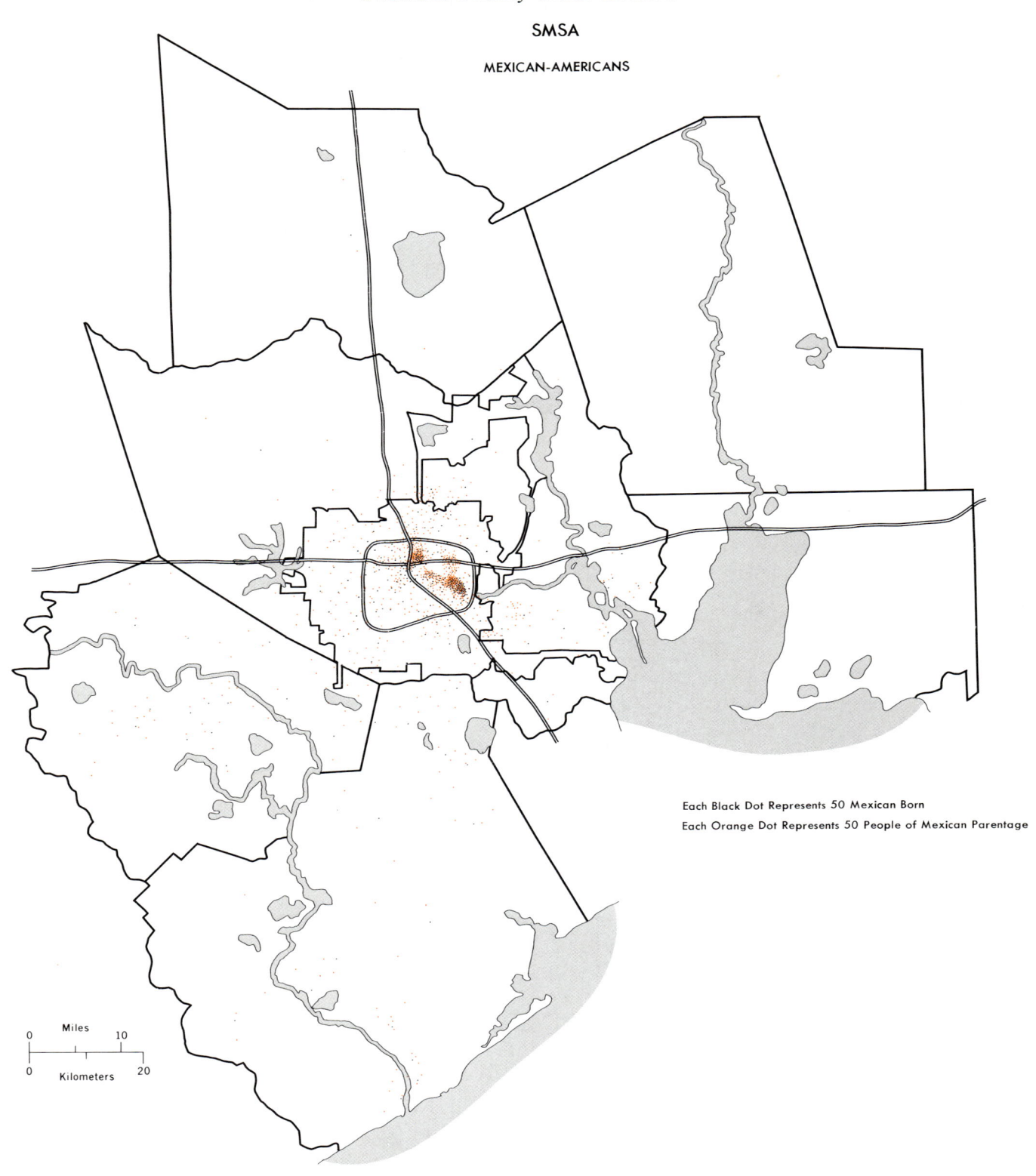

MEXICAN-AMERICANS

Each Black Dot Represents 50 Mexican Born
Each Orange Dot Represents 50 People of Mexican Parentage

people per square mile (610 per square kilometer), the lowest central-city density among the SMSAs mapped in the atlas. Although the inclusion of nonresidential areas in the gross densities mapped means that actual population densities in some parts of the city are higher than the densities indicated on the map, the fact remains that Houston is a low-density city, largely as a result of the dispersed, single-family housing that was in demand during the period when most of its housing was built. Individual tract densities vary from values rounding to zero density to 19,000 people per square mile (11,585 per square kilometer), but only 16 of Houston's 221 census tracts have densities equaling or exceeding 10,000 people per square mile (3,900 per square kilometer). They are all located in the old part of the city.

**Age and the Elderly.** The median age of the Houston SMSA population is 26 years. The Houston population is only slightly older, with a median age of 27. Individual tract medians range from 13 to 55 years (not graphed). Medians over 50 years are usually caused by institutionalized populations. This is not true in Houston, where the tract with the highest median has a small population (180), many of whom are old. In most of the SMSA median ages are below 30 years; exceptions are a few areas in Houston and the surrounding counties. Median ages below 20 years occur only in east-central Houston in a neighborhood with a relatively large Spanish-American population. Compared with other American metropolitan areas, both the SMSA and the central city have young populations.

People over 64 are infrequent in Houston and the SMSA; they comprise 6 percent of both the city and the SMSA populations. This proportion is low among the metropolitan areas included in the atlas, matched only by Washington, D.C. Tract percentages of the elderly vary from zero to 21. Dominantly rural tracts on the metropolitan periphery and a cluster of tracts at Houston's center have populations

*Twentieth-Century Cities: Houston*

SMSA

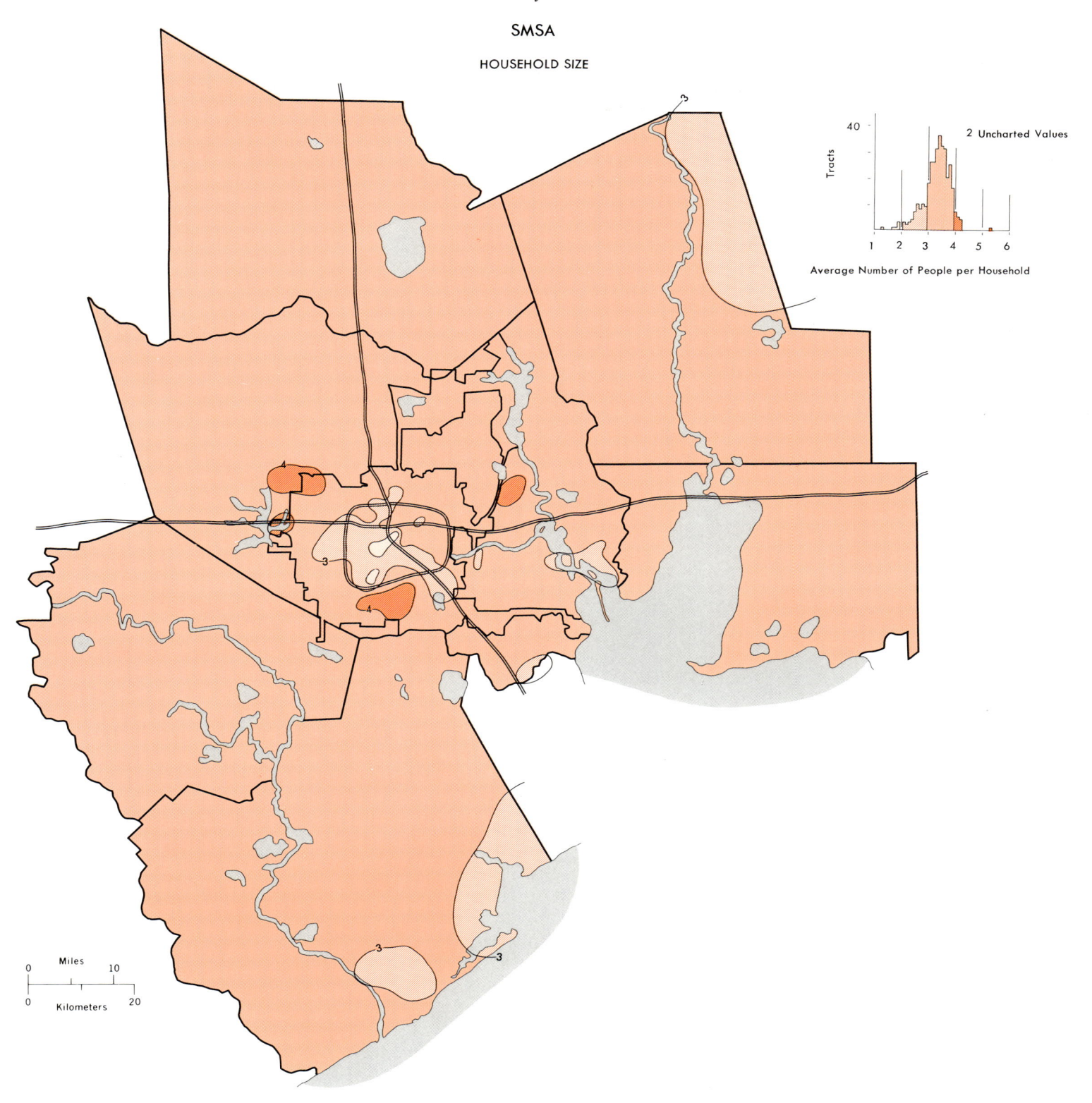

HOUSEHOLD SIZE

with more than 10 percent in the elderly group. Higher proportions of elderly in peripheral tracts result from out-migration of young people, whereas the concentrations of old people near the CBD are a response by elderly people of limited means to the inexpensive housing available there.

There are few differences between Houston and its SMSA because much of the city's growth is recent, it can expand its boundaries, and the populations of the outlying areas are sparse. More than is true in most metropolitan areas, the populations of the city and the SMSA are almost the same. Thus the two population pyramids are more similar than they usually are in American metropolitan areas.

**Sex Ratio.** The Houston SMSA has a more nearly equal balance of males and females than most metropolitan areas. There are 1.03 females for each male, which yields a sex ratio (males divided by females times 100) of 97. Typically, the central city is more female-dominant, with a sex ratio of 94, than the SMSA. Tract sex ratios range from 60 to 120 in the absence of unusual circumstances. In Houston there are a number of tracts with unusually high sex ratios. Several contain correctional institutions or military facilities.

**Negroes.** Houston's 317,000 blacks constitute the largest urban black community in the South. Blacks are 26 percent of the city population, and they are highly segregated, some 70 percent living in census tracts that are over 70 percent black. Blacks are concentrated in a broad belt running from south-central Houston into the north-central and northeastern parts of the city. Houston contains 83 percent of the SMSA's black population compared with its 62 percent share of the total population. (See SMSA map of black population on p. 387.)

**Spanish-Americans.** The Census Bureau estimates the number of Spanish-Americans in the city of Houston by counting those who

*Twentieth-Century Cities: Houston*

SMSA

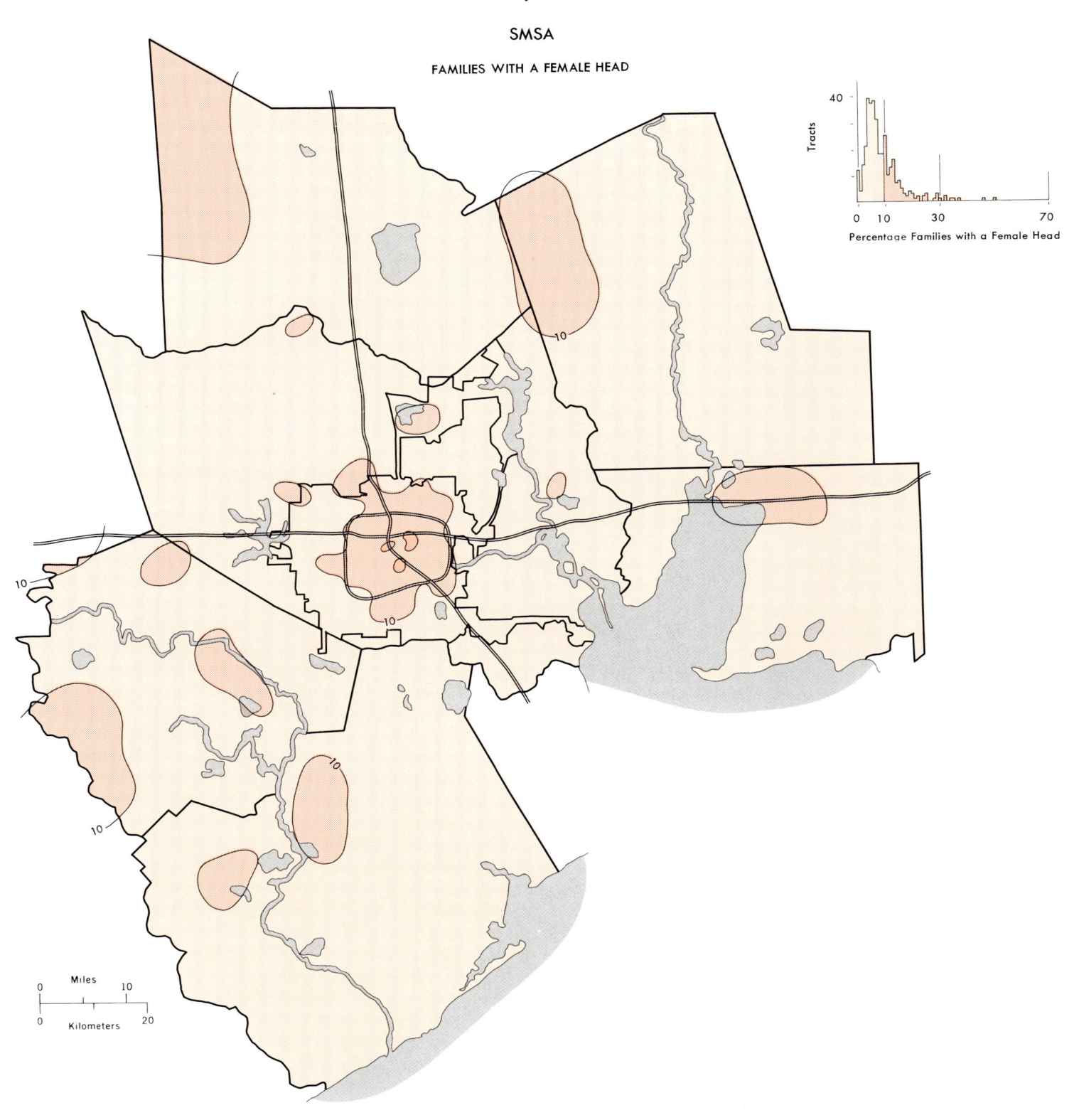

FAMILIES WITH A FEMALE HEAD

speak Spanish and adding to them non-Spanish speakers who have certain Spanish surnames. There are 150,000 Spanish-Americans in Houston by this reckoning, up 136 percent from the 1960 figure. The city's Spanish-Americans (11 percent of the total population) are located primarily in east-central Houston with outliers in scattered tracts in south-central Houston. As is often true in American cities, there is relatively little mingling of blacks and Spanish-Americans when mapped at the tract scale, and even less overlap would be evident were smaller statistical units used. Similarly, gradients between predominantly Spanish-American and predominantly Anglo-American neighborhoods are distinct. Of the SMSA's Spanish-Americans, 70 percent live in Houston compared with 62 percent of the total population. (SMSA map is on p. 395.)

Most of the SMSA's Spanish-Americans are of Mexican descent. Although foreign stock (foreign-born plus those with at least one foreign-born parent) from Central and South American nations constitutes 6,300 people, they are only 3 percent of the Spanish-American total of 212,000 in the SMSA. There are some 2,700 Cuban foreign stock and only 900 Puerto Ricans. The map of Mexican-Americans gives an incomplete picture of the SMSA's population of Mexican descent. Local residents make no distinction between recent Mexican immigrants and third- or fourth-generation native-born United States citizens of Mexican descent. Whereas there are 212,000 Spanish-Americans in the SMSA, there are only 65,000 of Mexican foreign stock (47,200 Mexican-born and 17,800 with at least one Mexican-born parent). Eighty percent of the Mexican-born and 72 percent of those with Mexican parentage live in Houston.

Mexican-Americans are by far the largest ethnic group in the Houston SMSA. German foreign stock is twice as numerous as any

*Twentieth-Century Cities: Houston*

SMSA

BLUE-COLLAR WORKERS

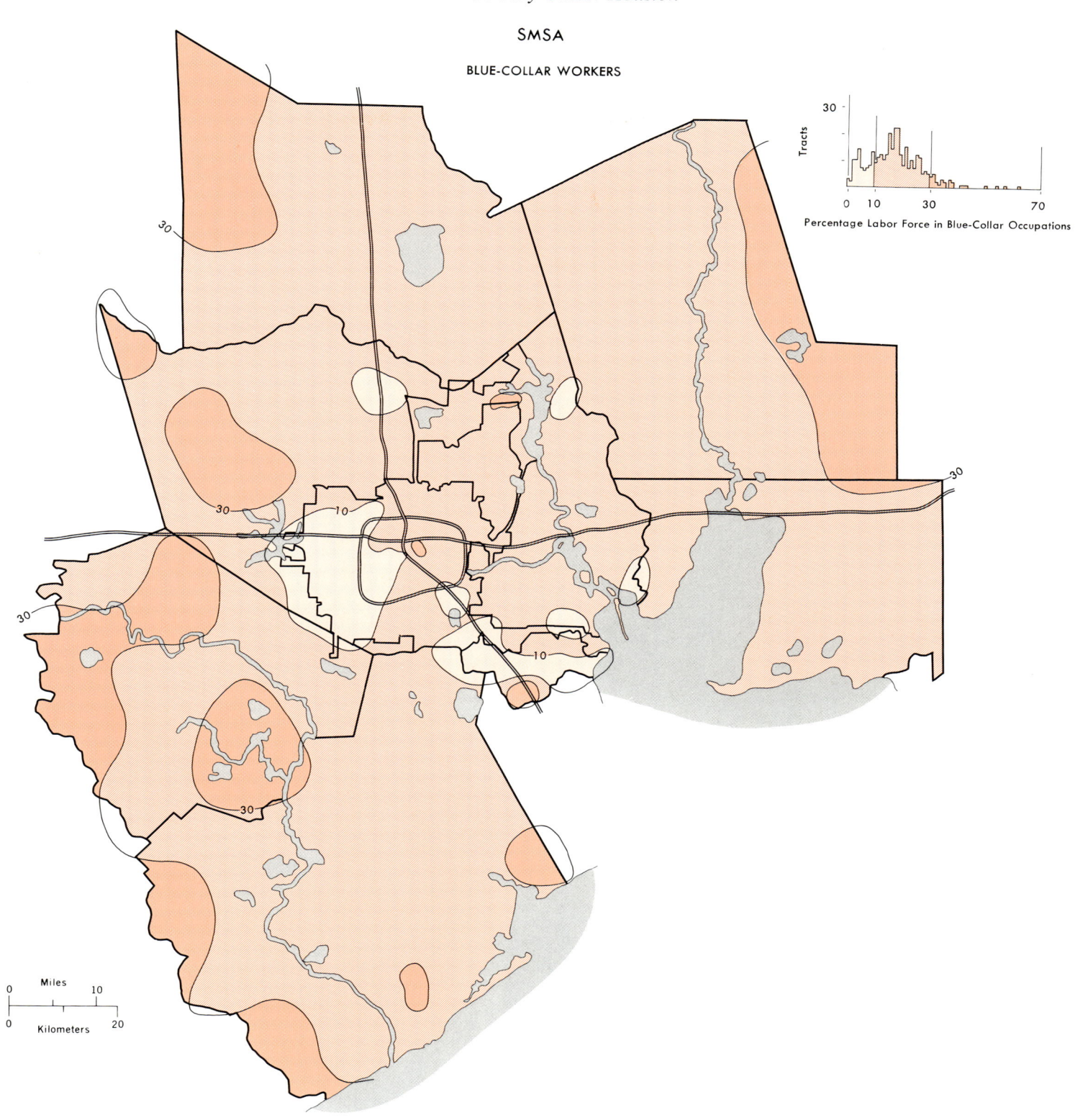

Percentage Labor Force in Blue-Collar Occupations

other group, but it comprises only 0.9 percent of the SMSA population. As was true of most Southern cities, Houston held little attraction for European immigrants in the early years, and its period of most rapid growth occurred after large-scale immigration ceased.

## SOCIOECONOMIC CHARACTERISTICS

**Household Size.** There are 3.2 people in the average SMSA household and 3.1 in the average Houston household. Central-city households are usually smaller than SMSA households, but the slight difference between the two in Houston reflects the general homogeneity of Houston and its suburbs. Household size is related to family life cycle. Small households are most frequent among young couples who have not started families and among old populations whose children have left home. Mean household sizes for tracts vary from 1.3 to 5.3 persons. The SMSA's smallest households are located southwest of the CBD along the axis between Rice University and the Astrodome. Mean households of fewer than 3 persons are common in the central area of Houston, except in heavily black and Spanish-American areas, where households are larger. Tract means of over 4 persons are uncommon in the SMSA, and the tract with the 5.3 mean is a statistical anomaly; it has only 6 families and thus is not mapped.

**Female Headship.** The Census Bureau defines female headship by the absence of a male spouse regardless of the sex of the household's principal breadwinner. Females head 10 percent of the SMSA's families and 12 percent of Houston's families. These families are concentrated somewhat in Houston, which contains 75 percent, compared with a 62 percent share of the total population. That degree of concentration is low compared with other SMSAs in the atlas.

*Twentieth-Century Cities: Houston*

SMSA

EXECUTIVES

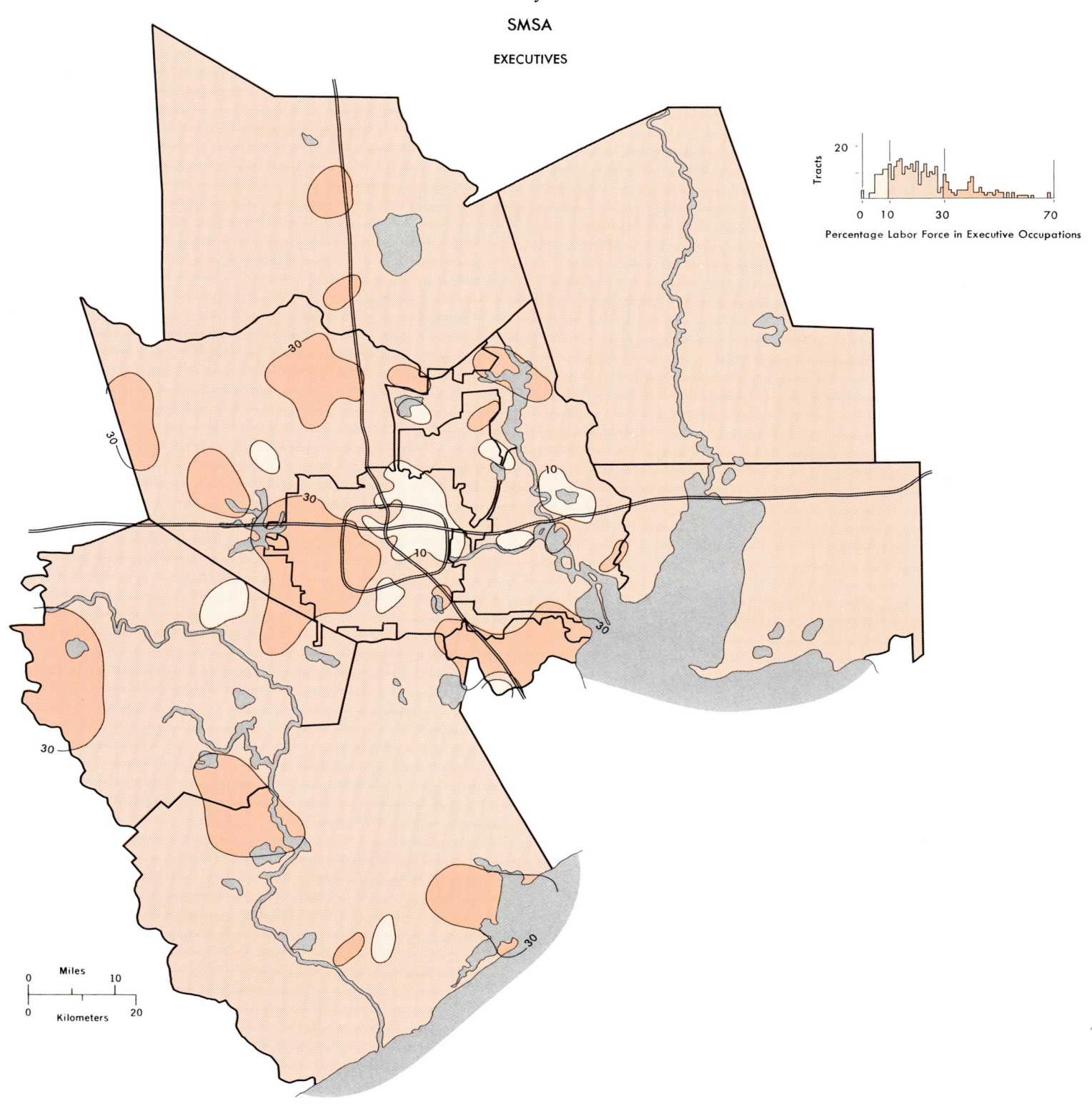

Households headed by females exceed 10 percent of tract families in much of central Houston, where a few tracts have proportions as high as·50 percent. The highest proportions of female headship occur in predominantly black neighborhoods. Females head 18 percent of Houston's black households but only 9 percent of the city's Spanish-American households.

**Occupations.** Thirteen percent of the SMSA's labor force work at blue-collar (laborers and operatives) jobs, and 24 percent classify themselves as executives (engineers, teachers, professionals, managers, proprietors, and administrators). The remaining 63 percent are service workers (36 percent) and clerical employees (27 percent). The breakdown for the city is: blue-collar, 12 percent; service, 35 percent; clerical, 30 percent; and executive, 23 percent. Thus the occupational structures of Houston and the entire SMSA are virtually identical.

Tract proportions of blue-collar workers vary from zero to 62 percent, although tracts where blue-collar workers are more than 30 percent of the labor force are rare; most are large, sparsely populated rural tracts. Much of the central area of the SMSA has blue-collar proportions between 10 and 30 percent except western Houston and southeastern Harris County.

Individual tracts have zero to 68 percent of their labor forces working in executive occupations, and in many places the map of executives reverses the map of blue-collar workers. The high-prestige area of western Houston has percentages well above 30, as does the southeastern Harris County area associated with the National Aeronautics and Space Agency complex. In heavily black northeastern Houston, few tracts have as much as 10 percent of their workers in executive ranks. Outside the city, tracts with more than 30 percent of their labor forces in executive jobs alternate with tracts where

212

*Twentieth-Century Cities: Houston*

## SMSA
### INCOME PER PERSON

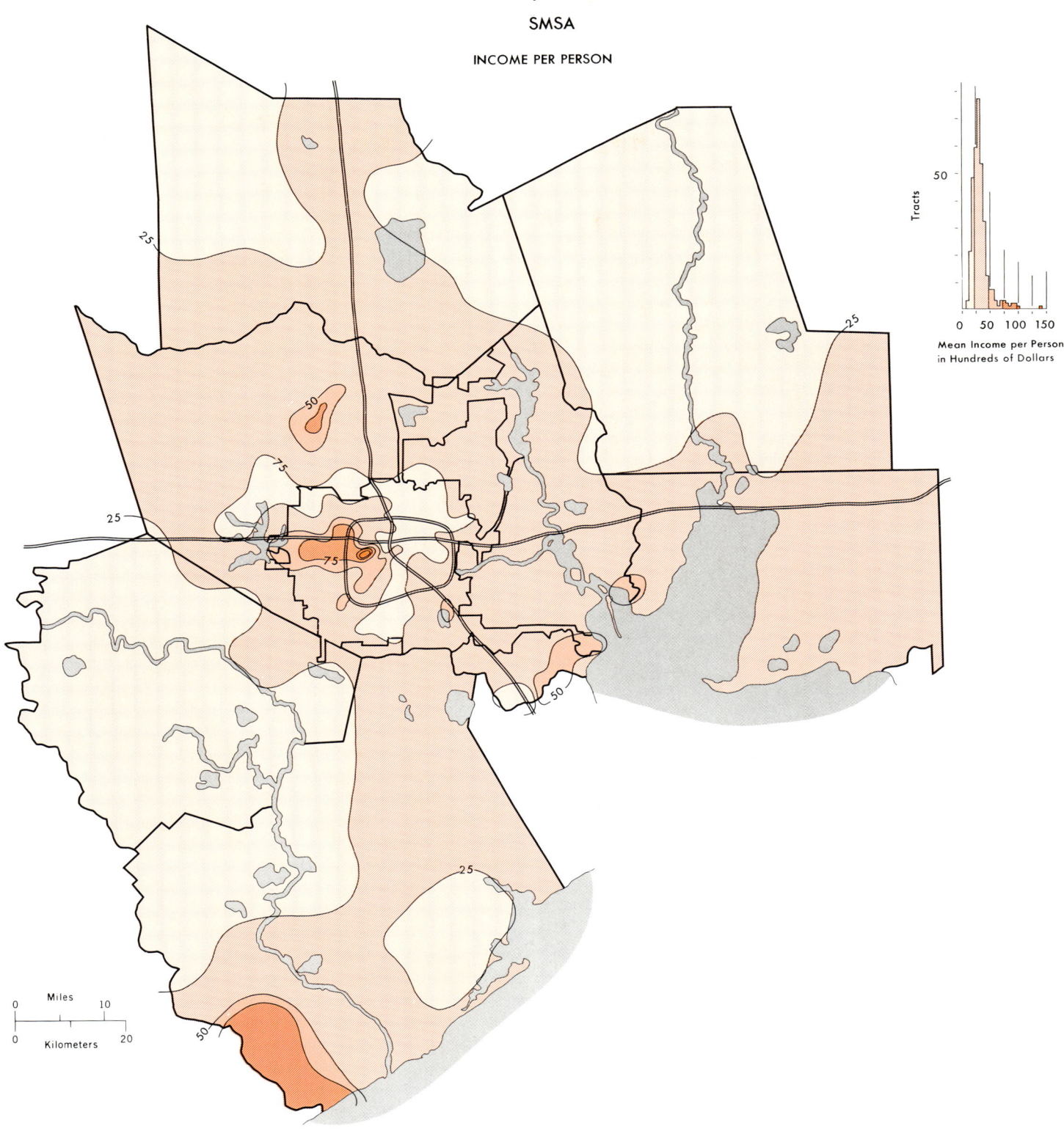

percentages are lower than 10 in a complicated pattern suggesting that there is significant socioeconomic differentiation among Houston's suburbs.

**Income.** Mean income per person in the Houston SMSA is $3,300 per year. Mean income per person in Houston is $3,400 per year. Usually incomes are lower in the central city than in the SMSA, and the reversal of this pattern in Houston emphasizes again the relative homogeneity of Houston and surrounding areas. Individual tract means vary from $1,000 to $14,000 per person annually. Incomes are below $2,500 throughout many of the peripheral rural areas where population is sparse. The largest concentration of low incomes occurs in the more densely populated area in south-central and northeastern Houston, with a westward extension outside Houston. Much of the area where incomes are less than $2,500 corresponds to Houston's predominantly black neighborhoods. The SMSA's highest incomes are concentrated on the west side of Houston with the peak west of the Houston CBD.

## TOPICS OF SPECIAL INTEREST IN THE HOUSTON REGION

**Population Change, 1960-1970.** (Histogram on p. 355.) The map of population change is produced by dividing each tract's 1970 population by its 1960 population. The quotient exceeds 1.0 if population increased over the decade, whereas it is a fractional value if population decreased. For the entire SMSA, the index of change is 1.39; for Houston it is 1.31. The metropolitan and city summary figures are based on population losses in tracts in and near downtown Houston and doubling, tripling, and quadrupling of population on the edge of Houston and in its suburbs. Rapid growth was most extensive

*Twentieth-Century Cities: Houston*

**SMSA**

POPULATION CHANGE, 1960-1970

(See Text)

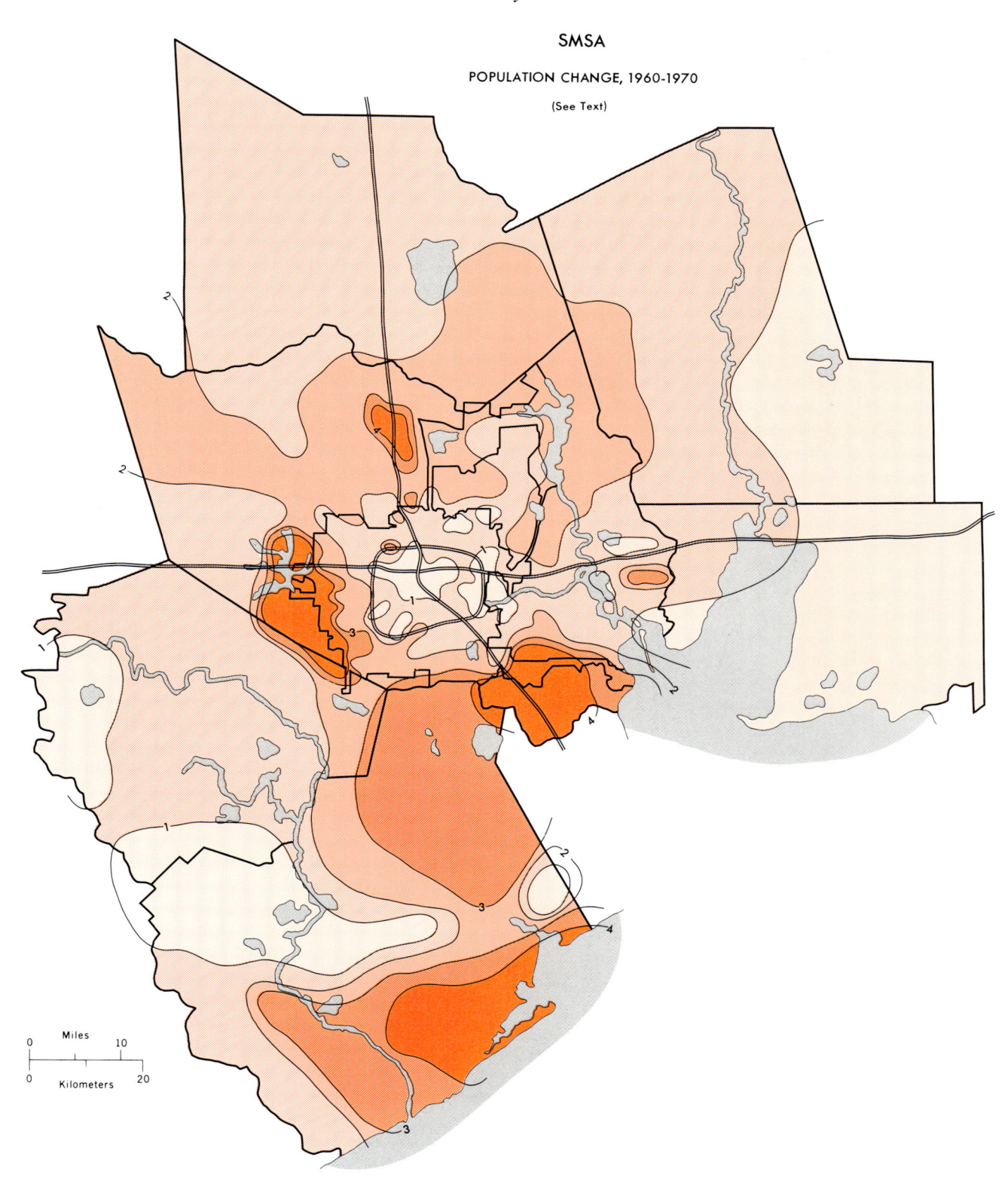

in Brazoria County during the 1960s, although greater numbers of people were involved in the increases in Harris County. More than doubling the population of an area during a decade often puts severe strain on local governments charged with providing such rapidly growing areas with public protection, sewers, water, and schools.

**Residential Change and New Housing.** In 1970, half the SMSA and city populations 5 years old and over lived in houses different from the dwellings they occupied in 1965. Such residential turnover is an index of transience and instability in some cities. In the Houston SMSA, some of the residential turnover in central-city Houston may be indicative of neighborhood instability, but elsewhere high rates of residential change from 1965 to 1970 reflect the movement of families into new housing. Many areas with high percentages of residential turnover correspond to areas where much if not most of the local housing stock was built from 1960 to March 1970. High rates of residential turnover in the Houston SMSA mean something quite different from similarly high rates in an eastern city, emphasizing once again the significant differences that exist among American metropolitan areas.

**Negroes and Spanish-Americans.** Houston has the largest urban black community in the South; the city's 317,000 blacks are 26 percent of the total city population. Houston contains 150,000 Spanish-Americans, and blacks and Spanish-Americans aggregate 38 percent of the city population. In combination, they dominate much of south and northeastern Houston, with little spillover into the suburbs. (SMSA maps are on pp. 387 and 395.) Blacks and Spanish-Americans

*Twentieth-Century Cities: Houston*

**SMSA**

RESIDENTIAL CHANGE, 1965-1970
(See Text)

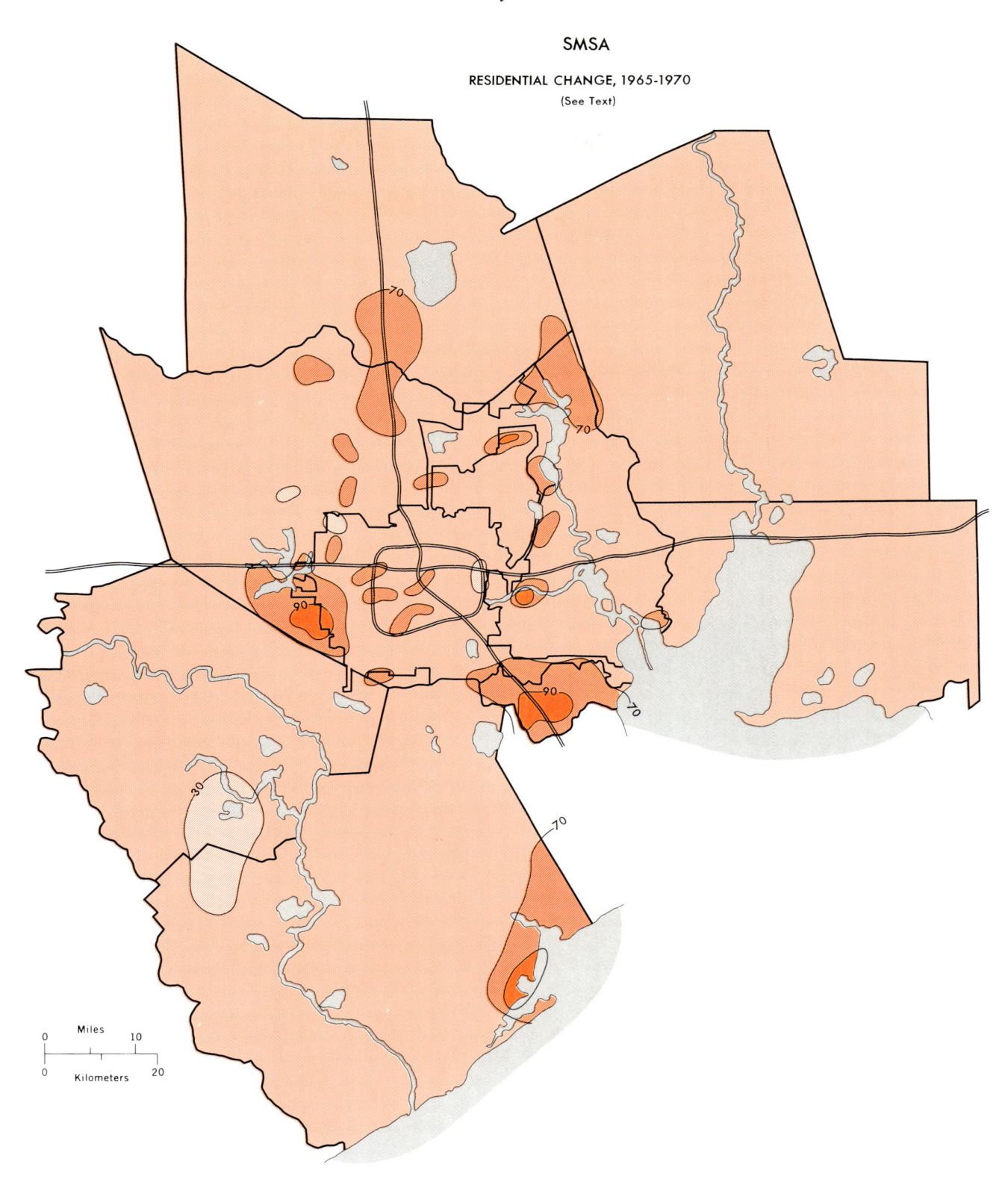

differ from the total population and from each other on several important dimensions. Whereas the mean household size for the entire city is 3.1 persons, Houston's average Spanish-American household has 4.1 persons and the average black household consists of 3.5 persons. But female headship is considerably more common among blacks than among Spanish-Americans, for 18 percent of Houston's black households are headed by females whereas only 9 percent of the Spanish-American households are.

Incomes also differ markedly. The mean family income for blacks is $7,000, well below the $9,300 mean for Spanish-American families, which in turn is well under the $13,200 mean for white families. Naturally, there are significant income and social differences within both the black and the Spanish-American communities, but the differences among white, black, and Spanish-American summary statistics indicate that Spanish-Americans and blacks especially still lack the skills and access to jobs that will provide them with incomes equal to those of whites.

**Poverty.** The consequence of limited participation in the job market and in prosperity generally is high levels of dependency and poverty in predominantly black and Spanish-Americans areas. In 1969 14 percent of all people in Houston had incomes below the poverty level, but blacks (93,200 persons or 54 percent of the poverty population) and Spanish-Americans (27,000 or 16 percent) are overrepresented in Houston's poverty population, blacks much more so than Spanish-Americans. The highest proportions of people below the poverty level occur where blacks are a significant minority if not a clear or overwhelming majority. Except for the tracts in Houston's northwest

## SMSA
### PERCENTAGE HOUSING BUILT 1960-1970

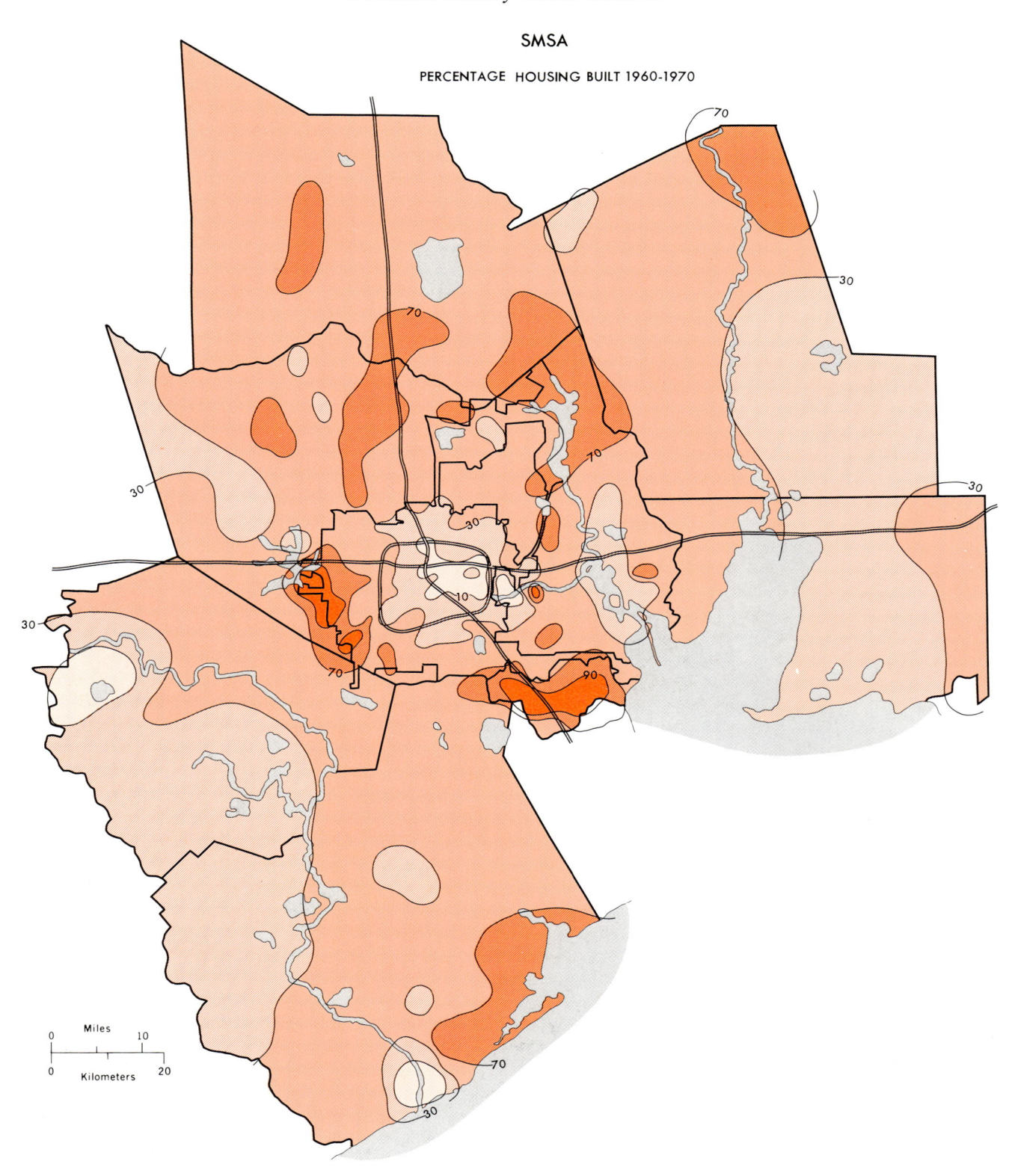

corner, no tract outside the black/Spanish-American area has more than 10 percent of its population below the poverty level.

---

The Houston metropolitan area is a new development in the evolution of American metropolitan regions. More of it was built in the 1950s and 1960s than any other SMSA in the atlas; it has faced fewer physical restraints on outward expansion than other metropolitan areas, and expansion has been less inhibited by zoning. As a result, it is the most spread-out city in the nation, settled at half the density of Los Angeles, the place that is usually cited as exhibit A in the indictment against urban sprawl. Houston sprawls twice as much as Los Angeles, yet it seems to work no worse than many other places.

Recent growth and the city's unusual capability of expanding its boundaries as settlement proceeds outward have produced a city and metropolitan area in which most of the city-suburb distinctions and dichotomies that are valid in other parts of the nation are inappropriate. With the glaring exception of black and Spanish-American minority groups, there are few statistical differences between Houston and the rest of Harris County. Perhaps the best hope the minority groups have for eventual full participation in Houston's social, economic, and political life is that in contrast to most other cities, they are not being relegated to an increasingly minority-dominated central city by the flight of prosperous whites to the suburbs.

*Twentieth-Century Cities: Houston*

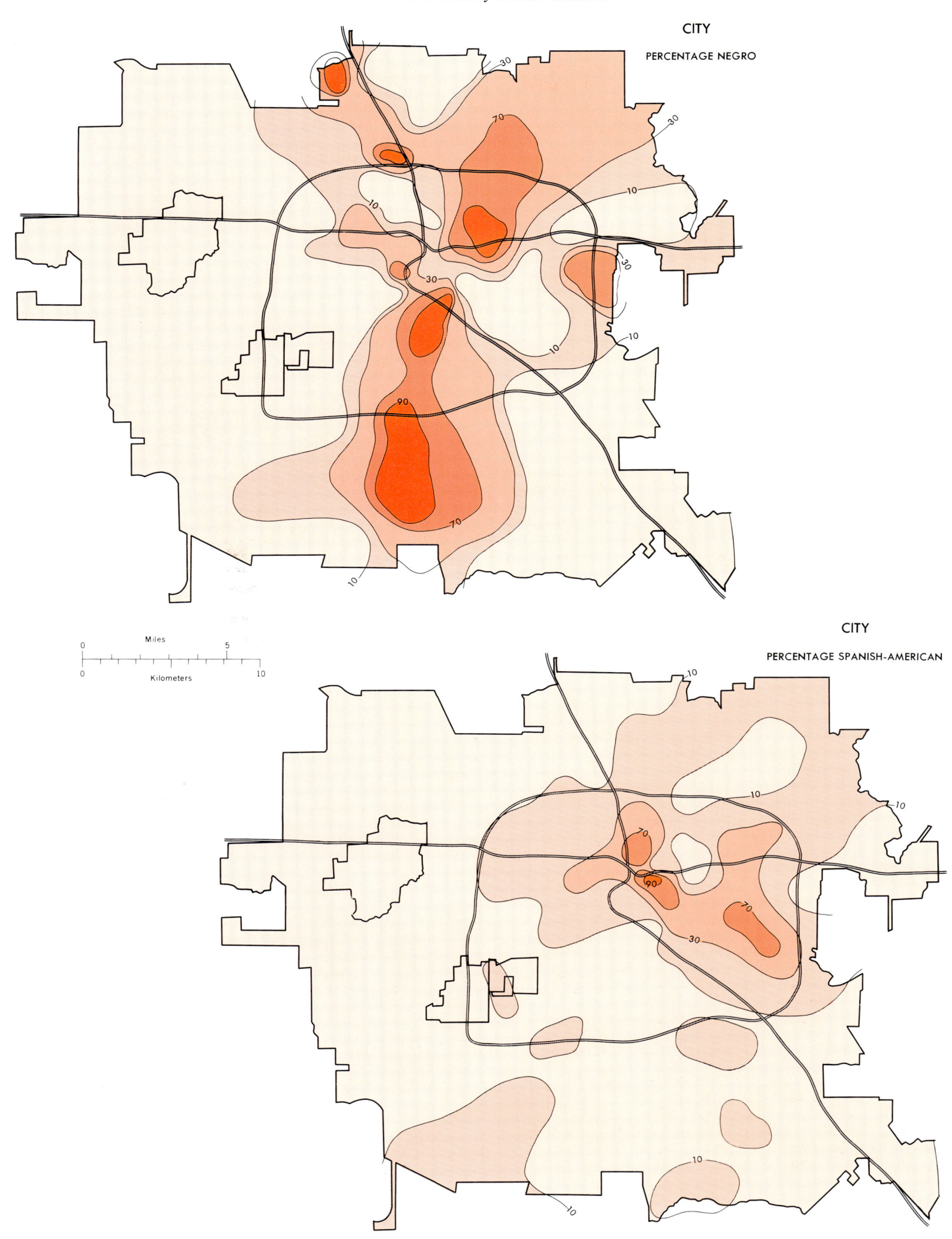

CITY
PERCENTAGE NEGRO

CITY
PERCENTAGE SPANISH-AMERICAN

*Twentieth-Century Cities: Houston*

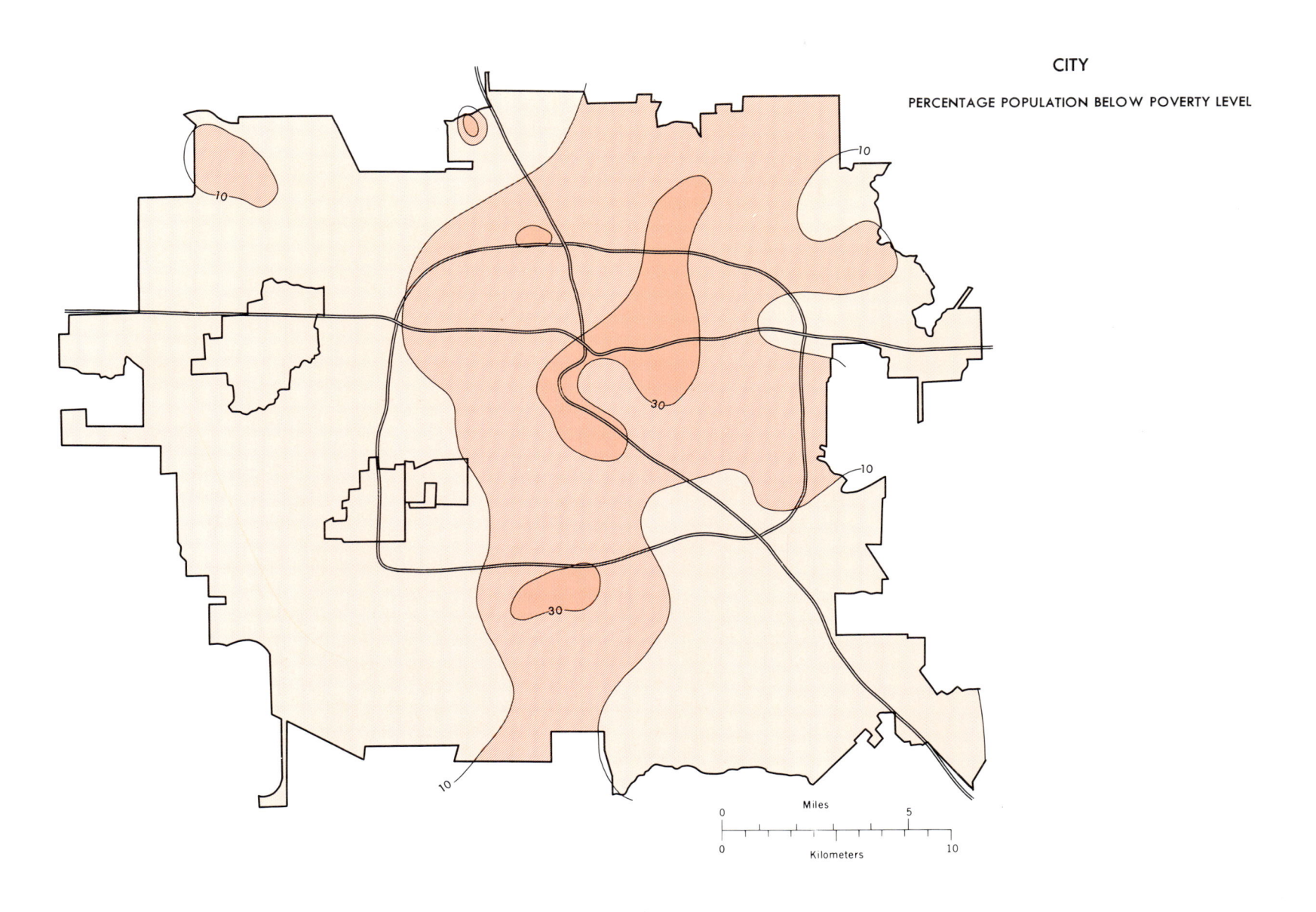

**CITY**

PERCENTAGE POPULATION BELOW POVERTY LEVEL

# CHAPTER 22

# Los Angeles

*Los Angeles may be the ultimate city of our age.*

CHRISTOPHER RAND, *Los Angeles:
The Ultimate City*, 1967

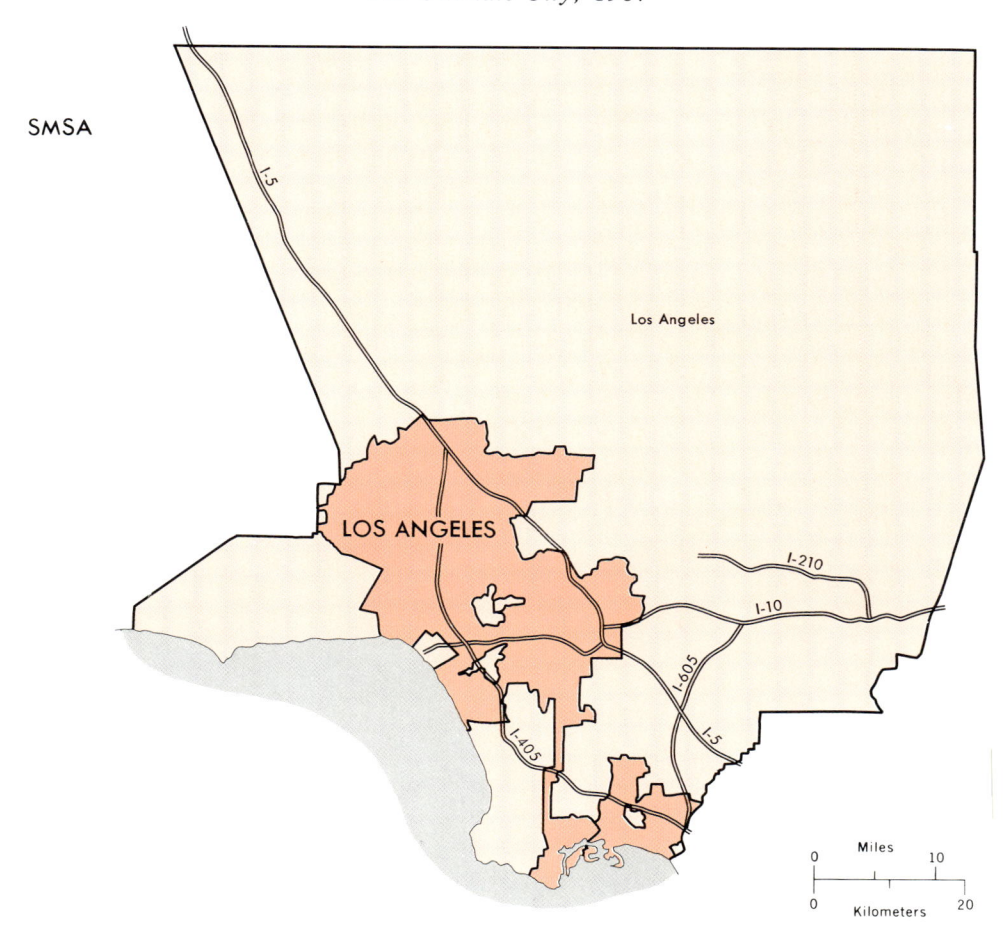

The Los Angeles-Long Beach Standard Metropolitan Statistical Area (SMSA) is the 2nd most populous in the nation. It has a population of 7,036,000; 2,816,000 (40 percent) live in Los Angeles and 359,000 (5 percent) live in Long Beach. The remaining 55 percent of the SMSA population lives in suburban communities or in the city's municipal enclaves. The Los Angeles-Long Beach SMSA is surrounded by 5 other SMSAs, and the aggregate population of the 6 SMSAs approaches 12,000,000 people. The Daily Urban System (DUS) defined by counties that have at least 5 percent of their labor forces working in Los Angeles County includes Orange, Riverside, San Bernardino, and Ventura counties (p. 221). It has a total population of 9,981,000 people and is the nation's 2nd most populous DUS. Most of the increase over the SMSA population is attributable to Orange County (the Anaheim-Santa Ana-Garden Grove SMSA has 1,420,000 people) and Riverside and San Bernardino counties (the San Bernardino-Riverside-Ontario SMSA has 1,143,000 people).

*Note:* All data are from the 1970 Censuses of Population and Housing unless otherwise indicated. Therefore the present tense refers to 1970 data except for income data which are from 1969. Cartographic conventions are explained in Chapter 1.

The southern California metropolitan complex developed recently and quickly. In 1900, there were only 102,000 people in Los Angeles whereas in New York there were 3,400,000 and in Chicago, 1,700,000. By 1940 Los Angeles had grown to 1,500,000 (p. 10). Between 1940 and 1970, 5 million people migrated to southern California. By 1970, the Los Angeles SMSA had nosed Chicago (6,978,000 people) out of 2nd place among American metropolitan areas. Although increases slowed somewhat toward the end of the 1960s, growth during the decade was identical to the national metropolitan increase of 16.6 percent. In contrast to the population of most central cities, the combined populations of Los Angeles-Long Beach increased 12 percent during the decade.

Los Angeles and Long Beach sprawl across a variety of landscapes ranging from sea level to elevations of more than 5,000 feet (1,525 meters). The area of original settlement near the Central Business District (CBD) is in the Los Angeles River Valley and is relatively flat and low-lying. Level terrain stretches south all the way to Long Beach, with the Dominguez Hills rising to elevations of over 1,000

*Twentieth-Century Cities: Los Angeles*

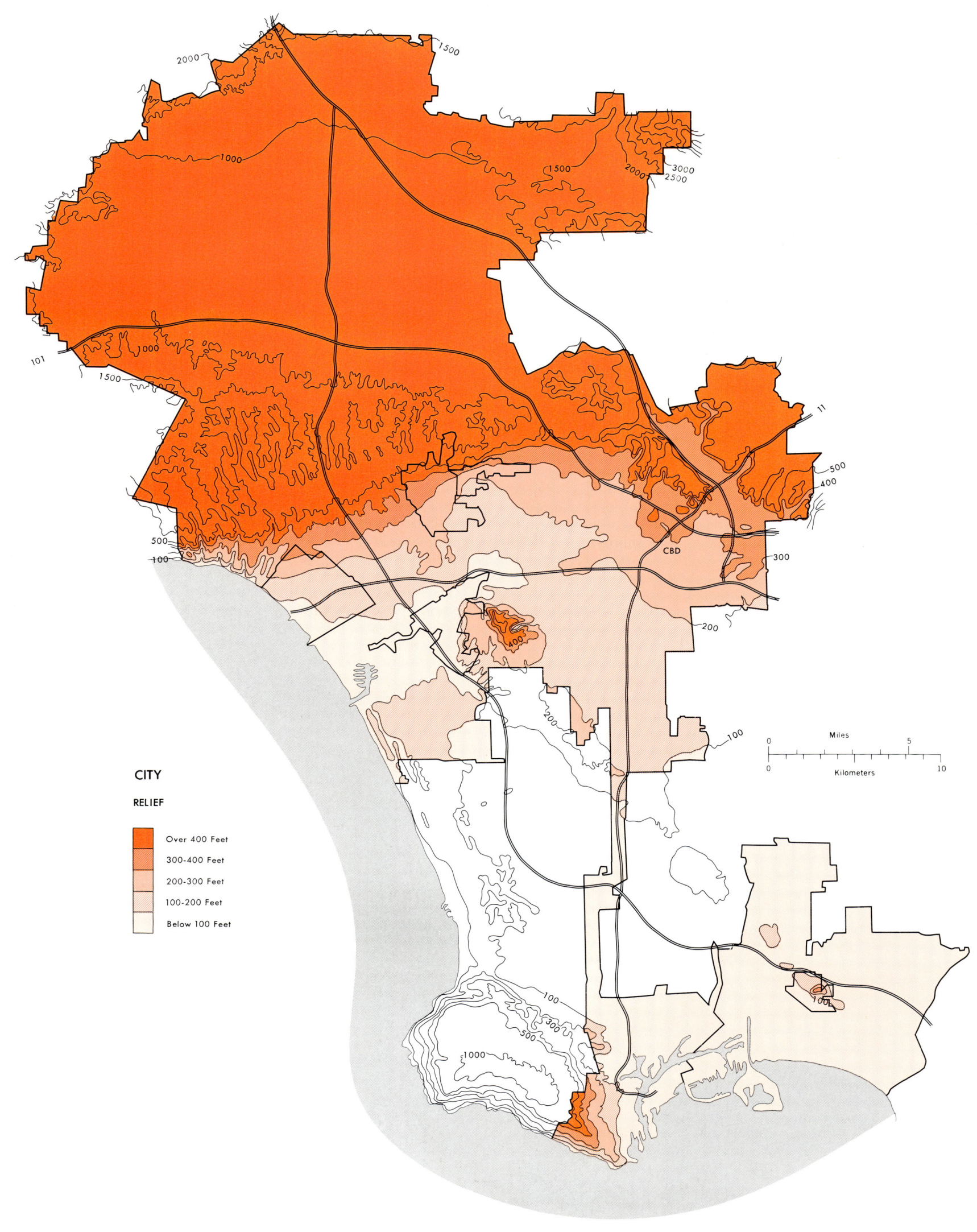

**CITY**

RELIEF

- Over 400 Feet
- 300-400 Feet
- 200-300 Feet
- 100-200 Feet
- Below 100 Feet

## Twentieth-Century Cities: Los Angeles

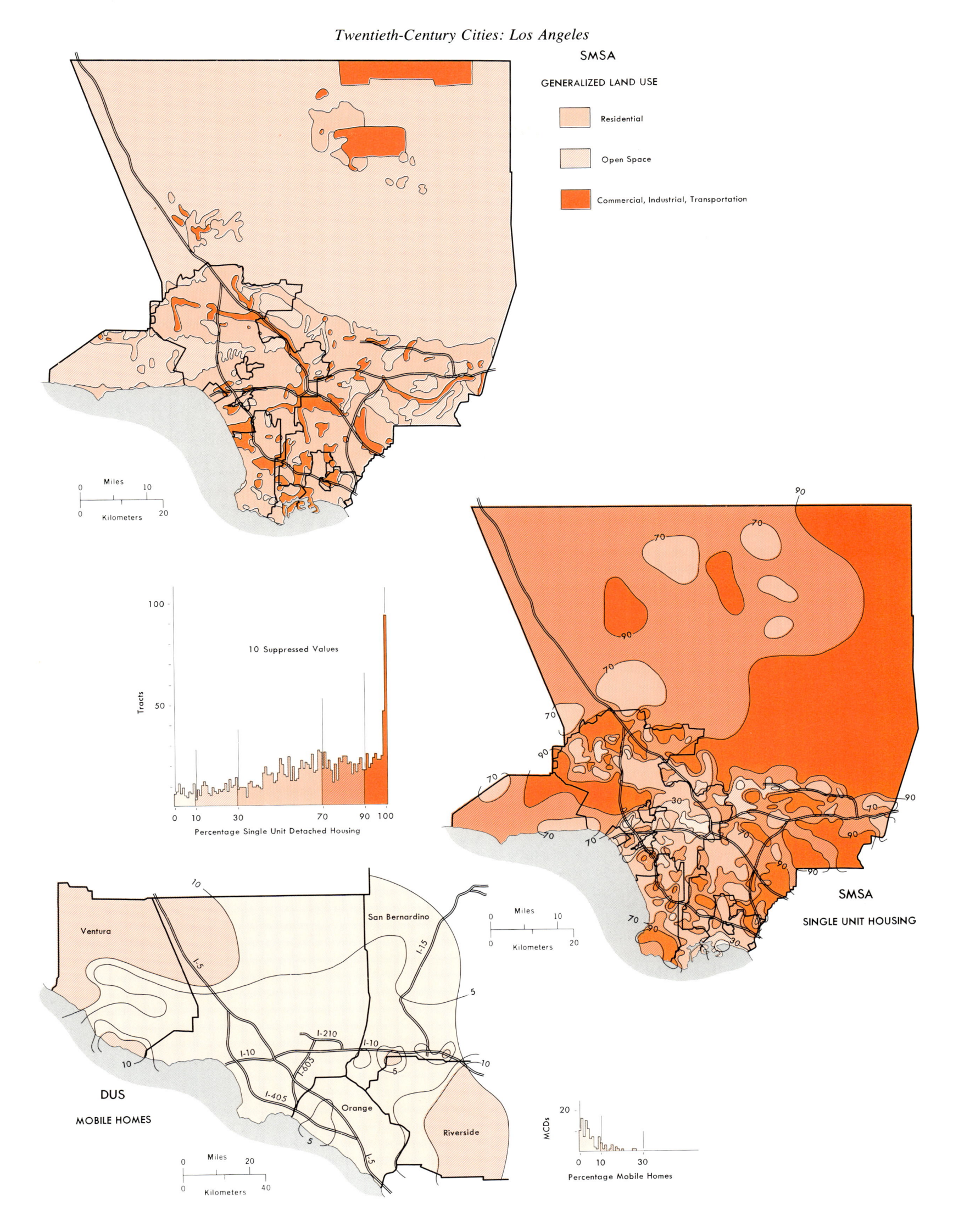

### SMSA
#### GENERALIZED LAND USE

- Residential
- Open Space
- Commercial, Industrial, Transportation

### SMSA
#### SINGLE UNIT HOUSING

### DUS
#### MOBILE HOMES

10 Suppressed Values

Percentage Single Unit Detached Housing

Percentage Mobile Homes

221

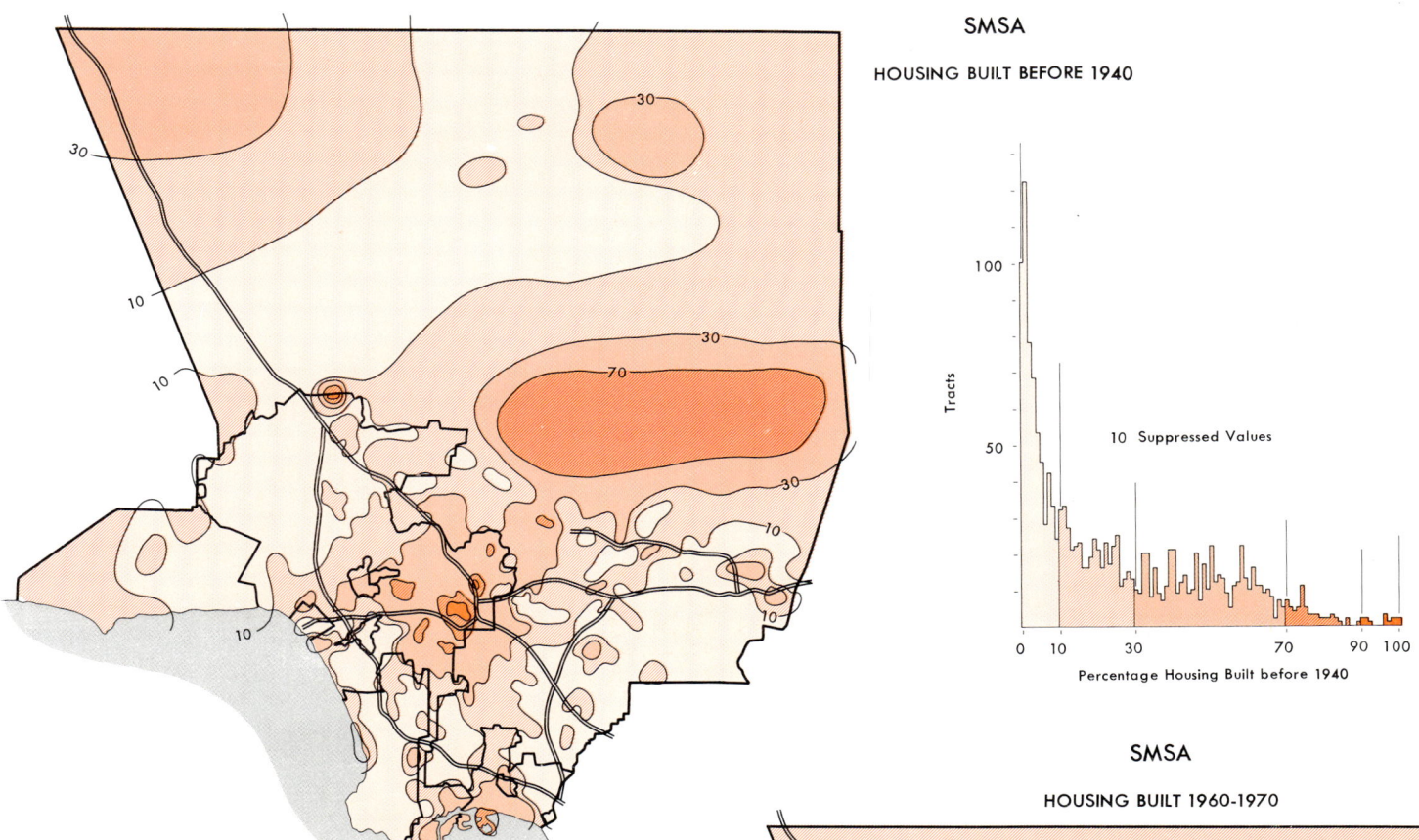

## Twentieth-Century Cities: Los Angeles

### SMSA
#### HOUSING BUILT BEFORE 1940

### SMSA
#### HOUSING BUILT 1960-1970

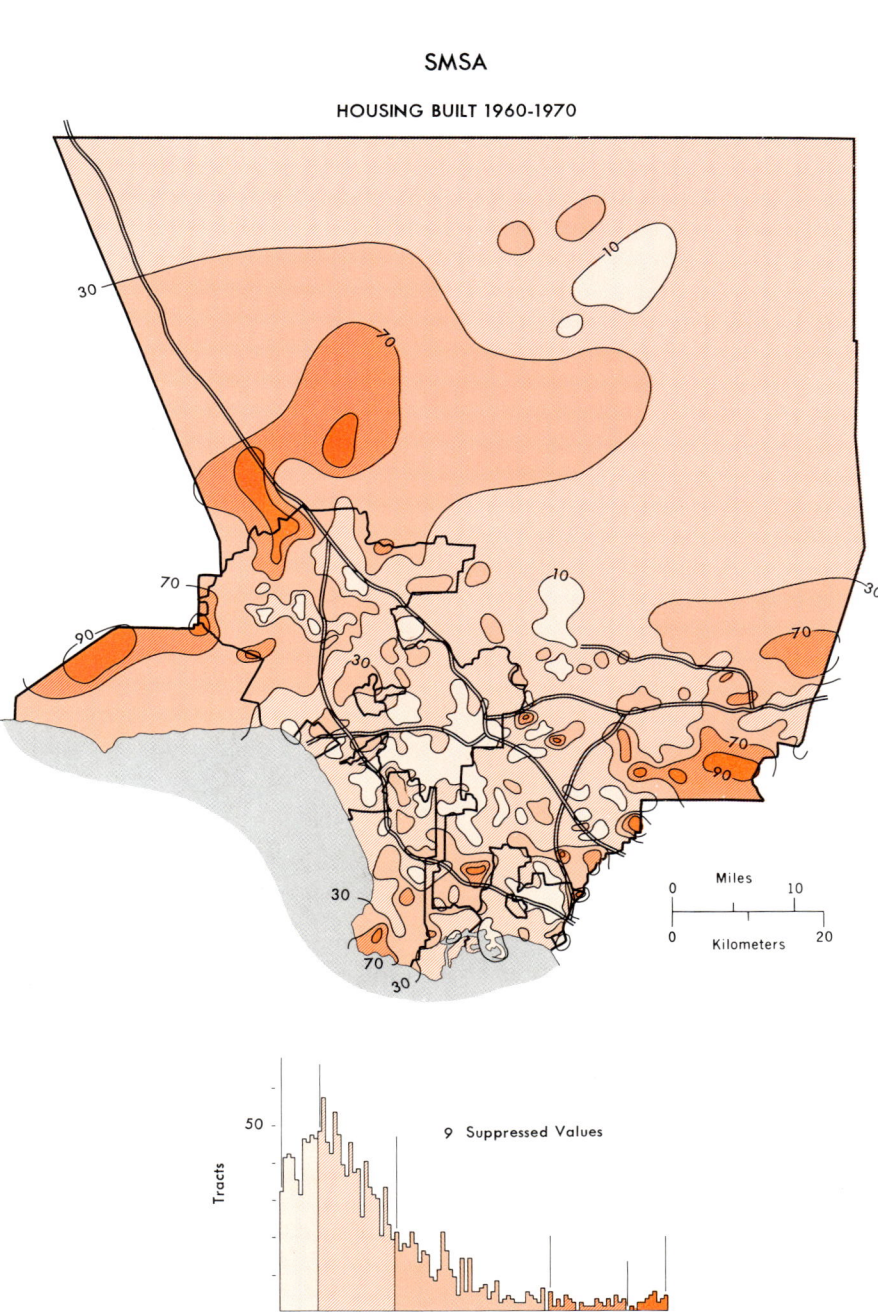

feet (300 meters) north of Long Beach. The foothills of the San Gabriel Mountains rise northeast of the CBD, and the Santa Monica Mountains reach elevations of 1,500 feet (460 meters) northwest of the downtown. A narrow gap between the two ranges connects the older parts of the city of Los Angeles with the San Fernando Valley, which comprises most of the northern part of the city. The Santa Susana Mountains are just north of the city boundary.

The city of Los Angeles expanded rapidly after 1900, absorbing formerly independent cities in the process. It began to import water from the Owens Valley east of the Sierra Nevada in 1913 and soon found it had more water than it could use. The surplus was offered to neighboring areas that were willing to be annexed. In the semiarid climate, the lure of assured water was attractive, and 49 separate annexations over a period of 15 years enlarged the city to 440 square miles. Ten independent cities and the San Fernando Valley were absorbed in the process. Some areas, such as West Hollywood, Beverly Hills, Santa Monica, and Culver City, chose not to be annexed, and they remain today as municipal enclaves within the city of Los Angeles.

Land use in the SMSA is determined by a combination of terrain and transportation. Most of the higher elevations are open space, although there is much residential and industrial land use in the Dominguez Hills, and the Santa Monicas are being penetrated on their flanks along the axes of the canyons. Ribbons of commercial, industrial, and transportation land use often appear along rail routes and freeways that frequently run parallel to each other. Much of the area along the Los Angeles-Long Beach boundary is given over to land use associated with the adjacent Los Angeles harbor and navy base. Low-density residential land use dominates most of the southern third of the SMSA, with open space and commercial/industrial land use scattered through the basically residential fabric. The middle and western parts of the SMSA are rugged to mountainous; much of the area is part of the Los Angeles National Forest, which is an important recreational resource for SMSA residents. The hills and mountains of the middle zone give way to the Mojave Desert in the northeastern quadrant. Settlement throughout most of the northern half of the SMSA is sparse to almost nonexistent except near military bases.

*Twentieth-Century Cities: Los Angeles*

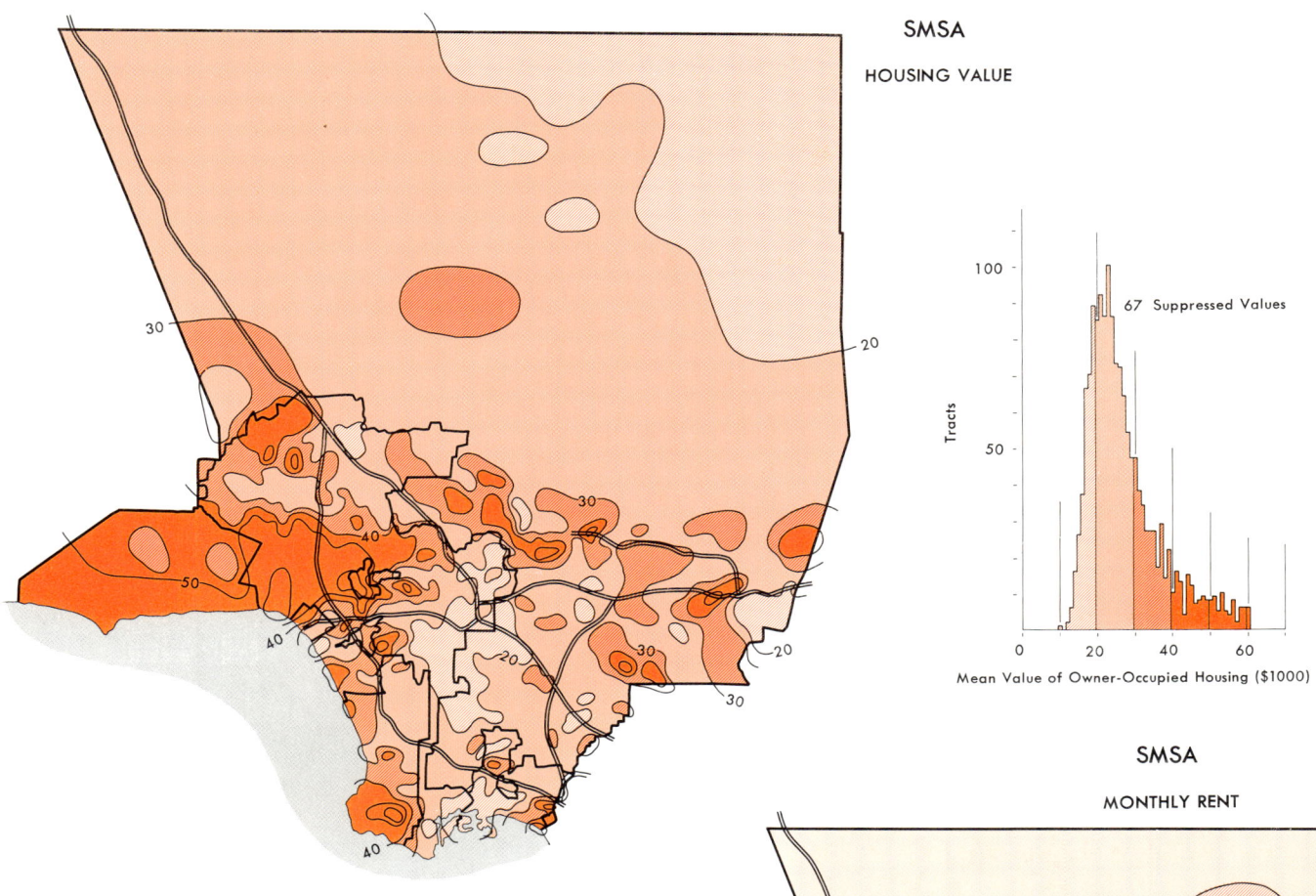

## HOUSING

**Housing Age.** Twenty-five percent of the SMSA's housing was built before 1940, 24 percent was built from 1940 through 1959, and the remaining 51 percent was built from 1960 to March 1970. The Los Angeles housing stock differs somewhat from the SMSA inventory: 32 percent is pre-1940, 23 percent dates from 1940 through 1959, and 45 percent from 1960 to March 1970. Los Angeles has 50 percent of the pre-1940 housing stock compared with its 42 percent share of all housing units, so old housing is only slightly concentrated in the city. Individual tract percentages of old housing vary from zero to 100, and most tracts are clustered in the lower half of the range, especially at the lower end. Tracts with more than 90 percent pre-1940 housing are rare, occurring only near downtown Los Angeles and in the northern San Fernando Valley. Percentages of older housing decrease outward from the Los Angeles core with some regularity, dropping to less than 10 percent outside central Los Angeles and away from the Los Angeles-Long Beach corridor. Proportions rise above general values in old settlements. The smallness of the areas where old housing exceeds 90 or even 70 percent suggests that most tracts have a mixture of housing, a suggestion reinforced by the shape of the new-housing distribution, which also has few tracts with proportions over 50 percent. The Los Angeles SMSA does not have the monolithic tracts of new housing often associated with it in popular accounts. Most tracts contain more of a mixture of pre-World War II and postwar housing than is true in eastern cities.

Tract percentages of housing built from 1960 to March 1970 range from zero to 100. The absence of wholesale similarities between the pre-1940 housing map and the map of 1960-1970 housing emphasizes once again the complexity of the region's stock. Although proportions of new housing are low in the south-central area of Los Angeles, and although proportions generally rise with distance from the CBD, there are numerous peaks and valleys in the surface caused by concentrations of new and old housing, which occur in equally small fragments. The most regular zones of housing age are in the almost uninhabited northern half of the SMSA.

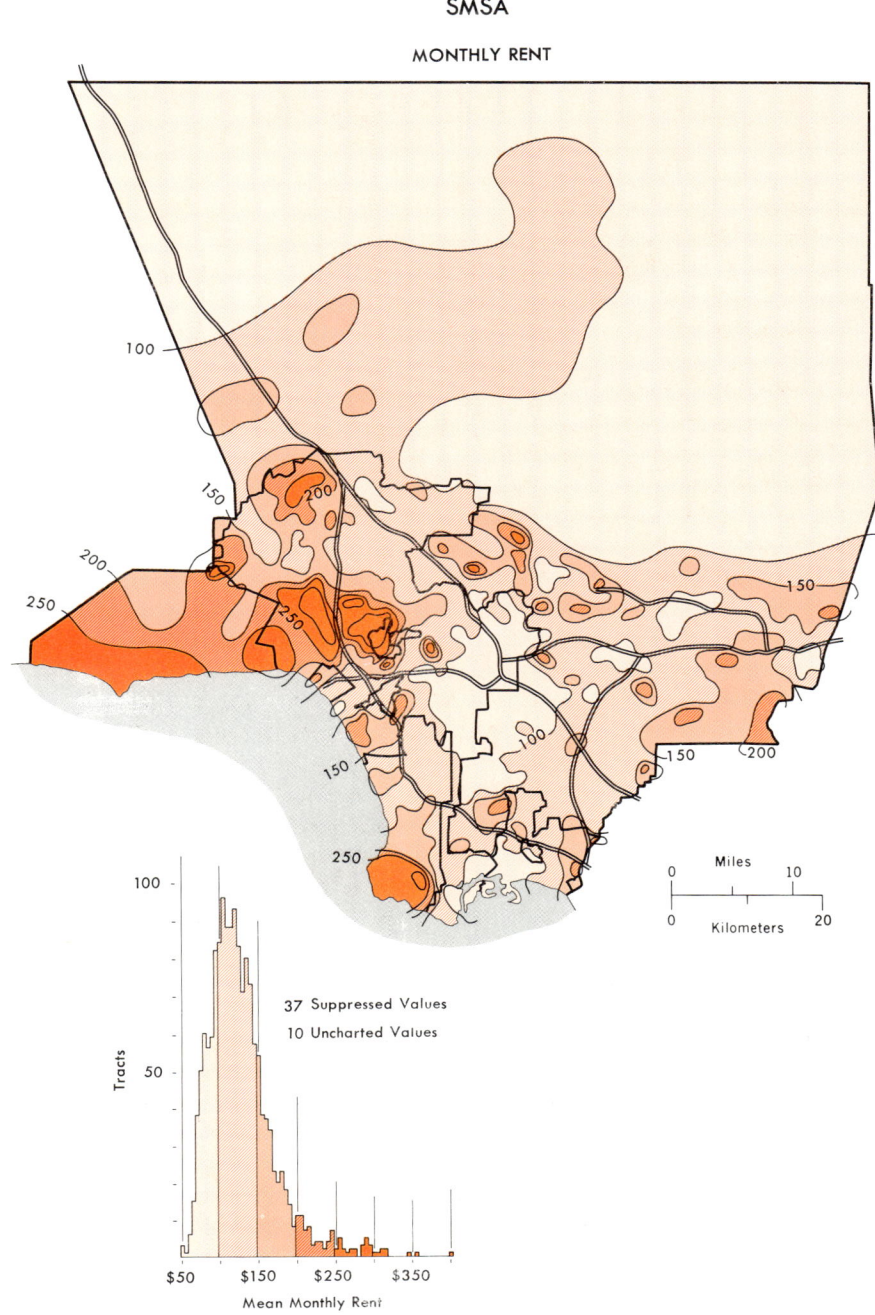

223

**Mobile Homes.** There are 85,400 mobile homes in the Los Angeles DUS which comprise 2.4 percent of the region's housing stock. Few municipalities have no mobile homes, but such housing is less than 5 percent of local inventories in Los Angeles and the immediate vicinity. There are 6,200 mobile homes in Los Angeles, which are 0.6 percent of all housing units. Mobile homes constitute 1.5 percent of the housing units in Los Angeles County, but they exceed 5 percent of local housing stocks only in the sparsely populated northern part of the county. Similarly, mobile homes are more prevalent in sparsely populated areas of Riverside (8.6 percent), San Bernardino (4.7 percent), and Ventura (4.2 percent) counties than they are in more densely settled Orange County (3.8 percent).

**Single-Unit Detached Housing.** Individual dwelling units make up 62 percent of the SMSA housing stock and 52 percent of the housing inventory in Los Angeles. Individual tract proportions range from zero to 100 percent; many more tracts are in the upper half than in the lower half of the range. The pattern of single-unit housing is complex, reflecting the existence of numerous independent centers of settlement. Tracts with proportions below 10 percent cluster near the CBDs of Los Angeles and Long Beach, but elsewhere in the SMSA patterns are irregular as a result of the region's complex settlement history. Most of the SMSA's multiple units are structures with 5 to 49 units (24 percent of the total housing stock). Large (50 or more units) structures provide only 4 percent of all housing; duplexes (4 percent) and 3- or 4-unit structures (6 percent) are also relatively unimportant. In Los Angeles, 30 percent of all housing units are located in structures with 5 to 49 units; 5 percent are in buildings with 50 or more units; another 5 percent are in duplexes; and 3- and 4-unit structures (8 percent) account for the rest.

**Housing Value and Rent.** The mean value of owner-occupied housing in the SMSA is $28,000, and the corresponding value for Los Angeles is $30,500. It is unusual for the central-city housing value to be higher than the SMSA mean, especially by a difference of $2,500. The anomaly results because the SMSA's peak housing values are inside rather than outside the city, a reversal of the pattern in most of the other SMSAs. Housing values in Los Angeles and the SMSA are high compared with other SMSAs. Tract mean values vary from $10,000 to $60,000. Once again, some regularities that appear in many American SMSAs are absent in the Los Angeles area. There is a core region astride the eastern boundary of the city where values are generally below $29,000. The more elevated locations in the San Gabriel foothills, the Santa Monicas, the Dominguez Hills, and the more scenic areas along the Pacific appear as high values on the map. Apart from those obvious variations, housing values rise and fall in a complicated pattern based on the local qualities of housing and the physical environment.

Monthly contract rents average $118 in the SMSA and $116 in Los Angeles. Individual tract means vary from $50 to over $500. The map of rents is similar in some respects to the map of housing values because areas that have high or low housing values also have high or low rents. The map of rents is not quite as broken up by high and low patches as is the housing-value map. However, it is far more complicated than the rent maps for most other SMSAs, even those for New York and Chicago (pp. 34 and 138).

## THE PEOPLE

**Population Density.** The overall population density of Los Angeles is 6,100 people per square mile (2,350 per square kilometer). Long Beach's density is 7,400 per square mile (2,850 per square kilometer). Individual tract densities range from 1,000 to 41,000 people per square mile (390 to 15,800 per square kilometer), although few tract densities exceed 20,000 people per square mile (7,700 per square kilometer). The inclusion of nonresidential areas in density calculations means that actual population densities in some parts of the city are higher than the gross densities mapped here. Densities over 10,000 people per square mile (3,860 per square kilometer) are largely concentrated in central Los Angeles and Long Beach. A few tract densities exceed 20,000 (7,700 per square kilometer). Outside these central areas, densities over 10,000 (3,860) are isolated occurrences. The low densities reflect the large proportion of urban growth in the Los Angeles area that occurred during the automobile era and the preferences of residents for low-rise, dispersed living. An SMSA map is on p. 316.

**Age and the Elderly.** There is little difference between Los Angeles and the entire SMSA in overall age-sex structure. The median age of the SMSA population is 29 years. The city median is slightly older at 30 years. The slightly larger 6- to 20-year-old age group in the SMSA pyramid indicates a normal preference of families with young children for suburban housing, but the similarities of the pyramids are more striking than the evident differences.

Tract medians vary from 12 to 70 years. Two groups of tracts have median ages under 20 years. The one located on the SMSA's eastern boundary consists of middle-class families with young children. The second cluster east of the corridor of Los Angeles extending south to Los Angeles Harbor is in an area occupied primarily by blacks. Median ages are high in central Los Angeles, especially in the West Hollywood, Beverly Hills, and Santa Monica areas. Although some of the SMSA's highest median ages are produced by institutions, the zone of high median ages in the SMSA center occurs "naturally" and is one of the many unusual features of the region. The highest median age (60) occurs in a tract in Long Beach that is populated almost exclusively by retired people.

People 64 years of age and older make up 9 percent of the SMSA's population and 10 percent of Los Angeles's people. Tract percentages vary from zero to 60, but in few tracts are more than 30 percent of the people in the over-64 category. The elderly consistently exceed 10 percent of tract populations in central Los Angeles, the eastern suburbs, and in central Long Beach. The northern part of the SMSA, where the elderly also exceed 10 percent of local populations, is sparsely populated.

**Sex Ratio.** There are 1.07 females for each male in the SMSA, which yields a female-dominant sex ratio (males divided by females times 100) of 94. In Los Angeles the sex ratio is almost the same, 93. The SMSA sex ratio patterns are related to population density and the locations of military facilities. Most densely settled parts of the region are female-dominant, as is usually true in metropolitan regions. Military bases raise sex ratios well over 100 in the northern half of the SMSA and in the vicinity of the U.S. Navy facilities in Long Beach. The 100 isopleth of male-female balance approximates the outer edge of the built-up residential area in the central part of the SMSA. It separates the female-dominant urban population from the rural population. Rural populations are often male-dominant even in the absence of military facilities such as those located in northern Los Angeles County.

**Negroes.** There are 522,597 blacks in Los Angeles and Long Beach. They comprise 16 percent of the combined populations of the cities. Although in the early part of the century blacks were widely scattered, neighborhoods once separate have now coalesced into a massive ghetto of 40 square miles that stretches southward 12 miles and eastward 3 to 7 miles from the CBD. Generally speaking, higher-income blacks live west of the Harbor Freeway, which bisects the black community; the areas east of the freeway are less affluent. Watts, scene of the 1969 disturbances, is the appendage immediately to the left of the map scale. (An SMSA map is on p. 388.)

*Twentieth-Century Cities: Los Angeles*

CITY

PEOPLE PER SQUARE MILE

Thousands of People per Square Mile

Nonresidential Areas

225

*Twentieth-Century Cities: Los Angeles*

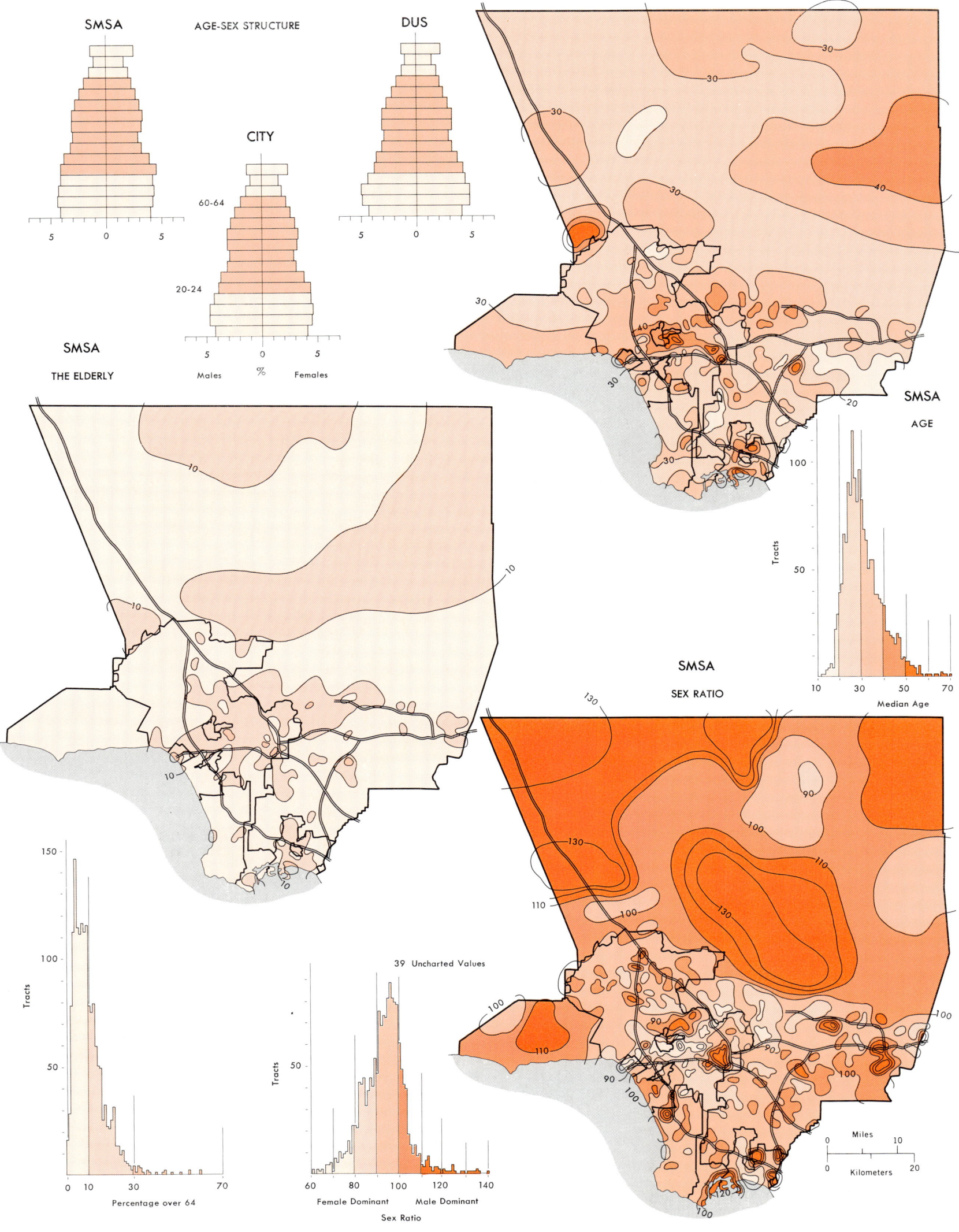

226

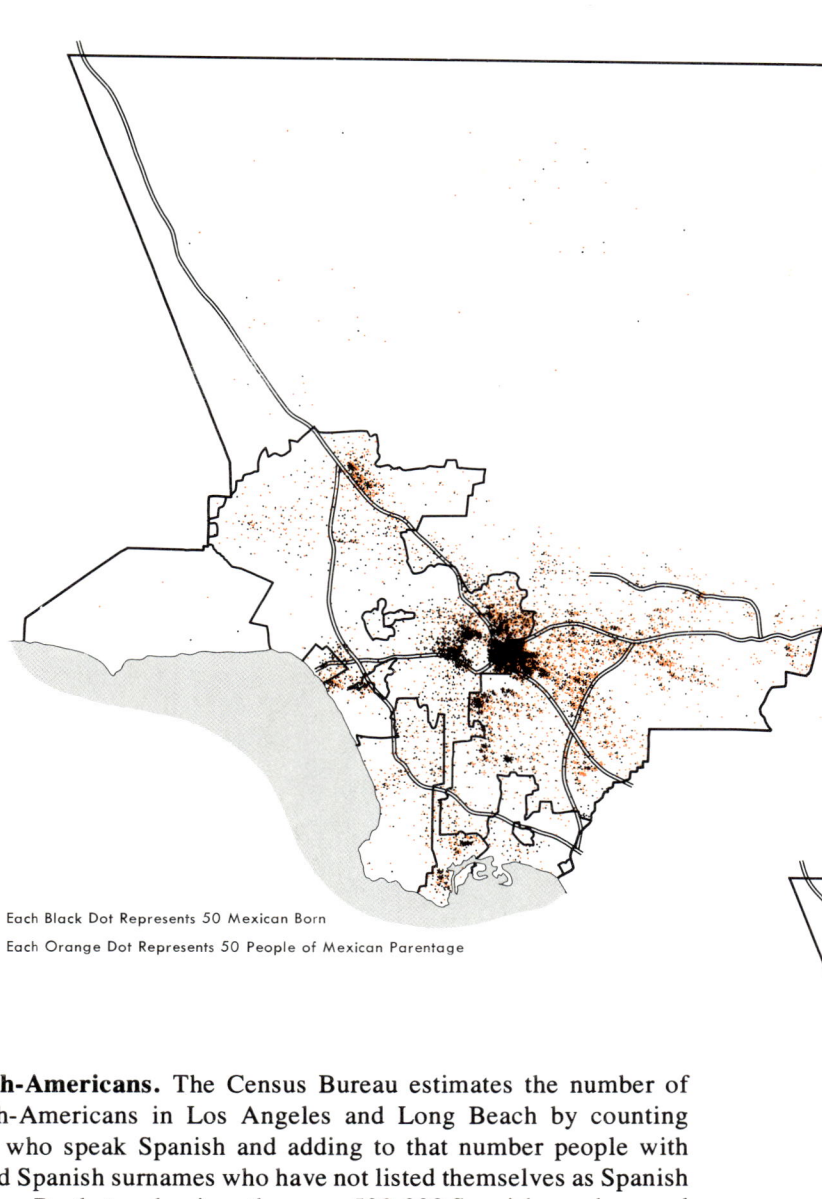

*Twentieth-Century Cities: Los Angeles*

SMSA

MEXICAN-AMERICANS

Each Black Dot Represents 50 Mexican Born
Each Orange Dot Represents 50 People of Mexican Parentage

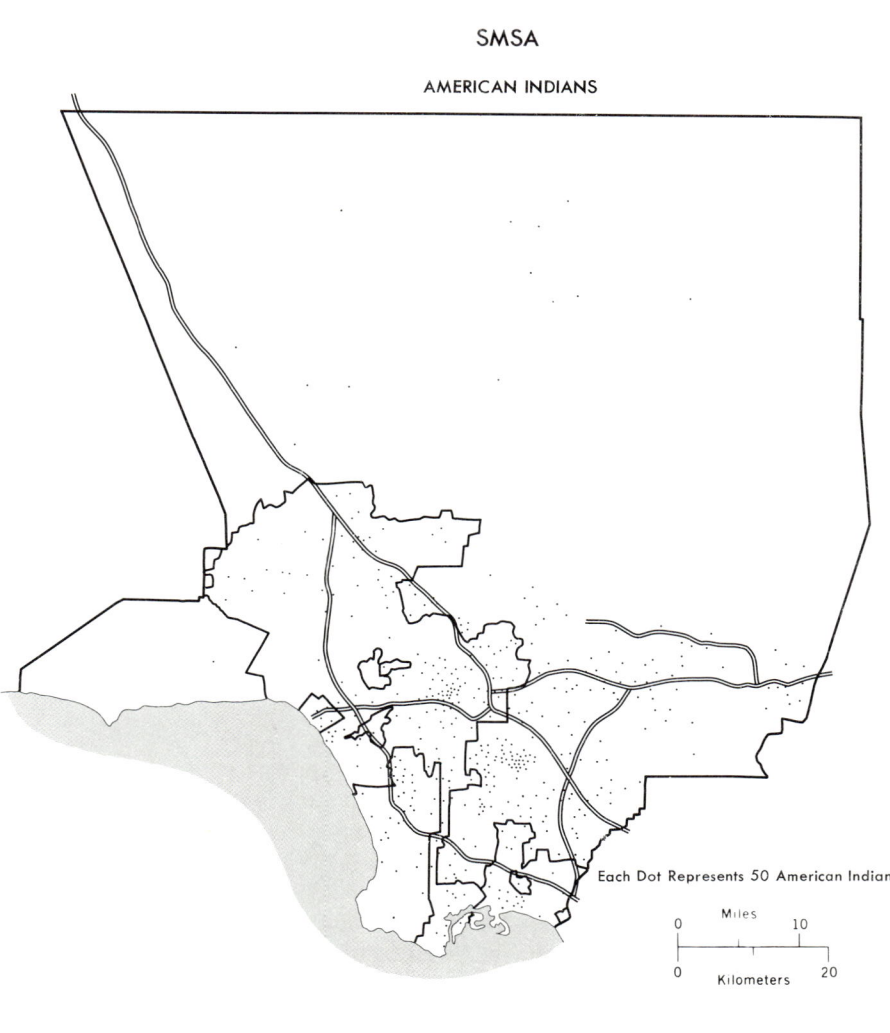

SMSA

AMERICAN INDIANS

Each Dot Represents 50 American Indians

**Spanish-Americans.** The Census Bureau estimates the number of Spanish-Americans in Los Angeles and Long Beach by counting people who speak Spanish and adding to that number people with selected Spanish surnames who have not listed themselves as Spanish speakers. By that reckoning, there are 503,000 Spanish speakers and 42,000 people with Spanish surnames, a total Spanish-American population of 545,000 or 17 percent of the cities' populations. The most intense concentrations of Hispanics occur northeast of the Los Angeles CBD, where a few tracts have Spanish-American populations exceeding 90 percent. There are also less intense concentrations in the southernmost extension of Los Angeles and in the San Fernando Valley on the north. The composition of the central cities' Spanish community breaks down as follows: Mexican foreign stock, 41.7 percent (228,000); indigenous Americans of Mexican descent, 42.3 percent (230,000); Central and South American foreign stock, 10.5 percent (57,000); Cuban foreign stock, 3.6 percent (20,000); and Puerto Ricans, 1.9 percent (10,000). (An SMSA map is on p. 396.)

**Mexican-Americans.** The Los Angeles SMSA's Mexican foreign stock numbers 207,000 Mexican-born and 303,000 with at least one Mexican-born parent. Mexican foreign stock is 7.2 percent of the SMSA population. Although some Mexican-Americans are scattered throughout the SMSA, the Mexican-American minority is especially concentrated around the Los Angeles downtown, especially on its east side. Half of the SMSA's Mexican-born and 40 percent of those of Mexican parentage reside within Los Angeles. Long Beach has few Mexican-Americans, its total Mexican stock aggregating but 1.5 percent of the Long Beach population. The Los Angeles Mexican-American population is the largest urban concentration in the world outside Mexico City.

**American Indians.** There are 24,500 American Indians in the Los Angeles SMSA according to the Census Bureau, but this is probably an underestimate. Indians are scattered throughout the metropolitan area and are not particularly concentrated in Los Angeles, which has 37 percent of the Indian population compared with 40 percent of the total population. Long Beach also has about as many as might be expected, given its share of the SMSA population. Aside from the slight clustering evident northwest of the Los Angeles CBD and south of the Mexican-American *barrio*, the SMSA's Indians show no tendency to concentrate in small areas.

**Chinese-Americans.** The census questionnaire requires that all nonwhite persons identify themselves as members of 1 of 8 "racial"

*Twentieth-Century Cities: Los Angeles*

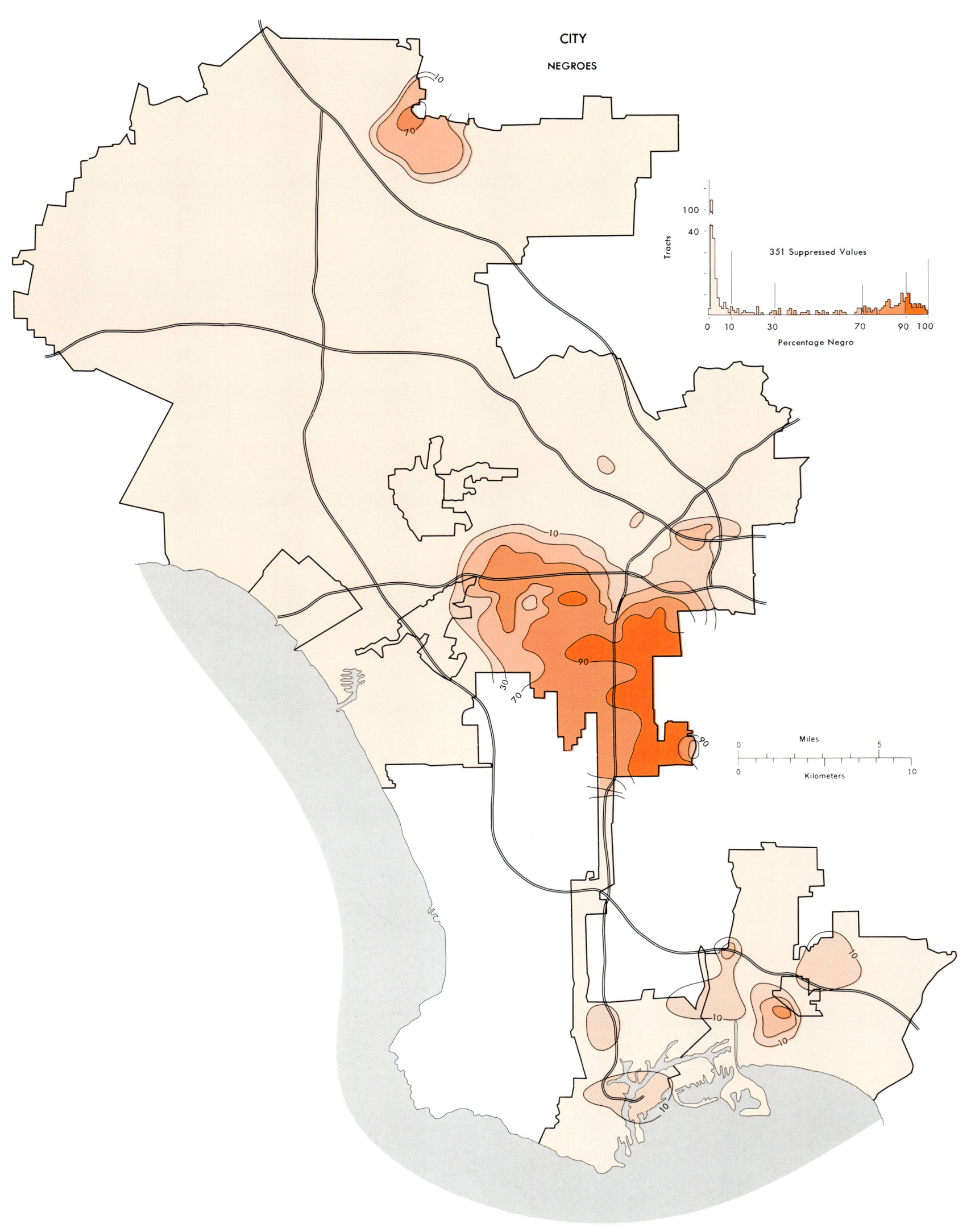

CITY

NEGROES

351 Suppressed Values

Percentage Negro

*Twentieth-Century Cities: Los Angeles*

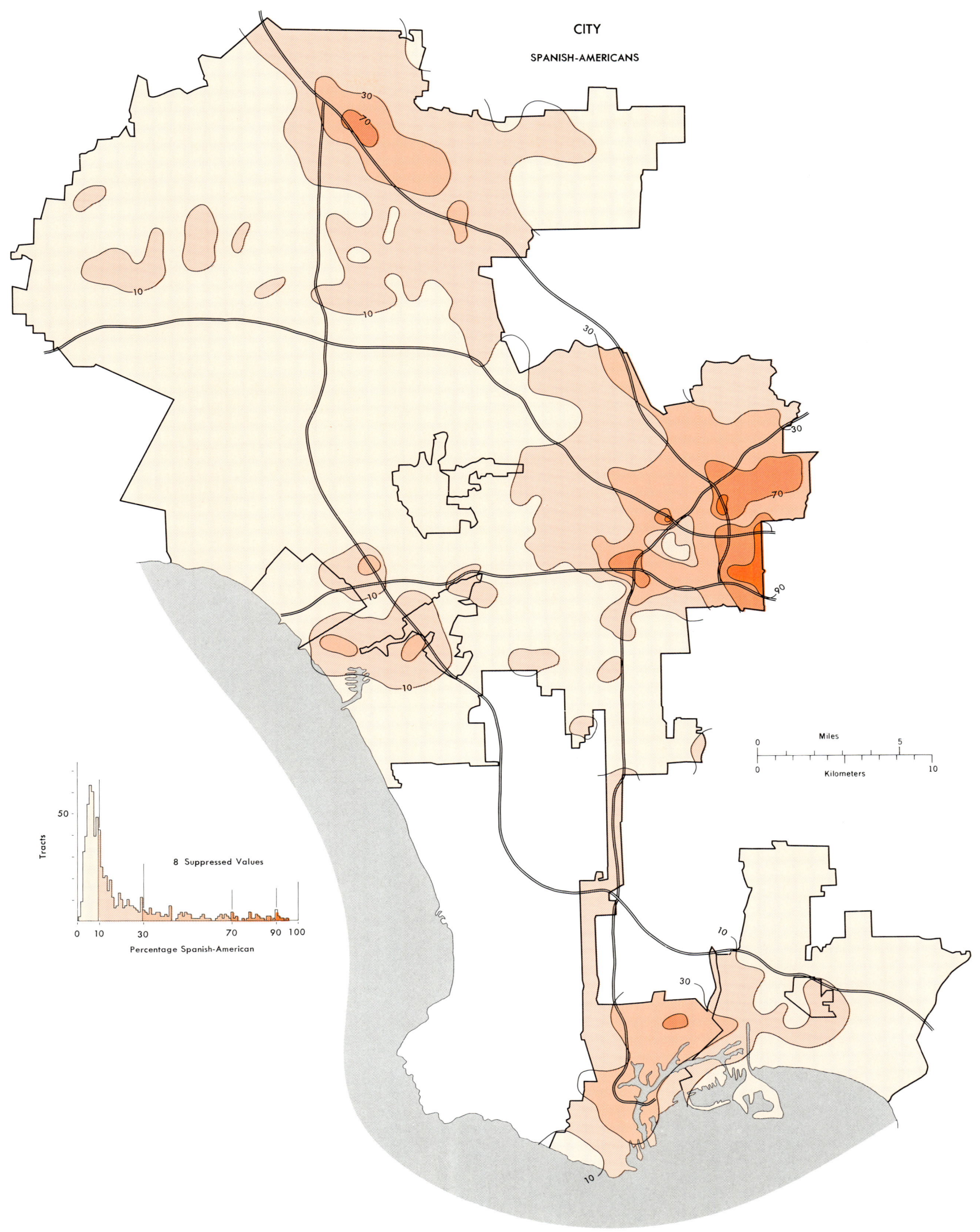

CITY

SPANISH-AMERICANS

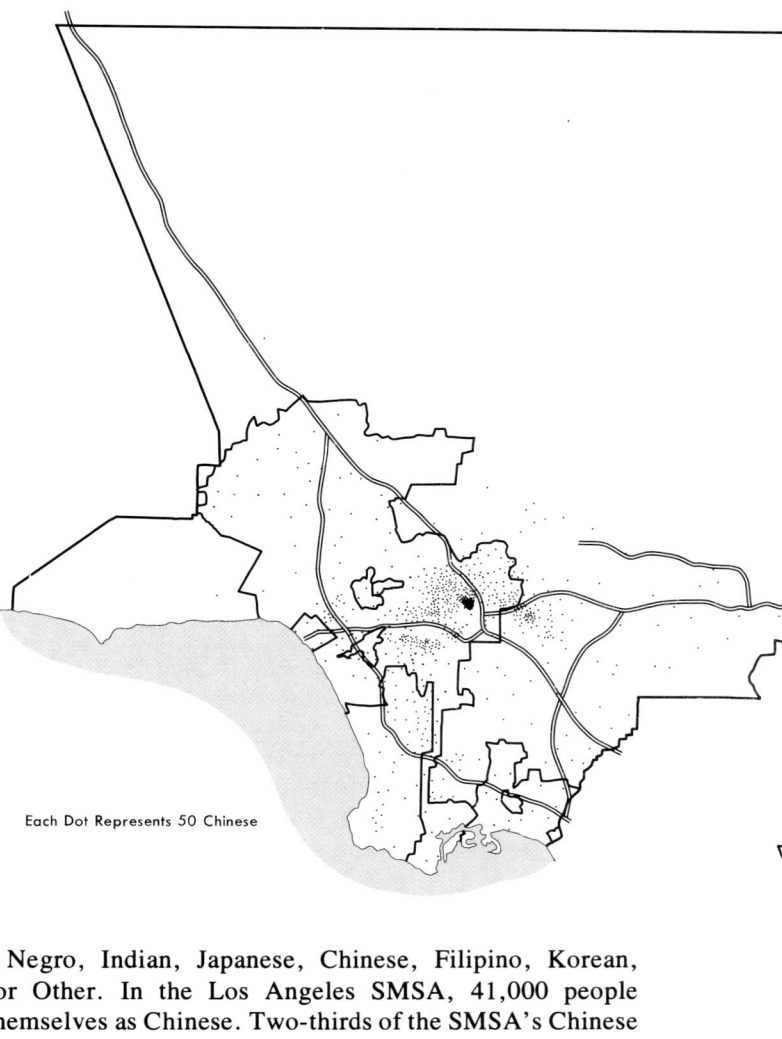

categories: Negro, Indian, Japanese, Chinese, Filipino, Korean, Hawaian, or Other. In the Los Angeles SMSA, 41,000 people identified themselves as Chinese. Two-thirds of the SMSA's Chinese live in Los Angeles, where many are concentrated in a small area north of the CBD.

**Japanese-Americans.** There are 104,000 Japanese-Americans in the SMSA, 53 percent of whom live in Los Angeles. Most of the central-city Japanese live northwest of the CBD, with an outlying cluster east of Santa Monica. Many of the Japanese living outside the city reside in the Gardena municipality located along the southward extension of Los Angeles. Before World War II, the Japanese community was centered on the "Little Tokyo" section in downtown Los Angeles. The Japanese who returned after the forcible resettlements in the interior during World War II dispersed more widely. Whereas Japanese supported themselves by gardening and other agricultural pursuits before World War II, they have moved rapidly into business and the professions since their return.

**Canadian-Americans.** There are 68,000 Canadian-born and 107,000 people with at least one Canadian-born parent in the Los Angeles SMSA. Canadian-Americans are distributed roughly in accordance with population density; 40 percent of the Canadian-born and 36 percent of those of Canadian parentage live in Los Angeles compared with the city's 40 percent share of the total population. Few Canadians live in neighborhoods dominated by blacks.

**German-Americans.** German foreign stock totals 129,000, of whom 41,000 are German-born. Aside from their avoidance of the SMSA's black neighborhoods, German-Americans are spread throughout the SMSA except in the sparsely inhabited north. Forty-five percent of the SMSA's German-born and 38 percent of the people of German parentage live in the city of Los Angeles.

**Russian-Americans.** Russian-Americans in the Los Angeles SMSA are usually Jews of Russian descent rather than ethnic Russians. The region is home to 1 of every 10 American Jews, and it has what is probably the third largest urban Jewish community in the world, after New York City and Tel Aviv. Many are second- or third-generation Americans, but there are 129,000 Russian foreign stock, of whom 33,000 are Russian-born. The Russian-American community is more concentrated in the city of Los Angeles and its enclaves than are other ethnic groups. Of the SMSA's Russian foreign stock, 69 percent of the Russian-born and 72 percent of the people of Russian parentage live in Los Angeles.

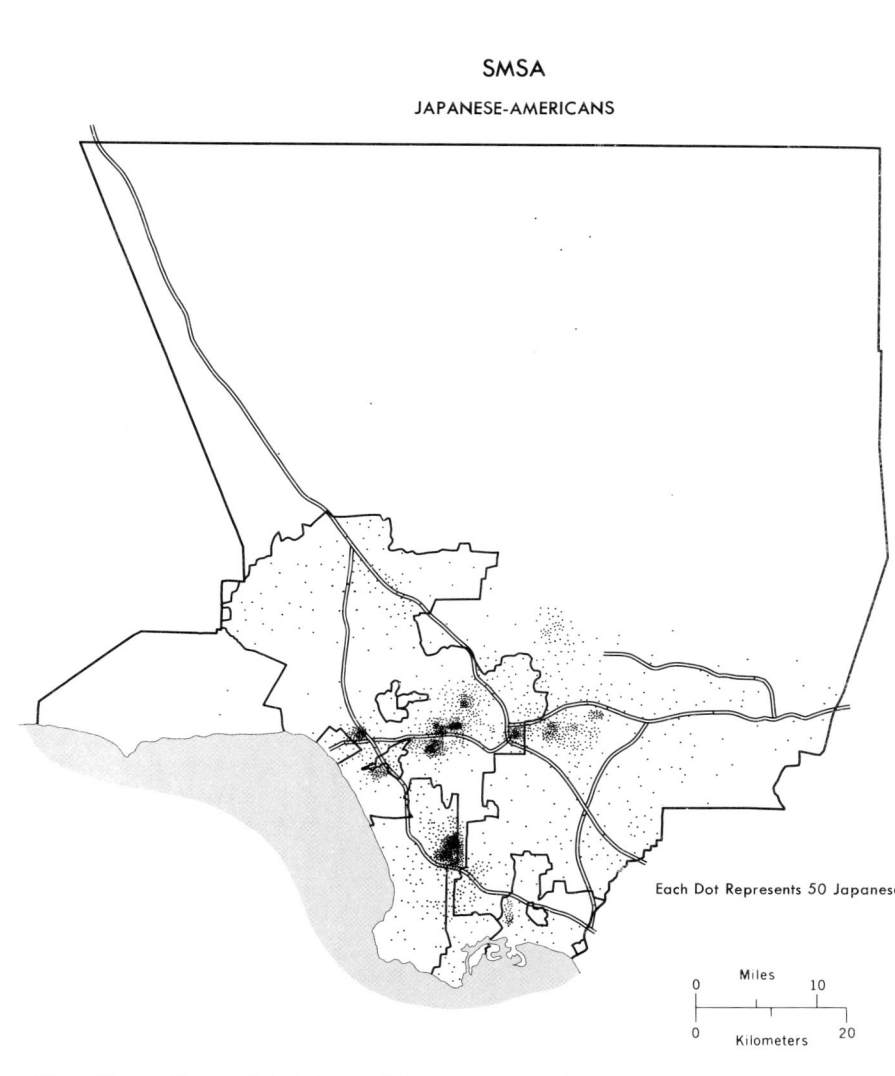

**Italian-Americans.** There are 112,000 Italian-Americans in the SMSA. Like the Canadian- and German-Americans, Italian-

*Twentieth-Century Cities: Los Angeles*

SMSA

CANADIAN-AMERICANS

Each Black Dot Represents 50 Canadian Born

Each Orange Dot Represents 50 People of Canadian Parentage

SMSA

GERMAN-AMERICANS

Each Black Dot Represents 50 German Born

Each Orange Dot Represents 50 People of German Parentage

SMSA

RUSSIAN-AMERICANS

Each Black Dot Represents 50 Russian Born

Each Orange Dot Represents 50 People of Russian Parentage

231

SMSA

ITALIAN-AMERICANS

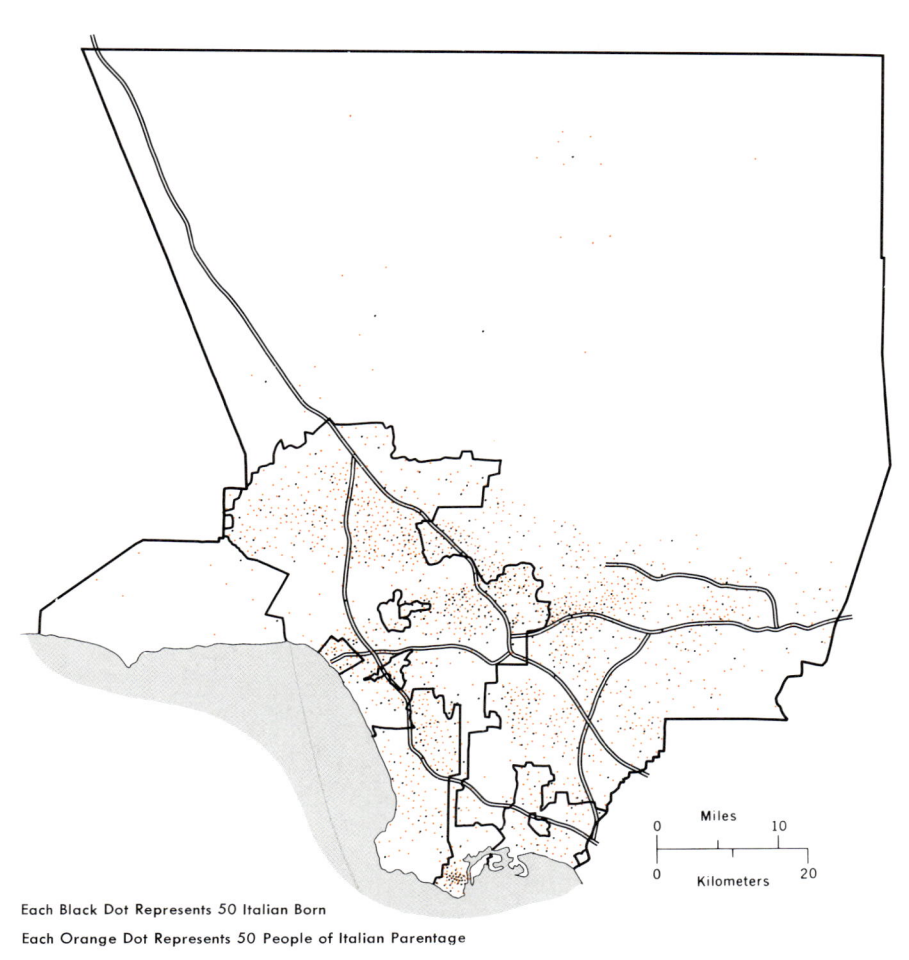

Each Black Dot Represents 50 Italian Born
Each Orange Dot Represents 50 People of Italian Parentage

Americans are distributed roughly in accordance with population density. Forty-six percent of the SMSA's 26,000 Italian-born live in Los Angeles, as do 40 percent of those of Italian parentage.

The racial and ethnic complexity of the Los Angeles SMSA belies its reputation as a metropolis populated by relocated Midwesterners where homogeneity reigns supreme. In addition to large numbers of Hispanics, blacks, Chinese, and Japanese, the region has significant numbers of Filipinos, Koreans, and European ethnics.

## SOCIOECONOMIC CHARACTERISTICS

**Household Size.** There are 2.8 people in the average SMSA household and 2.7 in the average Los Angeles household. The Los Angeles and San Francisco SMSAs have the lowest average household size of the SMSAs mapped in the atlas. Household size is closely related to family life cycle. Small households are most frequent where older populations whose children have established their own households and where young families that have not yet had children reside. Individual tract averages range from 1.1 to 5 people per household. Small households are concentrated in a broad zone that runs northeast-southwest through the SMSA. Large households prefer the San Fernando Valley on the north and the suburbs east of Los Angeles. The highest tract average is located in a heavily black area northwest of Long Beach. The average black household in the SMSA has 3.1 persons. The average Spanish-American household is even larger; it contains 3.7 persons.

**Female Headship.** The Census Bureau defines female headship by the absence of a male spouse regardless of the sex of the family's principal breadwinner. Females head 13 percent of the SMSA's families and 16 percent of the families in Los Angeles. Individual tract percentages vary from zero to 70. Female headship is slightly concentrated in Los Angeles and Long Beach; 53 percent of the families headed by females live in the two cities. Female headship is notably concentrated in black areas (p. 388). Of the black households

in the SMSA, 21 percent are headed by females. Among Spanish-Americans, female headship is 12 percent.

**Occupations.** Fifteen percent of the SMSA's labor force work at blue-collar (laborers and operatives) jobs and 24 percent classify themselves as executives (engineers, teachers, professionals, managers, proprietors, and administrators). The remaining 61 percent are service (32 percent) and clerical (29 percent) workers. The city's occupational structure is almost identical to the SMSA's.

Tract percentages of blue-collar workers range from zero to 55. Tracts with more than 30 percent of their labor forces in blue-collar occupations cluster in east-central and northern Los Angeles. Percentages are low in affluent west-central Los Angeles, along the Pacific coast, northeast of the downtown area, and in the southeastern part of the county.

Individual tracts have between zero and 68 percent of their labor forces in executive occupations. The map reverses the map of blue-collar workers in many places. Black and Spanish-American neighborhoods have few executives, whereas affluent parts of the SMSA often have more than 30 percent of their labor forces in blue-collar jobs.

**Income.** Mean income per person in the SMSA is $3,900 per year, and the corresponding figure for Los Angeles is $4,000. Individual tract means vary from $500 to $24,500. Incomes are below $2,500 in central Los Angeles, where blacks are concentrated, and in the areas immediately to the east, where Spanish-Americans are dominant. Incomes are generally high along the Pacific coast, but the most affluent area is in west-central Los Angeles west and north of Beverly Hills and West Hollywood, where the wealthy have built homes on the slopes and up the canyons of the Santa Monicas. A secondary zone of affluence is located northwest of the Los Angeles CBD on the slopes of the San Gabriels, and another is in southeastern Los Angeles County.

## TOPICS OF SPECIAL INTEREST IN THE LOS ANGELES-LONG BEACH REGION

**Residential Turnover.** In 1970, 46 percent of the SMSA's residents who were 5 years old or older were living in houses different from the ones they occupied in 1965. In many parts of the SMSA, residential turnover varies between 30 and 70 percent, but turnover exceeds 70 percent and even 90 percent in a number of areas. The high turnover in the sparsely settled northern, western, and eastern parts of the SMSA is caused by people moving into new housing. The turnover at scattered locations in central Los Angeles and in the suburbs east of the city often consists of shifting among existing dwellings, and in such areas, high rates of turnover may be indicative of instability.

**Public Transportation Use.** (Histogram on p. 332.) Only 5.5 percent of the SMSA labor force and 9.2 percent of the Los Angeles labor force take public transportation to work. Except for a few tiny outliers, tracts where more than 10 percent of the workers use public transportation are clustered in central Los Angeles. Given the size of the city and the SMSA, the dispersion of jobs, and the area's low population density, public transportation offers few workers reasonable alternatives to automobile commuting. The Los Angeles region had an excellent public transportation system that connected (and often created) the region's numerous scattered settlements, but it languished and died after World War II. Subsequent sprawl makes it unlikely that anything similar will be resurrected in the future.

**Households without Automobiles.** (Histogram on p. 340.) Fifteen percent of the SMSA's households and 20 percent of the households in Los Angeles do not have access to an automobile. Given the limited

*Twentieth-Century Cities: Los Angeles*

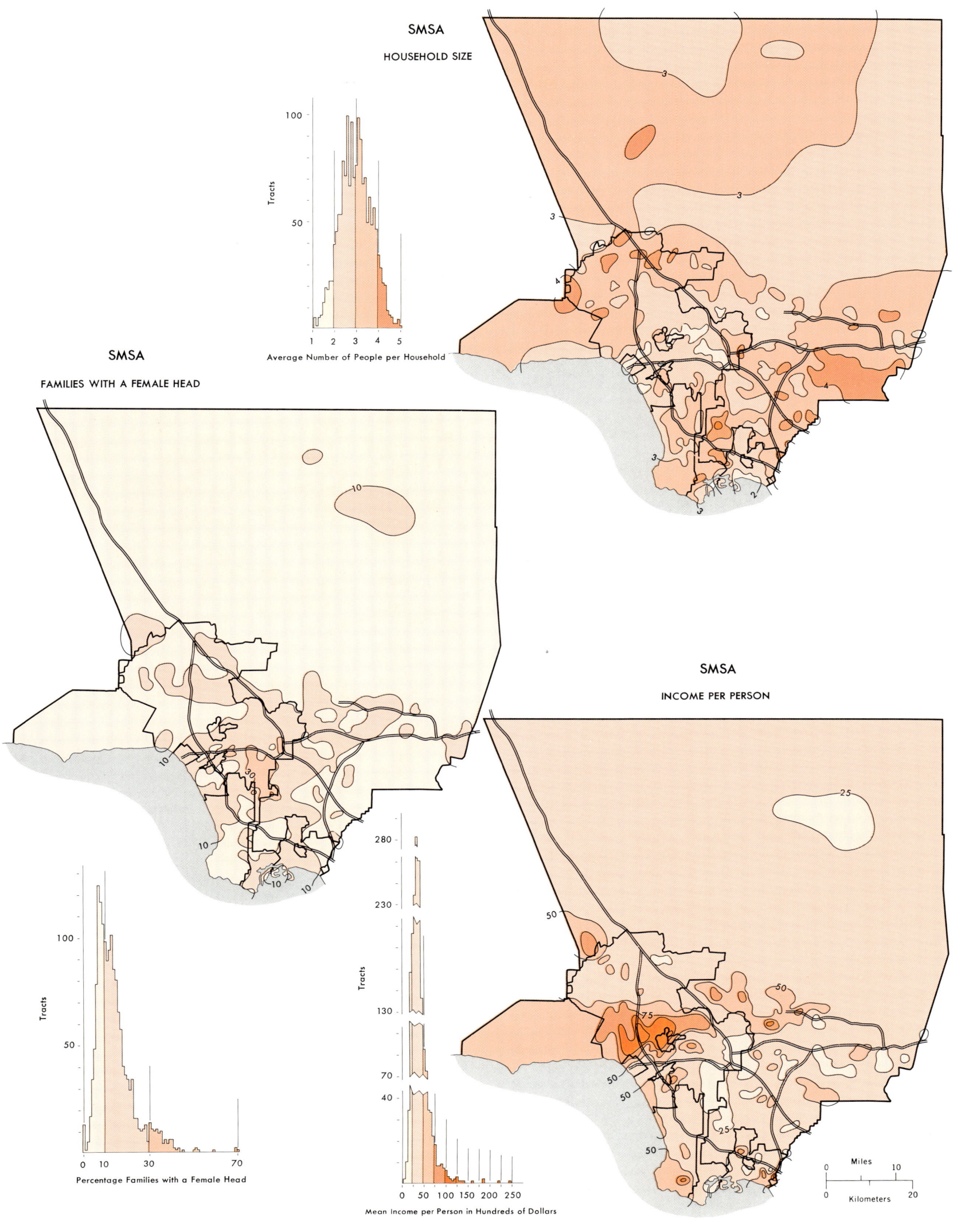

SMSA

HOUSEHOLD SIZE

Average Number of People per Household

SMSA

FAMILIES WITH A FEMALE HEAD

Percentage Families with a Female Head

SMSA

INCOME PER PERSON

Mean Income per Person in Hundreds of Dollars

233

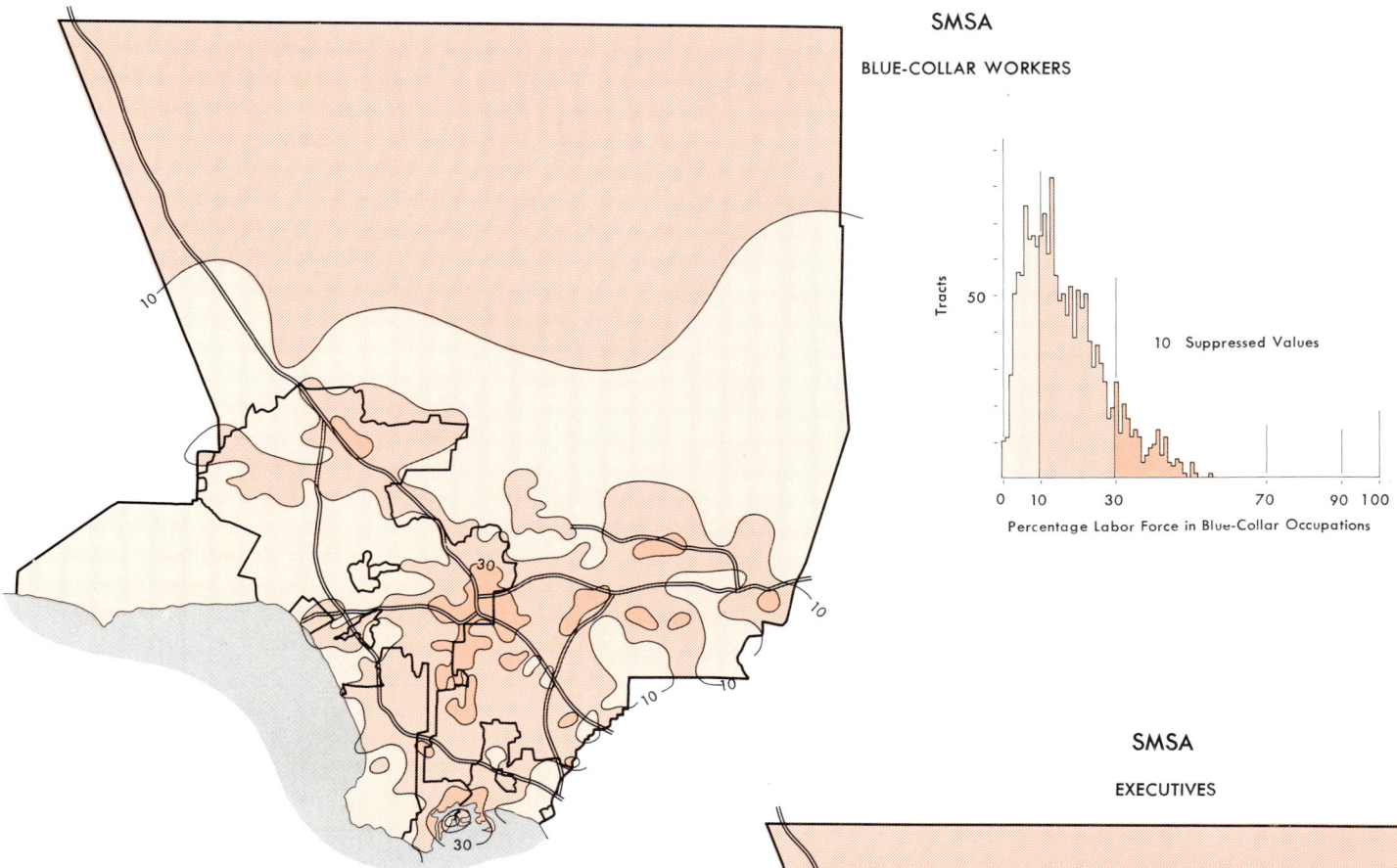

*Twentieth-Century Cities: Los Angeles*

SMSA

BLUE-COLLAR WORKERS

10 Suppressed Values

Percentage Labor Force in Blue-Collar Occupations

SMSA

EXECUTIVES

Percentage Labor Force in Executive Occupations

area served by efficient public transportation, not having the use of a car can be a serious handicap. Although percentages are highest in the core areas of Los Angeles and Long Beach, where public transportation is more effective than it is in outlying areas, there are many places located far from the core area where more than 10 percent of the households lack the personal mobility a car provides.

**Spanish-Americans.** (Histogram on p. 396; city map on p. 229.) The Census Bureau estimates the number of Spanish-Americans in Los Angeles by counting people who speak Spanish and adding to that number people with selected Spanish surnames who have not listed themselves as Spanish speakers. There are 1,289,311 Spanish-Americans in the SMSA, who comprise 18.3 percent of the total population. The Spanish-American minority is not as highly segregated as blacks (p. 388), but there are a number of heavily Hispanic areas in Los Angeles and the rest of the SMSA. Economically, Spanish-Americans are still behind whites; the mean family income for Spanish-Americans is $9,800 compared with $13,300 for whites. At the same time, Hispanics are somewhat better off than the SMSA's blacks, who have a mean family income of $8,500.

**The Poverty Population.** (Histogram on p. 420.) The incomes of 11 percent of the SMSA population (753,000 people) are below the poverty level. Of these, 292,000 are children under 18 years old. Although there are a number of areas where the poverty population exceeds 10 and occasionally 30 percent of tract totals, the largest concentration of people below the poverty level is in central Los Angeles and adjacent communities to the east, where the poverty area is generally coincident with heavily black and Spanish-American neighborhoods—24 percent of the SMSA's blacks and 15 percent of Spanish-Americans have incomes below the poverty level. Looked ~ther way, 24 percent of the SMSA's poverty population is black ~rcent is Spanish-American, whereas blacks make up only 11 ~e total population and Hispanics only 18 percent.

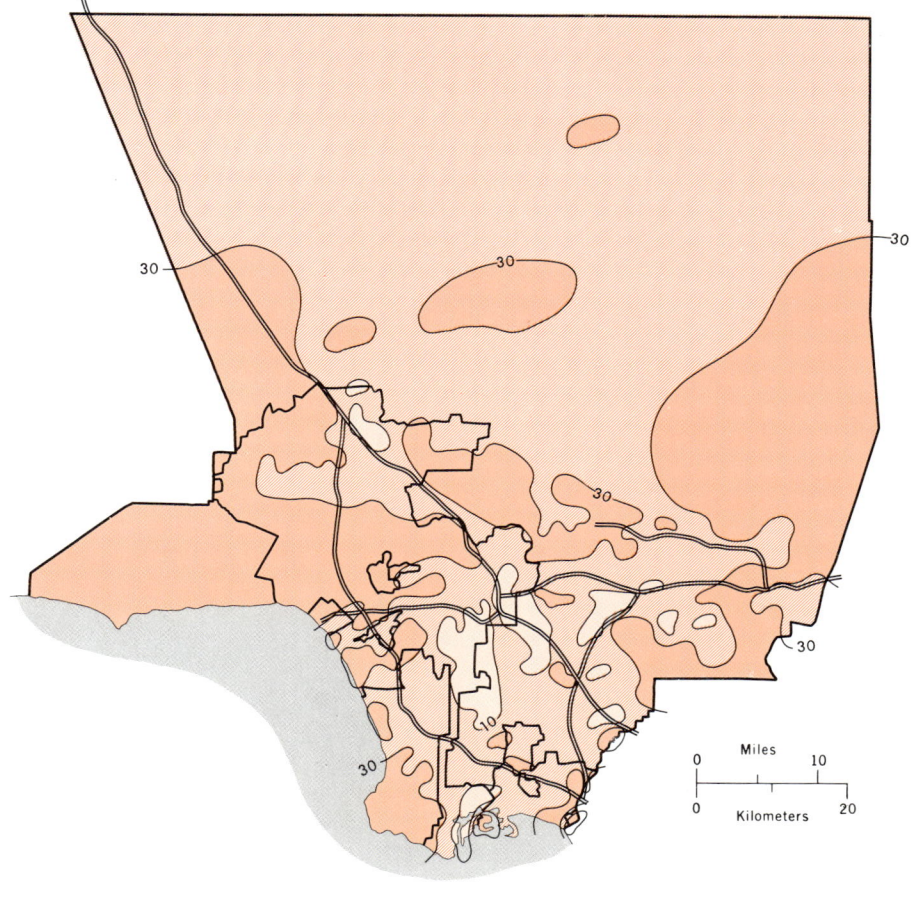

## Twentieth-Century Cities: Los Angeles

The Los Angeles metropolitan region is a massive, diverse, and extremely complicated urban area. The separate settlements we call suburbs, for want of a better term, are often individual places that started growing at different times for different reasons. Although Los Angeles and the numerous surrounding centers have now grown and coalesced into a single metropolitan system, the differences among them persist. Far from being the simple collection of suburbs and freeways in search of a city that it is often alleged to be, the Los Angeles region is a new urban form which is poorly understood. More than is true in other SMSAs, the relationships of population patterns to ecological differences are sharp and strong. Southern California offers a variety of climatic and topographic amenities, and the region's complex human geography is produced by people with different tastes choosing among them.

SMSA
PERCENTAGE LABOR FORCE TAKING PUBLIC TRANSPORTATION TO WORK

SMSA
RESIDENTIAL CHANGE, 1965-1970
(See Text)

SMSA
PERCENTAGE HOUSEHOLDS WITHOUT AN AUTOMOBILE

*Twentieth-Century Cities: Los Angeles*

SMSA

PERCENTAGE POPULATION BELOW POVERTY LEVEL

SMSA

PERCENTAGE SPANISH-AMERICAN

# CHAPTER 23

# Miami

*There are only two kinds of people in the United States: those living in Miami and those wanting to live in Miami.*

REAL ESTATE PROMOTER'S SLOGAN, 1925

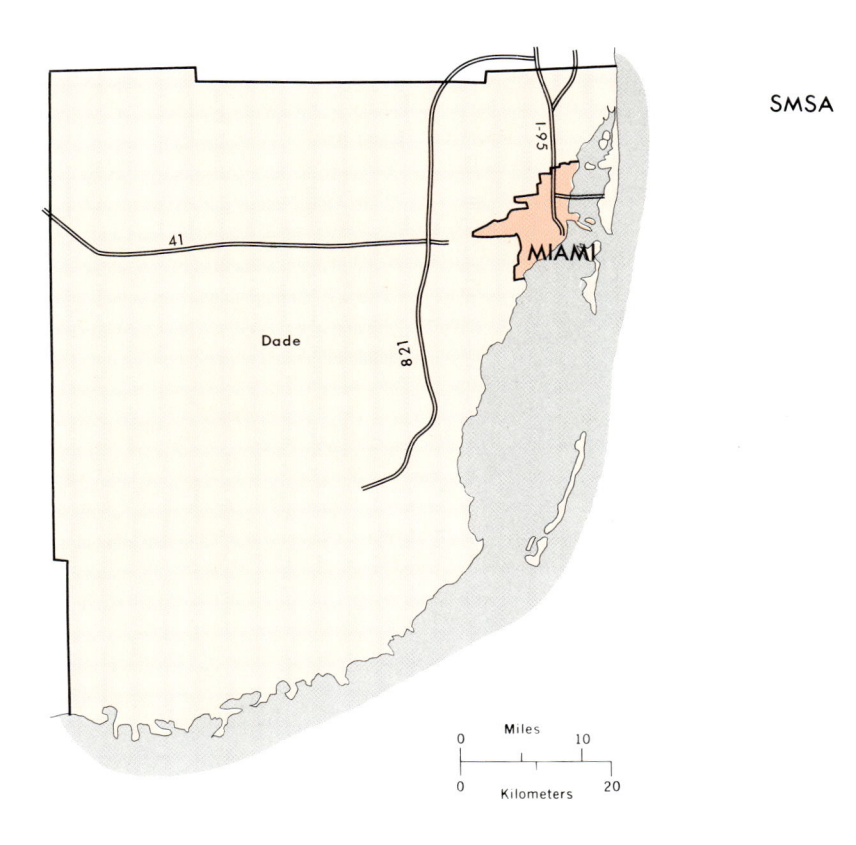

The Miami Standard Metropolitan Statistical Area (SMSA) is the 25th most populous SMSA in the nation with 1,268,000 people. Miami has a population of 335,000, which is 26 percent of the SMSA total. Almost all of the remaining 74 percent is divided among numerous small municipalities and unincorporated areas of Dade County. Although the SMSA includes all of Dade County, many parts of the county are almost completely uninhabited. The Daily Urban System (DUS) defined by counties that have at least 5 percent of their labor forces working in Dade County includes Dade and Broward counties (p. 238). Broward County (the Fort Lauderdale SMSA) has a population of 620,000 people; thus the total DUS population is 1,888,000, which makes it the 18th most populous DUS in the nation.

Settlement in Dade County began with a few villages and trading posts during the last quarter of the 19th century. By 1900, the county's total population was still less than 5,000 people. Pre-1900 settlements supported themselves by agriculture, especially by growing tomatoes and grapefruit. A freeze in the winter of 1894-1895 killed most of Florida's citrus except the crop in Dade County, which escaped the frost. The event alerted growers and developers to the possibilities of southern Florida, which they had previously largely ignored. A railroad was soon extended south, and Miami was incorporated in 1896. Miami boomed after World War I. The population rose from 29,500 in 1920 to 143,000 in 1925; it dropped to 110,500 in 1930 after the bursting of the real estate bubble in 1926, a disasterous hurricane, and the stock market crash of 1929. By 1940 a modest recovery was under way and the population had grown to 172,000 people. Growth has continued apace since (p. 10). The Miami population increased 15 percent from 1960 to 1970, a decade in which many central cities lost population. The SMSA population increased 36 percent in the 1960s, compared with a national metropolitan population increase of 17 percent. Three-fourths of the SMSA's increase resulted from immigration from other parts of the nation and from abroad.

Southern Florida is flat and only barely above sea level. Beach ridges 15 or 20 feet (4.5 to 6.0 meters) above sea level are the highest elevations in Miami. Behind the ridges, large areas are less than 5 feet (1.5 meters) above sea level. Most of the area outside the immediate vicinity of Miami and an extension of relatively high land to the

*Note:* All data are from the 1970 Censuses of Population and Housing unless otherwise indicated. Therefore the present tense refers to 1970 data except for income data which are from 1969. Cartographic conventions are explained in Chapter 1.

## Twentieth-Century Cities: Miami

**CITY**
RELIEF

- Over 20 Feet
- 15-20 Feet
- 10-15 Feet
- 5-10 Feet
- Below 5 Feet

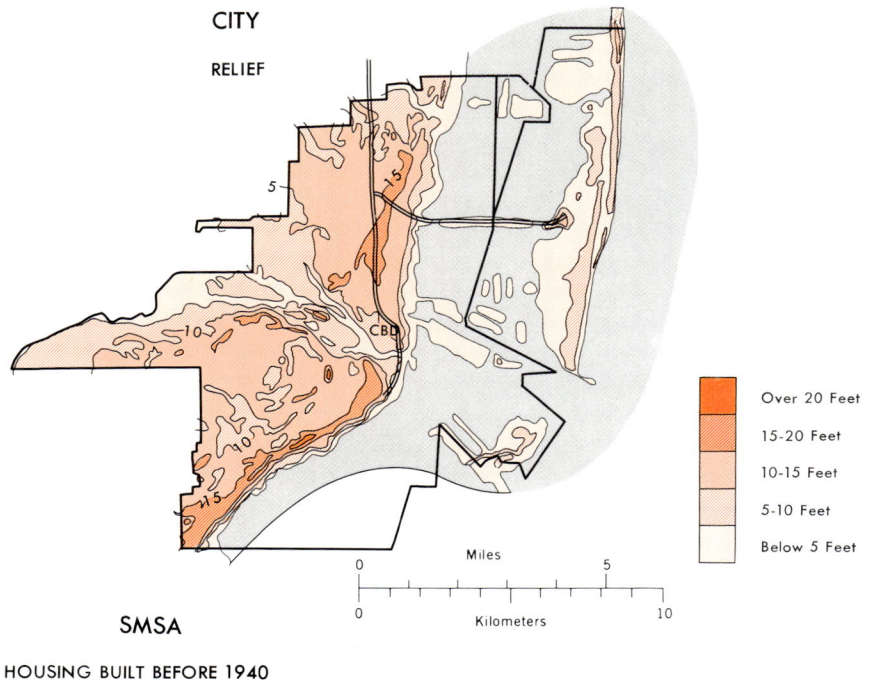

**SMSA**
HOUSING BUILT BEFORE 1940

**DUS**
MOBILE HOMES

**SMSA**
HOUSING BUILT 1960-1970

southwest consists of Everglades, an almost flat region flooded by heavy tropical rains in the summer. The Everglades would formerly impound the fresh rainwater, releasing it slowly and promoting a rich floristic, faunal, and aquatic "bloom" during the wet period. The numerous canals and drainage ditches dug into the Everglades over the last 80 years now threaten the viability of the area, since they lead the fresh water away so quickly that there is often little time for plant germination and aquatic egg hatches. Also the danger of winter fires has increased markedly and salt water has begun to intrude on southeastern coastal areas because of the lowered head of fresh water. Although none of these hazards to the Everglades are a direct threat to Miami, they demonstrate the catastrophic effects urbanization can have on delicate ecosystems.

Hurricanes are a more direct threat to Miami and other coastal cities in Florida. The increases in sea level caused by hurricane-force winds can and have inundated much of the region, causing immense damage. Since the last major hurricane, many housing units have been built along the coast in areas that are almost certain to be flooded in major hurricanes.

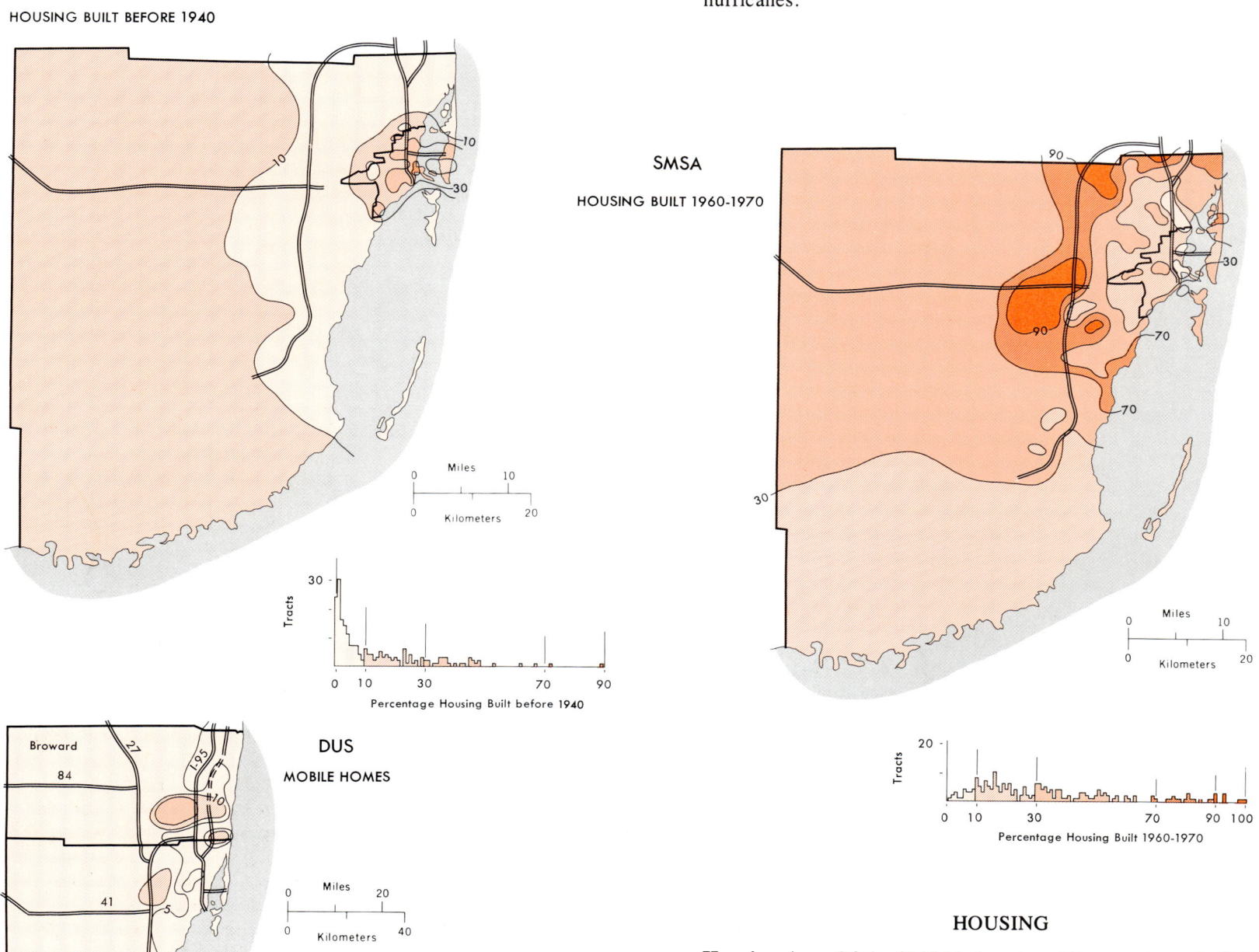

### HOUSING

**Housing Age.** Of the SMSA's housing, 15 percent was built before 1940, 52 percent from 1940 through 1959, and 33 percent from 1960 to March 1970. In Miami 30 percent was built before 1940, 51 percent from 1940 through 1959, and 19 percent from 1960 to March 1970. Miami contains 57 percent of the pre-1940 units, and Miami Beach (the municipality on the beach spit across Biscayne Bay which is politically separate from the City of Miami) has another 20 percent of the region's old housing. Individual tract percentages of old housing vary from zero to 89, most tracts having proportions below 30 percent. Most old housing is located in Miami and Miami Beach and their immediate vicinity. Old housing is less than 10 percent of tract inventories in a broad ring around Miami. Pre-1940 housing is more than 10 percent of tract stocks in the area west and south of Florida 826, but it is important to remember that this entire area consists of two tracts that together contain fewer than 1,000 housing units.

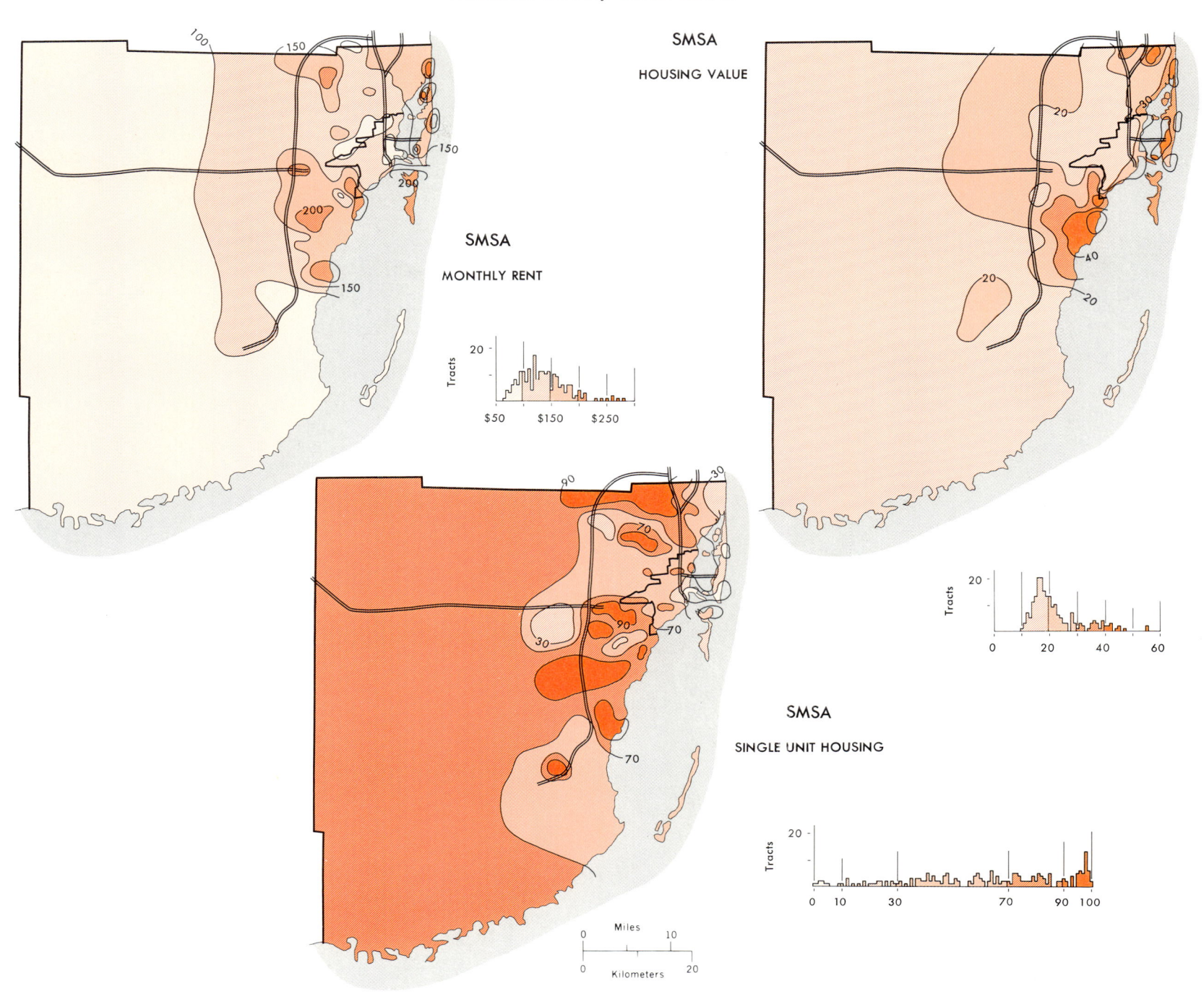

Tract percentages of housing built from 1960 to March 1970 range from zero to 100, with a relatively even distribution of tracts across that range. New housing comprises less than 10 percent of tract inventories throughout Miami and its northeastern and western suburbs. Proportions of new housing increase outward in an irregular ring around Miami, with maximum percentages located in northern Dade County and at the junction of Highways 41 and 826. The outer 70 percent isopleth is a good approximation of the edge of the densely settled area around Miami. Outside that line settlement drops almost to zero except to the south-southeast where settlement extends along Florida 826 to Homestead Air Force Base at its southern end. The area west and south of the western end of the expressway is, relative to the rest of the SMSA, virtually uninhabited.

**Mobile Homes.** There are 19,700 mobile homes in the Miami DUS. They constitute 2.8 percent of the region's housing stock. Many of the area's mobile homes are clustered in southeastern Broward County. In Broward County, mobile homes are 4 percent of all housing units. In Dade County, where mobile homes are 2.2 percent of all dwellings, mobile homes exceed 10 percent of tract totals on Miami's western and northern margins.

**Single-Unit Detached Housing.** Individual dwelling units make up 56 percent of the SMSA housing inventory. Another 42 percent of the region's units are in duplexes (6 percent), 3- and 4-unit buildings (4 percent), apartments with 5 to 49 units (22 percent), and large structures containing 50 or more dwellings (10 percent). The residual 2 percent are mobile homes. In Miami, 43 percent of all housing units are single, detached dwellings, and 57 percent occur in multiples. These are duplexes (10 percent), 3- and 4-unit structures (7 percent), 5- to 49-unit buildings (29 percent), and large multiples with 50 or more units (7 percent). The residual 4 percent are single-unit attached dwellings. Only 12 percent of the housing units in Miami Beach are single-unit detached dwellings. As would be expected in a resort city where land is at a premium, 47 percent of all units are in structures with 5 to 49 apartments and 34 percent are in buildings with 50 or more housing units. Much of the owner-occupied housing in Miami Beach is located on the man-made islands in Biscayne Bay.

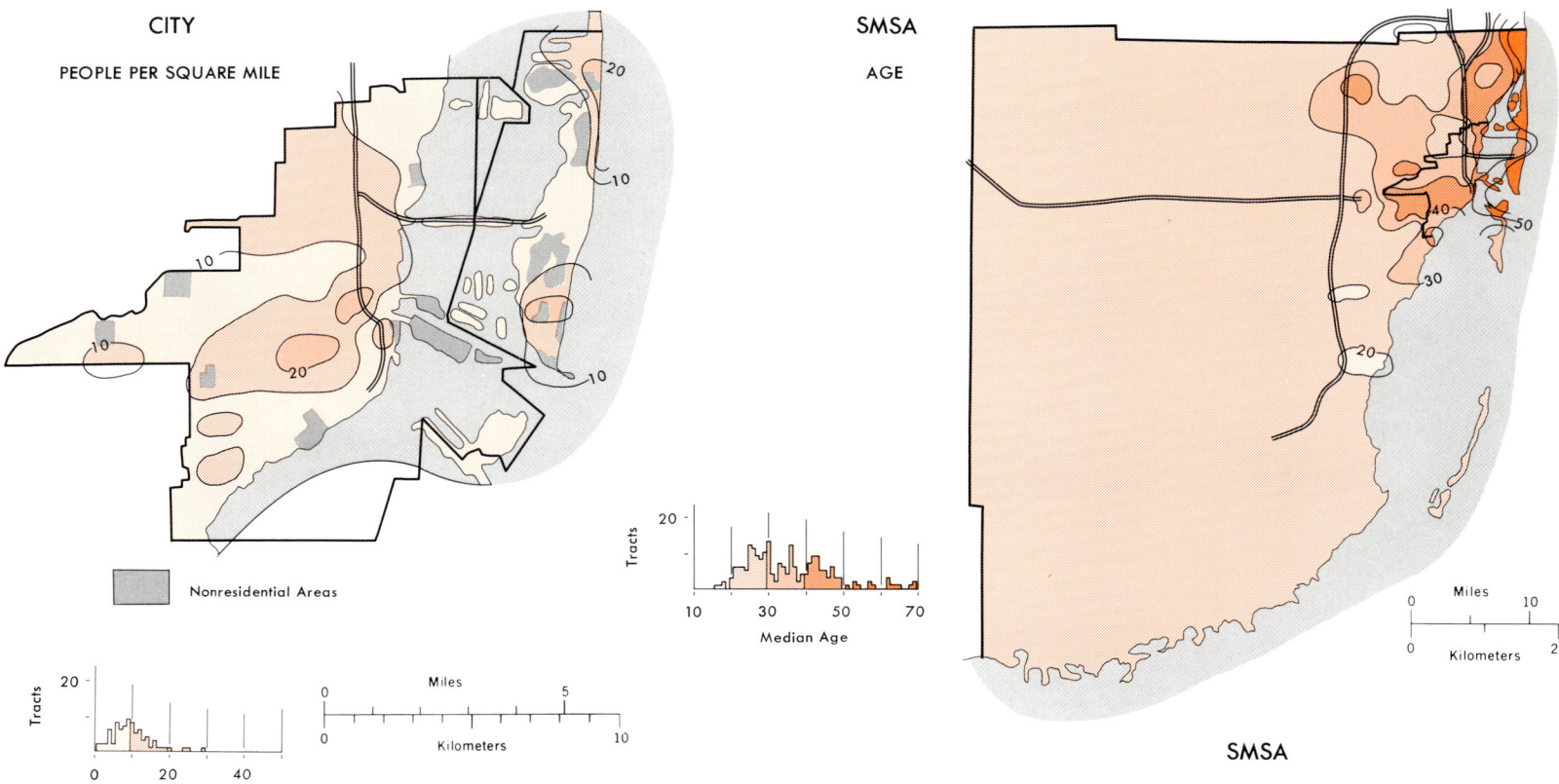

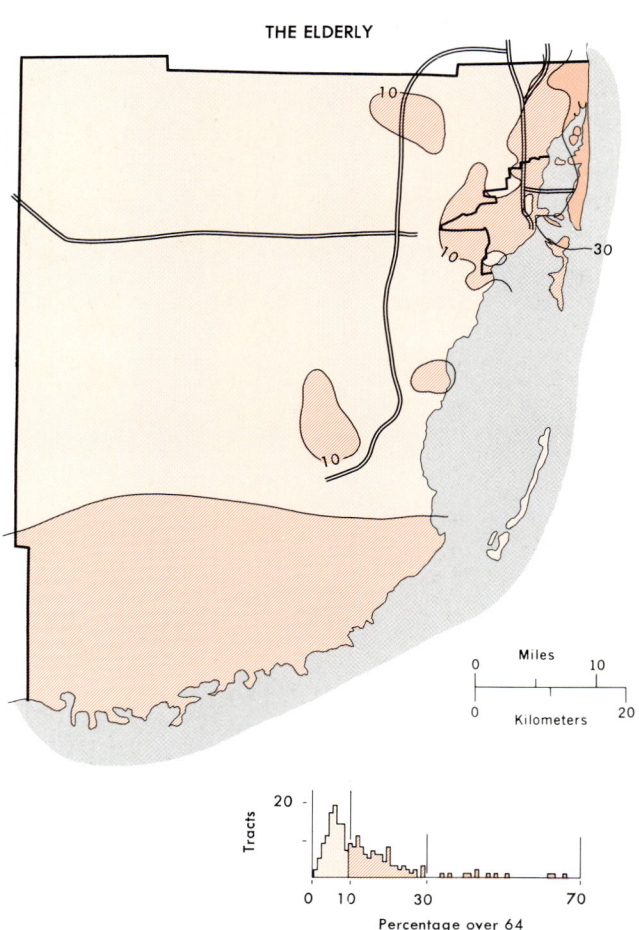

**Housing Value and Rent.** The mean value of owner-occupied housing in the SMSA is $23,000, and the corresponding figure for Miami is $19,000. The mean value of owner-occupied housing in Miami Beach is $41,000. Mean values in individual tracts vary from $10,000 to $55,000. Mean values below $20,000 are not differentiated on the map, but the lowest values occur in the Goulds-Perrine area near the end of Highway 826. Housing values in Miami are below $20,000 except along the bayshore. Expensive housing is spotted along Miami Beach, on the man-made islands in Biscayne Bay, and in northern Dade County. The region's most expensive housing is located in the coastal area of affluent Coral Gables, traditionally Miami's most prestigious suburb.

Mean monthly contract rents average $132 in the SMSA, $106 in Miami, and $167 in Miami Beach. The Miami Beach mean does not include transient hotel rents but does include hotel rents by permanent residents, many of whom live in old hotels. The SMSA mean rent is the second highest among the metropolitan areas mapped in the atlas, falling but one dollar behind the San Francisco SMSA's $133. Rents in the city of Miami are not especially high compared with other cities. Rents in central Miami and along its northwestern boundary are less than $100. Except for the sparsely inhabited west and south regions, the rest of the SMSA has mean monthly contract rents over $100 with the highest rents occurring in Miami Beach and the communities north of it, where some tracts have mean rents as high as $280. The area of coastal Coral Gables that has the SMSA's highest housing values contains virtually no rental units. Thus although rents are high in the Coral Gables area, the peak rents occur in and near Miami Beach.

## THE PEOPLE

**Population Density.** Miami's overall population density is 9,800 and Miami Beach's is 13,600 per square mile (3,800 and 5,250 per square kilometer). Individual tract densities vary from 1,000 to 29,000 per square mile (390 to 11,200 per square kilometer), although few tracts have densities exceeding 20,000 per square mile (7,700 per square kilometer). Because nonresidential areas are included in the density calculations, actual tract densities in some parts of the area are considerably higher than the gross densities mapped here. Three areas have densities over 20,000 per square mile (7,700 per square kilometer). Two are in Miami Beach and the other consists of two separate tracts in central Miami. The highest density occurs in a west-central Miami tract with a predominantly Cuban population. The influx of Cubans into Miami during the 1960s produced severe pressure on local housing stocks and led to crowding and densities in the Cuban areas that are uncharacteristic of the region as a whole. Because so much of Miami's growth occurred after World War II when single-family dwellings and inexpensive automobile transportation were in vogue, the city and the region are built and occupied at very low densities. (An SMSA map is on p. 316.)

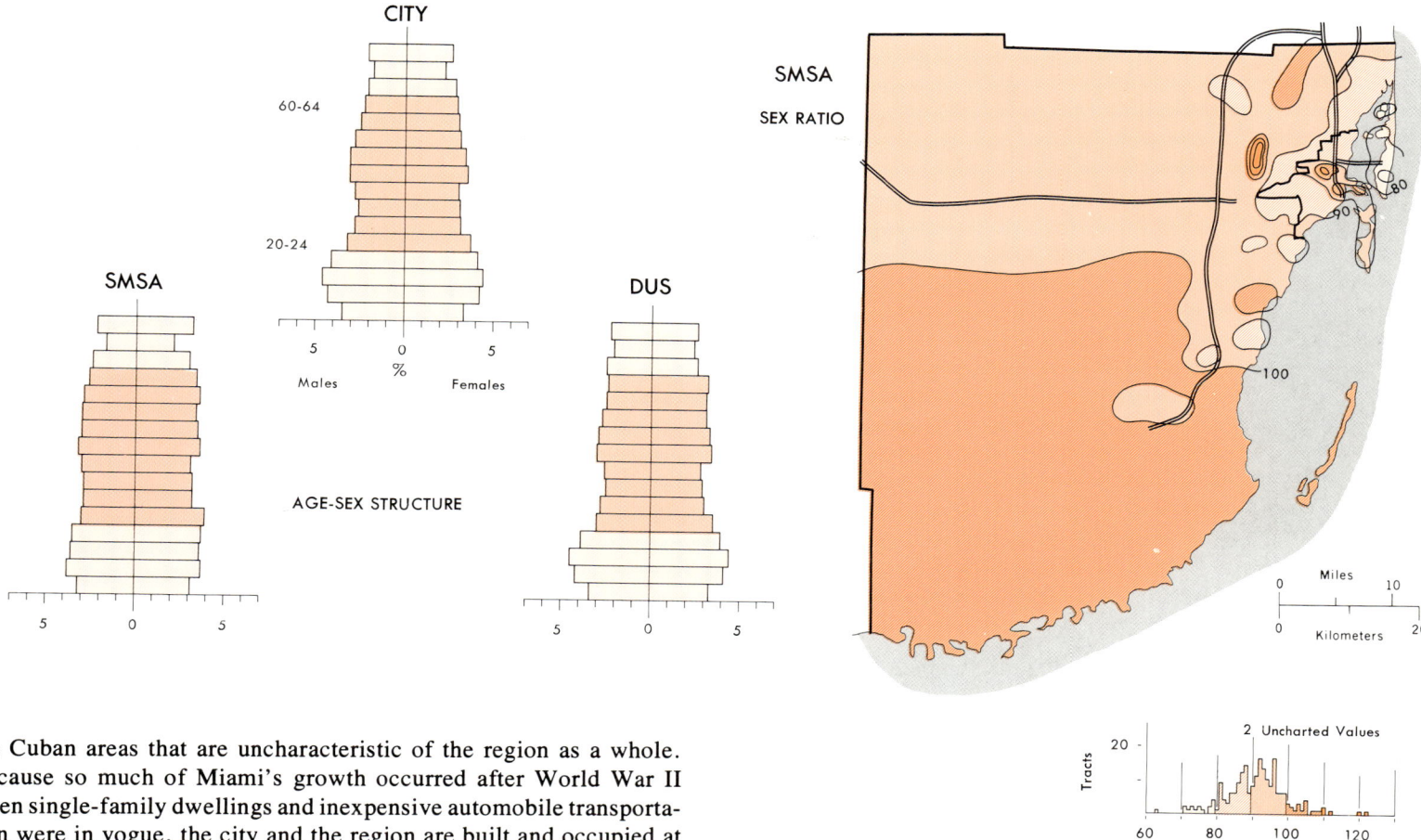

**Age and the Elderly.** With a median age of 34 years, the Miami SMSA has the oldest population of the SMSAs included in the atlas. In Miami, the median age of the population is 37 years and in Miami Beach it is 64 years. Miami's median age is easily the oldest among the central cities in the atlas, and Miami Beach's is in a class by itself. Median ages for individual tracts vary from 16 to 69 years, but there are few tracts below 20 years. The highest median ages are located in the two census tracts at the southern edge of Miami Beach. Many people who began to come to Miami Beach for vacations in the early decades of the century chose to retire there in mid-century, and the survivors comprise a unique population. Miami Beach and the coastal communities north of Miami Beach have median ages well over 50 years, which usually occur only among institutionalized populations in other parts of the nation. Median ages exceed 40 years in much of southern Miami and along the bayshore. Median ages are below 30 years in the predominantly black area of north-central Miami. Outside Miami, only the outer suburbs have median ages below 30 years.

People 64 years of age and older make up 14 percent of the SMSA population and 15 percent of Miami's people. Forty-nine percent of the Miami Beach population is over 64 years of age. Tract percentages of the elderly vary from 1 to 66; tracts with the highest percentages are located in southern Miami Beach. The elderly exceed 30 percent of tract populations throughout Miami Beach and the more northerly coastal communities. The elderly are more than 10 percent of tract populations in Miami, its northern suburbs, and most of Coral Gables, which is southwest of the city. Most of the rest of the SMSA has proportions below 10 percent.

The SMSA's population structure is the most unusual of the metropolitan areas included in the atlas, as is clearly evident in its population pyramid. It is in fact much more a column than a pyramid, since there is an almost even proportion of the population in all age cohorts. The city and DUS pyramids are only slightly more typical than the SMSA pyramid. Were it not for the black and Hispanic populations of Miami, however, the city pyramid would resemble the SMSA pyramid more closely, for a disproportionate number of the city's young people are black and Cuban.

**Sex Ratio.** There are 1.1 females for each male in the SMSA. yielding a female-dominant sex ratio (males divided by females times 100) of 90. Miami is more female-dominant than the SMSA with a sex ratio of 88. Miami Beach has 1.3 females for each male and a sex ratio of 77. Low sex ratios are to be expected in populations as old as those in Miami Beach and Miami, for female survival rates exceed male rates after young adulthood. Only a few areas of the SMSA are male-dominant. One is a run-down area located north of the Miami CBD and another is a tract containing a correctional institution west of the city. The remaining areas with sex ratios over 100 are areas dominated by young families except for the sparsely settled southern part of the SMSA, which has the slightly male-dominant population characteristic of largely rural areas.

**Negroes.** There are 76,000 blacks in Miami, who make up 23 percent of the city population. The city's blacks are highly segregated in the north-central part of the city, with one outlying tract on Miami's southwest side in the Coconut Grove neighborhood. The latter is the city's original area of black settlement. It was occupied initially by Bahamian blacks, skilled masons who were able to work coral and limestone. The Central and Brownsville-Liberty City ghetto areas in north-central Miami developed later, especially after 1950. Coconut Grove and the ghetto to the north are occupied by low-income blacks. Some of the SMSA's several suburban ghettos (p. 388) are dominated by middle-income blacks. There are but 320 blacks (0.4 percent of the population) in Miami Beach.

**Spanish-Americans.** The Census Bureau estimates the number of Hispanics in Miami by counting people who speak Spanish. By that reckoning there are 152,000 Spanish-Americans in Miami. Spanish-Americans exceed 30 percent of the population throughout most of the city, with percentages in the most intensely Spanish-American tracts approaching 90. There is virtually no Mexican foreign stock in Miami, but there is a small contingent of Puerto Ricans (6,700, or 4 percent of all Spanish-Americans) and a slightly larger group (8,900 or 6 percent) from Central and South America. Most of the remaining Hispanics are Cubans who began arriving in Miami shortly after the Cuban revolution. (SMSA map is on p. 396.)

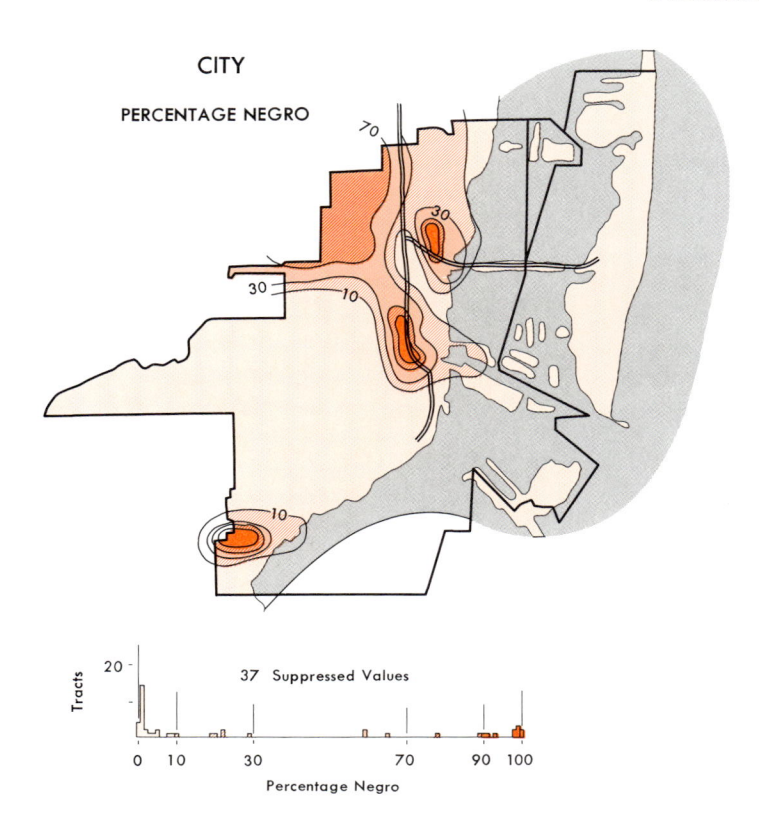

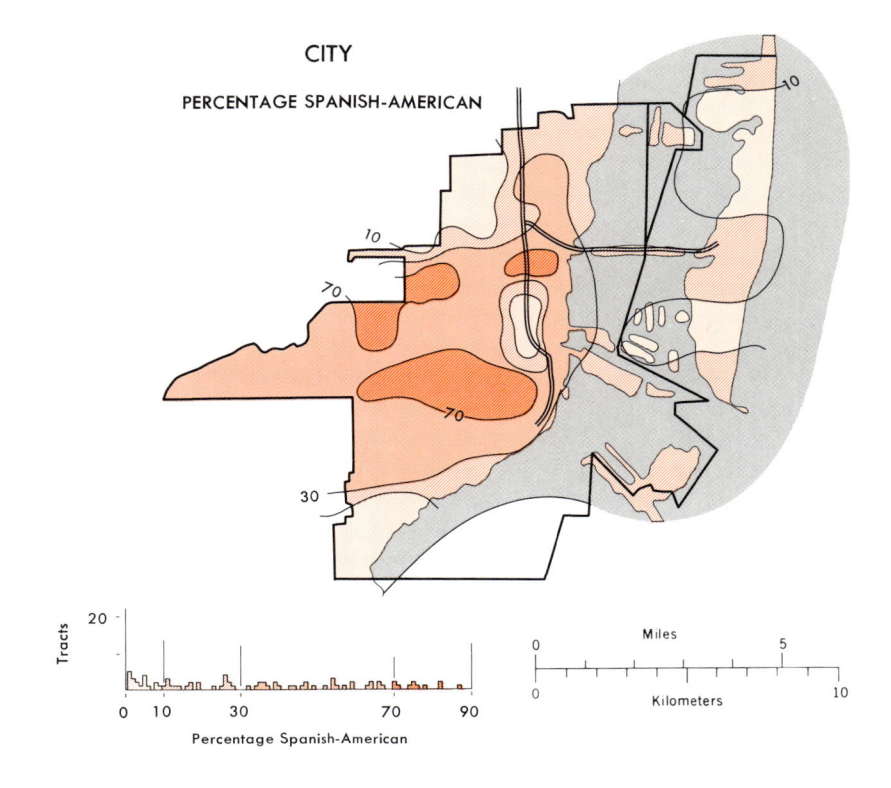

**Cuban-Americans.** Estimates of the actual number of Cubans in Miami vary. During the 1960s the federal government established a program to resettle in other parts of the nation the Cubans who were flooding into Miami. Subsequent to resettlement elsewhere, many Cubans have drifted back to Miami, drawn by the region's social and environmental attractions. The Census counted 109,000 Cuban-born and 13,700 people of Cuban parentage in 1970. The total Cuban foreign stock makes up 37 percent of Miami's population. At first Cubans were relegated to menial jobs, but since they were largely members of the prerevolutionary middle class, they quickly moved into trade, commerce, and the professions. Cubans now own almost a third of the businesses in Miami, and the mean income for Cuban families is well over $10,000. Few Cubans are dependent on public assistance; these few are the elderly and the disabled. Little Havana, in the heart of the Cuban community west of the Miami CBD, is an almost completely Cuban business area where many of the restaurants that formerly did business in Havana have been reconstituted.

**Jews.** During the 1920s Miami and Miami Beach became a popular winter vacation resort for New York's Jewish community, and as the population accustomed to vacationing there began to retire, large numbers decided to spend their retirement years in their favorite vacation spot. Old hotels that became less fashionable as newer and larger hotels were built northward along the beach (a process that continues today) were converted to residential apartments. The southern part of Miami Beach is now a geriatric ghetto, with a heavily Jewish population. Mapping Polish and Russian foreign stock is a good measure of the concentration, for few of the area's people of Polish and Russian descent are ethnic Russians or Poles. Most of the municipality of Miami Beach is over 30 percent Jewish, and one tract exceeds 50 percent. Inflation and fixed retirement incomes have proved disastrous for many south Miami Beach residents. Instead of golden years in the sun, too many face bleak years of struggling to survive on grossly inadequate incomes. In the three tracts that comprise the south end of Miami Beach, the income of 27 percent of the population is below the poverty level. Two-thirds of the total population in each of the tracts receives Social Security income.

Although the Miami metropolitan area developed too late to receive any of the influx of European immigrants that came to the United States in the late 19th and early 20th centuries, it has an unusual and stimulating ethnic mix. Little Havana has no counterpart in the United States, and Miami Beach has many shops, restaurants, and even hotels that cater primarily to a Jewish clientele. When Miami's blacks are added, the result is a great deal more human diversity than might at first be expected. However, only 3 percent of the SMSA's Spanish-Americans and 0.2 percent of its blacks live in Miami Beach compared with Miami Beach's 7 percent share of the SMSA population.

## SOCIOECONOMIC CHARACTERISTICS

**Household Size.** There are 2.9 people in the average SMSA household, 2.7 in the average Miami household, and 1.9 in the average Miami Beach household. On a tract basis, household sizes vary from 1.4 to 5.4 persons. Average household sizes under 2 persons are characteristic of tracts in Miami Beach and downtown Miami. Household sizes in the rest of Miami are between 2 and 3 people, except in the predominantly black area of north-central Miami where tract means larger than 3 persons prevail. The area south of Miami where household sizes exceed 4 and 5 persons are tracts with large populations of migrant laborers. The area where average household sizes exceed 4 persons along the SMSA's northern boundary is recently settled (p. 238) and occupied by families in their childbearing years.

**Female Headship.** The Census Bureau defines female headship by the absence of a male spouse regardless of the sex of the family's principal breadwinner. Of the families in the SMSA and in Miami, 17 percent are headed by females, as are 10 percent of the families in Miami Beach. Female headship exceeds 10 percent in Miami, Miami Beach, and in the suburban communities immediately north and west of Miami. Percentages of female headship increase to 30 in dominantly black areas in and near Miami. Of Miami's black households, 23 percent are headed by females. Female headship exceeds 10 percent south of Miami in the area where migrant laborers

**CITY**
CUBAN-AMERICANS

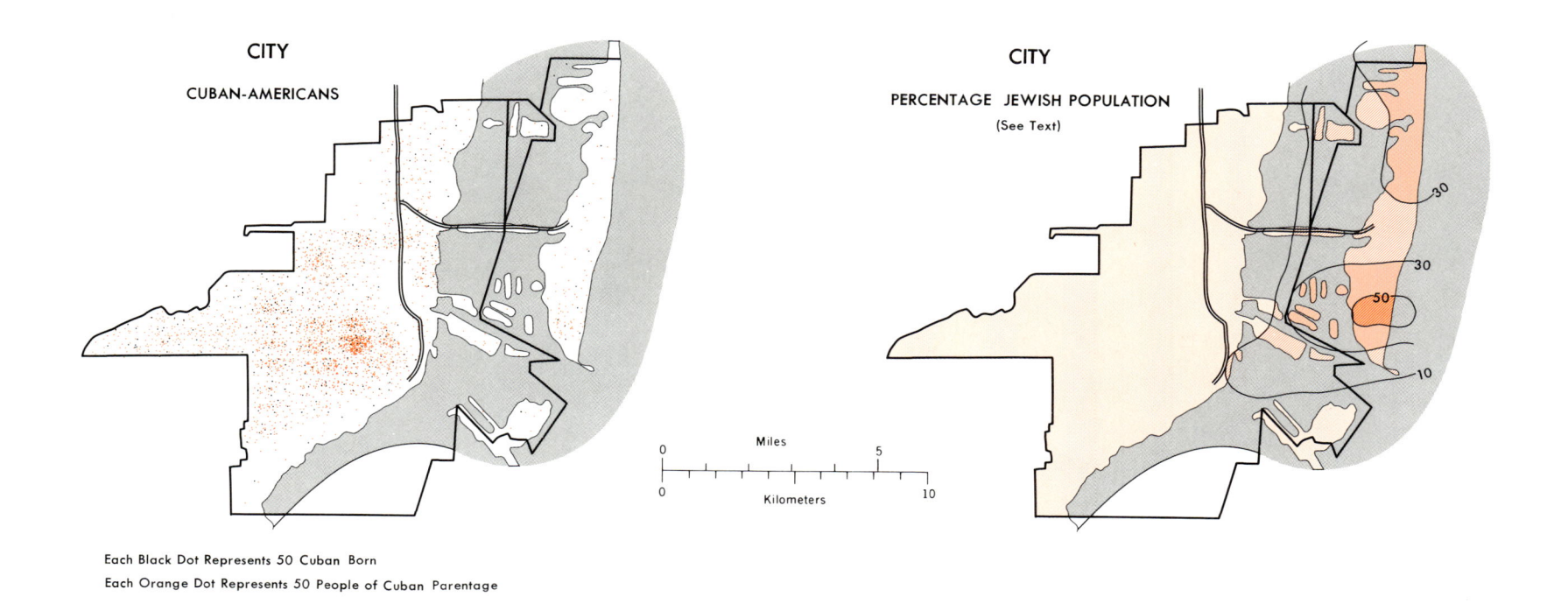

**CITY**
PERCENTAGE JEWISH POPULATION
(See Text)

Each Black Dot Represents 50 Cuban Born
Each Orange Dot Represents 50 People of Cuban Parentage

comprise significant percentages of tract populations. Some of the laborers are blacks and others are Mexican-Americans. It is likely that blacks contribute disproportionately to the higher rates of female headship, since female headship among Mexican-Americans is unusual.

**Occupations.** Of the SMSA's labor force, 14 percent work at blue-collar (laborers and operatives) jobs and 20 percent classify themselves as executives (engineers, teachers, professionals, managers, proprietors, and administrators). The remaining 66 percent are service workers (37 percent) and clerical employees (29 percent). The occupational breakdown for Miami is: blue-collar, 21 percent; service, 40 percent; clerical, 25 percent; and executive, 14 percent. In Miami Beach, 5 percent of the labor force work at blue-collar occupations, services employ 30 percent, clerical jobs occupy 38 percent, and 27 percent are executives.

Tract percentages of blue-collar workers range from 1 to 47. Blue-collar workers exceed 10 percent of tract labor forces in most of the metropolitan area except for the northern coastal suburbs, the beach communities, and Miami's western and southern suburbs. Percentages of blue-collar workers exceed 30 in northwestern Miami, and the blue-collar pattern extends across the municipal boundary into the northwestern suburbs; only in the northwestern sector are more than 10 percent of the suburban labor forces typically engaged in blue-collar occupations.

Between 2 and 56 percent of the labor forces in individual tracts work in executive occupations. Proportions are below 10 percent in the northwestern sector and in the fruit- and vegetable-growing areas south of Miami. Percentages exceed 30 in the suburbs south of Miami, in the northern part of Miami Beach, and in the beach and bayshore communities north of Miami Beach. In the southern part of Miami Beach, executives exceed 30 percent in the tract containing the man-made islands in Biscayne Bay.

**Income.** Mean income per person in the Miami SMSA is $3,500 per year. Miami's mean income per person is $2,800, and in Miami Beach it is $5,000. The high mean income for Miami Beach, in conjunction with the large poverty population living there, suggests that nonpoverty incomes in Miami Beach must be especially high. Indeed, the SMSA's highest income tract is the one composed of the man-made islands in Biscayne Bay, where the mean income per person is $10,500 per year. Incomes along the coast and bayshore exceed $5,000 per person per year except for the poor area of southern Miami Beach. Incomes below $2,500 are concentrated in the northwestern sector, especially in predominantly black neighborhoods. The region's lowest incomes are located in the fruit- and vegetable-growing area south of Miami, where incomes are $1,300 per person per year in the poorest tract and well below $2,500 in adjacent tracts.

TOPICS OF SPECIAL INTEREST IN THE MIAMI REGION

**Negroes.** (Histogram on p. 388.) There are 190,000 blacks in the SMSA; they are 15 percent of the total population. Blacks are highly segregated in the SMSA, but in contrast to many other highly segregated areas, blacks are not heavily concentrated in the SMSA's central city. Miami has 40 percent of the SMSA's blacks compared with its 26 percent share of the total population. Local residents recognize as many as 10 major black residential enclaves. The first black settlement in the area was in Coconut Grove in south Miami. When the railroad reached Miami in 1896, an area to the west of it in central Miami was set aside for blacks who worked for the railroad. The area eventually grew into the nucleus of Miami's largest ghetto. Separate black nuclei such as Carol City-Opa Locka to the north, and Richmond Heights-Perrine-Goulds and Homestead-Florida City on the south, remain distinct, although some merging is occurring in places where black enclaves are close together, such as Carol City-Opa Locka. There are social and economic differences among the black enclaves. Incomes are highest in Carol City and Richmond Heights, and lowest in Homestead-Florida City. Significant income differentials between whites and blacks persist. Mean family income for whites is $12,100 per year whereas the comparable figure for blacks is $6,800.

**Spanish-Americans.** (Histogram on p. 396.) The Census Bureau identifies Spanish-Americans in Florida by counting people who speak Spanish. Of the almost 300,000 Spanish speakers (24 percent of the SMSA population) 17,000 are Puerto Rican in origin and 26,000 are from Central and South America. With the exception of a population of indeterminate size composed of Mexican-American foreign stock and indigenous Mexican-Americans, most of the remainder of the Spanish-American population consists of Cuban

*Twentieth-Century Cities: Miami*

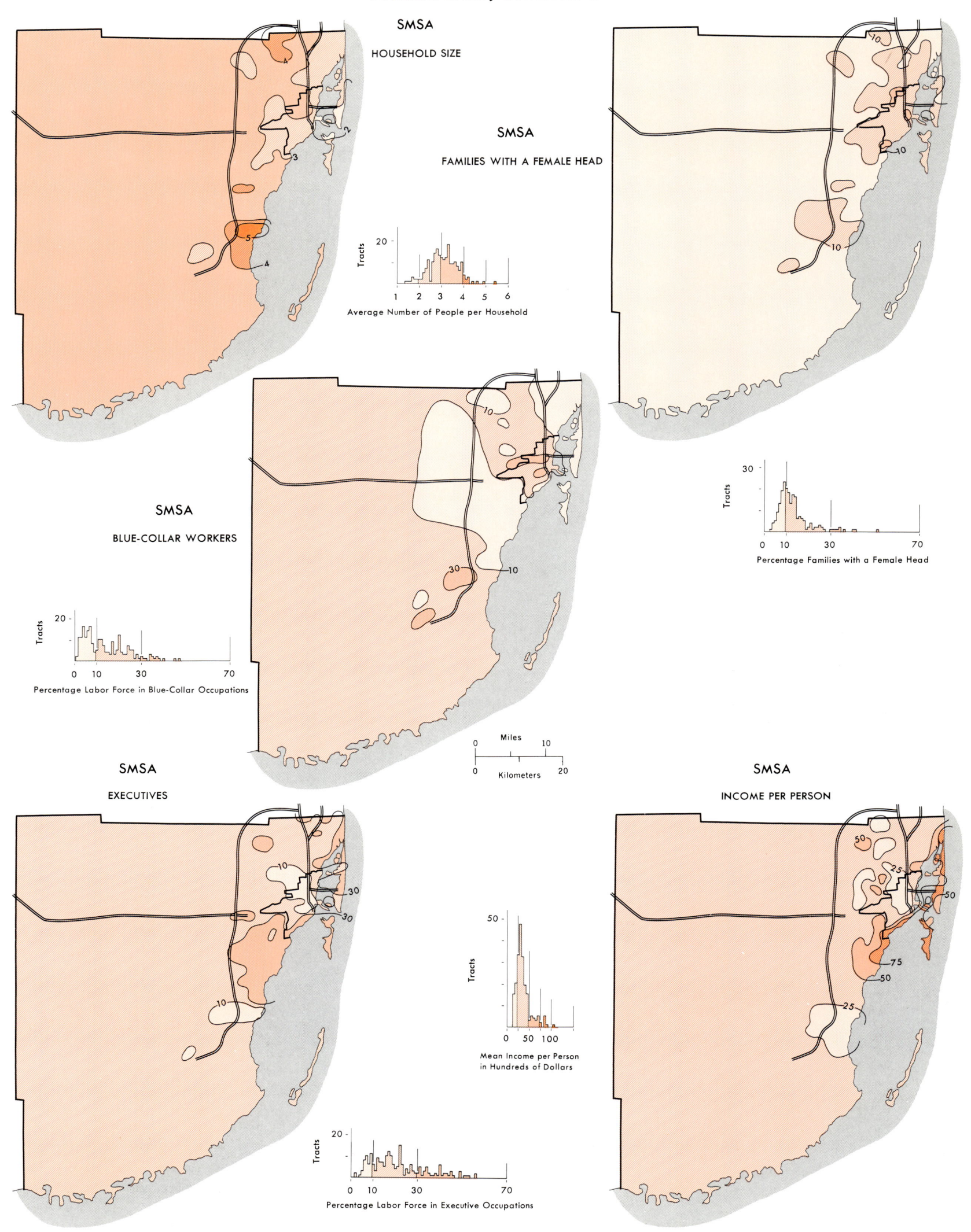

SMSA

HOUSEHOLD SIZE

Average Number of People per Household

SMSA

FAMILIES WITH A FEMALE HEAD

Percentage Families with a Female Head

SMSA

BLUE-COLLAR WORKERS

Percentage Labor Force in Blue-Collar Occupations

SMSA

EXECUTIVES

Percentage Labor Force in Executive Occupations

Mean Income per Person in Hundreds of Dollars

SMSA

INCOME PER PERSON

244

SMSA
THE ELDERLY

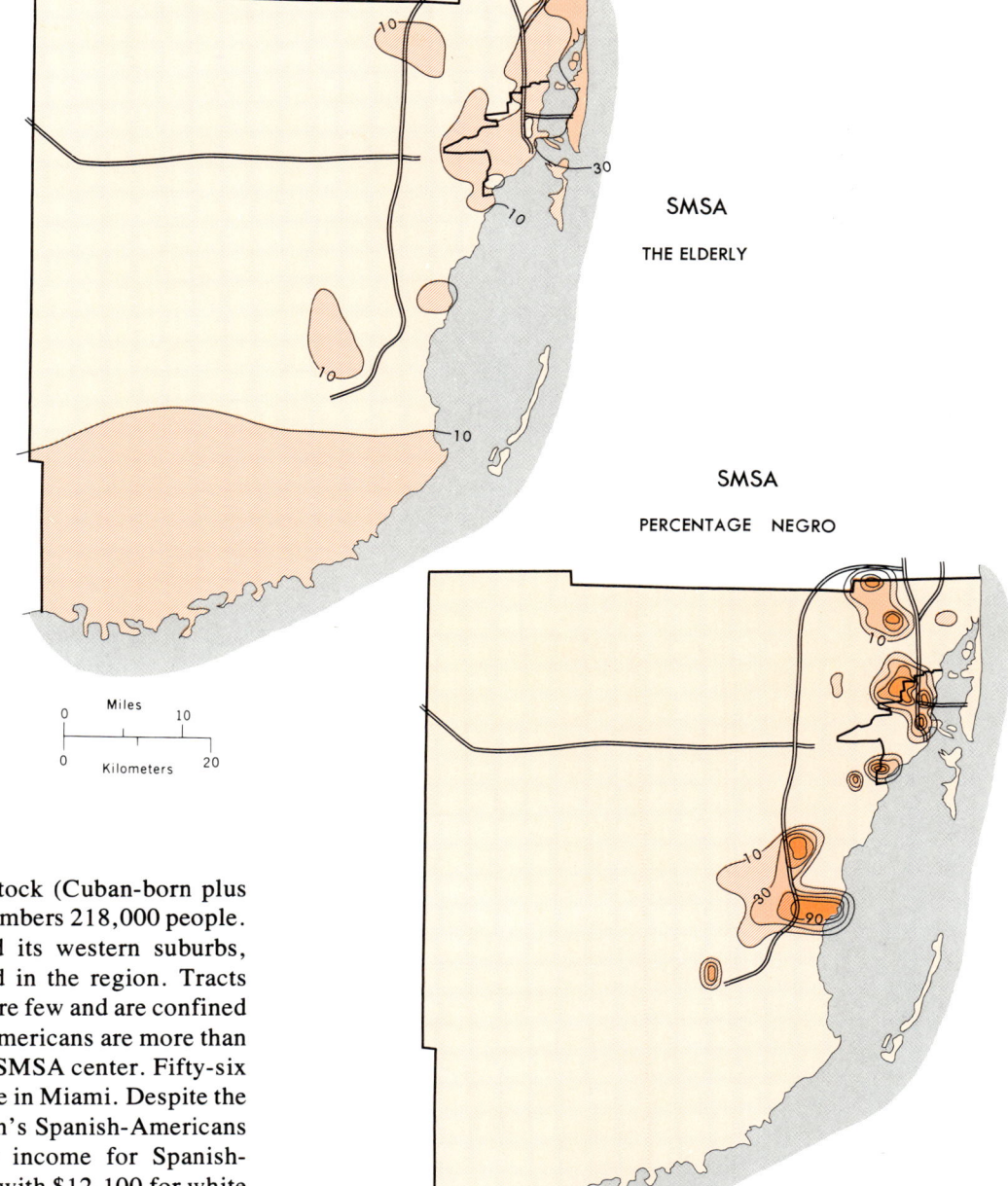

SMSA
PERCENTAGE NEGRO

refugees and their children. Cuban foreign stock (Cuban-born plus people with at least one Cuban-born parent) numbers 218,000 people. Most Spanish-Americans live in Miami and its western suburbs, although percentages over 10 are widespread in the region. Tracts where Spanish-Americans exceed 70 percent are few and are confined to Miami's Little Havana area. But Spanish-Americans are more than 30 percent of tract populations in much of the SMSA center. Fifty-six percent of the SMSA's Spanish-Americans live in Miami. Despite the fact that most have arrived recently, the region's Spanish-Americans are doing well economically. Mean family income for Spanish-Americans in the SMSA is $9,200, compared with $12,100 for white families and $6,800 for blacks. The quick success of the Cuban community, although not unexpected since the refugees are disproportionately drawn from Cuba's prerevolutionary middle class. has generated antagonism within the black community, where low incomes persist.

**Poverty.** (Histogram on p. 420.) Fourteen percent of the SMSA population, 20 percent of Miami's people, and 17 percent of the population of Miami Beach have incomes below the poverty level. The poverty population exceeds 10 percent of tract totals throughout Miami and Miami Beach, with a northern extension into suburban areas. More than 30 percent of the people in south Miami Beach, central Miami, and the predominantly black area of north-central Miami have incomes below the poverty level. The southern part of the SMSA also has a significant poverty population, with high concentrations in areas occupied by blacks and migrant laborers.

**Crowded Housing.** (Histogram on p. 292.) When housing units have more than 1 person per room, their occupants are usually crowded to an unhealthy, undersirable degree. Thirteen percent of the SMSA's housing units and 21 percent of Miami's dwellings are occupied by more than 1 person per room. Percentages of overcrowded units exceed 10 in most of the SMSA except for the affluent suburban areas of Coral Gables, the adjacent communities southwest of Miami, and the upper-class suburbs along the northern coast. Over 30 percent of all housing units are crowded in Miami's black ghetto and in some parts of the Cuban area. Overcrowding was especially acute in Little Havana during the early 1960s, but it abated toward the end of the decade as Cuban refugees established themselves economically. The migrant labor camps south of Miami are also evident as pockets of crowded housing. Almost half the housing in one tract is crowded, and in that tract, 28 percent of the tract's housing units have more than 1.5 people per room.

---

Miami strikes the uncritical eye as homogeneous and uninteresting, especially compared with the glittering opulence of the luxury hotels, restaurants, and nightclubs that line Miami Beach. Indeed, many visitors see no more of Miami than what is visible from the expressway connecting Miami Beach to the airport. The flat terrain and abundant vegetation contribute to an apparent homogeneity, for

*Twentieth-Century Cities: Miami*

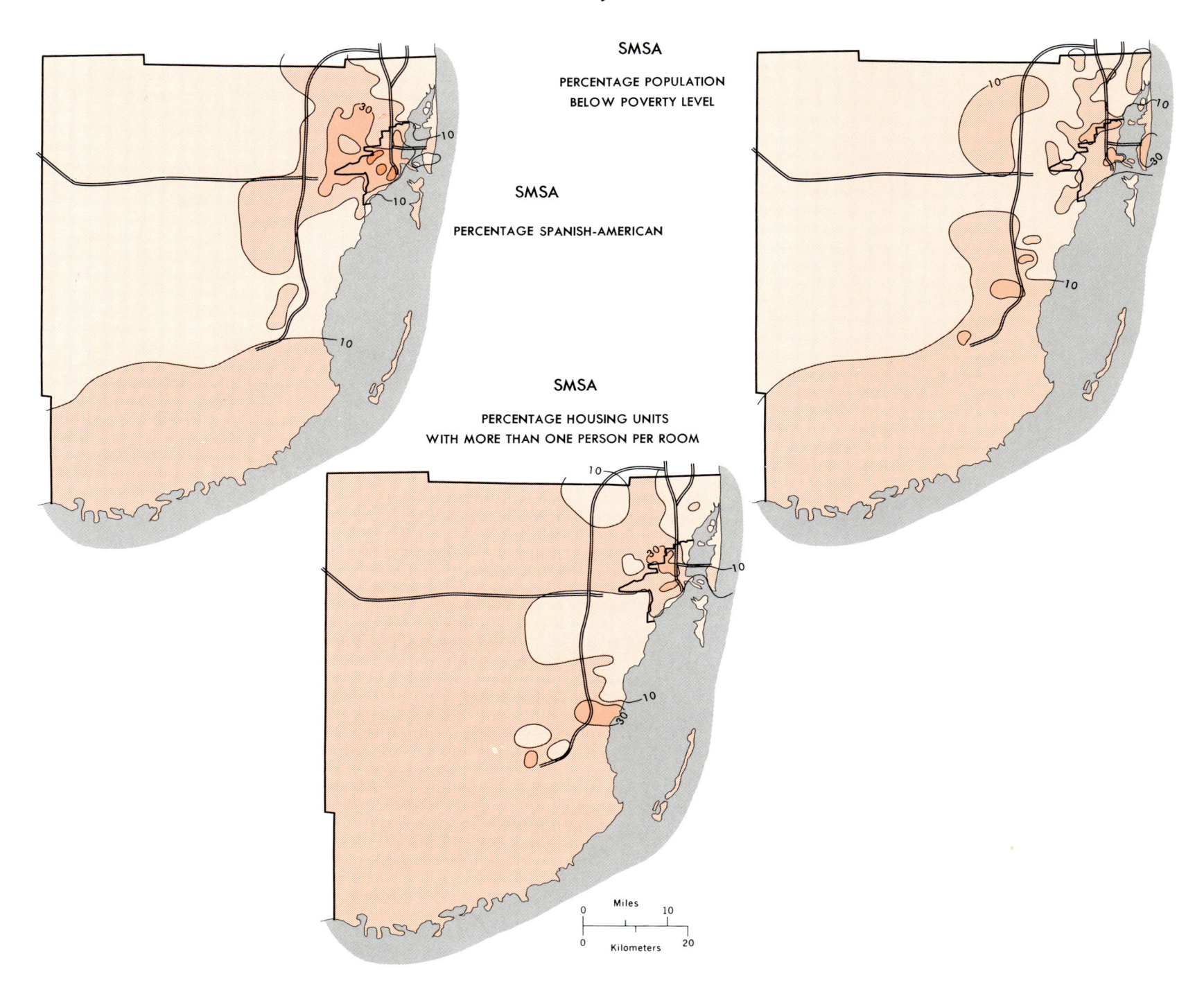

SMSA
PERCENTAGE POPULATION
BELOW POVERTY LEVEL

SMSA
PERCENTAGE SPANISH-AMERICAN

SMSA
PERCENTAGE HOUSING UNITS
WITH MORE THAN ONE PERSON PER ROOM

lush plantings and luxuriant wild vegetation mean that a house must be especially dilapidated or especially opulent to attract attention at first glance. Despite this surface sameness, Miami and its suburbs possess a great deal of ethnic and social diversity. Miami is in almost all respects the youngest city included in the atlas; it was largely undeveloped when Houston and Los Angeles were already booming. Despite its recent entrance into the American metropolitan arena, it is one of the nation's more complicated metropolitan regions.

CHAPTER 24

# Atlanta

*Atlanta has the nerve of a government mule. If it could suck as hard as it can blow,
it could bring the ocean to it and become a seaport.*

SAVANNAH PROVERB

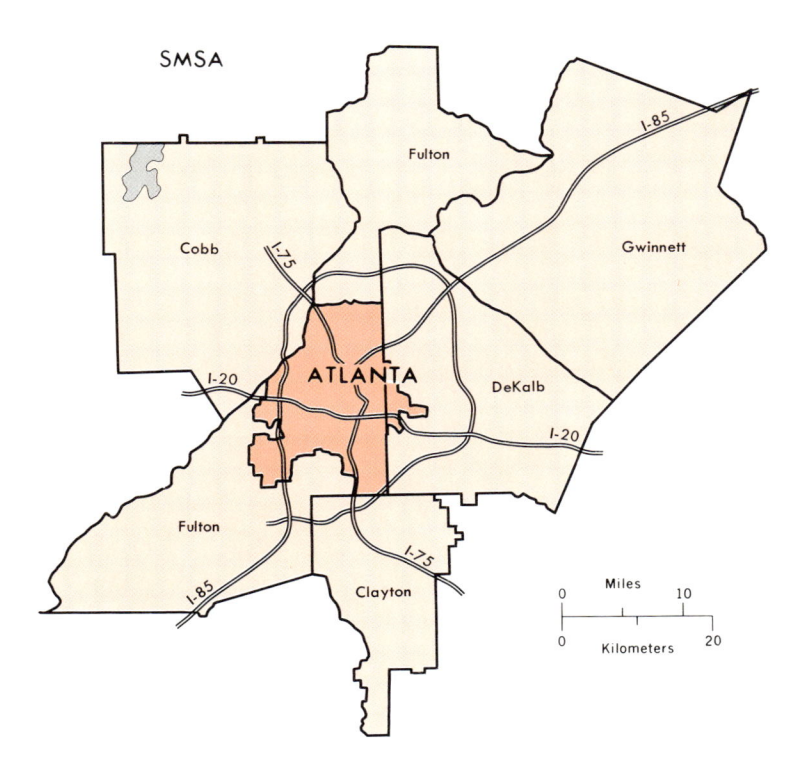

The Atlanta Standard Metropolitan Statistical Area (SMSA) is the nation's 20th most populous SMSA with 1,390,000 people. The population of the city of Atlanta is 497,000, or 36 percent of the SMSA total. The city crosses the boundary separating DeKalb and Fulton counties. Ninety percent of Atlanta's population lives in the Fulton County part of the city. An additional 27 percent of the SMSA population lives in DeKalb County outside Atlanta, and 11 percent lives in the rest of Fulton County. The remaining 26 percent of the SMSA total is divided among Clayton (7 percent), Cobb (14 percent), and Gwinnett (5 percent) counties. The Daily Urban System (DUS) defined by counties that have at least 5 percent of their labor forces working in DeKalb and Fulton counties includes all the SMSA counties and 24 additional Georgia counties (p. 248), which add 522,000 people to the SMSA population for a DUS total of 1,913,000. The region is the nation's 17th most populous DUS. The Atlanta commuting area is one of the largest in the nation.

Atlanta began as a rail center. By 1860, 15 railroads converged on the city, and it was already an important transportation hub and regional center. The city became an important Confederate supply base during the Civil War with machine shops, foundries, and arsenals complementing earlier rail-oriented activities. The Civil War almost destroyed the city for the Union armies sacked and burned it toward the war's close. Atlanta was rebuilt quickly after the Civil War, and the city's leaders continued their efforts to make Atlanta the regional metropolis for the southeastern United States. The city population reached 90,000 in 1900 (p. 10). Since then the city and the metropolitan area have continued to grow on the basis of Atlanta's role as a regional wholesaler and, more recently, on the basis of office activities that serve the region in its relations with the nation and the world. The population of the city increased slightly (2 percent) between 1960 and 1970, but the SMSA grew 37 percent during the same decade, compared with a national increase in metropolitan population of 17 percent.

Atlanta is located on the piedmont in gently rolling terrain. Few areas of the city are flat. However, there is little local relief; maximum differences in elevation within the city are less than 300 feet (90 meters). Like several other southern, inland cities, Atlanta's old core is situated on a drainage divide where it was convenient for the several railroads that stimulated early growth to meet. The city's rolling terrain is seldom steep enough to present barriers to movement in any direction, but it does present opportunities for differentiating neighborhoods and land uses.

Residential land uses have spread north, west, and east from the

*Note:* All data are from the 1970 Censuses of Population and Housing unless otherwise indicated. Therefore the present tense refers to 1970 data except for income data which are from 1969. Cartographic conventions are explained in Chapter 1.

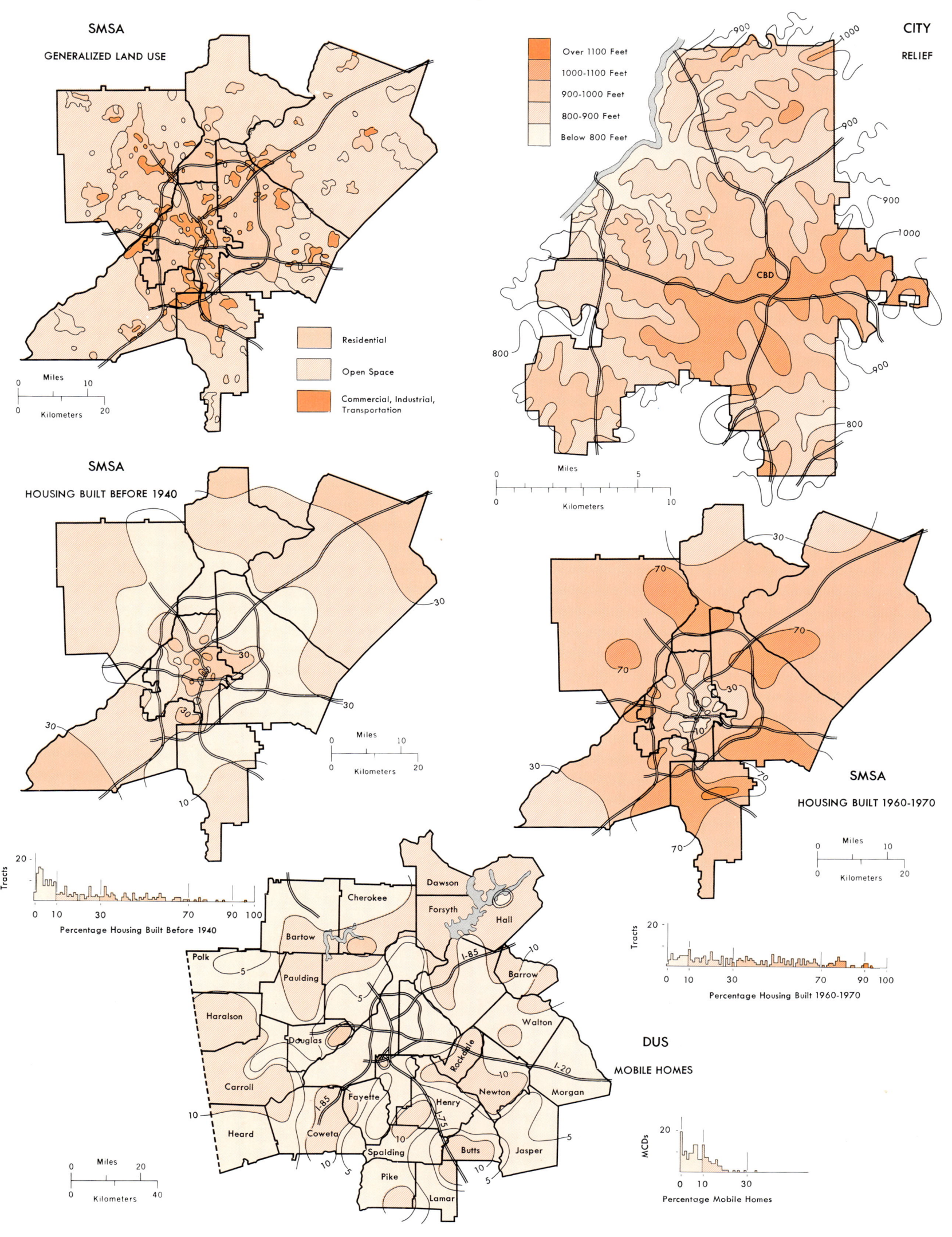

*Twentieth-Century Cities: Atlanta*

## SMSA
### GENERALIZED LAND USE

- Residential
- Open Space
- Commercial, Industrial, Transportation

## CITY
### RELIEF

- Over 1100 Feet
- 1000-1100 Feet
- 900-1000 Feet
- 800-900 Feet
- Below 800 Feet

## SMSA
### HOUSING BUILT BEFORE 1940

Percentage Housing Built Before 1940

## SMSA
### HOUSING BUILT 1960-1970

Percentage Housing Built 1960-1970

## DUS
### MOBILE HOMES

Percentage Mobile Homes

Counties: Dawson, Cherokee, Forsyth, Hall, Bartow, Polk, Paulding, Barrow, Haralson, Douglas, Walton, Carroll, Rockdale, Fayette, Newton, Morgan, Heard, Coweta, Henry, Butts, Jasper, Spalding, Pike, Lamar

248

*Twentieth-Century Cities: Atlanta*

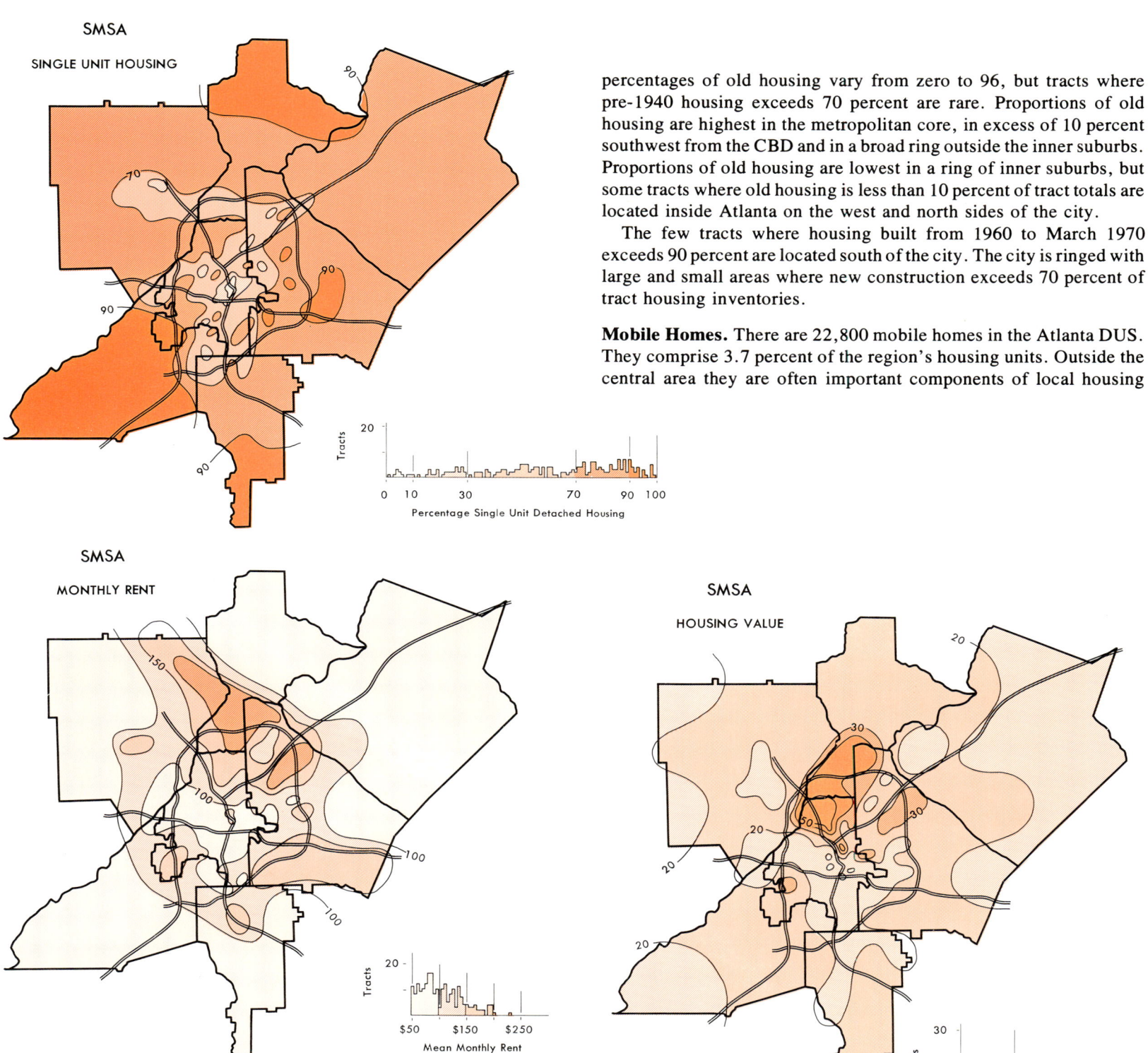

percentages of old housing vary from zero to 96, but tracts where pre-1940 housing exceeds 70 percent are rare. Proportions of old housing are highest in the metropolitan core, in excess of 10 percent southwest from the CBD and in a broad ring outside the inner suburbs. Proportions of old housing are lowest in a ring of inner suburbs, but some tracts where old housing is less than 10 percent of tract totals are located inside Atlanta on the west and north sides of the city.

The few tracts where housing built from 1960 to March 1970 exceeds 90 percent are located south of the city. The city is ringed with large and small areas where new construction exceeds 70 percent of tract housing inventories.

**Mobile Homes.** There are 22,800 mobile homes in the Atlanta DUS. They comprise 3.7 percent of the region's housing units. Outside the central area they are often important components of local housing

Central Business District (CBD) more rapidly than to the south. Industrial, commercial, and transportation land uses are concentrated in a north-south corridor paralleling rail routes into the city from the south, in the CBD area, and in the area northwest of the CBD, which also combines rail and industrial land uses. The industrial/commercial area on Atlanta's western boundary is a new industrial park. The similar area in east-central Cobb County is the industrial/military complex at Marietta (Lockheed Aircraft) and Dobbins Air Force Base.

## HOUSING

**Housing Age.** Of the SMSA's housing, 18 percent was built before 1940, 39 percent was built from 1940 through 1959, and 43 percent dates from 1960 to March 1970. In Atlanta, 30 percent was built before 1940, 43 percent from 1940 through 1959, and 27 percent from 1960 to March 1970. The Atlanta SMSA has a relatively low proportion of old housing, most of which is located in Atlanta. Tract

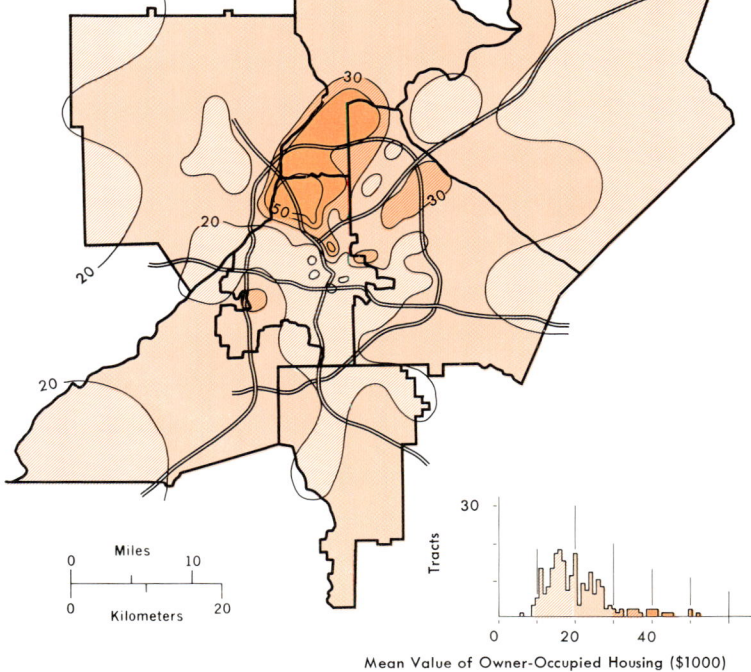

inventories. The 1,500 mobile homes in Cherokee County, for example, constitute 15 percent of the county's 9,800 housing units.

**Single-Unit Detached Housing.** (City map on p. 255.) Individual dwelling units make up 66 percent of the SMSA housing stock. Tract percentages exceed 30 in most of the SMSA except in the CBD and in scattered tracts around the downtown area. Within Atlanta, single-unit detached housing comprises 49 percent of the city's total housing, but even some of Atlanta's tracts have housing stocks in which detached housing exceeds 90 percent. The 34 percent of the SMSA housing that is not single-family detached dwellings consists of small proportions of duplex and 3- or 4-unit structures (6 percent), and many medium-sized (5- to 49-unit) structures (20 percent).

*Twentieth-Century Cities: Atlanta*

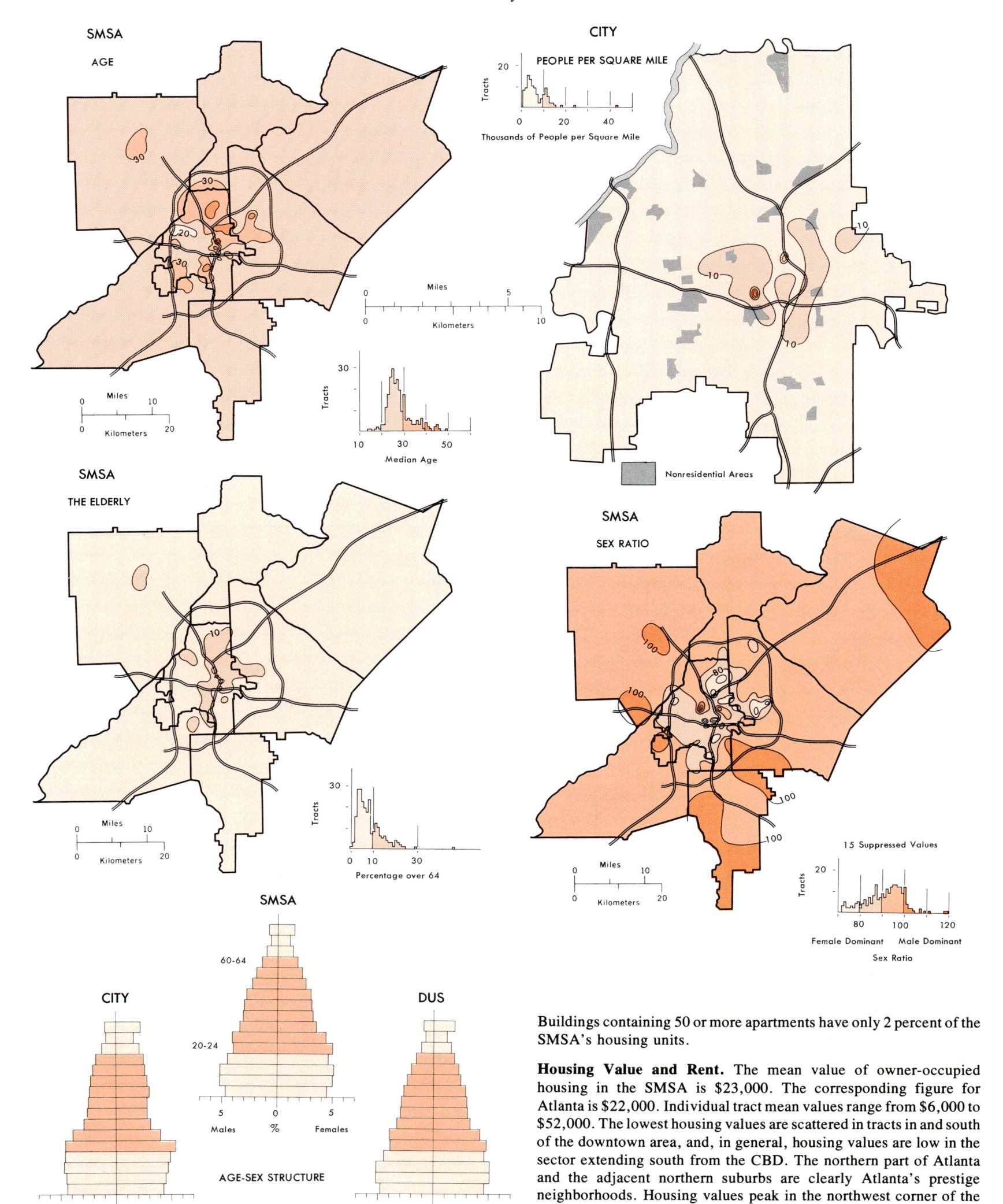

SMSA AGE

CITY PEOPLE PER SQUARE MILE

SMSA THE ELDERLY

SMSA SEX RATIO

CITY — SMSA AGE-SEX STRUCTURE — DUS

Buildings containing 50 or more apartments have only 2 percent of the SMSA's housing units.

**Housing Value and Rent.** The mean value of owner-occupied housing in the SMSA is $23,000. The corresponding figure for Atlanta is $22,000. Individual tract mean values range from $6,000 to $52,000. The lowest housing values are scattered in tracts in and south of the downtown area, and, in general, housing values are low in the sector extending south from the CBD. The northern part of Atlanta and the adjacent northern suburbs are clearly Atlanta's prestige neighborhoods. Housing values peak in the northwest corner of the city, and because the SMSA's highest-value housing is in the central

250

*Twentieth-Century Cities: Atlanta*

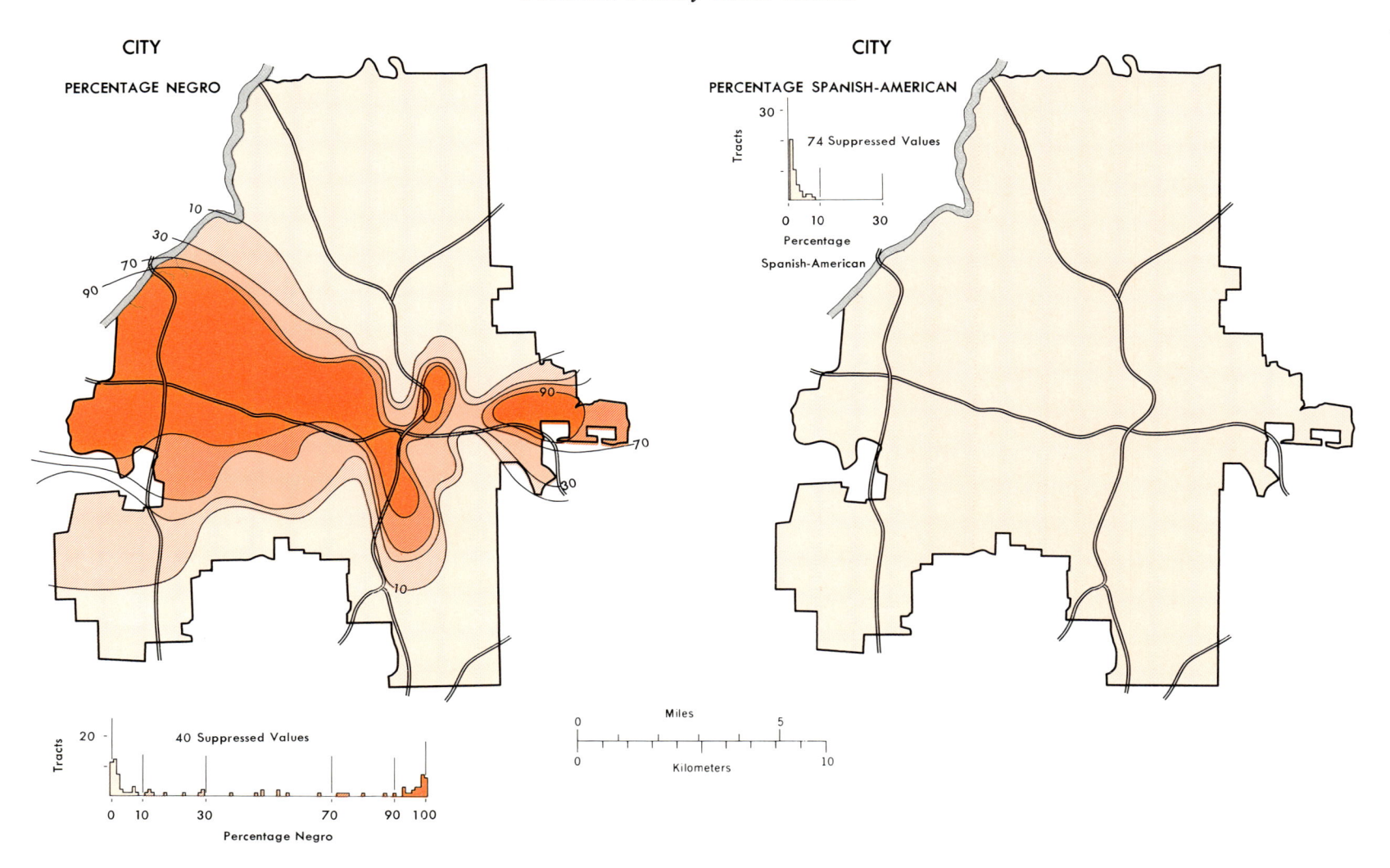

city, the difference between the city and SMSA means is unusually small. The area of low-value housing extending west from the CBD demarcates the area where blacks exceed 90 percent of tract populations.

Mean monthly contract rents average $107 for the SMSA and $91 in Atlanta. Individual tract means range from less than $50 (not plotted or mapped) to $235. The rent map is similar in some respects to the housing-value map, especially the higher rents to the north and the generally lower rents south of the CBD. The area of high mean rents extends farther to the northwest than does the area of high housing values, however, and a high-rent zone appears in southern DeKalb County that has no direct counterpart on the housing-value map.

## THE PEOPLE

**Population Density.** Atlanta's overall population density is 3,800 people per square mile (1,470 per square kilometer). Individual tract densities in the city range from 1,000 to 43,000 per square mile (390 to 16,600 per square kilometer). Densities over 15,000 per square mile (5,800 per square kilometer) are rare, and the highest density area is a tiny downtown tract consisting solely of a public housing project. Aside from that unusual circumstance, Atlanta is a low-density city. Most housing in the city was built after World War II when families preferred single-unit detached housing on large lots. (An SMSA map is on p. 316.)

**Age and the Elderly.** The median age of the Atlanta SMSA population is 26 years. The city population is slightly older on the average, with a median age of 27 years. Median ages are below 30 years for the SMSA's suburban tracts except those in the independent settlement of Marietta in north-central Cobb County. For the most part, tracts where median ages exceed 30 and, in some cases, 40 years are concentrated in Atlanta. Tracts in which median ages are less than 20 years are located in predominantly black areas of the city.

People 64 years of age and older make up 7 percent of the SMSA population and 9 percent of Atlanta's people. The patterns on the map of the elderly are different enough from those on the map of median age to suggest that high median ages are as much a function of the relative absence of young children as they are of disproportionate numbers of elderly people.

The contrasting age structures of the city and the entire SMSA are most clearly evident in the population pyramids. Atlanta has proportions of children and young adults similar to those of the SMSA as a whole, but there are relatively few adults in the 30- to 49-year-old cohorts in Atlanta compared with the SMSA. The difference reflects the selective out-migration of white families from the central city as they reach their child-raising years.

**Sex Ratio.** There are 1.07 females for each male in the SMSA, which yields a female-dominant sex ratio (males divided by females times 100) of 93. There are 1.13 females for each male in Atlanta, resulting in a city sex ratio of 89. Sex ratios exceed 100 in a few rural areas (usually slightly male-dominant) and in a few suburban areas where there are many families with young children. The most female-dominant tracts are located in predominantly black tracts near the city's center.

**Negroes.** There are 255,000 blacks in Atlanta. They make up 51 percent of the city population. Blacks numbered 186,000 in 1960, when they were 38 percent of the city's people. Atlanta now has one of the highest proportions of black population among large American cities. Atlanta's population increased by only 9,000 people between 1960 and 1970 in the face of a 69,000 increase in the black population. Thus white deaths and out-migration almost match black population increases. Before 1940 blacks were confined to three zones east, south, and west of the CBD. As black population and prosperity increased in the late 1940s, west-side black areas began encroaching on white neighborhoods. After some conflict, a gentlemen's

251

SMSA HOUSEHOLD SIZE

Average Number of People per Household

SMSA FAMILIES WITH A FEMALE HEAD

Percentage Families with a Female Head

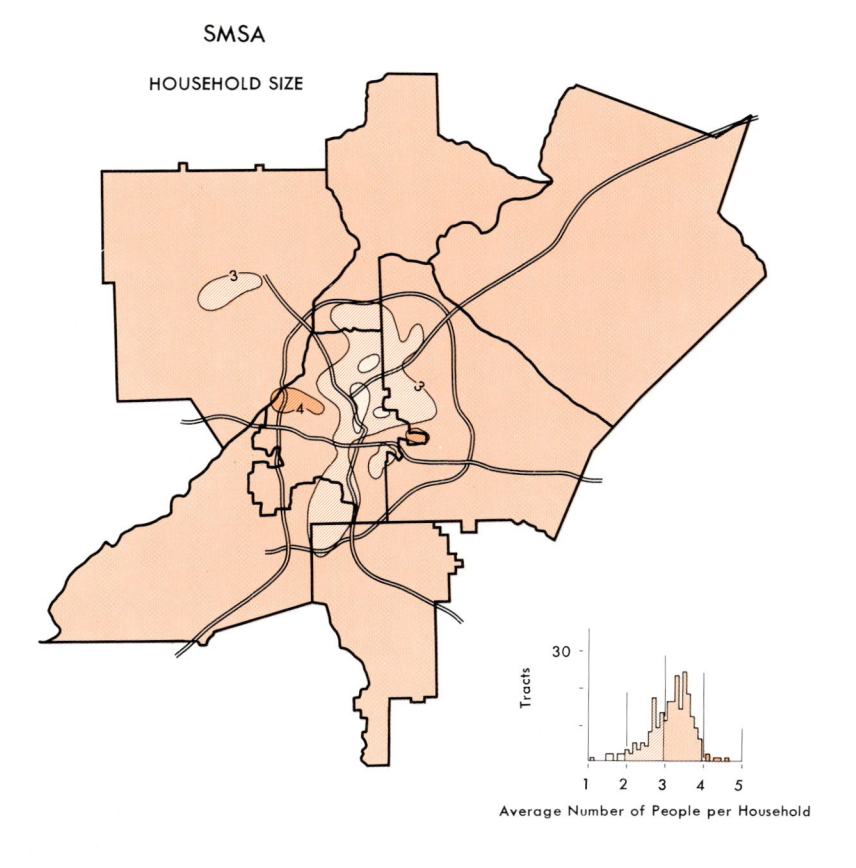

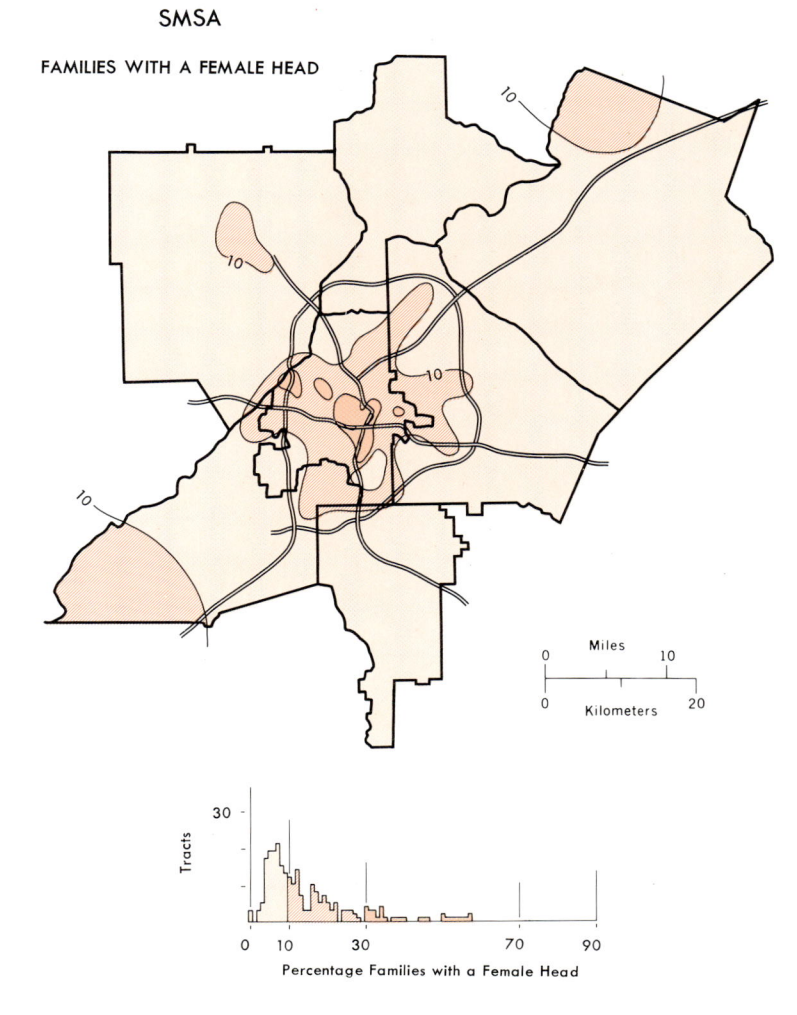

agreement was worked out in which blacks agreed not to move south in exchange for the freedom to move west. During the 1960s blacks also began to take over housing to the east in the DeKalb County part of the city. Atlanta remains sharply segregated along racial lines. Atlanta's black population and the neighborhoods they occupy are far from homogeneous. The city's most prestigious black neighborhood is Cascade Heights, located on the western boundary southwest of the CBD. The median income for black families in one tract there is $14,300, and several tracts have black median family incomes over $10,000. Such areas are atypical, however, for the overall median income for Atlanta's black families is $6,500 compared with $8,400 for all families in Atlanta. (An SMSA map of the black population is on p. 388.)

**Spanish-Americans.** The Census Bureau estimates the number of Hispanics in Atlanta by counting people who speak Spanish. By that reckoning there are 5,100 Spanish-Americans in the city, who comprise 1 percent of Atlanta's population. Most of the city's Hispanics are Americans of Mexican descent who are neither Mexican-born nor have at least one Mexican-born parent. There are few people of Mexican, Central and South American, or Puerto Rican stock, and only about 1,100 people of Cuban stock. In no tracts do Spanish-Americans exceed 10 percent of the population, and the most intense concentrations are located along Atlanta's eastern boundary just north of the city's extension into DeKalb County. There, 8 percent of one tract speaks Spanish. (An SMSA map is on p. 396.)

Atlanta, like most southern cities, has few people of European foreign stock. Foreign stock from the United Kingdom is the largest group in the SMSA, but it comprises only 0.6 percent of the SMSA population.

## SOCIOECONOMIC CHARACTERISTICS

**Household Size.** There are 3.2 people in the average SMSA household and 3 in the average Atlanta household. Individual tract averages vary from 1.1 to 4.6 people per household. Household sizes exceed 3 persons in most of the SMSA except in Marietta, in central Cobb County, and in Atlanta and some of the inner suburbs. Average household sizes exceeding 4 persons are characteristic of two tracts in predominantly black areas of Atlanta, reflecting the larger size (average, 3.6 persons) of the SMSA's black households. The SMSA's smallest average household sizes are located in tracts in and north of Atlanta's CBD.

**Female Headship.** The Census Bureau defines female headship by the absence of a male spouse regardless of the sex of the family's principal breadwinner. Using that definition, 13 percent of the SMSA's families and 22 percent of Atlanta's families are headed by females. Fifty-eight percent of the SMSA's families headed by females live in Atlanta compared with 36 percent of the total population. Individual tract percentages of female headship range from zero to 56, although proportions in most tracts are below 30 percent. High proportions of female headship are concentrated in Atlanta and especially in the city's black neighborhoods, where the highest proportions occur.

**Occupations.** Twelve percent of the SMSA's labor force work at blue-collar (laborers and operatives) jobs and 24 percent classify themselves as executives (engineers, teachers, professionals, managers, proprietors, and administrators). The remaining 64 percent is evenly divided between service and clerical workers. The corresponding breakdown for Atlanta is: blue-collar, 15 percent; service, 37 percent; clerical, 29 percent, and executive, 19 percent.

Blue-collar workers exceed 10 and even 30 percent of tract labor forces northeast of Atlanta. There are relatively few blue-collar workers in a diagonal belt running northeast to southeast across the SMSA that includes the northern part of Atlanta. In the central and southern parts of Atlanta and the western part of the CBD, most tracts have more than 10 percent of their labor forces in blue-collar jobs except for Atlanta's southwest corner and adjacent suburbs, and scattered tracts north and south of the city. Percentages of blue-collar workers exceed 30 in several predominantly black, central-city tracts.

In many parts of the SMSA the executive-occupation map almost reverses the map of blue-collar workers. The zone where executives exceed 30 percent corresponds to the area where blue-collar workers comprise less than 10 percent of tract residents. Socioeconomic differences among the predominantly black areas show up clearly on the map of executives. Less than 10 percent of tract labor forces engage in executive occupations in a predominantly black area extending northwest from downtown Atlanta, but more than 30 percent of tract residents engage in such occupations in an equally black area along Atlanta's western boundary.

**Income.** Mean income per person in the Atlanta SMSA is $3,500 per year, and mean income per person in Atlanta is $3,150 annually. Mean per person incomes for individual tracts vary from $500 to $15,000 per year, with only a few tracts having per capita incomes exceeding $7,500. Incomes are low on the southwestern and northeastern edges of the SMSA and in central Atlanta. The region's highest incomes are enjoyed by people living in northern Atlanta.

## TOPICS OF SPECIAL INTEREST IN THE ATLANTA REGION

**Income from Public Sources.** (Histogram on p. 428.) In the Atlanta SMSA, 2.2 percent of the total income received by all residents comes from Social Security and railroad retirement payments; 0.4 percent is public assistance and welfare payments. The two are combined here to show tract levels of payments from public sources. All tracts for which such payments exceed 5 percent of aggregate tract incomes are located near the metropolitan center, and tracts where public payments exceed 10 percent of all incomes are located in the dominantly black areas of Atlanta. Public payments exceed 30 percent of aggregate tract income in a single tract that contains only a public housing project and its dependent population.

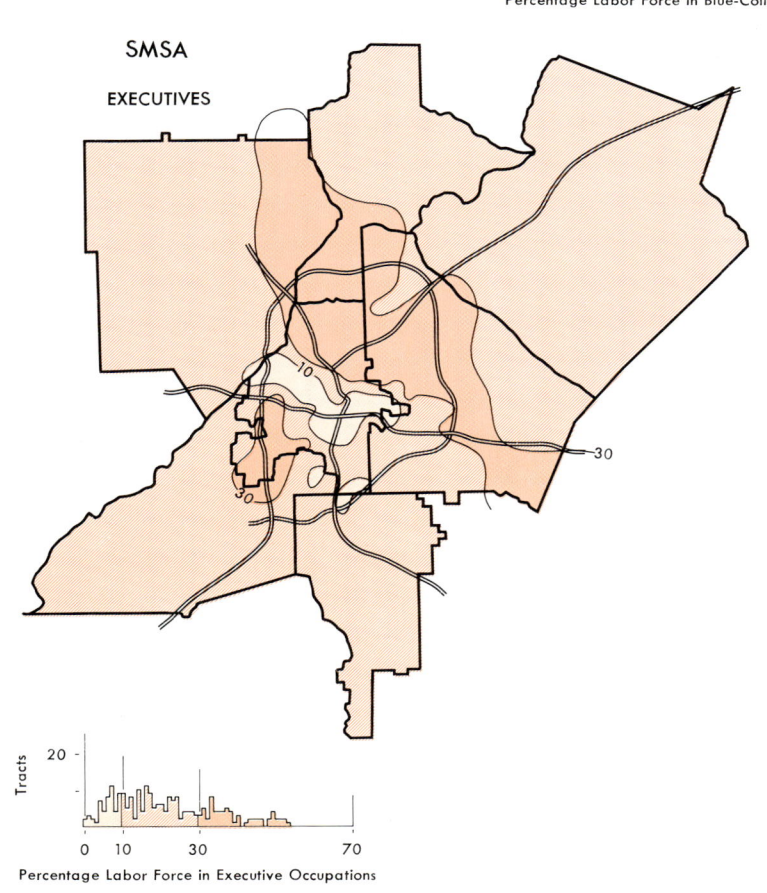

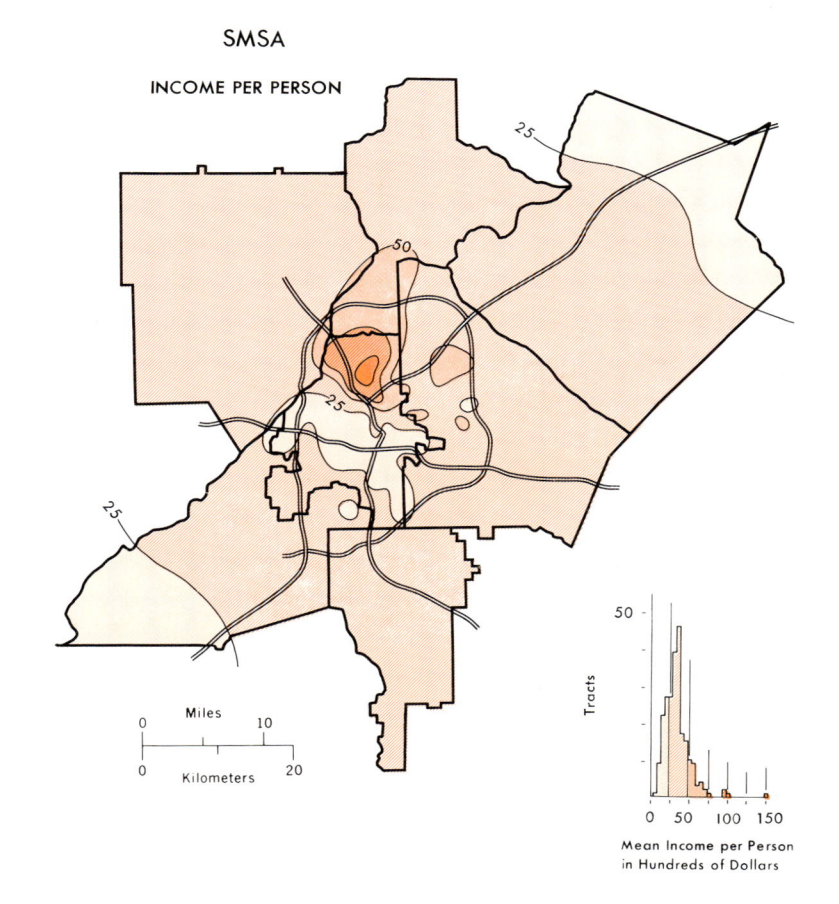

253

**20- to 21-Year-Olds in School.** (Histogram on p. 372.) Twenty-eight percent of the SMSA's people 20 and 21 years of age are enrolled in school, and 29 percent of Atlanta's 20- to 21-year-olds are in school. Tract percentages exceed 70 and 90 near several universities in central Atlanta, but they drop off to less than 10 percent in many adjacent tracts, especially in the southern part of the city. Proportions are high in the northern half of the city, where the SMSA's most affluent people live. The tract where enrollments exceed 90 percent in west-central DeKalb County is the location of Emory University. The area where enrollments exceed 30 percent of 20- to 21-year-olds in southwestern Atlanta includes some tracts with significant middle-income black populations, suggesting that participation in higher education depends as much on income and attitudes as it does on race.

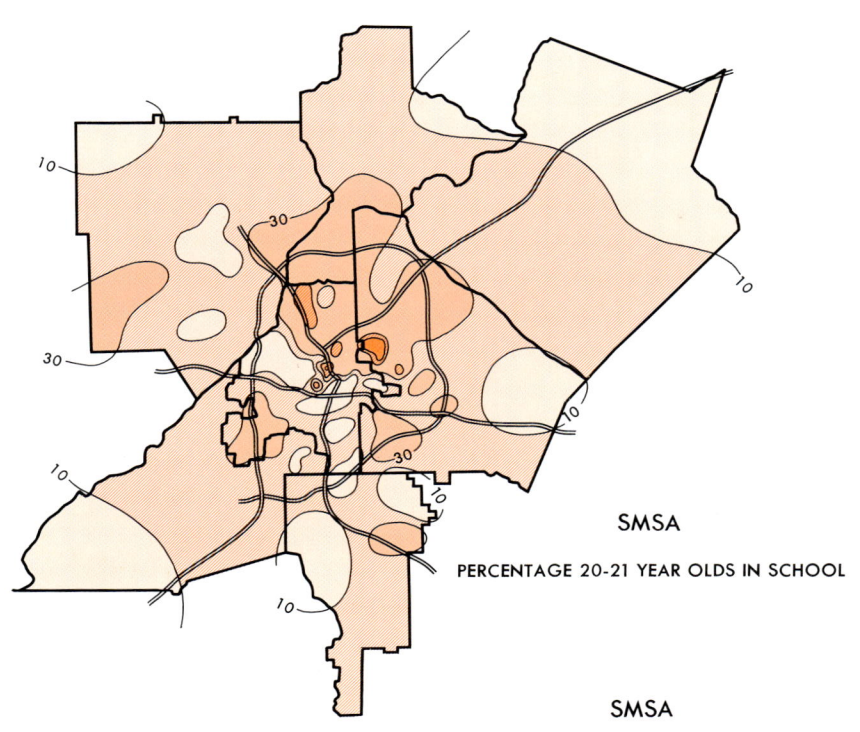

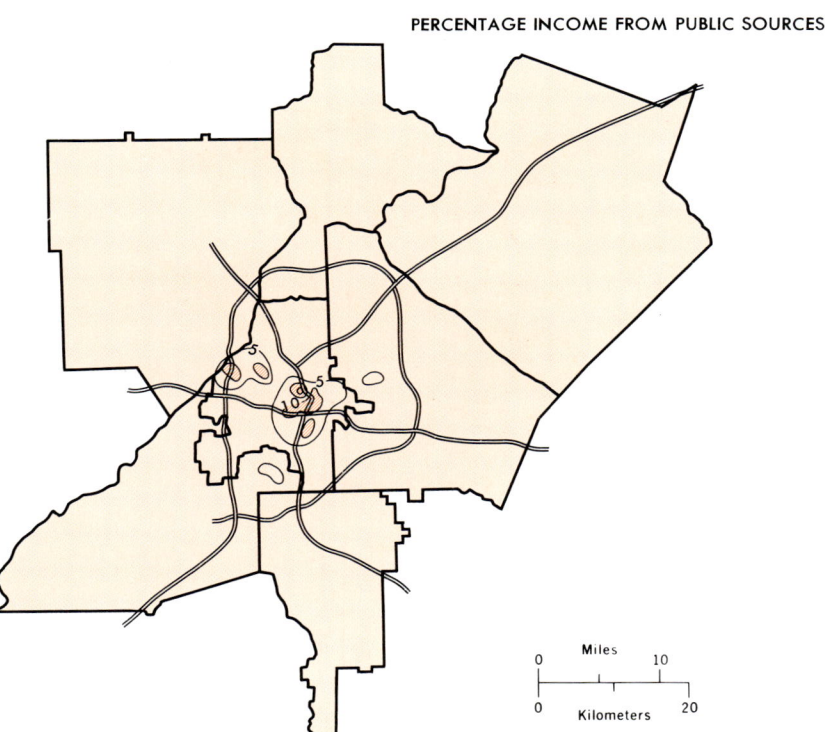

**Residential Change, 1965-1970.** In 1970, 59 percent of the SMSA's people over 5 years of age were living in houses different from the ones they occupied in 1965. In Atlanta, 44 percent were in different houses. Much of the apparent high residential turnover in suburban areas consists of people moving into newly built housing rather than neighborhood churning. Thus high rates of residential turnover in the suburbs should produce little of the disorganization sometimes associated with high rates of transience in old neighborhoods. In Atlanta, high proportions of residential change are clustered in tracts on the periphery of predominantly black areas, suggesting that the major generator of residential change in the city is the transition of housing from predominantly white to predominantly black occupancy.

**Crowded Housing.** (SMSA map on p. 292.) Dwellings in which there is more than 1 person per room are generally considered to be crowded. Segregation in the housing market combined with rapid increases in numbers of blacks has produced concentrations of crowded housing in black neighborhoods. In 1969, black residences housed 50 percent of Atlanta's residents, but they occupied only 20 percent of the city's residential area. There are 17,800 housing units with more than 1 person per room in Atlanta, and 13,800 (78 percent) of them are occupied by blacks.

**Single-Unit Detached Housing.** (SMSA map on p. 249.) Forty-nine percent of Atlanta's housing units are single-unit detached dwellings. Proportions are low in and near the CBD, and they rise with distance from the downtown. Concentrations of individual dwellings are most intense and widespread on the city's northern and southwestern sides. The city's stock of multiple-unit housing occurs primarily in medium-sized (5 to 49 units) apartment buildings, which contain 28 percent of Atlanta's housing stock. Duplex units account for 8 percent, and 3- and 4-unit structures comprise 9 percent of the city's housing. Large apartment buildings with 50 or more units furnish 6 percent of Atlanta's dwellings.

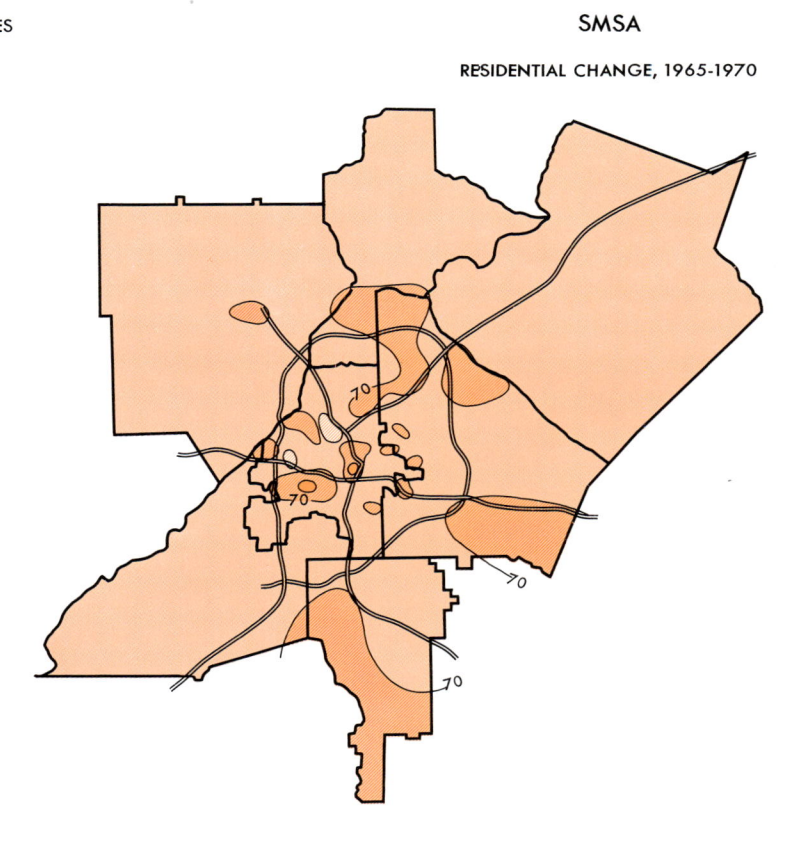

SMSA
PERCENTAGE 20-21 YEAR OLDS IN SCHOOL

SMSA
PERCENTAGE INCOME FROM PUBLIC SOURCES

SMSA
RESIDENTIAL CHANGE, 1965-1970

*Twentieth-Century Cities: Atlanta*

CITY

SINGLE UNIT HOUSING

CITY

PERCENTAGE HOUSEHOLDS WITHOUT AN AUTOMOBILE

CITY

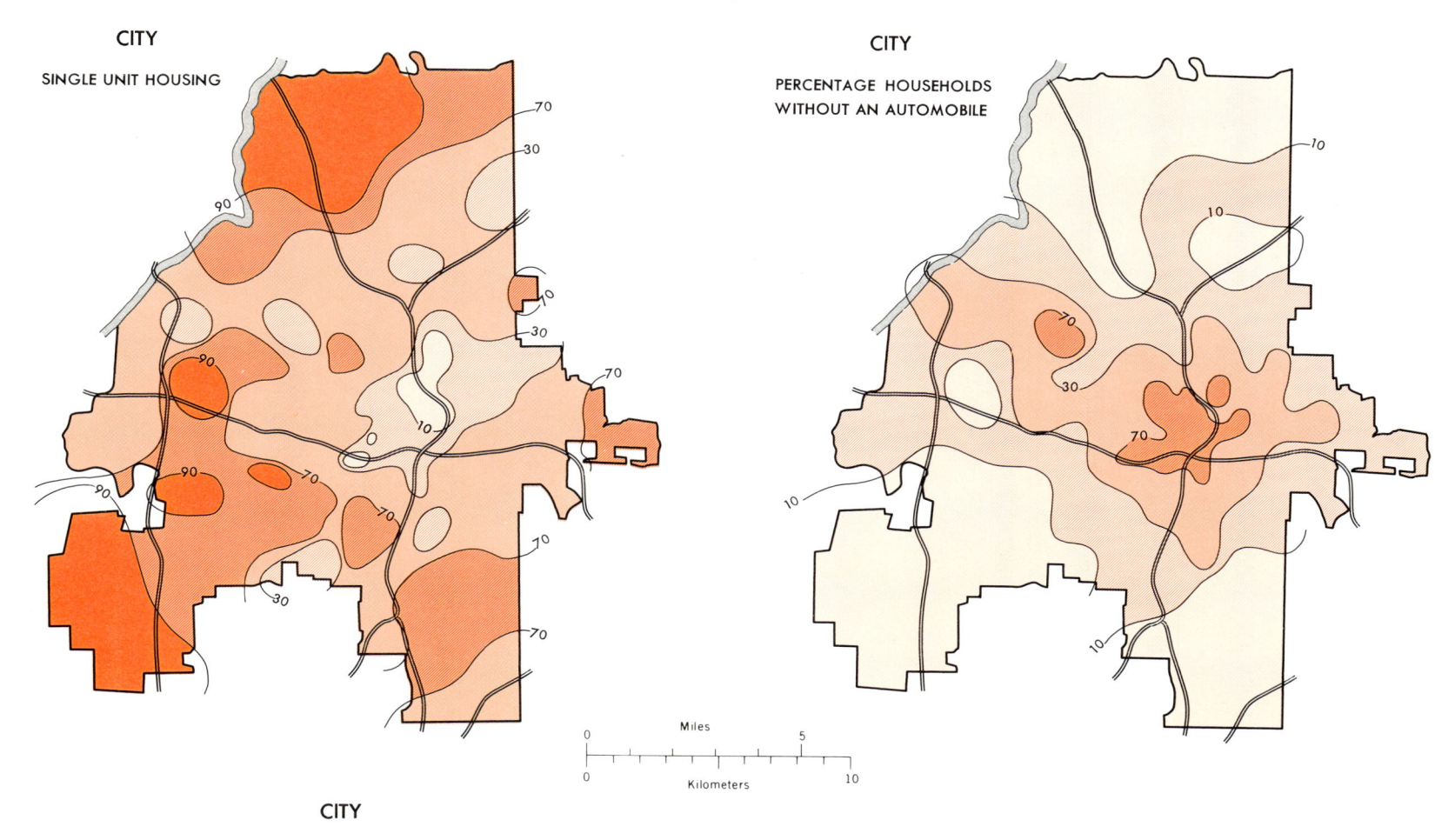

PERCENTAGE HOUSING UNITS WITH MORE THAN ONE PERSON PER ROOM

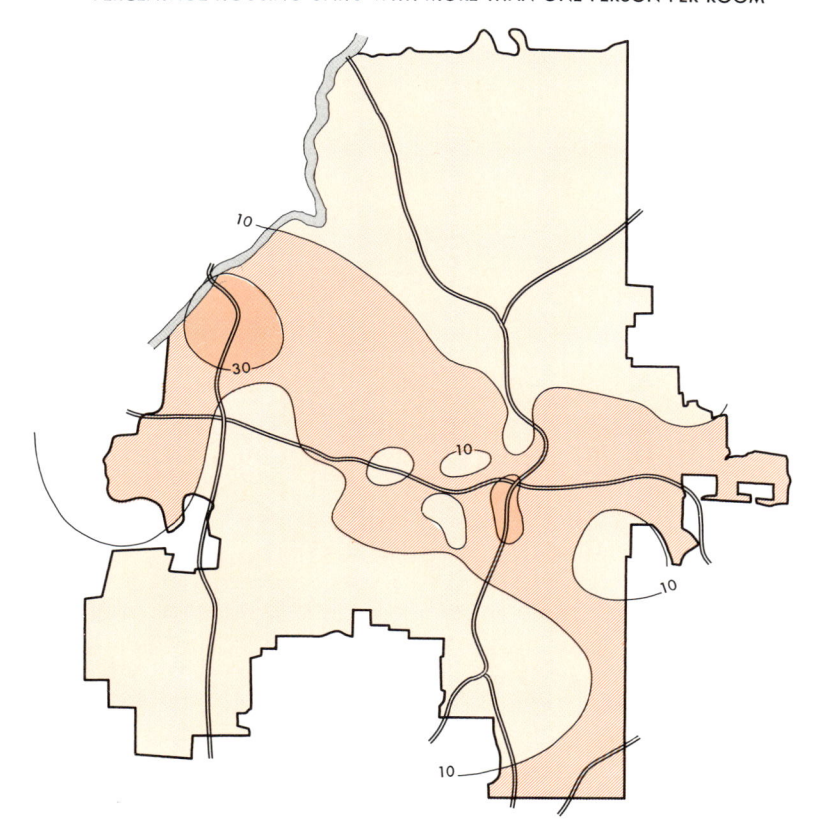

**Households without Automobiles.** (SMSA map on p. 340.) Twenty-nine percent of Atlanta's households (46,600) do not have an automobile available. Proportions of households without automobiles are highest in the downtown area. The people for whom the absence of automobile transportation is a serious handicap are probably those in the western sector of the city, where low rates of automobile availability combine with low incomes and long travel times to the city center.

Atlanta has long been the economic and cultural capital of the American southeast. That role retarded the city's growth relative to other metropolitan regions until after World War II because of the generally slow economic growth in the south. Since then the city and the metropolitan area have prospered with the rapid economic and urban growth of the South. Growth, development, and redevelopment in Atlanta have traditionally been guided by a small group of powerful individuals who were vitally concerned about the city's welfare. The tradition persists. A few major firms and their directors stimulated growth and redevelopment in downtown Atlanta. The continued concern of this influential group and their continued residence in Atlanta is the region's best guarantee that current and future problems will be addressed directly and intelligently.

# CHAPTER 25

# Washington, D.C.

*Physically, the city Washington most resembles is New Delhi. Both are artificial cities with broad shaded boulevards converging on traffic circles; both are characterized by massive stone piles in which the musty, sealing-wax business of government is conducted.*

RUSSELL BAKER, *An American in Washington*, 1961

The Washington Standard Metropolitan Statistical Area (SMSA) is the 7th most populous metropolitan area in the nation with 2,862,000 residents. The District of Columbia's 757,000 residents constitute 27 percent of the SMSA population. The remaining 73 percent is divided between Maryland (41 percent) and Virginia (32 percent) suburbs. Montgomery and Prince Georges counties have 18 and 23 percent of the SMSA total, and Fairfax (16 percent) and Arlington (6 percent) are the largest of the Virginia counties. Prince William and Loudon have 4 and 1 percent of the SMSA total respectively. The cities of Alexandria, Fairfax, and Falls Church are politically separate from Fairfax and Arlington counties; 4 percent of the SMSA population resides in Alexandria and 1 percent lives in Fairfax and Falls Church cities.

The Daily Urban System (DUS) defined by counties that have at least 5 percent of their labor forces working in the District, Arlington County, and Alexandria City includes the SMSA counties plus 4 additional counties in Maryland and 3 more in Virginia (p. 257). The DUS population is 3,347,000. Most of the 485,000 increase over the SMSA population consists of the population of Anne Arundel and Howard counties in Maryland. The DUS is the 8th most populous DUS in the nation.

*Note:* All data are from the 1970 Censuses of Population and Housing unless otherwise indicated. Therefore the present tense refers to 1970 data except for income data which are from 1969. Cartographic conventions are explained in Chapter 1.

The physiographic boundary between the coastal plain and the piedmont cuts through Washington, and the port of Georgetown was one of the region's early settlements. The present site of Washington was selected as the nation's capital in 1790. It was located near the center of the original 13 states and was accessible by ocean vessel to all parts of the new nation via Chesapeake Bay and the Potomac River. A decade of planning and construction preceded significant settlement, and as late as 1850 the District of Columbia had only 40,000 inhabitants—New York then had over half a million and Baltimore had 170,000. In many respects Washington remained a large village until the 1880s. The pace of life quickened during World War I, but as late as 1920 Washington was the nation's 14th largest city, and Buffalo, New York, had 70,000 more people than the nation's capital (p. 10). Since 1930 the city has grown as spectacularly as the federal government. The metropolitan area rose from 11th in the nation in 1960 to its current position of 7th by growing 37.8 percent during the decade, compared with a national metropolitan growth rate of 16.6 percent. The District's population peaked in 1950 at 802,000. It has since declined 6 percent.

The city and the federal government complex are located north of the confluence of the Potomac and the Anacostia rivers. The southeastern half of the District consists of a series of riverine terraces, several of which lie below the 100-foot (30-meter) contour and thus do not show on the map. Promontories on the 80-foot

## Twentieth-Century Cities: Washington, D.C.

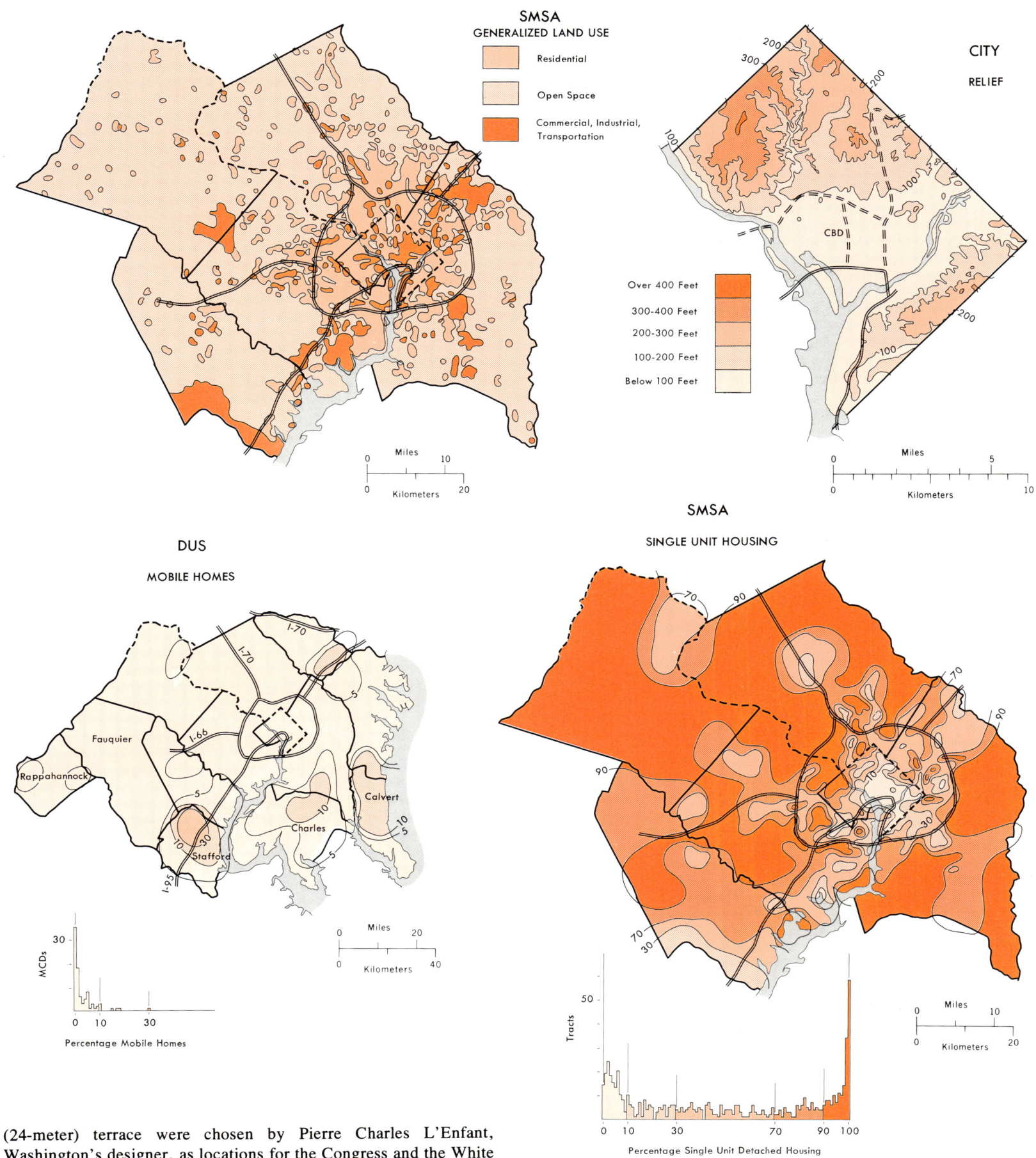

(24-meter) terrace were chosen by Pierre Charles L'Enfant, Washington's designer, as locations for the Congress and the White House. The city was laid out in a grid with broad diagonal avenues connecting the Capitol, the White House, and squares and circles reserved for monuments. The land rises to the northwest away from the confluence of the rivers. Rock Creek, flowing south into the Potomac, has eroded a deep gorge that has long been a barrier to movement between the east and west halves of the northern part of the city. From elevations of 400 feet (122 meters) in the western part of the District, the terrain continues to rise and becomes progressively more rolling in the western parts of the SMSA. The SMSA extends into the ridges and valleys of the Blue Ridge Mountains in central and western Loudon County.

Land uses in the commercial, industrial, and transportation category are usually governmental and institutional. Military facilities such as Quantico Marine Corps Base in southern Prince William County, Fort Belvoir in southeastern Fairfax County, and Bolling Air Force Base in central Prince Georges County are

*Twentieth-Century Cities: Washington, D.C.*

SMSA
HOUSING BUILT BEFORE 1940

Percentage Housing Built before 1940

SMSA
HOUSING BUILT 1960-1970

Percentage Housing Built 1960-1970

SMSA
HOUSING VALUE

42 Suppressed Values

Mean Value of Owner-Occupied Housing ($1000)

SMSA
MONTHLY RENT

21 Suppressed Values
7 Uncharted Values

Mean Monthly Rent

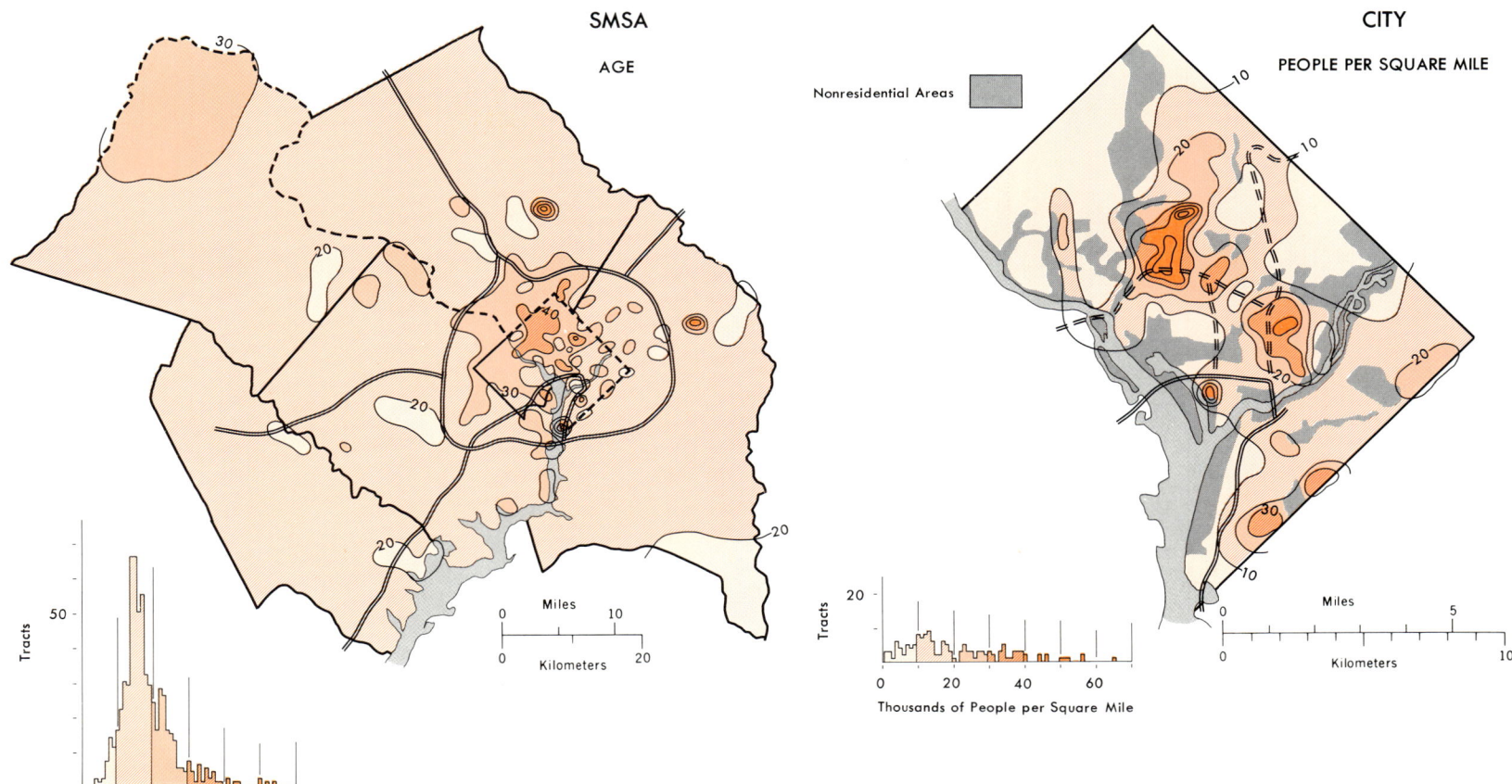

important land users. The large facility in northern Prince Georges County is the National Agricultural Research Center. Dulles Airport straddles the boundary between Fairfax and Loudon counties, and National Airport and Bolling Air Force Base occupy both sides of the Potomac just below its confluence with the Anacostia. Numerous additional government-related facilities are scattered throughout the District and the metropolitan area. Residential land uses have expanded more rapidly to the north and the southwest than they have to the east and southeast, although the earliest direction of residential expansion was northeast. Expansion to the southeast was restricted by the Anacostia River.

## HOUSING

**Housing Age.** Twenty-two percent of the SMSA housing was built before 1940, 40 percent was built from 1940 through 1959, and 38 percent dates from 1960 to March 1970. Washington's housing inventory is older; 47 percent was built before 1940, 37 percent was built from 1940 through 1959, and 16 percent dates from 1960 to March 1970. The large proportions of housing built since World War II in the District and in the SMSA attest to the recent and spectacular growth of the region.

The areas where proportions of old housing exceed 70 and in a few cases 90 percent are located in central Washington and in Alexandria, Virginia, along the Potomac to the south. The 30 percent isopleth outlines the pre-World War II axes of expansion northeast along U.S. 1 and north and south of the District. After a broad, irregular ring wherein old units make up less than 10 percent of tract inventories, the percentage of old housing begins to rise beyond the zone of recent growth.

New housing is clustered in scattered patches throughout the suburbs and in an urban renewal area in south-central Washington. Elsewhere in the city, housing built from 1960 to March 1970 rarely exceeds 10 percent of tract totals. Outside District boundaries, housing from the 1960s exceeds 30 percent of tract inventories, with frequent peaks to 70 or 90 percent, especially on the northern and

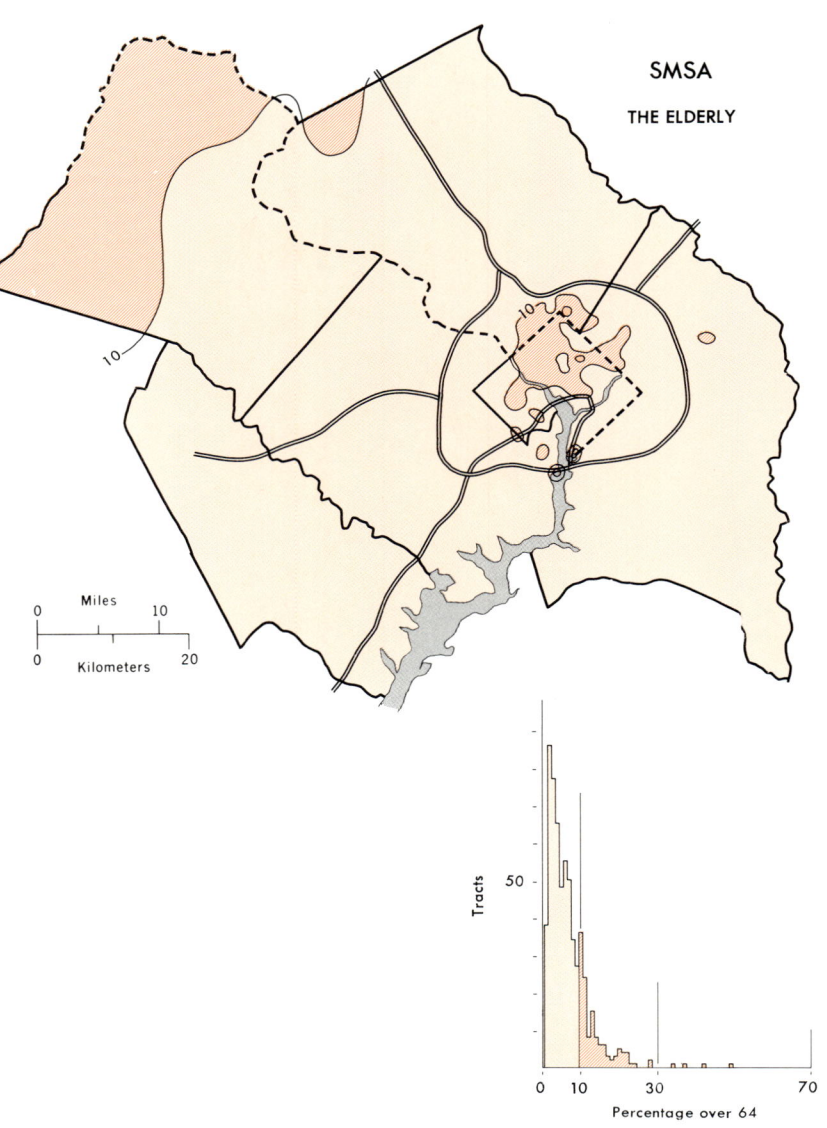

259

*Twentieth-Century Cities: Washington, D.C.*

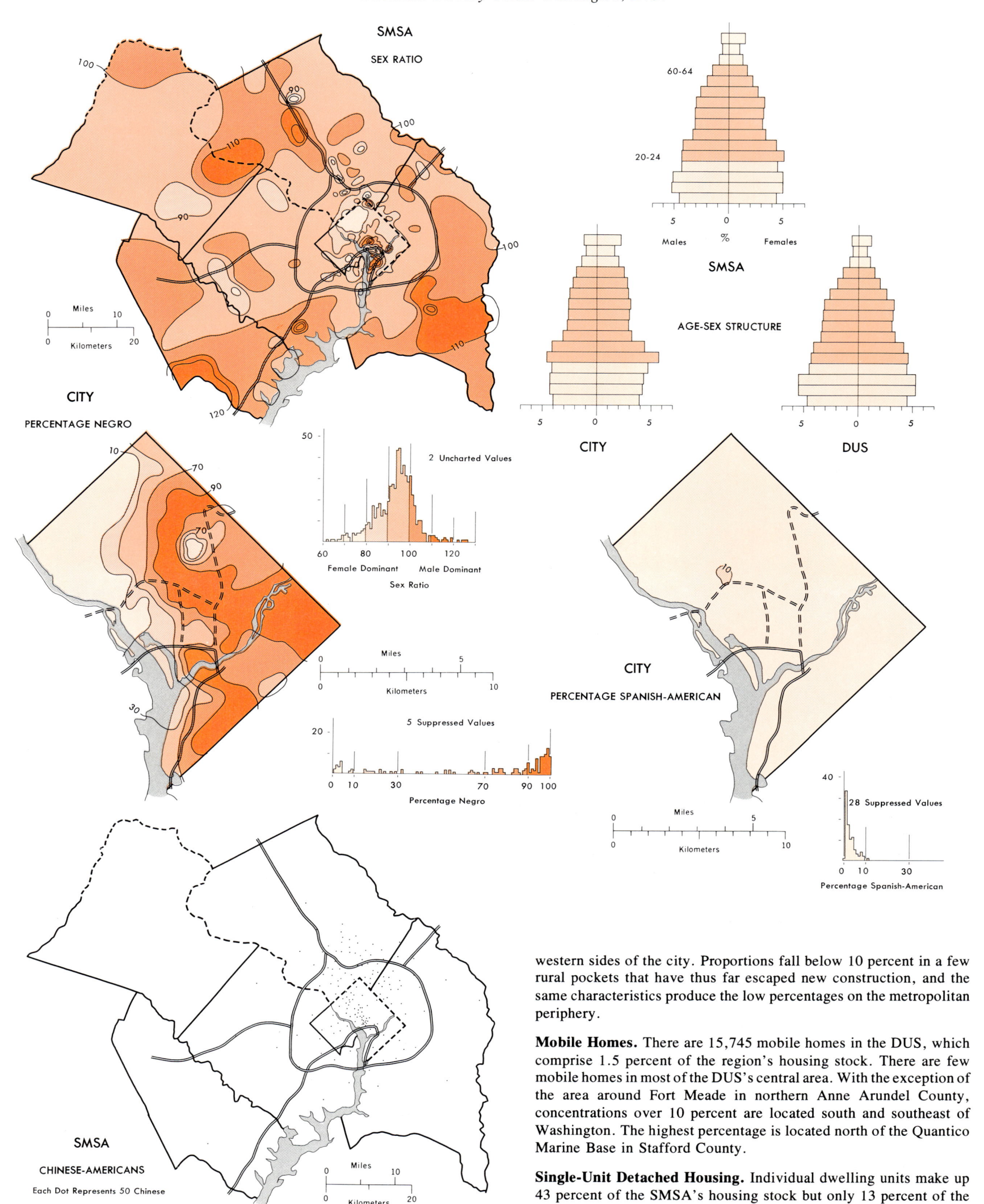

western sides of the city. Proportions fall below 10 percent in a few rural pockets that have thus far escaped new construction, and the same characteristics produce the low percentages on the metropolitan periphery.

**Mobile Homes.** There are 15,745 mobile homes in the DUS, which comprise 1.5 percent of the region's housing stock. There are few mobile homes in most of the DUS's central area. With the exception of the area around Fort Meade in northern Anne Arundel County, concentrations over 10 percent are located south and southeast of Washington. The highest percentage is located north of the Quantico Marine Base in Stafford County.

**Single-Unit Detached Housing.** Individual dwelling units make up 43 percent of the SMSA's housing stock but only 13 percent of the

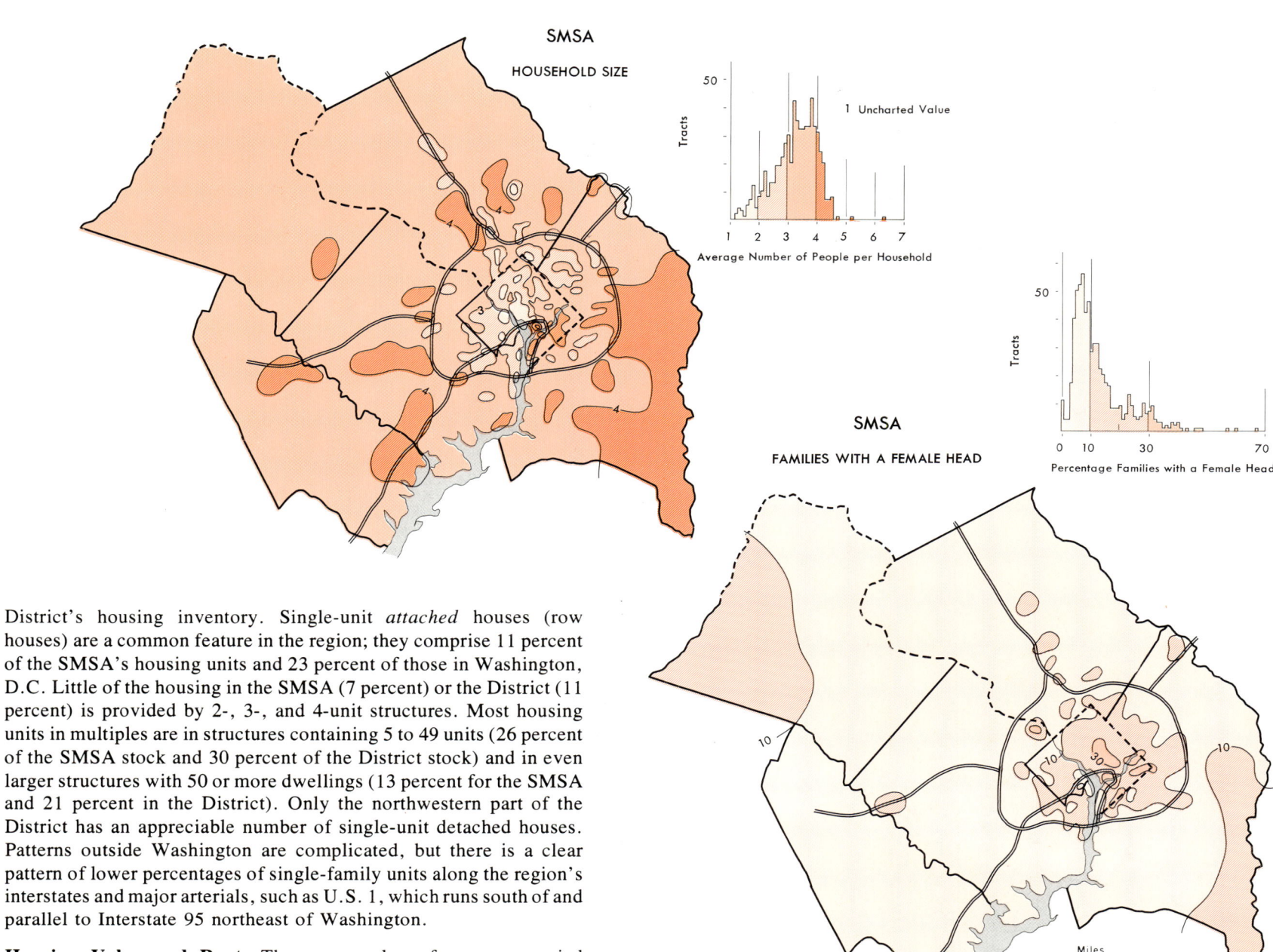

District's housing inventory. Single-unit *attached* houses (row houses) are a common feature in the region; they comprise 11 percent of the SMSA's housing units and 23 percent of those in Washington, D.C. Little of the housing in the SMSA (7 percent) or the District (11 percent) is provided by 2-, 3-, and 4-unit structures. Most housing units in multiples are in structures containing 5 to 49 units (26 percent of the SMSA stock and 30 percent of the District stock) and in even larger structures with 50 or more dwellings (13 percent for the SMSA and 21 percent in the District). Only the northwestern part of the District has an appreciable number of single-unit detached houses. Patterns outside Washington are complicated, but there is a clear pattern of lower percentages of single-family units along the region's interstates and major arterials, such as U.S. 1, which runs south of and parallel to Interstate 95 northeast of Washington.

**Housing Value and Rent.** The mean value of owner-occupied housing in the SMSA is $31,000, and the corresponding figure for Washington, D.C. is $27,000. Owner-occupied housing is expensive in the SMSA; only the New York City SMSA has a higher mean value ($32,000) among the SMSAs in the atlas. The mean value of owner-occupied housing in Washington is also high. Mean housing values for individual tracts vary from $10,000 to $57,000. There is a clear differentiation of high- and low-value housing in the SMSA. The eastern half of Washington and the eastern suburbs have low housing values; some tracts have maximum mean values in the high $30,000 range. Northwestern Washington and the northern and western suburbs have consistently higher mean values, some tracts inside and outside the District along the northwestern axis having mean values over $50,000. Northwestern Washington was firmly established as the city's prestige axis in the 1880s when wealthy families began to build houses northwest of Dupont Circle, but the trend in that direction was already evident early in the 19th century when the executive complex near the White House began to pull the center of the city west and north from its old center near Congress.

Mean monthly contract rents average $131 in the SMSA and $121 in Washington. Both are the highest respective SMSA and central-city rents among the regions mapped in the atlas. Individual tract mean rents vary from $55 to $355 (values over $300 are not charted). Although it differs in details, the map of mean rents has roughly the same pattern as the map of housing value, with generally higher rents on the north and west than on the east. The highest-cost rental units are located in tracts along the northwestern axis.

The spectacular growth of government employment and the consequent rapid growth and expansion of the Washington metropolitan area in the last several decades created housing demands that exceeded the local housing supply. Housing values and rents increased exorbitantly, especially in Washington's northern and western suburbs. Such pressure on limited housing stocks partially explains the high values and rents of the Washington region.

## THE PEOPLE

**Population Density.** Washington's overall population density is 12,300 people per square mile (4,750 per square kilometer). Individual tract densities vary from 1,000 to 65,000 people per square mile (390 to 25,000 per square kilometer), although tracts with densities over 40,000 per square mile (15,500 per square kilometer) are rare. Densities over 20,000 people per square mile (7,700 per square kilometer) are concentrated in the central part of the city, with small outliers of high density along the southeastern boundary. The highest densities are located north of the White House in north-central Washington, in the Capitol Hill area, and in the Southwest Renewal Area next to the tidal basin of the Potomac. (An SMSA map is on p. 316.)

## Twentieth-Century Cities: Washington, D.C.

**Age and the Elderly.** The median age of the SMSA population is 26 years and in Washington is 28. The difference between the city and the SMSA is attributable to the few young children in the District and the large numbers of young adults and the elderly, as indicated on the population pyramids. Median ages for individual tract populations vary from 14 to 64 years. Tracts with median ages over 50 years often contain institutionalized populations, for example the home for the elderly in the southern tip of Washington and the sanatorium in northern Price Georges County. The old population in east-central Montgomery County, however, are residents of the Leisure World retirement community. Old and young populations occur in patches, but the populations of the more prosperous, established areas on the city's northwest and west are generally older than the people who live on the east and the south.

People 64 years of age and older make up 6 percent of the SMSA's population and 9 percent of Washington's people. Both proportions are relatively low for an American metropolitan area. Proportions are especially low in the Maryland and Virginia suburbs, where only 1 person in 20 is over 64 years of age. At the tract level, percentages of the elderly range from 1 to 49; only a few tracts have percentages over 25. The elderly population is concentrated in Washington, which has 41 percent of the SMSA's elderly compared with its 27 percent share of the total population. Corresponding to the city's greater proportion of the elderly is its relative lack of young people. Comparisons of the Washington and SMSA population pyramids make it clear that most child-raising is done in the suburbs. Most of the children who live in Washington are black. The population aged 0 to 14 years is 89 percent black, whereas 71 percent of the District's total population is black.

**Sex Ratio.** There are 1.07 females for each male in the SMSA, which yields a female-dominant sex ratio (males divided by females times 100) of 94. Washington is more female-dominant than the entire SMSA. There are 1.15 females for each male resulting in a sex ratio of 87. Sex ratios vary from 60 to 120 in the absence of unusual circumstances. Many of the region's ratios over 120 are caused by military facilities and their male-dominant populations. Aside from such areas, males exceed females on the periphery of the region and in a few suburban tracts with many young children. Areas populated by young families are usually slightly male-dominant, for males usually exceed females in preadolescent populations. Higher female survival

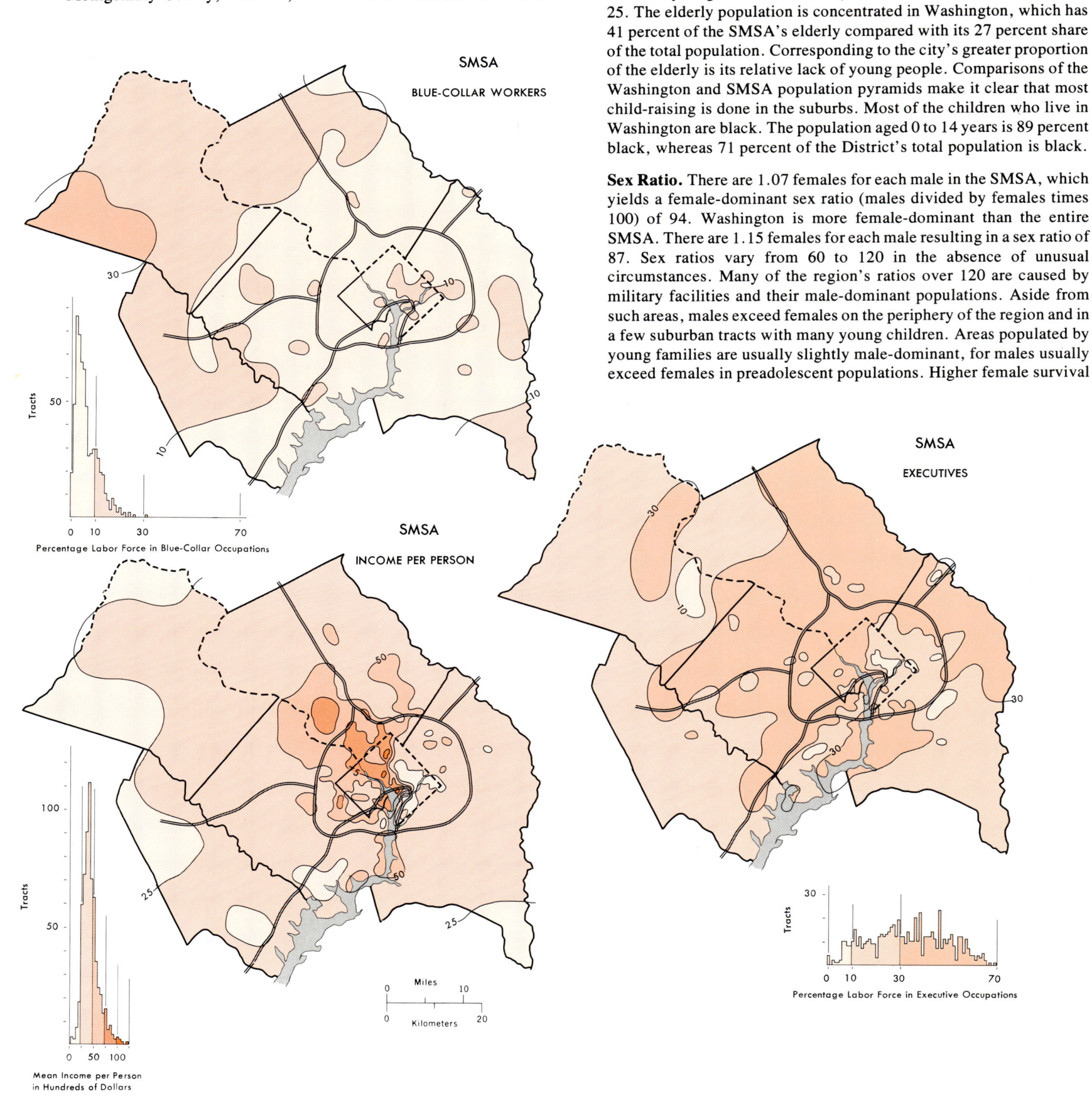

262

rates even the balance by young adulthood, and thereafter populations become progressively more female-dominant. Washington's low sex ratio is partially a function of its more female-dominant old population and partially a product of the selective migration of young adult females to the city.

**Negroes.** There are proportionally more blacks (71 percent) in Washington, D.C. than in any other major American city. Blacks are the majority or a large minority everywhere in the city except in the northwest. The gorge of Rock Creek and the parkway that occupies it still form a barrier between the heavily black eastern half of the city and the predominantly white northwest. Although blacks are moving to the suburbs, 76 percent of the SMSA's blacks still live in Washington compared with the city's 27 percent share of the total population. The isolated tract with less than 10 percent blacks in north-central Washington is the U.S. Soldiers Home. (An SMSA map is on p. 388.)

**Spanish-Americans.** The Census Bureau estimates the number of Hispanics in Washington by counting people who speak Spanish. By that reckoning there are 15,700 Spanish-Americans in the District who comprise 2.1 percent of its population. The most significant concentration of Hispanics is located in north-central Washington where a single tract exceeds 10 percent. Small numbers of Hispanics are scattered throughout the city. Most of the city's Spanish speakers are from Central and South America for there are only 1,200 Puerto Rican, 900 Cuban, and 600 Mexican foreign stock in the city. (An SMSA map is on p. 396.)

**Chinese-Americans.** The census questionnaire requires that all nonwhite persons identify themselves as members of 1 of 8 "racial" categories: Negro, Indian, Japanese, Chinese, Filipino, Korean, Hawaiian, or Other. In the Washington SMSA, 9,300 people identified themselves as Chinese. The Chinese are widely dispersed. Only 2,600 (31 percent) live in Washington. The city has a small Chinatown; but it is fading rapidly, and less than 10 percent of the Chinese community now lives there.

Washington was in many respects a large southern town until World War II, and as such it held few attractions for the European immigrants who settled in many northern cities. German, English, Central and

SMSA
PERCENTAGE NEGRO

SMSA
PERCENTAGE HOUSING UNITS WITH MORE THAN ONE PERSON PER ROOM

SMSA
PERCENTAGE HOUSEHOLDS WITHOUT AN AUTOMOBILE

*Twentieth-Century Cities: Washington, D.C.*

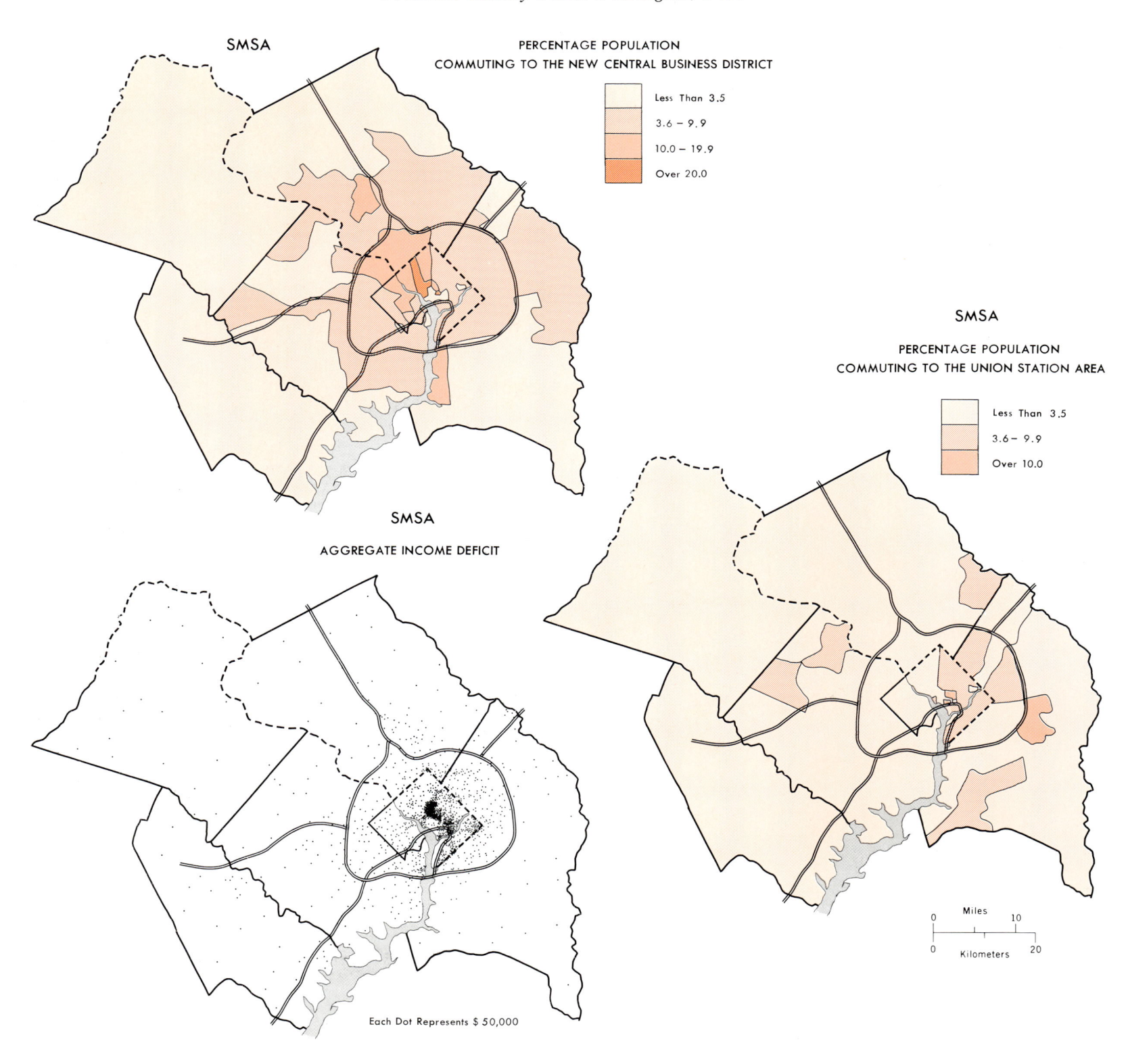

South American, Italian, Canadian, and Russian foreign stocks number from 40,000 to 29,000 people, but even the largest (the Germans) comprise no more than 1.3 percent of the SMSA population.

### SOCIOECONOMIC CHARACTERISTICS

**Household Size.** There are 3.1 people in the average SMSA household and 2.7 in the average Washington household. Household sizes for individual tracts vary from 1.2 to 6.3 people. The tract with the largest households is located in Washington's heavily black Southwest Renewal Area. The tract with an average household size of 5.2 people is located in a tiny, heavily black tract just east of the District's easternmost corner. Although it contains 2,500 people, the tract is too small to map. The average black household in the SMSA has 3.3 persons. Very small households are clustered in the center of the city, especially in and northwest of the downtown area. Households with fewer than 3 people dominate the western half of Washington and the inner Virginia suburbs. Households with more than 4 people are located in the outer suburbs, often in tracts where much of the housing stock was built from 1960 to March 1970 (p. 258).

**Female Headship.** The Census Bureau defines female headship by the absence of a male spouse, regardless of the sex of the family's breadwinner. Twelve percent of the SMSA's families and 25 percent of Washington's families are headed by females. Washington's percentage of female headship is highest of the central cities in the atlas. The city's high rate of female headship is mainly a function of its large black population, for 34,500 (84 percent) of the city's 41,000 families headed by females are black. Tract percentages of female headship vary from zero to 67. Female headship exceeds 10 percent throughout Washington and the inner suburbs except to the northwest. Proportions rise above 30 percent to the peak values in Washington's predominantly black neighborhoods.

**Occupations.** Six percent of the SMSA's labor force work at blue-collar (laborers and operatives) jobs and 33 percent classify themselves as executives (engineers, teachers, professionals, managers, proprietors, and administrators). The remaining 61 percent are service (29 percent) and clerical (32 percent) workers. The SMSA's proportions of service and clerical workers are typical for a metropolitan area, but the region has the smallest percentage of blue-collar workers and the largest percentage of executives of any of the SMSAs in the atlas, reflecting the region's heavy dependence on federal government employment. The occupational breakdown for Washington is: blue-collar, 8 percent; services, 36 percent; clerical, 32 percent; and executive, 24 percent.

From zero to 31 percent of tract labor forces are engaged in blue-collar occupations. Blue-collar workers exceed 10 percent of tract labor forces in the rural western part of the SMSA; the percentage exceeds 30 in a single sparsely populated tract in western Loudon County. Elsewhere in the SMSA proportions of blue-collar workers are low except in the heavily black areas of Washington and its eastern suburbs.

Individual tracts have between zero and 69 percent of their labor forces in executive occupations, and tracts are spread relatively evenly across the range. Eastern and southeastern Washington have few executives, and they are minor components of the labor forces in many of the tracts in southern Prince Georges County. Executives constitute more than 30 percent of the labor forces of most tracts in Arlington and Fairfax counties in Virginia and in Montgomery County, Maryland. Loudon and Prince William counties, as yet less densely populated with workers from Washington and the inner suburbs, have few tracts where executives exceed 30 percent of the labor force.

**Income.** Mean income per person in the Washington SMSA is $4,700 per year, and mean income per person in Washington is $3,850 per year. The SMSA income is the highest among the metropolitan areas in the atlas. The city's is high, but it is exceeded by incomes in Los Angeles ($4,000), San Francisco ($4,300), and Seattle ($4,100). Tract mean incomes vary from $500 to $12,000 per person per year. Low-income tracts are concentrated on the east side of Washington. Outlying low-income tracts are scattered east of Washington, to the south along the Potomac, and on the SMSA's western periphery. The SMSA's highest income tracts are located in northwest Washington, and the northwestern and western suburbs are generally considerably more prosperous than the region as a whole.

## TOPICS OF SPECIAL INTEREST IN THE WASHINGTON REGION

**Negroes.** (Histogram on p. 388.) The 24 percent of the SMSA's blacks who live outside the District of Columbia amount to 166,000 people. The major axis of black suburban expansion has been east into Prince Georges County. The county is now 14 percent black. Despite general occupational and income similarities between the county's suburban whites and blacks, a good deal of local segregation persists.

**Crowded Housing.** (Histogram on p. 292.) Housing units in which there is more than 1 person per room are usually considered overcrowded. In the Washington SMSA, 6 percent of all housing units have more than 1 person per room, as do 12 percent of the dwellings in the District of Columbia. Overcrowded housing is concentrated in Washington and the Maryland suburbs east of the city. Fifty-two percent of the SMSA's overcrowded units are located in Washington. The existence of a number of tracts on the metropolitan periphery where overcrowded units exceed 10 percent of tract housing inventories is a reminder that much of the nation's poor housing is located in rural areas.

**Income Deficit.** The aggregate amount by which incomes in the SMSA fell short of the poverty level in 1969 was $146,298,000. Fifty-three percent of that amount ($78,244,000) would have had to have been added to the 1969 incomes of Washington's poor to bring the poor in the city up to nonpoverty status. The deficit comes to $51 per capita in the SMSA and $103 in Washington, D.C. Although the region's deficit is clearly concentrated in Washington and especially in the city's black neighborhoods, the scattering of dots (each representing $50,000 of the deficit) throughout the region indicates that there are people with low incomes everywhere. Often the elderly have low enough incomes (even if they own valuable assets) to cause deficits in areas where they would not be expected.

**Commuting to the Central-City Area.** Commuting patterns in the SMSA highlight socioeconomic differences among the region's residents. The Central Business District (CBD) in Washington has been migrating to the northwest for decades, and the CBD's most desirable properties are now located in the vicinity of Connecticut Avenue and K Street, where numerous white-collar employers compete for office space. The proportions of tract labor forces commuting to the new CBD in the Connecticut and K Street area are clearly higher in the northwestern sector than in most other parts of the SMSA.

The Union Station area, which is a core of blue-collar and service employment (especially in the Government Printing Office), draws its workers from much different areas. Few of its workers come from the northwestern sector; high percentages come from the predominantly black areas of the District and from areas in Prince Georges County with significant black minorities. A number of workers also commute from western Fairfax County.

---

Washington is one of the most diverse cities in the nation. It has been a southern city during most of its existence, but northerners have now come to dominate the metropolitan area. It was planned and occupied before 1800, and some of its 160-foot wide avenues offer prospects that are almost Parisian. Yet the area's suburbs are new, most housing having been built since 1950. Sandwiched between the 18th-century core and the mid-20th-century suburbs are two other cities: a 19th-century city east of Rock Creek occupied by blacks of limited means and an early 20th-century city west of Rock Creek occupied by the region's wealthiest families. Each of these cities and many of the suburbs have their own social geography. Boundaries, and the social and economic stratification they demarcate, are sharp in Washington. The metropolitan area is as complex socioeconomically as many places are ethnically.

# PART III

## METROPOLITAN PROBLEMS: SIMILARITIES AND DIFFERENCES AMONG METROPOLITAN REGIONS

## Metropolitan Physical Environments

### CHAPTER 26

# Private Water Supplies

In the 1970 Census a 15 percent sample of households were asked: "Do you get water from a public system (city water department, etc.); an individual well; or some other source (a spring, creek, river, cistern, etc.)?" The resulting data underlie this map series, which shows the generalized distribution of nonpublic water supplies by minor civil divisions (municipalities, towns, villages, townships, etc.). The variable is mapped for the 20 most populous Daily Urban Systems (DUSs) in the nation. Each DUS consists of a central city or cities and the surrounding counties that have at least 5 percent of their labor forces working in the core.

In the nation as a whole, 18.5 percent of all year-round housing units have individual water supplies. The rest are served by piped water systems. Public water systems serve more dwellings inside metropolitan areas; 9 percent of the units within Standard Metropolitan Statistical Areas (SMSAs) have individual water supplies. Of the 27,842,000 housing units in the 20 DUSs mapped in this chapter, 2,055,000 (7.4 percent) have private water supplies. Proportions in individual DUSs vary from 1 percent in the Los Angeles DUS to 19.4 percent in the Minneapolis-St. Paul DUS (see accompanying tabulation).

Percentage and Number of Year-Round Housing Units with Individual Water Supplies

| | | |
|---|---|---|
| Boston | 6.0% | 98,886 |
| New York-Northern New Jersey | 5.2 | 315,495 |
| Philadelphia | 9.3 | 142,496 |
| Hartford-Connecticut Valley | 18.4 | 168,671 |
| Baltimore | 12.6 | 82,492 |
| New Orleans | 5.0 | 19,297 |
| San Francisco-Oakland | 3.1 | 50,459 |
| Pittsburgh | 13.3 | 120,353 |
| St. Louis | 9.0 | 76,267 |
| Cleveland | 10.6 | 102,578 |
| Chicago | 6.3 | 157,027 |
| Detroit | 10.0 | 148,407 |
| Minneapolis-St. Paul | 19.4 | 129,829 |
| Seattle | 6.7 | 45,465 |
| Dallas-Fort Worth | 5.7 | 48,733 |
| Houston | 11.6 | 87,331 |
| Los Angeles | 1.0 | 36,767 |
| Miami | 3.9 | 27,471 |
| Atlanta | 15.0 | 92,105 |
| Washington, D.C. | 13.1 | 104,917 |

*Note:* All data are from the 1970 Censuses of Population and Housing unless otherwise indicated. Therefore the present tense refers to 1970 except for income data which are from 1969. Cartographic conventions are explained in Chapter 1. County names and other locational information are shown on the SMSA map at the beginning of each city chapter (6-25) and on the DUS map of mobile homes near the beginning of each city chapter.

Isolated houses usually draw water from wells. As rural land comes into the metropolitan orbit, changes occur that make such water supplies less reliable. Additional house construction means more streets, driveways, parking lots, and roofs, which waterproof the land surface, speed up surface runoff, and slow groundwater recharge. Lowered groundwater heads often become problems about the same time that contamination of individual wells from onsite sewage disposal occurs (see next chapter). The need for a public water supply depends on settlement density, local groundwater conditions, and the capability of local soils to tolerate onsite sewage disposal. But there are few places in the nation where high-density urban development, onsite sewage disposal, and individual water supplies are compatible in the long run.

Thus the maps of nonpublic water systems presented here trace the extent of the densely urbanized areas around each of the 20 metropolitan cores. Proportions of housing units with individual water supplies are low in the metropolitan centers. Typically the gradient between low and high proportions is sharp, and the histograms accompanying the maps are bimodal. High proportions of individual water supplies on the metropolitan peripheries are interrupted by the existence of municipal water-supply networks in outlying independent cities and towns. The series on private water supplies is an especially useful tool for forecasting the locations of future urban developments and future water-supply and sewage-disposal problems when it is examined in conjunction with the maps of private sewage disposal in the next chapter.

**Boston.** Boston was one of the nation's pioneers in organizing metropolitan water supplies. There is no large river to tap near the city, and groundwater resources are erratic. Boston area leaders organized and combined numerous small surface basins into a metropolitan system during the 19th century, and most places where private water supplies serve more than 10 percent of all households are located on the edge of the DUS.

**New York-Northern New Jersey.** The sheer size and the unmatched population densities of New York and Northern New Jersey produce unusual water-supply problems. The network of surface basins that feeds fresh water into the region's centers is extensive and elaborate. High population densities coupled with the nature of soils and bedrock leave no alternative to public water in much of the central part of the region and along New Jersey's coastal fringe. Gradients between low and high proportions of private water supplies are sharp except eastward into Long Island.

**Philadelphia.** There are extensive areas in the Philadelphia DUS where proportions of households with private water supplies exceed 70 and 90 percent, but these areas are usually sparsely populated (p. 310).

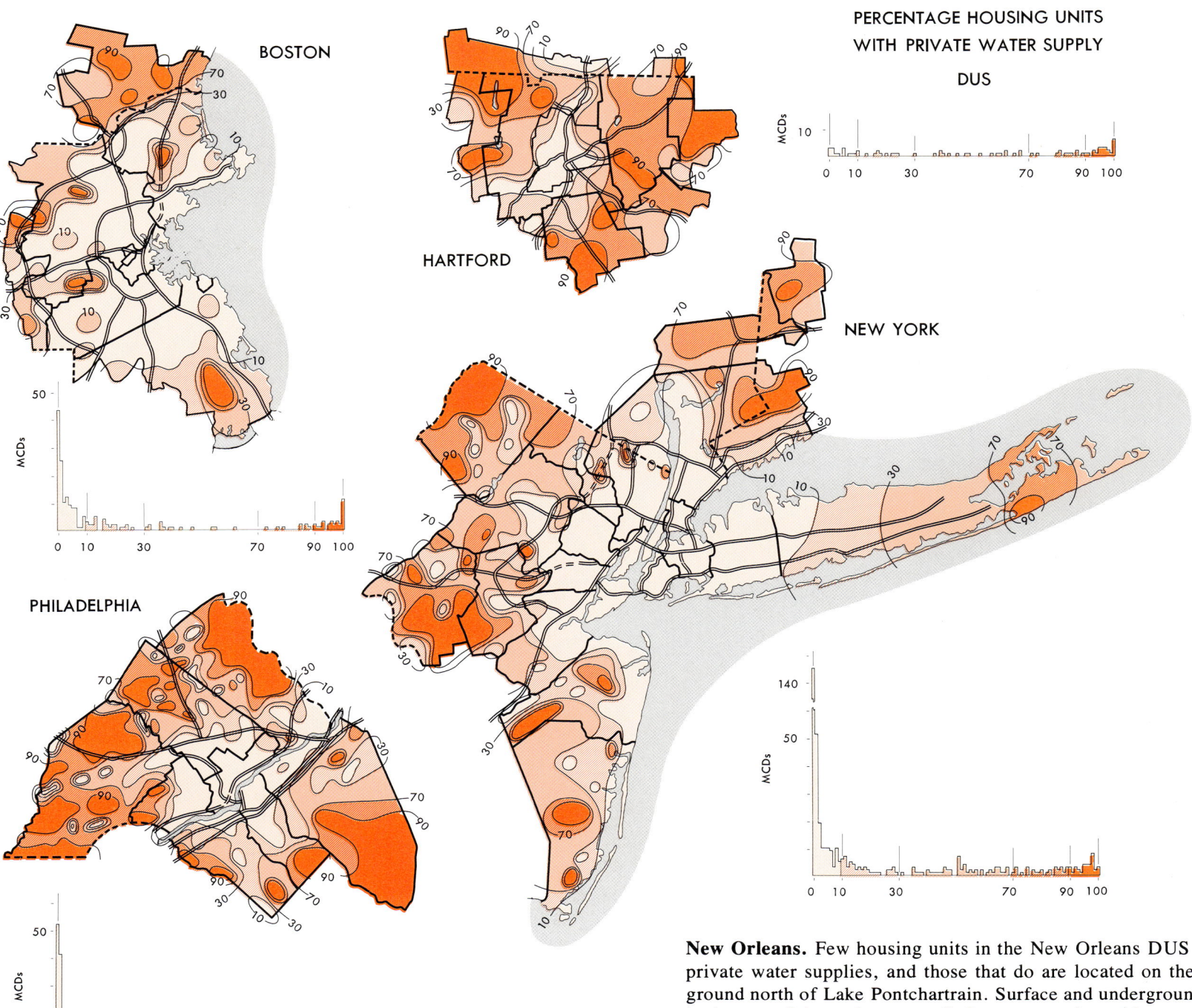

*Metropolitan Physical Environments: Private Water Supplies*

PERCENTAGE HOUSING UNITS
WITH PRIVATE WATER SUPPLY
DUS

**Hartford-Connecticut Valley.** The Hartford DUS has the 2nd highest proportion of housing units with private water supplies (18.4 percent) of the 20 DUSs included in the atlas. Its high proportion is related to the polynucleated settlement pattern in central Connecticut. The many small, separate water systems do not achieve the total penetration characteristic of areas where settlement is not as discontinuous. The large lot sizes and low densities characteristic of exurban settlement in the Hartford region make public water and sewer expensive, but private water and sewage disposal are correspondingly less risky than they would be at higher densities.

**Baltimore.** Settlement is spreading rapidly in parts of the Baltimore DUS that have neither public water nor public sewer (pp. 77, 275, and 351). Potential gaps between rapid, high-density development and public water connections are most probable in Carroll and Howard counties, where new development associated with Baltimore and Washington D.C. proceeds apace, and north of Baltimore, where suburban growth has already strained local groundwater resources and onsite sewage-disposal capacities.

**New Orleans.** Few housing units in the New Orleans DUS rely on private water supplies, and those that do are located on the higher ground north of Lake Pontchartrain. Surface and underground water in the rest of the region are unfit for consumption without extensive purification. Settlement in the near sea-level areas south of Lake Pontchartrain has often depended on diking and drainage, and public water and sewerage usually accompanied drainage projects.

**San Francisco-Oakland.** Surface fresh water is scarce to nonexistent in some parts of the Bay region, and groundwater supplies are limited, especially in relation to the region's 4,630,000 inhabitants. Thus individual water supplies are resorted to only on the DUS periphery, where settlement densities make expensive individual wells less costly than connection to distant public supplies.

**Pittsburgh.** A high proportion of the housing units in the Pittsburgh DUS (13.3 percent) have individual water sources because of the region's discontinuous settlement patterns and the inclusion of extensive rural areas in the DUS. Outside the core area where few units have private sources, the pattern is complex. The region's terrain is rugged. Most of the cities and towns lie in deeply incised stream valleys, and most of the uplands are sparsely settled. The cut-up nature of the region precludes the construction of regional water systems and leaves many areas without public water supplies where sharp differences in elevation outweigh horizontal proximity to water networks in valleys.

**St. Louis.** Private water supplies are in limited use in St. Louis City,

*Metropolitan Physical Environments: Private Water Supplies*

PERCENTAGE HOUSING UNITS WITH PRIVATE WATER SUPPLY

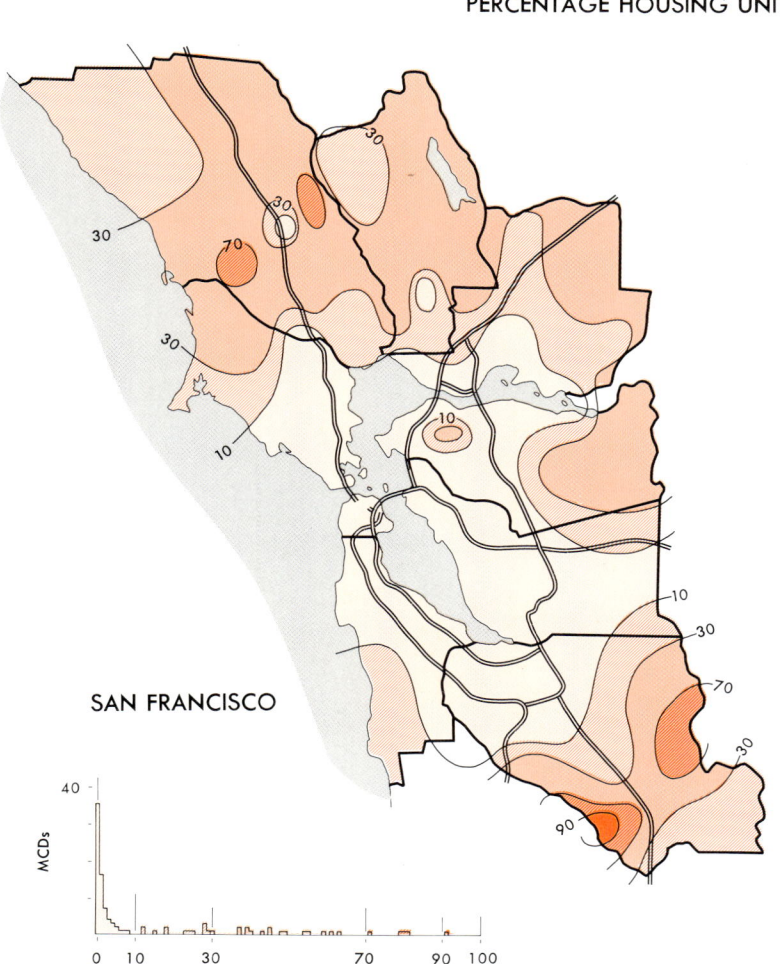

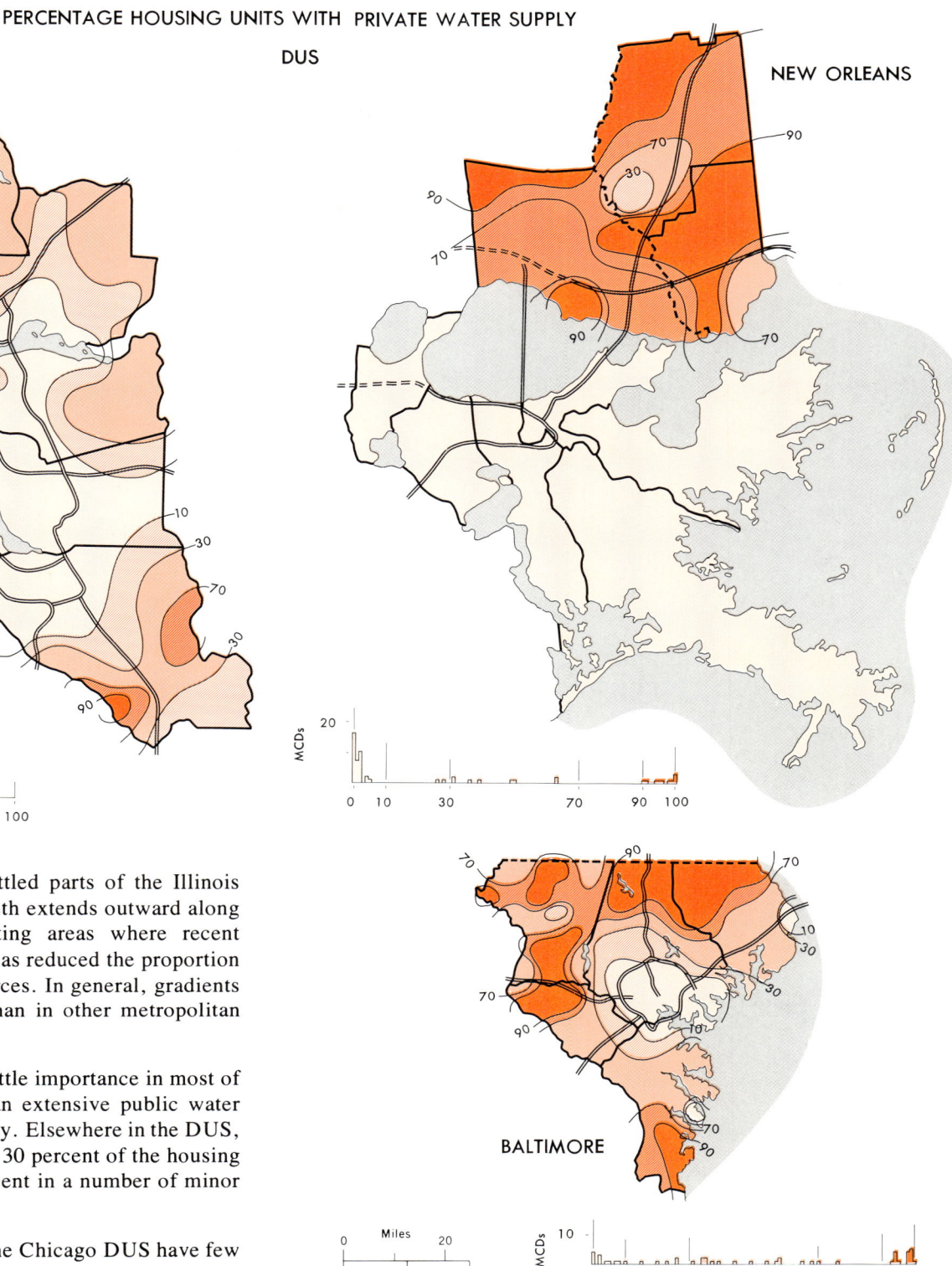

St. Louis County, and in the densely settled parts of the Illinois section of the DUS. The 70 percent isopleth extends outward along freeways in several directions, delineating areas where recent development tied to public water sources has reduced the proportion of housing units relying on individual sources. In general, gradients are more gentle in the St. Louis DUS than in other metropolitan regions.

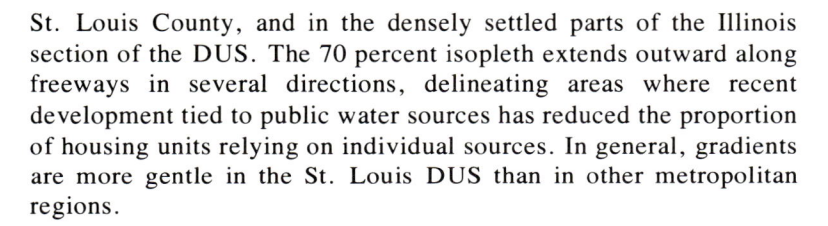

**Cleveland.** Private water supplies are of little importance in most of Cuyahoga County. A second area with an extensive public water network surrounds Akron in Summit County. Elsewhere in the DUS, individual water sources supply more than 30 percent of the housing units, with proportions rising over 90 percent in a number of minor civil divisions.

**Chicago.** The densely populated parts of the Chicago DUS have few or no individual water sources. Outside Chicago and the northwestern Indiana cities, reliance on individual water sources increases away from the metropolitan core, being common throughout all unincorporated parts of the DUS.

**Detroit.** Few housing units have individual water supplies in the central area of the Detroit DUS and along the river north of Lake St. Clair. The use of individual wells increases in importance outward from the central metropolitan area except where the municipal water systems of outlying towns produce pockets of low values. As in other midwestern metropolitan regions, the gradients from low to high proportions of private water supplies are more gentle than in other parts of the nation.

**Minneapolis-St. Paul.** The Twin Cities DUS has the highest proportion of individual wells and other private water sources of the 20 regions mapped in this chapter. The DUS is large and it includes much predominantly agricultural land. Water-supply patterns in the region are complex because of the numerous public water systems in many outlying towns and cities. Settlement densities are low in the Twin Cities region, and thus individual wells are less risky there than they might be in other areas.

**Seattle.** A relatively low proportion of housing units in the Seattle DUS use individual wells or other private water-supply sources even in the sparsely inhabited eastern part of the DUS. Minor civil divisions outside the more densely settled western part of the DUS are large, and the housing units located on their western margins that are connected to public water supplies outweigh the few interior units that have individual sources.

**Dallas-Fort Worth.** All minor civil divisions in the Dallas-Fort Worth DUS have some public water service. The Dallas-Fort Worth region has grown rapidly since World War II, and because extending incorporated areas is easy in Texas and because all incorporated areas

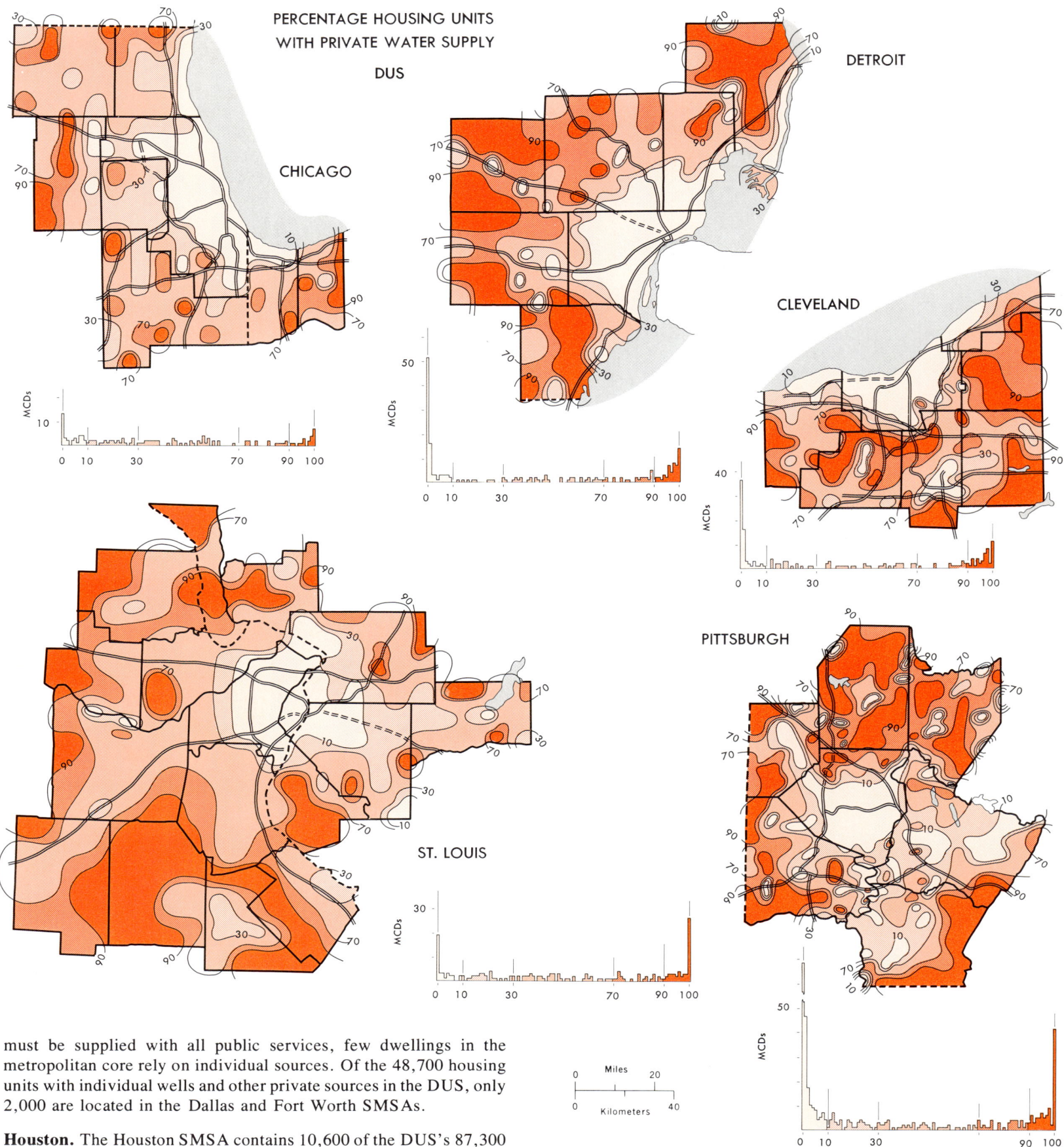

## Metropolitan Physical Environments: Private Water Supplies

### PERCENTAGE HOUSING UNITS WITH PRIVATE WATER SUPPLY

DUS

CHICAGO

DETROIT

CLEVELAND

ST. LOUIS

PITTSBURGH

must be supplied with all public services, few dwellings in the metropolitan core rely on individual sources. Of the 48,700 housing units with individual wells and other private sources in the DUS, only 2,000 are located in the Dallas and Fort Worth SMSAs.

**Houston.** The Houston SMSA contains 10,600 of the DUS's 87,300 housing units without public water service. Houston is unusual among large central cities in having over 2,200 dwellings (2.5 percent of the city's housing units) with individual water supplies. The continued existence of private water supplies within the city and the relatively high proportion in the SMSA are related to the large size of the SMSA and the continued expansion of Houston City.

**Los Angeles.** Few housing units in Los Angeles have individual wells because of the absence of groundwater resources in the semiarid region. Except for northern Ventura County and a few other isolated locations, the rest of the region relies on water imported into the region from distant sources and distributed through public networks. The availability of public water has been a more rigid control on development in the Los Angeles region than in any other area mapped in the atlas with the possible exception of metropolitan areas in Texas.

**Miami.** Groundwater supplies are abundant in the Miami region, although the diversion of Everglades drainage associated with large-scale development has progressively lowered water tables in the area. Most of the densely settled part of the DUS relies on water

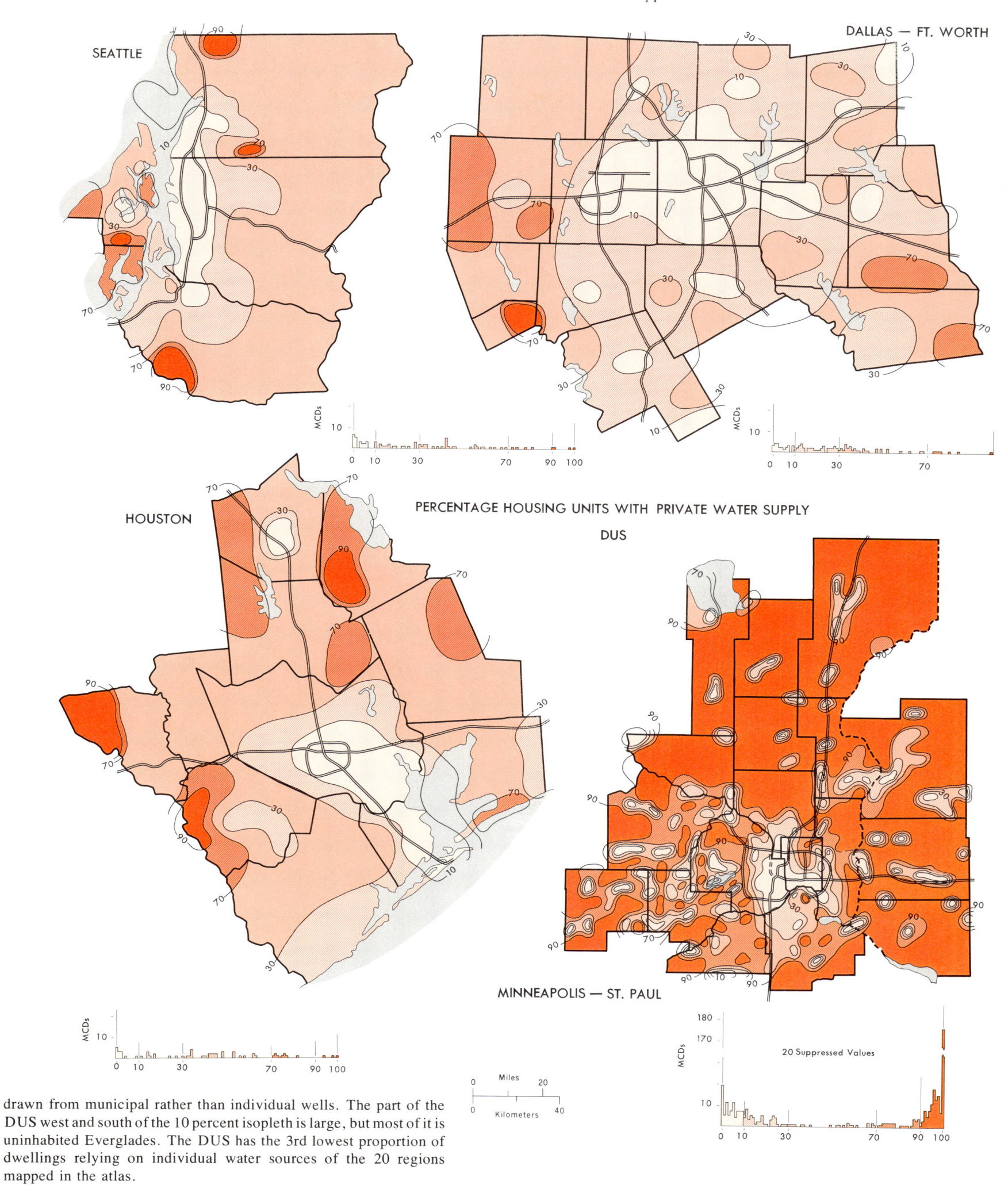

*Metropolitan Physical Environments: Private Water Supplies*

SEATTLE

DALLAS — FT. WORTH

HOUSTON

PERCENTAGE HOUSING UNITS WITH PRIVATE WATER SUPPLY

DUS

MINNEAPOLIS — ST. PAUL

20 Suppressed Values

drawn from municipal rather than individual wells. The part of the DUS west and south of the 10 percent isopleth is large, but most of it is uninhabited Everglades. The DUS has the 3rd lowest proportion of dwellings relying on individual water sources of the 20 regions mapped in the atlas.

**Atlanta.** Public water systems service a large area at the DUS core,

271

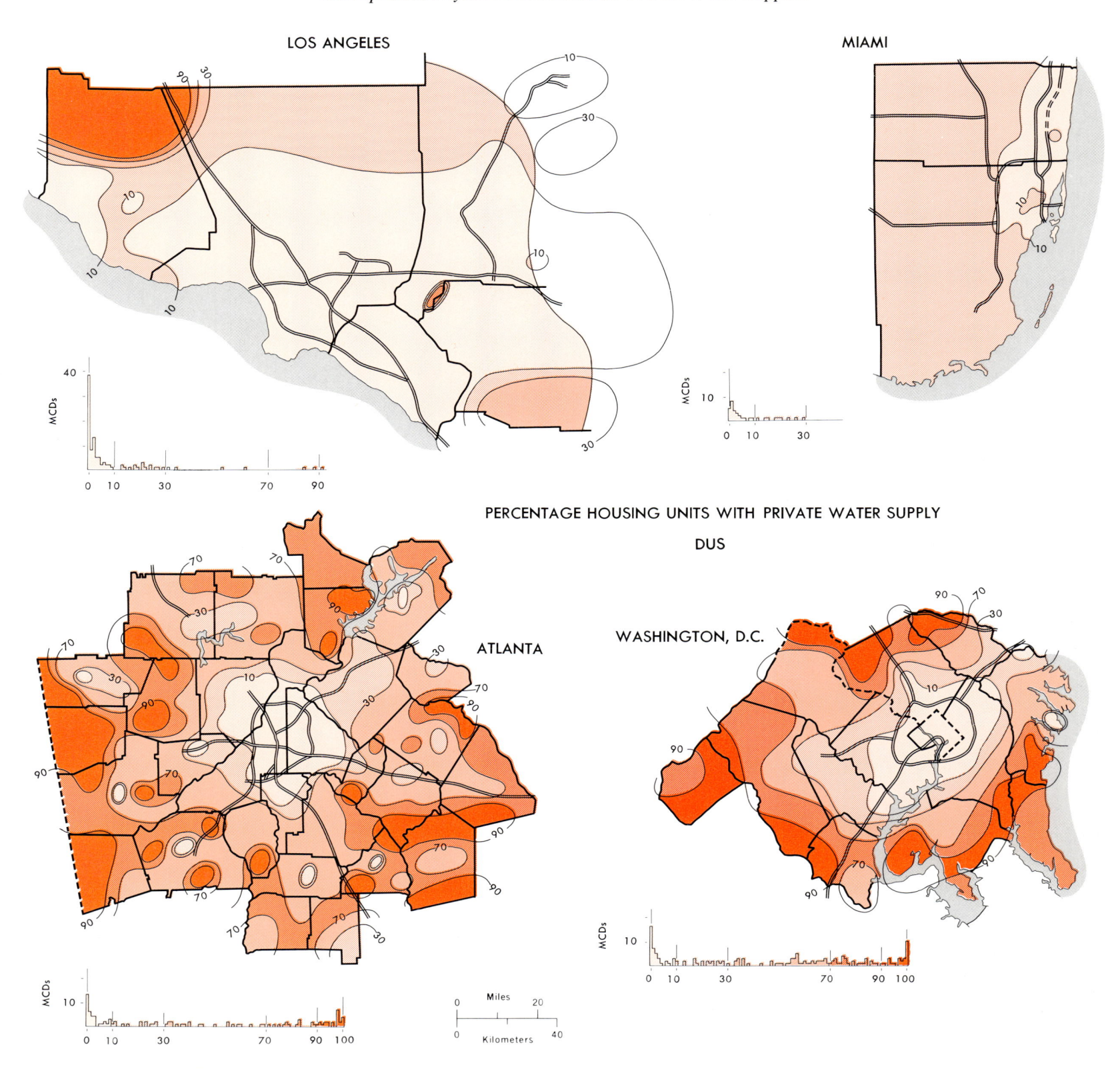

## Metropolitan Physical Environments: Private Water Supplies

LOS ANGELES

MIAMI

PERCENTAGE HOUSING UNITS WITH PRIVATE WATER SUPPLY

DUS

ATLANTA

WASHINGTON, D.C.

and reliance on individual wells and other sources increases slowly away from the core. The large proportion of the DUS housing units that relies on private wells is directly related to the large size of the DUS, for only 1,280 (1.4) percent of the DUS's 92,100 units with individual wells or other private water sources are located in the Atlanta SMSA, compared with its 73 percent share of the DUS population.

**Washington, D.C.** The proportion of dwellings relying on individual wells and other private water sources in the Washington DUS is high considering that a large fraction of the region's growth has occurred since World War II. Although most minor civil divisions not served by public networks lie on the region's periphery, lax zoning regulations in some of Washington's suburban counties have made the absence of public water (and sewage disposal) a chronic problem.

Throughout the nation, policies regarding connection to public utilities are becoming stricter. Local governments increasingly recognize the dangers of unrestricted construction that relies on individual wells. At the same time, they are becoming more sensitive to the costs of providing public utilities where settlement densities are low. The growing trend toward restricting development to areas served by public utilities and the phasing out of individual wells as public water becomes available suggest that reliance on individual wells and other private water sources should decrease. Gradients between areas served by public water systems and those drawing on private wells should become sharper in the future. As these trends continue, providing or withholding public water (and sewerage) will become an increasingly powerful means of enabling local governments to control the pace and location of development.

*Metropolitan Physical Environments*

CHAPTER 27

# Private Sewage Disposal

In the 1970 Census a 15 percent sample of households were asked; "Is this building connected to a public sewer?" Respondents had three choices: yes, connected to a public sewer; no, connected to a septic tank or cesspool; and no, use other means. The maps in this chapter show the proportion of each minor civil division's housing units that uses private (nonpublic) disposal methods. The variable is mapped for the 20 most populous Daily Urban Systems (DUSs) in the nation. Each DUS consists of a central employment core and the surrounding counties that have at least 5 percent of their labor forces working in the core.

In the United States, 28.8 percent of all year-round housing units use private sewage disposal. Units within Standard Metropolitan Statistical Areas (SMSAs) are better served by public networks than by private sources: only 17.9 percent of such units rely on private disposal methods. Of the 27,842,000 year-round housing units in the 20 DUSs, 4,503,000 (16.2 percent) use private sewage disposal. The DUS proportion is similar to the national SMSA proportion, and it is more than twice the percentage (7.4) that relies on private water supplies in the 20 DUSs (see previous chapter). Public sewer systems are generally less extensive than public water systems in and near America's large metropolitan areas. Water service is not cheap, but it is less expensive than sewer service. Faced with a choice between the two, municipalities choose water since public water decreases the hazards from well pollution caused by onsite sewage disposal.

Proportions of housing units using onsite disposal vary from 6 percent in the San Francisco DUS to 37.7 percent in the Miami DUS (see accompanying tabulation).

An isolated dwelling surrounded by porous soil can safely dispose of household sewage in a properly constructed septic tank. As housing densities rise, or if soil and drainage conditions prevent dispersal of waste materials, onsite disposal becomes unsafe and finally impossible. At typical suburban population densities, public sewer service is essential.

**Boston.** Public sewer systems are considerably less extensive than public water networks (p. 268) in the Boston DUS. Outside the metropolitan core, private sewer use is lowest directly west of Boston. The northern and southern parts of the DUS rely almost exclusively on individual disposal except in scattered locations. The difference (21.3 percent) between the proportion of housing units relying on individual water supplies (6 percent) and the proportion relying on onsite sewage disposal (27.3 percent) is one of the largest among the DUSs mapped here.

*Note:* All data are from the 1970 Censuses of Population and Housing unless otherwise indicated. Therefore the present tense refers to 1970 except for income data which are from 1969. Cartographic conventions are explained in Chapter 1. County names and other locational information are shown on the SMSA map at the beginning of each city chapter (6-25) and on the DUS map of mobile homes near the beginning of each city chapter.

**New York-Northern New Jersey.** Few units in the metropolitan core of the New York-New Jersey complex rely on private disposal. An exception is Richmond County, New York (Staten Island), where housing units using onsite disposal (p. 33) are being built in some areas. Public sewer and public water (p. 268) seem to be more closely linked on the New York side of the DUS than in New Jersey, where public water networks are geographically more extensive than public sewer systems.

Percentage and Number of Year-Round Housing Units with Private Sewage Disposal

| | | |
|---|---|---|
| Boston | 27.3% | 452,000 |
| New York-Northern New Jersey | 16.1 | 975,300 |
| Philadelphia | 11.8 | 181,600 |
| Hartford-Connecticut Valley | 32.4 | 296,600 |
| Baltimore | 18.4 | 119,900 |
| New Orleans | 10.7 | 40,900 |
| San Francisco-Oakland | 6.0 | 97,100 |
| Pittsburgh | 25.1 | 227,500 |
| St. Louis | 18.0 | 153,000 |
| Cleveland | 14.4 | 138,800 |
| Chicago | 7.2 | 177,800 |
| Detroit | 13.6 | 201,300 |
| Minneapolis-St. Paul | 17.9 | 120,000 |
| Seattle | 27.3 | 185,400 |
| Dallas-Fort Worth | 12.4 | 106,400 |
| Houston | 14.8 | 111,700 |
| Los Angeles | 8.4 | 299,700 |
| Miami | 37.7 | 262,300 |
| Atlanta | 33.9 | 208,200 |
| Washington, D.C. | 18.4 | 147,300 |

**Philadelphia.** Private sewage disposal methods are used intensively in large areas of the Philadelphia DUS, especially to the west and north. Proportions of housing units using onsite disposal rise and fall erratically between the core area served by public sewer and the unsewered periphery, depending on the location of cities and towns with collection and treatment systems. The difference between the proportions of units relying on onsite disposal (11.8 percent) and private water supplies (9.3 percent) is one of the smallest among the DUSs in the atlas. But the differences between the *maps* of private sewage disposal and private water supplies (p. 268) emphasize the fact that houses using individual wells may or may not have private sewers and vice versa.

**Hartford-Connecticut Valley.** Almost a third of the housing units in the Hartford DUS use onsite sewage-disposal techniques. The use of private disposal is spread relatively evenly throughout the region, for 26.8 percent of the dwellings in the SMSA rely on onsite disposal.

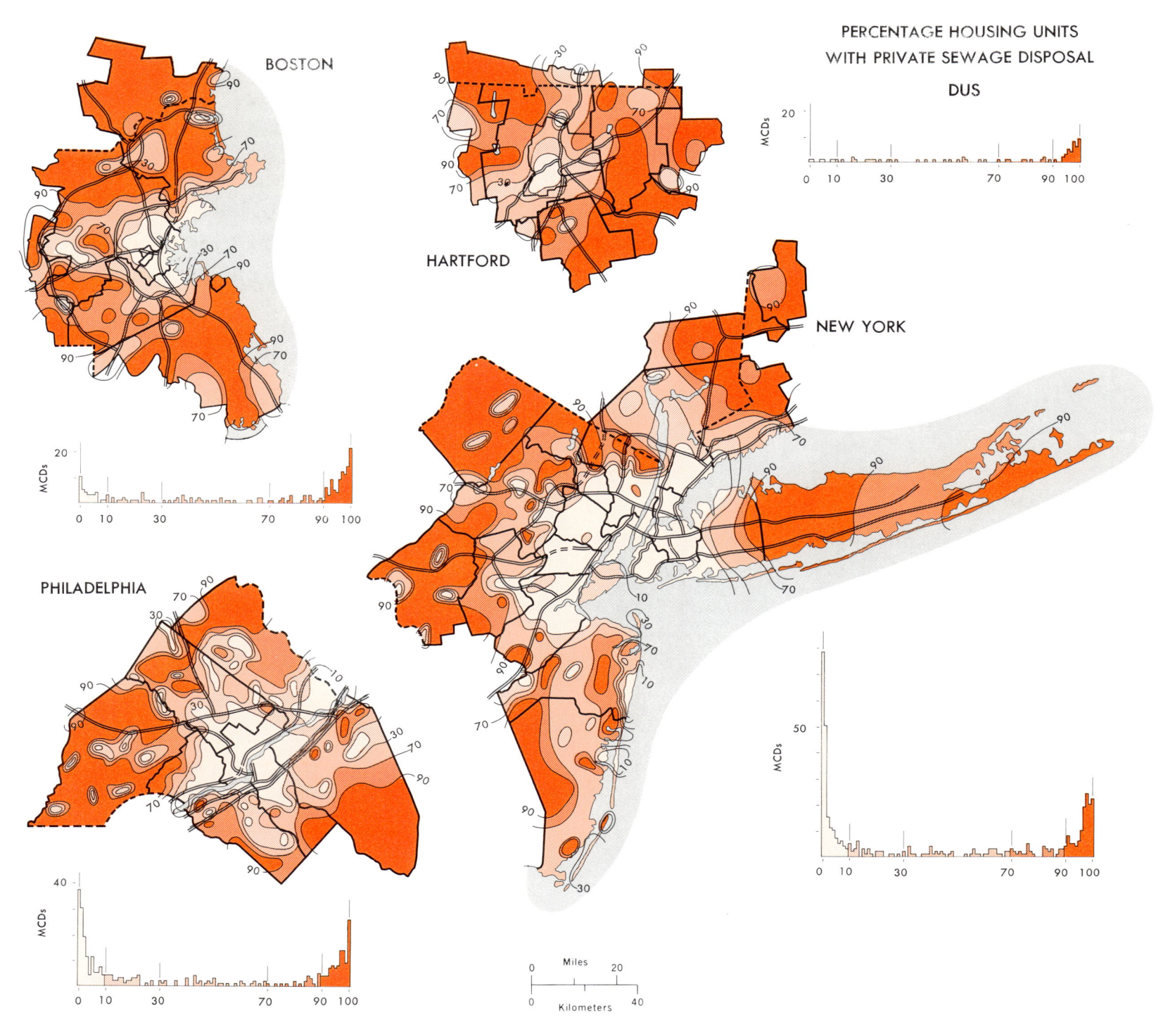

## Metropolitan Physical Environments: Private Sewage Disposal

PERCENTAGE HOUSING UNITS
WITH PRIVATE SEWAGE DISPOSAL

The high proportion of housing units with private sewage disposal is attributable to the urban and political fractionalization of the region and to its low population densities outside the Hartford core area.

**Baltimore.** Only in the minor civil divisions at the core of the Baltimore DUS do less than 10 percent of the housing units have private sewage disposal. Percentages are below 70 in most of the intensely developed axis stretching toward Washington on the southwest and Wilmington, Delaware on the northeast. Much of the sparsely populated northeastern part of the DUS relies almost exclusively on onsite disposal.

**New Orleans.** The relatively small number of dwellings in the New Orleans DUS that rely on private sewage disposal are located in the sparsely populated parts of the region. The New Orleans region, especially the area south of Lake Pontchartrain, is so near sea level (some parts are below sea level) that settlement depends on large-scale public drainage projects which usually provide public sewage disposal. Public drainage and sewer boards have considerable control over the location and timing of development in the low areas of the New Orleans DUS.

**San Francisco-Oakland.** Only 30,500 of the 97,100 units in the San Francisco DUS that rely on private disposal are located in the SMSA part of the region. Most of the SMSA is well served with public sewer because a large proportion of the region has been settled since World War II, when stringent regulations concerning onsite disposal have been in effect. Heavy reliance on private disposal is now confined to sparsely populated and isolated parts of the DUS.

**Pittsburgh.** Private sewage disposal is widespread in the Pittsburgh DUS outside the small core area that relies on public sewer systems. Of the 227,500 units that use onsite disposal, 157,700 (69.3 percent) are located within the SMSA. The rugged terrain in the DUS makes construction of large regional sewage systems difficult and expensive.

**St. Louis.** The pattern of private sewage disposal in the St. Louis DUS is similar to the pattern of private water supplies (p. 270). The proportion using onsite disposal techniques is generally higher than the proportion relying on individual wells throughout the region, and sewer networks are less extensive than water systems at the metropolitan core.

*Metropolitan Physical Environments: Private Sewage Disposal*

PERCENTAGE HOUSING UNITS WITH PRIVATE SEWAGE DISPOSAL
DUS

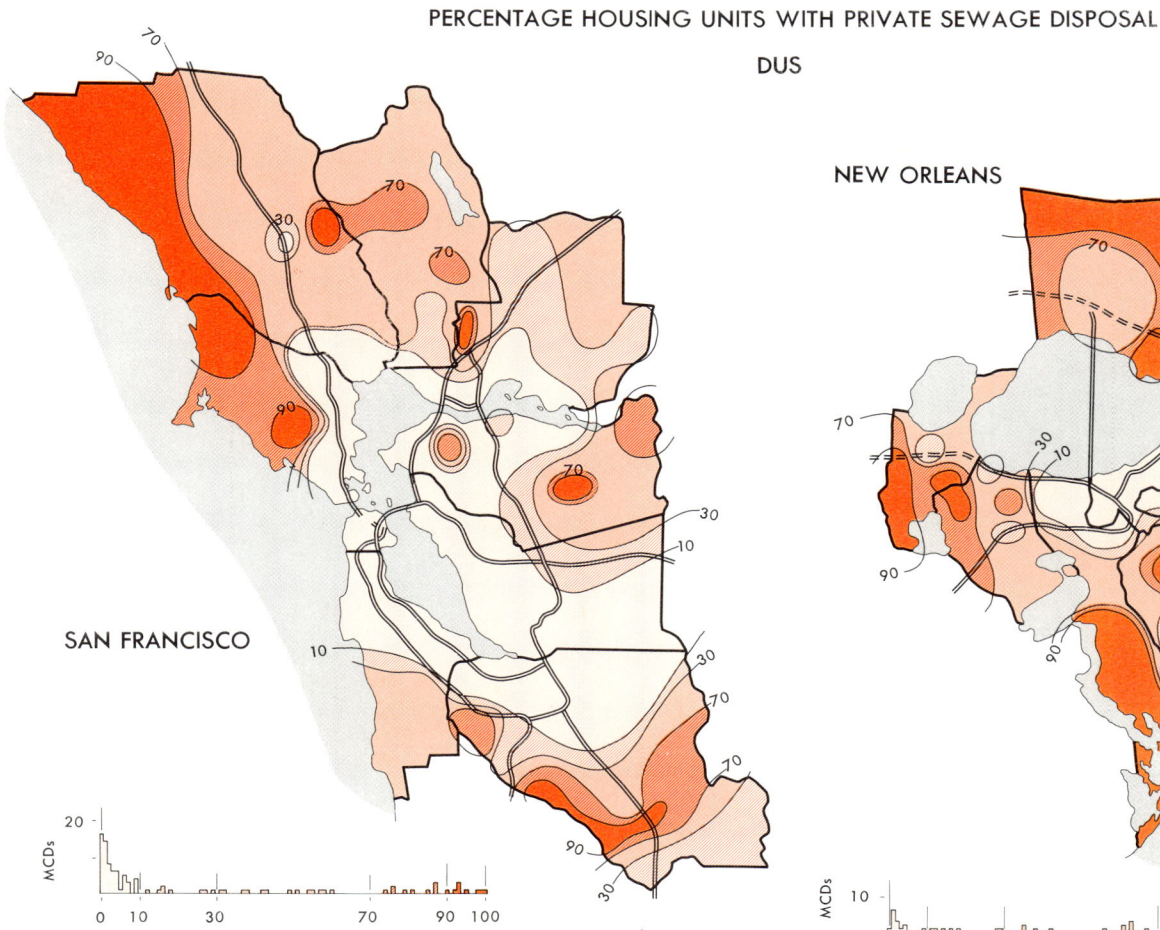

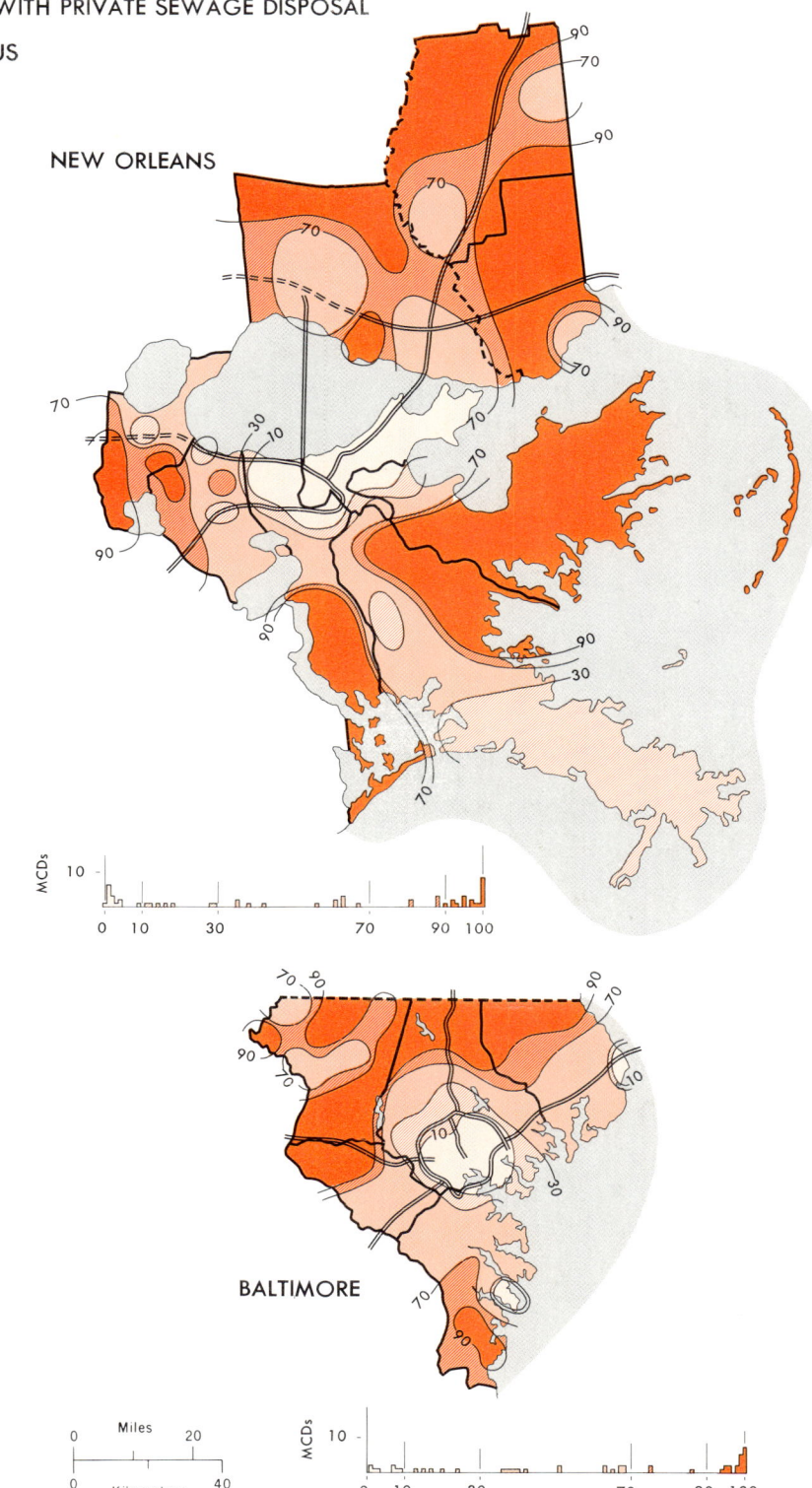

**Cleveland.** Cleveland and Akron have public disposal systems; onsite disposal is the rule rather than the exception in much of the rest of the region. Gradients between sewered and unsewered areas are gradual in the more densely settled parts of the region and sharp to the northeast.

**Chicago.** The proportion of the dwelling units using onsite disposal in the Chicago DUS is low compared with other DUSs in the East and Midwest. Also, sewer and water service areas are closely linked in the region. The map of private water supplies (p. 270) is virtually identical to the private sewage-disposal map, and the proportions are nearly identical at most locations on the maps.

**Detroit.** The pattern of private sewage disposal in the Detroit DUS is influenced by the history of settlement expansion in the region. Outlying areas rely heavily on private sewage disposal except along some of the region's freeways, where new housing developments have lowered percentages. As in the Chicago DUS, service areas for private sewage disposal and private water supplies (p. 270) are similar.

**Minneapolis-St. Paul.** The similarity between private sewage-disposal patterns and private water supplies (p. 271) noted in the Chicago and Detroit DUSs is also evident in the Minneapolis-St. Paul DUS. Most of the outlying centers that have municipal sewage disposal also have public water systems. Whereas it is common for the proportion of DUS housing units relying on onsite sewage disposal to be higher than the proportion using individual wells, in the Twin Cities DUS the difference is small: 19.4 percent use onsite disposal and 17.9 percent have private water supplies.

**Seattle.** Private sewage disposal is widespread in the Seattle DUS. The core areas within the 10 percent isopleths are small, but they encompass the bulk of the region's housing units because the settlement density is sparse throughout the rest of the DUS. The difference between the proportion of DUS dwellings with private sewage disposal (27.3 percent) and the proportion with private water supplies (6.7 percent) is considerable. Public water is available over a more extensive area along the coast than is public sewage disposal.

**Dallas-Fort Worth.** Percentages of units using private sewage disposal in minor civil divisions in the Dallas-Fort Worth DUS are evenly spread across the range from zero to 100. However, high-density places at the metropolitan cores contain large numbers of people, and the proportion of housing units (12.4 percent) that must rely on onsite sewage disposal is relatively low compared with some eastern and midwestern metropolitan regions. Because settlement density is so sparse in outlying counties, the difference between map areas and actual numbers of households in some categories is acute.

**Houston.** Private sewage disposal is least used in the eastern part of Harris County and in the Galveston area. The pattern of onsite sewage disposal is similar to that of private water sources (p. 271) except in

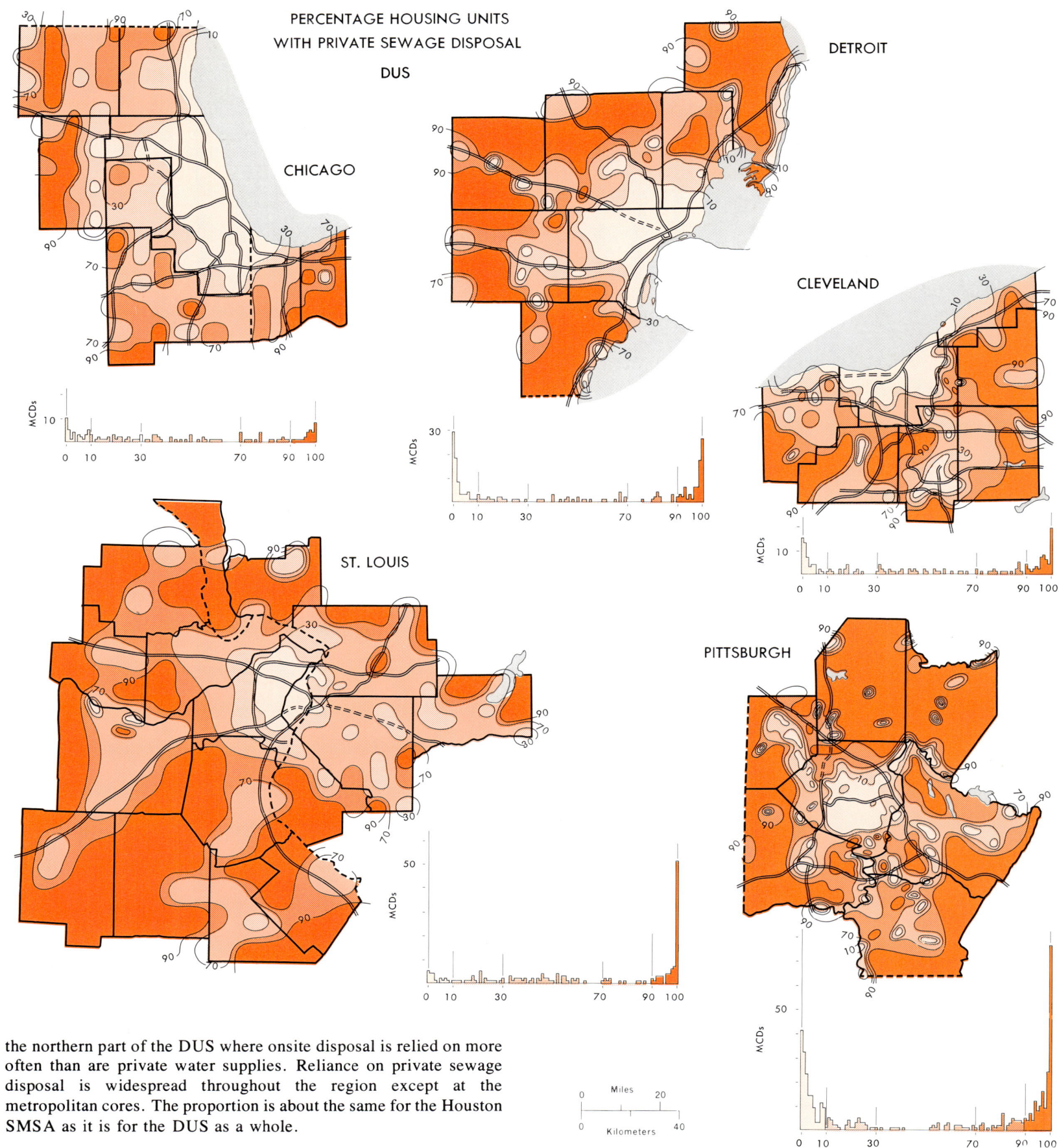

*Metropolitan Physical Environments: Private Sewage Disposal*

PERCENTAGE HOUSING UNITS WITH PRIVATE SEWAGE DISPOSAL
DUS

CHICAGO

DETROIT

CLEVELAND

ST. LOUIS

PITTSBURGH

the northern part of the DUS where onsite disposal is relied on more often than are private water supplies. Reliance on private sewage disposal is widespread throughout the region except at the metropolitan cores. The proportion is about the same for the Houston SMSA as it is for the DUS as a whole.

**Los Angeles.** Use of onsite sewage disposal in the Los Angeles DUS is largely confined to areas outside the densely populated parts of Los Angeles and Orange counties. The proportion of DUS dwellings using onsite disposal is low (8.4 percent) compared with other DUSs, but it contrasts sharply with the much smaller proportion (1 percent) using individual water supplies (p. 272). Such statistics are to be expected in a region where most of the water must be imported from distant sources and where a large proportion of residential development occurred after World War II, when regulations governing onsite disposal were stringent.

**Miami.** Proportionally more of the households in the Miami DUS use private sewage disposal than do households in any of the other DUSs in the atlas. Of the 262,300 dwellings in the DUS using onsite disposal, 38,700 are located in Miami and another 138,000 are located in Dade County outside Miami. The high proportion (37.7 percent) of DUS housing units relying on onsite disposal is sharply at odds with the small proportion (3.9 percent) using individual water supplies, but it is also a reason why individual wells (p. 272) would be unsafe in the densely settled parts of the DUS.

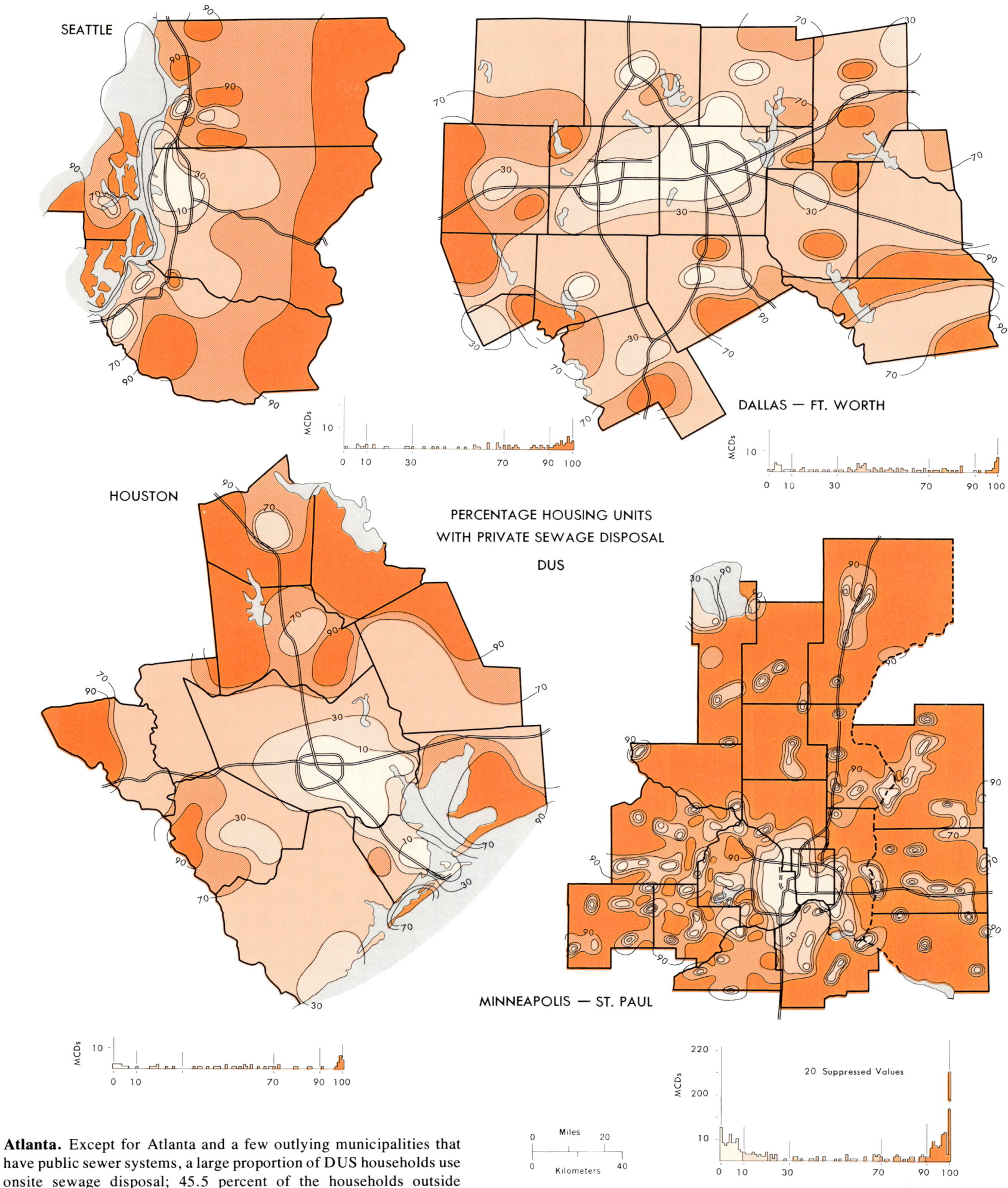

*Metropolitan Physical Environments: Private Sewage Disposal*

SEATTLE

DALLAS — FT. WORTH

HOUSTON

PERCENTAGE HOUSING UNITS
WITH PRIVATE SEWAGE DISPOSAL
DUS

MINNEAPOLIS — ST. PAUL

**Atlanta.** Except for Atlanta and a few outlying municipalities that have public sewer systems, a large proportion of DUS households use onsite sewage disposal; 45.5 percent of the households outside Atlanta rely on that method. The percentage of dwellings relying on onsite sewage disposal is higher than the proportion with private water supplies (p. 272) throughout the region.

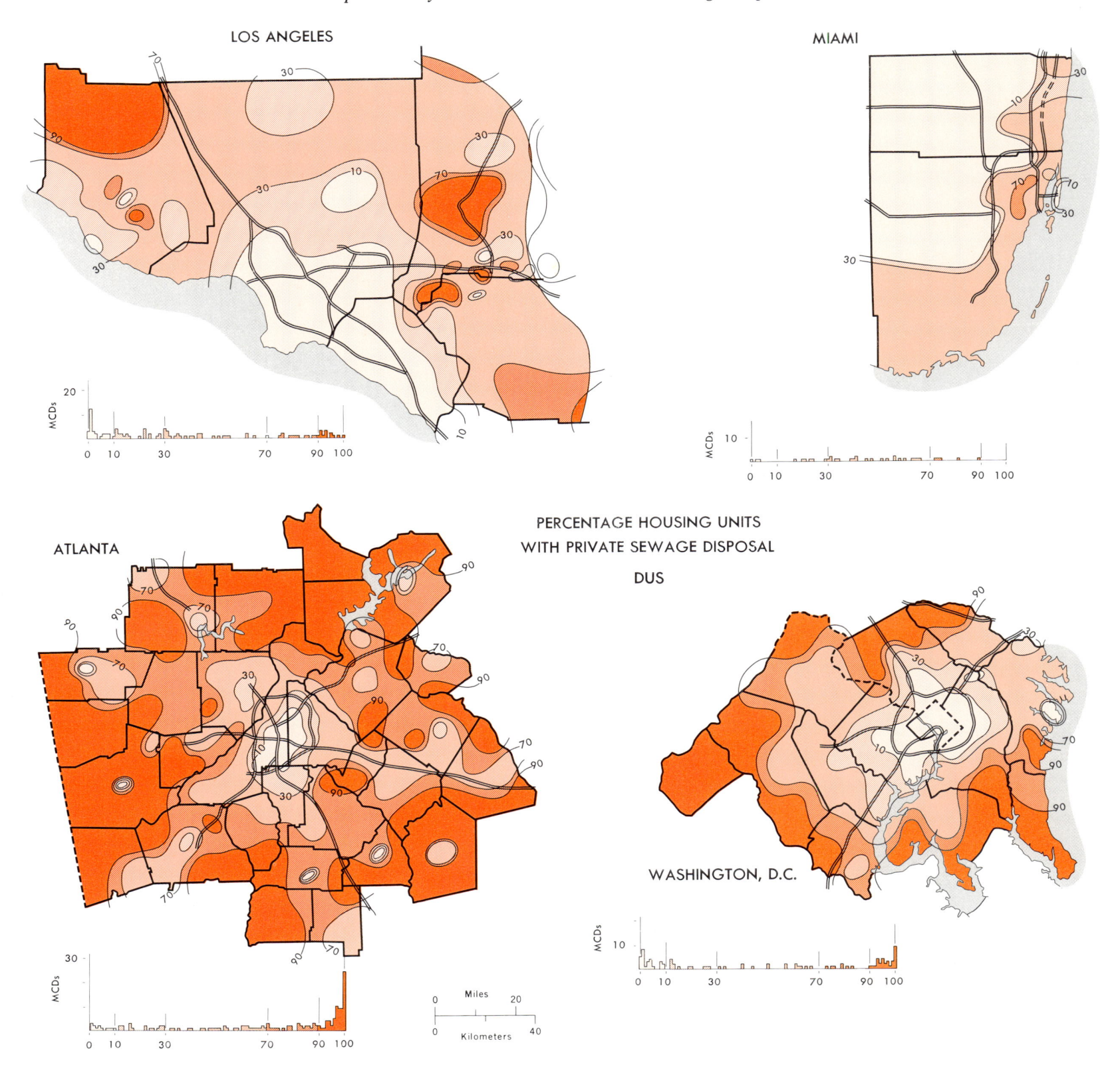

## Metropolitan Physical Environments: Private Sewage Disposal

LOS ANGELES

MIAMI

ATLANTA

PERCENTAGE HOUSING UNITS
WITH PRIVATE SEWAGE DISPOSAL
DUS

WASHINGTON, D.C.

**Washington D.C.** The proportion of households with private disposal increases regularly with distance from the metropolitan core. Proportions are lower at any given distance from Washington along major highways, and lower in Virginia than in Maryland suburbs. Providing adequate public sewage systems has been difficult in some Maryland counties. A moratorium on connections to public sewer—which was essentially a moratorium on new housing construction—was declared by several Prince Georges County municipalities in the early 1970s.

At typical suburban settlement densities, public sewer service is expensive to provide, and the cost per capita rises as settlement density decreases and distance to the treatment plant increases. Since public sewer service is essential for new suburban development, it has become highly influential if not fully determinative of the direction and timing of suburban development in many areas. A new sewer line into an undeveloped area is a strong incentive to build new subdivisions there, and the demand for new subdivisions is a strong rationale for extending sewer lines. The extension of public sewers has thus become one of the principal planning devices enabling municipalities and regional authorities to open certain areas for residential development while curtailing development in other areas.

*Open Space for Leisure Use*

CHAPTER 28

# Seasonal Housing Units

In the 1970 Census of Housing, enumerators attempted to inventory every dwelling in the nation and classify it according to its vacancy status and use. Vacant units were segregated into those temporarily vacant, those seasonally vacant, and those that house migratory workers. The results of this tabulation are the data used in this series, which maps vacant seasonal housing units by minor civil divisions (MCDs)—municipalities, villages, townships, etc. There is a map for each of the 20 most populous Daily Urban Systems (DUSs) in the nation. Each DUS consists of a central employment core and the surrounding counties that have at least 5 percent of their labor forces working in the core.

In the nation as a whole, about 1.1 percent of all housing units are seasonal dwellings used primarily for recreation. Relatively few of these units are located in Standard Metropolitan Statistical Areas (SMSAs). Even within the more populous DUS regions, seasonal dwellings are rare. There are 196,900 seasonal units in the 20 DUSs, but they amount to only 0.6 percent of the 28,312,000 dwellings in the 20 regions. The lack of amenities in and near some metropolitan areas and the inability of recreational uses to compete with industrial, commercial, and permanent residential uses in other places limit the number of recreational dwellings near the nation's most populous metropolises.

There are more seasonal dwellings within DUS boundaries in places that offer abundant climatic and terrain amenities, and that are close to mobile populations with relatively high incomes. Hence the number of seasonally vacant dwellings within a DUS is more a measure of the local supply of nearby recreational space than of demand for such space. The accompanying tabulation shows the number of households in the respective SMSAs that own a second home used at least part of the year. Significant differences between the number of households in an SMSA owning a second home and the number of vacant seasonal dwellings in the same DUS suggest correspondingly large movements of people beyond the DUS boundaries to recreational homesites. The proportion of all dwelling units that are seasonal is less than 2 percent of all housing units in all 20 DUSs.

Increased personal mobility attributable to better automobiles, the Interstate Highway System, and greater affluence contributes to the growing demand for seasonal dwellings. These developments have brought vast areas within easy weekend driving range of the nation's major metropolitan areas, thereby making it easier for city dwellers to make more frequent use of distant recreational dwellings than they could before 1960. Shorter work weeks and longer vacation periods have also helped stimulate demand, as has the adoption of flexible working hours by many firms. Energy shortages and lower speed limits should slow the trend toward consuming recreational resources at ever greater distances. Thus there may well be more rather than less pressure on recreational resources within DUSs in the years ahead. Accordingly, there could be a reduction in the number of vacant seasonal units within DUS boundaries. As families now owning recreational dwellings inside DUSs are faced with maintaining two dwellings as they enter their middle and later years, they may well decide to convert the recreational dwelling into a permanent residence. This has been occurring for several decades; many permanent dwellings at pleasant locations near metropolitan areas were formerly occupied seasonally.

|  | No. of Vacant Seasonal Units, DUS | No. of Households Owning a Second Home, SMSA |
|---|---|---|
| Boston | 31,575 | 65,660 |
| New York-Northern New Jersey | 88,065 | 172,375 |
| Philadelphia | 1,975 | 68,830 |
| Hartford-Connecticut Valley | 12,510 | 11,700 |
| Baltimore | 3,705 | 18,150 |
| New Orleans | 1,025 | 12,675 |
| San Francisco-Oakland | 1,915 | 52,080 |
| Pittsburgh | 3,065 | 29,875 |
| St. Louis | 2,890 | 25,055 |
| Cleveland | 1,335 | 18,595 |
| Chicago | 5,180 | 72,410 |
| Detroit | 1,255 | 75,270 |
| Minneapolis-St. Paul | 11,425 | 39,205 |
| Seattle | 2,850 | 27,645 |
| Dallas-Forth Worth | 1,295 | 30,510 |
| Houston | 1,560 | 33,405 |
| Los Angeles | 4,020 | 84,345 |
| Miami | 11,315 | 18,790 |
| Atlanta | 685 | 16,560 |
| Washington, D.C. | 4,295 | 44,485 |

**Boston.** In the Boston DUS, 1.9 percent of all housing units are seasonal dwellings. The comparatively large number of such units in the DUS suggests that many of the SMSA's 65,660 households with second homes have homes reasonably close to Boston. The coastal areas north and south of the metropolitan core are the sites of most seasonal units.

*Note:* All data are from the 1970 Censuses of Population and Housing unless otherwise indicated. Therefore the present tense refers to 1970 except for income data which are from 1969. Cartographic conventions are explained in Chapter 1. County names and other locational information are shown on the SMSA map at the beginning of each city chapter (6-25) and on the DUS map of mobile homes near the beginning of each city chapter.

*Open Space for Leisure Use: Seasonal Housing*

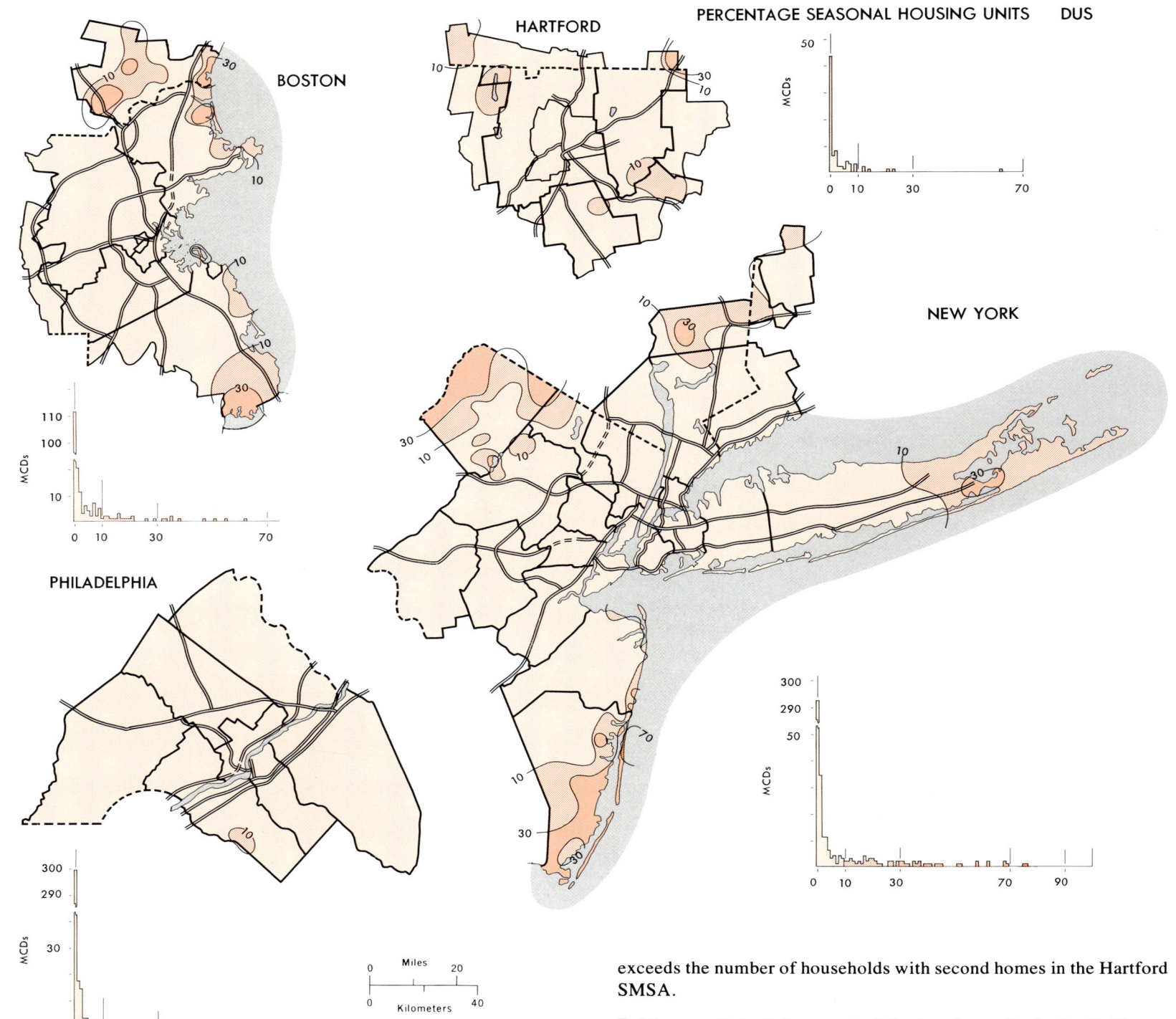

**New York-Northern New Jersey.** The 88,065 seasonal units in the New York DUS are 1.4 percent of the region's total housing stock. Seasonal units are located inland on the northern fringe of the DUS and along the New Jersey coast, with a third cluster on the eastern end of Long Island. The MCDs where seasonal dwellings exceed 70 percent of all housing units are located on the offshore beach bars in Ocean County, New Jersey.

**Philadelphia.** The Philadelphia DUS evidently offers few attractions for people desiring seasonal dwellings. The region has over 1,500,000 housing units, of which fewer than 2,000 are seasonal. Thus almost all of the 68,830 DUS residents (SMSA and DUS are coincident) who own second homes must travel outside the DUS to reach them. Many of the seasonal units on the New Jersey coast are owned by residents of the Philadelphia DUS.

**Hartford-Connecticut Valley.** The pressure New York and other northeastern metropolitan regions place on recreational resources in New England is evident in the seasonal-unit statistics for Hartford. The DUS contains the 3rd largest number of seasonal units among the 20 DUSs, and the number of seasonal units in the Hartford DUS exceeds the number of households with second homes in the Hartford SMSA.

**Baltimore.** Only 0.6 percent of the housing units in the Baltimore DUS (coincident with the SMSA) are seasonal dwellings. Therefore, most of the 18,150 DUS residents who own second homes must travel outside the region to reach them. The Baltimore DUS is underbounded; if it extended west into the Blue Ridge, the number of vacant seasonal units it contained would be larger than it is. Within existing DUS boundaries only southern Anne Arundel County contains MCDs in which seasonal units exceed 10 percent of local housing stocks.

**New Orleans.** The New Orleans DUS offers few attractive sites for seasonal dwellings. Most residents seek relief from hot temperatures and high humidity, both of which are inescapable throughout the DUS during much of the year.

**San Francisco-Oakland.** The San Francisco Bay Area offers residents a greater variety of ecological conditions than any other metropolitan region. In many respects, Bay Area residents can choose their favorite amenity location for the site of their permanent residence, and for that reason the small number (1,915) of vacant seasonal units in the DUS is not surprising. But the fact that over 52,000 Bay Area households own second homes suggests that at least some people may enjoy a change of scenery no matter how idyllic or varied the setting in which they reside.

*Open Space for Leisure Use: Seasonal Housing*

PERCENTAGE SEASONAL HOUSING UNITS
DUS

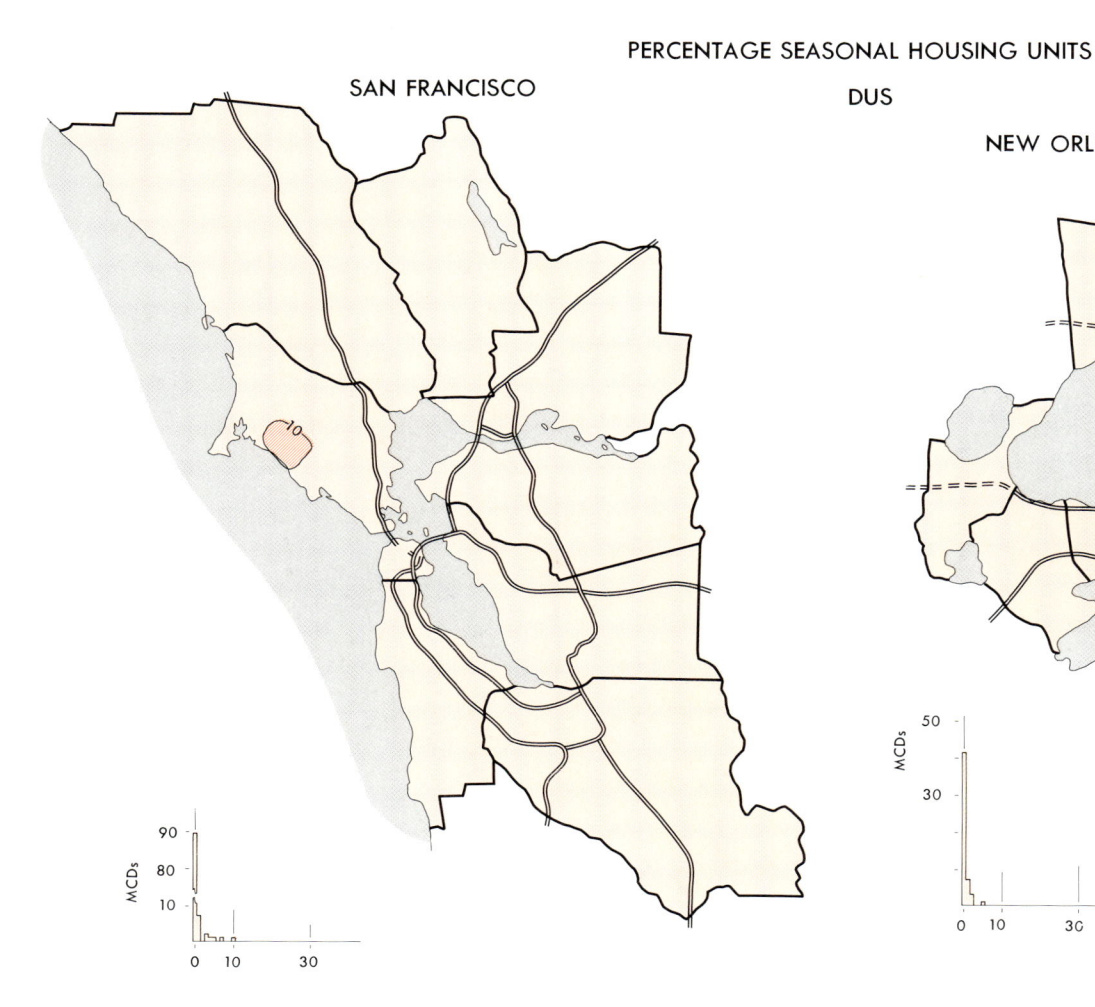

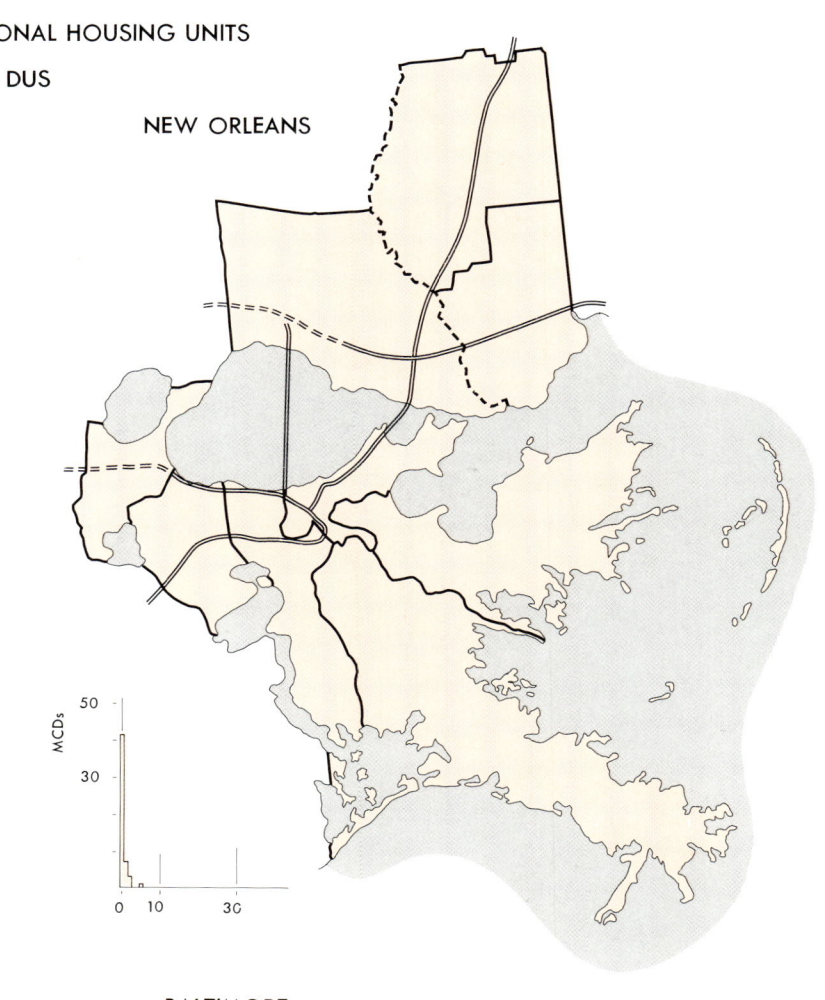

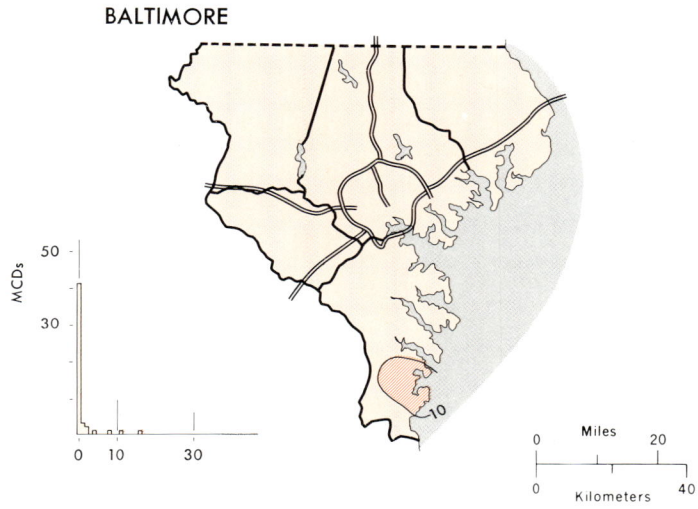

**Pittsburgh.** The deeply dissected Allegheny Plateau north and southeast of Pittsburgh contains small concentrations of seasonal dwellings. Most second homes owned by SMSA residents are located farther out from the metropolitan core in those general directions; even if all the DUS seasonal units were owned by SMSA residents with second homes, the DUS seasonal dwelling stock would satisfy but 10 percent of the SMSA "demand" for second homes.

**St. Louis.** Seasonal units in the St. Louis DUS are concentrated in Calhoun County, Illinois, and in Washington County, Missouri. Calhoun County lies between the Mississippi and Illinois rivers, and both the river bottoms and the uplands between them offer attractive sites for seasonal dwellings. Washington County is on the northern fringe of the Ozark Mountain region, which has long been a refuge for St. Louis residents seeking relief from the summer's heat and humidity. Although seasonal units in Calhoun and Washington counties as well as in other DUS locations are close at hand, the 2,890 seasonal units in the DUS are but a small fraction (11 percent) of the demand expressed in the form of the 25,055 SMSA residents who own second homes.

**Cleveland.** Most of the Lake Erie shore in the Cleveland DUS is occupied by industrial and permanent residential land uses. There are few seasonal dwellings in the entire DUS, and concentrations exceeding 10 percent of MCD units are located away from Lake Erie at inland locations where man-made lakes have produced amenity recreational sites. Thus most of the 18,595 second homes owned by SMSA residents lie outside the DUS. Northern Pennsylvania, western New York State, and Canada are preferred vacation-home locations for many residents of northeastern Ohio.

**Chicago.** Seasonal dwellings in the Chicago DUS exceed 10 percent of MCD housing units only near Fox Lake, in northwestern Lake County, Illinois. Permanent land uses outbid seasonal activities for locations on the Lake Michigan shore throughout the DUS, confining seasonal dwellings to interior locations such as Fox Lake and other glacial lakes in the northern part of the region. Many of the 72,410 second homes owned by Chicago SMSA residents are in Wisconsin, although some lie as far distant as northern Michigan and Minnesota.

**Detroit.** The pattern evident in Cleveland and Chicago is also characteristic of the Detroit DUS: seasonal units are concentrated in the interior rather than on the Great Lakes shores. One MCD on the St. Clair River has more than 10 percent seasonal dwellings, but most MCDs where proportions exceed 10 percent are located in morainic areas west and northwest of Detroit. The number of second homes owned by Detroit SMSA residents is larger than the number owned by Chicago SMSA residents despite the large difference (7.1 million versus 4.5 million) in population sizes. Even if all 1,255 seasonal units in the Detroit DUS were owned by SMSA residents, they would account for but 1.7 percent of the 75,270 second homes owned by SMSA households.

**Minneapolis-St. Paul.** The Twin Cities DUS contains a large number

281

*Open Space for Leisure Use: Seasonal Housing*

PERCENTAGE SEASONAL HOUSING UNITS
DUS

CHICAGO

DETROIT

CLEVELAND

ST. LOUIS

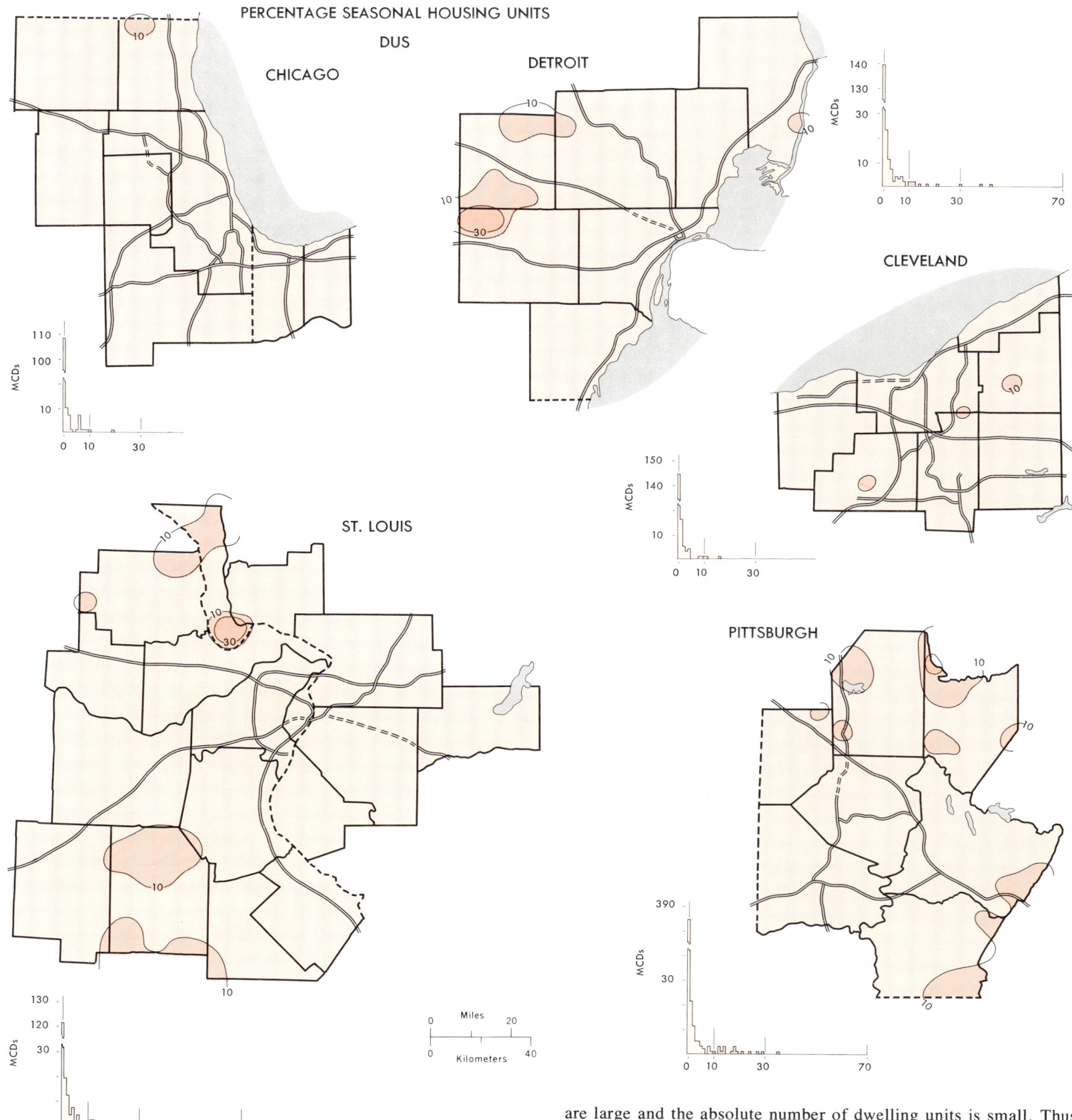

PITTSBURGH

of seasonal dwellings in relation to its population. Seasonal units exceed 10 percent of the housing units in many MCDs in the northern part of the region, with proportions in two MCDs exceeding 70 percent. The region's many glacial lakes and relatively poor soils discourage agriculture and make seasonal recreational land uses optimal in many places.

**Seattle.** Puget Sound and the Cascade Mountains have encouraged seasonal dwellings in the Seattle DUS. Although such units exceed 30 percent of the dwellings in the mountainous interior, the MCDs there are large and the absolute number of dwelling units is small. Thus more of the seasonal units in the DUS are located near Puget Sound. Although it might be thought that the site amenities available to many Seattle-area residents would decrease the demand for second residences, 27,645 households own second homes.

**Dallas-Fort Worth.** In none of the MCDs in the Dallas-Fort Worth DUS are more than 6 percent of the housing units classified as seasonal dwellings. Most of the region's seasonal units are adjacent to one of the man-made lakes in the DUS. Although 30,510 residents of the Dallas and Fort Worth SMSAs own second homes, most are located outside the DUS.

**Houston.** Like Dallas-Fort Worth, the Houston DUS offers few

282

*Open Space for Leisure Use: Seasonal Housing*

PERCENTAGE SEASONAL HOUSING UNITS
DUS

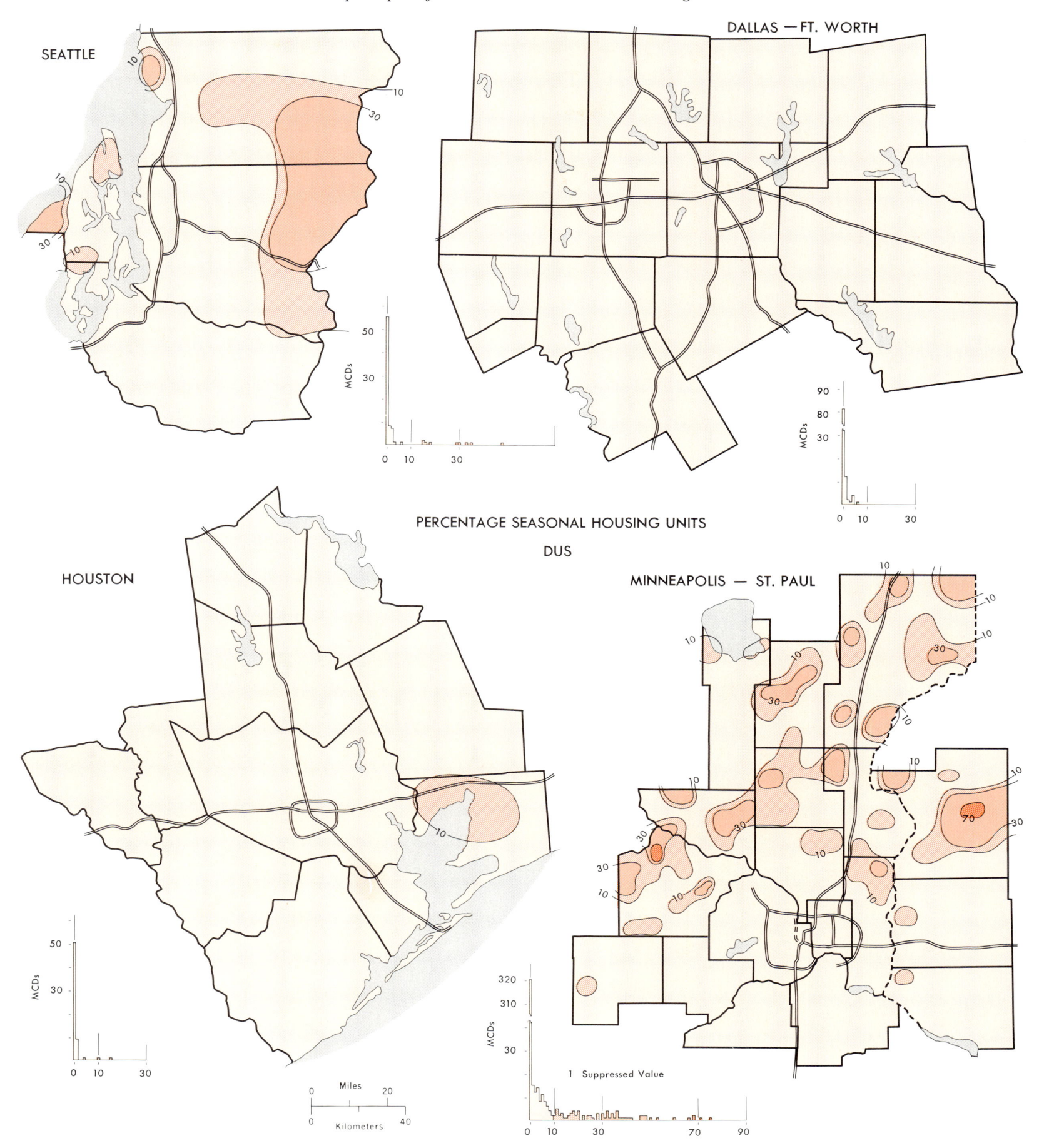

attractions for urbanites who desire seasonal homes. Proportions of seasonal units exceed 10 percent only in the two MCDs that flank Trinity Bay in Chambers County.

**Los Angeles.** The only MCD in the Los Angeles DUS in which seasonal dwellings exceed 10 percent of all housing units is located in the San Bernardino National Forest near Lake Arrowhead. With the exception of the Arrowhead concentration, the 4,020 seasonal units in the DUS are dispersed. The climatic and terrain amenities of the southern California region evidently do not dilute the demand for seasonal units, as measured by ownership of second homes that are used at least part of the year; 84,345 of the 2,432,000 households in the Los Angeles SMSA have second homes, compared with 72,410 of 2,184,000 in the Chicago SMSA.

*Open Space for Leisure Use: Seasonal Housing*

**Miami.** There are almost as many seasonal units in the Miami DUS as there are in the Twin Cities DUS, but whereas most seasonal units in the Twin Cities region are owned by local residents, many of the seasonally occupied units in Miami are owned by people in other parts of the nation. Miami's seasonal units are dispersed throughout the region, but percentages are slightly higher in Broward County than in the Dade County MCDs. The MCD with the highest proportion of seasonal units (8 percent) is Key Biscayne.

**Atlanta.** The Atlanta DUS has the smallest number of seasonal units of the 20 DUSs mapped in this series. The only MCD in which more than 10 percent of the housing units are in the seasonal category is located adjacent to Jackson Lake in southern Newton County. The Georgia countryside and even the large lakes in the northern part of the DUS are evidently unattractive to Atlanta residents who desire seasonal residences.

**Washington, D.C.** Most of the seasonal dwellings in the Washington DUS are located on the Chesapeake Bay shore. The Washington DUS extends into the Blue Ridge Mountains and the Shenandoah National Park on the west. The cluster of seasonal units in Rappahannock County is a precursor of more intensive development of recreational dwellings in that part of the DUS.

---

In most of the nation's most populous metropolitan regions there are few nearby sites suitable for seasonal dwellings, especially in relation to demand as measured by the number of SMSA households that own second homes they use part of the year. In the DUSs where seasonal dwellings are relatively numerous, it is impossible to determine whether these units are satisfying local demands. Given these qualifications, it is clear that the greatest *potential* for satisfying demands for amenity residential space within DUSs exists in the Boston, New York, Hartford, Minneapolis-St. Paul, and Miami regions.

*Housing in Metropolitan Areas*

CHAPTER 29

# Crowded Housing

In the 1970 Census, each head of household was asked how many rooms (excluding bathrooms, porches, foyers, etc.) he or she had in his or her living quarters. The number of persons occupying each household was also tabulated, and the calculations of average number of persons per household are the data used to produce the maps in this series. The percentage of households with more than 1 person per room is mapped for each Standard Metropolitan Statistical Area (SMSA) included in the 20 regions mapped here.

In the United States, 5,211,000 housing units (7.7 percent) have more than 1 person per room, a generally accepted measure of crowding. Crowding has declined absolutely and relatively since 1960, when 6,600,000 (11.5 percent) of the nation's households contained more than 1 person per room. Crowded housing is slightly more prevalent in nonmetropolitan than in metropolitan regions; 7.4 percent of all SMSA households are crowded, compared with 8.4 percent of all units outside SMSAs. Renter-occupied units are more often crowded than are owner-occupied units in the nation as a whole (10.8 percent versus 6.7 percent) and in SMSAs (10 percent versus 6.3 percent).

Within the 20 regions mapped here, 7.2 percent of all housing units are crowded. Proportions in individual SMSAs vary from 4.1 percent in Seattle to 13.3 percent in Miami. The percentages shown in the accompanying tabulation are for combined SMSAs when there is more than one SMSA in a region.

The relationship between crowding and behavior is unclear. Crowding is allegedly associated with physical and mental illness and social pathology. Crowding may also increase intra-family frictions because members simply cannot avoid getting in each other's way at times. Other analysts argue that people are not necessarily harmed by crowding, that when differences in income and social background are properly accounted for, people living in crowded houses and neighborhoods appear to be no worse off than those living at lower densities. Perhaps many of the psychological and physical pathologies associated with crowding in popular commentary are generally characteristic of low-income groups and are only more noticeable when circumstances force low-income people to live at high densities.

Crowding can be measured in several ways. Space requirements stated in square feet per person are useful for builders and housing inspectors, but it is difficult for census enumerators to make such measurements. Number of people per room ignores room size and life-styles, but it is a reasonably reliable measure of residential crowding.

*Note:* All data are from the 1970 Census of Population and Housing unless otherwise indicated. Therefore the present tense refers to 1970 except for income data which are from 1969. Cartographic conventions are explained in Chapter 1. County names and other locational information are shown on the SMSA map at the beginning of each city chapter (6-25) and on the DUS map of mobile homes near the beginning of each city chapter.

**Boston.** Crowded housing in the Boston SMSA is concentrated in the city of Boston (34 percent), especially in predominantly black parts of the city (pp. 25, 382). The outlying areas in which more than 10 percent of tract households are crowded are located in independent towns with aged housing stocks. Although crowded housing exceeds 10 percent of all units in only a few tracts, there are some units with more than 1 person per room throughout the SMSA.

Percentage of SMSA Housing Units with More Than
1 Person per Room

| | |
|---|---|
| Boston | 5.4 |
| New York-Northern New Jersey | 8.1 |
| Philadelphia | 5.3 |
| Hartford | 5.6 |
| Baltimore | 6.7 |
| New Orleans | 13.1 |
| San Francisco-Oakland | 5.9 |
| Pittsburgh | 5.8 |
| St. Louis | 9.5 |
| Cleveland | 5.3 |
| Chicago | 8.0 |
| Detroit | 7.6 |
| Minneapolis-St. Paul | 6.4 |
| Seattle | 4.1 |
| Dallas-Fort Worth | 7.8 |
| Houston | 9.9 |
| Los Angeles | 8.2 |
| Miami | 13.3 |
| Atlanta | 7.3 |
| Washington, D.C. | 6.6 |

**New York-Northern New Jersey.** The region consists of four SMSAs. Crowded housing is especially prevalent in the central cities of the SMSAs. Of all the crowded units in the region, 69 percent are located in New York City, where proportions of crowded households in some tracts exceed 50 percent.

**Philadelphia.** There are 81,600 housing units in the SMSA with more than 1 person per room; 40,650 (50 percent) are located in Philadelphia, where crowded conditions are experienced by more than a fifth of all households in some tracts. The scattered tracts where crowding exceeds 10 percent are mostly in old towns. The area over 10 percent on the eastern side of the SMSA is the Fort Dix military base.

**Hartford.** Concentrations of crowded households lie in the Connecticut River Valley in the region's oldest and largest towns. Of the SMSA's 11,600 crowded households, 5,200 (45 percent) are in Hartford. The neighborhoods where crowding is most intense in Hartford are occupied by blacks and Spanish-Americans (p. 65).

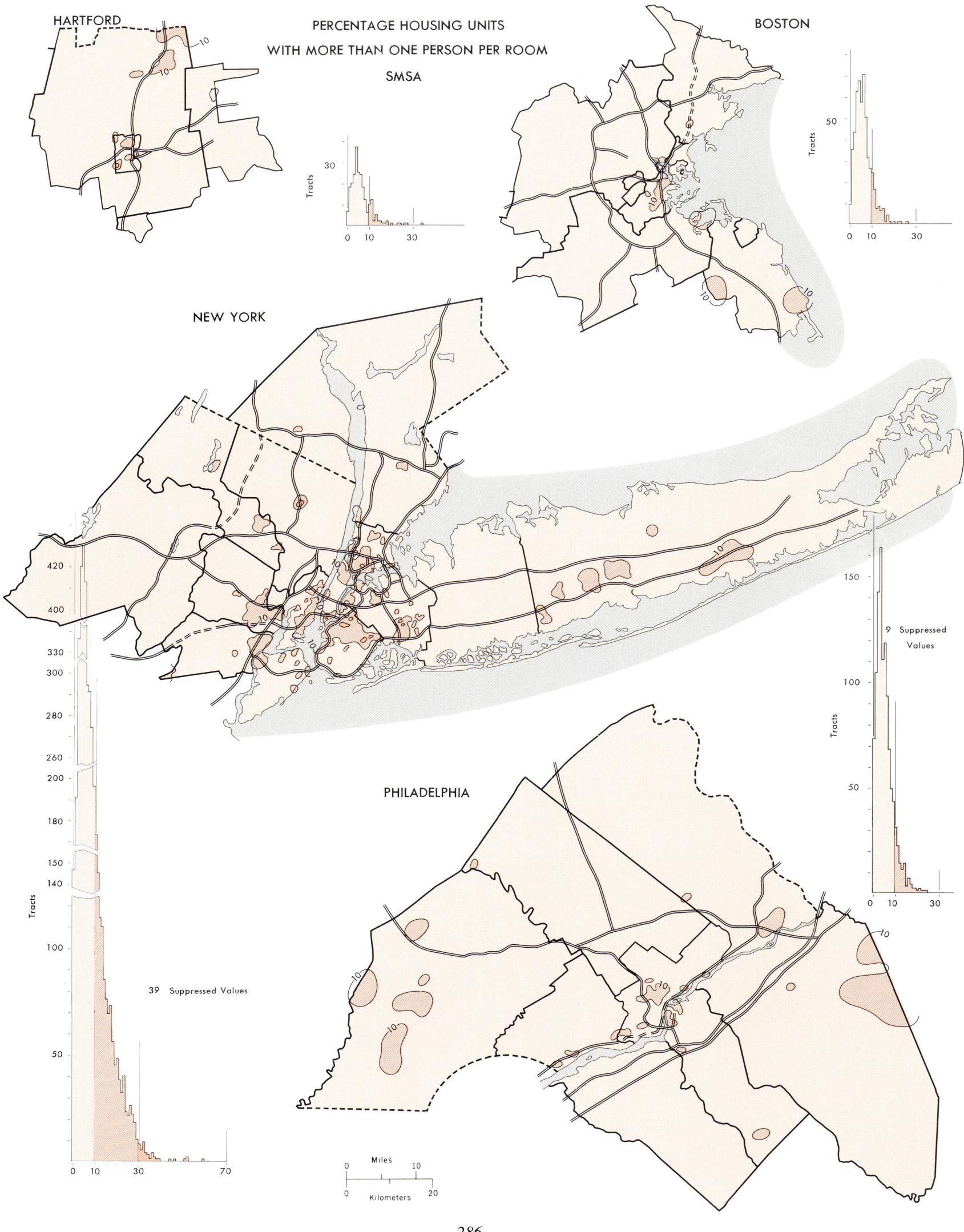

*Housing in Metropolitan Areas: Crowded Housing*

PERCENTAGE HOUSING UNITS
WITH MORE THAN ONE PERSON PER ROOM
SMSA

HARTFORD

BOSTON

NEW YORK

PHILADELPHIA

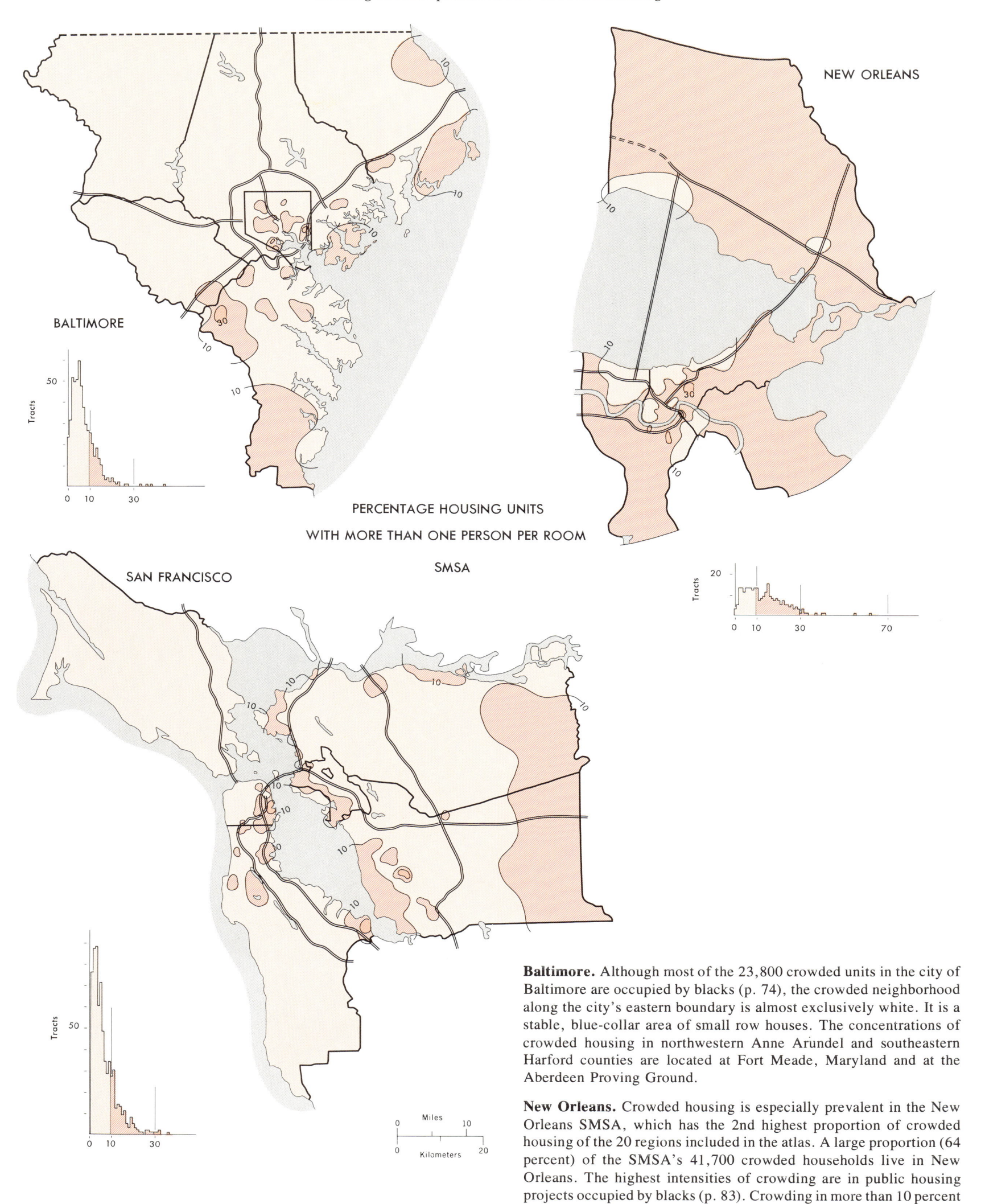

*Housing in Metropolitan Areas: Crowded Housing*

PERCENTAGE HOUSING UNITS
WITH MORE THAN ONE PERSON PER ROOM
SMSA

**Baltimore.** Although most of the 23,800 crowded units in the city of Baltimore are occupied by blacks (p. 74), the crowded neighborhood along the city's eastern boundary is almost exclusively white. It is a stable, blue-collar area of small row houses. The concentrations of crowded housing in northwestern Anne Arundel and southeastern Harford counties are located at Fort Meade, Maryland and at the Aberdeen Proving Ground.

**New Orleans.** Crowded housing is especially prevalent in the New Orleans SMSA, which has the 2nd highest proportion of crowded housing of the 20 regions included in the atlas. A large proportion (64 percent) of the SMSA's 41,700 crowded households live in New Orleans. The highest intensities of crowding are in public housing projects occupied by blacks (p. 83). Crowding in more than 10 percent

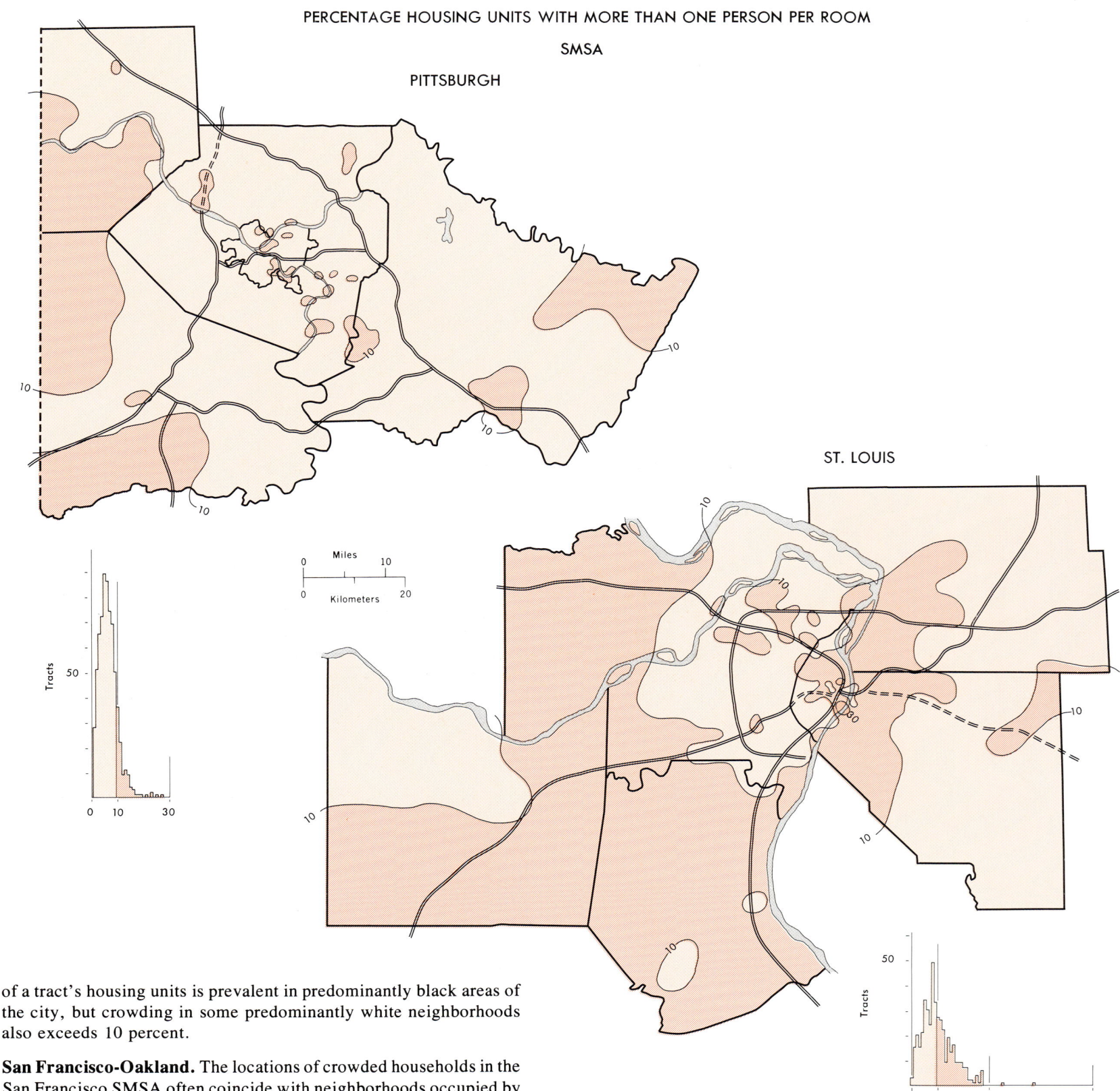

*Housing in Metropolitan Areas: Crowded Housing*

PERCENTAGE HOUSING UNITS WITH MORE THAN ONE PERSON PER ROOM
SMSA

of a tract's housing units is prevalent in predominantly black areas of the city, but crowding in some predominantly white neighborhoods also exceeds 10 percent.

**San Francisco-Oakland.** The locations of crowded households in the San Francisco SMSA often coincide with neighborhoods occupied by minority groups (pp. 94, 383, 391). The predominantly rural areas on the eastern and northern sides of the SMSA are exceptions, for they are predominantly white. Of the SMSA's 63,600 crowded households, 20,000 (31 percent) are located in San Francisco and 9,900 (16 percent) are located in Oakland.

**Pittsburgh.** Crowded housing in the Pittsburgh SMSA is a small-town and rural phenomenon; only 25 percent of the SMSA's 45,800 crowded units are located in Pittsburgh. The rest are scattered among the old mill towns along the Allegheny and Monongahela rivers and in outlying nonurban areas.

**St. Louis.** A relatively high proportion of the housing in the St. Louis SMSA has more than 1 person per room, and areas where crowded housing exceeds 10 percent dominate large areas of the map. Proportions are lower in the prosperous western and northwestern suburbs of St. Louis and east of the East St. Louis area. A third of the SMSA's 54,500 crowded units are located in St. Louis.

**Cleveland.** There are 34,300 crowded units in the Cleveland SMSA; 52 percent are located in Cleveland. Predominantly black areas on the city's east side have the highest concentrations of crowded housing (p. 131). In a few tracts there, crowded households exceed 20 percent of tract totals. But crowding also occurs in white neighborhoods, as is true in southwestern Cleveland.

**Chicago.** Tracts where the average number of persons per room exceeds 1 are scattered in several parts of the SMSA, but most (62

288

*Housing in Metropolitan Areas: Crowded Housing*

PERCENTAGE HOUSING UNITS
WITH MORE THAN ONE PERSON PER ROOM
SMSA

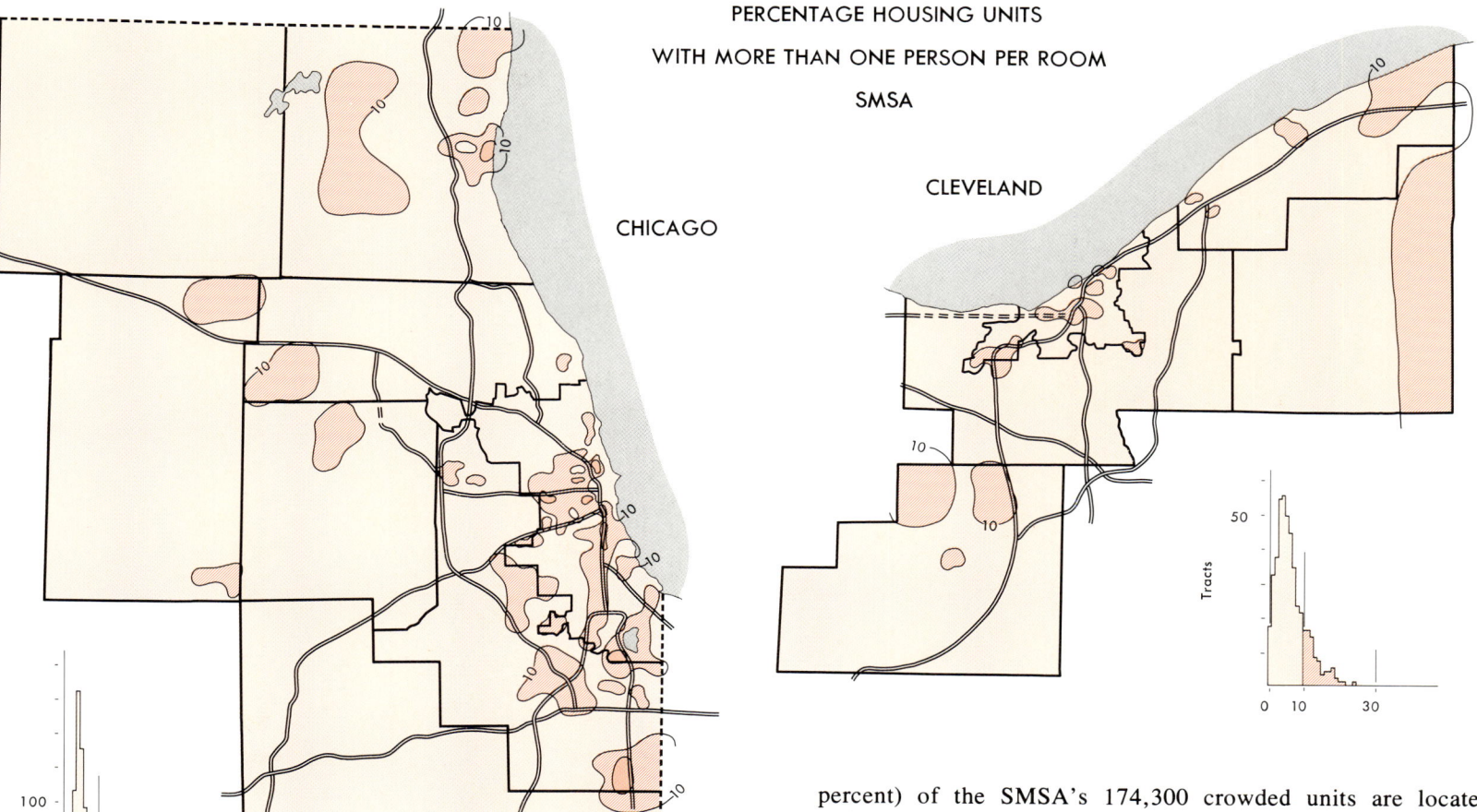

CHICAGO

CLEVELAND

DETROIT

percent) of the SMSA's 174,300 crowded units are located in Chicago. Also, the highest intensities of crowding are in the city. Over 60 percent of the units in the public housing projects next to Interstates 90 and 94 in south-central Chicago have more than 1 person per room. Within Chicago, areas where crowded housing exceeds 10 percent often coincide with areas occupied by low-income minority groups (pp. 140-141).

**Detroit.** Crowded households are more scattered in the Detroit SMSA than is usually true. Of the region's 96,050 crowded units, 38 percent are located in Detroit. Also, crowded housing is not associated as much with predominantly black neighborhoods (p. 153) as it often is in other SMSAs.

**Minneapolis-St. Paul.** Although a fairly large area of the Twin Cities SMSA has crowded households in excess of 10 percent, the proportion is low in the most densely settled parts of the region. Crowded housing is not especially concentrated in the central cities. Of the region's 35,800 crowded households, 6,900 (19 percent) are located in Minneapolis and 5,800 (16 percent) are located in St. Paul. The tract on St. Paul's northern boundary with 30 percent crowded households contains the University of Minnesota's married-student housing complex.

**Seattle.** The Seattle SMSA has the lowest proportion of households with more than 1 person per room of the 20 regions in the atlas. The few tracts where the proportion of such households exceeds 10 percent are sparsely populated. The SMSA's relatively young housing stock, the high incomes of its residents, and the high rates of home ownership contribute to the SMSA's low ratio of crowded units.

**Dallas-Fort Worth.** As indicated by the histogram for the combined Dallas and Fort Worth SMSAs, crowded housing in the region is more common than it is in most regions in the atlas. Crowded households occur in both rural and urban areas. There are 61,100 crowded units in the combined SMSAs; 24,550 (40 percent) are located in Dallas and 11,950 (20 percent) are located in Fort Worth. Crowding is highest in a heavily black area of west-central Dallas. The low proportions of crowded households in other parts of Dallas that are as predominantly black as the west-central area suggest that income, more than race, determines crowding (p. 189).

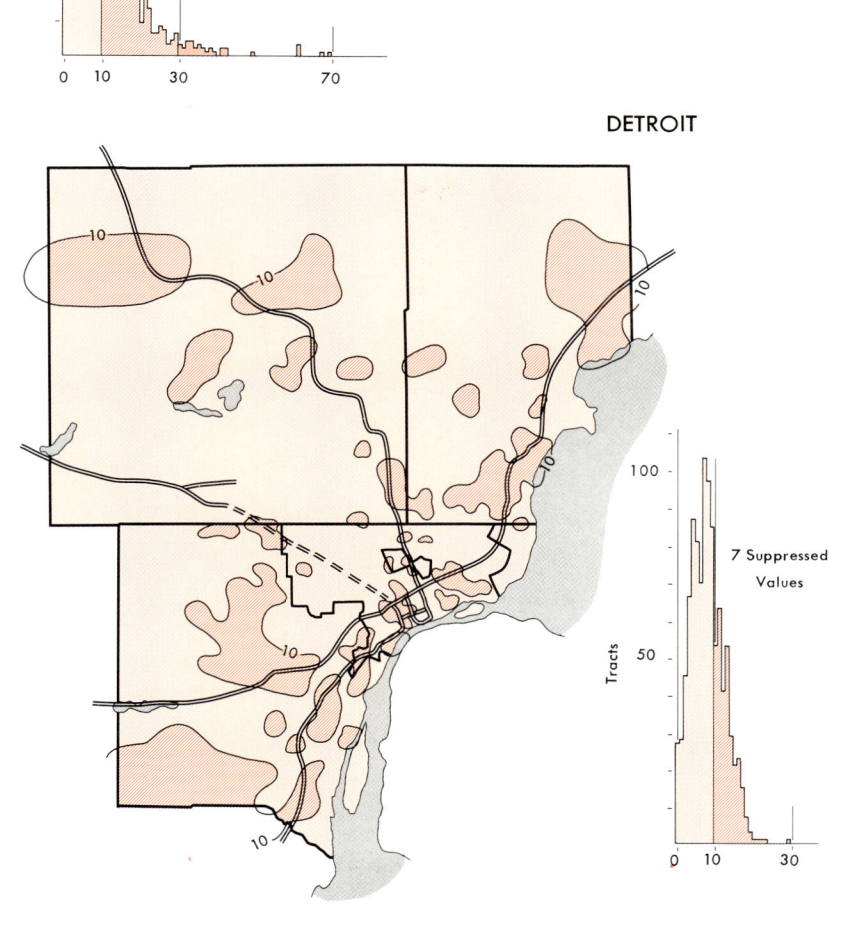

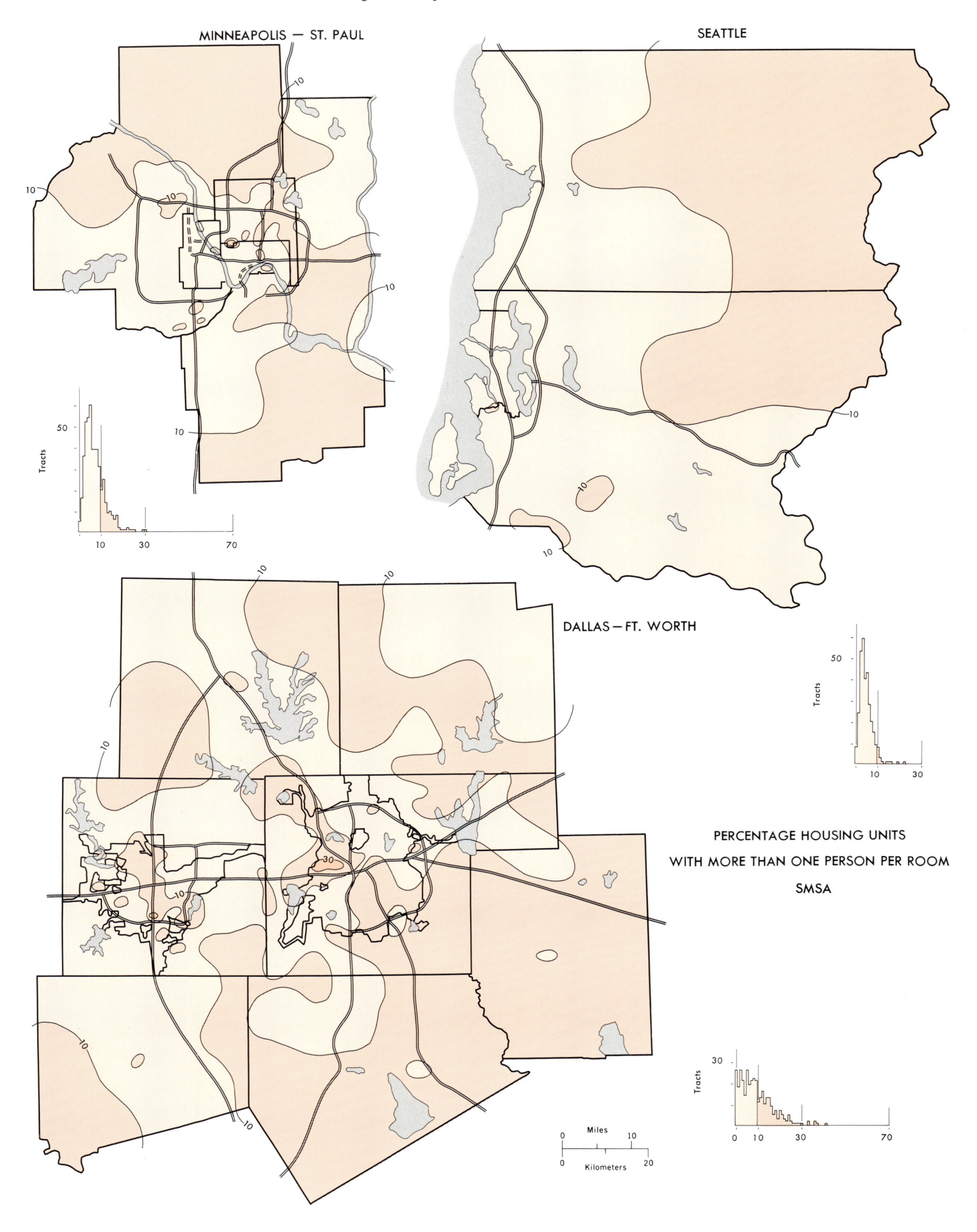

*Housing in Metropolitan Areas: Crowded Housing*

MINNEAPOLIS — ST. PAUL

SEATTLE

DALLAS — FT. WORTH

PERCENTAGE HOUSING UNITS
WITH MORE THAN ONE PERSON PER ROOM
SMSA

290

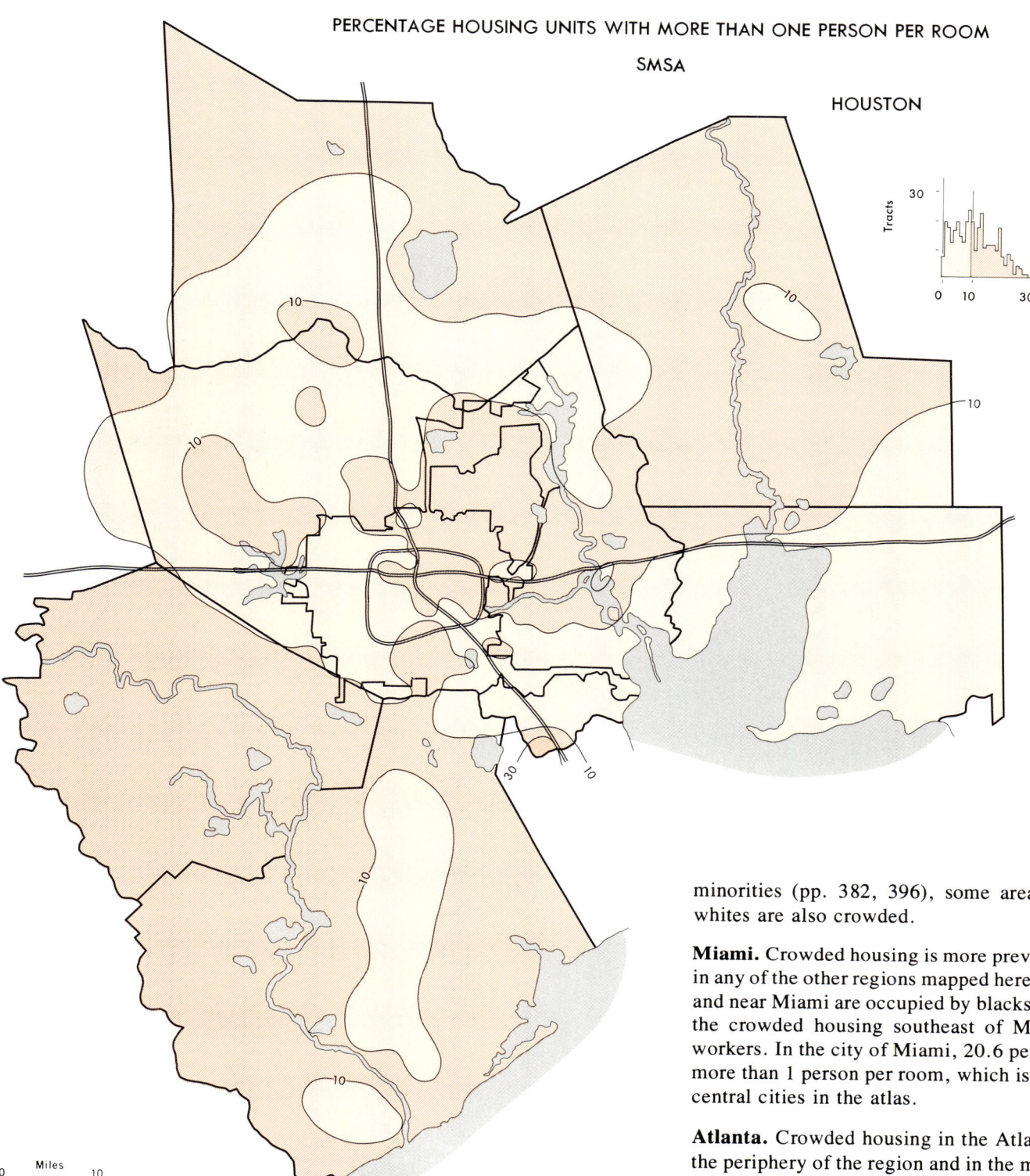

*Housing in Metropolitan Areas: Crowded Housing*

PERCENTAGE HOUSING UNITS WITH MORE THAN ONE PERSON PER ROOM
SMSA
HOUSTON

**Houston.** Almost 10 percent of the households in the Houston SMSA have more than 1 person per room, which is the 3rd highest proportion of crowding among the regions in the atlas. Crowded units exceed 10 percent of tract totals in many rural parts of the SMSA. Proportions are generally lower in the suburbs. The parts of the city where crowding exceeds 10 percent coincide well with areas occupied by low-income minority groups. (p. 207). Sixty-five percent of the SMSA's 60,500 crowded units are located in Houston.

**Los Angeles.** Concentrations of crowded housing are spread throughout the south-central part of the SMSA where old housing stocks in the area's many separate settlement centers attract low-income groups willing to occupy housing at high densities. Although much of the crowded housing occurs in areas occupied by minorities (pp. 382, 396), some areas occupied by lower-income whites are also crowded.

**Miami.** Crowded housing is more prevalent in the Miami SMSA than in any of the other regions mapped here. Many of the crowded units in and near Miami are occupied by blacks and Cuban refugees. Much of the crowded housing southeast of Miami is occupied by migrant workers. In the city of Miami, 20.6 percent of all housing units have more than 1 person per room, which is the highest proportion among central cities in the atlas.

**Atlanta.** Crowded housing in the Atlanta SMSA is concentrated on the periphery of the region and in the metropolitan core. Much of the central area where crowded households exceed 10 percent of tract totals coincides with heavily black parts of the city. The occurrence of crowding in areas occupied exclusively by whites and the absence of crowding in some tracts occupied by upper-income blacks makes it clear that the ability to purchase or rent spacious housing is more important than race in determining the degree of crowding in specific neighborhoods (p. 251).

**Washington, D.C.** Of the 62,050 crowded units in the SMSA, 31,450 (51 percent) are located in the District of Columbia where they are restricted to predominantly black neighborhoods (pp. 260, 388). Outside the central area, crowded housing occurs without regard to the racial composition of the population.

---

The coincidence of crowded housing and racial and ethnic minorities on almost all the maps in this series is striking but not wholly invariant. The fact that middle- and upper-income whites often occupy crowded housing suggests that the ability or inability to

*Housing in Metropolitan Areas: Crowded Housing*

MIAMI

LOS ANGELES

WASHINGTON, D.C.

PERCENTAGE HOUSING UNITS
WITH MORE THAN ONE PERSON PER ROOM
SMSA

ATLANTA

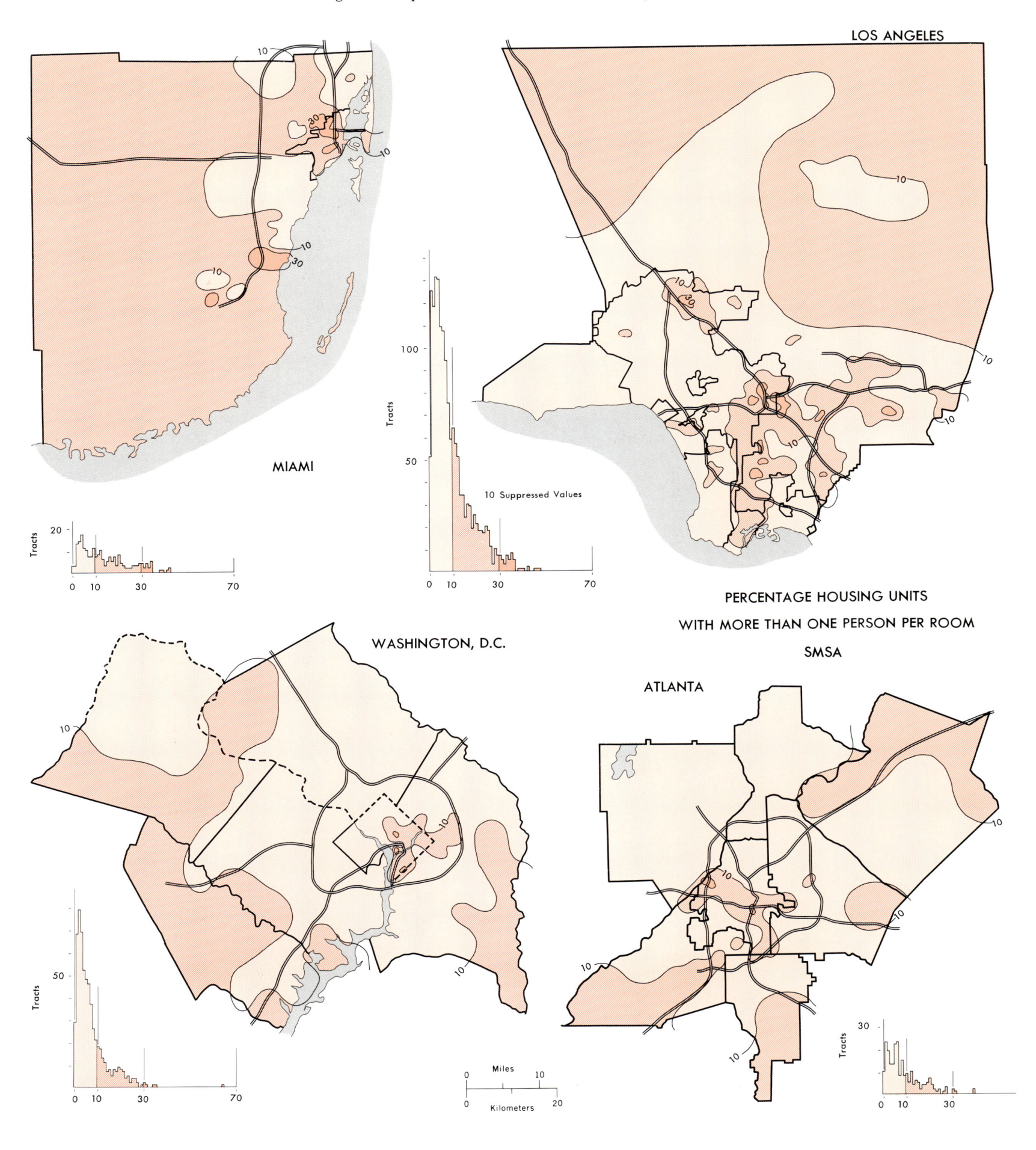

purchase or rent uncrowded housing is more important than race itself. The fact that black and Spanish-American incomes are sharply lower than white incomes explains the crowding usually observed in areas occupied by these minority groups.

*Housing in Metropolitan Areas*

CHAPTER 30

# Rent in Relation to Income

In the 1970 Census all household heads renting their living quarters were asked to specify the amount they paid for rent. Since a 20 percent sample of households were asked to specify their 1969 gross incomes, it is possible to cross-tabulate average 1969 incomes with average 1970 rents and determine the share of a household's income being expended for the quarters they occupy. The maps in this chapter show the proportion of census-tract households paying more than one-fourth of their 1969 incomes for rent. High proportions generally indicate concentrations of households having difficulty making ends meet.

In the nation 23.3 percent of the households occupying rental units pay 35 percent or more of their incomes for rent; 13.1 percent pay from 25 to 34 percent. Thus 36.4 percent of the nation's renting households have to spend more than one-fourth of their incomes on housing. Within the nation's Standard Metropolitan Statistical Areas (SMSAs), 6,599,000 (37.9 percent) of all households pay 25 percent or more of their incomes for rent. There are 9,876,000 rental units in the 20 regions mapped in this chapter. Of that number, 3,803,000 (38.5 percent) pay 25 percent or more of their incomes for rent. The proportion of households paying that percentage for rent in the central cities of the SMSAs mapped here is 39.2 percent.

Variations in the proportion of households paying one-fourth or more of their incomes for rental housing range from 34.3 percent in the Pittsburgh and Houston SMSAs to 52.8 percent in Miami (see accompanying tabulation). Proportions are usually a few percentage points higher in central cities than in entire SMSAs. Miami is an exception, for the large number of limited-income retiree renters in Miami Beach and elsewhere in the SMSA results in a higher proportion for the SMSA than for the central city.

Rent and income are usually correlated, but each can vary somewhat independently, making it difficult to interpret the ratio of rent to income without additional data. A household paying $70 of a $200 monthly income for rent, for example, is probably under greater financial strain than a household paying $350 of a $1,000 monthly income, despite the identical percentages. The latter will likely have more money left for discretionary purchases after rent and other necessities are paid. The former might have difficulty making ends meet even if rent were but 20 percent of its income. The rent-income ratio is sensitive to rents as well as to incomes, and both must be considered in determining whether rents exceeding 25 percent of incomes are creating financial stress.

*Note:* All data are from the 1970 Censuses of Population and Housing unless otherwise indicated. Therefore the present tense refers to 1970 except for income data which are from 1969. Cartographic conventions are explained in Chapter 1. County names and other locational information are shown on the SMSA map at the beginning of each city chapter (6-25) and on the DUS map of mobile homes near the beginning of each city chapter.

**Boston.** Households paying a fourth or more of their incomes for rent exceed 30 percent throughout the SMSA except for scattered tracts outside the core where proportions are lower. Such tracts are located in low-rent as well as in high-rent areas (p. 23). The tract in Essex County where households paying a fourth or more of their incomes for rent exceeds 70 percent has only 51 rental units, which are occupied by low-income households.

Percentage of Renting Households Paying a Fourth or More of Their Incomes for Rent

| Region | Central City(ies) | Entire SMSA |
| --- | --- | --- |
| Boston | 46.9 | 42.4 |
| New York | 35.7 | 36.1 |
| Jersey City | 33.0 | 31.2 |
| Newark | 43.1 | 38.7 |
| Paterson-Clifton-Passaic | 39.0 | 34.3 |
| Philadelphia | 39.2 | 36.6 |
| Hartford | 42.6 | 37.3 |
| Baltimore | 42.3 | 36.5 |
| New Orleans | 40.8 | 39.0 |
| San Francisco-Oakland | 46.6 | 45.1 |
| Pittsburgh | 41.0 | 34.3 |
| St. Louis | 38.6 | 37.0 |
| Cleveland | 36.0 | 34.9 |
| Chicago | 38.2 | 36.8 |
| Detroit | 37.9 | 36.3 |
| Minneapolis-St. Paul | 46.1 | 43.8 |
| Seattle | 45.9 | 42.1 |
| Dallas | 40.6 | 38.0 |
| Fort Worth | 35.2 | 33.9 |
| Houston | 37.0 | 34.3 |
| Los Angeles | 44.0 | 41.8 |
| Miami | 49.6 | 52.8 |
| Atlanta | 40.3 | 37.1 |
| Washington, D.C. | 38.0 | 34.6 |

**New York-Northern New Jersey.** Outlying areas where the proportion of households paying a fourth or more of their incomes for rent is below 30 percent are often affluent neighborhoods (p. 43) where people with large incomes are renting expensive units (p. 34). The tracts in the same category in Queens County are occupied by people with modest incomes. The central-city areas where less than 30 percent of the households pay a fourth or more of their incomes for rent are predominantly white (p. 38).

**Philadelphia.** Rent-income ratios are lowest in the west-central parts of the SMSA where moderate incomes (p. 59) combine with low rents

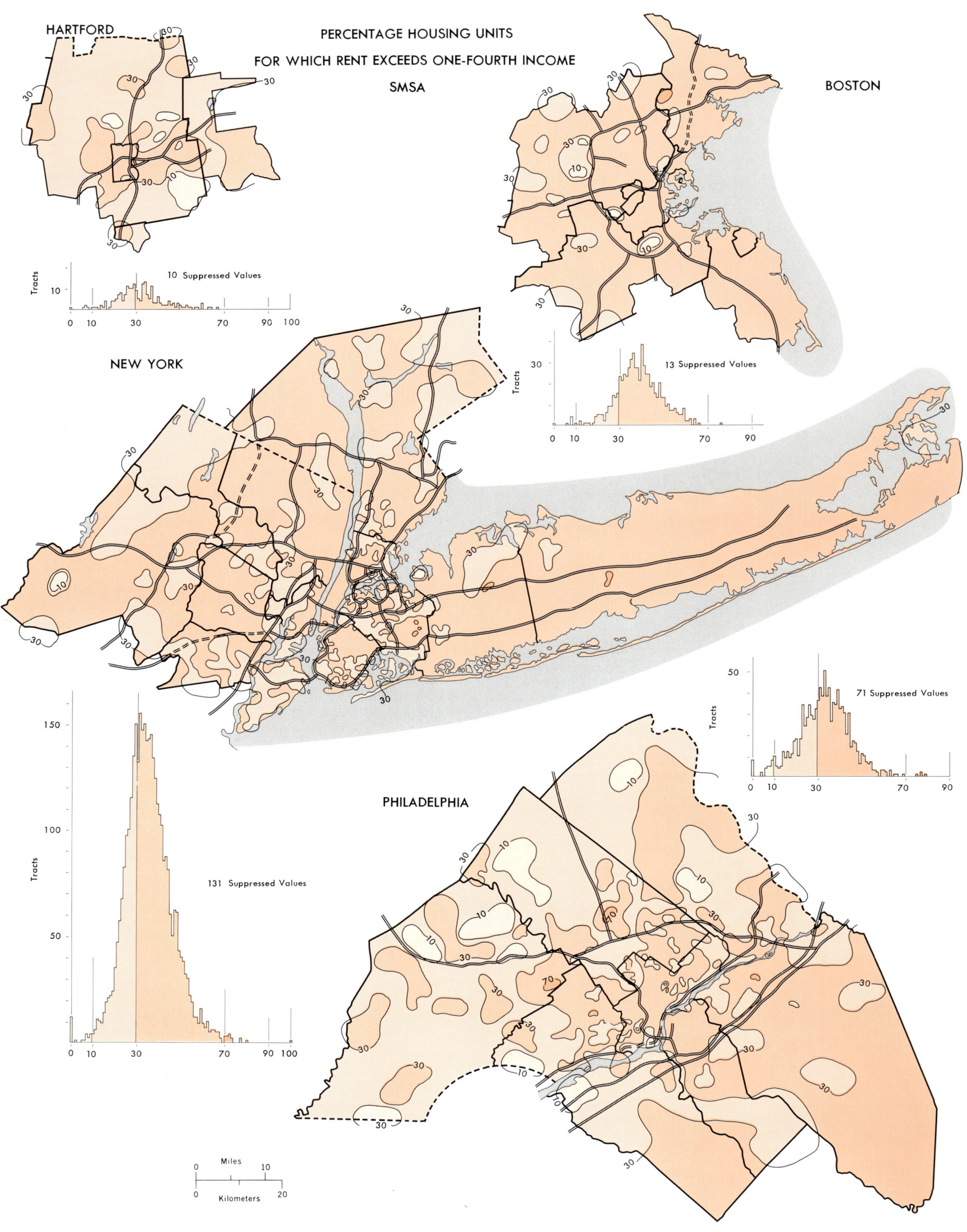

*Housing in Metropolitan Areas: Rent-Income Ratio*

PERCENTAGE HOUSING UNITS
FOR WHICH RENT EXCEEDS ONE-FOURTH INCOME
SMSA

HARTFORD

BOSTON

NEW YORK

PHILADELPHIA

*Housing in Metropolitan Areas: Rent-Income Ratio*

PERCENTAGE HOUSING UNITS FOR WHICH RENT EXCEEDS ONE-FOURTH INCOME

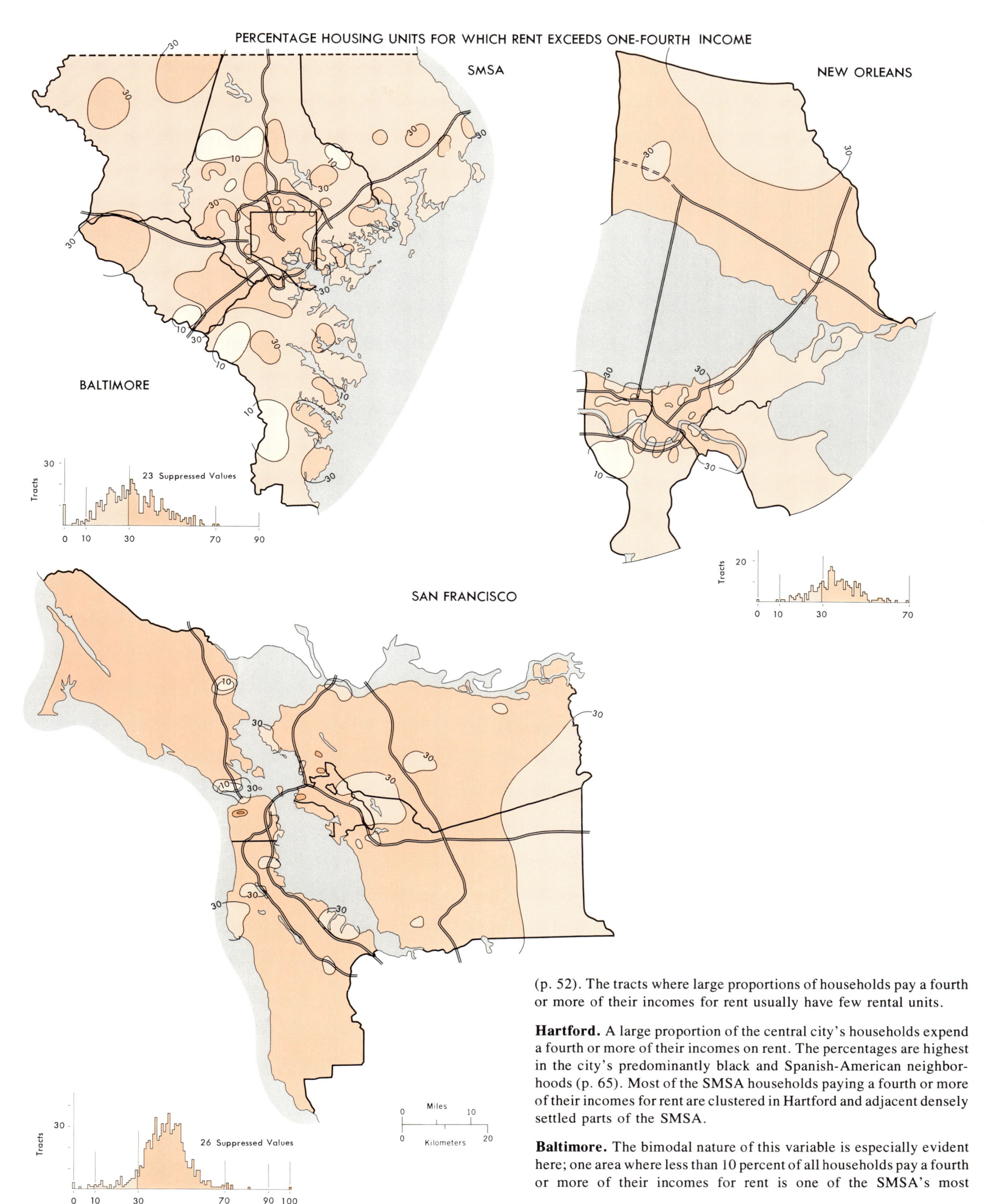

BALTIMORE SMSA

NEW ORLEANS

SAN FRANCISCO

(p. 52). The tracts where large proportions of households pay a fourth or more of their incomes for rent usually have few rental units.

**Hartford.** A large proportion of the central city's households expend a fourth or more of their incomes on rent. The percentages are highest in the city's predominantly black and Spanish-American neighborhoods (p. 65). Most of the SMSA households paying a fourth or more of their incomes for rent are clustered in Hartford and adjacent densely settled parts of the SMSA.

**Baltimore.** The bimodal nature of this variable is especially evident here; one area where less than 10 percent of all households pay a fourth or more of their incomes for rent is one of the SMSA's most

*Housing in Metropolitan Areas: Rent-Income Ratio*

PERCENTAGE HOUSING UNITS FOR WHICH RENT EXCEEDS ONE-FOURTH INCOME
SMSA

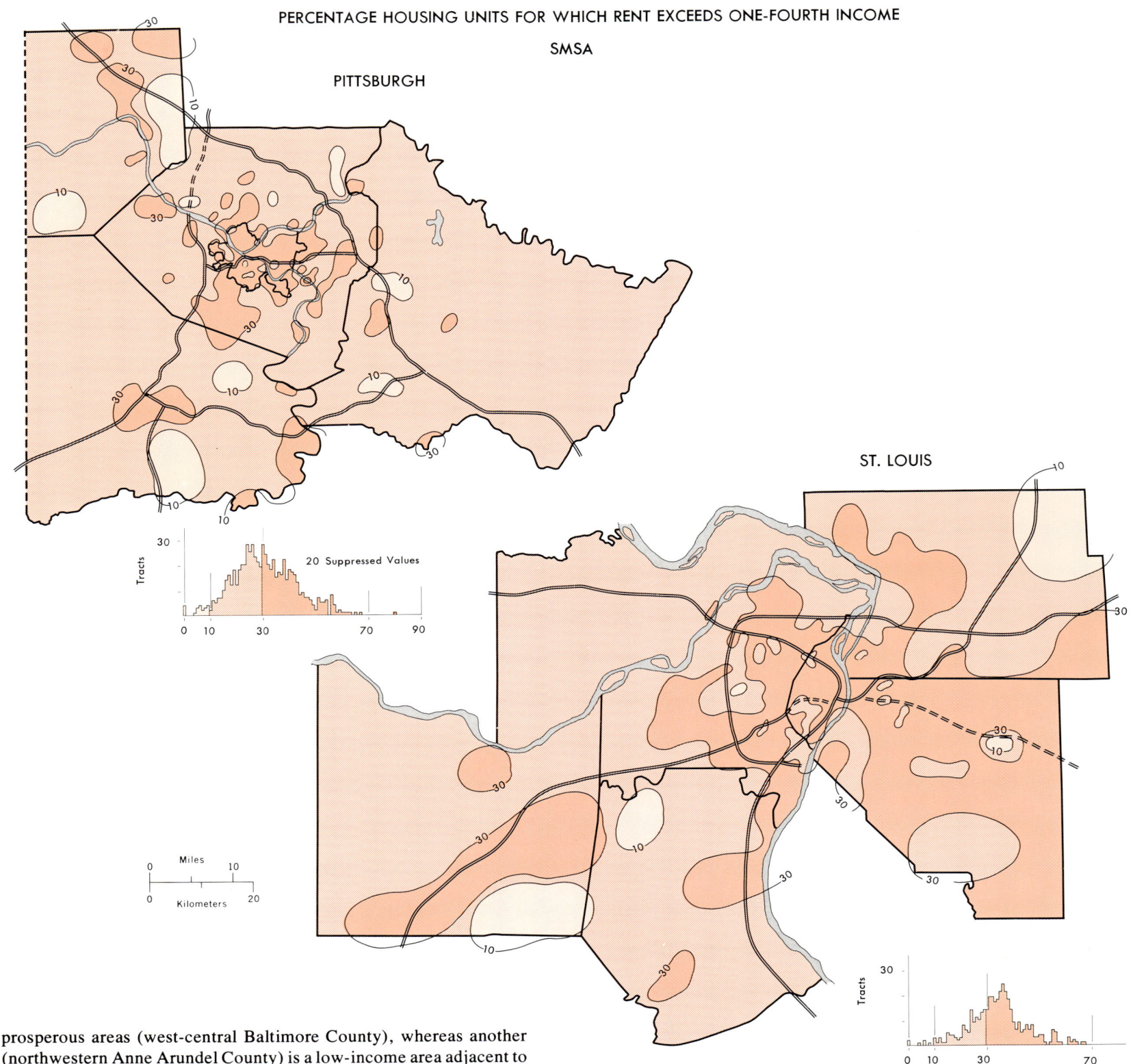

PITTSBURGH

ST. LOUIS

prosperous areas (west-central Baltimore County), whereas another (northwestern Anne Arundel County) is a low-income area adjacent to a military base (p. 76).

**New Orleans.** The proportion of households paying a fourth or more of their incomes for rent exceeds 30 percent throughout much of rural St. Tammany Parish, despite the low rents there (p. 81), because of low incomes (p. 85). An unusually high percentage (76.1) of SMSA households paying a fourth or more of their incomes for rent are located in New Orleans.

**San Francisco-Oakland.** Housing is comparatively expensive in the SMSA and its central cities (p. 92). Thus relatively high proportions of the residents who rent expend a fourth or more of their incomes on housing. Areas where such households make up less than 30 percent of tract households are usually financially well off (p. 100).

**Pittsburgh.** Comparatively low rents (p. 107) in the outlying areas of the SMSA keep the proportion of households paying a fourth or more of their incomes for rent below 30 percent in many places. Higher proportions are concentrated in Pittsburgh and its immediate suburbs, and in the settlements along the region's river valleys.

**St. Louis.** The 30 percent isopleth encloses more of the Illinois part of the SMSA than the Missouri part, although population densities (p. 312) are higher on the Missouri side. Rents (p. 119) are low in the areas where less than 10 percent of tract households pay a fourth or more of their incomes for rent, except for the tract west of St. Louis where both rents and incomes (p. 123) are high.

**Cleveland.** Although in some tracts in Cleveland's prosperous (p. 132) western suburbs less than 30 percent of the households pay a fourth or more of their incomes for rent, proportions exceed 30 percent in most of the affluent tracts as well as in the poverty areas in eastern Cleveland. Central-city proportions are lowest in the

*Housing in Metropolitan Areas: Rent-Income Ratio*

PERCENTAGE HOUSING UNITS

FOR WHICH RENT EXCEEDS ONE-FOURTH INCOME

SMSA

south-central area where households with modest incomes (p. 132) occupy low-cost rental units (p. 129).

**Chicago.** An unusually large percentage (75.2) of the SMSA's households paying a fourth or more of their incomes for rent are located in Chicago, where proportions are highest in the city's predominantly black neighborhoods (p. 385). In suburban areas, the 30 percent isopleth corresponds roughly to the $150 rent isopleth (p. 138).

**Detroit.** Despite high rents (p. 151) the proportion of households paying a fourth or more of their incomes for rent is low in affluent northeastern Wayne County. Elsewhere, such households constitute more than 30 percent of tract housing units except in outlying areas where rents are below $150.

**Minneapolis-St. Paul.** Households paying a fourth or more of their incomes for rent exceed 30 percent throughout most of the SMSA's central area except for northern Ramsey County where modest rents (p. 161) combine with above average incomes (p. 165). Tracts where households paying a fourth or more exceed 70 percent usually contain apartment buildings. Most households paying a fourth or more in such areas have incomes between $5,000 and $10,000, suggesting that the group paying especially high shares of their incomes for shelter may be young couples.

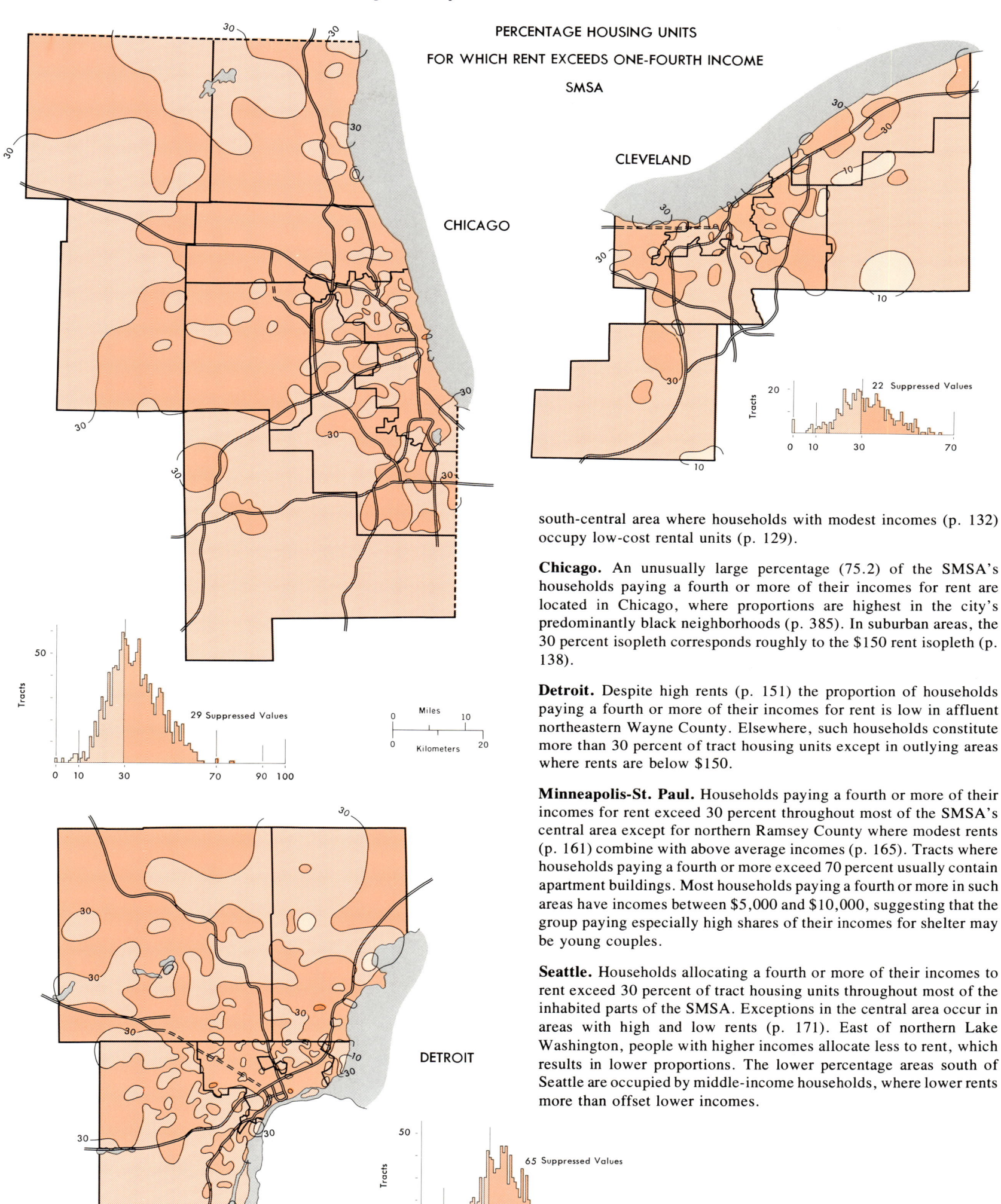

**Seattle.** Households allocating a fourth or more of their incomes to rent exceed 30 percent of tract housing units throughout most of the inhabited parts of the SMSA. Exceptions in the central area occur in areas with high and low rents (p. 171). East of northern Lake Washington, people with higher incomes allocate less to rent, which results in lower proportions. The lower percentage areas south of Seattle are occupied by middle-income households, where lower rents more than offset lower incomes.

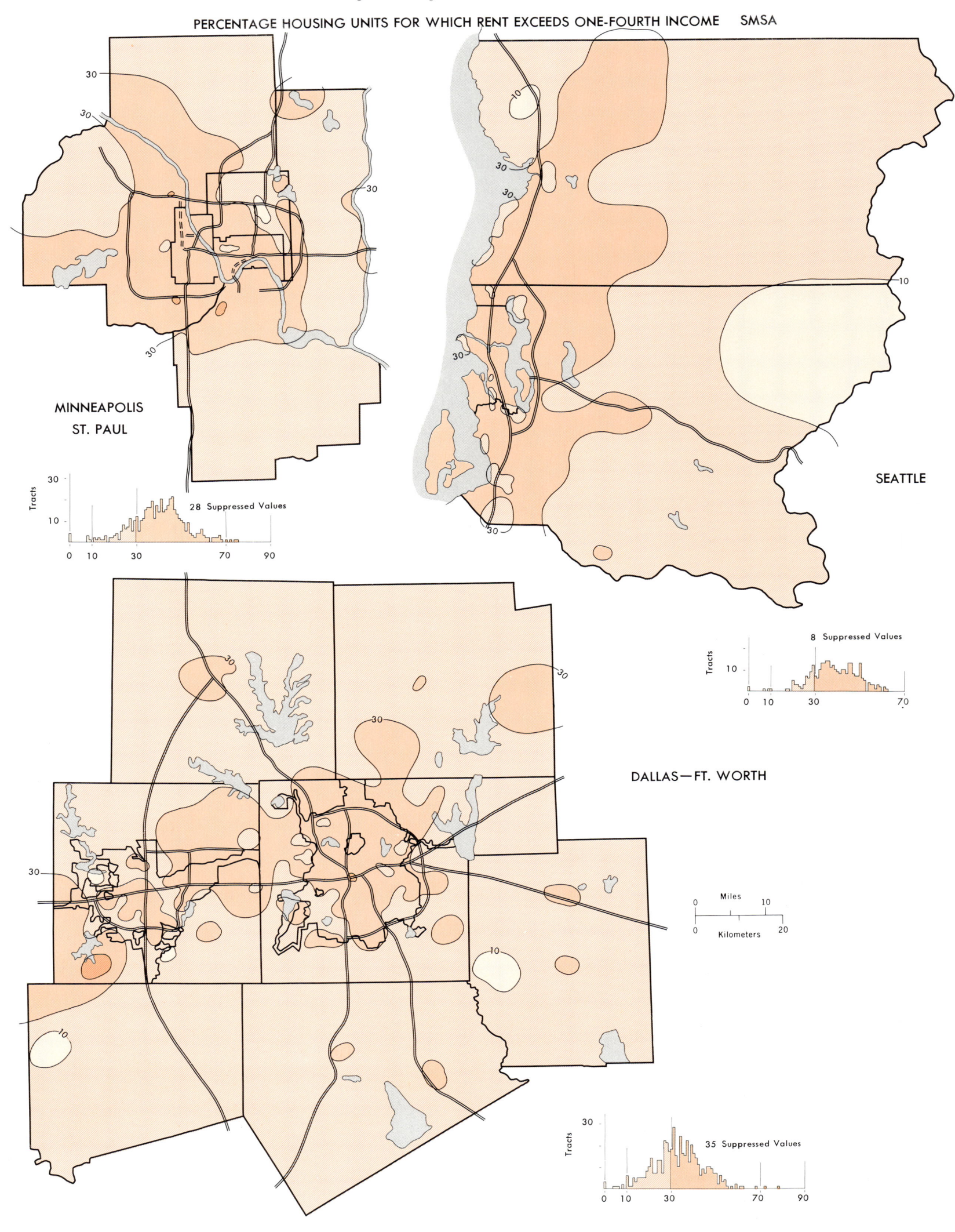

*Housing in Metropolitan Areas: Rent-Income Ratio*

PERCENTAGE HOUSING UNITS FOR WHICH RENT EXCEEDS ONE-FOURTH INCOME    SMSA

MINNEAPOLIS ST. PAUL

SEATTLE

DALLAS—FT. WORTH

*Housing in Metropolitan Areas: Rent-Income Ratio*

*Housing in Metropolitan Areas: Rent-Income Ratio*

PERCENTAGE HOUSING UNITS FOR WHICH RENT EXCEEDS ONE-FOURTH INCOME   SMSA

HOUSTON

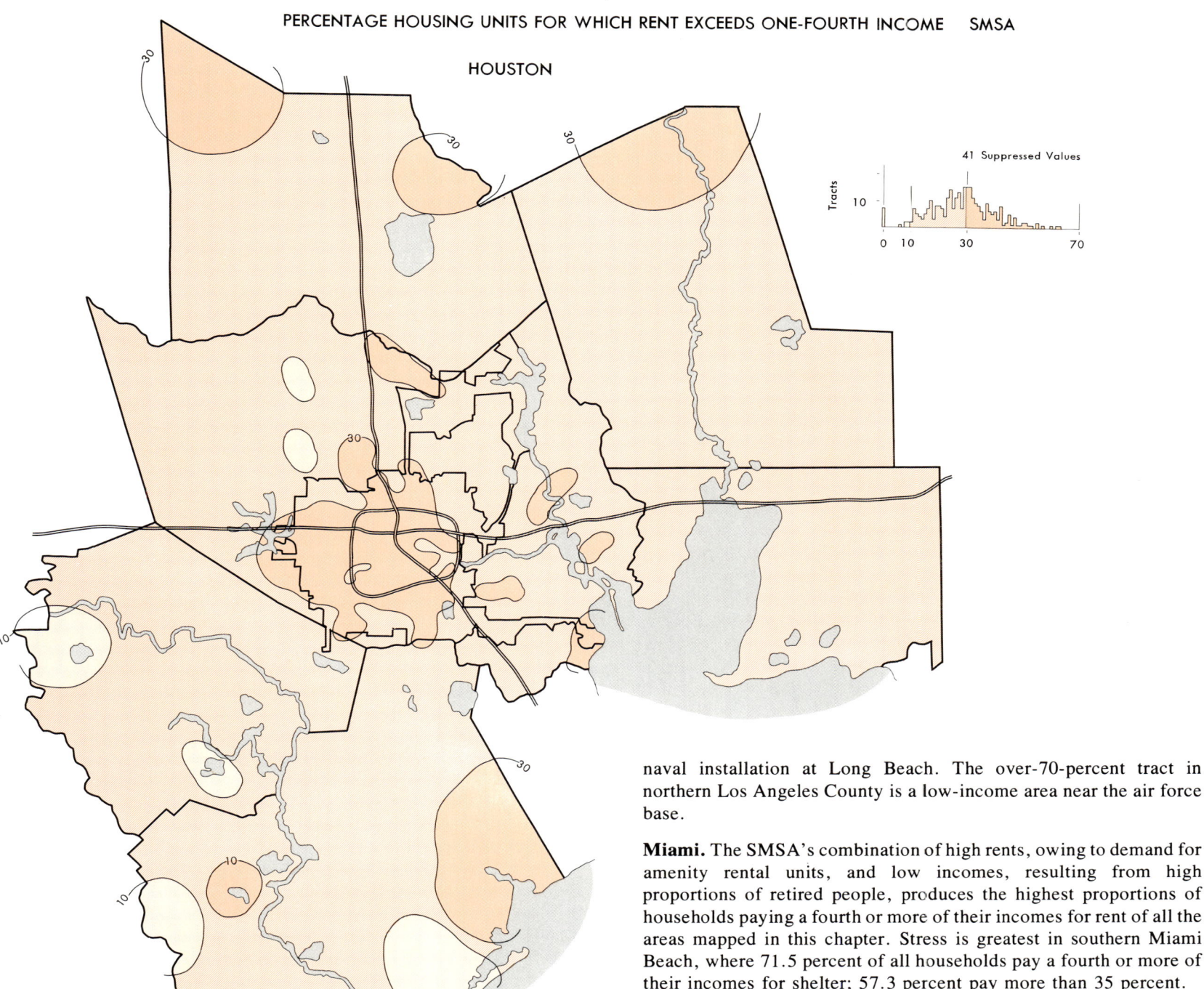

**Dallas-Fort Worth.** Rents are low in the SMSAs, but so are incomes. The central area where households paying a fourth or more of their incomes for rent exceed 30 percent corresponds roughly to the $100 rent isopleth (p. 185). Low rents in south-central Dallas do not compensate for the low incomes there (p. 194), which results in relatively high rent costs for the area's black residents (p. 194).

**Houston.** High proportions of households paying a fourth or more of their incomes for rent are produced by relatively costly rental housing (p. 203) on Houston's affluent west side and by low incomes (p. 213) on the city's east side. Outside the central area the pattern varies randomly; both incomes and rents are low.

**Los Angeles.** The percentage of households paying a fourth or more of their incomes for rent varies between 30 and 70 throughout most of the region. Sparsely populated areas have lower percentages, as does the naval installation at Long Beach. The over-70-percent tract in northern Los Angeles County is a low-income area near the air force base.

**Miami.** The SMSA's combination of high rents, owing to demand for amenity rental units, and low incomes, resulting from high proportions of retired people, produces the highest proportions of households paying a fourth or more of their incomes for rent of all the areas mapped in this chapter. Stress is greatest in southern Miami Beach, where 71.5 percent of all households pay a fourth or more of their incomes for shelter; 57.3 percent pay more than 35 percent.

**Atlanta.** Low rents outside the central part of the SMSA reduce the proportion of tract households paying a fourth or more of their incomes for rent to less than 30 percent. There is a close correspondence between the 30 percent isopleth and the $100 rent isopleth (p. 249).

**Washington, D.C.** Both rents (p. 258) and incomes (p. 262) are high throughout much of the SMSA. The pattern of households paying a fourth or more of their incomes for rent corresponds roughly to the $100 rent isopleth east and west of the District and to the $150 rent isopleth on its prosperous northern side.

---

Because the proportion of income allocated to rent depends on both incomes and rents, the maps of this variable show little of the clear central-city/suburban differentiation commonly evident in other variables. The low proportions of rental units in suburban areas and the fact that such units are often occupied by young couples with good prospects for increasing their incomes contrasts sharply with the kinds of people paying high proportions of their incomes for rent in central cities. There, rental units may be the rule rather than the exception, and the inhabitants are likely to have little hope of increasing their incomes or the quality of their housing in the future.

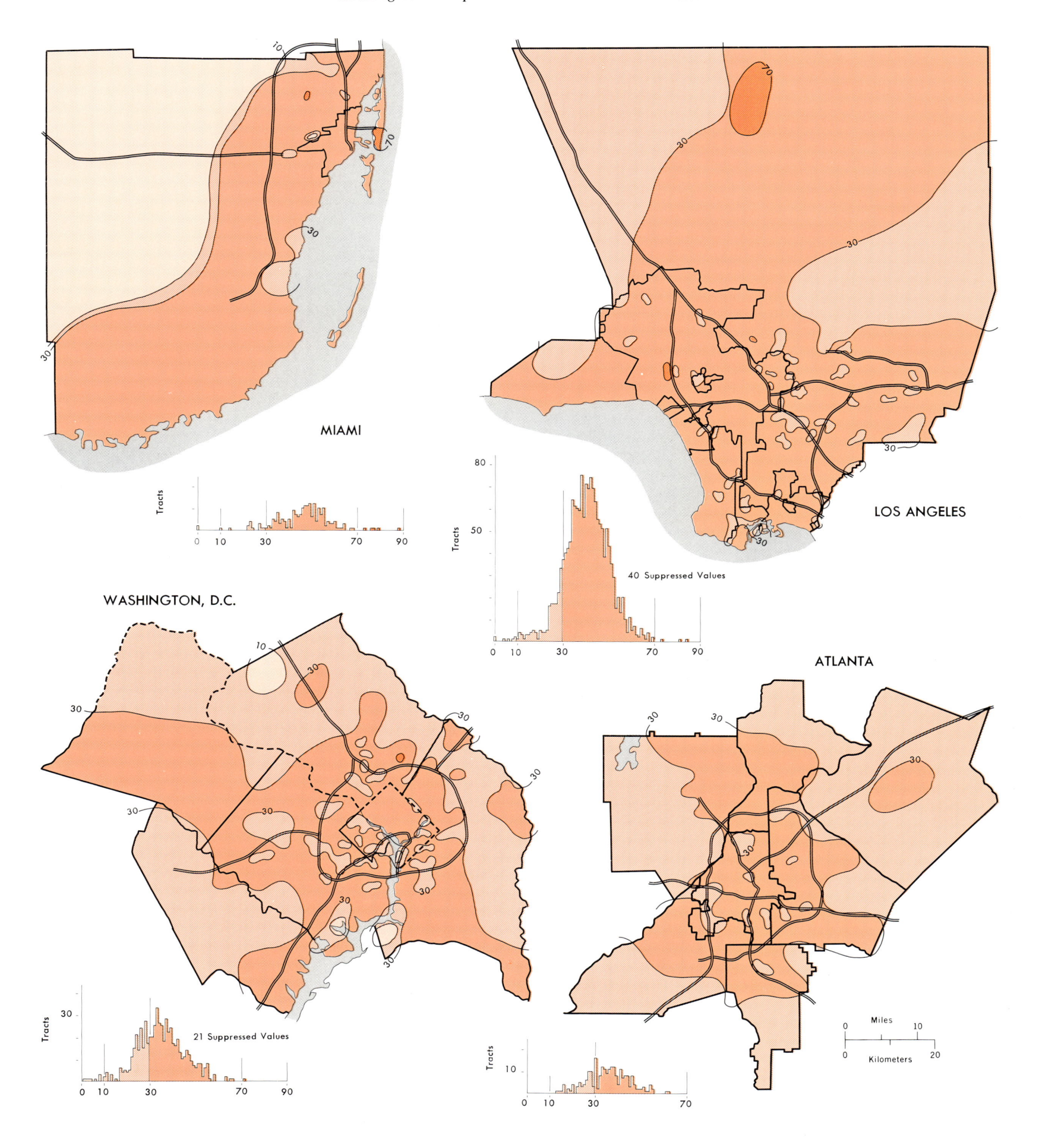

*Housing in Metropolitan Areas: Rent-Income Ratio*

MIAMI

LOS ANGELES

WASHINGTON, D.C.

ATLANTA

**PERCENTAGE HOUSING UNITS FOR WHICH RENT EXCEEDS ONE-FOURTH INCOME  SMSA**

*Housing in Metropolitan Areas*

## CHAPTER 31

# Housing Value and Income

In the 1970 Census all households in single-family dwellings were asked to estimate the amount their houses and lots would sell for if they were on the market. Since a 20 percent sample of households were also asked to give their 1969 incomes, it is possible to tabulate the incomes of households occupying units of different values. The maps in this chapter show the percentages of housing units worth more than $15,000 that are owned and occupied by households with 1969 incomes below $5,000.

There are 31,726,000 owner-occupied units in the nation. Of that number, 1,946,104 (6.1 percent) are worth more than $15,000 and are occupied by households with incomes below $5,000. Within the nation's Standard Metropolitan Statistical Areas (SMSAs), 1,417,000 (6.4 percent) of the owner-occupied single-family units fall into the same category. In the 24 SMSAs mapped in this chapter, 7.1 percent (706,800) of the 9,921,000 owner-occupied units are worth more than $15,000 and are occupied by households with incomes below $5,000 (see accompanying tabulation). Within the central cities of the SMSAs, the proportion of units with the specified value and income characteristics is 8.1 percent.

Low-income households occupying relatively costly units are usually spread throughout metropolitan areas rather than concentrated in central cities. Only in Minneapolis-St. Paul, New Orleans, and Dallas are as many as half such units located in central cities. In most SMSAs, two-thirds or more of the specified units lie outside central cities.

Homeowners with limited incomes relative to the value of their houses may or may not experience difficulties depending on circumstances. Income, as measured by the Census, does not include assets. Thus some people in relatively expensive housing may not be as badly off as their current cash incomes suggest. But for many low-income homeowners—especially the elderly—the house *is* the major asset, and keeping and maintaining it is increasingly difficult. Rising costs of maintenance and spiraling property taxes are especially troublesome to cope with when incomes are small and fixed. Elderly owners are often faced with the unappealing choice of letting property deteriorate or liquidating it in order to seek rental housing. To determine where such current and potential problems are located in the SMSAs, the owner-occupants likely to be facing the most severe combinations of low incomes and high housing values—those with incomes below $5,000 in dwellings worth more than $15,000—are mapped.

*Note:* All data are from the 1970 Censuses of Population and Housing unless otherwise indicated. Therefore the present tense refers to 1970 except for income data which are from 1969. Cartographic conventions are explained in Chapter 1. County names and other locational information are shown on the SMSA map at the beginning of each city chapter (6-25) and on the DUS map of mobile homes near the beginning of each city chapter.

**Boston.** Households with the characteristics specified above make up 8.4 percent of Boston's housing units and 6 percent of the entire SMSA inventory. Most tracts where such units exceed 10 percent of tract housing stocks are located in the SMSA's inner suburbs. Housing built before 1940 (p. 22) often exceeds 70 percent in such areas, and the proportion of people over 64 exceeds 10 percent (p. 24).

Number of Housing Units Worth More Than $15,000, Owned and Occupied by Households with Incomes below $5,000

| Region | Central City(ies) | Entire SMSA |
|---|---|---|
| Boston | 2,176 | 26,950 |
| New York | 30,000 | 80,450 |
| Jersey City | 550 | 1,850 |
| Newark | 800 | 19,000 |
| Paterson-Clifton-Passaic | 2,281 | 17,400 |
| Philadelphia | 7,000 | 33,000 |
| Hartford | 700 | 7,350 |
| Baltimore | 1,950 | 12,700 |
| New Orleans | 7,450 | 14,050 |
| San Francisco-Oakland | 21,300 | 55,700 |
| Pittsburgh | 3,200 | 20,550 |
| St. Louis | 4,100 | 19,950 |
| Cleveland | 7,950 | 29,700 |
| Chicago | 22,850 | 66,950 |
| Detroit | 17,200 | 51,550 |
| Minneapolis-St. Paul | 13,000 | 23,800 |
| Seattle | 11,150 | 22,350 |
| Dallas | 7,000 | 12,300 |
| Fort Worth | 1,950 | 4,200 |
| Houston | 6,950 | 11,450 |
| Los Angeles | 45,350 | 116,700 |
| Miami | 4,900 | 19,600 |
| Atlanta | 5,000 | 13,350 |
| Washington, D.C. | 7,900 | 25,450 |

**New York-Northern New Jersey.** The specified units are more numerous in suburban and exurban areas than in central cities throughout the region. As in Boston, there are some concentrations that correspond to areas with old housing (p. 32) and elderly populations (p. 36). The units mapped here are 10.3 percent of New York City's housing stock and 8.2 percent of the entire New York SMSA's units.

**Philadelphia.** Only 21.2 percent of the SMSA units worth more than $15,000 and occupied by households with incomes below $15,000 are located in Philadelphia. The rest are scattered throughout the SMSA, with proportions exceeding 10 percent in only a few areas. The

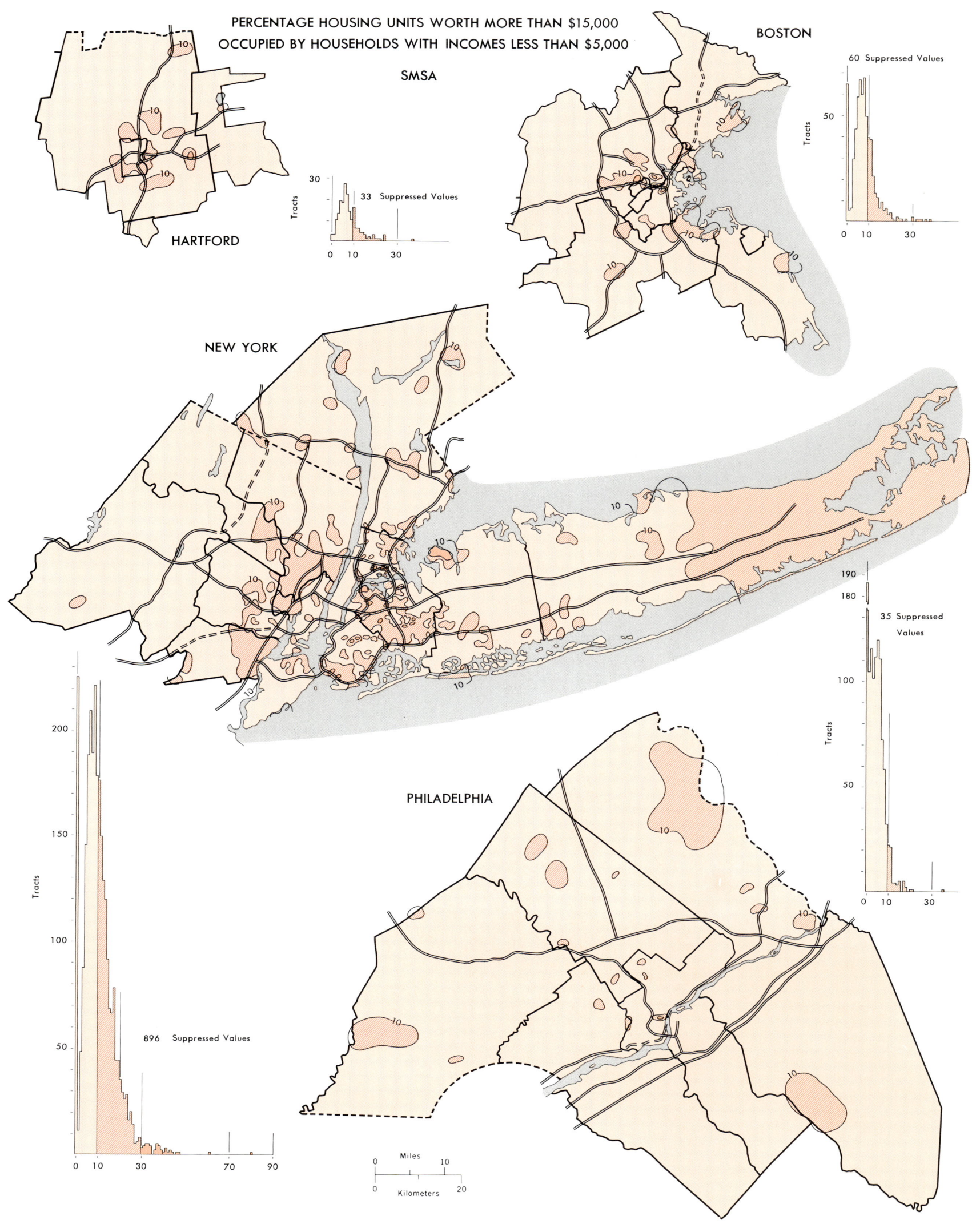

*Housing in Metropolitan Areas: Value-Income Ratio*

PERCENTAGE HOUSING UNITS WORTH MORE THAN $15,000
OCCUPIED BY HOUSEHOLDS WITH INCOMES LESS THAN $5,000

HARTFORD SMSA

BOSTON

NEW YORK

PHILADELPHIA

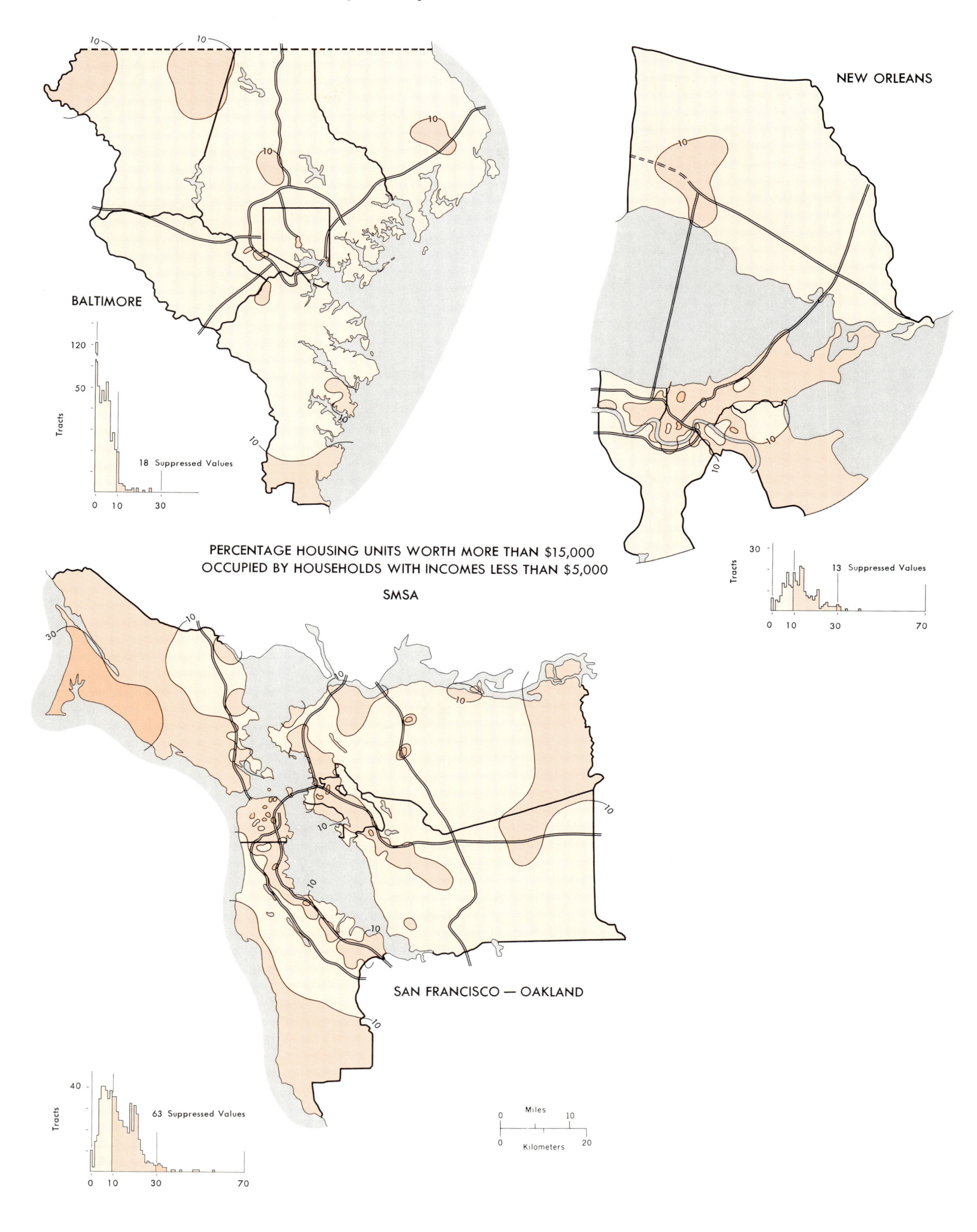

*Housing in Metropolitan Areas: Value-Income Ratio*

BALTIMORE

NEW ORLEANS

PERCENTAGE HOUSING UNITS WORTH MORE THAN $15,000
OCCUPIED BY HOUSEHOLDS WITH INCOMES LESS THAN $5,000
SMSA

SAN FRANCISCO — OAKLAND

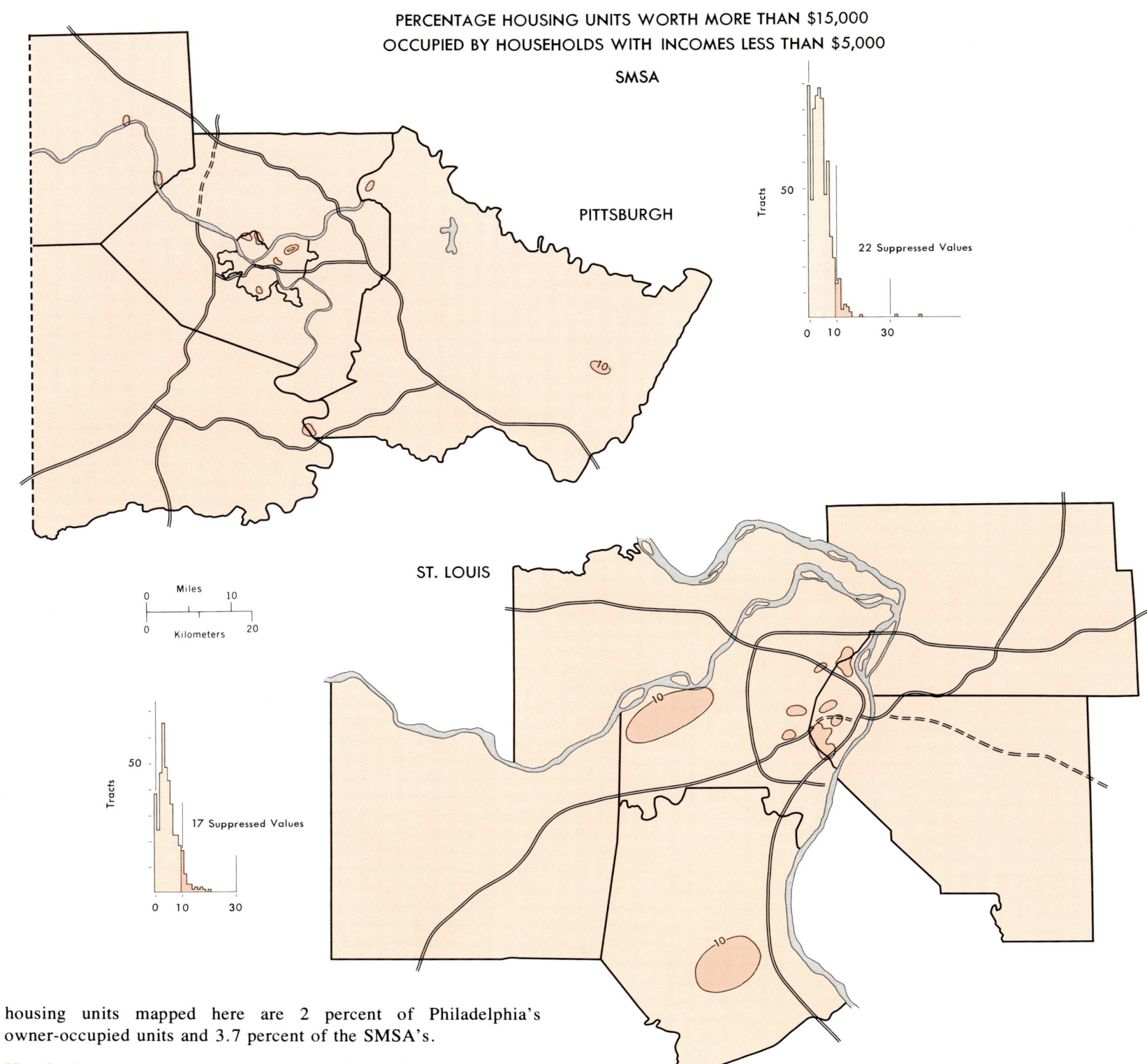

*Housing in Metropolitan Areas: Value-Income Ratio*

PERCENTAGE HOUSING UNITS WORTH MORE THAN $15,000
OCCUPIED BY HOUSEHOLDS WITH INCOMES LESS THAN $5,000

housing units mapped here are 2 percent of Philadelphia's owner-occupied units and 3.7 percent of the SMSA's.

**Hartford.** Low proportions of single-family dwellings (p. 64) and homeownership in Hartford reduce the number of units worth more than $15,000 and occupied by households with incomes below $5,000 to less than 10 percent of the SMSA total. Units with those characteristics are often located in parts of the SMSA where housing built before 1940 (p. 63) exceeds 30 percent of tract totals.

**Baltimore.** The housing units mapped here are only 1.7 percent of Baltimore's total housing units and 3.9 percent of the entire SMSA stock. Low income-to-value units are scattered throughout the city and SMSA, rarely exceeding 10 percent of tract housing inventories.

**New Orleans.** Just over half (53.3 percent) of the SMSA housing units worth more than $15,000 and occupied by households with incomes below $5,000 are located in New Orleans; 13.7 percent of the city units are in that category. Patterns of housing age (p. 80) suggest that such units may often be old dwellings occupied by elderly owners (p. 82) in areas where recent development has increased the prices of all units.

**San Francisco-Oakland.** In San Francisco 17.7 percent of all owner-occupied units are worth more than $15,000 and occupied by households with incomes below $5,000. The comparable proportion in Oakland is 15.6 percent, and it is 11.1 percent for the entire SMSA. The partial correspondence of areas where the units mapped here exceed 10 percent of tract housing units with concentrations of housing built before 1940 (p. 91) and high median ages (p. 93) implies that elderly households occupying older housing may produce the patterns on this map.

**Pittsburgh.** Tract proportions of owner-occupied dwellings worth more than $15,000 and occupied by households with incomes below $5,000 rarely exceed 10 percent except where old housing (p. 106) predominates. Most low income-to-value units are scattered throughout the region.

304

*Housing in Metropolitan Areas: Value-Income Ratio*

PERCENTAGE HOUSING UNITS WORTH MORE THAN $15,000
OCCUPIED BY HOUSEHOLDS WITH INCOMES LESS THAN $5,000
SMSA

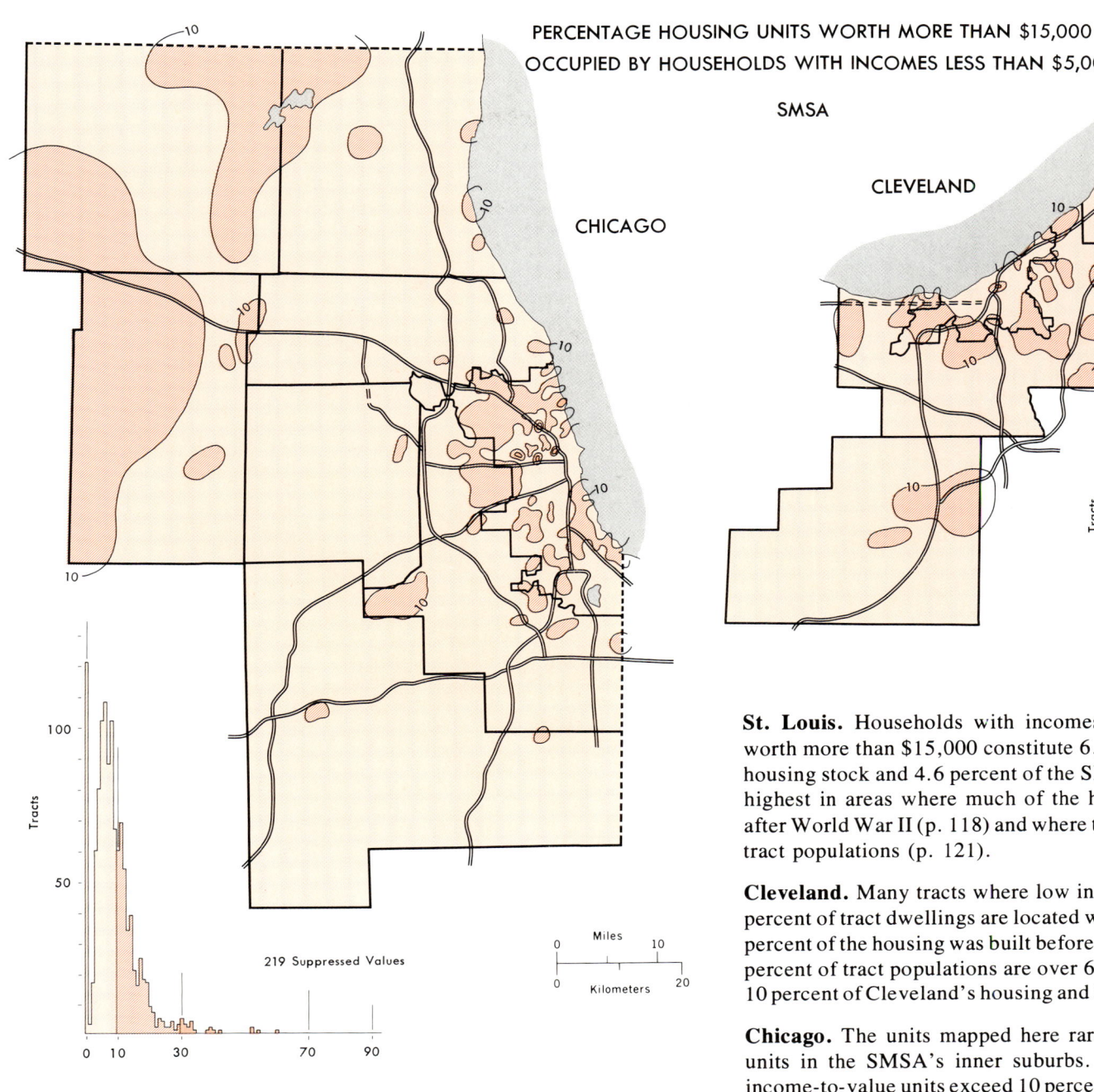

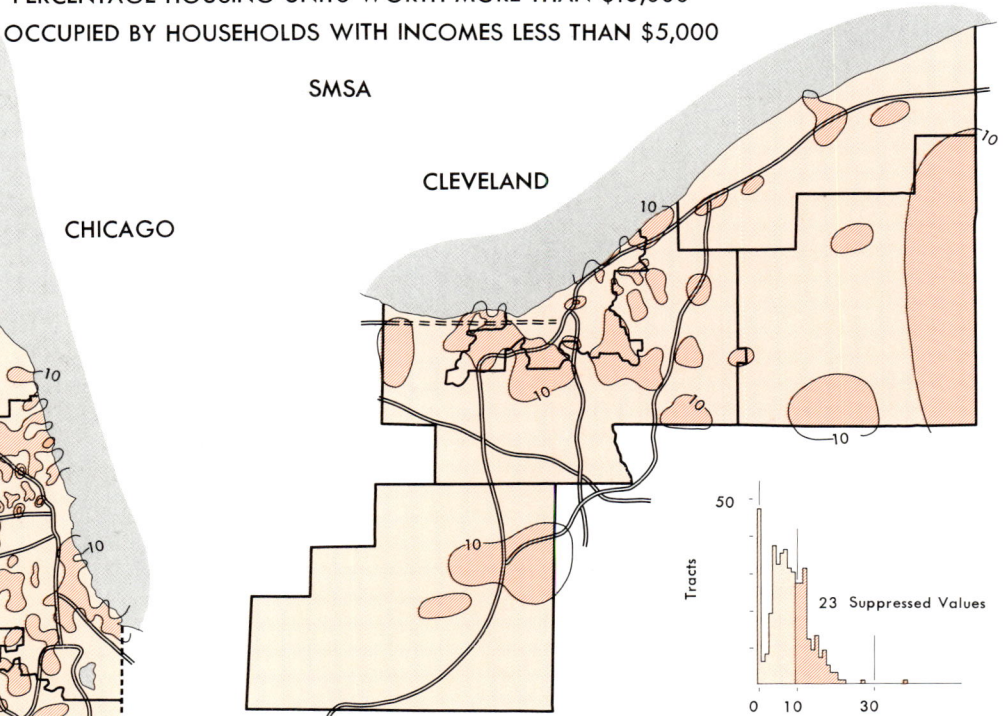

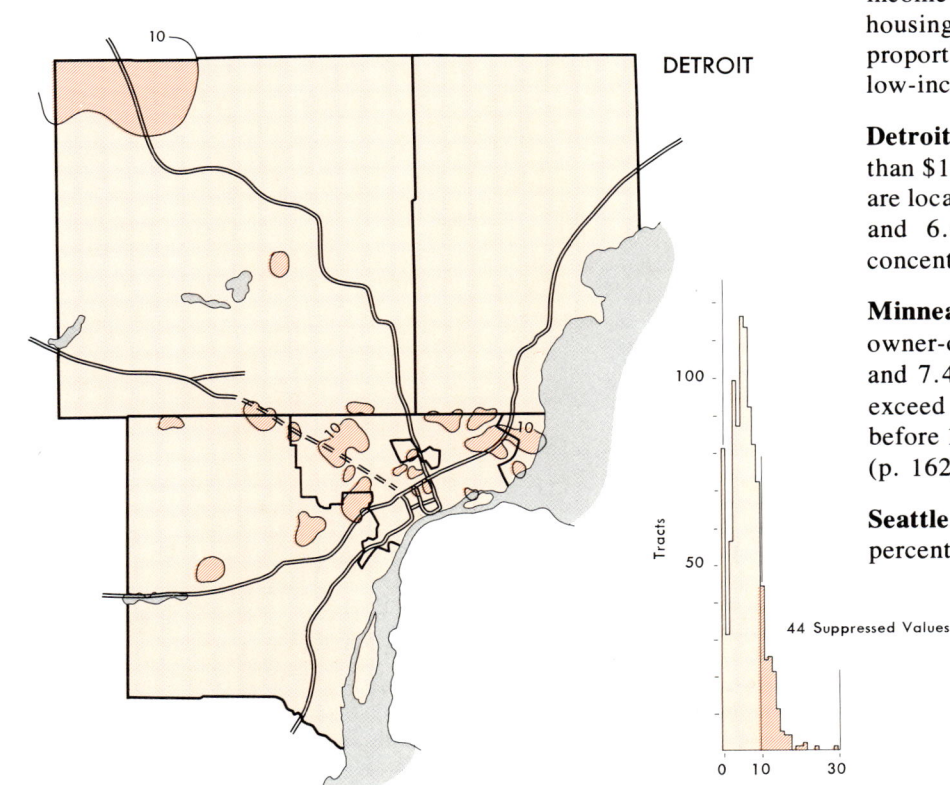

**St. Louis.** Households with incomes below $5,000 owning units worth more than $15,000 constitute 6.6 percent of the St. Louis City housing stock and 4.6 percent of the SMSA units. Concentrations are highest in areas where much of the housing was built immediately after World War II (p. 118) and where the elderly exceed 10 percent of tract populations (p. 121).

**Cleveland.** Many tracts where low income-to-value units exceed 10 percent of tract dwellings are located within areas where more than 30 percent of the housing was built before 1940 (p. 128) and more than 10 percent of tract populations are over 64 (p. 130). Such units make up 10 percent of Cleveland's housing and 8.7 percent of the SMSA stock.

**Chicago.** The units mapped here rarely exceed 10 percent of tract units in the SMSA's inner suburbs. Central-city areas where low income-to-value units exceed 10 percent are located in areas where the housing stock is relatively old (p. 137) and where there are significant proportions of elderly people (p. 139) except in the young, low-income area (p. 145) south of downtown Chicago.

**Detroit.** A third of the SMSA single-family dwellings worth more than $15,000 and owned by households with incomes below $5,000 are located in Detroit. Such units are 7.1 percent of Detroit's housing and 6.4 percent of the SMSA's. In Detroit and the SMSA, concentrations over 10 percent are rare.

**Minneapolis-St. Paul.** The specified units are 11.9 percent of the owner-occupied dwellings in Minneapolis, 9.8 percent in St. Paul, and 7.4 percent in the entire SMSA. Most tracts where such units exceed 10 percent are within the 70 percent isopleth of housing built before 1940 (p. 160) and the 10 percent isopleth of population over 64 (p. 162).

**Seattle.** Tracts where the units mapped in this chapter exceed 10 percent of all dwellings correspond closely to the 30 percent isopleth

*Housing in Metropolitan Areas: Value-Income Ratio*

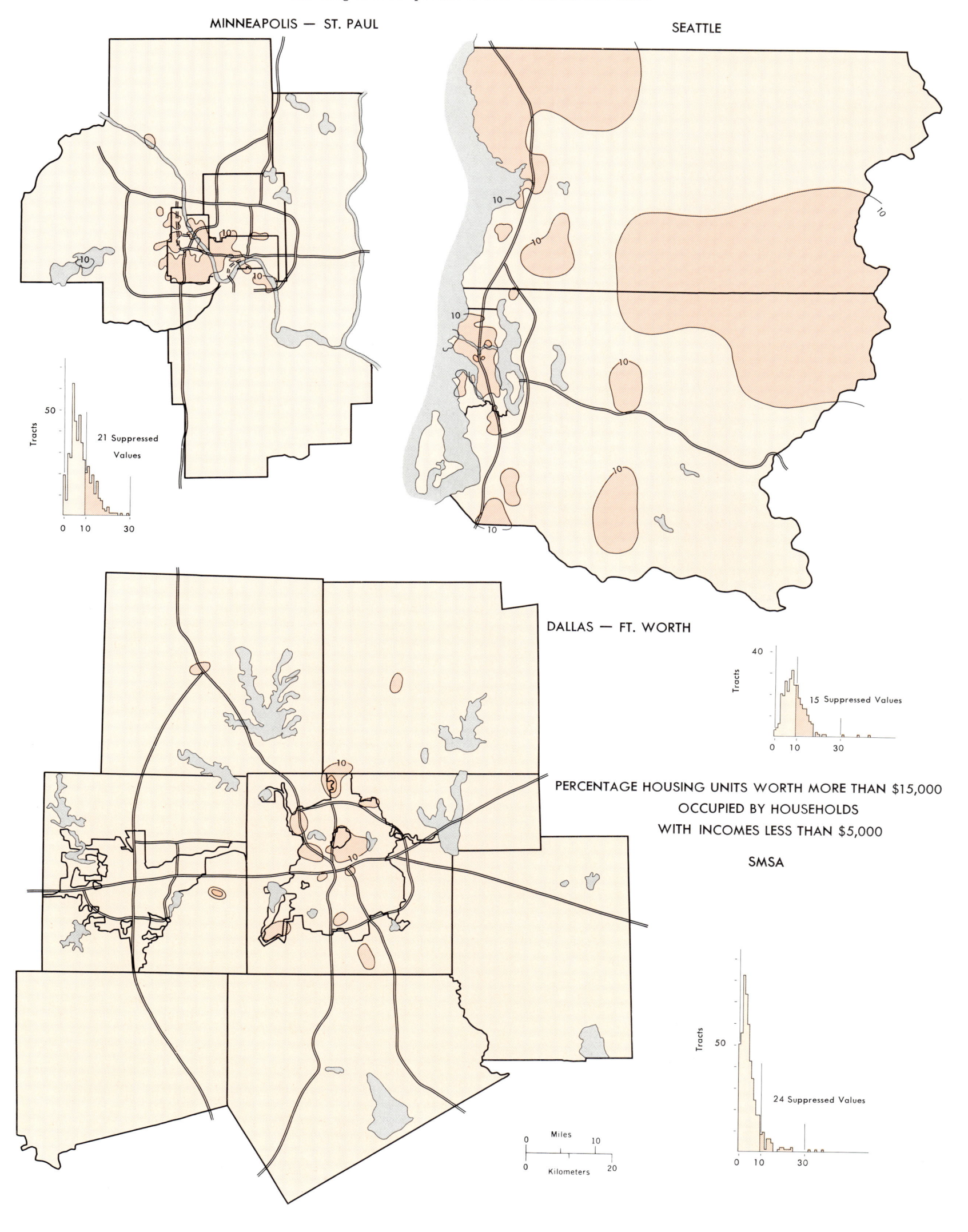

MINNEAPOLIS — ST. PAUL

SEATTLE

DALLAS — FT. WORTH

PERCENTAGE HOUSING UNITS WORTH MORE THAN $15,000 OCCUPIED BY HOUSEHOLDS WITH INCOMES LESS THAN $5,000

SMSA

*Housing in Metropolitan Areas: Value-Income Ratio*

PERCENTAGE HOUSING UNITS WORTH MORE THAN $15,000
OCCUPIED BY HOUSEHOLDS WITH INCOMES LESS THAN $5,000

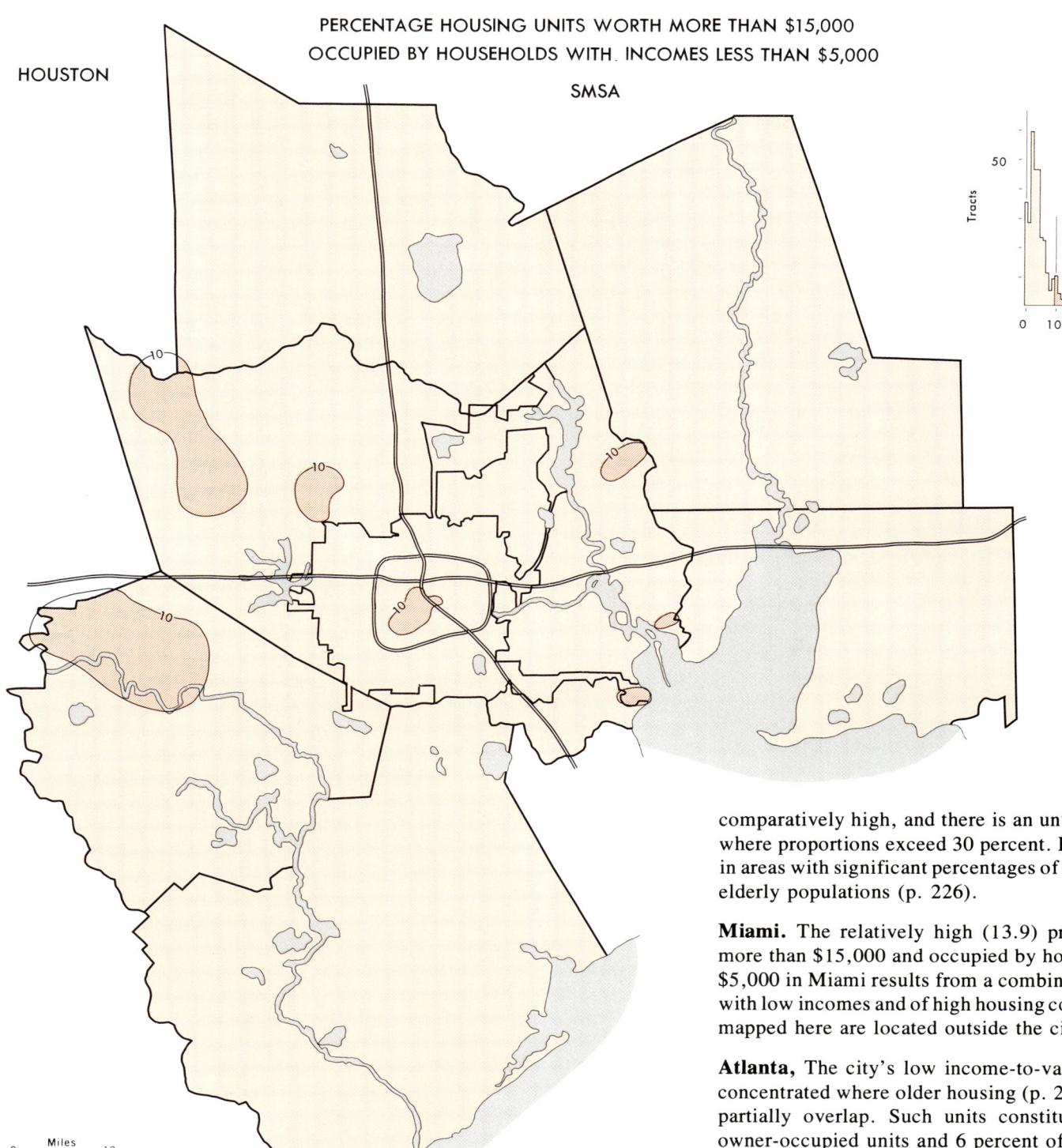

HOUSTON SMSA

of housing built before 1940 (p. 170) and the 10 percent isopleth of elderly population (p. 172).

**Dallas-Fort Worth.** Households with incomes below $5,000 and occupying dwellings worth more than $15,000 are scattered throughout the region; proportions rarely exceed 10 percent. Such units make up 4.6 percent of the owner-occupied dwellings in the Dallas SMSA and 2.9 percent of those in the Fort Worth SMSA.

**Houston.** The housing units worth more than $15,000 and owned by households with incomes below $5,000 are scattered throughout the city and the SMSA. They are often located in areas where housing built before 1940 predominates (p. 199). Over half the units with these characteristics are located within Houston's extensive boundaries.

**Los Angeles.** The proportions of units mapped in this chapter (12 percent in Los Angeles and 10.9 percent in the entire SMSA) are comparatively high, and there is an unusually large number of tracts where proportions exceed 30 percent. Proportions are generally high in areas with significant percentages of pre-1940 housing (p. 222) and elderly populations (p. 226).

**Miami.** The relatively high (13.9) proportion of dwellings worth more than $15,000 and occupied by households with incomes below $5,000 in Miami results from a combination of an elderly population with low incomes and of high housing costs. Three-fourths of the units mapped here are located outside the city of Miami.

**Atlanta,** The city's low income-to-value owner-occupied units are concentrated where older housing (p. 248) and low incomes (p. 253) partially overlap. Such units constitute 8.4 percent of Atlanta's owner-occupied units and 6 percent of the entire SMSA's.

**Washington, D.C.** Owner-occupied units worth more than $15,000 and occupied by households with incomes below $5,000 are 12.3 percent of the owner-occupied units in the District of Columbia and 6.6 percent of the SMSA units. In many parts of the SMSA, concentrations of such units correspond to concentrations of housing built before 1940 (p. 258) and of the elderly (p. 259).

---

The units mapped in this chapter are dispersed throughout central cities and metropolitan areas far more than is usually true of the variables mapped in the atlas. The correspondence of concentrations of units worth more than $15,000 and occupied by households with incomes below $5,000 with concentrations of housing built before 1940 and people over 64 suggests that the units mapped here are more often than not occupied by elderly people on fixed incomes trying to live out their days in housing purchased during their productive years. If the current incomes of these people are inadequate to maintain ownership or upkeep of their dwellings, the predictable results are forced sales, deterioration of the housing units, or, more probably, both.

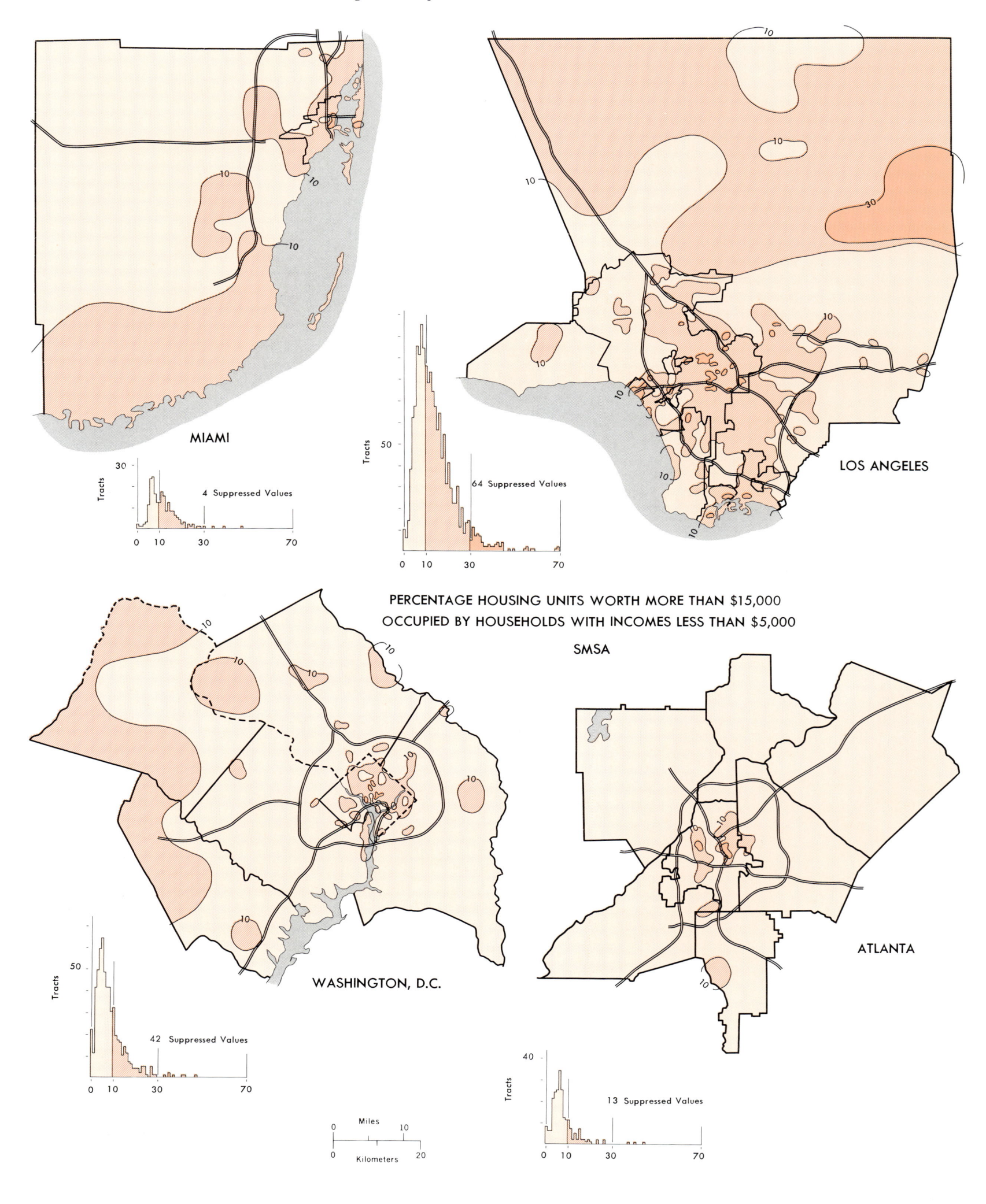

*Housing in Metropolitan Areas: Value-Income Ratio*

PERCENTAGE HOUSING UNITS WORTH MORE THAN $15,000
OCCUPIED BY HOUSEHOLDS WITH INCOMES LESS THAN $5,000
SMSA

MIAMI

LOS ANGELES

WASHINGTON, D.C.

ATLANTA

Transportation and Communication

## CHAPTER 32

# Population Density

Population density is seldom mapped, especially on a comparative basis, for the Census Bureau does not publish population densities for census tracts. The densities mapped here were calculated by dividing each census tract's population by its land area. Area measurements were obtained from local planning commissions and other agencies. When area measurements were not available, they were estimated with dot planimeters. Gross population densities were calculated and mapped in all instances. Even if a tract was known to consist largely of nonresidential area, its population was assumed to occupy the entire tract, because it is impossible to identify and measure nonresidential areas consistently. Thus the densities reported and mapped here underestimate actual densities on residential land.

The population density of the United States (including Alaska and Hawaii) is 58 people per square mile (22 per square kilometer). The land area of all Standard Metropolitan Statistical Areas (SMSAs) is 388,000 square miles (150,000 square kilometers). The 139,418,000 people living in SMSAs occupy that area at an average density of 360 people per square mile (140 per square kilometer). The 20 metropolitan regions mapped here contain 24 SMSAs with an aggregate land area of 58,575 square miles (22,620 square kilometers). The 24 SMSAs contain 67,997,000 people, for an overall density of 1,160 per square mile (450 per square kilometer). (See accompanying tabulation.) Density variations among and within metropolitan areas, and SMSA over- and underbounding make such summary statistics of limited value, but they provide a useful context in which to consider density differences among the 20 regions.

Metropolitan-area and central-city densities are largely dependent on the transportation technology available to urban residents during the period of the region's most rapid population growth. When walking was the only way to get to work and people had to live close to their jobs, densities were high, often exceeding 50,000 people per square mile (19,300 per square kilometer). As horse and later electric trolleys became available, urban residents could spread out and still get to work; densities of increments to older cities dropped accordingly. Automobiles provided even more mobility, making it possible to settle new places or add to old settlements at even lower densities. Thus an SMSA like Boston, which achieved a relatively large share of its current size earlier than other places, has a high population density whereas Houston, which has developed almost wholly during the automobile era, has a low density.

It is important to remember that SMSA population densities are dependent on county size, since SMSAs are defined on a county basis except in New England. For that reason, peak population densities in SMSAs are often as informative as overall SMSA densities. As indicated in the respective histograms, for example, peak densities in Boston approach 80,000 people per square mile (30,900 per square kilometer), whereas the highest densities in Houston are under 20,000 people per square mile (7,725 per square kilometer).

The uncharted values enumerated on the histograms are the number of tracts for which population density rounded to the nearest 1,000 people per square mile (390 per square kilometer) would be zero.

Population Density per Square Mile (per Square Kilometer)
| | | |
|---|---:|---:|
| Boston | 2,790 | (1,075) |
| New York-Northern New Jersey | 4,650 | (1,795) |
| Philadelphia | 1,355 | ( 525) |
| Hartford | 990 | ( 380) |
| Baltimore | 915 | ( 355) |
| New Orleans | 530 | ( 205) |
| San Francisco-Oakland | 1,255 | ( 485) |
| Pittsburgh | 790 | ( 305) |
| St. Louis | 575 | ( 220) |
| Cleveland | 1,360 | ( 525) |
| Chicago | 1,875 | ( 725) |
| Detroit | 2,155 | ( 830) |
| Minneapolis-St. Paul | 860 | ( 330) |
| Seattle | 335 | ( 130) |
| Dallas-Fort Worth | 375 | ( 145) |
| Houston | 315 | ( 120) |
| Los Angeles | 1,730 | ( 670) |
| Miami | 620 | ( 240) |
| Atlanta | 805 | ( 310) |
| Washington, D.C. | 1,215 | ( 470) |

**Boston.** Boston is underbounded, which partially accounts for its high SMSA density. But Boston is an old metropolitan region, and the high overall density of its central city (13,950 per square mile or 5,400 per square kilometer) is related to its age. City density is mapped on p. 23.

**New York-Northern New Jersey.** Competition for space in an old central city produces the highest population densities and the most extensive areas with high population densities in the nation. The overall density of New York City's five boroughs (mapped on p. 35) is 26,350 per square mile (10,175 per square kilometer).

**Philadelphia.** The area of the SMSA is slightly larger than the New York-Northern New Jersey region, but its smaller population yields a lower SMSA density. Densities are comparatively high in the older parts of the city (mapped on p. 53); the city has an overall density of 15,175 per square mile (5,860 per square kilometer).

**Hartford.** Hartford is an old settlement, but it is not large enough to generate the high densities that intense competition for space at the

*Note:* All data are from the 1970 Census of Population and Housing unless otherwise indicated. Therefore the present tense refers to 1970 except for income data which are from 1969. Cartographic conventions are explained in Chapter 1. County names and other locational information are shown on the SMSA map at the beginning of each city chapter (6-25) and on the DUS map of mobile homes near the beginning of each city chapter.

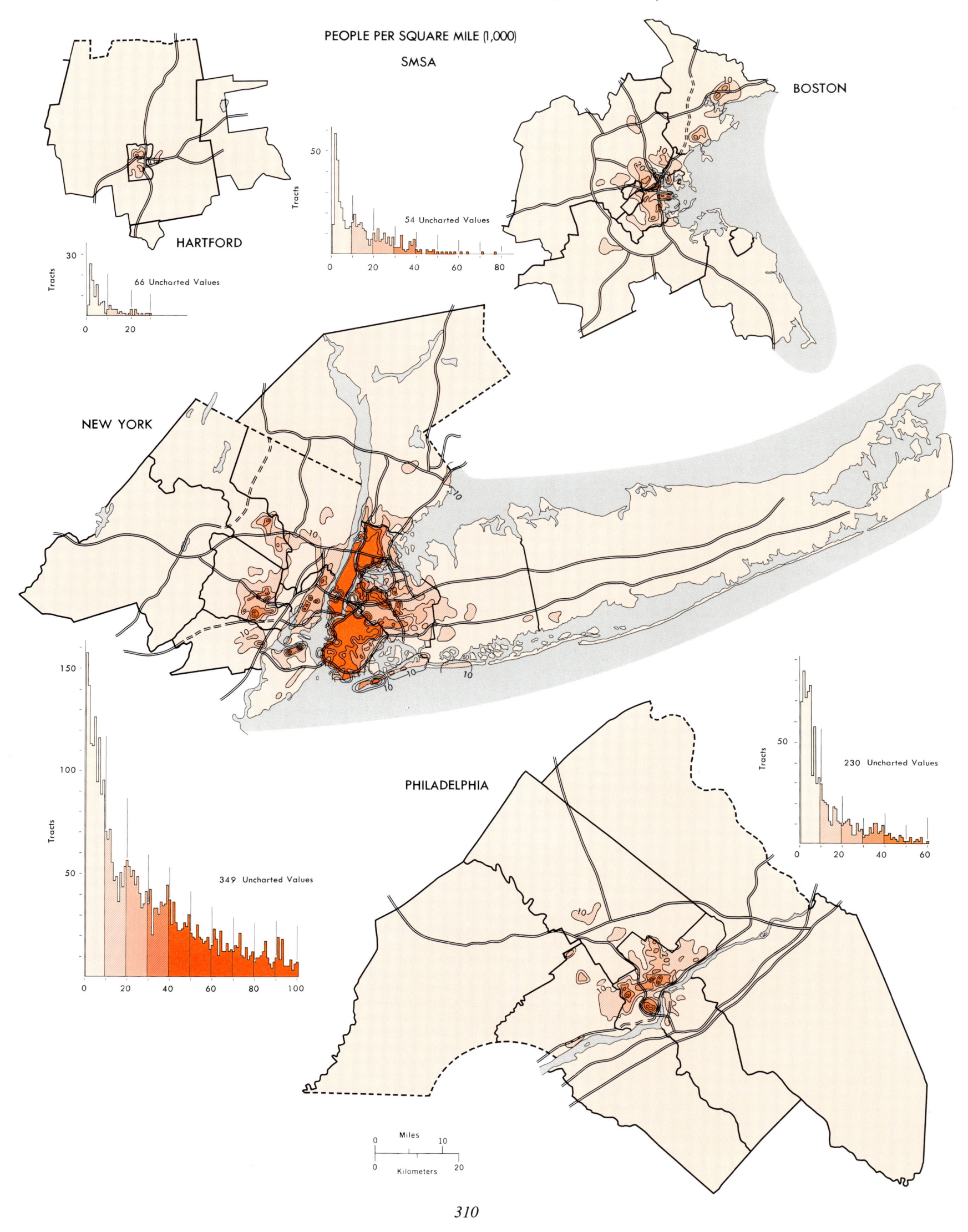

*Transportation and Communication: Population Density*

PEOPLE PER SQUARE MILE (1,000)
SMSA

HARTFORD

BOSTON

NEW YORK

PHILADELPHIA

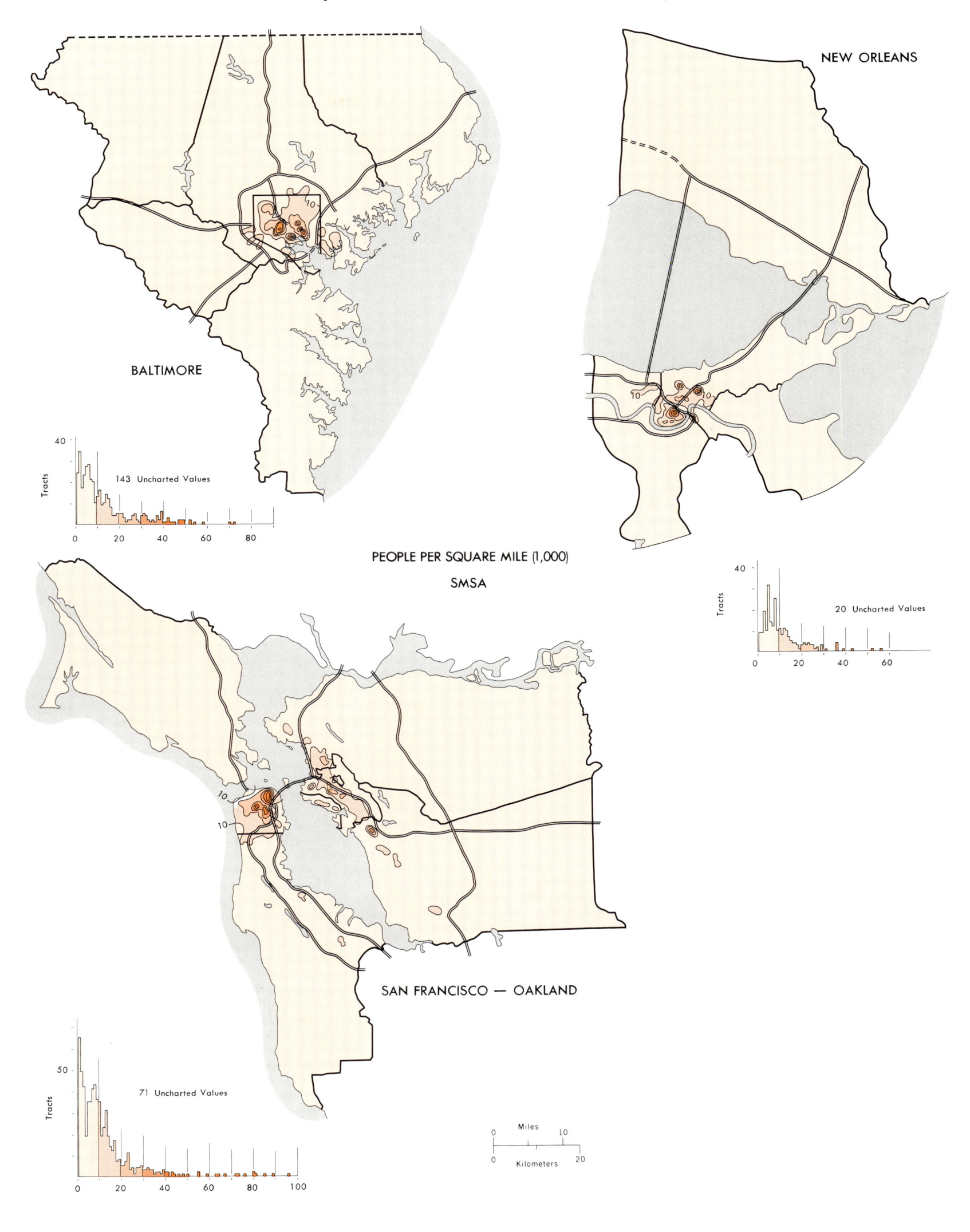

*Transportation and Communication: Population Density*

BALTIMORE

NEW ORLEANS

143 Uncharted Values

20 Uncharted Values

PEOPLE PER SQUARE MILE (1,000)
SMSA

SAN FRANCISCO — OAKLAND

71 Uncharted Values

311

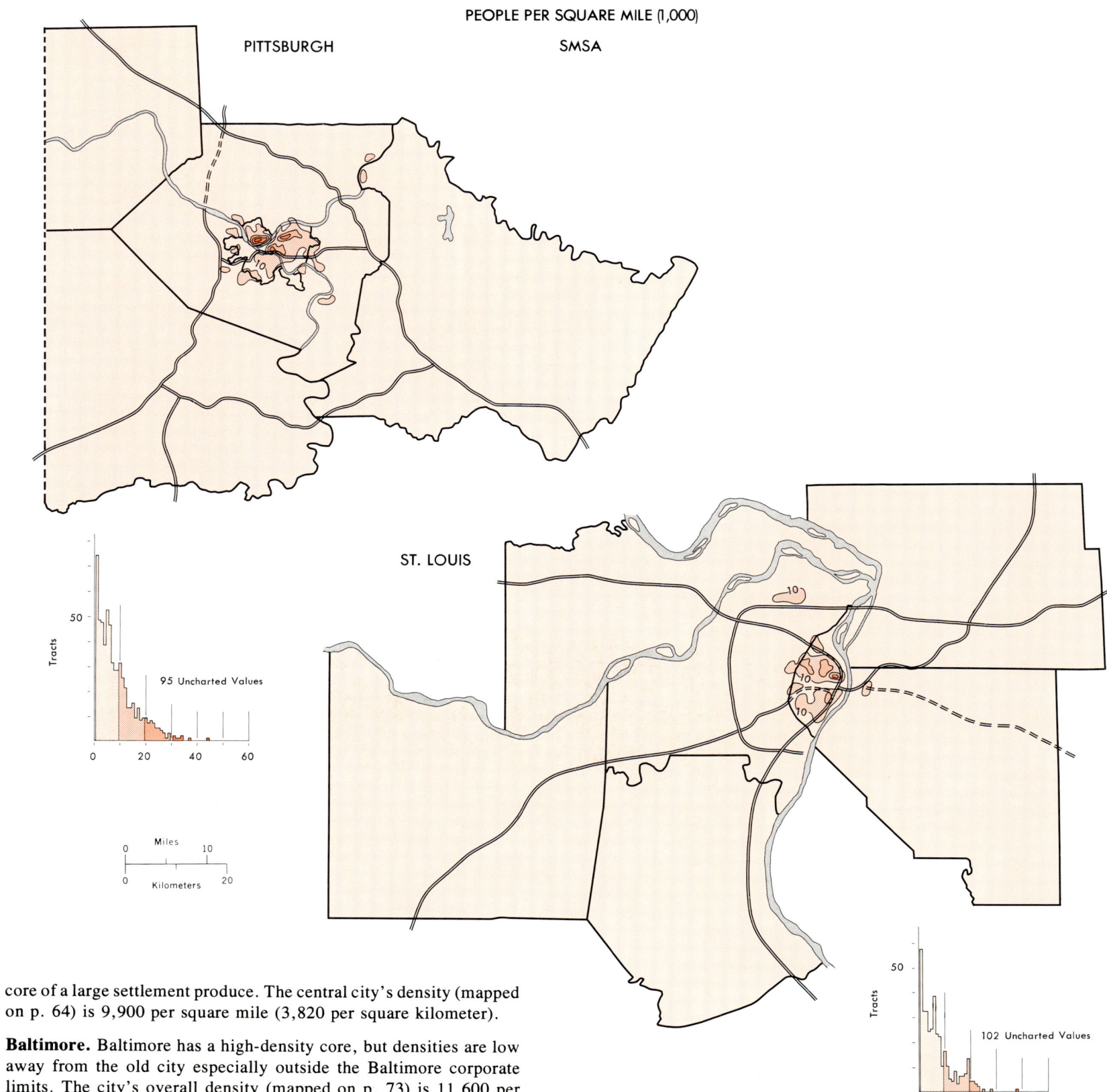

*Transportation and Communication: Population Density*

PEOPLE PER SQUARE MILE (1,000)

PITTSBURGH SMSA

ST. LOUIS

core of a large settlement produce. The central city's density (mapped on p. 64) is 9,900 per square mile (3,820 per square kilometer).

**Baltimore.** Baltimore has a high-density core, but densities are low away from the old city especially outside the Baltimore corporate limits. The city's overall density (mapped on p. 73) is 11,600 per square mile (4,465 per square kilometer).

**New Orleans.** Overall densities are low in the SMSA and in New Orleans City (3,000 per square mile or 1,160 per square kilometer) because both regions contain large unsettled areas of coastal wetlands. The overall averages are thus deceptive, and densities over 50,000 per square mile (19,300 per square kilometer) exist in a few places. The city is mapped on p. 82.

**San Francisco-Oakland.** San Francisco (overall density 15,765 people per square mile or 6,090 per square kilometer) is a 19th-century port, and for that reason some tracts are settled at high densities. Oakland's density is considerably lower, at 6,770 per square mile (2,615 per square kilometer). There are city maps on p. 93.

**Pittsburgh.** Densities over 10,000 per square mile (3,860 per square kilometer) are largely confined to the central city (map on p. 109), which has an overall density of 9,420 per square mile (3,640 per square kilometer). The outlying areas are industrial towns located in the region's narrow river valleys.

**St. Louis.** Densities over 25,000 per square mile (9,650 per square kilometer) are usually the sites of large public housing projects. The city's overall density (mapped on p. 120) is 10,165 per square mile (3,925 per square kilometer).

312

*Transportation and Communication: Population Density*

PEOPLE PER SQUARE MILE (1,000)
SMSA

CHICAGO

CLEVELAND

DETROIT

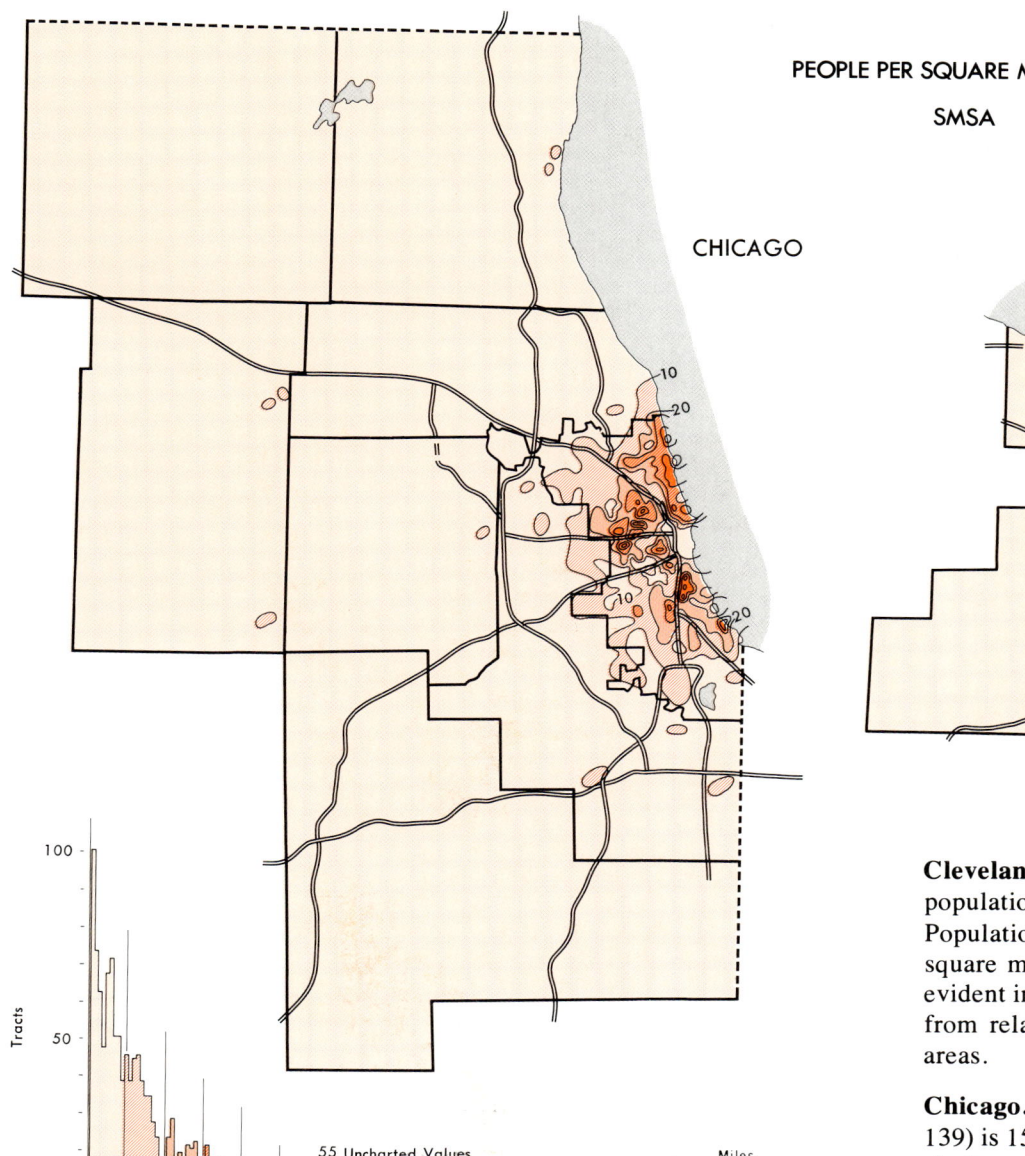

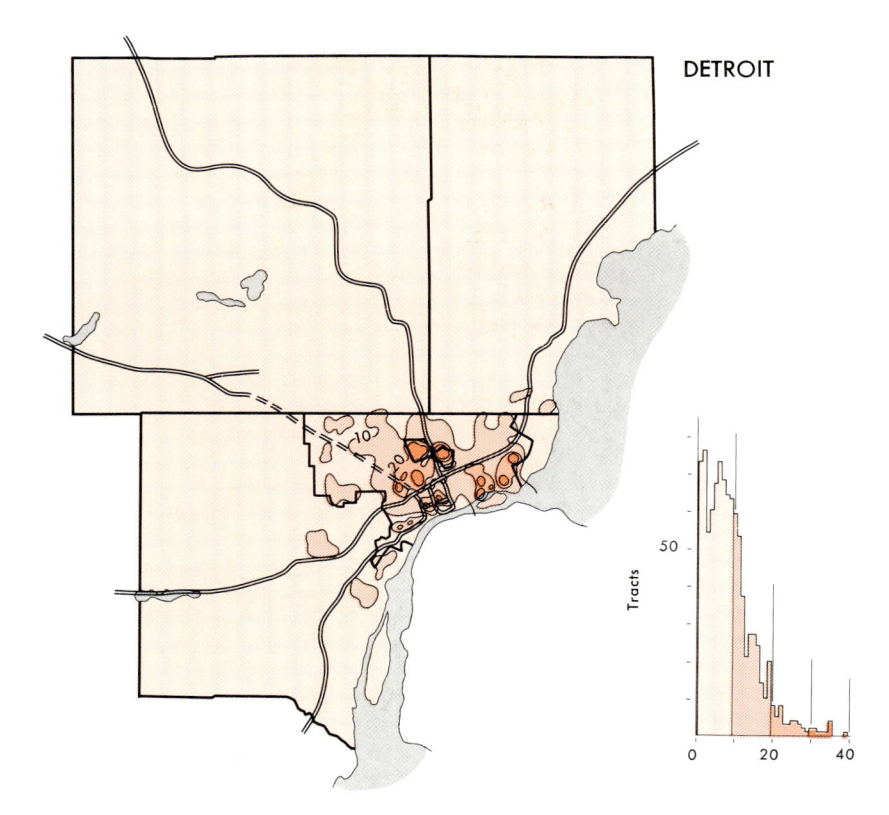

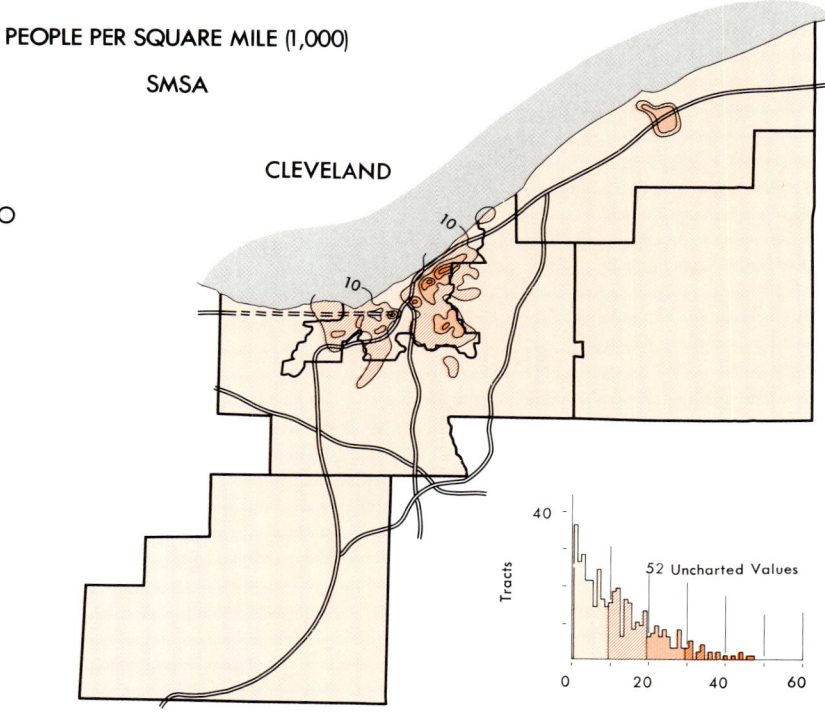

**Cleveland.** The SMSAs of the Midwest have relatively high population densities and correspondingly high peak densities. Population density in Cleveland (mapped on p. 120) is 9,895 per square mile (3,820 per square kilometer). The high SMSA density evident in Cleveland (and in the Chicago and Detroit SMSAs) results from relatively higher density settlement in suburban and exurban areas.

**Chicago.** Population density in the city of Chicago (mapped on p. 139) is 15,135 per square mile (5,845 per square kilometer), which is similar to Philadelphia's overall density. As in St. Louis, the highest densities occur in tracts containing public housing projects.

**Detroit.** Detroit is the youngest of the midwestern industrial metropolises. Its relatively high SMSA density is a result of underbounding. Population density in the city of Detroit (mapped on p. 152) is 10,970 per square mile (4,235 per square kilometer).

**Minneapolis-St. Paul.** Two distinct Central Business Districts and relatively abundant land during early settlement have produced low SMSA and central-city densities (mapped on p. 162) in the Twin Cities. The respective densities of Minneapolis and St. Paul are 7,885 and 5,935 people per square mile (3,045 and 2,290 per square kilometer).

**Seattle.** The SMSA's overall density is reduced by the sparsely populated eastern three-fourths of the SMSA. In Seattle, population density (mapped on p. 172) is 6,350 per square mile (2,450 per square kilometer).

**Dallas-Fort Worth.** Densities in the region are extremely low, reflecting recent settlement. The only densities over 20,000 per square mile (7,725 per square kilometer) occur in a small outlying town. The respective population densities of Dallas and Fort Worth are 3,180 and 1,920 per square mile (1,225 and 740 per square kilometer).

**Houston.** The SMSA has the lowest density of the 20 regions in the atlas, which is partially produced by overbounding. Low densities of recent settlement are equally important. The density of the central city (mapped on p. 204) is 2,840 per square mile (1,100 per square kilometer).

313

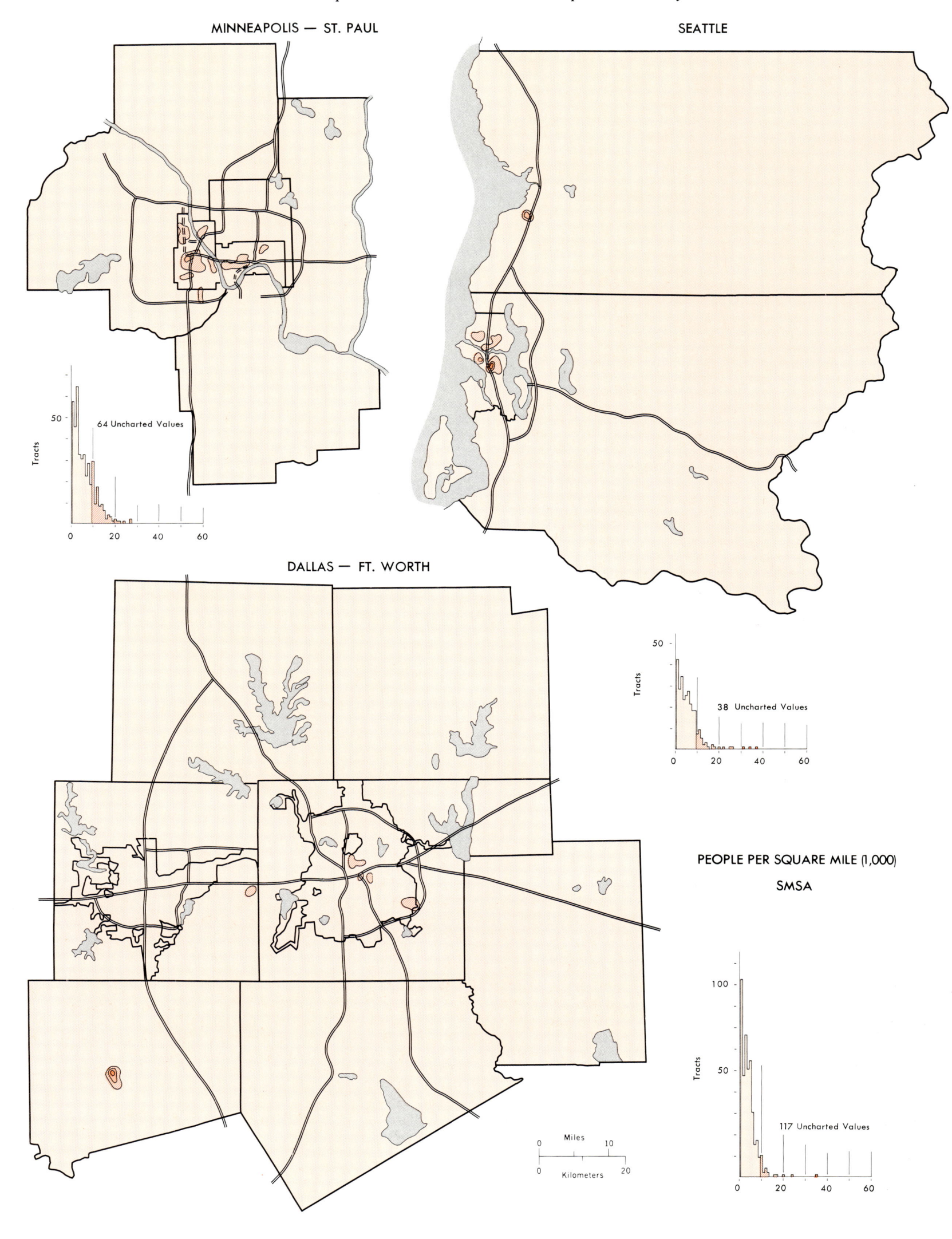

*Transportation and Communication: Population Density*

## MINNEAPOLIS — ST. PAUL

## SEATTLE

## DALLAS — FT. WORTH

**PEOPLE PER SQUARE MILE (1,000)**

SMSA

*Transportation and Communication: Population Density*

PEOPLE PER SQUARE MILE (1,000)

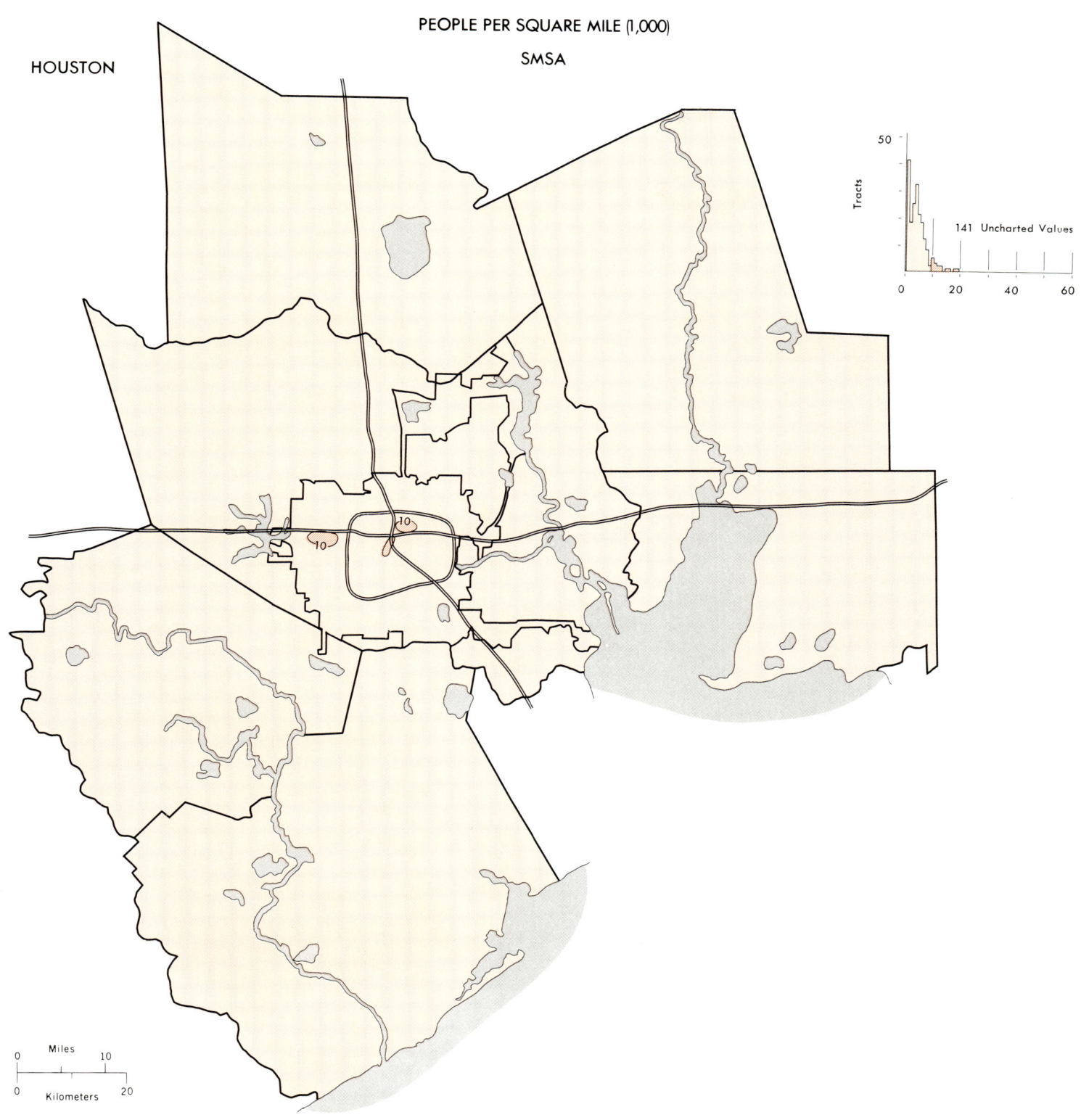

HOUSTON SMSA

**Los Angeles.** Despite its large area, the Los Angeles SMSA has a high population density, comparable to Chicago's. The difference between SMSA and city densities is relatively small, however. The city density (mapped on p. 225) is 6,060 per square mile (2,340 per square kilometer), reflecting its recent settlement.

**Miami.** A few tracts in Miami and Miami Beach have densities over 20,000 people per square mile (7,725 per square kilometer). Elsewhere in the SMSA densities are low. In Miami and Miami Beach, the respective population densities (mapped on p. 240) are 9,765 and 13,600 per square mile (3,770 and 5,250 per square kilometer).

**Atlanta.** Densities over 10,000 per square mile (3,860 per square kilometer) are confined to central Atlanta, reflecting the large proportion of growth in the city (mapped on p. 250) and SMSA that has occurred since World War II. The two highest-density tracts contain public housing projects. The city density is 3,785 people per square mile (1,495 per square kilometer).

**Washington, D.C.** The District of Columbia (mapped on p. 259) is a 19th-century city with an overall density (12,320 per square mile or 4,755 per square kilometer) appropriate to a city of that age. Many of the suburbs are post-World War II creations with low densities. The combination of the two yields a relatively high SMSA density.

---

The differences in average and peak population densities among metropolitan areas and central cities are striking. The effects of high and low densities on human behavior are unclear and controversial; but whatever the effect, the density differences mapped here document the complexity of the evolution of metropolitan settlement across the nation.

*315*

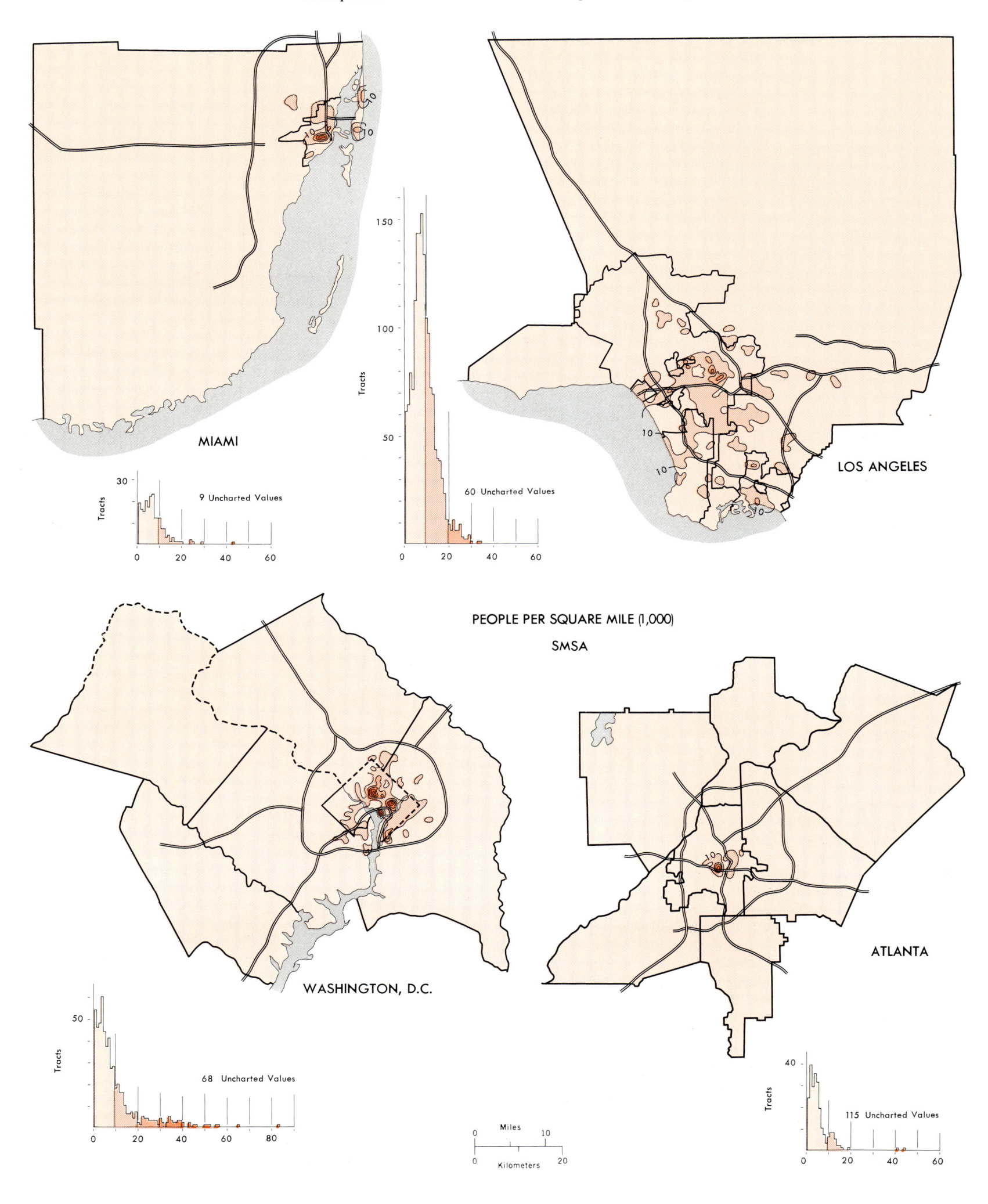

*Transportation and Communication: Population Density*

MIAMI

LOS ANGELES

PEOPLE PER SQUARE MILE (1,000)
SMSA

WASHINGTON, D.C.

ATLANTA

*Transportation and Communication*

CHAPTER 33

# Working in the Central Business District

In the 1970 Census a 15 percent sample of household heads reported the address of the place they worked during the previous week. Responses were processed to yield data on the number of workers in each census tract who worked in different parts of each Standard Metropolitan Statistical Area (SMSA). The numbers of people in each tract working in Central Business Districts (CBDs) were used to construct the maps in this series.

The CBD is often the single largest job center in a metropolitan area. Outlying and suburban centers employ more people than the CBD in aggregate, but individual dispersed employment centers are rarely as large as the CBD. The CBD is the preferred location for white-collar jobs, especially those of the managerial or professional kind shown on the maps of executive employment in the individual city chapters (6-25) of the atlas. Therefore metropolitan areas with high proportions of their labor forces in white-collar occupations usually have comparatively high percentages of their total labor forces working in the CBD. As the accompanying tabulation indicates, there is great variation in the proportions of the SMSAs' labor forces that work downtown.

The proportion of a tract's labor force that works in the CBD depends on its occupational structure and on the share of metropolitan white-collar jobs located in the CBD. The greater the proportion of the tract's labor force in managerial, technical, and professional occupations, and the greater the share of metropolitan employment in the CBD, the greater the likelihood that many of the tract's workers will commute to the CBD.

**Boston.** Most people working in the Boston CBD come from Boston, although the 5 percent isopleth extends well to the west and north of the city. Much of the post-World War II employment growth in the region has occurred along the SMSA's circumferential highway 128, and only a third of the SMSA jobs are now in Boston. If employment in Cambridge, Somerville, and Brookline were added, the employment share of that functional central city would be larger.

**New York-Northern New Jersey.** Commuting patterns in the New York region are complex. Commuting is shown within each of the four SMSAs comprising the region. Thus all commuting from New York tracts is to Manhattan (New York County), which was arbitrarily designated the CBD of the five Boroughs. The pull of New York employment in the New Jersey SMSAs is evident in the low percentages of employment in their respective CBDs and central cities, and in the proportions of New Jersey SMSA employees

*Note:* All data are from the 1970 Censuses of Population and Housing unless otherwise indicated. Therefore the present tense refers to 1970 except for income data which are from 1969. Cartographic conventions are explained in Chapter 1. County names and other locational information are shown on the SMSA map at the beginning of each city chapter (6-25) and on the DUS map of mobile homes near the beginning of each city chapter.

working outside the SMSAs, presumably in New York in many instances. In the Jersey City SMSA (Hudson County), 33 percent of the labor force works outside the SMSA. Proportions for the Newark SMSA (Essex, Morris, and Union counties) and the Paterson-Clifton-Passaic SMSA (Bergen and Passaic counties) are 18 percent and 30 percent. The histogram is plotted for the combined SMSAs.

Percentage of SMSA Residents Working in the Central City

| Region | CBD | Rest of the Central City |
|---|---|---|
| Boston | 7.1 | 26.2 |
| New York | 16.9 | 47.3 |
| Jersey City | 1.1 | 21.4 |
| Newark | 6.0 | 12.5 |
| Paterson-Clifton-Passaic | 1.4 | 15.0 |
| Philadelphia | 5.9 | 15.5 |
| Hartford | 6.5 | 25.7 |
| Baltimore | 5.5 | 39.3 |
| New Orleans | 17.4 | 42.3 |
| San Francisco-Oakland | 13.2 | 31.7 |
| Pittsburgh | 8.1 | 25.4 |
| St. Louis | 3.6 | 34.9 |
| Cleveland | 8.3 | 40.3 |
| Chicago | 7.5 | 40.4 |
| Detroit | 5.3 | 30.0 |
| Minneapolis-St. Paul | 11.7 | 43.4 |
| Seattle | 6.7 | 44.9 |
| Dallas | 10.1 | 53.8 |
| Fort Worth | 6.3 | 43.9 |
| Houston | 12.2 | 56.0 |
| Los Angeles | 4.0 | 37.1 |
| Miami | 4.2 | 30.6 |
| Atlanta | 9.0 | 40.5 |
| Washington, D.C. | 10.4 | 29.4 |

**Philadelphia.** Because much of Philadelphia is occupied by blue-collar workers with skills unsuited to the jobs available in the CBD, the regions of most intense commuting to the CBD are located in outlying parts of the city and in the northwestern suburbs, from which the Main Line of the old Pennsylvania Railroad provides good commuter rail service to the downtown area.

**Hartford.** The SMSA has many separate settlement and employment nuclei. Thus the Hartford CBD attracts relatively few of the SMSA workers, and most of the workers who do come to the CBD commute from nearby locations.

**Baltimore.** The most intense commuting to CBD jobs in the SMSA occurs from the northern part of the city and the inner northern

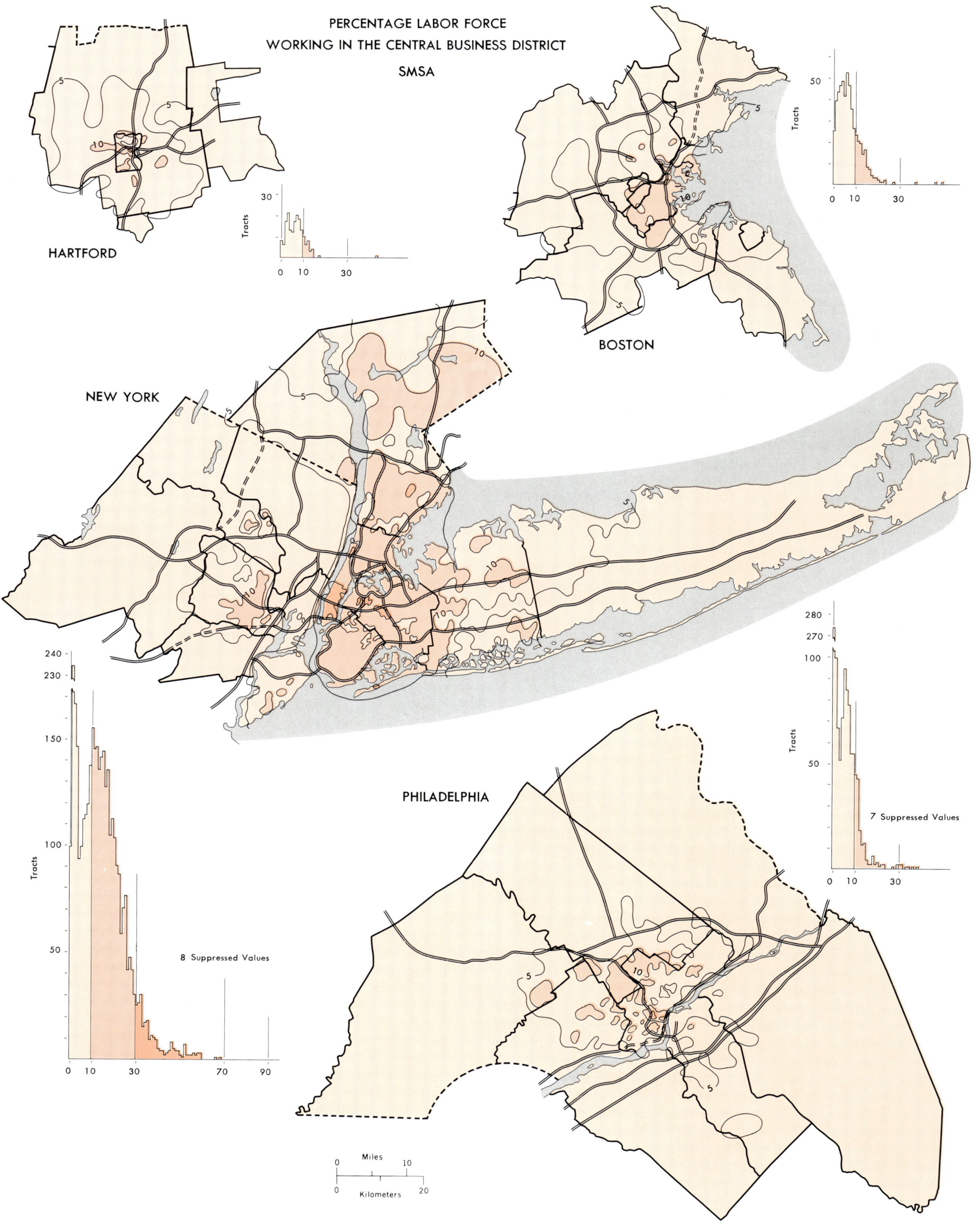

*Transportation and Communication: Working in the CBD*

PERCENTAGE LABOR FORCE
WORKING IN THE CENTRAL BUSINESS DISTRICT
SMSA

HARTFORD

BOSTON

NEW YORK

PHILADELPHIA

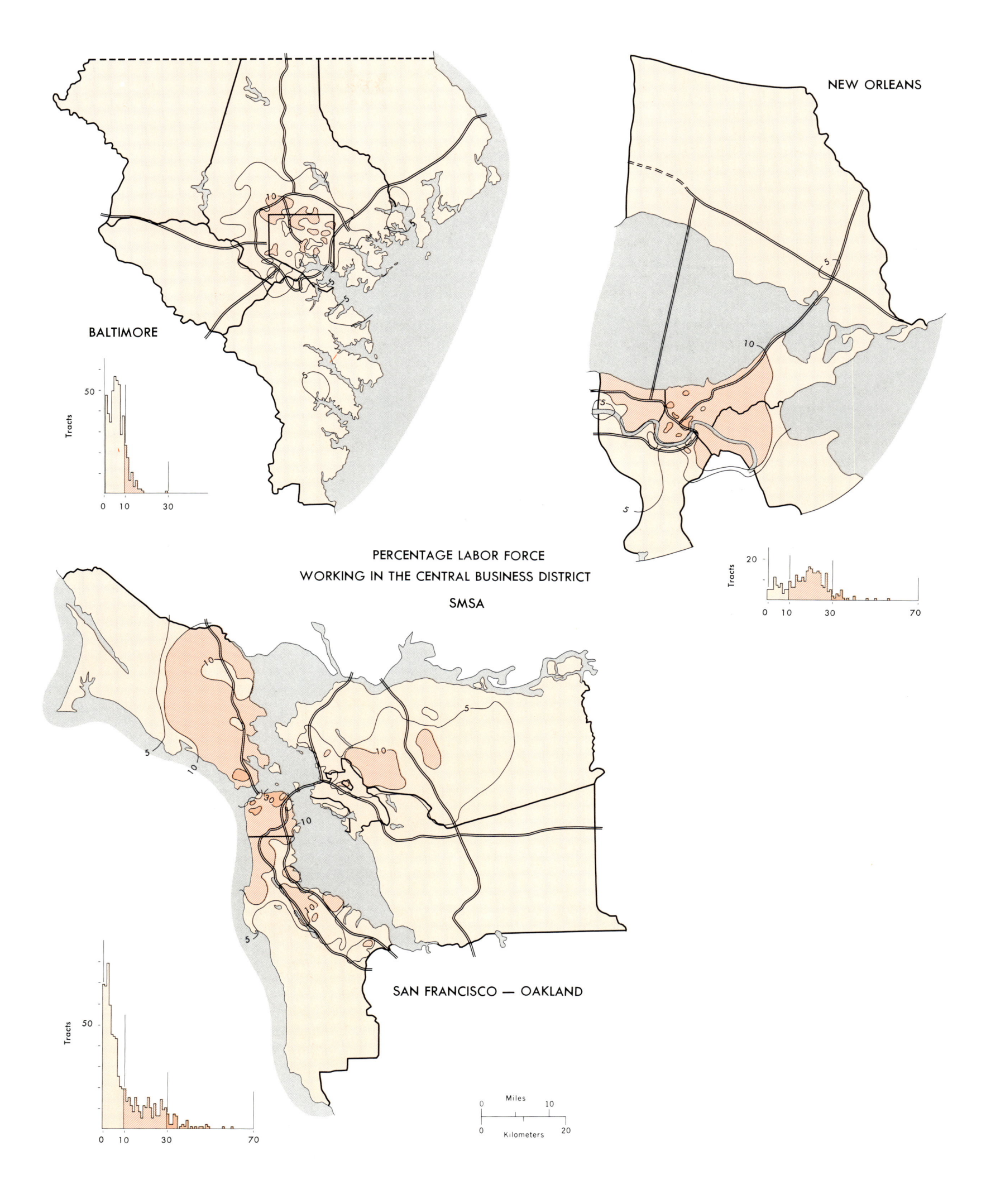

## Transportation and Communication: Working in the CBD

**BALTIMORE**

**NEW ORLEANS**

**PERCENTAGE LABOR FORCE WORKING IN THE CENTRAL BUSINESS DISTRICT**
**SMSA**

**SAN FRANCISCO — OAKLAND**

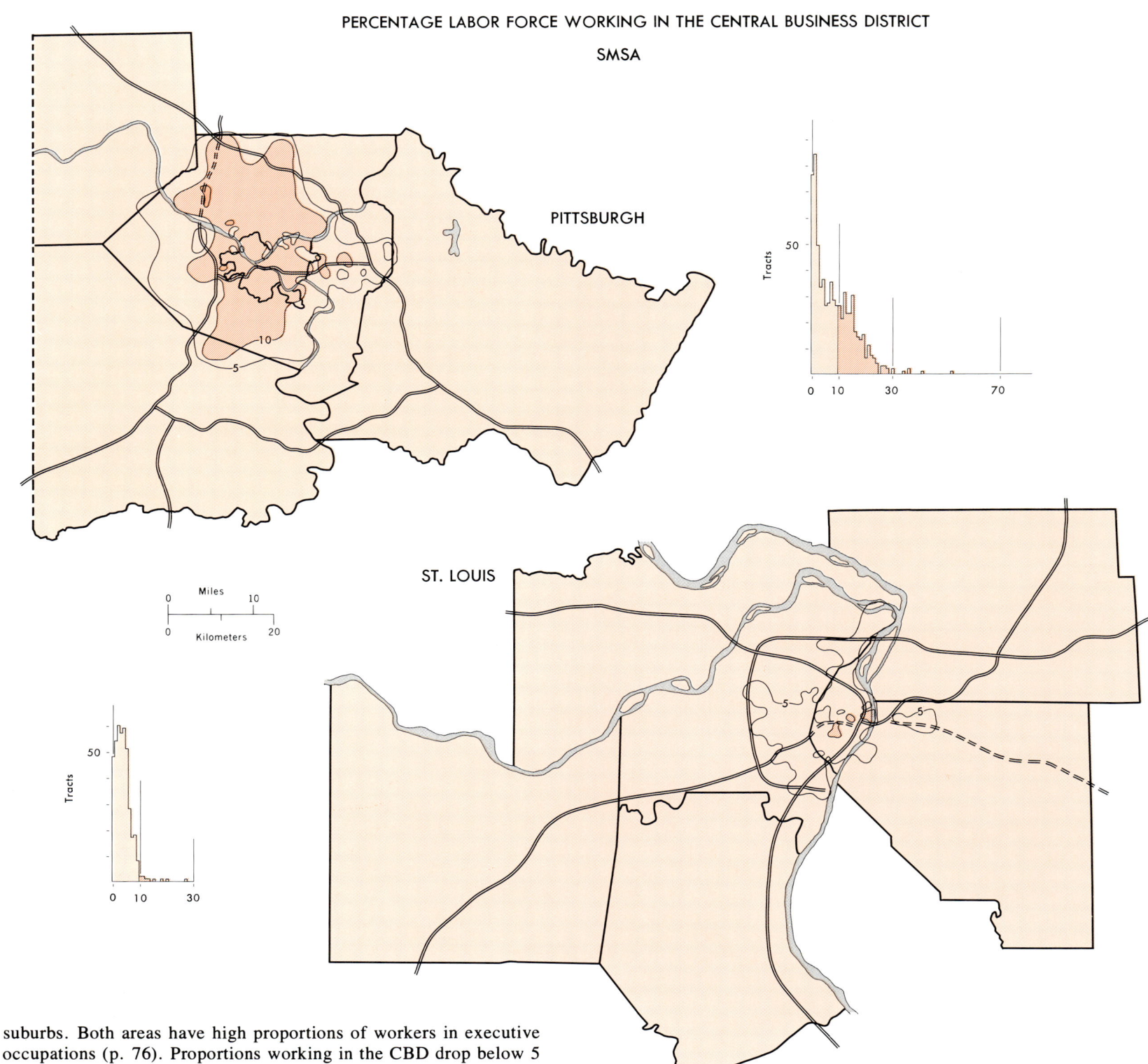

## Transportation and Communication: Working in the CBD

PERCENTAGE LABOR FORCE WORKING IN THE CENTRAL BUSINESS DISTRICT
SMSA

suburbs. Both areas have high proportions of workers in executive occupations (p. 76). Proportions working in the CBD drop below 5 percent in some heavily black areas of the city (p. 383).

**New Orleans.** The New Orleans CBD and New Orleans City have retained a comparatively high proportion of SMSA employment. CBD workers come from most of the settled portions of the SMSA. The importance of highway access is evident in the area where commuting to the CBD exceeds 5 percent at the junction of Interstates 12 and 59.

**San Francisco-Oakland.** The map and the histogram show commuting to the San Francisco CBD only. There is much cross-commuting in the Bay Area, and commuting to the two CBDs could not be shown on the same map. Of the SMSA labor force, 11.3 percent works in the San Francisco CBD and 21.5 percent works in the rest of San Francisco; 1.9 percent of the SMSA labor force works in the Oakland CBD and 10.2 percent in the rest of Oakland. The pull of the San Francisco CBD extends well to the north, east, and south, with some tracts east of Oakland sending more than 10 percent of their workers to downtown San Francisco.

**Pittsburgh.** The CBD draws workers from areas north and south of the city where proportions of the labor force in executive occupations are high (p. 112). Although the CBD retains a comparatively high share of the SMSA jobs, the rest of Pittsburgh has relatively few, resulting in a low proportion of SMSA jobs for the city.

**St. Louis.** The St. Louis CBD has the lowest proportion of SMSA employment of any single-centered region in the atlas. Much of the SMSA office employment has moved to western suburbs of the city, leaving few job opportunities in the downtown area.

**Cleveland.** The CBD draws many of its workers from upper-income areas on the city's eastern boundary such as Shaker Heights and Cleveland Heights. Others come from the city's west side. Proportions drop below 5 percent in the predominantly black neighborhood on Cleveland's east side (p. 385).

*Transportation and Communication: Working in the CBD*

PERCENTAGE LABOR FORCE
WORKING IN THE CENTRAL BUSINESS DISTRICT
SMSA

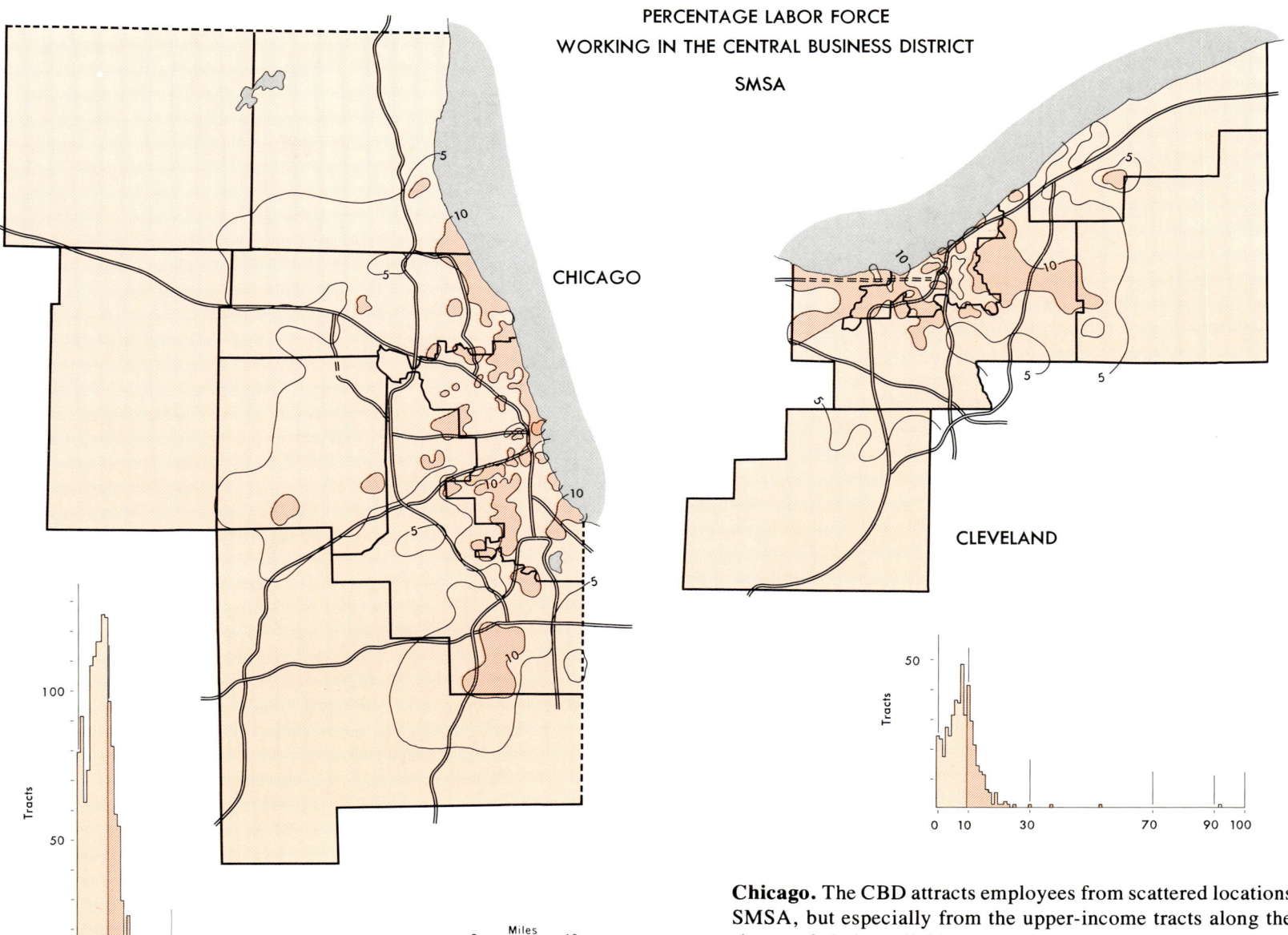

**Chicago.** The CBD attracts employees from scattered locations in the SMSA, but especially from the upper-income tracts along the north shore of Lake Michigan. The 5 percent isopleth encloses a comparatively large commuter shed that is less tied to freeway locations than might be true in other SMSAs without the commuter rail service the Chicago SMSA enjoys.

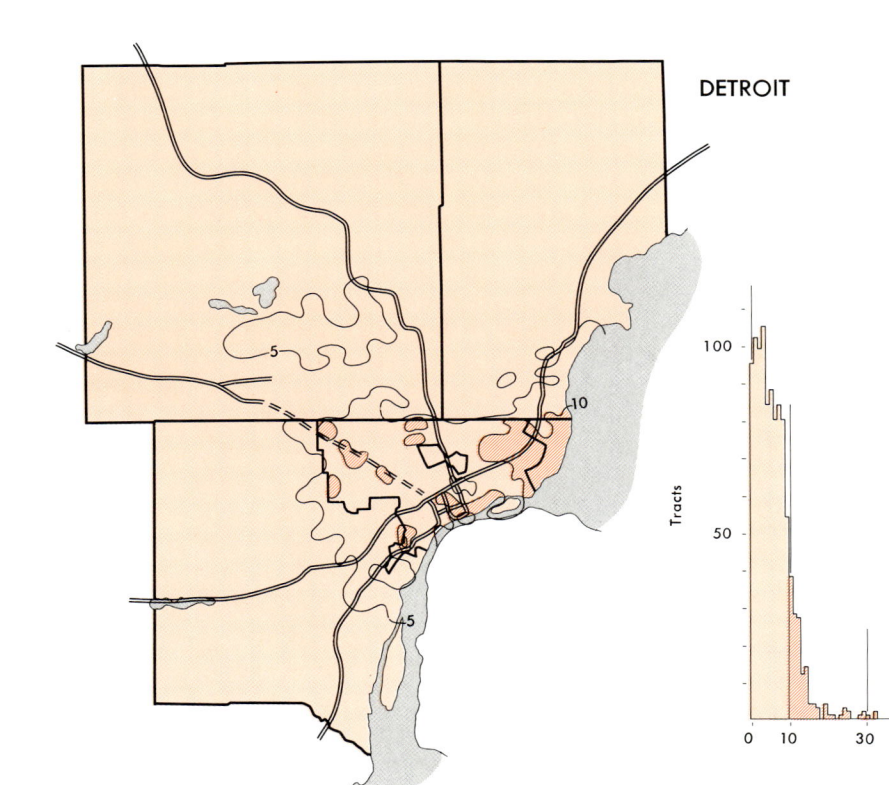

**Detroit.** The links between the CBD and communities occupied by upper-income workers in executive occupations (pp. 155-156) are especially evident in the Detroit SMSA, where the Pointe communities on Lake St. Clair and the upper-income area of central Monroe County are important sources of commuters to the CBD.

**Minneapolis-St. Paul.** The commuter sheds of the two CBDs just fail to overlap, and thus both were mapped. The Minneapolis CBD attracts 7.3 percent of the SMSA labor force, and 26.6 percent works in the rest of Minneapolis. Corresponding proportions for St. Paul are 4.4 and 16.8 percent.

**Seattle.** The Seattle CBD draws most of its workers from the northern part of the city and from the upper-income, white-collar (pp. 175-176) residential communities on Mercer Island and the east side of Lake Washington. The CBD and the city contain just over half of the SMSA jobs.

**Dallas-Fort Worth.** The Dallas and Fort Worth SMSAs have distinct commuting sheds. Worker exchanges between the two SMSAs are few; 2.9 percent of the Dallas SMSA labor force works outside the SMSA, as does 10.5 percent of the Fort Worth SMSA force. Both

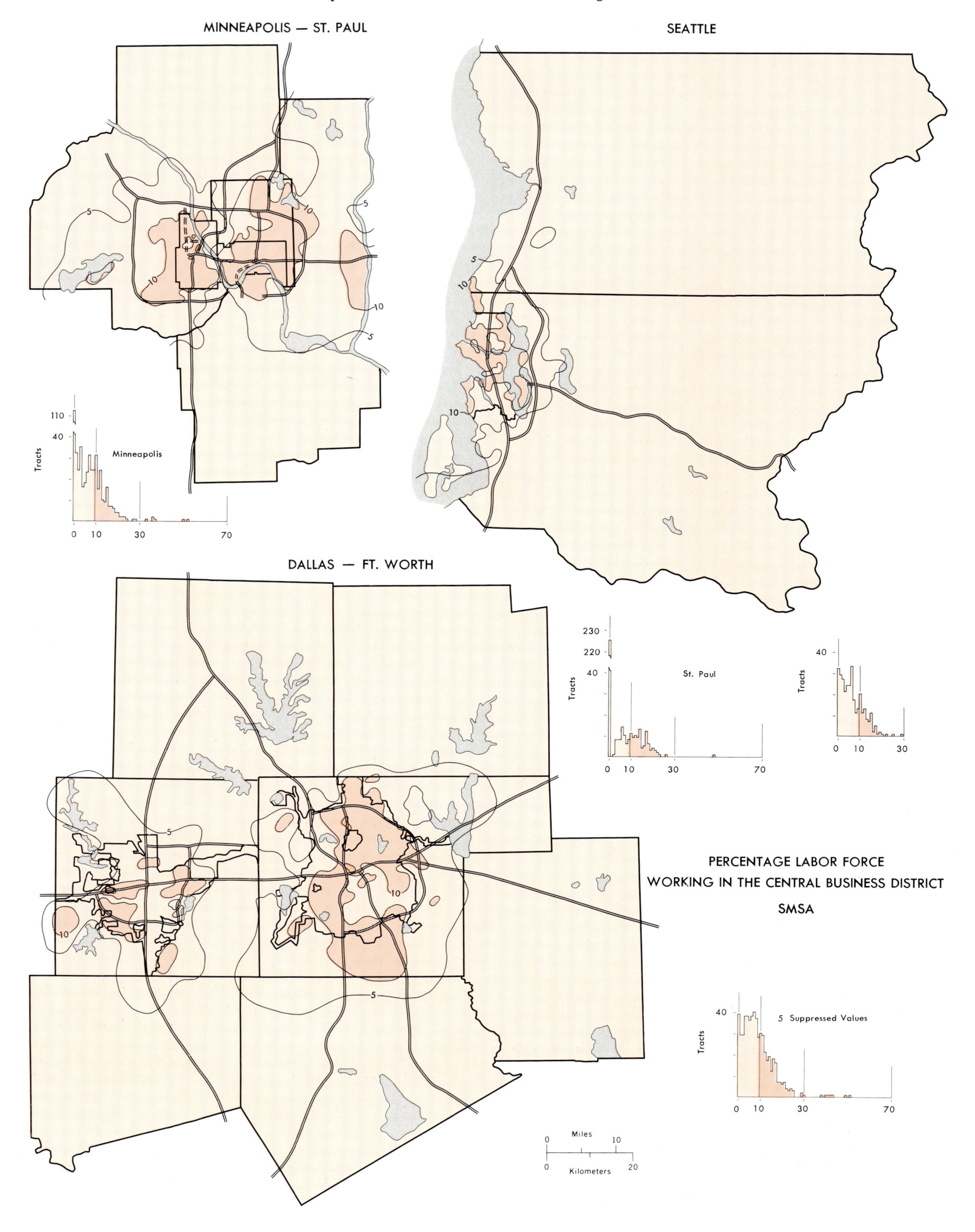

*Transportation and Communication: Working in the CBD*

MINNEAPOLIS — ST. PAUL

SEATTLE

DALLAS — FT. WORTH

PERCENTAGE LABOR FORCE
WORKING IN THE CENTRAL BUSINESS DISTRICT
SMSA

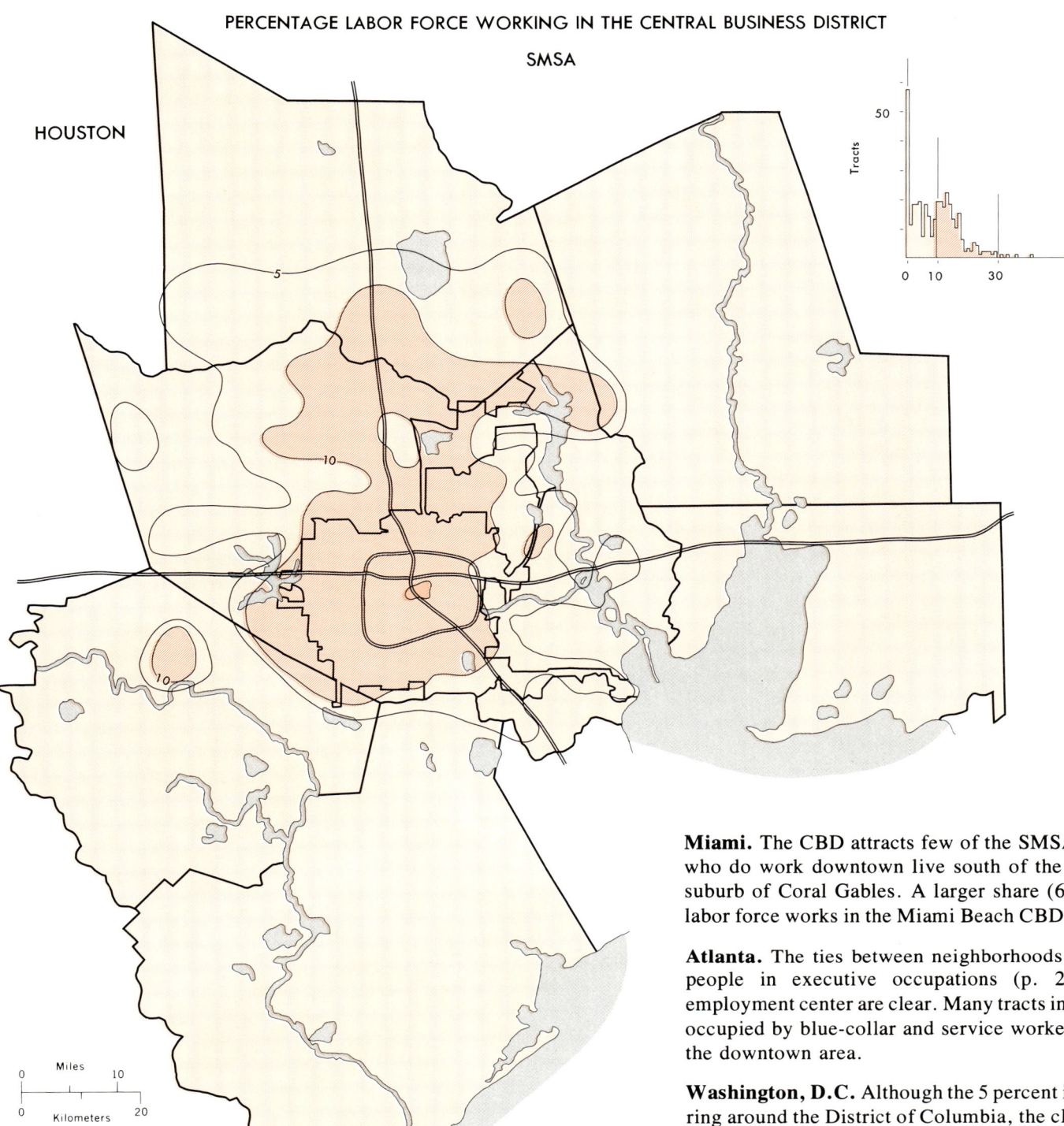

## Transportation and Communication: Working in the CBD

### PERCENTAGE LABOR FORCE WORKING IN THE CENTRAL BUSINESS DISTRICT
#### SMSA

HOUSTON

central cities, but especially Dallas, retain large proportions of the SMSA labor force because Texas cities can annex adjacent territory that would be suburban in other states.

**Houston.** The central city has the highest proportion of SMSA employment of the areas mapped in the atlas. As is true in Dallas and Fort Worth, Houston's ability to expand its municipal boundaries almost at will enables it to incorporate outlying employment centers. The percentages of CBD workers coming from predominantly black and Spanish-American neighborhoods (pp. 387, 395) are comparatively high in Houston.

**Los Angeles.** Dispersed employment opportunities in the SMSA leave the CBD a small share of total employment, and the area from which the CBD draws many of its workers is heavily Spanish-American (p. 396). Many of the business establishments in the downtown area cater to Spanish-Americans.

**Miami.** The CBD attracts few of the SMSA workers. Most of those who do work downtown live south of the CBD and in the affluent suburb of Coral Gables. A larger share (6.6 percent) of the SMSA labor force works in the Miami Beach CBD than in the Miami CBD.

**Atlanta.** The ties between neighborhoods with high proportions of people in executive occupations (p. 253) and the downtown employment center are clear. Many tracts in and near the CBD that are occupied by blue-collar and service workers send few employees to the downtown area.

**Washington, D.C.** Although the 5 percent isopleth forms an irregular ring around the District of Columbia, the clear axis of more intensive commuting to the CBD is from the affluent northwest. The policy of dispersing federal employment to suburban locations since World War II has left the District with a small share of SMSA jobs.

---

CBD employment is a critical element of two metropolitan problems. The economic viability of downtown areas is heavily dependent on the number of people working there, for large shares of CBD business are now done with CBD employees rather than with people who come from outlying areas specifically to shop. Thus no central city can view absolute and relative losses of CBD employment with equanimity.

The absolute and relative size of CBD employment is also a partial determinant of the viability of public transportation. The CBD is often the metropolitan destination that is easiest to reach by public transportation and in many instances the only destination being served by efficient public transit. Population density (Chapter 32), the proportion of the labor force working in the CBD, and the percentage of the labor force using public transportation (Chapter 34) are inseparable considerations in determining whether even heavily subsidized public transportation is worthwhile.

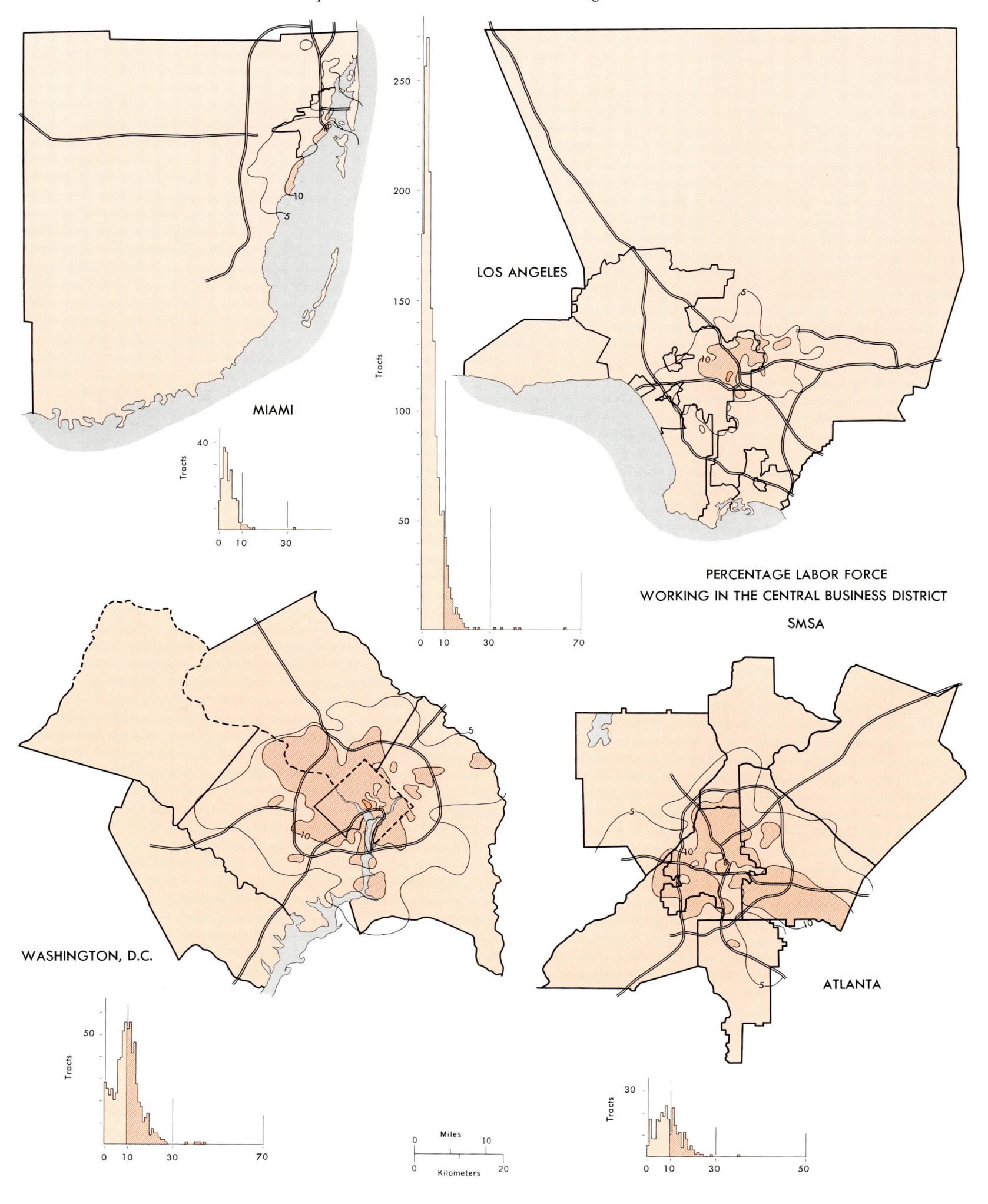

*Transportation and Communication: Working in the CBD*

MIAMI

LOS ANGELES

PERCENTAGE LABOR FORCE
WORKING IN THE CENTRAL BUSINESS DISTRICT
SMSA

WASHINGTON, D.C.

ATLANTA

*Transportation and Communication*

CHAPTER 34

# Public Transportation to Work

In the 1970 Census a 15 percent sample of all workers were asked how they traveled to work in the previous week. The number taking a bus or streetcar, subway or elevated train, or rail transportation in each tract is mapped here as a percentage of the tract's labor force for the Standard Metropolitan Statistical Areas (SMSAs) included in the nation's 20 most populous metropolitan regions.

People who take public transportation to work are a minority in the national labor force. Of all workers who reported their means of travel, 77.7 percent use automobile transportation (66 percent were drivers and 11.7 percent were passengers during the reference week). Public transportation conveys 8.4 percent of the nation's workers to their jobs; 5.5 percent travel by bus or streetcar, 2.3 percent move by subway or elevated, and 0.6 percent commute by rail. The residual consists of 7.4 percent who walk to work, 0.4 percent who take taxicabs, and 6.1 percent who either work at home or did not report their means of transportation to work. Public transportation use for commuting is slightly higher in the nation's metropolitan areas, where 11.6 percent of the labor force in all SMSAs relies on it in the following forms: bus and streetcar, 7.5 percent; elevated, 3.3 percent; and rail, 0.8 percent. The use of public transportation in the 20 most populous metropolitan regions mapped in the atlas is higher than the national and the metropolitan averages. Of the 25,212,000 workers in the 20 regions, 5,102,000 (20.2 percent) use public transportation. Proportions using public transit in individual SMSAs vary from well below 10 percent in places like Houston and Los Angeles to 22.9 percent in Chicago and 46.9 percent in the New York, New York SMSA (see accompanying tabulation).

The proportion of the labor force using public transportation at a place is related to the size of the place and thus the population density at its center. Other things being equal, the larger a metropolitan area's population, the higher the population density at its core. The higher the central-area density, the more viable and necessary public transportation is, for density of potential users is the critical determinant of whether public transit can be provided. Also, the higher the proportions of the city and SMSA labor forces working downtown (mapped in the previous chapter), the greater the need for and use of public transportation, which usually serves the Central Business District (CBD) better than other destinations. Automobile ownership rates (Chapter 35) are usually low in neighborhoods where public transportation use is comparatively high.

**Boston.** The SMSA's public-transit patrons use bus (11.5 percent) and subway and elevated trains (7.8 percent) to get to and from work. Ridership exceeds 30 percent in the core area of Boston, Cambridge, and Somerville. The 10 percent isopleth encloses a comparatively large area.

**New York-Northern New Jersey.** The region's public transportation complex serves an extensive region on both sides of the Hudson. Difficulties and expenses of automobile ownership and storage at the regional core produce high patronage rates and make commuting to the high-density core (pp. 310, 318) from distant locations via public transportation attractive over a large area. Public transportation is

Percentage of the Labor Force Taking
Public Transportation to Work

| Region | Central City(ies) | Entire SMSA |
|---|---|---|
| Boston | 38.3 | 19.3 |
| New York | 60.6 | 46.9 |
| Jersey City | 41.7 | 35.3 |
| Newark | 37.6 | 18.2 |
| Paterson-Clifton-Passaic | 14.9 | 14.2 |
| Philadelphia | 37.0 | 20.4 |
| Hartford | 26.0 | 9.7 |
| Baltimore | 25.7 | 13.0 |
| New Orleans | 30.5 | 19.8 |
| San Francisco-Oakland | 29.6 | 15.2 |
| Pittsburgh | 29.2 | 14.3 |
| St. Louis | 20.2 | 7.5 |
| Cleveland | 22.0 | 13.2 |
| Chicago | 35.8 | 22.9 |
| Detroit | 18.1 | 8.0 |
| Minneapolis-St. Paul | 16.8 | 8.9 |
| Seattle | 14.6 | 6.9 |
| Dallas | 10.4 | 6.2 |
| Fort Worth | 4.5 | 2.5 |
| Houston | 7.6 | 5.2 |
| Los Angeles | 9.2 | 5.5 |
| Miami | 16.8 | 8.8 |
| Atlanta | 20.6 | 8.9 |
| Washington, D.C. | 35.6 | 15.5 |

more intensely used in the Jersey City (Hudson County) and Newark (Essex, Morris, and Union counties) central cities and SMSAs than it is in dispersed, multicentered Paterson-Clifton-Passaic (Bergen and Passaic counties).

**Philadelphia.** Transit use is high in Philadelphia, exceeding 30 percent in much of the central part of the city. Of the 380,800 workers using public transportation in the SMSA, 274,300 (72 percent) live in

*Note:* All data are from the 1970 Censuses of Population and Housing unless otherwise indicated. Therefore the present tense refers to 1970 except for income data which are from 1969. Cartographic conventions are explained in Chapter 1. County names and other locational information are shown on the SMSA map at the beginning of each city chapter (6-25) and on the DUS map of mobile homes near the beginning of each city chapter.

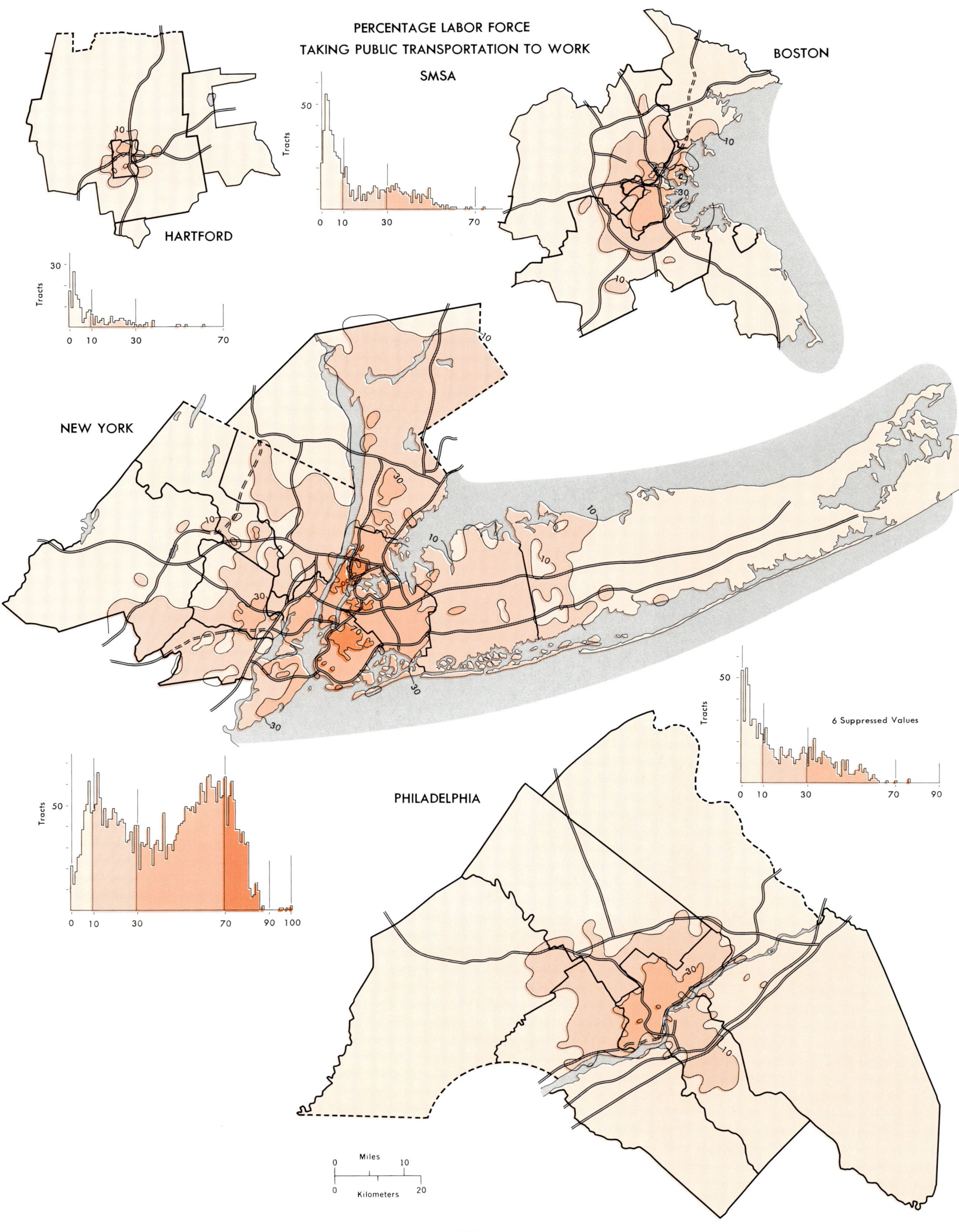

*Transportation and Communication: Public Transportation Use*

## PERCENTAGE LABOR FORCE TAKING PUBLIC TRANSPORTATION TO WORK
### SMSA

HARTFORD

BOSTON

NEW YORK

PHILADELPHIA

6 Suppressed Values

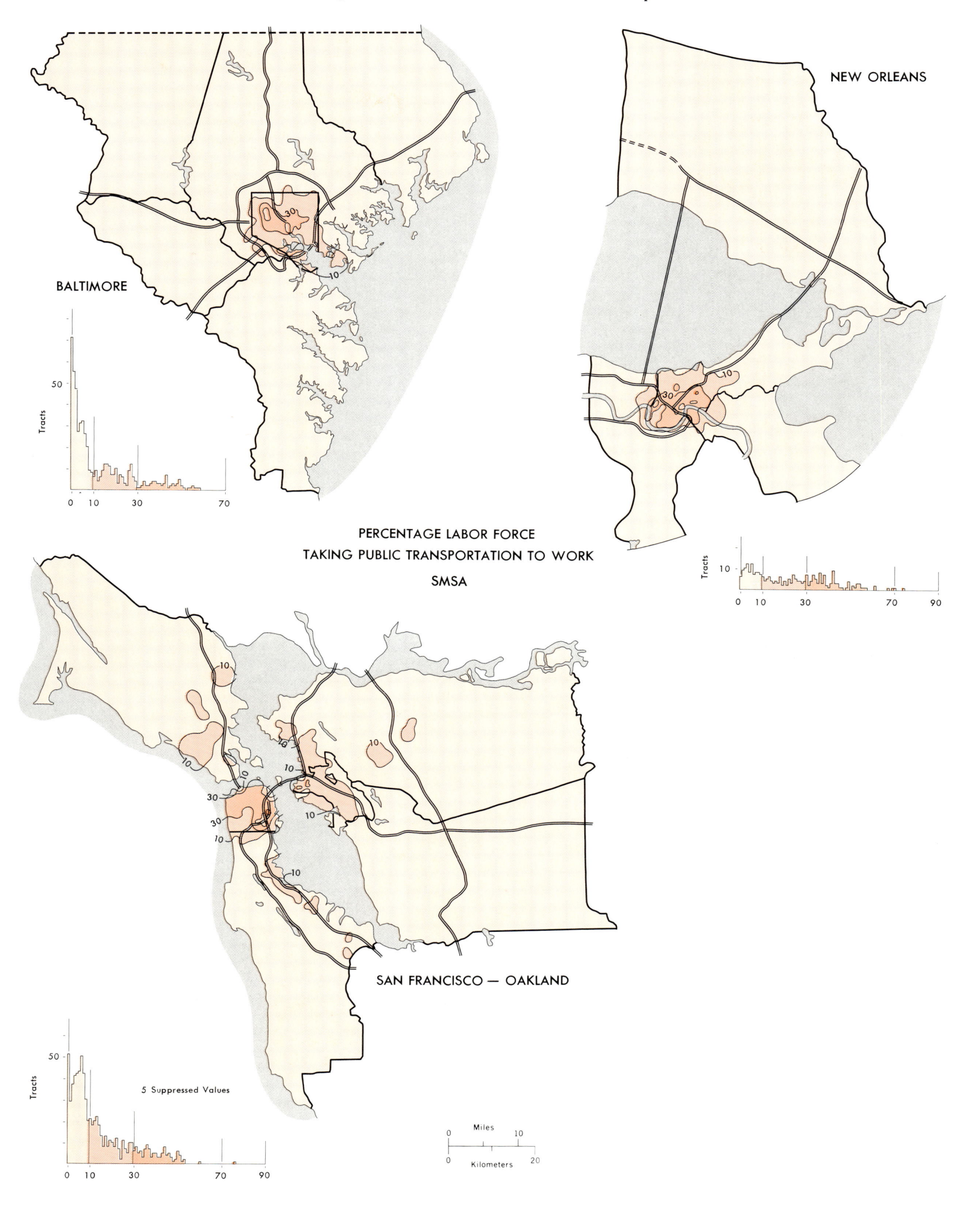

*Transportation and Communication: Public Transportation Use*

BALTIMORE

NEW ORLEANS

PERCENTAGE LABOR FORCE
TAKING PUBLIC TRANSPORTATION TO WORK
SMSA

SAN FRANCISCO — OAKLAND

5 Suppressed Values

*Transportation and Communication: Public Transportation Use*

PERCENTAGE LABOR FORCE TAKING PUBLIC TRANSPORTATION TO WORK

PITTSBURGH SMSA

ST. LOUIS

Philadelphia. Rail commuter service extends to the northwest and southeast.

**Hartford.** A majority (63.5 percent) of the workers using public transportation in the SMSA live in Hartford. The difficulty of providing good public transporation for the many dispersed employment centers in the region results in a comparatively low percentage of transit use for a northeastern SMSA.

**Baltimore.** Few workers outside Baltimore use public transportation; 82.9 percent of the SMSA transit patrons live inside the city, where public transit serves only a fourth of the labor force.

**New Orleans.** The central city retains a comparatively high proportion of SMSA jobs (p. 317), and public transportation use in New Orleans and the SMSA is high, given the city's population density (p. 311). Eighty-seven percent of those using public transportation for work trips live in New Orleans.

**San Francisco-Oakland.** The Bay Area's unusual commuting patterns (p. 319) produce an irregular map of public transportation use. More workers (35.5 percent) in San Francisco use public transportation than in Oakland (16.5 percent).

**Pittsburgh.** Nearly 1 of 3 Pittsburgh workers commutes via public transportation. The area where at least 10 percent of tract workers use public transit extends well beyond the Pittsburgh municipal boundary. Among the regions mapped, the SMSA has the highest proportion (55.1 percent) of public transit users living outside the central city.

**St. Louis.** Most (68.8 percent) people who use public transit for commuting live in St. Louis. Even there public transit serves only 1 of 5 workers. The low proportion of SMSA jobs in St. Louis and its CBD (p. 320) makes center-oriented transportation ineffective.

**Cleveland.** Public transit provides good commuter service beyond Cleveland's municipal boundaries; 42.2 percent of those using public

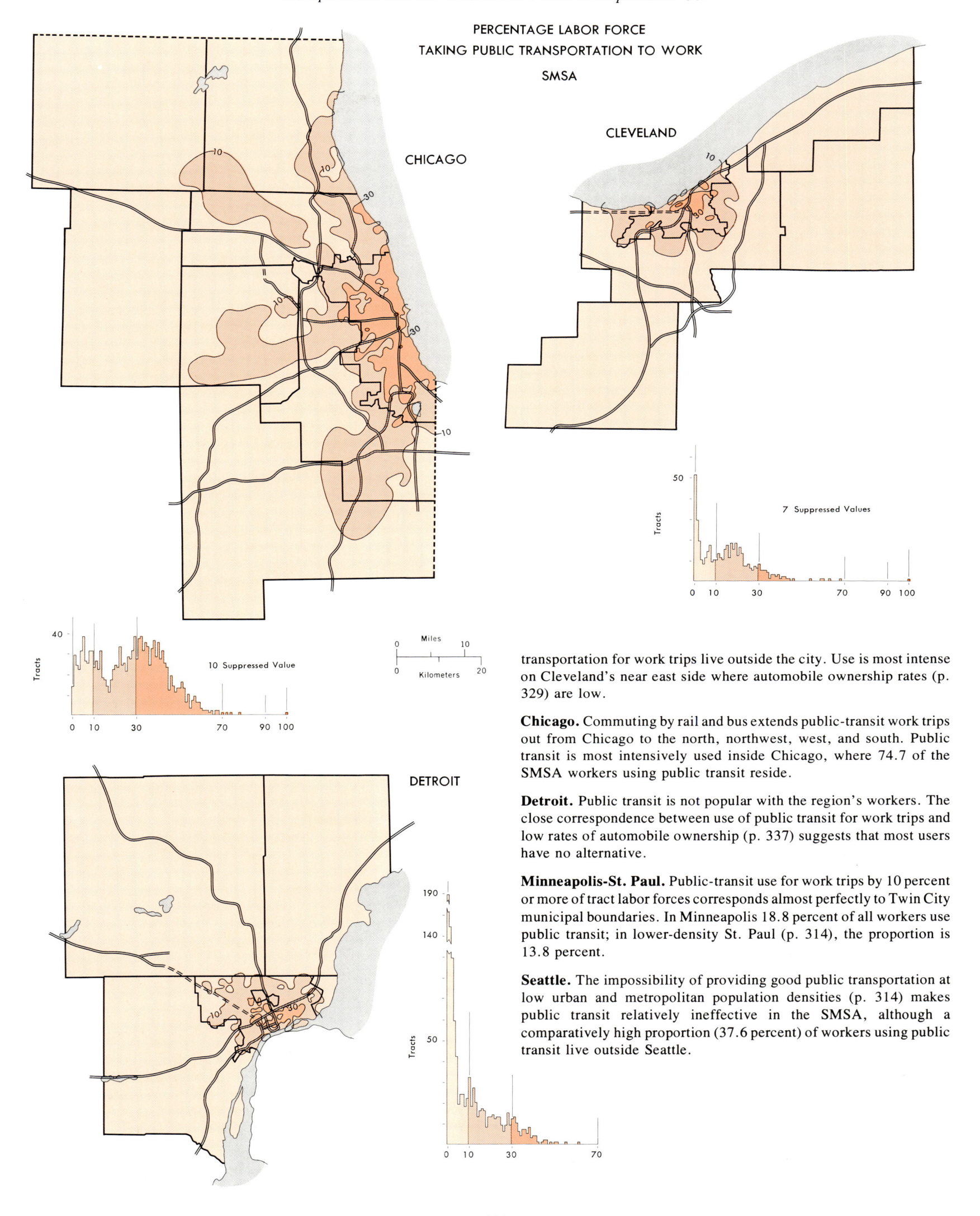

*Transportation and Communication: Public Transportation Use*

PERCENTAGE LABOR FORCE
TAKING PUBLIC TRANSPORTATION TO WORK
SMSA

transportation for work trips live outside the city. Use is most intense on Cleveland's near east side where automobile ownership rates (p. 329) are low.

**Chicago.** Commuting by rail and bus extends public-transit work trips out from Chicago to the north, northwest, west, and south. Public transit is most intensively used inside Chicago, where 74.7 of the SMSA workers using public transit reside.

**Detroit.** Public transit is not popular with the region's workers. The close correspondence between use of public transit for work trips and low rates of automobile ownership (p. 337) suggests that most users have no alternative.

**Minneapolis-St. Paul.** Public-transit use for work trips by 10 percent or more of tract labor forces corresponds almost perfectly to Twin City municipal boundaries. In Minneapolis 18.8 percent of all workers use public transit; in lower-density St. Paul (p. 314), the proportion is 13.8 percent.

**Seattle.** The impossibility of providing good public transportation at low urban and metropolitan population densities (p. 314) makes public transit relatively ineffective in the SMSA, although a comparatively high proportion (37.6 percent) of workers using public transit live outside Seattle.

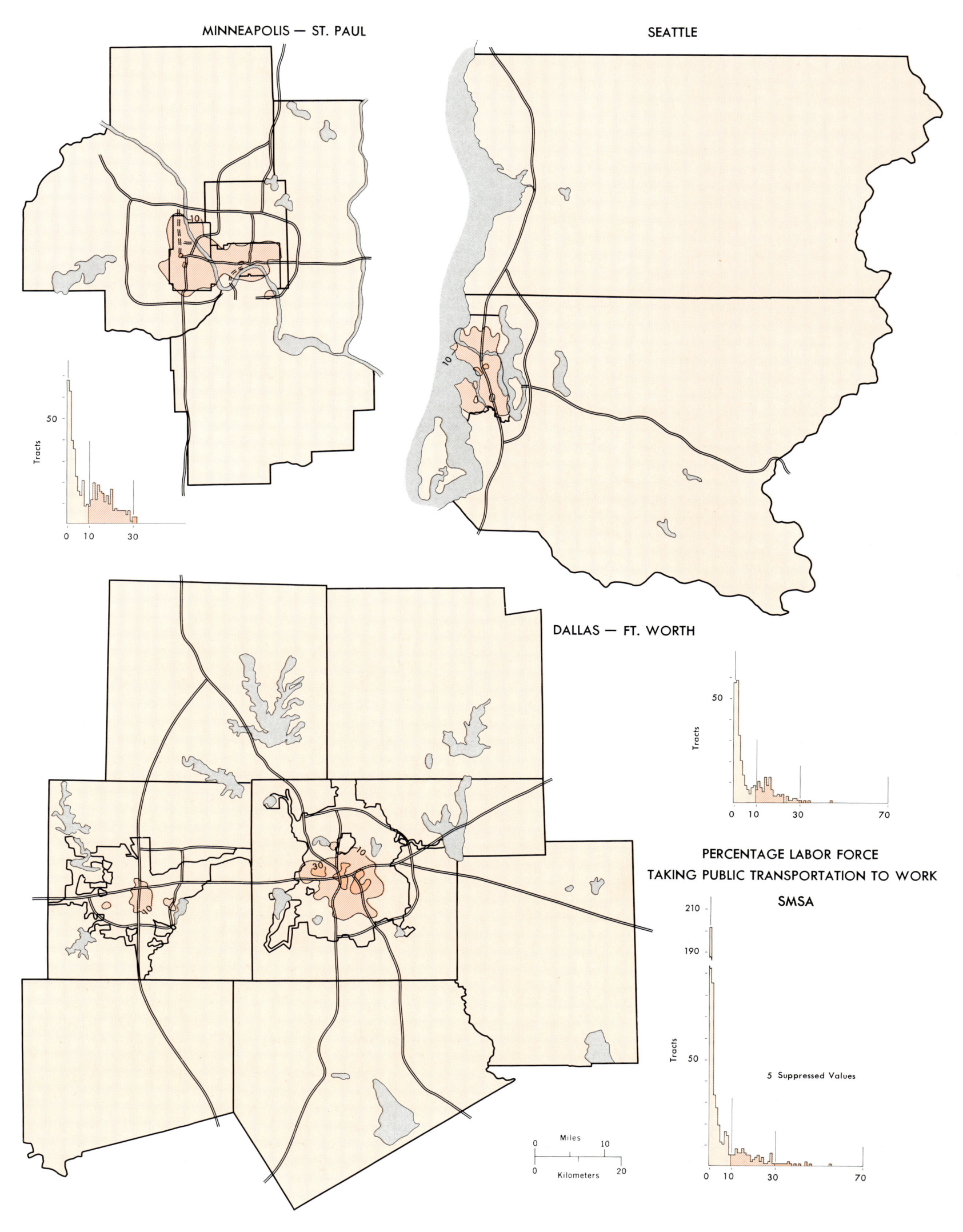

*Transportation and Communication: Public Transportation Use*

MINNEAPOLIS — ST. PAUL

SEATTLE

DALLAS — FT. WORTH

PERCENTAGE LABOR FORCE
TAKING PUBLIC TRANSPORTATION TO WORK

SMSA

5 Suppressed Values

330

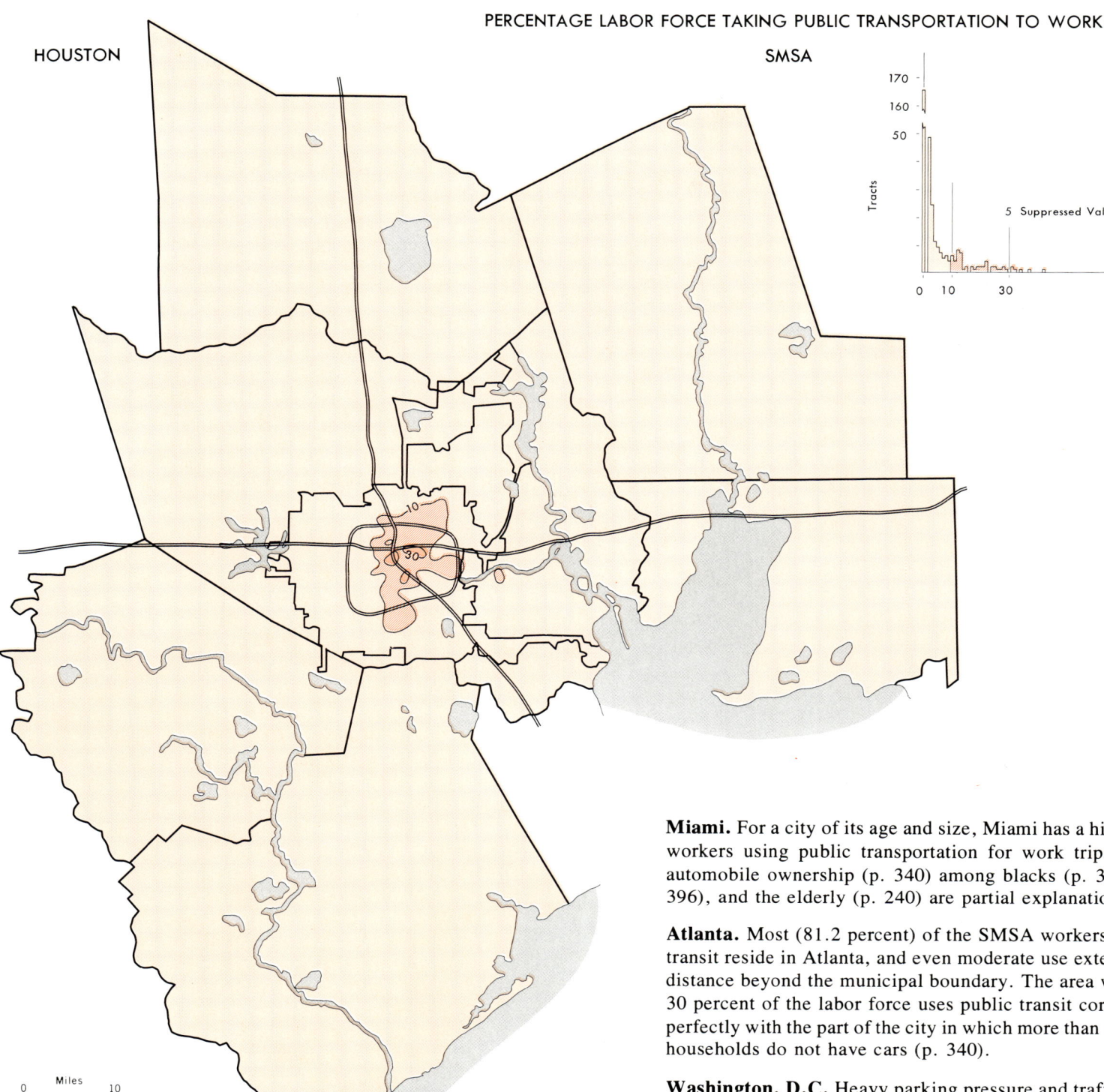

*Transportation and Communication: Public Transportation Use*

PERCENTAGE LABOR FORCE TAKING PUBLIC TRANSPORTATION TO WORK

HOUSTON SMSA

**Dallas-Fort Worth.** Overall rates of transit use for work trips are comparatively low in the SMSAs, and such use is especially concentrated in the relatively overbounded central cities; 94.7 percent of the Dallas SMSA workers using public transportation reside in Dallas. The corresponding percentage for Fort Worth is 92.6.

**Houston.** Very low population density (p. 315) precludes widespread commuting by public transportation in both the SMSA and the city. Only areas with low rates of automobile ownership (p. 339) generate even modest numbers of public-transit work trips.

**Los Angeles.** Overall transit use for work trips in the SMSA is low. There are secondary areas of transit use in Santa Monica and Long Beach, but the primary focus is on the Los Angeles CBD. That area draws heavily from predominantly Spanish-American neighborhoods (p. 396) where automobile ownership rates (p. 340) are low.

**Miami.** For a city of its age and size, Miami has a high proportion of workers using public transportation for work trips. Low rates of automobile ownership (p. 340) among blacks (p. 388), Cubans (p. 396), and the elderly (p. 240) are partial explanations.

**Atlanta.** Most (81.2 percent) of the SMSA workers who use public transit reside in Atlanta, and even moderate use extends only a short distance beyond the municipal boundary. The area where more than 30 percent of the labor force uses public transit corresponds almost perfectly with the part of the city in which more than 30 percent of the households do not have cars (p. 340).

**Washington, D.C.** Heavy parking pressure and traffic congestion in downtown Washington make public transit to work an attractive option throughout the District of Columbia and into the Maryland and Virginia suburbs. The proportions of workers using public transit for work trips are comparatively high in the District and the SMSA.

---

If public transportation can compete with the automobile for work trips anywhere, it ought to be able to do so in the nation's largest metropolitan regions. Population densities are high and there are large numbers of jobs in the core areas served by public transit. The generally low rates of public transit use shown in this chapter, and the close correspondence between public-transit use and areas of low automobile ownership (mapped in the following chapter), suggest that public transportation managers should concentrate on retaining as many of their existing patrons as possible. Decreasing population densities, increasing dispersal of employment, and increasing rates of automobile ownership (up from 77 percent of all families in 1960 to 82 percent in 1970) suggest that public transportation will have to be especially innovative and efficient to attract potential patrons now using private automobiles.

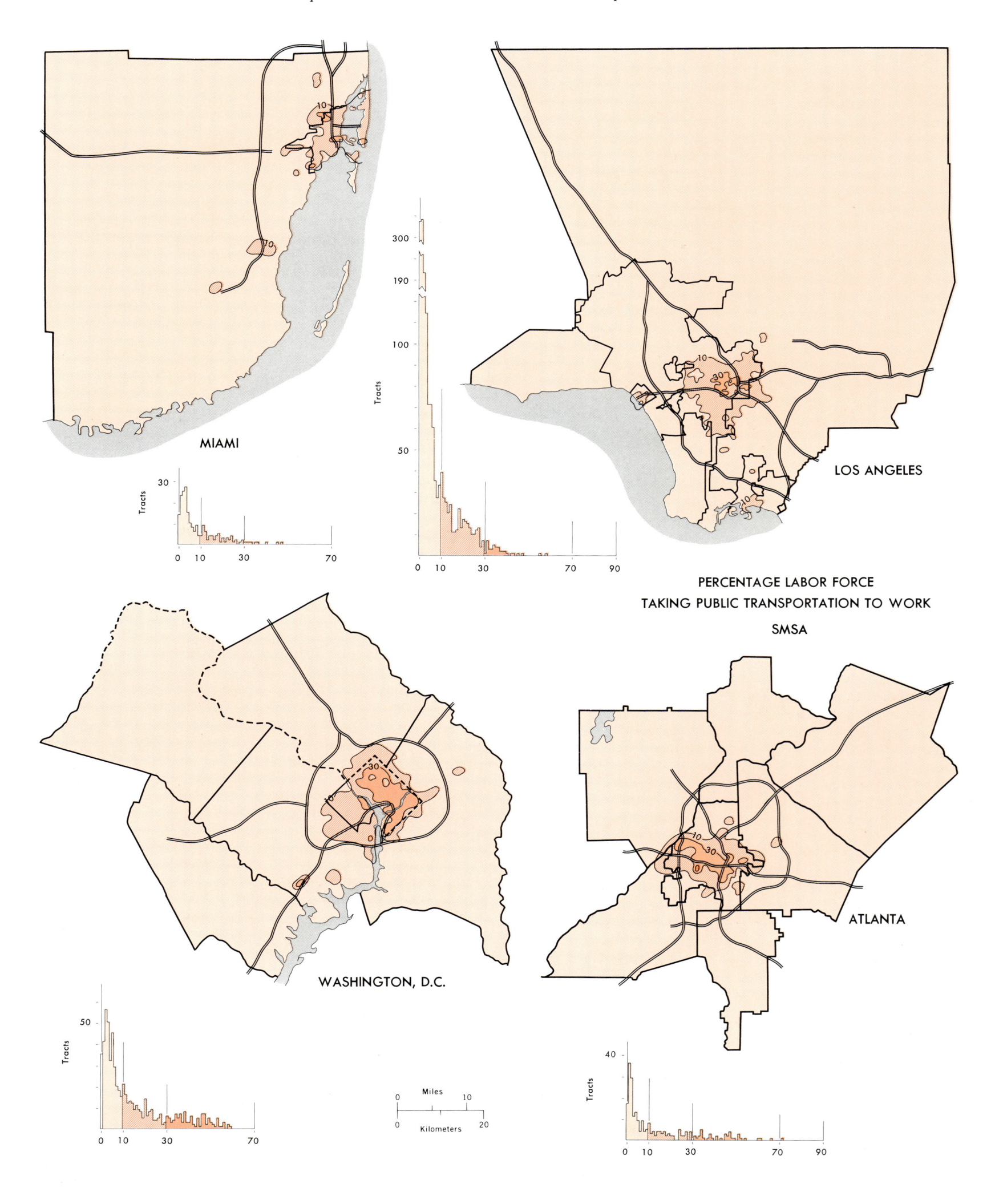

*Transportation and Communication: Public Transportation Use*

MIAMI

LOS ANGELES

PERCENTAGE LABOR FORCE
TAKING PUBLIC TRANSPORTATION TO WORK
SMSA

WASHINGTON, D.C.

ATLANTA

*Transportation and Communication*

CHAPTER 35

# Households without Automobiles

In the 1970 Census of Housing, a 15 percent sample of occupied households were asked "How many passenger automobiles are owned or regularly used by members of your household?" The possible responses included "none," and the maps in this chapter show the proportion of tract households that responded by checking "none" in each of the Standard Metropolitan Statistical Areas (SMSAs) in the nation's 20 most populous metropolitan regions.

Nationally, 11,081,000 (17.5 percent) of America's 63,445,000 occupied households do not have automobiles. The proportion is slightly higher (18.6 percent) in the nation's SMSAs and significantly higher (28.4 percent) in the central cities of the SMSAs (see accompanying tabulation). In the 20 regions mapped here, 23.4 percent of all households do not have cars. Automobile ownership is on the increase. Twenty-three percent of America's families did not own an automobile in 1960, and 41 percent were without automobiles in 1950.

The personal mobility provided by increased automobile ownership has improved many aspects of metropolitan life. But the more society in general depends on automobile transportation, the greater the disadvantage experienced by people without cars. To the extent that locations for facilities are chosen on the assumption that everyone has an automobile, people without one will have difficulty obtaining goods, services, jobs, and social contacts. Immobility can be particularly acute for the elderly and for unskilled, low-income groups whose services are not in demand in downtown areas (Chapter 33) and who must therefore seek jobs at dispersed locations poorly served by public transit (Chapter 34).

Automobile ownership depends largely on income, which in turn is related to education, occupation, race, etc. By and large, low rates of automobile ownership are symptoms rather than causes of poverty, but the handicap that lack of an automobile often imposes in some places is an important dimension of metropolitan problems. Rates of automobile unavailability are higher in central cities than in SMSAs as a whole, but public transportation is more accessible in and near the cores of SMSAs than farther out. Thus the people most seriously disadvantaged by the unavailability of an automobile are those in outlying areas where overall unavailability rates are low and those living in inner-city areas who cannot reach suburban job opportunities.

**Boston.** Boston's proportion of households without an automobile is 2nd highest of the central cities mapped here. Automobile unavailability is also widespread in the inner parts of the SMSA outside Boston. The areas where unavailability is high correspond closely to areas where use of public transportation to get to work is comparatively high (p. 326).

**New York-Northern New Jersey.** Low incomes are not the sole explanation for the large proportions of New York City households without automobiles. The expense of providing secure storage for an automobile in the region's high-density core is a deterrent to ownership even for middle- and upper-income households. The extent to which parking costs and congestion are deterrents to automobile use becomes evident when the unavailability map is compared with the

Percentage of Households without an Automobile

| Region | Central City(ies) | Entire SMSA |
|---|---|---|
| Boston | 46.7 | 24.0 |
| New York | 57.5 | 44.9 |
| Jersey City | 45.8 | 26.4 |
| Newark | 51.5 | 21.6 |
| Paterson-Clifton-Passaic | 35.7 | 13.9 |
| Philadelphia | 39.7 | 23.3 |
| Hartford | 37.7 | 14.7 |
| Baltimore | 41.1 | 23.3 |
| New Orleans | 37.3 | 26.4 |
| San Francisco-Oakland | 35.4 | 19.3 |
| Pittsburgh | 37.8 | 20.5 |
| St. Louis | 38.1 | 18.0 |
| Cleveland | 31.7 | 17.1 |
| Chicago | 39.3 | 24.3 |
| Detroit | 28.0 | 14.8 |
| Minneapolis-St. Paul | 25.3 | 14.2 |
| Seattle | 22.8 | 13.4 |
| Dallas | 14.1 | 11.0 |
| Fort Worth | 13.3 | 9.2 |
| Houston | 14.1 | 11.6 |
| Los Angeles | 20.1 | 15.1 |
| Miami | 28.5 | 19.6 |
| Atlanta | 28.7 | 14.3 |
| Washington, D.C. | 44.2 | 18.5 |

public-transportation map (p. 326). The 10 percent isopleth of automobile unavailability lies well inside the 10 percent isopleth for public-transit trips to work. Thus some households in suburban areas own cars they do not use for commuting.

**Philadelphia.** Three-fourths of the SMSA households without automobiles are located in Philadelphia. Secondary areas where unavailability is high are scattered throughout the region at the sites of small cities and towns. As in the New York region, the degree to

*Note:* All data are from the 1970 Censuses of Population and Housing unless otherwise indicated. Therefore the present tense refers to 1970 except for income data which are from 1969. Cartographic conventions are explained in Chapter 1. County names and other locational information are shown on the SMSA map at the beginning of each city chapter (6-25) and on the DUS map of mobile homes near the beginning of each city chapter.

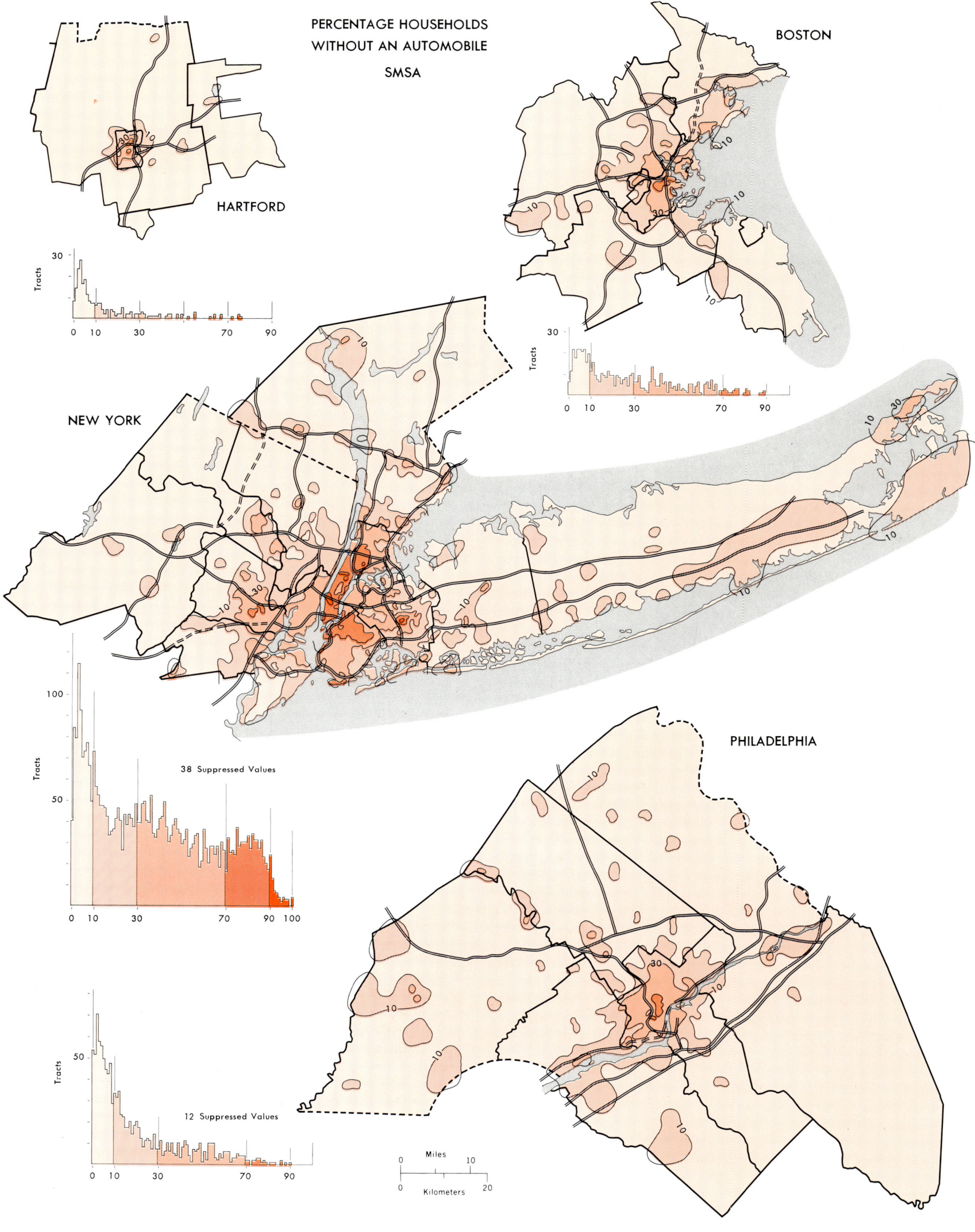

*Transportation and Communication: Households without Automobiles*

PERCENTAGE HOUSEHOLDS
WITHOUT AN AUTOMOBILE
SMSA

HARTFORD

BOSTON

NEW YORK

38 Suppressed Values

PHILADELPHIA

12 Suppressed Values

334

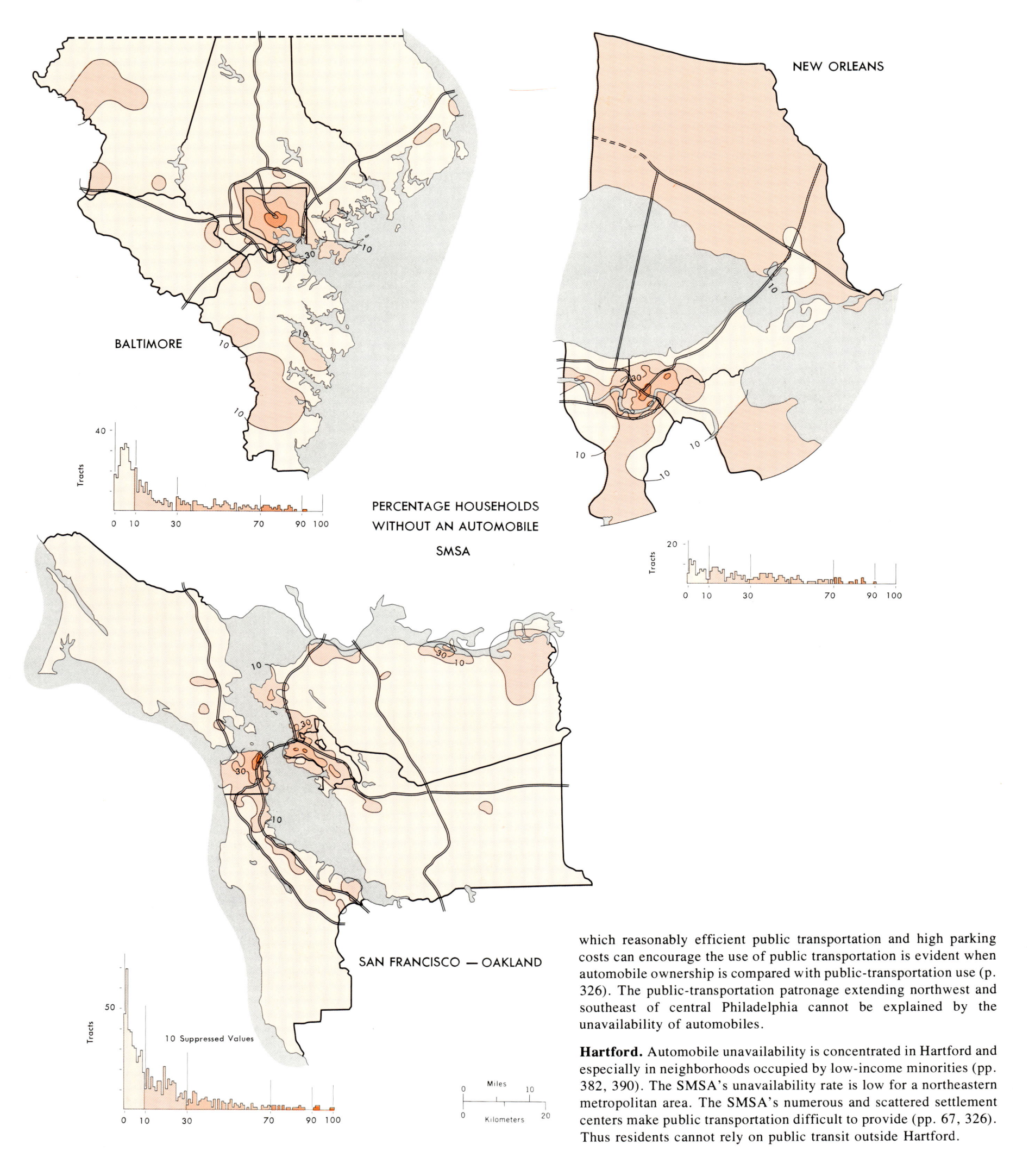

## Transportation and Communication: Households without Automobiles

BALTIMORE

NEW ORLEANS

PERCENTAGE HOUSEHOLDS
WITHOUT AN AUTOMOBILE
SMSA

SAN FRANCISCO — OAKLAND

10 Suppressed Values

which reasonably efficient public transportation and high parking costs can encourage the use of public transportation is evident when automobile ownership is compared with public-transportation use (p. 326). The public-transportation patronage extending northwest and southeast of central Philadelphia cannot be explained by the unavailability of automobiles.

**Hartford.** Automobile unavailability is concentrated in Hartford and especially in neighborhoods occupied by low-income minorities (pp. 382, 390). The SMSA's unavailability rate is low for a northeastern metropolitan area. The SMSA's numerous and scattered settlement centers make public transportation difficult to provide (pp. 67, 326). Thus residents cannot rely on public transit outside Hartford.

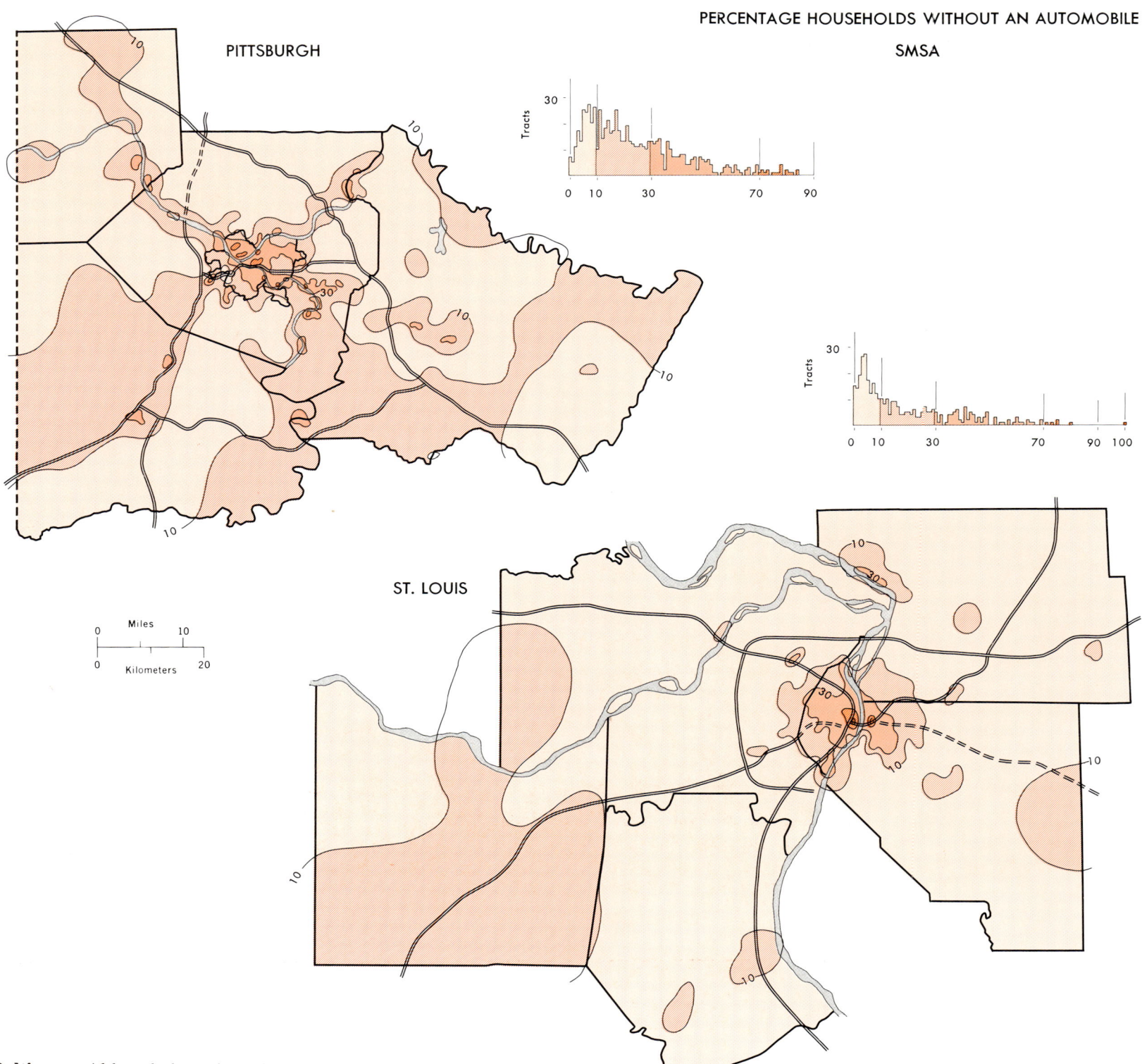

*Transportation and Communication: Households without Automobiles*

PERCENTAGE HOUSEHOLDS WITHOUT AN AUTOMOBILE
SMSA

**Baltimore.** Although throughout the SMSA there are scattered tracts where automobile unavailability exceeds 10 percent, 81.8 percent of the SMSA households without automobiles are located in Baltimore, where unavailability is highest in the city's predominantly black neighborhoods (p. 383).

**New Orleans.** Automobile unavailability is high throughout the settled portions of New Orleans except for the affluent neighborhoods in the northern and southwestern parts of the city. Many more central-city than suburban households lack cars, for New Orleans contains 84.6 percent of the SMSA households without cars.

**San Francisco-Oakland.** Automobile unavailability is higher (39.6 percent) in San Francisco than it is in Oakland (26.7 percent). Areas where more than 10 percent of households are without automobiles are scattered in settlement centers in the Bay Area, but households without cars outside San Francisco and Oakland aggregate only 26.5 percent of all SMSA households without automobiles. San Francisco contains 55.7 percent of the SMSA households without automobiles, and Oakland contains 17.6 percent.

**Pittsburgh.** High rates of automobile unavailability are usually a central-city phenomenon, as indeed they are in Pittsburgh, where over a third of the households lack cars. But automobile unavailability is also evident in small towns and rural areas; 56.8 percent of SMSA households without automobiles are located outside Pittsburgh.

**St. Louis.** Most households without automobiles are located in St. Louis and East St. Louis, Illinois. The area encompassed by the 10 percent unavailability isopleth is larger than that enclosed by the 10 percent public-transportation isopleth (p. 328). Immobility may therefore be more serious in the inner suburbs of St. Louis than in similar parts of other SMSAs.

**Cleveland.** The area inside the 30 percent unavailability isopleth is considerably larger than the area inside the 30 percent public-transportation isopleth (p. 329), suggesting that immobility may be an

336

*Transportation and Communication: Households without Automobiles*

PERCENTAGE HOUSEHOLDS WITHOUT AN AUTOMOBILE
SMSA

CHICAGO

CLEVELAND

DETROIT

especially serious problem in Cleveland's black community (p. 385). Most (70.7 percent) of the SMSA households without automobiles are located in Cleveland.

**Chicago.** High population density (p. 313), consequent higher costs of storage, and a large, low-income minority population (pp. 385, 383) combine to make an automobile too dear for many central-city households. Cars are scarce in scattered outlying towns and cities such as Elgin and Aurora in Kane County, but 84.2 percent of the SMSA households without automobiles are located in Chicago. As in other large, high-density cities, public transportation use (p. 329) extends outward into areas where automobiles are common.

**Detroit.** Automobile unavailability is comparatively low in Detroit and the region. The outlying areas where unavailability exceeds 10 percent are town centers where goods and services are within walking distance.

**Minneapolis-St. Paul.** Only 15.3 percent of the SMSA households without an automobile lie outside the two cities. Automobile unavailability, like public-transportation use (p. 330), corresponds closely to the Minneapolis and St. Paul city limits. In Minneapolis, 27.2 percent of the households lack automobiles, and in St. Paul the proportion is 22.2 percent.

**Seattle.** Automobile unavailability peaks in Seattle's downtown area

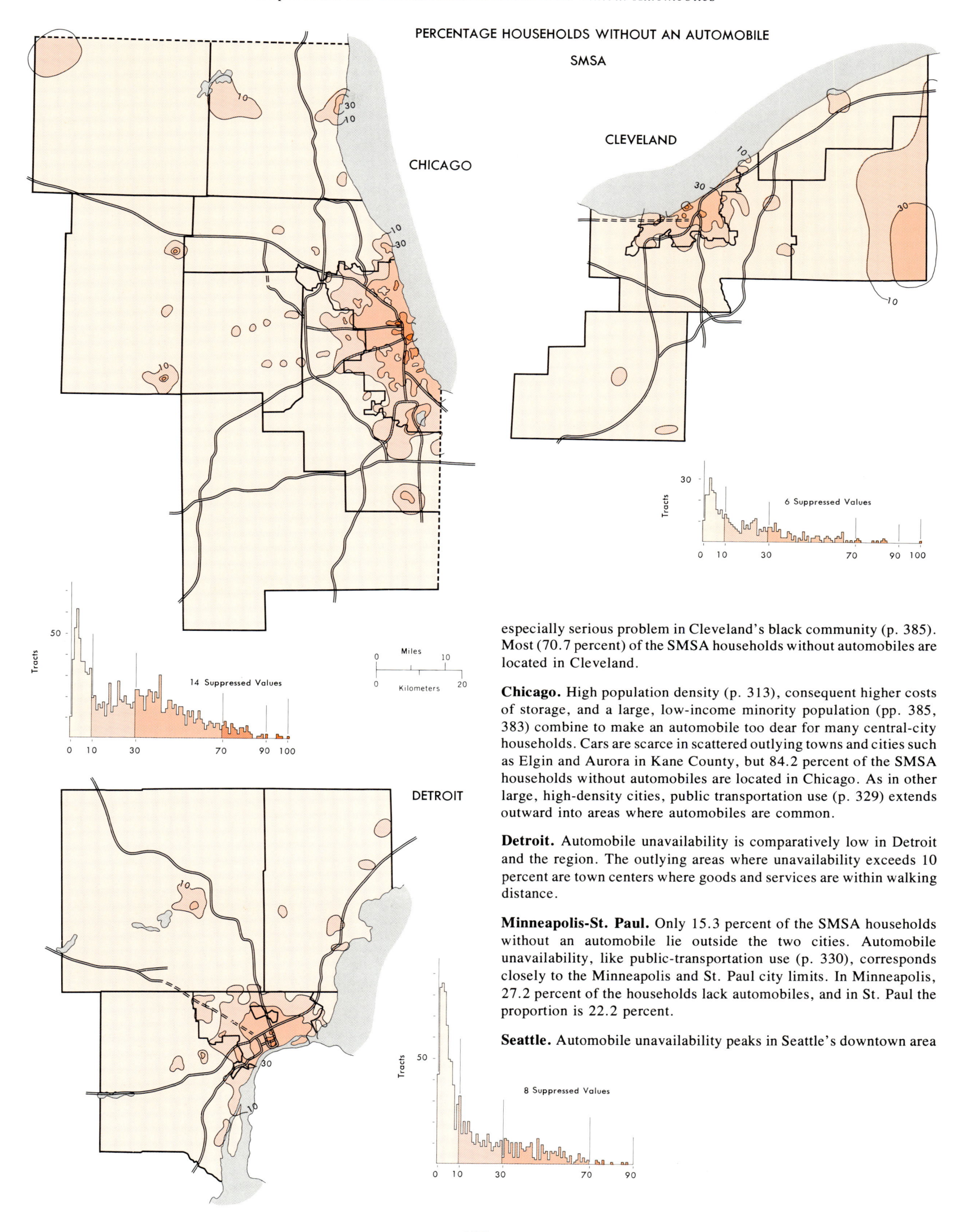

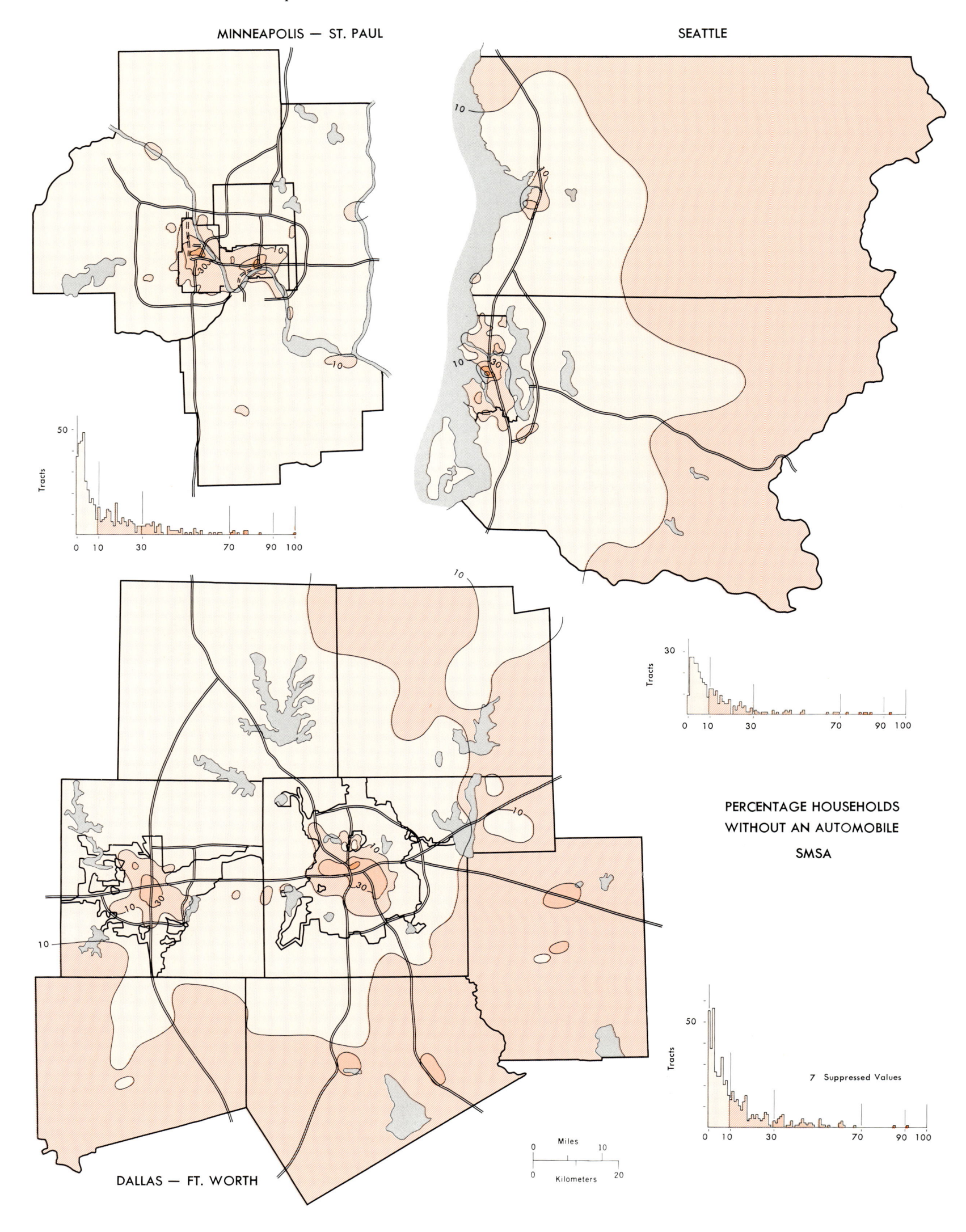

*Transportation and Communication: Households without Automobiles*

MINNEAPOLIS — ST. PAUL

SEATTLE

DALLAS — FT. WORTH

PERCENTAGE HOUSEHOLDS
WITHOUT AN AUTOMOBILE
SMSA

7 Suppressed Values

*Transportation and Communication: Households without Automobiles*

HOUSTON

PERCENTAGE HOUSEHOLDS WITHOUT AN AUTOMOBILE
SMSA

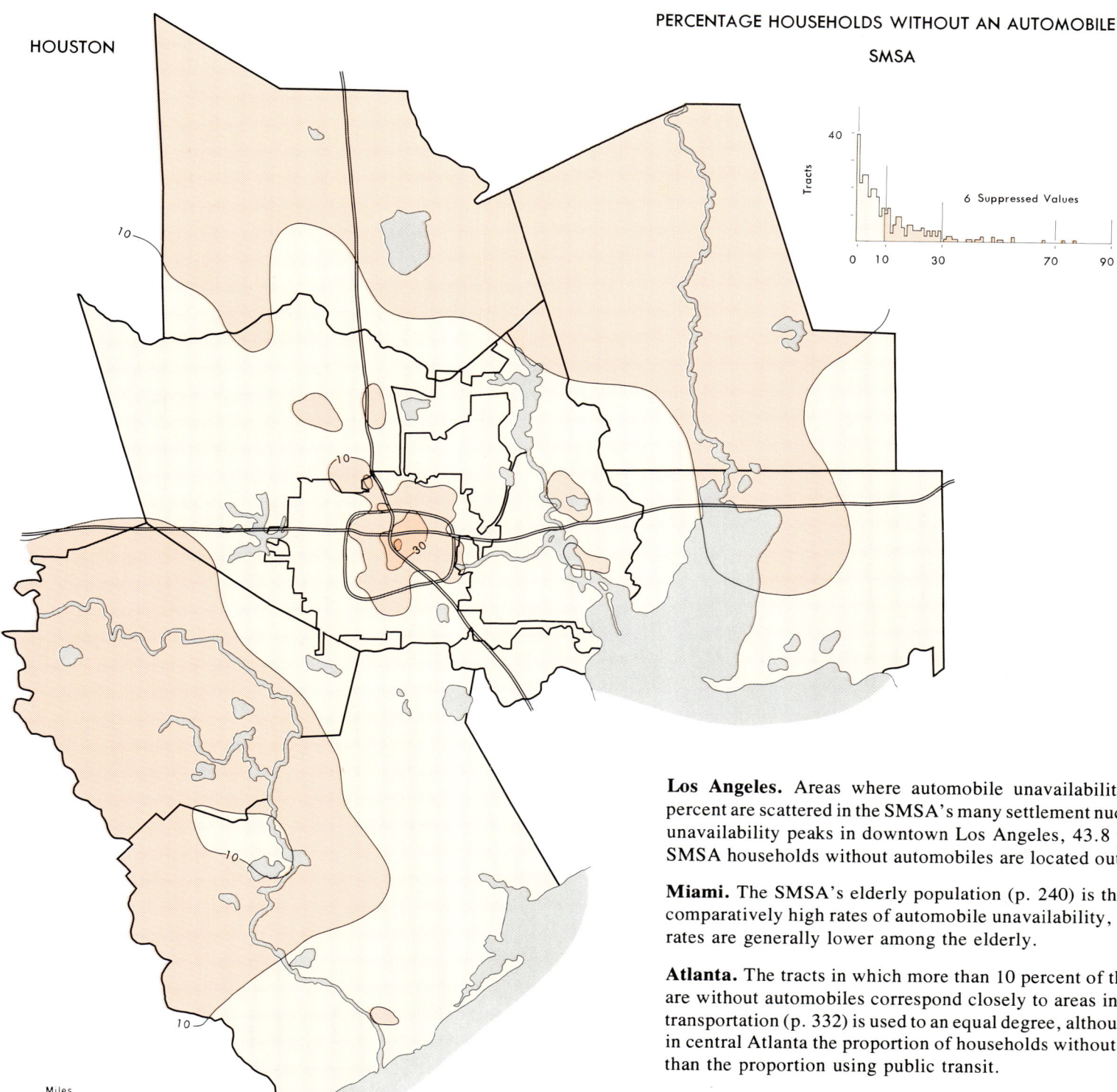

and drops sharply away from the Central Business District. The tracts where unavailability exceeds 30 percent in west-central Snohomish County are located in Everett.

**Dallas-Fort Worth.** The lowest rates of automobile unavailability among the 20 regions mapped in the atlas occur in the Texas cities, especially in Fort Worth. Although unavailability is highest in the central cities and especially disproportionate to public-transit use (p. 330) in Fort Worth, a fourth of each SMSA's households without automobiles are located outside the central cities.

**Houston.** Although most Houston households have automobiles, those that do not may be especially immobile because of the ineffective public transportation in the city (p. 331). The same can be said of the households without cars in the sparsely populated rural areas on the north and southwest.

**Los Angeles.** Areas where automobile unavailability exceeds 10 percent are scattered in the SMSA's many settlement nuclei. Although unavailability peaks in downtown Los Angeles, 43.8 percent of the SMSA households without automobiles are located outside the city.

**Miami.** The SMSA's elderly population (p. 240) is the cause of the comparatively high rates of automobile unavailability, for ownership rates are generally lower among the elderly.

**Atlanta.** The tracts in which more than 10 percent of the households are without automobiles correspond closely to areas in which public transportation (p. 332) is used to an equal degree, although in any tract in central Atlanta the proportion of households without a car is larger than the proportion using public transit.

**Washington, D.C.** Automobile unavailability is especially high in the District of Columbia, although the 10 percent isopleth extends into the Virginia and Maryland suburbs to match the 10 percent isopleth of public-transit use for trips to work (p. 332). Households without automobiles that are located outside the District are 30.2 percent of the SMSA total.

---

The relations between public-transit use and households without automobiles are circularly causal. The same conditions of high density and low incomes that prevent people from owning cars encourage satisfactory public transportation. At the same time, households without automobiles that must have access to a metropolitan area's goods and services—especially the elderly—have few options except to reside where public transportation is available. To a large degree, public transportation serves a captive market. Serious transporation problems result when needs for mobility and public-transportation service are out of geographical phase, and such imbalances are most serious in outlying areas where both automobile unavailability and public-transit use are low.

*Transportation and Communication: Households without Automobiles*

MIAMI

LOS ANGELES

PERCENTAGE HOUSEHOLDS
WITHOUT AN AUTOMOBILE

SMSA

WASHINGTON, D.C.

ATLANTA

*Transportation and Communication*

CHAPTER 36

# Households without Telephones

In the 1970 Census all household heads were asked "Is there a telephone on which people in your living quarters can be called?" Responses to the question are mapped in this chapter as the percentage of each tract's households that have no telephone. The maps probably underestimate the proportion of households without telephones *in* their living quarters, for even a pay station shared by several households might be counted by all the living units that share it.

The telephone has now become widely used. In 1950, 38 percent of the nation's households were without telephones, and in 1960, 22 percent still lacked service. Only 13 percent of the nation's households are now without telephone service. Many of these households are located in sparsely populated rural areas. Households lacking telephones constitute 10.9 percent of all households in Standard Metropolitan Statistical Areas (SMSA). In the 20 metropolitan regions mapped in the atlas, 10.6 percent of the households cannot be reached by telephone (see accompanying tabulation).

Telephone service has become a way of life if not a necessity of life for most Americans. Coordinating business and family activities would be impossible without it. The social impact of the telephone is poorly understood, and little is known about the ways residential subscribers use telephones. Thus it is difficult to specify the disadvantages of not having a telephone. Surprising proportions of households in some central cities and metropolitan areas do not have telephones.

Households without telephone service are more prominent in central cities than in SMSAs as a whole. Of all the households without telephones in the 24 SMSAs comprising the 20 regions mapped here, 67 percent are located in the central cities of the SMSAs.

**Boston.** Households without telephone service are clustered in the core of the SMSA. Overall, telephone unavailability in Boston is low compared with other northeastern SMSAs. Outlying areas where households lacking telephones exceed 10 percent are the centers of small cities and towns such as Waltham, on the west, and Lynn, to the north.

**New York-Northern New Jersey.** Households without telephone service are unusually frequent in the region's central cities and unusually rare in suburban areas, suggesting that telephone service is a necessity outside the region's core; only 9.3 percent of the New York SMSA's households outside New York City lack telephones. In New York City and the other central cities, high proportions of households without telephones are in areas populated by low-income minority groups (pp. 382, 390).

*Note:* All data are from the 1970 Census of Population and Housing unless otherwise indicated. Therefore the present tense refers to 1970 except for income data which are from 1969. Cartographic conventions are explained in Chapter 1. County names and other locational information are shown on the SMSA map at the beginning of each city chapter (6-25) and on the DUS map of mobile homes near the beginning of each city chapter.

**Philadelphia.** Places where households lacking telephones exceed 10 percent of tract totals are scattered in rural areas on the SMSA periphery and in small cities. The core area where over 30 percent of the households have no telephone corresponds roughly with the SMSA's lowest income region (p. 59). Although the cost of telephone service is moderate, service is evidently not worth the price below an indeterminate income threshold.

**Hartford.** Only 3,550 (2.3 percent) of the 108,750 SMSA households located outside the city of Hartford lack telephones. Few SMSA

Percentage of Households without Telephone Service

| Region | Central City(ies) | Entire SMSA |
|---|---|---|
| Boston | 15.7 | 7.5 |
| New York | 17.9 | 14.4 |
| Jersey City | 22.9 | 19.4 |
| Newark | 29.9 | 10.9 |
| Paterson-Clifton-Passaic | 22.4 | 6.8 |
| Philadelphia | 14.3 | 9.5 |
| Hartford | 20.1 | 7.1 |
| Baltimore | 19.0 | 12.2 |
| New Orleans | 15.8 | 13.1 |
| San Francisco-Oakland | 12.9 | 8.8 |
| Pittsburgh | 8.8 | 5.9 |
| St. Louis | 16.5 | 10.4 |
| Cleveland | 13.6 | 7.2 |
| Chicago | 16.2 | 10.6 |
| Detroit | 12.8 | 7.8 |
| Minneapolis-St. Paul | 6.6 | 4.2 |
| Seattle | 9.6 | 8.3 |
| Dallas | 13.7 | 13.6 |
| Fort Worth | 13.6 | 11.5 |
| Houston | 13.9 | 13.8 |
| Los Angeles | 12.1 | 10.9 |
| Miami | 23.6 | 14.6 |
| Atlanta | 17.1 | 10.9 |
| Washington, D.C. | 12.5 | 7.5 |

suburbanites lack the means or desire for telephone service. Within Hartford, households without telephones cluster near the Central Business District (CBD) and in nearby areas occupied by minority groups (pp. 390, 398).

**Baltimore.** Telephone unavailability is low in suburban areas; from there it increases inward toward the city center and outward toward the SMSA periphery. Although areas on the periphery where unavailability exceeds 10 percent are large, they are sparsely populated; 72.2 percent of the SMSA households lacking telephone service are located in Baltimore.

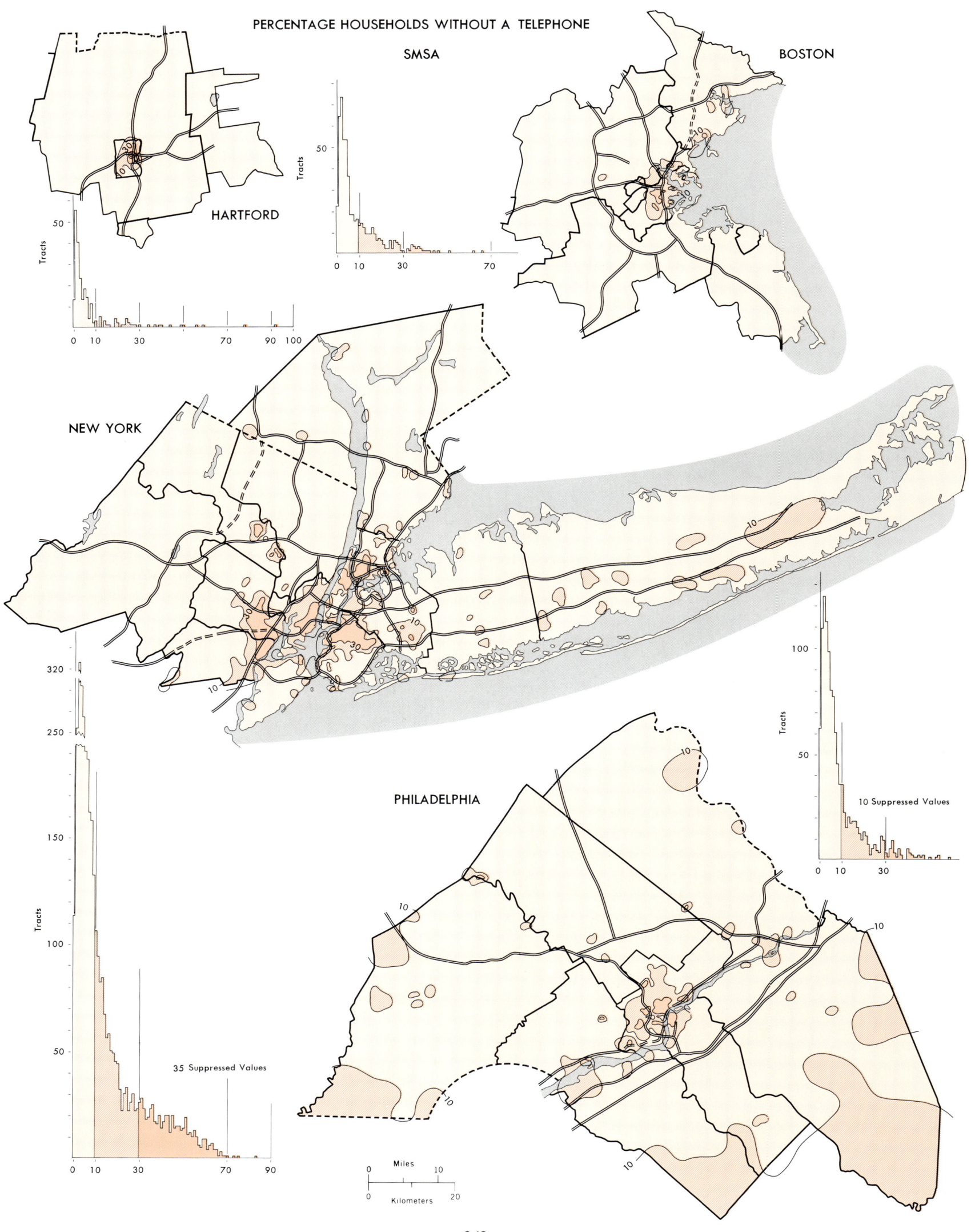

*Transportation and Communication: Households without Telephones*

PERCENTAGE HOUSEHOLDS WITHOUT A TELEPHONE

SMSA

HARTFORD

BOSTON

NEW YORK

PHILADELPHIA

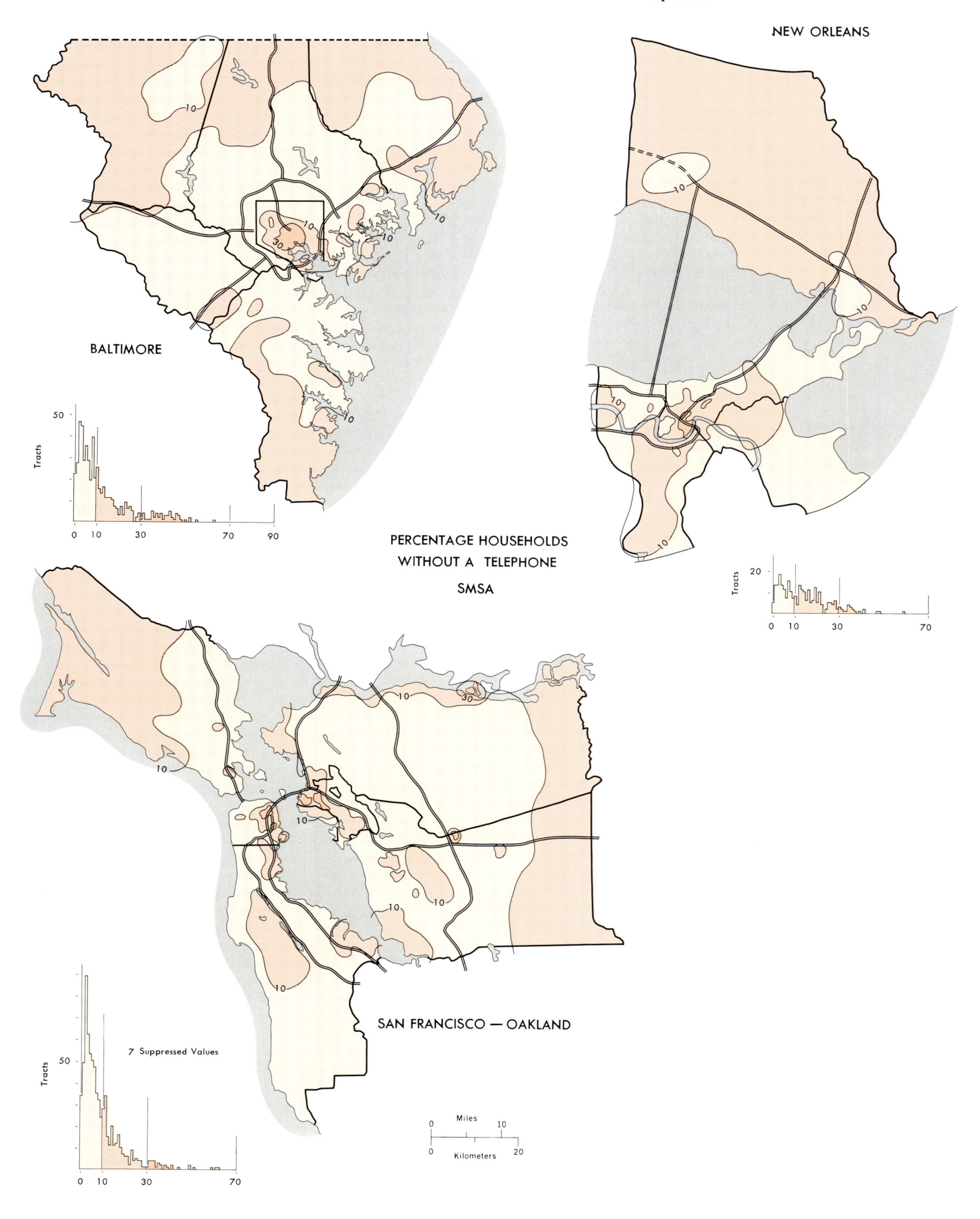

*Transportation and Communication: Households without Telephones*

BALTIMORE

NEW ORLEANS

PERCENTAGE HOUSEHOLDS
WITHOUT A TELEPHONE
SMSA

SAN FRANCISCO — OAKLAND

7 Suppressed Values

343

*Transportation and Communication: Households without Telephones*

PERCENTAGE HOUSEHOLDS WITHOUT A TELEPHONE
SMSA

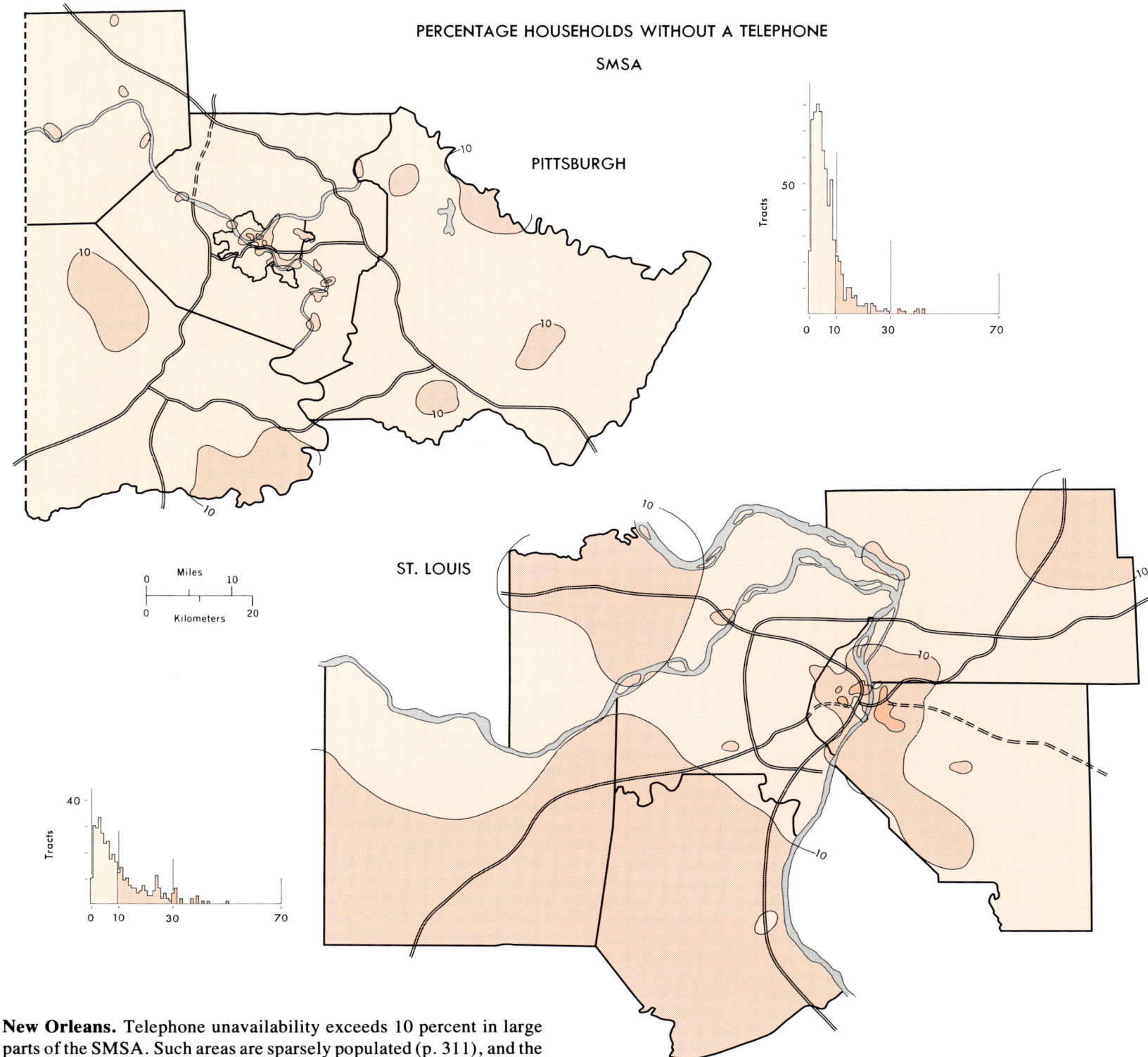

**New Orleans.** Telephone unavailability exceeds 10 percent in large parts of the SMSA. Such areas are sparsely populated (p. 311), and the proportion of SMSA households lacking telephone service within them is low (27.8) relative to the areas. But the problems of being without telephone service may be more serious in rural areas than they are in central cities, for neighbors and opportunities for personal communication are more dispersed.

**San Francisco-Oakland.** A comparatively low (58.7 percent) proportion of the SMSA households lacking telephone service are located in the two central cities. The rest are located in the SMSA's rural areas and small towns. Areas where unavailability exceeds 10 percent correspond in some instances to places occupied by low-income minority (pp. 383, 391) groups.

**Pittsburgh.** An unusually low proportion of Pittsburgh's households are without telephone service. Of the 44,900 households without service in the SMSA, only 15,700 (35 percent) are located in the central city. The remainder are concentrated in the small cities and towns in the region's river valleys and are scattered in predominantly rural areas.

**St. Louis.** Over half (53.5 percent) of the SMSA households without telephones are located outside the city of St. Louis. Telephone unavailability is especially widespread in the more rural parts of the SMSA, although the areas in Illinois occupied by people with low incomes (p. 123) have high rates of unavailability.

**Cleveland.** Most (71.1 percent) of the SMSA households without telephones are concentrated in Cleveland, where unavailability is highest in predominantly black neighborhoods (p. 385). The area where telephone and automobile (p. 337) unavailability is high on the east side of the SMSA contains a large poverty population (p. 417).

**Chicago.** The bulk (79.5 percent) of the SMSA households without telephones are located in Chicago. Proportions of households without telephones are considerably higher in the city's west-side black ghetto and nearby Spanish-American areas (pp. 385, 393) than they are in the

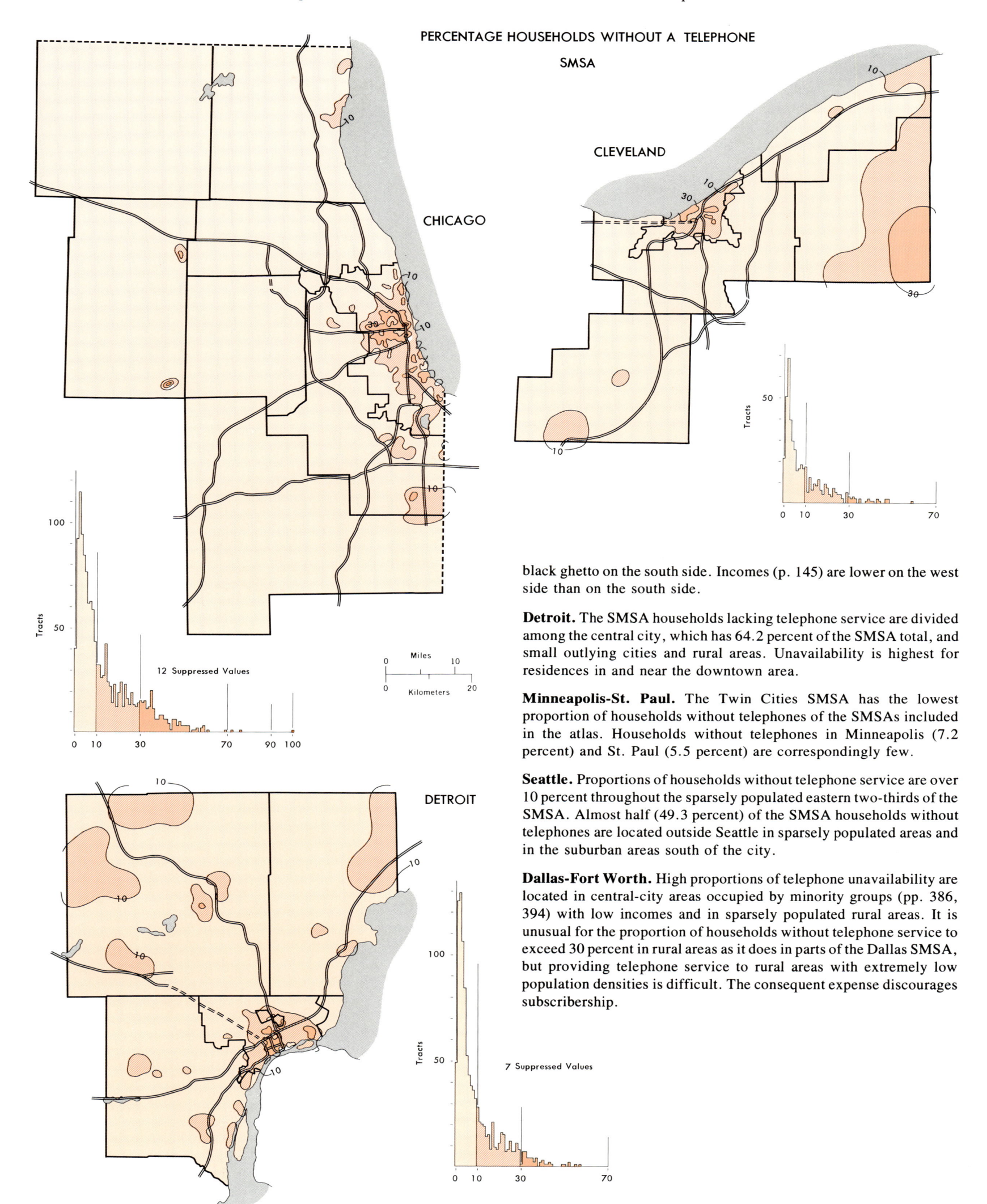

*Transportation and Communication: Households without Telephones*

PERCENTAGE HOUSEHOLDS WITHOUT A TELEPHONE
SMSA

black ghetto on the south side. Incomes (p. 145) are lower on the west side than on the south side.

**Detroit.** The SMSA households lacking telephone service are divided among the central city, which has 64.2 percent of the SMSA total, and small outlying cities and rural areas. Unavailability is highest for residences in and near the downtown area.

**Minneapolis-St. Paul.** The Twin Cities SMSA has the lowest proportion of households without telephones of the SMSAs included in the atlas. Households without telephones in Minneapolis (7.2 percent) and St. Paul (5.5 percent) are correspondingly few.

**Seattle.** Proportions of households without telephone service are over 10 percent throughout the sparsely populated eastern two-thirds of the SMSA. Almost half (49.3 percent) of the SMSA households without telephones are located outside Seattle in sparsely populated areas and in the suburban areas south of the city.

**Dallas-Fort Worth.** High proportions of telephone unavailability are located in central-city areas occupied by minority groups (pp. 386, 394) with low incomes and in sparsely populated rural areas. It is unusual for the proportion of households without telephone service to exceed 30 percent in rural areas as it does in parts of the Dallas SMSA, but providing telephone service to rural areas with extremely low population densities is difficult. The consequent expense discourages subscribership.

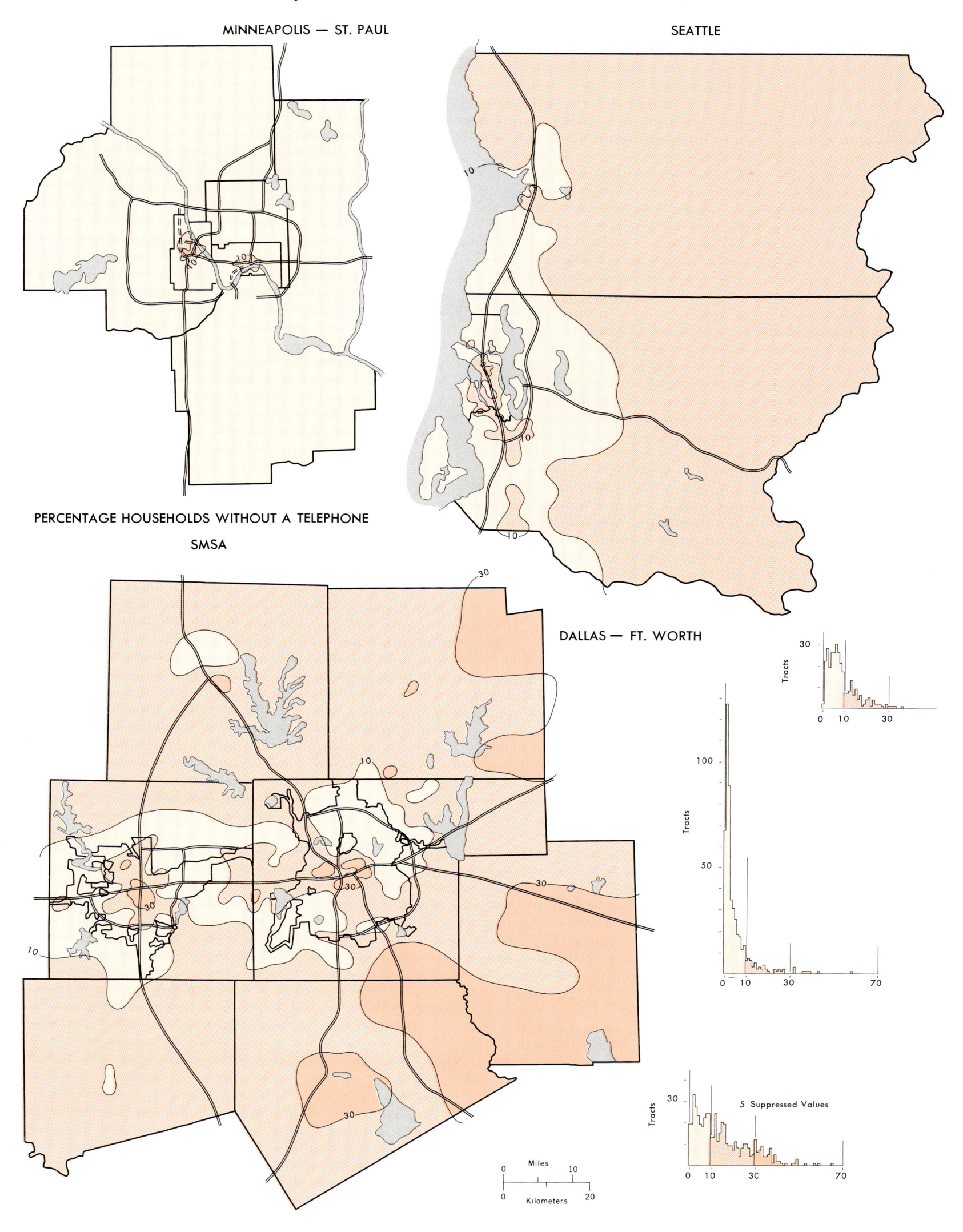

*Transportation and Communication: Households without Telephones*

MINNEAPOLIS — ST. PAUL

SEATTLE

PERCENTAGE HOUSEHOLDS WITHOUT A TELEPHONE
SMSA

DALLAS — FT. WORTH

5 Suppressed Values

346

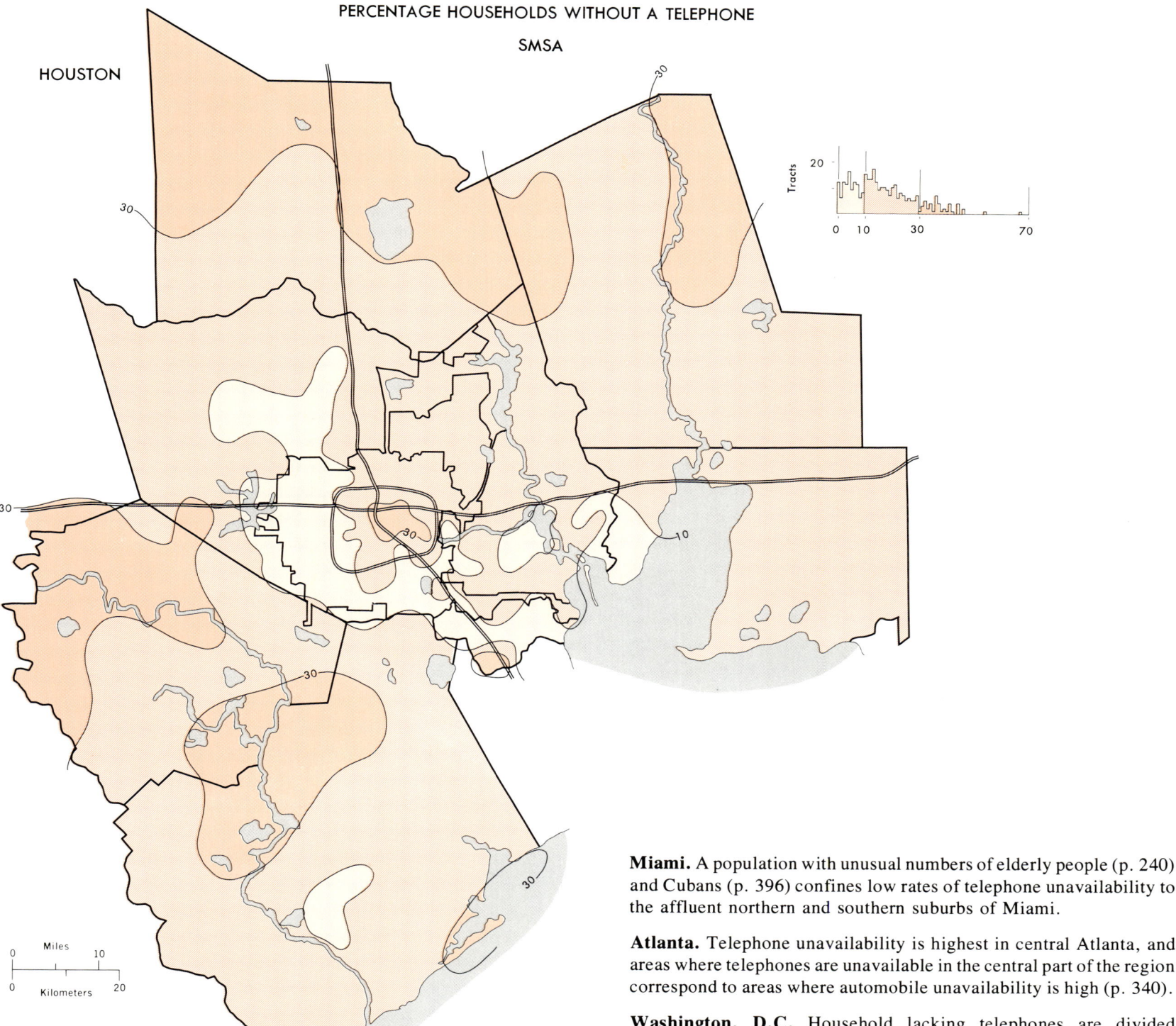

*Transportation and Communication: Households without Telephones*

PERCENTAGE HOUSEHOLDS WITHOUT A TELEPHONE

SMSA

HOUSTON

**Houston.** Households lacking telephones are concentrated in central Houston, although, as in Dallas-Fort Worth, proportions on the sparsely settled SMSA periphery are also high. Just over a third (35.2 percent) of the SMSA households without telephone service are located outside Houston. High proportions of telephone unavailability in Houston occur in areas occupied by Spanish-Americans (p. 395).

**Los Angeles.** Neighborhoods occupied by Spanish-Americans (p. 396) have the highest proportions of households without telephone service. Areas where more than 10 percent of tract households lack telephone service sprawl throughout the center of the region without regard to municipal boundaries. Because unavailability is high throughout the central area and in the sparsely populated north, over half (53.2 percent) of the SMSA households without telephones lie outside the city of Los Angeles.

**Miami.** A population with unusual numbers of elderly people (p. 240) and Cubans (p. 396) confines low rates of telephone unavailability to the affluent northern and southern suburbs of Miami.

**Atlanta.** Telephone unavailability is highest in central Atlanta, and areas where telephones are unavailable in the central part of the region correspond to areas where automobile unavailability is high (p. 340).

**Washington, D.C.** Household lacking telephones are divided between low-income (p. 262) central-city and inner-suburban areas, and outlying rural areas; 49.3 percent of the SMSA households without telephone service are located outside the District of Columbia.

---

In most places, households without telephones are located in low-income areas of central cities or in outlying rural parts of SMSAs. Central-city areas where telephone unavailability is high often correspond closely to areas where automobile unavailability is high (Chapter 35). Such is not true on the SMSA peripheries, where telephone unavailability is often higher than automobile unavailability, especially in the western and southern SMSAs with low population densities. Evidently, personal mobility is more important than interpersonal communication in sparsely populated areas. The absolute numbers of households lacking telephone service in sparsely populated areas is small, but the comparative disadvantages the households experience can be serious. The numerous opportunities for face-to-face contact in central-city areas where telephone unavailability is high are not available on the metropolitan periphery.

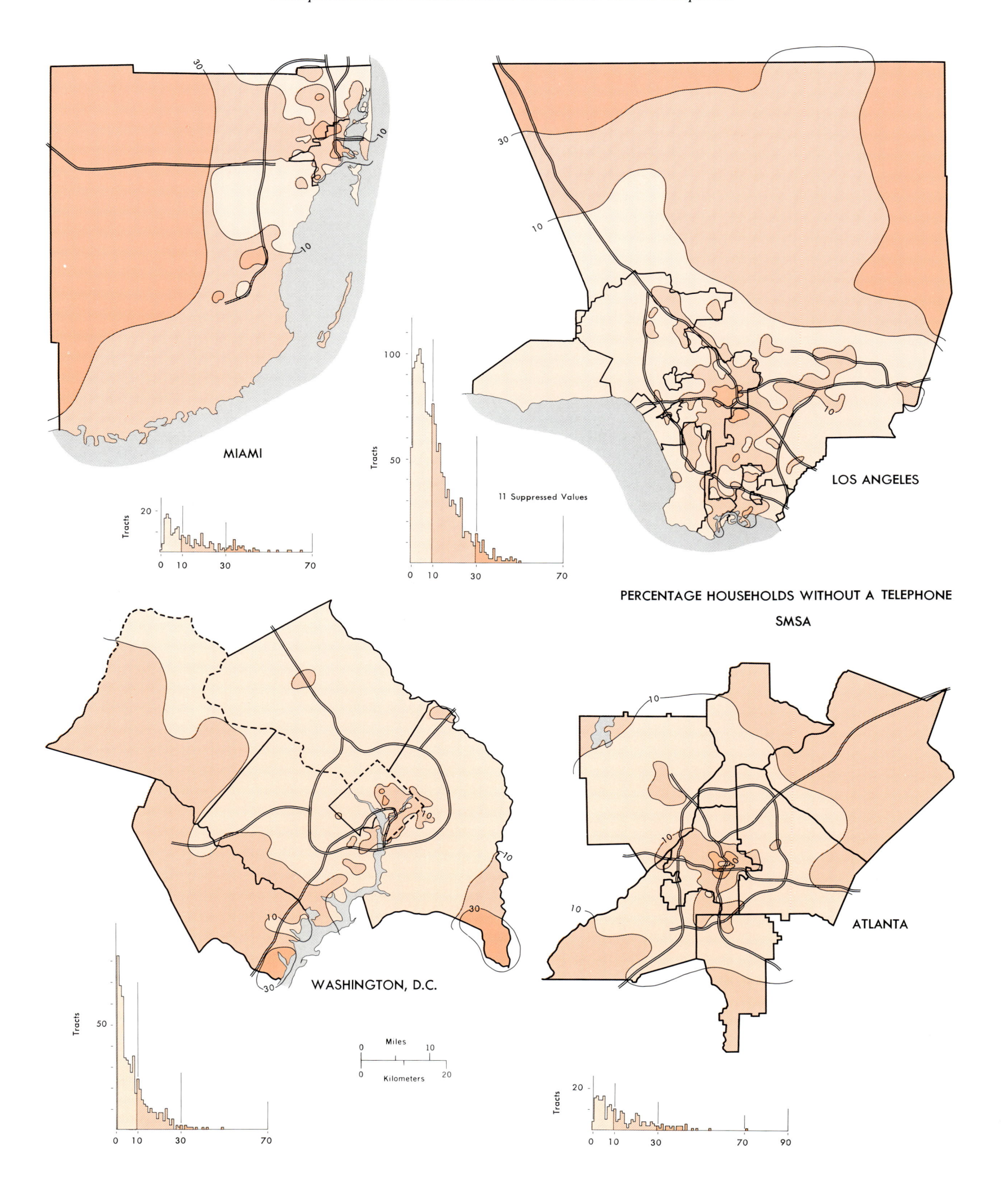

*Transportation and Communication: Households without Telephones*

MIAMI

LOS ANGELES

PERCENTAGE HOUSEHOLDS WITHOUT A TELEPHONE
SMSA

WASHINGTON, D.C.

ATLANTA

348

*Metropolitan Growth*

CHAPTER 37

# Population Change, 1960-1970

The maps in this chapter show estimated changes from 1960 to 1970 in total population and population density by census tract. Each tract's 1970 population is divided by its 1960 population. A ratio of 1.0 results when the 1960 populations and 1970 populations are identical. Ratios of less than 1.0 indicate population decline during the decade, whereas ratios in excess of 1.0 result when tract population increased from 1960 to 1970. The ratios also indicate changes in population density. If a tract's ratio is 2.0, population density and population size doubled between the two Censuses (see accompanying tabulation).

The ratios mapped in the 24 Standard Metropolitan Statistical Areas (SMSAs) are estimates rather than precise calculations. Census tract boundaries changed greatly in some SMSAs from 1960 to 1970, and much estimating was necessary to produce maps for these areas. The general procedure was to try to make 1960 tracts comparable to 1970 tracts. When tract boundary changes had occurred between the two Censuses, 1960 populations were allocated to 1970 tracts on the basis of land area. That is, a 1960 tract split into two tracts in the 1970 Census would have its 1960 population divided proportional to the areas of the 1970 tracts. In places where wholesale revision of tract boundaries rather than simple splits occurred, the same procedure was followed. Given the generalization procedures described in Chapter 1 and the scale at which the maps are presented, they are reasonably accurate. But the assumption of uniform population density inherent in the estimating procedure described above may occasionally produce spurious results, especially in suburban and outlying areas. Where census tracts are large, the assumption that population density throughout the tract was identical in 1960 is often unwarranted.

There are significant variations in growth patterns of SMSAs and their central cities among the regions mapped, from the Pittsburgh SMSA, which just failed to hold its population size (it rounds to 1.0), to Houston, which is 40 percent larger than it was in 1960. Most central cities are declining, except those in the South and Southwest. Since most central cities are losing population in the face of SMSA growth, population increases are largest in suburban areas.

**Boston.** The city population decreased by 56,000 people during the last decade while the entire SMSA increased by 267,000. Population density increases are moderate throughout the SMSA except where new housing construction (p. 22) near freeways has drawn enough new residents to double and even triple tract populations.

*Note:* All data are from the 1970 Censuses of Population and Housing unless otherwise indicated. Therefore the present tense refers to 1970 except for income data which are from 1969. Cartographic conventions are explained in Chapter 1. County names and other locational information are shown on the SMSA map at the beginning of each city chapter (6-25) and on the DUS map of mobile homes near the beginning of each city chapter.

**New York-Northern New Jersey.** Population and density are generally declining in the region's central cities and increasing moderately outside them. Exceptions are the sharp increases evident in north-central Long Island, western New Jersey, Staten Island (Richmond County), and in small areas of New York City. As is often true of small central-city areas showing major population increases, New York City's tracts where population is increasing contain new public housing built in urban-renewal areas.

Population and Population Density Change, 1960 to 1970

| Region | Central City(ies) | Entire SMSA |
|---|---|---|
| Boston | 0.92 | 1.06 |
| New York | 1.01 | 1.08 |
| Jersey City | 0.94 | 0.99 |
| Newark | 0.94 | 1.10 |
| Paterson-Clifton-Passaic | 1.00 | 1.14 |
| Philadelphia | 0.97 | 1.11 |
| Hartford | 0.97 | 1.21 |
| Baltimore | 0.96 | 1.15 |
| New Orleans | 0.95 | 1.15 |
| San Francisco-Oakland | 0.97 | 1.17 |
| Pittsburgh | 0.86 | 1.00 |
| St. Louis | 0.83 | 1.12 |
| Cleveland | 0.86 | 1.08 |
| Chicago | 0.95 | 1.12 |
| Detroit | 0.91 | 1.12 |
| Minneapolis-St. Paul | 0.93 | 1.22 |
| Seattle | 0.95 | 1.29 |
| Dallas | 1.24 | 1.39 |
| Fort Worth | 1.10 | 1.33 |
| Houston | 1.31 | 1.40 |
| Los Angeles | 1.13 | 1.17 |
| Miami | 1.15 | 1.36 |
| Atlanta | 1.02 | 1.37 |
| Washington, D.C. | 0.99 | 1.38 |

**Philadelphia.** Population increases are largest in the outer suburbs of Philadelphia, especially in New Jersey which has begun to attract suburban growth as close-in areas suitable for development in Pennsylvania fill up. Philadelphia's population has decreased 52,500 since 1960, whereas the population of the entire SMSA increased by 480,000 people.

**Hartford.** The central city's relative and absolute decrease (4,200) since 1960 has been small. The SMSA's growth (116,000 people) has occurred at moderate levels throughout the region except in East Hartford, where population has increased fivefold in some tracts.

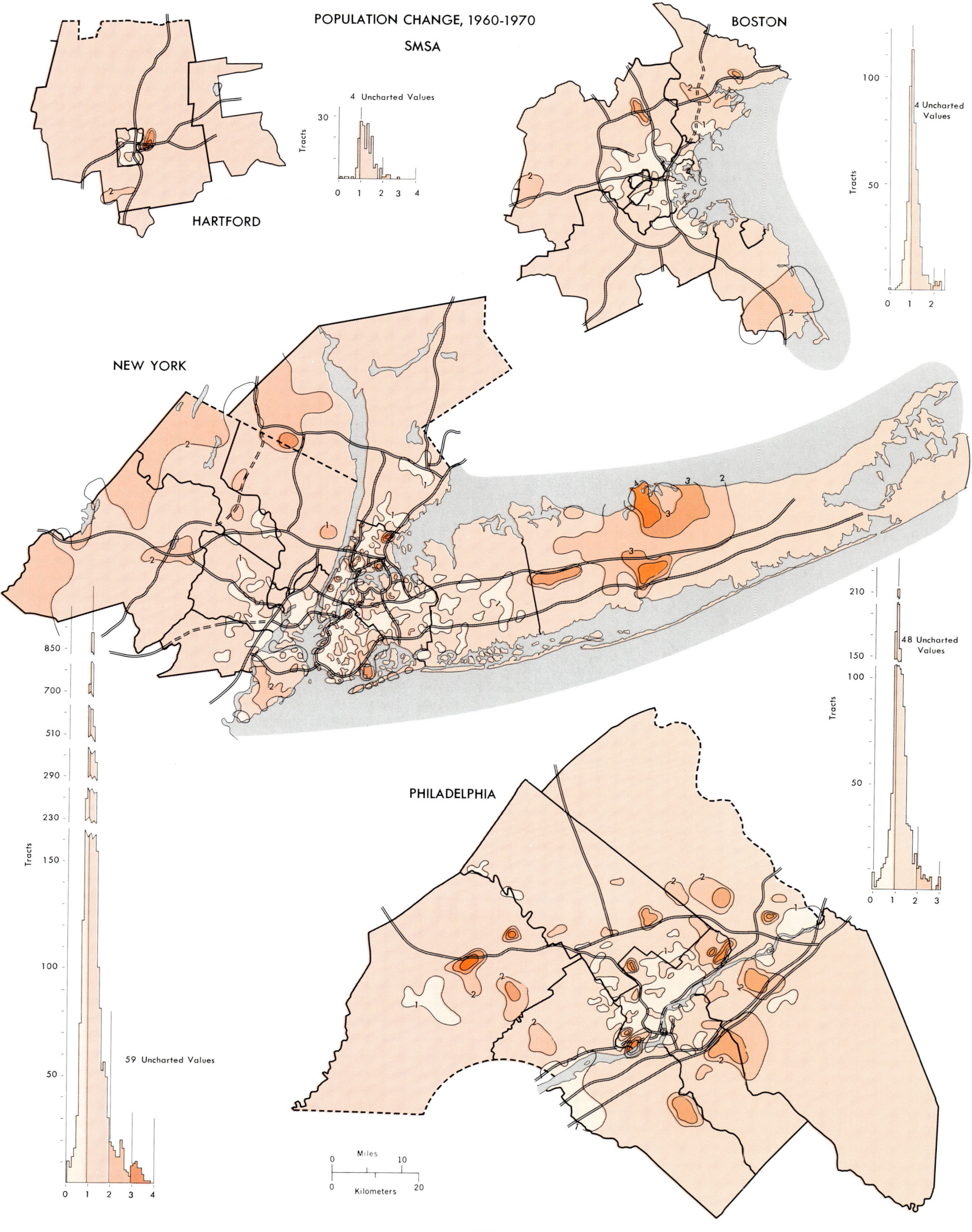

*Metropolitan Growth: Population Change*

POPULATION CHANGE, 1960-1970
SMSA

HARTFORD

BOSTON

NEW YORK

PHILADELPHIA

350

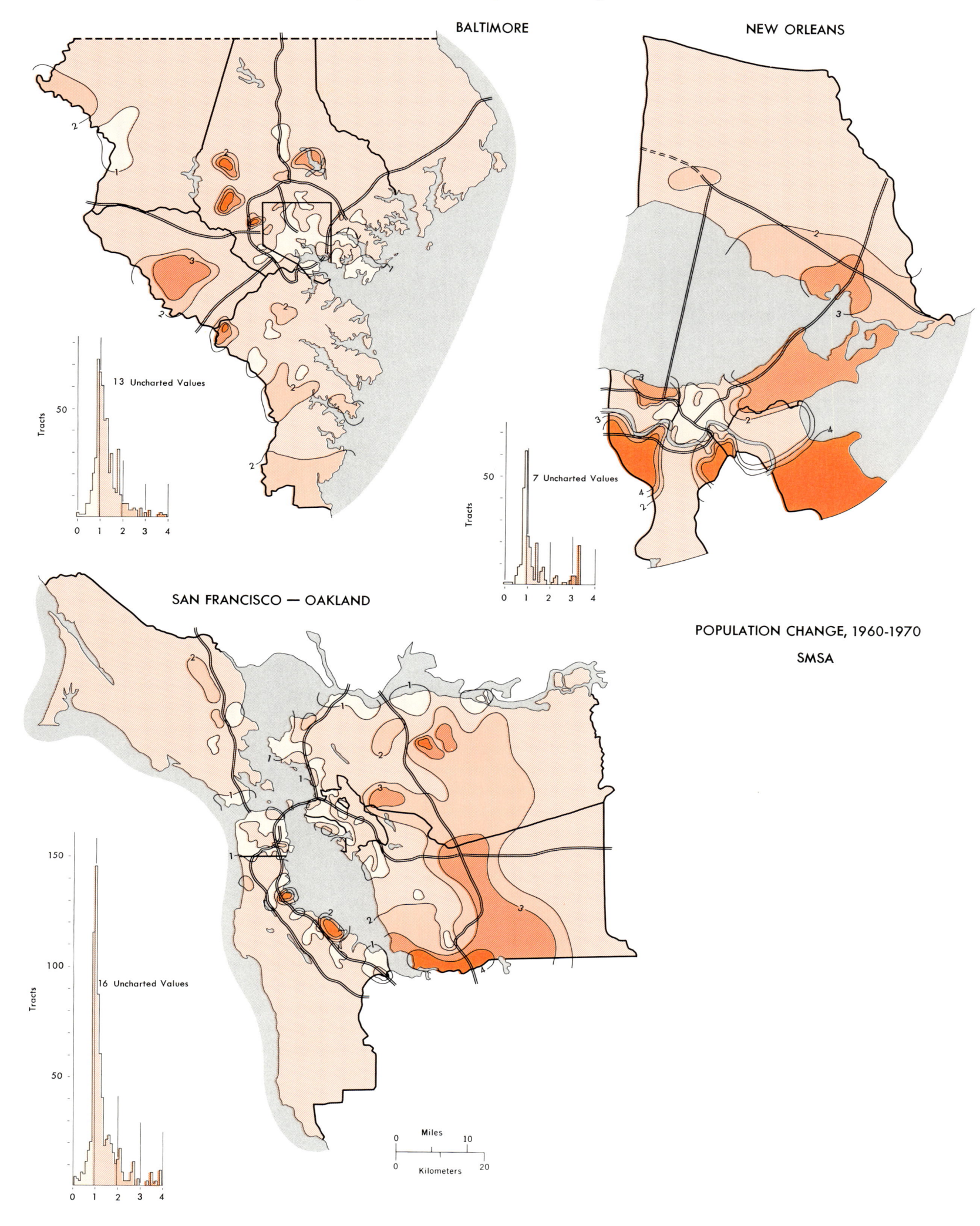

*Metropolitan Growth: Population Change*

BALTIMORE

NEW ORLEANS

SAN FRANCISCO — OAKLAND

POPULATION CHANGE, 1960-1970

SMSA

*Metropolitan Growth: Population Change*

POPULATION CHANGE, 1960-1970
SMSA

PITTSBURGH

ST. LOUIS

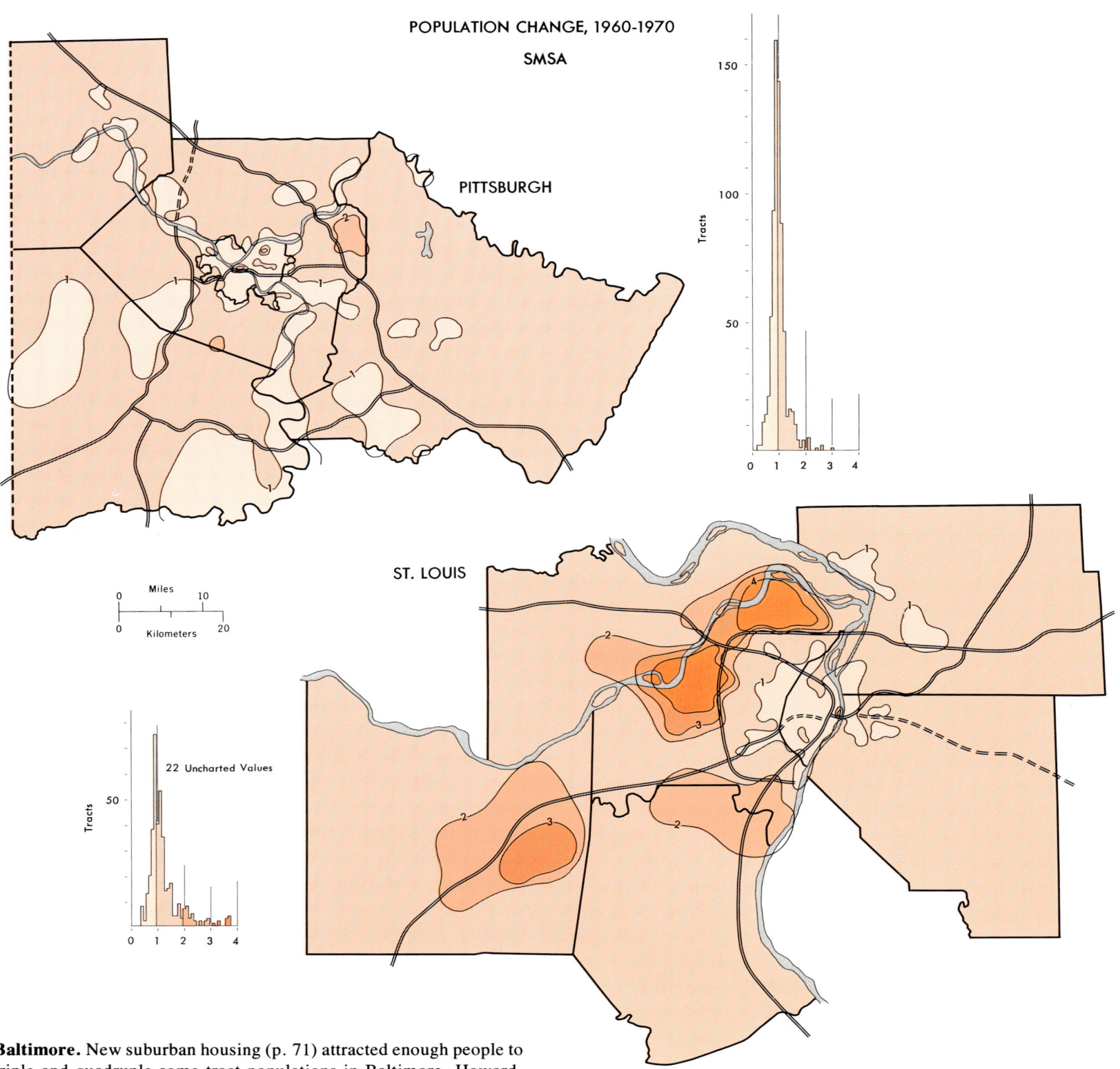

**Baltimore.** New suburban housing (p. 71) attracted enough people to triple and quadruple some tract populations in Baltimore, Howard, and Anne Arundel counties. The high growth areas in Howard and eastern Anne Arundel counties are as much tied to Washington D.C. as they are to Baltimore.

**New Orleans.** Some renewal areas near the downtown have lost as much as half their populations. Central-city population losses (p. 86) have been partially offset by gains in the northwest, northeast, and southeastern parts of the city, where new housing was still being built in the 1960s (p. 80). The completion of Interstate 10 across Lake Pontchartrain has produced a tripling of population in southeastern St. Tammany Parish.

**San Francisco-Oakland.** The region's most rapid population increases are occurring in central Alameda and Contra Costa counties and along the southwestern Bay shore. Growth along the Bay shore is larger in absolute numbers than that occurring east of the Bay because of the smaller 1960 base in central Alameda and Contra Costa counties. Absolute population declines in San Francisco (25,000) and Oakland (6,000) are small in the face of the SMSA's 460,000-person population increase.

**Pittsburgh.** The SMSA has the dubious distinction of being the only large metropolitan area in the nation showing a population decrease during the 1960s. The absolute decrease was small (4,070 people), but the selective out-migration of young people from the central city and the SMSA that produced it bodes ill for the region's future.

**St. Louis.** The population of St. Louis has declined by 128,000 people (17 percent) since 1960, the largest decrease occurring among the central cities mapped in the atlas. Areas with shrinking populations extend beyond the municipal boundary in several directions. Central-area losses are more than offset by rapid growth in western and northwestern suburban areas.

**Cleveland.** The central-city population has decreased 14 percent

*352*

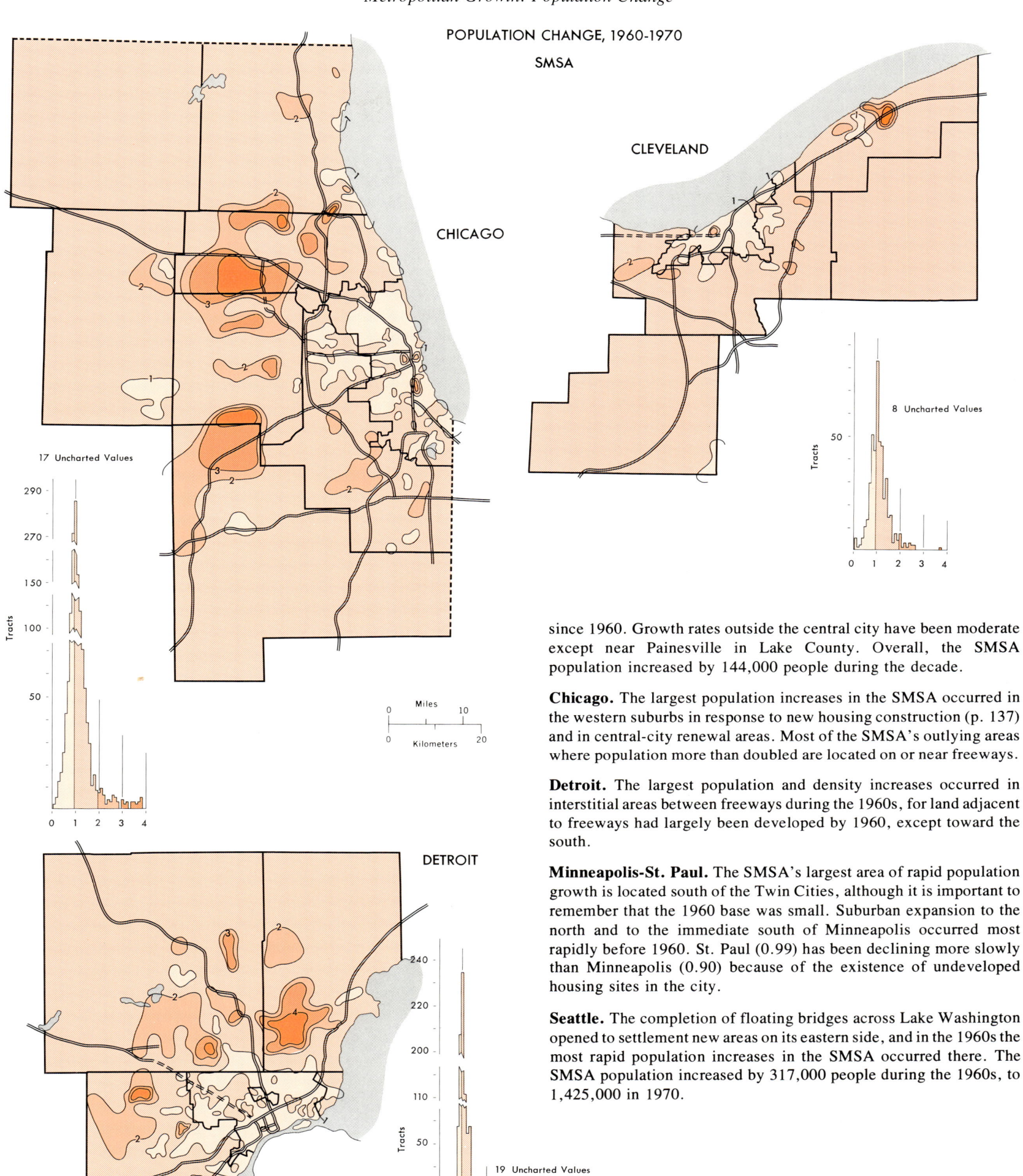

*Metropolitan Growth: Population Change*

POPULATION CHANGE, 1960-1970
SMSA

since 1960. Growth rates outside the central city have been moderate except near Painesville in Lake County. Overall, the SMSA population increased by 144,000 people during the decade.

**Chicago.** The largest population increases in the SMSA occurred in the western suburbs in response to new housing construction (p. 137) and in central-city renewal areas. Most of the SMSA's outlying areas where population more than doubled are located on or near freeways.

**Detroit.** The largest population and density increases occurred in interstitial areas between freeways during the 1960s, for land adjacent to freeways had largely been developed by 1960, except toward the south.

**Minneapolis-St. Paul.** The SMSA's largest area of rapid population growth is located south of the Twin Cities, although it is important to remember that the 1960 base was small. Suburban expansion to the north and to the immediate south of Minneapolis occurred most rapidly before 1960. St. Paul (0.99) has been declining more slowly than Minneapolis (0.90) because of the existence of undeveloped housing sites in the city.

**Seattle.** The completion of floating bridges across Lake Washington opened to settlement new areas on its eastern side, and in the 1960s the most rapid population increases in the SMSA occurred there. The SMSA population increased by 317,000 people during the 1960s, to 1,425,000 in 1970.

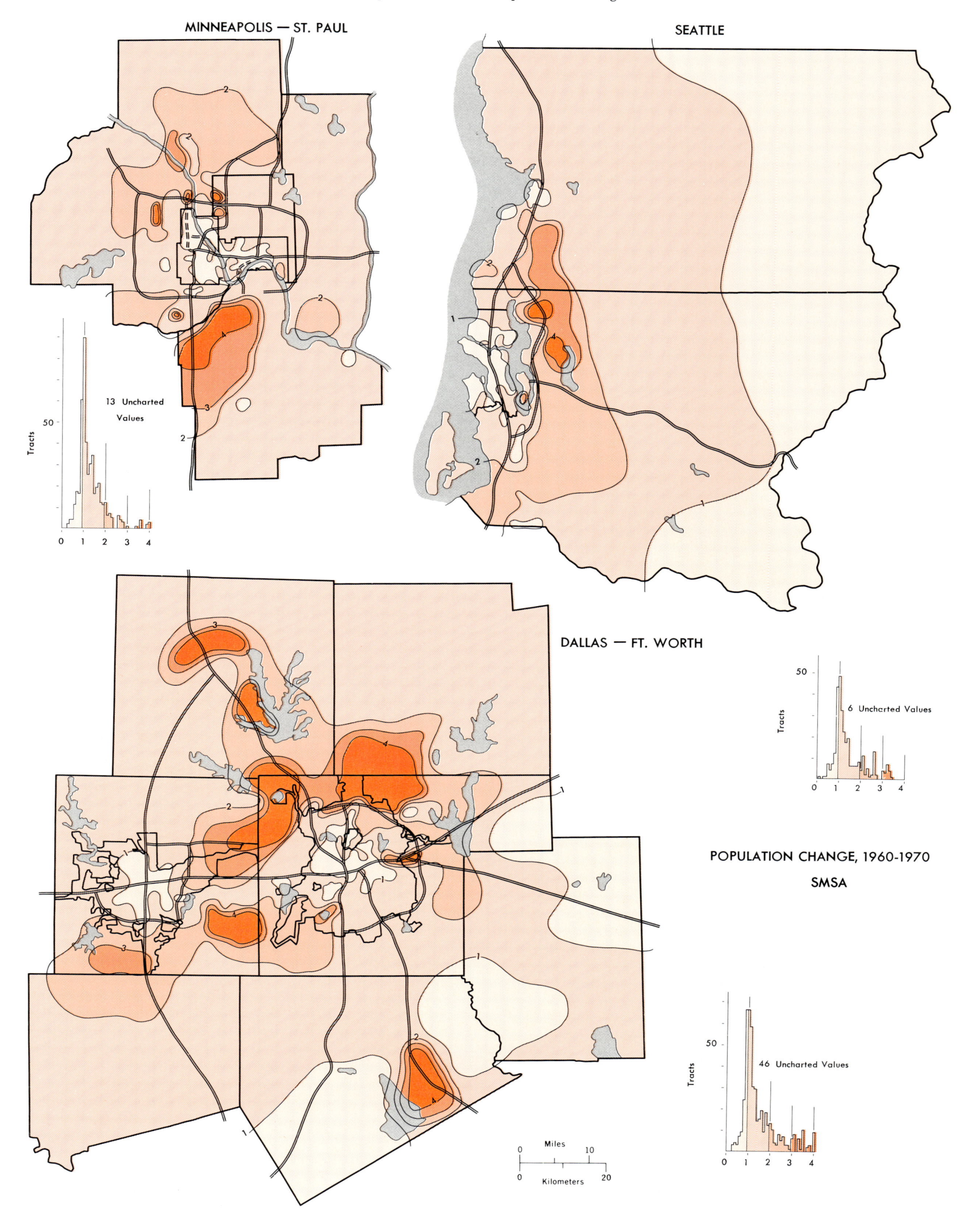

*Metropolitan Growth: Population Change*

MINNEAPOLIS — ST. PAUL

SEATTLE

DALLAS — FT. WORTH

POPULATION CHANGE, 1960-1970

SMSA

354

## Metropolitan Growth: Population Change

### POPULATION CHANGE, 1960–1970
### HOUSTON SMSA

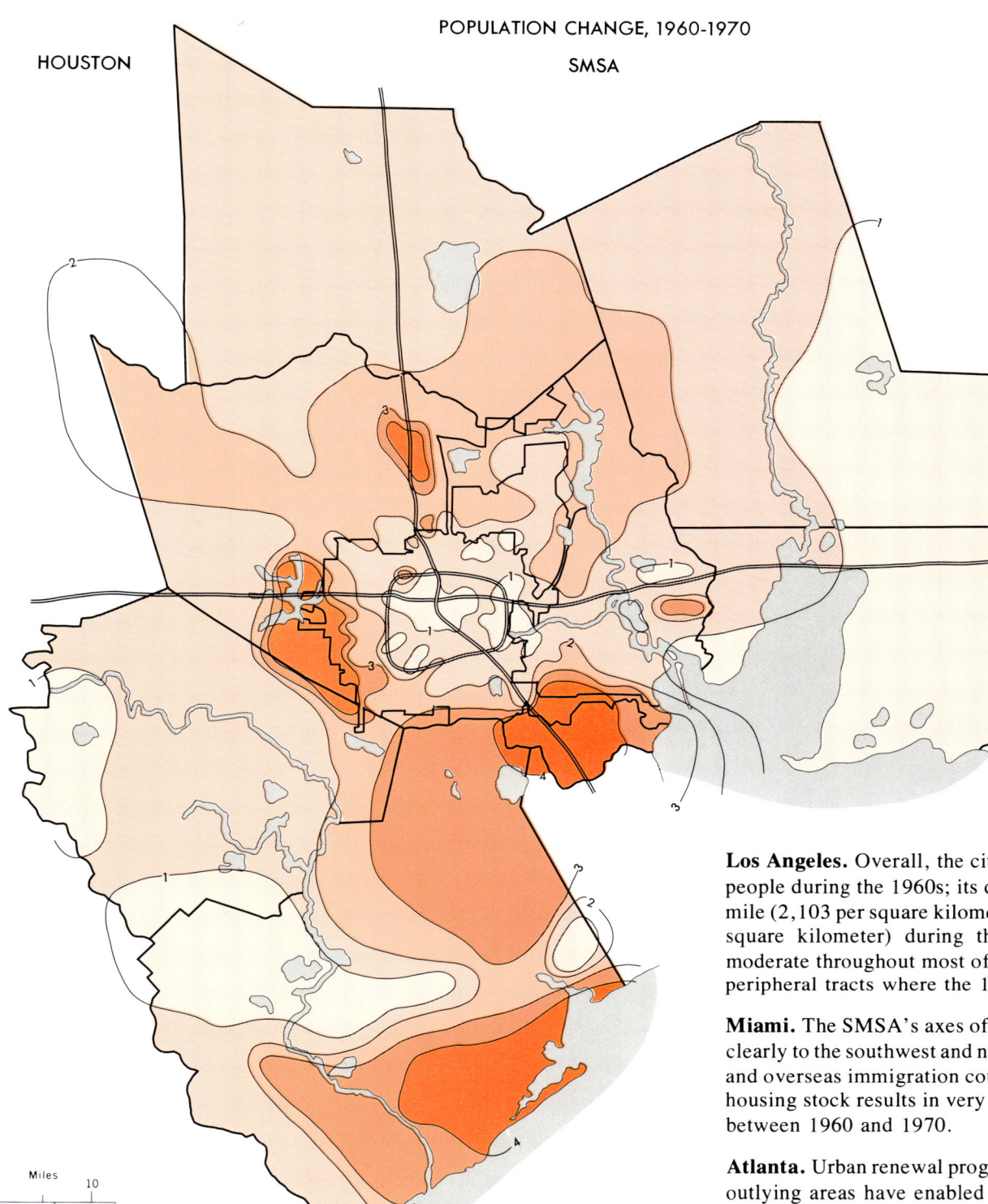

**Dallas-Fort Worth.** Large SMSA population increases in Dallas and Fort Worth are reflected in sharp population increases in several parts of the region. Texas cities can annex territory easily and thus encompass growing areas. Both Dallas and Fort Worth would have increased their populations even without the people living in annexed areas, indicating that growth is a region-wide phenomenon even though central-city rates are lower than the increases in suburban areas.

**Houston.** The SMSA has had the largest relative population increase of the metropolitan areas in the atlas. Within the region, increases have been sharpest in the prestige residential areas (p. 202) west of the city, near the Manned Space Center southeast of the city, and along the coast in Brazoria County. Of the 295,000 increase in Houston's population since 1960, 259,000 occurred within the area of the 1960 boundaries and 36,000 were added by annexation.

**Los Angeles.** Overall, the city of Los Angeles increased by 331,000 people during the 1960s; its density increased from 5,450 per square mile (2,103 per square kilometer) to 6,060 per square mile (2,340 per square kilometer) during the decade. Population increases were moderate throughout most of the area; the sharpest increases were in peripheral tracts where the 1960 base was small.

**Miami.** The SMSA's axes of suburban growth during the 1960s were clearly to the southwest and northwest of the city. Continued domestic and overseas immigration coupled with the region's relatively young housing stock results in very few tracts in which population declined between 1960 and 1970.

**Atlanta.** Urban renewal programs and modest population increases in outlying areas have enabled Atlanta to avoid a population decrease since 1960, although the increase amounted to only 10,000 people. The SMSA's growth is among the largest in the nation, reflecting its position as the economic hub of the southeastern United States.

**Washington, D.C.** Continued expansion of federal government employment during the 1960s spurred spectacular growth throughout Washington's suburban areas. The absolute size of the SMSA population increase (785,000 people) is exceeded only by increases in the New York and Los Angeles SMSAs, which had 1960 base populations 3 and 5 times larger than Washington's.

---

Density decreases in many central cities and increases in their suburban areas are decreasing population density differentials in SMSAs, although large density differences persist (Chapter 32). Nationally, limited convergence is evident between older and younger cities. The central-city densities of eastern and midwestern cities are declining at the same time that densities in western and southern cities are rising. Over the long run, some of the sharp density differences among the nation's largest cities and SMSAs may decrease.

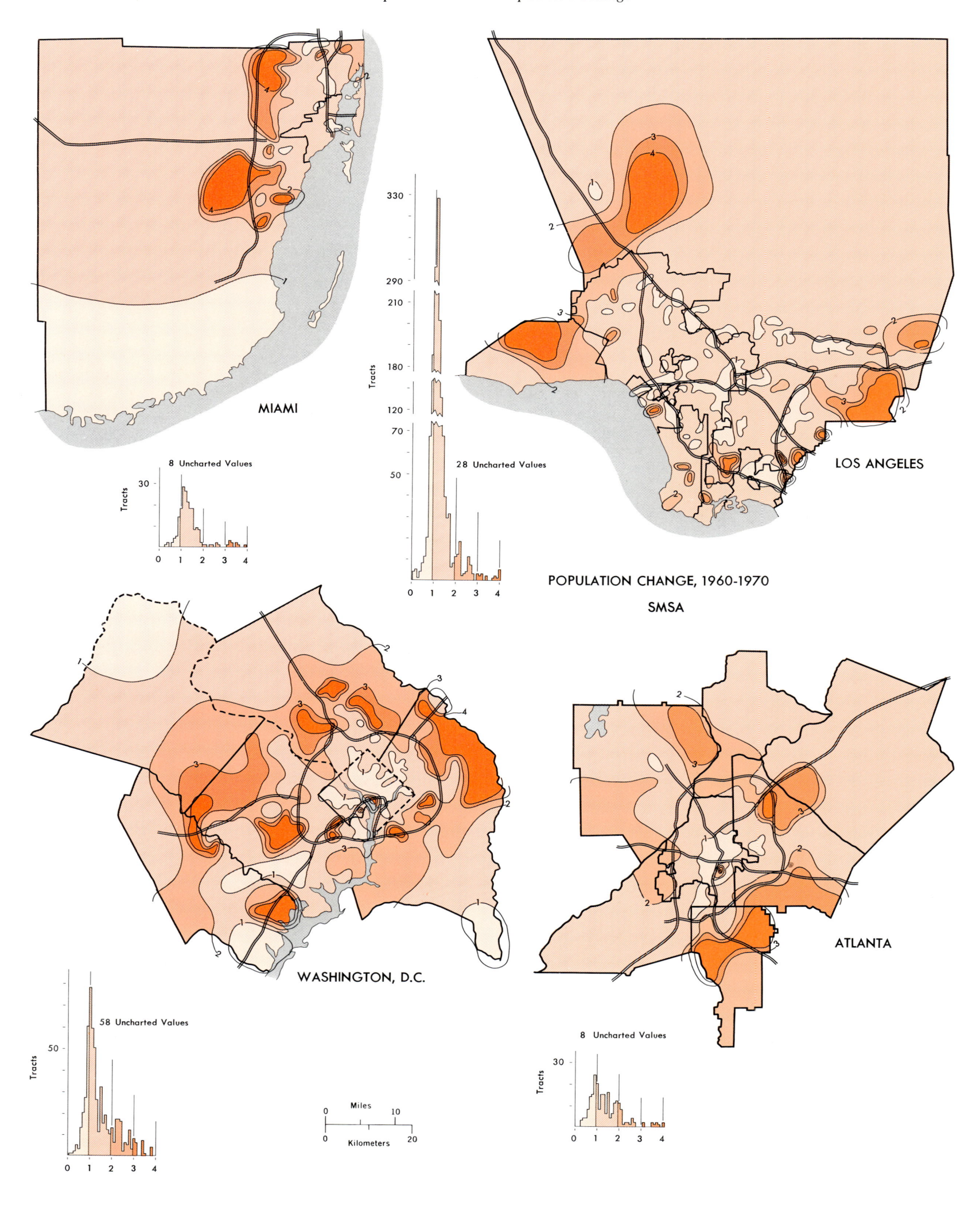

*Metropolitan Growth: Population Change*

MIAMI

LOS ANGELES

POPULATION CHANGE, 1960-1970
SMSA

WASHINGTON, D.C.

ATLANTA

*Education*

## CHAPTER 38

# Parochial School Enrollment

In the 1970 Census of Population, school enrollment data were gathered for a 15 percent sample of the population. It is possible to differentiate public, parochial, and other private school enrollments by school level (elementary, secondary, and college). These statistics are the basis of the maps in this chapter, which show the percentage of elementary school (grades 1-8) students enrolled in parochial schools in central cities.

The nation's elementary school enrollment amounts to 33,210,000 students, of whom 3,371,000 (10.2 percent) attend parochial schools. The rest (88.4 percent) attend public schools except for the 1.4 percent who go to private, nonparochial schools. Of the 22,662,000 students residing in Standard Metropolitan Statistical Areas (SMSAs) 2,849,000 (12.6 percent) attend parochial schools. In all central cities within SMSAs, parochial schools serve 14.6 percent of the elementary school students; private nonparochial schools provide instruction for 1.9 percent, and public schools serve the residual 83.5 percent (see accompanying tabulation).

Within the central cities mapped in this chapter, 744,000 (19 percent) of the 3,912,000 students attending elementary schools go to parochial schools. The remainder attend public (78.6 percent) or private nonparochial schools (2.4 percent). Parochial schools are a far from negligible component of central-city educational facilities. Although often more than half the parochial student enrollees in an SMSA reside in suburbs, the ways parochial schools are related to other phenomena of central-city life make it appropriate to map their enrollments at the central-city scale.

Parochial schools (mostly Roman Catholic parish elementary schools) enroll significant proportions of elementary school children in most central cities in the Northeast and Midwest. Public schools shoulder more of the educational burden in the West and South. Private nonparochial schools are of minor importance in most cities except in the South. In both North and South, parochial and private nonparochial schools provide an alternative to mandated race and class integration in addition to satisfying desires for religious and high-quality education. Thus parochial school attendance is closely related to ethnic and racial patterns and to neighborhood succession within cities.

**Boston.** Parochial school enrollments are highest in Boston's dominantly Italian North End (p. 26) and lowest in black neighborhoods (p. 25). Neighborhoods where parochial enrollments exceed 30 percent outside the North End and north Boston contain considerable numbers of Irish-Americans, emphasizing the degree to which parochial schools are predominantly Roman Catholic.

*Note:* All data are from the 1970 Censuses of Population and Housing unless otherwise indicated. Therefore the present tense refers to 1970 except for income data which are from 1969. Cartographic conventions are explained in Chapter 1. County names and other locational information are shown on the SMSA map at the beginning of each city chapter (6-25) and on the DUS map of mobile homes near the beginning of each city chapter.

**New York City.** Parochial school enrollments are highest in areas occupied by Roman Catholic ethnic groups (pp. 40-42) and lowest in predominantly black neighborhoods (p. 38). Enrollments are not especially high in Spanish-American areas (p. 38). Tracts where parochial enrollments exceed 90 percent are located in predominantly Italian-American areas in southern Manhattan and east-central Bronx County.

Percentage of Total Elementary School Enrollment

| City | Parochial Schools | Private Nonparochial Schools |
|---|---|---|
| Boston | 25.7 | 3.8 |
| New York City | 23.9 | 3.3 |
| Philadelphia | 33.7 | 2.4 |
| Hartford | 14.1 | 1.3 |
| Baltimore | 12.6 | 1.7 |
| New Orleans | 19.7 | 4.9 |
| San Francisco | 19.6 | 3.3 |
| Oakland | 11.0 | 1.4 |
| Pittsburgh | 33.9 | 2.1 |
| St. Louis | 18.9 | 1.3 |
| Cleveland | 17.8 | 0.6 |
| Chicago | 23.0 | 1.6 |
| Detroit | 18.7 | 0.8 |
| Minneapolis | 18.4 | 1.0 |
| St. Paul | 33.6 | 1.2 |
| Seattle | 11.7 | 2.1 |
| Dallas | 5.0 | 2.4 |
| Houston | 4.7 | 1.5 |
| Los Angeles | 10.6 | 2.9 |
| Miami | 6.9 | 5.1 |
| Atlanta | 1.9 | 3.8 |
| Washington, D.C. | 6.7 | 3.6 |

**Philadelphia.** The heavily Polish-American areas on Philadelphia's near northeast side (p. 55) and the dominantly Italian-American neighborhood (p. 56) have high parochial school enrollments. The highest proportions are in schools in the Polish area. Philadelphia is heavily dependent upon parochial schools; only Pittsburgh and St. Paul parochial school enrollments are proportionally equivalent. Because of Philadelphia's large population, the absolute size (96,500 students) of the parochial elementary enrollment is 3rd largest after New York and Chicago enrollments.

**Hartford.** The city has but 3,160 parochial elementary school students who are a small proportion of total elementary enrollments. As in other eastern cities, enrollments are concentrated in neighborhoods occupied by Roman Catholic minorities and sparse in areas occupied by low-income minority groups (p. 65). As is true in New

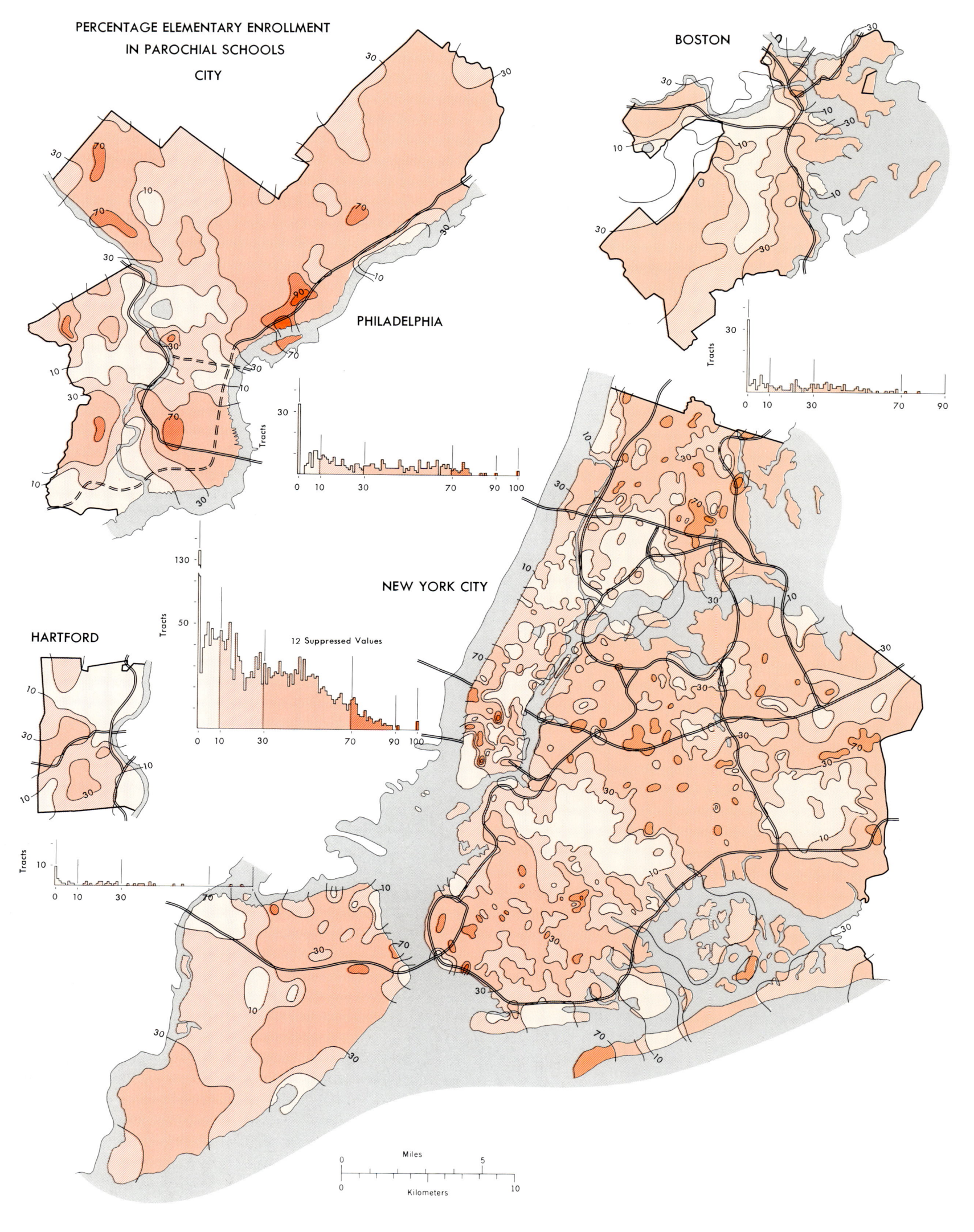

*Education: Parochial School Enrollment*

PERCENTAGE ELEMENTARY ENROLLMENT
IN PAROCHIAL SCHOOLS
CITY

BOSTON

PHILADELPHIA

HARTFORD

NEW YORK CITY

358

*Education: Parochial School Enrollment*

PERCENTAGE ELEMENTARY ENROLLMENT IN PAROCHIAL SCHOOLS CITY

BALTIMORE

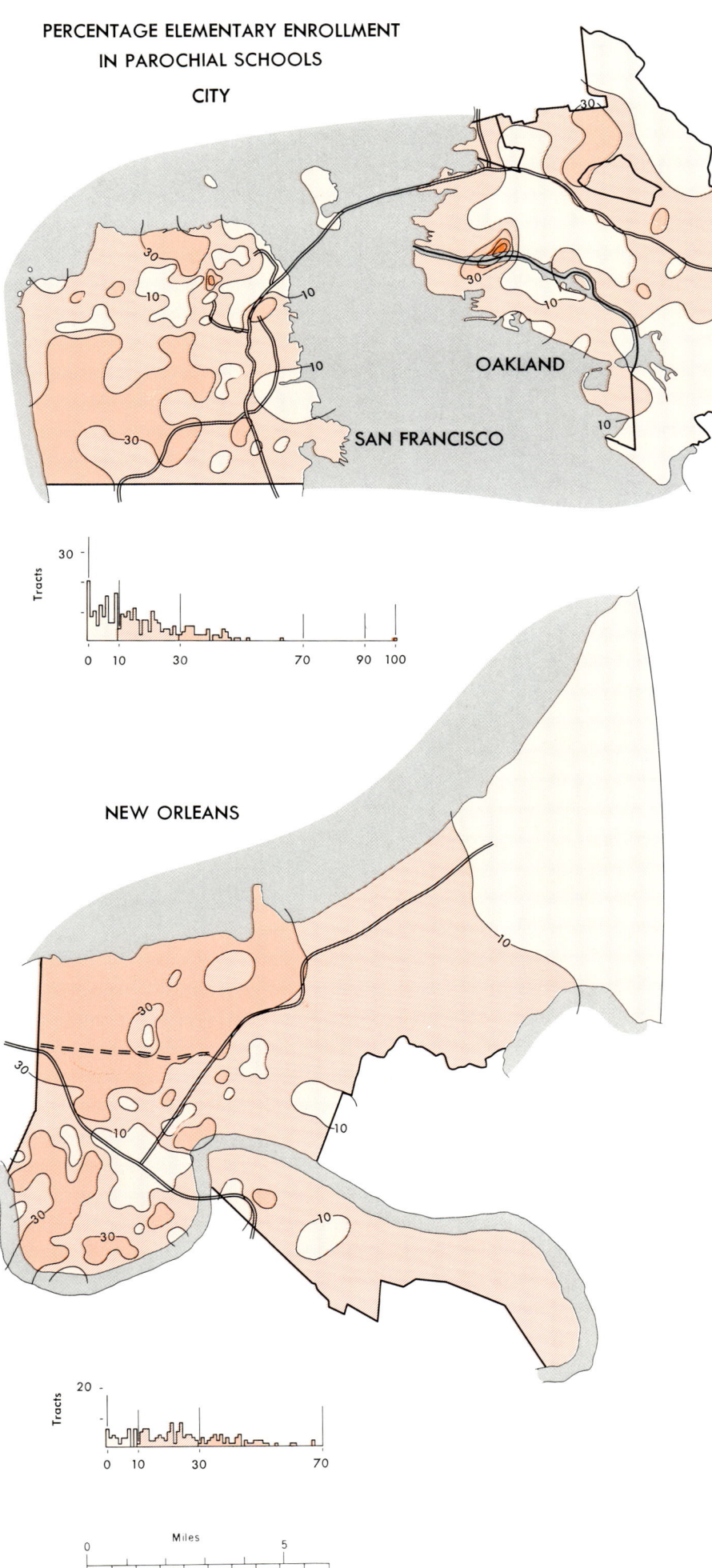

NEW ORLEANS

York City, enrollments are not especially high in Spanish-American neighborhoods, suggesting that the incomes and therefore the ability of ethnic groups to support independent schooling may be as much an element of parochial school enrollment as are concentrations of Catholic ethnic groups.

**Baltimore.** Parochial school enrollments are inversely related to the proportions of tract residents that are black (p. 74). Enrollments are highest in the ethnic neighborhoods on Baltimore's east side.

**New Orleans.** The city has comparatively high enrollments for a southern city, with 19,900 students attending parochial schools. Parochial enrollments are generally few in low-income areas of the city, which is not to say they are always high in upper-income areas. But this is true in New Orleans; parochial enrollments are high in the affluent northern and southwestern parts of the city (p. 85), where the city's heavily Catholic middle class is concentrated.

**San Francisco-Oakland.** Overall attendance in parochial schools is higher in San Francisco than in Oakland. The Oakland tract in which 100 percent attend parochial schools contains a significant Mexican-American population and only 29 elementary school students. Although some areas with Spanish-American populations (p. 94) are also areas with moderate parochial enrollments, parochial school enrollments are low in the most intensely Spanish-American neighborhoods.

**Pittsburgh.** The city has the largest proportion of its elementary students enrolled in parochial schools of the cities mapped here, although Philadelphia and St. Paul have nearly equal proportions. The usual inverse relationship between parochial enrollments and black population concentrations breaks down in Pittsburgh, for some predominantly black areas (p. 110) also have moderate or high parochial school enrollments. In all, 24,270 students attend parochial schools in the city.

**St. Louis.** Selective out-migration of young families has left St. Louis with a small proportion (22.9 percent) of the SMSA parochial school enrollment. Evidently, many parish parochial schools have migrated outward with their parishoners. Enrollments are low in the predominantly black areas of the city (p. 121).

**Cleveland.** Parochial enrollments are low in the predominantly black areas (p. 131) on Cleveland's east side, but they are also low in the low-income areas (p. 132) west of the Central Business District. As in

*Education: Parochial School Enrollment*

PERCENTAGE ELEMENTARY ENROLLMENT
IN PAROCHIAL SCHOOLS
CITY

PITTSBURGH

CLEVELAND

CHICAGO

ST. LOUIS

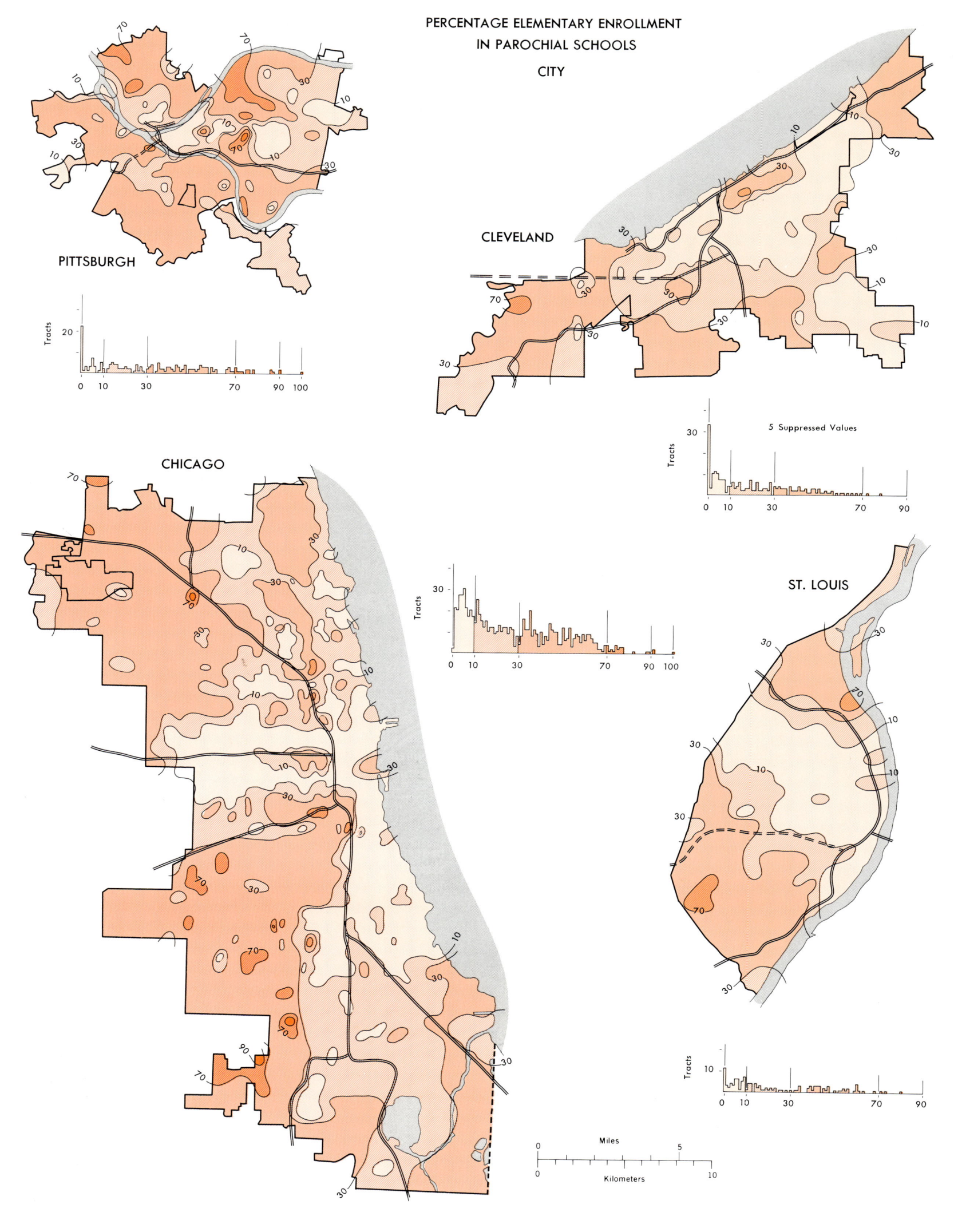

360

*Education: Parochial School Enrollment*

PERCENTAGE ELEMENTARY ENROLLMENT IN PAROCHIAL SCHOOLS
CITY

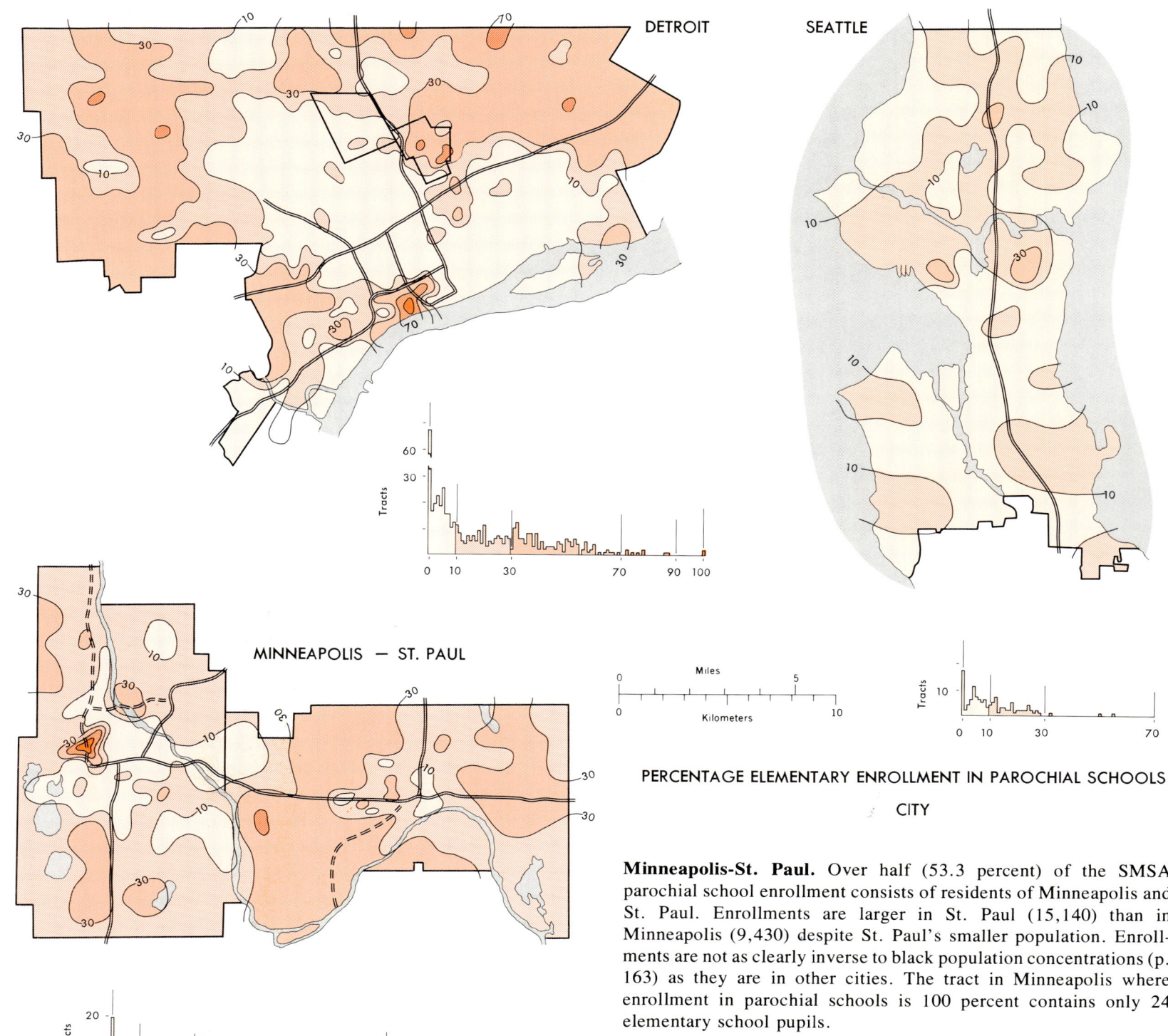

St. Louis, a relatively low proportion (29.6 percent) of the SMSA parochial school students reside in the central city.

**Chicago.** Almost half (48.9 percent) of the SMSA parochial elementary enrollment is located in Chicago. As in other cities, enrollments in predominantly black areas (p. 140) are low, but in contrast to most other cities, enrollments in the Spanish-American neighborhood (p. 141) southwest of the Central Business District exceed 30 percent of the elementary school population. Parochial enrollment peaks in southwestern Chicago occur in areas occupied by Irish and Polish ethnic groups (pp. 142-143).

**Detroit.** The city's 41,500 parochial elementary school students are spread around the periphery of the city for the most part. The peak value occurs in a tract with a large Spanish-American population (p. 153), where all 100 children attending elementary schools are enrolled in parochial schools.

**Minneapolis-St. Paul.** Over half (53.3 percent) of the SMSA parochial school enrollment consists of residents of Minneapolis and St. Paul. Enrollments are larger in St. Paul (15,140) than in Minneapolis (9,430) despite St. Paul's smaller population. Enrollments are not as clearly inverse to black population concentrations (p. 163) as they are in other cities. The tract in Minneapolis where enrollment in parochial schools is 100 percent contains only 24 elementary school pupils.

**Seattle.** Comparatively few of the city's elementary students attend parochial schools, and there is no clear association of parochial school enrollments, race (p. 173), and income (p. 175).

**Dallas.** The city has the 3rd lowest proportion of elementary students in parochial schools of the cities mapped in this chapter. Some areas where parochial school enrollments exceed 10 percent are located in areas occupied by Spanish-Americans, but others are not. Because of its large size and ability to expand its municipal boundaries, Dallas contains 68.4 percent of the SMSA parochial elementary enrollment.

**Houston.** Only 9,980 of the city's 214,100 elementary school students attend parochial schools. For the most part, areas where parochial elementary enrollments exceed 10 percent are located in areas containing some Spanish-American people, somewhat removed from the areas of most intense Spanish-American occupancy (p. 207).

**Los Angeles.** The proportion of elementary students attending parochial schools is comparatively low in the city, and areas where attendance exceeds 10 percent show no clear correspondence to maps of race (p. 228) or income (p. 233). There is a slight similarity

361

*Education: Parochial School Enrollment*

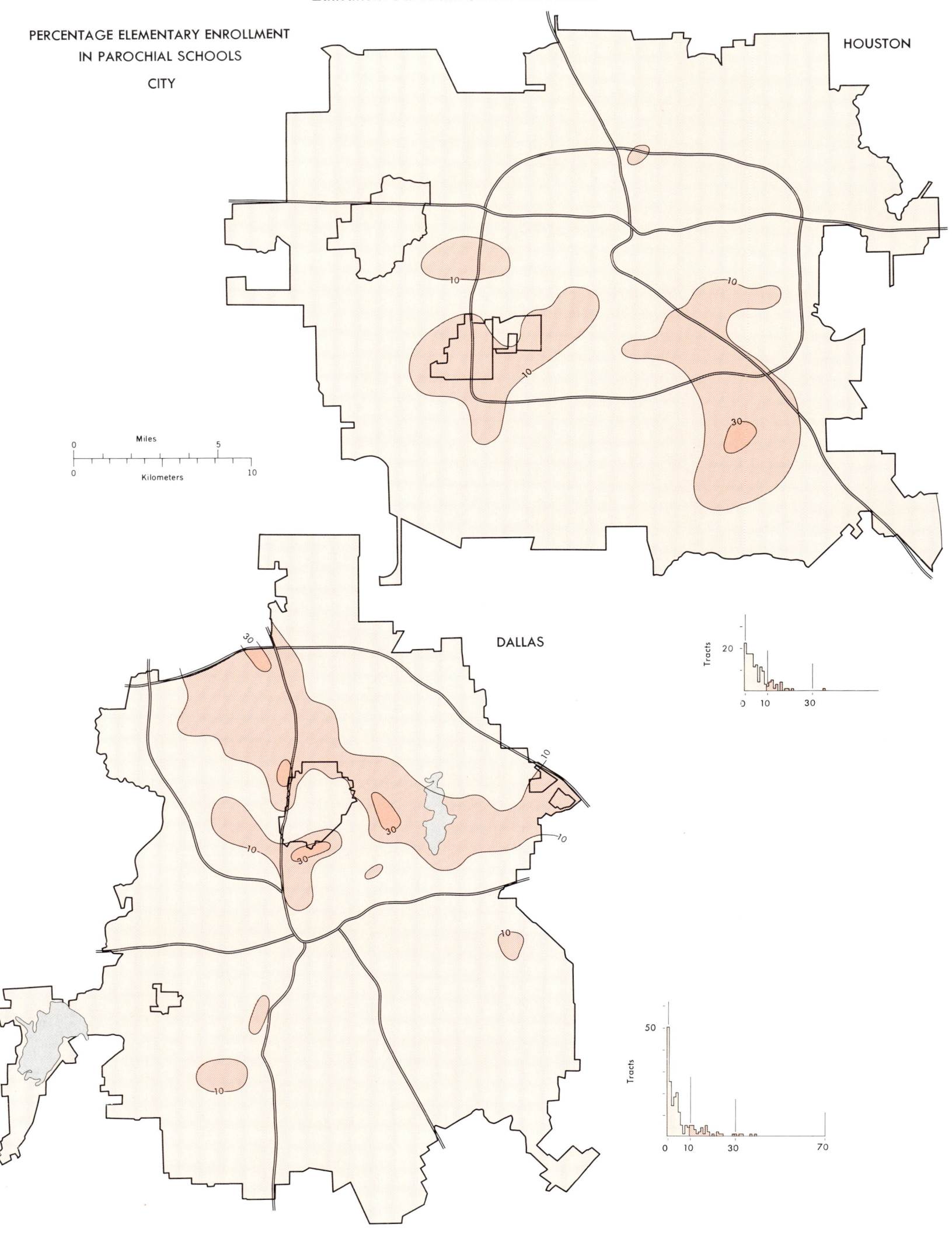

PERCENTAGE ELEMENTARY ENROLLMENT
IN PAROCHIAL SCHOOLS
CITY

HOUSTON

DALLAS

*Education: Parochial School Enrollment*

*Education: Parochial School Enrollment*

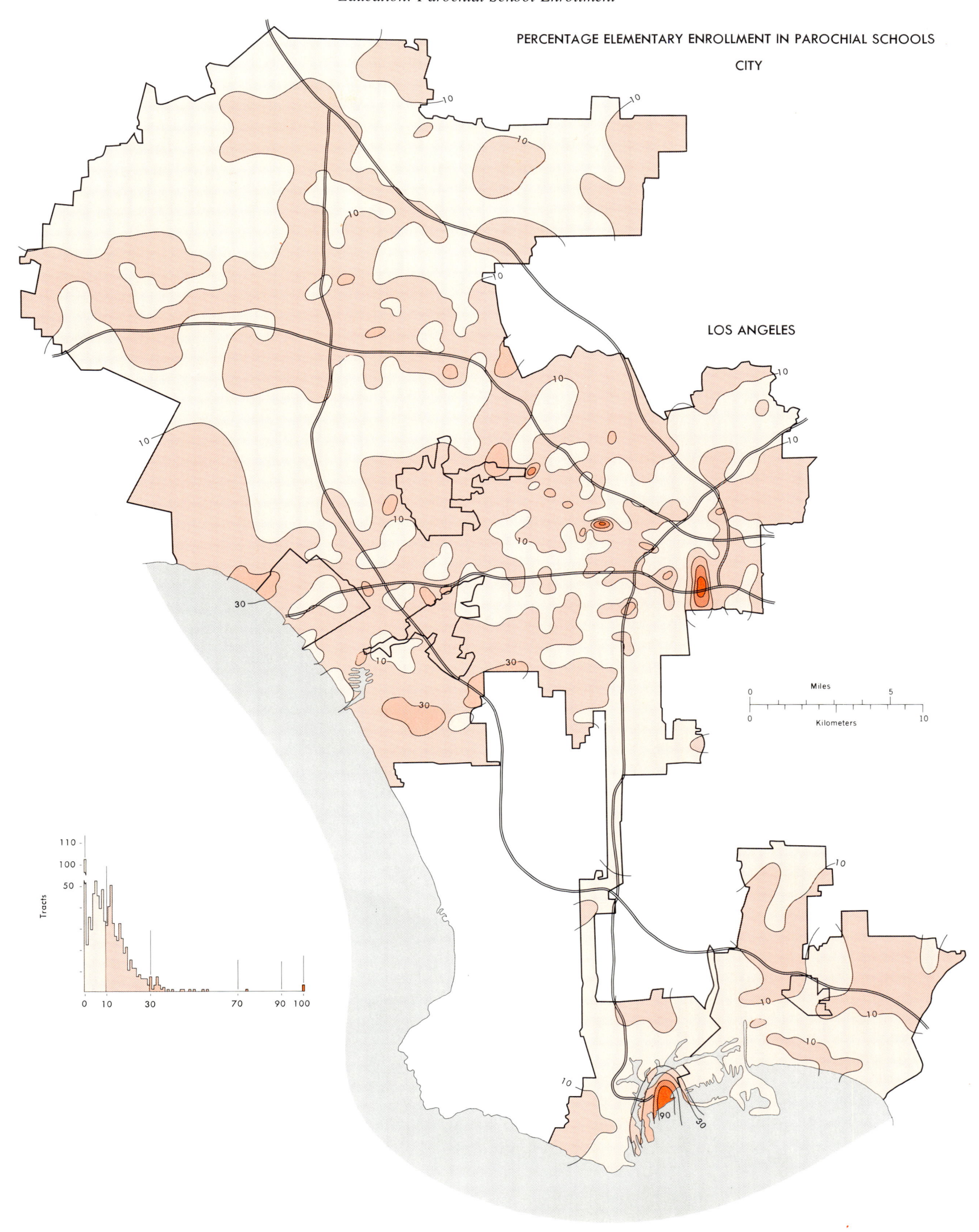

PERCENTAGE ELEMENTARY ENROLLMENT IN PAROCHIAL SCHOOLS
CITY

LOS ANGELES

*Education: Parochial School Enrollment*

MIAMI

ATLANTA

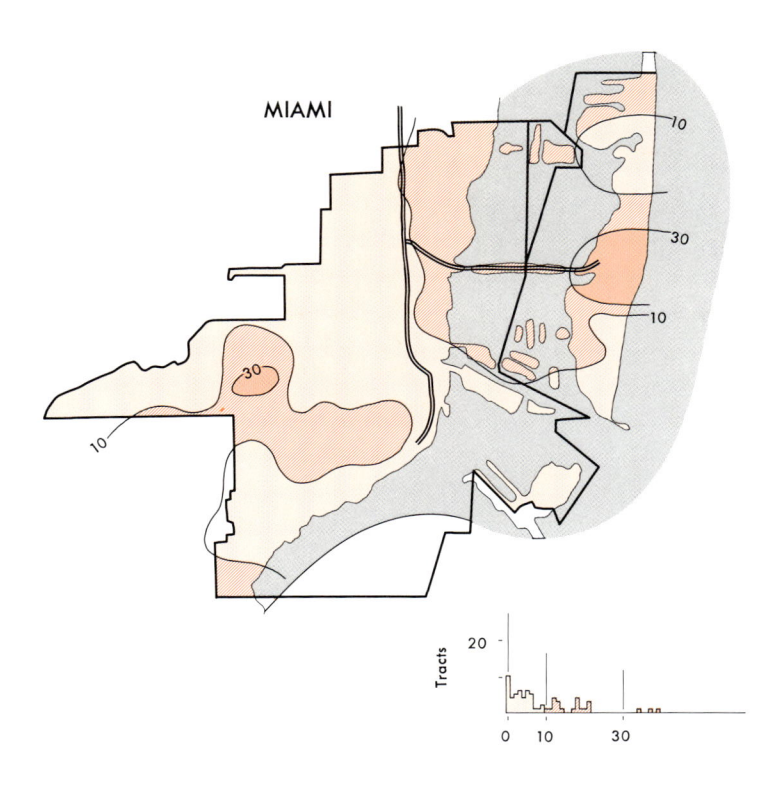

PERCENTAGE ELEMENTARY ENROLLMENT IN PAROCHIAL SCHOOLS
CITY

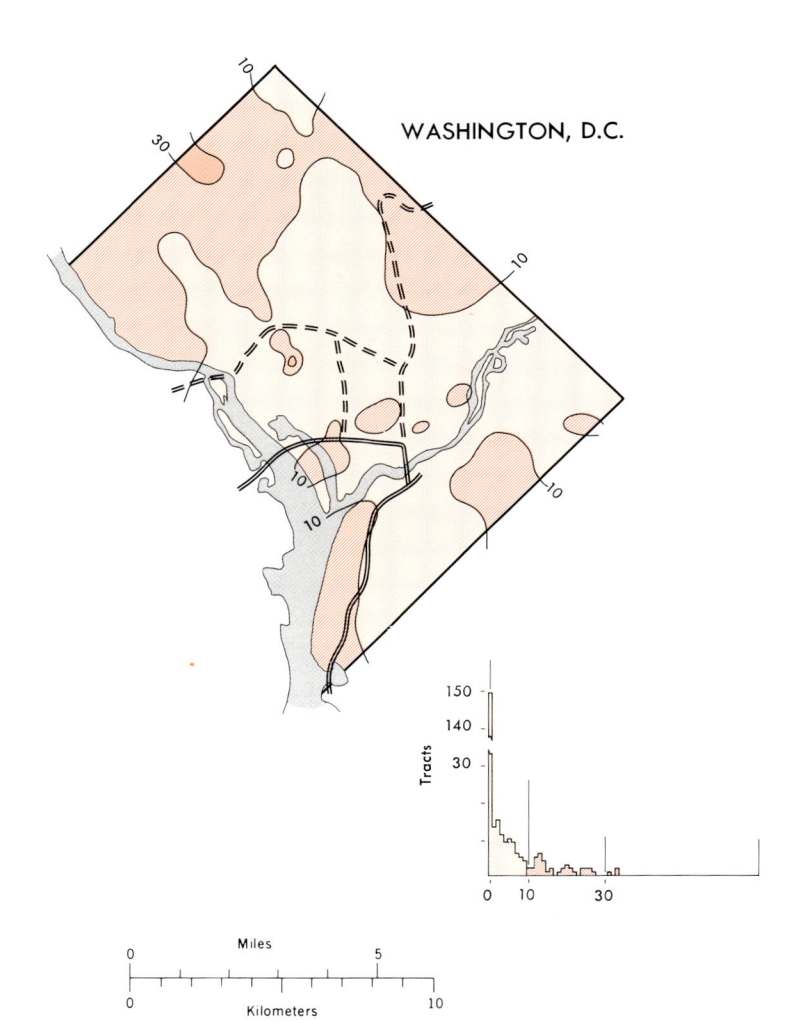

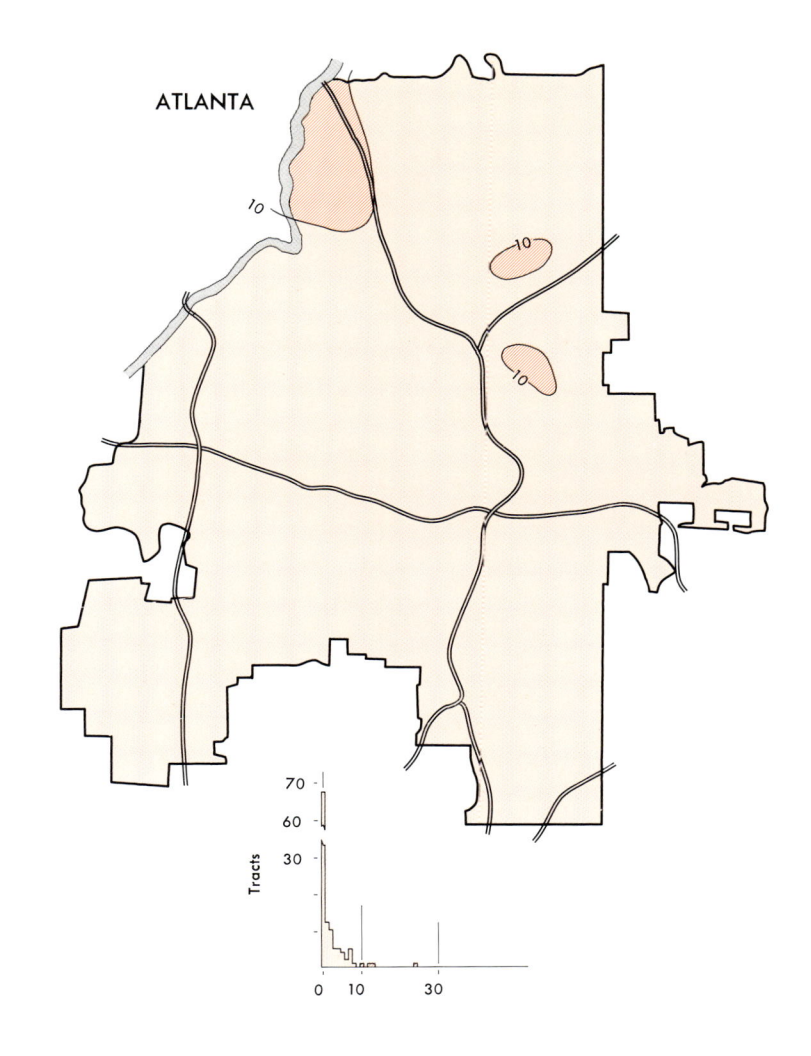

WASHINGTON, D.C.

between the enrollment map and the map of Italian-Americans (p. 232). The four tracts with high proportions have small populations.

**Miami.** Few (2,830) elementary students are enrolled in parochial schools in Miami, and almost as many (2,100) students are enrolled in private nonparochial schools. Parochial enrollments are often coincident with areas containing large Spanish-American populations (p. 242). Miami is underbounded, which partially explains the low proportion (19.9 percent) of SMSA parochial school enrollment in the city.

**Atlanta.** The city's parochial elementary enrollment (1,395) is the lowest among the cities mapped in this chapter and is also low relative to total population. Private nonparochial enrollment (2,825) is over twice as large as parochial enrollment.

**Washington, D.C.** Most (81.6 percent) of the SMSA's parochial elementary enrollment occurs outside the District of Columbia. The 7,420 elementary parochial students in the District live in black (p. 260) as well as predominantly white neighborhoods. There are 4,025 elementary students attending private nonparochial schools.

---

Parochial school enrollments are not universal in the nation's central cities, but the schools make important contributions to education in many places and are virtually indispensible in some cities. The key to the occurrence and persistence of parochial education seems to be ethnic groups that lack an anticlerical bias, value religious education, and have the financial ability to support parish schools. The role parochial schools play in overall city life is ambiguous. They are often an alternative to forced racial integration and its attendant disruptions in public schools; thus they preserve racial segregation. At the same time, they may help keep young, white households from migrating out of the city by providing that alternative. Whether cities benefit or lose on balance is not clear.

*Education*

CHAPTER 39

# 20- and 21-Year Olds in School

In the 1970 Census of Population, age was recorded for each person enumerated, and regular school or college attendance was tabulated for a 15 percent sample of individuals. From these data the Census Bureau calculated and reported the percentage of 20- and 21-year-olds attending school. These data are mapped by census tracts to produce the maps in this chapter.

There are 2,043,000 20- and 21-year-olds in the nation, of whom 30.1 percent (627,000) are attending school regularly. Within Standard Metropolitan Statistical Areas (SMSAs), the proportion attending school is 31.5 percent. In the central cities of SMSAs, 33.4 percent of 20- and 21-year-olds are going to school. Higher percentages in SMSAs and central cities reflect both the concentration of educational institutions in metropolitan areas and their cores and the higher participation in postsecondary education in these areas. Students attending school away from home are counted as residents of the places where they study, and high proportions of 20- and 21-year-olds in school occur in census tracts containing colleges with resident student populations (see accompanying tabulation).

Variations among SMSAs in the percentages of young adults attending school or college are usually small. Boston, with its plethora of colleges and universities, has the highest SMSA and central-city percentages. Houston has the smallest proportion of 20- and 21-year-olds in school among the SMSAs, and the same age group in Newark has the lowest central-city attendance.

Away from the immediate vicinity of educational institutions, there is a high geographical correspondence between young adults in college and socioeconomic status. Postsecondary schooling is expensive in terms of current outlays for tuition, books, and fees, and in terms of income forgone while attending school. Middle- and upper-income families can better afford the costs and lost earnings than can poorer families.

**Boston.** Proportions of young adults attending school are highest in the affluent areas west and northwest of Boston, although percentages are comparatively high throughout the SMSA. The over-90-percent tract in northern Norfolk County marks the location of Wellesley College. The high-participation tract on the coast is an area with upper-income residents.

**New York-Northern New Jersey.** Attendance is low in most central-city tracts, from whence it rises to peaks in outer suburban areas and then declines toward the SMSA peripheries. Living at home and commuting to school can reduce the costs of college education.

*Note:* All data are from the 1970 Censuses of Population and Housing unless otherwise indicated. Therefore the present tense refers to 1970 except for income data which are from 1969. Cartographic conventions are explained in Chapter 1. County names and other locational information are shown on the SMSA map at the beginning of each city chapter (6-25) and on the DUS map of mobile homes near the beginning of each city chapter.

Thus qualified central-city and suburban residents find it easier to attend college than do qualified people in peripheral areas, where colleges are not nearby. Participation rates are lowest in predominantly black and Spanish-American areas of central cities (p. 38).

**Philadelphia.** Participation in education by 20- and 21-year-olds is generally high in suburban areas with peaks above 70 percent in affluent areas (p. 59). The series of peaks above 90 percent west of Philadelphia are main-line college communities such as Haverford, Bryn Mawr, and Villanova. The peak just west of Interstate 76 in Philadelphia is the Drexel/University of Pennsylvania complex.

Percentage of 20- and 21-year-olds Attending School

| Region | Central City(ies) | Entire SMSA |
|---|---|---|
| Boston | 43.9 | 45.6 |
| New York | 32.5 | 30.0 |
| Jersey City | 31.0 | 27.5 |
| Newark | 33.7 | 17.7 |
| Paterson-Clifton-Passaic | 35.8 | 24.4 |
| Philadelphia | 27.5 | 26.6 |
| Hartford | 33.6 | 31.0 |
| Baltimore | 26.4 | 23.6 |
| New Orleans | 28.9 | 33.9 |
| San Francisco-Oakland | 34.6 | 32.3 |
| Pittsburgh | 33.7 | 43.1 |
| St. Louis | 28.0 | 24.7 |
| Cleveland | 28.3 | 20.7 |
| Chicago | 28.2 | 26.4 |
| Detroit | 24.9 | 22.6 |
| Minneapolis-St. Paul | 25.4 | 40.7 |
| Seattle | 34.4 | 45.4 |
| Dallas | 27.4 | 20.4 |
| Fort Worth | 29.0 | 27.7 |
| Houston | 24.1 | 26.8 |
| Los Angeles | 31.6 | 34.5 |
| Miami | 31.5 | 27.0 |
| Atlanta | 27.5 | 29.5 |
| Washington, D.C. | 30.5 | 34.6 |

**Hartford.** The University of Connecticut at Storrs on the east and Central Connecticut State College south of Hartford cause peaks among generally high values in the SMSA. A combination of affluence (p. 66) and students attracted to St. Joseph College and the University of Hartford produces the peak west of the city.

**Baltimore.** Overall participation in education is low in the SMSA compared with other East Coast metropolitan areas. Most tracts where proportions exceed 70 percent contain colleges or universities.

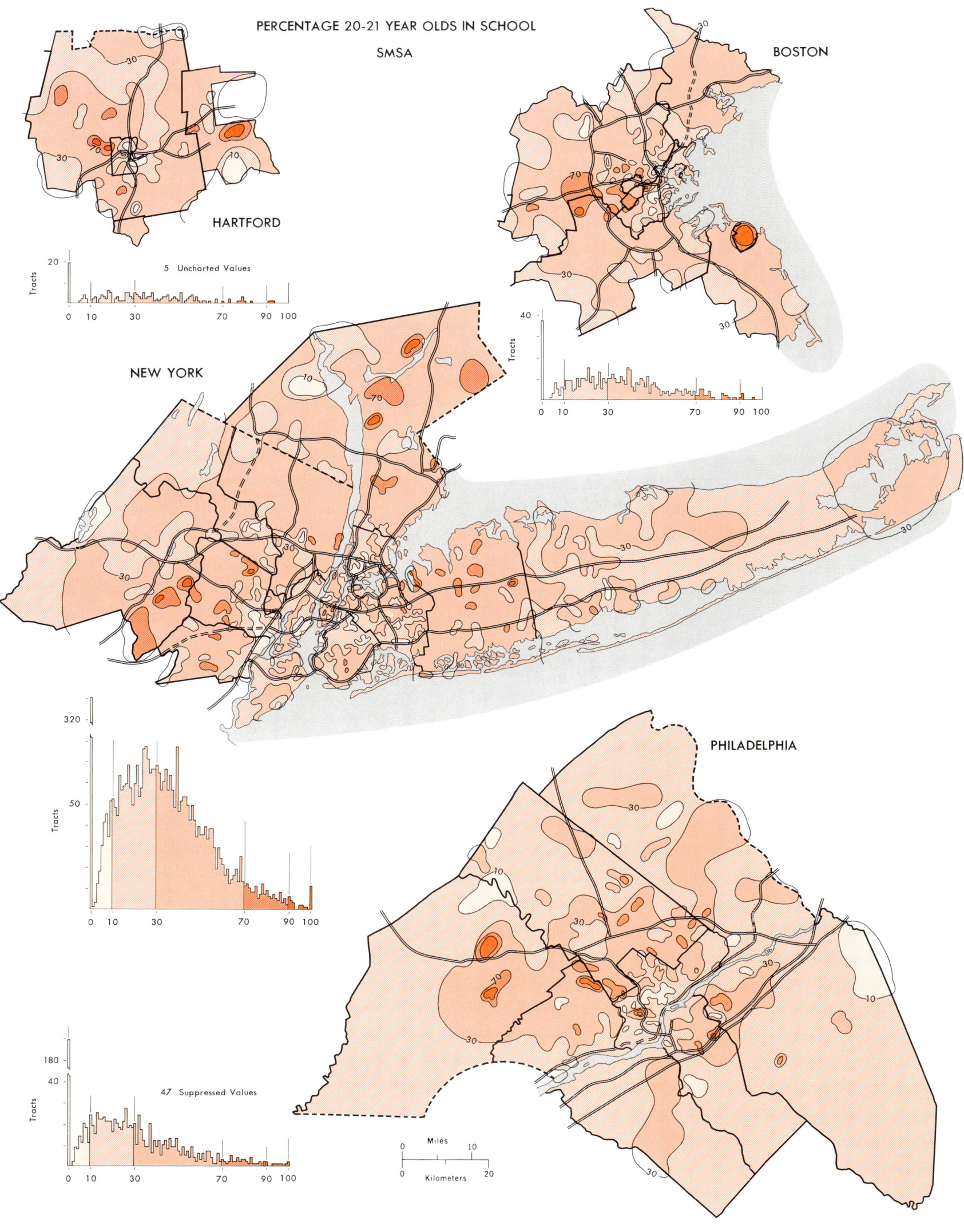

*Education: Young Adults in School*

PERCENTAGE 20-21 YEAR OLDS IN SCHOOL
SMSA

HARTFORD

BOSTON

NEW YORK

PHILADELPHIA

366

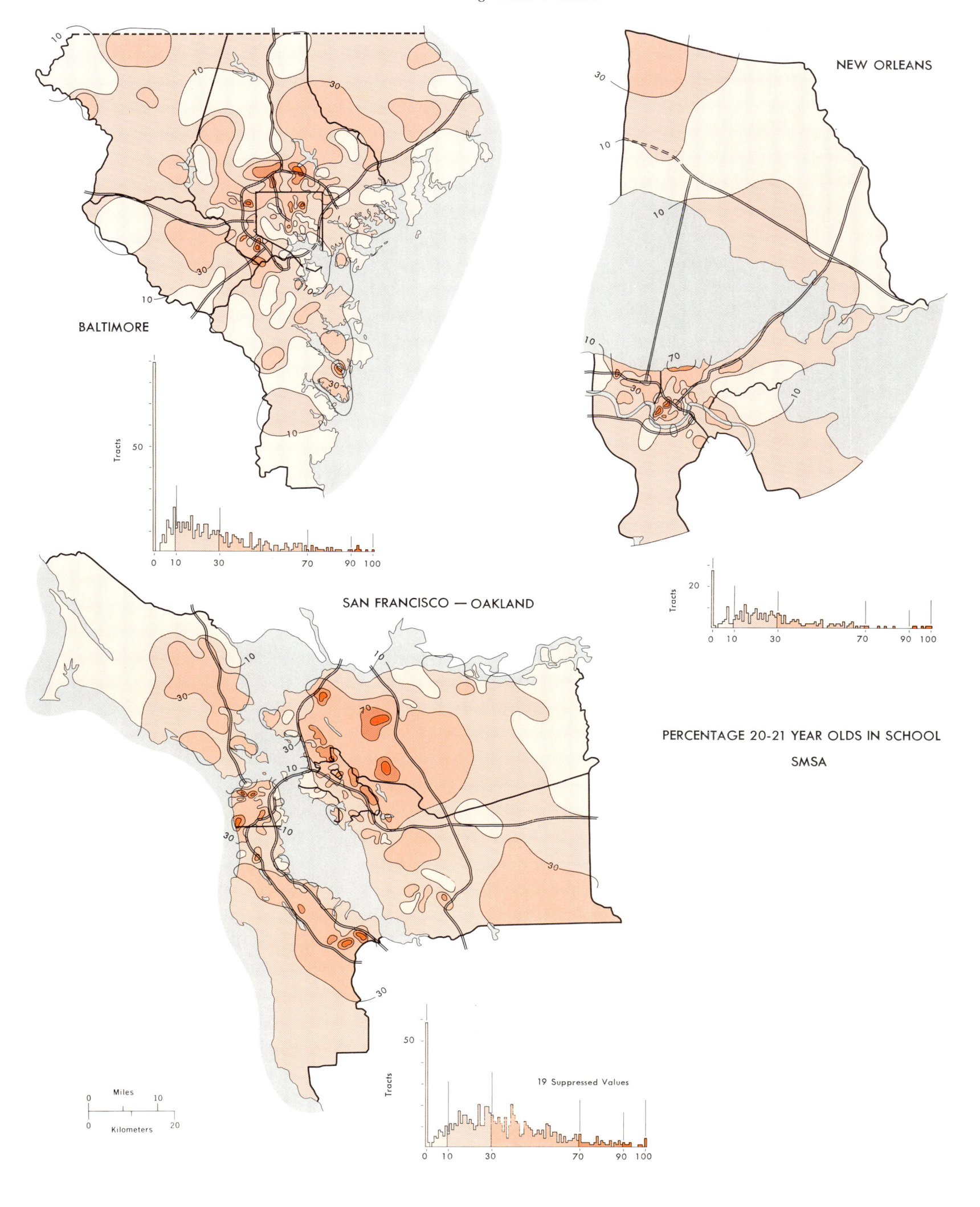

*Education: Young Adults in School*

BALTIMORE

NEW ORLEANS

SAN FRANCISCO — OAKLAND

PERCENTAGE 20-21 YEAR OLDS IN SCHOOL

SMSA

19 Suppressed Values

*Education: Young Adults in School*

PERCENTAGE 20-21 YEAR OLDS IN SCHOOL
SMSA

PITTSBURGH

ST. LOUIS

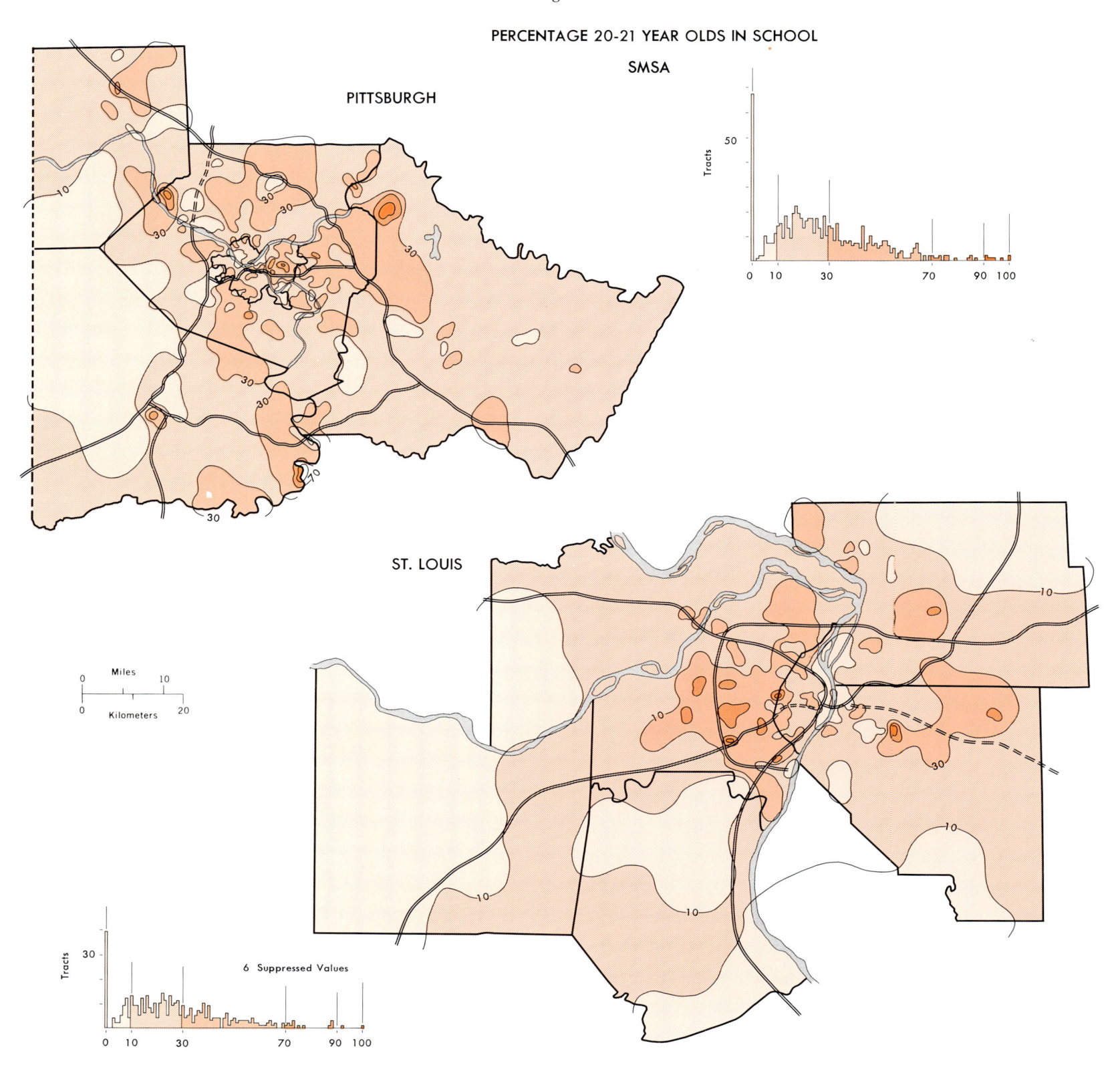

**New Orleans.** Colleges are often located in affluent neighborhoods, which makes it difficult to distinguish the influence of proximity from that of prosperity in producing high enrollments. This is true in New Orleans, where Louisiana State University at New Orleans, Xavier University, and Tulane and Loyola universities (north to south in Orleans County) appear as high percentages in affluent neighborhoods (p. 85).

**San Francisco-Oakland.** Participation is generally above 30 percent in affluent areas (p. 100) and below 10 percent in areas containing large numbers of blacks and Spanish-Americans (pp. 383, 391) and in outlying rural areas. Most of the tracts where participation exceeds 70 percent contain colleges or universities.

**Pittsburgh.** The link between parental socioeconomic status and college attendance is evident in the correspondence of many areas where enrollment exceeds 30 percent of the 20- and 21-year-old population with areas where employment in executive occupations (p. 112) exceeds 30 percent.

**St. Louis.** Overall attendance rates are low in the SMSA and in St. Louis. Rates are highest in the western suburbs, although there, as throughout the rest of the SMSA, proportions over 70 percent usually mark the locations of colleges or universities.

**Cleveland.** College enrollments are lowest in Cleveland's predominantly black areas (p. 385) where they are zero percent of the 20- and 21-year-olds in many tracts. Participation is generally highest in the western suburbs because of high incomes and incentives. Several colleges in the same area produce the peak values.

**Chicago.** Colleges in Lake Forest (Lake County) and Evanston (just

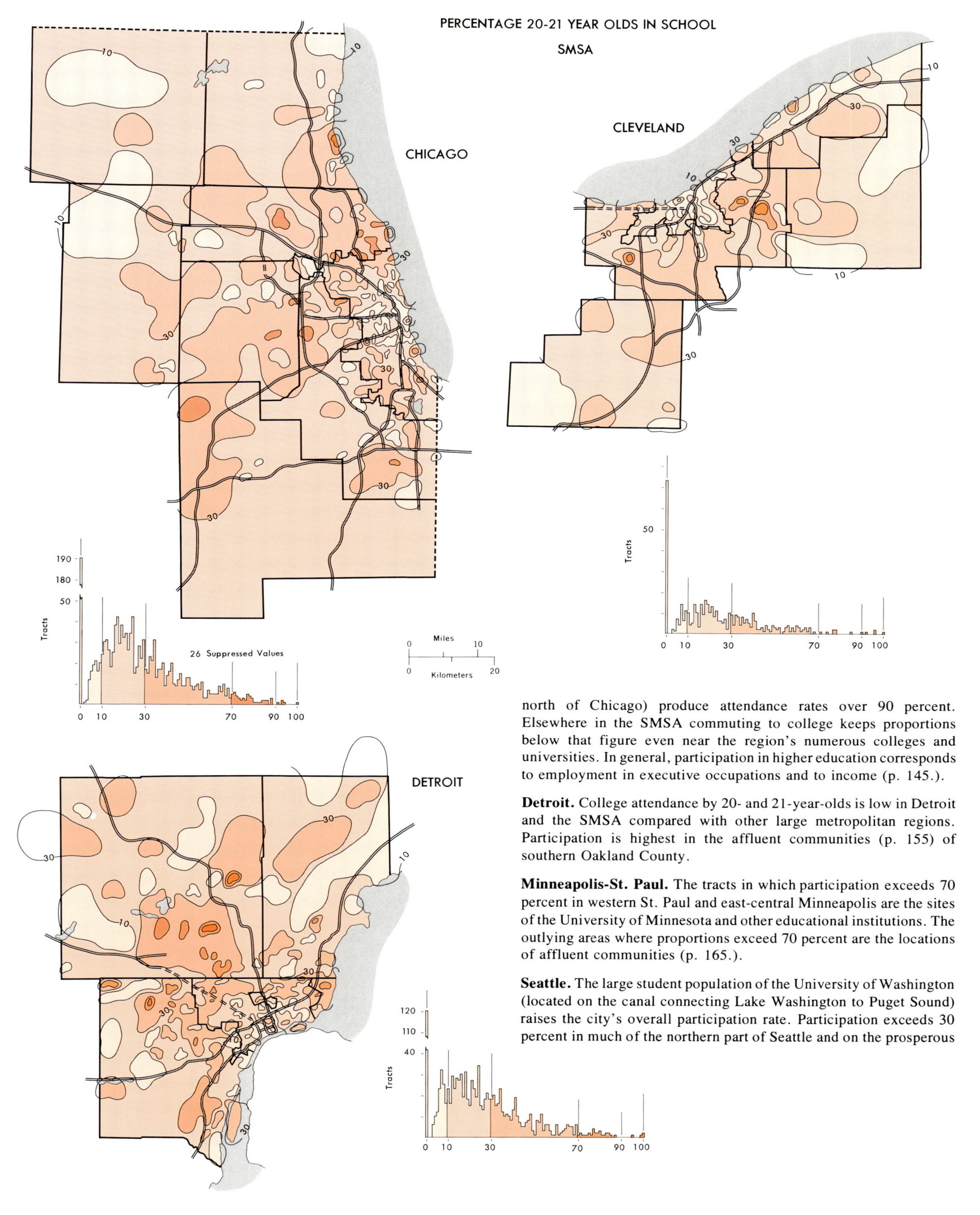

*Education: Young Adults in School*

## PERCENTAGE 20-21 YEAR OLDS IN SCHOOL
### SMSA

north of Chicago) produce attendance rates over 90 percent. Elsewhere in the SMSA commuting to college keeps proportions below that figure even near the region's numerous colleges and universities. In general, participation in higher education corresponds to employment in executive occupations and to income (p. 145.).

**Detroit.** College attendance by 20- and 21-year-olds is low in Detroit and the SMSA compared with other large metropolitan regions. Participation is highest in the affluent communities (p. 155) of southern Oakland County.

**Minneapolis-St. Paul.** The tracts in which participation exceeds 70 percent in western St. Paul and east-central Minneapolis are the sites of the University of Minnesota and other educational institutions. The outlying areas where proportions exceed 70 percent are the locations of affluent communities (p. 165.).

**Seattle.** The large student population of the University of Washington (located on the canal connecting Lake Washington to Puget Sound) raises the city's overall participation rate. Participation exceeds 30 percent in much of the northern part of Seattle and on the prosperous

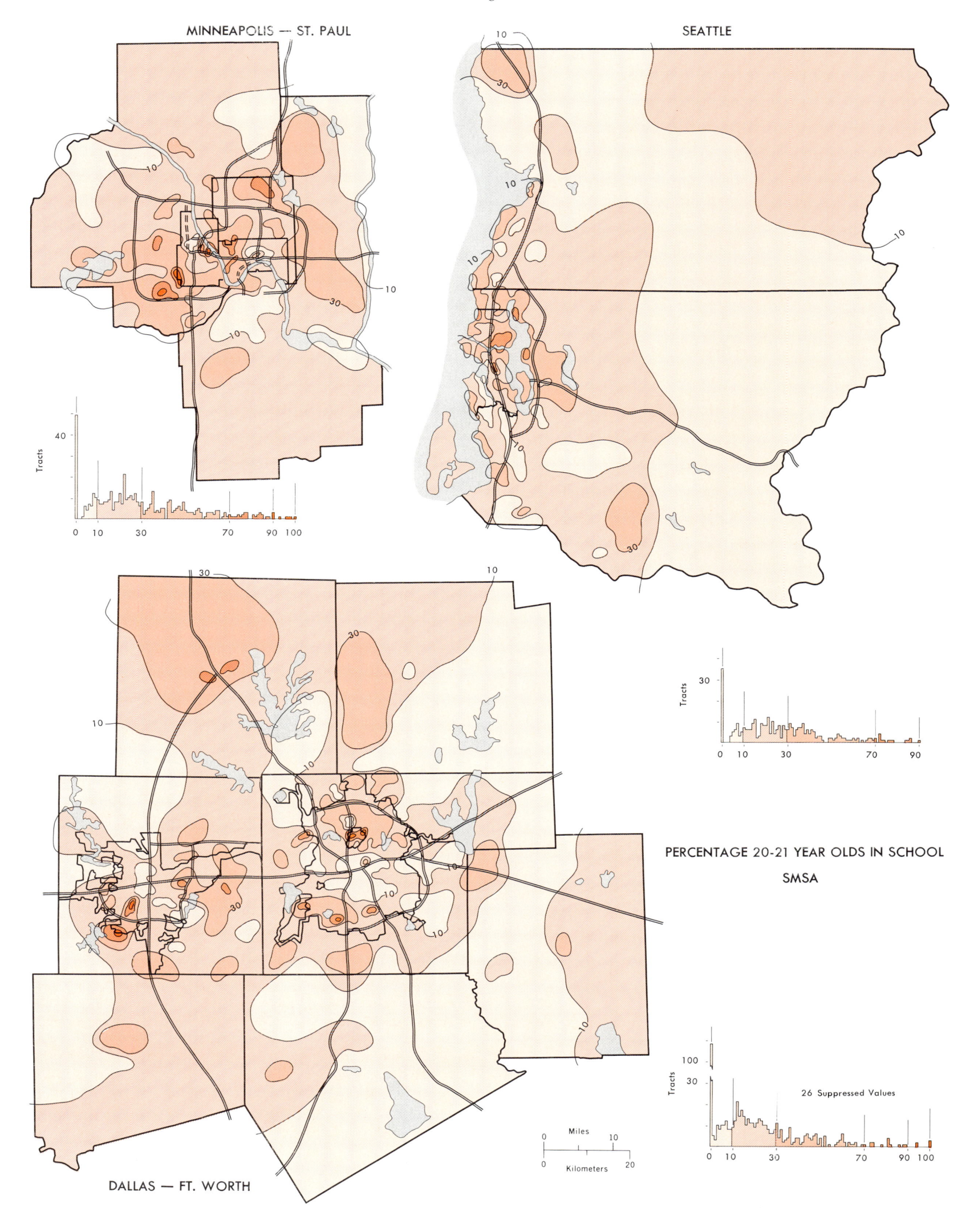

*Education: Young Adults in School*

MINNEAPOLIS — ST. PAUL

SEATTLE

DALLAS — FT. WORTH

PERCENTAGE 20-21 YEAR OLDS IN SCHOOL

SMSA

26 Suppressed Values

370

Education: Young Adults in School

PERCENTAGE 20-21 YEAR OLDS IN SCHOOL
SMSA

HOUSTON

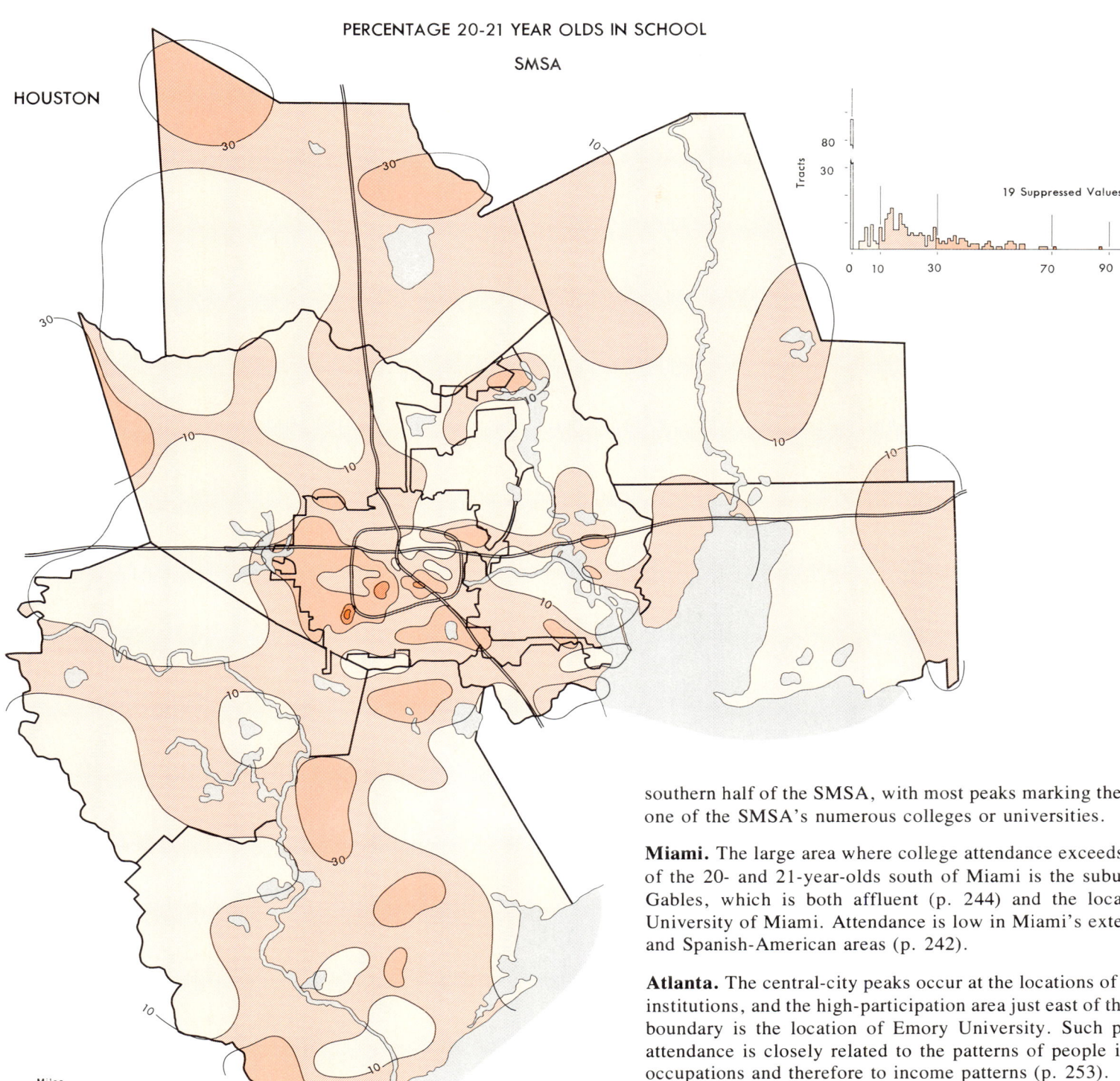

western side of Lake Washington. It is notably lower in southern Seattle and the southern suburbs.

**Dallas-Fort Worth.** Participation is generally low in black and Spanish-American neighborhoods (pp. 189-190), but there are some exceptions. Attendance is highest near Texas Christian University in southwestern Fort Worth and near Southern Methodist University in north-central Dallas.

**Houston.** Participation in education seems to be somewhat lower in Spanish-American than in black areas of the region (p. 207), but it is lower in both than in the upper-income areas on Houston's west side. Overall participation rates are low in the outlying parts of the SMSA.

**Los Angeles.** Few 20- and 21-year-olds in the sparsely populated northern part of the region attend school except near military facilities, which often provide extension courses in cooperation with local colleges and universities. Enrollments are generally high in the southern half of the SMSA, with most peaks marking the location of one of the SMSA's numerous colleges or universities.

**Miami.** The large area where college attendance exceeds 70 percent of the 20- and 21-year-olds south of Miami is the suburb of Coral Gables, which is both affluent (p. 244) and the location of the University of Miami. Attendance is low in Miami's extensive black and Spanish-American areas (p. 242).

**Atlanta.** The central-city peaks occur at the locations of educational institutions, and the high-participation area just east of the municipal boundary is the location of Emory University. Such peaks aside, attendance is closely related to the patterns of people in executive occupations and therefore to income patterns (p. 253).

**Washington, D.C.** Compared with other metropolitan areas, attendance in the SMSA's black neighborhoods (p. 388) is generally higher than usual. The relatively high incomes of many black civil servants and the existence of nearby colleges, some of which are predominantly black, help promote participation by the SMSA's blacks.

---

The repeated geographical association of college attendance, prosperity, and the availability of local opportunities for higher education is striking evidence that higher education and the higher incomes that result from it are not viable options for many poor families. Because low incomes occur disproportionately among blacks and other minority groups, they are usually the metropolitan groups with the lowest participation rates. The role of income in producing high and low enrollments is critical, but the close association between enrollment and executive occupations evident in many SMSAs suggests that income alone (which is, of course, closely related to occupation) is not the whole story. Attitudes toward education and the role models that parents provide are also important determinants of school enrollments.

371

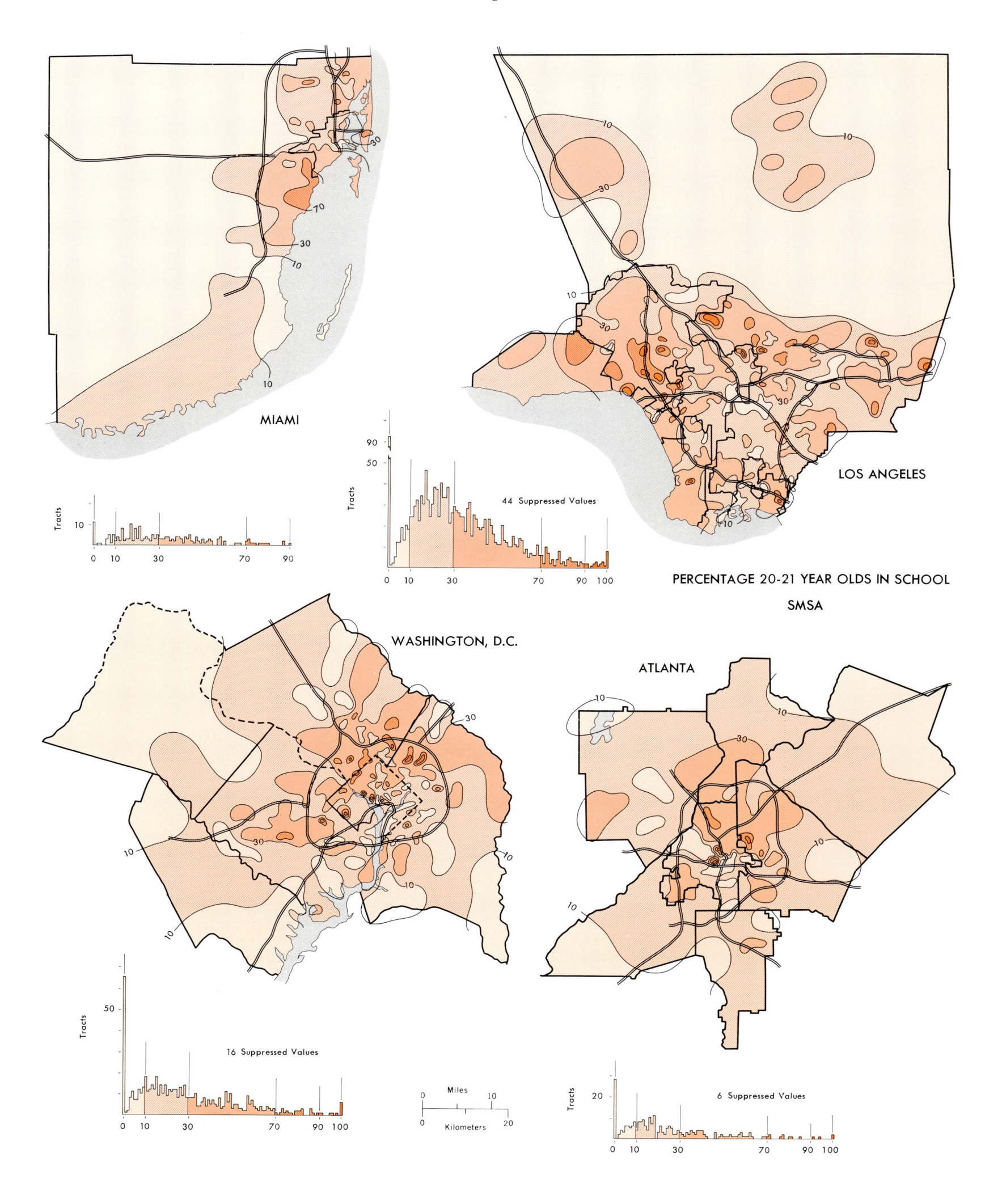

*Education: Young Adults in School*

MIAMI

LOS ANGELES

PERCENTAGE 20-21 YEAR OLDS IN SCHOOL
SMSA

WASHINGTON, D.C.

ATLANTA

*Public Health*

CHAPTER 40

# Immature Births

The Censuses of Population and Housing make no direct measurements of health or health care. Few of the variables in the Censuses are directly related to public health. An attempt to provide some measure of general health conditions and accessibility to health care has been made here by mapping the proportions of all live births under 2,500 grams (5 pounds, 8 ounces) in cities for which tract or other small-area data are available.

Birth weights under 2,500 grams are frequently associated with low incomes and the timing and quantity of medical care received by the mother during pregnancy. A study of 1963 birth weights demonstrated that 10.4 percent of the infants born to women in families with incomes below $3,000 were immature (under 2,500 grams) whereas only 6.8 percent of the births to women whose family incomes exceeded $10,000 were immature.* In every income category, immature births were more frequent among blacks than among whites or the total population. The same study showed that a clear positive relationship existed between the time medical care began and birth weight. Among mothers who received care starting in the first trimester of pregnancy, 6.7 percent of all births were low weight; among those beginning care in the third trimester, 8.6 percent of the births were immature. Immature births to mothers receiving no medical care were 11.5 percent of all live births.

Although there are statistical and conceptual hazards in making inferences from the proportion of immature births occurring in a single year or over a two-or three-year period for small areas, the general sensitivity of birth weights to incomes and to levels of medical care make them a useful index for a preliminary mapping of health-care access in American cities. The data mapped in this chapter were gathered from local and state health agencies and vital statistics registrars. They are therefore from different years and in one instance (New York City) are aggregated by health districts rather than census tracts. Appropriate details are provided in each city's annotation.

In 1971 there were 3,556,000 live births in the nation; 274,000 (7.7 percent) of these babies weighed less than 2,500 grams.† Of the children born to white mothers, 6.6 percent were immature whereas 13.4 percent of the nation's black infants weighed less than 2,500 grams at birth. There were 2,424,000 births within the nation's Standard Metropolitan Statistical Areas (SMSAs), of which 189,000 (7.8 percent) were immature. The proportion of low-weight births among blacks (13.6 percent) is higher than the white proportion (6.6 percent), as it is nationally. In the cities in this atlas for which birth-weight data are available, proportions of immature births vary from 13.1 percent in Washington, D.C. to 7 percent in St. Paul, Minnesota (see accompanying tabulation). Other things being equal, places with large low-income minority populations have high proportions of immature births.

Percentage Live Births under 2,500 Grams

| | |
|---|---|
| Boston | ND |
| New York City | 9.7 |
| Philadelphia | 11.3 |
| Hartford | ND |
| Baltimore | 10.6 |
| New Orleans | 11.5 |
| San Francisco | 7.2 |
| Oakland | 10.3 |
| Pittsburgh | 10.1 |
| St. Louis | 11.3 |
| Cleveland | 11.3 |
| Chicago | 11.4 |
| Detroit | ND |
| Minneapolis | 8.3 |
| St. Paul | 7.0 |
| Seattle | 7.7 |
| Dallas | 10.0 |
| Houston | 8.7 |
| Los Angeles | ND |
| Miami | ND |
| Atlanta | 10.7 |
| Washington, D.C. | 13.1 |

**Boston.** Data on birth weights are unavailable.

**New York City.** The data are mapped for the 260 health areas used by the Department of Health of the City of New York. The major clusters where immature births (1970 data) exceed 10 percent of health area totals are located in areas occupied by blacks (p. 382) and Spanish-Americans (p. 390). Incomes in such areas are usually low (p. 47), and significant proportions of their populations have incomes below the poverty level (p. 414).

**Philadelphia.** Immature births (1971 data) exceed 10 percent of all births in census tracts in the predominantly black neighborhoods of the city, but similar proportions of immature births are also evident in some predominantly white parts of south Philadelphia where incomes are low and income deficits (p. 430) are large.

**Hartford.** Data on birth weights are unavailable.

*Note:* Unless otherwise indicated, the present tense refers to the year or years specified in the annotation for each city. Cartographic conventions are explained in Chapter 1. County names and other locational information are shown on the SMSA map at the beginning of each city chapter (6-25) and on the DUS map of mobile homes near the beginning of each city chapter.

*Mary Grace Kovar, *Variations in Birth Weight: 1963 Legitimate Live Births*. Washington: U.S. Government Printing Office, 1968. National Center for Health Statistics, Series 22, Number 8.

†National Center for Health Statistics. *Vital Statistics of the United States, 1971*. Washington: U.S. Government Printing Office, 1975.

*Public Health: Immature Births*

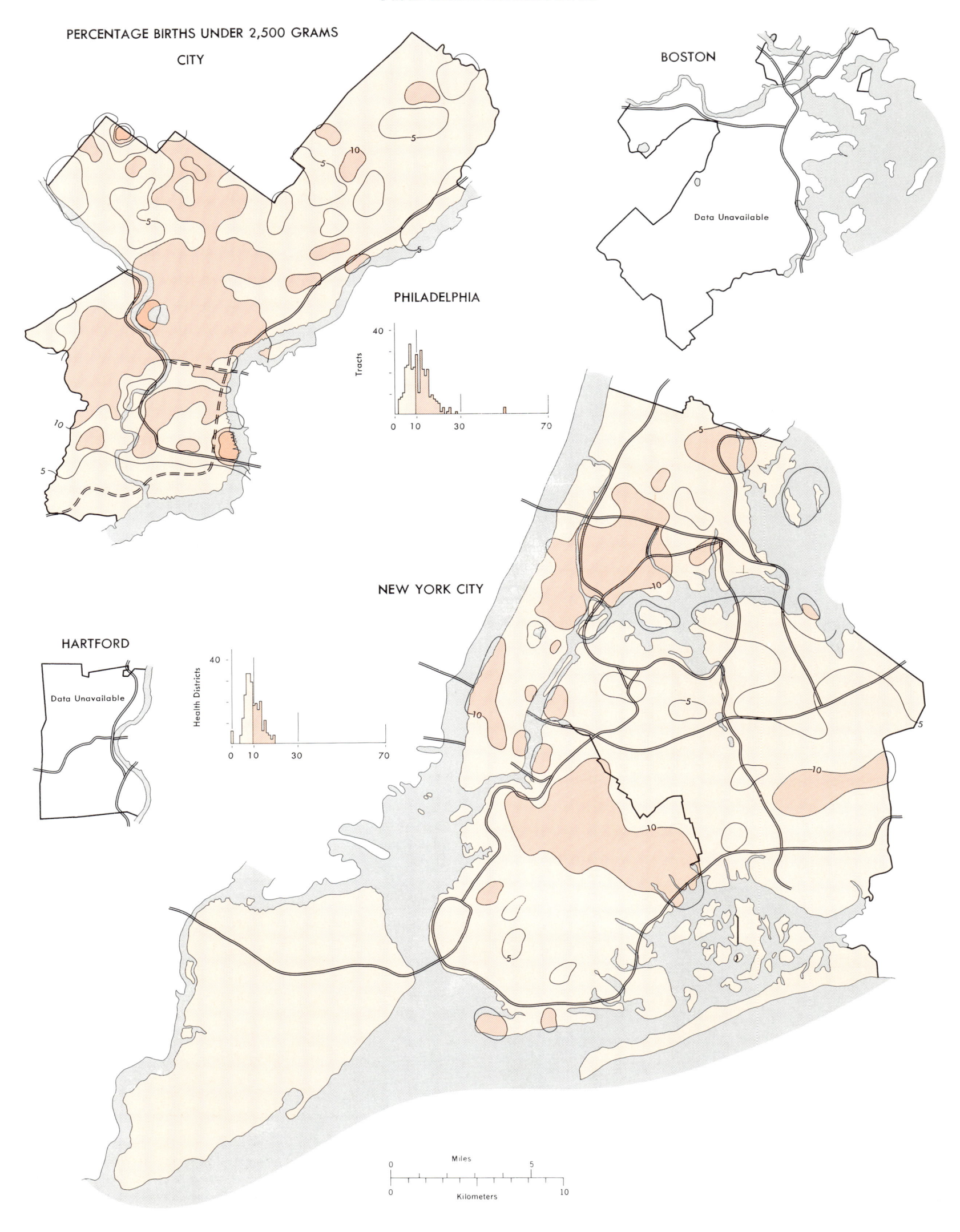

PERCENTAGE BIRTHS UNDER 2,500 GRAMS
CITY

BOSTON

PHILADELPHIA

HARTFORD

NEW YORK CITY

*Public Health: Immature Births*

PERCENTAGE BIRTHS UNDER 2,500 GRAMS

CITY

SAN FRANCISCO

OAKLAND

BALTIMORE

NEW ORLEANS

**Baltimore.** Immature births in 1971 are mapped by census tract. Almost all tracts in which births under 2,500 grams exceed 10 percent of all live births are located in predominantly black parts of the city (p. 74). Immaturity data by race are not available, but the nonwhite neonatal (the first 30 days of life) mortality rate of 19.9 per 1,000 live births compared with the white rate of 12 per 1,000 live births is suggestive of the race-specific immaturity rates, for low birth weight is predisposing to neonatal mortality.

**New Orleans.** Immature births in calendar year 1970 are mapped by census tract. The city has the highest proportion of immature births among cities mapped in this chapter. High proportions of low-weight births correspond closely to areas occupied by blacks (p. 83) with low incomes (p. 85). The neighborhoods occupied by prosperous blacks in the northern part of the city have low proportions of immature births. Whereas low-weight births are 7.5 percent of all white births, they are 14.4 percent of all black births.

**San Francisco-Oakland.** Immature births (1970-1972 data) are concentrated in black neighborhoods (p. 94) in San Francisco, where 12.4 percent of all black infants weighed less than 2,500 grams at birth, whereas only 6.6 percent of newborn white infants were that small. Data in Oakland are for 1970 only and no racial breakdown is available. The concentration of high rates in the city's black neighborhoods suggests that race-specific data for Oakland would be similar to the San Francisco statistics.

**Pittsburgh.** Comparatively high proportions of births under 2,500 grams (mapped here for 1970-1972) are concentrated primarily, but not exclusively, in parts of the city with significant black minorities (p. 110). In 1972, only 6 percent of white infants weighed less than 2,500 grams at birth, whereas 14.8 percent of nonwhite infants were immature.

**St. Louis.** Most of the tracts where low-weight births exceed 10 percent of all 1972 births are located in predominantly black parts of the city (p. 121), except for the extension southward along the Mississippi which demarcates a low-income area (p. 126). Race-specific immature birth data are not available.

**Cleveland.** Of the 1,770 immature births to Cleveland residents in 1970, 1,055 (60 percent) were to black mothers and 40 percent were to white mothers. Blacks comprise 38 percent of the city population. Whereas 8.3 percent of all newborn white infants weighed less than

375

*Public Health: Immature Births*

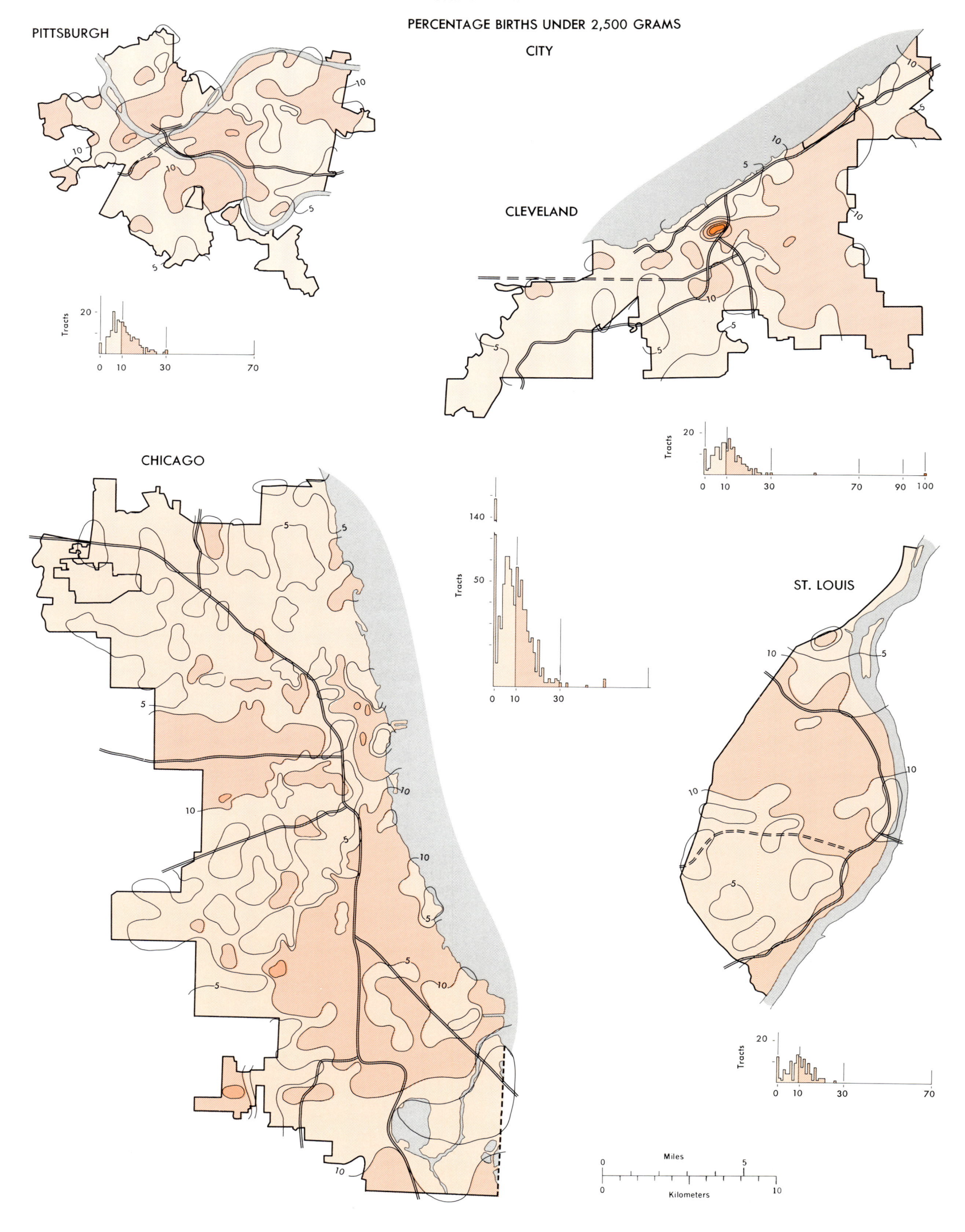

PERCENTAGE BIRTHS UNDER 2,500 GRAMS

CITY

PITTSBURGH

CLEVELAND

CHICAGO

ST. LOUIS

376

## Public Health: Immature Births

PERCENTAGE BIRTHS UNDER 2,500 GRAMS

CITY

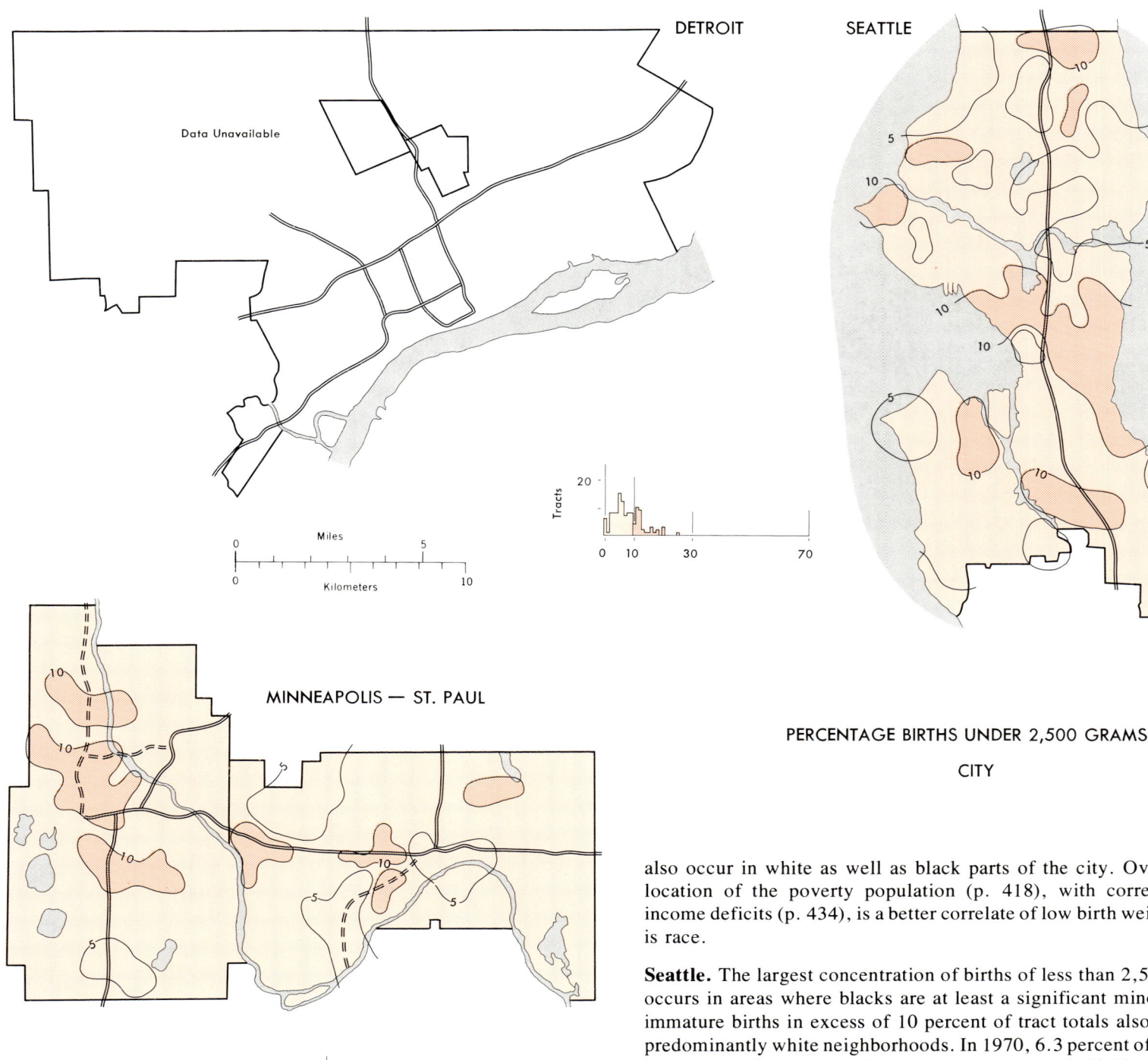

2,500 grams, the proportion among black newborns was 15 percent. The tract with 100 percent immature births had but 2 births in 1970.

**Chicago.** In 1972, 66 percent of the low-weight infants born in Chicago were black and 31 percent were white. The residual 3 percent were members of other racial groups. Thus low-weight births are concentrated in predominantly black areas of the city (p. 140), although one area where immature births exceed 10 percent of tract totals along Lake Michigan on the city's north side has a Spanish-American majority (p. 141).

**Detroit.** Data on birth weights are unavailable.

**Minneapolis-St. Paul.** Immature births (1969-1971) in Minneapolis are concentrated in several clusters that partially overlap black neighborhoods (p. 163). In St. Paul, immature births (1971 data only) also occur in white as well as black parts of the city. Overall, the location of the poverty population (p. 418), with corresponding income deficits (p. 434), is a better correlate of low birth weights than is race.

**Seattle.** The largest concentration of births of less than 2,500 grams occurs in areas where blacks are at least a significant minority, but immature births in excess of 10 percent of tract totals also occur in predominantly white neighborhoods. In 1970, 6.3 percent of all white births were immature, whereas 14.8 percent of all black infants weighed less than 2,500 grams.

**Dallas.** Immature births (1970 data) are concentrated in the city's black neighborhoods (p. 189) but much less so in areas occupied by Spanish-Americans (p. 190). The proportions of infants weighing less than 2,500 grams at birth for whites, blacks, and Spanish-Americans are 7, 15.5, and 8 percent respectively.

**Houston.** As in Dallas, high proportions of immature births (1970 data) are clustered in the city's black neighborhoods but less so in areas occupied by Spanish-Americans (p. 207). Income (p. 213) and especially poverty-level income (p. 218) are closely associated with high proportions of low-weight births.

**Los Angeles.** Data on birth weights are unavailable.

**Miami.** Data on birth weights are unavailable.

**Atlanta.** The correspondence of low-weight births in 1971 with the parts of Atlanta occupied by blacks (p. 251) with low incomes (p. 253) is especially striking. Race-specific data are unavailable, but the close correspondence in other cities of race and immature births suggests a high rate among blacks.

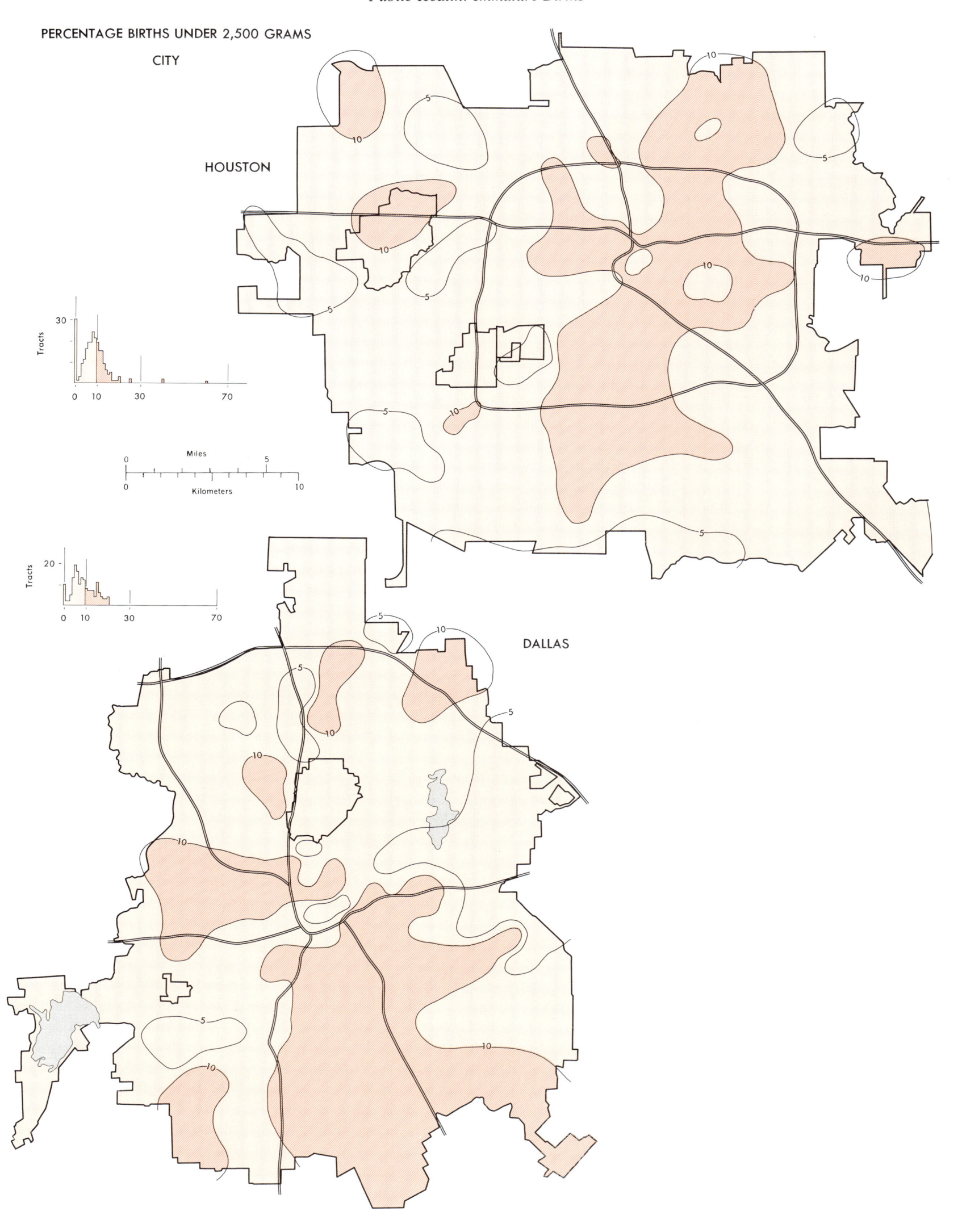

PERCENTAGE BIRTHS UNDER 2,500 GRAMS
CITY

HOUSTON

DALLAS

*Public Health: Immature Births*

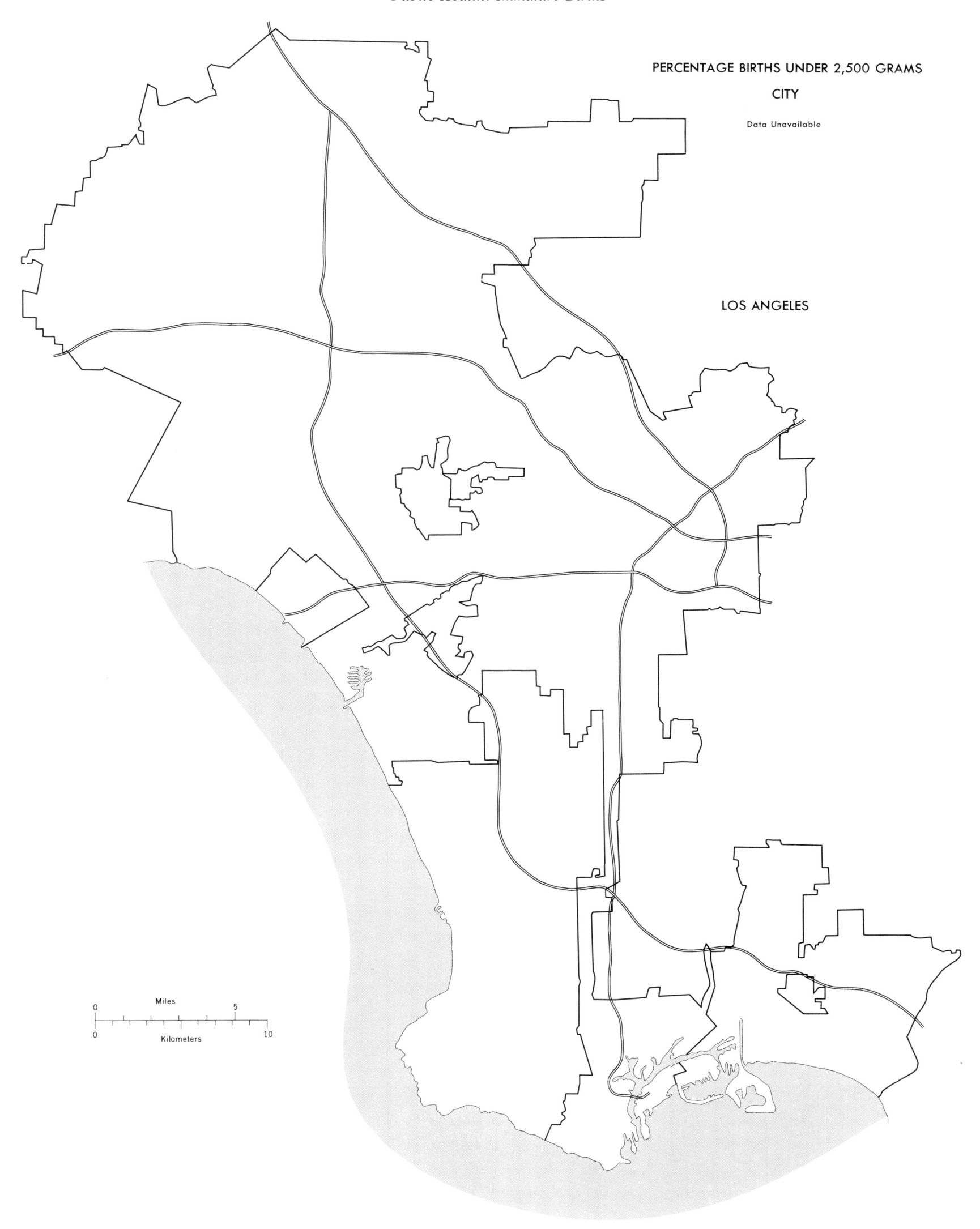

PERCENTAGE BIRTHS UNDER 2,500 GRAMS
CITY

Data Unavailable

LOS ANGELES

## Public Health: Immature Births

### MIAMI
Data Unavailable

### ATLANTA

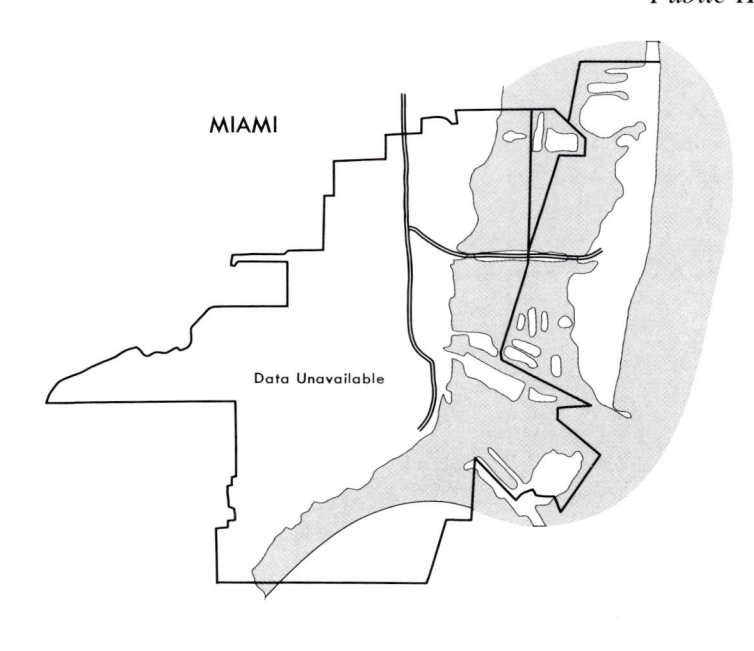

### PERCENTAGE BIRTHS UNDER 2,500 GRAMS
### CITY

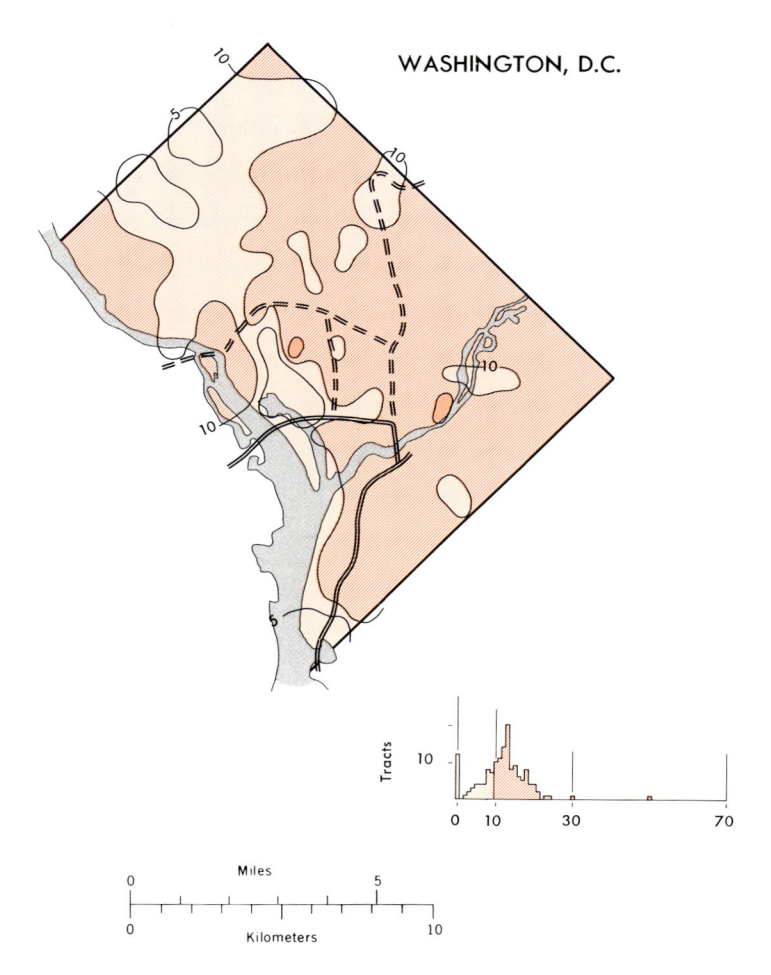

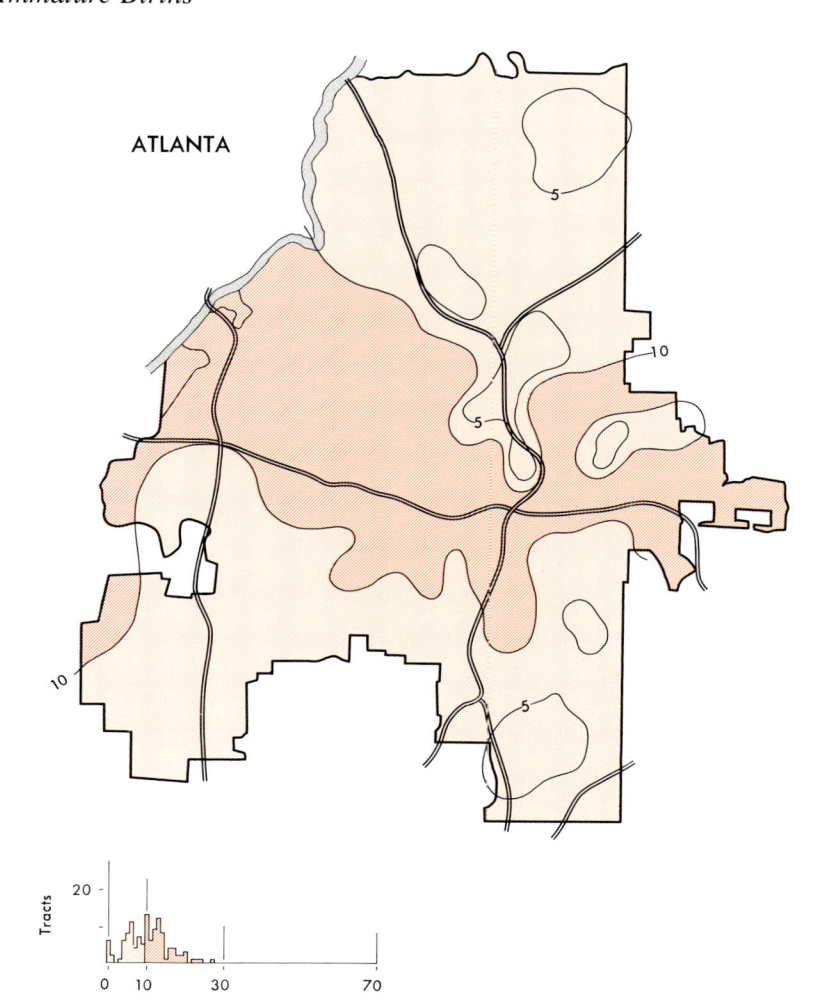

### WASHINGTON, D.C.

**Washington, D.C.** Only the city's affluent, predominantly white northwest has general immaturity rates under 10 percent of total resident births. In 1970, 13.7 percent of newborn black infants weighed less than 2,500 grams, whereas only 8.8 percent of all white infants were low-weight at birth. Because blacks are a large majority (71 percent) of the population of the District of Columbia and because most remaining white residents are older than the black population, 92 percent of the immature births in the city were to black mothers.

---

The consistent correspondence between black minority concentrations and high proportions of immature births is a product of generally low incomes and poor access to prenatal care. The lower age of mothers when bearing their first child is also a factor. Where blacks have middle-class incomes, as they do in parts of New Orleans, Atlanta, and other cities, the tracts they occupy have immature birthrates similar to those of tracts occupied by middle-class whites. Be that as it may, the high proportions of low-weight births in black and other low-income areas of cities are doubly troublesome. Not only do they indicate inadequate levels of health care among adult populations, but they also mean that a significant proportion of an already disadvantaged population begins life with an additional handicap.

## Socioeconomic Segregation

CHAPTER 41

# Negroes and New Single-Family Housing

In the 1970 Census each individual specified his or her race. These data were used to prepare the maps in this chapter, which show the percentage of the population that is black in the 20 metropolitan regions mapped in the atlas. Maps of black population for most of the central cities in the 20 regions appear in Chapters 6-25. One of every 9 Americans (11.1 percent) is black. The aggregate population in Standard Metropolitan Statistical Areas (SMSAs) is 11.7 percent black. In the central cities of SMSAs, blacks comprise 20.6 percent of the population. In the SMSAs mapped here, blacks make up 14.9 percent of the total population and 28.5 percent of the population within central cities (see accompanying tabulation).

Percentage of Negro Population

| Region | Central City(ies) | Entire SMSA |
|---|---|---|
| Boston | 16.3 | 4.6 |
| New York | 21.1 | 16.3 |
| Jersey City | 21.0 | 10.0 |
| Newark | 54.2 | 18.8 |
| Paterson-Clifton-Passaic | 17.4 | 5.5 |
| Philadelphia | 33.6 | 17.5 |
| Hartford | 27.9 | 7.6 |
| Baltimore | 46.4 | 23.7 |
| New Orleans | 45.0 | 31.0 |
| San Francisco-Oakland | 20.5 | 10.6 |
| Pittsburgh | 20.2 | 7.1 |
| St. Louis | 40.9 | 16.0 |
| Cleveland | 38.3 | 16.1 |
| Chicago | 32.7 | 17.6 |
| Detroit | 43.7 | 18.0 |
| Minneapolis-St. Paul | 4.0 | 1.8 |
| Seattle | 7.1 | 2.9 |
| Dallas | 24.9 | 15.9 |
| Fort Worth | 10.8 | 19.9 |
| Houston | 25.7 | 19.3 |
| Los Angeles | 17.9 | 10.8 |
| Miami | 22.7 | 15.0 |
| Atlanta | 51.3 | 22.3 |
| Washington, D.C. | 71.1 | 24.6 |

Nationally some 8,134,000 single-family dwellings were built from 1960 to March 1970, of which 388,000 (4.8 percent) are owned and occupied by blacks. Black ownership of new units is lower in SMSAs, at 4.2 percent of the housing built from 1960 to March 1970, but higher (8.5 percent) in the central cities of SMSAs. In the SMSAs

*Note:* All data are from the 1970 Censuses of Population and Housing unless otherwise indicated. Therefore the present tense refers to 1970 except for income data which are from 1969. Cartographic conventions are explained in Chapter 1. County names and other locational information are shown on the SMSA map at the beginning of each city chapter (6-25) and on the DUS map of mobile homes near the beginning of each city chapter.

mapped here, 2.1 percent of the single-family units built from 1960 to March 1970 are owned and occupied by blacks, as are 4.9 percent of the central-city units (see accompanying tabulation).

Number of Single-Family Dwellings Built 1960 to March 1970, Owned and Occupied by Negroes

| Region | Central City(ies) | Entire SMSA |
|---|---|---|
| Boston | 245 | 565 |
| New York | 2,700 | 7,310 |
| Jersey City | 65 | 65 |
| Newark | 20 | 1,215 |
| Paterson-Clifton-Passaic | 10 | 345 |
| Philadelphia | 1,350 | 5,670 |
| Hartford | 55 | 420 |
| Baltimore | 550 | 2,870 |
| New Orleans | 1,960 | 4,550 |
| San Francisco-Oakland | 1,585 | 4,305 |
| Pittsburgh | 410 | 1,065 |
| St. Louis | 820 | 1,840 |
| Cleveland | 1,415 | 2,060 |
| Chicago | 9,660 | 13,850 |
| Detroit | 3,055 | 5,895 |
| Minneapolis-St. Paul | 80 | 255 |
| Seattle | 620 | 985 |
| Dallas | 4.300 | 5,580 |
| Fort Worth | 2,015 | 2,185 |
| Houston | 7,440 | 10,225 |
| Los Angeles | 2,460 | 7,845 |
| Miami | 830 | 4,385 |
| Atlanta | 6,945 | 8,728 |
| Washington, D.C. | 2,067 | 9,158 |

On the maps that follow, a black dot is overprinted for each five single-family dwellings built from 1960 to March 1970 that are owned and occupied by blacks. The suppression of tract-level data when there are few blacks in a tract makes it impossible to complete the maps in some places. Thus the maps should be viewed cautiously and in conjunction with the table above, which is based on summary data for which suppression is not a problem.

**Boston.** Boston's blacks who own and occupy new housing live toward the edge of the predominantly black area, which is true in many other cities as well. The black-owned and black-occupied units are 1.2 percent of the new housing built in the city and 0.4 percent of the SMSA's new units. In suburban areas, 64 dots representing 320 units are missing because of suppressions.

**New York-Northern New Jersey.** Blacks own and occupy 10.1 percent of the New York City units built from 1960 to March 1970. In a few suburban places, blacks have acquired new housing in areas where they constitute less than 10 percent of tract populations.

*Socioeconomic Segregation: Negroes*

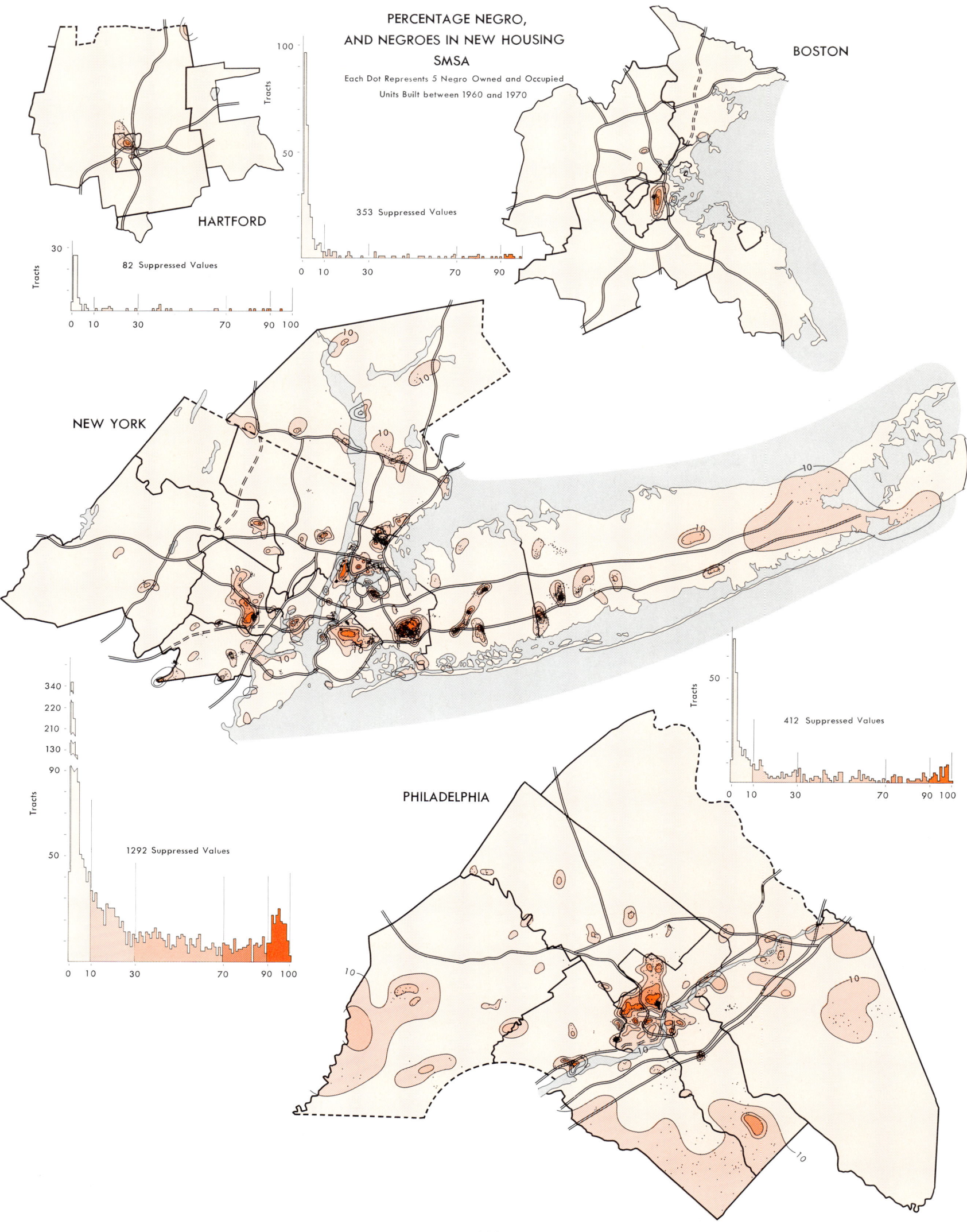

PERCENTAGE NEGRO, AND NEGROES IN NEW HOUSING
SMSA
Each Dot Represents 5 Negro Owned and Occupied
Units Built between 1960 and 1970

HARTFORD

BOSTON

NEW YORK

PHILADELPHIA

*Socioeconomic Segregation: Negroes*

BALTIMORE

NEW ORLEANS

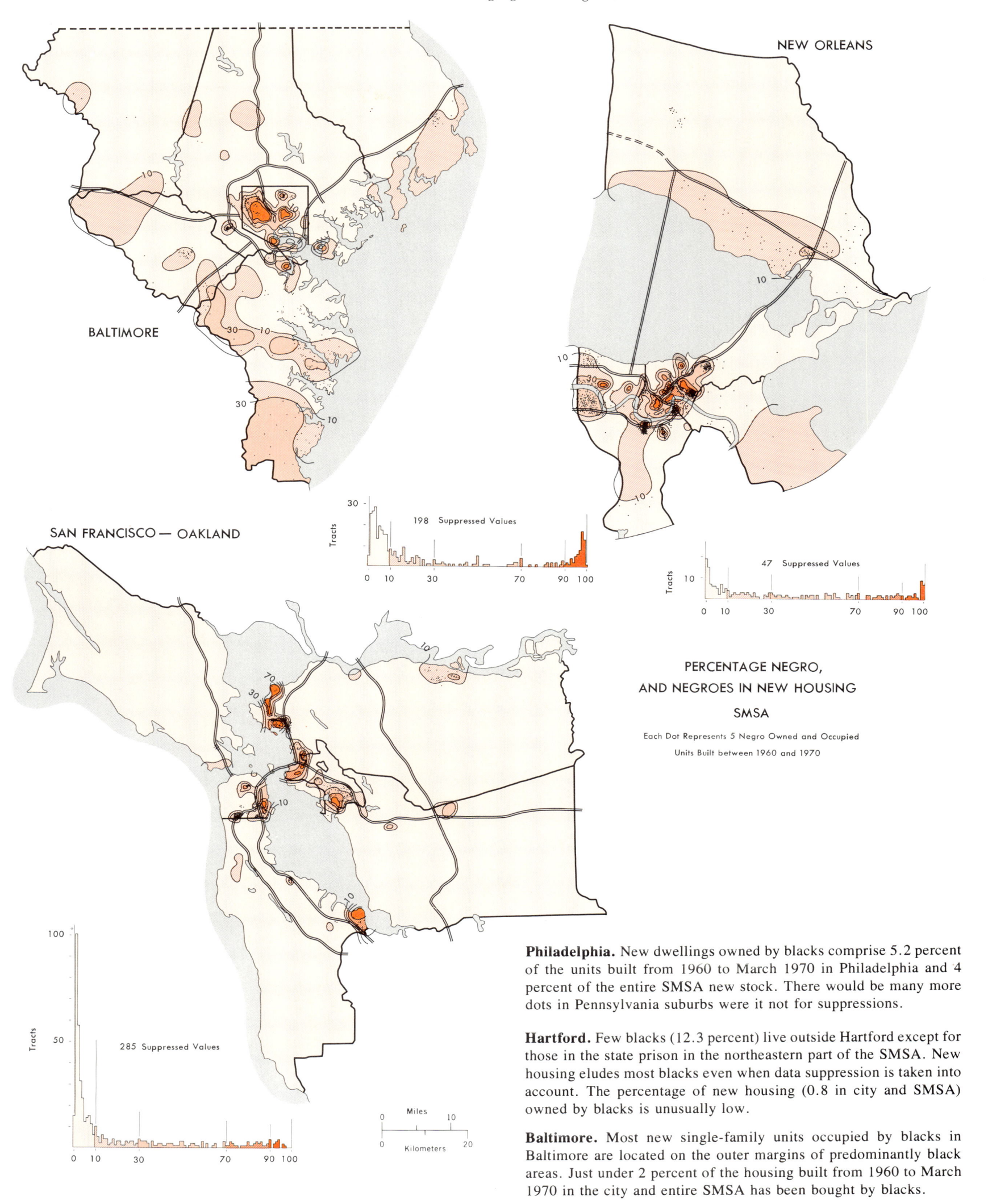

SAN FRANCISCO — OAKLAND

PERCENTAGE NEGRO,
AND NEGROES IN NEW HOUSING
SMSA

Each Dot Represents 5 Negro Owned and Occupied
Units Built between 1960 and 1970

**Philadelphia.** New dwellings owned by blacks comprise 5.2 percent of the units built from 1960 to March 1970 in Philadelphia and 4 percent of the entire SMSA new stock. There would be many more dots in Pennsylvania suburbs were it not for suppressions.

**Hartford.** Few blacks (12.3 percent) live outside Hartford except for those in the state prison in the northeastern part of the SMSA. New housing eludes most blacks even when data suppression is taken into account. The percentage of new housing (0.8 in city and SMSA) owned by blacks is unusually low.

**Baltimore.** Most new single-family units occupied by blacks in Baltimore are located on the outer margins of predominantly black areas. Just under 2 percent of the housing built from 1960 to March 1970 in the city and entire SMSA has been bought by blacks.

## Socioeconomic Segregation: Negroes

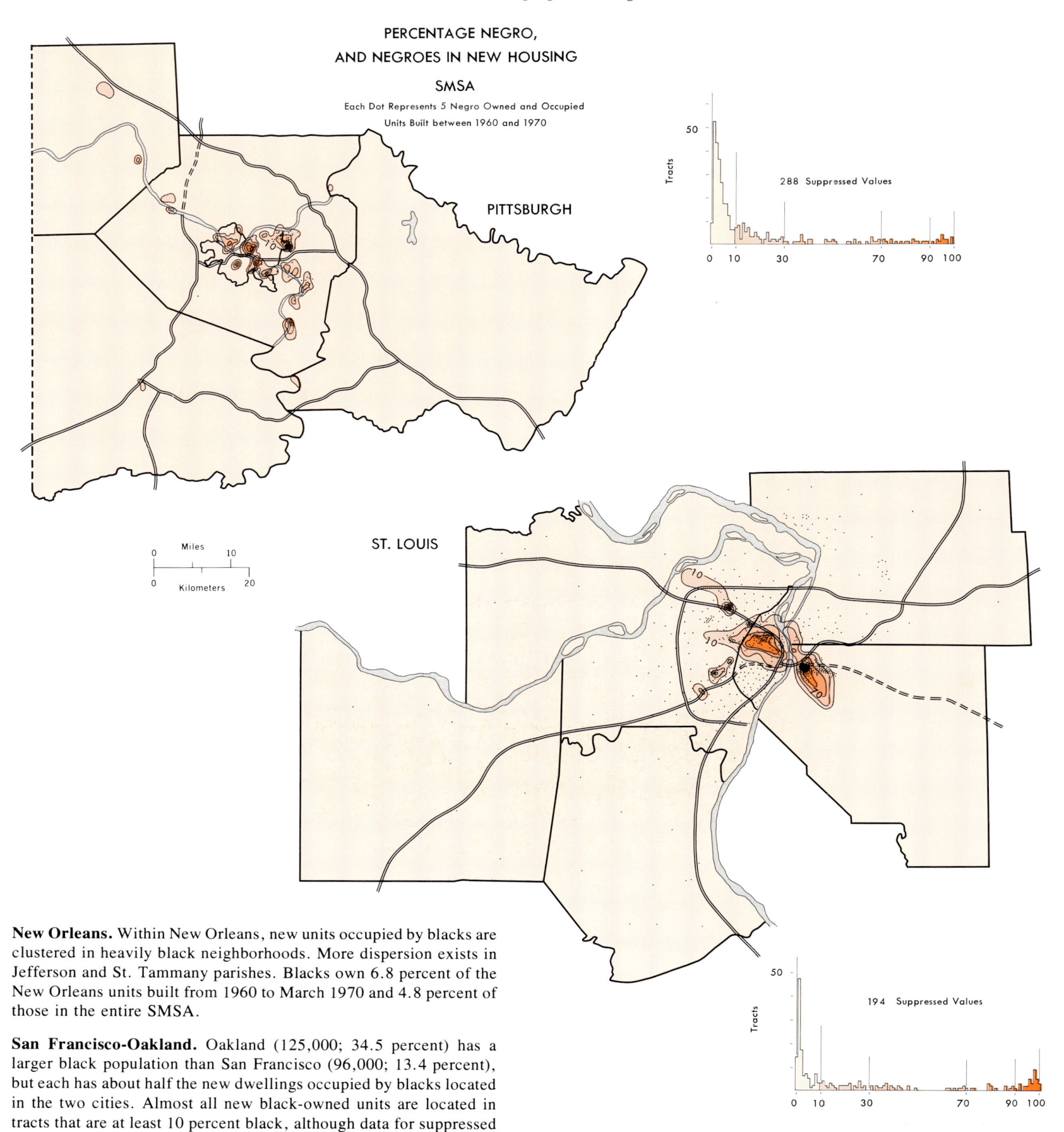

### PERCENTAGE NEGRO, AND NEGROES IN NEW HOUSING

SMSA

Each Dot Represents 5 Negro Owned and Occupied Units Built between 1960 and 1970

**New Orleans.** Within New Orleans, new units occupied by blacks are clustered in heavily black neighborhoods. More dispersion exists in Jefferson and St. Tammany parishes. Blacks own 6.8 percent of the New Orleans units built from 1960 to March 1970 and 4.8 percent of those in the entire SMSA.

**San Francisco-Oakland.** Oakland (125,000; 34.5 percent) has a larger black population than San Francisco (96,000; 13.4 percent), but each has about half the new dwellings occupied by blacks located in the two cities. Almost all new black-owned units are located in tracts that are at least 10 percent black, although data for suppressed tracts indicate greater dispersion.

**Pittsburgh.** Few (3,300) single-family units were built in the city in the 1960s, but blacks own 12.4 percent of those that were erected. Outside the city, new units owned by blacks (1.5 percent of the units built from 1960 to March 1970) seem to be confined to places where blacks constitute at least 10 percent of the population, although about 80 dots in outlying areas are missing because of data suppression.

**St. Louis.** Although two-thirds of the SMSA blacks live in St. Louis, 44.5 percent of the new single-family houses owned by blacks are located outside the city. Some are clustered in the East St. Louis, Illinois area, but an unusual number are scattered in the suburbs. Data suppression is minor.

**Cleveland.** The majority (68.7 percent) of the new one-family houses owned by blacks are located in southeastern Cleveland, but a few are scattered throughout the SMSA. Blacks own 9.3 percent of the new single-family units in Cleveland and 1.6 percent of those in the entire SMSA. Few data are suppressed.

*Socioeconomic Segregation: Negroes*

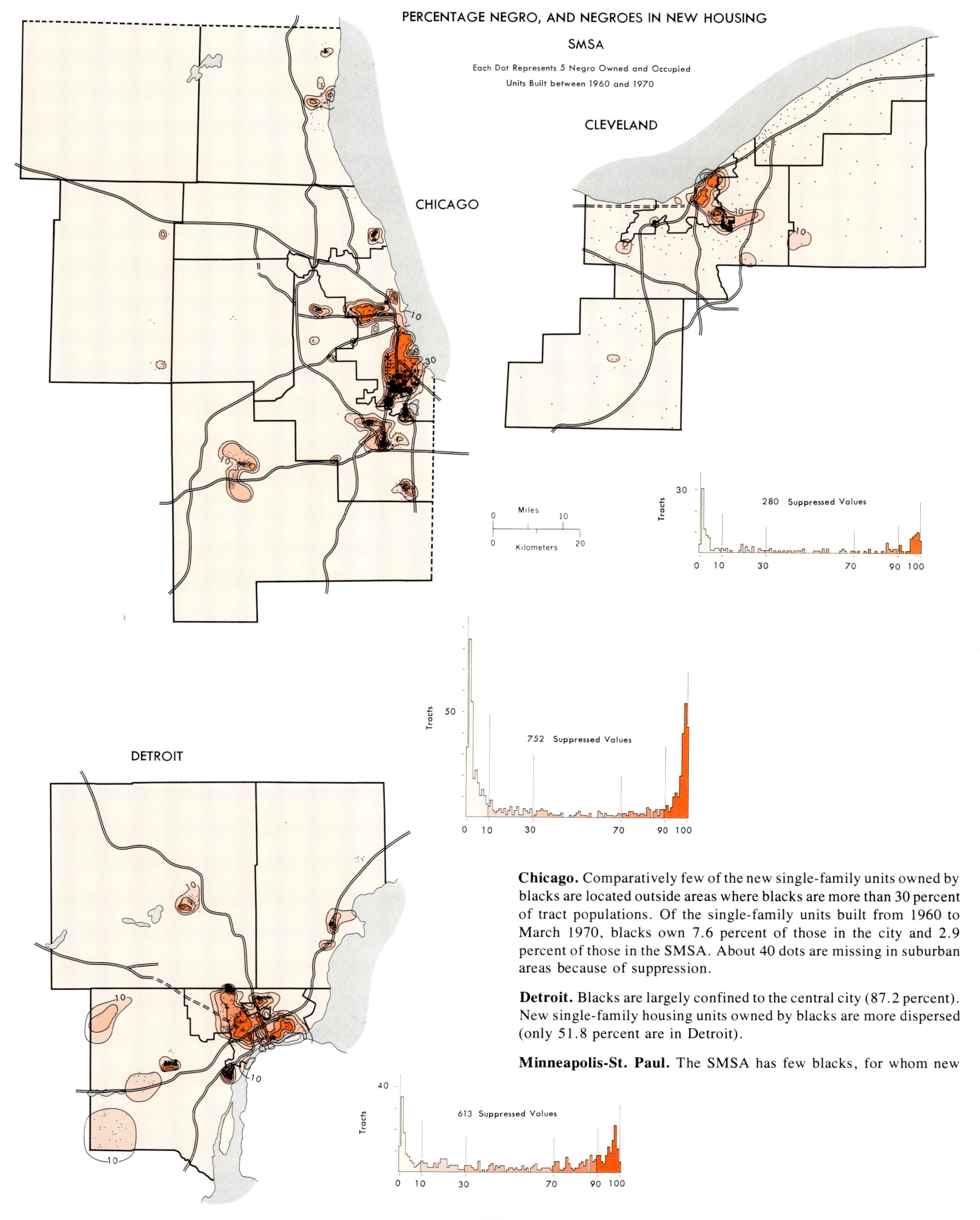

PERCENTAGE NEGRO, AND NEGROES IN NEW HOUSING

SMSA

Each Dot Represents 5 Negro Owned and Occupied
Units Built between 1960 and 1970

CLEVELAND

CHICAGO

DETROIT

**Chicago.** Comparatively few of the new single-family units owned by blacks are located outside areas where blacks are more than 30 percent of tract populations. Of the single-family units built from 1960 to March 1970, blacks own 7.6 percent of those in the city and 2.9 percent of those in the SMSA. About 40 dots are missing in suburban areas because of suppression.

**Detroit.** Blacks are largely confined to the central city (87.2 percent). New single-family housing units owned by blacks are more dispersed (only 51.8 percent are in Detroit).

**Minneapolis-St. Paul.** The SMSA has few blacks, for whom new

*Socioeconomic Segregation: Negroes*

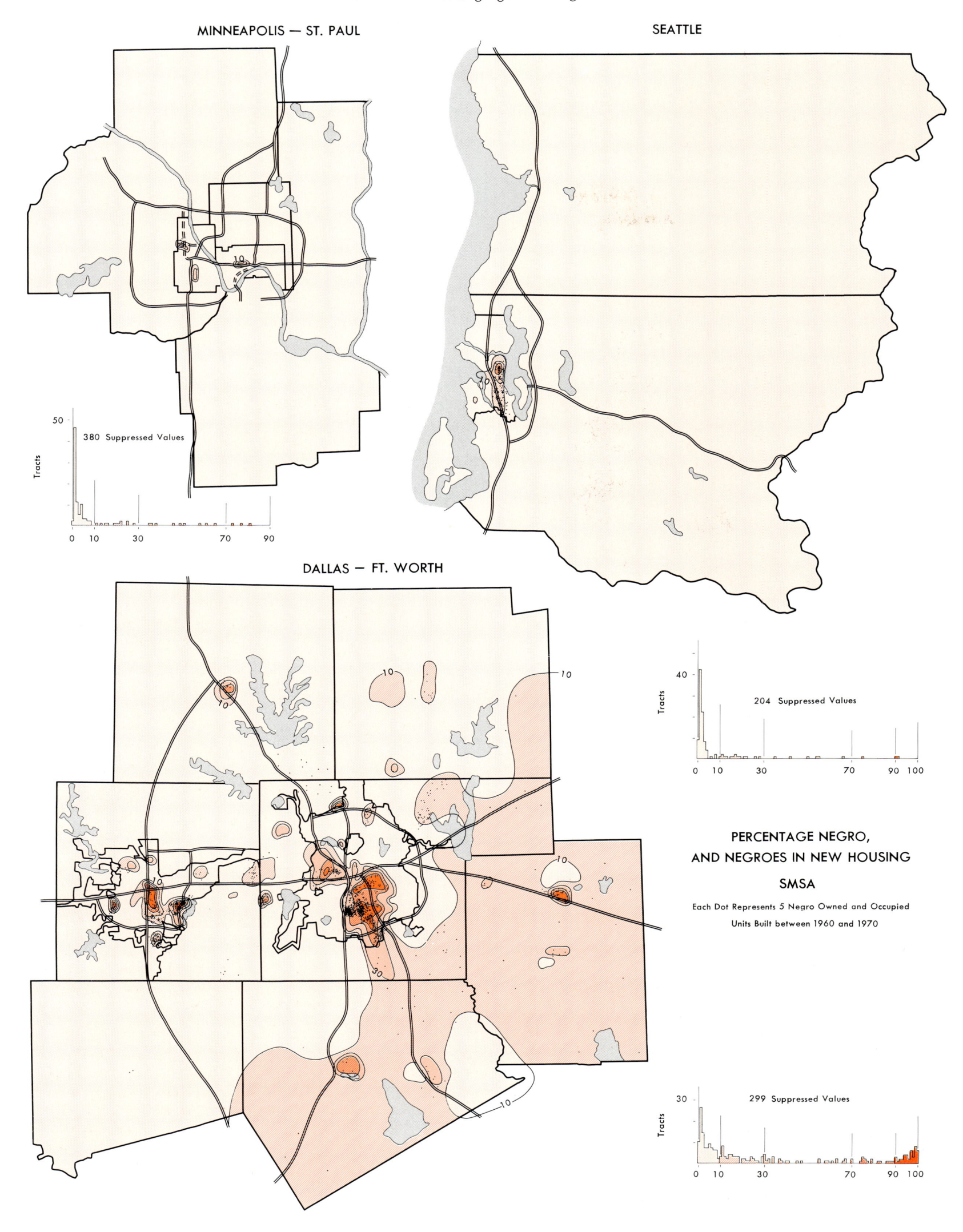

MINNEAPOLIS — ST. PAUL

SEATTLE

DALLAS — FT. WORTH

PERCENTAGE NEGRO,
AND NEGROES IN NEW HOUSING
SMSA

Each Dot Represents 5 Negro Owned and Occupied
Units Built between 1960 and 1970

## Socioeconomic Segregation: Negroes

### PERCENTAGE NEGRO, AND NEGROES IN NEW HOUSING

SMSA
Each Dot Represents 5 Negro Owned and Occupied
Units Built between 1960 and 1970

HOUSTON

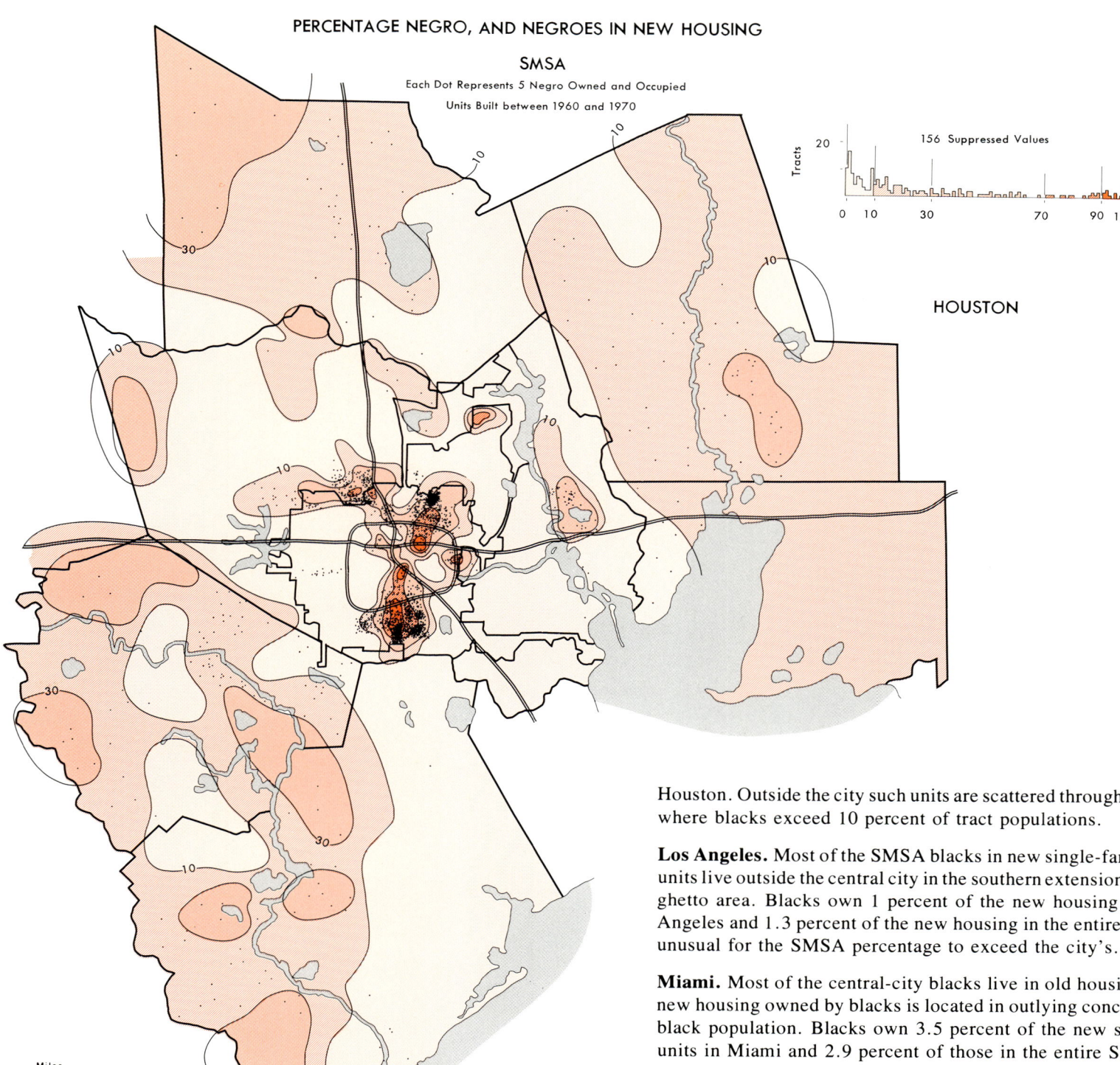

housing is almost unobtainable. They own but 0.2 percent of the single-family units built from 1960 to March 1970 in both central cities and the SMSA. Suppressions preclude mapping their locations.

**Seattle.** Blacks own and occupy 1.2 percent of the new single-family units in the city and 0.6 percent of those in the entire SMSA. Suppressions make it impossible to locate the 365 units outside Seattle.

**Dallas-Fort Worth.** Blacks own and occupy the following proportions of new units in the region: Dallas, 4.1 percent; Dallas SMSA, 2.7 percent; Fort Worth, 6.8 percent; Fort Worth SMSA, 2.5 percent. New black-owned units are scattered in rural areas.

**Houston.** Most (72.8 percent) of the single-family units built from 1960 to March 1970 and owned and occupied by blacks are located in Houston. Outside the city such units are scattered throughout the areas where blacks exceed 10 percent of tract populations.

**Los Angeles.** Most of the SMSA blacks in new single-family housing units live outside the central city in the southern extension of the major ghetto area. Blacks own 1 percent of the new housing built in Los Angeles and 1.3 percent of the new housing in the entire SMSA. It is unusual for the SMSA percentage to exceed the city's.

**Miami.** Most of the central-city blacks live in old housing, for most new housing owned by blacks is located in outlying concentrations of black population. Blacks own 3.5 percent of the new single-family units in Miami and 2.9 percent of those in the entire SMSA.

**Atlanta.** Almost 7,000 (15.2 percent) of the single-family units built from 1960 to March 1970 in the central city are owned and occupied by blacks. Of those erected in the entire SMSA, blacks own 4.5 percent. New units owned by blacks are notably absent in the northern part of Atlanta, compared with the rest of the city.

**Washington, D.C.** Most (72.5 percent) new single-family units owned by black occupants are located in Washington's eastern suburbs, although the absolute number and the proportion (4.7 percent) of new units inside the District of Columbia occupied by black owners are comparatively high.

---

Continued racial segregation in American metropolitan areas is evident in the sharp gradients between predominantly white and predominantly black areas in most SMSAs, and in the small numbers of blacks able to obtain new housing, most of which is located in predominantly white neighborhoods. Low incomes among blacks are a major impediment to participation in the general housing market, but white resistance to residential integration also maintains separate housing markets for blacks and whites.

*Socioeconomic Segregation: Negroes*

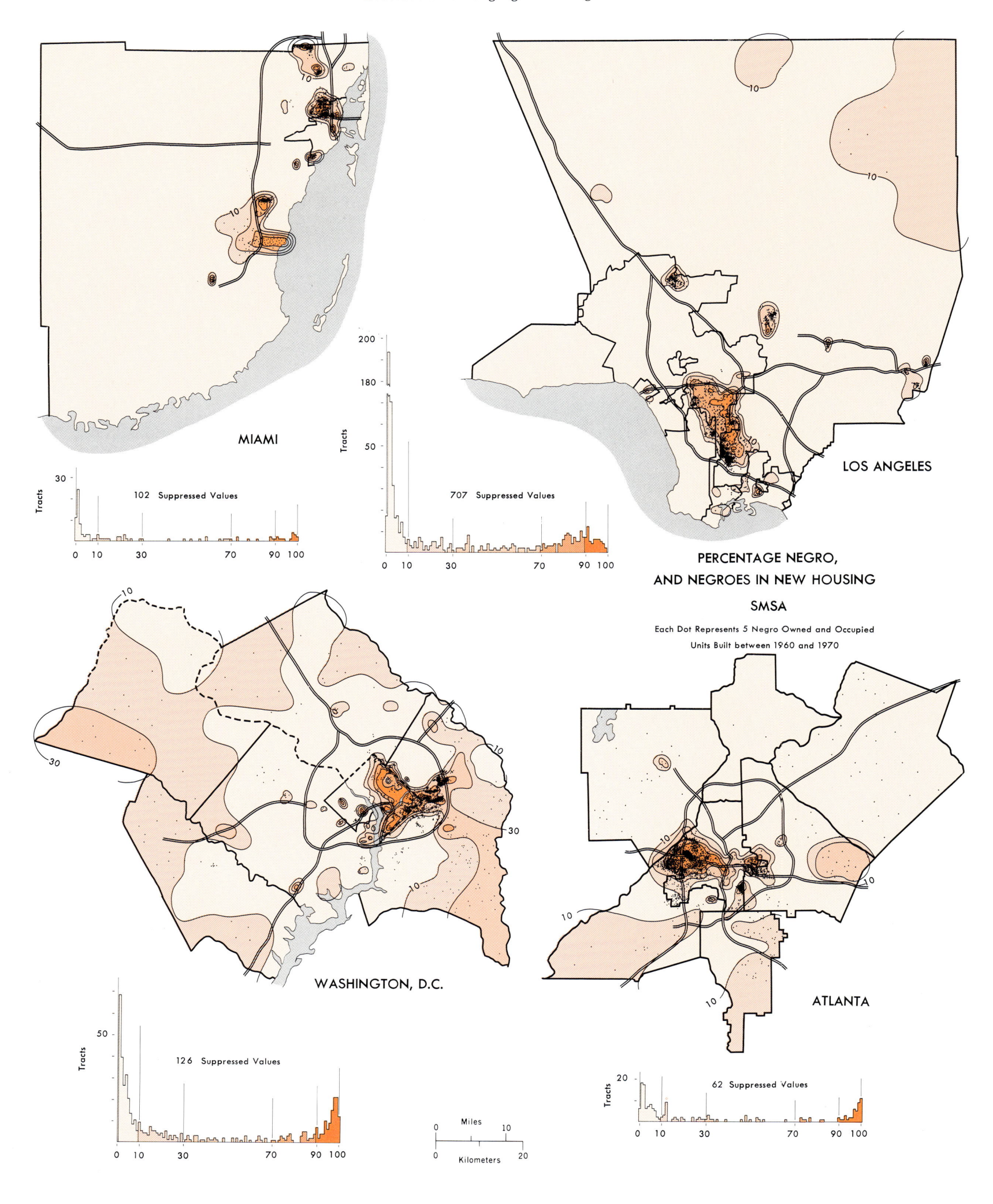

MIAMI

LOS ANGELES

102 Suppressed Values

707 Suppressed Values

PERCENTAGE NEGRO,
AND NEGROES IN NEW HOUSING

SMSA

Each Dot Represents 5 Negro Owned and Occupied
Units Built between 1960 and 1970

WASHINGTON, D.C.

ATLANTA

126 Suppressed Values

62 Suppressed Values

## Socioeconomic Segregation

## CHAPTER 42

# Spanish-Americans

In the 1970 Census of Population, Spanish-Americans—the nation's 2nd largest minority group—were identified by different characteristics in different places. In 42 states and the District of Columbia, Spanish-Americans were estimated by counting Spanish speakers. In California, Arizona, New Mexico, Colorado, and Texas, non-Spanish-speaking persons with selected Spanish surnames were added to those speaking Spanish to produce the estimate. In New Jersey, New York, and Pennsylvania, Puerto Rican stock as well as Spanish speakers were enumerated. Spanish speakers in the 42 states and Spanish speakers plus nonspeakers with Spanish surnames in the 5 southwestern states are mapped here at the SMSA scale. (See discussions of Spanish-Americans in Chapters 6-25.)

As defined above, there are 10,115,000 Spanish-Americans in the nation who comprise 5 percent of the total population. Spanish-Americans are concentrated in Standard Metropolitan Statistical Areas (SMSAs); the 8,470,000 Spanish-Americans who reside in SMSAs are 83.7 percent of the nation's Spanish-American population and 6.1 percent of the aggregate SMSA population. In contrast, 68.6 percent of the total population resides in SMSAs. Over half (51.2 percent) of the nation's Spanish-Americans live in central cities of SMSAs. There they are 8.1 percent of all central-city residents.

Proportions of Spanish-Americans vary from less than 1 percent in some cities and SMSAs to 23.6 percent in the Miami SMSA and 45.3 percent in Miami, where many Cuban refugees live. The nation's largest Spanish-American communities are located in the New York SMSA (1,392,000), the Los Angeles SMSA (1,289,000), and the San Francisco SMSA (364,000). (See accompanying tabulation.)

**Boston.** The SMSA's 36,200 Spanish-Americans are scattered in small numbers throughout much of the region, as indicated by the peak at the left side of the histogram and the large number of suppressed tracts. The few tracts where Spanish-Americans exceed 10 percent of the total population are located in Boston. Half of the SMSA's Spanish-American population lives in Boston (p. 25).

**New York-Northern New Jersey.** The region's SMSAs have the largest (1,620,000) Hispanic minority in the nation, although it is a heterogeneous group composed of Spanish speakers from several parts of the world. Of the New York City SMSA's Spanish-Americans, 91.9 percent (1,279,000) live in the central city's five boroughs (p. 38).

**Philadelphia.** There are 83,500 Spanish-Americans in the Philadelphia SMSA, about half of whom are of Puerto Rican birth or parentage. The most intense concentrations of Spanish-Americans are located in central Philadelphia and in Camden, New Jersey, just across the Delaware River. The 131 Spanish-Americans in southern Burlington County are all of Puerto Rican stock.

Percentage of Spanish-Americans

| Region | Central City(ies) | Entire SMSA |
|---|---|---|
| Boston | 2.8 | 1.3 |
| New York | 16.2 | 12.0 |
| Jersey City | 9.1 | 14.7 |
| Newark | 12.0 | 4.7 |
| Paterson-Clifton-Passaic | 10.3 | 3.9 |
| Philadelphia | 2.3 | 1.7 |
| Hartford | 7.6 | 2.4 |
| Baltimore | 1.0 | 1.0 |
| New Orleans | 4.4 | 4.2 |
| San Francisco-Oakland | 12.7 | 11.7 |
| Pittsburgh | 0.5 | 0.4 |
| St. Louis | 1.0 | 1.0 |
| Cleveland | 1.9 | 1.0 |
| Chicago | 7.4 | 4.7 |
| Detroit | 1.8 | 1.3 |
| Minneapolis-St. Paul | 1.4 | 0.9 |
| Seattle | 2.0 | 1.7 |
| Dallas | 8.0 | 6.5 |
| Fort Worth | 8.5 | 5.8 |
| Houston | 12.2 | 10.7 |
| Los Angeles | 18.4 | 18.3 |
| Miami | 45.3 | 23.6 |
| Atlanta | 1.0 | 1.0 |
| Washington, D.C. | 2.1 | 2.5 |

**Hartford.** There are 15,700 Spanish-Americans in the SMSA, of whom 11,900 (76.2 percent) reside in Hartford, where the community is concentrated in and near the downtown area (p. 65). Most (60 percent) of the region's Spanish-Americans are Puerto Rican stock, although there are about 1,600 people of Cuban birth or parentage in the SMSA.

**Baltimore.** The SMSA's 19,000 Spanish-Americans are scattered in small numbers throughout most of the SMSA; 44.5 percent live in Baltimore as do 43.7 percent of all the SMSA's people. Most of the SMSA's Spanish-Americans are of Central and South American, Cuban, and indigenous United States origin. Only 2,450 (13 percent) are of Puerto Rican birth or parentage.

**New Orleans.** Concentrations of Spanish-Americans in excess of 10 percent of tract populations are scattered in New Orleans, where 26,400 (59.4 percent) of the SMSA's 44,400 Hispanics reside. Because of the port's historic ties with Latin America, a large share of the SMSA's Hispanics are of Central and South American stock.

*Note:* All data are from the 1970 Censuses of Population and Housing unless otherwise indicated. Therefore the present tense refers to 1970 except for income data which are from 1969. Cartographic conventions are explained in Chapter 1. County names and other locational information are shown on the SMSA map at the beginning of each city chapter (6-25) and on the DUS map of mobile homes near the beginning of each city chapter.

## Socioeconomic Segregation: Spanish-Americans

HARTFORD

BOSTON

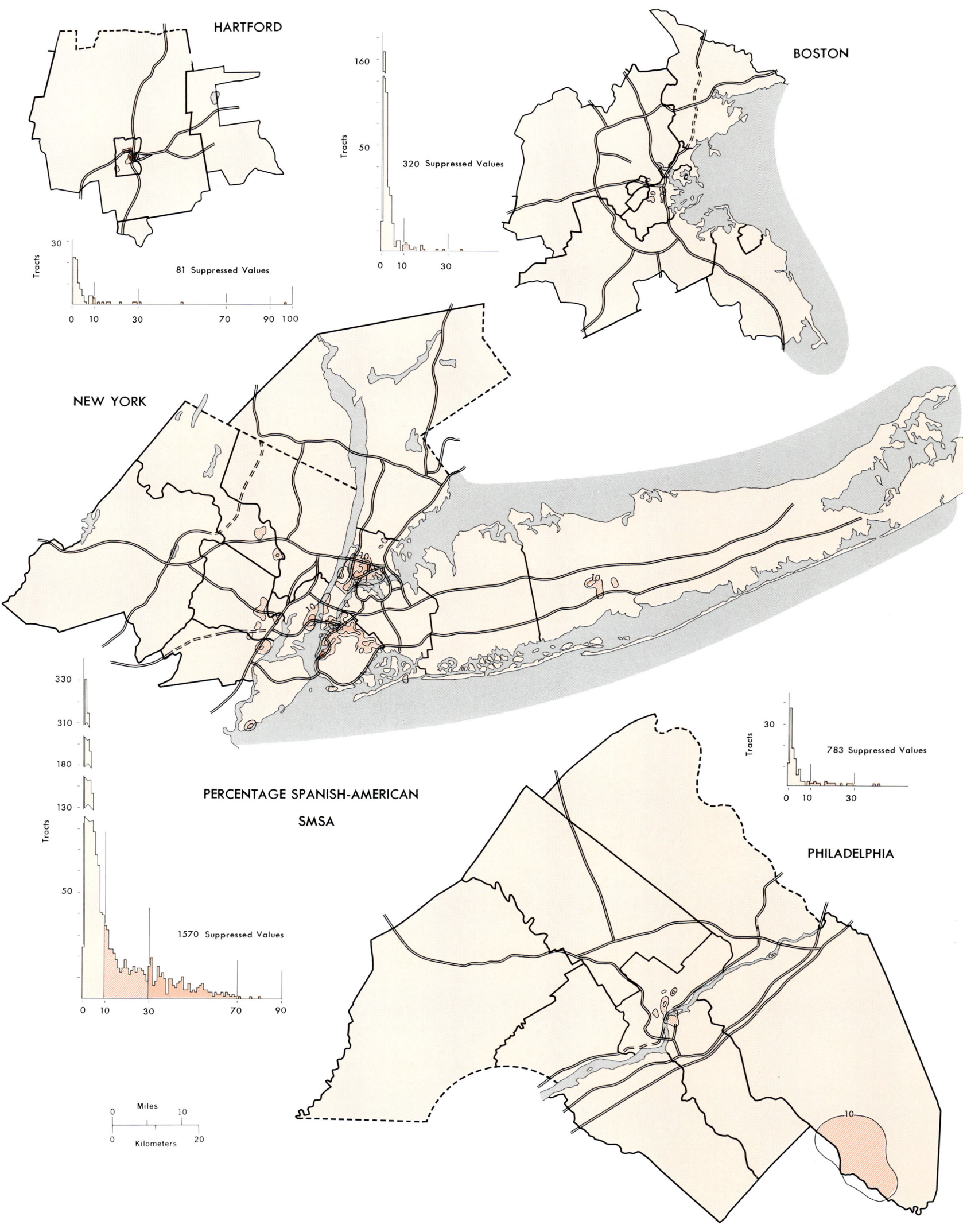

NEW YORK

PERCENTAGE SPANISH-AMERICAN SMSA

PHILADELPHIA

81 Suppressed Values

320 Suppressed Values

1570 Suppressed Values

783 Suppressed Values

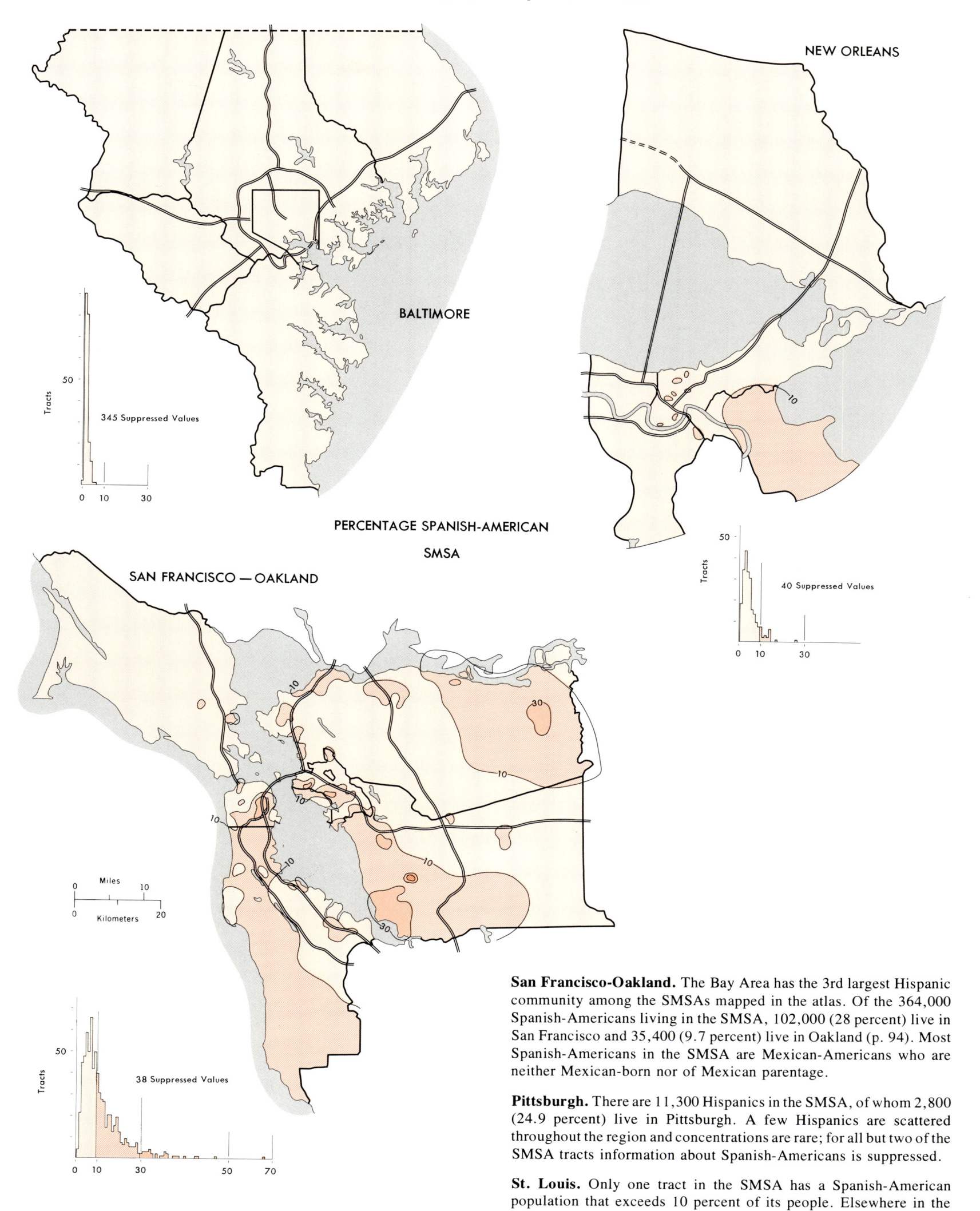

*Socioeconomic Segregation: Spanish-Americans*

PERCENTAGE SPANISH-AMERICAN
SMSA

**San Francisco-Oakland.** The Bay Area has the 3rd largest Hispanic community among the SMSAs mapped in the atlas. Of the 364,000 Spanish-Americans living in the SMSA, 102,000 (28 percent) live in San Francisco and 35,400 (9.7 percent) live in Oakland (p. 94). Most Spanish-Americans in the SMSA are Mexican-Americans who are neither Mexican-born nor of Mexican parentage.

**Pittsburgh.** There are 11,300 Hispanics in the SMSA, of whom 2,800 (24.9 percent) live in Pittsburgh. A few Hispanics are scattered throughout the region and concentrations are rare; for all but two of the SMSA tracts information about Spanish-Americans is suppressed.

**St. Louis.** Only one tract in the SMSA has a Spanish-American population that exceeds 10 percent of its people. Elsewhere in the

## Socioeconomic Segregation: Spanish-Americans

PERCENTAGE SPANISH-AMERICAN SMSA

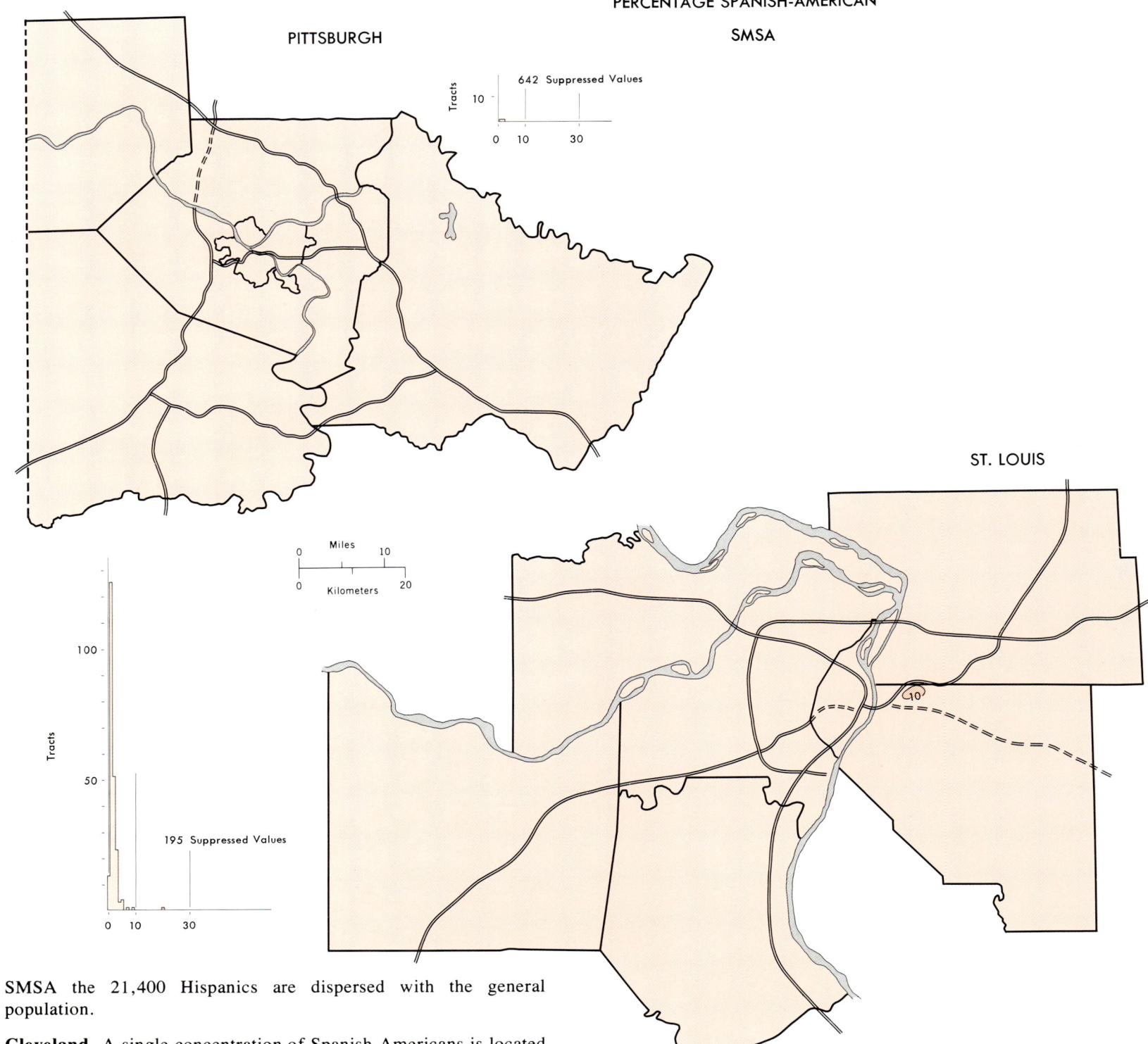

PITTSBURGH

ST. LOUIS

SMSA the 21,400 Hispanics are dispersed with the general population.

**Cleveland.** A single concentration of Spanish-Americans is located west of the Cleveland Central Business District. In the rest of the SMSA, Hispanics are scattered; 14,000 (65.6 percent) of the SMSA's 21,300 Spanish-Americans reside in Cleveland (p. 131). Over 40 percent of the SMSA's Hispanics are of Puerto Rican stock.

**Chicago.** The SMSA has the 4th largest Hispanic minority of cities in the atlas, after New York, Los Angeles, and San Francisco. The SMSA's Hispanics are concentrated in Chicago, where 247,300 (75.6 percent) live. About a third of the SMSA's Hispanics are Mexican-Americans. The remainder are Puerto Rican stock (26 percent), Americans of Mexican descent (26 percent), Central and South American stock (9 percent), and Cuban stock (6 percent). Central-city Hispanics are heavily concentrated in two predominantly Spanish-American neighborhoods, one dominantly Mexican, the other Puerto Rican; Cubans are well distributed in the city's north side (p. 141).

**Detroit.** The SMSA's 56,300 Spanish-Americans are dispersed in small numbers throughout the region with a concentration southwest of the Central Business District (p. 153). Slightly less than half (48 percent) of the SMSA's Hispanics live in Detroit.

**Minneapolis-St. Paul.** There are 16,700 Spanish-Americans in the Twin Cities SMSA, of whom 3,900 (23.6 percent) live in Minneapolis and 6,500 (39 percent) live in St. Paul. The most important Spanish-American community is located in St. Paul just south of the Mississippi River (p. 163). Most of the SMSA's Hispanics are Mexican-Americans or people of Central and South American stock. There are few people of Puerto Rican and Cuban stock. The Spanish-American minority in St. Paul is 2.1 percent of the city population.

**Seattle.** There are 24,200 Hispanics in the SMSA, of whom about 18,000 (74.5 percent) are native-born Americans of Mexican descent. Another 2,600 (10.7 percent) are Mexican foreign stock. There are few people of Puerto Rican or Cuban stock. For the most part, the SMSA's Hispanics are scattered in small numbers throughout the city

## Socioeconomic Segregation: Spanish-Americans

PERCENTAGE SPANISH-AMERICAN SMSA

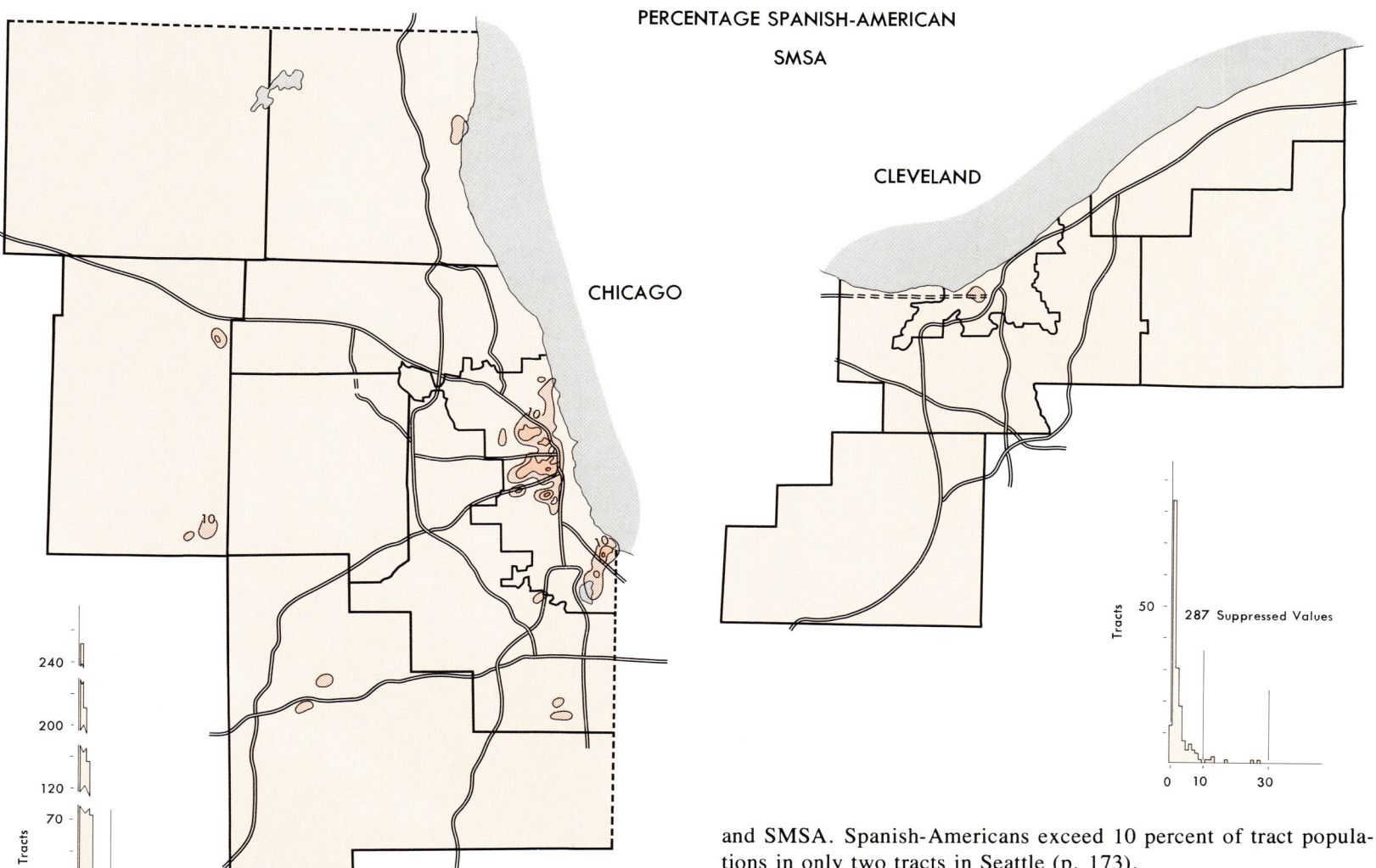

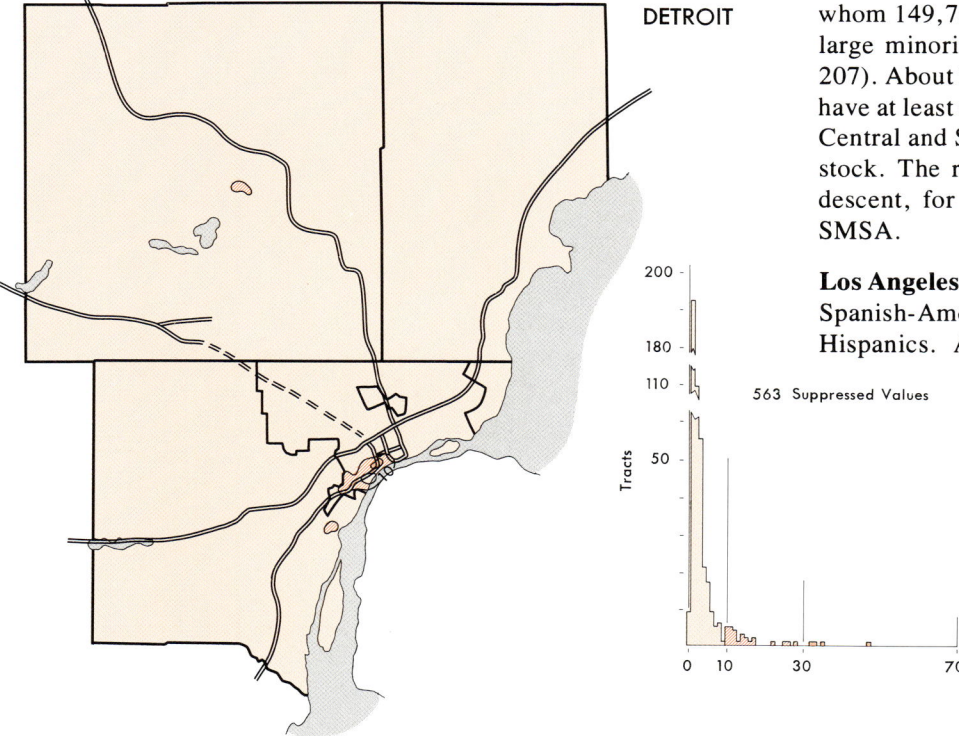

and SMSA. Spanish-Americans exceed 10 percent of tract populations in only two tracts in Seattle (p. 173).

**Dallas-Fort Worth.** There are 101,200 Spanish-Americans in the Dallas SMSA and 44,300 in the Fort Worth SMSA. Together they comprise 6.3 percent of the combined SMSA populations. The 67,900 Hispanics in Dallas and the 33,400 in Fort Worth are 8 and 8.5 percent of the respective cities' populations. There are few people of Puerto Rican or Cuban stock among the Hispanic population. Almost all the region's Spanish-Americans are native-born Americans of Mexican descent or people of Mexican birth or parentage.

**Houston.** There are 212,400 Spanish-Americans in the SMSA, of whom 149,700 (70.5 percent) live in Houston, where Hispanics are a large minority in most of the northeastern quadrant of the city (p. 207). About 30 percent of the SMSA's Hispanics are Mexican-born or have at least one Mexican-born parent (p. 208), about 3 percent are of Central and South American stock, and just over 1 percent are Cuban stock. The remaining two-thirds are native Americans of Mexican descent, for there are but 880 people of Puerto Rican stock in the SMSA.

**Los Angeles.** The Los Angeles metropolitan community of 1,289,000 Spanish-Americans is 2nd in size only to New York's 1,390,000 Hispanics. Almost 1 of 5 of the SMSA's residents is Spanish-

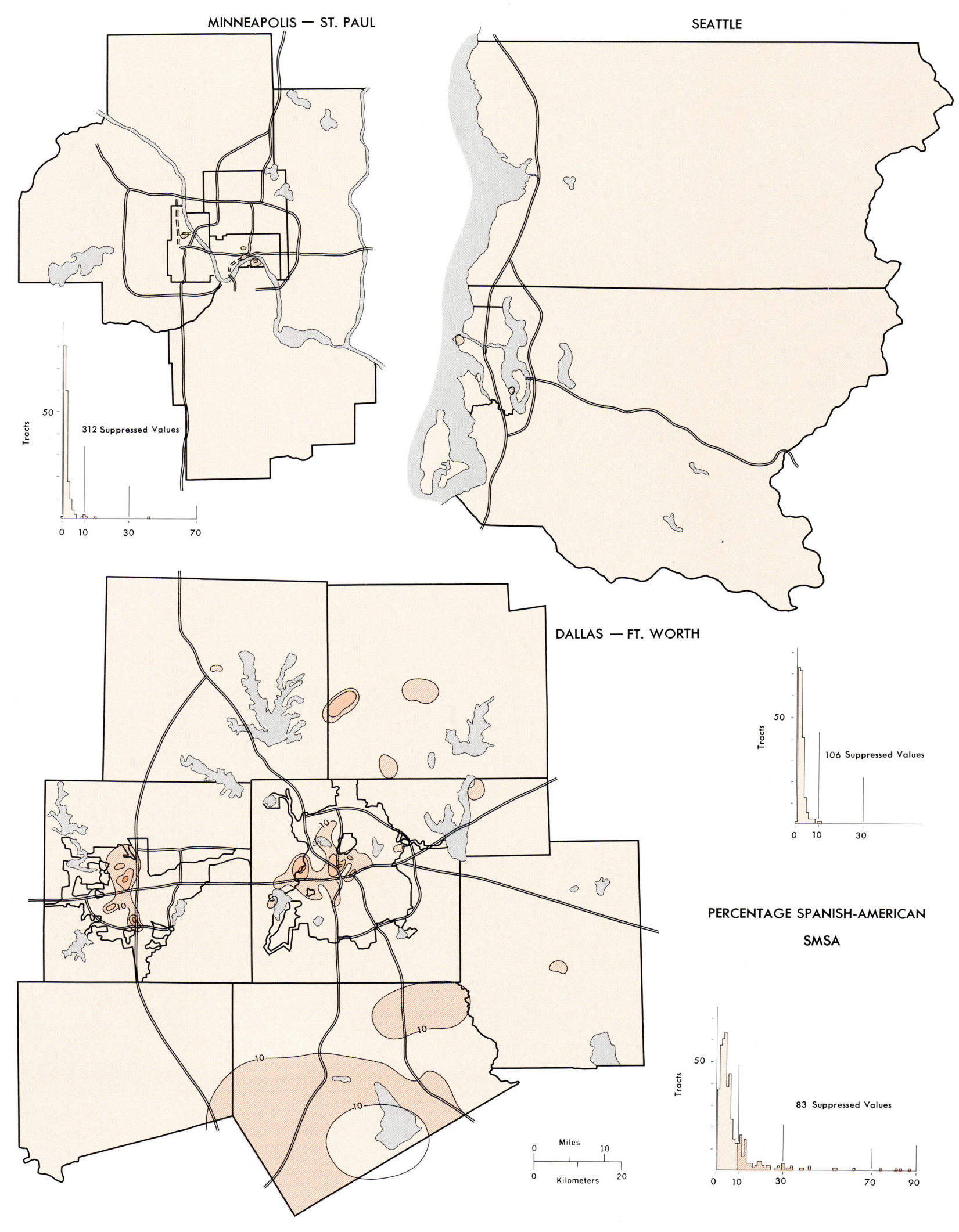

*Socioeconomic Segregation: Spanish-Americans*

MINNEAPOLIS — ST. PAUL

SEATTLE

DALLAS — FT. WORTH

PERCENTAGE SPANISH-AMERICAN

SMSA

312 Suppressed Values

106 Suppressed Values

83 Suppressed Values

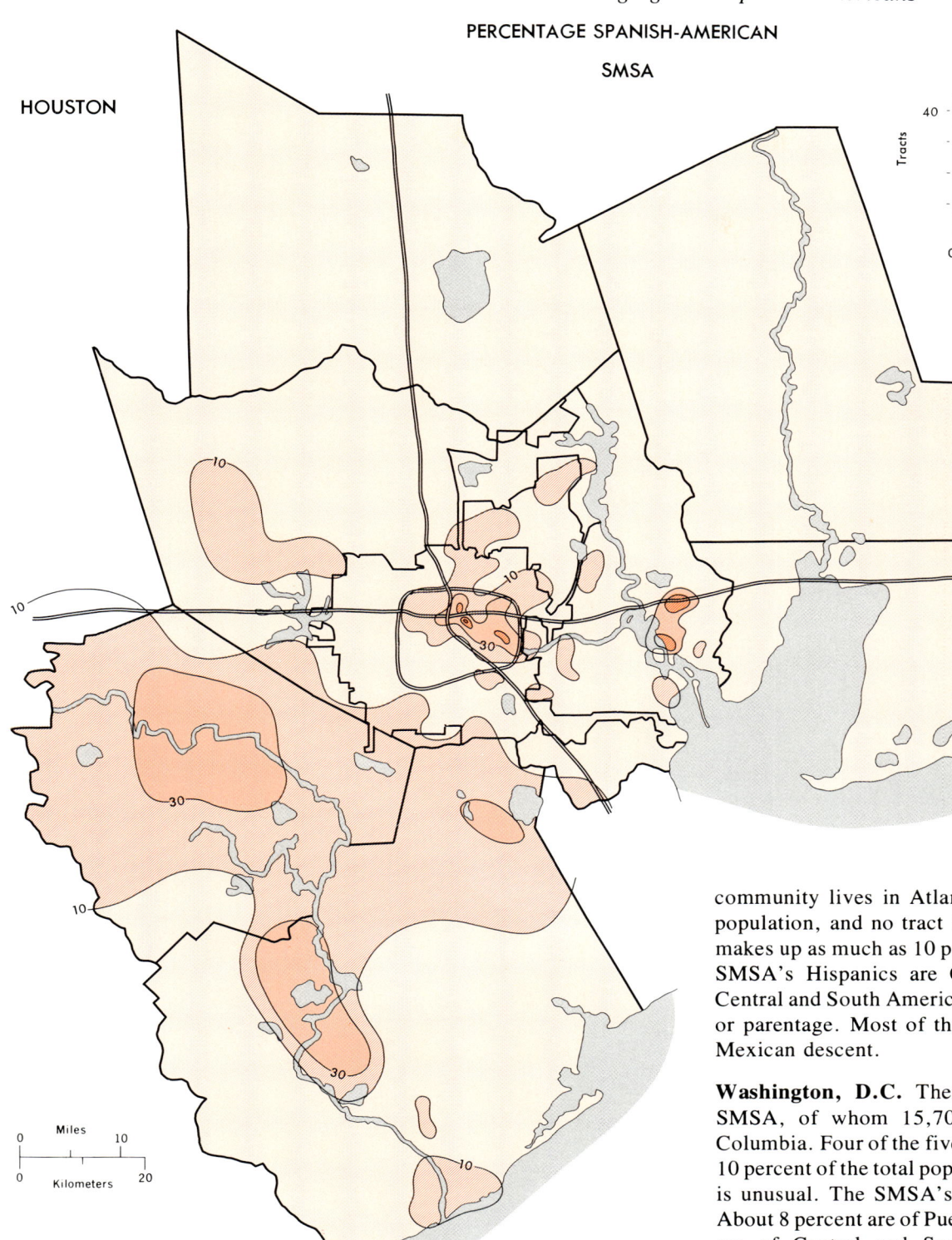

*Socioeconomic Segregation: Spanish-Americans*

PERCENTAGE SPANISH-AMERICAN

SMSA

HOUSTON

community lives in Atlanta compared with 36 percent of the total population, and no tract in the SMSA has a Hispanic minority that makes up as much as 10 percent of its population. About a fifth of the SMSA's Hispanics are Cuban stock, and another fifth are from Central and South America. About 7 percent are of Puerto Rican birth or parentage. Most of the remainder are native-born Americans of Mexican descent.

**Washington, D.C.** There are 70,900 Spanish-Americans in the SMSA, of whom 15,700 (22.2 percent) live in the District of Columbia. Four of the five tracts in which Spanish-Americans exceed 10 percent of the total population are located in suburban areas, which is unusual. The SMSA's Hispanic component is of diverse origin. About 8 percent are of Puerto Rican birth or parentage, and 43 percent are of Central and South American stock. Mexican-Americans constitute about 6 percent of the Hispanic community and Cuban-Americans are about 10 percent. Spanish-Americans in the SMSA are reasonably well off, with median family incomes of $12,160 compared with $12,900 for all SMSA families. The median for Spanish-American families residing in the District of Columbia ($9,600) is well under the median for all Spanish-American families.

American, which is proportionally 2nd only to the Miami SMSA's ratio of almost 1 in 4. Los Angeles is the place of residence for 40 percent of the SMSA Hispanics. The SMSA's Spanish-Americans are dispersed throughout most of the settled parts of the SMSA with the highest concentrations near downtown Los Angeles (p. 229). Most of the region's Hispanics are Mexican-Americans (p. 227).

**Miami.** The influx of refugees from Cuba in the late 1950s and in the 1960s has given the Miami SMSA the highest proportion of Spanish-Americans of the metropolitan areas mapped in the atlas. Just over half the SMSA's Hispanics live in Miami, where Cubans dominate neighborhoods west of the downtown area (pp. 242-243). Although Cuban refugees dominate the Hispanic community, there are 25,600 people of Central and South American stock in the SMSA, as well as 17,400 people of Puerto Rican birth or parentage.

**Atlanta.** Few of the SMSA's 13,800 Spanish-Americans are concentrated in small areas of the SMSA; 37 percent of the Hispanic

The nation's Spanish-Americans are a diverse collection of peoples from different places. Although their incomes are generally lower than those of the general population and although Spanish-Americans often suffer many of the disabilities produced by low incomes, making inferences about the characteristics of individual Hispanic communities from these general conditions is risky. Spanish speakers and non-Spanish speakers with certain Spanish names may be refugees from the Civil War in Spain, migrant laborers of Mexican descent, wealthy Cuban expatriates, recent immigrants from Puerto Rico, or Americans of Mexican descent whose families have lived in the United States for a century or more.

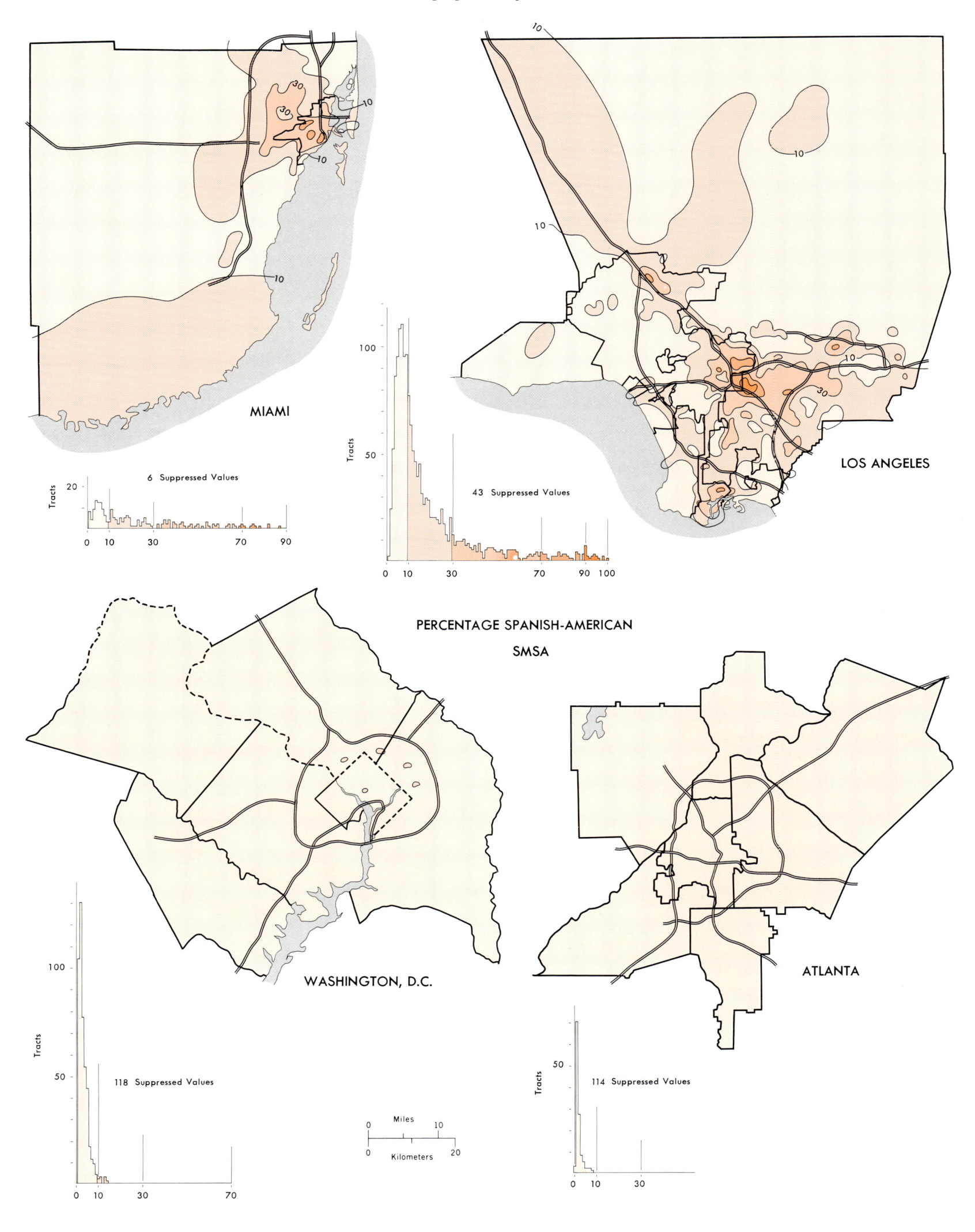

*Socioeconomic Segregation: Spanish-Americans*

MIAMI

LOS ANGELES

PERCENTAGE SPANISH-AMERICAN
SMSA

WASHINGTON, D.C.

ATLANTA

*Employment and Poverty*

CHAPTER 43

# Females in the Labor Force

In the 1970 Census of Population, a 20 percent sample of people 14 years old and older were asked whether they had worked or sought work during the previous week. The percentage of women 16 years old and older in the labor force was calculated from responses to the question. The proportion of adult (16 or over) females in each census tract who are working or seeking work is mapped here for the Standard Metropolitan Statistical Areas (SMSAs) included in the atlas.

There are 73,852,000 women 16 years old and older in the nation, of whom 30,547,000 (41.4 percent) are in the labor force. Participation rates are only slightly higher (42.8 percent) in the nation's SMSAs and in the central cities of all SMSAs (44.4 percent). Female participation in the national labor force increased sharply during the last 20 years. In 1960, 37.8 percent of the females 16 years of age and older were members of the labor force, and in 1950 the proportion stood at 33.9 percent. During the same 20-year period the proportion of adult males in the labor force has declined. In 1950, 86.8 percent of the nation's males 16 years old and older were labor-force members, whereas the proportion in 1970 was 80.6 percent. Female participation in the labor force peaks in the 20- to 24-year age group (57.5 percent in 1970) before family formation typically begins. The large numbers of children born in the years after World War II began entering the labor force in 1960-1961. The decline in male participation was caused by larger school enrollments for longer periods among young males and by early retirements among older males. Aside from such demographic and educational influences, the acceptance of women in jobs formerly closed to them has increased female participation in the labor force in almost all age groups during the last decade.

Female labor-force participation varies little from the national and the national metropolitan averages in most SMSAs mapped here. It is highest in the Washington SMSA and lowest in the Pittsburgh SMSA. Participation in the District of Columbia and in the city of Pittsburgh is correspondingly high and low (see accompanying tabulation). In general, participation is high in populations of young, single people and low among old populations. The different economic bases of different metropolitan areas (e.g., manufacturing versus services) are also influential.

**Boston.** Few tracts in the SMSA have female participation rates over 70 percent or under 30 percent. Some of the outlying tracts with low participation rates contain public institutions. Participation rates are highest in downtown tracts containing large numbers of young, single women.

*Note:* All data are from the 1970 Censuses of Population and Housing unless otherwise indicated. Therefore the present tense refers to 1970 except for income data which are from 1969. Cartographic conventions are explained in Chapter 1. County names and other locational information are shown on the SMSA map at the beginning of each city chapter (6-25) and on the DUS map of mobile homes near the beginning of each city chapter.

**New York-Northern New Jersey.** Low participation rates occur in predominantly black (p. 38) areas and in affluent, predominantly white neighborhoods (p. 43). Examples of the former are in northwestern Kings, southern Bronx, and southern Essex counties; the tracts in northern Nassau and Suffolk counties are examples of the latter. The large proportions of minority groups and an older population produce the region's generally low participation rates.

Percentage of Adult Females in the Labor Force

| Region | Central City(ies) | Entire SMSA |
|---|---|---|
| Boston | 47.8 | 45.3 |
| New York | 42.2 | 41.5 |
| Jersey City | 43.9 | 44.5 |
| Newark | 44.5 | 43.9 |
| Paterson-Clifton-Passaic | 45.0 | 43.8 |
| Philadelphia | 43.3 | 41.8 |
| Hartford | 51.6 | 48.3 |
| Baltimore | 45.6 | 43.7 |
| New Orleans | 40.0 | 38.4 |
| San Francisco-Oakland | 48.2 | 45.1 |
| Pittsburgh | 37.8 | 34.0 |
| St. Louis | 44.2 | 42.1 |
| Cleveland | 43.0 | 42.2 |
| Chicago | 46.7 | 45.2 |
| Detroit | 41.7 | 40.0 |
| Minneapolis-St. Paul | 49.6 | 48.9 |
| Seattle | 47.5 | 44.2 |
| Dallas | 52.0 | 49.3 |
| Fort Worth | 45.1 | 44.3 |
| Houston | 46.9 | 43.6 |
| Los Angeles | 46.2 | 44.6 |
| Miami | 48.8 | 44.0 |
| Atlanta | 51.0 | 48.8 |
| Washington, D.C. | 55.9 | 50.3 |

**Philadelphia.** Tracts where participation is less than 10 percent are scattered in the inner suburbs and central city. The tract where participation is 100 percent contains but 5 females 16 years old and older, all of whom are in the labor force.

**Hartford.** Female labor-force participation is high in the SMSA and in Hartford because of the unusual number of young women (p. 64) attracted to Hartford by jobs in the insurance industry and state government. Participation is highest in neighborhoods just west of the downtown area and lowest in areas occupied by blacks and Hispanics (p. 65).

**Baltimore.** Female participation in the labor force is lower than average near some of the SMSA's military facilities and in the affluent

*Employment and Poverty: The Female Labor Force*

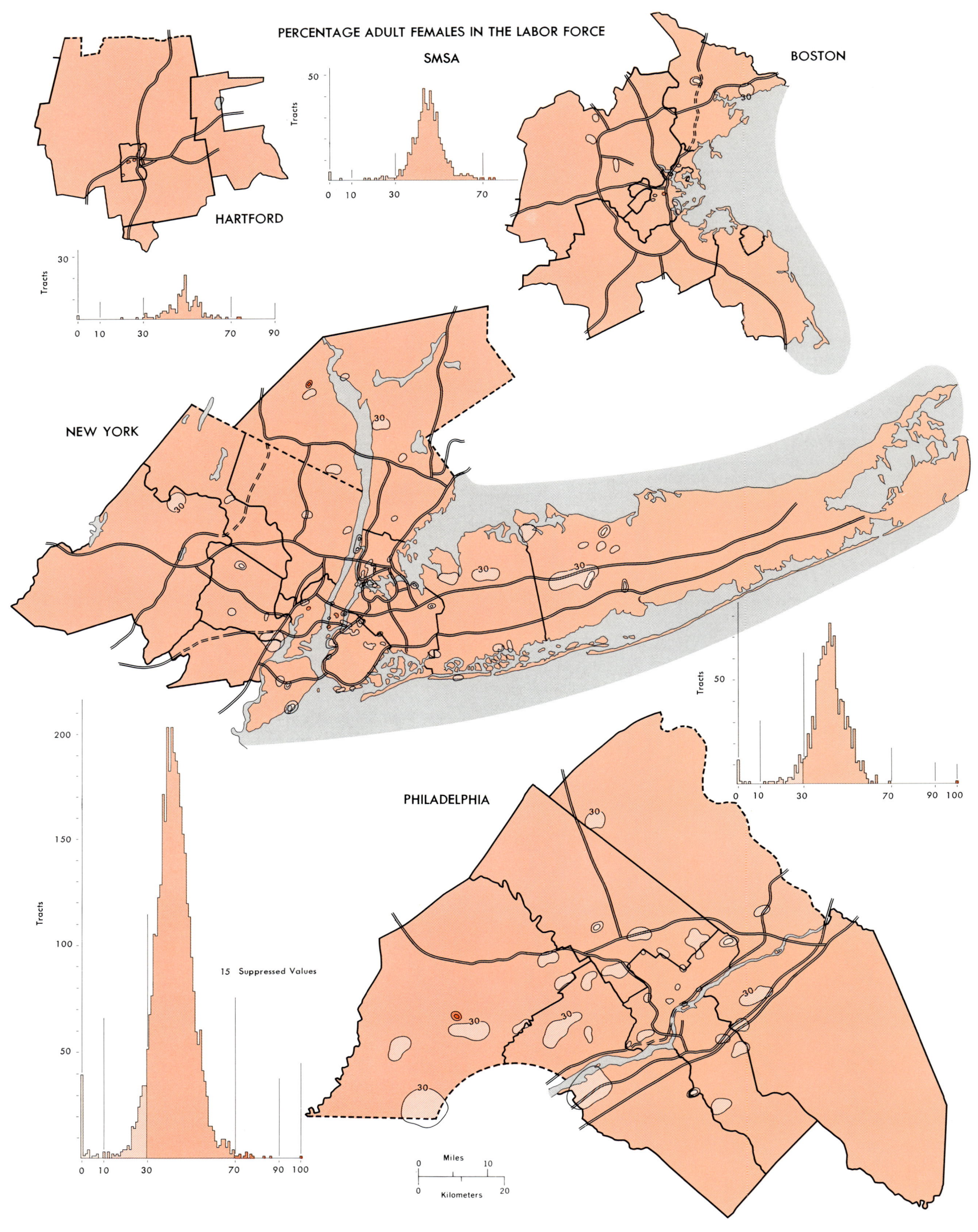

PERCENTAGE ADULT FEMALES IN THE LABOR FORCE

SMSA

BOSTON

HARTFORD

NEW YORK

PHILADELPHIA

15 Suppressed Values

398

*Employment and Poverty: The Female Labor Force*

BALTIMORE

NEW ORLEANS

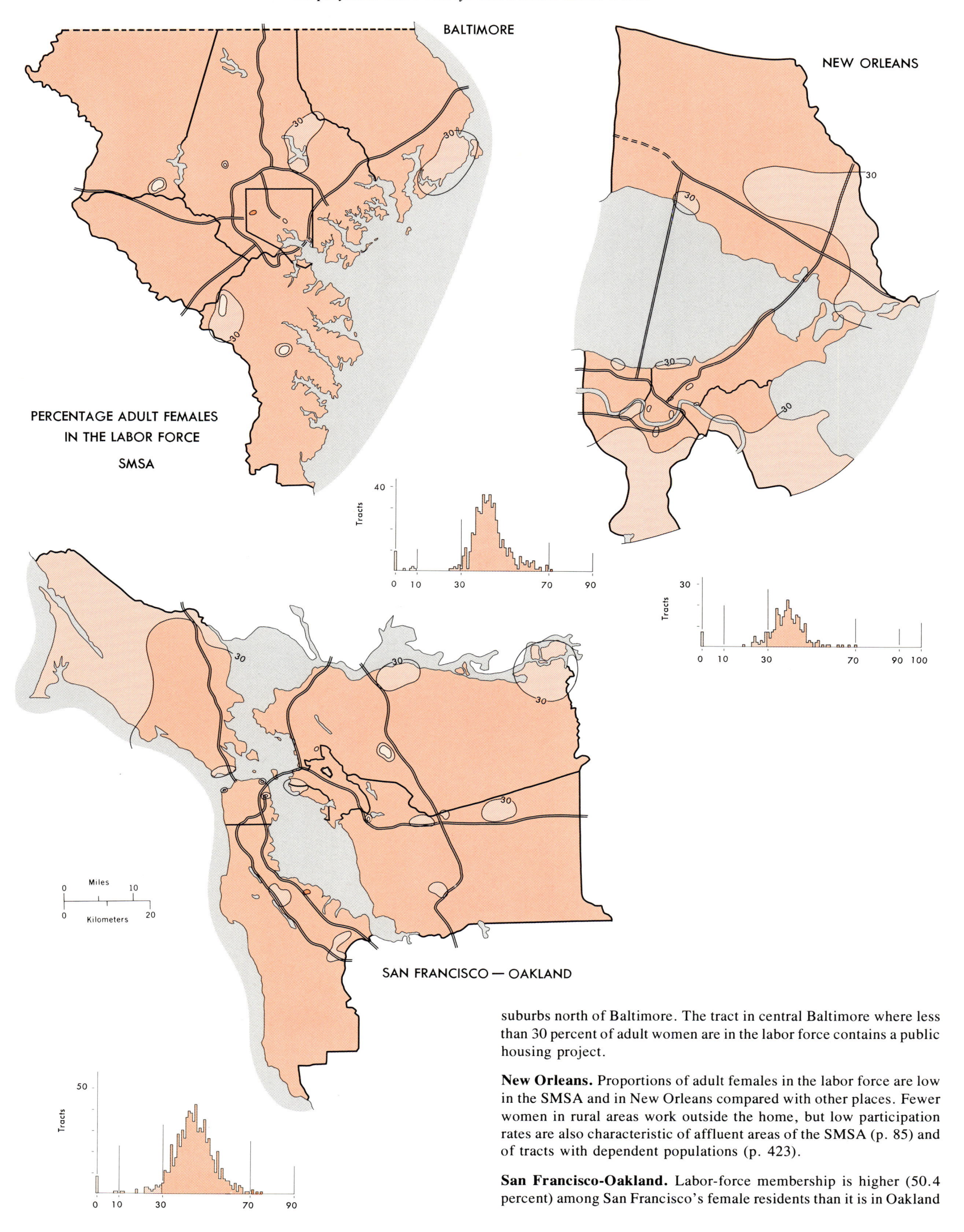

PERCENTAGE ADULT FEMALES
IN THE LABOR FORCE
SMSA

SAN FRANCISCO — OAKLAND

suburbs north of Baltimore. The tract in central Baltimore where less than 30 percent of adult women are in the labor force contains a public housing project.

**New Orleans.** Proportions of adult females in the labor force are low in the SMSA and in New Orleans compared with other places. Fewer women in rural areas work outside the home, but low participation rates are also characteristic of affluent areas of the SMSA (p. 85) and of tracts with dependent populations (p. 423).

**San Francisco-Oakland.** Labor-force membership is higher (50.4 percent) among San Francisco's female residents than it is in Oakland

*Employment and Poverty: The Female Labor Force*

PERCENTAGE ADULT FEMALES IN THE LABOR FORCE

PITTSBURGH

SMSA

ST. LOUIS

(43.6 percent), reflecting the larger numbers of young women in San Francisco and San Francisco's more service-oriented economy (p. 93). Low participation rates are sometimes associated with old populations (p. 93), and the large retirement community near Walnut Creek in Contra Costa County is especially evident on the map.

**Pittsburgh.** The SMSA population is unusually old (p. 109), producing in the city of Pittsburgh the lowest rates of labor-force membership among adult females of cities in the atlas. Participation is especially low in sparsely populated rural areas.

**St. Louis.** Proportions of adult females in the labor forces are lowest in peripheral rural areas. Other low percentages occur in the affluent suburbs (p. 123) west of St. Louis and in St. Louis and East St. Louis, Illinois tracts occupied by unskilled minority groups (pp. 384, 392).

**Cleveland.** Low labor-force participation among females occurs in affluent and poor parts of the SMSA (p. 132). The highest rates occur in tracts located on the city's northeast side and in the northeast suburbs.

**Chicago.** A number of tracts near the Central Business District have rates of female labor-force participation over 70 percent. Such tracts are often occupied by affluent professionals. Gradients to tracts where skills and labor-force membership are low are steep. Within the 30 to 70 percent category, tracts with proportions over 50 percent are clustered in the outer city and inner suburbs.

**Detroit.** Overall proportions of females in the labor force are low in the SMSA and Detroit. Several outlying areas where participation is low are affluent neighborhoods where financial incentives for females to enter the labor force are low.

**Minneapolis-St. Paul.** The influx of young people (p. 162) from other parts of Minnesota and from surrounding states produces high proportions of adult females in the labor force. In Minneapolis, 51.1 percent of that group are working, and in St. Paul, 47.3 percent are employed. Outer-city and inner-suburban areas have the highest proportions within the 30 to 70 percent category.

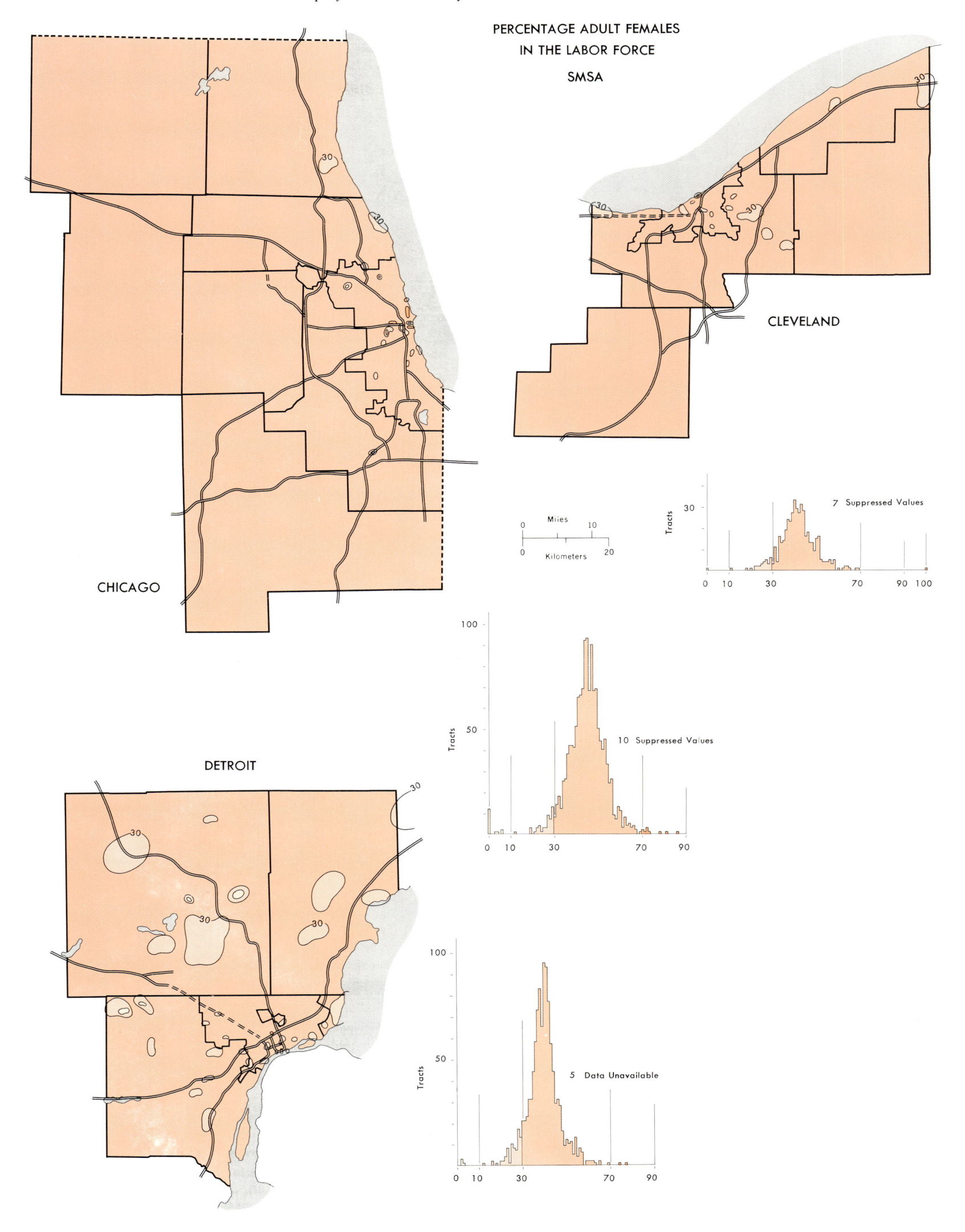

*Employment and Poverty: The Female Labor Force*

PERCENTAGE ADULT FEMALES
IN THE LABOR FORCE
SMSA

CLEVELAND

CHICAGO

DETROIT

401

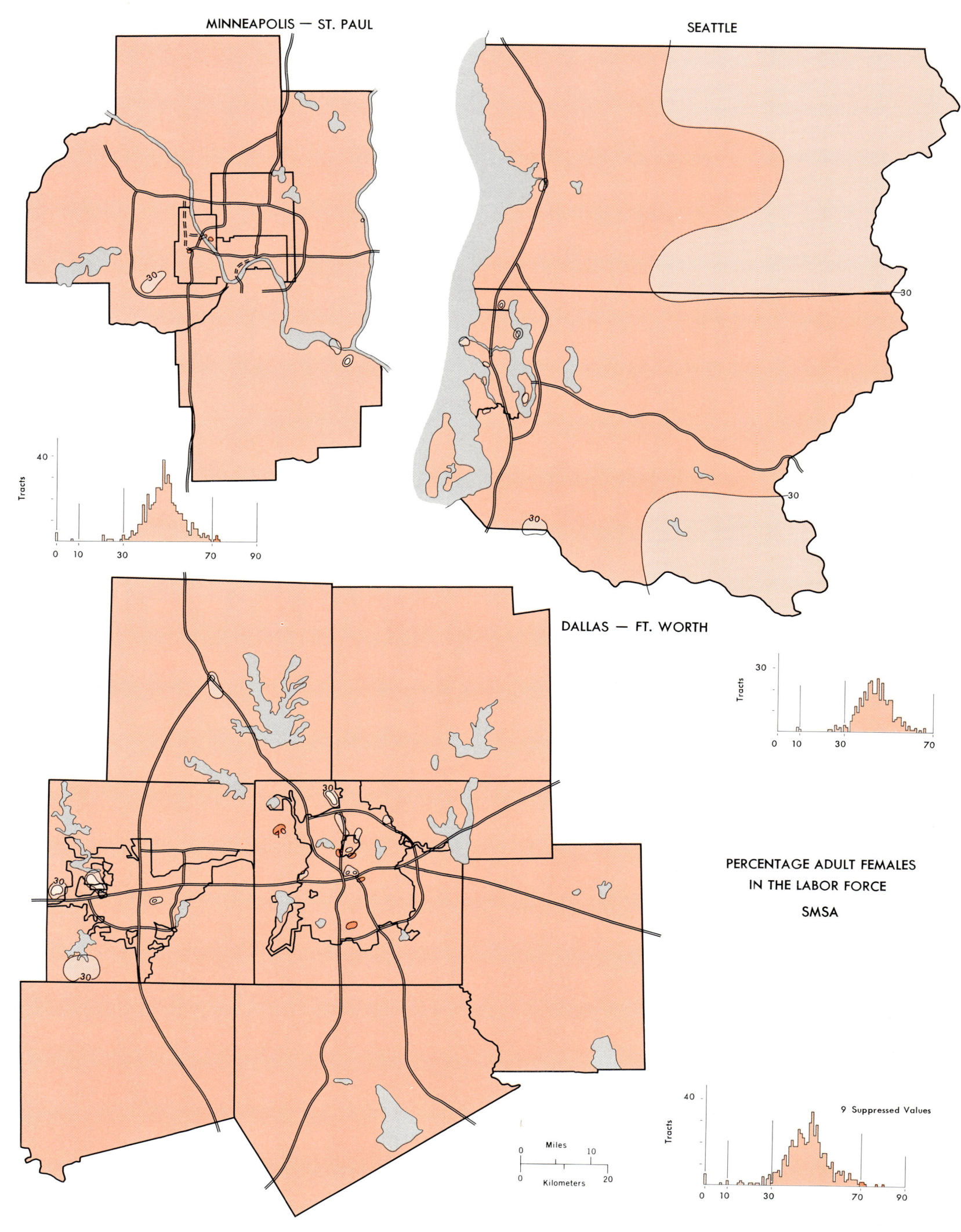

*Employment and Poverty: The Female Labor Force*

MINNEAPOLIS — ST. PAUL

SEATTLE

DALLAS — FT. WORTH

PERCENTAGE ADULT FEMALES
IN THE LABOR FORCE
SMSA

*Employment and Poverty: The Female Labor Force*

PERCENTAGE ADULT FEMALES IN THE LABOR FORCE
SMSA

HOUSTON

variations in female labor-force membership are small and extreme percentages are rare. The tract in Long Beach with 100 percent participation is a military base; the 100 percent tract in northern Los Angeles contains only 50 women, all of whom work.

**Miami.** Low proportions of females in the labor force are concentrated in areas dominated by the elderly (p. 240). An exception is the large tract south of Miami, where the presence of numerous families with young children depresses labor-force participation to 29 percent.

**Atlanta.** Participation rates under 30 percent are in tracts on the city's affluent north side and in nearby suburbs. The low-percentage tract at the city center is the site of a public housing project occupied by a dependent population (p. 428).

**Washington, D.C.** The SMSA and the District of Columbia have the highest participation rates of the places mapped here. Proportions exceed 70 percent in a number of tracts at the metropolitan core, and tracts with proportions of less than 30 percent are comparatively rare. The region's high participation rates are results of unusually large numbers of young females (p. 260) attracted by federal employment opportunities.

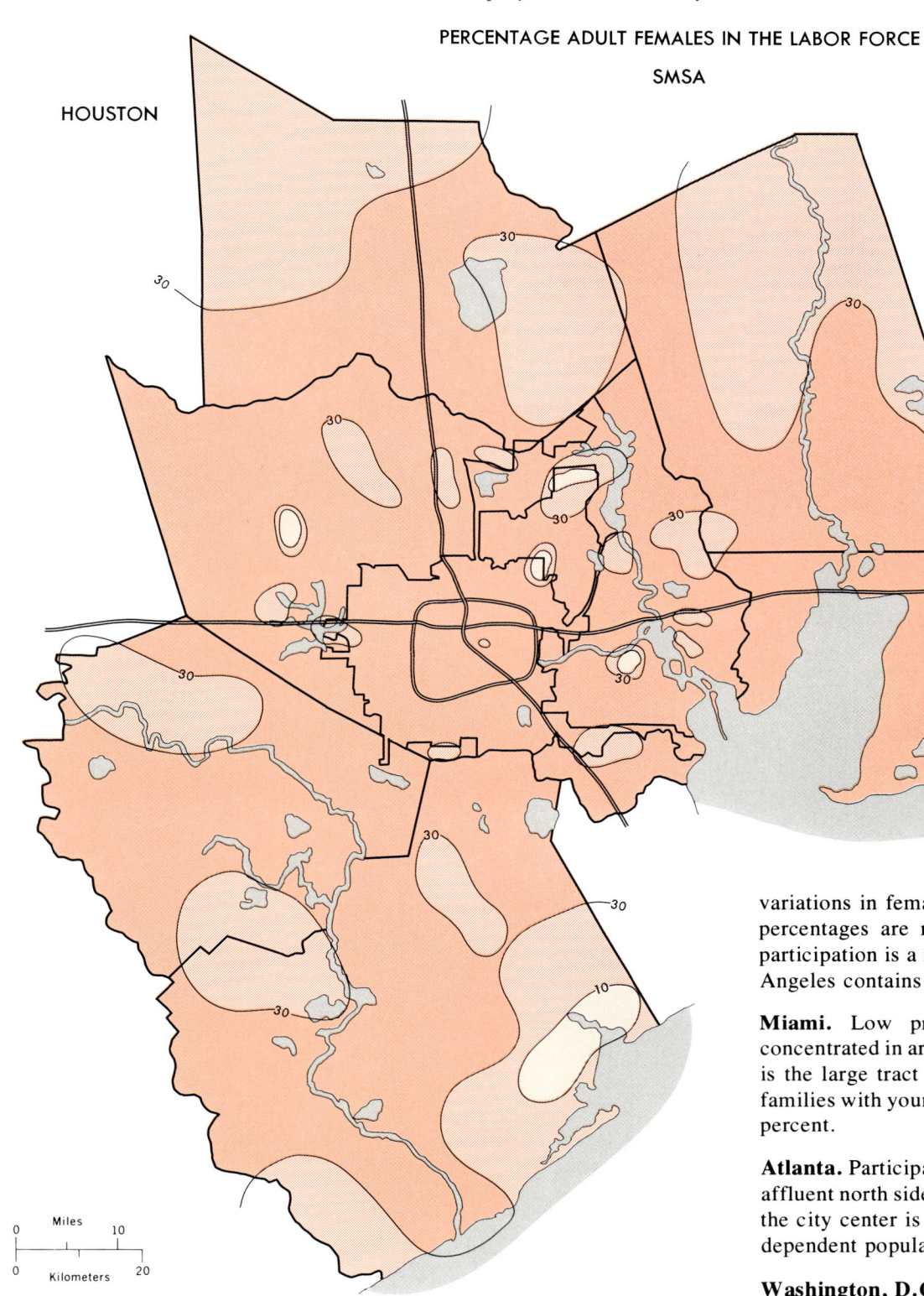

**Seattle.** The lack of employment opportunities accounts for the low participation rates in the eastern part of the SMSA. Throughout the coastal areas of the region, participation rates vary from 40 to 60 percent; they exceed 50 percent in most of central Seattle.

**Dallas-Fort Worth.** The unusually high proportion of Dallas females in the labor force is related to the SMSA's young population (p. 188) and recent growth. The Fort Worth SMSA, which has experienced slower growth, has lower participation rates.

**Houston.** For a young, rapidly growing SMSA, Houston has low rates of female labor-force membership. The SMSA's overall rate is depressed by low values in outlying areas where jobs are scarce. Closer to the SMSA center, low rates occur in affluent as well as in poor areas (p. 213).

**Los Angeles.** Considering the age and diversity of the SMSA,

---

Female participation in the labor force varies with skills, job opportunities, and financial pressures to work. Dependent females in central cities often lack the skills needed to enter the labor force profitably, and low participation rates result. At the other extreme, females in affluent neighborhoods often feel little need to seek employment. High participation rates are usually concentrated in outlying parts of central cities and in inner suburbs where financial pressures, adequate skills, and decreasing numbers of young children needing maternal attention create optimal conditions for participation.

*Employment and Poverty: The Female Labor Force*

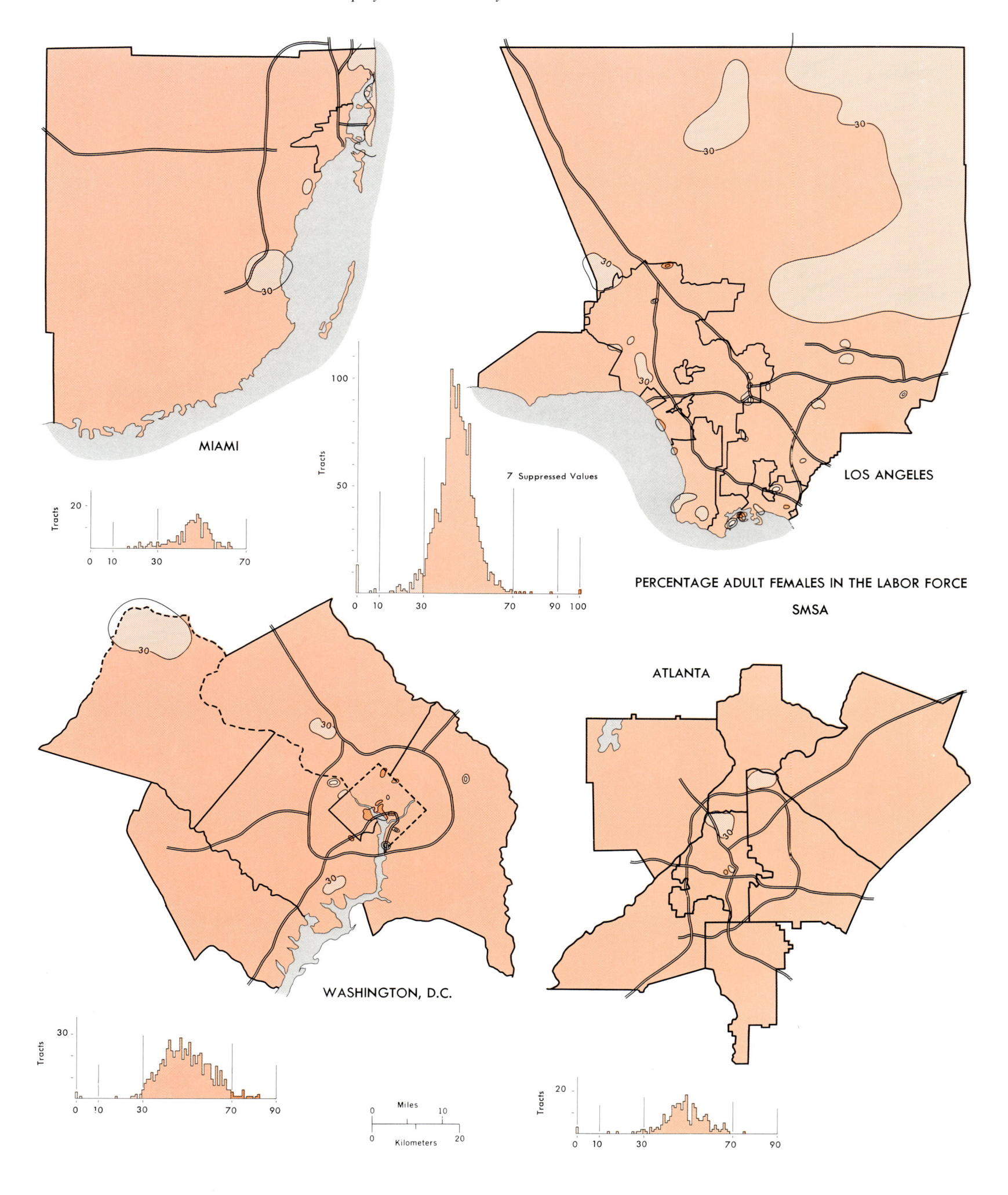

MIAMI

LOS ANGELES

PERCENTAGE ADULT FEMALES IN THE LABOR FORCE

SMSA

ATLANTA

WASHINGTON, D.C.

7 Suppressed Values

404

*Employment and Poverty*

## CHAPTER 44

# Unemployed Males

In the 1970 Census a 15 percent sample of individuals 14 years of age and older were asked whether they had a job or business from which they had been temporarily absent or laid off during the previous week. Responses were processed to yield the percentages of males 16 years old and older who were in the labor force and were unemployed. The percentages are mapped here at the tract level for each Standard Metropolitan Statistical Area (SMSA) included in the atlas.

Nationally, there are 49,549,000 adult males in the civilian labor force, of whom 1,925,000 (3.9 percent) are unemployed. Male unemployment in the nation's SMSAs (3.8 percent) is nearly identical to the national rate. Unemployment is slightly more prevalent in the central cities of the nation's SMSAs, where 4.4 percent of the adult-male civilian labor force is out of work (see accompanying tabulation).

Percentage of Unemployed Males
in the Civilian Labor Force

| Region | Central City(ies) | Entire SMSA |
|---|---|---|
| Boston | 4.8 | 3.5 |
| New York | 3.9 | 3.5 |
| Jersey City | 3.8 | 3.8 |
| Newark | 5.6 | 3.0 |
| Paterson-Clifton-Passaic | 3.6 | 2.9 |
| Philadelphia | 4.5 | 3.3 |
| Hartford | 4.7 | 2.8 |
| Baltimore | 4.3 | 3.0 |
| New Orleans | 5.5 | 4.6 |
| San Francisco-Oakland | 7.4 | 5.6 |
| Pittsburgh | 5.4 | 3.9 |
| St. Louis | 6.5 | 4.5 |
| Cleveland | 5.4 | 3.2 |
| Chicago | 4.1 | 3.0 |
| Detroit | 6.9 | 5.3 |
| Minneapolis-St. Paul | 4.0 | 3.1 |
| Seattle | 8.8 | 7.9 |
| Dallas | 2.9 | 2.6 |
| Fort Worth | 3.4 | 3.0 |
| Houston | 2.6 | 2.4 |
| Los Angeles | 7.0 | 6.0 |
| Miami | 4.0 | 3.3 |
| Atlanta | 3.4 | 2.4 |
| Washington, D.C. | 3.9 | 2.4 |

Unemployment rates are sensitive to national, regional, and local economic trends, making generalization through time from data

*Note:* All data are from the 1970 Censuses of Population and Housing unless otherwise indicated. Therefore the present tense refers to 1970 except for income data which are from 1969. Cartographic conventions are explained in Chapter 1. County names and other locational information are shown on the SMSA map at the beginning of each city chapter (6-25) and on the DUS map of mobile homes near the beginning of each city chapter.

collected for a single week risky. But comparative rates among different places should not change too much from year to year despite changes in absolute values. Areas where unemployment is relatively low on a given date are likely to continue to have relatively low unemployment, even if absolute rates rise overall, for general increases in unemployment will produce even larger increases elsewhere.

At any time, unemployment is highest among the people least equipped by training and education to hold jobs. Unemployment rates of blacks, for example, are typically almost double those of whites. Nationally, 6.3 percent of the black males and 5.8 percent of the Spanish-American males in the civilian labor force are unemployed compared with 3.6 percent of white males. Thus, other things being equal, SMSAs and cities with large minority populations will have higher unemployment rates, although the general relationship is often modified by local trends in individual industries. Seattle has few blacks, for example, but unemployment is high because of layoffs at Boeing Aircraft Company, one of the SMSA's largest employers. On the other hand, unemployment in Washington, D.C. is at the national average despite the high population of blacks resident in the city, for the federal government and numerous local industries offer many job opportunities for the city's blacks.

**Boston.** Unemployment exceeds 5 percent in the northern half of Boston, in adjacent areas at the metropolitan core, and in outlying towns and cities. The highest unemployment rates occur in black neighborhoods (p. 382). Unemployment is 7.1 percent among Boston's black males and 6.5 percent for blacks in the SMSA civilian labor force. Rates for Spanish-Americans are 9.4 and 6.5 percent.

**New York-Northern New Jersey.** Most tracts where unemployment exceeds 5 and 10 percent are located in central-city areas, although some outlying areas have rates over 5 percent. In the New York SMSA, 76.6 percent of the unemployed are located in New York City compared with 68.2 percent of the total population; central-city concentration is slight. In New York City, the unemployment rate for blacks (5.4 percent) is higher than the rate for the total population, and high unemployment tracts are concentrated in black neighborhoods (p. 382). Unemployment among New York City's Spanish-American males is 6.2 percent.

**Philadelphia.** Unemployment among SMSA blacks is 6.5 percent; in Philadelphia it is 6.7 percent, which accounts for the high rates in black neighborhoods (p. 382). Among Spanish-Americans, unemployment is 8.9 percent in Philadelphia and 7.7 percent in the entire SMSA. The large area on the eastern side of the SMSA where unemployment exceeds 5 percent is sparsely populated.

**Hartford.** Unemployment is low in the SMSA in contrast to the central city. Of the SMSA's 4,830 unemployed males, 1,840 (37.3

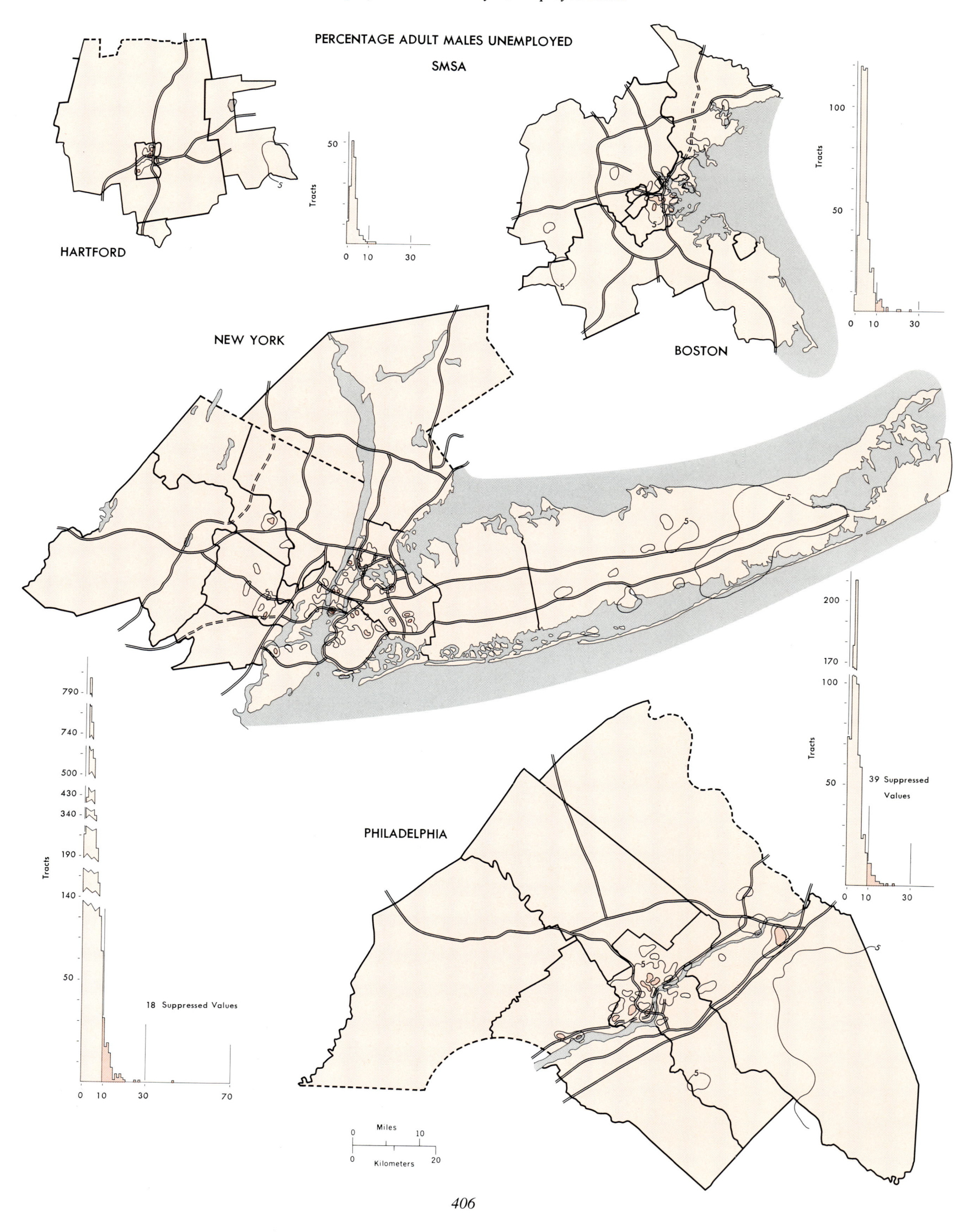

*Employment and Poverty: Unemployed Males*

PERCENTAGE ADULT MALES UNEMPLOYED
SMSA

HARTFORD

BOSTON

NEW YORK

PHILADELPHIA

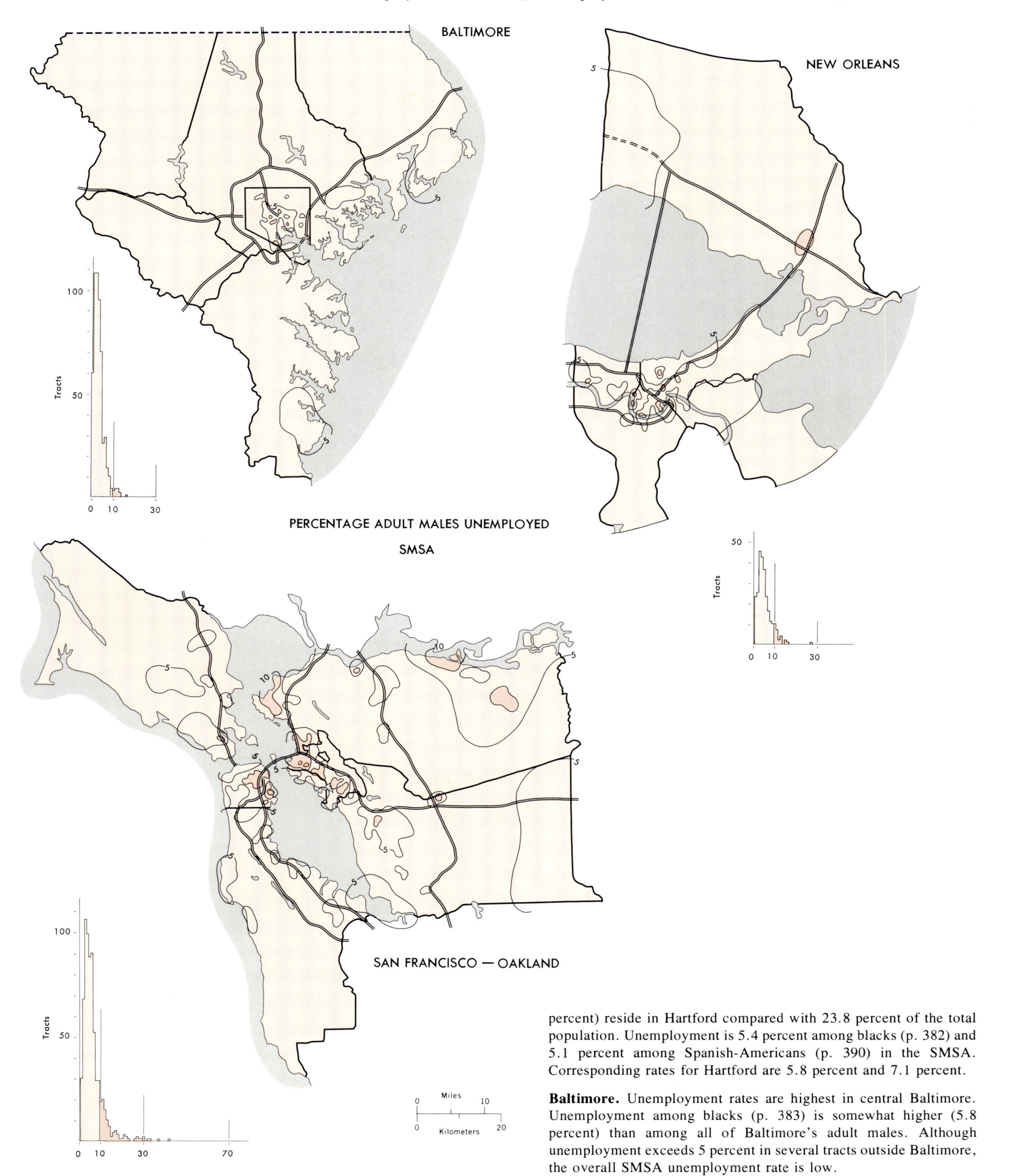

*Employment and Poverty: Unemployed Males*

PERCENTAGE ADULT MALES UNEMPLOYED
SMSA

percent) reside in Hartford compared with 23.8 percent of the total population. Unemployment is 5.4 percent among blacks (p. 382) and 5.1 percent among Spanish-Americans (p. 390) in the SMSA. Corresponding rates for Hartford are 5.8 percent and 7.1 percent.

**Baltimore.** Unemployment rates are highest in central Baltimore. Unemployment among blacks (p. 383) is somewhat higher (5.8 percent) than among all of Baltimore's adult males. Although unemployment exceeds 5 percent in several tracts outside Baltimore, the overall SMSA unemployment rate is low.

*Employment and Poverty: Unemployed Males*

PERCENTAGE ADULT MALES UNEMPLOYED
SMSA

PITTSBURGH

ST. LOUIS

**New Orleans.** Unemployment in New Orleans and the SMSA is higher than average for metropolitan areas, and blacks are disproportionately represented among the unemployed; 52 percent of the unemployed in New Orleans are black, as are 40 percent in the entire SMSA, whereas blacks are 45 percent of the city population and 31 percent of the SMSA population. The majority (63.6 percent) of the unemployed live in New Orleans, although rates over 5 percent are common in Jefferson and St. Tammany parishes.

**San Francisco-Oakland.** Both central cities and the entire SMSA have unusually high unemployment, especially in areas where blacks (p. 383) and Spanish-Americans (p. 391) are numerous. In some tracts, a third of the male labor force is out of work. Among black males, unemployment stands at 11.4 percent in San Francisco, 11.6 percent in Oakland, and 11 percent over the entire SMSA. Statistics for Spanish-Americans are 8.3, 8.2, and 6.3 percent.

**Pittsburgh.** Of the SMSA's unemployed, 29 percent live in Pittsburgh, compared with 22 percent of the total population who live there. The rest of the unemployed are scattered through sparsely settled areas and among the SMSA's outlying settlement centers. Unemployment rates for blacks are almost twice those of the total population in Pittsburgh; in the SMSA as a whole they are over twice the rate for all male workers.

**St. Louis.** Male unemployment in St. Louis is exceeded only by male unemployment in Los Angeles, San Francisco, and Seattle. Cutbacks in defense contracting are partially responsible for high rates in St. Louis and the three cities with higher rates. Unemployment is high in predominantly black parts of St. Louis, but large numbers of workers in East St. Louis are also jobless.

**Cleveland.** The parts of Cleveland where unemployment exceeds 5 percent are in predominantly black neighborhoods (p. 385). Although tracts exceeding 5 percent are rare outside Cleveland, 44 percent of the unemployed live outside the city of Cleveland.

**Chicago.** Although Chicago and the SMSA have comparatively low unemployment rates, the absolute numbers of unemployed in Chicago (35,250) and in the rest of the SMSA (19,750) are large.

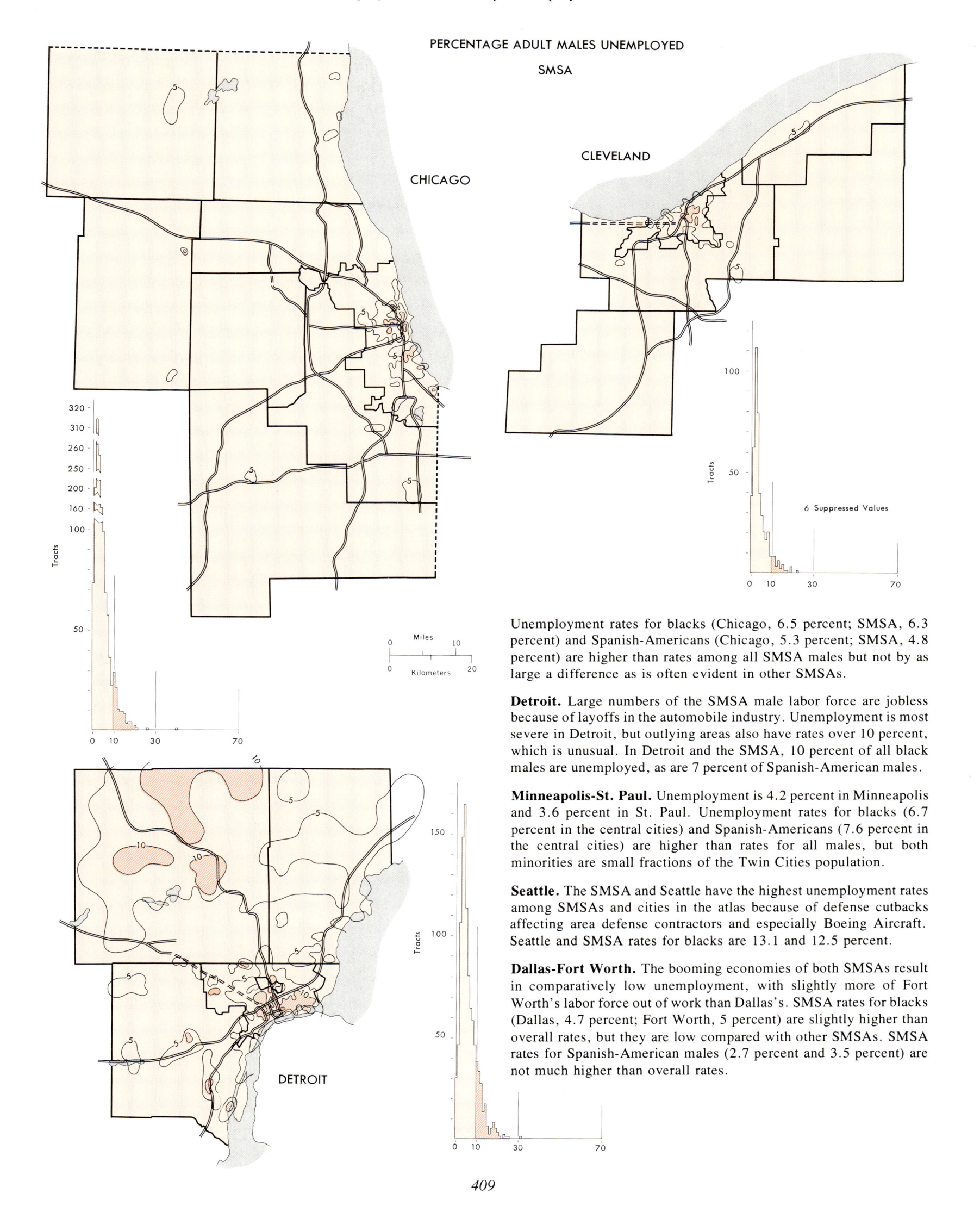

*Employment and Poverty: Unemployed Males*

PERCENTAGE ADULT MALES UNEMPLOYED
SMSA

CHICAGO

CLEVELAND

DETROIT

Unemployment rates for blacks (Chicago, 6.5 percent; SMSA, 6.3 percent) and Spanish-Americans (Chicago, 5.3 percent; SMSA, 4.8 percent) are higher than rates among all SMSA males but not by as large a difference as is often evident in other SMSAs.

**Detroit.** Large numbers of the SMSA male labor force are jobless because of layoffs in the automobile industry. Unemployment is most severe in Detroit, but outlying areas also have rates over 10 percent, which is unusual. In Detroit and the SMSA, 10 percent of all black males are unemployed, as are 7 percent of Spanish-American males.

**Minneapolis-St. Paul.** Unemployment is 4.2 percent in Minneapolis and 3.6 percent in St. Paul. Unemployment rates for blacks (6.7 percent in the central cities) and Spanish-Americans (7.6 percent in the central cities) are higher than rates for all males, but both minorities are small fractions of the Twin Cities population.

**Seattle.** The SMSA and Seattle have the highest unemployment rates among SMSAs and cities in the atlas because of defense cutbacks affecting area defense contractors and especially Boeing Aircraft. Seattle and SMSA rates for blacks are 13.1 and 12.5 percent.

**Dallas-Fort Worth.** The booming economies of both SMSAs result in comparatively low unemployment, with slightly more of Fort Worth's labor force out of work than Dallas's. SMSA rates for blacks (Dallas, 4.7 percent; Fort Worth, 5 percent) are slightly higher than overall rates, but they are low compared with other SMSAs. SMSA rates for Spanish-American males (2.7 percent and 3.5 percent) are not much higher than overall rates.

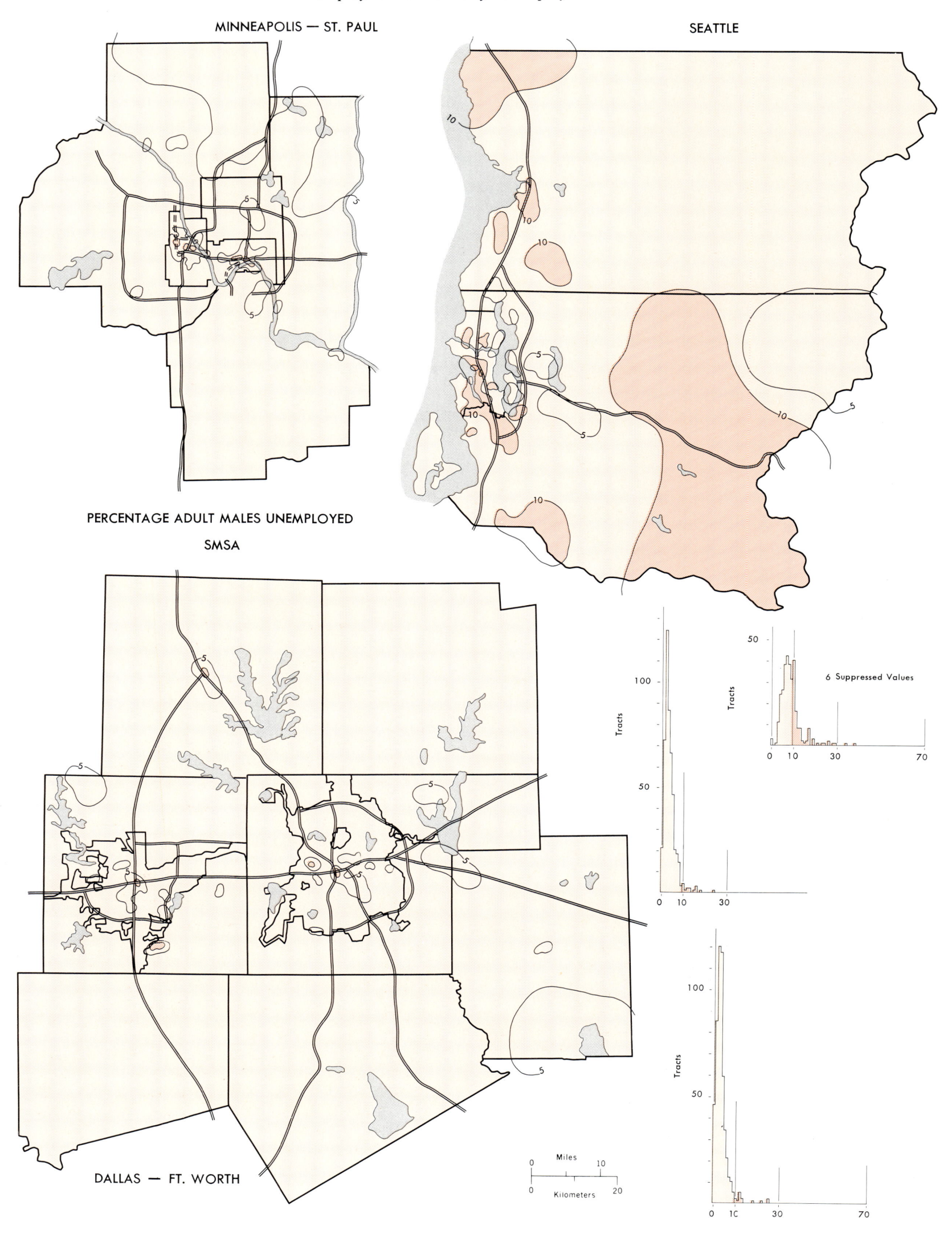

*Employment and Poverty: Unemployed Males*

MINNEAPOLIS — ST. PAUL

SEATTLE

PERCENTAGE ADULT MALES UNEMPLOYED

SMSA

DALLAS — FT. WORTH

410

*Employment and Poverty: Unemployed Males*

PERCENTAGE ADULT MALES UNEMPLOYED

SMSA

HOUSTON

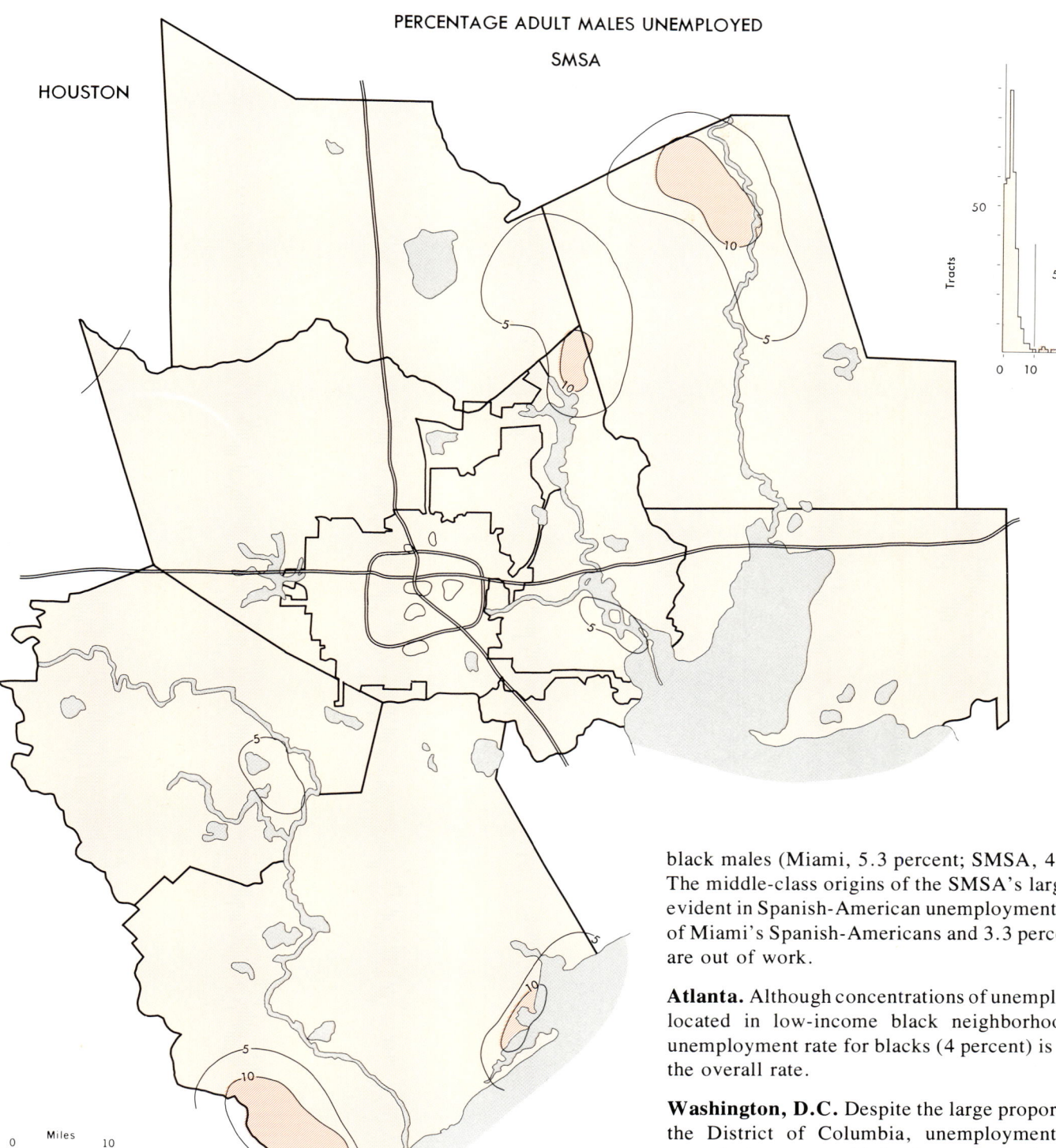

**Houston.** The SMSA unemployment rate is second lowest among the SMSAs in the atlas, and Houston's rate is lowest among the central cities. Tracts with unemployment rates over 10 percent are confined to the metropolitan periphery. Houston's rates for blacks (3.8 percent) and Spanish-Americans (2.7 percent) are unusually low also.

**Los Angeles.** Like other West Coast SMSAs, Los Angeles has high unemployment rates overall and even higher rates among its black minority. In Los Angeles, 10.6 percent of the black males are unemployed, as are 10.2 percent in the entire SMSA. Spanish-American rates (7.4 percent in Los Angeles, 6.6 percent for the entire SMSA) are not markedly different from total population rates. High tract rates are especially evident in predominantly black areas (p. 388).

**Miami.** Overall unemployment rates are low in the SMSA; joblessness exceeds 10 percent in only one census tract. Rates for black males (Miami, 5.3 percent; SMSA, 4.2 percent) are also low. The middle-class origins of the SMSA's large Cuban community are evident in Spanish-American unemployment figures; only 3.4 percent of Miami's Spanish-Americans and 3.3 percent of those in the SMSA are out of work.

**Atlanta.** Although concentrations of unemployed males in Atlanta are located in low-income black neighborhoods (p. 396), Atlanta's unemployment rate for blacks (4 percent) is only slightly higher than the overall rate.

**Washington, D.C.** Despite the large proportion of blacks residing in the District of Columbia, unemployment is below the national central-city average. Federal agencies and private firms offer jobs for almost all strata of Washington and SMSA society, resulting in low overall unemployment rates and comparatively low rates among blacks (4.3 percent in the District; 3.9 percent for the entire SMSA).

---

When reading maps of unemployment and studying variations in unemployment rates from place to place, it is especially important to avoid assuming that the problems of the unemployed are not serious where unemployment rates are low. An unemployed worker is as unemployed if he is 1 of 1,000 workers as he is if he is 1 of 10 members of the labor force.

Unemployment rates are almost universally higher for blacks and Spanish-Americans than they are for the total population. But the comparatively low rates for blacks in southern SMSAs and for Spanish-Americans in Texas SMSAs suggest that unemployment may be a result of recent migration (as among blacks and Spanish-Americans in northern and western SMSAs). Because southern SMSAs are growing more rapidly than SMSAs in other parts of the nation, however, the causes of low black and Spanish-American unemployment are difficult to specify.

*411*

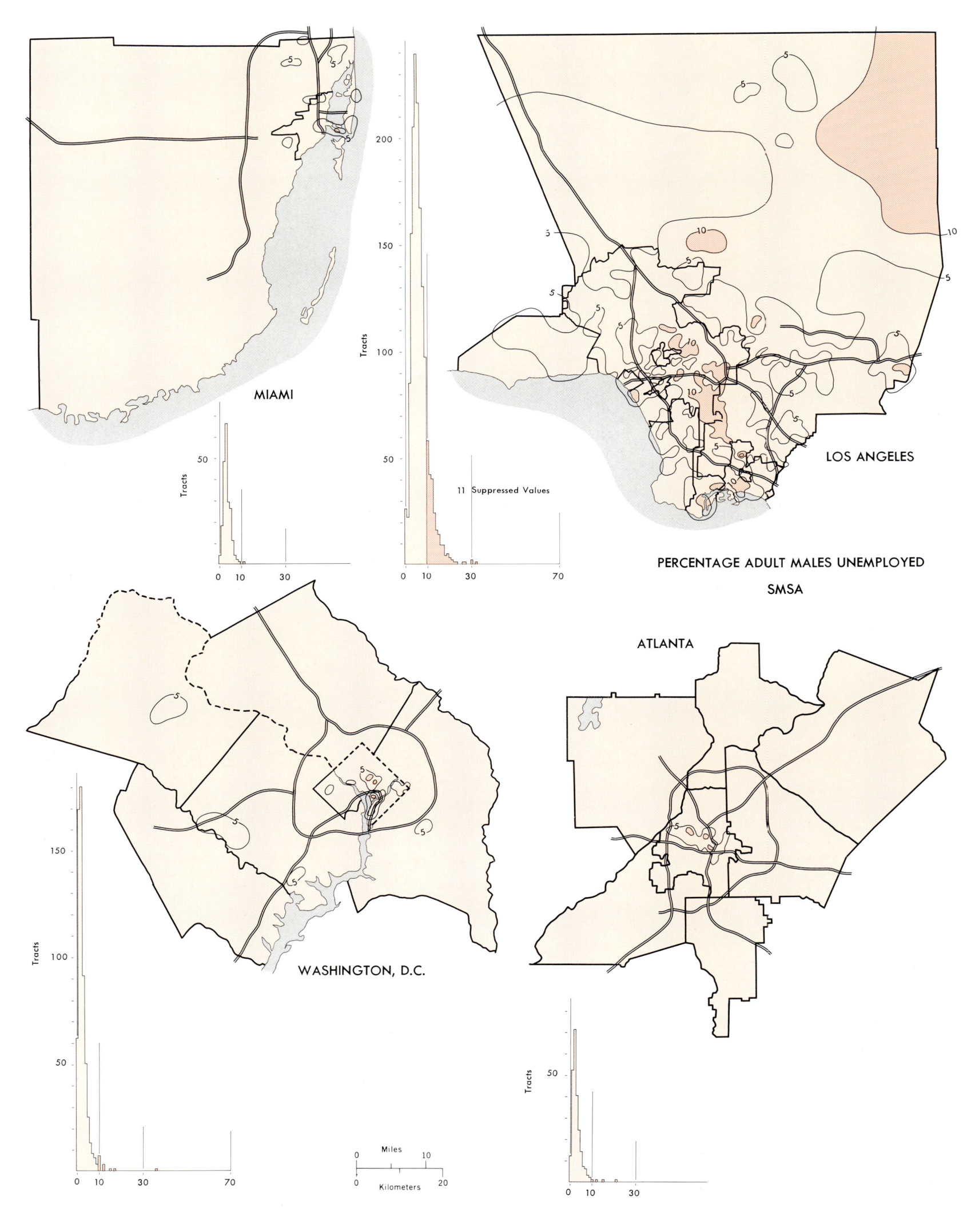

*Employment and Poverty: Unemployed Males*

MIAMI

LOS ANGELES

11 Suppressed Values

PERCENTAGE ADULT MALES UNEMPLOYED
SMSA

ATLANTA

WASHINGTON, D.C.

*Employment and Poverty*

CHAPTER 45

# The Poverty Population

Data from the 1970 Census of Population on family status and income were processed by the Bureau of the Census to yield the number of persons whose 1969 incomes were inadequate to meet estimated basic needs. This poverty level is updated annually to reflect changes in the Consumer Price Index. In 1969, the poverty threshold ranged from $1,834 for an unrelated individual, through $3,743 for a nonfarm family of 4, to $6,034 for a family of 7 or more people. In this chapter, the proportions of all persons whose individual incomes do not equal or exceed the poverty level or who live in families with incomes below the poverty threshold are mapped for census tracts in the 24 Standard Metropolitan Statistical Areas (SMSAs) included in the atlas.

In the nation as a whole, 27,125,000 people (13.7 percent of the population) have incomes below the poverty level or live in families with such incomes. Within SMSAs, 11.2 percent of the population have incomes below the poverty threshold. Of the nation's poverty population, 15,252,000 (56.2 percent) reside in SMSAs compared with 68.6 percent of the total population. Thus in contrast to most variables mapped in the atlas, poverty is more prevalent in nonmetropolitan areas than it is in SMSAs. Within central cities of SMSAs, 14.9 percent of all persons have incomes below the poverty threshold. In the 24 SMSAs mapped in this chapter, 10.1 percent of the people have incomes below the poverty level, as do 15.4 percent of the central-city residents (see accompanying tabulation).

The nation's poverty population consists of 5,945,000 unrelated individuals and 21,180,000 people living in families. Whereas the 21,180,000 in families are 10.7 percent of the nation's family population, the 5,945,000 unrelated individuals are 37 percent of the people in that category in the nation. Unrelated individuals over 64 years of age are especially afflicted by poverty; 48.5 percent of the unrelated individuals below the poverty level are 64 or older. Poverty status among the elderly is not restricted to unrelated individuals, for 25.6 percent of all people 64 years of age or older have incomes below the poverty cutoff.

Blacks and Spanish-Americans are also disproportionately represented in the poverty population. Whereas blacks are 11.1 percent of the nation's population, they comprise 28.3 percent of the poverty population; 35 percent of all blacks in the nation have incomes below the poverty level. Spanish-Americans make up 4.5 percent of the general population and 7.9 percent of the nation's poverty population; 23.5 percent of all Spanish-Americans are poor by the poverty-income criteria.

**Boston.** Poverty populations are concentrated at the metropolitan core and in the centers of outlying towns. Blacks comprise 29.5 percent of Boston's poverty population, and Spanish-Americans make up 6.3 percent.

**New York-Northern New Jersey.** Concentrations of the poverty population are highest in predominantly black and Spanish-American neighborhoods (pp. 382, 390). In the New York, New York SMSA, 23.6 percent of all blacks have incomes below the poverty threshold, as do 34.4 percent of the Spanish-Americans. Poverty among blacks and Spanish-Americans in the region's other SMSAs is also high.

Percentage of the Population below the Poverty Level

| Region | Central City(ies) | Entire SMSA |
|---|---|---|
| Boston | 16.2 | 8.5 |
| New York | 13.6 | 11.9 |
| Jersey City | 13.7 | 11.9 |
| Newark | 22.5 | 9.1 |
| Paterson-Clifton-Passaic | 12.6 | 5.8 |
| Philadelphia | 15.4 | 10.0 |
| Hartford | 17.0 | 6.9 |
| Baltimore | 18.4 | 11.3 |
| New Orleans | 26.8 | 20.2 |
| San Francisco-Oakland | 14.5 | 10.0 |
| Pittsburgh | 15.4 | 9.5 |
| St. Louis | 20.3 | 10.9 |
| Cleveland | 17.3 | 9.0 |
| Chicago | 14.5 | 9.3 |
| Detroit | 14.9 | 8.5 |
| Minneapolis-St. Paul | 10.6 | 6.7 |
| Seattle | 10.3 | 7.5 |
| Dallas | 13.5 | 11.3 |
| Fort Worth | 13.9 | 10.4 |
| Houston | 14.1 | 12.6 |
| Los Angeles | 13.3 | 10.9 |
| Miami | 20.6 | 14.2 |
| Atlanta | 19.8 | 11.7 |
| Washington, D.C. | 17.0 | 8.3 |

**Philadelphia.** Tracts where over 10 percent of the population is below the poverty level are scattered throughout the SMSA, with especially large areas of New Jersey having such proportions. Most of the outlying poverty areas are sparsely populated; 62.2 percent of the SMSA poverty population lives in Philadelphia, where 1 black out of 4 has an income below the poverty cutoff.

**Hartford.** Whereas blacks are 23.8 percent of Hartford's population, they are 42 percent of the city's poverty population. Thus concentrations of people with incomes below the poverty level are most intense in black neighborhoods (p. 382). Another 19.4 percent of the city's poverty population is Spanish-American.

*Note:* All data are from the 1970 Censuses of Population and Housing unless otherwise indicated. Therefore the present tense refers to 1970 except for income data which are from 1969. Cartographic conventions are explained in Chapter 1. County names and other locational information are shown on the SMSA map at the beginning of each city chapter (6-25) and on the DUS map of mobile homes near the beginning of each city chapter.

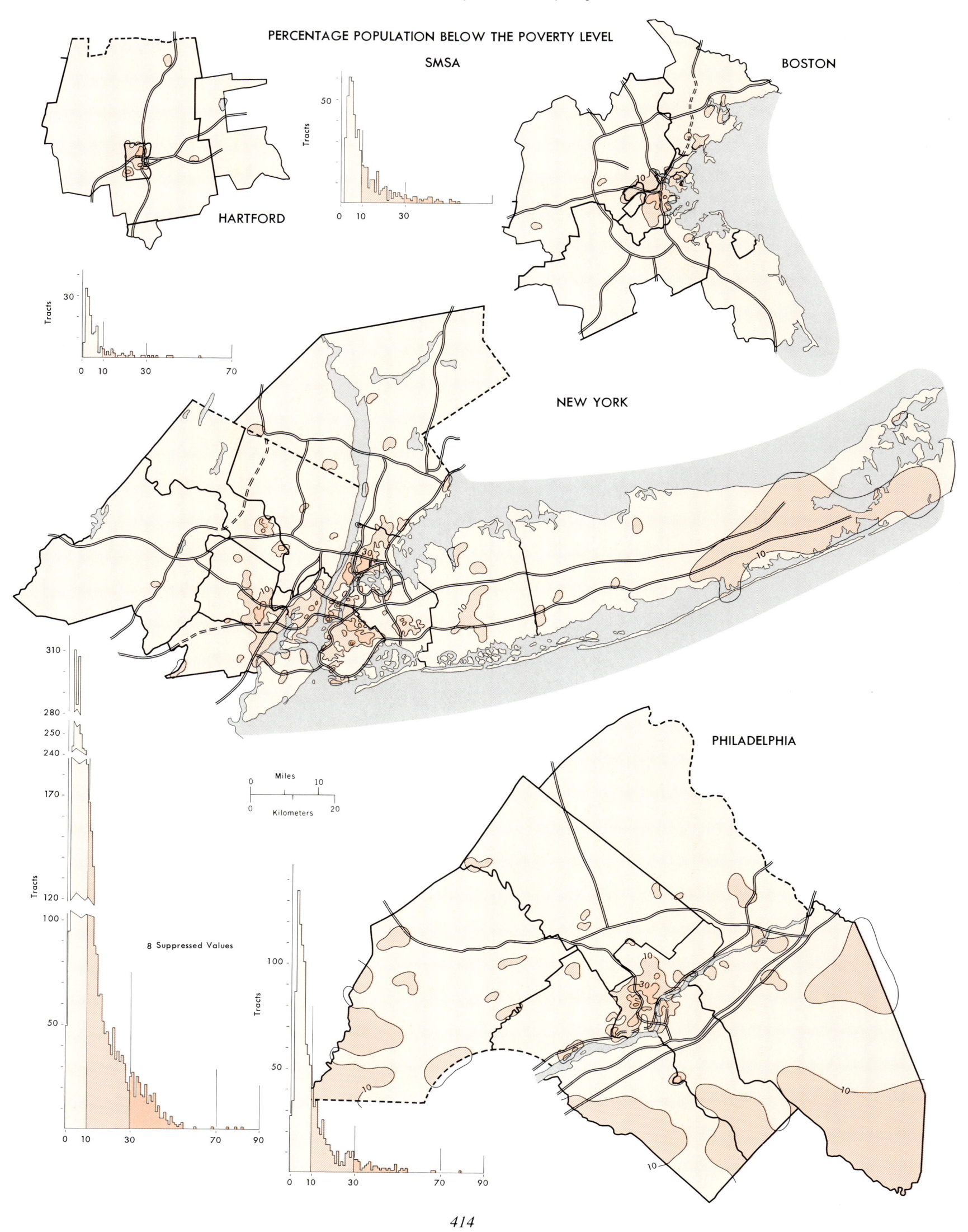

*Employment and Poverty: The Poverty Population*

PERCENTAGE POPULATION BELOW THE POVERTY LEVEL
SMSA

HARTFORD

BOSTON

NEW YORK

PHILADELPHIA

8 Suppressed Values

414

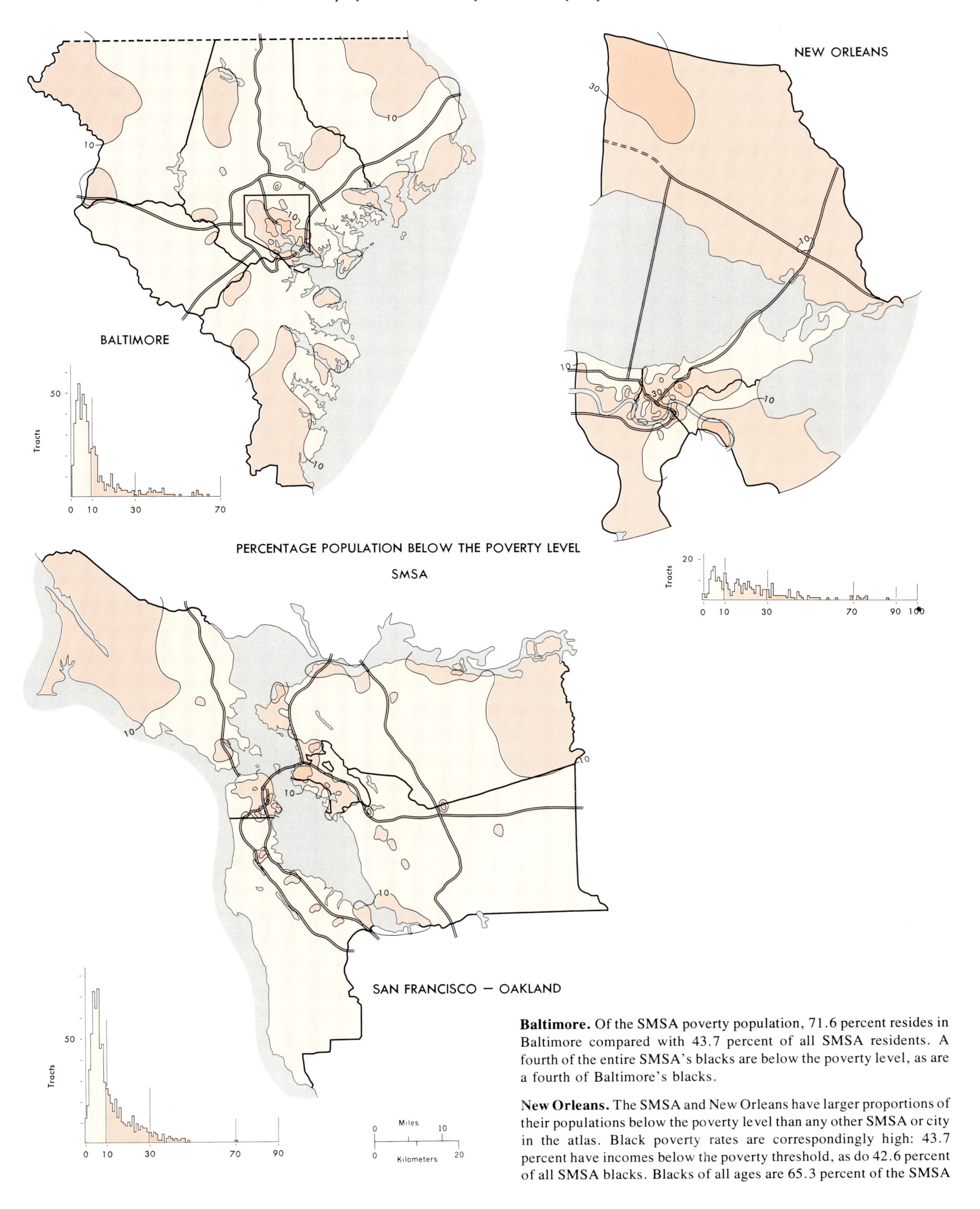

*Employment and Poverty: The Poverty Population*

BALTIMORE

PERCENTAGE POPULATION BELOW THE POVERTY LEVEL
SMSA

NEW ORLEANS

SAN FRANCISCO — OAKLAND

**Baltimore.** Of the SMSA poverty population, 71.6 percent resides in Baltimore compared with 43.7 percent of all SMSA residents. A fourth of the entire SMSA's blacks are below the poverty level, as are a fourth of Baltimore's blacks.

**New Orleans.** The SMSA and New Orleans have larger proportions of their populations below the poverty level than any other SMSA or city in the atlas. Black poverty rates are correspondingly high: 43.7 percent have incomes below the poverty threshold, as do 42.6 percent of all SMSA blacks. Blacks of all ages are 65.3 percent of the SMSA

*Employment and Poverty: The Poverty Population*

PERCENTAGE POPULATION BELOW THE POVERTY LEVEL
SMSA

poverty population. Whites 64 or older are another 7.3 percent, which means that only 27.4 percent of the poverty population is neither black nor elderly.

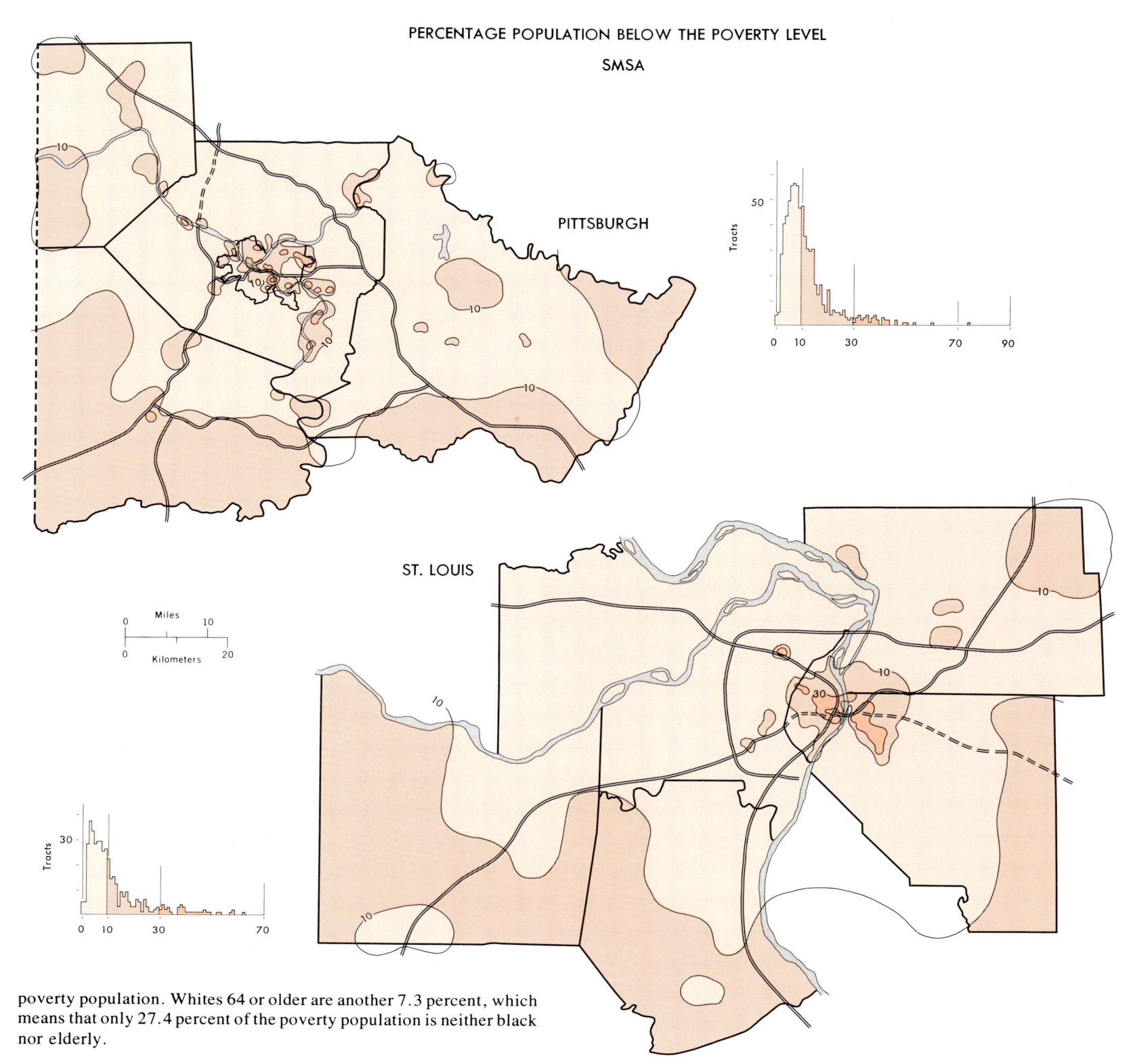

**San Francisco-Oakland.** In San Francisco 14 percent of the people have incomes below the poverty level, and in Oakland 16.6 percent are below the cutoff. Just under half (48.4 percent) of the SMSA poverty population lives outside San Francisco and Oakland, but concentrations over 10 percent of tract populations are scattered. Spanish-Americans comprise 13.2 percent of the poverty population compared with 11.7 percent of all SMSA residents. Blacks are 24.9 percent of those with poverty incomes compared with 10.6 percent of the total population.

**Pittsburgh.** The SMSA population has a comparatively high median age and a large number of elderly people (p. 109). A fourth of the SMSA poverty population consists of people 64 years old or older, and blacks under 64 constitute a fifth of the poverty group.

**St. Louis.** St. Louis has the 4th highest proportion of people with incomes below the poverty level of central cities in the atlas. Of the city's poverty population, 63.4 percent are blacks and 13.1 percent are nonblacks over 64. Similar poverty levels with similar component populations extend into East St. Louis and Illinois.

**Cleveland.** Poverty populations in excess of 10 percent of tract totals are confined to Cleveland and vicinity; 70 percent of the SMSA poverty population resides in Cleveland, and concentrations are highest in heavily black parts of the city (p. 385).

**Chicago.** Although outlying concentrations exist, 76 percent of those with incomes below the poverty threshold live in Chicago compared with 48.2 percent of the total population. The most intense concentrations occur in black neighborhoods (p. 385). In Chicago, only 22.8 percent of the poverty population is not elderly, black, or Spanish-American.

**Detroit.** The proportion of people with incomes below the poverty level peaks in central Detroit, but there are a number of outlying

*Employment and Poverty: The Poverty Population*

PERCENTAGE POPULATION BELOW THE POVERTY LEVEL
SMSA

CHICAGO

CLEVELAND

DETROIT

concentrations. Some of the outlying clusters mark the locations of black minorities (p. 385), but others occur in tracts with few or no blacks.

**Minneapolis-St. Paul.** The SMSA has the smallest proportion of its population below the poverty threshold of metropolitan areas mapped here, and St. Paul (9.5 percent) has the smallest percentage among central cities. In Minneapolis, 12 percent are below the cutoff.

**Seattle.** Limited economic opportunities and elderly populations produce high poverty rates in isolated interior parts of the SMSA. Poverty is less frequent along the coast except in Seattle. There, 13,300 (25 percent) of the city's 53,200 people with incomes below the poverty level are over 64 years of age.

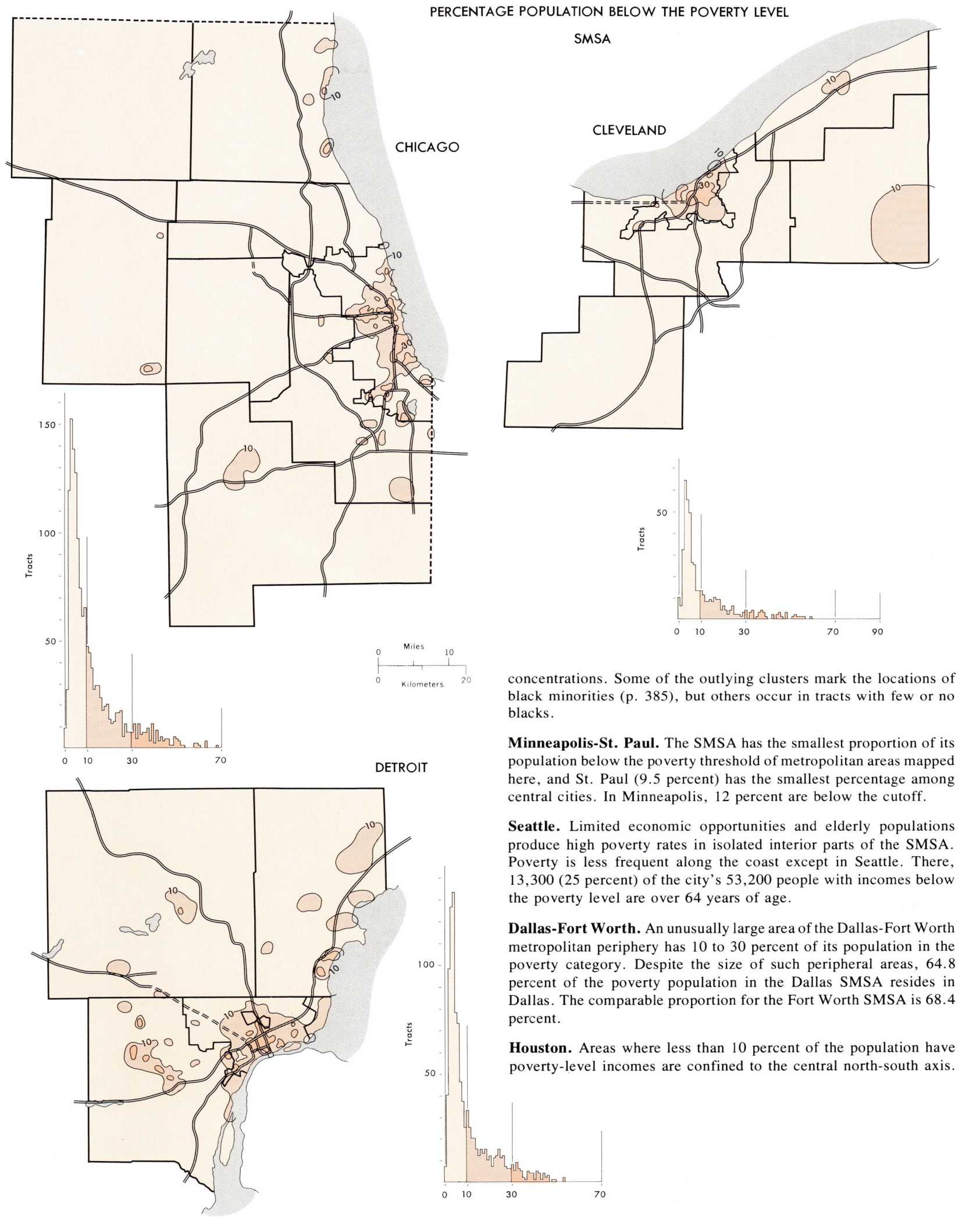

**Dallas-Fort Worth.** An unusually large area of the Dallas-Fort Worth metropolitan periphery has 10 to 30 percent of its population in the poverty category. Despite the size of such peripheral areas, 64.8 percent of the poverty population in the Dallas SMSA resides in Dallas. The comparable proportion for the Fort Worth SMSA is 68.4 percent.

**Houston.** Areas where less than 10 percent of the population have poverty-level incomes are confined to the central north-south axis.

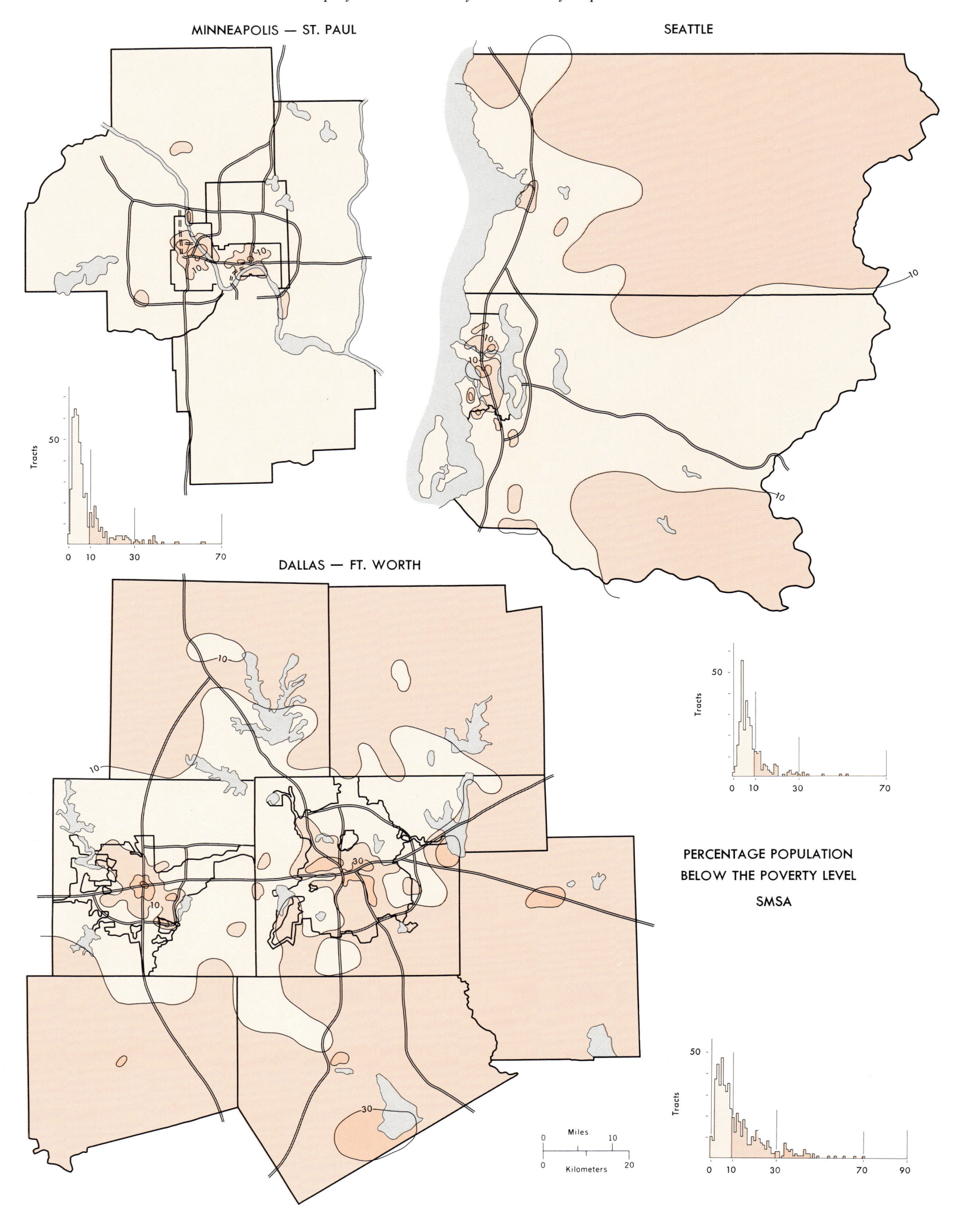

*Employment and Poverty: The Poverty Population*

MINNEAPOLIS — ST. PAUL

SEATTLE

DALLAS — FT. WORTH

PERCENTAGE POPULATION
BELOW THE POVERTY LEVEL
SMSA

*Employment and Poverty: The Poverty Population*

PERCENTAGE POPULATION BELOW THE POVERTY LEVEL
SMSA

HOUSTON

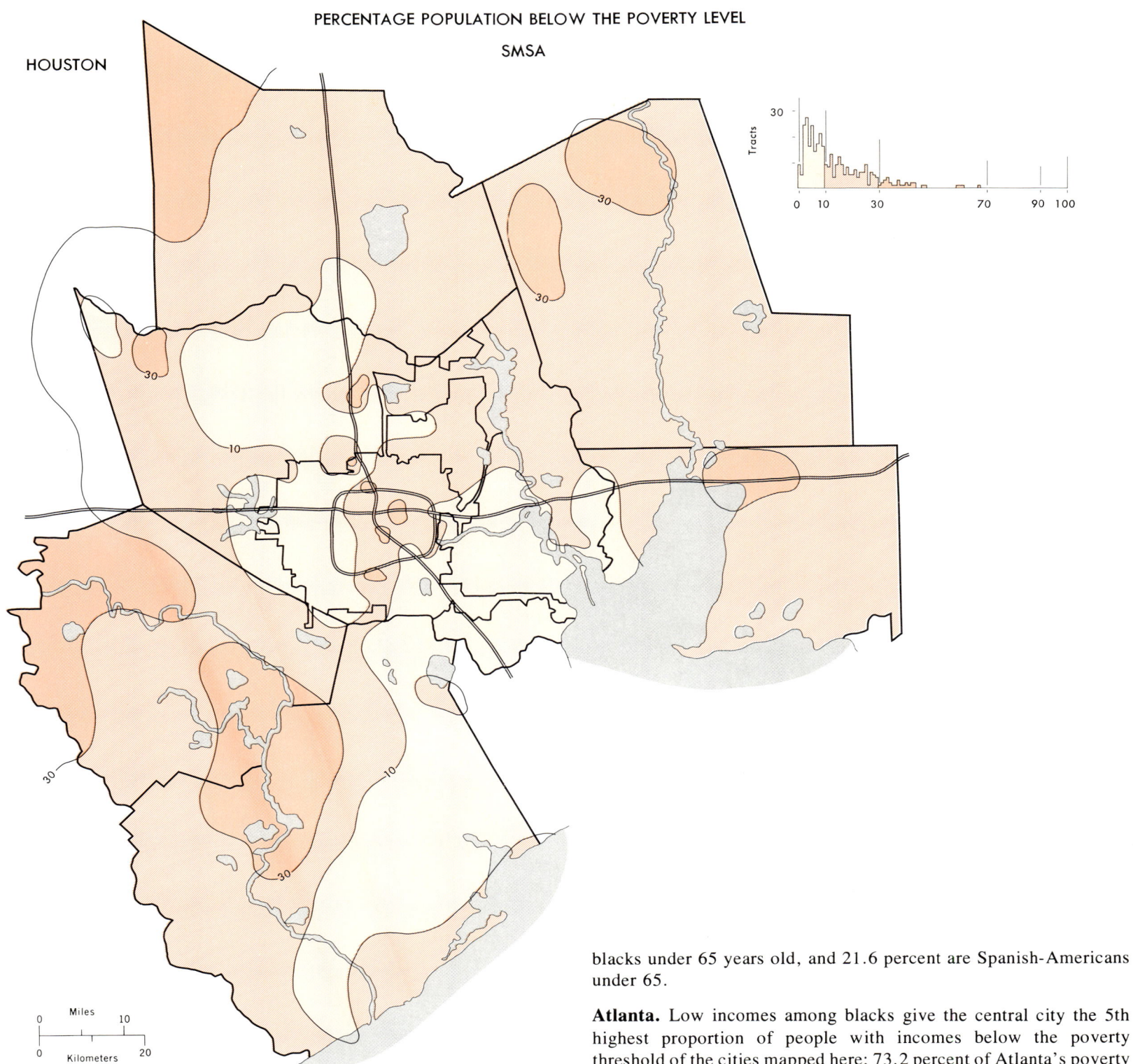

The SMSA has the 3rd largest proportion of people with incomes below the poverty level among metropolitan areas in the atlas. Poverty is especially prevalent among the SMSA's blacks (31.1 percent) and Spanish-Americans (18.2 percent).

**Los Angeles.** Concentrations of the poverty population are most intense in predominantly black (p. 388) and Spanish-American (p. 396) areas. Of the SMSA's 763,000 blacks, 180,000 (23.6 percent) have incomes below the poverty level, as do 14.7 percent of the SMSA's 1,289,000 Spanish-Americans.

**Miami.** The SMSA has the 2nd highest proportions of people with poverty-level incomes among places mapped in the atlas. Of the SMSA's 177,900 people with poverty-level incomes, 40,400 (22.7 percent) are over 64 years of age. Another 31.5 percent are blacks under 65 years old, and 21.6 percent are Spanish-Americans under 65.

**Atlanta.** Low incomes among blacks give the central city the 5th highest proportion of people with incomes below the poverty threshold of the cities mapped here; 73.2 percent of Atlanta's poverty population is black. In the SMSA, 28.9 percent of all blacks are in the poverty category.

**Washington, D.C.** Of the 123,100 people with poverty-level incomes in the District of Columbia, 102,700 (83.4 percent) are blacks. A fifth of the city's black residents have poverty-level incomes. Poverty rates among suburban blacks (p. 388) are considerably lower than central-city proportions.

---

In many metropolitan areas and central cities, skin color and age are closely related to poverty. Blacks and the elderly constitute as much as 85 percent of the poverty population in some places and more than 50 percent in most places. Although public assistance funds and Social Security payments are expended primarily on those groups (see the next chapter), high proportions of people with poverty-level incomes persist in the centers of metropolitan areas and on the metropolitan periphery.

419

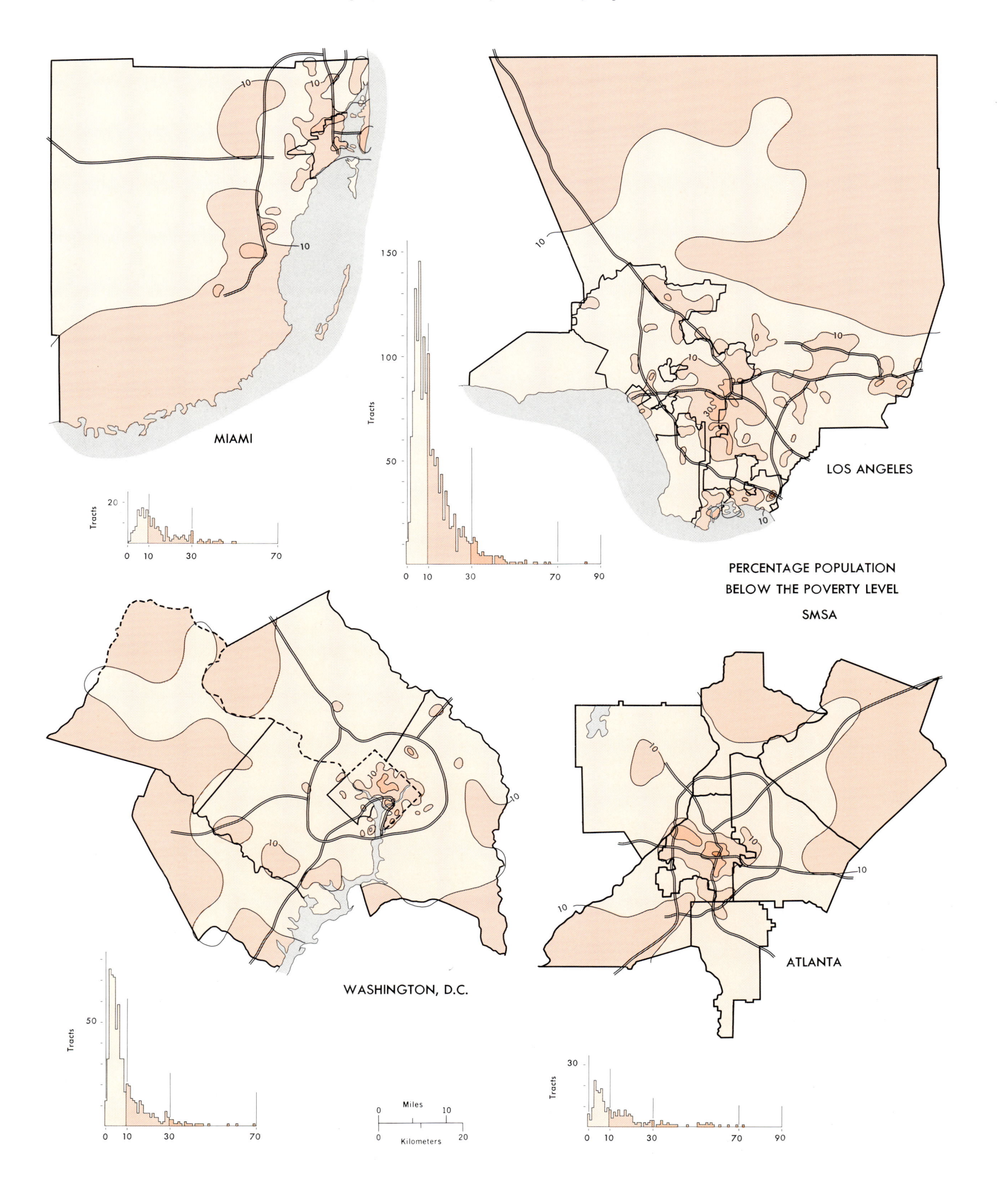

# Employment and Poverty: The Poverty Population

MIAMI

LOS ANGELES

PERCENTAGE POPULATION
BELOW THE POVERTY LEVEL
SMSA

WASHINGTON, D.C.

ATLANTA

*Employment and Poverty*

## CHAPTER 46

# Income from Public Payments

In the 1970 Census of Population, a 20 percent sample of people 14 years of age and older listed their 1969 money income by source, including income from Social Security, the government-operated railroad retirement system, and public assistance (including welfare). The maps in this chapter show the proportions of tract incomes received as Social Security, railroad retirement benefits, and public assistance. Disbursements from federal, state, and local programs for medical care and expenses are not included. Retirement and public assistance payments (both also referred to as *transfer* payments) are mapped for each of the 24 Standard Metropolitan Statistical Areas (SMSAs) included in the atlas.

In 1969, 4.2 percent of the nation's aggregate personal income came from Social Security (including railroad) retirement benefits (3.5 percent) and public assistance (0.7 percent) payments. Within the nation's SMSAs, 3.8 percent of all personal income came from such sources (3.1 percent from retirement payments and 0.7 percent in the form of public assistance). Public payments comprise a larger share of personal incomes in central cities, where 3.8 percent of all such income consists of retirement benefits and 1.1 percent consists of assistance payments, for a total transfer-fund share of 4.9 percent.

Proportions of income from public sources vary from a high of 8.5 percent in the city of Newark to a low of 1.6 percent in the Washington, D.C. SMSA. Social Security and railroad retirement payments are made largely to retired people (survivor benefits are paid to nonelderly), so places with old populations receive larger than usual percentages of their incomes from public sources. Dependent populations (often including the aged) that are larger than average generate higher than average proportions of payments from public assistance programs (see accompanying tabulation).

**Boston.** For the SMSA, 3.1 percent of the transfer payments mapped here are retirement benefits and 0.7 percent are public assistance disbursements. The corresponding breakdown for Boston is 4.1 and 2.6 percent. Although the largest concentration of transfer payments is in Boston, only 31.4 percent of the SMSA transfer payments are received by Boston residents.

**New York-Northern New Jersey.** Most places where transfer payments exceed 10 percent of total tract incomes are located in metropolitan cores. Newark's high proportion of transfer payments is caused by unusually large public assistance disbursements (4.7 percent of the city's aggregate income). In the rest of the region, city and SMSA assistance payments are not unusually high.

*Note:* All data are from the 1970 Censuses of Population and Housing unless otherwise indicated. Therefore the present tense refers to 1970 except for income data which are from 1969. Cartographic conventions are explained in Chapter 1. County names and other locational information are shown on the SMSA map at the beginning of each city chapter (6-25) and on the DUS map of mobile homes near the beginning of each city chapter.

**Philadelphia.** Retirement payments in Philadelphia are 4.4 percent of the city's aggregate income, and public assistance amounts to 1.6 percent. Although there are few tracts where transfer payments exceed 10 percent of tract incomes outside Philadelphia and Camden, a third of such payments in the SMSA are made to Philadelphia residents compared with the city's 40 percent share of the total population.

Percentage of Income from Public Payments

| Region | Central City(ies) | Entire SMSA |
| --- | --- | --- |
| Boston | 6.7 | 4.8 |
| New York | 5.4 | 4.4 |
| Jersey City | 6.1 | 5.4 |
| Newark | 8.5 | 3.8 |
| Paterson-Clifton-Passaic | 5.4 | 3.2 |
| Philadelphia | 6.0 | 4.2 |
| Hartford | 6.2 | 3.4 |
| Baltimore | 5.8 | 3.6 |
| New Orleans | 5.4 | 4.2 |
| San Francisco-Oakland | 5.3 | 3.7 |
| Pittsburgh | 7.1 | 5.1 |
| St. Louis | 7.3 | 4.1 |
| Cleveland | 5.9 | 3.5 |
| Chicago | 4.9 | 3.4 |
| Detroit | 6.0 | 3.5 |
| Minneapolis-St. Paul | 6.0 | 3.5 |
| Seattle | 4.6 | 3.3 |
| Dallas | 2.7 | 2.5 |
| Fort Worth | 3.7 | 3.0 |
| Houston | 2.5 | 2.4 |
| Los Angeles | 4.3 | 4.0 |
| Miami | 5.6 | 4.6 |
| Atlanta | 3.9 | 2.5 |
| Washington, D.C. | 2.9 | 1.6 |

**Hartford.** Public assistance makes up a comparatively high proportion (2.1 percent) of Hartford's personal income. In the entire SMSA, most (2.8 percent) transfer payments are retirement benefits; public assistance income is 0.7 percent of the SMSA total.

**Baltimore.** Most (4.4 percent of the city income) of the transfer payments received in Baltimore are retirement benefits; assistance disbursements total 1.4 percent. Corresponding proportions for the entire SMSA are 3 percent and 0.6 percent. Tracts where public payments exceed 10 percent of aggregate personal incomes are located in Baltimore's predominantly black neighborhoods (p. 383).

**New Orleans.** Public payments in New Orleans are not high, especially considering the city's large poverty population (p. 415). In

*Employment and Poverty: Public Payments*

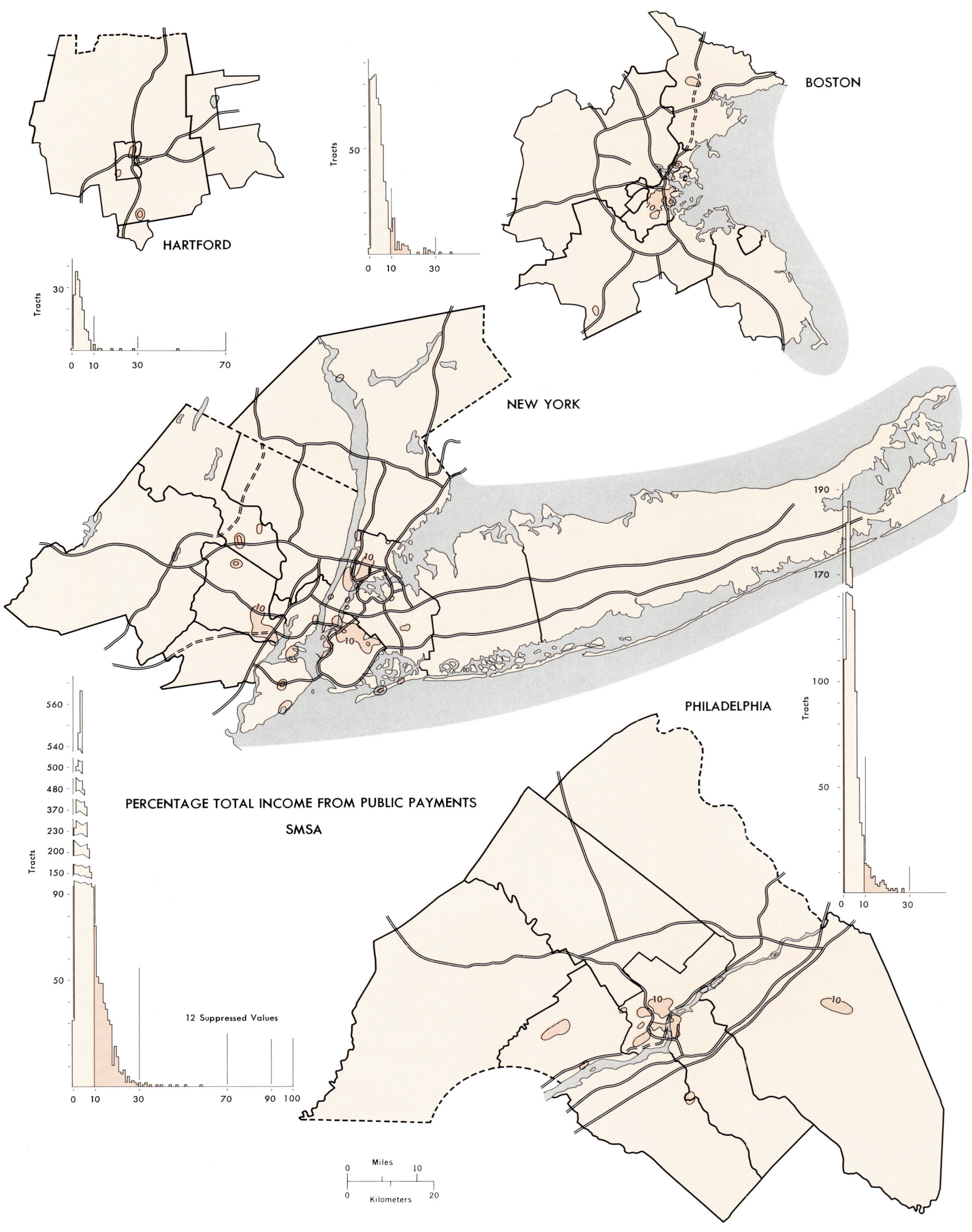

HARTFORD

BOSTON

NEW YORK

PERCENTAGE TOTAL INCOME FROM PUBLIC PAYMENTS
SMSA

PHILADELPHIA

12 Suppressed Values

*Employment and Poverty: Public Payments*

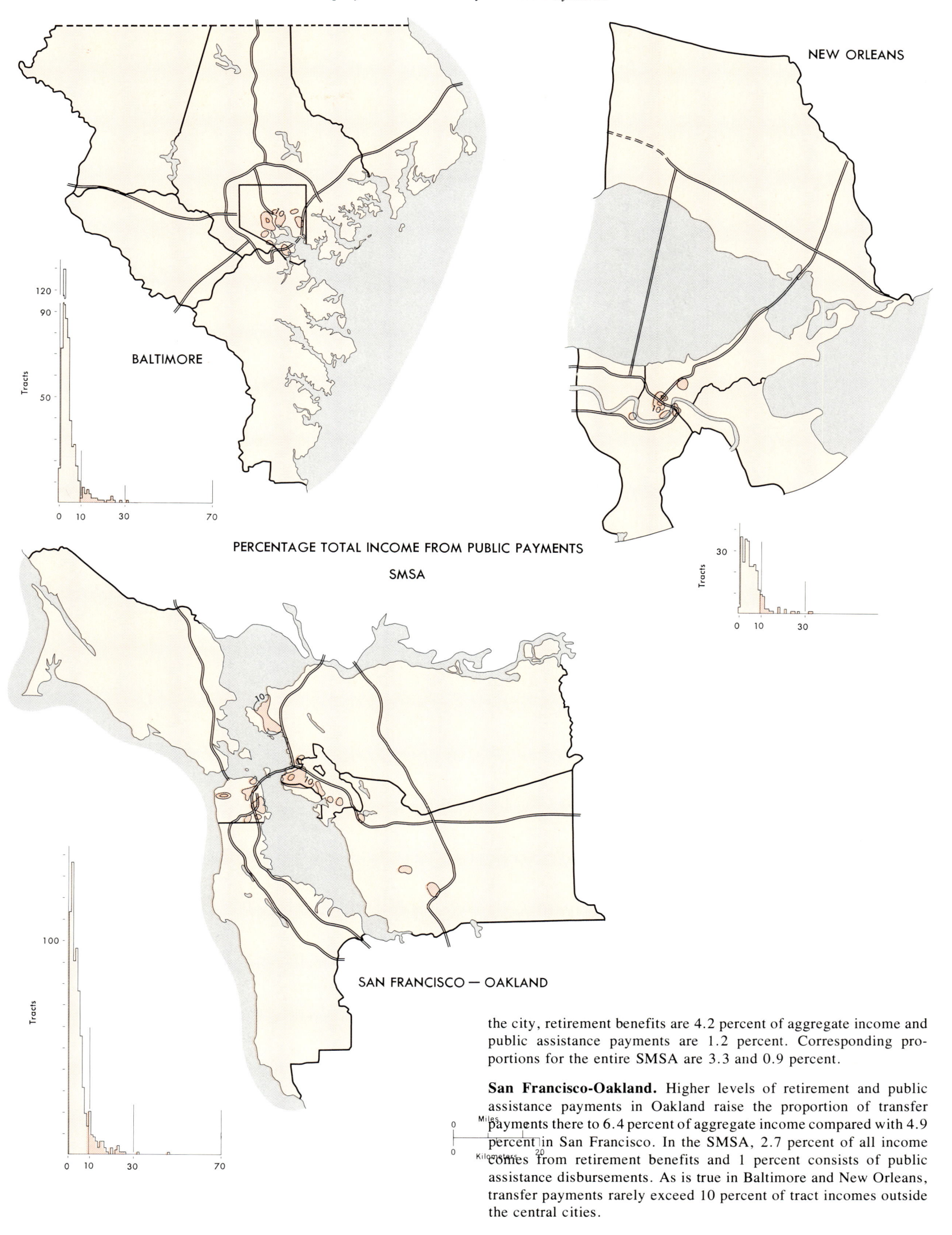

BALTIMORE

NEW ORLEANS

PERCENTAGE TOTAL INCOME FROM PUBLIC PAYMENTS
SMSA

SAN FRANCISCO — OAKLAND

the city, retirement benefits are 4.2 percent of aggregate income and public assistance payments are 1.2 percent. Corresponding proportions for the entire SMSA are 3.3 and 0.9 percent.

**San Francisco-Oakland.** Higher levels of retirement and public assistance payments in Oakland raise the proportion of transfer payments there to 6.4 percent of aggregate income compared with 4.9 percent in San Francisco. In the SMSA, 2.7 percent of all income comes from retirement benefits and 1 percent consists of public assistance disbursements. As is true in Baltimore and New Orleans, transfer payments rarely exceed 10 percent of tract incomes outside the central cities.

*Employment and Poverty: Public Payments*

PERCENTAGE TOTAL INCOME FROM PUBLIC PAYMENTS

SMSA

**Pittsburgh.** Out-migration of young people from the SMSA and the consequent high median age of the remaining population result in the 2nd highest level of retirement payments (4.3 percent of the aggregate SMSA income) among the SMSAs in the atlas. In Pittsburgh, retirement benefits are 5.3 percent of all income. The SMSA's many separate settlements are apparent in the scattered tracts where transfer payments exceed 10 percent of tract incomes.

**St. Louis.** The central city, with 6 percent of its aggregate income from retirement benefits and 1.3 percent from public assistance payments, has the largest proportion of transfer payments among places in the atlas. The tract in Madison County, Illinois, where public payments exceed 30 percent contains an institutionalized population.

**Cleveland.** Although public assistance payments account for the largest shares of tract incomes within Cleveland, such payments are only slightly concentrated there; 47.3 percent of such funds accrue to residents of Cleveland, with the balance going to people in the rest of the SMSA. In Cleveland, 4.6 percent of all income is retirement benefits, and 1.3 percent comes from public assistance. The SMSA breakdown is 3.1 and 0.5 percent.

**Chicago.** Transfer payments are not as concentrated in Chicago as is the poverty population (p. 417), but they are disproportionate to the population; city residents make up 48.2 percent of the SMSA population but they receive 62.7 percent of the SMSA public assistance payments. In Chicago, 3.7 percent of all income consists of retirement benefits and 1.2 percent comes from public assistance.

**Detroit.** In the central city, 4.7 percent of the aggregate income consists of retirement benefits and 1.3 percent is derived from assistance. The SMSA breakdown is 2.9 and 0.6 percent. The tract where such payments exceed 30 percent of tract income contains a state hospital.

**Minneapolis-St. Paul.** In Minneapolis, 5.1 percent of all personal income consists of retirement benefits and 1.2 percent is public assistance payments. Corresponding statistics for St. Paul are 4.6 and

*Employment and Poverty: Public Payments*

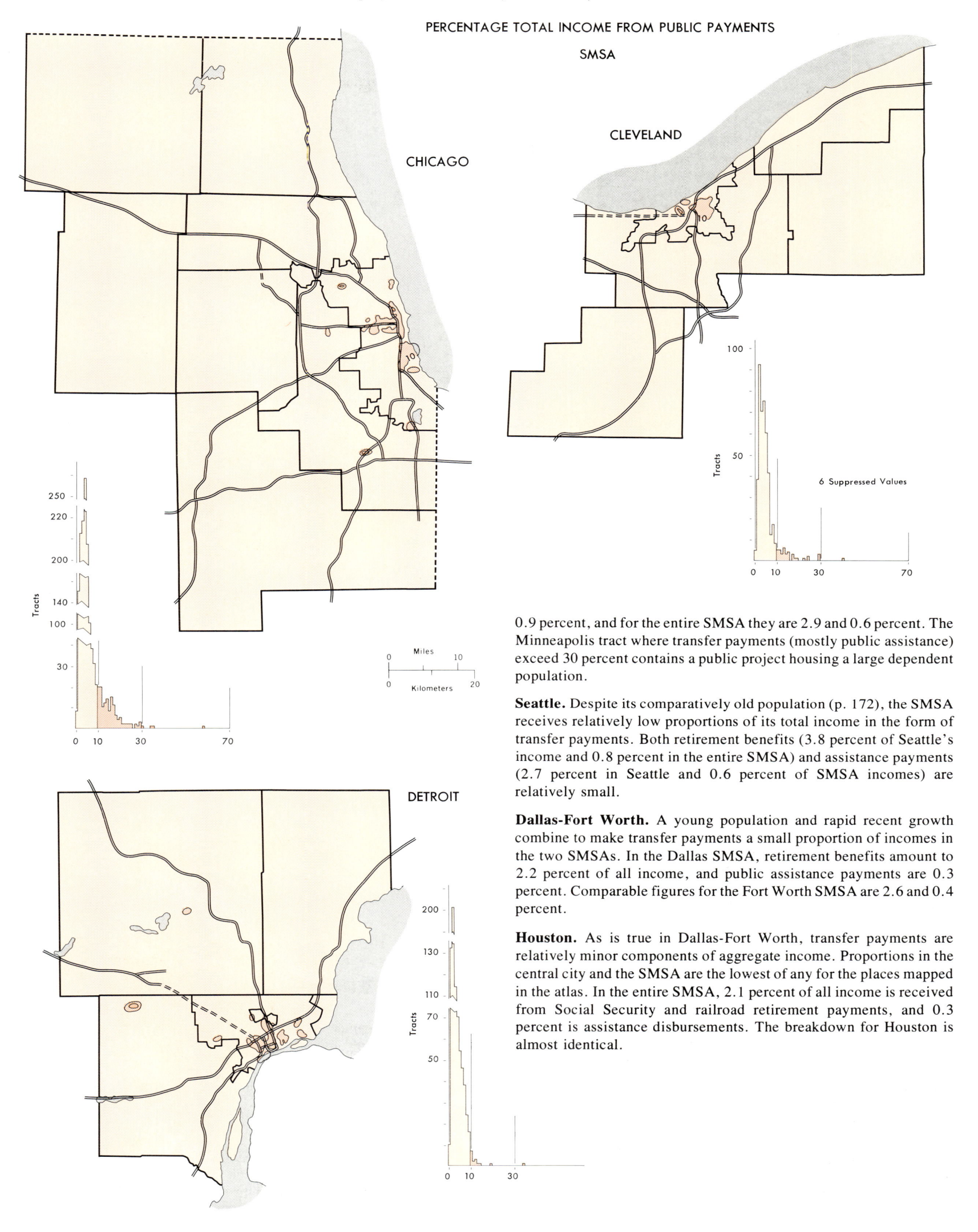

PERCENTAGE TOTAL INCOME FROM PUBLIC PAYMENTS
SMSA

CHICAGO

CLEVELAND

DETROIT

0.9 percent, and for the entire SMSA they are 2.9 and 0.6 percent. The Minneapolis tract where transfer payments (mostly public assistance) exceed 30 percent contains a public project housing a large dependent population.

**Seattle.** Despite its comparatively old population (p. 172), the SMSA receives relatively low proportions of its total income in the form of transfer payments. Both retirement benefits (3.8 percent of Seattle's income and 0.8 percent in the entire SMSA) and assistance payments (2.7 percent in Seattle and 0.6 percent of SMSA incomes) are relatively small.

**Dallas-Fort Worth.** A young population and rapid recent growth combine to make transfer payments a small proportion of incomes in the two SMSAs. In the Dallas SMSA, retirement benefits amount to 2.2 percent of all income, and public assistance payments are 0.3 percent. Comparable figures for the Fort Worth SMSA are 2.6 and 0.4 percent.

**Houston.** As is true in Dallas-Fort Worth, transfer payments are relatively minor components of aggregate income. Proportions in the central city and the SMSA are the lowest of any for the places mapped in the atlas. In the entire SMSA, 2.1 percent of all income is received from Social Security and railroad retirement payments, and 0.3 percent is assistance disbursements. The breakdown for Houston is almost identical.

*Employment and Poverty: Public Payments*

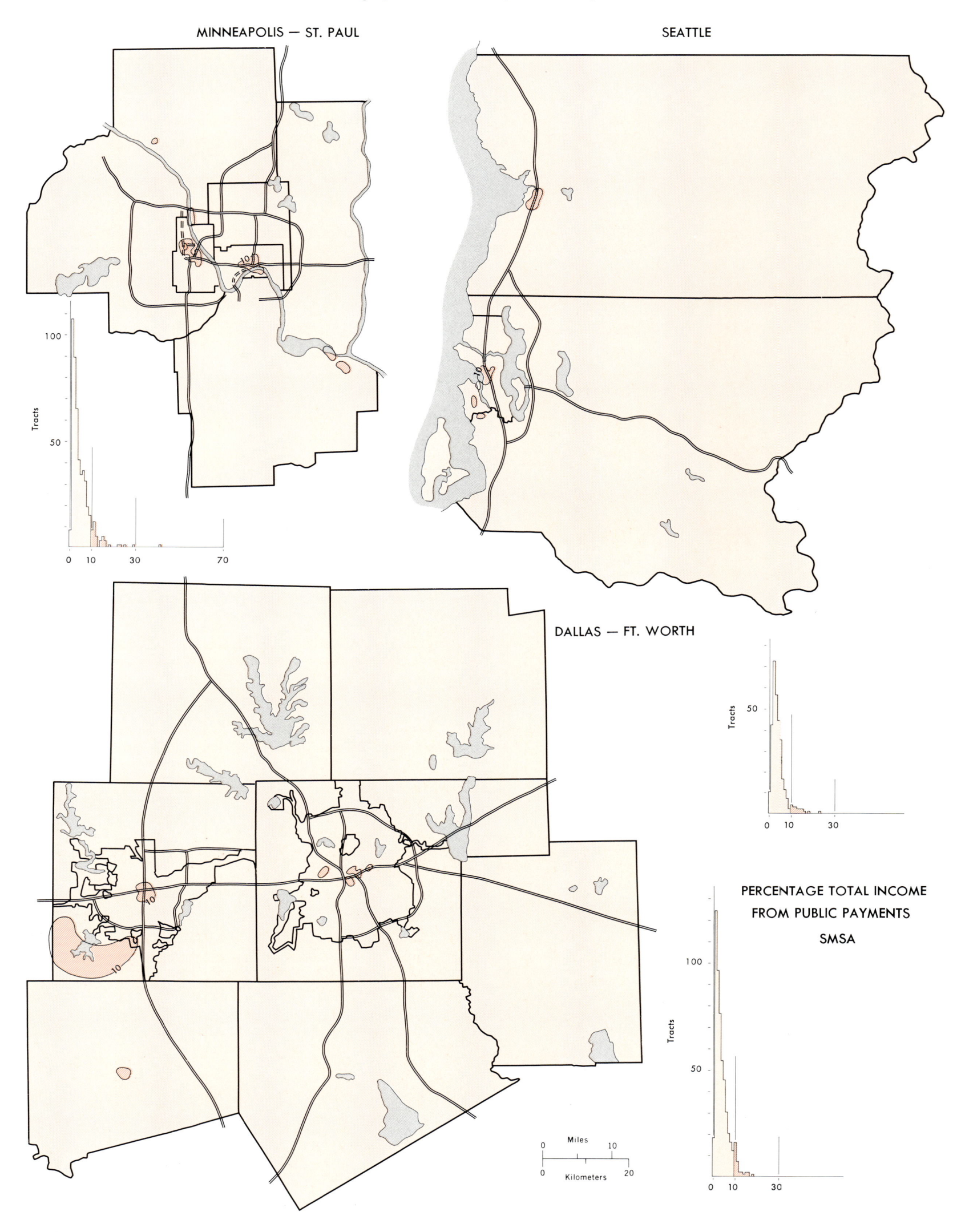

MINNEAPOLIS — ST. PAUL

SEATTLE

DALLAS — FT. WORTH

PERCENTAGE TOTAL INCOME FROM PUBLIC PAYMENTS

SMSA

*Employment and Poverty: Public Payments*

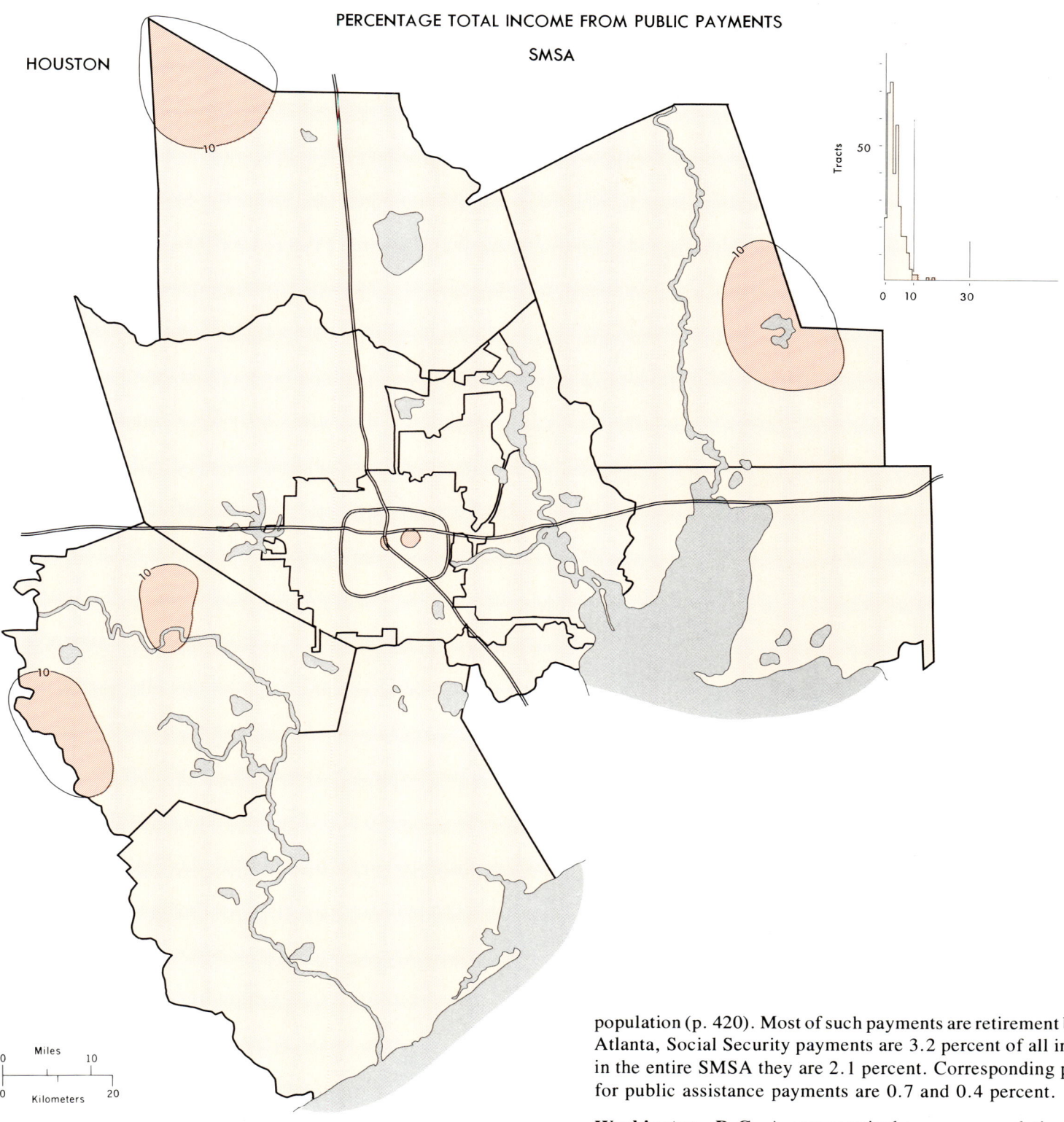

PERCENTAGE TOTAL INCOME FROM PUBLIC PAYMENTS

HOUSTON SMSA

**Los Angeles.** Tracts where public assistance payments exceed 10 percent of tract incomes are heavily concentrated in black and Spanish-American neighborhoods (pp. 388, 396). In Los Angeles, 2.9 percent of all income consists of retirement benefits and 1.4 percent comes from assistance. Comparable statistics for the entire SMSA are 2.8 and 1.2 percent.

**Miami.** Despite the large numbers of old people in Miami and the SMSA (p. 240), Social Security benefits (4.3 percent in Miami and 4.1 percent for the entire SMSA) are not an unusually large source of income. Assistance payments are also low at 1.3 percent in Miami and 0.5 percent for the SMSA. In Miami Beach, 10.7 percent of the aggregate income is received in the form of retirement benefits.

**Atlanta.** Tracts in which more than 10 percent of all income consists of transfer payments correlate closely with the SMSA poverty population (p. 420). Most of such payments are retirement benefits. In Atlanta, Social Security payments are 3.2 percent of all income, and in the entire SMSA they are 2.1 percent. Corresponding proportions for public assistance payments are 0.7 and 0.4 percent.

**Washington, D.C.** A comparatively young population and large numbers of blacks, many of whom in the past have worked at jobs not covered by Social Security, result in low levels of public payments in the SMSA and in Washington. In the District of Columbia, 2.2 percent of all income consists of retirement payments and 0.7 percent comes from assistance payments. The breakdown for the entire SMSA is 1.3 and 0.3 percent.

---

Retirement benefits and assistance payments help alleviate the distress of the elderly and the minority groups that are usually overrepresented in the poverty population, but the poverty population mapped in Chapter 45 and the income deficits mapped in Chapter 47 exist *despite* the retirement and assistance programs mapped in this chapter. Also, even if transfer payments were increased enough to eliminate income deficits, the underlying inability of the elderly and dependent populations to care for themselves, of which poverty is only one symptom, would remain.

427

*Employment and Poverty: Public Payments*

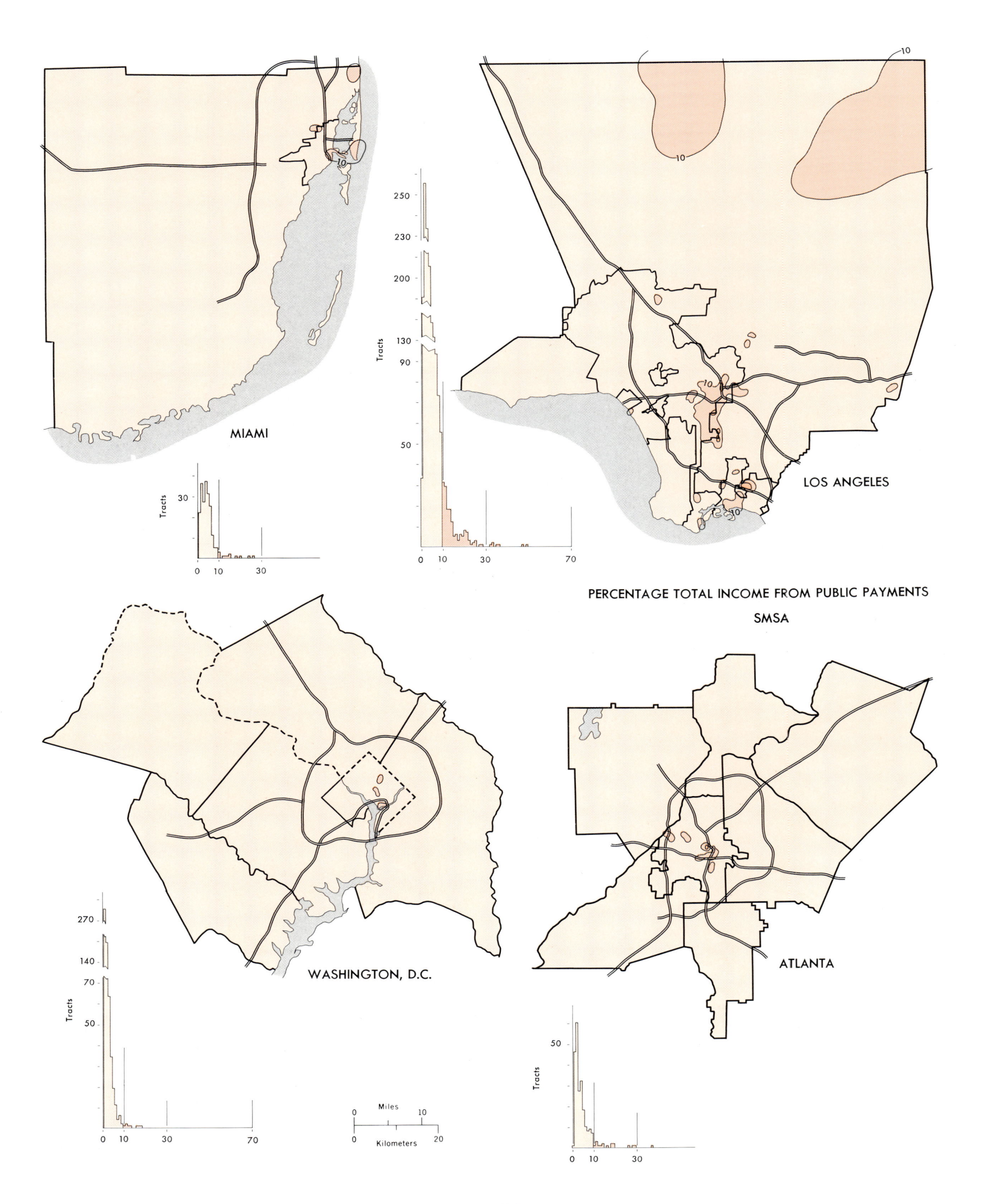

MIAMI

LOS ANGELES

PERCENTAGE TOTAL INCOME FROM PUBLIC PAYMENTS
SMSA

WASHINGTON, D.C.

ATLANTA

*Employment and Poverty*

CHAPTER 47

# Income Deficits

Income statistics gathered in the 1970 Census of Population make it possible to determine how much 1969 incomes fell short of 1969 poverty thresholds (see beginning of Chapter 45 for definition). The maps in this chapter show the locations of income deficits by means of dots, each of which represents $50,000 that would have to be added to 1969 incomes of the poverty population at each place to eliminate officially defined poverty. The maps were prepared by summarizing the aggregate income deficit for each census tract and placing the appropriate number of dots within the tract.

In the nation as a whole, the incomes of the poverty population fall $14.082 billion short of the poverty threshold. The aggregate deficit amounts to about $70 for every American. The low incomes of unrelated individuals are responsible for a disproportionate share of the deficit. Whereas unrelated individuals are only 6.1 percent of the nation's people, the aggregate incomes of these individuals are $5.660 billion (40.2 percent of the aggregate deficit) short of the poverty threshold. The remaining 60 percent of the income shortfall occurs in family incomes.

Income deficits in the nation's Standard Metropolitan Statistical Areas (SMSAs) total $8.456 billion, or 60.1 percent of the national shortfall. Since 68.6 percent of the national population resides in these SMSAs, income deficits are somewhat underrepresented in the nation's metropolitan areas. In SMSAs, 43.6 percent of the shortfall is in the incomes of unrelated individuals, and 56.4 percent consists of family income deficits. The per capita (total population) deficit in SMSAs is $62.

The per capita shortfall is larger ($84) in the central cities of SMSAs, where the aggregate deficit of $5.250 billion constitutes 37.3 percent of the national shortfall compared with the 31.4 percent of the nation's population residing in SMSA central cities. Of the $5.250 billion, $2.856 billion (54.4 percent) represents deficits in family incomes and $2.395 billion (45.6 percent) is the shortfall among the incomes of unrelated individuals (see accompanying tabulation).

Per capita deficits are large in cities with unusually large numbers of the elderly and dependent minority groups. They are smallest in places with youthful populations and rapidly expanding economies that create jobs at adequate wages for people who elsewhere might be unemployed.

**Boston.** The SMSA income deficit totals $140 million, of which $60 million (43 percent) occurs among residents of the city of Boston. Deficits are most concentrated in Boston and immediately adjacent places, but some dots are scattered throughout the SMSA. The occurrence of dots representing income shortfalls in affluent areas where one might not expect to find them usually signals populations of elderly people on limited retirement incomes.

**New York-Northern New Jersey.** The scale of some problems in the nation's largest metropolitan complex is evident in the size of the income deficit in the four SMSAs; it is $962 million, of which $784 million (82 percent) occurs in the New York, New York SMSA. Although income deficits are most serious and most concentrated in New York City, per capita deficits in the region are highest in the city

Per Capita Income Deficit

| Region | Central City(ies) | Entire SMSA |
|---|---|---|
| Boston | $93 | $51 |
| New York | 84 | 68 |
| Jersey City | 76 | 66 |
| Newark | 108 | 49 |
| Paterson-Clifton-Passaic | 66 | 34 |
| Philadelphia | 88 | 58 |
| Hartford | 99 | 41 |
| Baltimore | 102 | 63 |
| New Orleans | 144 | 107 |
| San Francisco-Oakland | 96 | 64 |
| Pittsburgh | 85 | 52 |
| St. Louis | 111 | 60 |
| Cleveland | 102 | 54 |
| Chicago | 79 | 52 |
| Detroit | 83 | 48 |
| Minneapolis-St. Paul | 65 | 40 |
| Seattle | 66 | 46 |
| Dallas | 68 | 57 |
| Fort Worth | 70 | 53 |
| Houston | 74 | 65 |
| Los Angeles | 78 | 63 |
| Miami | 120 | 82 |
| Atlanta | 110 | 62 |
| Washington, D.C. | 103 | 51 |

of Newark. The areas most seriously affected by income deficits in the region correspond closely to areas occupied by blacks and Spanish-Americans (pp. 382, 390).

**Philadelphia.** Another $279 million would be needed by the poverty population to eliminate poverty in the SMSA, of which $172 million (62 percent) would have to be added to the incomes of Philadelphia's poor to eliminate poverty there. Although the city's deficit is concentrated in black neighborhoods (p. 382), there is also a large income deficit in the predominantly Italian area south of downtown Philadelphia (p. 56).

**Hartford.** The SMSA aggregate deficit is $27 million, of which $16

*Note:* All data are from the 1970 Censuses of Population and Housing unless otherwise indicated. Therefore the present tense refers to 1970 except for income data which are from 1969. Cartographic conventions are explained in Chapter 1. County names and other locational information are shown on the SMSA map at the beginning of each city chapter (6-25) and on the DUS map of mobile homes near the beginning of each city chapter.

*Employment and Poverty: Income Deficits*

AGGREGATE INCOME DEFICIT, 1969

SMSA

Each Dot Represents $50,000

HARTFORD

BOSTON

NEW YORK

PHILADELPHIA

*Employment and Poverty: Income Deficits*

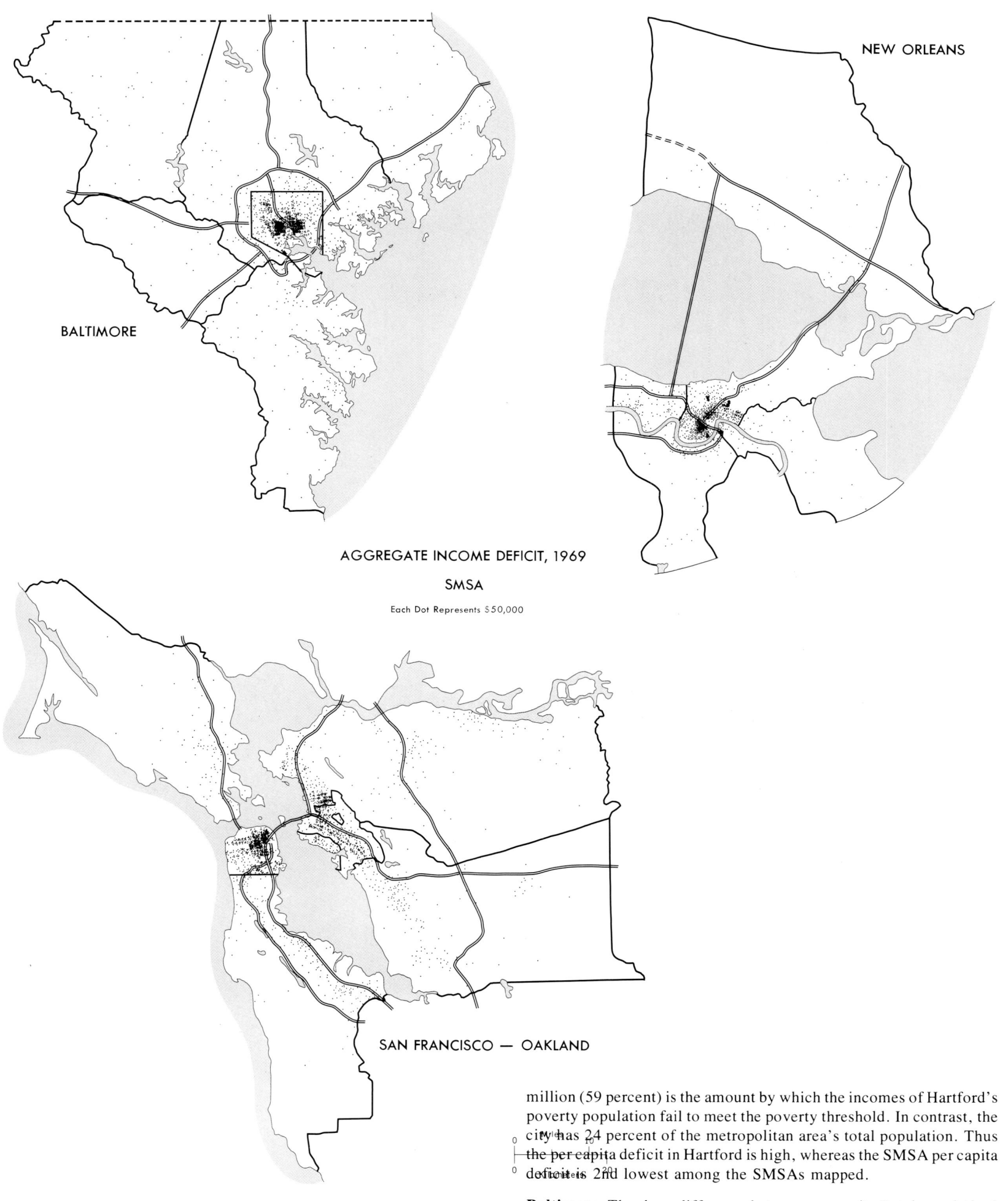

BALTIMORE

NEW ORLEANS

AGGREGATE INCOME DEFICIT, 1969
SMSA
Each Dot Represents $50,000

SAN FRANCISCO — OAKLAND

million (59 percent) is the amount by which the incomes of Hartford's poverty population fail to meet the poverty threshold. In contrast, the city has 24 percent of the metropolitan area's total population. Thus the per capita deficit in Hartford is high, whereas the SMSA per capita deficit is 2nd lowest among the SMSAs mapped.

**Baltimore.** The sharp difference between per capita (total population) deficits in Baltimore and for the entire SMSA results from a high concentration of deficit incomes in the central city; 71 percent of the SMSA deficit occurs in Baltimore compared with the 44 percent share

431

*Employment and Poverty: Income Deficits*

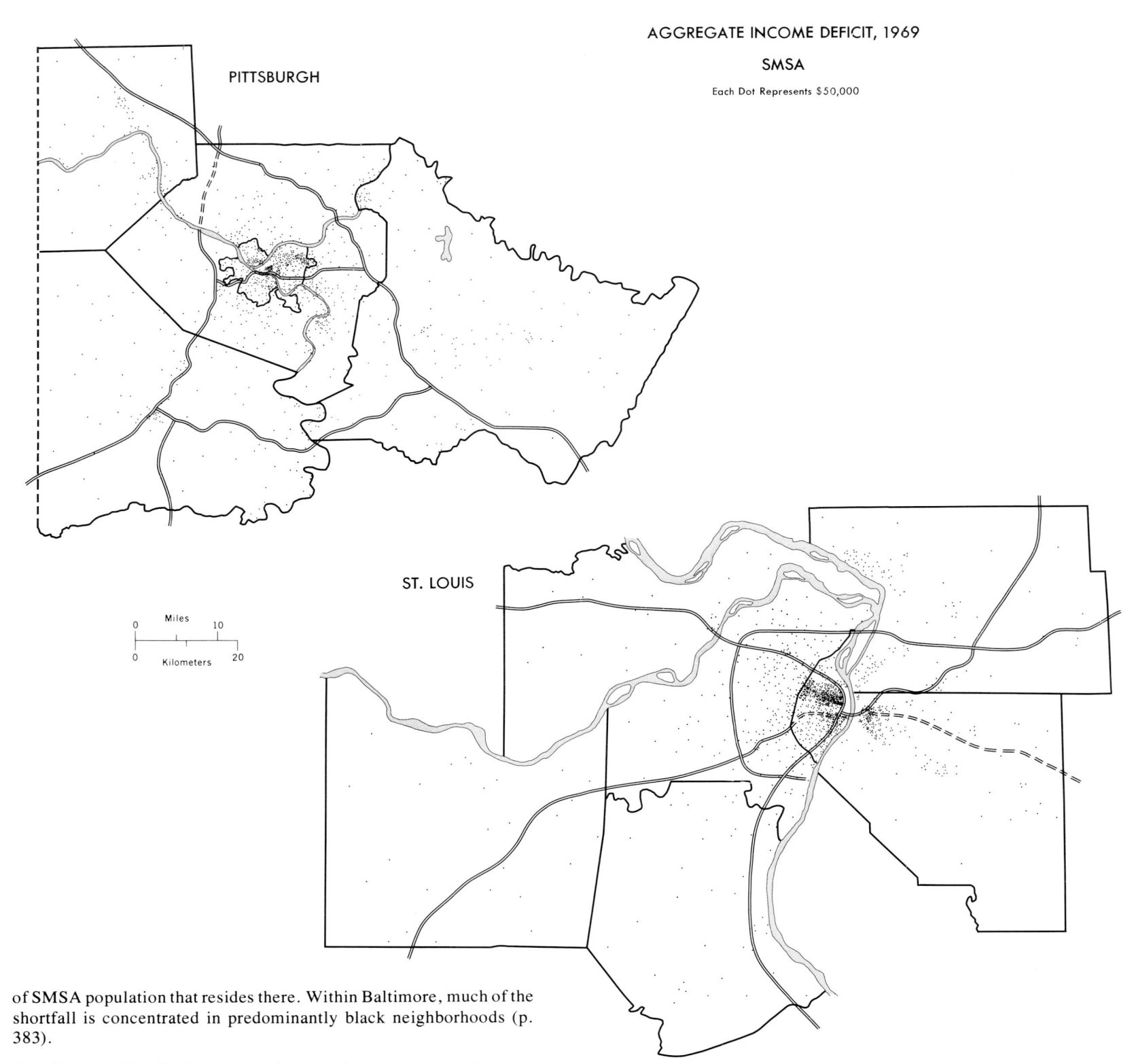

AGGREGATE INCOME DEFICIT, 1969

SMSA

Each Dot Represents $50,000

PITTSBURGH

ST. LOUIS

of SMSA population that resides there. Within Baltimore, much of the shortfall is concentrated in predominantly black neighborhoods (p. 383).

**New Orleans.** The SMSA and the city have the largest per capita (total population) shortfalls among places in the atlas. The SMSA total shortfall is $112 million, of which $85 million (76 percent) is located in New Orleans. Central New Orleans is most seriously affected by shortfalls, but the locations of several outlying housing projects with low-income, dependent occupants are evident in the small, dense clusters of dots around the main New Orleans core.

**San Francisco-Oakland.** The total income shortfall in the SMSA is $199 million, of which $69 million (35 percent) represents San Francisco's deficit and $35 million (18 percent) is Oakland's. The major deficit area outside San Francisco and Oakland occurs in Berkeley, just north of Oakland, where a large student population produces a cluster of dots. Although some of the neighborhoods where deficits are concentrated in San Francisco and Oakland are occupied by blacks and Spanish-Americans (pp. 383, 391), the correspondence between minority status and income shortfalls is not as striking as it is in some other cities such as New York.

**Pittsburgh.** Income deficits are scattered in the SMSA owing to the elderly population dispersed among the region's many settlements and rural areas, and the comparatively small (22 percent) proportion of the SMSA population residing in Pittsburgh. The SMSA total deficit is $125 million, of which $44 million (35 percent) would have to be added to the incomes of Pittsburgh's poor to eliminate poverty there.

**St. Louis.** The central city has an unusually large per capita (total population) income shortfall which is especially concentrated in the city's black neighborhoods (p. 384). A disproportionately large share (49 percent) of the aggregate SMSA deficit is concentrated in St. Louis compared with the 26 percent of the SMSA population residing there, which results in the large difference between the per capita deficits in St. Louis and the SMSA. The total SMSA deficit is $125 million.

*Employment and Poverty: Income Deficits*

AGGREGATE INCOME DEFICIT, 1969

SMSA

Each Dot Represents $50,000

CHICAGO

CLEVELAND

DETROIT

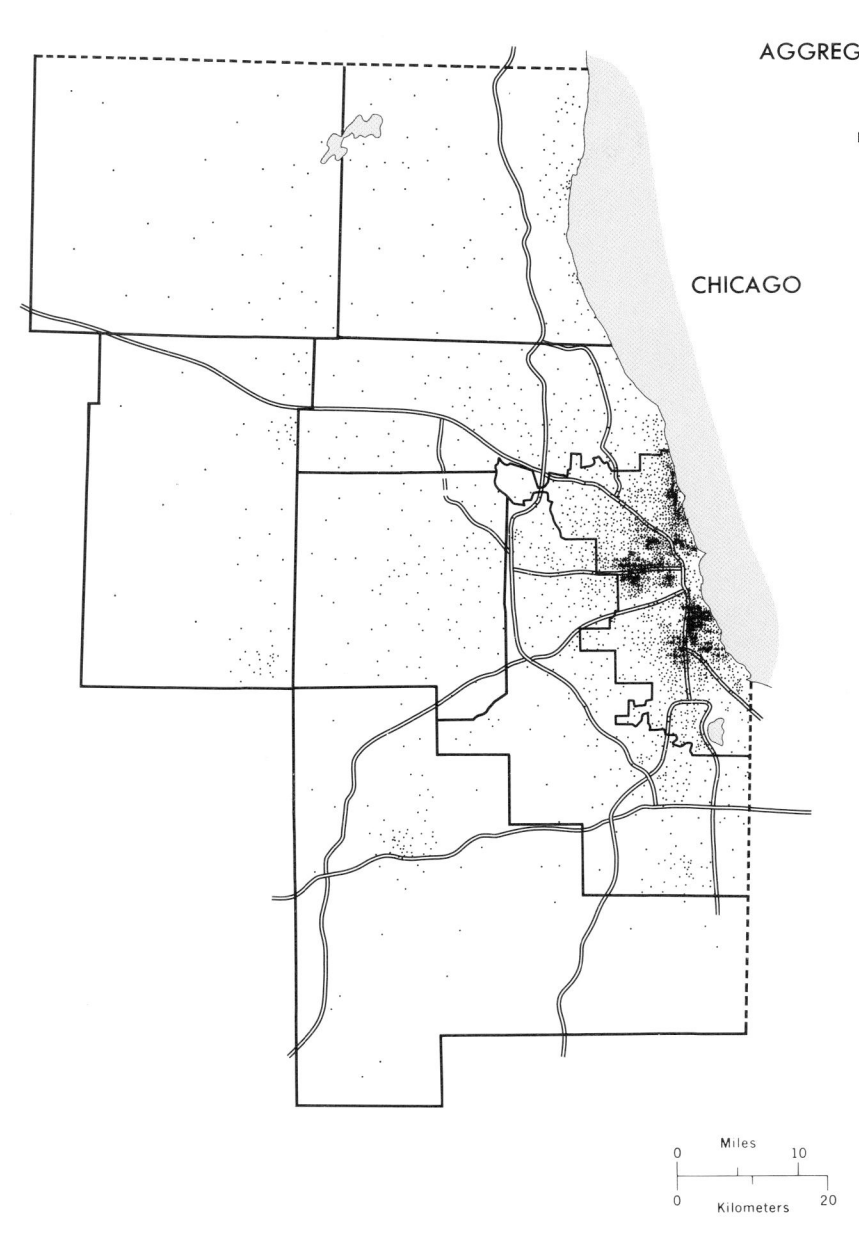

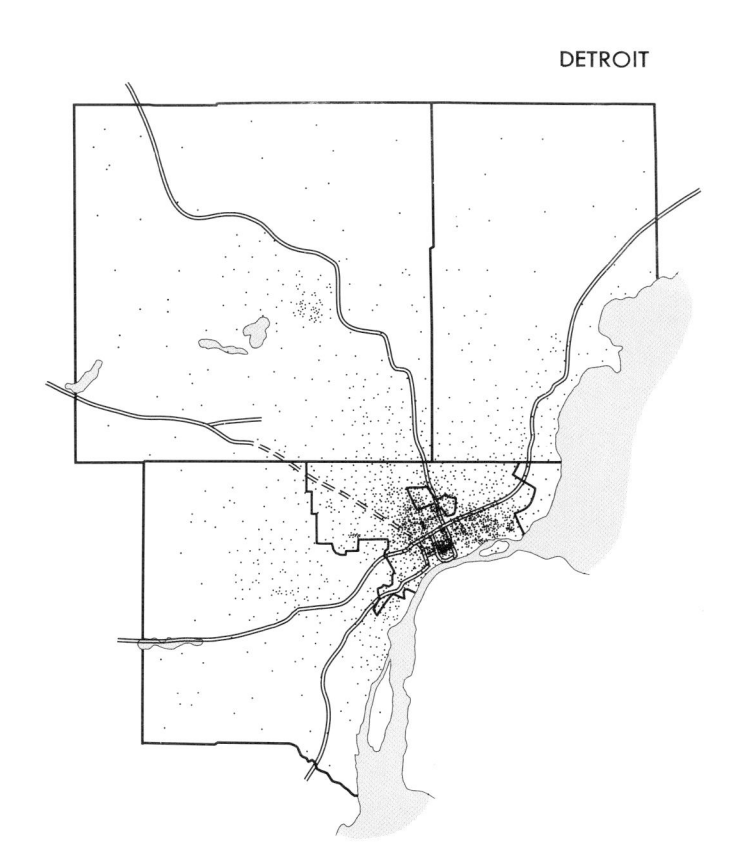

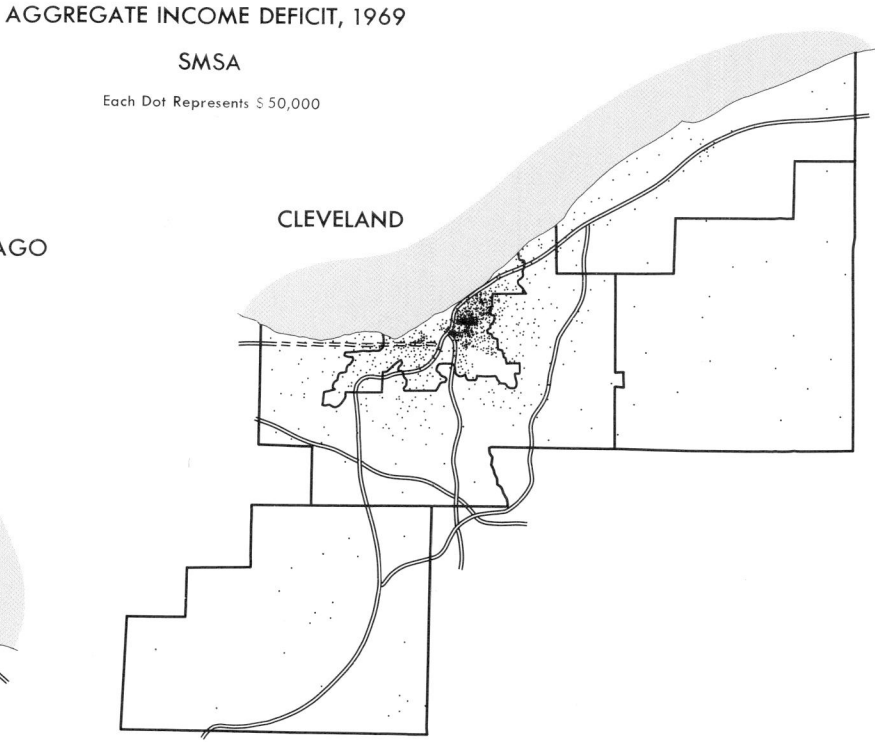

**Cleveland.** The total income shortfall in the SMSA is $111 million, of which $76 million (68 percent) is the amount of the income deficit in Cleveland. The concentration of income shortfalls in the northern part of the city's black community (p. 385) and the absence of income deficits in Cleveland's southeastern corner, which also has a large black population, point up the major socioeconomic differences that often exist among blacks within a city or SMSA.

**Chicago.** SMSA and central-city per capita (total population) deficits are low, but the region's large population means that the absolute size of its income deficit ($360 million) is large; $265 million (74 percent) of the deficit is located in Chicago. The city's two major black ghettos (p. 385) have high concentrations of the deficit. The elongated cluster of dots near Lake Michigan in north Chicago results from a concentration in that area of elderly people (p. 139) and Spanish-Americans (p. 393).

**Detroit.** The aggregate income shortfall of the SMSA is $202 million. Of that amount, $126 million (62 percent of the SMSA total) would have to be added to the incomes of Detroit's poor to eliminate poverty there, compared with the 36 percent of the SMSA population that lives in the city. Although the central-city deficit is concentrated in black neighborhoods (p. 385), no clusters of dots appear at the locations of suburban black communities.

**Minneapolis-St. Paul.** The SMSA income deficit is 2nd smallest, on a per capita basis, of the metropolitan areas mapped here. Per capita deficits are $72 in Minneapolis and $55 in St. Paul. Of the total SMSA shortfall of $71 million, $31 million (44 percent) is the gap between current incomes of the poverty population and nonpoverty status in Minneapolis, and $17 million (24 percent) is the shortfall in St. Paul. In Minneapolis, the shortfall is concentrated in and near the Central Business District rather than in areas occupied by black minorities.

**Seattle.** As is true in the Twin Cities, the deficit in Seattle is more closely associated with elderly and other white dependent groups than with racial minorities. Of the SMSA total deficit of $65 million, $35 million (54 percent) is located in Seattle, where the most intense concentration occurs near the Central Business District among elderly, male-dominant populations (p. 172).

**Dallas-Fort Worth.** Central-city and SMSA per capita (total

*Employment and Poverty: Income Deficits*

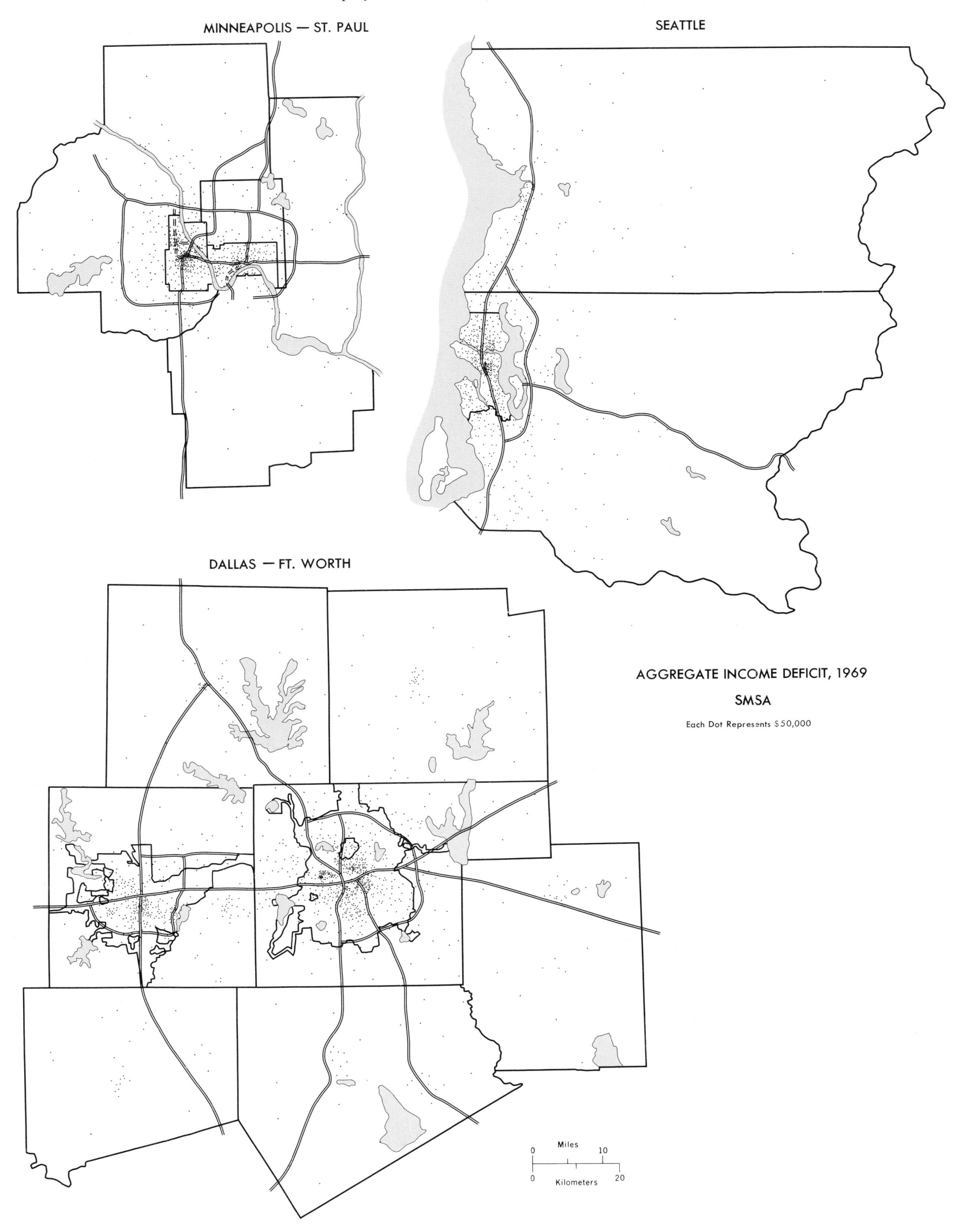

MINNEAPOLIS — ST. PAUL

SEATTLE

DALLAS — FT. WORTH

AGGREGATE INCOME DEFICIT, 1969

SMSA

Each Dot Represents $50,000

*Employment and Poverty: Income Deficits*

AGGREGATE INCOME DEFICIT, 1969

SMSA

Each Dot Represents $50,000

HOUSTON

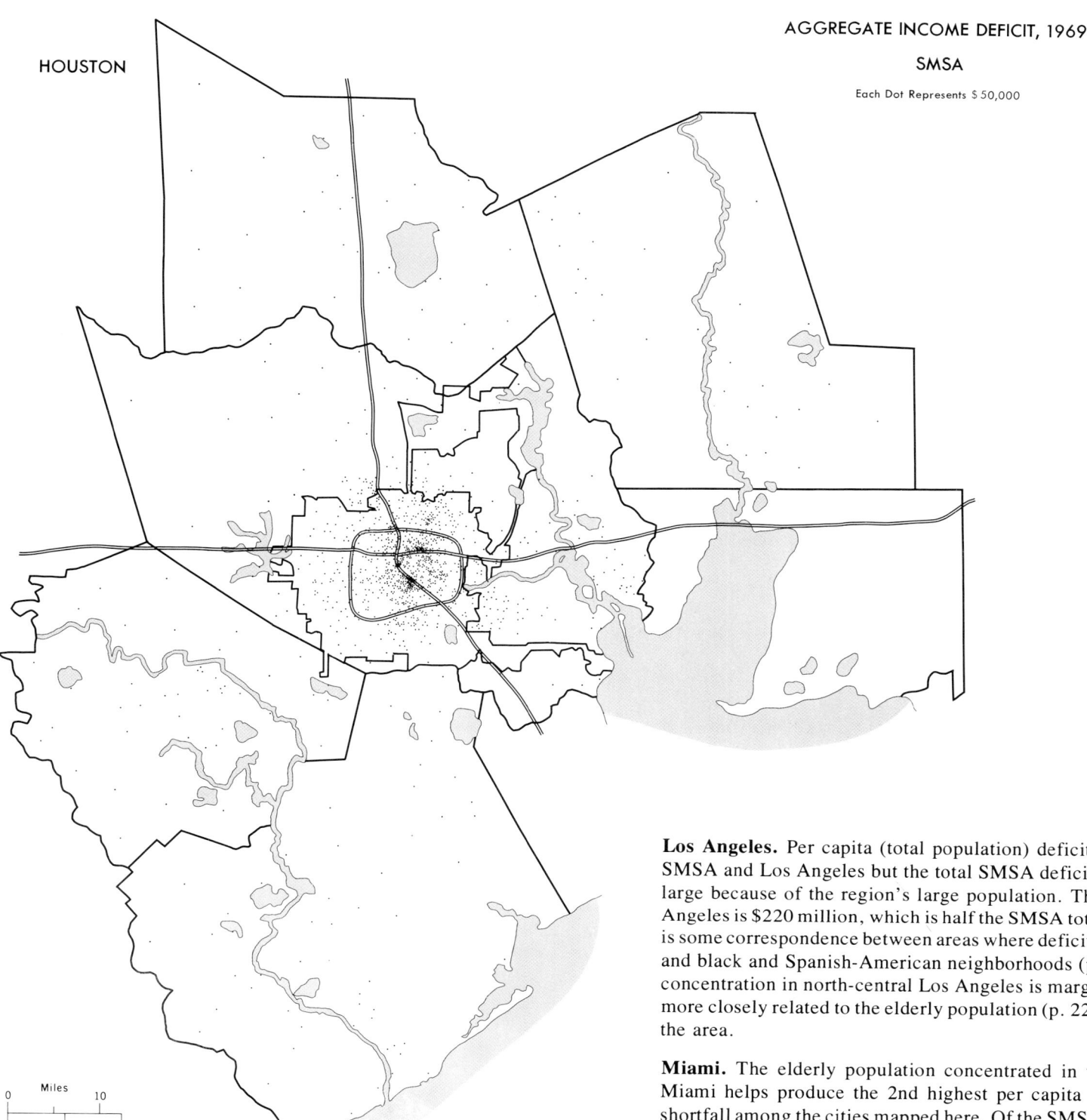

population) deficits are about the same in both metropolitan areas. The total deficit for the two SMSAs is $129 million, of which $89 million (69 percent) is located in the Dallas SMSA and $57 million (44 percent) is the shortfall in the city of Dallas. The deficit in the Fort Worth SMSA is $40 million (31 percent of the regional total), of which $28 million (22 percent of the regional total) is the gap between current incomes of the poverty population and the absence of poverty in Fort Worth.

**Houston.** The SMSA aggregate deficit is $129 million, of which $92 million (71 percent) is the income shortfall in Houston. The central-city deficit is concentrated in the inner parts of Houston's black and Spanish-American neighborhoods (pp. 387, 395). In outlying areas, some of the income shortfall occurs among blacks and Spanish-Americans and some of it represents poverty-level incomes of the elderly (pp. 205-206).

**Los Angeles.** Per capita (total population) deficits are small in the SMSA and Los Angeles but the total SMSA deficit ($442 million) is large because of the region's large population. The shortfall in Los Angeles is $220 million, which is half the SMSA total. Although there is some correspondence between areas where deficits are concentrated and black and Spanish-American neighborhoods (pp. 388, 396), the concentration in north-central Los Angeles is marginal to both and is more closely related to the elderly population (p. 226) concentrated in the area.

**Miami.** The elderly population concentrated in the SMSA and in Miami helps produce the 2nd highest per capita (total population) shortfall among the cities mapped here. Of the SMSA total shortfall of $103 million, $40 million (39 percent) is in Miami and $11 million (11 percent) is the deficit in Miami Beach, where a low-income, elderly population is concentrated. The remaining half of the deficit is scattered among Miami's suburbs. The per capita deficit in Miami Beach is $129.

**Atlanta.** Atlanta's large poverty population produces a high per capita (total population) deficit, but the concentration of the group with poverty incomes in the central city results in a low SMSA deficit on a per capita basis. The SMSA total deficit is $87 million, of which $55 million (63 percent) is the difference between current incomes of the poor and the elimination of officially defined poverty in Atlanta.

**Washington, D.C.** The aggregate income shortfall of the SMSA is $146 million, of which $78 million (53 percent) is the amount that would have to be added to the incomes of Washington, D.C.'s poor to eliminate poverty. Within the city, the deficit is heavily concentrated in the census tracts north of downtown Washington that are occupied by low-income blacks (p. 388) and a mixed population of the elderly and low-income whites (pp. 259, 262).

*Employment and Poverty: Income Deficits*

MIAMI

LOS ANGELES

AGGREGATE INCOME DEFICIT, 1969

SMSA

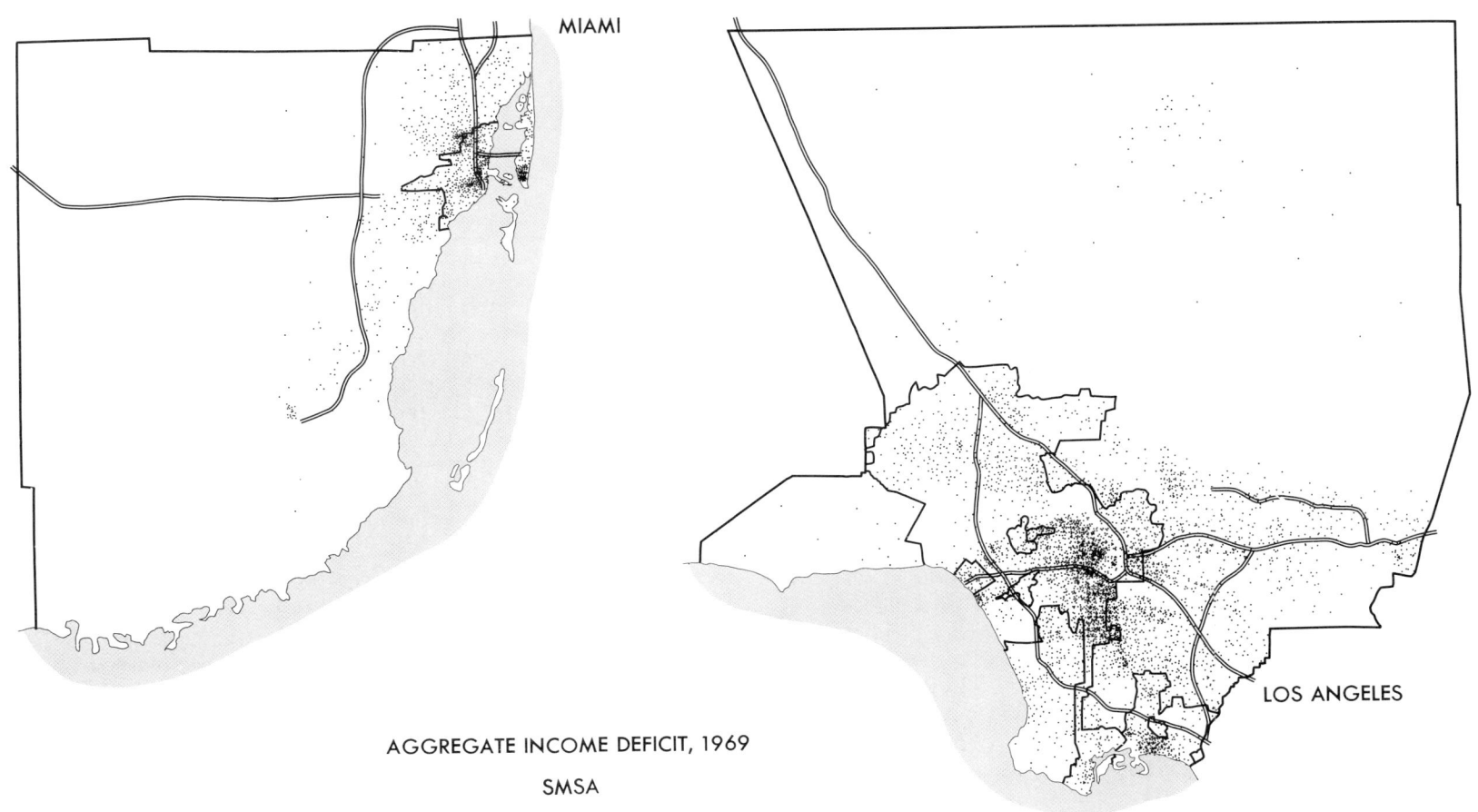

Each Dot Represents $50,000

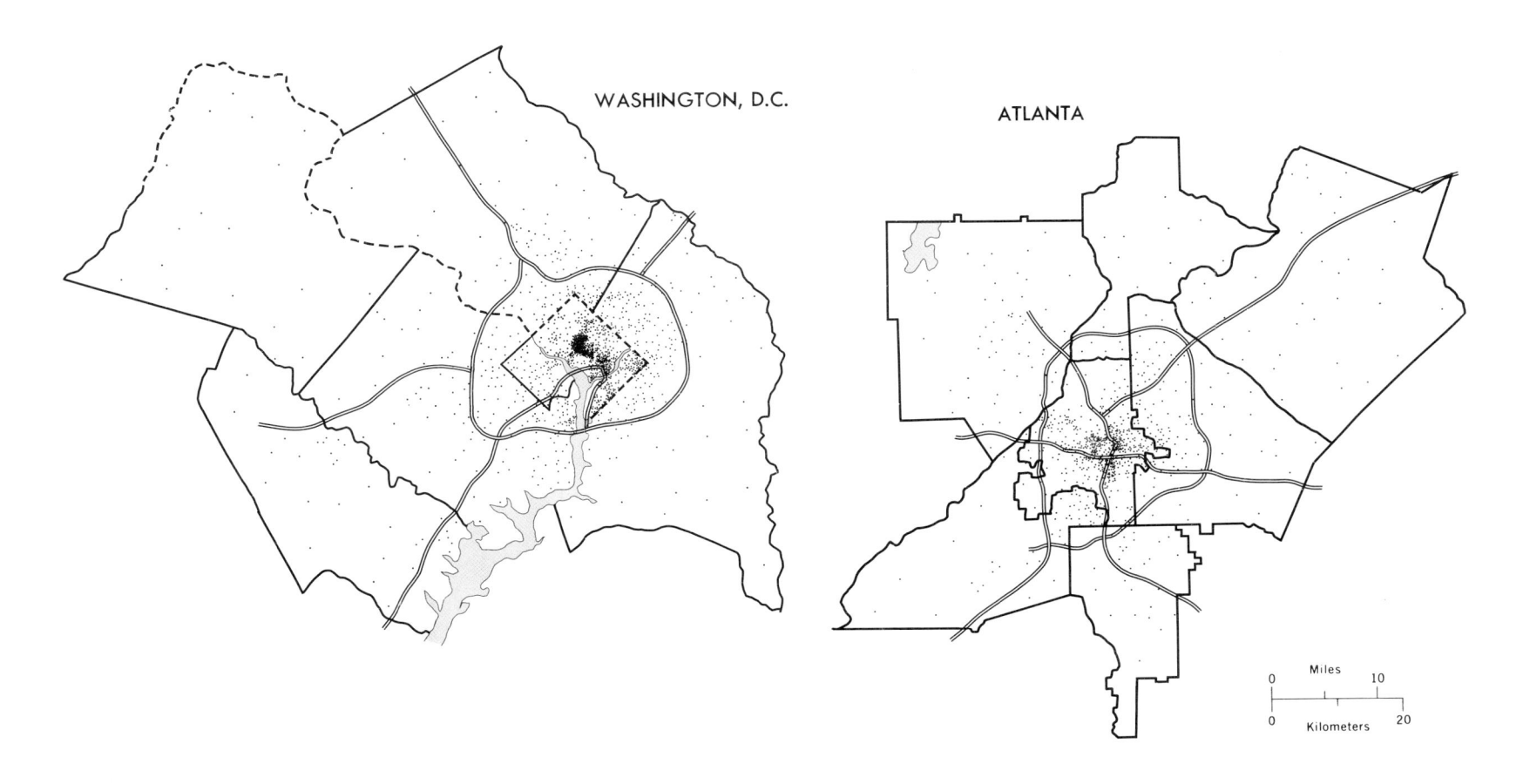

WASHINGTON, D.C.

ATLANTA

Income deficits persist in the face of large expenditures (Chapter 46) designed to eliminate poverty and despite the massive social programs of the 1960s devoted to the same goal. Thus it appears that inadequate incomes are a more intractable problem than policy makers once believed them to be. There is no denying that poverty exists in the nation's metropolitan areas even if it is imperfectly measured by the techniques in this and previous chapters. Nor can it be denied that transfer payments to the poverty population help alleviate the distress poverty causes. But the problem that underlies income deficits and the numerous secondary problems caused by inadequate incomes is the inability of many people to earn and accumulate adequate personal resources in our quasiprivate economy. A mechanism that would solve that problem remains elusive.

*Urban Renewal and Redevelopment*

CHAPTER 48

# Long-Term Housing Vacancies

Abandoned housing began appearing in American cities with increasing frequency during the 1960s. As noted in Chapter 4, some analysts view abandonment as the normal end state of the least competitive dwellings in an oversupplied housing market. According to this view, housing scarcities during the late 1940s and the 1950s and the slum clearance and urban renewal programs of the 1950s and early 1960s curtailed abandonment. When these processes had run their courses, abandonment began to appear after 1965. Other observers see abandonment as a result of the cumulative effects of poverty, racism, neglect, and exploitation. They view abandonment as a cancer that spreads by undermining the confidence of residents, owners, and landlords, thereby promoting abandonment of larger and larger areas.

Abandonment is difficult to define. To the extent that the word should designate units permanently withdrawn from the housing market, abandonment is difficult to measure, for abandonment is a gradual process that follows long-term vacancies and high vacancy rates in rental housing. Some impression of the extent of housing abandonment can be derived from 1970 census data on the number of housing units vacant one year or more. Vacant units are not necessarily abandoned, but in the competitive housing markets characteristic of most central cities, vacancies of a year's duration may signal uncertainties in the minds of landlords and prospective tenants regarding the future. Vacant units are mapped for the central cities of 22 of the Standard Metropolitan Statistical Areas (SMSAs) included in the atlas by placing one dot on the map for every five housing units vacant for a year or more. Suppression of tract-level data often results in differences between summary statistics (see accompanying tabulation) and the number of dots plotted.

In absolute terms there are more long-term vacancies outside than inside SMSAs despite the location of 68 percent of the nation's total housing stock inside SMSAs. The long-term trend of rural depopulation has resulted in the greater prevalence of abandonment outside metropolitan areas. Even though there are fewer abandoned units inside than outside SMSAs, the problem of abandoned housing is more serious in SMSAs because they are places where population is usually increasing and where crowded housing (Chapter 29) can be a problem. Long-term vacancies suggestive of property abandonment are, however, closely related to population decreases at the local as well as the national scale. Within SMSAs, over two-thirds of the long-term vacancies are located in central cities compared with the central cities' 50 percent share of all metropolitan housing. Population decreases are occurring in many central cities, and in most places housing abandonment is concentrated in neighborhoods where population decreases between 1960 and 1970 were greatest (Chapter 37). Preliminary inspection of abandonment maps made it clear that long-term vacancies are scattered in suburban areas whereas they are often highly clustered in central cities. Thus vacancies are mapped for central cities because of the importance of such clustering in promoting pessimism about neighborhood prospects.

Housing Units Vacant One Year or More

| City | Number of Units | Percentage of City Housing Stock |
|---|---|---|
| Boston | 2,110 | 0.9 |
| New York | 9,940 | 0.3 |
| Philadelphia | 6,790 | 1.0 |
| Hartford | 105 | 0.2 |
| Baltimore | 2,635 | 0.9 |
| New Orleans | 1,740 | 0.8 |
| San Francisco | 980 | 0.3 |
| Oakland | 520 | 0.4 |
| Pittsburgh | 2,320 | 1.2 |
| St. Louis | 2,850 | 1.2 |
| Cleveland | 2,395 | 0.9 |
| Chicago | 7,490 | 0.6 |
| Detroit | 3,780 | 0.7 |
| Minneapolis | 420 | 0.3 |
| St. Paul | 355 | 0.3 |
| Seattle | 985 | 0.4 |
| Dallas | 1,725 | 0.6 |
| Houston | 3,960 | 0.9 |
| Los Angeles | 3,010 | 0.3 |
| Miami | 240 | 0.2 |
| Atlanta | 500 | 0.3 |
| Washington, D.C. | 1,695 | 0.6 |

Long-term vacancies are numerous enough to suggest that abandonment is occurring in three of the four cities of the nation's historic metropolitan core (Boston, New York City, and Philadelphia). Few units have been vacant a year or more in Hartford. The early 19th-century port cities (Baltimore, New Orleans, and San Francisco) differ with respect to long-term vacancies. Abandonment is a problem in Baltimore and New Orleans, whereas long-term vacancies are infrequent enough in the Bay Area to suggest that housing abandonment is a minor problem, if it exists at all. The nation's 19th-century river and lake ports and inland centers have differing proportions of long-term vacancies depending on their ages. Pittsburgh, St. Louis, Cleveland, Chicago, and Detroit all have enough units vacant for a year or more to suggest that abandonment is occurring. Minneapolis, St. Paul, and Seattle have few long-term

*Note:* All data are from the 1970 Censuses of Population and Housing unless otherwise indicated. Therefore the present tense refers to 1970 except for income data which are from 1969. Cartographic conventions are explained in Chapter 1. County names and other locational information are shown on the SMSA map at the beginning of each city chapter (6-25) and on the DUS map of mobile homes near the beginning of each city chapter.

*Urban Renewal and Redevelopment: Vacant Housing*

**HOUSING UNITS VACANT ONE YEAR OR MORE
CITY**

Each Dot Represents 5 Vacant Units

BOSTON

PHILADELPHIA

HARTFORD

NEW YORK CITY

*Urban Renewal and Redevelopment: Vacant Housing*

**HOUSING UNITS VACANT ONE YEAR OR MORE**

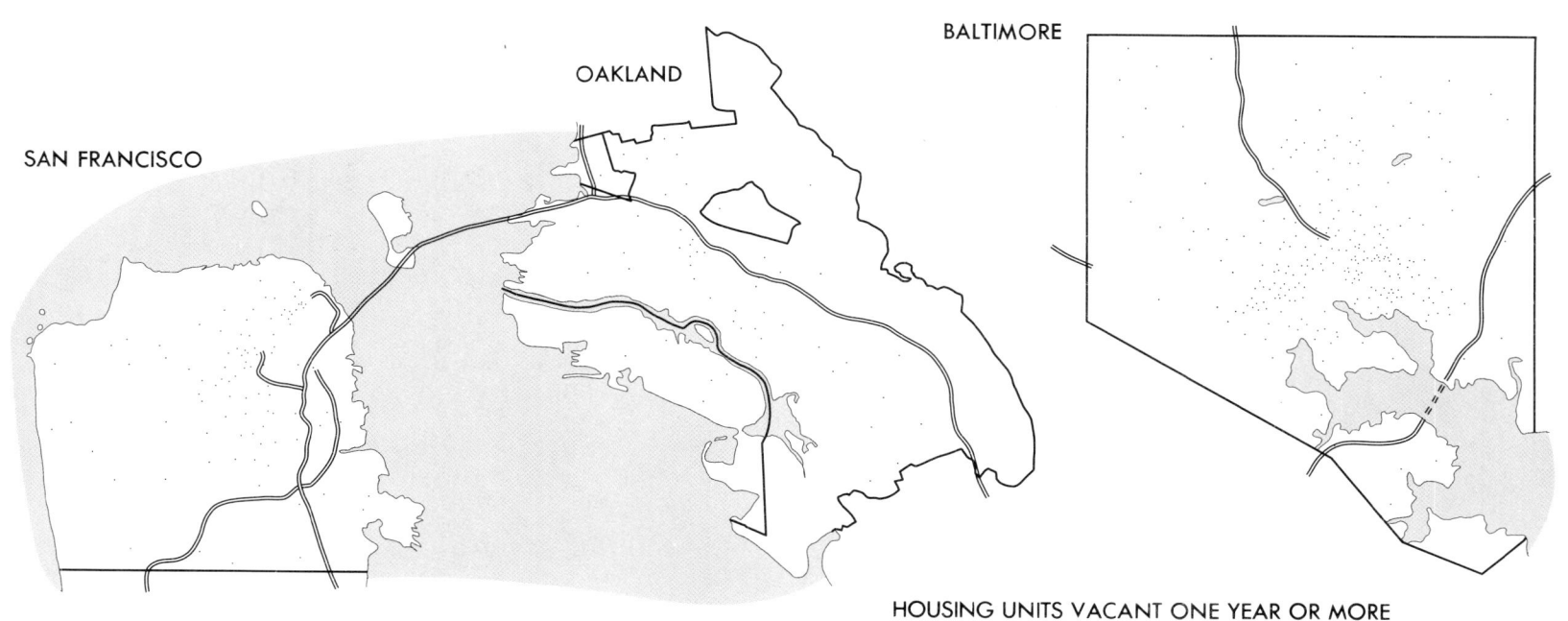

**CITY**

Each Dot Represents 5 Vacant Units

vacancies, and those that do exist are such small proportions of city housing inventories that abandonment is unlikely. Of the cities that have achieved most of their growth during the 20th century, long-term vacancies should be rare because housing units are newer and the population is usually growing more rapidly than it is in older cities, thus increasing the demand for housing. Exceptions occur in Dallas, Houston, and Washington, D.C., where some abandonment is evidently in progress in older parts of the cities. Long-term vacancies are infrequent in Los Angeles, Miami and Atlanta.

**Boston.** The majority of the long-term vacancies in Boston are located in the predominantly black part of the city (p. 25). Since housing in these areas is often crowded (p. 286), the concentration of vacancies there is indicative of probable abandonment. Population is decreasing in the center of the Boston SMSA (p. 350), but the area of decrease extends beyond the parts of the city where abandonment is occurring.

**New York City.** Long-term vacancies are clustered somewhat in Bronx and New York counties and along the boundary between Kings and Queens counties. Numerous suppressions result in much lower numbers of units vacant a year or more than might be expected given the publicity housing abandonment there has received. Discrepancies between independent estimates of abandonment and the number of long-term vacancies indicate that vacancies counted by the Census are poor estimators of abandonment in New York City although they may be useful ways of identifying the places where abandonment is beginning.

**Philadelphia.** North of the Central Business District, long-term vacancies are located in predominantly black parts of the city (p. 54) and along the expanding frontier of areas occupied by blacks. As is true in other eastern cities, long-term vacancies are common in areas where population density (p. 53) is high and where housing is crowded (p. 286), although population in such areas is decreasing (p. 350).

**Hartford.** Despite the existence in Hartford of comparatively large minority populations (p. 65) and urban renewal programs that have affected a large share of the central-city area (p. 68), there are few long-term vacancies. Suppression of tract-level data results in the absence of 12 dots from the map.

**Baltimore.** Extensive urban renewal in central Baltimore has been responsible for some of the long-term vacancies that exist. Landlords and tenants uncertain about when structures will be acquired for renewal of highways are unwilling to maintain and occupy them. Most of the long-term vacancies mapped here are located in predominantly black parts of the city (p. 74) and areas where population is decreasing (p. 351).

**New Orleans.** Long-term vacancies are scattered about the older part of the city (p. 80). There is little clustering of abandoned units

439

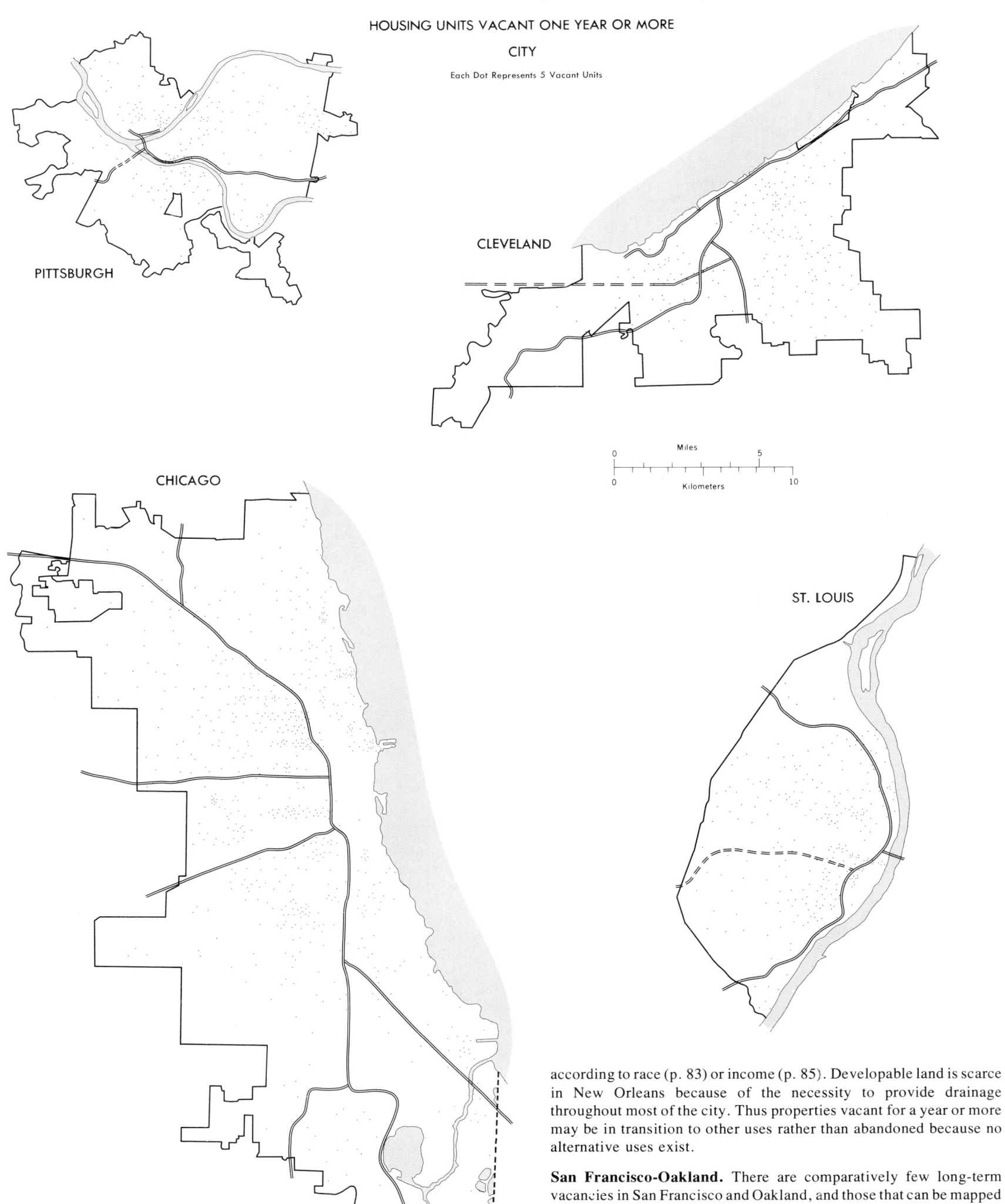

*Urban Renewal and Redevelopment: Vacant Housing*

HOUSING UNITS VACANT ONE YEAR OR MORE

CITY

Each Dot Represents 5 Vacant Units

PITTSBURGH

CLEVELAND

CHICAGO

ST. LOUIS

according to race (p. 83) or income (p. 85). Developable land is scarce in New Orleans because of the necessity to provide drainage throughout most of the city. Thus properties vacant for a year or more may be in transition to other uses rather than abandoned because no alternative uses exist.

**San Francisco-Oakland.** There are comparatively few long-term vacancies in San Francisco and Oakland, and those that can be mapped are scattered in a way that suggests little correspondence to race (p. 94), income (p. 100), or population change (p. 351).

*Urban Renewal and Redevelopment: Vacant Housing*

HOUSING UNITS VACANT ONE YEAR OR MORE
CITY

Each Dot Represents 5 Vacant Units

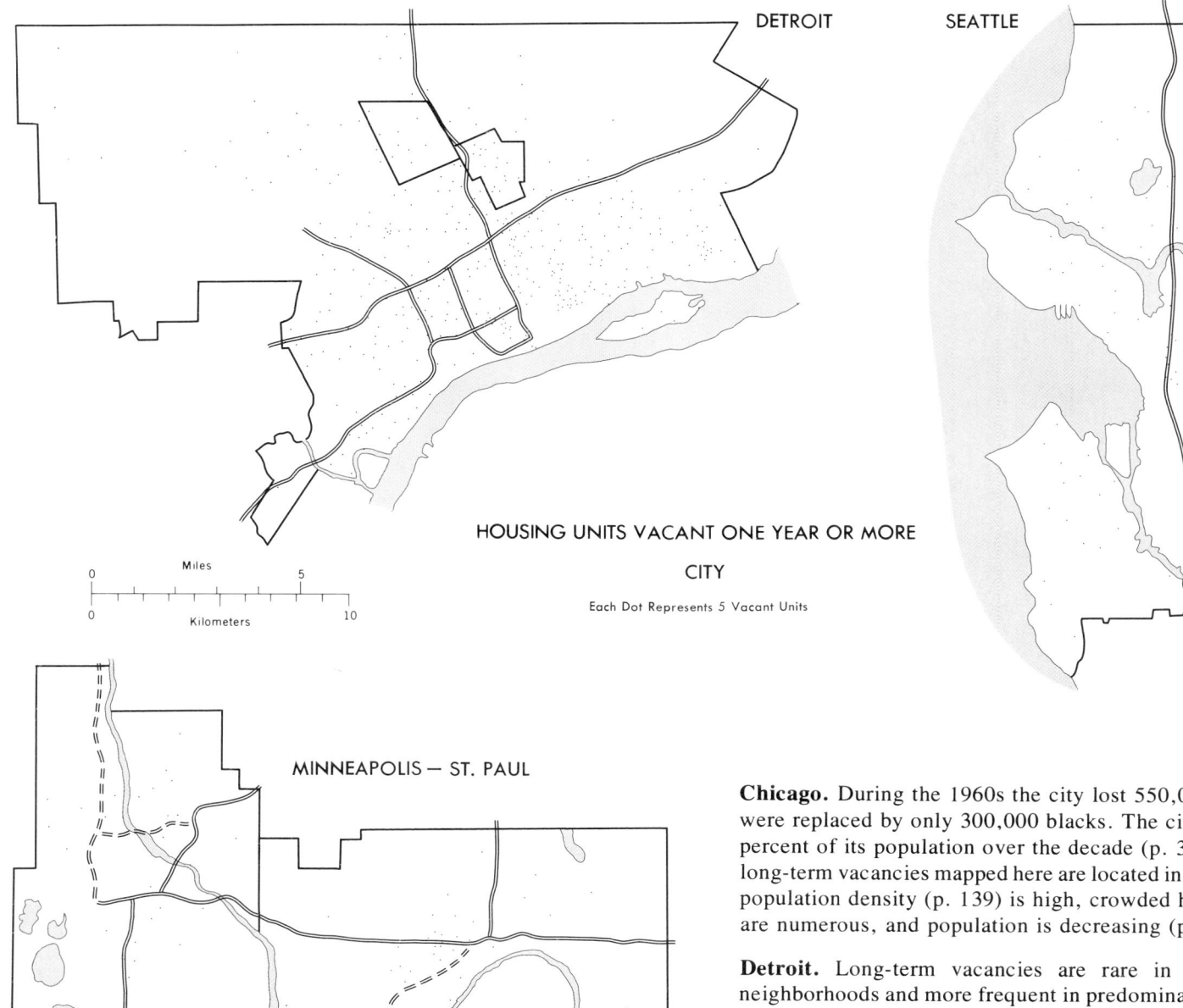

**Pittsburgh.** The SMSA and Pittsburgh are losing population (p. 352), and some abandonment of housing might therefore be expected. The problem, to the extent that it is reflected in long-term vacancies, does not appear to be serious in Pittsburgh. Clustering of mappable vacancies is minimal, and there is little systematic variation in their locations.

**St. Louis.** The city has the highest proportion of long-term vacancies among the places mapped here. In some parts of the city, as many as one-fifth of all standing units are vacant. Many of the vacant units are located in the city's black ghetto (p. 121), but large numbers are located in predominantly-white neighborhoods. Low incomes (p. 126), old housing (p. 125), and population decreases (p. 352) are more closely associated with long-term vacancies than is race.

**Cleveland.** Long-term vacancies are especially concentrated in predominantly black neighborhoods (p. 313). More than is often true in other cities, long-term vacancies are associated with the turmoil attendant upon rapid transition of neighborhoods from predominantly white to predominantly black and with population decrease (p. 353). Incomes in the area where mappable long-term vacancies are most frequent are low (p. 132).

**Chicago.** During the 1960s the city lost 550,000 white people who were replaced by only 300,000 blacks. The city as a whole lost 5.2 percent of its population over the decade (p. 353), and many of the long-term vacancies mapped here are located in parts of the city where population density (p. 139) is high, crowded housing units (p. 289) are numerous, and population is decreasing (p. 353).

**Detroit.** Long-term vacancies are rare in predominantly white neighborhoods and more frequent in predominantly black parts of the city (p. 153). Thus such vacancies may be closely related to racial transitions, as they are in other midwestern cities.

**Minneapolis-St. Paul.** Less than half the long-term vacancies in the Twin Cities are mappable because of suppression of tract-level vacancy data on the tapes from which the maps were prepared. The locations of the vacancies that can be mapped indicate that units vacant for a year or more are located in older parts of the two cities where population is decreasing. Vacancies are more closely related to age of housing and out-migration than to racial transition.

**Seattle.** The city has few vacant units, and those that do exist and are mappable (under half the total) are generally scattered, with a slight concentration in the city's black neighborhoods (p. 173). Suppressions are less frequent in the black area than in the rest of the city, so mapping all the units vacant a year or more would produce a more even distribution.

**Dallas.** Although the proportion of housing units vacant a year or more is not as high as it is in eastern cities with abandonment problems, it is higher than the proportion in midwestern cities and other southern cities where housing is not being abandoned. Mappable long-term vacancies are largely confined to the parts of the city with the oldest housing stocks (p. 183) where population is decreasing (p. 364). Constant expansion and relatively high incomes are simply making some older housing unattractive to people who can afford more attractive alternatives.

**Houston.** As in Dallas, the number of long-term vacancies and the proportion of the total housing stock they constitute are higher than

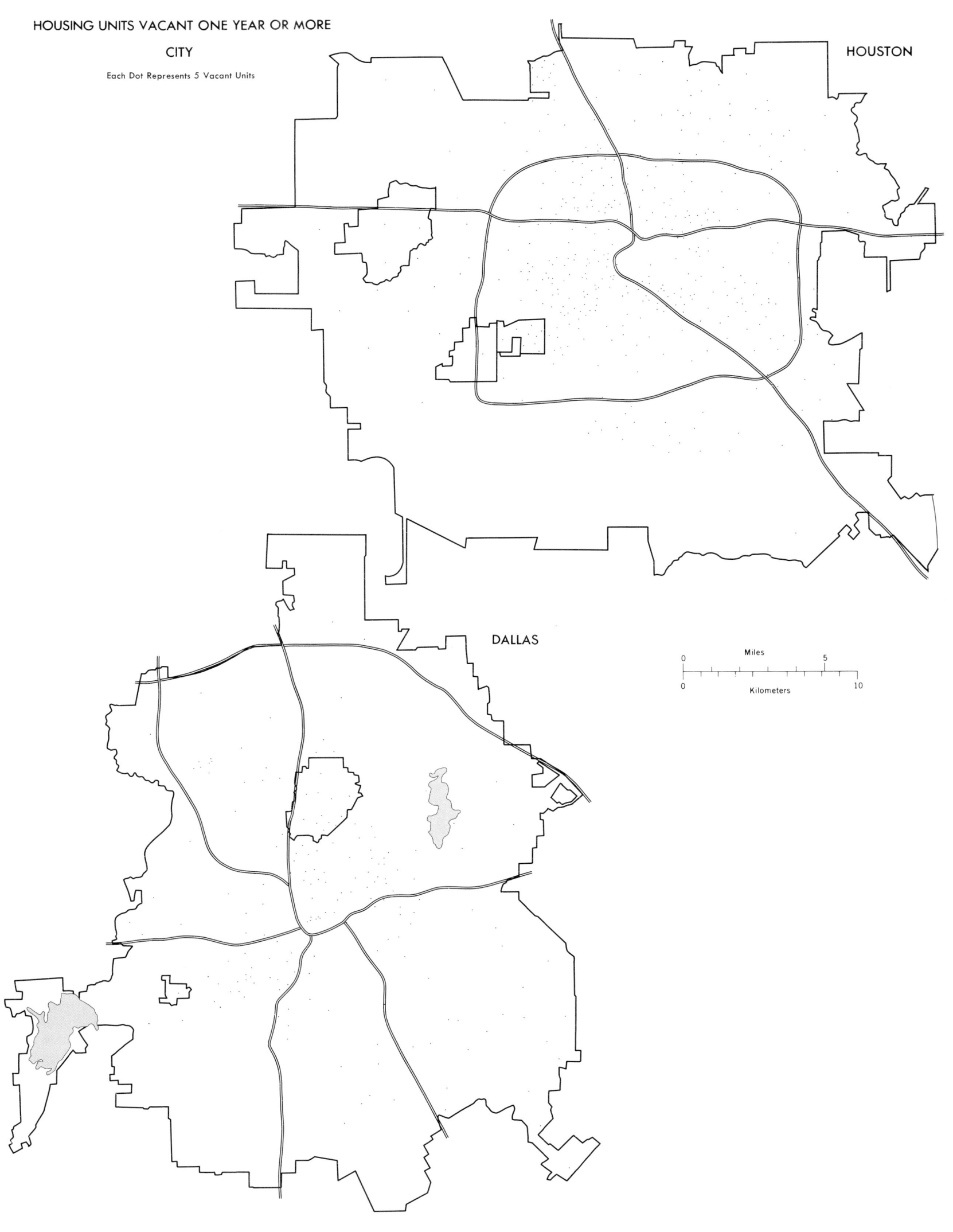

*Urban Renewal and Redevelopment: Vacant Housing*

**HOUSING UNITS VACANT ONE YEAR OR MORE**
CITY

Each Dot Represents 5 Vacant Units

HOUSTON

DALLAS

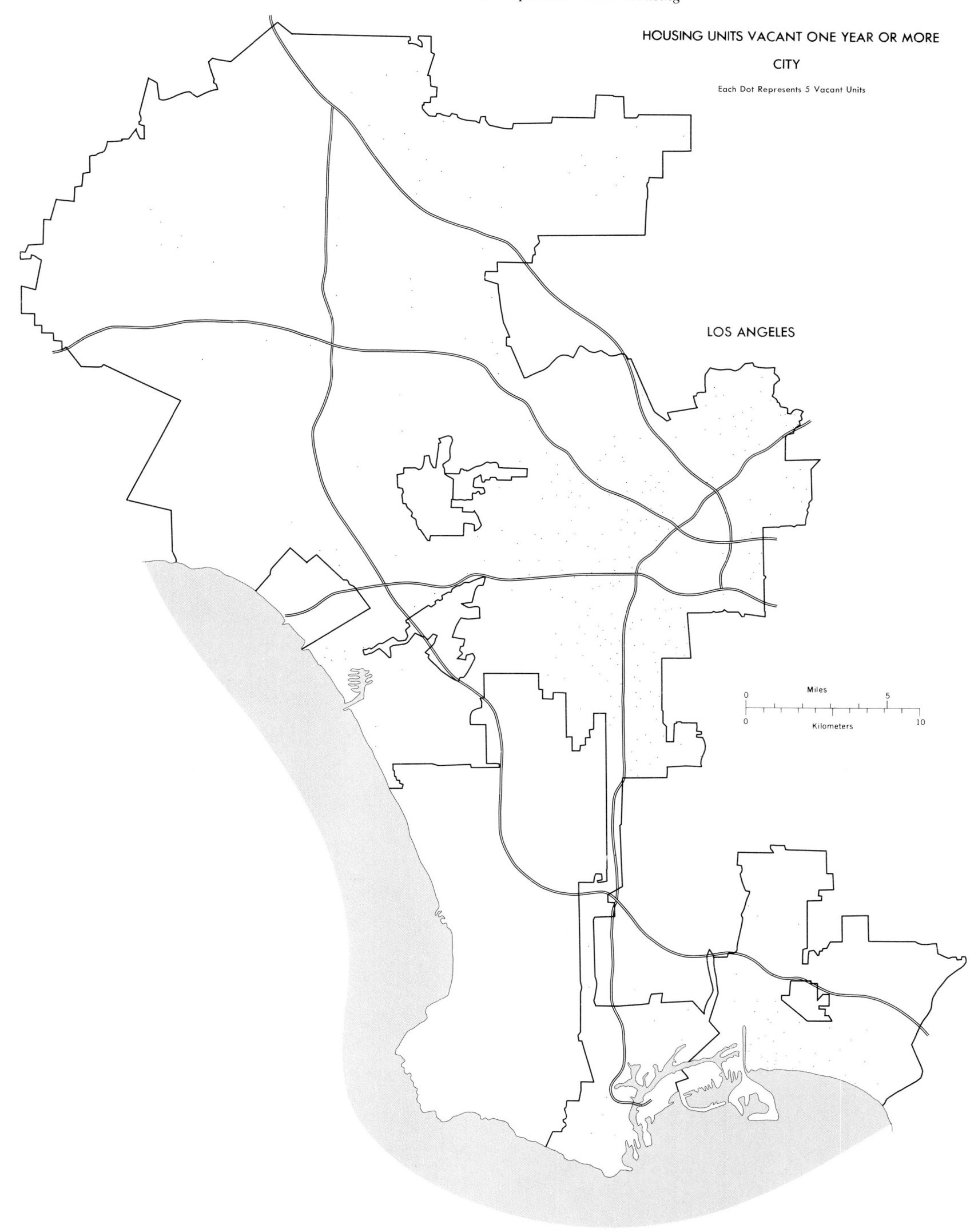

*Urban Renewal and Redevelopment: Vacant Housing*

HOUSING UNITS VACANT ONE YEAR OR MORE

CITY

Each Dot Represents 5 Vacant Units

LOS ANGELES

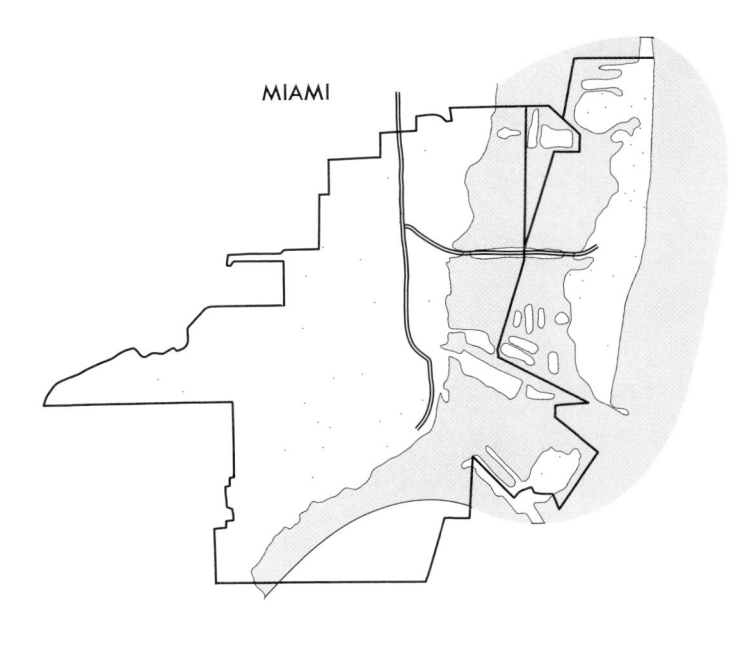

*Urban Renewal and Redevelopment: Vacant Housing*

**HOUSING UNITS VACANT ONE YEAR OR MORE**

**CITY**

Each Dot Represents 5 Vacant Units

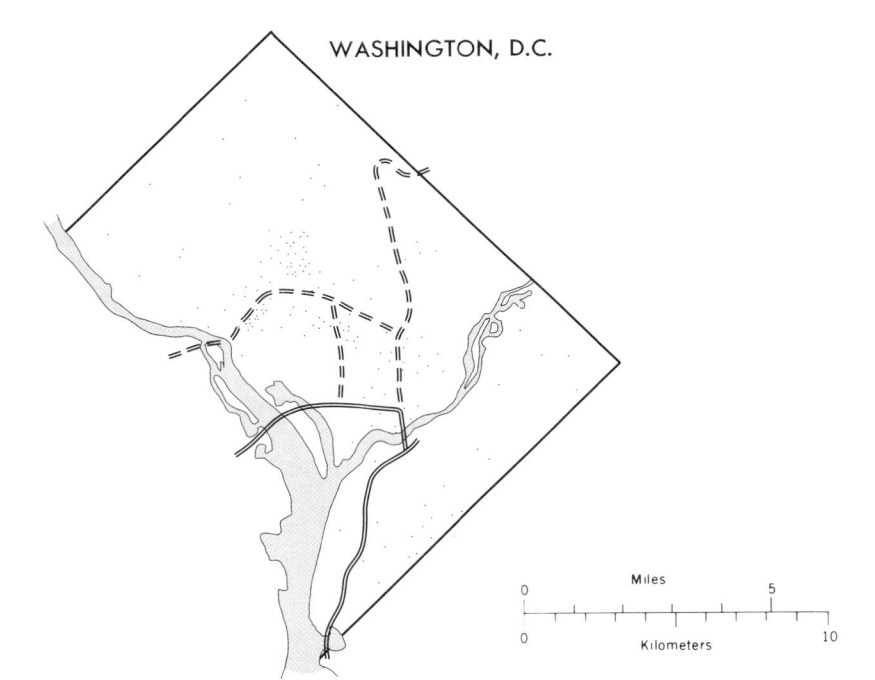

might be expected given the low proportion of old housing (p. 199) in the city and the pace of overall population growth. Most of the units vacant a year or more are located in the part of the central city where population decreased from 1960 to 1970 (p. 355), indicating that out-migration that cuts across racial and ethnic lines (p. 207) is responsible for the abandonment.

**Los Angeles.** The number of long-term vacancies in Los Angeles is large, but so is the city's housing stock. Thus the proportion of units vacant for a year or more is low. Very few of the units are mappable because most occur in tracts where the number of long-term vacancies is so small that the data are suppressed.

**Miami.** Only half the housing units vacant a year or more are mapped here because of the suppression of tract-level data. There are few vacancies and little abandonment of housing in the city's thriving housing market.

**Atlanta.** The few mappable (46 percent of the total) long-term vacancies in Atlanta betray little systematic variation with other socioeconomic characteristics. The city is growing rapidly, and vacant units are more often than not being held off the market pending a change to more lucrative land uses.

**Washington, D.C.** Suppressions make it impossible to map more than a small fraction of the units vacant for a year or more. Those that are mappable cluster in an area of population decrease (p. 356) in north-central Washington that has also undergone racial transition during the 1960s.

---

Long-term vacancies and the housing abandonment they demarcate or foretell are produced by causes as complex as the series of variables mapped in the second half of the atlas. More than any other variable, the number of vacant or abandoned units represents a collective judgment by owner, landlord, and prospective occupant about the long-term future of the places where abandonment is occurring. Their combined assessments produce first population decrease and finally abandonment.

# PART IV
# POLICY REQUISITES FOR AMERICAN METROPOLITAN REGIONS

# CHAPTER 49

# National, State, and Local Policy Considerations

### THE END AND THE BEGINNING

The nation's metropolitan regions have undergone three decades of wrenching change since World War II, and in one way or another the effects of that change are evident in every map in the atlas. Three decades of almost constant growth and expansion produced the widespread impression that continued metropolitan growth was inevitable. But history and common sense suggest that this is naïve. The late 1960s and early 1970s were especially turbulent and traumatic as civil disorders erupted in metropolitan areas, a deep recession dashed unrealistic expectations for unlimited prosperity, and energy shortages raised the price of mobility. Over the long run, the primal forces in American society, economy, and geography wield a pervasive and unrelenting influence that can be ignored or negated only temporarily.

The abandonment of housing and even of entire neighborhoods in the central cities of some older metropolitan areas makes it doubly clear that urban places are not exempt from the same processes of obsolescence and abandonment that previously depopulated many rural parts of the nation. Such abandonment and the slowed growth of metropolitan regions since 1970 leave us wondering whether the decade of the 1970s signals the beginning of the end for large tracts of urban territory or whether such changes are merely a healthy transition to lower-density land uses in an ongoing process of metropolitan development and redevelopment. Above all, the conditions of the nation's great cities lead us to seek the primal forces in American metropolitan life and intelligent social responses to the problems those forces create.

In this final chapter, we summarize certain features of postwar city-building, outline certain facts about the nation's urban life, pose certain dilemmas that develop when the distinctions between problems of people and problems of places are not clear, and identify the major obstacles inside government that prevent effective public response to problems in cities.

### THE POST-WORLD WAR II ERA HAS ENDED . . .

In 1945 middle-class America sprang free of the bonds imposed by years of depression and war. Withheld goods could once again be bought. Persons forceably relocated by unemployment, military service, and wartime needs could settle where they chose. Overcrowded housing with its grim wartime memories could be abandoned for fresh suburban opportunities. Marriages and families too long delayed were finally possible.

The postwar boom began in fits and starts, but it soon affected every person and place in the nation. Record rates of new housing construction meant a massive extension of built-up urban areas. After the war, people simply needed more housing at the places where they wanted to live. But they sought more than housing; symbols were involved as well. The suburb and the quest for status continued to shape the American personality, just as the frontier had once shaped the nation's psyche. Owning real estate has always held a special charm for immigrant Americans; most of them came from Europe where land ownership signified status, wealth, and a sense of freedom. In America the dream could be realized, usually with little difficulty. For example, the federal and state tax codes actually promoted demand for new housing by allowing householders to take mortgage interest and property taxes as deductions from income in calculating taxable income. The Federal Housing Administration promoted house buying by providing mortgage insurance for up to 95 percent of the home purchase price. Meanwhile veterans were willingly coaxed into the housing market as the Veterans Administration began writing mortgage insurance for veterans covering 100 percent of the purchase price of their new houses.

The new housing was erected at the edge of previously built-up areas, so the steady relocation of middle-class new house buyers meant a steady reduction in middle-class population densities and purchasing power, especially near the urban core. New suburban housing attracted households from all segments of the prewar housing stock, but middle-class households that had been cramped into rent-controlled apartments in aging neighborhoods next to downtown had special incentives and extra financial resources to make the long jump to the suburbs. Suburban vitality plus the departure of nearby purchasing power left the downtowns temporarily off balance. Years of maintenance neglected during depression and war had left them with a seedy appearance — dirty, congested, obsolete, depressing — symbols of days best forgotten.

Meanwhile suburban new home buyers carried to the suburbs something more than their purchasing power. They also relocated their reproductive potential. Young suburban families soon created an unprecedented baby boom, while older folks were left behind near the core, eventually to die. Half of the population redistribution toward the suburbs resulted from migration, the other half from the difference between births and deaths in suburbs versus urban cores. The annual national birth count soared from 2.9 million in 1945 to about 4.3 million in each of the peak years 1959-1961 (1974 *Statistical Abstract*, p. 51),* spurred by fashion, optimism, and perhaps an unconscious attempt to justify the materialistic drives that propelled these children and grandchildren of immigrants to new cars, new houses, and new suburbs "for the children."

Economic expansion was steady except for several short business recessions of the late 1940s and the 1950s. But the long-term performance of the economy saw per capita gross national product (GNP), in current dollars, rise steadily, from $1,058 in 1945 to $6,127 in 1973. In constant dollars, per capita production of goods and services more than doubled (1974 *Stat. Abs.*, pp. 5, 373, 376).

*Published by the U.S. Government Printing Office in 1974.

The index of output per man hour in manufacturing (1967 = 100) went from 64.4 in 1950 to 127.5 in 1973 (1974 *Stat. Abs.*, p. 357). The index of farm output per man hour (1967 = 100) rose from 35 in 1940 to 133 in 1973 (1974 *Stat. Abs.*, p. 614). Meanwhile the United States population rose over 50 percent, from 140 million in 1945 to almost 212 million by 1974 (1974 *Stat. Abs.*, p. 5). Until the recession of the mid-1970s, the postwar period was an era of spectacular increases in population and economic production.

The vastly improved efficiency of the economy could be traced in part to extraordinary rates of capital formation. In manufacturing industries the real net value of equipment, structures, and inventories in 1958 rose from $105 billion in 1950 to $230 billion in 1973 (1974 *Stat. Abs.*, p. 716). In communication, domestic telephone companies alone saw their book cost of plant rise from $11 billion in 1950 to over $73 billion in 1972 (1974 *Stat. Abs.*, p. 498). The 42,500-mile national system of interstate highways was begun and largely completed after 1954, at an eventual cost of several million dollars per mile. High rates of saving and capital formation accompanied prosperity and guaranteed its continuation. Heavy investment in transportation and communication systems helped raise overall economic efficiency. Information flows could substitute for the movement of people and goods. Inventories could be cut. Less was needed, more went further. Short-term and one-shot efficiencies were so great in fact that the nation could engage in a major war for years while cutting taxes, keeping interest rates low, and sustaining ever higher levels of per capita goods and service production. But the episode is now over. A new era has begun.

## . . . BUT TROUBLESOME FACTS REMAIN

The annual GNP is the market value of goods and certain services produced by the national economy each year. GNP along with GNP per capita have been used since the 1930s as principal measures of the performance of the national economy. As a measure of performance, GNP emphasizes the throughput of goods and services. It says nothing about national assets or the long-term picture of national wealth. GNP gives an annual income statement but no balance sheet.

Additionally the nation's attention to GNP as the thermometer for national economic health diverts attention from other concerns about society and the environments in which we live. By defining the quality of life in income or product terms, we tend to term as "problems" the failure of the GNP and GNP per capita to rise fast enough, the failure of some individuals or groups to obtain a pro-rata share of the GNP, or the success of some elements in the population at capturing more than an average or "fair" share. "Success" for each unit in the population often reduces to maintaining or increasing its share of the national income. To be a failure has come to mean being economically poor; to be poor as an individual, a neighborhood, a city, or a state is now defined as failing to attain a pro-rata share of the GNP. The job of the nation, as well as of the productive-consumptive units in it — individuals, households, firms, even government and quasigovernment agencies — has been to "get ahead" and to "stay ahead." It is much like a race run by all but without a goal or even a clearly marked track in which losing means finishing behind middle position.

Although it is unclear where the economy and society are heading, it is easier than ever before to get there. Since World War II the United States has installed a thoroughly modern transportation system, headed by the interstate highway system and the national fleet of 2,400 aircraft operated by scheduled air carriers. In the same period the nation's basic housing stock for the remainder of the century was constructed. Of the 69 million housing units in 1970 over 41 million were built from 1940 onward. Many of them replaced obsolete units, but the majority represented net additions to the national housing stock (1974 *Stat. Abs.*, p. 687). Meanwhile as central-city infilling and suburban house building proceeded at a frantic pace, the United States labor force grew by about 50 percent. The suburban development cycle gathered momentum as the new job centers attracted residential developers and as prosperous suburban households in turn attracted shopping and retail service centers. New jobs settled largely in the midst of suburban workers and customers, along unplanned highway strips, in planned highway strips, and in planned retail, office, or industrial clusters and parks.

Most of the adult population of the year 2000 has already been born, but the bulge of persons added to the national population between 1945 and 1975 will move like a platoon through the society. Persons born between 1930 and 1945 will continue to be in relatively short supply, while the 1945 to 1965 cohort will always be crowded. The postwar babies began life in crowded maternity wards and crowded grade schools; they continued on to crowded high schools and colleges. Large numbers tried to enter a glutted job market during the recession of the 1970s. They will always uncomfortably outnumber the new housing and job opportunities available to them, and when they retire, they will overload the Social Security system and eventually the cemeteries. The high birthrate anomaly of the postwar era will have meant permanent competitive disadvantages for its children, just as the birth troughs of the 1930s and the 1970s will have conferred special advantages for the lucky few.

For a system in which competitive position is important, generational differences take on a profound meaning. Recently inflation has compounded the special advantages for the owners of appreciating assets and the disadvantages for the wage and salary earners. High rates of price and wage inflation are coupled with progressively structured federal and state income tax schedules so that as a worker's pay rises 10 percent, the taxes he pays usually rise much faster, perhaps 15 percent. This happens because the tax rates on incremental income are higher than those on base income. A greater share of gross income diverted to taxes means a greater consumption of publicly provided goods and services and a corresponding reduction in the proportion of purchases of goods and services from the private sector. This steady and automatic diversion of an "inflation dividend" into the public purse effectively muffles public debate over long-term incremental needs for public services and diversion from the private sector of labor, capital, energy, and other resources needed to produce them. There is no public debate, especially at the state level. In municipalities, meanwhile, the price and quantity of services expand briskly, while funding must be squeezed out of the property tax or from state and federal treasuries. Unless tax rates are cut there is proportionately more money available automatically for state and local governmental services. They may be needed. There may be problems. But there should be more convincing public debate over definition of the problems and how they should be tackled.

## PROBLEMS OF PEOPLE VS. PROBLEMS OF PLACES

The kinds of suffering that lead to public outcry and eventual governmental response affect only a small fraction of the population at one time, but it is usually the same individuals, households, and groups that incur repeated punishment. Because our elected officials represent territories, and our general governments (federal, state, municipal) and special governments (districts) exercise jurisdiction over geographical areas rather than over interest groups or populations irrespective of where they live, the nation tends to define certain public problems as problems of *areas* rather than of the *people* who live there. Areas seem permanent while people come and go. Because of this habit of thought, the mere *concentration* of the symptoms of a problem often captures center stage, and the dispersal of a problem (poverty, public housing, crime) may be accepted as a palliative, if not a solution. Indeed when a problem becomes general to all areas, people tend to accept its presence as normal and gradually redefine their standards or expectations. To be sure, a vividly described geographical concentration of burglaries makes a greater impact on the public mind than does a report that crime rates increased nationwide. It also suggests that an effort to cut burglary should start where rates are highest. If we must begin somewhere, troubled places seem to present themselves as good starting points.

But whether programs are deployed in concrete ways on a map, or more abstractly through society and its institutions, two dilemmas remain for national urban policy. The first dilemma occurs when "justifiable expectations" are based on average rewards. If rewards for the peer group vary widely on either side of the average, it is impossible to eliminate feelings of relative deprivation on the part of persons or groups who fall below the average. In fact the only way to eliminate such deprivation for those below the average would be to eliminate any variation among persons in the rewards themselves. Then all would get the same, almost guaranteeing that incentives would lag, eventually bringing the averages down, perhaps triggering some form of absolute incremental deprivation.

A second public-policy dilemma develops when an ambitious person migrates from a poor region to a prosperous one. His move will depress the income average in his former home if his productivity and income there were above the local average. But the move may also pull down the income average in his new locale. His income might be higher than before, but lower than average in the new locale. Both regions may consider themselves worse off as a result of the move, but the migrant may reckon that he is better off. What is good for the individual in his estimation is bad for the group. Is this a problem? Can it be solved?

The nation has tended recently to pose issues such as these as problems that somehow ought to be solved. Public discussion of these issues in these terms encourages people to expect solutions. Failure to produce the promised results leads to disappointment and cynicism. In retrospect, solutions often can be seen as nothing more than social or economic shock absorbers, deployed during times when rapid rates of change exceed response times possible. People get accustomed to normal rates of change. Distress develops when rates increase or decrease, whether we are concerned with the birthrate, and death rate, the prime interest rate, the unemployment rate, the foreign immigration rate, the suburbanization rate, the household formation rate, the capital formation rate, or whatever. Sharp changes in rates cause concern, implying as they do a less predictable future.

Americans would like to be able to predict that their per capita consumption of goods and services will continue to rise, yet goods and services suppliers are experiencing increasing difficulty in filling jobs with reliable, productive workers. Increasing numbers of college-educated middle-class Americans seek the status, the pay, and the job protection offered by government employment. Yet all citizens seem to resent the steadily increasing fraction of their paychecks that is diverted to pay for these government services, usually provided in the name of solving problems.

Some families have responded to these economic pressures by keeping their households small and by increasing labor-force participation. Since the early 1960s, fewer and fewer babies have been born each year and the fraction of married women in the labor force has risen. Yet despite these trends there was a stability of sorts in labor-force participation. Between 1948 and 1975 adult employment fluctuated between 53 and 57 percent of the adult noninstitutional population. The average was 55.4 percent for the 28-year period, and in 1975 it was 55.2 percent, or about the average. For the country as a whole, 55 percent support themselves plus the other 45 percent; 214 million are supported by 86 million. Another 11 million worked part-time in 1975. Of all people with work experience during a year, less than 60 percent work year round. Thus although some elements in the population try to enter the labor force, other elements seem to be moving out, evidence perhaps of continued variety in values and goals in society.

These facts blur the usual distinction between independent and dependent populations, and between voluntary unemployment and involuntary unemployment. We usually point to the young and the elderly and label them as dependent populations; but many are productive members of the labor force, and many elderly are substantially wealthy. Almost half the persons aged 16 to 65 are voluntarily outside the labor force. Thus even though the birth shortages of the 1930s and 1970s and the birth surpluses of the 1950s and 1960s send shock waves through the population, the labor force, and the dependent population, society seems capable of adjusting to ever-changing circumstances. Perhaps the only "problem" that develops is rapid rates of change. Fashion and discretion may regulate whether one's productive activities take place inside or outside the paid labor force.

During periods of rapid rates of change, inequalities persist, perhaps as an inevitable consequence of changing tastes. In public debates over progress and poverty the discussion centers on material things and the means of access to them. Relative deprivation is measured in material terms. If relative deprivation becomes the measure of inequality, and if deprivation is measured only in terms of what people cannot get, supplying these wants cannot solve the problem of inequality or relative deprivation. For just as one set of needs is met, another rises as fashions change. To make matters worse, the increase of equal employment opportunities at the individual level probably yields greater inequality of rewards between families. If unusually talented women were the biggest losers from sex discrimination in the labor market, the biggest winners were average males and their families. Thus equal employment opportunities and affirmative action for individuals on the one hand, and socioeconomic equality for households on the other, are probably incompatible goals.

## OBSTACLES TO EFFECTIVE GOVERNMENT RESPONSE TO URBAN PROBLEMS

Two main obstacles stand in the way of effective government response to urban problems. First, uniform national policies designed and controlled by Washington must be made sensitive to local peculiarities. Second, ways must be found to ensure that the primary beneficiaries of urban programs are the clients rather than the program agencies and their staffs. Let us examine these issues in turn.

The United States as a matter of constitutional law is a collection of 50 sovereign states, internally subdivided to administer their internal affairs at the county level (in most states), through county-surrogates, as are found in Alaska's Judicial Districts, or through villages, towns, and cities in the two states that have no internal counties — Connecticut and Rhode Island. States also provide for the creation of general municipal governments for urban places. Most matters that directly affect people's daily lives manifest themselves at the local level and perhaps could be tackled there. But county and municipal governments frequently have lacked the will or the ready resources to respond to the urgent needs of local constituents. Consequently, federal programs have emerged in response to a full range of issues: environmental protection, outdoor recreation, housing, transportation, land use, education, health, law enforcement, racial and ethnic integration, employment and income maintenance, and urban development.

An unavoidable tension develops as national programs are created and deployed to solve local urban problems. The national urban policy must be uniform across the country, but program implementation and administrative rule-making must respect local differences. Yet if the same national program probably cannot succeed equally well in every locality, neither does the record promise that localities are able and willing to tackle their local problems by themselves without a prod from Washington.

It is certainly possible that state and local governments can be more sensitive to local distinctions; but like other governments they also can be notoriously ineffective in their use of resources. For one thing, the rise of professionalism in government service can mean better training and higher professional standards, but it can also mean that an agency created to tackle and solve a problem may end up paying less attention to its clients and more to its survival and prosperity as an agency. Commonly in the private sector, unhappy clients and customers can take their business elsewhere. Public agencies and their staffs are usually insulated from such competitive checks on performance and often operate remote from voters and elected officials.

The resources consumed by states and localities to produce their services have grown to a magnitude that makes these governments one of the major components of the American economy. From 1954 to 1974 state and local purchases of goods and services expanded from $27 billion to $192 billion (current dollars), increasing from 7.4 to 13.7 percent of the GNP. During the same period the number of state and local employees grew from 4.6 million to 11.6 million persons, or to about 1 in 7 nonagricultural workers in the United States.

Our thinking about the productivity of state and local government, and our expectations for it, are colored by the well-known record in the private sector. Productivity growth in the private sector has sustained high levels of living and material comforts. Private sector productivity growth (measured in constant terms) averaged about 2.5 percent annually from 1900 to 1947. Since then it has grown about 3 percent per year. Although the rate slowed a bit in the late 1960s, hourly production per worker is *four times* what it was 50 years ago.*

But with government employment accounting for a steadily increasing fraction of the work force, the nation can no longer look solely to the private sector for productivity increases that will improve economic well-being, if that is the goal. Greater productivity must come increasingly from state and local governments.

What is the meaning of productivity in government? The concept of productivity implies a ratio of the quantity and/or quality of results (output) to the resources (input) invested to achieve them. Government productivity has two facets: effectiveness and efficiency. *Effectiveness* means the extent to which government programs achieve their objectives. This definition assumes that what governments set out to do is based on judgments of the relative importance and cost of meeting public needs. Perceptions of need, in turn, are supposedly based on demands and expectations of voters, the consumers who express themselves through the political process (CED, 1976, p. 14). *Efficiency* concerns the way resources are combined and used to carry out government programs and activities at minimum cost. Efficiency is measured in several ways: with output per man hour, with capital-output ratios, or in terms of least-cost combinations of resources to do a specific set of jobs.

Improving productivity means raising the ratio of outputs to inputs, that is, providing more effective services at the same cost or the same services at lower cost. The inputs are the goods and services purchased by government from individuals (mainly public employees) and from outside organizations (mainly private firms). They are measured in conventional terms: man hours, machine time, or money costs per unit (CED, 1976, pp. 14-15). The definition of inputs gets more complicated when it includes contributions of the client, for example, the ability and motivation of a student, or the environment in which the service is performed, for example, the classroom and background of the student.

The outputs or results of government activity are even harder to evaluate, blurred as they are by the career agendas of the bureaus and personnel that purvey publicly provided services, by the needs and expectations of clients whose wants are partly regulated by what they think they can get, and by the competing interests within the voting community who often see the public sector as a competitor of the private sector. It is the voter's pocketbook that is emptied in support of both.

But these are not the only issues that overwhelm our tenuous grasp of the urban illness and prospective cures or prevent effective governmental response. Operating outside the market, remunerated but nonessential ineffective work may continue indefinitely if unchecked. And with ever more resources available automatically, the checks probably will never be self-imposed. Perhaps an increasing fraction of health, welfare, and educational services currently provided for hire by professionals, paraprofessionals, and would-be professionals should come from volunteers within communities as they care for themselves and strengthen their unity.

Meanwhile, as the public sector expands its enterprises, wealth is redistributing itself among age cohorts as the elderly see their houses appreciate at rapid rates, as middle-aged people, increasingly with two incomes per family, see their incomes rise rapidly, and as a crowded generation from the postwar baby boom finds college unrelated to job prospects and job prospects slimmer than at any time since the 1930s. The middle-aged bought housing with little or no down payment at an earlier time when real costs of materials, construction labor, and energy were cheap. Young people often have great difficulty assembling the down payment needed for a house purchase, but they also question the commitments, stabilities, and family orientation that house purchases imply. Like Aesop's fable of the Fox and the Grapes they may decide they do not want what they cannot get. Hence, asset accumulation rates are currently quite different for different age groups. Meanwhile persons born after 1945 lack many of the incentives and opportunities of the generation that preceded them.

Because it is becoming much more expensive to discard and replace cars, houses, neighborhoods, and perhaps cities, a maintenance trend seems under way, not just in personal consumption but also in the use of factories, warehouses, and equipment. These changes imply much more stability in our cities in the next 25 years than there was in the past 25.

As middle-aged adults reach the material prosperity defined as a goal by their Depression-conditioned elders, the young, unable to compete economically, start new fashions in nonmaterial or at least nonmarket realms, in natural foods, co-ops, used clothing, self-help housing and furnishings, volunteered services, and noncommercial entertainments. Officially they are poor because of low cash incomes and an absence of wealth (except, perhaps, distant inheritances). They represent an increasing fraction of young adult Americans, and their circumstances and outlook call into serious question the official definitions of poverty and level of living in contemporary America.

Thus the post-World War II era of city building may be over, but its passing may also mean a need to alter sharply our measures of what is right and what is wrong with our settlements. It is one thing to say that rampant materialism is an anachronism. It is quite another to observe that a significant fraction of contemporary Americans lack the knowledge, skills, and other cultural equipment needed to *regulate* their wants and needs, and to *acquire* what they need to live lives free of frustration and absolute deprivation.

## POLICY CONSIDERATIONS

In conclusion let us turn to the maps themselves and consider their implications for urban public policy in the decade ahead. The maps describe the inequalities that remain from place to place in our 20 major metropolitan regions despite programs of the New Deal, the

---

*Committee for Economic Development. *Improving Productivity in State and Local Government*. New York: CED, 1976. pp. 11-12.

Fair Deal, the New Frontier, the Great Society, and the recent New Federalism. Sometimes the regions of severe suffering relocated. Usually the intensity of want, deprivation, or genuine pain diminished. Nevertheless, geographical inequalities remain on the maps, reflecting the persistence of inequalities throughout American society.

But to talk of the inequalities within society is to traffic in abstractions. For policy purposes it helps to consider real people living in real places — the places described on these maps. By today's standards some of these areas are highly desirable places in which to live, while others are not. Because these places are such tangible manifestations of the inequalities in American society, attempts to eliminate inequalities often take the form of efforts to diminish the differences among neighborhoods and living environments within the United States. Examples include the racial and economic integration of housing, the extension of transit systems, busing of school children, and income maintenance programs and special employment services in areas of low income and high unemployment. As these efforts continue, one set of forces favors great restraint, conceding the inequalities but arguing that in a free society with freedom of movement and association people will move, like-minded groups will form, and some persons will tend to be excluded from places they would like to enter.

The central issue in the controversy has been joined in two recent treatises on moral philosophy: *A Theory of Justice* by John Rawls and *Anarchy, State and Utopia* by Robert Nozick. According to James S. Coleman,* both works treat the difficult questions raised by the persistence of inequalities in contemporary society. Rawls discusses the question of what is a just distribution in society, or indeed whether inequalities are justified in society and, if so, what kinds and amounts of inequality. His answer is that inequalities are justified only to the extent that they benefit the least advantaged members of society. Hence because some inequalities of location or resources — that is, of power — may yield higher productivity and thus greater benefit to all, they may be justified by Rawls's principle.

Nozick, on the other hand, argues that most inequalities arise not by the edict of central authorities but from individuals' innate or acquired differences in capabilities, skills, and other resources. Whereas Rawls assumes that these resources and their fruits are community property and that individuals have no right to them, Nozick argues that each person is entitled to what he has justly acquired. As Coleman observes, these positions express both the principal argument for regarding equality as the only just distribution and the principal argument for regarding inequalities as justified and equality as an artificially imposed state.

These two extreme positions are useful because they help illustrate what is gained or lost by moving in either direction. By moving toward absolute equality we lose individual liberty to the central authorities that impose equality in each realm. Yet by moving back too far in the direction of individual liberty, we forfeit equality in favor of the accident of birth reinforced by environment, the market, and the institution of private property.

How then should we interpret what the maps show us? Their general subject is the inequality from place to place in the living conditions for people. The basic sources of inequality are probably similar from city to city and from neighborhood to neighborhood, yet each set of cities manifests its geographical patterns of inequality in distinctive ways. The Nation's Historic Cities present one aspect, the Nineteenth-Century Ports present another. The Inland Centers and Ports across the Midwest present still another variety of American metropolitan settlement, different from cities growing up in earlier or later eras but as a group having much in common in their internal spatial organization. The Twentieth-Century Cities are still another breed. The experiences of older places may not directly pertain to them.

If we mentally superimpose the maps for any city, or for any set of similar cities, the *impoverished environments* are seen to pile up in one class of neighborhood while *environments of power* come into focus elsewhere. The spatial inequalities that exist in these composite mental maps represent environments largely insulated from one another. This separation will eventually promote further inequalities whatever the source of the initial differences, disadvantages, and separations.

Consider the case of individuals and developers who want to spread metropolitan settlement beyond the edge of the continuously built-up urban area (Chapters 26 and 27). By today's standards of taste these exurban locales are highly prized by those who can obtain them. Yet their present cost is exorbitant when essential services are extended into these extravagant appendages of our Daily Urban Systems. After several decades of public debate Americans have finally decided that the costs to future generations of uncontrolled spatial extension of urban areas today are unacceptable. Instead the carefully staged deployment of water and sewer systems defines development limits and modulates their extension. Meanwhile superior highways have linked the amenities of small-town life with burgeoning suburban job opportunities, promoting net migration from the metropolitan areas into the zones between them. These movements illustrate how the surfaces of inequality continue to relocate as the mobile, the informed, and the powerful discover, define, and take advantage of new opportunities and by their very actions set fashions for others to try to imitate. But they also illustrate how the concept of the Daily Urban System starts to break down just as it is defined and comes into use. Not only do an increasing number of jobs lack a fixed place of work and thereby lack a journey to work, but the Daily Urban System is increasingly spread out, more and more a multicentered *settlement field*. As the daily work trip becomes harder to use as the definitive element in the Daily Urban System, work itself begins to recede from its central position in contemporary life while the time and space devoted to leisure and recreational activities steadily expand. The Daily Urban System is joined by the weekly urban system as increasing numbers of the privileged head each weekend to the mountains, the seashore, the lake, or the desert for recreational settings different from weekday routines (Chapter 28).

In sum, as long as there is change in society and as long as there is freedom of movement, people individually and in aggregates will create geographical environments of power at one set of places and impoverished environments elsewhere. For some this will be labeled an unwanted outcome of an otherwise desirable process. For others, to the degree that the geographical inequalities are thought to promote still greater inequalities, the situation cries for correction and a debate will continue over the appropriate countervailing public response.

The debate will follow the lines developed by Rawls and Nozick, whether the subject is inequality in housing environments (Chapters 29-31), in personal mobility and communications opportunities (Chapters 32-36), or even in population and housing density (Chapter 37). Population densities inside our Daily Urban Systems at any period of time during the 20th century have tended to move toward a critical density. Densities higher than the critical density have moved down; those below have risen. Meanwhile the critical density itself has steadily declined.

Despite the performance of the averages — of population density or of any other attribute — variation or inequality persists on both sides of the average. The inequality persists partly because of habit or personal preference, partly because people lack the means to change their situation to another they consider more desirable. The meaning of the inequality will depend on local standards of need, adequacy, and desirability, and these vary from city to city, from neighborhood to neighborhood, from household to household, and from person to

---

*James S. Coleman. "Rawls, Nozick, and Educational Equality." *The Public Interest*. No. 43 (Spring 1976), pp. 121-128.

person. Usually we have no established standards, such as the U.S. Recommended Daily Allowance for Vitamin A. Instead we are left with ethical beliefs, moral arguments, and political debates. As the maps on education (Chapters 38-39), public health (Chapter 40), racial and ethnic segregation (Chapters 41-42), or economic welfare (Chapters 43-47) show, geographical inequalities persist despite the achievement of absolute gains by individuals and by entire groups. This fact is brutally apparent in the persistence and relocation of black ghettos. When aggressive, ambitious, and upwardly mobile families attempt to leave the ghetto behind, it follows them, surrounding them.

Large geographical areas of poverty correspond to impoverished environments. One of the outcomes of the impoverished environment is a deficiency of money incomes. Merely filling the income gap treats only the symptom of a larger, deeper problem. Supplying only money cannot provide the continuous nurturing needed to put youngsters on their feet as self-sufficient individuals in a quasiprivate economy. A recent proposed solution would disperse the impoverished from their impoverished environments and resettle them within the environments of power. Busing of school children out of certain inner-city neighborhoods is one such dispersal effort. The public provision of low- and moderate-income suburban housing is another. The privileged populations normally resent these direct intrusions into their preserves and unleash their political power to emasculate these programs. James Coleman suggests an alternative that has application to many fields of urban public policy. Rather than allowing the impoverished to be left behind or crushed in the exercise of complete freedom by the powerful, or withdrawing individual rights from the strong, the purposeful, and the successful and using a central authority to reassign them to the impoverished, a third route is suggested. That is, rather than withdrawing rights from those who have the economic power to exercise them effectively, society can enlarge the range of choice available to others. Such an effort can increase equality by adding to the lower end of the distribution rather than by diminishing inequality by directly taking something away from the top.

With busing, rather than ignore the present inequalities or shift suburban children to inner-city schools, such a policy would allow any child in a metropolitan area the right to transfer to a school of his choice, so long as the receiving school has a smaller proportion of his race than the school he leaves. For housing and urban renewal (Chapter 48) such a policy would not emphasize the dispersal of low-income housing into suburban areas but would recognize that many public purposes would be served if central-city housing and redevelopment authorities were to begin a massive rebuilding of obsolete neighborhoods, not solely for the poor but instead for middle- and upper-income families. If our concern for improving the plight of the poor is genuine, then the enrichment of impoverished environments seems a much more promising strategy than does a frontal attack on the environments of power.

# APPENDIX A

# Location Maps

SMSA Maps pp. 455-461    City Maps pp. 462-468

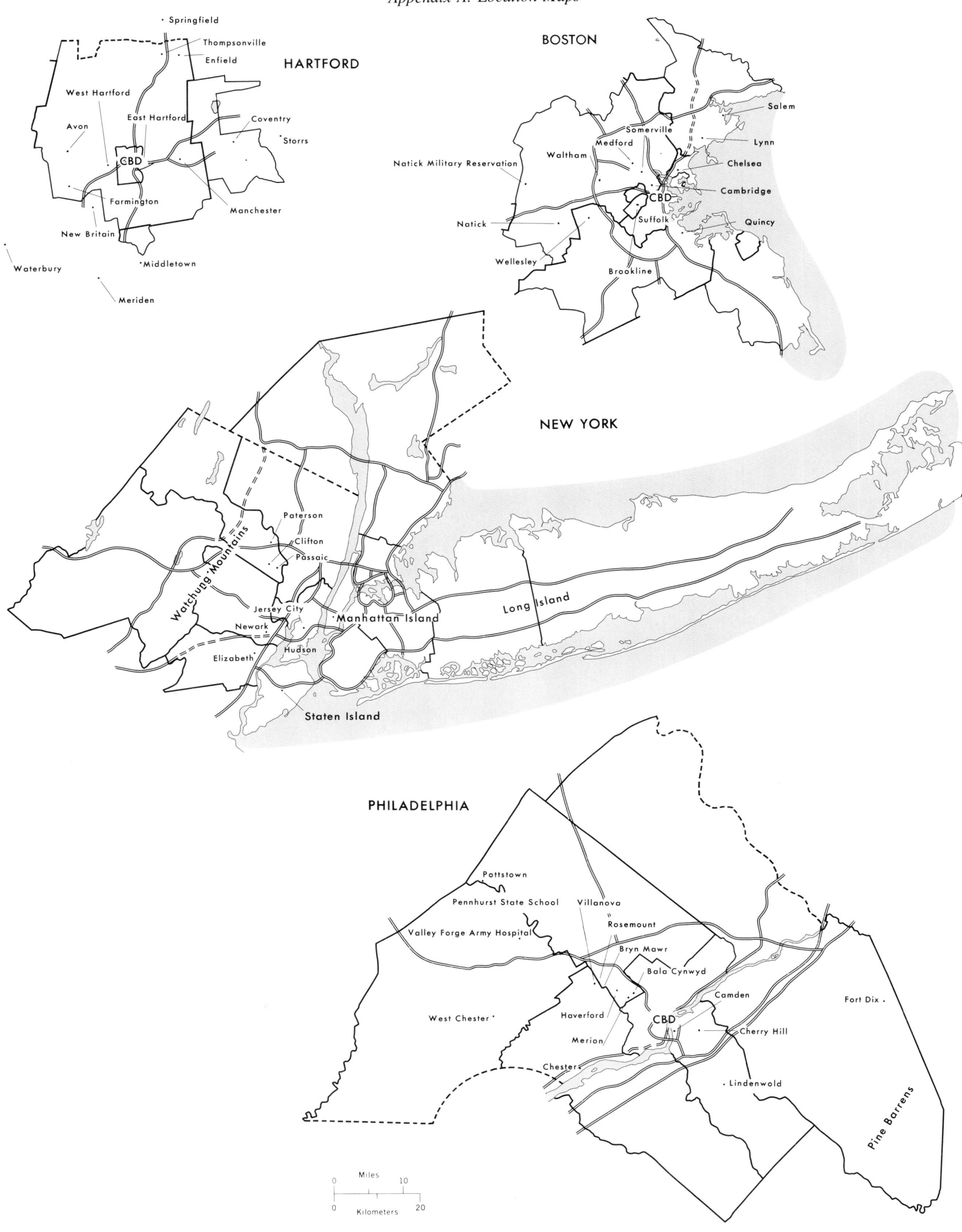

Appendix A: Location Maps

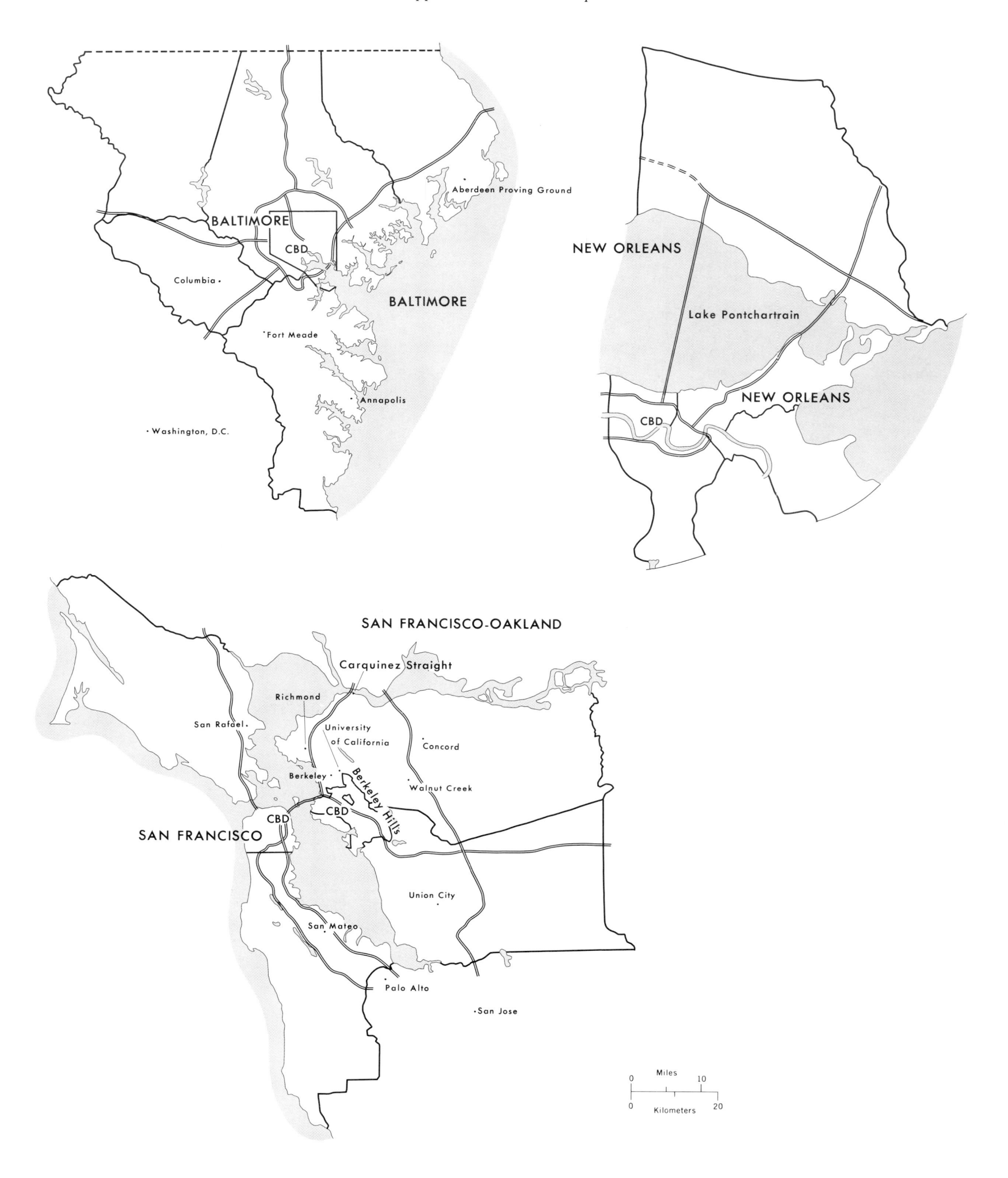

*Appendix A: Location Maps*

456

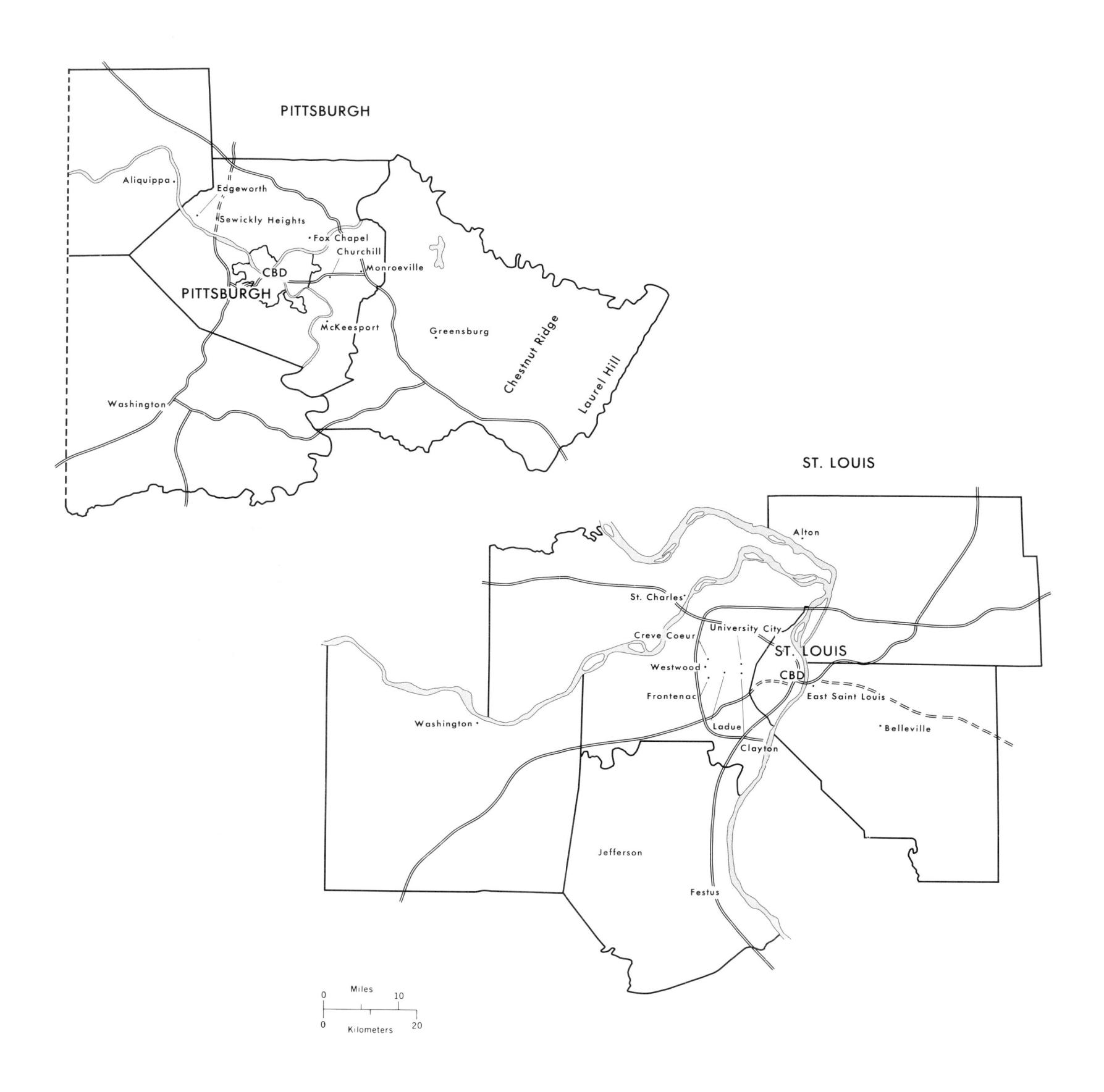

*Appendix A: Location Maps*

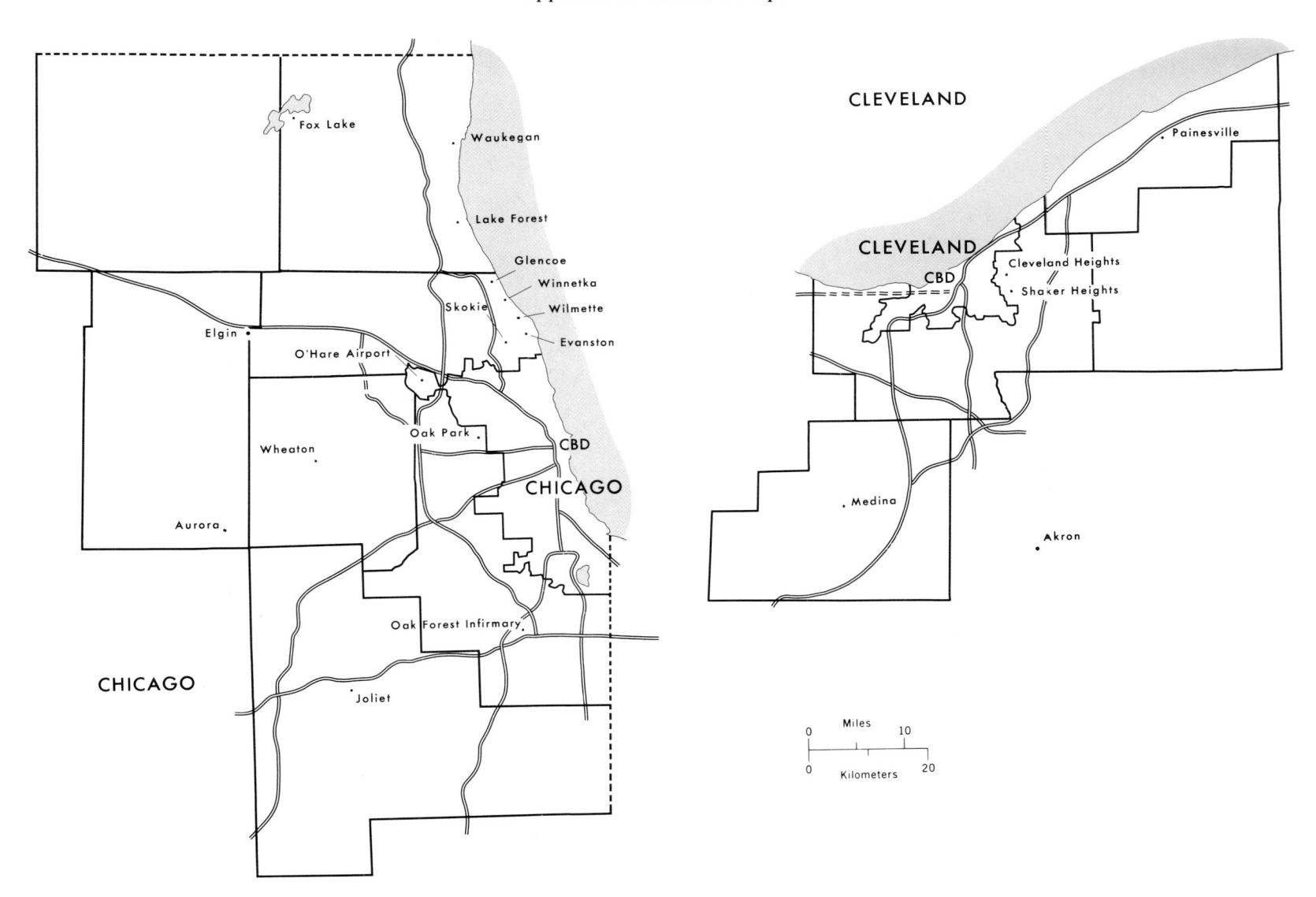

Appendix A: Location Maps

458

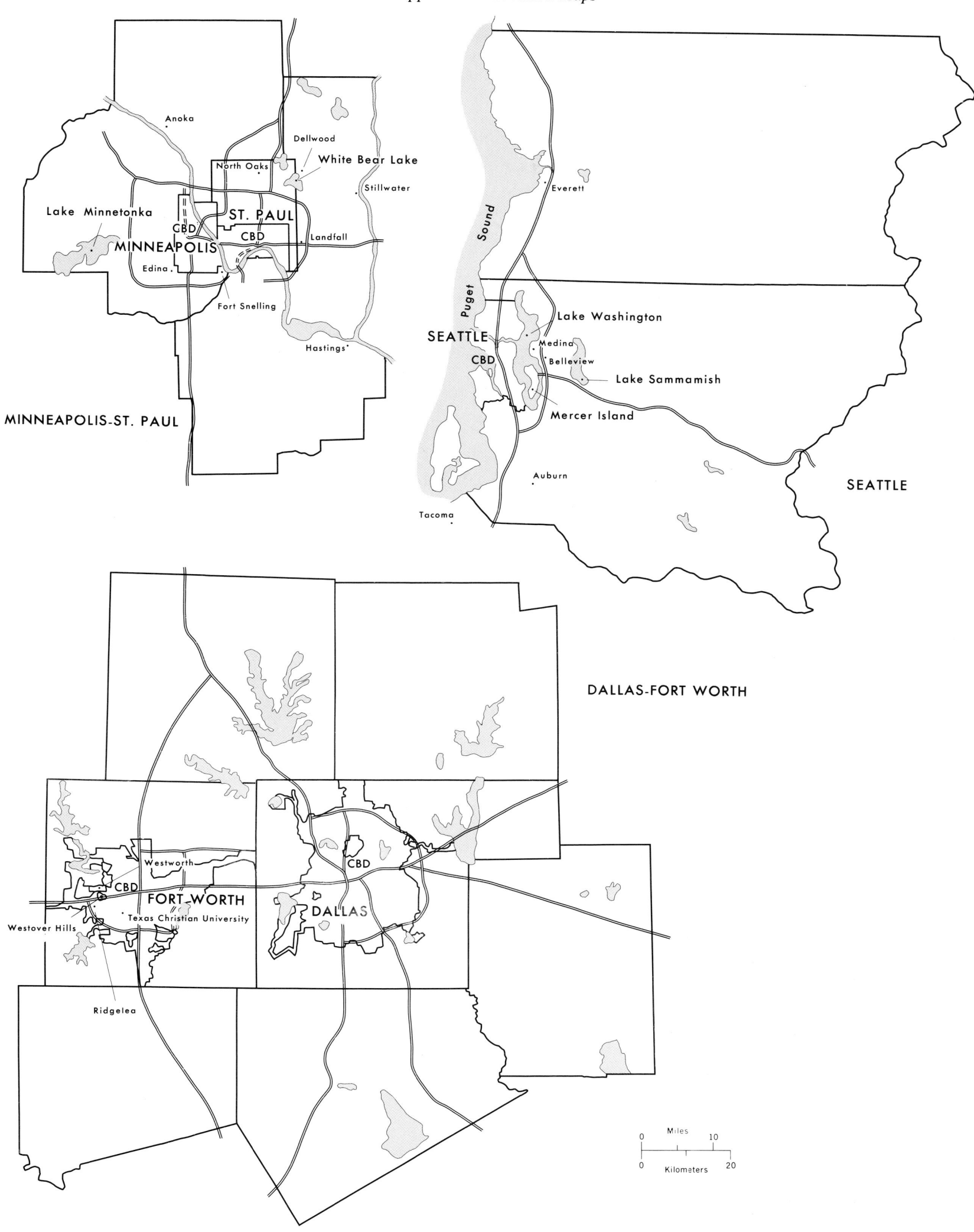

*Appendix A: Location Maps*

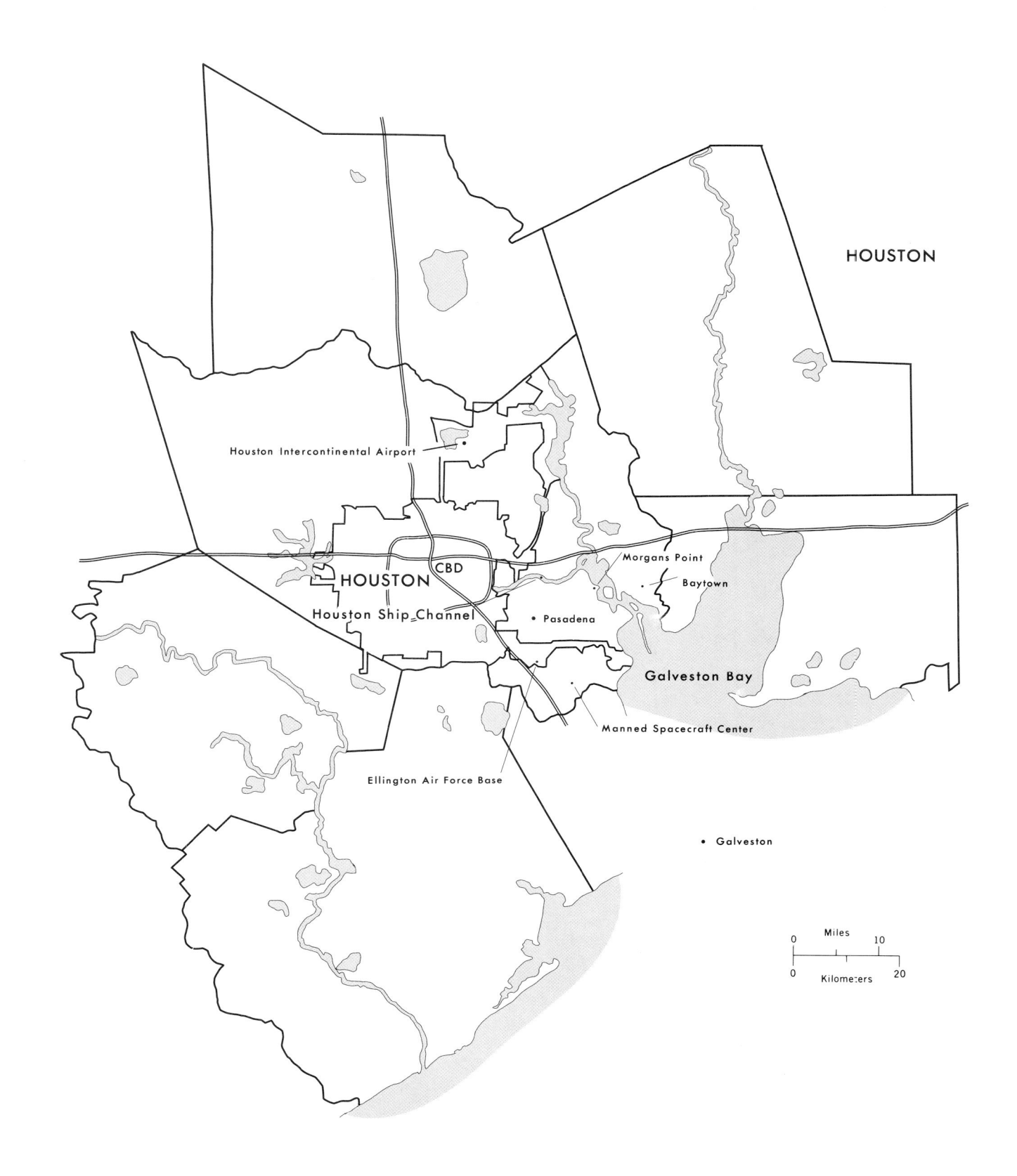

*Appendix A: Location Maps*

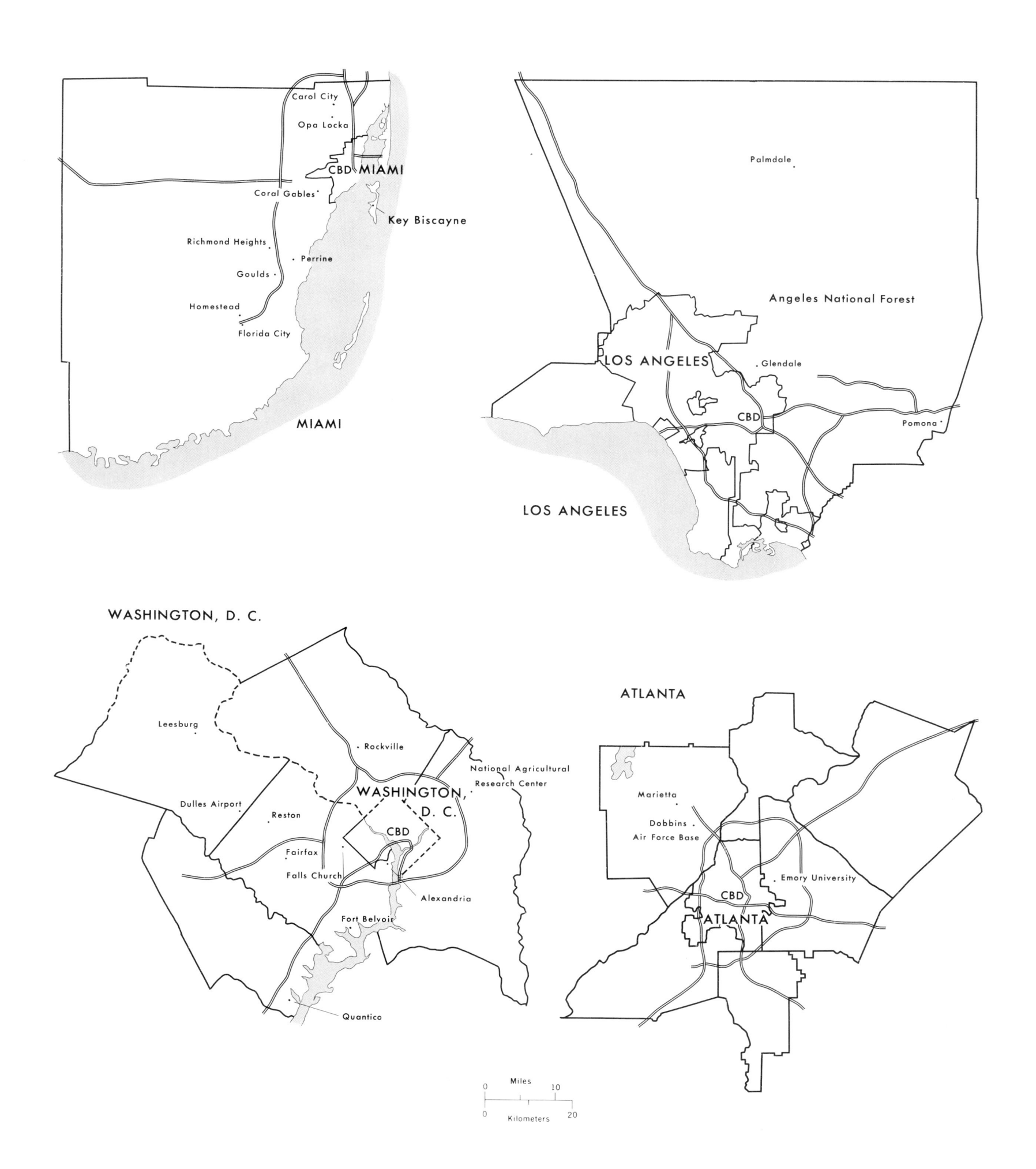

*Appendix A: Location Maps*

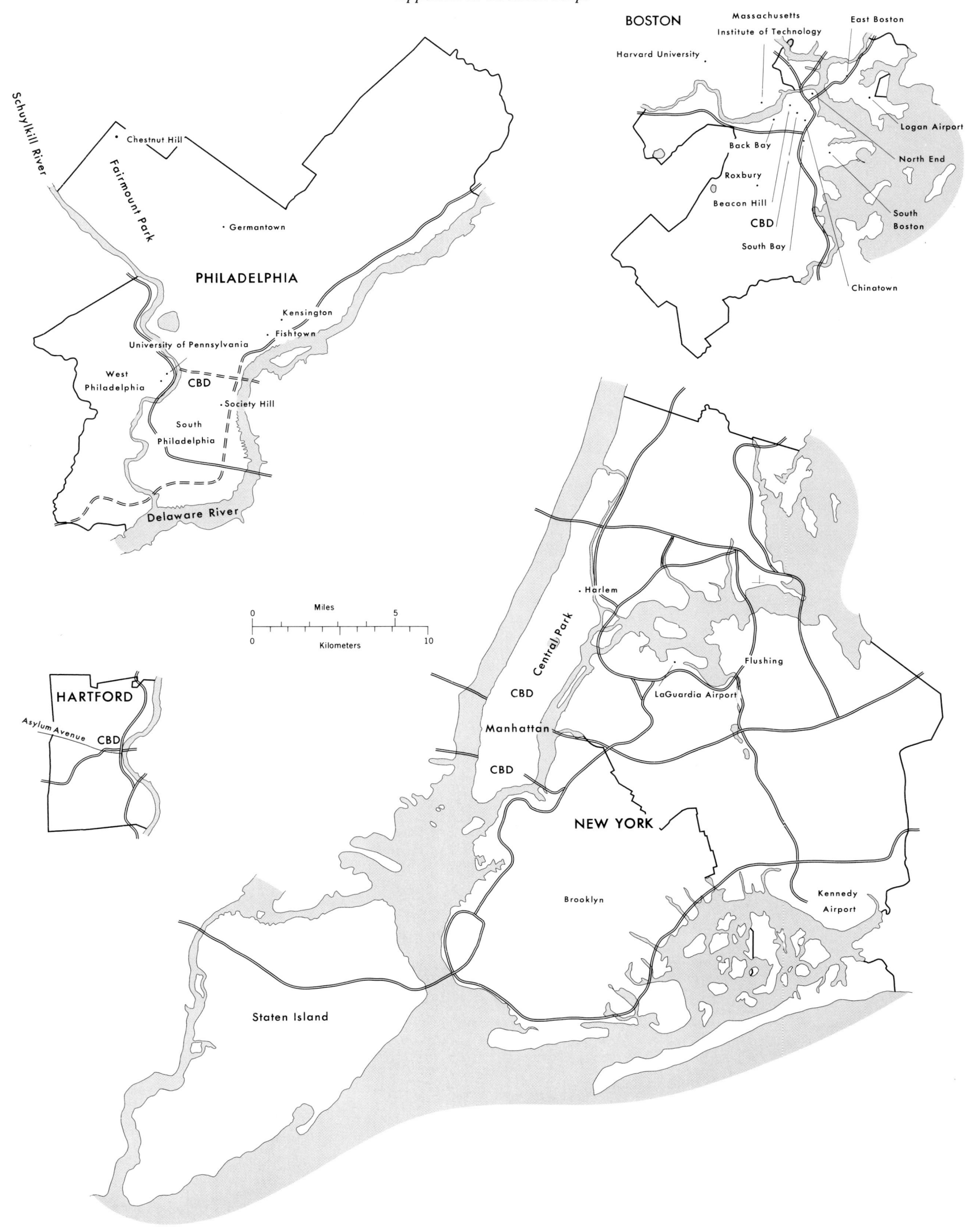

*Appendix A: Location Maps*

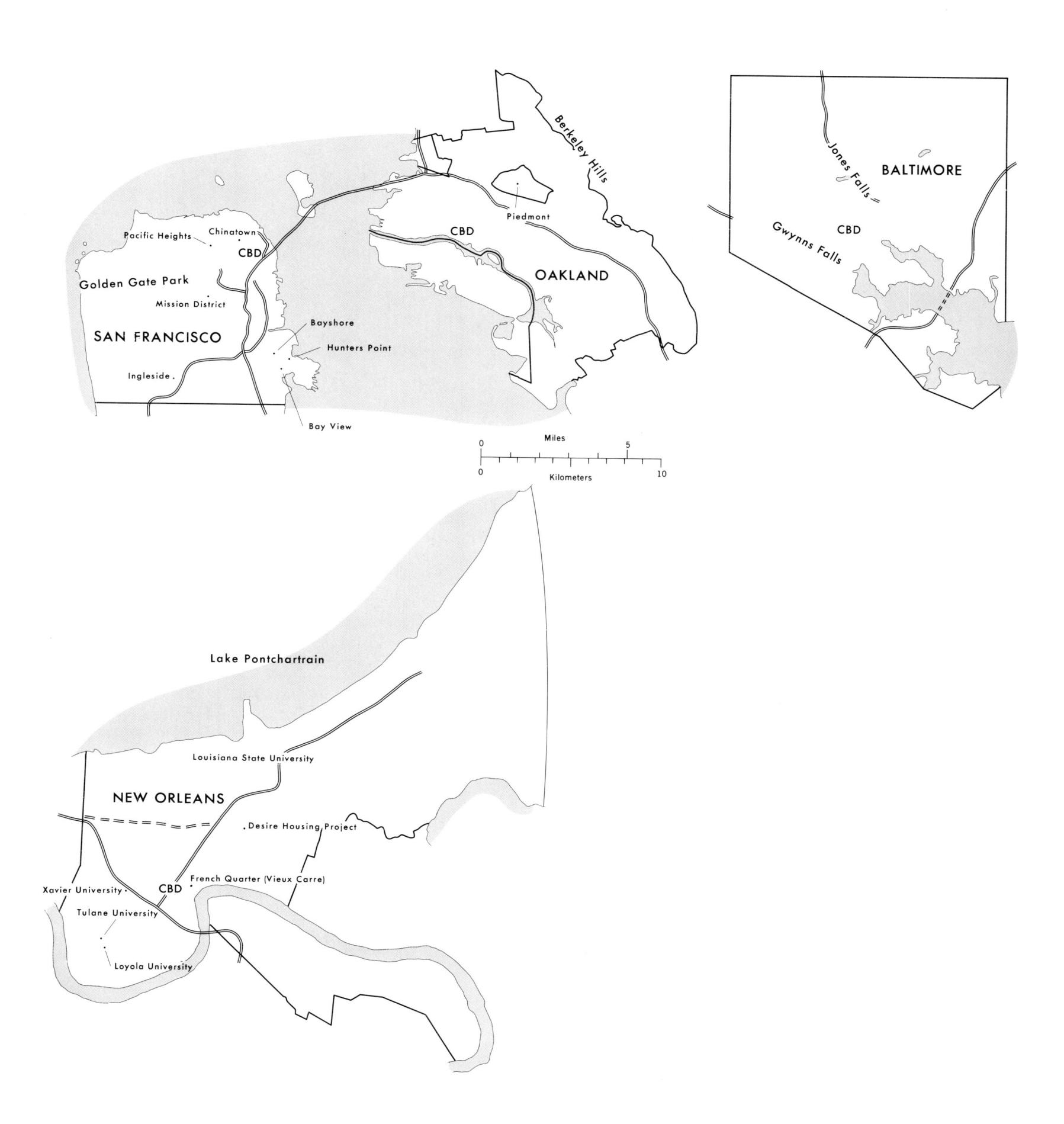

*Appendix A: Location Maps*

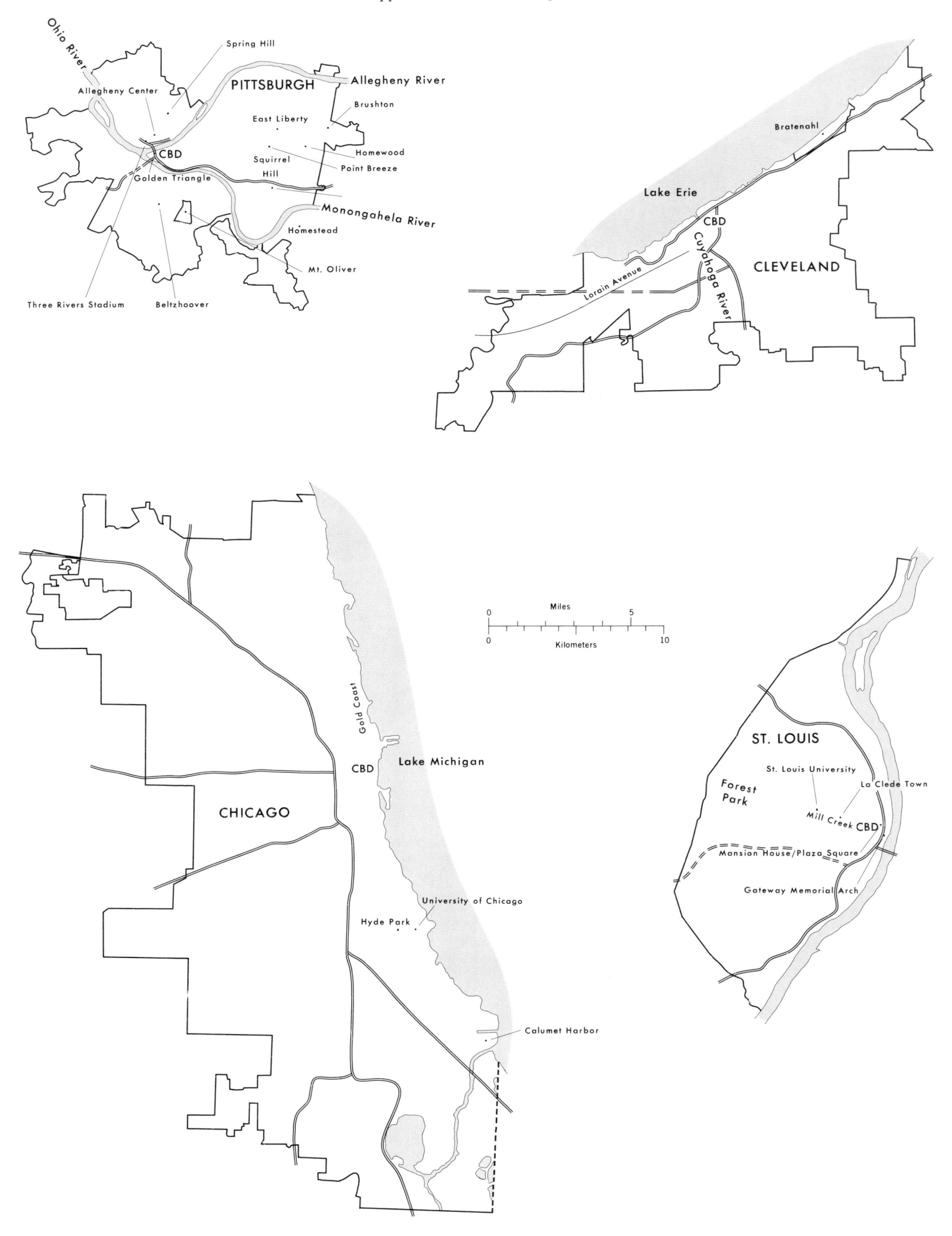

*Appendix A: Location Maps*

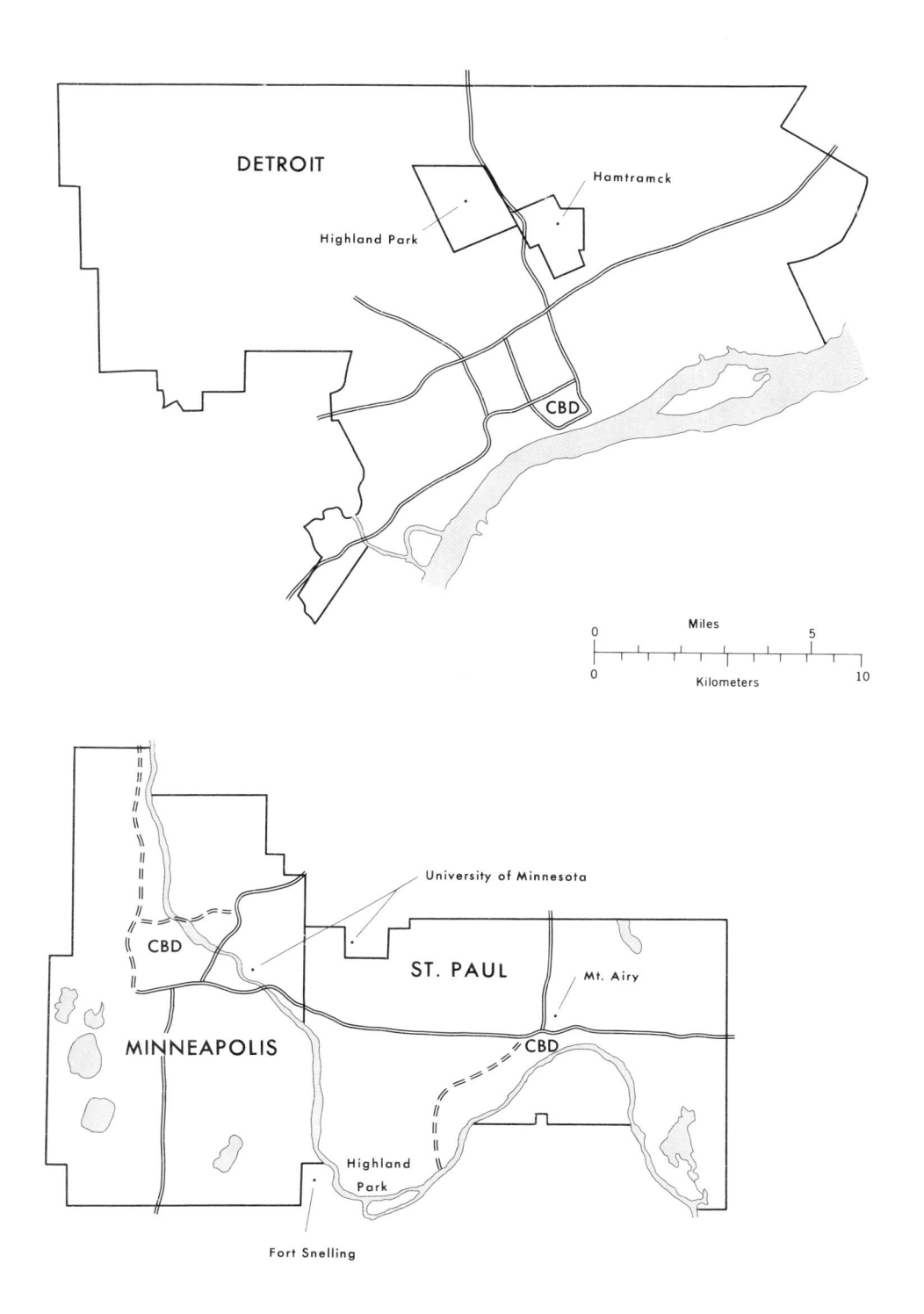

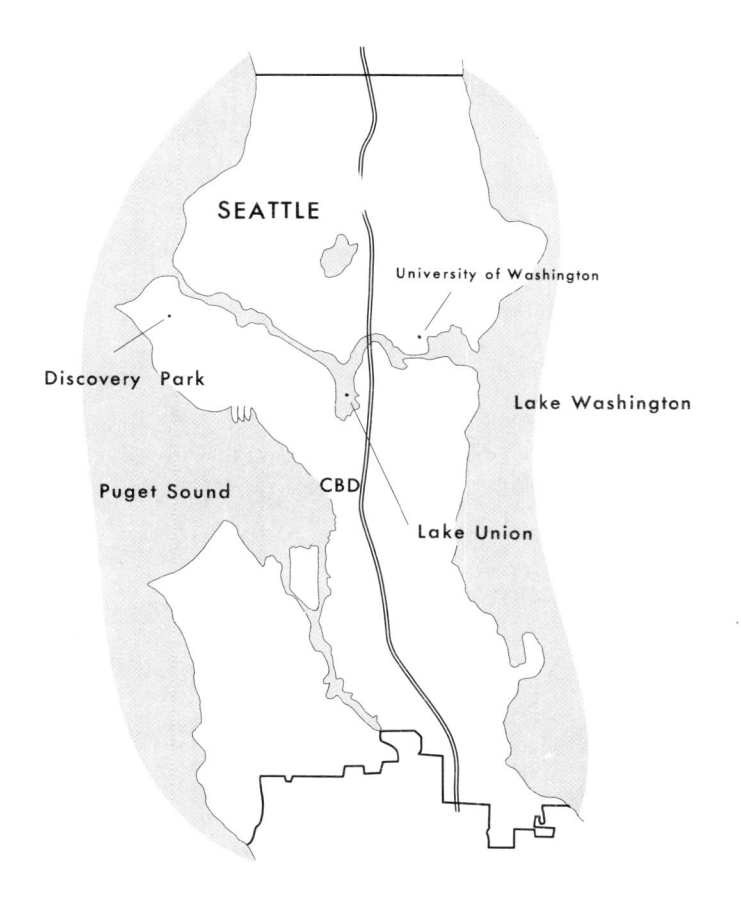

*Appendix A: Location Maps*

465

Appendix A: Location Maps

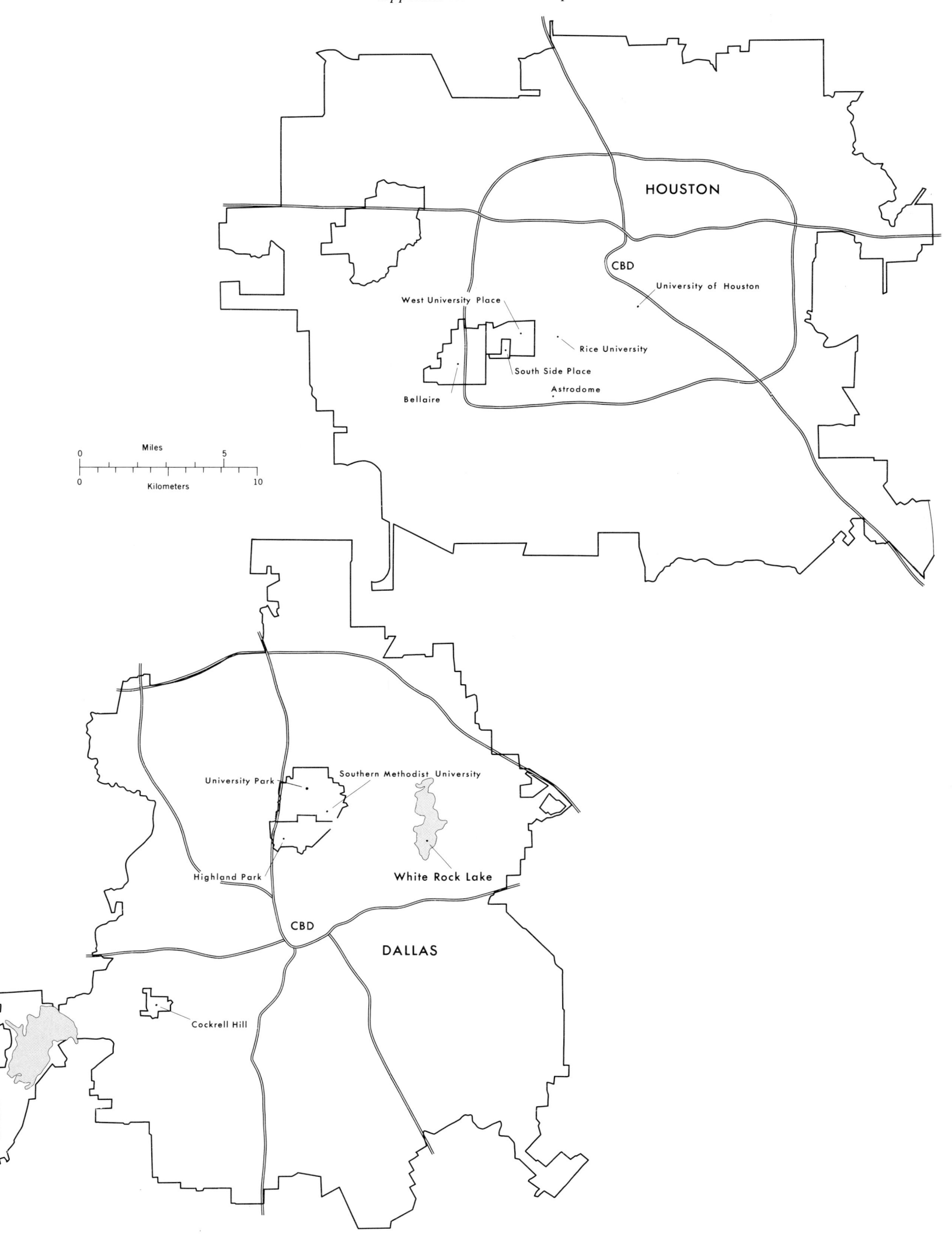

466

*Appendix A: Location Maps*

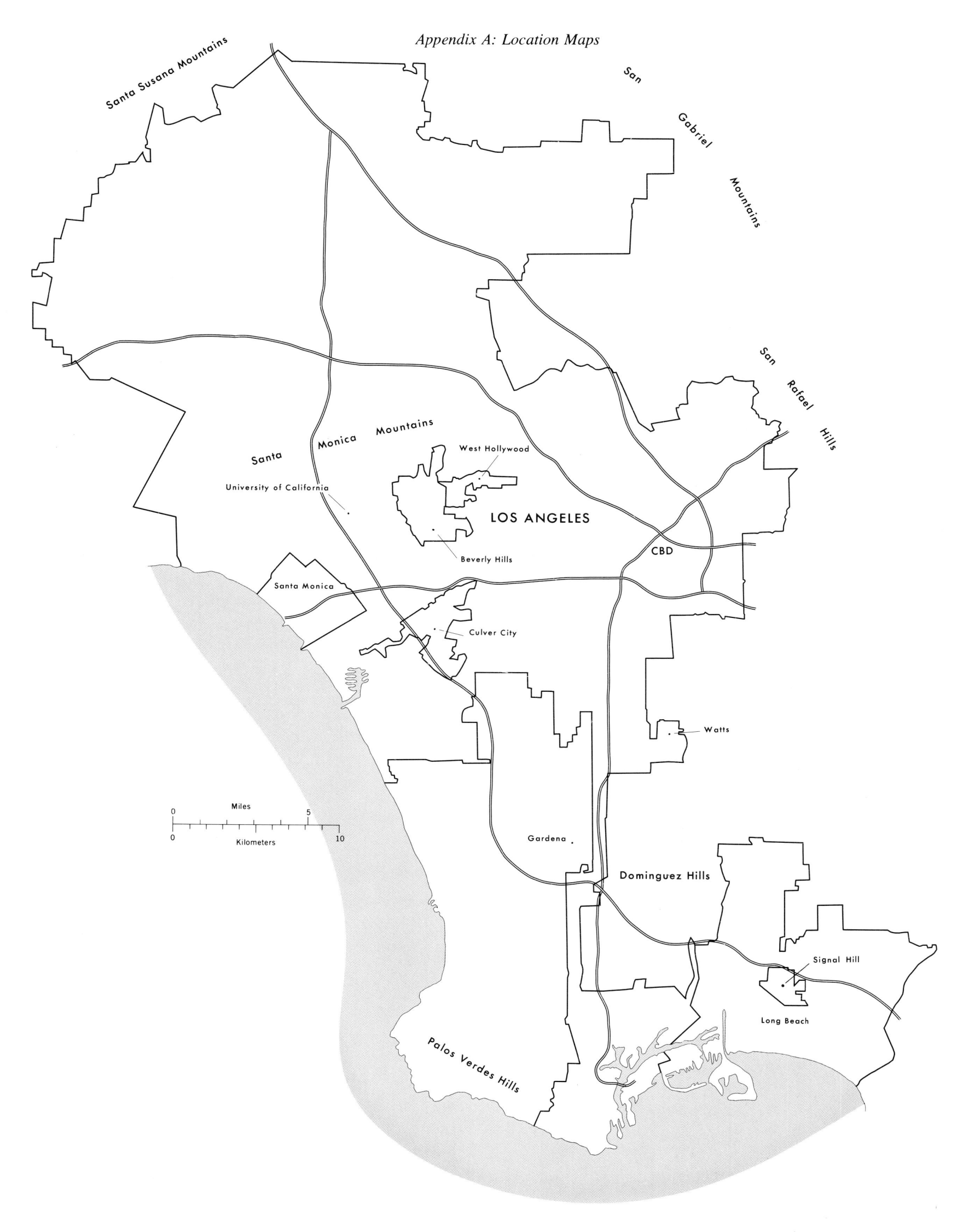

*Appendix A: Location Maps*

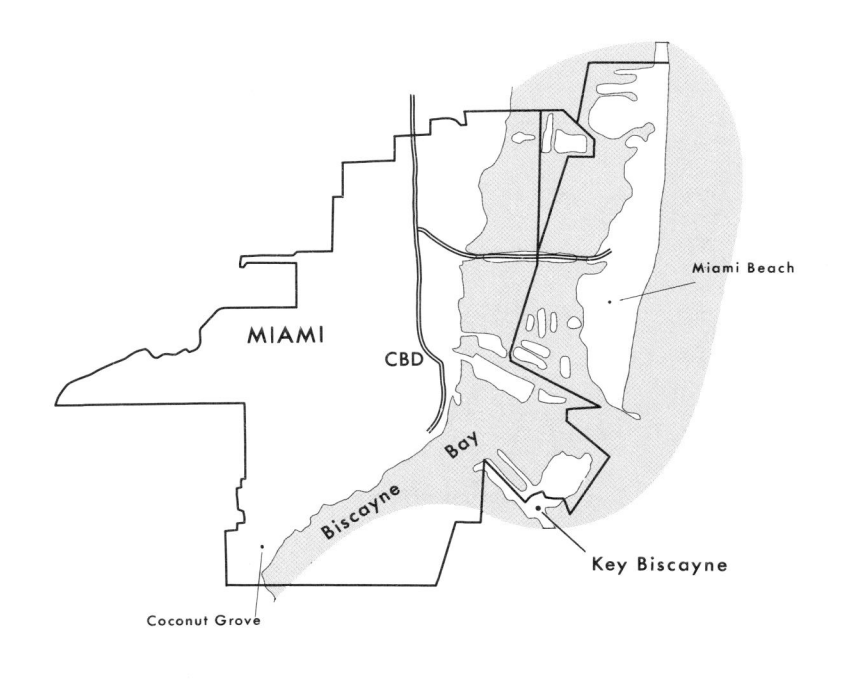

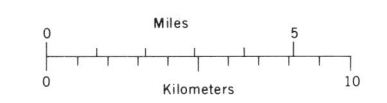

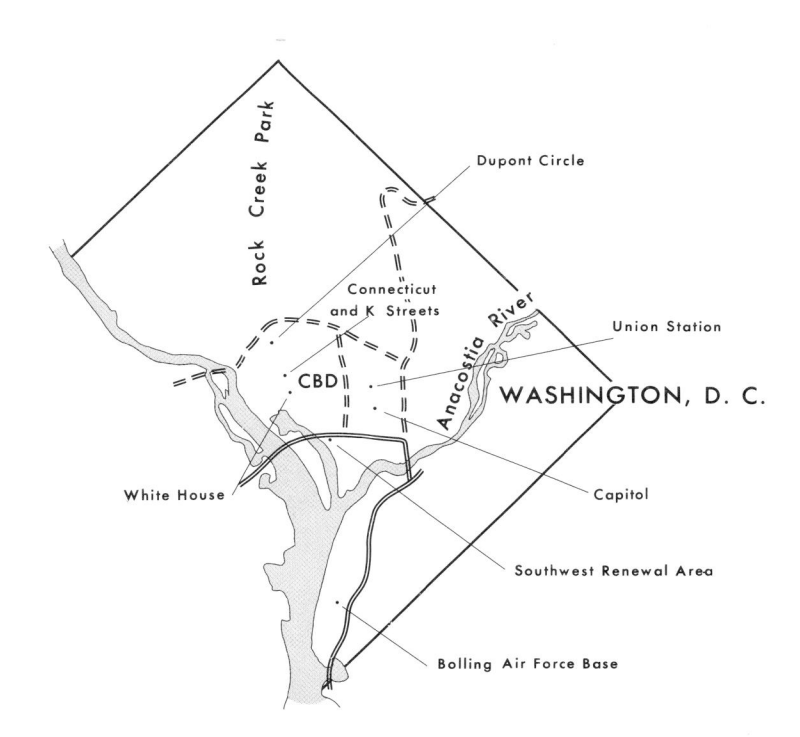

# APPENDIX B

Data Tables for Part II

# Data Tables for Part II

*Note:* Quotation marks (″) in these tables indicate that the statistical unit identified by the intersection of place and region (for example, Oakland-SMSA) does not exist. Thus the population of Oakland (362,000) is included in the population of the San Francisco-Oakland SMSA (3,100,000), which appears above the quotation marks in the Oakland-SMSA cell.

| Area | Population, 1970 (Thousands) | | |
|---|---|---|---|
| | **City** | **SMSA** | **DUS** |
| Boston | 641 | 2,754 | 3,855 |
| New York | 7,895 | 9,019 | 17,454 |
| Jersey City | 261 | 609 | ″ |
| Newark | 382 | 1,857 | ″ |
| Paterson | 145 | 1,359 | ″ |
| Clifton | 82 | ″ | ″ |
| Passaic | 55 | ″ | ″ |
| Philadelphia | 1,949 | 4,818 | 4,818 |
| Hartford | 158 | 664 | 1,190 |
| Baltimore | 906 | 2,071 | 2,071 |
| New Orleans | 593 | 1,046 | 1,170 |
| San Francisco | 716 | 3,110 | 4,631 |
| Oakland | 362 | ″ | ″ |
| Pittsburgh | 520 | 2,401 | 2,760 |
| St. Louis | 622 | 2,363 | 2,542 |
| Cleveland | 751 | 2,064 | 3,000 |
| Chicago | 3,367 | 6,979 | 7,611 |
| Detroit | 1,511 | 4,200 | 4,736 |
| Minneapolis | 434 | 1,814 | 2,123 |
| St. Paul | 310 | ″ | ″ |
| Seattle | 531 | 1,422 | 1,937 |
| Everett | 54 | ″ | ″ |
| Dallas | 844 | 1,556 | 2,504 |
| Fort Worth | 393 | 762 | ″ |
| Houston | 1,233 | 1,985 | 2,230 |
| Los Angeles | 2,816 | 7,032 | 9,981 |
| Long Beach | 359 | ″ | ″ |
| Miami | 335 | 1,286 | 1,188 |
| Atlanta | 479 | 1,390 | 1,913 |
| Washington, D.C. | 757 | 2,861 | 3,347 |

*Appendix B: Data Tables for Part II*

| Area | Land Area, 1970 Square Miles (Kilometers) | | | | | |
|---|---|---|---|---|---|---|
| | **City** | | **SMSA** | | **DUS** | |
| Boston | 46 | ( 119) | 987 | ( 2,256) | 2,240 | ( 6,267) |
| New York | 300 | ( 777) | 2,136 | ( 5,532) | 6,587 | ( 9,289) |
| Jersey City | 15 | ( 39) | 47 | ( 122) | " | ( " ) |
| Newark | 24 | ( 62) | 701 | ( 1,815) | " | ( " ) |
| Paterson | 8 | ( 21) | 427 | ( 1,106) | " | ( " ) |
| Clifton | 12 | ( 31) | " | ( " ) | " | ( " ) |
| Passaic | 3 | ( 8) | " | ( " ) | " | ( " ) |
| Philadelphia | 129 | ( 334) | 3,553 | ( 9,201) | 3,553 | ( 9,201) |
| Hartford | 17 | ( 44) | 672 | ( 1,740) | 1,588 | ( 4,112) |
| Baltimore | 78 | ( 202) | 2,259 | ( 5,850) | 2,259 | ( 5,850) |
| New Orleans | 198 | ( 512) | 1,975 | ( 5,114) | 4,828 | (12,503) |
| San Francisco | 45 | ( 116) | 2,478 | ( 6,417) | 6,994 | (18,112) |
| Oakland | 53 | ( 137) | " | ( " ) | " | ( " ) |
| Pittsburgh | 55 | ( 142) | 3,049 | ( 7,896) | 5,300 | (13,726) |
| St. Louis | 61 | ( 158) | 4,118 | (10,665) | 9,085 | (23,528) |
| Cleveland | 76 | ( 197) | 1,519 | ( 3,934) | 2,917 | ( 7,554) |
| Chicago | 223 | ( 576) | 3,719 | ( 9,631) | 4,567 | (12,060) |
| Detroit | 138 | ( 357) | 1,952 | ( 5,055) | 4,526 | (11,721) |
| Minneapolis | 55 | ( 142) | 2,107 | ( 5,461) | 10,024 | (25,960) |
| St. Paul | 52 | ( 135) | " | ( " ) | " | ( " ) |
| Seattle | 84 | ( 218) | 4,229 | (10,952) | 6,507 | (16,851) |
| Everett | 29 | ( 75) | " | ( " ) | " | ( " ) |
| Dallas | 266 | ( 689) | 4,564 | (11,820) | 12,391 | (32,090) |
| Fort Worth | 205 | ( 531) | 1,607 | ( 4,162) | " | ( " ) |
| Houston | 434 | (1,124) | 6,286 | (16,279) | 9,886 | (25,602) |
| Los Angeles | 464 | (1,202) | 4,069 | (10,538) | 34,007 | (88,070) |
| Long Beach | 49 | ( 127) | " | ( " ) | " | ( " ) |
| Miami | 34 | ( 88) | 2,042 | ( 5,288) | 3,261 | ( 8,445) |
| Atlanta | 132 | ( 342) | 1,727 | ( 4,472) | 8,719 | (22,580) |
| Washington, D.C. | 61 | ( 158) | 2,532 | ( 6,557) | 4,839 | (12,532) |

| Area | Housing Built before 1940 | | Housing Built 1940–1959 | | Housing Built 1960–1970 | | Percentage Mobile Homes | | | Percentage Single-Unit Detached | |
|---|---|---|---|---|---|---|---|---|---|---|---|
| | **City** | **SMSA** | **City** | **SMSA** | **City** | **SMSA** | **City** | **SMSA** | **DUS** | **City** | **SMSA** |
| Boston | 77.2 | 63.8 | 13.7 | 22.1 | 9.1 | 14.1 | 0.1 | 0.2 | 0.7 | 11.8 | 42.3 |
| New York | 62.1 | 53.8 | 24.4 | 29.8 | 13.5 | 16.4 | 0.0 | 0.1 | 0.1 | 7.9 | 25.1 |
| Jersey City | 78.9 | 77.2 | 13.5 | 13.4 | 7.6 | 9.4 | 0.0 | 0.2 | " | 6.7 | 9.5 |
| Newark | 68.4 | 51.9 | 22.9 | 30.8 | 8.7 | 17.3 | 0.0 | 0.1 | " | 7.9 | 46.4 |
| Paterson | 70.5 | 44.1 | 19.1 | 38.1 | 10.4 | 17.8 | 0.0 | 0.3 | " | 14.1 | 54.2 |
| Clifton | 44.0 | " | 45.2 | " | 10.7 | " | 0.0 | " | " | 49.8 | " |
| Passaic | 75.7 | " | 15.8 | " | 8.4 | " | 0.0 | " | " | 13.8 | " |
| Philadelphia | 69.5 | 51.4 | 20.1 | 30.0 | 10.4 | 18.6 | 0.1 | 0.7 | 0.7 | 6.6 | 36.5 |
| Hartford | 67.0 | 39.6 | 21.4 | 35.8 | 11.7 | 24.6 | 0.0 | 0.4 | 0.8 | 11.7 | 55.7 |
| Baltimore | 60.0 | 39.6 | 30.9 | 37.5 | 10.1 | 22.9 | 0.1 | 1.2 | 1.2 | 12.1 | 39.7 |
| New Orleans | 49.6 | 34.2 | 36.5 | 38.4 | 13.8 | 27.4 | 0.3 | 1.4 | 2.5 | 36.7 | 52.3 |
| San Francisco | 66.9 | 24.7 | 23.5 | 38.5 | 9.6 | 36.8 | 0.0 | 0.8 | 1.1 | 16.9 | 52.2 |
| Oakland | 53.3 | " | 29.6 | " | 17.1 | " | 0.1 | " | " | 47.3 | " |
| Pittsburgh | 74.4 | 54.4 | 18.4 | 31.0 | 7.2 | 14.6 | 0.0 | 1.1 | 1.7 | 39.5 | 65.7 |
| St. Louis | 73.8 | 41.6 | 19.8 | 34.2 | 6.5 | 24.2 | 0.0 | 2.2 | 2.8 | 32.5 | 64.6 |
| Cleveland | 73.4 | 45.9 | 20.9 | 34.5 | 5.7 | 19.6 | 0.3 | 0.8 | 1.2 | 36.5 | 57.7 |
| Chicago | 66.5 | 48.4 | 22.9 | 30.6 | 10.6 | 21.0 | 0.1 | 0.7 | 0.8 | 21.8 | 44.8 |
| Detroit | 61.8 | 37.3 | 34.1 | 43.2 | 4.1 | 19.5 | 0.1 | 1.2 | 1.4 | 53.1 | 69.2 |
| Minneapolis | 68.1 | 39.1 | 19.1 | 31.9 | 12.7 | 29.0 | 0.0 | 1.2 | 1.9 | 45.4 | 62.5 |
| St. Paul | 62.4 | " | 22.8 | " | 14.8 | " | 0.0 | " | " | 51.9 | " |
| Seattle | 47.6 | 30.0 | 36.2 | 35.8 | 16.2 | 34.1 | 0.4 | 2.5 | 2.9 | 58.7 | 69.5 |
| Everett | 44.3 | " | 33.2 | " | 22.5 | " | 1.3 | " | " | 67.9 | " |
| Dallas | 18.1 | 17.7 | 47.4 | 42.9 | 34.5 | 39.4 | 0.7 | 1.8 | 2.2 | 59.6 | 68.4 |
| Fort Worth | 26.7 | 19.1 | 51.9 | 46.7 | 21.4 | 34.1 | 0.9 | 2.5 | " | 73.8 | 76.6 |
| Houston | 17.3 | 15.3 | 49.2 | 47.0 | 33.5 | 37.8 | 1.2 | 2.2 | 2.4 | 64.8 | 71.2 |
| Los Angeles | 32.2 | 25.3 | 45.3 | 50.6 | 22.5 | 24.1 | 0.6 | 1.5 | 2.4 | 49.2 | 58.2 |
| Long Beach | 31.6 | " | 49.4 | " | 19.0 | " | 1.2 | " | " | 48.2 | " |
| Miami | 29.9 | 14.5 | 50.9 | 52.2 | 19.2 | 33.3 | 1.3 | 2.2 | 2.8 | 41.2 | 53.9 |
| Atlanta | 20.3 | 18.1 | 43.0 | 38.7 | 26.7 | 43.2 | 0.4 | 1.8 | 3.7 | 47.3 | 63.0 |
| Washington, D.C. | 47.0 | 21.2 | 37.3 | 40.9 | 15.8 | 37.9 | 0.1 | 0.6 | 1.5 | 13.3 | 43.0 |

*Appendix B: Data Tables for Part II*

| Area | Mean Value Owner-Occupied Housing City | SMSA | Mean Monthly Contract Rent City | SMSA | Population Density per Square Mile (Kilometer) City | | SMSA | |
|---|---|---|---|---|---|---|---|---|
| Boston | 20,700 | 27,200 | 111 | 117 | 13,936 | ( 5,381) | 2,791 | (1,078) |
| New York | 28,000 | 31,200 | 114 | 116 | 26,345 | (10,173) | 5,419 | (2,092) |
| Jersey City | 17,200 | 21,500 | 95 | 99 | 17,242 | ( 6,658) | 12,851 | (4,962) |
| Newark | 18,100 | 31,000 | 101 | 120 | 16,252 | ( 6,276) | 2,654 | (1,025) |
| Paterson | 20,900 | 33,300 | 99 | 128 | 17,241 | ( 6,657) | 3,181 | (1,228) |
| Clifton | 29,300 | " | 113 | " | 6,986 | ( 2,698) | " | ( " ) |
| Passaic | 25,500 | " | 96 | " | 17,226 | ( 6,652) | " | ( " ) |
| Philadelphia | 13,500 | 17,700 | 89 | 100 | 15,175 | ( 5,860) | 1,357 | ( 524) |
| Hartford | 22,400 | 28,300 | 109 | 119 | 9,081 | ( 3,507) | 989 | ( 382) |
| Baltimore | 11,600 | 18,200 | 94 | 101 | 11,568 | ( 4,462) | 917 | ( 354) |
| New Orleans | 25,200 | 23,300 | 75 | 81 | 3,011 | ( 1,163) | 530 | ( 205) |
| San Francisco | 30,700 | 30,000 | 113 | 133 | 15,764 | ( 6,087) | 1,254 | ( 484) |
| Oakland | 24,900 | " | 110 | " | 6,771 | ( 2,615) | " | ( " ) |
| Pittsburgh | 14,900 | 17,100 | 94 | 85 | 9,422 | ( 3,638) | 788 | ( 304) |
| St. Louis | 14,200 | 18,700 | 74 | 88 | 10,167 | ( 3,926) | 574 | ( 222) |
| Cleveland | 17,400 | 25,600 | 81 | 105 | 9,893 | ( 3,820) | 1,359 | ( 525) |
| Chicago | 22,800 | 27,600 | 113 | 121 | 15,136 | ( 5,845) | 1,876 | ( 724) |
| Detroit | 16,100 | 22,500 | 86 | 107 | 10,968 | ( 4,235) | 2,154 | ( 832) |
| Minneapolis | 19,600 | 24,000 | 108 | 121 | 7,884 | ( 3,044) | 861 | ( 332) |
| St. Paul | 20,500 | " | 101 | " | 5,933 | ( 2,291) | " | ( " ) |
| Seattle | 22,700 | 24,500 | 109 | 115 | 6,350 | ( 2,452) | 337 | ( 130) |
| Everett | 19,700 | " | 100 | " | 1,830 | ( 707) | " | ( " ) |
| Dallas | 20,700 | 19,900 | 119 | 116 | 3,179 | ( 1,228) | 341 | ( 132) |
| Fort Worth | 14,400 | 15,700 | 96 | 103 | 1,919 | ( 741) | 474 | ( 183) |
| Houston | 18,300 | 18,000 | 107 | 105 | 2,841 | ( 1,097) | 316 | ( 122) |
| Los Angeles | 30,500 | 28,200 | 116 | 118 | 6,060 | ( 2,340) | 1,730 | ( 668) |
| Long Beach | 25,900 | " | 107 | " | 7,369 | ( 2,845) | " | ( " ) |
| Miami | 18,800 | 22,700 | 106 | 132 | 9,763 | ( 3,770) | 621 | ( 240) |
| Atlanta | 21,600 | 23,300 | 91 | 107 | 3,783 | ( 1,461) | 805 | ( 311) |
| Washington, D.C. | 26,700 | 30,700 | 121 | 131 | 12,321 | ( 4,758) | 1,217 | ( 470) |

| Area | Median Age City | SMSA | Percentage over 64 City | SMSA | Sex Ratio City | SMSA | Percentage Negro City | SMSA | Percentage Spanish-American City | SMSA |
|---|---|---|---|---|---|---|---|---|---|---|
| Boston | 28 | 29 | 12.8 | 11.3 | 85 | 90 | 16.3 | 4.6 | 2.8 | 1.3 |
| New York | 32 | 32 | 12.1 | 10.9 | 88 | 90 | 21.1 | 16.3 | 16.2 | 12.0 |
| Jersey City | 31 | 33 | 11.3 | 11.4 | 90 | 91 | 11.3 | 10.1 | 9.1 | 14.7 |
| Newark | 26 | 31 | 8.0 | 9.9 | 90 | 91 | 8.0 | 18.8 | 12.0 | 4.7 |
| Paterson | 29 | 32 | 11.3 | 9.7 | 90 | 92 | 11.3 | 5.5 | 12.5 | 3.9 |
| Clifton | 38 | " | 11.8 | " | 90 | " | 11.8 | " | 1.5 | " |
| Passaic | 33 | " | 12.4 | " | 90 | " | 12.4 | " | 17.9 | " |
| Philadelphia | 27 | 29 | 7.8 | 9.7 | 99 | 93 | 7.8 | 17.5 | 2.3 | 1.7 |
| Hartford | 28 | 29 | 11.1 | 9.3 | 89 | 93 | 11.1 | 7.6 | 7.6 | 2.4 |
| Baltimore | 29 | 28 | 10.6 | 8.4 | 90 | 95 | 10.6 | 23.7 | 1.0 | 1.0 |
| New Orleans | 28 | 26 | 10.7 | 8.4 | 87 | 91 | 10.7 | 31.0 | 4.4 | 4.2 |
| San Francisco | 34 | 30 | 14.0 | 9.6 | 93 | 97 | 14.0 | 10.6 | 14.2 | 11.7 |
| Oakland | 32 | " | 13.3 | " | 92 | " | 13.3 | " | 9.8 | " |
| Pittsburgh | 34 | 32 | 13.5 | 10.7 | 87 | 92 | 13.5 | 7.1 | 0.5 | 0.4 |
| St. Louis | 32 | 27 | 14.7 | 10.6 | 84 | 91 | 14.7 | 16.0 | 1.0 | 1.0 |
| Cleveland | 29 | 29 | 10.6 | 9.2 | 90 | 92 | 10.6 | 16.1 | 1.9 | 1.0 |
| Chicago | 30 | 28 | 10.6 | 8.9 | 91 | 94 | 10.6 | 17.6 | 7.4 | 4.7 |
| Detroit | 29 | 27 | 11.5 | 8.1 | 92 | 95 | 11.5 | 18.0 | 1.8 | 1.3 |
| Minneapolis | 29 | 26 | 15.0 | 8.7 | 84 | 93 | 15.0 | 1.8 | 0.9 | 0.9 |
| St. Paul | 28 | " | 13.8 | " | 88 | " | 13.8 | " | 2.1 | " |
| Seattle | 32 | 28 | 13.1 | 8.5 | 92 | 96 | 13.1 | 7.1 | 2.0 | 1.7 |
| Everett | 29 | " | 11.9 | " | 94 | " | 11.9 | " | 0.1 | " |
| Dallas | 27 | 26 | 7.9 | 7.2 | 91 | 93 | 7.9 | 15.9 | 8.0 | 6.5 |
| Fort Worth | 28 | 27 | 9.6 | 7.6 | 93 | 96 | 9.6 | 10.8 | 8.5 | 5.8 |
| Houston | 27 | 26 | 6.4 | 6.1 | 94 | 97 | 6.4 | 19.3 | 12.2 | 10.7 |
| Los Angeles | 30 | 29 | 10.1 | 9.3 | 93 | 94 | 10.1 | 10.8 | 18.4 | 18.3 |
| Long Beach | 33 | " | 14.1 | " | 95 | " | 14.1 | " | 7.2 | " |
| Miami | 37 | 34 | 14.5 | 13.7 | 88 | 90 | 14.5 | 15.0 | 45.3 | 23.6 |
| Atlanta | 27 | 26 | 9.2 | 6.5 | 88 | 93 | 9.2 | 22.3 | 1.0 | 1.0 |
| Washington, D.C. | 28 | 26 | 9.4 | 6.0 | 87 | 94 | 9.4 | 24.6 | 2.1 | 2.5 |

*Appendix B: Data Tables for Part II*

| Area | American Indians City | SMSA | Japanese-Americans City | SMSA | Chinese-Americans City | SMSA | Mexican-Born City | SMSA |
|---|---|---|---|---|---|---|---|---|
| Boston | 1,047 | 2,132 | 645 | 2,593 | 7,007 | 12,025 | 157 | 540 |
| New York | 9,930 | 12,160 | 13,968 | 17,066 | 69,324 | 76,208 | 3,541 | 4,243 |
| Jersey City | 255 | 483 | 72 | 370 | 324 | 815 | 58 | 216 |
| Newark | 507 | 1,214 | 128 | 901 | 642 | 3,084 | 112 | 340 |
| Paterson | 192 | 655 | 43 | 1,396 | 157 | 1,807 | 17 | 233 |
| Clifton | 13 | " | 39 | " | 64 | " | 0 | " |
| Passaic | 57 | " | 45 | " | 78 | " | 0 | " |
| Philadelphia | 1,961 | 3,631 | 1,199 | 3,358 | 2,874 | 4,882 | 126 | 431 |
| Hartford | 241 | 432 | 100 | 329 | 135 | 364 | 11 | 56 |
| Baltimore | 1,740 | 2,553 | 394 | 1,252 | 1,071 | 2,000 | 106 | 164 |
| New Orleans | 463 | 885 | 292 | 481 | 513 | 774 | 595 | 824 |
| San Francisco | 2,900 | 12,011 | 11,705 | 32,463 | 58,696 | 88,108 | 8,022 | 25,831 |
| Oakland | 2,890 | " | 2,405 | " | 11,355 | " | 3,977 | " |
| Pittsburgh | 333 | 847 | 352 | 1,028 | 806 | 1,627 | 115 | 414 |
| St. Louis | 675 | 1,931 | 359 | 1,442 | 511 | 1,578 | 481 | 1,074 |
| Cleveland | 1,183 | 1,750 | 534 | 1,810 | 740 | 1,621 | 221 | 423 |
| Chicago | 6,575 | 8,996 | 10,833 | 15,292 | 9,357 | 12,653 | 38,771 | 47,397 |
| Detroit | 2,914 | 5,683 | 982 | 2,720 | 1,966 | 3,889 | 2,914 | 4,031 |
| Minneapolis | 5,829 | 9,582 | 686 | 1,965 | 855 | 1,985 | 167 | 723 |
| St. Paul | 1,906 | " | 241 | " | 273 | " | 365 | " |
| Seattle | 4,123 | 9,496 | 9,986 | 13,872 | 6,621 | 7,434 | 342 | 479 |
| Everett | 521 | " | 69 | " | 32 | " | 0 | " |
| Dallas | 3,437 | 5,022 | 572 | 868 | 525 | 863 | 5,504 | 6,723 |
| Fort Worth | 863 | 1,610 | 205 | 373 | 145 | 245 | 2,805 | 3,127 |
| Houston | 2,403 | 3,215 | 975 | 1,350 | 3,047 | 3,708 | 14,241 | 17,787 |
| Los Angeles | 9,172 | 24,509 | 54,878 | 104,078 | 27,345 | 40,978 | 104,045 | 206,831 |
| Long Beach | 1,172 | " | 3,223 | " | 712 | 1,852 | " | 3,507 |
| Miami | 286 | 1,085 | 188 | 809 | 626 | 1,271 | 367 | 960 |
| Atlanta | 365 | 893 | 163 | 578 | 369 | 697 | 43 | 118 |
| Washington, D.C. | 956 | 3,300 | 651 | 4,662 | 2,582 | 8,298 | 246 | 948 |

| Area | Mexican Parentage City | SMSA | Canadian-Born City | SMSA | Canadian Parentage City | SMSA | Irish-Born City | SMSA |
|---|---|---|---|---|---|---|---|---|
| Boston | 172 | 682 | 10,772 | 58,896 | 25,561 | 156,513 | 12,362 | 25,957 |
| New York | 4,352 | 5,629 | 20,545 | 32,675 | 30,019 | 59,798 | 68,778 | 84,442 |
| Jersey City | 39 | 216 | 386 | 927 | 804 | 1,943 | 1,772 | 3,320 |
| Newark | 88 | 588 | 467 | 5,179 | 436 | 10,502 | 860 | 5,652 |
| Paterson | 15 | 424 | 162 | 4,049 | 335 | 8,371 | 189 | 4,454 |
| Clifton | 12 | " | 132 | " | 433 | " | 198 | " |
| Passaic | 0 | " | 96 | " | 153 | " | 48 | " |
| Philadelphia | 343 | 1,529 | 2,387 | 8,359 | 4,797 | 19,969 | 6,060 | 11,998 |
| Hartford | 12 | 139 | 3,996 | 9,928 | 5,854 | 26,499 | 1,261 | 2,863 |
| Baltimore | 238 | 608 | 813 | 2,384 | 1,732 | 6,706 | 433 | 1,197 |
| New Orleans | 919 | 1,525 | 337 | 666 | 1,170 | 1,997 | 164 | 293 |
| San Francisco | 10,497 | 44,388 | 4,484 | 22,213 | 7,595 | 43,435 | 4,420 | 7,209 |
| Oakland | 5,514 | " | 1,960 | " | 3,843 | " | 544 | 2,555 |
| Pittsburgh | 225 | 1,087 | 579 | 2,550 | 1,244 | 6,644 | 1,125 | 2,346 |
| St. Louis | 647 | 2,540 | 251 | 2,076 | 948 | 6,307 | 498 | 1,158 |
| Cleveland | 550 | 1,084 | 1,385 | 6,146 | 3,213 | 14,726 | 1,370 | 3,076 |
| Chicago | 43,326 | 60,255 | 7,005 | 18,092 | 15,123 | 46,303 | 13,766 | 18,832 |
| Detroit | 5,488 | 10,013 | 22,031 | 68,357 | 36,613 | 152,626 | 1,600 | 3,301 |
| Minneapolis | 498 | 2,807 | 1,564 | 5,952 | 6,781 | 24,550 | 140 | 705 |
| St. Paul | 1,401 | " | 1,075 | " | 4,347 | " | 358 | " |
| Seattle | 854 | 2,113 | 8,521 | 19,446 | 19,187 | 50.794 | 517 | 966 |
| Everett | 75 | " | 765 | " | 2,150 | " | 23 | " |
| Dallas | 14,223 | 19,342 | 1,053 | 1,749 | 2,670 | 4,458 | 146 | 191 |
| Fort Worth | 7,819 | 9,212 | 279 | 607 | 1,069 | 2,234 | 74 | 80 |
| Houston | 34,113 | 47,156 | 1,751 | 2,610 | 3,823 | 6,003 | 372 | 399 |
| Los Angeles | 118,648 | 302,511 | 27,282 | 67,807 | 38,126 | 106,922 | 3,052 | 7,260 |
| Long Beach | 3,507 | " | 3,506 | " | 6,914 | " | 480 | " |
| Miami | 184 | 1,575 | 1,632 | 8,273 | 1,845 | 11,203 | 242 | 1,020 |
| Atlanta | 196 | 458 | 372 | 1,260 | 798 | 3,827 | 79 | 273 |
| Washington, D.C. | 365 | 2,378 | 1,087 | 6,263 | 2,827 | 18,823 | 506 | 1,816 |

*Appendix B: Data Tables for Part II*

| Area | Irish Parentage City | Irish Parentage SMSA | German-Born City | German-Born SMSA | German Parentage City | German Parentage SMSA | Polish-Born City | Polish-Born SMSA |
|---|---|---|---|---|---|---|---|---|
| Boston | 39,354 | 121,367 | 1,944 | 7,752 | 3,818 | 17,445 | 3,319 | 8,999 |
| New York | 151,844 | 572,778 | 98,336 | 140,970 | 111,704 | 203,782 | 119,604 | 137,407 |
| Jersey City | 8,128 | 15,831 | 1,425 | 5,111 | 4,301 | 12,498 | 3,318 | 7,084 |
| Newark | 3,277 | 38,660 | 961 | 18,033 | 2,470 | 37,282 | 1,800 | 13,599 |
| Paterson | 1,132 | 23,617 | 935 | 18,352 | 1,579 | 37,398 | 1,573 | 12,713 |
| Clifton | 1,017 | ″ | 1,182 | ″ | 2,065 | ″ | 1,556 | ″ |
| Passaic | 297 | ″ | 428 | ″ | 679 | ″ | 2,500 | ″ |
| Philadelphia | 32,492 | 71,795 | 10,849 | 26,255 | 26,604 | 73,821 | 11,116 | 17,322 |
| Hartford | 2,996 | 13,172 | 604 | 3,361 | 1,007 | 8,600 | 2,641 | 6,033 |
| Baltimore | 3,334 | 7,724 | 2,607 | 7,636 | 11,871 | 29,015 | 2,969 | 4,631 |
| New Orleans | 1,046 | 1,576 | 660 | 1,307 | 3,310 | 5,497 | 372 | 482 |
| San Francisco | 12,270 | 28,535 | 8,041 | 23,711 | 11,569 | 46,404 | 1,848 | 4,693 |
| Oakland | 2,555 | ″ | 2,098 | ″ | 4,652 | ″ | 526 | ″ |
| Pittsburgh | 6,633 | 20,859 | 2,180 | 7,126 | 13,271 | 46,300 | 3,363 | 9,717 |
| St. Louis | 3,462 | 9,901 | 2,267 | 7,800 | 15,368 | 47,293 | 739 | 2,544 |
| Cleveland | 4,803 | 13,669 | 4,076 | 12,391 | 12,279 | 40,740 | 6,234 | 13,305 |
| Chicago | 42,646 | 72,682 | 31,430 | 58,080 | 67,983 | 166,507 | 55,711 | 69,426 |
| Detroit | 5,299 | 14,920 | 7,065 | 20,076 | 23,118 | 68,871 | 17,268 | 33,705 |
| Minneapolis | 1,645 | 6,876 | 1,508 | 5,724 | 10,839 | 42,707 | 1,080 | 2,703 |
| St. Paul | 2,676 | ″ | 1,333 | ″ | 11,217 | ″ | 770 | ″ |
| Seattle | 3,194 | 5,954 | 2,775 | 6,604 | 8,934 | 21,058 | 672 | 977 |
| Everett | 182 | ″ | 234 | ″ | 878 | ″ | 32 | ″ |
| Dallas | 1,058 | 1,648 | 1,649 | 2,574 | 408 | 7,749 | 426 | 549 |
| Fort Worth | 615 | 894 | 449 | 861 | 1,896 | 3,663 | 107 | 123 |
| Houston | 1,536 | 2,041 | 2,279 | 3,467 | 8,455 | 14,157 | 779 | 941 |
| Los Angeles | 11,076 | 28,177 | 18,436 | 40,802 | 33,263 | 88,634 | 14,419 | 20,912 |
| Long Beach | 1,898 | ″ | 1,563 | ″ | 5,826 | ″ | 449 | ″ |
| Miami | 1,143 | 5,500 | 1,274 | 6,557 | 2,236 | 12,934 | 1,289 | 10,275 |
| Atlanta | 666 | 1,568 | 535 | 2,065 | 1,362 | 5,100 | 224 | 478 |
| Washington, D.C. | 3,047 | 11,825 | 1,809 | 12,825 | 3,833 | 25,227 | 795 | 3,172 |

| Area | Polish Parentage City | Polish Parentage SMSA | Russian-Born City | Russian-Born SMSA | Russian Parentage City | Russian Parentage SMSA | Italian-Born City | Italian-Born SMSA |
|---|---|---|---|---|---|---|---|---|
| Boston | 5,688 | 26,817 | 6,012 | 17,525 | 10,776 | 59,441 | 14,990 | 48,969 |
| New York | 172,715 | 248,224 | 117,363 | 132,620 | 276,555 | 380,153 | 212,160 | 279,874 |
| Jersey City | 7,887 | 20,249 | 1,054 | 2,544 | 2,769 | 6,950 | 7,089 | 20,804 |
| Newark | 4,415 | 42,334 | 1,653 | 10,170 | 2,187 | 34,951 | 8,049 | 32,312 |
| Paterson | 1,932 | 38,504 | 1,209 | 6,637 | 1,715 | 25,970 | 6,990 | 32,583 |
| Clifton | 4,873 | ″ | 879 | ″ | 2,209 | ″ | 2,035 | ″ |
| Passaic | 3,252 | ″ | 1,069 | ″ | 2,033 | ″ | 1,149 | ″ |
| Philadelphia | 15,526 | 70,491 | 23,349 | 29,902 | 55,450 | 90,551 | 25,629 | 47,277 |
| Hartford | 3,058 | 18,095 | 1,365 | 3,036 | 1,567 | 9,662 | 5,092 | 11,307 |
| Baltimore | 11,169 | 22,977 | 3,369 | 5,355 | 9,375 | 21,542 | 3,331 | 5,921 |
| New Orleans | 860 | 1,215 | 301 | 369 | 1,278 | 1,756 | 1,189 | 1,871 |
| San Francisco | 3,478 | 10,901 | 6,502 | 10,136 | 7,101 | 21,217 | 9,746 | 23,139 |
| Oakland | 810 | ″ | 609 | ″ | 1,781 | ″ | 2,261 | ″ |
| Pittsburgh | 14,081 | 54,556 | 2,563 | 3,886 | 8,614 | 18,350 | 6,968 | 26,581 |
| St. Louis | 2,757 | 10,638 | 490 | 3,206 | 964 | 11,694 | 2,555 | 4,932 |
| Cleveland | 16,585 | 48,180 | 2,383 | 8,510 | 3,172 | 20,200 | 6,057 | 15,158 |
| Chicago | 136,244 | 214,563 | 22,640 | 28,697 | 41,539 | 76,138 | 32,539 | 53,351 |
| Detroit | 50,868 | 125,938 | 6,391 | 13,330 | 9,333 | 34,003 | 11,461 | 27,048 |
| Minneapolis | 4,600 | 13,183 | 1,254 | 3,322 | 2,399 | 10,313 | 242 | 1,146 |
| St. Paul | 2,934 | ″ | 873 | ″ | 2,213 | ″ | 490 | ″ |
| Seattle | 1,741 | 3,363 | 1,269 | 1,709 | 3,156 | 7,197 | 1,501 | 2,317 |
| Everett | 58 | ″ | 8 | ″ | 165 | ″ | 17 | ″ |
| Dallas | 1,644 | 2,149 | 492 | 558 | 2,239 | 3,016 | 299 | 423 |
| Fort Worth | 537 | 838 | 103 | 129 | 541 | 796 | 114 | 146 |
| Houston | 3,034 | 4,117 | 730 | 868 | 3,357 | 3,984 | 931 | 1,061 |
| Los Angeles | 27,241 | 47,376 | 22,661 | 32,583 | 62,829 | 96,110 | 12,149 | 26,344 |
| Long Beach | 1,618 | ″ | 593 | ″ | 2,223 | ″ | 689 | ″ |
| Miami | 1,720 | 13,720 | 1,447 | 20,038 | 3,377 | 36,057 | 1,388 | 5,419 |
| Atlanta | 640 | 1,912 | 312 | 564 | 1,435 | 3,160 | 159 | 419 |
| Washington, D.C. | 1,992 | 14,476 | 1,460 | 4,929 | 4,137 | 23,975 | 1,650 | 6,188 |

*Appendix B: Data Tables for Part II*

| Area | Italian Parentage City | Italian Parentage SMSA | Persons per Household City | Persons per Household SMSA | Percentage Female Headship City | Percentage Female Headship SMSA | Percentage Blue-Collar City | Percentage Blue-Collar SMSA | Percentage Service City | Percentage Service SMSA |
|---|---|---|---|---|---|---|---|---|---|---|
| Boston | 29,985 | 143,380 | 2.8 | 3.1 | 22.6 | 13.5 | 12.7 | 11.7 | 36.0 | 32.1 |
| New York | 470,453 | 724,897 | 2.9 | 2.9 | 17.3 | 14.5 | 12.7 | 11.7 | 31.9 | 31.9 |
| Jersey City | 17,961 | 47,473 | 2.9 | 2.9 | 18.8 | 15.7 | 20.4 | 22.9 | 35.1 | 33.4 |
| Newark | 19,210 | 107,055 | 3.1 | 3.1 | 27.2 | 13.1 | 30.2 | 16.9 | 37.2 | 30.9 |
| Paterson | 11,255 | 104,848 | 3.0 | 3.2 | 19.3 | 9.4 | 33.4 | 15.3 | 33.5 | 29.7 |
| Clifton | 6,515 | " | 2.9 | " | 9.0 | " | 18.2 | " | 30.3 | " |
| Passaic | 2,263 | " | 2.8 | " | 17.3 | " | 31.1 | " | 31.1 | " |
| Philadelphia | 78,155 | 181,973 | 3.0 | 3.2 | 22.2 | 10.8 | 18.8 | 16.9 | 36.1 | 33.6 |
| Hartford | 5,936 | 27,384 | 2.7 | 3.2 | 19.0 | 13.0 | 20.7 | 14.0 | 35.5 | 30.7 |
| Baltimore | 9,652 | 23,223 | 3.1 | 3.2 | 21.8 | 13.6 | 18.4 | 15.1 | 39.7 | 35.8 |
| New Orleans | 8,850 | 15,904 | 3.0 | 3.2 | 21.6 | 15.9 | 12.2 | 12.2 | 39.4 | 37.8 |
| San Francisco | 19,294 | 65,633 | 2.3 | 2.8 | 16.6 | 12.0 | 9.4 | 10.6 | 35.5 | 33.2 |
| Oakland | 5,214 | " | 2.5 | " | 17.7 | " | 13.2 | " | 35.9 | " |
| Pittsburgh | 18,293 | 93,579 | 2.8 | 3.1 | 18.1 | 11.0 | 13.3 | 16.5 | 39.9 | 36.8 |
| St. Louis | 6,488 | 19,219 | 2.8 | 3.2 | 21.3 | 11.5 | 20.4 | 15.8 | 39.7 | 35.2 |
| Cleveland | 11,636 | 47,488 | 3.0 | 3.1 | 19.4 | 11.7 | 25.5 | 18.2 | 39.3 | 33.8 |
| Chicago | 65,103 | 143,644 | 2.7 | 3.1 | 17.8 | 12.1 | 19.4 | 16.0 | 34.8 | 33.1 |
| Detroit | 18,915 | 66,008 | 3.0 | 3.3 | 18.1 | 11.2 | 23.8 | 18.8 | 37.1 | 35.5 |
| Minneapolis | 1,153 | 6,193 | 2.6 | 3.2 | 15.7 | 9.4 | 13.8 | 12.8 | 34.7 | 33.0 |
| St. Paul | 2,173 | " | 2.9 | " | 13.7 | " | 13.8 | " | 35.2 | " |
| Seattle | 4,321 | 8,673 | 2.5 | 2.9 | 12.8 | 9.2 | 10.3 | 11.2 | 34.1 | 34.7 |
| Everett | 134 | " | 2.8 | " | 10.8 | " | 16.4 | " | 40.9 | " |
| Dallas | 2,072 | 3,152 | 3.0 | 3.1 | 13.7 | 10.7 | 12.9 | 13.5 | 32.9 | 32.5 |
| Fort Worth | 594 | 1,179 | 3.0 | 3.1 | 12.1 | 9.0 | 16.8 | 16.1 | 34.8 | 33.8 |
| Houston | 5,386 | 7,088 | 3.1 | 3.2 | 12.3 | 10.1 | 12.4 | 13.4 | 35.4 | 35.8 |
| Los Angeles | 33,959 | 85,752 | 2.7 | 2.8 | 16.1 | 13.3 | 14.7 | 15.3 | 30.5 | 31.8 |
| Long Beach | 2,977 | " | 2.4 | " | 13.4 | " | 12.2 | " | 34.9 | " |
| Miami | 2,263 | 15,819 | 2.7 | 2.9 | 17.3 | 12.6 | 21.1 | 14.5 | 40.1 | 36.8 |
| Atlanta | 668 | 2,248 | 3.0 | 3.2 | 21.7 | 12.5 | 14.9 | 11.9 | 37.4 | 32.1 |
| Washington, D.C. | 3,007 | 25,157 | 2.7 | 3.1 | 25.3 | 12.5 | 7.8 | 5.7 | 36.4 | 28.6 |

| Area | Percentage Clerical City | Percentage Clerical SMSA | Percentage Executive City | Percentage Executive SMSA | Income per Capita City | Income per Capita SMSA |
|---|---|---|---|---|---|---|
| Boston | 32.5 | 30.6 | 18.7 | 25.6 | 3,098 | 3,713 |
| New York | 34.4 | 32.9 | 21.0 | 23.4 | 3,735 | 3,921 |
| Jersey City | 31.1 | 29.7 | 13.5 | 14.1 | 3,067 | 3,203 |
| Newark | 22.4 | 28.5 | 10.2 | 23.8 | 2,498 | 3,961 |
| Paterson | 21.9 | 30.2 | 11.2 | 24.9 | 2,881 | 4,214 |
| Clifton | 30.7 | " | 20.8 | " | 4,261 | " |
| Passaic | 23.7 | " | 14.1 | " | 3,231 | " |
| Philadelphia | 29.2 | 28.3 | 15.9 | 21.2 | 3,040 | 3,418 |
| Hartford | 29.5 | 30.6 | 14.3 | 24.7 | 3,112 | 3,926 |
| Baltimore | 26.3 | 27.7 | 15.6 | 21.4 | 2,885 | 3,332 |
| New Orleans | 27.6 | 27.8 | 20.8 | 22.1 | 2,718 | 2,814 |
| San Francisco | 36.1 | 31.2 | 22.0 | 24.9 | 4,289 | 4,121 |
| Oakland | 30.3 | " | 20.6 | " | 3,650 | " |
| Pittsburgh | 28.6 | 26.1 | 18.2 | 20.6 | 3,135 | 3,195 |
| St. Louis | 26.7 | 27.8 | 13.2 | 21.2 | 2,772 | 3,437 |
| Cleveland | 23.9 | 27.5 | 11.3 | 20.6 | 2,848 | 3,674 |
| Chicago | 30.1 | 20.0 | 15.7 | 21.0 | 3,420 | 3,826 |
| Detroit | 25.1 | 25.8 | 14.0 | 19.9 | 3,226 | 3,738 |
| Minneapolis | 29.4 | 31.6 | 19.9 | 24.8 | 3,495 | 3,630 |
| St. Paul | 30.6 | " | 20.5 | " | 3,465 | " |
| Seattle | 31.0 | 28.2 | 24.6 | 26.0 | 4,079 | 3,857 |
| Everett | 24.1 | " | 18.6 | " | 3,396 | " |
| Dallas | 31.7 | 30.5 | 22.5 | 23.5 | 3,736 | 3,553 |
| Fort Worth | 26.9 | 27.2 | 21.4 | 22.8 | 3,269 | 3,298 |
| Houston | 29.1 | 27.2 | 23.1 | 23.6 | 3,394 | 3,313 |
| Los Angeles | 20.0 | 29.0 | 24.8 | 23.9 | 3,976 | 3,883 |
| Long Beach | 29.6 | " | 23.3 | " | 3,983 | " |
| Miami | 25.1 | 28.6 | 13.7 | 20.2 | 2,844 | 3,467 |
| Atlanta | 28.7 | 32.0 | 19.1 | 24.0 | 3,162 | 3,494 |
| Washington, D.C. | 32.1 | 32.6 | 23.6 | 33.0 | 3,859 | 4,273 |

# APPENDIX C

# Technical Notes for Cartographers

# Technical Notes for Cartographers

This atlas is somewhat unusual because it was conceived, designed, and produced by subject-matter specialists rather than by cartographers. Although we have tried throughout to adhere to the canons of cartographic lore, subject-matter considerations and cartographic orthodoxy were not always compatible. Accordingly, this appendix presents a brief summary of our rationale for selecting the scales, format, cartographic techniques, and production methods used in the atlas.

## TARGET AUDIENCE

As preliminary plans for the atlas proceeded, two overriding design considerations emerged. First, the atlas was to be a teaching and reference tool that would inform its readers about conditions in the nation's most populous metropolitan regions. Second, the primary audience would be nonspecialists as well as colleagues in the geographic and urban affairs professions. The entire Comparative Metropolitan Analysis Project was based on the assumption that the people who would benefit most from the atlas and the project's other publications were the business community, the interested citizens, the public officials, the planning commission staffs, the congressional assistants—in short the people who determine short-run and long-term policies affecting the nation's metropolitan regions as part of their daily work. Such people operate in a knowledge vacuum with regard to comparative geographical information on American cities.

Having decided early that intelligent nongeographers were a major part of our target audience, several constraints followed. The variables selected for mapping had to be easy to understand and interpret and simultaneously illustrative of important policy questions. Much of the target audience has neither the time nor the background to tease out the intricacies inherent in a complex statistical analysis of social, economic, and housing variables for a metropolitan region. By the same token, the cartographic techniques used to portray the simple variables selected had to be readily accessible to people with limited map-reading ability.

## ORIENTATION AND SCALE

Finally, the editor set some additional criteria that affected design and execution. Foremost was the decision that all maps of a given type of region (for example, SMSAs) would be presented at the same scale. Comparing maps of different cities projected at different scales is tricky even for a skilled map reader. Asking nonexperts to do so is unfair. The editor also decided that all maps would be oriented with north at the top of the page, as normally read, and that the largest map would have to fit on a single atlas page.

These orientation and scale criteria governed the trim size of the atlas, and it quickly became clear that the central-city map of Los Angeles-Long Beach was the largest selected for inclusion. The cost of binding books larger than this atlas dictated that the binding edge not exceed 13 inches (33 centimeters). Since Los Angeles-Long Beach would fit the page area at a scale of 1:250,000, that scale was selected for central-city maps. To maximize the number of maps that could be viewed simultaneously, smaller scales were chosen for larger regions. At 1:1,000,000, the Houston Standard Metropolitan Statistical Area (SMSA) just fits on one of the atlas pages. Daily Urban Systems (DUSs) would present few fit problems at scales larger than the 1:2,000,000 selected for them, but at larger scales they would use more space than their subject matter justifies.

## ORGANIZATION

The ideal way to present the information contained in this atlas would be in a three-dimensional matrix in which the rows were places, the columns were variables, and the third dimension of depth contained maps of different scales. In such a format, people interested in places could observe maps across the rows and examine all the variables mapped for a place. People interested in a specific variable and the way it differed in occurrence and intensity from place to place could satisfy their curiosity by looking up and down the columns. Anyone interested in more or less detail regarding a specific variable at a specific place could move in and out along the third dimension to see maps at different geographical scales.

Short of renting a vacant airplane hanger, mounting maps in such a format, and erecting scaffolding that would enable people to move through the three-dimensional "atlas" at will, the ideal cannot be realized in a single bound volume. Having had a more or less conventional, bound atlas in mind from the outset, some compromises were necessary. Part II was designed to serve the interests of those wanting information about specific places. Each chapter brings together over 20 maps of basic socioeconomic variables for each of the metropolitan regions included in the atlas. The comparative section (Part III) makes it possible for people interested in specific topics to see how they vary from place to place. The problem of making maps available at different scales of generalization according to the user's specific needs has, with a few exceptions, not been solved. The scale that seemed most appropriate for each variable mapped was selected and the map is presented at that scale.

Because we could not present results in a three-dimensional format in which readers could move about, the placement of maps on pages and the relationships of the pages to each other were especially important. On the one hand, it was desirable to have as many maps on two facing pages as possible to maximize the number of topics or cities that could be viewed simultaneously. On the other hand, it was desirable to have a map and its accompanying text close together. The two goals conflict, for space used for text cannot be used for maps, and vice versa.

When push came to shove, text was usually shoved to maximize the

*Appendix C: Technical Notes for Cartographers*

number of maps visible simultaneously. As much as was possible, pages were laid out to make related maps visible at the same time and thereby facilitate the intended comparisons, for the major value of the atlas lies in the comparisons of cities with similar and different histories.

To that end, a sequence was adopted for the organization of the chapters in Part II and the maps in each chapter of Part III. The arrangement of maps reflects an implicit theory of American metropolitan evolution. Boston, New York-Northern New Jersey, Philadelphia, and Hartford are old (17th-century) cities of the nation's traditional eastern core. Baltimore, New Orleans, and San Francisco are major ports that arose during the 19th century. Pittsburgh, St. Louis, Cleveland, Chicago, Detroit, Minneapolis-St. Paul, and Seattle appear next in sequence. They are all inland or coastal locations that grew rapidly during the 19th century as a result of water and rail interconnections with other parts of the nation. The last six places—Dallas-Fort Worth, Houston, Los Angeles, Miami, Atlanta, and Washington, D.C.—are all creatures of the 20th century; the rapid, sustained growth that made them great cities has occurred since 1900.

Places within these subgroups are usually more similar to each other with respect to a particular variable than they are to cities in other subgroups, suggesting that the selection of subgroups based on the ages and locations of places and the arrangement of maps by such subgroups is a reasonable procedure.

## CARTOGRAPHIC TECHNIQUES

The small size at which the maps were to be projected made it impossible to include census tract boundaries on the final maps. Moreover, we felt that census tracts are arbitrary statistical units which should not be reified by retention of their boundaries. Purpose as well as scale dictated that the maps be generalized, for we concluded that the target audience would be more interested in broad patterns than in local details. Taken together, these considerations seemed to make a compelling case for isopleth mapping. Most of the maps in the atlas show patterns by means of shaded isopleths that are in turn based on percentages or other simple calculations.

Tract centroids were "eyeballed" on the basis of tract shape and area, and the interpolations of isolines between centroids (done manually by the chief cartographer) were based on the assumption that changes from place to place were linear. As explained in Chapter 1, isolated high or low values that seemed to be anomalous were often eliminated, and indeed the assumption of linear change was sometimes modified, especially for large, sparsely populated tracts on the peripheries of metropolitan regions, where it is reasonable to assume that most of the tract population resides in the parts of the tract nearest the metropolitan center. Thus a good deal of judgment was involved in the mapping process, both in the interpolation and in the editing of the interpolated maps. Departures from the assumptions of linearity were checked with other sources when possible, and on the whole, the density of control points (tract centroids) on the final maps is such that they are accurate. Overall, we feel that our generalization procedures have struck a reasonable compromise between two indefensible extremes: blind adherence to assumptions known to be inaccurate at the outset and pushing the data about at will to make the maps look as they "ought" to.

Not all variables were appropriate for isopleth mapping. For phenomena that occur erratically or in small numbers we have relied on dot-distribution maps. If American Indians were mapped as percentages of tract populations, for example, little of interest would result because Indians are usually small percentages of tract populations even where they are relatively numerous. Dots give a much more accurate impression of where Indians are located in our large cities.

We had originally hoped to print the atlas in four colors. A different color scheme would have been used for shading the isopleths, for water, and so forth. As the final outlines of the atlas emerged and costs of platemaking and printing were computed, it became obvious that four colors would be too expensive and we would have to make do with two. For the most part, the use of two colors causes no serious problems. We deliberately used five values of orange that are difficult to distinguish from each other at first glance. The isopleth generalization technique assumes continuous variation from high to low statistical values, and the five orange values reinforce the idea of continuous variation. The use of alternating dot and line screens to produce the different values makes it possible for readers interested in detail rather than general impressions to distinguish different values on close examination.

The literature on the meaning and perception of color in cartography is inconclusive. We chose orange because it seemed to us to have the fewest latent connotations. Blue would have made the information printed in black harder to read and it is generally associated with water. Green does not vitiate black as much, but it is associated with vegetation. Red is laden with cultural connotations. Yellow was disagreeable to many people we consulted, in addition to which comparatively few values are distinguishable between zero and 100 percent. The orange selected seemed to strike a balance of legibility, lack of implicit connotation, and tolerance in large doses. Because the same color scheme was to be used throughout the atlas tolerance became an important consideration.

Selection of the five-class breakdown for percentage variables is explained in Chapter 1. The retention of the same color scheme for these five classes throughout the atlas was dictated by the target audience. A single color scheme was used so that once it was learned, it could be relied upon for the entire work.

Most isopleth maps are accompanied by histograms. The fact that area on a map often bears little relation to the number of people occupying it is one of the vexations of mapping human geographical phenomena. The only solution seems to be to transform maps into areal cartograms. These work reasonably well when shapes are maintained and contiguity is forgone, as in Figure 2.4. However, the distortion they would wreak on most metropolitan areas was such that transformations were dismissed from consideration fairly quickly. The inclusion of histograms that provide information on the number of tracts—and therefore the number of people—in each category seemed to be the optimal strategy for preventing readers from equating map area in each category with the number of people in each category.

The project steering committee was consulted frequently during the design stages of the atlas, and the decisions described above were subjects of lengthy weighings of pros and cons and, not infrequently, impassioned oratory. Although a different pair of directors, a different steering committee, and a different chief cartographer might have made somewhat different choices, we are reasonably confident that another group starting with the same objectives would have made similar if not identical decisions.

## PRODUCTION

Producing the atlas required the design and execution of over 1,000 maps and over 750 graphs that were to be spread over some 400 atlas pages. Major economies in production were effected by preparing a number of page modules containing from one to six maps and using them repetitively.

The numerous advances in computer graphics and cartography that have occurred in the last few years were barely on the horizon when the atlas was being planned in 1971 and 1972. The advice the steering committee received from most people was to rely on manual production techniques. Therefore variables selected for mapping were converted to hard copy and then transferred manually to base maps.

## Appendix C: Technical Notes for Cartographers

The atlas relies on 60 base maps, 3 at different scales for each of the 20 cities. Data compilation bases were derived from metropolitan-area tract maps and minor civil division maps that accompany printed census reports. In addition, 60 separate political boundary overlays and another 60 overlays showing water features and highways were prepared. Bases and overlays were drafted at four or five times final production scale.

Isoline and dot-distribution overlays were interpolated by the chief cartographer and his assistants. Because the atlas compares patterns among the 20 metropolitan areas, standard isopleth and dot values were used throughout. The extreme values of most topics mapped with isopleths were of greatest interest, and since these topics are normally mapped in percentages, isopleths were interpolated at 10, 30, 70, and 90 percent. Dot values of one dot for 50 people on ethnic group maps and one dot for 10 dwellings on housing-condition maps were established. The histograms accompanying isopleth maps were drafted at five times final production scale.

The edited overlays were reduced to final production size, as were the boundary and location cue overlays. Atlas pages were then scribed as single units, with pages containing from one to six maps and their related histograms. Isopleths were scribed on one overlay, and the photographically reduced histogram negatives were stripped into the same overlay. Because political boundaries, water features, and highways were invariant from base to base, those overlays were composed photographically at a considerable saving in cartographic time.

Color separations were produced by double exposure of Keuffel & Esser photosensitive peelcoats through the isopleth/histogram and political-boundary overlays. Orange prints in five values (10, 20, 40, 60, and 100 percent), and black prints in two values (10 and 100 percent). Thus five-color separation negatives were made for the five orange values and one separation was made for water features, which print 10 percent black. A separate lettering overlay was prepared using stick-up typography.

The negative for the 100 percent black areas was compiled by multiple contact exposure of the lettering negative, the data/histogram negative, the political-boundary negative, and the location-cue negative to duplicating film. The usual products delivered to the printer thus consisted of seven negatives, five for production of the orange plate negative and two for exposure to the black plate negative. Pages containing one or more dot maps were produced in much the same way, except that a separate dot negative was prepared. Pages with isopleth maps and dot maps in both colors thus required nine exposures, whereas pages with black dots required but three exposures.

The 30 percent black used to show nonresidential areas on the central-city population density map at the beginning of each chapter (except Dallas-Fort Worth) in Part II was produced by making a separate negative for exposure with a 30 percent screen on the black negative for pages containing such maps. An identical positive was used as a holdout on the orange plate negative for these pages, so that only the 30 percent black printed.

The printer prepared color proofs of each page, which provided the final check for errors before platemaking. All scribing films, photographic films, and peelcoats used in production were of 0.0075 inch (0.19 mm.) thickness and were punched for pin registration. Thus the negatives supplied to the printer were in almost perfect register.

Many production economies were realized because only the data overlays and histograms varied over the 60 standard base maps. The comparative nature of the work imposed certain constraints, but they were offset by the benefits of frequent repetition of bases and standardization of symbols.

# GLOSSARY and INDEX/GAZETTEER

# Glossary

Most of the terms and definitions in the glossary are adapted or taken from the U.S. Bureau of the Census's *1970 Census Users' Guide* published by the U.S. Government Printing Office in 1970, since the 1970 Censuses of Population and Housing are the major data sources used in the atlas. Terms are generally listed as they appear in the body of the atlas. Thus *Median Age* is defined under *M* not *A*.

*Age.* Usually determined in completed years as of the time of enumeration from replies to a question on the month and year of birth.

*Age, Median.* See *Median Age*.

*American, Canadian-, German-, Irish-, Italian-, Mexican-, Polish-,* or *Russian-.* See *Canadian-American, German-American, etc.* See also, *Foreign Stock*.

*American, Chinese-* or *Japanese-.* See *Race*.

*American Indian.* See *Race*.

*Area, Metropolitan, Standard Metropolitan Statistical, Urban, Urbanized.* See *Metropolitan Area, Standard Metropolitan Statistical Area, Urban Area, Urbanized Area*.

*Automobile Availability.* Occupied units are classified as having an automobile available if someone in the household owns or has the regular use of an automobile, including company cars regularly kept at home.

*Barrio.* A district or neighborhood of a city or town in Spanish-speaking nations. The Spanish-speaking neighborhoods of American cities in the Southwest.

*Black.* See *Race*.

*Blue-Collar Worker.* Defined here as laborers and operatives.

*Canadian-American.* A person of Canadian birth or parentage. See *Foreign Stock*.

*CBD.* See *Central Business District*.

*Census County Division.* In 21 states for which *Minor Civil Divisions* are not suitable for presenting statistics, the Census Bureau has established relatively permanent statistical units designated Census County Divisions.

*Census Tract.* Small, relatively permanent areas into which large cities and adjacent areas are divided for purposes of providing comparable small-area statistics. The average tract has about 4,000 residents.

*Central Business District* (abbreviation: *CBD*). Usually the downtown retail trade area of a city.

*Central City.* The largest city in a Standard Metropolitan Statistical Area is always a central city. One or more additional cities may also be central cities.

*Chinese-American.* See *Race*.

*Clerical Worker.* Defined here as wholesale and retail trade workers, bookkeepers, secretaries, and other clerical workers.

*Code, ZIP.* See *ZIP Code*.

*College.* Defined here as junior or community colleges, regular 4-year colleges, and graduate or professional schools.

*Consumer Price Index.* An annual or monthly number series reporting in ratios of base-year retail prices the changes in the cost of living of a person or group of persons purchasing an identical set of consumer goods and services.

*Contract Rent.* The monthly dollar rent agreed upon for occupied units or asked for vacant units regardless of any furnishings, utilities, or services that are included. See also *Gross Rent*.

*County.* The primary political divisions of the states, except in Louisiana, where such divisions are called parishes, and in Alaska, where 29 census divisions are used as county equivalents, and in Connecticut and Rhode Island, where counties have no legal existence; villages, towns, and cities are the primary divisions of these two states. A number of cities (for example, Baltimore, St. Louis, Philadelphia, San Francisco, and New Orleans) are independent of any county and thereby constitute primary divisions within the states.

*Daily Urban System* (abbreviation: *DUS*). The central employment core of a metropolitan area and the surrounding counties that have at least 5 percent of their resident labor forces working in the employment core. The employment core consists of the county or counties in which the central city or cities are located. In metropolitan regions wholly or partially in the New England states (Connecticut, Maine, Massachusetts, New Hampshire, and Rhode Island), the central employment cores were defined for the atlas by the Census Bureau through the courtesy of Mr. Richard Forstall. They usually consist of the central city and the political units contiguous to it. New England Daily Urban Systems are defined on the basis of townships rather than counties. Thus each township that has at least 5 percent of its resident labor force working in the central employment core is included in that core city's Daily Urban System.

*Density, Population.* See *Population Density*.

*District, Central Business.* See *Central Business District*.

*Division, Census County* or *Minor Civil.* See *Census County Division* and *Minor Civil Division*.

*DUS.* See *Daily Urban System*.

*Employment Core.* The county or counties in which the central city or cities of a Daily Urban System are located. In Daily Urban Systems wholly or partially in the New England states (Connecticut, Maine, Massachusetts, New Hampshire, and Rhode Island), the central employment cores were defined for the atlas by the Census Bureau through the courtesy of Mr. Richard Forstall. They usually consist of the central city and the political units contiguous to it. New England Daily Urban Systems are defined on the basis of townships rather than counties. Thus each township that has at least 5 percent of its resident labor force working in the central employment core is included in that core's Daily Urban System.

*Executives.* Defined here as engineers, teachers, professionals, managers, proprietors, and administrators.

*Family.* Two or more people living in the same household who are related by blood, marriage, or adoption.

*Family Head.* A household head living with one or more persons related to him or her by blood, marriage, or adoption.

*Female Headship.* Households in which the head was reported to be a female. Because of the way the Census Bureau determines headship (see *Household Head*) a household headed by a female is by definition one in which a husband is absent.

*Foreign-Born Population.* Persons born outside the United States who were not United States citizens at the time of birth by virtue of the citizenship of their parent(s).

*Foreign Parentage.* United States natives, one or both of whose parents are foreign-born.

*Foreign Stock.* The native population of foreign parentage plus the foreign-born population. Foreign stock is classified by country of origin.

*German-American.* A person of German birth or parentage. See *Foreign Stock.*

*Gross Rent.* The *Contract Rent* plus the average cost of utilities (water, electricity, gas) and fuels, to the extent that they are paid for by the renter or by a relative, welfare agency, or friend.

*Group Quarters.* All persons who are not members of households are counted as living in group quarters. Quarters occupied by 5 or more persons unrelated to the head of the household or by 6 or more unrelated persons are also called group quarters.

*Head, Household* or *Family.* See *Household Head* or *Family Head.*

*Hispanics.* See *Spanish-Americans.*

*Household.* All persons occupying a single housing unit are referred to as a household unless they are designated as living in group quarters. See *Group Quarters.*

*Household Head.* One person in each household is designated as the head, that is, the person who was reported as the head by the members of the household. However, if a married woman living with her husband was reported as the head, her husband is considered as head for the purpose of simplifying tabulations.

*Housing, Single-Family (Unit), Single-Unit Attached,* and *Single-Unit Detached.* See *Single-Family Housing (Unit), Single-Unit Attached Housing,* and *Single-Unit Detached Housing.*

*Housing Units.* All living quarters located in a statistical unit, including both occupied and vacant housing. Used interchangeably with *Housing Inventory* and *Housing Stock.* A housing unit exists when the occupants of apartments, groups of rooms, or single rooms live and eat separately from any other persons in the structure and there is either direct access to the unit from outside or through a common hall or complete kitchen facilities for the occupants' exclusive use.

*Housing Units, Vacant or Occupied.* See *Occupied Housing Unit* and *Vacant Housing Unit.*

*Housing Value.* The respondent's estimate of how much the property would sell for on the current market or, for vacant units, the asking price at the time of enumeration. Value was requested only for single-family houses (detached or attached) that were owner-occupied or vacant for sale and that were situated on properties of fewer than ten acres (4.05 hectares).

*Immature Birth.* A live birth in which the infant weighs 2,500 grams (5.5 pounds) or less at birth.

*Income.* Requested from all persons 14 years of age or older for the preceding calendar year, even if they had no income. Income for a statistical unit is the sum of the dollar amounts respondents reported receiving.

*Income Deficit.* The difference between the aggregate income of the poverty population and the aggregate poverty level for the identical population in a given statistical unit. The amount of money that would have to be added to the incomes of the poverty population to eliminate officially defined poverty within the statistical unit.

*Income per Capita.* Calculated by dividing the aggregate income of all persons in a statistical unit by the number of people in the unit.

*Incorporated Place.* Political units incorporated as cities, boroughs, villages, or towns (except in New England, New York, and Wisconsin).

*Indian, American.* See *Race.*

*Individual, Primary* or *Unrelated.* See *Primary Individual* or *Unrelated Individual.*

*Infant Mortality.* Death of a child within the first year after live birth. Usually expressed as a rate per 1,000 or 10,000 live births.

*Institutionalized Population.* Residents of mental hospitals, homes for the aged, and inmates of institutions such as prisons.

*Inventory, Housing.* See *Housing Units.*

*Irish-American.* A person of Irish birth or parentage. See *Foreign Stock.*

*Italian-American.* A person of Italian birth or parentage. See *Foreign stock.*

*Japanese-American.* See *Race.*

*Labor Force.* Employed persons, people unemployed but seeking work, and members of the armed forces.

*Land, Made.* See *Made Land.*

*Land Use.* The dominant use (residential, industrial/commercial/transportation, or open space/agricultural) to which parcels of land are devoted.

*Made Land.* Land created by filling bays or rivers.

*MCD.* See *Minor Civil Division.*

*Median Age.* The age that divides a population into two equal parts, one-half below that age, the other above.

*Megalopolis.* Literally, "great city." The term used by the geographer Jean Gottmann *(Megalopolis: The Urbanized Northeastern Seaboard of the United States.* Cambridge: MIT Press, 1961, p. 4) to refer to the coalescing fabric of metropolitan areas stretching from Boston, Massachusetts, to Washington, D.C. It distinguished such linked collections of cities from single metropolitan (literally, "mother city") areas. The term was first used by a group of ancient Greeks planning a new city-state in the Peloponnesus, who hoped their new city would become the largest in Greece. It did not.

*Metropolitan Area.* A city and its surrounding territory, without further specific definition or precise delimitation in terms of political boundaries. Used interchangeably with *Metropolitan Region, Urban Area,* and *Urban Region.* It is not synonymous with *Standard Metropolitan Statistical Area.*

*Metropolitan Network.* The reciprocal connections of the national and international systems of cities for business, social, and political purposes as measured by flows of goods, people, and information.

*Metropolitan Region.* A city and its surrounding territory, without further specific definition or precise delimitation in terms of political boundaries. Used interchangeably with *Metropolitan Area, Urban Area,* and *Urban Region.*

*Metropolitan System.* See *Metropolitan Network.*

*Mexican-American.* A person of Mexican birth or parentage. See *Foreign Stock.*

*Minor Civil Division* (abbreviation: *MCD).* The primary political and administrative subdivisions of counties or parishes. May be villages, towns, cities, boroughs, etc.

*Mobile Home.* A trailer or similar unit movable from place to place even if it is resting on a temporary or permanent foundation.

*Glossary*

*Mortality, Infant* or *Neonatal.* See *Infant Mortality, Neonatal Mortality.*

*Municipality.* All active governmental units officially designated cities, boroughs, villages, or towns (except in New England, New York, and Wisconsin). Municipalities generally correspond to the incorporated places recognized in the Population and Housing Censuses.

*Native Parentage.* Native persons, both of whose parents are also natives of the United States.

*Native Population.* Persons born in the United States, Puerto Rico, or a possession of the United States. Also persons who, although they were born in a foreign country or at sea, have at least one native-American parent.

*Negro.* See *Race.*

*Neonatal Mortality.* Death of a child within the first 30 days after live birth. Usually expressed as a rate per 1,000 or 10,000 live births.

*Network, Metropolitan.* See *Metropolitan Network.*

*Occupation.* Employed persons reported the occupation at which they worked the most hours during the week preceding the Census. The unemployed reported their last occupation.

*Occupied Housing Unit.* A unit is considered occupied if it is the usual residence of the person(s) living in it at the time of enumeration.

*Onsite Sewage Disposal.* See *Private (Individual) Sewage Disposal.*

*Overbounded.* A city, Standard Metropolitan Statistical Area, or other politically defined unit is said to be overbounded if its political boundaries extend well beyond the places and areas that are closely linked to the urban area's nucleus.

*Owner-Occupied Housing.* A housing unit is classified as owner-occupied if the respondent living in the unit reports that he or she currently owns or is buying it.

*Parentage.* Responses to questions about birthplace (country) of mother and father are used to classify the native population into two categories: native of native parentage and native of foreign or mixed parentage.

*Parentage, Native.* See *Native Parentage.*

*Parish.* See *County.*

*Parochial School.* A school controlled and supported mainly by a religious organization.

*Persons per Room.* Calculated by dividing the number of persons in the household by the number of rooms in the housing unit it occupies. Bathrooms, halls, foyers, porches, and balconies are not counted as rooms.

*Place.* A concentration of population regardless of the existence of legally prescribed units, powers, or governmental functions.

*Place, Incorporated, Unincorporated,* or *Urban.* See *Incorporated Place, Unincorporated Place,* or *Urban Place.*

*Place of Work.* Recorded for people who worked during the week preceding the Census. Persons who worked at more than one job reported the place of work for the job at which they worked the most hours. Persons who traveled in their work or worked in more than one place reported where they began work, if they reported to a central headquarters, or where they worked the most hours.

*Polish-American.* A person of Polish birth or parentage. See *Foreign Stock.*

*Population.* The population of a geographical area or statistical unit comprises all persons whose usual place of residence at the time of the Census was in that area or unit.

*Population Change.* The increase or decrease in population for a statistical unit from 1960 to 1970. As mapped in the atlas, population change is calculated by dividing the 1970 population of a statistical unit by its estimated 1960 population. If the 1970 population is larger than the 1960 population, a number greater than 1.0 results; if the statistical unit has lost population, the quotient is less than 1.0.

*Population Density.* The number of people per square mile or square kilometer of land area. Land area includes dry land, land temporarily or partially covered by water, streams less than 0.125 miles (0.20 kilometers) wide, and lakes, reservoirs, and ponds of fewer than 40 acres (16.2 hectares).

*Poverty Level.* In 1970 families and unrelated individuals were classified as being above or below the poverty level on the basis of a poverty index developed by a federal interagency committee in 1969. This index takes into account such factors as family size, number of children, and farm-nonfarm residence, as well as the amount of money income. The poverty level is based on an "economy" food plan designed by the Department of Agriculture for "emergency or temporary use when funds are low." The definition assumes that a family is classified as poor if its total money income amounts to less than three times the cost of the "economy" food plan. These cutoff levels are updated every year to reflect changes in the Consumer Price Index.

In 1969 some of the poverty thresholds were:
Unrelated individuals, $1,834;
All families, $3,388;
Families containing 2 persons, $2,364;
Families containing 6 persons, $4,921.

*Poverty Population.* The number of primary individuals with incomes below the poverty level and the number of people living in families or households with incomes below the poverty level.

*Primary Individual.* A household head living alone or with nonrelatives only.

*Private (Individual) Sewage Disposal.* Housing units that use septic tanks, cesspools, or other nonpublic forms of sewage disposal are classified as having individual sewage disposal systems. Used interchangeably with *Onsite Sewage Disposal.*

*Private (Individual) Water Supply.* Housing units that receive water from individual wells that are on the property of the housing unit and that serve 5 or fewer housing units are considered to be private water supplies, as are water sources such as springs, creeks, and rivers.

*Public Payments.* Income received from Social Security retirement, survivor, and disability payments, from the railroad retirement program, and from public assistance and welfare programs. Does not include payments from private pension or disability plans.

*Public Sewage Disposal.* A city, county sanitary district, neighborhood, or subdivision sewer system.

*Public Transportation.* Railroads, subways or elevateds, buses or streetcars, and taxicabs.

*Public Water Supply.* A publicly or privately owned system in which a common source supplies running water to more than 5 housing units.

*Race.* In the 1970 Census, people were asked to indicate their race by selecting one of the following: White, Negro or Black, Indian (American), Japanese, Chinese, Filipino, Hawaiian, Korean, or Other (to be specified). Persons who indicated racial mixture were classified according to the race of their father, if he was present in the household and if his race was one of the races the respondent listed. If the father's race could not be determined, the first race the person listed was used.

*Region, Metropolitan.* See *Metropolitan Region.*

*Rent.* Rent data were collected only for renter-occupied housing units rented for cash rent and for vacant units that were for rent, excluding one-family houses on properties of more than 10 acres (4.05 hectares). See *Contract Rent* and *Gross Rent.*

*Rent-Income Ratio.* Yearly gross rent expressed as a percentage of the total income reported by the family or primary individual

# Glossary

*occupying the unit for the previous year. Calculated only for renter-occupied units for which gross rent was tabulated.*

*Residence.* Each person enumerated was counted as an inhabitant of his or her usual place of abode, usually the place where he or she lived and slept. Persons in the armed forces, college students, crews of United States merchant vessels in harbor, crews of United States naval vessels not deployed to an overseas fleet, inmates of institutions, persons without a usual place of residence, and persons staying overnight at a mission, flophouse, jail, etc. were counted as inhabitants of the places where they were enumerated.

*Residence 5 Years Ago.* Ascertained for persons 5 years of age or older, who were asked to indicate if they lived in "this house" 5 years ago or in a "different house."

*Room, Persons per.* See *Persons per Room.*

*Russian-American.* A person of Russian birth or parentage. See *Foreign Stock.*

*Scale.* The scale of a map is the relationship between distance on the map and distance on the earth's surface. Thus a map with a scale of 1:62,500 is one on which one inch on the map represents 62,500 inches (one mile or 1.6 kilometers) on the earth's surface.

*Service Worker.* Defined here as private and personal service workers, food service workers, transportation workers, mechanics and repairmen, and certain craftsmen.

*Sewage Disposal, Onsite, Private, or Public.* See *Private (Individual) Sewage Disposal* and *Public Sewage Disposal.*

*Sex Ratio.* The number of males in a statistical unit divided by the number of females multiplied by 100. Thus sex ratios over 100 are male-dominant, whereas sex ratios below 100 are female-dominant.

*Single-Family Housing (Unit).* A housing unit containing a single household.

*Single-Unit Attached Housing.* Single-unit structures that have one or more walls extending from ground to roof separating them from adjoining structures — for example, a row house.

*Single-Unit Detached Housing.* Single-unit structures detached from any other house, that is, with open space on all four sides. Such structures are considered detached even if they have an adjoining private garage or contain a business unit.

*SMSA.* See *Standard Metropolitan Statistical Area.*

*Spanish-Americans.* In the 1970 Census the Spanish-American population was defined according to the sample an individual was enumerated in and by his or her state of residence.

> In New York, New Jersey, and Pennsylvania, persons of Puerto Rican Stock were counted.
> In the 5 southwestern states (Arizona, California, Colorado, New Mexico, and Texas) persons who spoke Spanish and persons who did not speak Spanish but had selected Spanish surnames were counted.
> In the remaining states, persons who spoke Spanish were counted as Spanish-Americans.

The maps of Spanish-Americans in the atlas are based on people who spoke Spanish except in Texas and California where people with selected Spanish surnames who did not speak Spanish were added to the Spanish speakers to obtain the data for the maps. There are many people of Mexican descent in the southwestern states who do not use the Spanish language, and counting non-Spanish speakers with Spanish surnames is one means of estimating the size of that specific group.

*Spanish Language Population.* Persons who reported Spanish as their mother tongue as well as persons in families in which the head or wife reported Spanish as his or her mother tongue.

*Standard Metropolitan Statistical Area* (abbreviation: *SMSA*). A county or group of counties containing at least one city (or twin cities) with population of 50,000 or more, plus adjacent counties (townships in New England) that are metropolitan in character and are economically and socially integrated with the central city or cities.

*Statistical Unit.* Any geographical area for which the Census Bureau aggregates census data. Examples are city blocks, census tracts, central cities, counties, states, etc.

*Stock, Foreign.* See *Foreign Stock.*

*Stock, Housing.* See *Housing Units.*

*Suppressed Values.* To avoid disclosing detailed information on individuals, the Census Bureau withholds data in certain categories when there are few individuals with a given characteristic in a statistical unit. The threshold number below which a given characteristic (for example, race) is suppressed depends on how much additional information accompanies the characteristic in question. Because the atlas maps were prepared from computer tapes containing very detailed cross-tabulations of variables, the suppression thresholds are higher than they are for printed census data where far fewer variables are tabulated. Many tract observations for percentage Negro and percentage Spanish-American are suppressed on our maps even though the data are not suppressed in printed tract reports.

*System, Daily Urban.* See *Daily Urban System.*

*System, Metropolitan.* See *Metropolitan Network.*

*Telephone Availability.* Occupied housing units are classified as having a telephone available if there is a telephone on which occupants can receive calls. It may be located in the housing unit or elsewhere, as in the hall of an apartment building, in another apartment, or in another building, so long as the occupant has access to it.

*Township.* Over 17,000 organized governments located in 16 states, including governments officially known as "towns" in New England, New York, and Wisconsin, as well as all governmental units officially called townships in other areas.

*Tract, Census.* See *Census Tract.*

*Transfer Payments.* Certain payments to individuals that do not correspond to any current contribution to production but are claims of one set of individuals against the income of another. Public assistance and Social Security benefits are examples.

*Transportation to Work.* People who worked during the week preceding the Census specified the principal mode of travel or type of conveyance they used to get to their places of work on the last day they worked.

*Underbounded.* A central city, Standard Metropolitan Statistical Area, or other politically defined urban unit is said to be underbounded if its political boundaries are too small to include all the places and areas that are closely linked to the central unit. Boston, for example, is said to be underbounded because it does not include Cambridge, Somerville, and Everett, which are contiguous, closely linked places that are economically and socially part of Boston.

*Unemployed.* Civilians 14 years old and over who were neither "at work" nor "with a job but not at work" during the 4 weeks preceding the Census, and who were available for work during the week preceding the Census.

*Unincorporated Place.* Densely settled population centers that are not incorporated. Each has a definite residential nucleus. Boundaries around unincorporated places are drawn by the Census Bureau to include, insofar as possible, all of the densely settled area.

*Unit, Statistical.* See *Statistical Unit.*

*Unit, Vacant Migratory or Vacant Seasonal.* See *Vacant Migratory Unit* or *Vacant Seasonal Unit.*

*Unrelated Individual.* A person not living with relatives but living in a household entirely alone or with one or more persons not related to him or her, or living in group quarters.

*Urban Area.* A city and its surrounding territory without further specific definition or precise delimitation in terms of political boundaries. Used interchangeably with *Metropolitan Area, Metropolitan Region,* and *Urban Region.* It is not synonymous with *Urbanized Area.*

*Urban Place.* All incorporated or unincorporated places of 2,500 population or more.

*Urban Population.* All persons living in:
>Places of 2,500 inhabitants or more incorporated as cities, boroughs, villages, and towns (except towns in New England, New York, and Wisconsin); plus
>The densely settled urban fringe, whether incorporated or unincorporated, of urbanized places; plus
>Unincorporated places of 2,500 or more inhabitants.

*Urban Renewal.* Usually refers to one of the federally financed programs for purchasing and clearing dilapidated areas of cities of their existing structures and selling the cleared properties to public agencies and private investors for the construction of new facilities. Early urban renewal programs emphasized massive clearing. Later programs were less comprehensive in conception and permitted spot renewal and the refurbishing of deteriorating but sound structures. "Urban renewal" is sometimes used more generally to refer to the ongoing process of city building and rebuilding, but the usual referent is the federal programs of the 1950s and 1960s.

*Urbanization.* The proportion of a nation's labor force living in urban places. The term also refers to increases in the percentage of a nation's population in urban places produced by migration, differential population increase, or both.

*Urbanized Area.* Contains a city (or twin cities) of 50,000 or more population (central city) plus the surrounding densely settled incorporated and unincorporated areas that meet certain criteria of population size or density. *Urbanized Area* is not synonymous with *Urban Area.*

*Vacant Housing Unit.* A unit was considered vacant if no persons were living in it at the time of enumeration. Also, units temporarily occupied by persons having a usual place of residence elsewhere were classified as vacant; units where the usual residents were only temporarily absent were not classified as vacant.

*Vacant Migratory Units.* Units for migratory workers employed in farm work during the crop season.

*Vacant Seasonal Units.* Vacant units intended for occupancy during only a season of the year, for example, units for summer or winter recreational use or units for herders or loggers.

*Vacant Year-Round Units.* Vacant units intended for occupancy at any time of the year even if used only occasionally throughout the year.

*Value-Income Ratio.* The value of the unit in relation to the total income reported by the family or primary individual for the preceding year. Calculated for owner-occupied units only.

*Water Supply, Private* and *Public.* See *Private (Individual) Water Supply* and *Public Water Supply.*

*White.* See *Race.*

*Year Structure Built.* Housing units are classified by the year the structure in which they are located was built, that is, the year in which the respondent or occupant reported the original construction was completed. Later remodeling, additions, and conversions do not change the unit's age.

*ZIP Code.* From Zone Improvement Plan. Five-digit postal codes used to designate small towns or zones within metropolitan areas. Some census data are now available by ZIP Code areas.

# Index/Gazetteer

Page numbers in Roman type refer to text discussions of the topics indicated. Boldface page numbers refer to maps.

Abandoned housing, 437–44
Aberdeen Proving Ground, **456**
sex ratio, 74
Age, *see* Median age
of housing, definition (Year Structure Built), 489
individual, Census enumeration, 485
Age-sex structure, city, DUS, SMSA
Atlanta, **250,** 251
Baltimore, **73,** 74
Boston, **24,** 26
Chicago, 138–41, **140**
Cleveland, 129–31, **130**
Dallas-Forth Worth, 187–9, **187**
Detroit, 152, 153–4
Hartford, **64,** 65–6
Houston, **206,** 208–9
Los Angeles, 224, **226**
Miami, 241, **241**
Minneapolis-St. Paul, **162,** 164
New Orleans, **83,** 84-5
New York, 32–4, **37**
Philadelphia, 52, **53**
Pittsburgh, 108, **109**
St. Louis, **121,** 123
and migration, 13–4
San Francisco, **93,** 96–7
Seattle, **173,** 173–4
Washington, D.C., **260,** 262–3
Air-passenger traffic flows, 10–1, **11**
Akron, Ohio, 127, **458**
Alexandria, Va., 256, **461**
Aliquippa, Pa., **457**
Allegheny Center (Pittsburgh), **464**
Allegheny River, **464**
Alton, Ill., 118, **457**
Amenities and metropolitan growth, 9
American Indians
Chicago, 141, **141**
Dallas-Forth Worth SMSAs, 189, **190**
data tabulation, **474**
Detroit SMSA, **154,** 155
Los Angeles SMSA, 227, **227**
Minneapolis-St. Paul SMSA, **163,** 164
San Francisco-Oakland SMSA, **97,** 98
Anacostia River, **468**
Annapolis, Md., 71, 75, **456**
Anoka, Minn., **459**
Antisnob law (Mass.), 29
Area of cities, SMSAs, DUSs, 472
Areas
metropolitan, definition, 486
urban, definition, 488
urbanized, definition, 489
Arlington Heights housing project (Pittsburgh), 113
Astrodome Stadium (Houston), 205, 211, **466**
Asylum Avenue (Hartford), 63, 67, **462**
Atlanta
age-sex structure, **250,** 251
automobiles, households without, 255, **255**
base map, **248, 468**
births, immature, 377, **380**

housing and housing units
crowded, 254, **255**
single-unit detached, 249–50, **255**
vacant, 444, **444**
Negroes, **251,** 251–2
median family income, 252
population, 247, 471
density, **250,** 251
*1850-1940,* **10**
relief, 247, **248**
school enrollment, parochial, 364, **364**
Spanish-Americans, **251,** 252
Atlanta DUS
age-sex structure, **250,** 251
base map, **248**
composition, 247, **248**
housing units, seasonal, 284, **284**
mobile homes, **248,** 249
population, 247, 471
sewage disposal, private, 277, **278**
water supply, private, 271–2, **272**
Atlanta SMSA
age-sex structure, **250,** 251
automobiles, households without, 339, **340**
base map, **247, 461**
blue-collar workers, 252–3, **253**
CBD employment, 323, **324**
clerical workers, 252
Dobbins Air Force Base, 249, **461**
elderly population, **250,** 251
executives, 252–3, **253**
female headship, 252, **252**
female labor force, 403, **404**
household size, 252, **252**
housing
built before *1940,* **248,** 249
built *1960–1970,* **248,** 249
crowded, 291, **292**
multiple-unit, 249–50
rent, mean monthly, **249,** 251
rent/income ratio, 299, **300**
single-unit detached, **249,** 249–50
value, mean, **249,** 250–1
value/income ratio, 307, **308**
income
deficit, 435, **436**
per person per year, 253, **253**
from public payments, 253, **254,** 427, **428**
land use, **248,** 249
Mariette, Ga., 249, 252, **461**
median age, **250,** 251
in national metropolitan system, 10–1, **11**
Negroes, 387, **388**
in new single-unit housing, 387, **388**
occupations, 252-3. *See also* blue-collar workers, clerical workers, executives, service workers
population, 247, 471
change, *1960–1970,* 355, **356**
density, 315, **316**
*1950–1970,* **10**
poverty population, 419, **420**

public transportation use, 331, **332**
residential change, *1965–1970,* 254, **254**
school enrollments, 20-21 year olds, 254, **254,** 371, **372**
service workers, 252
sex ratio, **250,** 251
Spanish-Americans, 395, **396**
telephones, households without, 347, **348**
unemployment, male, 411, **412**
Atlas
cartographic conventions and techniques, 204, 479–81
data
sampling rates, 17
substitutions, 19
design principles, 479–81
maps and text, 479–80
complementarity, 2
organization, 1–2, 14, 479
and urban theory, 480
policy considerations, 450–1
production techniques, 480–1
purposes, 1, 479–81
technical notes, 479–81
Auburn, Wash., **459**
Aurora, Ill., **458**
Automobiles, households without, 333–340
Atlanta, 255, **255**
SMSA, 339–340, **340**
Baltimore SMSA, 78, **78, 335,** 336
Boston SMSA, 333, **334**
Chicago SMSA, 337, **337**
Cleveland SMSA, 336, **337**
Dallas-Fort Worth SMSAs, **338,** 339
data tabulation, 333
definition, 485
Detroit, 158, **158**
SMSA, 337, **337**
Hartford SMSA, **334,** 335
Houston SMSA, 339, **339**
Los Angeles SMSA, 232–4, **235, 339, 340**
Miami SMSA, 339, **340**
Minneapolis-St. Paul SMSA, 167, **167,** 337, **338**
New Orleans SMSA, **86,** 88, **335,** 336
New York-Northern New Jersey SMSAs, 333, **334**
Philadelphia SMSA, 333-5, **334**
Pittsburgh SMSA, 336, **336**
and poverty, 333
and public transportation use, 331–9
St. Louis SMSA, 336, **336**
San Francisco SMSA, **335,** 336
Seattle SMSA, 337–9, **338**
in SMSAs, 333
in United States, 333
Washington, D.C. SMSA, **263,** 339, **340**
Avon, Conn., 67, **455**

Baby boom, postwar, 447
Back Bay (Boston), **462**
Bala Cynwyd, Pa., 57, **455**

Baltimore
age-sex structure, **73,** 74
base map, **71, 463**
births, immature, 375, **375**
Cuban-Americans, 75
ground rent, 73
housing units, seasonal, 439, **439**
Mexican-Americans, 75
Negroes, 74, **74**
population, 70, 471
density, **73,** 74
*1790-1940,* **10**
Puerto Rican stock, 75
relief, 70, **71**
row houses, 72
school enrollment, parochial, 359, **359**
Spanish-Americans, **74,** 74–5
Baltimore DUS
age-sex structure, **73,** 74
base map, **72**
composition, 70
housing units, seasonal, 280, **281**
mobile homes, 72, **72**
population, 70, 471
sewage disposal, private, 274, **275**
water supply, private, 268, **269**
Baltimore SMSA
age-sex structure, **73,** 74
automobiles, households without, 78, **78, 335,** 336
base map, **70, 456**
blue-collar workers, 75, **76**
CBD employment, 317–20, **319**
clerical workers, 75
elderly population, **73,** 74
executives, 75–6, **76**
female headship, 75, **75**
female labor force, 397–9, **399**
Gwynns Falls, 70, **463**
household size, 75, **75**
housing
age, 71
built before *1940,* 71, **71**
built *1960–1970,* 71, **71**
crowded, 286, **287**
rent, mean monthly, **72,** 72–3
rent/income ratio, 78, **78, 295,** 295–6
single-unit detached, 72, **72**
vacant, 439, **439**
value, mean, **72,** 72–3
value/income ratio, **303,** 304
income
deficit, **431,** 431–2
per person per year, 76, **76**
from public payments, 421, **423**
Jones Falls, 70, **463**
land use, 71, **71**
median age, **73,** 74
in national metropolitan system, 10–1, **11**
Negroes, 383, **383**
in new single-unit housing, 77, 78, 383, **383**
occupations, 75–6. *See also* blue-collar workers, clerical workers, executives, service workers

*491*

# Index

population, 70, 471
   change, *1960–1970,* **77,** 77–8, **351,** 352
   density, **311,** 312
   *1950–1970,* **10**
poverty population, 415, **415**
public transportation use, **327,** 328
school enrollments, 20–21 year olds, 365, **367**
service workers, 75
sewage disposal, private, **77,** 77–8
sex ratio, **73,** 74
Spanish-Americans, 389, **391**
telephones, households without, 341, **343**
unemployment, male, 407, **407**
*Barrio,* 485
Base maps, atlas, 481
Bay Area Rapid Transit (BART), 102
Bay View neighborhood (San Francisco), 97, **463**
Bayshore (San Francisco), **463**
Baytown (Houston), 202, **460**
Beacon Hill (Boston), 29, **462**
Bellaire (Houston), **466**
Belleville, Ill., 118, **457**
Bellevue, Wash., 171, **459**
Beltzhoover (Pittsburgh), 110, **464**
Berkeley, Cal., **456**
Berkeley Hills, 92, **456, 463**
Berry, Brian J. L., 12
Beverly Hills, Cal., 224, **467**
Birmingham, Mich., 153, **458**
Births, immature, 15, 373–80
   Atlanta, 377, **380**
   Baltimore, 375, **375**
   Chicago, **376,** 377
   Cleveland, 375–7, **376**
   Dallas, 377, **378**
   data tabulation, 373
   definition, 486
   Houston, 377, **378**
   Minneapolis, 377, **377**
   New Orleans, 375, **375**
   New York City, 373, **374**
   Oakland, 375, **375**
   Philadelphia, 373, **374**
   Pittsburgh, 375, **376**
   St. Louis, 375, **376**
   St. Paul, 377, **377**
   San Francisco, 375, **375**
   Seattle, 377, **377**
   in SMSAs, 373
   in United States, 373
   Washington, D.C., 380, **380**
Biscayne Bay (Miami), **468**
Blacks (Negroes), Census enumeration, 485
Bloomfield Hill, Mich., 153, **458**
Blue-collar workers
   Atlanta SMSA, 252–3, **253**
   Baltimore SMSA, 75, **76**
   Boston SMSA, **27,** 29
   Chicago SMSA, **145,** 146
   Cleveland SMSA, **132,** 133
   Dallas-Fort Worth SMSAs, 191–2, **193**
   data tabulation, 476
   definition, 485
   Detroit, **156,** 157
   Hartford SMSA, **66,** 67
   Houston SMSA, **211,** 212
   Los Angeles SMSA, 232, **234**
   Miami SMSA, 243, **244**
   Minneapolis-St. Paul SMSA, **165,** 165–6
   New Orleans, SMSA, **85,** 87
   New York-Northern New Jersey SMSAs, 41–2, **44**
   Philadelphia SMSA, 56–7, **58**
   Pittsburgh SMSA, **112,** 113, **114,** 114–5
   St. Louis SMSA, **124,** 125
   San Francisco-Oakland SMSA, 99–100, **99**
   Seattle SMSA, **176,** 177
   Washington, D.C. SMSA, **262,** 265
Boeing Aircraft Company (Seattle), 169
Bolling Air Force Base (Washington, D.C.), 257, 259, **468**
Boston
   age-sex structure, **24,** 26

base map, **22, 462**
Beacon Hill, 29, **462**
Chinatown, 26, **462**
East Boston, **462**
   Italian-Americans, 28
housing units, vacant, **438,** 439
Negroes, **25,** 26
North End, **462**
   Italian-Americans, 28
population, 21, 471
   change, recent, 21
   density, **23,** 25
   in 19th century, 21
   *1790–1940,* **10**
relief, 21, **22**
school enrollment, parochial, 357, **358**
Spanish-Americans, **25,** 26
underbounding, 21
Boston DUS
   age-sex structure, **24,** 26
   base map, **22**
   composition, 21, 22
   housing units, seasonal, 279, **280**
   mobile homes, **22,** 23
   population, 21, 70, 471
   sewage disposal, private, 273, **274**
   water supply, private, 267, **268**
Boston SMSA
   age-sex structure, **24,** 26
   automobiles, households without, 333, **334**
   base map, **21, 455**
   blue-collar workers, **27,** 29
   Canadian-Americans, **25,** 26–7
   CBD employment, 317, **318**
   Chinese-Americans, **25,** 26
   elderly population, **24,** 26
   executives, **27,** 29
   female headship, **27,** 29
   female labor force, 397, **398**
   household size, **27,** 29
   housing
      age, 22
      built before *1940,* **22,** 22–3
      built *1960–1970,* **22,** 22–3
      closed suburban, **28,** 29
      crowded, 285, **286**
      rent, mean monthly, 23, **24**
      rent/income ratio, 293, **294**
      single-unit detached, 23, **23**
      value, mean, **23,** 24
      value/income ratio, 301, **302**
   income
      deficit, 429, **430**
      per person per year, **27,** 29
      from public payments, 421, **422**
   Irish-Americans, **25,** 26
   Italian-Americans, **26,** 28
   land use, **22,** 22
   median age, **24,** 26
   metropolitan government, 29
   in national metropolitan system, 10–1, **11**
   Negroes, 28, **28,** 381, **382**
      in new single-unit housing, 381, **382**
   occupations, 29. *See also* blue-collar workers, clerical workers, executives, service workers
   political fragmentation, 29, **29**
   population, 21, 471
      change, *1960–1970,* 349, **350**
      density, 309, **310**
      *1950–1970,* **10**
   poverty population, 413, **414**
   public transportation use, 325, **326**
   restrictive zoning, **28,** 29
   Russian-Americans, **26,** 27
   school enrollments, 20-21 year olds, 365, **366**
   sex ratio, **24,** 26
   Spanish-Americans, 389, **390**
   tax burdens, **28,** 29
   telephones, households without, 341, **342**
   unemployment, male, 405, **406**
   Boundaries, political, cartographic symbols for, 4
Bratenahl, Ohio, 129, **464**

Brookline, Mass., **455**
   Irish-Americans in, 26
Brooklyn (New York City), **462**
Brushton (Pittsburgh), 110, **464**
Bryn Mawr, Pa., 49, 57, 365, **455**
Bus service areas (Hartford SMSA), **67,** 68
Busing, 452
Calumet Harbor (Chicago), 144, **464**
Cambridge, Mass., **455**
Camden, N.J., 56, **455**
   female headship, 56
Canadian-Americans
   Boston SMSA, **25,** 26–7
   Canadian-born
      data tabulation, 474
   Canadian parentage
      data tabulation, 474
   definition, 485
   French
      Waltham, Mass., 27
   Hartford SMSA, **65,** 66
   Los Angeles SMSA, 230, **231**
   Lynn, Mass., 27
   Medford, Mass., 27
   Somerville, Mass., 27
Capital formation, postwar era, 448
Capitol, United States (Washington, D.C.), **468**
Carol City (Miami SMSA), 243, **461**
Carquinez Straight (San Francisco SMSA), 90–1, **456**
Cartographic conventions, 2–4
Cartographic techniques, Appendix C
Cascade Mountains, 168
   barrier to eastward connections from Seattle, 169
CBD (Central Business District), definition, 485
CBD employment, 317–324
   Atlanta SMSA, 323, **324**
   Baltimore SMSA, 317–320, **319**
   Boston SMSA, 317, **318**
   Chicago SMSA, 147, **148,** 321, **321**
   Cleveland SMSA, 320, **321**
   Dallas-Fort Worth SMSAs, 321–3, **322**
   data tabulation, 317
   definition, 485
   Detroit SMSA, 321, **321**
   Hartford SMSA, 317, **318**
   Houston SMSA, 323, **323**
   Los Angeles SMSA, 323, **324**
   Miami SMSA, 323, **324**
   Minneapolis-St. Paul SMSA, 321, **322**
   New Orleans SMSA, 319, 320
   New York-Northern New Jersey SMSAs, 317, **318**
   Philadelphia SMSA, 317, **318**
   Pittsburgh SMSA, 320, **320**
   and public transportation use, 325, 331
   St. Louis SMSA, 320, **320**
   San Francisco-Oakland SMSA, 319, 320
   Seattle SMSA, 321, **322**
   Washington, D.C. SMSA, 323, **324**
Census tracts, definition, 485
*Census Users' Guide, 1970,* 17
Censuses of Population and Housing, *1970,* 17
   data
      for city blocks, 18
      collection procedures, 18
      reliability, 19
   Fourth Count Summary Tapes, 19
   questions, 17
      sampling rates, 17-18
   Second Count Summary Tapes, 19
Center for Community Change and National Urban League, 12
Central cities
   definition, 485
   map scale, 4
   of 20 largest DUSs, populations to *1970,* **10**
Central Connecticut State College, 365
Central Park (New York), **462**

Central and South American stock, 389–395
Chelsea (Boston), **455**
Cherry Hill, N.J., 49, 51, **455**
Chester, Pa., **455**
Chestnut Hill (Philadelphia), 49, 57, **462**
Chestnut Ridge (Pittsburgh SMSA), **457**
Chicago
   age-sex structure, 138–141, **140**
   base map, **136, 464**
   births, immature, **376,** 377
   Chinatown, 142
   competition with St. Louis, 116
   female headship, 146, **148**
   housing
      abandonment, 12
      multiple-unit, 136
      vacant, **440,** 441
   Hyde Park, 141
   Mexican-Americans, 141
   Negroes, **140,** 141
   population, 70, 135, 471
      density, 138, **139**
      *1840–1940,* **10**
   Puerto Rican stock, 141
   relief, 136, **136**
   residential change, *1965–1970,* 147, **147**
   school enrollment, parochial, 147, 147–8, **360,** 361
   Spanish-Americans, 141, **141**
   University of, 141, 147
   walking to work, **146,** 147
Chicago DUS
   age-sex structure, 138–41, **140**
   base map, **136**
   composition, 135
   housing units, seasonal, 281, **282**
   mobile homes, 136, **136**
   population, 70, 135, 471
   sewage disposal, private, 275, **276**
   water supply, private, 269, **270**
Chicago SMSA
   age-sex structure, 138–41, **140**
   American Indians, 141, **141**
   automobiles, households without, 337, **337**
   base map, **135, 458**
   blue-collar workers, **145,** 146
   Calumet Harbor, 144, **464**
   CBD employment, 147, **148,** 321, **321**
   Chinese-Americans, 142, **142**
   clerical workers, 146
   elderly population, 138–141, **139**
   Evanston, Ill., 146, 368, **458**
   executives, **145,** 146
   female headship, **144,** 146
   female labor force, 400, **401**
   German-Americans, 142, **143**
   Glencoe, 146, **458**
   Gold Coast, 138, **464**
   household size, **144,** 146
   housing
      age, 136
      built before *1940,* 136, **137**
      built *1960–1970,* 136, **137**
      crowded, 288–9, **289**
      multiple-unit, 136
      rent, mean monthly, 138, **138**
      rent/income ratio, 297, **297**
      single-unit detached, 136, **137**
      value, mean, 136-8, **138**
      value/income ratio, 305, **305**
   income
      deficit, 433, **433**
      per person per year, **145,** 146–7
      public payments, 424, **425**
   Irish-Americans, 142, **142**
   Italian-Americans, 143, **144**
   Japanese-Americans, 142, **142**
   median age, 138–40, **139**
   in national metropolitan system, 10–1, **11**
   Negroes, 385, **385**
      in new single-unit housing, 385, **385**
   Oak Forest Infirmary, 140, **458**
   occupations, 146. *See also* blue-collar workers, clerical workers, executives, service workers

*492*

# Index

Polish-Americans, 142–4, **143**
population, 70, 135, 471
    change, *1960–1970*, 353, **353**
    density, 313, **313**
    *1950–1970*, **10**
poverty population, 416, **417**
public transportation use, 329, **329**
residential change, *1965–1970*, **146**, 147
Russian-Americans, **143**, 144
    Jews versus ethnic Russians, 144
school enrollments, 20-21 year olds, 368–9, **369**
service workers, 146
sex ratio, **140**, 140–1
Spanish-Americans, 392, **393**
telephones, households without, 344–5, **345**
unemployment, male, 408–9, **409**
urban renewal, private, 136
Wilmett, 146, **458**
Winnetka, 146, **458**
Chinese-Americans
    Boston SMSA, **25**, 26
    Census enumeration, 485, 487
    Chicago SMSA, 142, **142**
    data tabulation, 474
    Los Angeles SMSA, 227–30, **230**
    New York-Northern New Jersey SMSAs, 37, **39**
    San Francisco-Oakland SMSA, **95**, 97–8
    Seattle SMSA, **174**, 176
Churchill, Pa., 108, **457**
Cities
    city age and urban problems, 11
    competition and interdependence, 9
    criteria for inclusion in atlas, 8
    diversity and variety, 1, 8
    economic and symbolic importance, 7–8
    education in, 14
    employment and poverty, 15
    evolution and growth, 14, 447
        in agrarian era, 9
        and economic development, 9
        in future, 15, 450
        *1960–1970*, 349–355: data tabulation, 349
        theory, 480
        and transportation technology, 9
    growth prospects and urban problems, 11
    housing, 14
    human needs, 15
    images, 8
    information sources, 16
    in national life, 8
    neighborhood life cycles, 12, 15
    open space, 14
    physical environment, 14
    policy uniformity, 1
    public health, 15
    rapid growth period and urban problems, 11
    socioeconomic segregation, 15
    transportation and communication, 14
    urban renewal, 15
City, central, definition, 485
Class intervals on maps, 3, 480
Clayton, Mo., 126, **457**
Clerical workers
    Atlanta SMSA, 252
    Baltimore SMSA, 75
    Chicago SMSA, 146
    Cleveland SMSA, 133
    Dallas-Fort Worth SMSAs, 191–2
    data tabulation, 476
    definition, 485
    Detroit SMSA, 157
    Hartford SMSA, 67
    Houston SMSA, 212–3
    Los Angeles SMSA, 232
    Miami SMSA, 243
    Minneapolis-St. Paul SMSA, 165
    New Orleans SMSA, 87
    Pittsburgh SMSA, 113
    St. Louis SMSA, 125
    San Francisco SMSA, 99–100
    Seattle SMSA, 177
    Washington, D.C. SMSA, 265

Cleveland
    age-sex structure, 129–31, **130**
    base map, **128**, 464
    births, immature, 375–7, **376**
    crime, 133–4, **134**
    housing
        crowded, 134, **134**
        vacant, **440**, 441
    industrial areas, 133, **133**
    Italian-Americans, 133, **133**
    Lorain Avenue, 131, **464**
    Negroes, **131**
    population, 70, 127, 471
        density, 129, **130**
        *1830–1940*, **10**
    Puerto Rican stock, 131
    relief, 127, **128**
    school enrollment, parochial, 359–61, **360**
    Spanish-Americans, 131, **131**
    voting patterns, 134, **134**
Cleveland DUS
    age-sex structure, 129–31, **130**
    Akron, Ohio, 127, **458**
    base map, **127**
    composition, 127
    housing units, seasonal, 281, **282**
    mobile homes, 128, **128**
    population, 127, 471
    sewage disposal, private, 275, **276**
    water supply, private, 269, **270**
Cleveland Heights, **458**
Cleveland SMSA
    age-sex structure, 129–31, **130**
    automobiles, households without, 336, **337**
    base map, **127**, **458**
    blue-collar workers, **132**, 133
    Bratenahl, 129, **464**
    CBD employment, 320, **321**
    clerical workers, 133
    Cuyahoga River Valley, 127, **464**
    elderly population, 129–30, **130**
    executives, **132**, 133
    female headship, 131, **132**
    female labor force, 400, **401**
    household size, 131, **132**
    housing
        age, 128
        built before *1940*, 128, **128**
        built *1960–1970*, 128, **128**
        crowded, 288, **289**
        rent, mean monthly, 129, **129**
        rent/income ratio, 296–7, **297**
        single-unit detached, 128–9, **129**
        value, mean, 129, **129**
        value/income ratio, 305, **305**
    income
        deficit, 433, **433**
        per person per year, **132**, 133
        from public payments, 424, **425**
    Lorain, Ohio, 127
    median age, 129, **130**
    in national metropolitan system, 10–1, **11**
    Negroes, 384, **385**
        in new single-unit housing, 384, **385**
    occupations, 133. *See also* blue-collar workers, clerical workers, executives, service workers
    political fragmentation, 134, **134**
    population, 70, 127, 471
        change, *1960–1970*, 352–3, **353**
        density, 313, **313**
        *1950–1970*, **10**
    poverty population, 416, **417**
    public transportation use, 328–9, **329**
    school enrollments, 20-21-year-olds, 368, **369**
    service workers, 133
    sex ratio, 130, **130**
    Shaker Heights, 129, **458**
    Spanish-Americans, 392, **393**
    telephones, households without, 344, **345**
    unemployment, male, 408, **409**
Clifton, N.J., **455**
Clinton Valley State Hospital (Detroit SMSA), 154

Closed suburban housing (Boston SMSA), 28–9
Cockrell Hill (Dallas), **466**
Coconut Grove (Miami), 241, 243, **468**
Coleman, James S., 452
College, definition, 485
    enrollments, 365–371
Color scheme for maps, 3, 480
Columbia, Md., 71, **456**
Columbia Point (Boston), Negroes in, 26
Commentary, complementarity with maps, 2
Committee for Economic Development, 450
Commuting (Washington, D.C.), **264**, 265, **468**
Comparative advantages and urban growth, 9
Comparative Metropolitan Analysis Project, 479
Competition among metropolitan areas, 9
Concord, Cal., **456**
Connecticut and K Streets (Washington, D.C.), 264, **468**
Consumer Price Index, 413
    definition, 485
Coral Gables, Fla., 240, 241, 371, **461**
Core, employment, definition, 485
Corporate headquarters in metropolitan regions, 7
County, definition, 485
County boundaries, cartographic symbols for, 4
*County and City Data Book, 1972*, 17
County Divisions, Census, 485
Coventry, Conn., 68, **455**
Creve Couer, Mo., 122, 126, **457**
Crowded housing, 14. *See also* Housing, crowded, and individual SMSA entries
Cuban-Americans, 389–395
    Baltimore, 75
    Dallas-Forth Worth SMSAs, 189
    Houston, 210
    Los Angeles, 227
    Miami, 242, **243**, 245
    New Orleans, 86
    San Francisco-Oakland, 98
    Washington, D.C., 263
Culver City, Cal., 222, **467**
Cuyahoga River Valley, 127, **464**

Daily Urban System
    definition, 485
    obsolescence, 451
    map scale, 4
    20 largest, **2**, 7
        area aggregate, 5
        commercial and economic affairs, importance in, 7–8
        composition, 7
        population aggregate, 7
        population cartogram, **8**
Dallas
    annexation power, 196
    base map, **466**
    births, immature, 377, **378**
    housing units, vacant, 441, **442**
    school enrollment, parochial, 361, **362**
Dallas-Fort Worth
    age-sex structure, **187**, 187–9
    Cuban-Americans, 189
    Mexican-Americans, 189
    population, 181, 471
    *1880–1940*, **10**
    Puerto Rican stock, 189
Dallas-Fort Worth DUS
    age-sex structure, **187**, 187–9
    base map, **184**
    composition, 181
    housing units, seasonal, 282, **283**
    mobile homes, **184**, 186
    population, 181, 471
    sewage disposal, private, 275, **277**
    water supply, private, 269–70, **271**
Dallas-Fort Worth SMSAs
    age-sex structure, **187**, 187–9
    American Indians, 189, **190**
    automobiles, households without, **338**, 339

    base map, **181**, **459**
    blue-collar workers, 191–2, **193**
    CBD employment, 321–3, **322**
    clerical workers, 191–2
    elderly population, 187, **188**
    executives, 191–2, **193**
    female headship, 191, **192**
    female labor force, **402**, 403
    Highland Park, 186, **466**
    household size, 191, **191**
    housing
        age, 182–4
        built before *1940*, 182–4, **183**
        built *1960–1970*, 182–4, **183**
        crowded, 289, **290**
        multiple-unit, 186
        rent, mean monthly, **185**, 186
        rent/income ratio, **298**, 299
        single-unit detached, **184**, 186
        value, mean, **185**, 186
        value/income ratio, **306**, 307
    income
        deficit, 196, **196**, 433–5, **434**
        per person per year, 192, **194**
        from public payments, 425, **426**
    median age, 187, **188**
    in national metropolitan system, 10–1, **11**
    Negroes, 189, **189**, 192, **194**, 386, 387
        in new single-unit housing, 192, **195**, **386**, 387
    occupations, 191–2. *See also* blue-collar workers, clerical workers, executives, service workers
    population 181, 471
        change, *1960–1970*, **354**, 355
        density, **186**, 186–7, 313, **314**
        *1950–1970*, **10**
    poverty population, 417, **418**
    public transportation use, **330**, 331
    relief, 182, **182**
    Ridgelea, 186, **459**
    school enrollments, 20-21 year olds, **370**, 371
    service workers, 191–2
    sex ratio, 187–9, **187**
    Spanish-Americans, 189, **190**, 393, **394**
    telephones, households without, 345, **346**
    unemployment, male, 409–11, **410**
    University Park, 186, **466**
    Westover Hills, 186, **459**
    Westworth, 192, **459**
Data, census
    appropriateness for atlas, 19
    bias toward places, 14
    collection and processing, 18–9
    drawbacks, 19
    hidden theories, 16
    versus local sources, 17
    reliability, 19
    sample rates, 17
    sources, 17
    substitution, 19
    suppression, 4
Deficit, income, *see* Income deficit
Delaware River, **462**
Dellwood (Minneapolis-St. Paul SMSA), 166, **459**
Density of population
    data tabulation, 473
    definition, 487
Dependent populations, 449
Desire Housing Project (New Orleans), 84, 86–7, 88, **463**
Detroit
    age-sex structure, **152**, 153–4
    automobiles, households without, 158, **158**
    base map, **150**, **465**
    housing units, vacant, 441, **441**
    Mexican-Americans, 155
    Negroes, **153**, 154
    population, 149, 471
        density, **152**, 153
        *1820–1940*, **10**
    Puerto Rican stock, 155
    relief, 150, **150**

493

# Index

school enrollment, parochial, 361, **361**
Spanish-Americans, **153,** 154–5
unemployment, male, **156,** 158
Detroit DUS
  age-sex structure, **152,** 153–4
  base map, **150**
  composition, 149
  housing units, seasonal, 281, **282**
  mobile homes, **150,** 151
  population, 149, 471
  sewage disposal, private, 275, **276**
  water supply, private, 269, **270**
Detroit House of Corrections, 154, 158, **458**
Detroit SMSA
  age-sex structure, **152,** 153–4
  American Indians, **154,** 155
  automobiles, households without, 337, **337**
  base map, **149, 458**
  Birmingham, 153, **458**
  Bloomfield Hills, 153, **458**
  blue-collar workers, **156,** 157
  CBD employment, 321, **321**
  clerical workers, 157
  Clinton Valley State Hospital, 154
  elderly population, **152,** 153–4
  executives, **156,** 157
  female headship, **155,** 157
  female labor force, 400, **401**
  Grosse Pointe, 153, **458**
  Hamtramck, 151, 153, 154, 155, 158, **465**
  Highland Park, 151, 154, 158, **465**
  household size, **155,** 156
  housing
    age, 151
    built before *1940,* **150,** 151
    built *1960–1970,* **150,** 151
    crowded, 289, **289**
    multiple-unit, 153
    rent, mean monthly, **151,** 153
    rent/income ratio, 297, **297**
    single-unit detached, **151,** 151–2
    value, mean, **151,** 153
    value/income ratio, 305, **305**
  income
    deficit, 433, **433**
    family, mean, **156,** 158
    per person per year, **155,** 157–8
    from public payments, 424, **425**
  Inkster, 158, **458**
  Italian-Americans, **154,** 155
  land use, 150, **150**
  median age, **152,** 153–4
  in national metropolitan system, 10–1, **11**
  Negroes, **157,** 158, 385, **385**
    in new single-unit housing, 385, **385**
  Northland Shopping Center, 154, **458**
  Northville State Hospital, 158, **458**
  occupations, 157. *See also* blue collar workers, clerical workers, executives, service workers
  Polish-Americans, **154,** 154–5
  population, 149, 471
    change, *1960–1970,* **157,** 158, 353, **353**
    density, 313, **313**
    *1950–1970,* **10**
  poverty population, 416–7, **417**
  public transportation use, 329, **329**
  residential change, *1965–1970,* **157,** 158
  Romeo, 157, **458**
  school enrollments, 20-21 year olds, 369, **369**
  Selfridge Air Force Base, 154, **458**
  service workers, 157
  sex ratio, **152,** 154
  Spanish-Americans, 392, **393**
  telephones, households without, 345, **345**
  unemployment, male, 409, **409**
*Directory of Federal Statistics for Local Areas, 1966,* 17
*Directory of Federal Statistics for States, 1967,* 17
*Directory of Non-Federal Statistics for States and Local Areas: A Guide to Sources, 1969,* 17

Discovery Park (Seattle), 174, **465**
Diversity, urban, 1
Division, minor civil, definition, 486
Dobbins Air Force Base (Atlanta), 249, **461**
Dominguez Hills (Los Angeles), 219, 222, 224, **467**
Dot distribution maps, 480
  generalization, 4
Drexel University (Philadelphia), 365
Dulles International Airport (Washington D.C. SMSA), 259, **461**
Duluth-Superior SMSA, overbounding, 6
Dupont Circle, (Washington, D.C.) **468**

East Boston, 28, **462**
East Hartford, 64, **455**
East Liberty (Pittsburgh), 110, **464**
East St. Louis, **457**
Easterlin, Richard A., 15
Echelon Mall, N.J., 49
Economic development
  role in city development, 9
  and urbanization in U.S., 5
Edgeworth (Pittsburgh SMSA), 113, **457**
Edina (Minneapolis-St. Paul SMSA), **459**
Education
  school enrollment, parochial, 357–364
  school enrollments 20-21 year olds, 365-372
Elderly population
  Atlanta SMSA, **250,** 251
  Baltimore SMSA, **73,** 74
  Boston SMSA, **24,** 26
  central-city versus suburban residents, 33
  Chicago SMSA, 138–9, **139**
  Cleveland SMSA, 130, **130**
  Dallas-Fort Worth SMSAs, 187, **188**
  data tabulation, 473
  Detroit SMSA, **152,** 153–4
  Hartford SMSA, **64,** 65
  Houston SMSA, **206,** 208–9
  income deficits, 429
  Los Angeles SMSA, 224, **226**
  Miami SMSA, **240,** 241, 245
  Minneapolis-St. Paul SMSA, **162,** 164
  New Orleans SMSA, **82,** 84
  New York-Northern New Jersey SMSAs, 32–4, **36**
  Philadelphia SMSA, 52, **53**
  Pittsburgh, 113, 113–4
  Pittsburgh SMSA, 108, **109**
  poverty status, 413–9
  St. Louis SMSA, **121,** 123
  San Francisco SMSA, **93,** 96–7
  Seattle SMSA, **172,** 173–4
  Washington, D.C. SMSA, **259,** 262
Elgin, Ill., **458**
Elizabeth, N.J., **455**
Ellington Air Force Base (Houston SMSA), 203, **460**
Emory Univ. (Atlanta SMSA), 371, **461**
Employment
  in CBD, 317–24
  female labor force, 397–403
  government, 450
  in metropolitan core
    definition, 485
  unemployment, male, 405–11
Enfield, Conn., 65, **455**
Environments, impoverished versus those with power, 451
Eras, urban and metropolitan
  post-World War II, 447
  underlying theory, 480
Ethnicity and parochial school enrollments, 357–64
Evanston, Ill. (Chicago SMSA), 146, 368, **458**
Everett, Washington, 178, **459**
Executives
  Atlanta SMSA, 252–3, **253**
  Baltimore SMSA, 75–6, **76**
  Boston SMSA, **27,** 29
  Chicago SMSA, **145,** 146
  Cleveland SMSA, **132,** 133
  commuting in Baltimore-Washington area, 75–6

Dallas-Fort Worth SMSAs, 191–2, **193**
  data tabulation, 476
  definition, 486
  Detroit SMSA, **156,** 157
  Hartford SMSA, **66,** 67
  Houston SMSA, **212,** 212–3
  Los Angeles SMSA, 232, **234**
  Miami SMSA, 243, **244**
  Minneapolis-St. Paul SMSA, **165,** 165–6
  New Orleans SMSA, **85,** 87–8
  New York-Northern New Jersey SMSAs, 41–2, **44**
  Philadelphia SMSA, 56–7, **58**
    Valley Forge Army Hospital, 57
  Pittsburgh SMSA, **112,** 113
  St. Louis SMSA, **124,** 125
  San Francisco SMSA, **99,** 99–100
  Seattle SMSA, **176,** 177
  Washington, D.C. SMSA, **262,** 265

Fairfax, Va., 256, **461**
Fairmount Park (Philadelphia), **462**
Falls Church, Va., 256, **461**
Family, Census definition, 486
Farmington Town, Conn., 67, **455**
Federal Housing Administration, 447
Female headship
  Atlanta SMSA, 252, **252**
  Baltimore SMSA, 75, **75**
  Boston SMSA, **27,** 29
  Chicago, 148, **148**
    SMSA, **144,** 146
  Cleveland SMSA, 131, **132**
  Dallas-Fort Worth SMSAs, 191, **192**
  data tabulation, 476
  definition, 486
  Detroit SMSA, **155,** 157
  Hartford SMSA, **66,** 67
  Houston SMSA, **210,** 211–2
  Los Angeles SMSA, 232, **233**
  Miami SMSA, 242–3, **244**
  Minneapolis-St. Paul SMSA, **164,** 165
  New Orleans, **87,** 88
    Desire Housing Project, 87
    SMSA, **84,** 87
  New York-Northern New Jersey SMSAs, 41, **43**
  Philadelphia SMSA, 55–6, **57**
    Camden, N.J., 56
  Pittsburgh SMSA, **111,** 113
  St. Louis SMSA, **122,** 124
  San Francisco SMSA, **98,** 99
  Seattle SMSA, **175,** 176
  Washington, D.C. SMSA, **261,** 264–5
Female labor force, 15, 397–403
  Atlanta SMSA, 403, **404**
  Baltimore SMSA, 397–9, **399**
  Boston SMSA, 397, **398**
  Chicago SMSA, 400, **401**
  Cleveland SMSA, 400, **401**
  Dallas-Fort Worth SMSAs, **402,** 403
  data tabulation, 397
  definition, 397
  Detroit SMSA, 400, **401**
  Hartford SMSA, 397, **398**
  Houston SMSA, 403, **403**
  Los Angeles SMSA, 403, **404**
  Miami SMSA, 403, **404**
  Minneapolis-St. Paul SMSA, 400, **402**
  New Orleans SMSA, 399, **399**
  New York-Northern New Jersey SMSAs, 397, **398**
  Philadelphia SMSA, 397, **398**
  Pittsburgh SMSA, 400, **400**
  St. Louis SMSA, 400, **400**
  San Francisco SMSA, **399,** 399–400
  Seattle SMSA, **402,** 403
  in SMSAs, 397
  in United States, 397
  Washington D.C. SMSA, 403, **404**
Festus, Mo., **457**
Filipino Census enumeration, 487
Fillmore district (San Francisco), 97
Filter-down housing process, 13
Fishtown (Philadelphia), **462**
Florida City (Miami SMSA), 243, 261
Flushing neighborhood (New York), **462**

Japanese-Americans in, 37
Foreign-born, *see* Foreign stock
Foreign stock
  definition, 486
  foreign-born, definition, 486
  foreign parentage, definition, 486
Forest Park, (St. Louis), 122, **464**
Fort Belvoir, Va., 257, **461**
Fort Dix, N.J., 52, **455**
Fort Lawton, Wash., 174, **465**
Fort Meade, Md., 260, **456**
  blacks in new housing, 78
  income per person per year, 77
  mobile homes, 72
  rents, mean monthly, 74
  sex ratio, 74
Fort Snelling (Minneapolis-St. Paul SMSA), 459, **465**
Fourth Count Summary Tapes (Census), 19
Fox Chapel (Pittsburgh SMSA), 113, 457
Fox Lake, Ill., **458**
French Quarter (New Orleans), 84, 88, 463
Frontenac, Mo., 122, 457

Galveston, Texas, 200, **460**
Galveston Bay, **460**
Gardena, Cal., 230, **467**
Gateway Memorial Arch (St. Louis), 464
Generalization of maps, 3
German-Americans
  Chicago SMSA, 142, **143**
  definition, 486
  German-born, data tabulation, 475
  German parentage, data tabulation, 475
  Los Angeles SMSA, 230, **231**
  New York SMSA, 38–9, **40**
  Jews versus ethnic Germans, 39
Germantown (Philadelphia), **462**
Glencoe, Ill., 146, **458**
Gold Coast (Chicago), 138, **464**
Golden Gate Park (San Francisco), 98, **463**
Golden Triangle (Pittsburgh), 115, **464**
Gottmann, Jean, 6, 486
Goulds (Miami SMSA), 240, 243, **461**
Government employment, 450
Government programs, effectiveness and efficiency, 480
Greater Hartford Process, 68
Greensburg, Pa., **457**
Gross National Product
  definition, 448
  *1945* and *1973,* 447
Gross rent, definition, 486
Grosse Pointe, Mich., 153, **458**
Ground rent, Baltimore, 73
Group quarters, definition, 486
Gwynns Falls (Baltimore), 70, **463**

Hamtramck, Mich., 151, 154, 155, 158, **465**
Harlem (New York City), **462**
Hartford
  age-sex structure, **64,** 65
  Asylum Avenue area, 63
  base map, **63, 462**
  housing
    multiple-unit, 63
    projects for elderly, **67,** 68
    vacant, **438,** 439
  Negroes, 65, 66
  population, 62, 471
    density, **64,** 64–5
    *1790–1940,* **10**
  relief, 62, **63**
  school enrollment, parochial, 357–9, **358**
  Spanish-Americans, **65,** 66
Hartford-Connecticut Valley DUS
  age-sex structure, **64,** 65
  base map, **63**
  composition, 62
  housing units, seasonal, 280, **280**
  mobile homes, 63, **63**
  population, 62, 471
  sewage disposal, private, 273–4, **274**
  water supply, private, 268, **268**
Hartford SMSA
  age-sex structure, **64,** 65

494

# Index

automobiles, households without, **334**, 335
Avon Town, 67, **455**
base map, **62, 455**
blue-collar workers, **66**, 67
bus service areas, **67**, 68
Canadian-Americans, **65**, 66
CBD employment, 317, **318**
clerical workers, 67
Coventry, 68, **455**
East Hartford, 64, **455**
elderly population, **64**, 65
executives, **66**, 67
female headship, **66**, 67
female labor force, 397, **398**
Greater Hartford Process, 68
household size, **66**, 67
housing
   age, 63
   built before *1940*, 63, **63**
   built *1960–1970*, 63, **63**
   crowded, 285, **286**
   multiple-unit, 63
   rent, mean monthly, 63-4, **64**
   rent/income ratio, **294**, 295
   single-unit detached, 63, **64**
   value, mean, 63, **64**
   value/income ratio, **302**, 304
income
   deficit, 429–31, **430**
   per person per year, **66**, 67
   from public payments, 421, **422**
Italian-Americans, **65**, 66
land use, 62, **63**
median age, **64**, 65
in national metropolitan system, 10–1, **11**
Negroes, 66, **68, 382**, 383
   in new single-unit housing, **382**, 383
occupations, 67. *See also* blue-collar workers, clerical workers, executives, service workers
Polish-Americans, **65**, 66–7
population, 62, 471
   change, *1960–1970*, 349, **350**
   density, 309–12, **310**
   *1950–1970*, **10**
poverty population, 413, **414**
public transportation use, **326**, 328
school enrollments, 20-21 year olds, 365, **366**
service workers, 67
sex ratio, **64**, 65–6
Spanish-Americans, 389, **390**
telephones, households without, 341, **342**
underbounding, 62
unemployment, male, 405–7, **406**
urban development, *1970*, 68, **68**
West Hartford, 67, **455**
Harvard Univ., 462
Hastings, Minn., **459**
Haverford, Pa., 365, **455**
Hawaiians, Census enumeration, 487
Head, family, definition, 486
Head, household, definition, 486
Headquarters, corporate, concentration in metropolitan region, 7
Headship, female, definition, 486
Highland Park (Dallas), 186, **466**
Highland Park, Mich., 151, 154, 158, **465**
Highland Park (St. Paul), 165, **465**
Hill District (Pittsburgh), 110
Histogram, 480
   convention for noting data suppression, 4
   use with maps, 2–3
   vertical scales, 4
Homestead (Pittsburgh), **464**
Homestead Air Force Base (Miami SMSA), 239, **461**
Homewood (Pittsburgh), 110, **464**
Household, definition, 486
Household head, definition, 486
Household size
   Atlanta SMSA, 252, **252**
   Baltimore SMSA, 75, **75**
   Boston SMSA, **27**, 29
   Chicago SMSA, **144**, 146
   Cleveland SMSA, 131, **132**
   Dallas-Fort Worth SMSAs, 191, **191**

data tabulation, 476
Detroit SMSA, **155**, 156
Hartford SMSA, **66**, 67
   Springfield, Mass., 67
Houston SMSA, **209**, 211
   Negro and Spanish-American, 215
Los Angeles SMSA, 232, **233**
Miami SMSA, 242, **244**
Minneapolis-St. Paul SMSA, **164**, 165
New Orleans SMSA, **84**, 86–7
New York-Northern New Jersey SMSAs, 41, **42**
Philadelphia SMSA, 55, **56**
   Pennhurst State School, 55
Pittsburgh SMSA, **111**, 113
St. Louis SMSA, **122**, 124
San Francisco SMSA, **98**, 99
Seattle SMSA, **175**, 176
Washington, D.C. SMSA, **261**, 264
Housing
abandoned, 12, 15, 437–44, 447
   definition, 437
   explanation, alternation, 12, 13
   and vacancy chains, 12
age
   Atlanta SMSA, 249
   Baltimore SMSA, 71
   Boston SMSA, 22
   Chicago SMSA, 136
   Cleveland SMSA, 128
   Dallas-Fort Worth SMSAs, 182–4
   definition (Year Structure Built), 489
   Detroit SMSA, 151
   Hartford SMSA, 63
   Houston SMSA, 202–3
   Los Angeles SMSA, 223
   Miami SMSA, 238–9
   Minneapolis-St. Paul SMSA, 160–1
   New Orleans, SMSA, 83
   New York-Northern New Jersey SMSAs, 31–2
   Philadelphia SMSA, 49
   Pittsburgh SMSA, 106–7
   St. Louis SMSA, 118–20
   San Francisco SMSA, 90–2
   Seattle SMSA, 169–70
   value/income ratios, 301–8
   Washington, D.C. SMSA, 259–60
built before *1940*
   Atlanta SMSA, **248**, 249
   Baltimore SMSA, 71, **71**
   Boston SMSA, **22**, 22–3
   Chicago SMSA, 136, **137**
   Cleveland SMSA, **128**, 128
   Dallas-Fort Worth SMSAs, 182–3 **183**
   data tabulation, 472
   Detroit SMSA, **150**, 151
   Hartford SMSA, 63, **63**
   Houston SMSA, **199**, 202–3
   Los Angeles SMSA, 220, **222**
   Miami SMSA, **238**, 238–9
   Minneapolis-St. Paul SMSA, **160**, 161–3
   New Orleans SMSA, **80**, 83
   New York-Northern New Jersey SMSAs, 31–2, **32**
   Philadelphia SMSA, 49, **50**
   Pittsburgh SMSA, **106**, 106–7 115, **115**
   St. Louis, **125**, 126; SMSA, **118**, 118–9
   San Francisco SMSA, 90–2, **91**
   Seattle SMSA, 169–70, **170**
   Washington, D.C. SMSA, **258**, 259–60
built *1940–1970*, 448
built *1960–1970*
   Atlanta SMSA, **248**, 249
   Baltimore SMSA, 71, **71**
   Boston SMSA, **22**, 22–3
   Chicago SMSA, 136, **137**
   Cleveland SMSA, 128, **128**
   Dallas-Fort Worth SMSAs, 182–3, **183**
   data tabulation, 472
   Detroit SMSA, **150**, 151
   Hartford SMSA, 63, **63**
   Houston SMSA, **200**, 202–3, 214, **216**
   Los Angeles SMSA, 220, **222**

Miami SMSA, **238**, 238–ᵃ
Minneapolis-St. Paul SMSA, **160**, 160-3
New Orleans SMSA, **80**, 83
New York-Northern New Jersey SMSAs, 31–2, **33**
Philadelphia SMSA, 49, **50**
Pittsburgh SMSA, **106**, 106–7
St. Louis, **125**, 126; SMSA, **118**, 118–9
San Francisco SMSA, 90–2, **91**
Seattle SMSA, 169–70, **170**
single-family, Negro occupancy, 381–7
Washington, D.C. SMSA, **258**, 259–60
crowded
   Atlanta, 254, **255**; SMSA, **292**
   Baltimore SMSA, **287**
   Boston SMSA, 285, **286**
   Chicago SMSA, 288–9, **289**
   Cleveland, 134, **134**; SMSA, 288, **289**
   Dallas-Fort Worth SMSAs, 289, **290**
   data tabulation, 285
   Detroit SMSA, 289, **289**
   Hartford SMSA, 285, **286**
   Houston SMSA, 291, **291**
   Los Angeles SMSA, 291, **292**
   Miami SMSA, 245, **246**, 291, **292**
   Minneapolis-St. Paul SMSA, 289, **290**
   New Orleans SMSA, **287**, 287–8
   New York, 45–6, **47**
   New York-Northern New Jersey SMSAs, 285, **286**
   Philadelphia SMSA, 285, **286**
   Pittsburgh SMSA, 288, **288**
   St. Louis SMSA, 288, **288**
   San Francisco SMSA, **287**, 288
   Seattle SMSA, 289, **290**
   in SMSAs, 285
   and social pathology, 285
   in U.S., 285
   Washington, D.C. SMSA, **263**, 265, 291, **292**
demand changes, U.S. *1960–1970*, 13
filter-down process, 13
inventory, changes, *1960–1970*, 13
inventory, definition, 486
mobile homes
   data tabulation, 472
   definition, 486
multiple-unit
   Atlanta SMSA, 249–50
   Chicago SMSA, 136
   Dallas-Fort Worth SMSAs, 126
   Detroit SMSA, 153
   Hartford SMSA, 63
   Houston SMSA, 203–5
   Los Angeles SMSA, 224
   Miami SMSA, 239–40
   New Orleans, 84
   Philadelphia, 49
   Pittsburgh, 107–8
   San Francisco SMSA, 95
   Seattle SMSA, 171
   Washington, D.C. SMSA, 260–1
new
   federal incentives, 447
   Negro occupancy, 381–7
occupied, definition, 487
owner-occupied
   definition, 487
   mean value, data tabulation, 473
projects
   Hartford, **67**, 68
rent, mean monthly
   Atlanta SMSA, **249**, 250–1
   Baltimore SMSA, **72**, 72–4
   Boston SMSA, **23**, 24
   Chicago SMSA, 136-8, **138**
   Cleveland SMSA, 129, **129**
   Dallas-Fort Worth SMSAs, **185**, 186
   data tabulation, 473
   Detroit SMSA, **151**, 153
   Hartford SMSA, 63–4, **64**
   Houston SMSA, **203**, 205–6
   Los Angeles SMSA, **223**, 224
   Miami SMSA, **239**, 240

Minneapolis-St. Paul SMSA, **161**, 163
New Orleans SMSA, **81**, 84
New York-Northern New Jersey SMSAs, 32, **34**
Philadelphia SMSA, 49–51, **52**
Pittsburgh SMSA, **107**, 108
St. Louis SMSA, **119**, 122
San Francisco SMSA, **92**, 95–6
Seattle SMSA, 171, **171**
Washington, D.C. SMSA, **258**, 261
rent/income ratio, 293–300
   Atlanta SMSA, 299, **300**
   Baltimore SMSA, 78, **78**, **295**, 295–6
   Boston SMSA, 293, **294**
   Chicago SMSA, **297**
   Cleveland SMSA, 296–7, **297**
   Dallas-Fort Worth SMSAs, **298**, 299
   data tabulation, 293
   Detroit SMSA, **297**
   Hartford SMSA, **294**, 295
   Houston SMSA, 299, **299**
   Los Angeles SMSA, 299, **300**
   Miami SMSA, 299, **300**
   Minneapolis-St. Paul SMSA, 297, **298**
   New Orleans SMSA, **295**, 296
   New York-Northern New Jersey SMSAs, 293, **294**
   Philadelphia SMSA, 293–4, **294**
   Pittsburgh SMSA, 296, **296**
   St. Louis SMSA, 296, **296**
   San Francisco SMSA, **295**, 296
   Seattle SMSA, **298**
   in SMSAs, 293
   in U.S., 293
   Washington, D.C. SMSA, 299, **300**
seasonal, 279–84
   Atlanta DUS, 284, **284**
   Baltimore DUS, 280, **281**
   Boston DUS, 279, **280**
   Chicago DUS, 281, **282**
   Cleveland DUS, 281, **282**
   Dallas-Fort Worth DUS, 282, **283**
   data tabulation, 279
   definition (Vacant Seasonal Units), 489
   Detroit DUS, 281, **282**
   Hartford-Connecticut Valley DUS, 280, **280**
   Houston DUS, 282–3, **283**
   Los Angeles DUS, 283, **284**
   Miami DUS, 284, **284**
   Minneapolis-St. Paul DUS, 281–2, **283**
   New Orleans DUS, 280, **281**
   New York-Northern New Jersey DUS, 280, **280**
   Philadelphia DUS, 280, **280**
   Pittsburgh DUS, 281, **282**
   St. Louis DUS, 281, **282**
   San Francisco-Oakland DUS, 280, **281**
   Seattle DUS, 282, **283**
   second-home ownership, 279
   in 20 largest DUSs, 279
   in U.S., 279
   Washington, D.C. DUS, 284, **284**
single-family, definition, **488**
single-unit attached, definition, 488
single-unit detached
   Atlanta, 254, **255**: SMSA, **249**, 249–50
   Baltimore SMSA, 72, **72**
   Boston SMSA, 23, **23**
   Chicago SMSA, 136, **137**
   Cleveland SMSA, 128–9, **129**
   Dallas-Fort Worth SMSAs, **184**, 186
   data tabulation, 472
   definition, 488
   Detroit SMSA, **151**, 151–3
   Hartford SMSA, 63, **64**
   Houston SMSA, **201**, 203–5
   Los Angeles SMSA, **221**, 224
   Miami SMSA, **239**, 239–40
   Minneapolis-St. Paul SMSA, **161**, 163
   New Orleans SMSA, **81**, 84
   New York-Northern New Jersey SMSAs, 32, **35**

## Index

Philadelphia SMSA, 49, **51**
Pittsburgh SMSA, 107–8, **108**
St. Louis SMSA, **117,** 121–2
San Francisco SMSA, **92,** 95
Seattle SMSA, **170,** 171
Washington, D.C. SMSA, **257,** 260–1
supply changes, U.S., *1960–1970,* 13
unit, definition, 486
vacant, 15, 437–44
  Atlanta, 444, **444**
  Baltimore, 439, **439**
  Boston, **438,** 439
  in central cities, 437
  Chicago, **440,** 441
  Cleveland, **440,** 441
  Dallas, 441, **442**
  data tabulation, 437
  definition, 489
  Detroit, 441, **441**
  Hartford, **438,** 439
  Houston, 441–4, **442**
  Long Beach, **443,** 444
  Los Angeles, **443,** 444
  Miami, 444, **444**
  Minneapolis, 441, **441**
  New Orleans, **439,** 439–40
  New York, **438,** 439
  Oakland, **439,** 440
  Philadelphia, 57, **59, 438,** 439
  Pittsburgh, **440,** 441
  and population change, *1960–1970,* 437–444
  St. Louis, **440,** 441
  St. Paul, 441, **441**
  San Francisco, **439,** 440
  Seattle, 441, **441**
  in SMSAs, 437
  in U.S., 437
  Washington, D.C., 444, **444**
vacant migratory, definition, 489
value, mean
  Atlanta, **249,** 250–1
  Baltimore SMSA, **72,** 72–4
  Boston SMSA, **23,** 24
  Chicago SMSA, 136–8, **138**
  Cleveland SMSA, 129, **129**
  Dallas-Fort Worth SMSAs, **185,** 186
  data tabulation, 473
  definition, 486
  Detroit SMSA, **151,** 153
  Hartford SMSA, 63, **64**
  Houston SMSA, **202,** 205–6
  Los Angeles SMSA, **223,** 224
  Miami SMSA, **239,** 240
  Minneapolis-St. Paul SMSA, **161,** 163
  New Orleans SMSA, **81,** 84
  New York-Northern New Jersey SMSAs, 32, **34**
  Philadelphia, 57–8, **59**
  SMSA, 49–51, **51**
  Pittsburgh SMSA, 107, **107**
  St. Louis SMSA, **119,** 122
  San Francisco SMSA, **92,** 95–6
  Seattle SMSA, 171, **171**
  Washington, D.C. SMSA, **258,** 261
value/income ratio, 301
  Atlanta SMSA, 307, **308**
  Baltimore SMSA, **303,** 304
  Boston SMSA, 301, **302**
  Chicago SMSA, 305, **305**
  Cleveland SMSA, 305, **305**
  Dallas-Fort Worth SMSAs, **306,** 307
  data tabulation, 301
  Detroit SMSA, 305, **305**
  Hartford SMSA, **302,** 304
  Houston SMSA, 307, **307**
  Los Angeles SMSA, 307, **308**
  Miami SMSA, 307, **308**
  Minneapolis-St. Paul SMSA, 167, **167,** 305, **306**
  New Orleans SMSA, **303,** 304
  New York-Northeren New Jersey SMSAs, 301, **302**
  Philadelphia SMSA, 301–4, **302**
  Pittsburgh SMSA, 304, **304**

St. Louis SMSA, **304,** 305
San Francisco SMSA, **303,** 304
Seattle SMSA, 305–7, **306**
in SMSAs, 301
in U.S., 301
Washington, D.C. SMSA, 307, **308**
Housing and Urban Development Act of *1968,* 14
Houston
  age-sex structure, **206,** 208–9
  Astrodome Stadium, 205, 211, **466**
  base map, **198, 466**
  births, immature, 377, **378**
  Cuban-Americans, 200
  extraterritorial control, 202
  housing
    multiple-unit, 203–5
    vacant, 441–4, **442**
  land-use regulation, 201–2
  Negroes, **207,** 209, 214–5, **217**
  population, 199, 471
    density, **204,** 206–8
    *1850–1940,* **10**
  poverty population, 215–6, **218**
  Puerto Rican stock, 210
  relief, **198,** 200
  Rice Univ., 211, **466**
  school enrollment, parochial, 361, **362**
  Spanish-Americans, **207,** 209–10, 214–5, **217**
Houston DUS
  age-sex structure, **206,** 208–9
  base map, **201**
  composition, 199
  Galveston, 200, **460**
  housing units, seasonal, 282–3, **283**
  mobile homes, **201,** 203
  population, 199, 471
  sewage disposal, private, 275–6, **277**
  water supply, private, 270, **271**
Houston Ship Channel, 200, 201, 203, **460**
Houston SMSA
  age-sex structure, **206,** 208–9
  automobiles, households without, 339, **339**
  base map, **197, 460**
  Baytown, 202, **460**
  blue-collar workers, **211,** 212–3
  CBD employment, 323, **323**
  clerical workers, 212–3
  elderly population, **206,** 208–9
  Ellington Air Force Base, 203, **460**
  executives, **212,** 212–3
  female headship, **210,** 211–2
  female labor force, 403, **403**
  household size, **209,** 211
    Negro and Spanish-American, 215
  housing
    age, 202–3
    built before *1940,* **199,** 202–3
    built *1960–1970,* **200,** 202–3, **216**
    crowded, 291, **291**
    multiple-unit, 203–5
    rent, mean monthly, **203,** 205–6
    rent/income ratio, 299, **299**
    single-unit, **201,** 203–4
    value, mean, **202,** 205–6
    value/income ratio, 307, **307**
  income
    deficit, 435, **435**
    per person per year, 213, **213:**
      Negro and Spanish-American, 215
    from public payments, 425, **427**
  Intercontinental Airport, 202, **460**
  land use, **198,** 200–1
  Manned Spacecraft Center, 203, 205, 206, **460**
  median age, **205,** 208
  Mexican-Americans, **208,** 210
  Morgans Point, 202, **460**
  in national metropolitan system, 10–1, **11**
  Negroes, 387, **387**
    in new single-unit housing, 387, **387**
  occupations, 212–3. *See also* blue-collar workers, clerical workers, executives, service workers

St. Louis SMSA, **304,** 305
San Francisco SMSA, **303,** 304
Seattle SMSA, 305–7, **306**
Pasadena, 205, **460**
population, 199, 471
  change, *1960–1970,* 213–4, **214,** 355, **355**
  density, 313, **315**
  *1950–1970,* **10**
  poverty population, 417–9, **419**
  public transportation use, 331, **331**
  residential change, *1965–1970,* 214, **215**
  school enrollments, 20-21 year olds, 371, **371**
  service workers, 212–3
  sex ratio, **204,** 209
  Spanish-Americans, 393, **395**
  telephones, households without, 347, **347**
  unemployed males, 411, **411**
Hunter's Point (San Francisco), 96, 97, **463**
Hyde Park (Chicago), 141, **464**

Immature births, *see* Births, immature
Income
  and birth weight, 373–80
  Census enumeration, 486
  deficit, 15, 429–35
    Atlanta SMSA, 435, **436**
    Baltimore SMSA, **431,** 431–2
    Boston SMSA, 429, **430**
    Chicago SMSA, 433, **433**
    Cleveland SMSA, 433, **433**
    Dallas-Fort Worth SMSAs, 196, **196,** 433–5, **434**
    data tabulation, 429
    definition, 486
    Detroit SMSA, 433, **433**
    Hartford SMSA, 429–31, **430**
    Houston SMSA, 435, **435**
    Los Angeles SMSA, 435, **436**
    Miami SMSA, 435, **436**
    Minneapolis-St. Paul SMSA, 433, **434**
    New Orleans SMSA, **431,** 432
    New York-Northern New Jersey SMSAs, 429, **430**
    Philadelphia SMSA, 429, **430**
    Pittsburgh SMSA, 432, **432**
    St. Louis SMSA, 432, **432**
    San Francisco SMSA, **431,** 432
    Seattle SMSA, 433, **434**
    in SMSAs, 429
    in U.S., 429
    Washington, D.C. SMSA, **264,** 265, 435, **436**
  mean family
    Detroit SMSA, **156,** 158
    Los Angeles, Spanish-American, 234
    Pittsburgh SMSA, **114,** 114–5
  per person per year
    Atlanta SMSA, 253, **253**
    Baltimore SMSA, 76, **76**
    Boston SMSA, **27, 28,** 29
    Chicago SMSA, **145,** 146–7
    Cleveland SMSA, **132,** 133
    Dallas-Fort Worth SMSAs, 192, **194**
    data tabulation, 475
    definition, 486
    Detroit SMSA, **155,** 157
    Hartford SMSA, **66,** 67
    Houston SMSA, 213, **213;** Negro and Spanish-American, 215
    Los Angeles SMSA, 232, **233**
    Miami SMSA, 243, **244**
    Minneapolis-St. Paul SMSA, **165,** 166
    New Orleans SMSA, **85,** 88
    New York SMSA, 45–6, **47**
    New York-Northern New Jersey SMSAs, 42–3, **43**
    Philadelphia SMSA, 57, **59, 60;** and race, 57
    Pittsburgh SMSA, **112,** 113; and occupation, 114–5
    St. Louis, 123, 125–6, **126**
    San Francisco SMSA, 100, **100**
    Seattle SMSA, 175, **175**

Washington, D.C. SMSA, **262,** 265
from public payments, 15, 421–7
  Atlanta SMSA, 253, **254,** 427, **428**
  Baltimore SMSA, 421, **423**
  Boston SMSA, 421, **422**
  Chicago SMSA, 424, **425**
  Cleveland SMSA, 424, **425**
  Dallas-Fort Worth SMSAs, 425, **426**
  data tabulation, 421
  definition, 487
  Detroit SMSA, 424, **425**
  Hartford SMSA, 421, **422**
  Houston SMSA, 425, **427**
  Los Angeles SMSA, 427, **428**
  Miami SMSA, 427, **428**
  Minneapolis-St. Paul SMSA, 424–5, **426**
  New Orleans SMSA, 421–3, **423**
  New York-Northern New Jersey SMSAs, 421, **422**
  Philadelphia SMSA, 421, **422**
  Pittsburgh SMSA, 424, **424**
  St. Louis SMSA, 424, **424**
  San Francisco SMSA, 423, **423**
  Seattle SMSA, **178,** 179, 425, 426
  in SMSAs, 421
  in U.S., 421
  Washington, D.C. SMSA, 427, **428**
and telephone use, 347
Indians, *see* American Indians
Indicators
  definition, 14
  economic, 16
  housing, 14
  socioeconomic, 1, 16
Individual
  primary, definition, 487
  unrelated, definition, 488
Inequality
  geographical, 451–2
    strategy for reducing, 452
  among people, 449
  among places, 450–1
Infant mortality, *see* Mortality
Inflation, 448
Information flows and metropolitan interdependence, 10–1
Ingleside (San Francisco), 100, 101, **463**
Inkster, Mich., 158, **458**
Institutionalized population, definition, 486
Interdependence among metropolitan areas, 9–10, **11**
  measuring, 10–1
Inventory, housing, *see* Housing inventory
Irish-Americans
  Boston SMSA, **25,** 26
  Brookline, Mass., 26
  Chicago SMSA, 142, **142**
  definition, 486
  Irish-born, data tabulation, 474
  Irish parentage, data tabulation, 475
  New York SMSA, 37–8, **40**
  Somerville, Mass., 26
Isopleth
  definition, 3
  technique, 480
Italian-Americans
  Boston SMSA, **26,** 28
    East End, 28
    North End, 26
  Chicago SMSA, **143,** 144
  Cleveland, 133, **133**
  definition, 486
  Detroit SMSA, **154,** 155
  Hartford SMSA, **65,** 66
  Italian-born, data tabulation, 475
  Italian parentage, data tabulation, 476
  Los Angeles SMSA, 230–2, **232**
  New York SMSA, 40, **42**
  Philadelphia SMSA, 52, **56**
  parochial school enrollments, 58
  Pittsburgh SMSA, **110,** 111
  San Francisco SMSA, **97,** 98

Japanese-Americans
  Census enumeration, 486

496

# Index

Chicago SMSA, 142, **142**
  data tabulation, 474
  Los Angeles SMSA, 230, **230**
  New York SMSA, 37, **39**
    Flushing neighborhood, 37
  San Francisco-Oakland SMSA, **96**, 98
  Seattle SMSA, **174**, 176
Jersey City, **455**
Jews
  Chicago SMSA
    enumerated as Russian-Americans, 144
  Los Angeles
    enumerated as Russian-Americans, 230
  Miami, 242, **243**
  New York SMSA, 40
    enumerated as German foreign stock, 39
    enumerated as Polish foreign stock, 39
    enumerated as Russian foreign stock, 39–40
  Philadelphia SMSA
    enumerated as Russian-Americans, 52
Joliet, Ill., **458**
Jones Falls (Baltimore), 70, **463**

Kennedy Airport, **462**
Kensington (Philadelphia), **462**
Key Biscayne (Miami SMSA), **461, 468**
Koreans, Census enumeration, 487
Kovar, Mary Grace, 373

Labor force
  definition, 486
  female participation, 397–403
  occupational structure, data tabulation, 476
  participation rates, *1948* and *1975*, 449
  unemployment, definition, 488. *See also* Unemployment, males
La Clede Town (St. Louis), 120, 123, **464**
Ladue, Mo., 122, 126, **457**
La Guardia Airport (New York City), **462**
Lake Forest, Ill. 368, **458**
Lake Minnetonka (Minneapolis-St. Paul SMSA), 163, 165, 168, **459**
Lake Ponchartrain (New Orleans SMSA), **456**
Lake Sammamish, (Seattle SMSA), **459**
Lake Union, 178, **465**
Lake Washington, 178, **459, 465**
  bridges and population growth, 179
  housing age in Seattle SMSA, 170
  and housing values, 171
  mobility in Seattle, 169
Lake Washington Ship Canal, 178
Land area, data tabulation, 472
Land use
  Atlanta SMSA, 247–9, **248**
  Baltimore SMSA, 70–1, **71**
  Boston SMSA, 22, **22**
  definition, 486
  Detroit SMSA, 150, **150**
  Hartford SMSA, 62, **63**
  Houston SMSA, **198**, 200–1
  Los Angeles SMSA, **221**, 222
  Minneapolis-St. Paul SMSA, 160, **160**
  New Orleans SMSA, **80**, 83
  Philadelphia SMSA, 48–9, **49**
  Pittsburgh SMSA, 105–6, **106**
    compared to St. Louis, 118
  St. Louis SMSA, **117**, 118
    compared to Pittsburgh, 118
  San Francisco SMSA, 90, **90**
  Seattle SMSA, 169, **169**
  Washington, D.C. SMSA, **257**, 257–9
Landfall Trailer Park (Minneapolis-St. Paul SMSA), 166, **459**
Laurel Hill (Pittsburgh), 105–6, **457**
Leesburg, Va., **461**
Lindenwold, N.J., 49, 51, **455**
Locational information, 4
  for DUS maps, 4
Logan Airport, **462**

Long Beach, **467**
  housing units, vacant, **443**, 444
  Negroes, 224, **228**
  population, 218, 471
    density, 224, **225**
  relief, 219–20, **220**
  school enrollment, parochial, 361–4, **363**
  Spanish-Americans, 227, **229**
Long Island (New York SMSA), **455**
Lorain, Ohio, 127
Lorain Avenue (Cleveland), 131, **464**
Los Angeles
  age-sex structure, 224, **226**
  base map, **220, 467**
  Cuban-Americans, 227
  housing
    multiple-unit, 224
    vacant, **443**, 444
  Negroes, 224, **228**
  population, 219, 471
    density, 224, **225**
    *1850–1940*, 10
  Puerto Rican stock, 227
  relief, **220**, 221–2
  Russian-Americans
    Jews versus ethnic Russians, 230
  San Gabriel Mts., 222, 224, **466**
  Santa Monica Mts., 222, 224, **466**
  Santa Susana Mts., 222, **466**
  school enrollment, parochial, 361–4, **363**
  Spanish-Americans, 227, **229**
  Watts, 224, **466**
Los Angeles DUS
  age-sex structure, 224, **226**
  base map, **221**
  composition, 219
  housing units, seasonal, 283, **284**
  mobile homes, **221**, 224
  population, 219, 471
  sewage disposal, private, 276, **278**
  water supply, private, 270, **272**
Los Angeles National Forest, **461**
Los Angeles SMSA
  age-sex structure, 224, **226**
  American Indians, 227, **227**
  automobiles, households without, 232–3, **235**, 339, **340**
  base map, **219, 461**
  Beverly Hills, 224, **467**
  blue-collar workers, 232, **234**
  Canadian-Americans, 230, **231**
  CBD employment, 323, **324**
  Chinese-Americans, 227–30, **230**
  clerical workers, 236
  Culver City, 222, **467**
  Dominguez Hills, 219, 222, 224, **467**
  elderly population, 224, **226**
  executives, 232, **234**
  female headship, 232, **233**
  female labor force, 403, **404**
  Gardena, 230, **467**
  German-Americans, 230, **231**
  household size, 232, **233**
  housing
    age, 223
    built before *1940*, 222, 223, **236**
    built *1960–1970*, **222**, 223
    crowded, 291, **292**
    multiple-unit, 224
    rent, mean monthly, **223**, 224
    rent/income ratio, 299, **300**
    single-unit detached, **221**, 224
    value, mean, **223**, 224
    value/income ratio, 307, **308**
  income
    deficit, 435, **436**
    per person per year, 232, **233**
    from public payments, 427, **428**
  Italian-Americans, 230–1, **232**
  Japanese-Americans, 230, **230**
  land use, **221**, 222
  median age, 224, **226**
  Mexican-Americans, 227, **227**
  in national metropolitan system, 10–1, **11**
  Negroes, 387, **388**
    in new single-unit housing, 387, **388**

occupations, 232. *See also* blue-collar workers, clerical workers, executives, service workers
population, 219, 471
  change, *1960–1970*, 355, **356**
  density, 315, **316**
  *1950–1970*, 10
poverty population, 234, **236**, 419, **420**
public transportation use, 232, **235**, 331, **332**
residential change, *1965–1970*, 232, **235**
Russian-Americans, 230, **231**
Santa Monica, 222, 224, **467**
school enrollments, 20–21 year olds, 371, **372**
service workers, 232
sex ratio, 224, **226**
Spanish-Americans, 227, **236**, 393–5, 396
telephones, households without, 347, **348**
unemployment, males, 411, **412**
West Hollywood, 222, 224, **455**
Louisiana State Univ. (New Orleans), 368, **463**
Loyola Univ. (New Orleans), 88, 365, **463**
Lynn, Mass., **455**
  Canadian-Americans in, 27

McKeesport, Pa., **457**
Made land, definition, 486
Mail-out/mail-back system (Censuses, 1970), 18
Manchester, Conn., 62, 65, **455**
  Italian-Americans, 66
Manhattan Island (New York City), **455, 462**
Manned Spacecraft Center (Houston), 203, 205, 206, **460**
Mansion Home Project (St. Louis), 120, **464**
Manufacturing era and urban growth in U.S., 9
Manufacturing productivity, 448
Maps
  accuracy and reliability, 19
  cartographic techniques, 480
  central-city, 4
    scale, 4
  class intervals, 3, 480
  color scheme, 3, 480
  conventions, 2–4
  cross-referencing in text, 2
  Daily Urban System
    scale, 4
  design, 479–81
  dot distribution, 4, 480
  generalization, 3, 480
  and histograms, 480
  isopleth, 3, 4
  location, 4
  and policy considerations, 480–1
  reading, 2
  scale, 4, 479
    definition, 488
    population cartograms, 7
  Standard Metropolitan Statistical Area, 4
    scale, 4
  symbols, 2–4
  and text placement, 479–80
  valid inference from, 3
Marietta, Ga., 249, 252, **461**
Massachusetts Institute of Technology, (Boston SMSA), **462**
Medford, Mass., **455**
  Canadian-Americans in, 27
Median age
  Atlanta SMSA, **250**, 251
  Baltimore SMSA, **73**, 74
  Boston SMSA, 24, 26
  Chicago SMSA, 138–40, **139**
  Cleveland SMSA, 129–30, **130**
  Dallas-Fort Worth SMSAs, 187, **188**
  data tabulation, 473
  definition, 486
  Detroit SMSA, **152**, 153–4
  Hartford SMSA, **64**, 65
  Houston, SMSA, **205**, 208

Los Angeles SMSA, 224, **226**
Miami SMSA, **240**, 241
Minneapolis-St. Paul SMSA, **162**, 164
and neighborhood transition, 52
New Orleans SMSA, **82**, 84
New York-Northern New Jersey SMSAs, 32–4, **36**
and out-migration of young people, 52
Philadelphia SMSA, 52, **53**
Pittsburgh SMSA, 108, **109, 113**, 113–4
St. Louis SMSA, **120**, 123
San Francisco SMSA, **93**, 96–7
Seattle SMSA, **172**, 173–4
Washington, D.C. SMSA, **259**, 262
Medical care (prenatal) and immature births, 373
Medina, Ohio, **458**
Medina, Wash., 178, **459**
Megalopolis, definition, 6, 486
Mercer Island (Washington), **459**
  housing value, 171
Meriden, Conn., 62, **455**
Merion, Pa., 57, **455**
Metropolitan areas
  competition and interdependence, 9
  criteria for inclusion in atlas, 8
  definition, 5, 6, 486
  land-use productivity, 7
  population change and migration, 13
  role in national life, 4
Metropolitan districts, 5
Metropolitan eras in U.S., 9
Metropolitan government
  Boston, 29
  Minneapolis-St. Paul, 167
Metropolitan growth and economic evolution in U.S., 9
Metropolitan life, role of places and people, 1
Metropolitan network, definition, 486
Metropolitan population, *1790–1970*, 10
Metropolitan region, definition, 486
Mexican-Americans, 389–95
  Baltimore, 75
  Chicago, 141
  Dallas, 189
  definition, 486
  Detroit, 155
  Houston SMSA, **208**, 210
  Los Angeles SMSA, 227, **227**
  Mexican-born, data tabulation, 474
  Mexican parentage, data tabulation, 474
  San Francisco-Oakland SMSA, **96**, 98
  Washington, D.C., 263
Miami
  age-sex structure, 241, **241**
  base map, **238, 468**
  Coconut Grove, 241, 243, **468**
  Cuban-Americans, 242, **243**, 245
  Jews, 242, **243**
  housing
    multiple-unit, 239–40
    vacant, 444, **444**
  Negroes, 241, **242**
  population, 237, 471
    density, 240, **240**
    *1900–1940*, 10
  Puerto Rican stock, 241–2
  relief, 237–8, **238**
  school enrollment, parochial, 364, **364**
  Spanish-Americans, 241–2, **242**
    mean family income, 245
Miami Beach, 238, **468**
Miami DUS
  age-sex structure, 241, **241**
  base map, **238**
  composition, 237
  housing units, seasonal, 284, **284**
  mobile homes, **238**, 239
  population, 237, 471
  sewage disposal, private, 276, **278**
  water supply, private, 270–1, **272**
Miami SMSA
  age-sex structure, 241, **241**
  automobiles, households without, 339, **340**
  base map, **237, 461**
  blue-collar workers, 243, **244**

497

# Index

Carol City, 243, **461**
CBD employment, 323, **324**
clerical workers, 243
Coral Gables, 240, 241, **461**
elderly population, **240**, 241, 245, **245**
executives, 243, **244**
female headship, 242–3, **244**
female labor force, 403, **404**
Florida City, 243, **461**
Goulds, 240, 243, **461**
Homestead Air Force Base, 239, **461**
household size, 242, **244**
housing
  age, 238–9
  built before *1940*, **238**, 238–9
  built *1960–1970*, **238**, 238–9
  crowded, 245, **246**, 291, **292**
  multiple-unit, 239–40
  rent, mean monthly, **239**, 240
  rent/income ratio, 299, **300**
  single-unit detached, **239**, 239–40
  value, mean, **239**, 240
  value/income ratio, 307, **308**
income
  deficit, 435, **436**
  per person per year, 243, **244**
  from public payments, 427, **428**
median age, **240**, 241
Miami Beach, 238, **468**
in national metropolitan system, 10–1, **11**
Negroes, 243, **245**, 387, **388**
  in new single-unit housing, 387, **388**
occupations, 243. *See also* blue-collar workers, clerical workers, executives, service workers
Opa-Rocka, 243, **461**
Perrine, 240–3, **461**
population, 237, 471
  change, *1960–1970*, 355, **356**
  density, 315, **316**
  *1950–1970*, **10**
poverty population, 245, **246**, 419, **420**
public transportation use, 331, **332**
Puerto Rican stock, 243
Richmond Heights, 243, **461**
school enrollment, 20-21 year olds, 371 **372**
service workers, 243
sex ratio, 241, **241**
Spanish-Americans, 243–4, **246**, 395, **396**
telephones, households without, 347, **348**
unemployment, males, 411, **412**
Middletown, Conn., 62, **455**
Migration
  and population change, 13
  role in causing urban problems, 13–4
  socioeconomic consequences, 449
Mill Creek renewal area (St. Louis), 120, 122, 126, **464**
Minneapolis-St. Paul
  age-sex structure, **162**, 164
  base map, **160**, **465**
  births, immature, 377, **377**
  housing units, vacant, 441, **441**
  Lake Minnetonka, 163, 165, 166, **459**
  Mount Airy Housing Project, 165, **465**
  Negroes, **163**, 164
  population, 159, 471
    density, **162**, 163–4
    *1850–1940*, **10**
  relief, 159–60, **160**
  school enrollment, parochial, 361, **361**
  Spanish-Americans, **163**, 164
Minneapolis-St. Paul DUS
  age-sex structure, **162**, 164
  base map, **161**
  composition, 159
  housing units, seasonal, 281–2, **283**
  mobile homes, **161**, 163
  population, 159, 471
  sewage disposal, private, 275, **277**
  water supply, private, 269, **271**
Minneapolis-St. Paul SMSA
  age-sex structure, **162**, 164
  American Indians, **163**, 164
  automobiles, households without, 167, **167**, 337, **338**

base map, **159**, **459**
blue-collar workers, **165**, 165–6
CBD employment, 321, **322**
clerical workers, 165
Dellwood, 166, **459**
elderly population, **162**, 164
executives, **165**, 165–6
female headship, **164**, 165
female labor force, 400, **402**
Highland Park neighborhood, 165, **465**
household size, **164**, 165
housing
  age, 160–1
  built before *1940*, **160**, 160–1
  built *1960–1970*, **160**, 160–1
  crowded, 289, **290**
  rent, mean monthly, **161**, 163
  rent/income ratio, 297, **298**
  single-unit detached, **161**, 163
  value, mean, **161**, 163
  value/income ratio, 167, **167**, 305, **306**
income
  deficit, 433, **434**
  per person per year, **165**, 166
  from public payments, 424–5, **426**
land use, 160, **160**
Landfall Trailer Park, 166, **459**
median age, **162**, 164
metropolitan government, 167
in national metropolitan system, 10–1, **11**
Negroes, 385–7, **386**
  in new single-unit housing, 385–7, **386**
North Oaks, 163, 166, **459**
occupations, 165. *See also* blue-collar workers, clerical workers, executives, service workers
population, 159, 471
  change, *1960–1970*, 353, **354**
  density, 166–7, **167**, 313, **314**
  *1950–1970*, **10**
poverty population, 417, **418**
public transportation use, 166, **166**, 328, **330**
residential change, *1965–1970*, 166, **166**
school enrollments, 20-21 year olds, 369, **370**
service workers, 165
sex ratio, **162**, 164
Spanish-Americans, 392, **394**
telephones, households without, 345, **346**
unemployment, male, 409, **410**
White Bear Lake, 166, **459**
Minor civil divisions
  basis for histograms, 4
  definition, 486
Minority population, birth weights, 373–80
Mission District (San Francisco), 96, **463**
  Spanish-Americans, 97
Mobile homes
  Atlanta DUS, **248**, 249
  Baltimore DUS, 72, **72**
  Boston DUS, **22**, 23
  Chicago DUS, 136, **136**
  Cleveland DUS, 128, **128**
  Dallas-Fort Worth DUS, **184**, 186
  data tabulation, 472
  Detroit DUS, **150**, 151
  Hartford-Connecticut Valley DUS, 63, **63**
  Houston DUS, **201**, 203
  Los Angeles DUS, **221**, 224
  Miami DUS, **238**, 239
  Minneapolis-St. Paul DUS, **161**, 163
  New Jersey Pine Barrens, 32
  New Orleans DUS, **81**, 83–4
  New York-Northern New Jersey DUS, 32, **33**
  Philadelphia DUS, 49, **50**, **106**, 107
  St. Louis DUS, **119**, 121
  San Francisco-Oakland DUS, **91**, 95
  Seattle DUS, **169**, 171
  Washington, D.C. DUS, **257**, 260
Monongahela River, **464**
Monroeville, Pa., **457**
Morgans Point (Houston SMSA), 202, **460**
Morrison, Peter A., 13

Mortality, infant and neonatal, 487
Mount Airy Housing Project (St. Paul), 165, **465**
Mt. Oliver (Pittsburgh), **464**
Municipal boundaries, cartographic conventions, 4
Municipality, definition, 487

Natick, Mass., **455**
  U.S. Army installation, 26
National Agricultural Research Center (Washington, D.C. SMSA), 259, **461**
National Airport (Washington, D.C. SMSA), 259
National Center for Health Statistics, 373
*National Survey of Housing Abandonment*, 12
National Urban League, housing abandonment hypothesis, 12
Native parentage, definition, 487
Native population, definition, 487
Needs, human, in American cities, 1, 15
Negroes, 15, 381–8
  Atlanta, 251, 251–2
    median family income, 252
    SMSA, 387, **388**: in new single-unit housing, 387, **388**
  Baltimore, 74, **74**
    SMSA, **383**, **383**: in new single-unit housing, 77, **78**, 383, **383**
  Boston, **25**, 26
    Columbia Point, 26
    SMSA, **28**, 29, 381, **382**: in new single-unit housing, 381, **382**
    South Bay, 26
  Census enumeration, 487
  Chicago, **140**, 141
    SMSA, 385, **385**: in new single-unit housing, 385, **385**
  Cleveland, 131, **131**
    SMSA, 384, **385**: in new single-unit housing, 384, **385**
  Dallas-Fort Worth SMSAs, 189, **189**, 192, **194**, **386**, 387
    in new single-unit housing, 192, **195**, **386**, 387
  data tabulation, 381, 473
  Detroit, **153**, 154
    SMSA, **157**, 158, 385, **385**: in new single-unit housing, 385, **385**
  Hartford, **65**, 66
    SMSA, 68, **68**, **382**, 383: in new single-unit housing, **382**, 383
  Houston, **207**, 209, 214–5, **217**
    SMSA, 387, **387**: in new single-unit housing, 387, **387**
  Long Beach, 224, **228**
  Los Angeles, 224, **228**
    SMSA, 387, **388**: in new single-unit housing, 387, **388**
  Miami, 241, **242**
    SMSA, 243, **245**, 387, **388**: in new single-unit housing, 387, **388**
  Minneapolis, **163**, 164
  Minneapolis-St. Paul SMSA, 385–7, **386**
    in new single-unit housing, 385–7, **386**
  New Orleans, **83**, 85–6
    SMSA, **383**, 384: in new single-unit housing, **383**, 384
  in new single-family housing, data tabulation, 381
  New York
    diversity and origins, 36
    SMSA, 36, **38**, 381, **382**: in new single-unit housing, 381, **382**
  Oakland, **94**, 97
  Philadelphia, 52, **54**
    median family income, *1969*, 52
    SMSA, 61, **61**, **382**, 383: in new single-unit housing, **382**, 383
  Pittsburgh, **110**, 110–1, 115, **115**
    SMSA, 384, **384**: in new single-unit housing, 384, **384**
    among poverty population, 413–9
  Roxbury (Boston), 26
  St. Louis, **121**, 123, **125**, 126
    migration, *1960–1970*, 13

  SMSA, 384, **384**: in new single-unit housing, 384, **384**
  St. Paul, **163**, 164
  San Francisco, **94**, 97
  San Francisco-Oakland SMSA, 100, **100**, **383**, 384
    in new single-unit housing, 101, **101**, **383**, 384
  Seattle, **173**, 174
    SMSA, **178**, 179, **386**, 387: in new single-unit housing, **386**, 387
  in SMSAs, 381
  unemployment, male, 405–11
  in U.S., 381
  Washington, D.C., **260**, 263
    SMSA, **263**, 265, 387, **388**: in new single-unit housing, 387, **388**
Neighborhood life cycles, 12, 15
Neonatal mortality, *see* Mortality
Network, metropolitan, *see* Metropolitan network
New Britain, Conn., **455**
New Haven, Conn., 62
New London, Conn., 62
New Orleans
  age-sex structure, **83**, 84–5
  base map, **80**, **462**
  births, immature, 375, **375**
  Cuban-Americans, 86
  Desire Housing Project, 84, **463**
  female headship, **87**, 88
  French Quarter, 88, **463**
  household size, Desire Housing project, 86–7
  housing
    multiple-unit, 84
    vacant units, **439**, 439–40
  Loyola Univ., 88, **463**
  Negroes, **83**, 85–6
  population, 79, 471
    change, *1960–1970*, **86**, 88: Desire Housing Project, 88
    density, **82**, 84: Desire Housing Project, 84
    *1810–1940*, **10**
  poverty population, **87**, 88
  Puerto Rican stock, 86
  relief, 79-83, **80**
  school enrollment, parochial, 359, **359**
  Spanish-Americans, **83**, 86
  Tulane Univ., 88, **463**
  Univ. of New Orleans, 88, **463**
New Orleans DUS
  age-sex structure, **83**, 84–5
  base map, **81**
  composition, 79
  housing units, seasonal, 280, **281**
  mobile homes, **81**, 83–4
  population, 79, 471
  sewage disposal, private, 274, **275**
  water supply, private, 268, **269**
New Orleans SMSA
  age-sex structure, **83**, 84–5
  automobiles, households without, **86**, 88, 335, **336**
  base map, **79**, **456**
  blue-collar workers, **85**, 87
  CBD employment, 319, **320**
  clerical workers, 87
  elderly population, **82**, 84
  executives, **85**, 88
  female headship, **84**, 87
  female labor force, 399, **399**
  French Quarter, 84, **463**
  household size, **84**, 86–7
  housing
    age, 83
    built before *1940*, **80**, 83
    built *1960–1970*, **80**, 83
    crowded, 286–7, **287**
    rent, mean monthly, **81**, 84
    rent/income ratio, **295**, 296
    single-unit detached, **81**, 84
    value, mean, **81**, 84
    value/income ratio, **303**, 304
  income
    deficit, **431**, 432

# Index

per person per year, **85**, 88
  from public payments, 421–3, **423**
land use, **80**, 83
median age, **82**, 84
in national metropolitan system, 10–1, **11**
Negroes, **383**, 384
  in new single-unit housing, **383**, 384
occupations, 87. *See also* blue-collar workers, clerical workers, executives, service workers
population, 79, 471
  change, *1960–1970*, **86**, 88, **351**, 352
  density, **311**, 312
  *1950–1970*, **10**
poverty population, **415**, 415–6
public transportation use, **327**, 328
school enrollments, 20-21 year olds, **87**, 88, **367**, 368
service workers, 87
sex ratio, **82**, 85
Spanish-Americans, 389, **391**
telephones, households without, **343**, 344
unemployment, male, **407**, 408
New York
  age-sex structure, 32–4, **37**
  base map, **31**, **462**
  births, immature, **373**, **374**
  Chinatown, 37
  housing units, vacant, **438**, 439
  Polish-Americans, Jews versus ethnic Poles, 39
  population, 30, 471
    density, 32, **35**
    *1790–1940*, **10**
    under *18*, 43–5, **45**
  relief, 30–1, **31**
  school enrollment, parochial, 357, **358**
New York-Northern New Jersey DUS
  age-sex structure, 32–4, **37**
  base map, **33**
  composition, 30
  housing units, seasonal, 280, **280**
  mobile homes, 32, **33**
  population, 30, 471
  sewage disposal, private, 273, **274**
  water supply, private, 267, **268**
New York-Northern New Jersey SMSAs
  age-sex structure, 32–4, **37**
  automobiles, households without, 333, **334**
  base map, **30**, **455**
  blue-collar workers, 41–2, **44**
  CBD employment, 317, **318**
  Chinese-Americans, 37, **39**
  composition, 30
  elderly population, 32–3, **36**
  executives, 41–2, **44**
  female headship, 41, **43**
  female labor force, 397, **398**
  German-Americans, 38–9, **40**
    Jews versus ethnic Germans, 39
  household size, 41, **42**
  housing
    age, 31–2
    built before *1940*, 31–2, **32**
    built *1960–1970*, 31–2, **33**
    crowded, 45–6, **47**, 285, **286**
    rent, mean monthly, 32, **34**
    rent/income ratio, 293, **294**
    single-unit detached, 32, **35**
    value, mean, 32, **34**
    value/income ratio, 301, **302**
  income
    deficit, 429, **430**
    per person per year, 42–3, **43**, 45–6, **47**
    from public payments, 421, **422**
  international role, 30
  Irish-Americans, 37–8, **40**
  Italian-Americans, 40, **42**
  Japanese-Americans, 37, **39**
    in Flushing neighborhood, 37
  median age, 32–3, **36**
  in national metropolitan system, 10–1, **11**
  Negroes, 36, **38**, 381, **382**
    diversity and origins, 36
    in new single-unit housing, 381, **382**

occupations, 41–2. *See also* blue-collar workers, clerical workers, executives, service workers
Polish-Americans, 39, **41**
population, 30, 471
  change, *1960–1970*, 349, **350**
  density, 32, **46**, 309, **310**
  *1950–1970*, **10**
poverty population, 413, **414**
public transportation use, 325, **326**
Russian-Americans, 39–40, **41**
  Jews versus ethnic Russians, 39–40
school enrollments, 20-21 year olds, 365 **366**
sex ratio, 34, **37**
Spanish-Americans, 36–7, **38**, 389, **390**
  diversity and origins, 37
telephones, households without, 341, **342**
unemployment, male, 405, **406**
Newark, N.J., **455**
Newton, Mass., Russian-Americans in, 28
North Beach (San Francisco), 98
North End (Boston), **462**
North Oaks (Minneapolis-St. Paul SMSA), 163, 166, **459**
Northland Shopping Center (Detroit SMSA), 154, **458**
Northville State Hospital (Detroit SMSA), 158, **458**
Nozick, Robert, 451

Oak Forest Infirmary (Chicago DUS), 140, **458**
Oak Park, Ill., **458**
Oakland, *see* San Francisco-Oakland entries
  base map, **90**, **463**
  births, immature, 375, **375**
  housing units, vacant, **439**, 440
  Negroes, **94**, 97
  population, 89, 471
    density, **93**, 96
  relief, 90, **90**
  school enrollment, parochial, 359, **359**
  Spanish-Americans, **94**, 97
Occupational structure
  CBD labor force, 317
  data tabulation, 476
  and urbanization in U.S., 5
Occupations
  Atlanta SMSA, 252–3
  Baltimore SMSA, 75–6
  Boston SMSA, 29
  Census enumeration, 487
  Chicago SMSA, 146
  Cleveland SMSA, 133
  Dallas-Fort Worth SMSAs, 191–2
  Detroit SMSA, 157
  Hartford SMSA, 67
  Houston SMSA, 212–3
  Los Angeles SMSA, 232
  Miami SMSA, 243
  Minneapolis-St. Paul SMSA, 165
  New Orleans SMSA, 87
  New York-Northern New Jersey SMSAs, 41–2
  Philadelphia SMSA, 56–7
  Pittsburgh SMSA, 113
    and income per person per year, 114–5
  St. Louis SMSA, 125
  San Francisco SMSA, 99–100
  Seattle SMSA, 177
  Washington, D.C. SMSA, 265
Occupied housing unit, *see* Housing, occupied
O'Hare Airport (Chicago), **458**
Ohio River (Pittsburgh), **464**
Onsite sewage disposal, definition, 487
Opa-Locka, Fla., 243, **461**
Open space, 14
Overbounding, definition, 487
  SMSA, 6

Pacific Heights (San Francisco), **463**
Painesville, Ohio, **458**
Palmdale, Fla., **461**
Palo Alto, Cal., **456**

Palos Verdes Hills (Los Angeles), **467**
Parentage, definition, 487
  foreign, definition, 486
  native, definition, 487
Parish, definition, 487
Parochial school
  definition, 487
  enrollments, 14
  Philadelphia, 58
Pasadena (Houston), 200, **460**
Passaic, N.J., **455**
Paterson, N.J., **455**
Payments, public, definition, 487
Payments, transfer, definition, 488
Pennhurst State School (Philadelphia SMSA), **455**
Perrine (Miami SMSA), 240, 243, **461**
Persons per houshold, data tabulation, 476
Persons per room, definition, 487
Philadelphia
  age-sex structure, 52, **53**
  base map, **49**, **462**
  births, immature, 373, **374**
  Chestnut Hill, 49, 57, **462**
  housing
    multiple-unit, 49
    vacant, 57, **59**, **438**, 439: housing abandonment, 57
    value, mean, 57–8, **59**
  Negroes, 52, **54**
  population, 48, 471
    density, 51–2, **53**
    *1790–1940*, **10**
  relief, 48–9, **49**
  row houses, 49
  school enrollment, parochial, 58, **60**, 357, **358**
    Italian-American, 58
    Polish-American, 58
  Society Hill renewal area, 57–8
  Spanish-Americans, 52, **54**
  urban homestead program, 57
Philadelphia DUS
  age-sex structure, 52, **53**
  base map, **50**
  composition, 48
  housing units, seasonal, 280, **280**
  mobile homes, 49, **50**
  population, 48, 471
  sewage disposal, private, 273, **274**
  water supply, private, 267, **268**
Philadelphia SMSA
  age-sex structure, 52, **53**
  automobiles, households without, 333–5, **334**
  base map, **48**, **455**
  blue-collar workers, 56, **58**
  Bryn Mawr, 49, **455**
  CBD employment, 317, **318**
  elderly population, 52, **53**
  executives, 56, **58**
  female headship, 55–6, **57**
    Camden, N.J., 56
  female labor force, 397, **398**
  household size, 55, **56**
  housing
    age, 49
    built before *1940*, 49, **50**
    built *1960–1970*, 49, **50**
    crowded, 285, **286**
    rent, mean monthly, 49–51, **52**
    rent/income ratio, 293–5, **294**
    single-unit detached, 49, **51**
    value, mean, 49–50, **51**
    value/income ratio, 301–4, **302**
  income
    deficit, 429, **430**
    per person per year, 57, **59**, **60**: in Main Line communities, 57
    from public payments, 421, **422**
  Italian-Americans, 52, **56**
  land use, 48–9, **49**
  Main Line communities, 49, **455**
    housing values and rents, 49–51
  median age, 52, **53**
  in national metropolitan system, 10–1, **11**

Negroes, 61, **61**, **382**, 383
  in new single-unit housing, **382**, 383
occupations, 56–7. *See also* blue-collar workers, clerical workers, executives, service workers
Polish-Americans, 52, **55**
population, 48, 471
  change, *1960–1970*, 58–61, **60**, 349, **350**
  density, 309, **310**
  *1950–1970*, **10**
poverty population, 413, **414**
public transportation use, 325–8, **326**
Rosemount, 49, **455**
Russian-Americans, 52, **55**
  Jews versus ethnic Russians, 52
school enrollments, 20-21 year olds, 365, **366**
sex ratio, 52, **54**
Spanish-Americans, 389, **390**
telephones, households without, 341, **342**
unemployment, male, 405, **406**
Villanova, 49, **455**
Physical environment
  sewage disposal, private, 273–8
  water supply, private, 267–72
Piedmont, Cal., 100, **463**
Pine Barrens, N.J., **455**
  income, 57
  mobile homes, 32
Pittsburgh
  age-sex structure, 108–10, **109**
  base map, **106**, **464**
  Beltzhoover, 110, **464**
  births, immature, 375, **376**
  Brushton, 110, **464**
  East Liberty, 110, **464**
  elderly population, 108, **113**
  Hill District, 110
  Homewood, 110, **464**
  housing
    multiple-unit, 107–8
    vacant, **440**, 441
  Negroes, 110, **110**, 115, **115**
  Point Breeze, 108, **464**
  population, 105, 471
    density, 108, **109**
    *1800–1940*, **10**
  relief, 105–6, **106**
    and settlement pattern, 115
  school enrollment, parochial, 359, **360**
  Spanish-Americans, **110**, 111
  Spring Hill, 108, **464**
  Squirrel Hill, 108, **113**, **464**
Pittsburgh DUS
  age-sex structure, 108–10, **109**
  base map, **106**
  composition, 105
  housing units, seasonal, 281, **282**
  mobile homes, **106**, 107
  population, 105, 471
  sewage disposal, private, 274, **276**
  water supply, private, 268, **270**
Pittsburgh SMSA
  age-sex structure, 108–10, **109**
  Arlington Heights housing project, 113
  automobiles, households without, 336, **336**
  base map, **105**, **457**
  blue-collar workers, **112**, 113, **114**, 114–5
  CBD employment, 320, **320**
  Churchill, 108, **457**
  clerical workers, 113
  Edgeworth, 113, **457**
  elderly population, 108, **109**
  executives, **112**, 113
  female headship, **111**, 113
  female labor force, 400, **400**
  Fox Chapel, 113, **457**
  household size, **111**, 113
  housing
    age, 106–7
    built before *1940*, **106**, 106–7, 115, **115**
    built *1960–1970*, **106**, 106–7
    crowded, 288, **288**

## Index

rent, mean monthly, **107**, 108
rent/income ratio, 296, **296**
single-unit detached, 107–8, **108**
value, mean, **107**, 108
value/income ratio, 304, **304**
income
  deficit, 432, **432**
  mean family, **114**, 114–5
  per person per year, **112**, 113
  from public payments, 424, **424**
Italian-Americans, **110**, 111
land use, compared to St. Louis, 118
Laurel Hill, 106, **457**
median age, 108, **109, 113**, 113–4
in national metropolitan system, 10–1, **11**
Negroes, 384, **384**
  in new single-unit housing, 384, **384**
occupations, 113. *See also* blue-collar workers, clerical workers, executives, service workers
Polish-Americans, **110**, 111
population, 105, 471
  change, *1960–1970*, 352, **352**
  decrease, *1960–1970*, 105
  density, 312, **312**
  *1950–1970*, **10**
poverty population, 416, **416**
public transportation use, 328, **328**
school enrollments, 20-21 year olds, 367, **368**
service workers, 117
Sewickley Heights, 113, **457**
sex ratio, 108–10, **109**
Spanish-Americans, 391, **392**
telephones, households without, 344, **344**
unemployment, male, 408, **408**
Places
  definition, 487
    incorporated, 486
    unincorporated, 488
    urban, 489
  inequalities among, 450–1
  and problems, 488–9
  of work, definition, 487
Plaza Square Project (St. Louis), 120, **464**
Point Breeze (Pittsburgh), 108, **464**
Policy, urban and metropolitan
  and comparative analysis, 16
  dilemmas, 449
  federal government role, 449
  and geographical inequalities, 451
  strategy for reducing, 452
  obstacles to effective policy, 449
  unformity, 1
Polish-Americans
  Chicago SMSA, 142–4, **143**
  definition, 487
  Detroit SMSA, **154**, 155
  Hartford SMSA, **65**, 66–7
  New York SMSA, 39, **41**
    Jews versus ethnic Poles, 39
  Philadelphia SMSA, 52, **55**
    parochial school enrollments, 58
  Pittsburgh SMSA, **110**, 111–3
  Polish-born, data tabulation, 475
  Polish parentage, data tabulation, 475
Political boundaries, cartographic conventions, 4
Political fragmentation
  Boston SMSA, 29, **29**
  Cleveland SMSA, 134, **134**
Pomona, Cal., **461**
Pontiac, Mich., **458**
Population
  central cities
    to *1970*, 471
    *1970* data tabulation, 10
  change, 14
  and housing vacancies, 437–44
  change, *1960–1970*, 349–56
    Atlanta SMSA, 355, **356**
    Baltimore SMSA, 77, **77, 351**, 352
    Boston SMSA, 349, **350**
    Chicago SMSA, 353, **353**
    Cleveland SMSA, 352, **353**
    Dallas-Fort Worth SMSAs, **354**, 355

data tabulation, 349
definition, 487
Detroit SMSA, **157**, 158, 353, **353**
Hartford SMSA, 349, **350**
Houston SMSA, 213–4, **214**, 355, **355**
Los Angeles SMSA, 355, **356**
Miami SMSA, 355, **356**
Minneapolis-St. Paul SMSA, 353, **354**
New Orleans, **86**, 88: SMSA, **351**, 352
New York-Northern New Jersey SMSAs, 349, **350**
Philadelphia SMSA, 58–61, **60**, 349, **350**
Pittsburgh SMSA, 352, **352**
St. Louis SMSA, 352, **352**
San Francisco SMSA, **351**, 352
Seattle SMSA, **178**, 179, 353, **354**
Washington, D.C. SMSA, 355, **356**
density, 14, 309–16
  Atlanta, **250**, 251: SMSA, 315, **316**
  Baltimore, **73**, 74: SMSA, **311**, 312
  Boston, **23**, 25: SMSA, 309, **310**
  change, *1960–1970*, SMSAs, 349–55
  Chicago, 138, **139**: SMSA, 313, **313**
  Cleveland, 129, **130**: SMSA, 313, **313**
  convergence, 451
  Dallas-Fort Worth SMSAs, **186**, 186–7, 313, **314**
  data tabulation, SMSAs, 309, 473
  definition, 487
  Detroit, **152**, 153: SMSA, 313, **313**
  Hartford, **64**, 64–5: SMSA, 309–12, **310**
  Houston, **204**, 206–8: SMSA, 313, **315**
  and human behavior, 315
  Long Beach, 224, **225**
  Los Angeles, 224, **225**: SMSA, 315, **316**
  Miami, 240, **240**: SMSA, 315, **316**
  Minneapolis, **162**, 163–4
  Minneapolis-St. Paul SMSA, 166–7, **167**, 313, **314**
  and municipal services costs, 187
  New Orleans, **82**, 84: SMSA, **311**, 312
  New York, 32, **35**: SMSA, 45, **46**, 309, **310**
  Oakland, **93**, 96
  Philadelphia, 51–2, **53**: SMSA, 309, **310**; South Philadelphia, 51; West Philadelphia, 51
  Pittsburgh, 108, **109**: SMSA, 312, **312**
  St. Louis, **120**, 123: SMSA, 312, **312**
  St. Paul, **162**, 163–4
  San Francisco, **93**, 96: SMSA, **311**, 312
  Seattle, 171–3, **172**: SMSA, 313, **314**
  in SMSAs, 309
  and social pathology, 45
  and transportation technology, 309
  in U.S., 309
  Washington, D.C., **259**, 261: SMSA, 315, **316**
DUS, *1970*, data tabulation, 471
institutionalized, definition, 486
metropolitan, *1790–1970*, **10**
native, definition, 487
of places, definition, 487
poverty, *see* Poverty population
in SMSAs
  *1970*, data tabulation, 471
  to *1970*, **10**
under *18*, New York City, 43–4, **45**
urban
  definition, 489
  and rural U.S., 6
Postwar (World War II) era, 447
  capital formation, 448
Pottstown, Pa., **455**
Poverty
  and automobile ownership, 333
  definition, 14, 487
  income deficit, 429–35
  population, 15, 413–9
    Atlanta SMSA, 419, **420**
    Baltimore SMSA, 415, **415**
    Boston SMSA, 413, **414**
    Chicago SMSA, 416, **417**

Cleveland SMSA, 416, **417**
Dallas-Fort Worth SMSAs, 417, **418**
data tabulation, 413
definition, 487
Detroit SMSA, 416–7, **417**
Hartford SMSA, 413, **414**
Houston, 215–6, **218**, 417–9, **419**: Negro and Spanish-American components, 215–6
Los Angeles SMSA, 234, **236**, 415, **420**
Miami SMSA, 245, **246**. 419. **420**
Minneapolis-St. Paul SMSA, 417, **418**
New Orleans, **87**, 88: SMSA, **415**, 415–6
New York-Northern New Jersey SMSAs, 413, **414**
Philadelphia SMSA, 413, **414**
Pittsburgh SMSA, 416, **416**
St. Louis SMSA, 416, **416**
San Francisco SMSA, **415**. 416
Seattle SMSA, **177**, 178–9, 417, **418**
in SMSAs, 413
in U.S., 413
Washington, D.C. SMSA, 419, **420**
Price Index, Consumer, definition, 485
Primary individual, definition, 487
Private sewer system, 14
  definition, 487
Private water supplies, 14
  definition, 487
Problems, metropolitan and urban, 12–5
  *in* cities versus *of* cities, 5, 14
  collective self-confidence, 11
  important determinants, 11
  and mirgration, selective, 13–4
  people versus places, 14, 448
  places versus people, 14, 448
  policy uniformity, 1
  and solutions, 12–5, 449
    prerequisite, 14
  and values, 15
Productivity, 448–50
Pruitt-Igoe Projects (St. Louis), 122, 123
Public assistance payments, 421–7
Public health, 373–80
Public payments, 421–7
  definition, 487
Public sector growth, 450
Public sewage disposal, definition, 487
Public transportation, definition, 487
Public transportation use, 14, 325–31
  Atlanta SMSA, 331, **332**
  and automobile ownership, 331
  Baltimore SMSA, **327**, 328
  Boston SMSA, 325, **326**
  Chicago SMSA, 329, **329**
  Cleveland SMSA, 328–9, **329**
  Dallas-Fort Worth SMSAs, **330**, 331
  data tabulation, 325
  Detroit SMSA, 329, **329**
  Hartford SMSA, **326**, 328
  Houston SMSA, 331, **331**
  Los Angeles SMSA, 232, **235**, 331, **332**
  Miami SMSA, 331, **332**
  Minneapolis-St. Paul SMSA, 166, **166**, 329, 330
  New Orleans SMSA, **327**, 328
  New York-Northern New Jersey SMSAs, 325, **326**
  Philadelphia SMSA, 325–8, **326**
  Pittsburgh SMSA, 328, **328**
  St. Louis SMSA, 328, **328**
  San Francisco-Oakland SMSA, 101–2, **102**, 327, 328
  Seattle SMSA, 329, **330**
  in SMSAs, 325
  in U.S., 325
  Washington, D.C. SMSA, 331, **332**
Public water supply, definition, 487
Puerto Rican stock, 389–95
  Baltimore, 75
  Boston, 26
  Chicago, 141
  Cleveland, 131
  Dallas, 189
  Detroit, 155
  Hartford, 66

Houston, 210
Los Angeles, 227
Miami, 241–2
  SMSA, 243
New Orleans, 86
New York City, 37
Philadelphia, 52
San Francisco, 98
Washington, D.C. 263
Puget Sound, 459

Quality of life
  in American cities, 1
  Cleveland and suburbs, 134
  and Gross Natinal Product, 448
  St. Louis, **125**, 126
Quantico Military Base, Va., 257, 260 **461**
Quincy Mass., 29, 455, **455**

Race, Census enumeration, 487
Railroads, and urban growth in U.S., 9
Rawls, John, 451
Recessions, *1940s* and *1950s*, 447
Region, metropolitan, definition, 486
Relief
  Atlanta, 247, **248**
  Baltimore, 70–1, **71**
  Boston, 21–2, **22**
  Chicago, 136, **136**
  Cleveland, 127, **128**
  Dallas-Fort Worth SMSAs, 182, **182**
  Detroit, 149, **150**
  Hartford, 62, **63**
  Houston, **198**, 200
  Long Beach, 219–22, **220**
  Los Angeles, 219–22, **220**
  Miami, 237–8, **238**
  Minneapolis, 159–60, **160**
  New Orleans, 79–83, **80**
  New York, 30–1, **31**
  Oakland, 90, **90**
  Philadelphia, 48, **49**
  Pittsburgh, 105–6, **106**
  St. Louis, 116–8, **117**
  St. Paul, 159–60, **160**
  San Francisco, 90, **90**
  Seattle, 169, **169**
  Washington, D.C., 256, **257**
Renewal, urban, *see* Urban renewal
Rent
  Census enumeration, 487
  contract, definition, 485
  gross, definition, 486
  mean monthly, data tabulation, 473
Rent/income ratio, 14, 293–300
  definition, 487
Residence, definition, 488
Residential change, *1965–1970*
  Atlanta SMSA, 254, **254**
  Chicago SMSA, **146**, 147, **147**
  definition, 488
  Detroit SMSA, **157**, 158
  Houston SMSA, 214, **215**
  Los Angeles SMSA, 232, **235**
  Minneapolis-St. Paul SMSA, 166, **166**
Residential quality, St. Louis, 126, **126**
Reston, Va., **461**
Restrictive zoning, Boston SMSA, **28**, 29
Retirement benefits, railroad and Social Security, 421–7
Rice Univ. (Houston), 211, **466**
Richmond, Cal., 101, **456**
Richmond Heights (Miami SMSA), 243, **461**
Ridgelea (Fort Worth), 186, **459**
Rock Creek (Washington, D.C.), 257, **468**
Rockville, Md., **461**
Romeo, Mich., 157, **458**
Rosemount, Pa., 49, 57, **455**
Row houses
  Baltimore, 72
  Philadelphia, 49
  San Francisco, 95
  Washington, D.C., 261
Roxbury (Boston), **462**
  Negroes in, 26
  Russian-Americans in, 28

# Index

Russian-Americans
  Boston SMSA, **26.** 144
  Chicago SMSA, **143,** 144
    Jews versus ethnic Russians, 144
  definition, 488
  Los Angeles SMSA, 230, **231**
    Jews versus ethnic Russians, 230
  New York SMSA, 39–40, **41**
    Jews versus ethnic Russians, 39–40
  Newton, Mass., 28
  Philadelphia SMSA, 52, **55**
    Jews versus ethnic Russians, 52
  Roxbury (Boston), 28
  Russian-born, data tabulation, 475
  Russian parentage, data tabulation, 475

St. Charles, Mo., 118, **457**
St. Clair Shores, Mich., **458**
St. Joseph College (Hartford), 365
St. Louis
  age-sex structure, **121,** 123
  base map, **117, 464**
  Belleville, Ill., 118, **457**
  births, immature, 375, **376**
  competition with Chicago, 116
  Forest Park, 122, **464**
  housing
    built before *1940,* **125,** 126
    built *1960–1970,* **125,** 126
    vacant, **440,** 441
  income per person per year, 125–6, **126**
  La Clede Town, 120, 123, **464**
  land use, compared to Pittsburgh, 118
  Mansion Home Project, 120, **464**
  Mill Creek, 120, 122, 126, **464**
  Negroes, **121,** 123, **125,** 126
    migration, *1960–1970,* 13
  Plaza Square Project, 120, **464**
  population, 116, 471
    density, **120,** 123
    growth and decline, *1950–1970,* 13
    *1830–1940,* **10**
  Pruitt-Igoe Projects, 122, 123
  quality of life, **125,** 126
  relief, **117,** 117–8
  residential quality, 126, **126**
  St. Louis Univ., **464**
  school enrollment, parochial, 359, **360**
  Spanish-Americans, **121,** 123–4
St. Louis DUS
  age-sex structure, **121,** 123
  base map, 119
  composition, 116
  housing units, seasonal, 281, **282**
  mobile homes, **119,** 121
  population, 116, 471
  sewage disposal, private, 274, **276**
  water supply, private, 268–9, **270**
St. Louis SMSA
  age-sex structure, **121,** 123
  Alton, 118, **457**
  automobiles, households without, 336, **336**
  base map, **111, 457**
  blue-collar workers, **124,** 125
  CBD employment, 320, **320**
  Clayton, Mo., 126, **457**
  clerical workers, 125
  Creve Couer, 122, 126, **457**
  elderly population, **121,** 123
  executives, **124,** 125
  female headship, **122,** 124
  female labor force, 400, **400**
  Frontenac, 122, **457**
  household size, **122,** 124
  housing
    age, 118–20
    built before *1940,* **118,** 118–20
    built *1960–1970,* **118,** 118–20
    crowded, 288, **288**
    rent, mean monthly, **119,** 122
    rent/income ratio, 296, **296**
    single-unit detached, **117,** 121–2
    value, mean, **119,** 122
    value/income ratio, **304,** 305
  income
    deficit, 432, **432**

per person per year, **123,** 125–6
from public payments, 424, **424**
Ladue, 122, 126, **457**
land use, **117,** 118
median age, **120,** 122
in national metropolitan system, 10–1, **11**
Negroes, 384, **384**
  in new single-unit housing, 384, **384**
occupations, 125. *See also* blue-collar workers, clerical workers, executives, service workers
population, 116, 471
  change, *1960–1970,* 352, **352**
  decrease, *1960s,* 13
  density, 312, **312**
  *1950–1970,* **10**
poverty population, 416, **416**
public transportation use, 328, **328**
St. Charles, 118, **457**
school enrollments, 20-21 year olds, 368, **368**
service workers, 125
sex ratio, **120,** 123
Spanish-Americans, 391–2, **392**
telephones, households without, 344, **344**
unemployment, male, 408, **408**
Westwood, 126, **457**
St. Paul
  base map, **160,** 465
  births, immature, 377, **377**
  housing units, vacant, 441, **441**
  Negroes, **163,** 164
  population, 159, 471
    density, **162,** 163–4
    relief, 159–60, **160**
  school enrollment, parochial, 361, **361**
  Spanish-Americans, **163,** 164
Salem, Mass., **455**
Sammamish Lake
  and housing values, 171
  and rents, mean monthly, 171
Sampling rates, Census, 17
San Francisco-Oakland
  age-sex structure, **93,** 96–7
  base map, **90, 463**
  Bay View neighborhood, 97, **463**
  births, immature, 375, **375**
  Chinatown, **95,** 96, 98
  Chinese-Americans, **95,** 97–8
  Cuban-Americans, 98
  Fillmore district, 97
  Golden Gate Park, 98, **463**
  housing
    multiple-unit, 95
    vacant, **439,** 440
  Hunter's Point, 96, 97, **463**
  Ingleside neighborhood, 101, **463**
  Mission district, 96, **463**
  Negroes, **94,** 97
  population, 89, 471
    density, **93,** 96
    *1860–1940,* **10**
  Puerto Rican stock, 98
  relief, 90, **90**
  row houses, 95
  school enrollment, parochial, 359, **359**
  Spanish-Americans, **94,** 97
  unemployment, male, 100-1, **101**
San Francisco-Oakland DUS
  age-sex structure, **93,** 96–7
  base map, **91**
  composition, 89
  housing units, seasonal, 280, **281**
  mobile homes, **91,** 95
  population, 89, 471
  sewage disposal, private, 274, **275**
  water supply, private, 268, **269**
San Francisco-Oakland SMSA
  age-sex structure, **93,** 96–7
  American Indians, **97,** 98
  automobiles, households without, **335,** 336
  base map, **89, 456**
  Bay Area Rapid Transit (BART), 102
  Berkeley Hills, 92, **463**
  blue-collar workers, **99,** 99–100
  Carquinez Straight, 90–1, **456**

CBD employment, **319,** 320
Chinese-Americans, **95,** 97–8
clerical workers, 99–100
ecological variety, 90
elderly population, **93,** 96–7
executives, **99,** 99–100
female headship, **98,** 99
female labor force, **399,** 399–400
household size, **98,** 99
housing
  age, 90–2
  built before *1940,* 90–2, **91**
  built *1960*–1970, 90–2, **91**
  crowded, **287,** 288
  multiple-unit, 95
  rent, mean monthly, **92,** 95–6
  rent/income ratio, **295,** 296
  single-unit detached, **92,** 95
  value, mean, **92,** 95–6
  value/income ratio, **303,** 304
income
  deficit, **431,** 432
  per person per year, 100, **100**
  from public payments, 423, **423**
Italian-Americans, **97,** 98
Japanese-Americans, **96,** 98
land use, 90, **90**
median age, **93,** 96–7
Mexican-Americans, **96,** 98
in national metropolitan system, 10–1, **11**
Negroes, 100, **100, 383,** 384
  in new single-unit housing, 101, **101, 383,** 384
North Beach, 98
occupations, 99–100. *See also* blue-collar workers, clerical workers, executives, service workers
Piedmont, 100, **463**
population, 89, 471
  change, *1960–1970,* **351,** 352
  density, **311,** 312
  *1950–1970,* **10**
poverty population, **415,** 416
public transportation use, 101–2, **102, 327,** 328
Richmond, 101, **456**
school enrollments, 20-21 year olds, **367,** 368
service workers, 99–100
sex ratio, **94,** 97
Spanish-Americans, 391, **391**
  median family income, 100
telephones, households without, **343,** 344
unemployment, male, **407,** 408
Union City, 98, **456**
Univ. of California-Berkeley, 99–100, **456**
Walnut Creek, 96, **456**
San Gabriel Mts. (Los Angeles), 222, 224, **466**
San Jose, Cal., **456**
San Mateo, Cal., **456**
San Raphael, Cal., **456**
San Raphael Hills (Los Angeles), **467**
Santa Monica Mts. (Los Angeles), 222, 224, **467**
Santa Susana Mts. (Los Angeles), 222, **466**
Scale, cartographic, 4, 479
  definition, 488
  and generalizations, 3
School enrollment, parochial, 357–64
  Atlanta, 364, **364**
  Baltimore, 359, **359**
  Boston, 357, **358**
  Chicago, **147,** 147–8, **360,** 361
  Cleveland, 359–61, **360**
  Dallas, 361, **362**
  data tabulation, 357
  Detroit, 361
  and ethnicity, 357–64
  Hartford, 357–9, **358**
  Houston, 361, **362**
  Long Beach, 361–4, **363**
  Los Angeles, 361–4, **363**
  Miami, 364, **364**
  Minneapolis, 361, **361**

New Orleans, 359, **359**
New York, 357, **358**
Oakland, 359, **359**
Philadelphia, 58, **60,** 357, **358**
Pittsburgh, 359, **360**
St. Louis, 359, **360**
St. Paul, 361, **361**
San Francisco, 359, **359**
Seattle, 361, **361**
in SMSAs, 357
in U.S., 357
Washington, D.C., 364, **364**
School enrollments, 20-21 year olds, 14, 365–71
  Atlanta SMSA, 254, 254, 371, **372**
  Baltimore SMSA, 365, **367**
  Boston SMSA, 365, **366**
  Chicago SMSA, 368–9, **369**
  Cleveland SMSA, 368, **368**
  Dallas-Fort Worth SMSAs, **370,** 371
  data tabulation, 365
  Detroit SMSA, 369, **369**
  Hartford SMSA, 365, **366**
  Houston SMSA, 371, **371**
  Los Angeles SMSA, 371, **372**
  Miami SMSA, 371, **372**
  Minneapolis-St. Paul SMSA, 369, **370**
  New Orleans SMSA, **87,** 88, 367, **368**
  New York-Northern New Jersey SMSAs, 365, **366**
  Philadelphia SMSA, 365, **366**
  Pittsburgh SMSA, 368, **368**
  St. Louis SMSA, 368, **368**
  San Francisco SMSA, **367,** 368
  Seattle SMSA, 369–71, **370**
  in SMSAs, 365
  in U.S., 365
  Washington, D.C. SMSA, 371, **372**
School, parochial, definition, 487
Schuylkill River (Philadelphia), **462**
Seasonal homes, definition, 14, (Vacant Seasonal Unit), 489
Seattle
  age-sex structure, **173,** 173–4
  base map, **169, 465**
  births, immature, 377, **377**
  Discovery Park, 174, **465**
  Fort Lawton, 174, **465**
  housing
    multiple-unit, 171
    vacant, 441, **441**
  Negroes, **173,** 174
  population, 168, 471
    density, 171–2, **172**
    *1870–1940,* **10**
  rail connections to East, 168
  relief, 169, **169**
  school enrollment, parochial, 361, **361**
  Skid Road, 174
  Spanish-Americans, **173,** 174–5
Seattle DUS
  age-sex structure, **173,** 173–4
  base map, **169**
  composition, 168
  housing units, seasonal, 282, **283**
  mobile homes, **169,** 171
  population, 168, 471
  sewage disposal, private, 275, **277**
  water supply, private, 269, **271**
Seattle SMSA
  age-sex structure, **173,** 173–4
  automobiles, households without, 337–9, **338**
  base map, **168, 459**
  blue-collar workers, **176,** 177
  CBD employment, 321, **322**
  Chinese-Americans, **174,** 176
  clerical workers, 177
  elderly population, **172,** 173–4
  Everett, 178, **459**
  executives, **176,** 177
  female headship, **175,** 176–7
  female labor force, **402,** 403
  household size, **175,** 176
  housing
    age, 169–70

501

## Index

built before *1940*, 169–71, **170**
built *1960–1970*, 169–71, **170**
crowded, 289, **290**
multiple-unit, 171
rent, mean montly, 171, **171**
rent/income ratio, 297, **298**
single-unit detached, **170**, 171
value, mean, 171, **171**
value/income ratio, 305–7, **306**
income
  deficit, 433, **434**
  per person per year, **175**, 178
  from public payments, **178**, 179, 425, **426**
Japanese-Americans, **174**, 176
Lake Union, 178, **459**
Lake Washington, 178, **459**
Lake Washington Ship Canal, 178, **465**
land use, 169, **169**
median age, **172**, 173–4
Medina, Wash., 178
in national metropolitan system, 10–1 **11**
Negroes, **178**, 179, **386**, 387
  in new single-unit housing, **386**, 387
occupations, 177. *See also* blue-collar workers, clerical workers, executives, service workers
population, 168, 471
  change, *1960–1970*, **178**, 179, 353, **354**
  density, 313, **314**
  *1950–1970*, **10**
poverty population, **177**, 178, 417, **418**
public transportation use, 329, **330**
school enrollments, 20-21 year olds, 369–71, **370**
service workers, 171
sex ratio, **172**, 174
Spanish-Americans, 392–3, **394**
telephones, households without, 345 **346**
unemployment, male, 409, **410**
Second Count Summary Tapes (Census), 19
Second-home ownership, 279–84
Segregation
  Negroes, 381–7
  persistence, 452
  Spanish-Americans, 389–96
Selfridge Air Force Base (Detroit), 154, **458**
Service workers
  Atlanta SMSA, 252
  Baltimore SMSA, 75
  Chicago SMSA, 146
  Cleveland SMSA, 133
  Dallas-Fort Worth SMSAs, 191–2
  data tabulation, 476
  definition, 488
  Detroit SMSA, 157
  Hartford SMSA, 67
  Houston SMSA, 212–3
  Los Angeles SMSA, 232
  and metropolitan growth in U.S., 9
  Miami SMSA, 243
  Minneapolis-St. Paul SMSA, 165
  New Orleans SMSA, 87
  Pittsburgh SMSA, 113
  St. Louis SMSA, 125
  San Francisco SMSA, 99–100
  Seattle SMSA, 177
  Washington, D.C. SMSA, 265
Sewage disposal, onsite, definition, 487
Sewage disposal, private, 273–8
  Atlanta DUS, 277, **278**
  Baltimore DUS, 274, **275**
    SMSA, 77, **77**
  Boston DUS, 273, **274**
  Chicago DUS, 275, **276**
  Cleveland DUS, 275, **276**
  Dallas-Fort Worth DUS, 275, **277**
  data tabulation, 273
  definition, 487
  Detroit DUS, 275, **276**
  Hartford-Connecticut Valley DUS, 273–4, **274**
  Houston DUS, 275–6, **277**
  Los Angeles DUS, 276, **278**
  Miami DUS, 276, **278**

Minneapolis-St. Paul DUS, 275, **277**
New Orleans DUS, 274, **275**
New York-Northern New Jersey DUS, 273, **274**
Philadelphia DUS, 273, **274**
Pittsburgh DUS, 274, **276**
St. Louis DUS, 274, **276**
San Francisco-Oakland DUS, 274, **275**
Seattle DUS, 275, **277**
in SMSAs, 273
in 20 largest DUSs, 273
in U.S., 273
Washington, D.C. DUS, 278, **278**
Sewage disposal, public, definition, 487
Sewickley Heights (Pittsburgh SMSA), 113, **457**
Sex ratio
  Atlanta SMSA, **250**, 251
  Baltimore SMSA, **73**, 74
  Boston SMSA, **24**, 26
  Chicago SMSA, **140**, 140–1
  Cleveland SMSA, **130**, 130–1
  Dallas-Fort Worth SMSAs, **187**, 187–9
  data tabulation, 473
  definition, 488
  Detroit SMSA, **152**, 154
  Hartford SMSA, **64**, 65–6
  Houston SMSA, **204**, 209
  Los Angeles SMSA, 224, **226**
  Miami SMSA, 241, **241**
  Minneapolis-St. Paul SMSA, **162**, 164
  New Orleans SMSA, **82**, 85
  New York-Northern New Jersey SMSAs, 34, **37**
  Philadelphia SMSA, 52, **54**
    Fort Dix, N.J., 52
  Pittsburgh SMSA, 108–10, **109**
  St. Louis SMSA, **120**, 123
  San Francisco SMSA, **94**, 97
  Seattle SMSA, **172**, 174
  Washington, D.C. SMSA, **260**, 262–3
Shaker Heights (Cleveland SMSA), 129, **458**
Shorelines, cartographic conventions for, 4
Signal Hill, Cal., **467**
Single-family housing, definition, 488
Single-unit attached housing
  Baltimore, 72
  definition, 488
Single-unit deteached, *see* Housing, single-unit detached
Skid Road (Seattle), 174
Skokie, Ill., **458**
Social Security payments, 421–7
Society Hill (Philadelphia), **462**
Socioeconomic segregation
  Negroes, 381–8
  Spanish-Americans, 389–95
Socioeconomics status and college enrollments, 365
Somerville, Mass., **455**
  Canadian-Americans in, 27
  Irish-Americans in, 26
South Bay (Boston), 462
  Negroes in, 26
South Boston, **462**
South Philadelphia, 51, **462**
South Side Plan (Houston), **466**
Southern Methodist Univ., 371
Southwest Renewal area (Washington, D.C.), 261, 264, **468**
Spanish-Americans, 15, 389-98
  Atlanta, **251**, 252
    SMSA, 395, **396**
  Baltimore, **74**, 74–5
    SMSA, 389, **391**
  births, immature, 373–80
  Boston, **25**, 26
    SMSA, 389, **390**
  Census enumeration, 488
  Chicago, 141, **141**
    SMSA, 392, **393**
  Cleveland, 131, **131**
    SMSA, 392, **393**
  Dallas-Fort Worth SMSAs, 189, **190**, 393, **394**
  data suppression, 4

data tabulation, SMSAs, 389, 473
definition, 389
Detroit, 153, 154–5
  SMSA, 392, **393**
Hartford, **65**, 66
  SMSA, 389, **390**
Houston, **207**, 209–11, 214–5, **217**
  SMSA, 393, **395**
Long Beach, 227, **229**
Los Angeles, 227, **229**
  SMSA, 234, **236**, 393–5, **396**
Miami, 241–2, **242**
  mean family income, 245
  SMSA, 243–5, **246**, **395**, 396
Minneapolis, **163**, 164
Minneapolis-St. Paul SMSA, 392, **394**
New Orleans, **83**, 86
  SMSA, 389, **391**
New York SMSA, 36–7, **38**, 389, **390**
  diversity and origins, 37
Oakland, **94**, 97
Philadelphia, 52, **54**
  SMSA, 389, **390**
Pittsburgh, **110**, 111
  SMSA, 391, **392**
  among poverty population, 413–9
St. Louis, **121**, 123–4
  SMSA, 391–2, **392**
St. Paul, **163**, 164
San Francisco, **94**, 97
  SMSA, 391, **391**
Seattle, **173**, 174–5
  SMSA, 392–3, **394**
in SMSAs, 389
unemployed males, 405–11
in U.S., 389
Washington, D.C., **260**, 263
  SMSA, 295, **296**
Spanish-language population, definition, 488
Specialization and urban growth, 9
Spring Hill (Pittsburgh), 108, **464**
Springfield, Mass., 62, **455**
  household size, 67
Square miles, cities, SMSAs, DUSs, data tabulation, 472
Squirrel Hill (Pittsburgh), 108, 113, **464**
Standard Metropolitan Statistical Area (SMSA)
  aggregate area and population in U.S, 5
  definition, 5, 488
  map scale, 4
  in *1970*, **7**
  in *1960* and *1970* Censuses, 5
  size disparities, 5–6
  within 20 largest DUSs
    population, *1950–1970*, **10**
State boundaries, cartographic conventions for, 4
Staten Island, **455**, **462**
*Statistical Abstract of the U.S.*, 17, 447, 448
Statistical units
  definition, 488
  Census, 18
Stillwater, Minn., **459**
Stock, *see* Foreign stock
Storrs, Conn., **455**
Substitutions, 19
Suburbs and central cities in postwar era, 447
Suppressed values
  description, 488
  notation convention, 4
  tract data, 4

Tacoma SMSA, **459**
  population, 168
Tax burdens, Boston SMSA, **28**, 29
Tax rates and publicly provided services, 448
Telephone calls, as measures of metropolitan interdependence, 10–1
Telephones, households without, 341–8
  Atlanta SMSA, 347, **348**
  Baltimore SMSA, 341, **343**
  Boston SMSA, 341, **342**
  Chicago SMSA, 344–5, **345**
  Cleveland SMSA, 344, **345**

Dallas-Fort Worth SMSAs, 345, **346**
  data tabulation, 341
  definition, 488
  Detroit SMSA, 345, **345**
  Hartford SMSA, 341, **342**
  Houston SMSA, 347, **347**
  Los Angeles SMSA, 347, **348**
  Miami SMSA, 347, **348**
  Minneapolis-St. Paul SMSA, 345, **346**
  New Orleans SMSA, **343**, 344
  New York-Northern New Jersey SMSAs, 341, **342**
  Philadelphia SMSA, 341, **342**
  Pittsburgh SMSA, 344, **344**
  St. Louis SMSA, 344, **344**
  San Francisco SMSA, **343**, 344
  Seattle SMSA, 345, **346**
  in SMSAs, 341
  in U.S., 341
  Washington, D.C. SMSA, 347, **348**
Texas Christian Univ. (Dallas), 371, **459**
Thompsonville, Conn., 65, **455**
Three Rivers Stadium (Pittsburgh), **464**
Township, definition, 488
Tracts, census
  arbitrary statistical units, 480
  basis for histograms, 2
  definition, 485
  population
    average, 3, 18
    disparities, 3
  size (area) disparities, 3
Transfer payments, 421
  definition, 488
Transportation
  and population density, 309
  public
    and CBD employment, 323–4
    definition, 487
    to work, 325–32
  role in city development, 9
  and telephone use, 347
Tulane, Univ. (New Orleans), 88, 365, **463**

Underbounding, definition, 488
  of SMSAs, 6
Unemployment, male, 15, 405–11
  Atlanta SMSA, 411, **412**
  Baltimore SMSA, 407, **407**
  Boston SMSA, 405, **406**
  Chicago SMSA, 408–9, **409**
  Cleveland SMSA, 408, **409**
  Dallas-Fort Worth SMSAs, 409–11, **410**
  date tabulation, 405
  definition, 488
  Detroit, **156**, 158, 409, **409**
  Hartford SMSA, 405–7, **406**
  Houston SMSA, 411, **411**
  Los Angeles SMSA, 411, **412**
  Miami SMSA, 411, **412**
  Minneapolis-St. Paul SMSA, 409, **410**
  New Orleans SMSA, **407**, 408
  New York-Northern New Jersey SMSAs, 405, **406**
  Philadelphia SMSA, 405, **406**
  Pittsburgh SMSA, 408, **408**
  St. Louis SMSA, 408, **408**
  San Francisco-Oakland, 100–1, **101**
    SMSA, **407**, 408
  Seattle SMSA, 409, **410**
  in SMSAs, 405
  in U.S., 405
  Washington, D.C. SMSA, 411, **412**
Unincorporated place, definition, 488
Union City, Cal., 98, **456**
Union Station (Washington, D.C.), 265, **468**
U.S. Bureau of the Census, 17
U.S. Department of Health, Education and Welfare, 16
Univ. of California-Berkeley, 99–100, **456**
Univ. of California-Los Angeles, **467**
Univ. of Chicago, 141, 147, **464**
Univ. of Connecticut, 365
Univ. of Houston, **466**
Univ. of Miami, 371

# Index

Univ. of Minnesota, 369, **465**
Univ. of New Orleans, 88
Univ. of Pennsylvania, 365, **462**
Univ. of Washington, 369, **465**
University Park (Dallas), 186, **466**
Unrelated individuals, definition, 488
Urban area, definition, 488
Urban development, Hartford SMSA, 68, **68**
Urban growth
    and comparative advantage, 9
    and immigration, 13
    and natural increase, 13
    and self-confidence, 11
    and sewage disposal systems, 278
    and urban problems, 11
    and water supply, 272
Urban homestead program, Philadelphia, 57
Urban League, *see* National Urban League
Urban place, definition, 489
Urban population, 6
    definition, 489
Urban renewal, 15
    definition, 489
    Hartford SMSA, 68
    housing units, abandoned, 437–44
    Philadelphia, Society Hill area, 57–8
    private
        Chicago, 136
        New York City, 32
    Washington, D.C., 261
*Urban Wilderness, The: A History of the American City,* 1
Urbanization
    American population, 5
    definition, 489
    and economic development in U.S., 5, 9
    U.S., after *1840,* 5
    U.S., *1790–1970,* 6
Urbanized areas
    aggregate area and population, *1970,* 5
    definition, 489
    patterns in U.S., 5

Vacancy chains, 12
    directionality, 13
Vacant housing, 15, 437–44
    definition, 489
    Philadelphia, 57
Vacant migratory units, definition, 489
Valley Forge Army Hospital (Philadelphia SMSA), 57, **455**
Value, housing, definition, 486
Value/income ratio, 14, 301–8
    definition, 489
Veterans Administration, 447
Vieux Carre (New Orleans), **463**

Villanova (Philadelphia SMSA), 49, 57, 365, **455**
Voting patterns, Cleveland, 134, **134**

Walking to work, Chicago, **146,** 147
Walnut Creek, Cal., 96, **456**
Waltham, Mass., **455**
    Canadian-Americans (French) in, 27
Warner, Sam Bass, Jr., 1
Washington, D.C.
    age-sex structure, **260,** 262–3
    base map, **257, 468**
    births, immature, 380, **380**
    Cuban-Americans, 263
    housing
        multiple-unit, 260–1
        vacant, 444, **444**
    location relative to Baltimore, 70
    Mexican-Americans, 263
    Negroes, **260,** 263
    population, 256, 471
        density, **259,** 261
        *1800–1940,* **10**
    Puerto Rican stock, 263
    relief, 256–7, **257**
    Rock Creek, 257, **468**
    row houses, 261
    school enrollment, parochial, 364, **364**
    Southwest Renewal area, 261, 264, **468**
    Spanish-Americans, **260,** 263
Washington, D.C. DUS
    age-sex structure, **260,** 262–3
    base map, **257**
    composition, 256
    housing units, seasonal, 284, **284**
    mobile homes, **257,** 260
    population, 256, 471
    sewage disposal, private, 278, **278**
    water supply, private, 272, **272**
Washington, D.C. SMSA
    age-sex structure, **260,** 262–3
    Alexandria, Va., 256, **461**
    automobiles, households without, **263,** 265, 339, **340**
    base map, **256, 461**
    blue-collar workers, **262,** 265
    Bolling Air Force Base, 257, 259, **468**
    CBD employment, 323, **324**
    clerical workers, 265
    commuting to 14th and K area, **264,** 265
    commuting to Union Station area, **264,** 265
    Dulles International Airport, 259, **461**
    elderly population, **259,** 262
    executives, **262,** 265
    Fairfax, Va., 256, **461**
    Falls Church, Va., 256, **461**

female headship, **261,** 264–5
female labor force, 403, **404**
Fort Belvoir, Va., 257, **461**
Fort Meade, 260, **461**
household size, **261,** 264
housing
    age, 259–60
    built before *1940,* **258,** 259–60
    built *1960–1970,* **258,** 259–60
    crowded, **263,** 265, 291, **292**
    multiple-unit, 260–1
    rent, mean monthly, **258,** 261
    rent/income ratio, 299, **300**
    single-unit detached, **257,** 260–1
    value, mean, **258,** 261
    value/income ratio, 307, **308**
income
    deficit, **264,** 265, 435, **436**
    per person per year, **262,** 265
    from public payments, 427, **428**
land use, **257,** 257–9
median age, **259,** 262
National Agricultural Research Center, 259, **461**
National Airport, 259
in national metropolitan system, 10–1, **11**
Negroes, **263,** 265, 387, 388
    in new single-unit housing, 387, **388**
occupations, 265. *See also* blue-collar workers, clerical workers, executives, service workers
population, 256, 471
    change, *1960–1970,* 355, **356**
    density, 315, **316**
    *1950–1970,* **10**
poverty population, 419, **420**
public transportation use, 331, **332**
Quantico Military Base, 257, 260, **461**
school enrollments, 20-21 year olds, 371, **372**
service workers, 265
sex ratio, **260,** 262–3
Spanish-Americans, 395, **396**
telephones, households without, 347, **348**
unemployment, male, 411, **412**
Washington, Mo., **457**
Washington, Pa., **457**
Watchung Mts. (New Jersey), **455**
    and settlement patterns, 31
Water bodies, screening, 4
Water supply, private, 267–272
    Atlanta DUS, 271–2, **272**
    Baltimore DUS, 268, **269**
    Boston DUS, 267, **268**
    Chicago DUS, 269, **270**
    Cleveland DUS, 269, **270**

    Dallas-Fort Worth DUS, 269–70, **271**
    data tabulation, 267
    definition, 489
    Detroit DUS, 269, **270**
    and future urban development, 267, 272
    Hartford-Connecticut Valley DUS, 268, **268**
    Houston DUS, 270, **271**
    Los Angeles DUS, 270, **272**
    Miami DUS, 270–1, **272**
    Minneapolis-St. Paul DUS, 269, **271**
    New Orleans DUS, 268, **269**
    New York-Northern New Jersey DUS, 267, **268**
    Philadelphia DUS, 267, **268**
    Pittsburgh DUS, 268, **270**
    St. Louis DUS, 268–9, **270**
    San Francisco-Oakland DUS, 268, **269**
    Seattle DUS, 269, **271**
    in SMSAs, 267
    in 20 largest DUSs, 267
    in U.S., 267
    Washington, D.C. DUS, 272, **272**
Water supply, public, definition, 487
Waterbury, Conn., 62, **455**
Watts (Los Angeles), 224, **467**
Waukegan, Ill., **458**
Welfare payments, 421–7
Wellesley, Mass., **455**
Wellesley College, 365
West Chester, Pa., **455**
West Hartford, Conn., 67, **455**
West Hollywood (Los Angeles SMSA), 222, 224, **467**
West Philadelphia, 51, **462**
West University Place (Houston), **466**
Westover Hills (Fort Worth), 186, **459**
Westwood, Mo., 126, **457**
Westworth (Dallas-Fort Worth SMSA), 192, **459**
Wheaton, Ill., **458**
White (race), Census enumeration, 487
White Bear Lake (Minneapolis-St. Paul SMSA), 166, **459**
White House (Washington, D.C.), **468**
White Rock Lake (Dallas), **466**
Wilmette, Ill., 146, **458**
Winnetka, Ill., 146, **458**
Work, place of Census definition, 487
Working in the CBD, 14, 317–24

Xavier Univ. (New Orleans), 368, **463**

Young adults in school, 365–371

ZIP Code, definition, 489